S0-ACB-924

A BIBLIOGRAPHY OF BRITISH INDUSTRIAL RELATIONS

A BIBLIOGRAPHY OF BRITISH INDUSTRIAL RELATIONS

G. S. BAIN and G. B. WOOLVEN

CAMBRIDGE UNIVERSITY PRESS

CAMBRIDGE

LONDON · NEW YORK · MELBOURNE

Published by the Syndics of the Cambridge University Press
The Pitt Building, Trumpington Street, Cambridge CB2 1RP
Bentley House, 200 Euston Road, London NW1 2DB
32 East 57th Street, New York, NY 10022, USA
296 Beaconsfield Parade, Middle Park, Melbourne 3206, Australia

First published 1979

Printed in Great Britain by
Western Printing Services Ltd, Bristol

Library of Congress Cataloguing in Publication Data
Bain, George Sayers.
A bibliography of British industrial relations.
1. Industrial relations – Great Britain – Bibliography.
I. Woolven, G. B., joint author. II. Title.
Z7164.L1B26 [HD8391] 016.331'0941 76–53516
ISBN 0 521 21547 1

SHORT CONTENTS

CONTENTS

Part One

General

Part Two

Employees: Industrial Attitudes and Behaviour

Part Three

Employee Organisation

Part Four

Employers and their Organisation

Part Five

Labour–Management Relations

Part Six

The Labour Force, Labour Markets, and Conditions of Employment

Part Seven

The State and its Agencies

PREFACE

The aim of this bibliography is to bring together all the secondary source material, except that of an ephemeral or strictly propagandist nature, published in English between 1880 and 1970 on British industrial relations. It includes books, pamphlets, articles in learned and professional journals, theses, and government reports. The subject is broadly defined to cover not only the traditional topics of trade unionism and labour–management relations but also those aspects of other fields which are relevant to the study of any aspect of job regulation – the process of making and administering the rules which regulate or control employment relationships. It follows that the bibliography recognises the interdisciplinary nature of industrial relations, and it includes relevant material from such disciplines as industrial psychology, industrial sociology, labour economics, labour history, labour law, personnel management, and social administration.

The bibliography has a lengthy history. A preliminary collection of references was begun under George Bain's direction in 1967 by John Pimlott, then a research assistant at Nuffield College, Oxford, and now a Staff Tutor in Industrial Relations and Economics at the University of Southampton. But the compilation began in earnest in October 1969 when George Bain and Gillian Woolven joined forces and the latter assumed the responsibility for undertaking the basic search for references. Work continued full-time until December 1972 and part-time until July 1976 when the typescript was sent to the publisher. Although neither of us was a bibliographical innocent when the project began, we greatly underestimated the size of the task we had set ourselves. Indeed, if we had fully appreciated at the outset the amount of time and effort which would be required to complete the bibliography, we would never have begun it. But, as Martin and McIntyre have noted, 'those who seek to compile bibliographies bring their cares upon themselves, and have a duty to conceal them, as best they can, from their readers'.[1] Hence rather than burden the reader with all the trials and tribulations we encountered in our work, we turn to the happy duty of acknowledging the help and encouragement which we received from various individuals and institutions.

Much useful advice was received from the members of the British Universities Industrial Relations Association, the Society for the Study of Labour History, and the Industrial Law Society, who replied to our circular letter seeking comments and suggestions on the proposed nature and scope of the bibliography, and many valuable references were gleaned from the questionnaire which we sent to trade unions, employers' associations, and various union-employer organisations. We are greatly indebted to all those who replied. We are also indebted to all those from whose previous work we benefited – the compilers of the bibliographies which we ransacked for references – and to Dr Joyce Bellamy and Professor John Saville of the University of Hull for providing us with much useful information from their files prior to the publication of the first volume of their *Dictionary of Labour Biography*.

We are most grateful to Pat Back, Greg Bamber, John Bennett, Julia Harrison, Christine Kennedy, Carolyn Shercliff, and Helen Smith for checking many of the references; to Brian Hillery, Aidan Kelly, and Arthur Maltby for helping with Irish sources; to the staffs of numerous libraries, both in Britain and abroad, who answered letters and telephone calls concerning such references; and to the staffs of the principal libraries used in undertaking the search – the British Library, the British Library of Political and Economic Science, the Bodleian Library, Nuffield College Library, the Library of the Oxford Union (by permission of the President), Manchester City Libraries, the University of Manchester and the University of Manchester Institute of Science and Technology Libraries, Manchester Business School Library,

[1] G. H. Martin and S. McIntyre, *A Bibliography of British and Irish Municipal History*, I (Leicester: Leicester University Press, 1972), ix.

and the University of Warwick Library – who facilitated our work by their kind assistance.

The tedious but essential work of maintaining the voluminous correspondence and of typing the manuscript was undertaken by Mrs Freeborn and her staff of Hunts Typing Bureau, Oxford, and by Annemarie Flanders, Anne Heape, Wendy Hudlass, Muriel Stanley, and Hilary Williams of the Social Science Research Council's Industrial Relations Research Unit at the University of Warwick. Our thanks are due to all these people.

Once the first draft of the manuscript had been typed, various sections were sent to specialists in the fields concerned. We greatly benefited from the comments and criticisms of Dr W. R. Garside of the University of Birmingham; Mr Jim Durcan of Nuffield College, Oxford; Professor V. George of the University of Kent; Mr Andrew Gottschalk of the London Business School; Dr Paul O'Higgins of Christ's College, Cambridge; and Mr M. E. Rose of the University of Manchester. Several colleagues at Warwick – Steve Anderman, William Brown, Hugh Clegg, Richard Hyman, and Barry Thomas – also gave us the benefit of their advice.

The bibliography was made possible by the generosity of the Social Science Research Council. It gave a grant for the first three years of the project and later provided support from the budget of its Industrial Relations Research Unit at the University of Warwick. We are particularly grateful to the SSRC's Management and Industrial Relations Committee who made the original recommendation to support the project. Our thanks must also be given to the University of Manchester Institute of Science and Technology for administering the grant.

We are under no illusion that we have compiled a perfect bibliography, and we accept responsibility for the errors it contains. Some of these became apparent at the final stage of proofreading and could not conveniently be removed. For example, a few publications, especially parliamentary papers which are often variously described in official and other lists, are entered twice. To some extent this duplication is functional, as such publications are often listed in each of two appropriate sections of the bibliography. All known duplicates are indicated in the index by an asterisk. There are undoubtedly other errors, and also omissions, for, as Sidney Webb noted many years ago, 'any attempt to make a complete guide to the study of even the narrowest field of human knowledge is perverse and doomed to failure'.[1] So we should be grateful if readers would draw to our attention any errors or omissions which they detect. We can then make these good in the supplements which we plan to publish from time to time (the first will probably be issued in 1980–81), and in this way make the bibliography a more comprehensive and accurate guide to the literature within its scope.

GEORGE BAIN
GILLIAN WOOLVEN

1 'Introduction', *A London Bibliography of the Social Sciences*, I (London: London School of Economics and Political Science, 1931), vii.

PERIODICAL TITLES AND ABBREVIATIONS

Abbreviation	Title
ABS Bull.	*ABS Bulletin* (Association of Broadcasting Staffs)
ALGES Bull.	*ALGES Bulletin* (Association of Local Government Engineers and Surveyors)
A.Sc.W. J.	*A.Sc.W. Journal* (Association of Scientific Workers)
ASSET	*ASSET* (Association of Supervisory Staffs, Executives and Technicians)
Aberd. Univ. Rev.	*Aberdeen University Review*
Acad. Polit. Sci. Proc.	*Academy of Political Science Proceedings*
Accting. Res.	*Accounting Research*
Acctnt. Mag.	*Accountant's Magazine*
Adm. Sci. Q.	*Administrative Science Quarterly*
Administration	*Administration* (Dublin)
Adult Educ.	*Adult Education*
Advmt. Sci.	*Advancement of Science*
Agric. Hist. Rev.	*Agricultural History Review*
Agriculture	*Agriculture*
Almoner	*Almoner*
Am. Anthrop.	*American Anthropology*
Am. Econ. Rev.	*American Economic Review*
Am. Hist. Rev.	*American History Review*
Am. J. Econ. Sociol.	*American Journal of Economics and Sociology*
Am. J. Sociol.	*American Journal of Sociology*
Am. Neptune	*American Neptune*
Am. Polit. Sci. Rev.	*American Political Science Review*
Amat. Hist.	*Amateur Historian*
Angl.-Dan. J.	*Anglo-Danish Journal*
Angles. Antiq. Soc. Field Club Trans.	*Anglesey Antiquarian Society and Field Club Transactions*
Ann. Am. Acad. Polit. Soc. Sci.	*Annals of the American Academy of Political and Social Science*
Ann. Collect. Econ.	*Annals of Collective Economy*
Antiq. J.	*Antiquaries Journal*
Appl. Statist.	*Applied Statistics*
Aquarius	*Aquarius*
Arbit. J.	*Arbitration Journal*
Archaeol. Ael.	*Archaeologia Aeliana* (Society of Antiquaries of Newcastle-upon-Tyne)
Archaeol. Cambrensis	*Archaeologia Cambrensis* (Cambrian Archaeological Association)
Archaeol. Cant.	*Archaeologia Cantiana*
Archaeologia	*Archaeologia*
Archit. Archaeol. Soc. Durham Northumb. Trans.	*Architectural and Archaeological Society of Durham and Northumberland Transactions*
Archives	*Archives*
Ars Quat. Coron.	*Ars Quatuor Coronatorum* (Masonic Lodge Quatuor Coronati No. 2706)

Asian Labour	*Asian Labour*
Ass. Ind. Med. Offr. Trans.	*Association of Industrial Medical Officers Transactions*
Assd. Archit. Soc. Rep. Pap.	*Associated Architectural Societies Reports and Papers*
Assist. Librar.	*Assistant Librarian*
Atl. Mon.	*Atlantic Monthly*
Aust. J. Polit. Hist.	*Australian Journal of Politics and History*
Authors' Lodge No. 3456 Trans.	*Authors' Lodge No. 3456 Transactions* (Masonic)
BBC Staff Ass. Bull.	*BBC Staff Association Bulletin*
Banker	*Banker*
Bankers' Mag.	*Bankers' Magazine*
Bedford. Hist. Rec. Soc. Octavo Publs.	*Bedfordshire Historical Record Society Octavo Publications*
Berks. Archaeol. J.	*Berkshire Archaeological Journal*
Bett. Bus.	*Better Business*
Bibl. Soc. Trans.	*Bibliographical Society Transactions*
Board Celt. Studies Bull.	*Board of Celtic Studies Bulletin*
Board of Trade J.	*Board of Trade Journal*
Br. Archaeol. Ass. J.	*British Archaeological Association Journal*
Br. Dent. J.	*British Dental Journal*
Br. J. Adm. Law	*British Journal of Administrative Law*
Br. J. Educ. Psychol.	*British Journal of Educational Psychology*
Br. J. Educ. Studies	*British Journal of Educational Studies*
Br. J. Ind. Med.	*British Journal of Industrial Medicine*
Br. J. Ind. Relat.	*British Journal of Industrial Relations*
Br. J. Ind. Saf.	*British Journal of Industrial Safety*
Br. J. Med. Educ.	*British Journal of Medical Education*
Br. J. Oral Surg.	*British Journal of Oral Surgery*
Br. J. Psychol.	*British Journal of Psychology*
Br. J. Sociol.	*British Journal of Sociology*
Br. Med. J.	*British Medical Journal*
Br. Mgmt. Rev.	*British Management Review*
Br. Q. Rev.	*British Quarterly Review*
Br. Univ. A.	*British Universities Annual*
Brad. Antiq.	*Bradford Antiquary*
Brew. Guard.	*Brewers' Guardian*
Brew. J.	*Brewers' Journal*
Bris. Glouc. Archaeol. Soc. Trans.	*Bristol and Gloucestershire Archaeological Society Transactions*
British Book News	*British Book News*
Bull. Trim. Ass. Int. Lutte Chôm.	*Bulletin Trimestriel de l'Association Internationale pour la Lutte Contre le Chômage*
Bulletin	*Bulletin* (British Library of Political Science)
Bus. Hist.	*Business History*
Bus. Hist. Rev.	*Business History Review*
Bus. Hist. Soc. Bull.	*Business History Society Bulletin*
Caern. Hist. Soc. Trans.	*Caernarvonshire Historical Society Transactions*
Cah. Bruges	*Cahiers de Bruges*
Calif. Mgmt. Rev.	*California Management Review*
Camb. Hist. J.	*Cambridge Historical Journal*
Camb. J.	*Cambridge Journal*
Camb. Law J.	*Cambridge Law Journal*
Can. J. Econ. Polit. Sci.	*Canadian Journal of Economics and Political Science*
Car. Res. Advis. Centre J.	*Careers Research Advisory Centre Journal*
Ceredigion	*Ceredigion* (Journal of the Cardiganshire Antiquarian Society)
Cert. Acctnt. J.	*Certified Accountants' Journal*
Char. Orgn. Rev.	*Charity Organisation Review*
Chart. Survey.	*Chartered Surveyor*
Chautauquan	*Chautauquan*
Chem. Drugg.	*Chemist and Druggist*

Ches. N. Wales Archit. Archaeol. Hist. Soc. J.	*Chester and North Wales Architectural, Archaeological and Historic Society Journal*
Child	*Child*
Chiropodist	*Chiropodist*
Christus Rex	*Christus Rex*
Civ. Serv. Argus	*Civil Service Argus*
Cloth. Inst. J.	*Clothing Institute Journal*
Co-existence	*Co-existence*
Collns. Hist. Staffs.	*Collections for a History of Staffordshire*
Columb. J. Wld. Bus.	*Columbia Journal of World Business*
Columb. Law Rev.	*Columbia Law Review*
Commonwealth	*Commonwealth*
Communist Int.	*Communist International*
Communist Rev.	*Communist Review*
Comp. Polit.	*Comparative Politics*
Comp. Studies Soc. Hist.	*Comparative Studies in Society and History*
Composer	*Composer*
Contemp. Rev.	*Contemporary Review*
Cornell Law Q.	*Cornell Law Quarterly*
Cost Acc.	*Cost Accountant*
Current Econ. Comment	*Current Economic Comment*
Dance & Dancers	*Dance & Dancers*
Dent. Hlth.	*Dental Health*
Derby. Archaeol. Nat. Hist. Soc. J.	*Derbyshire Archaeological and Natural History Society Journal*
Derby. Misc.	*Derbyshire Miscellany*
Devon. Ass. Advmt. Sci. Lit. Art Rep. Trans.	*Devonshire Association for the Advancement of Science, Literature and Art Report and Transactions*
Distr. Bank Rev.	*District Bank Review*
Dors. Nat. Hist. Archaeol. Soc. Proc.	*Dorset Natural History and Archaeological Society Proceedings*
Dublin Rev.	*Dublin Review*
Durham Univ. J.	*Durham University Journal*
Durham Univ. Phil. Soc. Proc.	*Durham University Philosophical Society Proceedings*
E. Herts Archaeol. Soc. Trans.	*East Herts Archaeological Society Transactions*
E. Rid. Antiq. Soc. Trans.	*East Riding Antiquarian Society Transactions*
Eccles Distr. Hist. Soc. Trans.	*Eccles and Distrist Historical Society Transactions*
Econ. Dev. Cult. Change	*Economic Development and Cultural Change*
Econ. Hist.	*Economic History*
Econ. Hist. Rev.	*Economic History Review*
Econ. J.	*Economic Journal*
Econ. Rec.	*Economic Record*
Econ. Rev.	*Economic Review*
Econ. Studies	*Economic Studies* (formerly *Journal of Economic Studies*)
Economica	*Economica*
Edinb. Med. J.	*Edinburgh Medical Journal*
Edinb. Rev.	*Edinburgh Review*
Electl. Rev.	*Electrical Review*
Electl. Superv.	*Electrical Supervisor*
Engineering	*Engineering*
Engl. Hist. Rev.	*English Historical Review*
Engl. Rev.	*English Review*
Envir. Engng.	*Environmental Engineering*
Essex Rev.	*Essex Review*
Eug. Rev.	*Eugenics Review*
Europ. Econ. Polit. Survey	*European Economic and Political Survey*
Explor. Entrepren. Hist.	*Explorations in Entrepreneurial History*
Farm Econ.	*Farm Economist*
Finanzarchiv	*Finanzarchiv*

Flints. Hist. Soc. Publs.	*Flintshire Historical Society Publications*
Fmr. Club J.	*Farmers' Club Journal*
Folk-lore	*Folk-lore*
Foreign Aff.	*Foreign Affairs*
Fortn. Rev.	*Fortnightly Review*
Fortnightly	*Fortnightly*
Fun. Dir.	*Funeral Director*
Gdn. Cities Tn. Plann.	*Garden Cities & Town Planning*
Geogrl. Mag.	*Geographical Magazine*
Good Words	*Good Words*
Hamps. Field Club Archaeol. Soc. Pap. Proc.	*Hampshire Field Club and Archaeological Society Papers and Proceedings*
Harv. Bus. Rev.	*Harvard Business Review*
Higher Educ. Rev.	*Higher Education Review*
Highway	*Highway: A Journal of Adult Education*
Hist. J.	*Historical Journal*
Hist. Soc. Lanc. Chesh. Trans.	*Historic Society of Lancashire and Cheshire Transactions*
Hist. Studies	*History Studies* (Buckland)
Hist. Today	*History Today*
Historian	*Historian*
History	*History*
Hlth. Soc. Welf.	*Health and Social Welfare*
Hon. Soc. Cymm. Trans.	*Honourable Society of Cymmrodorion Transactions*
Hospital	*Hospital*
Hug. Soc. Lond. Proc.	*Huguenot Society of London Proceedings*
Hum. Factor	*Human Factor*
Hum. Relat.	*Human Relations*
Hunter Archaeol. Soc. Trans.	*Hunter Archaeological Society Transactions*
Huntington Libr. Q.	*Huntington Library Quarterly*
I.M.A. Journal	*I.M.A. Journal* (Institutional Management Association)
IMF Staff Pap.	*IMF Staff Papers* (International Monetary Fund)
Ind. Labor Relat. Rev.	*Industrial and Labor Relations Review*
Ind. Law Rev.	*Industrial Law Review*
Ind. Law Soc. Bull.	*Industrial Law Society Bulletin*
Ind. Relat.	*Industrial Relations*
Ind. Relat. J.	*Industrial Relations Journal*
Ind. Relat. Res. Bull.	*Industrial Relations Research Bulletin* (Engineering Employers' Federation)
Ind. Saf. Surv.	*Industrial Safety Survey*
Ind. Tutor	*Industrial Tutor*
Indep. Rev.	*Independent Review*
India Q.	*India Quarterly*
Indian Econ. J.	*Indian Economic Journal*
Indian J. Econ.	*Indian Journal of Economics*
Indian J. Ind. Relat.	*Indian Journal of Industrial Relations*
Indian J. Labour Econ.	*Indian Journal of Labour Economics*
Ins. Act. Soc. Glasg. Trans.	*Insurance and Actuarial Society of Glasgow Transactions*
Inst. Actuar. Students' Soc. J.	*Institute of Actuaries Students' Society Journal*
Inst. Bankers J.	*Institute of Bankers Journal*
Inst. Br. Geogr. Publs.	*Institute of British Geographers Publications*
Inst. Hist. Res. Bull.	*Institute of Historical Research Bulletin*
Inst. Mar. Engrs. Trans.	*Institute of Marine Engineers Transactions*
Inst. Transp. J.	*Institute of Transport Journal*
Instn. Chem. Engrs. Trans.	*Institution of Chemical Engineers Transactions*
Instn. Engrs. Shipbldrs. Scotl. Trans.	*Institution of Engineers and Shipbuilders in Scotland Transactions*
Instn. Loco. Engrs. J.	*Institution of Locomotive Engineers Journal*
Instn. Wat. Engrs. J.	*Institution of Water Engineers Journal*

Int. Aff.	*International Affairs* (Moscow)
Int. Comp. Law Q.	*International and Comparative Law Quarterly*
Int. Inst. Labour Studies Bull.	*International Institute for Labour Studies Bulletin*
Int. J. Comp. Sociol.	*International Journal of Comparative Sociology*
Int. J. Nurs. Studies	*International Journal of Nursing Studies*
Int. J. Opin. Att. Res.	*International Journal of Opinion and Attitude Research*
Int. Labour Rev.	*International Labour Review*
Int. Rev. for Soc. Hist.	*International Review for Social History*
Int. Rev. of Soc. Hist.	*International Review of Social History*
Int. Soc. Sci. J.	*International Social Science Journal*
Int. Social. J.	*International Socialist Journal*
International	*International*
Irish Econ.	*Irish Economist*
Irish Hist. Studies	*Irish Historical Studies*
Isle Man Nat. Hist. Antiq. Soc. Proc.	*Isle of Man Natural History and Antiquarian Society Proceedings*
J. Agric. Econ.	*Journal of Agricultural Economics*
J. Am. Soc. Sci. Ass.	*Journal of the American Social Science Association*
J. Am. Statist. Ass.	*Journal of the American Statistical Association*
J. Appl. Psychol.	*Journal of Applied Psychology*
J. Br. Studies	*Journal of British Studies*
J. Bus. Law	*Journal of Business Law*
J. Common Mkt. Studies	*Journal of Common Market Studies*
J. Comp. Legisl.	*Journal of Comparative Legislation*
J. Contemp. Hist.	*Journal of Contemporary History*
J. Econ. Bus. Hist.	*Journal of Economic and Business History*
J. Econ. Hist.	*Journal of Economic History*
J. Econ. Studies	*Journal of Economic Studies*
J. Educ. Adm. Hist.	*Journal of Educational Administration and History*
J. H.M. Cust. Exc.	*Journal of H.M. Customs and Excise*
J. Hosp. Pharm.	*Journal of Hospital Pharmacy*
J. Ind. Econ.	*Journal of Industrial Economics*
J. Ind. Relat.	*Journal of Industrial Relations*
J. Inst. Bankers Ir.	*Journal of the Institute of Bankers in Ireland*
J. Inst. Lands. Archit.	*Journal of the Institute of Landscape Architects*
J. Law Econ.	*Journal of Law and Economics*
J. Leeds Univ. Min. Soc.	*Journal of the Leeds University Mining Society*
J. Med. Hist.	*Journal of Medical History*
J. Ment. Sci.	*Journal of Mental Science*
J. Mgmt. Studies	*Journal of Management Studies*
J. Mod. Hist.	*Journal of Modern History*
J. Polit.	*Journal of Politics*
J. Polit. Econ.	*Journal of Political Economy*
J. Publ. Adm.	*Journal of Public Administration* (later *Public Administration*)
J. Soc. Chirop.	*Journal of the Society of Chiropodists*
J. Soc. Sci.	*Journal of Social Science*
J. St. Med.	*Journal of State Medicine*
J. Transp. Econ. Policy	*Journal of Transport Economics and Policy*
J. Transp. Hist.	*Journal of Transport History*
Jew. Hist. Soc. Engl. Trans.	*Jewish Historical Society of England Transactions*
Journal	*Journal* (Institute of Journalists)
Journalist	*Journalist* (National Union of Journalists)
Kyklos	*Kyklos*
Kyoto Univ. Econ. Rev.	*Kyoto University Economic Review*
Labor Hist.	*Labor History*
Labor Law J.	*Labor Law Journal*
Labour Hist.	*Labour History*

Labour Mag.	*Labour Magazine*
Lanc. Chesh. Antiq. Soc. Trans.	*Lancashire and Cheshire Antiquarian Society Transactions*
Lancet	*Lancet*
Law Mag. Law Rev.	*Law Magazine and Law Review*
Leic. Lit. Phil. Soc. Trans.	*Leicester Literary and Philosophical Society Transactions*
Libr. Ass. Rec.	*Library Association Record*
Libr. Assist.	*Library Assistant*
Librn. Bk. World	*Librarian and Book World*
Lincs. Hist.	*Lincolnshire Historian* (Lincolnshire Local History Society)
Lincs. Mag.	*Lincolnshire Magazine* (Lindsey Local History Society)
Listener	*Listener*
Lloyds Bank Rev.	*Lloyds Bank Review*
Lodge Res. No. 2429 Leic. Trans.	*Lodge of Research No. 2429 Leicester Transactions* (Masonic)
Lond. Camb. Econ. (Serv.) Bull.	*London and Cambridge Economic (Service) Bulletin*
Lond. Middx. Archaeol. Soc. Trans.	*London and Middlesex Archaeological Society Transactions*
Lond. Q. Holb. Rev.	*London Quarterly and Holborn Review*
London Soc. J.	*London Society Journal*
Lough. J. Soc. Studies	*Loughborough Journal of Social Studies*
Louis. Law Rev.	*Louisiana Law Review*
Lpool. Econ. Statist. Soc. Trans.	*Liverpool Economic and Statistical Society Transactions*
Mac. Mag.	*Macmillan's Magazine*
Manchr. Sch.	*Manchester School*
Manchr. Statist. Soc. Trans.	*Manchester Statistical Society Transactions*
Mamp. Appl. Psychol.	*Manpower and Applied Psychology*
Mar. Mirror	*Mariner's Mirror* (Society for Nautical Research)
Marx Meml. Libr. Q. Bull.	*Marx Memorial Library Quarterly Bulletin*
Marxism Today	*Marxism Today*
Marxist Q.	*Marxist Quarterly*
Med. J. Aust.	*Medical Journal of Australia*
Med. Offr.	*Medical Officer*
Med. Wld.	*Medical World*
Mem. Proc. Manchr. Lit. Phil. Soc.	*Memoirs and Proceedings of the Manchester Literary and Philosophical Society*
Merion. Hist. Rec. Soc. J.	*Merioneth Historical Record Society Journal*
Mers. Ass. Mason. Res. Trans.	*Merseyside Association for Masonic Research Transactions*
Method. Times	*Methodist Times*
Mgmt. Int.	*Management International*
Mgmt. Today	*Management Today*
Millg. M.	*Millgate Monthly*
Middx. Archaeol. Soc. Trans.	*Middlesex Archaeological Society Transactions*
Min. Electl. Mech. Engr.	*Mining Electrical and Mechanical Engineer*
Minerva	*Minerva*
Minist. Labour Gaz.	*Ministry of Labour Gazette*
Misc. Lat.	*Miscellanea Latomorum*
Mod. Law Rev.	*Modern Law Review*
Month	*Month*
Mon. Labor Rev.	*Monthly Labor Review*
Mon. Music. Rec.	*Monthly Musical Record*
Mon. Rev.	*Monthly Review*
Mon. Rev. Lond. Joint City Midl. Bank	*Monthly Review of London Joint City and Midland Bank*
Moor. Wall Street	*Moorgate and Wall Street*
Mot. Trad.	*Motor Trader*
Music. Times	*Musical Times*
Musicians' J.	*Musicians' Journal*
Mys. Univ. Half-y. J.	*Mysore University Half-yearly Journal*
N. Am. Rev.	*North American Review*
NE. Group Study Labour Hist. Bull.	*North East Group for the Study of Labour History Bulletin*

Natn. Inst. Econ. Rev.	*National Institute Economic Review*
Natn. Inst. Ind. Psychol. J.	*National Institute of Industrial Psychology Journal*
Natn. Libr. Wales J.	*National Library of Wales Journal*
Natn. Prov. Bank Rev.	*National Provincial Bank Review*
Natn. Rev.	*National Review*
Natsopa J.	*Natsopa Journal*
Nature	*Nature*
Naut. Mag.	*Nautical Magazine*
Neath Antiq. Soc. Trans.	*Neath Antiquarian Society Transactions*
New Left Rev.	*New Left Review*
New Reas.	*New Reasoner*
New Rev.	*New Review*
New Soc.	*New Society*
New States.	*New Statesman*
Newc. Soc. Trans.	*Newcomen Society Transactions*
News Br. Coun. Staff Ass.	*News from the British Council Staff Association*
Nineteenth Century	*Nineteenth Century (and After)*
Northamps. Past Pres.	*Northamptonshire Past and Present*
Norw. Sci. Goss. Club Rep. Proc.	*Norwich Science Gossip Club Report of Proceedings*
Notes	*Notes* (Association of Head Postmasters)
Notes Quer.	*Notes and Queries*
Notts. Install. Mast. Lodge No. 3593 Trans.	*Notts. Installed Masters' Lodge No. 3593 Transactions* (Masonic)
Nth. Hist.	*Northern History*
Nurs. Times	*Nursing Times*
Occup. Psychol.	*Occupational Psychology*
Off. Archit. Plann.	*Official Architecture and Planning*
Oil Gas Fir.	*Oil & Gas Firing*
Old Corn.	*Old Cornwall*
Old Edinb. Club Book	*Old Edinburgh Club Book*
Old Staff. Soc. Trans.	*Old Stafford Society Transactions*
Oper. Bldr.	*Operative Builder*
Operat. Res. Q.	*Operational Research Quarterly*
Optician	*Optician*
Oxf. Econ. Pap.	*Oxford Economic Papers*
Oxf. Univ. Inst. (Econ.) Statist. Bull.	*Oxford University Institute of (Economics and) Statistics Bulletin*
Oxoniensia	*Oxoniensia*
PEP Broad.	*PEP Broadsheet*
Pers. Mgmt.	*Personnel Management*
Pers. Psychol.	*Personnel Psychology*
Peterb. Nat. Hist. Sci. Archaeol. Soc. A. Rep.	*Peterborough Natural History, Scientific and Archaeological Society Annual Report*
Physiotherapy	*Physiotherapy*
Planning	*Planning*
Plebs	*Plebs*
Plym. Instn. Devon Corn. Nat. Hist. Soc. A. Rep. Trans.	*Plymouth Institution and Devon and Cornwall Natural History Society Annual Report and Transactions*
Polit. Q.	*Political Quarterly*
Polit. Sci. Q.	*Political Science Quarterly*
Polit. Studies	*Political Studies*
Politico	*Politico*
Populat. Studies	*Population Studies*
Pos. Rev.	*Positivist Review*
Prim. Method. Q. Rev.	*Primitive Methodist Quarterly Review*
Pris. Serv. J.	*Prison Service Journal*
Probation	*Probation*
Prof. Engr.	*Professional Engineer*

Prof. Geogr.	*Professional Geographer*
Progress	*Progress*
Progress Civic Soc. Ind.	*Progress, Civil, Social, Industrial: Organ of the British Institute of Social Service*
Publ. Adm.	*Public Administration*
Publ. Adm. (Sydney)	*Public Administration* (Sydney)
Publ. Fin.	*Public Finance*
Publ. Offr.	*Public Officer*
Puritan	*Puritan*
Parl. Aff.	*Parliamentary Affairs*
Past Pres.	*Past and Present*
Q. J. Econ.	*Quarterly Journal of Economics*
Q. J. Int. Ass. Unempl.	*Quarterly Journal of the International Association on Unemployment*
Q. Rev.	*Quarterly Review*
Q. Rev. Econ. Bus.	*Quarterly Review of Economics and Business*
Qual. Engr.	*Quality Engineer*
R. Corn. Polytech. Soc. Rep.	*Royal Cornwall Polytechnic Society Report*
R. Hist. Soc. Trans.	*Royal Historical Society Transactions*
R. Inst. Br. Archit. J.	*Royal Institute of British Architects* (later *RIBA Journal*)
R. Inst. Publ. Hlth. Hyg. J.	*Royal Institute of Public Health and Hygiene Journal*
R. Instn. Chart. Survey. J.	*Royal Institution of Chartered Surveyors Journal*
R. Instn. Chart. Survey. Trans.	*Royal Institution of Chartered Surveyors Transactions*
R. Instn. Corn. J.	*Royal Institution of Cornwall Journal*
R. Phil. Soc. Glasg. Proc.	*Royal Philosophical Society of Glasgow Proceedings*
R. Sanit. Inst. J.	*Royal Sanitary Institute Journal*
R. Soc. Arts J.	*(Royal) Society of Arts Journal*
R. Soc. Med. Proc.	*Royal Society of Medicine Proceedings*
R. Statist. Soc. J.	*Royal Statistical Society Journal*
RIBA J.	*RIBA Journal* (formerly *Royal Institute of British Architects Journal*)
Race	*Race*
Rec. Bucks.	*Records of Buckinghamshire*
Red Tape	*Red Tape*
Reg. Studies	*Regional Studies*
Relat. Ind.	*Relations Industrielles*
Res Publ.	*Res Publica*
Rev. Econ. Prog.	*Review of Economic Progress*
Rev. Econ. Statist.	*Review of Economics and Statistics*
Rev. Econ. Studies	*Review of Economic Studies*
Rev. Polit.	*Review of Politics*
Rev. Revs.	*Review of Reviews*
Review	*Review* (Society of Telecommunication Engineers)
Review	*Review* (United Trade Press)
Right Angle	*Right Angle*
Roch. Lit. Soc. Trans.	*Rochdale Literary Society Transactions*
Round Table	*Round Table*
S. Afr. J. Econ.	*South African Journal of Economics*
S. Shields Archaeol. Hist. Soc. Pap.	*South Shields Archaeological and Historical Society Papers*
S.-West. Soc. Sci. Q.	*Southwestern Social Science Quarterly*
Scand. Econ. Hist. Rev.	*Scandinavian Economic History Review*
Schoolmaster	*Schoolmaster*
Sci. Bus.	*Scientific Business*
Sci. Soc.	*Science and Society*
Sci. Wkr.	*Scientific Worker*
Scientia	*Scientia*
Scott. Geogr. Mag.	*Scottish Geographical Magazine*
Scott. Hist. Rev.	*Scottish Historical Review*
Scott. J. Polit. Econ.	*Scottish Journal of Political Economy*

Shrops. Archaeol. Soc. Trans.	*Shropshire Archaeological Society Transactions*
Soc. Antiq. Newc. Tyne Proc.	*Society of Antiquaries of Newcastle-upon-Tyne Proceedings*
Soc. Archit. J.	*Society of Architects Journal*
Soc. Clerks Urb. Distr. Counc. Off. J.	*Society of Clerks of Urban District Councils Official Journal*
Soc. Econ. Studies	*Social and Economic Studies*
Soc. Forces	*Social Forces*
Soc. Res.	*Social Research*
Soc. Sci.	*Social Science* (Philadelphia)
Soc. Serv. Rev.	*Social Service Review*
Soc. Study Labour Hist. Bull.	*Society for the Study of Labour History Bulletin*
Social. Reg.	*Socialist Register*
Social. Rev.	*Socialist Review*
Sociol. Rev.	*Sociological Review*
Sociology	*Sociology*
Som. Archaeol. Nat. Hist. Soc. Proc.	*Somersetshire Archaeological and Natural History Society Proceedings*
Som. Mast. Lodge No. 3746 Trans.	*Somerset Masters' Lodge No. 3746 Transactions* (Masonic)
St. George	*Saint George*
St. Service	*State Service*
Sth. Econ. J.	*Southern Economic Journal*
Statist. Soc. Inq. Soc. Ir. J.	*Statistical and Social Inquiry Society of Ireland Journal* (then *Dublin Statistical Society Journal*)
Supervisor	*Supervisor*
Survey. Instn. Trans.	*Surveyors Institution Transactions*
Sx. Archaeol. Colln.	*Sussex Archaeological Collections*
Sx. County Mag.	*Sussex County Magazine*
Sx. Notes Quer.	*Sussex Notes and Queries*
Taxes	*Taxes*
Tech. J.	*Technical Journal*
Text. Hist.	*Textile History*
Theosophist	*Theosophist*
Thores. Soc. Publs.	*Thoresby Society Publications*
Thoro. Soc. Trans.	*Thoroton Society Transactions*
Three Banks Rev.	*Three Banks Review*
Tijdschr. Econ. Soc. Geogr.	*Tijdschrift voor Economische en Sociale Geografie*
Trade Un. Regist.	*Trade Union Register*
Trans. Soc. Engrs.	*Transactions of the Society of Engineers*
Transp. Sal. Staff J.	*Transport Salaried Staff Journal*
Tribune	*Tribune*
Twentieth Century	*Twentieth Century*
U.S. Bur. Labor Bull.	*U.S. Bureau of Labor Bulletin*
Unit. Par. Mag.	*United Parish Magazine*
Univ. Birm. Hist. J.	*University of Birmingham Historical Journal*
Univ. Bull.	*University Bulletin*
Univ. Minn. Ind. Relat. Center Bull.	*University of Minnesota Industrial Relations Center Bulletin*
Univ. Qd. Law J.	*University of Queensland Law Journal*
Univ. Tor. Q.	*University of Toronto Quarterly*
Urb. Studies	*Urban Studies*
Vic. Studies	*Victorian Studies*
Vjschr. Soz. Wirt.	*Vierteljahrschrift für Sozial- und Wirtschaftsgeschichte*
Voc. Asp.	*Vocational Aspect of Secondary and Further Education*
Welsh. Hist. Rev.	*Welsh History Review*
Welt. Arch.	*Weltwirtschaftliches Archiv*
West. Econ. J.	*Western Economic Journal*
West. Polit. Q.	*Western Political Quarterly*
Westm. Bank Rev.	*Westminster Bank Review*
Westm. Rev.	*Westminster Review*
Whit. Bull.	*Whitley Bulletin*

Wilts. Mag.	*Wiltshire Magazine*
Wise. Rev.	*Wiseman Review*
Wld. Med.	*World Medicine*
Wool. Nat. Field Club Trans.	*Woolhope Naturalists' Field Club Transactions*
Yale Rev.	*Yale Review*
Yorks. Archaeol. J.	*Yorkshire Archaeological Journal*
Yorks. Bull. Econ. Soc. Res.	*Yorkshire Bulletin of Economic and Social Research*
Yorks. Dial. Soc. Trans.	*Yorkshire Dialect Society Transactions*
Yr. Bk. Educ.	*Year Book of Education*
Z. Angl. Am.	*Zeitschrift für Anglistik und Amerikanistik*

INTRODUCTION

Sidney Webb, one of the greatest students of industrial relations, was an ardent supporter of bibliographies. He urged would-be researchers

> to start by compiling a list of books, pamphlets, and reports bearing on the chosen subject. The mere survey of their titles, publication dates, and tables of contents is a necessary preliminary to every voyage of discovery after new truth. The second step is – not reading through these innumerable volumes, all of them more or less obsolescent or at any rate of exhausted fertility – but skipping lightly over their pages, pencil in hand, to note down all the hints and hypotheses, cavilling objections and irresponsible interrogations that will arise in the investigator's mind as he turns irreverently, or even mockingly, over the pages in which the craziest cranks have printed their fancies and venerable 'authorities' enshrined their 'standard' doctrines. Then, and not till then, is the researcher in a position effectively to begin his serious business of investigation for the discovery of new truth.[1]

In spite of Sidney Webb's advocacy of bibliographies, few have been published on British industrial relations, and most of those which do exist are very restricted in scope and less than comprehensive within their scope. The Society for the Study of Labour History, for example, has published a number of bibliographies in its *Bulletin*, but most of these are confined to sources on labour history; so is Frow and Katanka's *The History of British Trade Unionism: A Select Bibliography*. The Institute of Personnel Management periodically issues *Personnel Management: A Bibliography*, but it mainly lists recently published items and ignores several areas of interest to industrial relations specialists. Hepple, Neeson, and O'Higgins, *A Bibliography of the Literature on British and Irish Labour Law* (London: Mansell, 1975) is, as its title suggests, largely confined to the legal aspects of industrial relations. Allen's *International Bibliography of Trade Unionism* covers a wide range of countries and consequently is able to devote only a few pages to Britain. Gottschalk *et al.*'s *British Industrial Relations: An Annotated Bibliography* is a useful guide to the more recent literature, but is highly selective and contains few references to older works. In short, there is no comprehensive, retrospective bibliography of the literature on British industrial relations.

The present volume seeks to provide such a bibliography. It does so in an attempt to reduce inefficiency and ignorance. In the past, industrial relations specialists have had to spend a great deal of time and energy compiling bibliographies for their own use. In doing so, they have often unwittingly duplicated the efforts of others, and, duplicated or not, their efforts have often been unsatisfactory. For the literature on industrial relations is published in a wide variety of forms and in the journals of a multitude of disciplines and organisations, and a single individual, or even a research team, has rarely had the resources to search all these sources thoroughly. Thanks to the Social Science Research Council, the necessary resources have now been provided.

Anyone who sets out to compile a bibliography is confronted with three basic questions. How to define its scope? How to obtain the references? And how to arrange them? If a bibliography is to be of maximum use, it must make clear how these questions have been answered.

SCOPE

Subject scope

Industrial relations has no universally agreed definition of its scope and content. The subject has not been characterised, like some other fields of study, by a central body of analytical concepts and systematic theories. Instead, it has borrowed concepts, theories, and techniques from a wide

[1] 'Introduction', *A London Bibliography of the Social Sciences*, I (London: London School of Economics and Political Science, 1931), v.

range of disciplines, including anthropology, economics, history, law, political science, psychology, and sociology. This eclecticism has made the subject's boundaries uncertain and unstable. They have tended at one time or another, as Chamberlain has observed, to include 'all of those whose interests are touched by labor, whether we think of labor as a functional task, the agent who performs the function, an informal primary society of which he is a part, the formal organizations based on him and his counterparts, a social class, an historical force, a political party, or the subject of governmental regulations'.[2]

A bibliography covering all aspects of the phenomenon of labour would be of enormous length. It would also be of doubtful utility. For labour 'is at one and the same time so universal in its presence and yet so varied in its significance', to quote Chamberlain once again, that 'as a single enveloping interest it is without content, and no more useful in organizing knowledge than would be, for example, the effort to relate the study of money in whatever context it is found'.[3] If the study of industrial relations is to proceed in a coherent fashion, and if a bibliography of its literature is to be of manageable length, then its definition must specify a general problem or an analytical focus around which learning can be meaningfully organised.

In this bibliography the subject of industrial relations is defined as the study of *all* aspects of job regulation – the process of making and administering the rules which regulate or control employment relationships.[4] This definition fully recognises the interdisciplinary nature of industrial relations; it does not regard any of the contributing disciplines as having a monopoly of the truth. At the same time, it specifies a quite distinct field of study whose boundaries are not coterminous with those of any single discipline or combination of disciplines. Indeed, as defined here, industrial relations is both narrower and broader in scope than those subjects, such as industrial sociology, industrial psychology, and labour economics, upon which it draws. It is narrower than these subjects because they are interested in explaining phenomena other than job regulation; it is broader because no other subject is interested in, or capable of, explaining all aspects of job regulation. Thus the bibliography includes literature from all of the disciplines which contribute to industrial relations but not all of the literature from any of them.

In addition, by emphasising job regulation as the central concern of industrial relations and thereby raising the fundamental question of *who* regulates *what* and *how*, the definition stresses the political nature of industrial relations phenomena and suggests that they can be fully comprehended only by taking into account the distribution of power within industry and within the wider society. It rejects the idea that the various aspects of job regulation can necessarily be explained by examining a narrowly conceived set of 'industrial relations variables'. All aspects of human behaviour and the environment in which it occurs must be treated as being *potentially* related to job regulation. But the bibliography includes only that literature which demonstrates that its subject matter is *actually* related to job regulation.

Geographical and linguistic scope

The bibliography includes that literature which relates to England, Wales, Scotland, and Northern Ireland. It also includes material on what is now the Republic of Ireland, but it cannot claim to be as comprehensive here as for the other countries. The title of the bibliography reflects this incompleteness by referring only to British industrial relations.

Although the borders of the above countries are more precise than the conceptual boundaries of 'job regulation', the geographical scope of the bibliography is not entirely unproblematical. Not all studies of industrial relations deal with a single country. Many of them adopt a comparative perspective, and many of these include the United Kingdom within their purview. But they often do so only in a cursory fashion. The International Labour Office, for example, publishes numerous works which are primarily concerned with developing countries but which make passing comparisons

[2] Neil W. Chamberlain, 'Issues for the Future', *Proceedings of the Thirteenth Annual Meeting of the Industrial Relations Research Association*, ed. Gerald G. Somers (Madison, Wisconsin: IRRA, 1961), 101.

[3] Ibid., 103.

[4] This definition obviously derives from the work of Dunlop and Flanders. See John T. Dunlop, *Industrial Relations Systems* (New York: Holt, 1958), and Allan Flanders, *Industrial Relations: What is Wrong with the System?* (London: Faber, 1965). Their work has been attacked because it relies upon the much-criticised notion that industrial relations phenomena constitute a 'social system'. See the sources discussed in G. S. Bain and H. A. Clegg, 'A Strategy for Industrial Relations Research in Great Britain', *British Journal of Industrial Relations*, XII (March 1974), 91–113. The weaknesses of the systems concept are not an argument against defining industrial relations in terms of job regulation, however, for the two ideas are not mutually dependent; the one can be advanced without the other. And the concept of job regulation is put forward here quite independently of the notion of a 'system' of industrial relations.

with the United Kingdom as the 'prototype' industrial nation. Such works are excluded from this bibliography, but comparative works which deal with the United Kingdom in a systematic and detailed way are included.

In contrast with comparative works which deal with industrial relations in more than one country, there are others, such as general theoretical works and works dealing with the methodology and teaching of the subject, which are virtually 'countryless'. In general, these works have been excluded from this bibliography unless they explicitly draw upon British experience; for example, Dunlop's *Industrial Relations Systems* is included, but Walton and McKersie's *A Behavioral Theory of Labor Negotiations* (New York: McGraw-Hill, 1965) is excluded. To have done otherwise would have produced a bibliography of unmanageable length and of a non-British character. In any case, the major theoretical works in industrial relations are generally well known to scholars in the field, and details about them can easily be obtained from a number of existing bibliographies and from such sources as the *Library Catalog of the New York State School of Industrial and Labor Relations, Cornell University* (Boston: G. K. Hall, 1967–).

Regardless of whether a work deals with the United Kingdom in isolation or in conjunction with other countries, it is included in this bibliography only if it appears in English. To have included even the major foreign-language publications on British industrial relations would have demanded a wider range of linguistic skills – at least French, German, Italian, Russian, and Swedish – than those possessed by the present compilers, would have resulted in a partial and superficial coverage of the relevant literature, and would have greatly increased the length of the bibliography. In short, if there is a case for bringing together the foreign-language publications on British industrial relations, it is a specialist task which must be undertaken by another bibliography.

Chronological scope

The bibliography includes literature published between 1880 and 1970 inclusively. Material published after 1970 will be listed in supplements which will be issued from time to time. Material published before 1880 is generally of a different character from later material: it is amorphous and tends to be difficult to separate from the general historical and philosophical material of the period. It is also much more difficult to trace because the subject catalogue of the British Library begins only in 1880. Hence listing material published before 1880, like that published in foreign languages, is a specialist task for a separate bibliography.

Occasionally, however, titles published before 1880 and after 1970 have been included. The reports of the Royal Commission on the Organization and Rules of Trade Unions and Other Associations (1867–9) and the Royal Commission on Labour Laws (1874–5) are listed even though they were published before 1880. And where a work has been published in numerous editions, as have many legal texts and commentaries, the first edition is mentioned even if it is pre-1880. Similarly, all the reports of the National Board for Prices and Incomes are listed even though some of them were published in 1971.

Categories of material

The bibliography covers a variety of forms of publication. It has attempted to include all printed books which are relevant, including collections and individual contributions to collections. Where appropriate, separate entries have been made for individual chapters in general works. The coverage of printed pamphlets, which can be identified in the bibliography by their pagination, is much more selective. Only the more substantial of these have been included; those of an ephemeral and strictly propagandist nature have been excluded.

In general, only articles, including major review articles but not short reviews, in 'learned' journals broadly defined have been included. But there are certain exceptions to this rule. A number of important articles on various aspects of British industrial relations were published during the late nineteenth and early twentieth centuries in such 'general' periodicals as the *Contemporary Review* and the *English Review*, and these have been included. Relevant articles in *New Society*, which, strictly, does not fall within the range of journals to be scanned, were included because of their coverage of research in progress or recently completed. The more substantial articles in bank reviews were also included, as were selected historical articles in union journals. But, in general, articles in trade union and employer association journals, house journals, and trade journals; newspapers and popular journals; such business and professional journals as *Personnel Management*, *Industrial Society*, and *Management Today*; such weeklies as *The Economist*, the *New Statesman*, and the *Spectator*; and such monthlies as *Socialist Commentary*, *Labour Monthly*, and *Crossbow* have been excluded. A more precise idea of the range of journals which the bibliography covers can be obtained from the preceding list of periodical titles.

Official publications on British industrial relations are voluminous. As well as British and Irish government publications, such as the reports of royal commissions, courts of inquiry, the

National Board for Prices and Incomes, the Commission on Industrial Relations, special parliamentary and departmental committees, and selected publications of various ministries and departments, the bibliography has included the relevant publications of such international bodies as the United Nations, the International Labour Office, and the Organisation for Economic Co-operation and Development. Routine periodical reports of government bodies, such as articles in the *Department of Employment Gazette*, annual reports, and statistical returns,[5] have generally been excluded; so have the reports of the proceedings of both Houses of Parliament; reports of judicial proceedings (but not case books on labour law); bills, acts, statutory instruments, wages regulation orders, administrative circulars, and consultative documents; the awards of the Industrial Court; the decisions of industrial tribunals, the National Insurance Commissioners, and the Registrar of Friendly Societies and Trade Unions; and the reports of such agencies as the Civil Service Arbitration Tribunal, the National Arbitration Tribunal, and the Industrial Disputes Tribunal.[6]

Trade unions, employers' associations, and joint organisations produce a wide range of 'primary' materials, including general business and legal papers, financial statements, and correspondence; rule books and constitutions; minutes of meetings; proceedings of conferences; periodic reports of various committees and officers; newspapers and journals;[7] press releases; collective agreements; and miscellaneous ephemera such as broadsheets presenting an organisation's case in a dispute and pamphlets discussing various aspects of an organisation's policy. Such material has been excluded from the bibliography.[8] Also excluded are primary materials produced by individual firms: documents concerned with apprenticeship and training schemes and pension and welfare arrangements; contracts of service; minutes of meetings and negotiations with trade unions; correspondence with trade unions; staff handbooks; house journals;[9] and reports on various aspects of a company's industrial relations policy.

But the official histories and anniversary souvenirs of trade unions, employers' associations, and union-employer organisations have generally been included; so have such significant union publications as the Trades Union Congress's *Trade Union Structure and Closer Unity*. Similarly, selected publications of political parties, such as the report of the Labour Party's Working Party on Industrial Democracy, the Conservative Party's *Fair Deal at Work*, and the Liberal Party's *Partners at Work*, have been included, but not ephemeral material such as election manifestos and propaganda broadsheets.[10]

All unpublished material, except theses and dissertations accepted for higher degrees, has generally been excluded; so have synopses of reports and documents. Also excluded are all iconographic, photographic, and cinematic materials; gramophone records and tapes; music and songs; and novels, plays, poems, and other fictional writing. But biographies and autobiographies have been included, particularly those of trade union leaders and those of workers describing their conditions of work.

METHOD OF COMPILATION

Having indicated the nature of the references included in the bibliography, the next task is to explain how they were obtained. To begin with,

[5] But more discursive statistical works have been included. See Part One, II of this bibliography. See also G. S. Bain and G. B. Woolven, 'The Primary Materials of British Industrial Relations', *British Journal of Industrial Relations*, IX (November 1971), 402–4 for a discussion of guides to labour statistics.

[6] See Bain and Woolven (1971), ibid., 399–402, for a discussion of the bibliographical guides to state records and reports. Further information about many of the British government publications listed in this bibliography can be found in P. and G. Ford, *Select List of British Parliamentary Papers 1833–1899* (Oxford: Blackwell, 1953); *idem, A Breviate of Parliamentary Papers* (Oxford: Blackwell, 1951–61) which covers the period 1900–54 in three volumes; and P. and G. Ford and Diana Marshallsay, *Select List of British Parliamentary Papers 1955–1964* (Shannon: Irish University Press, 1970).

[7] See R. Harrison, G. B. Woolven, and R. Duncan, *The Warwick Guide to British Labour Periodicals, 1790–1970* (Hassocks: Harvester Press, 1977).

[8] See Bain and Woolven (1971), op. cit., 392–9, for a discussion of the bibliographical guides to the records and reports of trade unions, employers' associations, joint organisations, and individual firms.

[9] See *British House Journals*, published by the British Association of Industrial Editors in 1956 and 1962; the first edition contains a list of almost eight hundred journals, while the second edition has over one thousand entries. The *Newspaper Press Directory* (1846–) also contains a list of house journals; for example, the 1968 edition lists approximately two thousand of them.

[10] Some of this material is listed in a *Bibliography* published by the Labour Party in 1967 and in G. B. Woolven, *Publications of the Independent Labour Party 1893–1932* (Sheffield: Society for the Study of Labour History, 1977), and some of it is reproduced in F. W. S. Craig (comp.), *British General Election Manifestos, 1918–1966* (Chichester: Political Reference Publications, 1970).

an outline of the proposed nature and scope of the bibliography was sent to the members of the British Universities Industrial Relations Association, the Society for the Study of Labour History, and the Industrial Law Society, as well as other selected individuals and organisations, asking for comments and suggestions. Their replies were analysed and comments on particular aspects were collected together for future reference. They prompted various modifications in the proposed scope of the bibliography and proved most useful in guiding the compilation in many of the more difficult areas.

The next step was to make a list of the major sources of industrial relations literature.[11] Then a systematic search of these sources was begun. The main periodicals in the field were scanned. The major bibliographies, indexes, and library catalogues (e.g. *A London Bibliography of the Social Sciences*; the *British National Bibliography*; the *Library Catalog of the New York State School of Industrial and Labor Relations, Cornell University*; the *International Bibliography of Sociology*; and the *Index to Economic Journals*) were examined, as were a vast number of smaller bibliographies on various aspects of industrial relations and related subjects. Finally, in order to obtain details of publications not readily available through existing sources, a questionnaire was sent to approximately six thousand trade unions, professional associations, employers' associations, and union-employer organisations requesting information regarding material published about them.

Bibliographies, indexes, library catalogues, and questionnaire replies are not infallible guides to the literature which they list; on the contrary, they often contain errors and inconsistencies. Hence once the various sources had been combed, many of the resulting references had to be checked further to complete bibliographical descriptions, to remove doubts about the accuracy of information provided, or to ascertain the contents when titles did not give a sufficiently clear indication of whether the work came within the scope of the bibliography or of the subject heading under which it should be classified.

References were checked either by obtaining a 'second opinion' from a reputable source such as the *British National Bibliography*, the Library of Congress *National Union Catalog*, and the catalogues of the British Library and the British Library of Political and Economic Science; or by personal examination in a wide variety of libraries in London, Oxford, and Manchester; or through correspondence with authors, publishers, librarians, and others. At the end, however, a number of references remained unverified. Many of these were excluded from the bibliography for they appeared to be abbreviated or incorrect descriptions of works already included, extracts from such works, or announcements of projects which had never been completed. Unverified references which did not appear to fall into any of these categories and which possessed enough detail to suggest that they actually represented published works were included, however, in the hope that others might know of them and supply details which could be included in future supplements to the bibliography. Undoubtedly, errors remain. But they should not be so numerous or so gross as to hinder users of the bibliography from finding what they want.

[11] Many of these sources are given in G. S. Bain and G. B. Woolven, 'The Literature of Labour Economics and Industrial Relations: A Guide To Its Sources', *Industrial Relations Journal*, 1 (Summer 1970), 30–42.

ARRANGEMENT AND USE

Once the references had been accumulated and verified, the final stage of the compilation began: the arrangement of the entries. To begin with, they were grouped into broad subject categories. These categories were then subdivided, resubdivided, and rearranged until the detailed scheme described in the contents pages of this bibliography finally emerged. A classification scheme and the literature it classifies are mutually dependent; the one influences the other. On the one hand, the classification scheme used here has tried to respect the interdisciplinary nature of industrial relations by using categories which reflect as little as possible the assumptions and methodologies of the particular disciplines from which the literature stems. On the other hand, the classification scheme has tried to avoid forcing the literature into categories in which it does not comfortably fit.

Within subject classes two basic ways of arranging entries were considered: alphabetically by author and chronologically by date of publication. Those who commented on the proposed nature and scope of the bibliography were about equally divided as to the merits of the two systems. The compilers finally decided to arrange the entries within each subject class by year of publication and, within year of publication, alphabetically by author. Since an author index is provided, a chronological arrangement provides a useful additional perspective of the literature. The author index includes single authors, joint authors, names of corporate bodies when acting as authors, compilers, translators, contributors to collections, and chairmen of government committees and commissions when the reports of these bodies might be identified by the chairman's name. The index sometimes gives more information about authors, including titles acquired as at 1970, than do individual entries in the bibliography.

The entries are numbered in sequence throughout the bibliography and, where an entry covers more than one subject, its serial number has been used to make the necessary cross-references. Cross-references from one section of the bibliography to particular items in another section (e.g. *See also*: 129, 351, and 876) appear at the end of sections; cross-references between entire sections of the bibliography (e.g. See also Part Six, II, D, 2, and Part Six, III, B) appear at the beginning of sections. Some sections also have an introductory note which indicates their scope and how they relate to other sections of the bibliography. Anyone using the bibliography should, in Ottley's phrase, 'examine the genus as well as the species'.[12] In other words, the user should examine not only the section dealing with the subject in question but also the general sections from which that subject derives, not forgetting that Part One, IV lists numerous items which provide information on virtually every topic covered by the bibliography.

The form of entry for each item in the bibliography is a modified version of the standard catalogue entry according to the *Anglo-American Cataloging Rules*. A complete reference for a book or pamphlet gives details of author, title, place of publication, publisher, date of publication, pagination or number of volumes if more than one, and, where applicable, a series note. A complete reference for a periodical article gives details of author, title of article, title of periodical, series note where applicable, volume number, issue number, date of publication, and pagination.

The names of authors are given in full whenever possible; so are the titles of articles, books, pamphlets, and theses. The titles of periodicals are given in an abbreviated form based on principles suggested by the British Standards Institution,[13] and a list of the abbreviations used is provided at the beginning of the bibliography. Where the author and the publisher are the same, as with many publications of corporate bodies such as the Trades Union Congress, the author's name is not normally repeated in full in the imprint as publisher. Her (His) Majesty's Stationery Office and the United States Government Printing Office are usually abbreviated as H.M.S.O. and U.S.G.P.O. when they appear in the imprint of a work. If the place of publication on the publisher is unknown, the information is simply omitted; the abbreviations 'n.p.' and 'n.pub.' are not used. In those few entries where no publication date at all could be provided, the abbreviation 'n.d.' is used. If a work is part of a series, the details of the series are given in round brackets. The abbreviations 'n.s.' and 'o.s.' are used before the volume number of a periodical to indicate 'new series' and 'old series'.

UPPER CASE roman numerals are used to indicate the specific volume number of a work or periodical; lower case roman numerals are used to indicate the number of preliminary pages in a work. Arabic numerals are used to indicate the total number of volumes in a given work, the number of pages of text, and the issue number of a periodical. Square brackets are used to indicate information (e.g. name of author, date or place of publication, publisher) which has been supplied by the compilers of the bibliography.

In a bibliography in which the entries within each subject class are arranged chronologically, each entry must be placed under a particular year. But the date of publication cannot always be precisely established. It is expressed in one of the following ways:

1890 indicates that the date of publication is given and is correct.

[1890?91] indicates that the date of publication is either 1890 or 1891.

[1890–91] in the case of a multi-volume work indicates that publication spanned these years.[14]

1890 [i.e. 1891] indicates that the date of publication is given as 1890 in the book but that it was actually published in 1891.

[1890] indicates that although the date of publication is not given in the book, it is certain from internal or other evidence that the book was in fact published in 1890.

[1890?] indicates that there is some evidence to suggest that 1890 is a possible date of publication but it is not certain.

[189–] indicates that the date of publication is within the decade.

[*c.* 1890] indicates that the date of publication is within a narrow range of years on either side of 1890.

[12] George Ottley, *A Bibliography of British Railway History* (London: Allen and Unwin, 1965), 17.

[13] See *Recommendations for the Abbreviation of Titles of Periodicals*, BS4148 (London: B.S.I., 1967).

[14] This form occurs particularly in relation to theses, many of which have been taken from Aslib's *Index to Theses Accepted for Higher Degrees in the Universities of Great Britain and Ireland*. As each volume of this work covers theses accepted in a particular academic year it has for the most part been necessary to give the date o a thesis in this form.

[*c.* 1890?] indicates that there is little evidence for the date of publication but that it is within a fairly wide range of years on either side of 1890.

[19—] and [19—?] are two special cases of the above forms. [19—] indicates that there is little evidence for the date of publication but that it is within a fairly wide range of years after 1900. Similarly, [19—?] indicates that the date of publication is within a fairly wide range of years around the turn of the century.

Dates are ordered as follows: [1890], [1890?], [*c.* 1890], and [*c.* 1890?] are all filed as 1890; [1890?91] and [1890–91] are filed after 1890 and before 1891; 1890 [i.e. 1891] is filed as 1891; [189–] is filed before 1890; similarly, [19—] and [19—?] are filed before 1900; those few publications which are completely undated are filed before all others in their section of the bibliography. In filing periodicals only the year of publication is considered; the day, month, etc. are ignored.

The word-by-word system of alphabetization is used for filing references within year of publication and for ordering entries in the author index.[15] Anonymous works are filed under the first word of the title (ignoring the definite or indefinite article); the abbreviation 'Anon.' is not used. Where pseudonyms have been used, the author's true name, where known, is given in square brackets.

Annotations are used to note the qualification or position of an author of, for example, an autobiography or an official union history; the relationship of a work to other works (e.g. sequels and replies); a change of title; the individual titles of a multi-volume work; the circumstances of writing (e.g. a memorial lecture); the contents of a work by several authors; and the translator of a work. Annotations are also used to elaborate a title which is not sufficiently clear or explicit.

[15] See British Standards Institution, *Specification for Alphabetical Arrangement and the Filing Order of Numerals and Symbols*, BS1749 (London: B.S.I., 1969).

Finally, wherever possible, the different editions of a work are given in an annotation. Bibliographical details are given only when they differ from those of the main edition. If a work describes itself as 'second edition', it is noted as such even if, strictly speaking, it is only a reissue.

No locations are given. The sheer bulk of the work would have made their listing an enormous task. In any case, the majority of the works included in this bibliography can be found in the British Library and in the British Library of Political and Economic Science; further locations of periodicals are given in the *British Union Catalogue of Periodicals* and various regional lists held by major libraries.

No attempt was made to evaluate the works described or to abstract their contents; such tasks were beyond the resources and competency of the compilers. In any case, the objective of the bibliography is not to tell those who are interested in British industrial relations what they should read but to inform them of what they may read if they so desire. It attempts within its scope to be as comprehensive as possible. It may be regarded as a master bibliography from which more specialised bibliographies, classified and annotated as desired, may be derived.

Although comprehensive in nature, the bibliography does not claim to be complete. For bibliographical research is subject to the law of diminishing returns: there comes a time when tracing obscure references is more trouble and expense than it is worth. Nevertheless, the present bibliography is more comprehensive than any other on the same subject. And while it will not relieve the researcher of the need to 'break his own way for himself', to end this introduction as it began by quoting Sidney Webb, the bibliography should 'shorten the labour and smooth the path' of all those who are interested in British industrial relations.[16]

[16] Op. cit., vii.

PART ONE

GENERAL

I. BIBLIOGRAPHIES, GUIDES, AND ARCHIVAL SOURCES

This section includes not only general bibliographies on industrial relations but also those which are concerned with a particular aspect of the subject. Surveys of research and opinion are classified with the subject to which they pertain.

1 **Welch**, Charles. *The bibliography of the livery companies of the City of London.* London: J. Bale, 1890. 7p.

2 **Peddie**, Robert Alec. 'Bibliography.' Webb, S. and Webb, B. *The history of trade unionism.* London: Longmans, Green, 1894. p. 499–543.

3 **Hopkinson**, Austin and **Bowley**, Arthur Lyon. 'Bibliography of wage statistics in the United Kingdom in the nineteenth century.' *Econ. Rev.*, VIII, 4 (October 1898), 504–20.

Includes details of the collection of trade union publications presented to the British Library of Political Science by S. and B. Webb.

4 **Marot**, H. *A handbook of labor literature in the English language.* Philadelphia, 1899. 96p.

5 **National Anti-Sweating League.** *A short bibliography of 'sweating', and a list of the principal works, and references to the legal minimum wage.* London, 1906. 24p.

6 **Taylor**, Fanny Isabel. *A bibliography of unemployment and the unemployed.* London: P. S. King, 1909. xix, 71p. (London School of Economics and Political Science. Studies in economics and political science. Bibliographies 1.)

Preface by Sidney Webb.

7 **Welsh Bibliographical Society.** *A bibliography of Robert Owen, the socialist, 1771–1858.* Aberystwyth: the Society, 1914. 54p.

Second edition, revised and enlarged. 1925.

8 **Papworth**, Lucy Wyatt and **Zimmern**, Dorothy M. *Women in industry: a bibliography.* London: Women's Industrial Council, 1915. viii, 107p.

9 **Zimand**, Savel. *Representation in industry: a bibliography on workshop committees, Whitley Councils, industrial democracy, etc.* New York: Public Library, Economics Division, Public Affairs Information Service, 1920. 22p.

10 **Zimand**, Savel. *Modern social movements: descriptive summaries and bibliographies.* New York: H. W. Wilson, 1921. vi, 260p.

Prepared under the auspices of the Bureau of Industrial Research.

Contents include 'Trade unionism', 'The cooperative movement', 'Proposed experiments in industrial democracy', 'Guild socialism', 'Syndicalism'.

11 **British Library of Political Science.** 'Bibliography on unemployment.' *Bulletin*, 17 (February 1922), 22–8. (Select bibliographies 18.)

12 *Labour: a catalogue of rare books, pamphlets and periodicals relating to the Chartist movement, communism . . . trade unions and kindred subjects.* London, 1922. 82p.

13 **Hamilton**, J. 'Some old union records.' *Plebs*, XV, 1 (January 1923), 22–3.

14 **International Labour Office.** *Bibliography of unemployment.* Geneva, 1926. 155p. (Studies and reports, series C, 12.)

Second edition. 1930. viii, 217p.

15 **Conover**, Helen Field. *A bibliography of bibliographies of trade unions.* Washington: Library of Congress, 1937. 18p.

16 **Massie**, Joseph. *Bibliography of the collection of books and tracts on commerce, currency and Poor Law, 1557 to 1763, formed by Joseph Massie.* London: G. Harding's Bookshop, 1937. 173p.

17 **Chamberlin**, Waldo. *Industrial relations in wartime: Great Britain, 1914–1918. Annotated bibliography of materials in the Hoover Library on War, Revolution, and Peace.* Stanford, Calif.: Stanford U.P.; London: Humphrey Milford, Oxford U.P., 1940. x, 239p.

18 **Taylor**, Hasseltine Byrd. *Sutro Collection: bibliography of books and pamphlets on the English Poor Laws, 1639–1890.* San Francisco: Sutro Branch, California State Library, 1940. iii, 53 leaves. (Occasional papers. Bibliographical series 2.)

19 **Guttsman**, Wilhelm Leo. *British social services: a selection of books, pamphlets and documents: an exhibition arranged by the National Book League in association with the National Council of Social Service.* Cambridge: Cambridge U.P., 1951. 54p.

20 **Richardson**, John Henry. 'British industrial relations: a bibliographical survey.' *British Book News* (October 1951), 639–43.

21 **International Labour Office**. *Bibliography on labour law*. Geneva: I.L.O., 1953. 83p. (Bibliographical contributions 8.)
Cumulative supplement, 1–2. 1955.
Revised edition. 1958. 104p. (Bibliographical contributions 13.)

22 **Gulick**, Charles Adams, **Ockert**, Roy A. and **Wallace**, Raymond J. *History and theories of working class movements: a select bibliography*. Berkeley, Calif.: University of California, Bureau of Business and Economic Research and Institute of Industrial Relations, 1955. 364p.

23 **International Labour Office**. *Bibliography on industrial relations*. Geneva: I.L.O., 1955. iii, 103p. (Bibliographical contributions 10.)

24 **Meier**, Deborah W. *Foreign trade unions: a bibliographic review*. Chicago: Industrial Relations Center, University of Chicago, 1955. iii, 174p.

25 **International Labour Office**. *Bibliography on workers' education*. Geneva: I.L.O., 1956. ii, 41p. (Bibliographical contributions 11.)

26 **International Labour Office**. *Bibliography on vocational training*. Geneva: I.L.O., 1957. iii, 39p. (Bibliographical contributions 12.)

27 **Turner**, J. *Trade unions: a union list of books*. Eccles: Public Library, 1957. 15p.
Published on behalf of the libraries of Altrincham, Eccles, Sale, Salford, and Swinton and Pendlebury. 100 references.

28 **Benge**, Ronald Charles. *Technical and vocational education in the United Kingdom: a bibliographical survey*. Paris: Unesco, 1958. 51p. (Unesco educational studies and documents 27.)

29 **International Labour Office**. *Bibliography on co-operation*. Geneva: I.L.O., 1958. ii, 128p. (Bibliographical contributions 14.)
Revised edition, 1964. (Bibliographical contributions 23.)

30 **International Labour Office**. *Bibliography on non-manual workers*. Geneva: I.L.O., 1959. 68p. (Bibliographical contributions 18.)

31 **Pollard**, Sidney. 'Sources for trade union history.' *Amat. Hist.*, IV, 5 (Autumn 1959), 177–81.

32 **University of London**. Library. *Robert Owen, 1771–1858: catalogue of an exhibition of printed books, held in the Library of the University of London, October–December 1958*. London, 1959. 40p.

33 **Hobsbawm**, Eric John Ernest. 'Records of the trade union movement.' *Archives*, IV, 23 (Lady Day 1960), 129–37.

34 **International Labour Office**. *Bibliography on vocational guidance*. Geneva: I.L.O., 1961. ii, 37p. (Bibliographical contributions 21.)

35 **Large**, Marion. 'Library sources in labour history. 2. Birmingham Local Collection.' *Soc. Study Labour Hist. Bull.*, 3 (Autumn 1961), 13–15.

36 **Brophy**, Jacqueline (comp.). 'Bibliography of British labor and radical journals 1880–1914.' *Labor Hist.*, III, 1 (Winter 1962), 103–26.

37 **Line**, M. B. 'Library sources in labour history: Southampton University.' *Soc. Study Labour Hist. Bull.*, 4 (Spring 1962), 55.

38 **Pelling**, Henry Mathison. 'Manuscript sources of British labour history in the United States.' *Soc. Study Labour Hist. Bull.*, 5 (Autumn 1962), 39–40.

39 **Saville**, John. 'Henry George and the British labour movement: a select bibliography with commentary.' *Soc. Study Labour Hist. Bull.*, 5 (Autumn 1962), 18–26.

40 **Sellers**, Ian. 'Library sources of labour history: City of Liverpool Picton Reference Library, Record Office.' *Soc. Study Labour Hist. Bull.*, 5 (Autumn 1962), 42–3.

41 **Williams**, James Eccles. 'Labour in the coalfields: a critical bibliography.' *Soc. Study Labour Hist. Bull.*, 4 (Spring 1962), 24–32.
Rejoinders by A. R. Griffin and R. Frankenburg published in *Bull.*, 5 (Autumn 1962), 44–6 and 47–9.
Reply by J. E. Williams, 49–54.

42 **Bakewell**, Kenneth Graham Bartlett. *Productivity in British industry*. London: Library Association, 1963. 29p. (Special subject list 41.)

43 **Dunsmore**, Michael. 'Library sources for labour history: Bradford reform societies, 1835–68. MSS in Bradford Reference Library.' *Soc. Study Labour Hist. Bull.*, 7 (Autumn 1963), 36–7.

44 **Houlton**, R. 'Two aspects of guild socialism: Penty and Hobson, and the building guilds. A select bibliography with commentary.' *Soc. Study Labour Hist. Bull.*, 7 (Autumn 1963), 23–8.

45 **International Labour Office**. *Bibliography on social security*. Geneva: I.L.O., 1963. v, 167p. (Bibliographical contributions 20.)

46 **Tsuzuki**, Chushichi. 'Japanese archives relating to British labour history.' *Soc. Study Labour Hist. Bull.*, 7 (Autumn 1963), 29–33; 8 (Spring 1964), 18–22.

47 **Chaloner**, William Henry. 'Labour conditions during the industrial revolution: a select bibliography, 1953–1963.' *Soc. Study Labour Hist. Bull.*, 8 (Spring 1964), 37–8.

48 **Guttsman**, Wilhelm Leo. 'Material on labour history in British libraries. 6. Sources on the history of the British labour movement in the British Library of Political and Economic Science.' *Soc. Study Labour Hist. Bull.*, 8 (Spring 1964), 23–30.

49 **Bain**, George Sayers and **Pollins**, Harold. 'The history of white-collar unions and industrial relations: a bibliography.' *Soc. Study Labour Hist. Bull.*, 11 (Autumn 1965), 20–65.

50 **International Labour Office**. *Bibliography of research sources on labour questions*. Geneva: I.L.O., 1965. vi, 129p. (Bibliographical contributions 24.)

51 **Leventhal**, Fred M. 'Notes on sources: [the George Howell collection, Bishopsgate Institute, London].' *Soc. Study Labour Hist. Bull.*, 10 (Spring 1965), 38–40.

52 **Mundle**, George F. *Industrial relations bibliographies: a check-list.* Champaign, Ill.: Institute of Labor and Industrial Relations, University of Illinois, 1965. iii, 54p. (Bibliographical contributions 8.)

53 **Parker**, S. R. *A bibliography of industrial sociology (including the sociology of occupations).* London: Polytechnic, 1965. 15p.

54 **Bakewell**, Kenneth Graham Bartlett. *How to find out: management and productivity. A guide to sources of information arranged according to the Universal Decimal Classification.* Oxford, London: Pergamon, 1966. x, 354p. (Commonwealth and international library. Libraries and technical information.)

Second edition. 1970. x, 389p.

55 **Gross**, Charles. *A bibliography of British municipal history, including gilds and parliamentary representation.* Leicester: Leicester U.P., 1966. Second edition.

First published as volume v of *Harvard historical studies* by Longmans, Green and Co., New York, 1897.

56 **Ottley**, George. *A bibliography of British railway history.* London: Allen and Unwin, 1965 [i.e. 1966]. 683p. Section H. 'Railway labour', p. 249–64.

57 **Armstrong**, D. *Short annotated bibliography [on manpower planning].* London: Tavistock Institute, 1967.

58 **Rowe**, David J. 'Local records for labour history.' *NE. Group Study Labour Hist. Bull.*, 1 (October 1967), 15–16.

59 **Allen**, Victor L. *International bibliography of trade unionism.* London: Merlin P., 1968. viii, 180p.

60 **Clarke**, J. F. and **Rowe**, David J. 'Local records for labour history: tape recordings.' *NE. Group Study Labour Hist. Bull.*, 2 (October 1968), 10–12.

Details of tape recording done by the Group including extracts from conversations with Sir William Lowther (President of N.U.M.), Will Richardson (Chairman of South Moor Miners' Lodge) on the General Strike and Charles Stirling (a boilermaker in his 80s, who worked for the Consett Iron Co. for over 60 years).

61 **Garside**, W. Richard. 'Labour problems in the Durham coalfield: a critical bibliography.' *NE. Group Study Labour Hist. Bull.*, 2 (October 1968), 18–22.

62 **Hunt**, Christopher John. 'A brief list of sources for the study of the labour history of the lead mining industry of the Northern Pennines.' *NE. Group Study Labour Hist. Bull.*, 2 (October 1968), 13–17.

63 **Institute of Personnel Management.** *Personnel management: a bibliography.* London, 1968. 153p.

Compiled by Carole Faubert.

Replaces earlier ones published in 1950 and 1962.

64 **National Book League.** *T.U.C. centenary, 1868–1968: books reflecting the social changes of the last century.* London: National Book League, 1968. 62p.

65 **Townroe**, Peter Michael. *Industrial location and regional economic policy: a selected bibliography.* Birmingham: University of Birmingham, Centre for Urban and Regional Studies, 1968. vii, 43p. (Occasional paper 2.)

66 **Winn**, Viola. 'Information resources.' Hutchings, D. (ed.). *Education for industry: Symposium on the Integration of Further Education and Industrial Training.* London: Longmans, 1968. p. 115–22.

67 **Clarke**, Ronald Oliver, **Fatchett**, D. J. and **Rothwell**, S. G. *Workers' participation and industrial democracy: a bibliography.* London: R. O. Clarke, 1969. 12p.

68 **Frow**, Ruth, **Frow**, Edmund and **Katanka**, Michael. *The history of British trade unionism: a select bibliography.* London: Historical Association, 1969. 44p. (Helps for students of history 76.)

69 **Gard**, R. M. 'Labour history of the railways in Durham and Northumberland to 1900: an introduction to sources and bibliography.' *NE. Group Study Labour Hist. Bull.*, 3 (October 1969), 17–23.

70 **Gottschalk**, Andrew W., **Whittingham**, T. G. and **Williams**, N. *British industrial relations: an annotated bibliography.* Nottingham: Department of Adult Education, University of Nottingham, [1969]. 72p.

71 **Grace**, Ray P. 'Publications by working class organisations in the North East during the General Strike.' *NE. Group Study Labour Hist. Bull.*, 3 (October 1969), 39–41.

A guide to a collection made by A. Mason.

72 **Lewis**, Christopher Gray (ed.). *Manpower planning: a bibliography.* London: English Universities P.; New York: American Elsevier Pub. Co., 1969. viii, 96p.

73 **Mason**, Antony. 'The General Strike in the North East: a bibliographical sketch.' *NE. Group Study Labour Hist. Bull.*, 3 (October 1969), 34–8.

74 **Organisation for Economic Co-operation and Development.** *Bibliography [of] international migration of manpower.* Paris: O.E.C.D., 1969.

75 **Bain**, George Sayers and **Woolven**, Gillian Beatrice. 'The literature of labour economics and industrial relations: a guide to its sources.' *Ind. Relat. J.* (Summer 1970), 30–42.

This paper forms part of a book *The use of economics literature* edited by J. Fletcher, Butterworths, 1971.

76 **Foster**, John. 'Labour in South Shields 1800–50: an interim bibliography.' *NE. Group Study Labour Hist. Bull.*, 4 (November 1970), 5–9.

77 **International Labour Office.** *Bibliography on women workers.* Geneva: I.L.O., 1970. iii, 252p. (Bibliographical contributions 26.)

II. GUIDES TO AND NATURE OF STATISTICAL SOURCES

Statistics on a particular subject are to be found with the subject. See also Part Six, II, D, 2; and Part Six, III, B.

78 **Bowley**, Arthur Lyon. 'The abstract of labour statistics, 1894–5.' *Econ. J.*, VI, 23 (September 1896), 465–70.

79 **Bowley**, Arthur Lyon. [Address to Section F of the British Association, York.] *R. Statist. Soc. J.*, LXIX, 3 (September 1906), 540–58.
Includes a discussion of labour statistics.

80 **Bowley**, Arthur Lyon. 'The improvement of official statistics.' *R. Statist. Soc. J.*, LXXI, 3 (September 1908), 459–79.
Discussion, p. 480–95.

81 **Bowley**, *Sir* Arthur Lyon. *The nature and purpose of the measurement of social phenomena.* London: King, 1915. viii, 241p.
Second edition. 1923.

82 **Bowley**, *Sir* Arthur Lyon. *Official statistics: what they contain and how to use them.* London: Oxford U.P., 1921. 63p. (World of to-day.)
Second edition. 1928. 72p.

83 *The facts of industry: the case for publicity.* London: Macmillan, 1926. 62p.
Compiled by a Committee under the Chairmanship of W. T. Layton, Editor of *The Economist.*
'Industrial relations', p. 11–33.
Survey of statistical information available.

84 **Pribram**, Karl. 'The scope of labour statistics.' *Int. Labour Rev.*, XIV, 4 (October 1926), 476–88.

85 **Nixon**, J. W. 'The measurement of "risk" in connection with labour statistics.' *Int. Labour Rev.*, XVII, 5 (May 1928), 633–50.

86 **Ainsworth**, Ralph B. 'The sources and nature of statistical information in special fields of statistics: United Kingdom labour statistics.' *R. Statist. Soc. J.*, Ser. A, CXIII, 1 (1950), 37–49.

87 **Ainsworth**, Ralph B. 'Labour statistics.' Kendall, M. G. (ed.). *The sources and nature of the statistics of the United Kingdom.* Vol. 1. London: Oliver and Boyd for the Royal Statistical Society, 1952. p. 75–86.

88 **United States**. Department of Labor. *Labor statistics series: United Kingdom.* Washington, 1952.

89 **Interdepartmental Committee on Social and Economic Research**. *Labour statistics: material collected by the Ministry of Labour and National Service.* London: H.M.S.O., 1958. vii, 78p. (Guides to official sources, 1.)
First issued 1948.
Revised 1950.

90 **Ministry of Labour**. 'Recent developments in Ministry of Labour statistics.' *Br. J. Ind. Relat.*, I, 3 (October 1963), 299–309.

91 **Phelps Brown**, Ernest Henry and **Browne**, Margaret H. 'Carroll D. Wright and the development of British labour statistics.' *Economica*, n.s., XXX, 119 (August 1963), 277–86.

92 **Oherlihy**, C. St J. 'Economic studies in Northern Ireland labour statistics.' *Statist. Soc. Inq. Soc. Ir. J.*, XXI, 2 (1963–64), 145–75.

93 **Buxton**, N. K. and **MacKay**, Donald Iain. 'Comparability of Ministry of Labour statistics of employment, 1923–64.' *Br. J. Ind. Relat.*, II, 3 (November 1964), 418–23.

94 **MacKay**, Donald Iain and **Buxton**, N. K. 'A view of regional labour statistics.' *R. Statist. Soc. J.*, Ser. A, CXXVIII, 2 (1965), 267–84.

See also: 3.

III. NATURE AND STUDY OF THE SUBJECT

As discussions on the nature of a subject tend to be theoretical, this section, unlike other parts of the bibliography, includes works which are primarily based on foreign experience but which are nevertheless relevant to the study of the subject in Britain.

95 **Webb**, Beatrice. 'Methods of investigation.' Sociological Society. *Sociological papers.* Vol. 3. London, New York: Macmillan, 1907. p. 345–51.
Abstract of discussion, p. 352–53.
The author's reply, p. 353–54.

96 **Webb**, Beatrice. *My apprenticeship.* London: Longmans, 1926. xiv, 458p.
Another edition. Harmondsworth: Penguin Books, 1938. (Pelican books A31.)
Second edition. Longmans, 1946. xii, 389p.
Revised, 1950.

97 **Miles**, George Herbert. 'Methods of research in industrial relations.' *Natn. Inst. Ind. Psychol. J.*, IV, 7 (July 1929), 373–8.
'Based on a paper read before the Cambridge Congress of the International Association for the Study and Improvement of Human Relations and Conditions in Industry.'

98 **Webb**, Sidney James and **Webb**, Beatrice. *Methods of social study.* London: Longmans, Green, 1932. vii, 263p.

99 **Hamilton**, Mary Agnes. *Sidney and Beatrice Webb: a study in contemporary biography.* London: Sampson Low, 1933. vi, 314p.

100 **Labour Research Department**. *Twenty-one years old.* London, 1933. 8p.

101 **Vannier**, Webster. 'The problem of social investigation: the method of Sidney and Beatrice Webb.' *Essays in social economics in honor of Jessica Blanche Peixotto*. Berkeley, Calif.: U. of California P., 1935. p. 321–36.

102 **Cole**, George Douglas Howard. 'Beatrice Webb as an economist.' *Econ. J.*, LIII, 212 (December 1943), 422–37.

Obituary.

103 **Hare**, Anthony Edward Christian. 'Industrial relations and economic theory.' *Econ. Rec.*, XIX, 36 (June 1943), 11–22.

104 **Cole**, Margaret Isabel. *Beatrice Webb*. London: Longmans, Green, 1945. 197p.

105 **Tawney**, Richard Henry. *Beatrice Webb, 1858–1943*. London: Humphrey Milford, 1945. 27p.

Reprinted from British Academy *Proceedings* xxix, 1943.

Reprinted in R. H. Tawney. *The attack and other papers*. London: Allen and Unwin, 1953. p. 101–28.

106 **University of Minnesota**, Industrial Relations Center. *Training and research in industrial relations: proceedings of a conference held May 25 and 26, 1945*. Minneapolis, 1945. 60p. (Bulletin 1.)

107 **Fraser**, John Munro. 'A psychodynamic approach to industrial relations.' *Occup. Psychol.*, XX, 3 (July 1946), 132–8. (Essays presented to Dr Myers, XXVI.)

'From a collection of essays by past and present members of the staff, presented on the Institute's 21st anniversary.'

108 **Nixon**, Edna. *John Hilton: the story of his life*. London: Allen and Unwin, 1946. 344p.

109 **Cole**, Margaret Isabel. 'Sidney Webb, 1859–1947.' *Makers of the labour movement*. London: Longmans, Green, 1948. p. 227–47.

110 **Feinsinger**, Nathan P. 'The contribution of the law to industrial relations research.' Industrial Relations Research Association. *Proceedings of the first annual meeting, Cleveland, Ohio, December 29–30, 1948*. p. 223–8.

Discussion, p. 229–33.

111 **Kerr**, Clark. 'Economic analysis and the study of industrial relations.' *Univ. Minn. Ind. Relat. Center Bull.*, 7 (April 1948), 12–16.

From the proceedings of the Third Annual Conference on Training and Research in Industrial Relations, May 22nd and 23rd, 1947.

Reprinted under the title 'The model of the trade union' in Bakke, E. W. and Kerr, C. (eds.). *Unions, management and the public*. New York: Harcourt, Brace, 1948.

112 **Kornhauser**, Arthur. 'The contribution of psychology to industrial relations research.' Industrial Relations Research Association. *Proceedings of the first annual meeting, Cleveland, Ohio, December 29–30, 1948*. p. 172–88.

Discussion, p. 229–33.

113 **Leiserson**, Avery. 'The role of political science in industrial relations research.' Industrial Relations Research Association. *Proceedings of the first annual meeting, Cleveland, Ohio, December 29–30, 1948*. p. 189–98.

Discussion, p. 229–33.

114 **Webb**, Beatrice. *Our partnership*. London: Longmans, Green, 1948. xiii, 543p.

Edited by Barbara Drake, Margaret I. Cole, etc.

On the earlier years of the marriage of Sidney and B. Webb.

Another issue. New York, 1948.

115 **Wright Mills**, C. 'The contribution of sociology to studies of industrial relations.' Industrial Relations Research Association. *Proceedings of the first annual meeting, Cleveland, Ohio, December 29–30, 1948*. p. 199–222.

Discussion, p. 229–33.

116 **Cole**, Margaret Isabel. 'Labour research.' Cole, M. I. (ed.). *The Webbs and their work*. London: Muller, 1949. p. 147–63.

117 **Woods**, H. D. (ed.). *The universities and industrial relations*. Montreal, 1949. 70p.

118 **Dunlop**, John Thomas and **Whyte**, William Foote. 'Framework for the analysis of industrial relations: two views.' *Ind. Labor Relat. Rev.*, III, 3 (April 1950), 383–401.

'This discussion developed from a conference sponsored by the Social Science Research Council. See Charles A. Myers and John G. Turnbull, Research on Labor Management Relations: Report of a Conference held on February 24–25, 1949, at the Industrial Relations Section, Princeton University, Princeton, New Jersey.' (New York: Social Science Research Council, 1949), pp. 10–17. The two papers are followed on p. 402–12 by comments by E. Wight Bakke, Douglass V. Brown, Lloyd H. Fisher, George C. Homans, Clark Kerr, and F. L. W. Richardson, jr.

119 **McConnell**, John W. 'Problems of method in the study of human relations.' *Ind. Labor Relat. Rev.*, III, 4 (July 1950), 548–60.

120 **Mumford**, Enid M. *An evaluation of participant observation as a research method for the study of work groups in industry*. 1950–51. (M.A. thesis, University of Liverpool.)

121 **Brown**, James Douglas. 'University research in industrial relations.' Industrial Relations Research Association. *Proceedings of the fifth annual meeting, December 1952*. p. 2–7.

Presidential address.

122 **Rodgers**, Brian. 'The Social Science Association, 1857–1886.' *Manchr. Sch.*, XX, 3 (September 1952), 283–210.

One of the earliest scientific societies to investigate trade unions and labour problems.

123 **Saville**, John. 'A note on the present position of working-class history.' *Yorks. Bull. Econ. Soc. Res.*, IV, 2 (September 1952), 125–32.

124 **Webb**, Beatrice. *Beatrice Webb's diaries, 1912–1924*. London: Longmans, Green, 1952. xxvi, 272p.

Edited by Margaret I. Cole.

125 **Fogarty**, Michael Patrick. *The function of an undergraduate department of industrial relations: an inaugural lecture*. Cardiff: U. of Wales P., 1953. 31p.

126 **Tawney**, Richard Henry. 'The Webbs and their work.' *The attack and other papers*. London: Allen and Unwin, 1953. p. 129–46.
Webb Memorial Lecture, May 1945.

127 **Musson**, Albert Edward. 'Writing trade-union history.' *Amat. Hist.*, I, 9 (December 1953–January 1954), 273–7.

128 **Dunlop**, John Thomas. 'Research in industrial relations: past and future.' Industrial Relations Research Association. *Proceedings of the seventh annual meeting, December 1954*. p. 92–101.
Discussion, p. 107–11.

129 **Webbink**, Paul. 'Methods and objectives of industrial relations research.' Industrial Relations Research Association. *Proceedings of the seventh annual meeting, December 1954*. p. 102–6.

130 **Cole**, Margaret Isabel. *Beatrice and Sidney Webb*. London: Fabian Society, 1955. 47p. (Fabian tract 297. Biographical series 15.)

131 **Smith**, John Harold. 'The scope of industrial relations.' *Br. J. Sociol.*, VI, 1 (March 1955), 80–5.
Review article.

132 **Webb**, Beatrice. *Beatrice Webb's diaries, 1924–1932*. London: Longmans, Green, 1956. xxv, 327p.
Edited with an introduction by Margaret Cole.

133 **Galenson**, Walter. 'Reflections on the writing of labor history.' *Ind. Labor. Relat. Rev.*, XI, 1 (October 1957), 85–95.

134 **Phillips**, W. A. P. 'The price of respectability: reflections on current trends in British trade union studies.' *Aust. J. Polit. Hist.*, II, 2 (May 1957), 204–17.

135 **Mumford**, Enid M. 'Participant observation in industry: an evaluation.' *Occup. Psychol.*, XXXII, 3 (July 1958), 153–61.
'The material on which this paper is based was collected during the course of an enquiry undertaken in the docks industry by the Department of Social Science of the University of Liverpool. The main report on this enquiry has been published in *The Dockworker* (Liverpool University Press, 1954).'

136 **Allen**, Victor L. 'The need for a sociology of labour.' *Br. J. Sociol.*, x, 3 (September 1959), 181–92.

137 **Scott**, William Henry. 'The aims of industrial sociology: some reflections.' *Br. J. Sociol.*, x, 3 (September 1959), 193–203.

138 **Ritt**, Laurence. *The Victorian conscience in action: the National Association for the Promotion of Social Science, 1857–1886*. 1959–60. (Dissertation, Columbia University.)

139 **Arram**, D. S. *A critical examination of the assumptions in some post-war British industrial sociology*. 1960–61. (M.A. thesis, University of Leeds.)

140 **Aronson**, Robert L., and others. *Essays on industrial relations research: problems and prospects*. Ann Arbor and Detroit: University of Michigan–Wayne State University, Institute of Labor and Industrial Relations, 1961.

141 **Backstrom**, Philip N. 'The British labor movement: a challenge to the young historian.' *Historian*, XXIV, 4 (August 1962), 415–22.

142 **Monaghan**, William. *Teaching programmes having a bearing on relations between employers and workers: joint missions in the United States and Europe*. Paris: Organisation for Economic Co-operation and Development, 1962. 120p.
United Kingdom, p. 47–60.

143 **Seear**, Nancy. 'Industrial research in Britain.' Welford, A. T., Argyle, M., Glass, D. V. and Morris, J. N. (eds.). *Society: problems and methods of study*. London: Routledge and Kegan Paul, 1962. p. 171–83.
Revised edition. 1967.

144 **Society for the Study of Labour History.** 'The teaching of labour history.' *Soc. Study Labour Hist. Bull.*, 4 (Spring 1962), 33–43; 5 (Autumn 1962), 3–8.

145 **Strachey**, Evelyn John St Loe. 'The Webbs.' *The strangled cry, and other unparliamentary papers*. London: Bodley Head, 1962. p. 183–9.
A talk on the B.B.C. Third Programme, 1960.

146 **Allen**, Victor L. 'Valuations and historical interpretation: a case study.' *Br. J. Sociol.*, XIV, 1 (March 1963), 48–58.
A criticism of the *History of trade unionism* by Sidney and Beatrice Webb.

147 **Behrend**, Hilde M. 'The field of industrial relations.' *Br. J. Ind. Relat.*, I, 3 (October 1963), 383–94.

148 **Windmuller**, John P. 'Model industrial relations systems.' Industrial Relations Research Association. *Proceedings of the sixteenth annual meeting, Boston, Massachusetts, December 27 and 28, 1963*. p. 60–75.

149 **Banks**, Joseph Ambrose. 'The sociology of work.' Fyrel, T. R. (ed.). *The frontiers of sociology*, London: Cohen and West, 1964. p. 13–27.

150 **Barbash**, Jack. 'The elements of industrial relations.' *Br. J. Ind. Relat.*, II, 1 (March 1964), 66–78.

151 **Hobsbawm**, Eric John Ernest. 'Trade union historiography.' *Soc. Study Labour Hist. Bull.*, 8 (Spring 1964), 31–6.

152 **Munby**, Lionel. 'Studying/writing working class history.' *Marxism Today*, VIII, 10 (October 1964), 309–13.

153 **McNulty**, Paul James. *Economics and the study of labor*. 1964–5. (Dissertation, Cornell University.)

154 **Brown**, Richard K. 'Participation, conflict and change in industry: a review of research in industrial sociology at the Department of Social Science, University of Liverpool.' *Sociol. Rev.*, n.s., XIII, 3 (November 1965), 273–95.

155 **Hagen**, Everett E. 'Some implications of personality theory for the theory of industrial relations.' *Ind. Labor Relat. Rev.*, XVIII, 3 (April 1965), 339–51.

A contribution to a Symposium on the Behavioral Sciences and Industrial Relations in this issue.

156 **Whyte**, William Foote. 'A field in search of a focus.' *Ind. Labor Relat. Rev.*, XVIII, 3 (April 1965), 305–22.

A contribution to a Symposium on the Behavioral Sciences and Industrial Relations in this issue.

157 **Briggs**, Asa. 'Trade-union history and labour history.' *Bus. Hist.*, VIII, 1 (January 1966), 39–47.

158 **Brunel**, Christopher and **Jackson**, Peter M. 'Notes on tokens as a source of information on the history of the labour & radical movement.' *Soc. Study Labour Hist. Bull.*, 13 (Autumn 1966), 26–36.

159 **Fox**, Alan. *Industrial sociology and industrial relations: an assessment of the contribution which industrial sociology can make towards understanding and resolving some of the problems now being considered by the Royal Commission.* London: H.M.S.O., 1966. v, 33p. (Royal Commission on Trade Unions and Employers' Associations. Research papers 3.)

160 **Thomason**, George. 'The teaching of industrial relations.' Pugh, D. (ed.). *The academic teaching of management.* Oxford: Blackwell, 1966. p. 59–65. (Association of Teachers of Management. Occasional papers 4.)

161 **Brown**, Richard K. 'Research and consultancy in industrial enterprises: a review of the contribution of the Tavistock Institute of Human Relations to the development of industrial sociology.' *Sociology*, I, 1 (January 1967), 33–60.

162 **Garside**, W. Richard. 'On writing trade union history, with special reference to the Durham Miners' Association, 1919–1947.' *NE. Group Study Labour Hist. Bull.*, 1 (October 1967), 8–10.

Summary of a paper read at Van Mildret College on 13 May 1967.

163 **Hameed**, Syed M. A. 'Theory and research in the field of industrial relations.' *Br. J. Ind. Relat.*, V, 2 (July 1967), 222–36.

164 **Hobsbawm**, Eric John Ernest. 'Essays in bibliography and criticism. LVIII. Trade union history.' *Econ. Hist. Rev.*, 2nd ser., XX, 2 (August 1967), 358–64.

165 **Labour History**. 'Symposium: what is labour history?' *Labour Hist.*, 12 (May 1967), 60–81.

Contributors: N. B. Nairn, J. A. La Nauze, D. W. Rawson, T. H. Irving, E. C. Fry.

166 **Muggeridge**, Kitty and **Adam**, Ruth. *Beatrice Webb: a life, 1858–1943.* London. Secker and Warburg, 1967. 272p.

167 **Parker**, Stanley Robert, and others. *The sociology of industry.* London: Allen and Unwin, 1967. 182p. (Studies in sociology 1.)

By S. R. Parker, R. K. Brown, J. Child and M. A. Smith.

168 **Saville**, John. 'The present position and prospects of labour history.' *NE. Group Study Labour Hist. Bull.*, 1 (October 1967), 4–6.

A paper read to the Group on 3 December 1966 at Rutherford College of Technology.

169 **Smith**, M. A. 'Scope and directions in industrial sociology.' Parker, S. R., and others. *The sociology of industry.* London: Allen and Unwin, 1967. p. 13–20.

170 **Walker**, Kenneth Frederick. 'The comparative study of industrial relations.' *Int. Inst. Labour Studies Bull.*, 3 (November 1967), 105–32.

Paper presented at the First World Congress of the International Industrial Relations Association.

171 **Pemble**, R. J. *The National Association for the Promotion of Social Science (1857–1885): a sociological analysis.* 1967–8. (M.A. thesis, University of Nottingham.)

172 **Bugler**, Jeremy. 'The new Oxford group.' *New Soc.*, XI, 281 (15 February 1968), 221–2.

Oxford academics in the field of industrial relations.

173 **Eldridge**, John E. T. 'The sociology of work: trends and counter-trends.' *Industrial disputes: essays in the sociology of industrial relations.* London: Routledge and Kegan Paul; New York: Humanities P., 1968. Appendix A, p. 229–35.

Based on a broadcast talk given in January 1966 in the B.B.C. study series 'The Sphere of the Sociologist'.

174 **Marsh**, Arthur I. 'Research and teaching in industrial relations: the United Kingdom experience.' *Int. Inst. Labour Studies Bull.*, 5 (November 1968), 64–78.

Summary of discussions on this and other papers, p. 108–35.

175 **McNulty**, Paul James. 'Labor problems and labor economics: the roots of an academic discipline.' *Labor Hist.*, IX, 2 (Spring 1968), 239–61.

176 **Simpson**, John. 'Scottish labour historiography: a progress report.' *Soc. Study Labour Hist. Bull.*, 17 (Autumn 1968), 29–32.

Review article.

177 **Gill**, John. 'One approach to the teaching of industrial relations.' *Br. J. Ind. Relat.*, VII, 2 (July 1969), 265–72.

178 **Margerison**, C. J. 'What do we mean by industrial relations? A behavioral science approach.' *Br. J. Ind. Relat.*, VII, 2 (July 1969), 273–86.

179 **Somers**, Gerald G. (ed.). *Essays in industrial relations theory.* Ames, Iowa: Iowa State U.P., 1969. xi, 200p.

180 **Walker**, Kenneth Frederick. 'Strategic factors in industrial relations systems: a

programme of international comparative industry studies.' *Int. Inst. Labour Studies Bull.*, 6 (June 1969), 187–209.

On the programme of the International Institute for Labour Studies.

181 **Williams**, Roger and **Guest**, David. 'Psychological research and industrial relations: a brief review.' *Occup. Psychol.*, XLIII, 3–4 (1969), 201–11.

182 **Banks**, Joseph Ambrose. *Marxist sociology in action: a sociological critique of the Marxist approach to industrial relations.* London: Faber, 1970. 324p. (Society today and tomorrow.)

Also Harrisburg, Pa.: Stackpole Books.

183 **Blain**, Alexander Nicholas John and **Gennard**, John. 'Industrial relations theory: a critical review.' *Br. J. Ind. Relat.*, VIII, 3 (November 1970), 389–407.

184 **Gray**, Sidney G. 'The Tavistock Institute of Human Relations.' Dicks, H. V. *Fifty years of the Tavistock Clinic.* London: Routledge and Kegan Paul, 1970.

185 **Whincup**, Michael Hynes. *Teaching industrial law.* Association of Teachers of Supervisory Studies, 1970. 11p. (Occasional paper 3.)

See also: 512.

IV. THE INDUSTRIAL RELATIONS SYSTEM: GENERAL WORKS

This section contains works of the following nature: those pertaining to more than one aspect of the industrial relations system, those comparing the British system with systems in other countries, those concerned with 'the labour problem', the place of labour in society, and similar philosophical questions. See also Part Three, III, A; Part Five, I; Part Five, IV, A; Part Five, V, A; and Part Seven, I.

A. GREAT BRITAIN

186 **Wall**, Walter William. *Labour, capital, and finance: essays on the great problems of the day, by 'Spectator'.*

Most of the essays were originally published in *The Financier*.

187 **Makepeace**, F. *Capital and labour.* London, 1881. 277p.

188 **Hart**, Mary H. *Papers on the labour question.* London, 1882–5. 4 pts. in 1.

Contents: 1. 'A brief sketch of the "Maison Leclaire" and its founder.'

2. 'A practical method of reconciling capital and labour.' 1885. 7p. Reprinted from the *Pall Mall Gazette*, February 18th, 1885.

3. 'Obstacles to industrial reform: a paper.' 1885.

4. 'The organisation of labour: a paper.'

189 **Toynbee**, Arnold. 'Industry and democracy.' *Lectures on the Industrial Revolution in England: popular addresses, notes and other fragments.* London: Rivingtons, 1884. p. 178–202.

'This Address was delivered in the earlier part of 1881, to audiences of working men at Newcastle, Chelsea, Bradford (where employers also were present), and Bolton.'

Later editions: 1887; London: Longmans, 1908; New York: Kelley, 1969.

190 **Beesly**, Edward Spencer. 'The education of public opinion.' Industrial Remuneration Conference. *The report of the proceedings and papers.* London: Cassell, 1885. p. 215–21.

Discussion, p. 240–50.

On the organisation of industry.

191 **Cherrie**, J. M. 'Our industrial system: its effects upon the well-being of the working classes.' Industrial Remuneration Conference. *The report of the proceedings and papers.* London: Cassell, 1885. p. 311–22.

Discussion, p. 323–35.

192 **Young**, Edmund J. *Literary and Historical Society, University College, Dublin. The labour question: an address delivered at the inaugural meeting of the session, November, 1885.* Dublin: printed by Browne and Nolan, 1885. 18p.

193 **Bumpus**, A. A. *The future of labour.* Loughborough, 1886. 31p.

194 **Oliphant**, James (ed.). *The claims of labour: a course of lectures delivered in Scotland in the Summer of 1886, on various aspects of the labour problem.* Edinburgh: Co-operative Printing Co., 1886. 275p.

195 **Manning**, Henry Edward, Cardinal, Archbishop of Westminster. *The rights and dignity of labour.* London: Burns and Oates, 1887. 24p.

'This Lecture, originally delivered in Leeds, has been recently revised for publication by his Eminence. It is this Lecture which is referred to by the Cardinal in his recent letter upon the Knights of Labour, and the views expressed in it may be taken to represent the settled opinions of his Eminence upon the relations between labour and capital.'

196 **Besant**, Annie. 'Industry under socialism.' Shaw, G. B. (ed.). *Fabian essays in socialism.* London: Walter Scott, 1889. p. 150–69.

Reprinted. 1908.

New editions. 1920, 1931.

197 **Gladstone**, William Ewart. *On the rights and responsibilities of labour.* London, 1890.

Reprinted from *Lloyd's News*.

198 **Wise**, Bernhard Ringrose. *The labour question, or social revolt and its causes: addresses.* Balmain, 1890. 11p.

199 **Gorst**, *Sir* John Eldon. *The labour question: a speech by Sir John Gorst, M.P., at Chatham, February 12th, 1891.* Birmingham: *Birmingham Daily Gazette*, 1891. 12p.

200 **Quarterly Review**. 'The conflict between capital and labour.' *Q. Rev.*, CLXXIII, 345 (July 1891), 253–78.

Review article.

201 **Universities' Settlement Association.** *The organization of industry: the report of a conference held at . . . Oxford . . . 1890.* Oxford, 1891. 61p.

202 **Hill,** James. *How to solve the labour problem.* London: W. Ridgway, 1892. 12p.

203 **Nicholson,** Joseph Shield. 'Capital and labour: their relative strength.' *Econ. J.*, II, 7 (September 1892), 478–90.

Draws practical conclusions from the calculations described in the paper 'The living capital of the United Kingdom.' *Econ. J.*, I, 1 (March 1891), 95–107.

Reprinted in *Strikes and social problems.* London: Black, 1896. p. 117–36.

204 **Sweeney,** Edward. *The labour question as it is, with its solution.* Liverpool: printed by S. R. Jones, 1892. 10p.

205 **Brooks,** George. *Industry and property: a plea for truth and honesty in economics, and for liberty and justice in social reform, being a discussion of present-day labour problems.* Halesworth: the author, 1892, 1894. 2v.

An abridgement. London: Sampson, Low, 1895. viii, 325p.

206 **Leppington,** C. H. d'E. 'Three solutions of the industrial problem.' *Char. Orgn. Rev.*, IX, 99 (April 1893), 121–6.

Signed C. H. d'E. L.

207 **Warren,** G. O. *Freedom. Rent, interest, profit and taxes, the true causes of wage-slavery, discussed and exploded. An address on the labour question, delivered before the Dublin Ethical Society on 16th November, 1893.* London: W. Reeves, 1893. 16p.

208 **Dyer,** Henry. *The evolution of industry.* London: Macmillan, 1895. xiii, 285p.

209 **Dunelm,** B. F. 'The organization of industry.' *Econ. Rev.*, IX, 2 (April 1899), 145–55.

'An address to the Macclesfield Branch of the Christian Social Union, Oct. 25, 1898.'

210 **Bosanquet,** Helen. *The strength of the people: a study in social economics.* London, New York: Macmillan, 1902. xii, 346p.

211 **Howell,** George. *Labour legislation, labour movements and labour leaders, 1800–1900.* London: Fisher Unwin, 1902. xxiii, 499p.

Second edition. 1905. 2v.

212 **Webb,** Sidney James. 'Social movements.' *The Cambridge Modern History. Volume XII. The latest age.* Cambridge: Cambridge U.P., 1910. p. 730–65.

213 **Babson,** Roger Ward. *The future of the working classes: economic facts for English employers and wage earners.* London: Effingham Wilson, 1913. 75p.

'Based on certain lectures delivered by the author at London and Paris in March and April, 1913.'

214 **Layton,** Walter Thomas, Baron Layton. *The relations of capital and labour.* London, Glasgow: Collins Clear Type P., 1914. 264p. (The Nation's library.)

215 **Norwood,** *Sir* Cyril. *The relations of capital, labour and the state: an address given to Bristol employers . . . with some letters bearing thereon.* Bristol: Arrowsmith, 1916. 39p.

216 **West Country Miner.** 'The abuse of labour.' *Engl. Rev.*, XXII (May 1916), 453–62.

217 **Browne,** *Sir* Benjamin C. 'The relations between capital and labour. II. The standpoint of capital.' Dawson, W. H. (ed.). *After-war problems.* London: Allen and Unwin, 1917. p. 170–84.

218 **Roberts,** George Henry. 'The relations between capital and labour. I. The standpoint of labour.' Dawson, W. H. (ed.). *After-war problems.* London: Allen and Unwin, 1917. p. 149–69.

219 **Chapman,** *Sir* Sydney John (ed.). *Labour and capital after the war, by various writers.* London: Murray, 1918. x, 280p.

Contributors: Dr H. Russell Wakefield, Bishop of Birmingham, J. R. Clynes, Lord Leverhulme, Adelaide Mary Anderson, R. H. Tawney, F. Dudley Docker, F. S. Button, Sir Hugh Bell, A. Susan Lawrence, B. Seebohm Rowntree, the editor.

Appendix: First Report of the Whitley Committee.

220 **Hichens,** William Lionel. *Some problems of modern industry, being the Watt Anniversary Lecture for 1918.* London: Nisbet, 1918. 61p.

221 **Macara,** *Sir* Charles Wright. *Capital and labour: a series of articles on conscription of wealth, the need for . . . the removal of labour unrest.* Ashton-under-Lyne, 1918. [10]p.

222 **Macara,** *Sir* Charles Wright. *Social and industrial reform.* Manchester: Sherratt and Hughes, 1918. 206p.

Seventh edition. 1919. 332p.

Eighth edition. 1920. 459p.

223 **Woods,** Frank Theodore, Bishop of Peterborough. *A new fellowship in industry: a speech.* London: S.P.C.K., 1918. 11p.

224 **Cooper,** William Ranson. *The claims of labour & of capital.* London: Constable, 1919. v, 82p.

225 **Hichens,** William Lionel. *The new spirit in industrial relations, being an address . . .* London: Nisbet, 1919. 31p.

226 **Reynard,** Hélène. 'The industrial situation.' *Econ. J.*, XXIX, 115 (September 1919), 290–301.

227 **United States.** Department of Labor. *Report of the Employers' Industrial Commission of the United States Department of Labor on British labor problems.* Washington, D.C.: U.S.G.P.O., 1919. 37p.

228 **United States.** National Civic Federation. Commission on Foreign Inquiry. *The labor situation in Great Britain and France.* New York: Dutton, 1919. x, 433p.

229 **Willcocks,** Mary Patricia. *Towards new horizons.* London, New York: John Lane, 1919. vii, 213p.

230 **Zimmern,** *Sir* Alfred Eckhard. 'Progress in industry.' *Nationality & governement; with other war-time essays.* London: Chatto and Windus, 1919. p. 172–203.

231 **Alden**, Percy, and others. *Labour and industry: a series of lectures*. Manchester: Manchester U.P.; London: Longmans, Green, 1920. viii, 293p. (Publications of the University of Manchester 137.)

A series of 12 lectures delivered at the Department of Industrial Administration in the College of Technology, University of Manchester, during 1919 and 1920.

232 **Askwith**, George Ranken. *Industrial problems and disputes*. London: Murray, 1920. x, 494p.

Another edition. New York: Harcourt, Brace, 1921. x, 494p.

233 **Gleason**, Arthur. *What the workers want: a study of British labor*. London: Allen and Unwin, 1920; New York: Harcourt, Brace and Howe. vii, 518p.

234 **Jones**, John Harry. *Social economics*. London: Methuen, 1920. x, 239p.

Second edition. 1922. xii, 239p.

235 **Voysey**, E. B. 'The human element in industry.' Alden, P., and others. *Labour and industry* . . . Manchester: Manchester U.P.; London: Longmans, Green, 1920. p. 113–29.

236 **Wootton**, Barbara. 'Classical principles and modern views of labour.' *Econ. J.*, XXX, 117 (March 1920), 46–60.

237 **Jones**, Walter. *Capital and labour: their duties and responsibilities*. London: King, 1921. viii, 168p.

238 **Orton**, William Aylott. *Labour in transition: a survey of British industrial history since 1914*. London: P. Allan, 1921. xxiv, 286p.

239 **Stone**, *Sir* Gilbert. *A history of labour*. London: Harrap, 1921. 415p.

240 **National Movement Towards a Christian Order of Industry and Commerce.** *Prospectus*. London, 1922. 10p.

241 **Emmott**, A., Baron. 'The relations of capital and labour.' *R. Statist. Soc. J.*, LXXXVI, 1 (January 1923), 1–21.

Presidential address, November 21, 1922.

242 **Price**, Langford Lovell Frederick Rice. 'Industrial policy.' *Econ. J.*, XXXIII, 131 (September 1923), 352–61.

243 **Robertson**, *Sir* Dennis Holme. *The control of industry*. London, Cambridge: Cambridge U.P., 1923. x, 169p. (Cambridge economic handbooks 4.)

Revised edition. 1928. x, 169p.

New edition. Welwyn: Nisbet; Cambridge: Cambridge U.P., 1960. xiii, 161p. By D. H. Robertson and S. R. Dennison.

244 **Barnes**, George Nicoll. *Industrial conflict: the way out. A study of the industrial problem in its practical aspects*. London: Pitman, 1924. xi, 100p.

245 **Brockway**, Archibald Fenner. *Make the workers free! The industrial policy of the I.L.P.* London: Independent Labour Party Publication Department, 1925. 14p.

246 **Burns**, Cecil Delisle. *Industry and civilisation*. London: Allen and Unwin; New York: Macmillan, 1925. 278p.

Appendix 1. 'The group-mind in trade unionism.' First published in the Journal of the National Institute of Industrial Psychology.

247 **Burns**, Cecil Delisle. *The philosophy of labour*. London: Allen and Unwin, 1925. 126p.

248 **Furniss**, Edgar Stephenson and **Guild**, Lawrence R. *Labor problems: a book of materials for their study*. Boston: Houghton Mifflin, 1925. x, 621p.

Reprinted. New York: Arno and The New York Times, 1969.

249 **Jones**, Henry Arthur. *What is capital? An inquiry into the meaning of the words 'capital' and 'labour'*. London: Eveleigh Nash, 1925. 72p.

250 **Williams**, Thomas George. *The main currents of social and industrial change, 1870–1924*. London: Pitman, 1925. viii, 314p.

Chap. VI. 'Trade cycles and unemployment.'

Chap. VII. 'Industrial conflict and conciliation.'

Chap. VIII. 'Industrial welfare.'

Chap. IX. 'The labour movement.'

Chap. X. 'Social welfare.'

With statistical appendices.

251 **Board of Trade**. *Survey of industrial relations*. London: H.M.S.O., 1926. v, 497p.

3rd vol. of the Reports of the Committee on Industry and Trade.

252 **Catlin**, Warren Benjamin. *The labor problem in the United States and Great Britain*. New York, London: Harper, 1926. x, 659p.

D.Phil. thesis, Columbia University.

Revised edition. 1935. xii, 765p.

253 **Hayward**, W. R. and **Johnson**, G. W. *The evolution of labour: past, present and future*. London: Duckworth, 1926. 223p.

254 **Rose**, Frank Herbert. *Our industrial jungle*. London: Faber and Gwyer, 1926. xxii, 178p.

255 **Manchester Guardian**. *Industrial relations*. Manchester: John Russell Scott, for the Manchester Guardian and Evening News Ltd., 1927. 36p.

A collection of articles.

256 **Spencer**, Malcolm (ed.). *The kingdom of God in industry*. London: Independent P., 1927. 92p.

Second edition. 1928. Issued by a Joint Social Council of the Churches.

257 **Clay**, Henry. 'The Liberal industrial report.' *Econ. J.*, XXXVIII, 150 (June 1928), 193–203.

Discusses 259.

258 **Hook**, Alfred. *The human factor in industry and politics: an appeal to the Churches*. London: King, 1928. xi, 211p.

259 **Liberal Party**. *Britan's industrial future; being the report of the Liberal industrial inquiry*. London: Benn, 1928. xxiv, 503p.

Book 3. 'Industrial relations', p. 143–242.

260 **Shields**, Bernard Francis. *The evolution of industrial organisation*. London: Pitman, 1928. xii, 296p.

Second edition. 1930. xv, 414p.

261 **International Industrial Relations Institute.** 1st Congress, Cambridge, 1928. *Report of first triennial congress held in Cambridge (England) July, 1928, on the subject of fundamental relationships between all sections of the industrial community.* The Hague, 1928–9. 2v. in 1.

Text chiefly in English, with some contributions in French or German.

Section I. Reports from countries, edited in the original languages for the members of the Congress.

Section II. The Cambridge proceedings.

262 **Clay,** *Sir* Henry. *The problem of industrial relations, and other lectures.* London: Macmillan, 1929. ix, 322p.

263 **Selekman,** Benjamin Morris and **Selekman,** Sylvia Kopald. *British industry today: a study of English trends in industrial relations.* New York, London: Harper, 1929. 290p.

264 **International Industrial Relations Institute.** *Rational organisation and industrial relations: a symposium of views from management, labour and the social sciences, contributed to the 1929 I.R.I. discussions meeting on the subject of human relations in a rationally organized industry.* The Hague, 1930. 279p.

Edited by M. L. Fleddérus. Chiefly in English with some contributions in French and German.

265 **Hilton,** John. *Industrial relations: inaugural lecture.* Cambridge: Cambridge U.P., 1931. 41p.

266 **Richardson,** John Henry. *Industrial relations in Great Britain.* Geneva: International Labour Office, 1933. xi, 272p. (Studies and reports, series A (Industrial Relations), 36.)

Second edition. 1938. xi, 290p.

267 **Richardson,** John Henry. 'Industrial relations.' British Association. *Britain in depression.* London: Pitman, 1935. p. 57–79.

268 **Kelsall,** Roger Keith and **Plaut,** Theodor. *Industrial relations in the modern state: an introductory survey.* London: Methuen, 1937. xii, 131p.

269 **Institute of Labour Management.** 'Industrial relations in Great Britain.' *Seventh International Management Congress, Washington, D.C., September 19th to September 23rd 1938. Personnel—General Management papers, part I.* Baltimore, Md.: Waverly P., 1938. p. 21–4.

270 **Richardson,** John Henry. 'Industrial relations.' British Association. Economic Science and Statistics Section. *Britain in recovery.* London: Pitman, 1938. p. 113–21.

271 **Rowntree,** Benjamin Seebohm. 'The modern labor problem.' *Wharton Assembly: addresses, 1938.* Philadelphia: U. of Pennsylvania P., 1938. p. 1–14.

272 **United States.** Commission on Industrial Relations in Great Britain and Sweden. *Report of the Commission on Industrial Relations in Great Britain, with appendices.* Washington: U.S.G.P.O., 1938. vii, 146p.

273 **Catherwood,** B. F. 'A synthesis of the British system of industrial and labour relations.' Gannett, F. E. and Catherwood, B. F. (eds.). *Industrial and labour relations in Great Britain: a symposium.* New York: the editors, 1939. p. 12–28.

274 **Clynes,** John Robert. 'The British Labour Party and industry.' Gannett, F. E. and Catherwood, B. F. (eds.). *Industrial and labour relations in Great Britain: a symposium.* New York: the editors, 1939. p. 270–80.

275 **Frey,** John Philip. 'A comparison of the American and British systems of industrial and labour relations.' Gannett, F. E. and Catherwood, B. F. (eds.). *Industrial and labour relations in Great Britain: a symposium.* New York: the editors, 1939. p. 333–44.

Author was President of the Metal Trades Department of the American Federation of Labor.

276 **Gannett,** Frank Ernest. 'How Britain handles her labour problem.' Gannett, F. E. and Catherwood, B. F. (eds.). *Industrial and labour relations in Great Britain: a symposium.* New York: the editors, 1939. p. 3–11.

277 **Gannett,** Frank Ernest and **Catherwood,** B. F. (eds.). *Industrial and labour relations in Great Britain: a symposium.* New York: the editors, 1939. xiv, 364p.

278 **Wolman,** Leo. 'Labour relations since the war.' Warren, R. B., Wolman, L. and Clay, H. *The state in society: a series of public lectures delivered under the auspices of McGill University, Montreal, January 23, 1939–February 10, 1939.* London, New York: Oxford U.P., 1940. p. 78–89.

279 **Ministry of Labour and National Service.** *Industrial relations handbook* . . . London: H.M.S.O., 1944. 260p.

Supplement 1. May 1947. 1947. 39p.
Supplement 2. January 1948. 1948. 30p.
Supplement 3. December 1949. 1950. 100p.
Supplement 4. 1951. 44p.
Revised editions, 1953, 1961, 1967.

280 **Kirkaldy,** Harold Stewart. *Industrial relations in conditions of full employment: an inaugural lecture* . . . Cambridge: Cambridge U.P., 1945. 26p.

281 **McGregor,** Alexander Grant. *Collective bargaining and decadence: the solution of Britain's gravest problem.* London: Pitman, 1946. 79p.

282 **Kirkaldy,** Harold Stewart. *The spirit of industrial relations: the Perin Memorial Lectures delivered at Jamshedpur in December 1946* . . . Bombay: Oxford U.P., 1947. xviii, 138p.

283 **British Association for Commercial and Industrial Education.** *The short road to industrial co-operation.* London, 1948. 92p.

284 **Shakespeare,** *Sir* Geoffrey Hithersay. *A new climate in industry.* London, 1948. 35p.

285 **Watson,** Peter. 'Industrial relations.' Berry, A. and Wilson, D. (eds.). *Conservative Oxford.* [Oxford?]: Oxford University Conservative Association, 1949. p. 45–8.

286 **Whyte**, William Hamilton. 'The future of industrial relations.' *Nineteenth Century*, CXLVI (November 1949), 304–10.

287 **Fraser**, Michael. *The worker in industry: a study of the Workers' Charter and the practical application of its proposals.* London: Conservative Political Centre, 1950. 71p.

288 **Wylie**, Tom. *A concise guide to industrial relations.* Birmingham: Birmingham Central Technical College, Students' Union, Industrial Administration Group, 1950. 34p.

Fifth revised edition. Birmingham: Institute of Supervisory Management, 1966. 65p.

289 **United States**. Research Council For Economic Security. *Studies in social security abroad: labor-management relations, Great Britain, France, Sweden.* Chicago, 1951. 21p. (Publication 79.)

290 **Albu**, Austen. 'The organisation of industry.' Crossman, R. H. S. (ed.). *New Fabian essays.* London: Turnstile P., 1952. p. 121–42.

291 **Flanders**, Allan David. 'Industrial relations.' Worswick, G. D. N. and Ady, P. H. (eds.). *The British economy 1945–1950.* Oxford: Clarendon P., 1952. p. 101–24.

292 **Briggs**, Asa. 'Social background.' Flanders, A. and Clegg, H. A. (eds.). *The system of industrial relations in Great Britain . . .* Oxford: Blackwell, 1954. p. 1–41.

293 **Flanders**, Allan David and **Clegg**, Hugh Armstrong (eds.). *The system of industrial relations in Great Britain: its history, law and institutions.* Oxford: Blackwell, 1954. viii, 380p.

Corrected impression, reprinted 1964.

1970 edition by H. A. Clegg.

294 **Richardson**, John Henry. *An introduction to the study of industrial relations.* London: Allen and Unwin, 1954. 442p.

295 **A Special Correspondent**. 'The malaise in industrial relations.' *Banker*, CII, 337 (February 1954), 79–86.

296 **Fitzgerald**, Mark J. *Britain: views on industrial relations.* Notre Dame, Ind.: U. of Notre Dame P., 1955. ix, 221p.

297 **Friedmann**, Georges. 'Some experiments in industrial and human relations.' *Int. Labour Rev.*, LXXI, 1 (January 1955), 79–87.

'. . . a preview of new matter prepared by the author for a further edition of his work *Problèmes humains du machinisme industriel*, which is to be published shortly (Paris, Gallimard) . . . Here he discusses a number of experiments carried out in French and British undertakings with the object of improving industrial relations.'

298 **Mortished**, R. J. P. 'Industrial relations.' *Administration*, IV, 2 (Summer 1956), 41–53.

299 **Garrett**, *Sir* A. W. *Changing industrial relations.* London, 1957. 26p.

300 **Marquand**, Hilary Adair. 'Industrial relations in Britain today.' *Labor Law J.*, VII, 6 (June 1957), 407–15.

301 **Badger**, Alfred Bowen. *Man in employment: the fundamental principles of industrial relations.* London: Booker, 1958. 320p.

Second edition. London: Macmillan; New York: St Martin's P., 1966. x, 422p.

302 **Dunlop**, John Thomas. *Industrial relations systems.* New York: Holt, 1958. xiii, 399p. (A Holt-Dryden book.)

303 **Ford**, Percy. *The economics of collective bargaining.* Oxford: Blackwell, 1958. xiv, 121p.

Second edition, revised. 1964. x, 141p.

304 **Hare**, Anthony Edward Christian. *The first principles of industrial relations.* London: Macmillan, 1958. vii, 145p.

Second edition. London: Macmillan; New York: St Martin's P., 1965. vii, 149p.

305 **Phelps Brown**, Ernest Henry. *The growth of British industrial relations: a study from the standpoint of 1906–14.* London: Macmillan; New York: St Martin's P., 1959. xxxvii, 414p.

Reprinted. 1965. (Papermacs 124.)

306 **Richardson**, John Henry. 'Some aspects of industrial relations.' *Indian J. Labour Econ.*, II, 1 (April 1959), 46–59.

Based on addresses which the author gave during the Convocation Week at Lucknow University and the Second All-India Labour Economics Conference at Agra.

307 **Kerr**, Clark, **Dunlop**, John Thomas, **Harbison**, Frederick Harris and **Myers**, Charles A. *Industrialism and industrial man: the problems of labor and management in economic growth.* Cambridge, Mass.: Harvard U.P., 1960. 331p.

Another edition. London: Heinemann, 1962. 317p. (Heinemann books on sociology.)

Second edition. New York: Oxford U.P., 1964. 263p. (A galaxy book.)

308 **Roberts**, Benjamin Charles. 'Industrial relations in an affluent society.' *Lloyds Bank Rev.*, n.s., 55 (January 1960), 29–40.

309 **Levine**, Solomon B. 'Our future industrial society: a global vision.' *Ind. Labor Relat. Rev.*, XIV, 4 (July 1961), 548–55.

A review article on *Industrialism and industrial man . . .* by C. Kerr, J. T. Dunlop, F. Harbison, and C. A. Myers.

310 **Meyers**, Frederic. 'A look at labor relations in Britain.' *Calif. Mgmt. Rev.*, III, 3 (Spring 1961), 16–27.

311 **Shanks**, Michael. *The stagnant society: a warning.* Harmondsworth: Penguin Books, 1961. 236p. (Penguin special S189.)

312 **Liberal Party**. *Industrial affairs: a report submitted to the Liberal Party by a committee under the chairmanship of Mr Peter McGregor, June 1962.* London: Liberal Publications Department, 1962. 52p.

313 **Roberts**, Benjamin Charles (ed.). *Industrial relations: contemporary problems and perspectives.* London: Methuen, 1962. xvi, 288p.

Revised edition. 1968.

314 **Ross**, Arthur Max. 'The new industrial relations in Britain.' *Labour Law. J.* XIII, 7 (July 1962), 492–501.

Reprinted in *Industrial Relations Research Association Spring meeting 1962.*

315 **Ross**, Arthur Max. 'Prosperity and British industrial relations.' *Ind. Relat.*, II, 2 (February 1963), 63–94.

316 **Industrial Relations Research Association**. 'Industrial relations in 1975: collective bargaining.' [Discussion.] Industrial Relations Research Association. *Proceedings of the seventeenth annual meeting, Chicago, Illinois, December 28 and 29, 1964*. p. 160–9.

Contribution by B. C. Roberts for Great Britain.

317 **Smith**, John Harold. 'Employers, workers, and unions.' *New Soc.*, III, 80 (9 April 1964), 16–17. (New issues 5.)

318 **Flanders**, Allan David. *Industrial relations: what is wrong with the system? An essay on its theory and future*. London: Faber, 1965. 63p.

A companion volume to *Collective bargaining: prescription for change*.

Also published by the Institute of Personnel Management, London, 1965, 63p.

Reprinted in *Management and unions: the theory and reform of industrial relations*. London: Faber, 1970. p. 83–128.

319 **Stuttard**, Charles Geoffrey. *An ABC of industrial relations*. London: Industrial Society, 1965.

320 **Sykes**, Andrew James Macintyre. 'The ideological basis of industrial relations in Great Britain.' *Mgmt. Int.*, 6 (1965), 65–72.

321 **Clarke**, Michael. *Industrial relations*. London: Industrial Society, 1966. vi, 36p. (Notes for managers 11.)

322 **Flanders**, Allan David. *The future of voluntarism in industrial relations*. London: Institute of Personnel Management, 1966. 8p. (Industrial relations series.)

'Sequel to *Industrial relations: what is wrong with the system?*'

Also published in *Personnel Management*, XLVIII, 378 (December 1966), i–viii.

323 **Larke**, W. M. 'Industrial relations.' *British Automation Conference, 1965: report of the meeting at Eastbourne, 7–10 November, 1965*. London: Institution of Production Engineers, 1966. p. 162–9.

The author was Adviser to the Board on Industrial Legislation and Sociological Development, Stewarts and Lloyds Ltd.

324 **Lerner**, Shirley W. 'Social and labour problems.' Prest, A. R. (ed.). *The U.K. economy: a manual of applied economics*. London: Weidenfeld and Nicolson, 1966. p. 191–242.

Title in *Contents* is 'Social and labour relations'.

Second edition. 1968. p. 183–227. Chapter entitled 'Social problems'.

325 **Oldfield**, Frederick Edwin. *New look industrial relations*. London: Mason Reed, 1966. 152p.

326 **Portus**, J. H. 'United States, Britain and Australia: some comparisons.' *J. Ind. Relat.*, VIII, 2 (July 1966), 111–27.

'This is a combination of two papers read to the first weekend convention of the Industrial Relations Society of South Australia in September, 1965.'

327 **Cannon**, Leslie. 'Human problems in industry. II. Current problems of industrial relations.' *R. Soc. Arts J.*, CXV, 5127 (February 1967), 163–71.

Cantor Lecture delivered 28 November 1966. Discussion, p. 171–5.

The author was General President of the Electrical Trades Union.

328 **Flanders**, Allan David. *Collective bargaining: prescription for change*. London: Faber, 1967. 80p.

'A companion piece and practical sequel' to *Industrial relations: what is wrong with the system?*

A revised version of written evidence submitted to the Royal Commission on Trade Unions and Employers' Associations in November 1966, subsequently published in *Selected written evidence submitted to the Royal Commission*, p. 542–80. The author's oral evidence to the Commission was published as *Minutes of evidence 62*.

Reprinted in *Management and unions: the theory and reform of industrial relations*. London: Faber, 1970. p. 155–211.

329 **Woodward**, Joan. 'Human problems in industry. I. The study of industrial behaviour.' *R. Soc. Arts J.*, CVX, 5127 (February 1967), 146–58.

Cantor Lecture delivered 21 November 1966. Discussion, p. 158–62.

330 **Macarthy**, Peter G. (ed.). 'The future of industrial relations in Western Europe: approaches and perspectives. II. Seminar discussion.' *Int. Inst. Labour Studies Bull.*, 4 (February 1968), 116–46.

A discussion of a lecture given by Jean-Daniel Reynaud. The lecture is printed in the same issue of the *Bulletin*, p. 86–115.

331 **Mortimer**, James Edward. *Industrial relations*. London: Heinemann for the Institute of Supervisory Management, 1968. 114p. (Supervisor's bookshelf.)

332 **Neal**, Leonard Francis and **Robertson**, Andrew. *The manager's guide to industrial relations*. London: Allen and Unwin, 1968. 151p. (Studies in management 3.)

333 **Reynaud**, Jean-Daniel. 'The future of industrial relations in Western Europe: approaches and perspectives. I. Public lecture. *Int. Inst. Labour Studies Bull.*, 4 (February 1968), 86–115.

A public lecture given in Geneva on 13 June 1967.

An analysis of a seminar on the subject matter of the lecture is given in the same issue of the *Bulletin*, p. 116–46.

334 **Robertson**, Norman and **Thomas**, J. L. *Trade unions and industrial relations*. London: Business Books, 1968. viii, 214p. ('Business management' books.)

335 **Wilson**, A. W. and **Hill**, Stanley R. *Industrial relations, law and economics*. London: Longmans, 1968. xi, 185p. (Supervisory series 3.)

A National Extension College course prepared in collaboration with the Institute of Supervisory Management.

336 **Armstrong**, Eric George Abbott. *Industrial relations: an introduction*. London: Harrap, 1969. viii, 211p.

337 **Coates**, Ken. 'The review of the year: storm centres of tomorrow.' *Trade Un. Regist.* (1969), 9–25.

338 **McCarthy**, William Edward John (ed.). *Industrial relations in Britain: a guide for management and unions*. London: Lyon, Grant and Green, 1969. vii, 151p. (Administrative Staff College, Henley, publication.)

339 **McCarthy**, William Edward John. 'Introduction: signs of change.' McCarthy, W. E. J. (ed.). *Industrial relations in Britain: a guide for management and unions*. London: Lyon, Grant and Green, 1969. p. 3–26.

340 **Neal**, Leonard Francis. 'Industrial relations in the '70's.' *Manchr. Statist. Soc. Trans.* (1969–70), 12p.

341 **Clegg**, Hugh Armstrong. *The system of industrial relations in Great Britain*. Oxford: Blackwell, 1970. xi, 484p.

1954 edition edited by A. Flanders and H. A. Clegg.

New edition. 1972.

342 **Flanders**, Allan David. *Management and unions: the theory and reform of industrial relations*. London: Faber, 1970. 317p.

343 **Grant**, Ronald Melville. *Industrial relations*. London: Ginn, 1970. 64p. (Manchester economics project. Satellite books 3.)

344 **McCarthy**, William Edward John. 'Industrial relations – the middle way.' *New Soc.*, XVI, 418 (1 October 1970), 590–1.

345 **McGregor**, Peter and **Lishman**, Gordon. *Participation in a competitive economy*. London: Liberal Publication Department, 1970. 24p. (Liberal focus 3.)

Title on cover: *The best of both worlds*.

346 **Stuttard**, Charles Geoffrey. *Problems at work*. London: Ginn; Melbourne [etc.]: Cheshire, 1970. 96p. (The world today.)

B. IRELAND

347 **Barry**, W. 'Labour and capital, limited.' *Dublin Rev.*, CXII (April 1893), 341–59.

348 **Kettle**, Thomas Michael. 'Labour and civilization.' *Dublin Rev.*, CLIV (April 1914), 355–71.

349 **Dale**, J. A. 'Labour problems in Northern Ireland.' *Int. Labour Rev.*, XI, 2 (February 1925), 229–38.

The author was Permanent Secretary, Ministry of Labour, Northern Ireland.

350 **O'Mahony**, David. *Industrial relations in Ireland: the background*. Dublin: Economic Research Institute, 1964. 56p. (Paper 19.)

351 **Hillery**, Patrick J. 'Industrial relations in the Republic of Ireland.' *Christus Rex*, XXI, 4 (October–December 1967), 305–10.

352 **Kavanagh**, James. 'The human side of industrial relations.' *Christus Rex*, XXI, 4 (October–December 1967), 338–42.

353 **McCarthy**, Charles. 'Industrial relations: the workers' view.' *Christus Rex*, XXI, 4 (October–December 1967), 358–64.

354 **O'Donnell**, Matthew. 'Industrial relations: a philosophical viewpoint.' *Christus Rex*, XXI, 4 (October–December 1967), 321–32.

355 **Walker**, Brian W. 'Industrial relations in Northern Ireland.' *Christus Rex*, XXI, 4 (October–December 1967), 311–20.

356 **Daly**, George F. A. *Industrial relations: comparative aspects, with particular reference to Ireland*. Cork: Mercier P., 1968. xiv, 344p.

357 **Carroll**, John F. 'A trade union view of industrial relations.' Irish Management Institute. *Industrial democracy: a symposium*. Dublin: the Institute, 1969. p. 49–55.

The author was General Vice-President of the Irish Transport and General Workers' Union.

PART TWO

EMPLOYEES: INDUSTRIAL ATTITUDES AND BEHAVIOUR

The memoirs and autobiographies of workers have generally been classified at Part Six, IV, A, 1, and Part Six, IV, A, 3 because they are primarily concerned with describing conditions of work. But they also contain material on workers' attitudes and behaviour.

I. GENERAL

This section includes general material on industrial sociology and industrial psychology (but see Part One, III for material on the contribution of sociology and psychology to the study of industrial relations), as well as on such subjects as work and leisure, the meaning of work, orientations to work, and the sociology of particular occupations. Material on social relationships at work and the social organisation of work is also included here; material on the more formal aspects of work group organisation is classified at Part Three, III, G, 9. Material dealing with the attitudes of supervisors towards their work is classified at Part Four, II, C. See also Part Six, II, A.

358 **Pear**, Tom Hatherley. 'The applications of psychology to industry.' Berriman, A. E., and others. *Industrial administration: a series of lectures*. Manchester: Manchester U.P.; London: Longmans, Green, 1920. p. 23–47.

359 **Watts**, F. *An introduction to the psychological problems of industry*. London: Allen and Unwin, 1921. 240p.

360 **Williams**, Whiting. *Horny hands and hampered elbows: the worker's mind in Western Europe*. London: Allen and Unwin, 1922. xi, 285p.

361 **Harrison**, Hubert Deacon. *Industrial psychology and the production of wealth*. London: Methuen, 1924. x, 184p.

362 **Sargant Florence**, Philip. *Economics of fatigue and unrest and the efficiency of labour in English and American industry*. London: Allen and Unwin; New York: Holt, 1924. 426p.

363 **Firth**, Violet Mary. *The psychology of the servant problem: a study in social relationships*. London: C. W. Daniel, 1925. 96p.

364 **Tilgher**, Adriano. *Work: what it has meant to men through the ages*. London: Harrap, 1931. xiv, 225p.

Translated by Dorothy Canfield Fisher.

Later published under the title *Homo faber: work through the ages*. Chicago: Regney, [1965?]. xix, 225p. (Gateway edition 6085.)

365 **Dataller**, Roger. 'The worker's point of view. XIV. The problem of allegiance.' *Hum. Factor*, VII, 5 (May 1933), 181–5.

Reprinted in *The worker's point of view: a symposium*. London: Woolf, 1933. p. 153–160.

366 **Stewart**, William Dale. *Some psychological aspects of employment in the coal-mining industry, with special reference to the Ayrshire coalfield in Scotland*. 1933. (B.Litt. thesis, University of Oxford.)

367 **Viteles**, Morris Simon. *Industrial psychology*. London: Cape, 1933. xviii, 652p.

Reprinted. 1962.

368 *The worker's point of view: a symposium*. London: Woolf, 1933. 160p.

Contains articles which appeared originally in *The Human Factor*, the journal of the National Institute of Industrial Psychology.

W. F. Watson. 'A working mechanic's view.'

J. H. Mitchell. 'A miner's view.'

J. Gibson. 'A plasterer's view.'

L. Katin. 'A compositor's view.'

T. H. Hargrave. 'Working conditions and morale.'

R. Dataller. 'The individual employer *versus* the joint stock corporation.'

369 **Brown**, Alfred Barratt. *The machine and the worker*. London: Nicholson and Watson, 1934. 215p. (University extension library.)

370 **Dickson**, M. G. 'The factory worker's philosophy.' *Sociol. Rev.*, XXVIII, 3 (July 1936), 295–312.

Based on the author's experiences as a labourer in a London factory, after graduating from Oxford.

371 **Whitehead**, Thomas North. *The industrial worker: a statistical study of human relations in a group of manual workers*. London: Oxford U.P., 1938. 2v.

Vol. 1. Text.

Vol. 2. Diagrams.

372 **Meyenberg**, F. L. 'An industrial employee – a lifelong apprentice.' *Occup. Psychol.*, XIII, 1 (January 1939), 52–8.

373 **Mass-Observation**. *War factory: a report.* London: Gollancz, 1943. 127p.
Editor of Mass-Observation: Tom Harrison.

374 **Smith**, May. *An introduction to industrial psychology.* London: Cassell, 1943. 264p.
Fifth edition. 1952. 295p.

375 **Oakley**, Charles Allen. *Men at work.* London: Hodder and Stoughton; U. of London P., 1945. xii, 301p.
On industrial psychology.

376 **Tenen**, Cora. *Adolescent attitudes to authority at work.* 1945. (M.A. thesis, University of Manchester).

377 **Marriott**, Reginald. *The importance of the attitudes of men and women workers in industry.* 1946. (M.Sc. thesis, University of Manchester.)

378 **Maule**, Harry Gordon and **Smith**, May. *Industrial psychology and the laundry trade.* London: Pitman, 1947. vii, 144p.

379 **Tenen**, Cora. 'Some problems of discipline among adolescents in factories.' *Occup. Psychol.*, XXI, 2 (April 1947), 75–81.

380 **British Association for the Advancement of Science**. 'Human factors in industry.' *Advmt. Sci.*, V, 17 (April 1948), 96–118.
Main contributions to a conference held on Saturday, May 8, 1948 at Leamington.
Summary of proceedings appeared in *Nature*, CLXI, p. 791.

381 **Davis**, Norah M. 'Attitudes to work among building operatives.' *Occup. Psychol.*, XXII, 2 (April 1948), 56–62.

382 **Gillespie**, James J. *Free expression in industry: a social-psychological study of work and leisure.* London: Pilot P., 1948. 167p.

383 **Political and Economic Planning**. 'The human factor in industry.' *Planning*, XIV, 279 (5 March 1948), 249–84.

384 **Zweig**, Ferdynand. *Men in the pits.* London: Gollancz, 1948. 177p.
Also Left Book Club edition.

385 **Cole**, Margaret Isabel. *Miners and the Board.* London: Fabian Publications and Gollancz, 1949. 25p. (Research series 134.)
'Based on the Report of a Fabian Research Group.'
Miners' attitudes to nationalisation.

386 **Wilson**, A. T. M. *Hospital nursing auxiliaries: notes on a background survey and job analysis.* London: Tavistock Publications, 1949. 32p.
Shorter version in *Hum. Relat.*, III (1950), 89–105.

387 **Taylor**, Gordon Rattray. *Are workers human?* London: Falcon P., 1950. 196p.
Boston: Houghton Mifflin, 1952. 273p.

388 **Woodward**, Joan. *Employment relations in a group of hospitals; a report of a survey by the Department of Social Science of the University of Liverpool.* London: Institute of Hospital Administration, 1950.

389 **Gabriel**, J. *An analysis of the emotional problems of teachers.* 1950–51. (Ph.D. thesis, University of London.)

390 **Chambers**. Eric Gordon. *Psychology and the industrial worker.* Cambridge: Cambridge U.P., 1951. 189p.

391 **Ferguson**, Thomas and **Cunnison**, James. *The young wage-earner: a study of Glasgow boys.* London, New York: Oxford U.P. for the Nuffield Foundation, 1951. x, 194p.

392 **Fraser**, John Munro. *Psychology: general, industrial, social.* London: Pitman, 1951. x, 310p.
Second edition. 1963. x, 336p.
Second edition, paperback. 1967.

393 **Lloyd**, Roger. 'The English navvy.' *Q. Rev.*, CCLXXXIX, 590 (October 1951), 500–9.

394 **Rice**, Albert Kenneth. 'The use of unrecognized cultural mechanisms in an expanding machine-shop, with a contribution to the theory of leadership. (The Glacier Project III.)' *Hum. Relat.*, IV, 2 (May 1951), 143–60.

395 **Trist**, Eric Lansdowne and **Bamforth**, K. W. 'Some social and psychological consequences of the longwall method of coal-getting: an examination of the psychological situation and defences of a work group in relation to the social structure and technological content of the work system.' *Hum. Relat.*, IV, 1 (February 1951), 3–38.

396 **Walker**, J. and **Marriott**, Reginald. 'A study of some attitudes to factory work.' *Occup. Psychol.*, XXV, 3 (July 1951), 181–91.

397 **Heron**, Alastair Arnold Carnegie. *A psychological study of occupational adjustment.* 1951–52. (Ph.D. thesis, University of London.)

398 **Kristy**, N. F. *Criteria of occupational success among Post Office counter clerks.* 1951–52. (Ph.D. thesis, University of London.)

399 **Bartlett,** *Sir* Frederic. 'The employment of the older worker.' Ministry of Labour and National Service. *The worker in industry.* London: H.M.S.O., 1952. p. 80–7.

400 **Handyside**, John Duncan. 'An estimate of the size of primary working groups in British industry.' *Occup. Psychol.*, XXVI, 2 (April 1952), 107–8.

401 **Zweig**, Ferdynand. *The British worker.* Harmondsworth: Penguin Books, 1952. 243p. (Pelican books A237.)

402 **Balfour**, William Campbell. 'Productivity and the worker.' *Br. J. Sociol.*, IV, 3 (September 1953), 257–65.

403 **Bond-Williams**, N. I. 'Informal workers' groups: an interim report on an industrial experiment.' *Br. Mgmt. Rev.*, XI, 4 (July 1953), 37–56.

404 **Denerley**, Ronald Alfred. 'Workers' attitudes towards an establishment scheme.' *Occup. Psychol.*, XXVII, 1 (January 1953), 1–10.

405 **Livingstone**, Elizabeth. 'Attitudes of women operatives to promotion.' *Occup. Psychol.*, XXVII, 4 (October 1953), 191–9.
'A report of a survey carried out in the course of the NIIP Foreman Research.'

406 **Greaves**, Mary Elsworth. *A psychological investigation into certain factors affecting attitudes towards work.* 1953–54. (M.A. thesis, University of London.)

407 **Lynch**, G. W. *An estimate of the extent of larceny in industry and the motivations of this phenomenon.* 1953–54. (M.Sc.(Econ.) thesis, University of London.)

408 **Wittermans**, E. *The social organisation of an industrial work group.* 1953–54. (M.A. thesis, University of London.)

409 **Balchin**, Nigel Martin. *The worker in modern industry.* London: Institute of Personnel Management, 1954. 14p. (Occasional papers 5.)

410 **Brown**, James Alexander Campbell. *The social psychology of industry.* Harmondsworth: Penguin, 1954. 310p. (Pelican book.)

411 **Department of Scientific and Industrial Research** and **Medical Research Council.** *First report of the Joint Committee on Human Relations in Industry, March 1953 to March 1954.* London: H.M.S.O., 1954. iv, 16p.

412 **Hearnshaw**, L. S. 'Attitudes to work.' *Occup. Psychol.*, XXVIII, 3 (July 1954), 129–39.
Chairman's Address to the Industrial Section of the British Psychological Society, London, 14 January 1954.

413 **Ling**, Thomas Mortimer. 'Major psychosocial problems of industry.' Ling, T. M. (ed.). *Mental health and human relations in industry.* London: H. K. Lewis, 1954. p. 7–25.

414 **Ling**, Thomas Mortimer. 'Research in mental health and human relations in industry.' Ling, T. M. (ed.). *Mental health and human relations in industry.* London: H. K. Lewis, 1954. p. 229–48.

415 **Ling**, Thomas Mortimer. 'A survey of the teaching of mental health and human relations in industry.' Ling, T. M. (ed.). *Mental health and human relations in industry.* London: H. K. Lewis, 1954. p. 205–28.

416 **Lloyd Davies**, T. A. 'Society and work.' Ling, T. M. (ed.). *Mental health and human relations in industry.* London: H. K. Lewis, 1954. p. 193–204.

417 **Richardson**, Stephen Alexander. *The social organization of British and United States merchant ships.* Ithaca, N.Y.: New York State School of Industrial and Labor Relations, 1954. xi, 122 leaves.
Mimeographed.

418 **Scott**, Jerome Fentress. 'Research in industrial management.' Ling, T. M. (ed.). *Mental health and human relations in industry.* London: H. K. Lewis, 1954. p. 177–92.

419 **Tredgold**, Roger Francis. 'Aggression in industry.' Ling, T. M. (ed.). *Mental health and human relations in industry.* London: H. K. Lewis, 1954. p. 69–82.

420 **Viteles**, Morris Simon. *Motivation and morale in industry.* London: Staples P., 1954. xvi, 510p.
New York: W. W. Norton. 1953.

421 **Wilson**, V. W. 'The individual and the group in industry.' Ling, T. M. (ed.). *Mental health and human relations in industry.* London: H. K. Lewis, 1954. p. 27–46.

422 **Sluckin**, W. *Criteria and circumstances of occupational success in co-operative employment at Newcastle-on-Tyne.* 1954–55. (Ph.D. thesis, University of London.)

423 **Burns**, Tom. 'The reference of conduct in small groups: cliques and cabals in occupational milieux.' *Hum. Relat.*, VIII, 4 (November 1955), 467–86.

424 **Bradney**, Pamela J. *The status system of a modern store.* 1955–56. (D.Phil. thesis, University of Oxford.)

425 **Haines**, D. B. *The small working group as a problem of management.* 1955–56. (M.Sc. (Econ.) thesis, University of London.)

426 **Dennis**, Norman, **Henriques**, Fernando and **Slaughter**, Clifford. *Coal is our life.* London: Eyre and Spottiswoode, 1956. 255p.

427 **Fogarty**, Michael Patrick. *Personality and group relations in industry.* London: Longmans, Green, 1956. ix, 341p.

428 **London Press Exchange, Ltd.** *Work in the welfare age.* London: London Press Exchange, 1956. 36p. (Papers dealing with subjects of general significance for the community 4.)
Contributions: W. H. Scott. 'Leadership in industry.' p. 7–16.
Victor Feather. 'A trade union view.' p. 17–22.
Daniel Bell. 'The evasion of work.' p. 23–30.
'What do workers want?: research report.' p. 31–6.

429 **Richardson**, Stephen Alexander. 'Organizational contrasts on British and American ships.' *Adm. Sci. Q.*, I, 2 (September 1956), 189–207.

430 **Wyatt**, Stanley, **Marriott**, Reginald and **Denerley**, Ronald Alfred. *A study of attitudes to factory work.* London: H.M.S.O., 1956. 115p. (Medical Research Council. Special reports 292.)

431 **Balchin**, Nigel Martin. 'The development of industry: its impact on the worker.' Thomson, D. C. (ed.). *Management, labour and community.* London: Pitman, 1957. p. 132–43.

432 **Bradney**, Pamela J. 'The joking relationship in industry.' *Hum. Relat.*, X, 2 (May 1957), 179–87.
Based on part of the research undertaken for a D.Phil. thesis, Oxford: *The status system of a modern store.*

433 **Herzberg**, Frederick, **Mausner**, Bernard, **Peterson**, Richard O. and **Capwell**, Dora F. *Job attitudes: review of research and opinion.* Pittsburgh, Penn.: Psychological Service of Pittsburgh, 1957.
'Literature review.'

434 **Horobin**, G. W. 'Community and occupation in the Hull fishing industry.' *Br. J. Sociol.*, VIII, 4 (December 1957), 343–56.

435 **Marsh**, Henry John. *People at work: essays and commentaries.* London: Industrial Welfare Society, 1957. vii, 68p.
Revised edition. 1959. xii, 74p.

436 **Thompson**, John William. *A factorial study of the values and attitudes of graduate teachers in training.* 1957. (M.Ed. thesis, University of Manchester.)

437 **Blain**, Isabel. *Comments on the job: views of employees in six companies. A study of data collected by Institute investigators during employee attitude surveys.* London: National Institute of Industrial Psychology, 1958. 20p. [Report 13.]

438 **Department of Scientific and Industrial Research** and **Medical Research Council.** *Final report of the Joint Committee on Human Relations in Industry 1954–57, and Report of the Joint Committee on Individual Efficiency in Industry 1953–57.* London: H.M.S.O., 1958. vi, 44p.
Chairmen: A. B. Waring; Sir Frederick Bartlett.

439 **Stephenson**, Richard M. 'Stratification, education and occupational orientation: a parallel study and review.' *Br. J. Sociol.*, IX, 1 (March 1958), 42–52.

440 **Cunnison**, Sheila. *Factors affecting the output of individuals in a group in an industrial situation.* 1959. (Ph.D. thesis, University of Manchester.)

441 **Fogarty**, Michael Patrick. 'On substitution between the goals of working groups.' *Br. J. Sociol.*, X, 1 (March 1959), 38–44.

442 **Lupton**, Tom. *Social factors influencing norms of production in British factories.* 1959. (Ph.D. thesis, University of Manchester.)

443 **Trist**, Eric Lansdowne and **Sofer**, Cyril. *Exploration in group relations: a residential conference held in September, 1957 by the University of Leicester and the Tavistock Institute of Human Relations.* Leicester: Leicester U.P., 1959. 68p.

444 **Andrews**, Anthony J. 'Advertising.' Todd, J. M. (ed.). *Work: Christian thought and practice; a symposium.* London: Darton, Longman and Todd; Baltimore, Md.: Helicon P., 1960. p. 72–82.
Personal account of an executive in a London advertising agency.

445 **Dominian**, Jack. 'The doctor.' Todd, J. M. (ed.). *Work: Christian thought and practice; a symposium.* London: Darton, Longman and Todd; Baltimore, Md.: Helicon P., 1960. p. 93–101.
Personal account.

446 **Foster**, John. 'Parish priest.' Todd, J. M. (ed.). *Work: Christian thought and practice; a symposium.* London: Darton, Longman and Todd; Baltimore, Md.: Helicon P., 1960. p. 102–12.
Personal account.

447 **Henriques**, Fernando. 'The miner and his lass.' *Twentieth Century,* CLXVII, 999 (May 1960), 405–12.

448 **McGlone**, John. 'The factory worker.' Todd, J. M. (ed.). *Work: Christian thought and practice; a symposium.* London: Darton, Longman and Todd; Baltimore, Md.: Helicon P., 1960. p. 48–54.
Personal account by a draughtsman in a factory in Glasgow.

449 **McGrath**, Patrick. 'The Englishman's work.' Todd, J. M. (ed.). *Work: Christian thought and practice; a symposium.* London: Darton, Longman and Todd; Baltimore, Md.: Helicon P., 1960. p. 27–43.

450 **Powell**, Robert. 'The agricultural worker.' Todd, J. M. (ed.). *Work: Christian thought and practice; a symposium.* London: Darton, Longman and Todd; Baltimore, Md.: Helicon P., 1960. p. 55–64.
Personal account of a farm manager in the Midlands.

451 **Rendel**, David. 'Government research.' Todd, J. M. (ed.). *Work: Christian thought and practice; a symposium.* London: Darton, Longman and Todd; Baltimore, Md.: Helicon P., 1960. p. 83–92.
Personal account of a research worker in aeronautics.

452 **Sheppard**, D. *A comparison of workers' and their employers' statements about the status of workers within an industry.* 1960. 3p. (Social Survey papers. Methodological series M.89.)

453 **Todd**, John Murray (ed.). *Work: Christian thought and practice; a symposium.* London: Darton, Longman and Todd; Baltimore, Md.: Helicon P., 1960. viii, 225p.

454 **Woodward**, Joan. *The saleswoman: a study of attitudes and behaviour in retail distribution.* London: Pitman, 1960. viii, 86p.

455 **Zweig**, Ferdynand. 'The new factory worker.' *Twentieth Century,* CLXVII, 999 (May 1960), 397–404.
Based on an inquiry originally to study the 'mutual impact of family life and industry', extended to social change, study of working and living conditions as affected by post-war development.

456 **Revans**, Reginald William. 'The measurement of supervisory attitudes.' *Manchr. Statist. Soc. Trans.* (1960–61), 32p.
The outlooks of ward sisters upon those with whom they work.

457 **Joseph**, Joyce. 'Research note on attitudes of 600 adolescent girls to work and marriage.' *Br. J. Sociol.*, XII, 2 (June 1961), 176–83.

458 **Sykes**, Andrew James Macintyre. *A comparison of the belief systems of three industrial groups.* 1961. (Ph.D. thesis, University of Glasgow.)

459 **Zweig**, Ferdynand. *The worker in an affluent society: family life and industry.* London: Heinemann, 1961. xvii, 268p. (Heinemann books on sociology.)

460 **Fraser**, John Munro. *Industrial psychology.* Oxford: Pergamon, 1962. ix, 181p. (Commonwealth and international library of science, technology and engineering 105.)

461 **Herbst**, P. G. *Autonomous group functioning: an exploration in behaviour theory and measurement.* London: Tavistock, 1962. xiii, 271p.
Based on an investigation in the British coal-mining industry.

462 **Lupton**, Tom. 'Behaviour in workshops.' *New Soc.*, 7 (15 November 1962), 13–15.

463 **Shimmin**, Sylvia. 'Extra-mural factors influencing behaviour at work.' *Occup. Psychol.*, XXXVI, 3 (July 1962), 124–31.
'Chairman's address to the Occupational Psychology Section of the British Psychological Society, delivered at a meeting held at Birkbeck College, London, on 16 February, 1962.'

464 **Sykes**, Andrew James Macintyre and **Bates**, James. 'A study of conflict between formal company policy and the interests of informal groups.' *Sociol. Rev.*, n.s., x, 3 (November 1962), 313–27.

465 **Tunstall**, Jeremy. *The fishermen.* London: MacGibbon and Kee, 1962. 294p.

466 **Cotgrove**, Stephen and **Parker**, Stanley Robert. 'Work and non-work.' *New Soc.*, II, 41 (11 July 1963), 18–19.
A review of recent studies.

467 **Fogarty**, Michael Patrick. *The rules of work.* London: Chapman, 1963. 299p.

468 **Gillis**, John S. and **Landsberger**, Henry A. 'The sense of responsibility among young workers. Part 3. Need achievement, job aspirations and life situation.' *Occup. Psychol.*, XXXVII, 2 (April 1963), 101–11.

469 **Goldthorpe**, John H. and **Lockwood**, David. 'Affluence and the British class structure.' *Sociol. Rev.*, n.s., XI, 2 (July 1963), 133–63.

470 **Klein**, Lisl. *The meaning of work.* London: Fabian Society, 1963. 21p. (Fabian tract 349.)

471 **Lupton**, Tom. *On the shop floor: two studies of workshop organization and output.* Oxford: Pergamon P., 1963. vii, 208p. (International series of monographs on social and behavioural sciences 2.)

472 **Raphael**, Winifred and **Zimmerman**, Michael William. *After the take over: a study of reactions of employees in a group of companies.* London: National Institute of Industrial Pyschology, 1963. 35p. (Reports 15.)

473 **Trist**, Eric Lansdowne, **Higgin**, G. W., **Murray**, H. and **Pollock**, A. B. *Organizational choice: capabilities of groups at the coal face under changing technologies: the loss, re-discovery and transformation of a work tradition.* London: Tavistock, 1963. xv, 332p.

474 **Acton Society Trust**. *Mergers.* London: the Trust, 1963–66. 3v.
1. *Mergers, past and present,* by R. Smith and D. Brooks.
2. *The human effects of mergers: the impact on managers,* by R. Stewart, P. Wingate and R. Smith.
3. *The human effects of mergers: the impact on the shop floor,* by D. Brooks and R. Smith.

475 **Cooper**, Robert C. *Leader's task relevance and subordinate behaviour in industrial work groups.* 1963–64. (Ph.D. thesis, University of Liverpool.)

476 **Cooper**, Robert. 'What makes a good work leader?' *New Soc.*, IV, 99 (20 August 1964), 11–13.

477 **Jones**, Kathleen. 'Social science teachers.' *New Soc.*, IV, 114 (3 December 1964), 15–16.

478 **Kelly**, Joe. 'The study of executive behaviour by activity sampling.' *Hum. Relat.*, XVII, 3 (August 1964), 277–88.

479 **Lupton**, Tom and **Cunnison**, Sheila. 'Workshop behaviour.' Gluckman, M. (ed.). *Closed systems and open minds . . .* Edinburgh, London: Oliver and Boyd, 1964. p. 103–28.

480 **Parker**, Stanley Robert. 'Type of work, friendship patterns, and leisure.' *Hum. Relat.*, XVII, 3 (August 1964), 215–19.

481 **Sykes**, Andrew James Macintyre. 'A study in changing the attitudes and stereotypes of industrial workers.' *Hum. Relat.*, XVII, 2 (May 1964), 143–54.
'. . . describes an attempt made to change the attitudes of hostility that certain workers held towards their foremen by changing the stereotype on which these attitudes were based.'

482 **Cotgrove**, Stephen. 'The relations between work and non-work among technicians.' *Sociol. Rev.*, n.s., XIII, 2 (July 1965), 121–9.

483 **Parker**, Stanley Robert. 'Work and non-work in three occupations.' *Sociol. Rev.*, n.s., XIII, 1 (March 1965), 65–75.
Bank employees, child care officers, youth employment officers.

484 **Close**, A. S. *A comparative study of work attitudes of married and single women in manual and clerical occupations.* 1965–66. (M.A. thesis, University of London.)

485 **Hollowell**, Peter Gilbert. *Some bases of job satisfaction in a mobile occupational group: an examination of the dimensions of satisfaction amongst lorry drivers.* 1965–66. (Ph.D. thesis, University of Wales, Cardiff.)

486 **Pendlebury**, A. C. *A study of work load, attitudes and behaviour of sales assistants.* 1965–66. (M.A. thesis, University of London.)

487 **Stockdale**, G. *A study of attitudes in an expanding textile company.* 1965–66. (M.Sc. Tech. thesis, University of Manchester.)

488 **Birmingham University**. Department of Extra-Mural Studies. *Social attitudes to work: a report by a sociology class under the guidance of Donald Macnair.* Birmingham: Institute of Supervisory Management, 1966. 38p.
Second edition, revised.
With an additional chapter by G. W. Howells.

489 **Box**, Steven and **Cotgrove**, Stephen. 'Scientific identity, occupational selection and role strain.' *Br. J. Sociol.*, XVII, 1 (March 1966), 20–8.

490 **Bucklow**, Maxine. 'A new role for the work group.' *Adm. Sci. Q.*, XI, 1 (June 1966), 59–78.

'This article discusses the role assigned to the work group to bring about desired changes in employee motivation, and suggests that the role proposed by the Tavistock Institute of Human Relations in London has been more successful than earlier approaches which derived largely from the Hawthorne studies.'

491 **Cunnison**, Sheila. *Wages and work allocation: a study of social relations in a garment workshop.* London: Tavistock Publications, 1966. xxvi, 291p.

492 **Cunnison**, Sheila. 'Work sharing and favouritism.' *New Soc.*, VIII, 212 (20 October 1966), 603–6.

From the author's *Wages and work allocation.*

493 **Daniel**, William Wentworth. 'A comparative consideration of two industrial work groups.' *Sociol. Rev.*, n.s., XIV, 1 (March 1966), 39–52.

494 **Foster**, J. G. *Loyalty in an expanding organisation.* 1966. (M.Sc. Tech. thesis, University of Manchester.)

495 **Goldthorpe**, John H. 'Attitudes and behaviour of car assembley workers: a deviant case and a theoretical critique.' *Br. J. Sociol.*, XVII, 3 (September 1966), 227–44.

496 **Institute of Supervisory Management.** *Social attitudes to work.* London: the Institute, 1966.

497 **Shimmin**, Sylvia. 'Concepts of work.' *Occup. Psychol.*, XL, 4 (October 1966), 195–201.

'Paper given at the first annual conference of the Social Psychology Section, British Psychological Society, at Oxford, July, 1966.'

498 **Sykes**, Andrew James Macintyre. 'Joking relationships in an industrial setting.' *Am. Anthrop.*, LXVIII, 1 (February 1966), 188–93.

'This paper describes a system of joking relationships that was found to exist between members of the male and female staff of a large Glasgow printing works.'

499 **Sykes**, Andrew James Macintyre. 'A study in attitude change.' *Occup. Psychol.*, XL, 1–2 (January–April 1966), 31–41.

'An attempt to change the attitudes of officers from the services towards trade unionism.'

500 **Barry**, B. A. *The normative regulation of behaviour in a research organisation.* 1966–67. (M.Sc. thesis, University of Wales, Cardiff.)

501 **Thomason**, George F. 'Managerial work roles and relationships.' *J. Mgmt. Studies*, III, 3 (October 1966), 270–84; IV, 1 (February 1967), 17–30.

'This paper presents the findings of a number of studies which were carried out by members of the Churchill College Management course . . . '

502 **Brown**, Richard K. 'Human relations and the work group.' Parker, S. R., and others. *The sociology of industry.* London: Allen and Unwin, 1967. p. 99–112.

503 **Cannon**, I. C. 'Ideology and occupational community: a study of compositors.' *Sociology*, I, 2 (May 1967), 165–85.

504 **Clark**, Stanley Carruthers. *The concept of alienation in industrial studies: a theoretical and methodological discussion.* 1967. 72p. (M.A. thesis, University of Manchester.)

505 **Cooper**, Robert and **Payne**, Roy. 'Extraversion and some aspects of work behaviour.' *Pers. Psychol.*, XX, 1 (1967), 45–57.

506 **Fox**, Alan. *An introduction to people and productivity.* Oxford, London: Pergamon, 1967. 18p. (Take home books; Productivity progress series.)

507 **Goldthorpe**, John H., **Lockwood**, David, **Bechhofer**, Frank and **Platt**, Jennifer. 'The affluent worker and the thesis of *embourgeoisement*: some preliminary research findings.' *Sociology*, I, 1 (January 1967), 11–31.

508 **Holmes**, Roger. 'The ownership of work: a psychological approach.' *Br. J. Ind. Relat.*, V, 1 (March 1967), 19–27.

509 **Ingham**, Geoffrey Keith. 'Organizational size, orientation to work and industrial behaviour.' *Sociology*, I, 3 (September 1967), 239–58.

510 **Mann**, Peter Henry. *Young men and work: a sociological enquiry.* Sheffield: Sheffield University, Department of Sociological Studies, 1967. 76 leaves.

A report to the Army Department, Ministry of Defence.

511 **Parker**, Stanley Robert. 'The subjective experience of work.' Parker, S. R., and others. *The sociology of industry.* London: Allen and Unwin, 1967. p. 147–57.

512 **Revans**, Reginald William. 'Quantitative methods and management research: a case – the sampling of shop-floor attitudes.' Mosson, T. M. (ed.). *Teaching the process of management: the proceedings of an international seminar.* London: Harrap, 1967. p. 153–75.

513 **Parker**, Stanley Robert. *Work and leisure: a study of their interrelation.* 1967–68. (Ph.D. thesis, University of London.)

514 **Redgrove**, J. A. *Work and the menstrual cycle.* 1967–68. (Ph.D. thesis, University of Birmingham.)

515 **Saunders**, G. R. *Relationship between personality and social factors and success as a sales representative, both of a petrol company and an animal food company.* 1967–68. (M.Sc. thesis, University of Aston.)

516 **Eldridge**, John E. T., and others. 'Status in steel: a group discussion.' Eldridge, J. E. T. *Industrial disputes: essays in the sociology of industrial relations.* London: Routledge and Kegan Paul; New York: Humanities P., 1968. Appendix C. p. 249–58.

Extracts from a tape-recorded group discussion between four blue-collar workers in a steel company, members of a W.E.A. class and two research workers.

517 **Goldthorpe**, John H., **Lockwood**, David, **Bechhofer**, Frank and **Platt**, Jennifer. *The affluent worker: industrial attitudes and behaviour.* London: Cambridge U.P., 1968. vii, 206p. (Cambridge studies in sociology 1.)

518 **Goldthorpe**, John H., **Lockwood**, David, **Bechhofer**, Frank and **Platt**, Jennifer. *The affluent worker: political attitudes and behaviour.* London: Cambridge U.P., 1968. vii, 94p. (Cambridge studies in sociology 2.)

519 **Hollowell**, Peter Gilbert. *The lorry driver.* London: Routledge and Kegan Paul, 1968. vii, 263p. (International library of sociology and social reconstruction.)

520 **Life**, Edward Andrew. *Behaviour in the working environment: an introduction to some recent thinking and research.* Henley-on-Thames: Administrative Staff College, 1968. 28p. (Occasional papers 10.)

521 **Millward**, Neil. 'Family status and behaviour at work.' *Sociol. Rev.*, n.s., XVI, 2 (July 1968), 149–64.

'. . . deals with the transitional period between leaving school and getting married of broadly working class young women . . . different arrangements by which these girls contribute to family income is an important factor in explaining their behaviour at work . . .'

522 **Williams**, Raymond. 'The meanings of work.' Fraser, R. (ed.). *Work: twenty personal accounts.* Harmondsworth: Penguin, 1968. p. 280–98.

523 **Bland**, C. S. *A study in attitudes in industrial apprentices to trade unions, social class and politics: an exploratory study into class consciousness.* 1968–69. (Ph.D. thesis, University of London.)

524 **Clegg**, N. C. *A study of the attitudes of National Coal Board craft apprentices and craftsmen in a college of further education towards home, work, college and aspects of these institutions.* 1968–69. (M.Ed. thesis, University of Leeds.)

525 **Hastings**, A. *The chartered accountant in industry: a study of values.* 1968–69. (Ph.D. thesis, University of Birmingham.)

526 **Heller**, Frank Alexander. *A study of attitudes and aspirations in an industrial setting.* 1968–69. (Ph.D. thesis, University of London.)

527 **Ingham**, Geoffrey Keith. *Organizational size, orientation to work, and industrial behaviour.* 1968–69. (Ph.D. thesis, University of Cambridge.)

528 **Salaman**, John Graeme. *Some sociological determinants of occupational communities.* 1968–69. (Ph.D. thesis, University of Cambridge.)

529 **Daniel**, William Wentworth. 'Industrial behaviour and orientation to work: a critique.' *J. Mgmt. Studies*, VI, 3 (October 1969), 366–375.

530 **Dunkerley**, David. *Techniques of analysis of executive behaviour.* 1969. (M.Sc. Econ. thesis, University of Wales, Cardiff.)

531 **Eldridge**, John E. T. 'The British blue-collar worker.' Dufty, N. F. (ed.). *The sociology of the blue-collar worker.* Leiden: Brill, 1969. p. 80–94.

532 **Eldridge**, John E. T. 'The British blue-collar worker.' *Int. J. Comp. Sociol.*, X, 1–2 (March–June 1969), 80–94.

533 **Foster**, Charles. *Building with men: an analysis of group behaviour and organization in a building firm.* London: Tavistock P., 1969. xv, 220p.

534 **Goldthorpe**, John H., **Lockwood**, David, **Bechhofer**, Frank and **Platt**, Jennifer. *The affluent worker in the class structure.* London: Cambridge U.P., 1969. viii, 239p. (Cambridge studies in sociology 3.)

535 **Ingham**, Geoffrey Keith. 'Plant size: political attitudes and behaviour.' *Sociol. Rev.*, n.s., XVII, 2 (July 1969), 235–49.

536 **Kelsall**, Roger Keith and **Kelsall**, Helen M. *The school teacher in England and the United States: the findings of empirical research.* Oxford: Pergamon, 1969. viii, 198p. (Commonwealth and international library. Education and educational research.)

537 **MacDonald**, Keith and **Nichols**, W. A. T. 'Employee involvement: a study of drawing offices.' *Sociology*, III, 2 (May 1969), 233–8.

Research note.

538 **Morgan**, David Hopcraft John. *Theoretical and conceptual problems in the study of social relations at work: an analysis of the differing definitions of women's roles in a Northern factory.* 1969. 408p. (Ph.D. thesis, University of Manchester.)

539 **Osuji**, O. N. *A study of the physical, psychological and sociological factors affecting industrial rehabilitees.* 1969. (Ph.D. thesis, Department of Management Sciences, University of Manchester Institute of Science and Technology.)

540 **Smith**, Peter B. 'Relationships between managers and their work associates.' *Adm. Sci. Q.*, XIV, 3 (September 1969), 338–45.

By P. B. Smith, David Moscow, Mel Berger, and Cary Cooper.

541 **Stuttard**, Charles Geoffrey. *Work is hell: an anatomy of workplace clichés.* London: Macdonald, 1969. 126p.

542 **Sykes**, Andrew James Macintyre. 'Navvies: their social relations.' *Sociology*, III, 2 (May 1969), 157–72.

543 **Sykes**, Andrew James Macintyre. 'Navvies: their work attitudes.' *Sociology*, III, 1 (January 1969), 21–35.

544 **Trist**, Eric Lansdowne and **Bamforth**, K. W. 'Technicism: some effects of material technology on managerial methods and on work situation and relationships.' Burns, T. (ed.). *Industrial man.* Harmondsworth: Penguin, 1969. p. 331–58.

Excerpt from 'Some social and psychological consequences of the longwall method of coal-getting.' *Hum. Relat.*, IV (1951), 3–38.

545 **Brown**, Richard and **Brannen**, Peter. 'Social relations and social perspectives amongst shipbuilding workers: a preliminary statement.' *Sociology*, IV, 1 (January 1970), 71–84; 2 (May 1970), 197–211.

546 **Chin**, K. K. F. *An examination into some aspects of women at work in clerical and manufacturing industries and their attitudes to job training, mobility and responsibility*. 1970. (M.Sc. dissertation, Department of Management Sciences, U.M.I.S.T.)

547 **Cotgrove**, Stephen Frederick and **Box**, Steven. *Science, industry and society: studies in the sociology of science*. London: Allen and Unwin, 1970. xii, 211p.

548 **Crompton**, Rosemary and **Wedderburn**, Dorothy. 'Technological constraints and workers' attitudes.' Woodward, J. (ed.). *Industrial organization: behaviour and control.* London: Oxford U.P., 1970. p. 203–33.

Based on material fully reported in the authors' *Workers' attitudes and technology: a case study*, Cambridge U.P., 1969.

549 **Davies**, J. G. W. 'What is occupational success?' *Occup. Psychol.*, XLIV (1970), 195–204.

Reprinted from *Occup. Psychol.*, XXIV (1950), 7–17.

550 **Davies**, J. G. W. 'What is occupational success? Postscript 1970.' *Occup. Psychol.*, XLIV (1970), 221–2.

551 **Dennis**, Norman, **Henriques**, Fernando and **Slaughter**, Clifford. 'An extreme occupation.' Butterworth, E and Weir, D. *The sociology of modern Britain: an introductory reader*. London: Fontana/Collins, 1970. p. 187–91.

Reprinted from *Coal is our life*. London: Eyre and Spottiswoode, 1956, p. 38, 44–5, 73–4, 76–7, 79–80.

552 **Goldthorpe**, John H. and **Lockwood**, David. 'The changing national class structure.' Butterworth, E. and Weir, D. *The sociology of modern Britain: an introductory reader*. London: Fontana/Collins, 1970. p. 206–13.

Reprinted from 'Affluence and the British class structure.' *Sociol. Rev.*, n.s., XI, 2 (July 1963), 133–63.

553 **Goldthorpe**, John H. 'Factory work.' Butterworth, E. and Weir, D. *The sociology of modern Britain: an introductory reader*. London: Fontana/Collins, 1970. p. 163–70.

Reprinted from 'Attitudes and behaviour of car assembly workers: a deviant case and a theoretical critique.' *Br. J. Sociol.*, XVII, 3 (September 1966), 227–40.

554 **Goldthorpe**, John H., **Lockwood**, David, **Bechhofer**, Frank and **Platt**, Jennifer. 'Industrial attitudes of affluent workers.' Worsley, P. (ed.). *Modern sociology: introductory readings*. Harmondsworth: Penguin, 1970. p. 235–8.

Excerpt from *The affluent worker: industrial attitudes and behaviour*. London: Cambridge U.P., 1968. p. 174–8.

555 **Ingham**, Geoffrey Keith. *Size of industrial organization and worker behaviour*. London: Cambridge U.P., 1970. 170p. (Cambridge papers in sociology 1.)

556 **Lane**, Michael. 'Publishing managers, publishing house organization and role conflict.' *Sociology*, IV, 3 (1970), 367–83.

557 **Lockwood**, David. 'The clerk.' Butterworth, E. and Weir, D. *The sociology of modern Britain: an introductory reader*. London: Fontana/Collins, 1970. p. 175–82.

Reprinted from D. Lockwood. *The black-coated worker*. London: Allen and Unwin, 1958. p. 89–95.

558 **Lupton**, Tom. 'Factory work.' Butterworth, E. and Weir, D. *The sociology of modern Britain: an introductory reader*. London: Fontana/Collins, 1970. p. 170–5.

Reprinted from T. Lupton. *On the shop floor*. Oxford: Pergamon P., 1963. p. 187–8, 195–9.

559 **MacFarlane**, James. 'Merchant seamen aboard ship: a study at the workplace.' *Ind. Relat. J.* (December 1970), 66–76.

560 **Mackenzie**, Gavin. 'The class situation of manual workers: the United States and Britain.' *Br. J. Sociol.*, XXI, 3 (September 1970), 333–42.

Review article.

561 **New Society**. *Work: a New Society social studies reader*. London: New Science Publications, [1970?]. 31p.

13 articles reprinted from *New Society*.

'Prepared mainly for use in schools and colleges . . .'

562 **Parker**, Stanley Robert. 'Work and leisure.' Butterworth, E. and Weir, D. *The sociology of modern Britain: an introductory reader*. London: Fontana/Collins, 1970. p. 191–4.

Reprinted from 'Work and non-work in three occupations.' *Sociol. Rev.* (March 1965), 65, 70–5.

563 **Reeves**, Joan Wynn. 'What is occupational success?' *Occup. Psychol.*, XLIV (1970), 213–17.

A shortened version of an article first published in *Occup. Psychol.*, XXIV (1950), 153–9.

564 **Reeves**, Joan Wynn. 'What is occupational success? Postscript 1970.' *Occup. Psychol.*, XLIV (1970), 219–20.

565 **Scott**, Donald. *The psychology of work*. London: Duckworth, 1970. x, 256p.

566 **Social Surveys (Gallup Poll) Limited.** *The attitude of seafarers to their employment: report submitted to the Committee of Inquiry into Shipping*. London: Board of Trade, 1970. 3v.

567 **South-Eastern Regional Hospital Board, Scotland.** *Junior hospital medical staff survey 1968/69: being a report to the South-Eastern Regional Hospital Board, Scotland, on material gathered during interviews with doctors in the post-registration house officer, senior house officer and registrar grades in the service of the region between October 1968 and April 1969*. Edinburgh: the Board, 1970. x, 74p.

By P. W. R. Petrie.

568 **Stott**, Mary Boole. 'What is occupational success?' *Occup. Psychol.*, XLIV (1970), 205–12.
Reprinted from *Occup. Psychol.*, XXIV (1950), 105–12.

569 **Timperley**, S. R. 'A study of a self-governing work group.' *Sociol. Rev.*, n.s., XVIII, 2 (July 1970), 259–81.
'This paper describes a study by a participant observer carried out in 1966 in a new airport in the United Kingdom.'

570 **Tunstall**, Jeremy. 'Work and social life of fishermen.' Worsley, P. (ed.). *Modern sociology: introductory readings.* Harmondsworth: Penguin, 1970. p. 239–44.
Excerpts from Jeremy Tunstall. *The fishermen.* London: MacGibbon and Kee, 1962. p. 89–94, 135–8.

See also: 120; 154; 161; 184.

II. MOTIVATION AND MORALE

This section includes the more sociological and psychological literature on such subjects as job satisfaction, incentives to work, and restriction of output. Many of the general works in Part Two, I also contain material on these topics. See Part Five, II for the literature dealing with trade union restrictions on output, and Part Six, III, G for literature on wage incentives.

571 **Williams**, Whiting. *Full up and fed up: the worker's mind in crowded Britain.* London: Allen and Unwin, 1922. ix, 324p.

572 **Myers**, Charles Samuel. 'Hindrances to output.' *Economica*, V, 15 (November 1925), 270–80.

573 **Angles**, A. 'Restriction of output.' *Natn. Inst. Ind. Psychol. J.*, III, 5 (January 1927), 248–51.

574 **Pear**, Tom Hatherley. *Fitness for work.* London: U. of London P., 1928. 187p.

575 **Miles**, George Herbert. *The 'will to work'.* London: Routledge, 1929. 79p. (Routledge introductions to modern knowledge 11.)

576 **Hargrave**, T. H. 'The worker's point of view. VIII. Working conditions and morale.' *Hum. Factor*, VI, 10 (October 1932), 382–4.
Reprinted in *The worker's point of view: a symposium.* London: Woolf, 1933. p. 145–9.

577 **Lee**, Christopher A. 'Some notes on incentives in industry.' *Hum. Factor*, VI, 5 (May 1932), 180–2.
'Contributed to a discussion on Incentives at the Centenary Meeting of the British Association in London, 1931.'

578 **Miles**, George Herbert. 'Effectiveness of labour incentives.' *Hum. Factor*, VI, 2 (February 1932), 52–8.
'A paper read at the Centenary Meeting of the British Association in London, 1931.'

579 **Miles**, George Herbert. *The problem of incentives in industry.* London: Pitman, 1932. 58p.
Three lectures given at the London School of Economics and Political Science under the Heath Clark Bequest to the National Institute of Industrial Psychology.

580 **Medical Research Council.** Industrial Health Research Board. *Incentives: some experimental studies.* London: H.M.S.O., 1935. (Report 72.)
By C. A. Mace.
Re-issued 1952.

581 **Jahoda**, Marie. 'Incentives to work: a study of unemployed adults in a special situation. *Occup. Psychol.*, XVI, 1 (January 1942), 20–30.

582 **Balchin**, Nigel. 'Satisfactions in work.' *Occup. Psychol.*, XXI, 3 (July 1947), 125–34.

583 **Urwick**, Lyndall Fownes. *Morale.* Manchester: Manchester Municipal College of Technology, Department of Industrial Administration, 1947. 38p. (Series of monographs on higher management 10.)

584 **Wright**, Peter. *Incentives to work.* London: Bureau of Current Affairs, 1947. 20p. (Current Affairs, 29.)
The author was editor of *Current Affairs.*

585 **Balchin**, Nigel. 'The nature of incentives.' *Nineteenth Century*, CXLIV (November 1948), 247–54.

586 **Brown**, Wilfred Banks Duncan and **Raphael**, Winifred Jessie Gertrude Spielman. *Managers, men and morale.* London: Macdonald and Evans, 1948. vii, 163p.

587 **Davis**, Norah M. *Incentives to work and their relation to health and efficiency with particular reference to workers in the building industry.* 1948. (Ph.D. thesis, University of London.)

588 **Mace**, C. A. 'Industrial incentives and morale.' *Nineteenth Century*, CXLIV (December 1948), 321–7.

589 **Mace**, C. A. 'Satisfactions in work.' *Occup. Psychol.*, XXII, 1 (January 1948), 5–19.
Chairman's Address to the Social Psychology Section of the British Psychological Society, 24 September 1947.

590 **Mace**, C. A. 'Satisfactions in work: a further comment.' *Occup. Psychol.*, XXII, 2 (April 1948), 103–4.

591 **Curle**, Adam. 'The sociological background to incentives.' *Occup. Psychol.*, XXIII, 1 (January 1949), 21–8.

592 **Mace**, C. A. 'Status and morale.' *Nineteenth Century*, CXLVI (September 1949), 169–73.
A comment on 'The missing incentive' by C. M. Woodhouse.

593 **Marriott**, Reginald. 'Size of working group and output.' *Occup. Psychol.*, XXIII, 1 (January 1949), 47–57.
A study resulting from an inquiry into the satisfaction of production workers in two motor-car factories.

594 **Phelps Brown**, Ernest Henry. 'Morale, military and industrial.' *Econ. J.*, LIX, 233 (March 1949), 40–55.

595 **Rowntree**, Benjamin Seebohm. 'Incentives and the "practical man".' *Nineteenth Century*, CXLV (March 1949), 163–72.

596 **Schuster**, *Sir* George. 'Some reflections on incentives.' *Nineteenth Century*, CXLV (February 1949), 94–102.

597 **Urwick**, Lyndall. 'The will to work.' *Nineteenth Century*, CXLV (January 1949), 12–21.

598 **Wilkins**, Leslie T. *Incentives and the young worker*. 9p. [Social Survey G. 34.]
Reprinted from *Occupational Psychology*, October 1949. Mimeographed.

599 **Woodhouse**, C. M. 'The missing incentive.' *Nineteenth Century*, CXLVI (August 1949), 88–99.

600 **Wilkins**, Leslie T. 'Incentives and the young male worker in England, with some notes on ranking methodology.' *Int. J. Opin. Attit. Res.*, IV (1950), 541–62.

601 **Heller**, Frank Alexander. 'Measuring motivation in industry.' *Occup. Psychol.*, XXVI, 2 (April 1952), 86–95.
The investigation was carried out in two hosiery firms in Leicester.

602 **Handyside**, John Duncan. 'Raising job satisfaction: a utilitarian approach.' *Occup. Psychol.*, XXVII, 2 (April 1953), 89–97.

603 **Hewitt**, David and **Parfit**, Jessie. 'A note on working morale and size of group.' *Occup. Psychol.*, XXVII, 1 (January 1953), 38–42.

604 **Ministry of Pensions and National Insurance**. *National insurance retirement pensions: reasons given for retiring or continuing work. Report of an enquiry by the Ministry.* London: H.M.S.O., 1954. 136p.

605 **Martin**, Alec Owen. *A study of some incentives in the acquisition of a manual skill.* 1954–55. (Ph.D. thesis, University of London.)

606 **Clewes**, Winston. *The human implications of work study*. London: Industrial Welfare Society, 1955. 13p.

607 **Revans**, Reginald William. 'Industrial morale and size of unit.' *Polit. Q.*, XXVII, 3 (July–September 1956), 303–11.
Reprinted in Galenson, W. and Lipset, S. M. (eds.). *Labor and trade unionism: an interdisciplinary reader.* New York, London: Wiley, 1960. p. 295–300.

608 **Revans**, Reginald William. 'Human relations, management and size.' Hugh-Jones, E. M. (ed.). *Human relations and modern management*. Amsterdam: North-Holland Publ. Co., 1958. p. 177–220.

609 **West**, V. V. H. *Changes in motivation in girls in the first two years of employment.* 1958–59. (M.A. thesis, University of London.)

610 **Entwistle**, Alison and **Reiners**, W. J. *Incentives in the building industry*. London: H.M.S.O., 1958 [i.e. 1959]. iv, 44p. (Department of Scientific and Industrial Research. Building Research Station. National building studies, special reports 28.)

611 **Bannister**, J. A. *Social factors in occupational satisfaction.* 1959–60. (M.A. thesis, University of Nottingham.)

612 **Dalziel**, Stuart and **Klein**, Lisl. *The human implications of work study: the case of Pakitt Ltd.* Stevenage: Human Sciences Unit, Warren Spring Laboratory, 1960. xiii, 81p.

613 **Friedmann**, Georges. *The anatomy of work: the implications of specialization.* London: Heinemann, 1961. xxiii, 203p. (Heinemann books on sociology.)
Translated by Wyatt Rawson.
Originally published as *Le travail en miettes.* Paris: Gallimard, 1956.
American edition, *The anatomy of work: labor leisure and the implications of automation.* Glencoe, Ill: Free P., 1961. 203p.
Reissued New York: Free P. of Glencoe, 1964. (Free Press paperback.)
Chap. IV. 'Towards job enlargement. B. British investigations.'

614 **Handyside**, John Duncan. 'Satisfactions and aspirations.' *Occup. Psychol.*, XXXV, 4 (October 1961), 213–44.
Chairman's Address to the Occupational Section of the British Psychological Society, 24 February 1961.

615 **Hickson**, D. J. 'Motives of workpeople who restrict their output.' *Occup. Psychol.*, XXXV, 3 (July 1961), 111–21.
'This paper is derived from a thesis presented for the degree of M.Sc. (Tech.) and later deposited in the library of the University of Manchester.'

616 **Walker**, Nigel David. *Morale in the Civil Service: a study of the desk worker*. Edinburgh: Edinburgh U.P., 1961. ix, 302p.

617 **Pym**, Denis L. A. *Differences between factory and office workers on a measure of occupational frustration.* 1961–62. (M.A. thesis, University of London.)

618 **Stephens**, Leslie. 'A case for job enlargement.' *New Soc.*, 2 (11 October 1962), 9–11.
The author was Director, Institute of Personnel Management.

619 **Park**, R. C. R. *A study of some of the social factors affecting labour productivity in coal mines.* 1962–63. (Ph.D. thesis, University of Edinburgh.)

620 **Speak**, Beatrice Mary. *A study of some differentiating characteristics of responders, partial-responders and non-responders to questionnaires on job satisfaction.* 1962–63. (Ph.D. thesis, University of London.)

621 **Pym**, Denis L. A. 'A study of frustration and aggression among factory and office workers.' *Occup. Psychol.*, XXXVII, 3 (July 1963), 165–79.

622 **Wilson**, Constance Shirley. *Social factors influencing industrial output: a sociological study of factories in N.W. Lancashire.* 1963. v, 564p. (Ph.D. thesis, University of Manchester.)

623 **Crichton**, Anne Olivia Janet and **Crawford**, Marion Phoebe. *Disappointed expectations? Report on a survey of professional and technical staff in the hospital service in Wales, 1963.* Whitchurch, Glam.: Welsh Hospital Board, Welsh Staff Advisory Committee, 1964. x, 110p.

624 **Daniel**, William Wentworth. 'Bakers' boredom.' *New Soc.*, IV, 112 (19 November 1964), 14–16.

625 **Handyside**, John Duncan and **Speak**, Mary. 'Job satisfaction: myths and realities.' *Br. J. Ind. Relat.*, II, 1 (March 1964), 57–65.

626 **Klein**, Lisl. 'Operators' attitudes to piecework.' *New Soc.*, IV, 94 (16 July 1964), 11–13.

627 **Parker**, Stanley Robert. *Work satisfaction: a review of the literature.* 1964. 14p. (Social Survey M. 115.)

628 **Pym**, Denis L. A. 'A manpower study: the chemist in research and development.' *Occup. Psychol.*, XXXVIII, 1 (January 1964), 1–35.

629 **Revans**, Reginald William. *Standards for morale: cause and effect in hospitals.* London: Oxford U.P. for the Nuffield Provincial Hospitals Trust, 1964. xvi, 134p.

630 **Speak**, Mary. 'Some characteristics of respondents, partial-respondents and non-respondents to questionnaires on job satisfaction.' *Occup. Psychol.*, XXXVIII, 3–4 (July–October 1964), 173–82.

631 **Pym**, Denis L. A. *Occupational changes and their relations with employee satisfactoriness and satisfaction.* 1964–65. (Ph.D. thesis, University of London.)

632 **Banks**, Olive and **Mumford**, Enid. 'Secrecy and strain in an English firm.' Scott, W. H. (ed.). *Office automation: administrative and human problems.* Paris: Organisation for Economic Co-operation and Development, 1965. p. 19–30.

633 **Combey**, P. G. and **Rackham**, J. J. 'Rewards and punishment in industry.' *New Soc.*, VI, 155 (16 September 1965), 15–17.

634 **Cumberland Preparation for Retirement Committee.** *Attitudes towards retirement: a summary of a survey among men between the ages of 50 and 55 years undertaken by the College of Further Education, Workington.* 1965. 14p.

635 **Dale**, A. J. 'Job satisfaction and organization among hospital domestic workers.' *Br. J. Ind. Relat.*, III, 2 (July 1965), 164–81.

636 **Hardin**, Einar. 'Perceived and actual change in job satisfaction.' *J. Appl. Psychol.*, XLIX, 5 (October 1965), 363–7.

637 **Sadler**, Philip John. *Leadership style, confidence in management and job satisfaction.* Berkhamsted, Herts.: Ashridge Management College, 1966. 25p. (Papers in management studies.)

638 **Van Beinum**, Hans J. J. *The morale of the Dublin busmen: a socio-diagnostic study of the Dublin city services of Coras Iompair Eireann.* Dublin: Mount Salus P., [1966?]. 94p.

639 **Kelly**, J. G. *Role, social origins and satisfaction of lay national teachers in Dublin City – a study in the sociology of occupation.* 1966–67. (M.Soc.Sc. thesis, National University of Ireland.)

640 **Haines**, John. 'Satisfaction in social work.' *New Soc.*, IX, 223 (5 January 1967), 17–18. 'Society at work.'

641 **British Institute of Management.** *Motivation and productivity conference held 1–2 August 1968.* London: B.I.M., 1968.

642 **Berry**, D. F. 'Applied research in motivation, performance and assessment.' Lamble, J. H. (ed.). *Men, machines and the social sciences.* Bristol: Bath U.P., 1969. p. 31–53.
Includes discussion of paper.

643 **Gorfin**, C. C. 'The suggestion scheme: a contribution to morale or an economic transaction?' *Br. J. Ind. Relat.*, VII, 3 (November 1969), 368–84.

644 **Hart**, Ian. 'Executive morale in the civil service.' *Administration*, XVII, 2 (Summer 1969), 142–71.
Based on the results of a survey by postal questionnaire.

645 **Hilgendorf**, E. L. and **Irving**, B. L. 'Job attitude research: a new conceptual and analytical model.' *Hum. Relat.*, XXII, 5 (October 1969), 415–26.
'Revised version of a paper presented to the 2nd Annual Conference of the Occupational Psychology Section of the British Psychological Society, January 1969, Loughborough.'

646 **Lim**, H. M. *A literature survey of job satisfaction and behaviour.* 1969. (M.Sc. thesis, Management Engineering Section, Imperial College of Science and Technology.)

647 **Ni Bhroin**, Noirin. *The motivation and productivity of young women workers.* Dublin: Irish National Productivity Committee, Development Division, 1969. xv, 151p. (Human sciences in industry, study 4.)

648 **Paul**, William James, **Robertson**, Keith B. and **Herzberg**, Frederick. 'Job enrichment pays off.' *Harv. Bus. Rev.* (March–April 1969), 61–78.
A report on five studies carried out in British companies.

649 **Vamplew**, C. and **Cotgrove**, Stephen. 'The impact of a productivity agreement on job satisfaction and motivation.' Lamble, J. H. (ed.). *Men, machines and the social sciences.* Bristol: Bath U.P., 1969. p. 72–86.
'Research report.'

650 **Forge**, Keith Warwick Cornish. *Morale of department store salespeople.* 1969–70. (M.Sc. thesis, University of Edinburgh.)

651 **Balchin**, Nigel. 'Satisfactions in work.' *Occup. Psychol.*, XLIV (1970), 165–73.
Reprinted from *Occup. Psychol.*, XXI (1947), 125–34.

652 **Hill**, Michael J. 'Are the work-shy a myth?' *New Soc.*, XVI, 409 (30 July 1970), 191–3. 'Out of work, 2.'

653 **Jacobsohn**, Daniel. *Attitudes towards work and retirement among older industrial workers in three firms.* 1970. (Ph.D. (Econ.) thesis, University of London.)

654 **Mace**, C. A. 'Satisfactions at work.' *Occup. Psychol.*, XLIV (1970), 175–85.
Reprinted, with references added, from *Occup. Psychol.*, XXII (1948), 5–19.

655 **Mumford**, Enid. 'Job satisfaction: a new approach derived from an old theory.' *Sociol. Rev.*, n.s., XVIII, 1 (March 1970), 71–101.

656 **Oakley**, Ann. 'Occupation housewife.' *New Soc.*, XVI, 411 (13 August 1970), 282–4.

657 **Paul**, William James and **Robertson**, Keith B. *Job enrichment and employee motivation.* London: Gower P., 1970. 119p. (Gower Press special study.)

658 **Smithers**, Alan and **Carlisle**, Sheila. 'Reluctant teachers.' *New Soc.*, XV, 388 (5 March 1970), 391–2.

659 **Wall**, Toby D. and **Stephenson**, Geoffrey M. 'Herzberg's two-factor theory of job attitudes: a critical evaluation and some fresh evidence.' *Ind. Relat. J.* (December 1970), 41–65.

660 **Wild**, Ray and **Ridgeway**, C. C. 'The structure of the work needs of female workers.' *Br. J. Ind. Relat.*, VIII, 1 (March 1970), 94–9.
'Research note.'

See also: 4799; 4946; 5016; 14,411.

III. ABSENTEEISM

See also Part Six, II, E, 5; and Part Six, IV, D.

661 **Collie**, *Sir* Robert John. *Malingering and feigned sickness.* London: Arnold, 1913. xii, 340p.
Assisted by Arthur H. Spicer.
Second edition, revised and enlarged. 1917. xvi, 664p.

662 **Jones**, Arthur Bassett and **Llewellyn**, Richard Llewellyn Jones. *Malingering, or the simulation of disease.* London: Heinemann, 1917. xxiii, 708p.
'With a chapter on malingering in relation to the eye, by W. M. Beaumont.'

663 **Vernon**, Horace Middleton and **Bedford**, Thomas. *A study of absenteeism in a group of ten collieries.* London: Medical Research Council, Industrial Fatigue Research Board, 1928. iv, 68p. (Report 51.)

664 **Medical Research Council.** *Two studies of absenteeism in coal mines.* London: H.M.S.O., 1931. 59p. (Industrial Health Research Board report 62.)
I. H. M. Vernon, T. Bedford and C. G. Warner. 'The absenteeism of miners in relation to short time and other conditions.'
II. T. Bedford and C. G. Warner. 'A study of absenteeism at certain Scottish collieries.'

665 **Garland**, T. O. 'The doctor's point of view. 1. One-day absenteeism.' *Hum. Factor*, X, 1 (January 1936), 23–8.

666 **Garland**, T. O. 'The doctor's point of view. 2. Always ill and never ill.' *Hum. Factor*, X, 2 (February 1936), 66–71.

667 **Garland**, T. O. 'The doctor's point of view. 3. Home environment as a factor in absenteeism of the factory girl.' *Hum. Factor*, X, 3 (March 1936), 99–105.

668 **Medical Research Council.** Industrial Health Research Board. *Sickness absence and labour wastage.* London: H.M.S.O., 1936. v, 70p. (Report 75.)
Part I. *Sickness absence: its measurement and incidence in clerical work and light occupations.* By May Smith and Margaret A. Leiper, with the co-operation of Millais Culpin.
Part II. *Labour wastage.* By Major Greenwood and May Smith.
Re-issued 1952.

669 **Chatterjee**, P. H. *Studies of labour wastage and sickness absence.* 1941. (Ph.D. thesis, University of London.)

670 **Raphael**, Winifred. 'Problems of war-time attendance.' *Occup. Psychol.*, XV, 2 (April 1941), 53–60.

671 **Gosden**, V. J. 'Absenteeism at a Midlands munition factory.' *Occup. Psychol.*, XVI, 3 (July 1942), 125–33.

672 **Medical Research Council.** Industrial Health Research Board. *Hours of work, lost time and labour wastage.* London: H.M.S.O., 1942. (Emergency report 2.)

673 **Ministry of Labour and National Service.** *The problem of absenteeism.* London: [the Mini-try?], 1942. 8p.

674 **Wells**, Frederick Arthur. 'Voluntary absenteeism in the cutlery trade.' *Rev. Econ. Studies*, IX, 2 (February 1942), 158–80.

675 **Medical Research Council.** Industrial Health Research Board. *A study of absenteeism among women.* London: H.M.S.O., 1943. 12p. (Emergency report 4.)
By Stanley Wyatt, R. Marriott and D. E. R. Hughes.

676 **Medical Research Council.** Industrial Health Research Board. *Absence from work, prevention of fatigue.* London: H.M.S.O., 1944. (Conditions for industrial health and efficiency pamphlet 2.)

677 **Medical Research Council.** Industrial Health Research Board. *The recording of sickness absence in industry (a preliminary report) by a sub-committee of the Industrial Health Research Board.* London: H.M.S.O., 1944. ii, 17p. (Report 85.)
Reprinted. 1948.

678 **Greenwell**, E. G. 'The young absentee.' *Occup. Psychol.*, XIX, 2 (April 1945), 71–5.

679 **Medical Research Council.** Industrial Health Research Board. *A study of certified sickness absence among women in industry.* London: H.M.S.O., 1945. 34p. (Report 86.)
By Stanley Wyatt.

680 **Medical Research Council.** Industrial Health Research Board. *Why is she away? The problem of sickness among women in industry.* London: H.M.S.O., 1945. (Conditions for industrial health and efficiency pamphlet 3.)

681 **Behrend**, Hilde M. *Absence under full employment.* 1951. (Ph.D. thesis, University of Birmingham.)

682 **Moos**, S. 'The statistics of absenteeism in coal mining.' *Manchr. Sch.*, XIX, 1 (January 1951), 89–108.

683 **Spratling**, F. H. and **Lloyd**, F. J. 'Personnel statistics and sickness-absence statistics.' *Publ. Adm.*, XXIX, 3 (Autumn 1951), 257–77.

A paper given before the Institute of Actuaries, 26 February 1951.

Reprinted in slightly modified form from the *Journal of the Institute of Actuaries.*

684 **Buzzard**, Richard Bethune and **Shaw**, W. J. 'An analysis of absence under a scheme of paid sick leave.' *Br. J. Ind. Med.*, IX, 4 (October 1952), 282–95.

685 **Denerley**, Ronald Alfred. 'Some effects of paid sick leave on sickness absence.' *Br. J. Ind. Med.*, IX, 4 (October 1952), 275–81.

686 **Acton Society Trust**. *Size and morale: a preliminary study of attendance at work in large and small units.* London, the Trust, 1953. 43p.

687 **Behrend**, Hilde M. 'Absence and labour turnover in a changing economic climate.' *Occup. Pyschol.*, XXVII, 2 (April 1953), 69–79.

Describes a follow-up study to H. Behrend, *Absence under full employment*, Monograph A3, University of Birmingham Studies in Economics and Society, 1951; and J. R. Long, *Labour turnover under full employment*, Monograph A2, University of Birmingham Studies in Economics and Society, 1951.

688 **Hill**, John Michael Meath and **Trist**, Eric Lansdowne. 'A consideration of industrial accidents as a means of withdrawal from the work situation: a study of their relation to other absences in an iron and steel works.' *Hum. Relat.*, VI, 4 (November 1953), 357–80.

Reprinted in Baker, F., and others (eds.). *Industrial organizations and health.* Vol. 1. London: Tavistock Publications, 1969. p. 292–319.

689 **Buzzard**, Richard Bethune. 'Attendance and absence in industry: the nature of the evidence.' *Br. J. Sociol.*, V, 3 (September 1954), 238–52.

The text of a paper read to the British Sociological Association on 11 November 1953.

690 **Liddell**, Francis Douglas Kelly. 'Attendance in the coal-mining industry.' *Br. J. Sociol.*, V, 1 (March 1954), 78–86.

Discusses work done by the Statistics Branch of the National Coal Board.

691 **Liddell**, Francis Douglas Kelly. 'The measurement of daily variations in absence.' *Appl. Statist.*, III, 2 (June 1954), 104–11.

Based on data obtained from a colliery.

692 **Moor**, Oswald. *How to reduce absenteeism by positive planning.* Ashford-in-Middlesex: Wodderspoon, 1954. 34p.

Also London: Blick Time Recorders, 1954.

693 **British Institute of Management.** *Absence from work: recording and analysis.* London: B.I.M., 1955. vii, 21p. (Personnel management series 6.)

694 **Hill**, John Michael Meath and **Trist**, Eric Lansdowne. 'Changes in accidents and other absences with length of service.' *Hum. Relat.*, VIII, 2 (May 1955), 121–52.

Reprinted with Emery, F. E. *Some characteristics of enterprises, and their leadership* as *Industrial accidents, sickness, and other absences.* Tavistock Pamphlet 4. 1962.

695 **Castle**, Peter F. C. 'Accidents, absence, and withdrawal from the work situation.' *Hum. Relat.*, IX, 2 (May 1956), 223–33.

696 **Acton Society Trust.** *Size and morale, part II: a further study of attendance at work in large and small units.* London: the Trust, 1957. 36p.

697 **Argyle**, Michael, **Gardner**, Godfrey and **Cioffi**, Frank. 'The measurement of supervisory methods.' *Hum. Relat.*, X, 4 (November 1957), 295–313.

'. . . the results of an investigation into the effects of different styles of first-line supervision on production and related variables . . . in eight electrical engineering factories in the United Kingdom.'

698 **Crowther**, John. 'Absence and turnover in the divisions of one company, 1950–1955.' *Occup. Psychol.*, XXXI, 4 (October 1957), 256–69.

699 **Shepherd**, R. D. and **Walker**, J. 'Absence and the physical conditions of work.' *Br. J. Ind. Med.*, XIV, 4 (October 1957), 266–74.

700 **Argyle**, Michael, **Gardner**, Godfrey and **Cioffi**, Frank. 'Supervisory methods related to productivity, absenteeism, and labour turnover.' *Hum. Relat.*, XI, 1 (February 1958), 23–40.

701 **Shepherd**, R. D. and **Walker**, J. 'Absence from work in relation to wage level and family responsibility.' *Br. J. Ind. Med.*, XV, 1 (January 1958), 52–61.

702 **Behrend**, Hilde. 'Voluntary absence from work.' *Int. Labour Rev.*, LXXIX, 2 (February 1959), 109–40.

703 **Industrial Welfare Society.** *The investigation and control of sickness absence.* London: the Society, 1959. 6p.

704 **Ashworth**, H. W. *National Health Insurance absenteeism in a Manchester general practice.* 1960–61. (M.D. thesis, University of Manchester.)

705 **Ashworth**, H. W. 'Sickness absence from work.' *Med. Wld*, XCV, 2 (August 1961), 97–104.

706 **British Institute of Management.** *Absence from work: incidence, cost and control.* London: B.I.M., 1961. x, 53p.

Results of survey projected in *Absence from work: recording and analysis*, 1955.

707 **De La Mare**, Gwynneth and **Sergean**, R. 'Two methods of studying changes in absence with age.' *Occup. Psychol.*, XXXV, 4 (October 1961), 245–52.

708 **Hill**, John Michael Meath and **Trist**, Eric Lansdowne. *Industrial accidents, sickness and other absences.* London: Tavistock Publications, 1962. 58p. (Tavistock pamphlets 4.)

709 **Buzzard**, Richard Bethune and **Liddell**, Francis Douglas Kelly. *Coalminers' attendance at work: the report of an investigation by a National Coal Board research team.* London: National Coal Board (Medical Service), 1963. 180p. (National Coal Board. Medical research memoranda 3.)

710 **Froggatt**, P. 'One-day absence in industry.' *Statist. Soc. Inq. Soc. Ir. J.*, XXI, 3 (1964–5), 166–77.
Discussion, 177–8.
In Belfast.

711 **Association of British Pharmaceutical Industry**. Office of Health Economics. *Work lost through sickness.* London: O.H.E., 1965. 33p.

712 **Cooper**, Robert and **Payne**, Roy. 'Age and absence: a longitudinal study in three firms.' *Occup. Psychol.*, XXXIX, 1 (January 1965), 31–5.

713 **Industrial Welfare Society**. *Attendance recording.* London: the Society, 1965. 17p.

714 **Ministry of Pensions and National Insurance**. *Digest of statistics analysing certificates of incapacity, June 1958–June 1961.* London: H.M.S.O., 1965. 35p.

715 **Handy**, L. J. and **Turner**, Herbert Arthur. 'Absenteeism in the mines.' *New Soc.*, VII, 184 (7 April 1966), 17–18.
'Society at work.'

716 **Ministry of Pensions and National Insurance**. *Report of an enquiry into the incidence of incapacity for work.* London: H.M.S.O., 1964–5 [i.e. 1966]. 2v.
Part I. *Scope and characteristics of employers' sick pay schemes.*
Part II. *Incidence of incapacity for work in different areas and occupations.*

717 **Owens**, A. Constance. 'Sick leave among railwaymen threatened by redundancy: a pilot study.' *Occup. Psychol.*, XL, 1–2 (January–April 1966), 43–52.

718 **Freeman**, N. H. M. *Industrial absenteeism as a social process.* 1966–7. (M.A. thesis, University of Nottingham.)

719 **Froggatt**, P. *Short-term absence from industry: a statistical and historical study.* 1966–7. (Ph.D. thesis, Queen's University, Belfast.)

720 **Hill**, Michael. 'Who stays home?' *New Soc.*, IX, 235 (30 March 1967), 459–60.

721 **Handy**, L. J. 'Absenteeism and attendance in the British coal-mining industry: an examination of post-war trends.' *Br. J. Ind. Relat.*, VI, 1 (March 1968), 27–50.

722 **Department of Health and Social Security**. *Digest of statistics analysing certificates of incapacity, June 1961–May 1964.* London: the Department, 1969. 223p.

723 **Taylor**, Peter John. *Absenteeism: causes and control.* London: Industrial Society, 1969. 30p. (Notes for managers 15.)

724 **Ayoub**, A. H. H. *Absenteeism among manual women workers in engineering: a case study.* 1970. (M.Sc. thesis, Department of Management Sciences, U.M.I.S.T.)

725 **Confederation of British Industry**. *Absenteeism: an analysis of the problem.* London: C.B.I., 1970. vi, 15p.

See also: 14,697.

IV. ATTITUDES TOWARDS INNOVATION AND CHANGE

Many of the general works in Part Two, I also discuss workers' attitudes to innovation and change. See also Part Five, II; and Part Six, II, D, 3. The voluminous literature on the nature and extent of automation is not included here. Much of the literature in English published between the late 1940s and 1965 on automation is listed and annotated in three volumes published by the School of Labor and Industrial Relations at Michigan State University under the main title *Economic and Social Implications of Automation.* Volume 1 was compiled by Gloria Cheek and published in 1958, while volumes 2 and 3 were compiled by Einar Hardin *et al.* and published in 1961 and 1967 respectively. Another useful source of information on automation is the series of bulletins published by the I.L.O. under the main title *Labour and Automation* (1964–).

726 **Katin**, Louis. 'The worker's point of view. III. Imagination and rationalization.' *Hum. Factor*, VI, 5 (May 1932), 183–6.
Reprinted in *The worker's point of view: a symposium.* London: Woolf, 1933. p. 131–6.

727 **Myers**, Charles Samuel. *Business rationalisation: its dangers and advantages considered from the psychological and social standpoints. Three lectures . . .* London: Pitman, 1932. vii, 76p.

728 **Sessions**, William H. 'The employer's point of view. I. Rationalization and the craftsman.' *Hum. Factor*, VII, 6 (June 1933), 212–17.
Discusses article by L. Katin in vol. VI, p. 183–6.

729 **Hazell**, Ralph C. 'A printer's viewpoint.' Williams, H. (ed.). *Man and the machine.* London: Routledge, 1935. p. 32–44.

730 **Banks**, Joseph Ambrose, **Halsey**, A. H. and **Scott**, William Henry. 'Sociological aspects of technical change in a steel plant.' International Sociological Association. *Transactions of the third world congress of sociology . . . 1956.* Vol. 2. London: the Association, 1956. p. 86–96.
An outline of the study published by Liverpool U.P. in 1956.

731 **Scott**, William Henry, **Banks**, Joseph Ambrose, **Halsey**, A. H. and **Lupton**, Tom.

Technical change and industrial relations: a study of the relations between technical change and the social structure of a large steelworks. Liverpool: Liverpool U.P., 1956. 336p. (Social research series.)

732 **Department of Scientific and Industrial Research.** *Men, steel and technical change.* London: H.M.S.O., 1957. 36p. (Problems of progress in industry 1.)

By the Industrial Research Section, Department of Social Science, University of Liverpool.

Prepared by Olive Banks and W. H. Scott.

733 **Organisation for European Economic Co-operation.** European Productivity Agency. *Inquiry into the attitudes of workers in the steel industry towards technological changes. 6. United Kingdom.* Paris: O.E.E.C., 1958. 116p. (Project 164.)

By University of Liverpool, Industrial Research Section.

734 **Organisation for Economic Co-operation and Development.** European Productivity Agency. *Steel workers and technical progress: a comparative report on six national studies.* Paris: O.E.C.D., 1959. 66p. (E.P.A. project 164. Industrial version 2.)

735 **Banks**, Olive. *The attitudes of steel workers to technical change.* Liverpool: Liverpool U.P., 1960. viii, 152p. (Social research series.)

736 **Chadwick-Jones**, John K. *The social and psychological effects of change in the tinplate industry of South-West Wales: a study of the handmill worker.* 1960–61. (Ph.D. thesis, University of Wales, Cardiff.)

737 **Banks**, Olive and **Mumford**, Enid. 'Automation stress in the office.' *New Soc.*, 7 (15 November 1962), 11–13.

738 **British Productivity Council.** *Industria change and human effects: edited text of papers given at the 1961 Factory Equipment Exhibition, London.* London: the Council, 1962. 20p. (Efficiency in today's factory 3.)

739 **Daniel**, William Wentworth. *A consideration of individual and group attitudes in an expanding and technically changing organisation.* 1963. (M.Sc. Tech. thesis, University of Manchester.)

740 **Marek**, J. *Social and psychological responses to changing environmental demands: a study of the effects of automation in two factories.* 1963. (Ph.D. thesis, University of London.)

741 **Revans**, Reginald William. 'Attitudes to innovation.' *New Soc.*, II, 47 (22 August 1963), 20–1.

742 **Zetie**, S. P. *A study of individual and group employee attitudes in an expanding and technically changing firm.* 1964. (M.Sc. Tech. thesis University of Manchester.)

743 **Touraine**, Alain, **Durand**, Claude, **Pecaut**, Daniel and **Willener**, Alfred. *Acceptance and resistance: a résumé by the Secretariat of OECD of 'Workers' attitudes to technical change' by Alain Touraine and associates.* Paris: O.E.C.D., 1965. 116p.

A publication of the Manpower and Social Affairs Directorate, Social Affairs Division.

744 **Touraine**, Alain, **Durand**, Claude, **Pecaut**, Daniel and **Willener**, Alfred. *Workers' attitudes to technical change: an integrated survey of research.* Paris: Organisation for Economic Co-operation and Development, 1965. 177p. (Industrial relations aspects of manpower policy 2.)

745 **Caddick**, D. I. *The introduction of electronic data processing equipment into offices; a comparative study of management policies and personnel adjustment.* 1965–6. (M.Sc. dissertation, University of London.)

746 **Ministry of Labour.** *Attitudes to efficiency in industry: report of a working party of officials.* London: H.M.S.O., 1966. iv, 35p.

747 **Brown**, Richard K. 'Technology, technical change and automation.' Parker, S. R., and others. *The sociology of industry.* London: Allen and Unwin, 1967. p. 113–25.

748 **Mumford**, Enid and **Banks**, Olive. *The computer and the clerk.* London: Routledge and Kegan Paul, 1967. xi, 252p. (British library of business studies.)

749 **Mumford**, Enid and **Ward**, Tom B. 'Managers and computers.' Butterworth, E. and Weir, D. (eds.). *The sociology of modern Britain: an introductory reader.* London: Fontana/Collins, 1970. p. 182–7.

Reprinted from 'How the computer changes management', *New Soc.* (23 September 1965.)

PART THREE

EMPLOYEE ORGANISATION

The concept of a 'trade union' is taken here in its widest sense to cover all organisations of employees which try by any means to influence and regulate the terms and conditions of employment of their members. More specifically, the literature on manual unions, white-collar unions, professional unions and associations, and staff associations as well as friendly societies, craft guilds, and livery companies is included.

I. CRAFT GUILDS AND LIVERY COMPANIES

See also Part Four, I; and Part Six, II, B, 3, a.

750 **Fox**, Francis Frederick. *Some account of the Ancient Fraternity of Merchant Taylors of Bristol*. Bristol: printed for private circulation, 1880. 147p.

Only 50 copies printed.

751 **Lambert**, George. *The Barbers' Company: a paper read before the British Archaeological Association . . . 1881*. London, 1881. 67p.

Second edition. London: Brettell, [1882?]. 67p.

752 **Compton**, Charles Henry. *The history of the Worshipful Company of Horners of London*. London: the Company, 1882. 18p.

Sixth edition. Collingridge, 1902. 20p.

753 **Campbell**, William. *History of the Incorporation of Cordiners in Glasgow*. Glasgow: R. Anderson, 1883. xi, 310p.

754 **Chaffers**, W. *History of English goldsmiths*. London, 1883. 267p.

755 **Pring**, James Hurly. *On the origin of gilds; with a notice of the ancient gild-hall of Taunton*. Taunton: J. F. Hammond, 1883. 24p.

756 **Rivington**, Charles Robert. 'The records of the Worshipful Company of Stationers.' *Lond. Middx. Archaeol. Soc. Trans.*, VI, I (1883), 280–340.

757 **Royal Commission on the Livery Companies of the City of London**. 1884. (C. 4073, 4073 – I, II, III, IV.)

Vol I. *Reports and memoranda, and the oral inquiry*.

Vol. II. *Returns of the Great Companies, in answer to the Commissioners' circular, and correspondence with reference thereto*.

Vol. III. *Returns of the Minor Companies, and correspondence with reference thereto*.

Vol. IV. *Mr. Hare's reports on the Charities of the twelve Great Companies, and charitable accounts*. By Thomas Hare.

Vol. V. *Reports as to the charities of the Minor Companies, charitable accounts, information with respect to guilds of foreign countries, abstracts of the Companies' returns and corporate and trust expenditure between 1870 and 1890*.

758 **Scott**, James Benjamin. *A short account of the Wheelwrights' Company*. London: printed for private circulation, 1884. 72p.

759 **Blakesley**, George Holmes. *The London Companies Commission: a comment on the majority report*. London: Kegan Paul, 1885. 63p.

760 **Edinburgh Review**. 'The City livery companies.' *Edinb. Rev.*, CLXII (July 1885), 181–204.

Review article on *The report of the Royal Commission appointed to inquire into the Livery Companies of the City of London*. 1884.

761 **Rae**, James. *The City of London livery companies . . . a lecture*. London: Marlborough, 1885. 23p.

762 **S.**, L. B. *The City Livery Companies and their corporate property*. London: Rivingtons, 1885. 71p.

763 **Dibdin**, *Sir* Lewis Tonna. *The Livery Companies of London, being a review of the Report of the Livery Companies' Commission*. London: Hamilton, Adams, 1886. 123p.

764 **Bain**, Ebenezer. *Merchant and craft guilds: history of the Aberdeen incorporated trades*. Aberdeen: Edmond and Spark, 1887. xii, 360p.

765 **Colston**, James. *The Guildry of Edinburgh: is it an incorporation? with introductory remarks concerning 'gilds'* . . . Edinburgh: R. Cameron, 1887. x, 208p.

766 **Humpherus**, Henry. *History of the origin and progress of the Company of Watermen and Lightermen of the River Thames, with numerous historical notes*. London: S. Prentice, 1887. 3v.

767 **Jupp**, Edward Basil. *An historical account of the Worshipful Company of Carpenters of the City of London.* London, 1848.
Second edition. London: Pickering and Chatto, 1887. xix, 676p.

768 **Lyons**, M. J. *The City companies.* London: Liberty and Property Defence League, 1887.
'A report of a lecture.'

769 **Seligman**, Edwin Robert Anderson. *Two chapters on the mediaeval guilds of England.* Baltimore: American Economic Association, 1887. 113p. (Publications, vol. 2, no. 5.)

770 **Milbourn**, T. (ed.). *The Vintners' Company, their muniments, plate, and eminent members, with some account of the Ward of Vintry.* 1888. 136p.
Issued for private circulation.
Revised and edited by T. Milbourn.

771 **Sawyer**, William Phillips. 'The Drapers' Company.' *Lond. Middx. Archaeol. Soc. Trans.*, VII, 1 (1888), 37–64.
A sketch of the history.

772 **Watford**, Cornelius. *Gilds: their origin, constitution, objects and later history.* London: G. Redway, 1888. xi, 272p.
New and enlarged edition.

773 **Fox**, Francis Frederick and **Taylor**, John. *Some account of the Guild of Weavers in Bristol.* Bristol: privately printed, 1889. 100p.
Only 50 copies printed.

774 **Noble**, Theophilus Charles. *A brief history of the Worshipful Company of Ironmongers, London, A.D. 1351–1889, with an appendix containing some account of the Blacksmiths' Company.* London: printed for private circulation only, 1889. viii, 74p.
Illustrations by G. Cruikshank and others.

775 **Shaw**, George. *Revived guild action, with a history of the movement for the registration of plumbers.* London: Simpkin, Marshall, 1889. 128p.
Second edition. 1889. 128p.

776 **Sherwell**, John William. *A descriptive and historical account of the Guild of Saddlers of the City of London.* London, 1889. xxiv, 240p.
Second edition. *The history of the Guild of Saddlers of the City of London*, revised and brought up to date by K. S. Laurie and A. F. G. Everitt. London: printed for private circulation, 1937. 230p.
Third edition, revised by K. S. Laurie. London: Saddlers' Company, 1956. 228p. Private circulation.

777 **Cunningham**, William. *Craft gilds: paper read at meeting of the Society for the Protection of Ancient Buildings, 25th June, 1890.* London, 1890. 23p.

778 **Daw**, Joseph. *A sketch of the early history of the Worshipful Company of Butchers.* London: the Company, 1890. 38p.
Reprinted, with additions.
First published 1869.

779 **Lambert**, George. *The Worshipful Company of Pattenmakers: a list of masters, wardens, court of assistants, and livery, with a "Short account of the patten" and "Two years in the chair".* London: printed for private circulation, 1890. 55p.

780 **Welch**, Charles. *A brief account of the Worshipful Company of Gardeners of London.* London: privately printed, 1890. 14p.

781 **Young**, Sidney (comp.). *The annals of the barber-surgeons of London.* London: Blades, East and Blades, 1890. xi, 623p.
With extracts from the records and facsimiles.

782 **Colston**. James. *The incorporated trades of Edinburgh; with an introductory chapter on the rise and progress of municipal government in Scotland.* Edinburgh: Colston, 1891. l, 237p.

783 **Hibbert**, Francis Aidan. *The influence and development of English gilds as illustrated by the history of the craft gilds of Shrewsbury.* Cambridge: Cambridge U.P., 1891. xii, 168p. (University of Cambridge. Thirlwall dissertation 1891.)

784 **Lambert**, Joseph Malet. *Two thousand years of gild life; or, An outline of the history and development of the gild system from early times, with special reference to its application to trade and industry, together with a full account of the gilds and trading companies of Kingston-upon-Hull, from the 14th to the 18th century.* Hull: Brown, 1891. xi, 414p.

785 **Stewart**, Horace. *History of the Company of Gold and Silver Wyre-Drawers, and of the origin and development of the industry which the Company represents.* London: printed for the Company, 1891. xvi, 140p.

786 **Hazlitt**, William Carew. *The livery companies of the City of London: their origin, character, development and social and political importance.* London: Sonnenschein, 1892. xiv, 692p.

787 **Webb**, Sidney James. *London's heritage in the City guilds.* 1892. 3p. (The Fabian municipal program, no. 2.)

788 **Christie**, James. *Some account of parish clerks, more especially of the Ancient Fraternity, Bretherne and Sisterne of S. Nicholas, now known as the Worshipful Company of Parish Clerks.* London: privately printed, 1893. xxii, 219p.
The author was Chaplain to the North-Eastern Hospital, Tottenham.

789 **Woolacott**, John Evans. *The curse of turtledom: exposé of the methods . . . of the Livery Companies.* London: Effingham Wilson, 1894. 111p.
Reprinted from the *Financial Times*.

790 **Cheyney**, Edward Potts (ed.). *English towns and gilds.* Philadelphia, 1895. 40p. (Philadelphia U. Transactions and reprints from the original sources of European history, vol. 2, no. 1.)

791 **Lambert**, George. *The Tin Plate Workers' Company with a short account of the discovery and manufacture of tin.* London, 1895. 40p.

792 **Ebblewhite**, Ernest Arthur. *A chronological history of the Worshipful Company of Tin Plate Workers, alias Wire Workers of the City of London, from the date of its incorporation to the present time*. London: privately printed, 1896. viii, 133p.

793 **Prideaux**, *Sir* W. S. *Memorials of the Goldsmiths' Company, being gleanings from their records between the years 1335 and 1815, with an introduction, and notes . . . by Sir W. S. Prideaux*. London: printed for private circulation, 1896. 2v.

794 **Sylvester**, Alfred Arthur (ed.). *The Corporation of the City of London and the first twelve of the great City Guilds*. London: Topographical and Pictorial Publishing Co., 1897. 377p.

795 **Mathews**, J. Douglass. 'History of the Innholders' Company.' *Lond. Middx. Archaeol. Soc. Trans.*, n.s., I, 2 (1898), 151–76.

796 **Ramsey**, William. *The Worshipful Company of Glass Sellers of London*. London: printed for the Company, 1898. 152p.

A history.

797 **Ashley**, William James. 'Professor Gross's "Gild merchant".' *Surveys, historic and economic*. London: Longmans, Green, 1900. p. 213–18.

See C. Gross. *The gild merchant: a contribution to British municipal history*. 1890.

798 **Berry**, Henry Fitzpatrick. *The records of the Dublin Gild of Merchants, known as the Gild of the Holy Trinity, 1438–1671*. Dublin, 1900.

Reprinted from the *Journal of the Proceedings of the Royal Society of Antiquaries of Ireland*.

799 **Welch**, Charles. 'Historical sketch of the Pewterers' Company.' *Lond. Middx. Archaeol. Soc. Trans.*, n.s., I, 3 (1900), 235–55.

800 **Welch**, Charles. *The history of the Worshipful Company of Gardeners*. 2nd ed. London: Blades, East and Blades, 1900. 52p.

801 **Shickle**, Charles William. *The guild of the merchant tailors in Bath*. Bath: Herald Office, 1902. 72p.

802 **Tingley**, J. C. 'Notes upon the craft guilds of Norwich with particular reference to the masons.' *Ars Quat. Coron.*, XI (1902), 197–204.

803 **Wadmore**, James Foster. *Some account of the Worshipful Company of Skinners of London, being the Guild or Fraternity of Corpus Christi*. London: the Company, 1902. x, 340p.

804 **Welch**, Charles. *History of the Worshipful Company of Pewterers of the City of London*. London: Blades, East and Blades, 1902. 2v.

805 **Bateson**, Mary (ed.). *Cambridge gild records*. Cambridge: Cambridge Antiquarian Society, 1903. xxxvii, 176p. (Publications. Octavo series, 39.)

806 **Berry**, Henry Fitzpatrick. *The Ancient Corporation of Barber-Surgeons, or Gild of St. Mary Magdelene, Dublin*. Dublin, 1903.

Reprinted from the *Journal of the Royal Society of Antiquaries of Ireland*.

807 **Heron**, Alexander. *The rise and progress of the Company of Merchants of Edinburgh, 1681–1902*. Edinburgh: Clark, 1903. xv, 400p.

808 **Jelf**, *Sir* Ernest Arthur. *Some London institutions of public importance in their legal aspects*. London: H. Cox, 1903. vii, 231p.

Edited with notes and an index by A. C. McBarnet.

809 **Latimer**, John. *History of the Society of Merchant Venturers of the City of Bristol, with some account of the anterior merchants' guilds*. Bristol: Arrowsmith, 1903. viii, 345p.

810 **Latimer**, John. 'The Mercers' and Linen Drapers' Company of Bristol.' *Bris. Glouc. Archaeol. Soc. Trans.*, XXVI, 2 (1903), 288–92.

811 **Norman**, Philip. *The ancient halls of the City Guilds, with some account of the history of the companies*. London: Bell, 1903. xi, 211p.

Illustrations by T. R. Way.

812 **Rivington**, Charles Robert. *1403–1903: a short account of the Worshipful Company of Stationers*. London: Waterlow and Layton, 1903. 69p.

813 **Thomson**, Daniel. *The weaver's craft: a history of the Weavers' Incorporation of Dunfermline*. Paisley: A. Gardner, 1903. 380p.

814 **Ditchfield**, Peter Hampson. *The city companies of London and their good works: a record of their history, charity and treasure*. London: Dent, 1904. xv, 354p.

815 **Unwin**, George. *Industrial organisation in the sixteenth and seventeenth centuries*. Oxford: Clarendon P., 1904. viii, 277p.

816 **Barrett**, Charles Raymond Booth. *The history of the Society of Apothecaries of London*. London: Elliot Stock, 1905. xxxix, 310p.

817 **Kramer**, Stella. *The English craft gilds and the government: an examination of the accepted theory regarding the decay of the craft gilds*. New York, 1905. 152p. (Columbia College. Studies in history, vol. 23, no. 4.)

818 **M'Ewan**, D. *Old Glasgow weavers: records of the Incorporation of Weavers*. Glasgow, 1905. 166p.

819 **Smythe**, William Dumville. *An historical account of the Worshipful Company of Girdlers, London*. London: Chiswick P., 1905. viii, 288p.

820 **Welch**, Charles. 'History and antiquities of the Worshipful Society of Apothecaries.' *Lond. Middx. Archaeol. Soc. Trans.*, n.s., I, 5 (1905), 438–50.

821 **Leader**, Robert Eadon. *History of the Company of Cutlers in Hallamshire, in the County of York*. Sheffield: Pawson and Brailsford, 1905–6. 2v.

822 **Poock**, Anselm. 'Trade societies in the middle ages.' *Manchr. Statist. Soc. Trans.* (1905–6), 87–128.

823 **Burkitt**, Edward Herbert. *A short history of the Worshipful Company of Curriers*. London, 1906. 72p.

Revised edition. 1923. 75p.

824 **Royal Society of Arts Journal.** 'Early history of the London guilds.' *R. Soc. Arts J.*, LIV, 2804 (17 August 1906), 933–5.

825 **Sebastian**, Lewis Boyd. *An old city company: a sketch of the history of the Skinners' Company of London.* London: Bedford P., 1906. 108p. (Sette of Odd Volumes. Privately printed Opuscula, no. 54.)

826 **Bobart**, Henry Hodgkinson. *A short account of the Company of Basket Makers . . . by the Clerk.* London, 1907. 7p.

827 *Hammermen of Edinburgh and their altar in St Giles Church.* Edinburgh: W. J. Hay, 1907. 294p.

828 **Crossweller**, William Thomas. *The Gardeners' Company: a short chronological history, 1605–1907.* London: privately printed, 1908. 52p.

829 **Mellows**, William Thomas. 'Markets, guilds and fairs of Peterborough.' *Peterb. Nat. Hist. Sci. Archaeol. Soc. A. Rep.* 37th (1908), 53–68.
Also published separately 1909.

830 **Unwin**, George. *The gilds and companies of London.* London: Methuen, 1908. xvi, 397p. (Antiquary's books.)
Second edition. 1925. xvi, 397p.
Third edition. London: Allen and Unwin, 1938. xvi, 401p.
Fourth edition, with a new introduction by William F. Kahl. London: Cass, 1963. xlvi, 401p.

831 **Pick**, S. Perkins. 'The guild merchant and other guilds and freemasonary.' *Lodge Res. No. 2429 Leic. Trans.* (1908–09), 54–70.

832 **Marwick**, *Sir* James David. *Edinburgh guilds and crafts: a sketch of the history of burgess-ship, guild brotherhood, and membership of crafts in the city.* Edinburgh: Scottish Burgh Records Society, 1909. xi, 258p.
Edited by R. Penwick.

833 **Robson**, John Stephenson. 'Some account of the Incorporated Company of Free Joiners of Newcastle-upon-Tyne.' *Archaeol. Ael.*, 3rd ser., v (1909), 170–96.

834 **Thomson**, Daniel. *The Dunfermline hammermen: a history of the incorporation of hammermen in Dunfermline; to which is appended a history of the Convener's Court of Dunfermline.* Paisley: A. Gardner, 1909. 259p.

835 **Welch**, Charles. *History of the Worshipful Company of Paviors of the City of London . . .* London: privately printed, 1909. 108p.

836 **Burgess**, Walter H. 'Mediaeval guilds.' *Plym. Instn. Devon Corn. Nat. Hist. Soc. A. Rep. Trans.*, xv (1909–15), 307–12.

837 **Holford**, Christopher. *A chat about the Broderers' Company, by an old boy and past master.* London: Allen, 1910. x, 314p.

838 **Rivington**, Charles Robert. 'The Stationers' Company.' *Lond. Middx. Archaeol. Soc. Trans.*, n.s., II, 1 (1910), 119–36.

839 **Bobart**, Henry Hodgkinson (comp.). *Records of the Basketmakers' Company.* London: Dunn, Collin, 1911. xi, 183p.
Facsimile reprint. London: Worshipful Company of Basketmakers, 1967.

840 **Dendy**, Frederick Walter. 'The struggle between the merchant and craft gilds of Newcastle in 1515.' *Archaeol. Ael.*, 3rd ser., VII (1911), 77–101.

841 **Simpson**, Frank. *Chester city guilds: the Barber-Surgeons Company.* Chester: G. R. Griffith, 1911. 106p.

842 **Simpson**, Frank. 'The City Gilds or Companies of Chester, with special reference to that of the barber-surgeons.' *Ches. N. Wales Archit. Archaeol. Hist. Soc. J.*, n.s., XVIII (1911), 98–203.

843 **Thornley**, John Charles and **Hastings**, George Woodyatt. *The Guilds of the City of London and their Liverymen, being an historical account of the various guilds of the City of London and their liverymen, compiled from authentic records.* London: London and Counties Press Association, 1911. x, 488p.

844 **Towse**, J. Wrench. 'The Worshipful Company of Fishmongers.' *Lond. Middx. Archaeol. Soc. Trans.*, n.s., II, 2 (1911), 195–210.

845 **Hotblack**, J. T. 'Norwich guilds.' *Norw. Sci. Goss. Club Rep. Proc.* (1911–12), 9–12.
Summary of Presidential Address.

846 **Barron**, E. Jackson. 'Notes on the history of the Armourers' and Brasiers' Company'. *Lond. Middx. Archaeol. Soc. Trans.*, n.s., II, 3 (1912), 300–19.

847 **Chanter**, J. F. 'The Exeter Goldsmiths' Guild.' *Devon. Ass. Advmt. Sci. Lit. Art. Rep. Trans.*, XLIV (1912), 438–79.

848 **Gould**, Arthur William. *History of the Worshipful Company of Fruiterers of the City of London.* Exeter: privately printed, 1912. xxvii, 151p.

849 **Haskins**, Charles. *The ancient trade guilds and companies of Salisbury.* Salisbury: Bennett, 1912. xxxvi, 423p.

850 **Lambert**, Joseph Malet. 'Trade gilds of Beverley.' *E. Rid. Antiq. Soc. Trans.*, XIX (1912), 91–109.

851 **Lumsden**, Harry and **Aitken**, P. H. *History of the hammermen of Glasgow: a study typical of Scottish craft life and organisation.* Paisley, 1912. xxv, 446p.

852 **Rosedale**, Honyel Gough. *A short history of the Worshipful Company of Horners.* London: Blades, East and Blades, 1912. 46p.

853 **Rose-Troup**, Frances. 'The Kalendars and the Exeter trade-gilds before the Reformation.' *Devon. Ass. Advmt. Sci. Lit. Art Rep. Trans.*, XLIV (1912), 406–30.

854 **Cunningham**, William. 'The guildry and trade incorporations in Scottish towns.' *R. Hist. Soc. Trans.*, 3rd ser., VII (1913), 1–24.

855 **Young**, Sidney. *The history of the Worshipful Company of Glass Sellers of London.* London: Barber, 1913. 76p.

856 **Marsh**, Bower (ed.). *Records of the Worshipful Company of Carpenters.* Oxford, 1913–39. 6v.
Vols. 5, 6 edited by John Ainsworth.

857 **Brown**, Albert. *The Worshipful Company of Tin Plate Workers alias Wire Workers and its connection with the tin-plate industries.* London, 1914. 34p.

858 **Cunningham**, William, Archdeacon of Ely. *Notes on the organisation of the mason's craft in England.* London: H. Milford, 1914. 11p.

Read at the International Historical Congress, April, 1913.

From the *Proceedings of the British Academy.*

859 **Jackson**, John. *Notes on the history and antiquities of the Worshipful Company of Coopers.* London, 1914. 20p.

860 **Pitt**, George Newton. *Notes on the history of the Armourers' & Brasiers' Company: an address.* London: R. Clay, 1914. 23p.

861 **Simpson**, Frank. 'The city gilds of Chester: the Smiths, Cutlers and Plumbers' Company.' *Ches. N. Wales Archit., Archaeol. Hist. Soc. J.*, n.s., XX (1914), 5–121.

862 **Johnson**, Arthur Henry. *The history of the Worshipful Company of the Drapers of London, preceded by an introduction on London and her gilds up to the close of the XVth century.* Oxford: Clarendon P., 1914–22. 5v.

863 **Ditchfield**, Peter Hampson. 'The Worshipful Company of Masons and its connection with freemasonry.' *Authors' Lodge No. 3456 Trans.*, I (1915), 89–96.

864 **Phillips**, Henry Laverock. *Annals of the Worshipful Company of Joiners.* Privately printed, 1915. v, 130p.

'Extracted from original documents.'

865 **Simpson**, Frank. 'The city gilds of Chester: the Skinners and Feltmakers' Company.' *Ches. N. Wales. Archit. Archaeol. Hist. Soc. J.*, n.s., XXI (1915), 77–149.

866 **Weston**, Francis. 'Some account of the Barbers' Company and the plate, pictures and charters at Barber-Surgeons' Hall, E.C.' *Br. Archaeol. Ass. J.*, n.s., XXI, 1 (March 1915), 17–56.

867 **Carr**, Thomas. 'The Worshipful Society of Apothecaries: a short sketch of the history of the Society.' *Ars Quat. Coron.*, XXIX (1916), 270–2.

868 **Welch**, Charles. *History of the Cutlers' Company of London and of the minor cutlery crafts, with biographical notices of early London cutlers.* London, 1916, 1923. 2v.

869 **Chanter**, J. F. 'The Barnstaple Goldsmiths' Guild, with some notes on the early history of the town.' *Devon. Ass. Advmt. Sci. Lit. Art Rep. Trans.*, XLIX (1917), 163–89.

870 **Conder**, Edward. 'The Worshipful Company of Masons of the City of London.' *Authors' Lodge No. 3456 Trans.*, II (1917), 166–71.

871 **Dodds**, Madeleine Hope. 'The Butchers' Company of Newcastle-upon-Tyne.' *Archaeol. Ael.*, 3rd ser., XIV (1917), 1–91.

872 **Hawkins**, James Harford. *History of the Worshipful Company of the Art or Mistery of Feltmakers of London.* London: Crowther and Goodman, 1917. viii, 172p.

873 **Hobson**, Samuel George. 'The genesis of national guilds.' *Contemp. Rev.*, CXI (March 1917), 366–74.

874 **Scott**, Jonathan French. 'Limitations of gild monopoly.' *Am. Hist. Rev.*, XXII, 3 (April 1917), 586–9.

875 **Wills**, Herbert Winkler. *The Worshipful Company of Armourers and Brasiers.* London, 1917.

Reprinted from *The Builder*, 21 September 1917.

876 **Knight**, A. Charles. 'The Tallow Chandlers' Company: its origin and a sketch of its history.' *Br. Archaeol. Ass. J.*, n.s., XXIV (December 1918), 173–216.

877 **Renard**, Georges. *Guilds in the Middle Ages.* London: Bell, 1918. xxv, 139p.

Translated by Dorothy Terry, and edited with an introduction by G. D. H. Cole.

878 **Simpson**, Frank, 'The City Guilds of Chester: the Bricklayers' Company.' *Ches. N. Wales Archit. Archaeol. Hist. Soc. J.*, n.s., XXII (1918), 55–90.

879 **Ashdown**, Charles Henry. *History of the Worshipful Company of Glaziers of the City of London, otherwise the Company of Glaziers and Painters of Glass.* London: the Company, 1919. 163p.

With contributory notes by Percy W. Berriman Tippetts.

880 **Salwey**, Theophilus John. 'Notes on some trade guilds at Ludlow.' *Ars Quat. Coron.*, XXXII (1919), 149–62.

881 **Power**, Eileen E. 'Historical revisions. XII. English craft gilds in the middle ages.' *History*, n.s., IV, 16 (January 1920), 211–14.

882 **Somers-Smith**, R. V. 'The Company of Grocers.' *Lond. Middx. Archaeol. Soc. Trans.*, n.s., IV, 3 (1920), 228–45.

883 **Warner**, *Sir* Frank. *The Weavers' Company: a short history.* London: Baynard P., [1920?]. 29p.

Printed for private circulation.

884 **Dendy**, Frederick Walter. *Three lectures delivered to the Literary and Philosophical Society, Newcastle-upon-Tyne, on old Newcastle, its suburbs, and gilds, and an essay on Northumberland.* Newcastle-upon-Tyne: Literary and Philosophical Society of Newcastle-upon-Tyne, 1921. 85p.

885 **Waldo**, Frederick Joseph. *The Worshipful Company of Plumbers: some points in the history and policy of an ancient City company.* London, 1921. 11p.

Second edition. *A short history of the Worshipful Company of Plumbers of the City of London.* 1923. 39p.

886 **Rosedale**, Honyel Gough. 'History of the gilds and freemasonry.' *Notts. Install. Mast. Lodge No. 3593 Trans.*, XI (1921), 105–9; XII (1922), 115–19.

887 **Berry**, Albert James. *Preston's progress through its gild; or, From field to factory.* Preston: G. Toulmin, 1922. xvi, 60p.

888 *History of the Worshipful Company of Innholders of the City of London*. London: privately printed, 1922. 71p.

889 **Dale**, Hylton Burleigh. *The Fellowship of Woodmongers: six centuries of the London coal trade*. London, 1923. 152p.

Reprinted from the *Coal Merchant and Skipper*.

890 **Englefield**, William Alexander Devereux. *The history of the Painter-Stainers Company of London*. London: Chapman and Dodd, 1924 [i.e. 1923]. 248p.

Re-issued with new introduction and supplementary index. 1936. 11, xvi, 13–252p.

891 **Muir**, Arthur. *Traditions and customs of the hammermen of Glasgow, and the insignia and relics of the Incorporation of Hammermen*. 1923. 58p.

Second edition. Glasgow: Jackson, 1929. x, 84p.

892 **Poole**, Herbert. 'Some notes on the trade companies of Kendal in the 16th and 17th centuries.' *Ars Quat. Coron.*, XXXVI (1923), 5–33.

893 **Rees**, Joseph Aubrey. *The Worshipful Company of Grocers, 1345–1923*. London, Sydney: Chapman and Dodd, 1923. 189p.

894 **Rivington**, Reginald Thurston. *The Worshipful Company of Stationers: a short account of its charter, hall, plate, registers & other matters connected with its history*. London: the Company, 1923. 15p.

Another edition. 1928. 14p.

895 **Rosedale**, Honyel Gough. 'Origins of gilds and freemasonry.' *Mers. Ass. Mason. Res. Trans.*, I (1923), 33–8.

Summary of a lecture.

896 **Sutton**, George F. 'Notes on the early history of the Worshipful Company of Leathersellers.' *Lond. Middx. Archaeol. Soc. Trans.*, n.s., V, 1 (1923), 14–27.

897 **Morton**, James Herbert. 'Livery companies of London.' *Lodge Res. No. 2429 Leic. Trans.* (1923–24), 150–63.

898 **Hodgson**, J. C. and **Wood**, H. M. 'The Merchants' Company of Alnwick.' *Archaeol. Ael.*, 3rd ser., XXI (1924), 16–37.

899 **Smith**, Joshua Toulmin. *English gilds: the original ordinances of more than one hundred early English gilds*. 1924. cxcix, 483p. (Early English Text Society. Original series 40.)

With a preliminary essay in five parts *On the history and development of gilds*, by Lujo Brentano.

Originally published, without the essay, 1870.

900 **Reade**, Hubert. 'Some account books of the first Lord Scudamore and of the Hereford craft guilds.' *Wool. Nat. Field Club Trans.* (1924–26), 119–33.

'The Hereford guild accounts', p. 130–3.

901 **Hibbert**, William Nembhard. *History of the Worshipful Company of Founders, of the City of London*. London: privately printed, 1925. xv, 315p.

902 **Stone**, Arthur Carlyon Stanley. *The Worshipful Company of Turners: its origin and history*. London: Lindley-Jones, 1925. vii, 337p.

903 **Daynes**, Gilbert William. 'The Company of Masons of the City of London.' *Lodge Res. No. 2429 Leic. Trans.* (1924–25), 135–49; (1925–26), 100–15.

904 **Berry**, Charles Walter. *The Worshipful Company of Tin Plate Workers alias Wire Workers and its connection with the wire industries*. London: Rixon and Arnold, 1926. 40p.

905 **Bibliographic Society**. 'The Stationers' Company's records.' *Bibl. Soc. Trans.*, n.s., VI, 4 (March 1926), 348–57.

A catalogue to the close of the eighteenth century of records at Stationers' Hall.

906 **Ditchfield**, Peter Hampson. *The story of the City Companies*. London: G. T. Foulis, 1926. 333p.

907 **Fitch**, Charles. *The history of the Worshipful Company of Pattenmakers*. Bungay: R. Clay, 1926. xii, 141p.

908 **Harris**, Mary Dormer. *The history of the Drapers' Company of Coventry*. Coventry: H. A. Smith, 1926. 38p.

909 **Baxter**, Peter (comp.). *The Shoemaker Incorporation of Perth, 1545 to 1927*. Perth: J. McKinlay, 1927. 224p.

910 **ffoulkes**, Charles. 'The Armourers' Company of London and the Greenwich School of Armourers.' *Archaeologia*, LXXVI (1927), 41–58.

911 **Knowles**, John A. 'Additional notes on the history of the Worshipful Company of Glaziers.' *Antiq. J.*, VII, 3 (July 1927), 282–93.

In response to the invitation in Charles H. Ashdown's *History of the Worshipful Company of Glaziers, otherwise the Company of Glaziers and Painters of Glass*. London: the Company, 1919.

912 **Knowles**, John A. 'Artistic craft guilds of the middle ages.' *R. Inst. Br. Archit. J.*, 3rd ser., XXXIV, 8 (19 February 1927), 263–71.

Comment, by Edward Warren, XXXIV, 10 (19 March 1927), 341.

Reply, by J. A. Knowles, XXXIV, 11 (2 April 1927), 371–2.

913 **Kramer**, Stella. *The English craft gilds: studies in their progress and decline*. New York: Columbia U.P., 1927. xi, 228p.

914 **Skillington**, Stephen Harry. *The certificates of three Leicester gilds, with an introduction and notes*. Leicester: E. Backus, 1927. 50p.

915 **Auden**, G. A. 'The Gild of Barber Surgeons of the City of York.' *R. Soc. Med. Proc.*, XXI (1927–28), 1400–6.

916 **Pybus**, F. C. 'The Company of Barber Surgeons and Tallow Chandlers of Newcastle-upon-Tyne.' *R. Soc. Med. Proc.*, XXII (1928–29), 287–96.

917 **Chambers**, Jonathan David. 'The Worshipful Company of Framework Knitters (1657–1778).' *Economica*, IX, 27 (November 1929), 296–329.

918 **Consitt**, Frances. *The history of the London Weavers' Company*. 1929. (B. Litt. thesis, University of Oxford.)

919 **Marshall**, T. H. 'Capitalism and the decline of the English gilds.' *Camb. Hist. J.*, III, 1 (1929), 23–33.
An inquiry into *The English craft gilds*, by Stella Kramer, Columbia U.P., 1927.

920 **Pearce**, Arthur. *The history of the Butchers' Company*. London: Meat Traders' Journal Co., 1929. xii, 280p.

921 **Skillington**, Stephen Harry. *The Leicester Gild of Tallow Chandlers*. Leicester, 1929. 15p.

922 **Webb**, John Joseph. *The Guilds of Dublin*. London: Benn, 1929. 298p.

923 **Court**, Thomas H. and **Von Rohr**, Moritz. 'Contributions to the history of the Worshipful Company of Spectaclemakers.' *Opt. Soc. Trans.*, XXXI, 2 (1929–30), 53–90.

924 **Cresswell**, Beatrix Feodore. *A short history of the Worshipful Company of Weavers, Fullers and Shearmen of the City and County of Exeter*. Exeter: W. Pollard, 1930. vi, 134p.

925 **Elkington**, George. *The Worshipful Company of Coopers: with notes and recollections, 1873 to 1930*. Margate: W. T. Parrett, 1930. 113p.

926 **Pitt**, Sydney Hewitt. *Some notes on the history of the Worshipful Company of Armourers and Brasiers*. London: privately printed, 1930. 47p.

927 **Rivington**, Charles Robert. *A brief account of the Worshipful Company of Stationers*. London: Boyle, Son and Watchurst, 1930. 12p.

928 **Blackham**, Robert James. *The soul of the city: London's Livery Companies, their storied past, their living present*. London: Sampson Low, 1931. xvi, 358p.

929 **Blades**, George Rowland, Baron Ebbisham. *The Worshipful Company of Gardeners of London*. London: the company, 1931. 19p.
Second edition. 1931. 19p.

930 **Incorporation of Bakers of Glasgow**. *The Incorporation of Bakers of Glasgow*. Glasgow: the Incorporation, 1931. 212p.
An historical account.
New edition.

931 **Mander**, Charles Henry Waterland. *A descriptive and historical account of the Guild of Cordwainers of the City of London*. London: printed for private circulation, 1931. 222p.

932 **Pitt**, Sydney Hewitt. *The Mistery of St. George of the Armorers*. London: Pelican P. for the author, 1931. 64p. (Sette of Odd Volumes. Opuscula 91.)
Printed for private circulation.
On the origin and growth of the Worshipful Company of Armourers and Brasiers of London.

933 **Goodale**, Sydney Frederick. 'Craft guilds and merchants' guilds, London.' *Som. Mast. Lodge No. 3746 Trans.*, V (1931–34), 230–4.

934 **Ebblewhite**, Ernest Arthur. *The Parish Clerks' Company and its charters; with a biographical calendar and an inventory of its property between 1610 and 1705*. London: privately printed, 1932. 117p.

935 **Phillips**, Frank Taverner. *A history of the Worshipful Company of Cooks, London*. London: privately printed, 1932. xxi, 207p.

936 **Pontifex**, Bryan. *The City of London livery companies*. London: 'City Press', 1932. 32p.

937 **Wall**, Cecil. *The London Apothecaries, their Society and their Hall*. London, 1932. 28p.

938 **Blackham**, Robert James. 'London's livery companies.' *Angl.-Dan. J.*, VIII, 30 (October 1933), 4–8.

939 **Consitt**, Frances. *The London Weavers' Company*. Oxford: Clarendon P., 1933.
Vol. I. *From the twelfth century to the close of the sixteenth century*. xi, 343p.

940 **Dale**, Marian K. 'The London Silkwomen of the fifteenth century.' *Econ. Hist. Rev.*, IV, 3 (October 1933), 324–35.
'. . . it is the purpose of this article to illustrate the usual practices among female participants in trade and industry at this time, and to show that although this mistery was not recognised as a definite gild, it was pursued on the lines of the craft gilds of male workers.'

941 **Elkington**, George. *The Coopers' Company and craft*. London: Sampson Low, 1933. ix, 310p.

942 **Lambert**, John James (ed.). *Records of the Skinners of London, Edward I to James I*. London, 1933. 429p.

943 **Thrupp**, Sylvia Lettice. *A short history of the Worshipful Company of Bakers of London*. London: the Company, 1933. xiii, 207p.

944 **Brewin**, Arthur H. 'History of the Worshipful Company of Dyers, London.' Society of Dyers and Colourists. *The Jubilee issue of the Society of Dyers & Colourists, 1884–1934*. Bradford: the Society, 1934. p. 7–15.

945 **Stevenson**, John H. *The Grocer Company of Glasgow, instituted 1789, incorporated 1796: a short history of the Company since its institution one hundred and forty-five years ago*. Glasgow: privately printed, 1934. 50p.

946 **Coach Makers' Company**. 'The Coach and Coach Harness Makers' Company.' *London Soc. J.*, 206 (April 1935), 58–63.

947 **Hendson**, Charles. 'The rules of a cobblers' gild at Helston in 1517.' *Essays in Cornish history*. Oxford: Clarendon P., 1935. p. 75–9.
Edited by A. L. Rowse and M. I. Henderson.

948 **Miscellanea Latomorum**. 'A Canterbury gild.' *Misc. Lat.*, n.s., XIX, 9 (June 1935), 129–33.
Notes on a Fellowship account book, 1657–1714.
Editorial.

949 *The Worshipful Company of Goldsmiths of the City of London*. London, 1935. 31p.
A descriptive pamphlet.

950 **Englefield**, William Alexander Devereux. 'Visit to the hall of the Painter-Stainers' Company.' *London Soc. J.*, 217 (March 1936), 45–7.
Account of the history of the company.

951 **Fisher**, Frederick Jack. *A short history of the Worshipful Company of Horners*. Croydon: privately printed, 1936. xiv, 138p.

952 **Seggie**, J. Stewart. *Corporation of Squaremen: short historical account*. Edinburgh, 1936. 12p.
Reprinted from *Scots Year Book*, 1935–36.

953 **Shelley**, Roland J. A. *Brief notes on the Wigan pewterers*. Wigan: T. Wall, 1936. 20p.
Reprinted from the *Wigan Observer*.

954 **Adams**, Arthur James. *The history of the Worshipful Company of Blacksmiths from early times until the year 1647. Being selected reproductions from the original books of the Company, an historical introduction, and many notes*. London: published privately, 1937. xiii, 66p.
. . . until the year 1785. London: Sylvan P., 1951. 207p.

955 **Garbett**, H. L. E. (ed.). 'The agreement with the shoemakers of Stafford, 1476.' *Old Staff. Soc. Trans. for 1936* (1937), 17–26.
Text and notes.

956 *A history of the Worshipful Company of Coachmakers and Coach Harness-Makers of London*. London: Chapel River P., 1937. ix, 102p.
Printed for private circulation.

957 **Lumsden**, Harry. *History of the Skinners, Furriers and Glovers of Glasgow: a study of a Scottish craft guild in its various relations*. Glasgow: Wylie, 1937. xxiv, 306p.

958 **Wall**, Cecil. *The history of the Surgeons' Company, 1745–1800*. London: Hutchinson's Scientific and Technical Publications, 1937. 256p.

959 **Bell**, Walter George. *A short history of the Worshipful Company of Tylers and Bricklayers of the City of London*. London: Montgomery, 1938. viii, 81p.

960 **Marwick**, William Hutton. 'The Incorporation of the Tailors of the Canongate.' *Old Edinb. Club Book*, XXII (1938), 91–131.

961 **Jones**, Philip Edmund. *The Worshipful Company of Poulters of the City of London: a short history*. London: Oxford U.P., 1939. 252p.
Second edition. 1965. 266p.

962 **Knoop**, Douglas and **Jones**, Gwilym Peredur. 'The London Masons' Company.' *Econ. Hist.*, III, 14 (February 1939), 157–66.

963 **Pontifex**, Bryan. *The City of London Livery Companies*. London: Methuen, 1939. viii, 93p.

964 **Ridge**, C. Harold (comp.). *Records of the Worshipful Company of Shipwrights. Vol. I. 1428–1780. Being an alphabetical digest of freemen and apprentices, etc. Compiled from the Company's records by C. Harold Ridge. With a short history of the Company by A. Charles Knight*. London: Phillimore, 1939. xvi, 261p.
Only 200 copies printed.

965 **Howard**, Alexander Liddon (comp.). *The Worshipful Company of Glass-Sellers of London, from its inception to the present day*. London: Worshipful Company of Glass-Sellers, 1940. 152p.
Compiled from various sources and re-edited.

966 **Dove**, Constance Winifred. *The old English gild system*. 1941. (M.A. thesis, University of Leeds.)

967 **Thrupp**, Sylvia L. 'Medieval gilds reconsidered.' *J. Econ. Hist.*, II, 2 (November 1942), 164–73.

968 **Hart**, Thomas. 'Glasgow trade guilds.' *R. Phil. Soc. Glasg. Proc.*, LXVII (1942–43), 65–86.

969 **Whiting**, Charles Edwin. 'The Durham trade gilds.' *Archit. Archaeol. Soc. Durham Northumb. Trans.*, IX (1942–44), 143–262; 265–416.

970 **Levy**, Hermann. 'The economic history of sickness and medical benefit before the Puritan Revolution.' *Econ. Hist. Rev.*, XIII, 1–2 (1943), 42–57.

971 **Pick**, Frederick Lomax. 'The English gild.' *Ars Quat. Coron.*, LVI (1943), 291–8.
Inaugural address, 1943.

972 **Pontifex**, Bryan. 'The city livery companies.' *Banker*, LXVI, 207 (April 1943), 21–5.
London.

973 **Foster**, *Sir* William. *A short history of the Worshipful Company of Coopers of London*. Cambridge: Cambridge U.P., 1944. viii, 147p.

974 **Pooley**, *Sir* Ernest Henry. *The guilds of the City of London*. London: Collins, 1945. 47p. (Britain in pictures. The British people in pictures.)

975 **Pick**, Frederick Lomax. 'Preston: the gild and the craft.' *Ars Quat. Coron.*, LIX (1946), 90–126.

976 **Ponting**, K. G. 'The weavers and fullers of Marlborough.' *Wilts. Mag.*, LIII, 190 (June 1949), 113–17.

977 **Harvey**, Alfred Salter. *The 'Trinity House' of Kingston upon Hull*. Hull: A. Brown for the Corporation of Hull Trinity House, 1950. 32p.

978 **Barnes**. L. Hickman and **Ellison-Macartney**, J. *A short history of the Grocers' Company, together with a description of the Grocers' Hall and the principal objects of interest therein*. London: Grocers' Company, 1950 [i.e. 1951]. viii, 78p.
For private circulation.
A revised and expanded version of an earlier pamphlet and catalogue by L. Hickman Barnes.

979 **Eltringham**, G. J. 'Salisbury companies and their ordinances, with particular reference to the woodworking crafts.' *Wilts. Mag.*, LIV, 195 (December 1951), 195–91.

A description of seventeenth-century documents in the archives of the Corporation of Salisbury.

980 *The Livery Companies of the City of London.* London: *City Press Newspaper*, 1951. 28p.

981 **Bennett**, Eric. *The Worshipful Company of Carmen of London: a short history.* London: Worshipful Company of Carmen; Simpkin Marshall, 1952. 181p.
Revised edition. London: Dawsons, 1961. 185p.

982 **Groombridge**, Margaret J. 'The city gilds of Chester.' *Ches. N. Wales Archit. Archaeol. Hist. Soc. J.*, n.s., XXXIX (1952), 93–108.

983 **Hollaender**, A. E. J. 'The archives of the Worshipful Company of Gunmakers of the City of London.' *Archives*, 8 (Michaelmas 1952), 8–19.

984 **Lindsay**, Matthew. *History of the Incorporation of Bonnetmakers and Dyers of Glasgow, 1597–1950.* Glasgow: Incorporation of Bonnetmakers and Dyers of Glasgow, 1952. 121p.
Sixth edition.
Previous edition 1930.

985 **Hodgson**, Sidney. *The Worshipful Company of Stationers and Newspaper Makers: notes on its origin and history, archives, portraits, plate, etc.* London: Stationers' Company, 1953. 15p.

986 **Mason**, John. *The history of Trinity House of Leith.* Glasgow: McKenzie Vincent, 1956. 194p.

987 **Barker**, Theodore Cardwell. *The Girdlers' Company: a second history.* London: Girdlers' Company, 1957. xv, 186p.
Private circulation.

988 **Gwilliam**, R. C. 'The Chester Tanners and Parliament, 1711–1717.' *Ches. N. Wales Archit. Archaeol. Hist. Soc. J.*, n.s., XLIV (1957), 41–9.
On a series of letters concerning the Tanners' Company's attempt to defeat certain parliamentary measures which affected their trade.

989 **Morgan**, B. G. *The King's Master Masons, 1245–1515.* 1957–58. (Ph.D. thesis, University of Liverpool.)

990 **Girtin**, Thomas. *The golden rain: a narrative history of the Clothworkers' Company, 1528–1958.* London: Clothworkers' Company, 1958. xii, 364p.
Private circulation.

991 **Kellett**, J. R. 'The breakdown of gild and corporation control over the handicraft and retail trade in London.' *Econ. Hist. Rev.*, 2nd ser., x, 3 (April 1958), 381–94.

992 **Harding**, F. J. W. 'The Company of Butchers and Fleshers of Durham.' *Archit. Archaeol. Soc. Durham Northumb. Trans.*, XI (1958–65), 93–100.

993 **Halcrow**, Elizabeth M. 'Records of the Bakers and Brewers of Newcastle upon Tyne at the Black Gate.' *Archaeol. Ael.*, 4th ser., XXXVII (1959), 327–32.

994 **Blagden**, Cyprian. *The Stationers' Company: a history, 1403–1959.* London: Allen and Unwin, 1960. 322p.

995 **Kahl**, William F. *The development of London livery companies: an historical essay and a select bibliography.* Boston, Mass.: Baker Library, Harvard Graduate School of Business Administration, 1960. viii, 104p. (Kress Library of Business and Economics. Publication 15.)

996 **Lloyd**, T. H. *The medieval gilds of Stratford-on-Avon and the timber-framed building industry.* 1960–61. (M.A. thesis, University of Birmingham.)

997 **Fox**, Levi. 'The Coventry guilds and trading companies with special reference to the position of women.' Birmingham Archaeological Society and the Dugdale Society. *Essays in honour of Philip B. Chatwin.* Oxford: printed for subscribers only by Vivian Ridler at the University Press, 1962. p. 13–26.

998 **Reddaway**, T. F. 'The London goldsmiths circa 1500.' *R. Hist. Soc. Trans.*, 5th ser., XII (1962), 49–62.
Worshipful Company of Goldsmiths.

999 **Warner**, Oliver Martin Wilson. *A history of the Innholders' Company.* London: Innholders' Society, 1962. xii, 123p.
Second history, revised and re-written.
See also *History of the Worshipful Company of Innholders of the City of London.* London: privately printed, 1922. 71p.

1000 **Wall**, Cecil and **Cameron**, Hector Charles. *A history of the Worshipful Society of Apothecaries of London: abstracted and arranged from the manuscript notes of the late Cecil Wall by the late H. Charles Cameron; revised, annotated, and edited by E. Ashworth Underwood.* London: Oxford U.P. for the Wellcome Historical Medical Museum.
Vol. 1. 1617–1815. 1963. xiv, 450p. (Wellcome Historical Medical Museum. Publications, new series, 8.)

1001 **Watson**, John Steven. *A history of the Salters' Company.* London: Oxford U.P., 1963, 161p.

1002 **Founders Company**. *Wardens' accounts of the Worshipful Company of Founders of the City of London, 1497–1681.* London: Athlone P., 1964. lviii, 491p.
Transcribed, calendared and edited by Guy Parsloe.

1003 **Girtin**, Thomas. *The triple crowns: a narrative history of the Drapers' Company, 1364–1964.* London: Hutchinson, 1964. 408p.
First edition. 1958. 408p.

1004 **Pinto**, Edward Henry. *The origins and history of the Worshipful Company of Furniture Makers, up to the end of 1963.* London: Worshipful Company of Furniture Makers, 1964. 39p.
Private circulation.

1005 **Steele**, Arnold Francis. *The Worshipful Company of Gardeners of London: a history of its revival, 1890–1960.* London: Worshipful Company of Gardeners, 1964. xi, 201p.

1006 **Warner**, Oliver Martin Wilson. *A history of the Tin Plate Workers alias Wire Workers Company of the City of London.* London: Tin Plate Workers alias Wire Workers Company, 1964. xi, 88p.

1007 **Champness**, Roland. *The Worshipful Company of Turners of London.* London: Lindley-Jones, 1966. x, 270p.
Private circulation.

1008 **Daynes**, John Norman. *A short history of the ancient Mistery of the Dyers of the City of London.* London: Worshipful Company of Dyers, 1966. 103p.
Private circulation.

1009 **Elrington**, C. R. 'Records of the Cordwainers' Society of Tewkesbury, 1562–1941.' *Bris. Glouc. Archaeol. Soc. Trans.*, LXXXV (1966), 164–74.

1010 **Phillips**, Frank Taverner. *A second history of the Worshipful Company of Cooks, London.* Kingston-upon-Thames: Worshipful Company of Cooks, 1966. xv, 159p.

1011 **Reddaway**, T. F. 'The livery companies of Tudor London.' *History*, n.s., LI, 173 (October 1966), 287–99.
'A talk given on Saturday, 16 April 1966, to the sixtieth annual conference of the Historical Association.'

1012 **Collins**, J. P. *The Vintners' Company of London in the earlier sixteenth century.* 1967–68. (M.Phil. thesis, University of Leeds.)

1013 **Storey**, Arthur. *Trinity House of Kingston upon Hull.* Hull: Hull Trinity House, 1967–69. 2v.
Vol. 1. 1967. 146p.
Vol. 2. 1969. 202p.

1014 **Alford**, Bernard William Ernest and **Barker**, Theodore Cardwell. *A history of the Carpenters Company.* London: Allen and Unwin, 1968. 271p.

1015 **Fox**, Adam. *A brief description of the Worshipful Company of Skinners.* London: Skinners' Company, 1968. 72p.
Revised edition. 'Privately printed for the Company.'
Previous edition 1956.

1016 **Mayer**, Edward. *The Curriers and the City of London: a history of the Worshipful Company of Curriers.* London: Curriers Company, 1968. xi, 212p.

1017 **Oxley**, James Edwin. *The fletchers and longbow stringmakers of London.* London: Worshipful Company of Fletchers, 1968. 160p.

1018 **Youings**, Joyce. *Tuckers Hall, Exeter: the history of a provincial city company through five centuries.* Exeter: University of Exeter; The Incorporation of Weavers, Fullers and Shearmen, 1968. xiv, 258p.

1019 **Bennett**, Eric. *The Worshipful Company of Wheelwrights of the City of London, 1670–1970.* Newton Abbot: David and Charles 1970. 171p.
Includes the charter and bylaws of the Company.

1020 **Gordon**, George. *The Shore Porters' Society of Aberdeen, 1498–1969.* Aberdeen: Alex. P. Reid, 1970. 127p.

1021 **Monier-Williams**, Randall. *The Tallow Chandlers of London.* London: Kaye and Ward.
Vol. 1. *The mystery in the making.* 1970. 96p.

1022 **Rowe**, David J. (ed.). *The records of the Company of Shipwrights of Newcastle-upon-Tyne, 1622–1967.* Gateshead: printed by Northumberland P., for the Society. 2v.
Vol. 1. 1970. 203p. Vol. 2. 1971. (Surtees Society. Publications vol. 181.)

1023 **Worshipful Company of Carmen of London.** *The Worshipful Company of Carmen of London tercentenary.* London: T.W.C.C. Publications, 1970. 42p.

See also: 1; 55; 1146; 1364; 9035; 9364; 12,640.

II. FRIENDLY SOCIETIES

See also Part Three, III, G, 6; Part Seven, VII, A; and Part Seven, IX, B.

1024 **Borthwick**, J., and others. *The Jackson prize essays on friendly societies.* Leeds, 1885. v, 114p.

1025 **Brabrook**, Edward William. 'The relation of the state to thrift: ten years' statistics of friendly societies and similar institutions.' *R. Statist. Soc. J.*, XLVIII, 1 (March 1885), 21–44.
Discussion, p. 45–53.

1026 **Hewat**, Archibald. *Friendly societies.* London: Layton, 1886. (Insurance and Actuarial Society. Transactions, Series 2, no. 4.)

1027 **Wilkinson**, John Frome. *The friendly society movement: its origin . . . and growth, its . . . influences.* London: Longmans, 1886. xvi, 229p.
Another edition. 1891. xvi, 239p.

1028 **Watson**, Reuben. *An essay on friendly societies and sick clubs.* London, 1888. 32p.

1029 **Wilkinson**, John Frome. *The mutual friendly and provident institutions of the working classes.* London, 1888. 52p.

1030 **Watson**, Reuben. *The causes of deficiences in friendly societies, and some remarks on hazardous occupations.* Manchester: J. Heywood, 1889. 24p.

1031 **Johnston**, Thomas, of Borrowstounness. *The records of an ancient friendly society: the Bo'ness United General Sea Box; two centuries and a half of local history.* Bo'ness: Proprietors of the *Falkirk Herald*, 1890, vii, 117p.
Reprinted from the *Falkirk Herald*.

1032 **Hardwick**, Charles. *The history, present position, and social importance of friendly societies.* Manchester: J. Heywood, 1893. xiv, 170p.
Third edition, revised.
Previous editions. 1859, 1869.

1033 **Dalton and District United Workmen's Association.** *Dalton and District United Workmen's Association: a review.* Dalton-in-Furness, 1894. 9p.

1034 **Wallace**, John Bruce. *Towards fraternal organisation: an explanation of the Brotherhood Trust.* London: Brotherhood Trust, 1894. 28p.
Second edition, revised.
Third edition, revised. 1894. 29p.
Another edition. 1895. 32p.

1035 **Brabrook**, Edward William. 'The progress of friendly societies and other institutions connected with the Friendly Societies Registry Office during the ten years 1884–94.' *R. Statist. Soc. J.*, LVIII, 2 (June 1895), 286–302.
With discussion, p. 321–6.
Read before the Royal Statistical Society, 23 April 1895.

1036 **Haldane**, Elizabeth S. 'Registered friendly societies for women.' *Natn. Rev.*, XXVIII, 166 (December 1896), 559–66.

1037 **Ludlow**, John M. 'Friendly societies and their congeners.' *Econ. Rev.*, VI, 4 (October 1896), 481–502.

1038 **Brabrook**, *Sir* Edward William. *Provident societies and industrial welfare.* London: Blackie, 1898. 224p. (Victorian era series.)

1039 **Toynbee**, H. V. 'The present position of the friendly societies.' *Nineteenth Century*, XLV, 168 (June 1899), 891–905.

1040 **Ludlow**, John M. 'Centenarian friendly societies.' *Contemp. Rev.*, LXXXII (October 1902), 546–54.

1041 **Pomeroy**, Eltweed. *The English friendly societies.* [New York?, 1902?] 8p.
Reprinted from *Arena*, January 1902.

1042 **Brabrook**, *Sir* Edward William. '[Address to Section F of the British Association, Southport, 1903].' *R. Statist. Soc. J.*, LXVI, 3 (September 1903), 603–16.

1043 **Millis**, W. F. *The Railway Benevolent Institution: its rise and progress from 1858 to 1897.* London, 1903. 182p.

1044 **Shairp**, Leslie V. 'The friendly society movement.' *Char. Orgn. Rev.*, n.s., XVI, 94 (October 1904), 199–206.

1045 **Brabrook**, *Sir* Edward William. 'On the progress of friendly societies and other institutions connected with the Friendly Societies Registry Office during the ten years 1894–1904.' *R. Statist. Soc. J.*, LXVIII, 2 (June 1905), 320–42.
With discussion, p. 342–52.
'Read before the Royal Statistical Society, 18th April, 1905.'

1046 **Riebenack**, Max. *Railway provident institutions in English speaking countries.* Philadelphia, 1905. 357, 31, [30]p.

1047 **Friendly Society of Iron Founders of England, Ireland and Wales**. *Century Souvenir.* Manchester, 1909.

1048 **Leveaux**, A. M. 'Friendly societies and their origin.' *Char. Orgn. Rev.*, n.s., XXV, 150 (June 1909), 294–304.
'Paper read at the Seventy-Seventh Annual Meeting of the Dunmow Friendly Society, held on Thursday, February 2, 1909.'

1049 **Fletcher**, J. M. J. 'Some records of an eighteenth century benefit society.' *Derby. Archaeol. Nat. Hist. Soc. J.*, XXXIII (1911), 221–34.
Tideswell Humane Friendly Indefatigable Union Society.

1050 **Bourne**, J. *A short history of friendly societies in general and of the Birmingham Ebenezer Provident Sick Society in particular.* [Birmingham], 1913. 14p.

1051 **Brabrook**, *Sir* Edward William. 'On the progress of friendly societies and other institutions connected with the Friendly Societies Registry Office during the ten years, 1904–1914.' *R. Statist. Soc. J.*, LXXXIII, 3 (May 1915), 414–33.
With discussion, p. 433–45.

1052 **Bushrod**, W. T. *The development of the great affiliated friendly societies from their humble and often obscure origins in the 18th century.* 1924. (M.A. thesis, University of Manchester.)

1053 **Campbell**, Richardson. *Provident and industrial institutions* . . . Manchester: Rechabite Buildings, [1925]. 282p.

1054 **Davis**, Paul. *The old friendly societies of Hull.* Hull: A. Brown, 1926. x, 69p.

1055 **Hine**, Richard. 'Friendly societies and their emblems.' *Dors. Nat. Hist. Archaeol. Soc. Proc.*, XLIX (1928), 114–24.

1056 **Maltby**, Herbert John Mason. 'Early Manchester and Salford friendly societies.' *Lanc. Chesh. Antiq. Soc. Trans.*, XLVI (1929), 32–40.

1057 **Eason**, A. H. *The story of the Fishmongers' & Poulterers' Institution: a century of work, 1827–1927.* London: printed by the Whitefriars P., 1930. viii, 96p., 12 plates.
The author was Secretary of the Institution.

1058 **Taylor**, Glen A. 'The early friendly societies of Neath.' *Neath Antiq. Soc. Trans.*, 2nd ser., III (1932–33), 42–4.

1059 **Brown**, Charles Hilton Leonard and **Taylor**, Joseph Andrew George. *Friendly societies.* Cambridge: Cambridge U.P., 1933. xii, 95p. (Institute of Actuaries Students' Society's consolidation of reading series 2.)

1060 **Friendly Society of Operative Stonemasons**. *Centenary souvenir.* 1933.

1061 **Maltby**, Herbert John Mason. 'Early Bradford Friendly Societies.' *Brad. Antiq.*, VII, n.s., V (1933), 17–28.

1062 **McPherson**, James Mackenzie. 'The Sea Box of Fraserburgh.' *Aberd. Univ. Rev.*, XXIX, 86 (Spring 1942), 123–8.
Seamen's friendly society, 18th–19th centuries.

1063 **Creasy**, John (comp.). *The printer's devil: an account of the history and objects of the Printers' Pension, Almshouse and Orphan Asylum Corporation.* London: Hutchinson, 1943. 95p.

Founded 1827.
Edited by Walter Hutchinson.

1064 **Lincoln**, John Abraham (ed.). *The way ahead: the strange case of the friendly societies.* London: National Conference of Friendly Societies, 1946. 68p.

1065 **Morgan**, Frederick Charles. 'Friendly societies in Herefordshire.' *Wool. Nat. Field Club Trans.*, XXXII (1946–48), 183–211.

1066 *The English friendly society movement.* Bridgetown, 1948. 19p. (Development and welfare in the West Indies. Bulletins 25.)

1067 **Morgan**, Frederick Charles. *Friendly societies in Herefordshire.* Hereford: Woolhope Naturalists Field Club, 1949. 29p.

1068 **Blake**, William Thomas Cann and **Moore**, Joseph Moreton. *Friendly societies.* Cambridge: Cambridge U.P. for the Institute of Actuaries and the Faculty of Actuaries, 1951. viii, 126p.
'Draft' published 1950, London, Edinburgh. 102p.

1069 **Wulcko**, Laurence Marriott. 'Some early friendly societies in Buckinghamshire.' *Notes Quer.*, CXCVI, 3 (February 3, 1951), 45–9; 4 (February 17, 1951), 68–71; 5 (March 3, 1951), 90–3; 6 (March 17, 1951), 124–8.
Reprinted Chalfont St Peter, Bucks.: the author, 1951. 16p. For private circulation.

1070 **Hobsbawm**, Eric John Ernest. 'Friendly societies.' *Amat. Hist.* III, 3 (Spring 1957), 95–101.

1071 **Gosden**, Peter Henry John Heather. *The development of friendly societies in England, 1815–1875.* 1959. (Ph.D. thesis, University of London.)

1072 **Barnett**, D. C. *Ideas of social welfare, 1780–1834, with special reference to friendly societies and allotment schemes.* 1961. (M.A. thesis, University of Nottingham.)

1073 **Gosden**, Peter Henry John Heather. *The friendly societies in England, 1815–1875.* Manchester: Manchester U.P., 1961. x, 262p.

1074 **Workers' Circle Friendly Society.** Central Committee. *The Circle golden jubilee, 1909–1959.* London: the Society, 1961. 36p.
In English and Yiddish.

1075 **Geddes**, Peter and **Holbrook**, John Philip. *Friendly societies: a text-book for actuarial students.* Cambridge: Cambridge U.P., for the Institute of Actuaries and the Faculty of Actuaries in Scotland, 1963. viii, 282p.

1076 **Treble**, James H. 'The attitudes of friendly societies towards the movement in Great Britain for state pensions, 1878–1908.' *Int. Rev. of Soc. Hist.*, XV, 2 (1970), 266–99.
'This article is a slightly extended version of a paper read at a meeting of Scottish Economic Historians at the University of Edinburgh, December 1969.'

See also: 1146; 8537; 9035.

III. TRADE UNIONS AND PROFESSIONAL ASSOCIATIONS

See also Part Five; and Part Seven, VII, B. Many of the works in Part Six, IV on conditions of employment also contain material on trade unionism.

A. GENERAL

This section includes the more general discussions and analyses of trade unionism as opposed to the general historical studies which appear in Part Three, III, B, 1, and the more specialised works on union growth, structure, government, and administration which appear in Part Three, III, G. See also Part One, IV; Part Five, I; and Part Seven, I.

1077 **A Shipowner.** *Free trade and trades' unionism.* London: Simpkin, Marshall, 1881. 68p.

1078 **Carlyle**, Thomas. *Last words of Thomas Carlyle on trades-unions, promoterism and the signs of the times.* Edinburgh: W. Paterson, 1882. 46p.
Editor's preface signed J.C.A., i.e. John Carlyle Aitken.

1079 **Trant**, William. *Trades unions: their origin and objects, influence and efficacy.* London: Kegan Paul, Trench, 1884. viii, 188p.
'... based upon the Essay for which the author obtained the £50 prize offered at the Trade Unions Congress in 1873 by the late Mr. Alexander Macdonald, M.P. Much new information and the latest statistics have been added to the work as it appeared in its original form.'

1080 **Burt**, Thomas. 'Trade unions and the working classes.' Co-operative Wholesale Society. *Annual and diary for the year 1885.* p. 374–8.

1081 **Howell**, George. 'Trade unions: their origin, rise, progress and work.' Co-operative Wholesale Society. *Annual and diary for the year 1885.* p. 352–9.

1082 **Burnett**, John. 'Trade unions as a means of improving the conditions of labour.' Oliphant, J. (ed.). *The claims of labour: a course of lectures delivered in Scotland in the summer of 1886, on various aspects of the labour problem.* Edinburgh: Co-operative Printing Co., 1886. p. 7–40.

1083 **Baernreither**, Joseph Maria. *English associations of working men.* London: Swan Sonnenschein, 1888. xv, 473p.
English edition, translated by Alice Taylor.
Enlarged and revised by the author.

1084 **Cummings**, Edward. 'The English trades-unions.' *Q.J. Econ.*, III (July 1889), 403–35; 526–8.

1085 **Donovan**, Robert. *Trades' unionism: its principles, its history and its uses.* Dublin: *The Nation* office, 1889. 24p.

1086 **Sterling**, J. *Trade unionism.* Glasgow, 1889. 56p.

1087 **Besant**, Annie. *The trades union movement.* London: Freethought Publishing Co., 1890. 29p.

1088 **Champion**, Henry Hyde. 'The Federation of Labour.' *New Rev.*, II, 13 (June 1890), 524–33.

1089 **Charteris**, Francis Wemyss, Earl of Wemyss and March. *Trade-unionism and free labour.* London, 1891. 11p.

1090 **McIver**, Lewis. *Trades unionism: an address to the electors, delivered by Mr. L. McIver, the Unionist Candidate for South Edinburgh.* Beaufort: A. Parker, 1891. 12p.

1901 **Mather**, William. *On trades unions.* West Gorton, 1891. 8p.

1092 **Quelch**, H. *Trade unionism, co-operation, and social democracy.* 1892. 16p.

1093 **Woods**, Robert Archey. 'The labor movement.' *English social movements.* London: Swan Sonnenschein, 1892. p. 1–37.

Based on a lecture given at Andover Seminary in the Spring Term under the Alumni Lectureship for the year 1890–1.

First published New York: Scribner, 1891.

1094 **Hobhouse**, Leonard Trelawney. *The labour movement.* London: Fisher Unwin, 1893. xii, 98p.

Second edition. 1898. xii, 98p.

Third edition, revised. New York: Macmillan, 1912. 159p.

1095 **Schulze-Gaevernitz**, Gerhart von. *Social peace: a study of the trade union movement in England.* London: Swan Sonnenschein, 1893. xx, 300p.

With a preface to the English edition.

Translated by C. M. Wicksteed.

Edited by G. Wallis.

1096 **Settle**, A. *The meaning of the labour movement.* Manchester, 1893. 15p.

1097 **Birks**, James. *Trades' unionism: criticism and a warning.* West Hartlepool: J. Gowland, 1894. 50p.

Reprinted 'from the Newcastle Weekly Chronicle, together with an outline of the correspondence discussion to which the article gave rise'.

1098 **Tillett**, Ben. 'The need of labour representation.' Galton, F. W. (ed.). *Workers on their industries.* London: Swan Sonnenschein, 1895 [i.e. 1894]. p. 212–26.

1099 **Cree**, Thomas S. *A criticism of the theory of trade unions: paper read before the Economic Guidance Section of the Philosophical Society of Glasgow, 12th November, 1890.* Glasgow: Bell and Bain, 1895. 50p.

Fourth edition.

Earlier editions. 1891, 1892.

1100 **Martyn**, C. E. D. *Trade-unionism: a lecture delivered to the Edinburgh Branch of the Bakers' National Federal Union.* [Dundee? 1895?] 15p.

1101 **Stobart**, Matthew. 'Wanted, a newer trade unionism.' *Westm. Rev.*, CXLIII, 1 (January 1895), 23–30.

1102 **Aveling**, Eleanor Marx. *The working-class movement in England.* London, 1896. 40p.

1103 **Nicholson**, Joseph Shield. 'Labour combinations and competition.' *Strikes and social problems.* London: Black, 1896. p. 22–44.

1104 **Rousiers**, Paul de. *The labour question in Britain.* London: Macmillan, 1896. xxvi, 393p.

Translated by F. L. D. Herbertson.

First published Paris, 1895.

1105 **Birks**, James. *Trade unionism in relation to wages.* London: Liberty Review Publ. Co., 1897. 32p.

1106 **Holland**, Henry Scott. 'The labour movement.' Christian Social Union. *Three addresses delivered at the Christian Social Union meeting at Bristol, December 1st, 1896.* Bristol: W. C. Hemmons, 1897.

1107 **Mallock**, William Hurrell. 'The buckjumping of labour.' *Nineteenth Century*, XLII, 247 (September 1897), 337–48.

1108 **Felton**, Katherine. 'Rousiers's theory of the evolution of the laborer.' *J. Polit. Econ.*, VI, 3 (June 1898), 380–95.

1109 **Taylor**, Benjamin. 'A study in trade unionism.' *Nineteenth Century*, XLIII, 254 (April 1898), 679–92.

1110 **Quarterly Review**. 'Trade unions in practice and theory.' *Q. Rev.*, CLXXXVII, 374 (April 1898), 332–56.

1111 **Maddison**, Fred. *The store, the workshop, and the trade union.* [Nottingham: Co-operative Printing Works, 1898?] 7p.

1112 **Cummings**, Edward. 'A collectivist philosophy of trade unionism.' *Q.J. Econ.*, XIII (January 1899), 151–86.

1113 **Lilley**, Alfred Leslie. 'Trade unionism.' Hocking, W. J. (ed.). *The Church and new century problems.* London: Wells Gardner, Darton, 1901. p. 137–54.

'Published under the auspices of the Christian Social Union.'

1114 **Davis**, William John. *Industrial combination: its progress, difficulties, and stability.* Birmingham, 1903. 23p.

1115 **Hutchinson**, James G. 'A working man's view of trade-unions.' *Nineteenth Century*, LIII, 312 (February 1903), 290–8.

1116 **Jones**, Thomas. *Social aspects of trade unionism: a speech*... Abergavenny: Owen, 1904. 32p.

1117 **Pratt**, Edwin A. *Trade unionism and British industry.* London: Murray, 1904. vii, 244p.

'A reprint of *The Times* articles on "The crisis in British industry", with an introduction.'

1118 **The Times**. *Trade unionism and British industry: a reprint of the* Times *articles on 'The crisis in British industry'.* London, 1904, vii, 244p.

1119 **Wardle**, George James. *The principle of association: a plea for trade unionism.* London, [1904?]. 15p.

1120 **Coleman**, C. 'The trade union movement.' *Char. Orgn. Rev.*, n.s., XVIII, 104 (August 1905), 80–8.
Read at a meeting of the Charity Organisation Society, 15 May, 1905.

1121 **Drage**, Geoffrey. *Trade unions.* London: Methuen, 1905. xii, 203p.

1122 **Walling**, William English. 'British and American trade unionism.' *Ann. Am. Acad. Polit. Soc. Sci.*, XXVI, 3 (November 1905), 721–39.

1123 **Biddulph**, D. Wright. 'History, use and abuse of trade unions.' *Westm. Rev.*, CLXV, 4 (April 1906), 401–14.

1124 **Ruegg**, Alfred Henry and **Cohen**, Herman Joseph. *The present and future of trade unions.* London: Clowes, 1906. 64p.

1125 **Bell**, Richard. *Trade unionism.* London, Edinburgh: Jack, 1907. 108p. (Social problems series 3.)
The author was Secretary of the Amalgamated Society of Railway Servants.

1126 *Organized labor and capital.* London: Moring, 1907. 226p. (William Bull lectures.)
Contents: 'The past', by Rev. Washington Gladden. 'The corporation', by Talcott Williams. 'The union', by Rev. George Hodges. 'The people', by Rev. F. G. Peabody.

1127 **Wilson**, Philip Whitwell. *Trade unionism.* London: C. H. Kelly, 1907. 10p. (Social tracts for the times 6.)

1128 **Pouget**, Émile. *The basis of trade unionism.* London: T. H. Keell, 1908. 19p. ('Voice of labour' pamphlet.)
Reprinted from *Freedom.*

1129 **Kelsall**, T. *The trade union struggle.* London, 1909. 12p.

1130 **Wilson**, Philip Whitwell. 'Trade unionism.' Crooks, W., and others. *Social ideals: papers on social subjects.* London: R. Culley, 1909. p. 19–26.
'An Address delivered at the Men's Meeting, Leysian Mission, London.'

1131 **Eliot**, Charles William. *The future of trades-unionism and capitalism in a democracy.* New York and London: Putnam, 1910. v, 128p.
Larwill lectures, 1909.

1132 **Lees-Smith**, Hastings Bernard. *Trade unionism.* London, 1910. 15p.

1133 **Aldred**, G. A. *Trade unionism and the class war.* London, 1911. 13p.

1134 **Carter**, George Reginald. *The modern tendency towards industrial combination in some spheres of British industry; its forms and developments; their causes and determinant circumstances.* 1911. (M.A. thesis, University of Wales, Aberystwyth.)

1135 **Clay**, *Sir* Arthur Temple Felix. *Syndicalism and labour: notes upon some aspects of social and industrial questions of the day.* London: Murray, 1911. xv, 230p.
Another edition. New York: Dutton, 1911. 230p.

1136 **Greenwood**, John Henry. *The theory and practice of trade unionism.* London: Fabian Society, 1911. 70p. (Fabian socialist series IX.)
Preface by Sidney Webb.

1137 **Allsopp**, H. 'The future of trade unionism.' *Econ. J.*, XXII, 85 (March 1912), 130–4.

1138 **Brownlie**, J. T. *Some dangers which threaten trade unionism.* London, [1912?]. 16p.

1139 **MacDonald**, James Ramsay. *Trade unions in danger.* London, 1912. 15p.

1140 *The tyranny of trade unions, by one who resents it.* London: E. Nash, 1912. 246p.

1141 **Clayton**, Joseph. *Trade unions.* London, Edinburgh: Jack; New York: Dodge Publishing Co., 1913. 93p. (The people's books.)

1142 **Cole**, George Douglas Howard and **Mellor**, William. *The greater unionism, with special reference to mining, building, engineering and shipbuilding, transport, and general labour, and to the position of the General Federation of Trade Unions.* Manchester: National Labour P., 1913. 20p.

1143 **Mackay**, Thomas. 'The methods of the new trade unionism.' *The dangers of democracy: studies in the economic questions of the day.* London: Murray, 1913. p. 12–48.
First published in the *Quarterly Review.*

1144 **Mackay**, Thomas. 'Trade unions in practice and theory.' *The dangers of democracy: studies in the economic questions of the day.* London: Murray, 1913. p. 49–89.
First published in the *Quarterly Review.*

1145 **Morton**, Alfred. *Why trade union labour fails.* London: St Stephen's P., 1913. 16p.

1146 **Robinson**, M. Fothergill. *The spirit of association, being some account of the gilds, friendly societies, co-operative movement and trade unions of Great Britain.* London: Murray, 1913. xii, 403p.

1147 **Harley**, John Hunter. 'Syndicalism and the labour situation.' *Contemp. Rev.*, CV (January 1914), 47–56.

1148 **Somerville**, Henry. *Trade-unionism.* London: Catholic Truth Society, 1914. 24p. (Catholic Social Guild series 23.)
Reissued 1914. (Catholic Social Guild pamphlets, series 3.)
Reissued 1914. (Publications of the Catholic Truth Society, vol. 100.)

1149 **Lloyd**, Charles Mostyn. *Trade unionism.* London: Black, 1915. vii, 244p. (Social workers' series.)
Second edition, revised and enlarged. 1921. viii, 291p.
Third edition, revised and enlarged. 1928. vii, 194p.

1150 **Workers' Educational Association.** Yorkshire District. *Trade union problems and policy.* Leeds, [1916?]. 31p.

1151 **Higgs**, Richard. *The failure of the labour movement.* Dover: Dover Printing and Publishing Co., 1917. 91p.

1152 **McLaine**, W. *Trade unionism at the cross-roads.* London: British Socialist Party, 1917. 16p.

1153 **Taylor**, J. R. 'Labour organization.' Furniss, H. Sanderson (ed.). *The industrial outlook.* London: Chatto and Windus, 1917. p. 106–69.

1154 **Cole**, George Douglas Howard. *An introduction to trade unionism: being a short study of the present position of trade unionism in Great Britain prepared for the Trade Union Survey of the Fabian Research Department.* London: Fabian Research Department; Allen and Unwin, 1918. vi, 128p. (Trade union series 4.)

Revised edition published in 1924 under the title *Organised labour* . . .

1155 **Cole**, George Douglas Howard. *Labour in the Commonwealth: a book for the younger generation.* London: Headley Bros., 1918. 223p. New York: Huebsch, 1919. 223p.

1156 **Engineer**. 'Trade unions.' *Natn. Rev.*, LXX, 419 (January 1918), 602–17.

1157 **Arnot**, Robert Page. *Trade unionism: a new model.* London: Independent Labour Party, 1919. 16p. (Pamphlets. New series, 19.)

1158 **Clynes**, John Robert. *The responsibility of trade unions in relation to industry* . . . London: Industrial Reconstruction Council, 1919. 15p.

'A lecture delivered before the Industrial Reconstruction Council . . . on . . . 19th February 1919 . . .'

1159 **Ruskin College, Oxford**. *The trade unions: organisation and action.* London, 1919. 75p.

A report of the proceedings at a national conference held under the auspices of Ruskin College at Coventry on May 30th and 31st 1919.

By J. T. Murphy, J. W. Muir and W. Graham.

1160 **Clynes**, John Robert. 'Organised labour in relation to industrial development.' Manchester University. *Labour and industry: a series of lectures.* Manchester: Manchester U.P.; London: Longmans, 1920. p. 247–265.

'A lecture given on Tuesday, March 2, 1920.'

1161 **Fisher**, Victor. 'Labour evolution and social revolution.' *Nineteenth Century*, LXXXVIII, 524 (October 1920), 595–606.

1162 **Appleton**, William Archibald. *What we want and where we are: facts not phrases.* London: Hodder and Stoughton, 1921. 221p.

Another edition. New York: G. H. Doran, 1922. 197p.

The author was Secretary of the General Federation of Trade Unions.

Contents: 'Phrases'; 'The relations of labour and capital'; 'Trade unionism'; 'Pertinent interrogations'; 'Unemployment: causes and remedies'; 'Labour unrest'; 'Strikes, wages and values'; 'Wages and methods'; 'Housing'; 'Education'; 'War and armies'; 'The soldier and labour'; 'Syndicalism'; 'Communism in Russia and Britain'; 'Co-partnership'; 'Trade and taxes'.

1163 **Bunting**, John Howard. *Is trade unionism sound? A suggestion for outflanking the power of capital.* London: Benn, 1921. x, 98p.

Second edition. 1922. x, 98p. Foreword by J. R. Clynes.

1164 **O'Brien**, George Augustine Thomas. *Labour organization.* London: Methuen, 1921. xi, 182p.

Revised 1921. xi, 180p.

1165 **Hopkinson**, Austin. 'Trade unions.' *Manchr. Statist. Soc. Trans.*, (1922–23), 33–44.

1166 **Blanshard**, Paul. *An outline of the British labor movement.* New York: George H. Doran, 1923. 174p.

Introduction by Arthur Henderson.

1167 **Cole**, George Douglas Howard. *British trade unionism: problems and policy. A syllabus for classes and students.* London: Labour Research Department, 1923. 31p. (Syllabus series 10.)

1168 *Labour's dynamic; being reports of speeches delivered at Labour Week in London, 1922* . . . London: Labour Publishing Co., 1923. 66p.

1169 *'Villadom' or, lower middle-class snobs, by 'one of them'. A plea for a middle-class trade union.* London: E. J. Larby, 1923. 10p.

1170 **Appleton**, William Archibald. *Trade unionism.* London: Hodder and Stoughton, 1924. 159p.

1171 **Burns**, Cecil Delisle. 'The group-mind in trade unionism.' *Nat. Inst. Ind. Psychol. J.*, II, 3 (July 1924), 116–24.

Later published in *Occup. Psychol.*, XVII, 2 (April 1943), 64–72.

1172 **Cole**, George Douglas Howard. *Organised labour: an introduction to trade unionism.* London: Allen and Unwin, 1924. xii, 182p.

A revised edition of *An introduction to trade unionism* . . . 1918.

1173 **Eddy**, George Sherwood. *The new world of labor.* London: Allen and Unwin, 1924. 216p.

Chap. V. 'The evolution of labor in the West.'

Chap. VI. 'The British labor movement.'

1174 **Oneal**, James. *Labor in England and America: a significant contrast.* New York, 1924. 16p.

1175 **Appleton**, William Archibald. *Trade unions: their past, present and future.* London: P. Allan, 1925. 183p. (Westminster library.)

1176 **Tawney**, Richard Henry. *The British labor movement.* New Haven, Conn.: Yale U.P., 1925. 189p. (Institute of Politics publications.)

1177 **Appleton**, William Archibald. 'Trade unionism: an explanation, a condemnation, and an entreaty.' *Nineteenth Century*, C, 593 (July 1926), 1–9.

1178 **Citrine**, Walter McLennan. *The trade union movement of Great Britain.* Amsterdam: International Federation of Trade Unions, 1926. 118, xp. (International trade union library 2–3.)

The author was Acting Secretary of the Trades Union Congress.

1179 **Holt-Thomas**, G. *The future of British industry and trades unionism.* London: Odhams P., 1926. 32p.

1180 **Hunter**, *Sir* George Burton and **Good**, E. T. *Trade unions and trade unionism.* London: Hutchinson, 1926. 61p.

1181 **Shadwell**, Arthur. *Trade union reform.* London: *The Times*, 1927. 24p.
Reprinted from *The Times.*
Second edition.

1182 **Citrine**, Walter McLennan. *Labour and the community.* London: Benn, 1928. 32p. (Self and society booklets 7.)

1183 **Jones**, Arthur Creech. *Trade unionism today.* London: Workers' Educational Association, 1928. vi, 90p. (W.E.A. outlines.)

1184 **Citrine**, Walter McLennan. *The future of trade unionism.* London, 1929. 12p.

1185 **Citrine**, Walter McLennan. *Trade unionism in modern industry.* London, 1929. 11p.

1186 **Sacred Congregation of the Council.** *Trade unions and employers' associations: the Catholic view.* Oxford, 1929. 23p.

1187 **Cunnison**, James. *Labour organization.* London: Pitman, 1930. vii, 272p. (Pitman's applied economics series.)

1188 **Suthers**, Robert B. 'The National Trade Union Club.' *Labour Mag.*, XI, 10 (February 1933), 499–53.

1189 **Engels**, Friedrich. *The British labour movement.* London: Lawrence, 1934. 46p.
Another edition. London: Lawrence and Wishart, 1941. 46p.
Articles from *The Labour Standard*, 1881.

1190 **Neumann**, Franz. *Trade unionism, democracy, dictatorship.* London, 1934. 94p. (Workers' Educational Trade Union Committee. W.E.T.U.C. sixpenny library 1.)

1191 **Murphy**, John Thomas. *Modern trade unionism: a study of the present tendencies and the future of trade unions in Britain.* London: Routledge, 1935. xvi, 199p. (New-world series.)

1192 **Petch**, Arthur William. *Trade unionism: what every worker should know.* London, [1935?]. 20p.

1193 **Ackroyd**, D. E. *The economic policy of trade unions in Great Britain in the post-war period, as illustrated by the proceedings of the Trades Union Congress.* 1936. (B.Litt. thesis, University of Oxford.)

1194 **Horner,** Arthur Lewis. *Trade unions and unity.* London, 1937. 14p.

1195 **Mahon**, John Augustus. *Trade unionism.* London: Gollancz, 1938. 95p. (New people's library 9.)
Also Left Book Club edition.

1196 **Cole**, George Douglas Howard. *British trade unionism to-day: a survey . . . with the collaboration of thirty trade union leaders and other experts.* London: Gollancz, 1939. 591p.
Reissued. London: Methuen, 1945. 591p.

1197 **Marquand**, Hilary Adair. 'Great Britain.' *Organized labour in four continents.* London, New York: Longmans, Green, 1939. p. 117–189.

1198 **Ware**, Norman J. 'Labor movements of Great Britain and the United States.' *Am. Econ. Rev.*, XXIX, 2 (June 1939), 237–45.

1199 **MacDonald**, Lois. 'Foreign labor movements.' Stein, E. and Davis, J. (eds.). *Labor problems in America.* New York: Farrar and Rinehart, 1940.

1200 **Citrine**, Walter McLennan. *British trade unions.* London: Collins, 1942. 47p. (Britain in pictures. The British people in pictures.)

1201 **Hutt**, George Allen. *Problems of trade unionism.* London: Lawrence and Wishart, 1942. 24p. (Marx House syllabus.)

1202 **Price**, John. *British trade unions.* London: Longmans, 1942. 44p. (British life and thought 12.)
Revised edition. London: Longmans, Green for the British Council, 1948. 47p.

1203 **Roper**, Joseph Igal. *Trade unionism and the new social order: a students' guide.* London: Workers' Educational Association, 1942. 32p. (W.E.A. study outline 6.)
Revised edition. W.E.A. and Workers' Educational Trade Union Committee, 1949. 40p. (Study outline 16.)

1204 **Common Wealth.** *Trade unions and common ownership.* London, 1943. 21p. (Pamphlets 202.)

1205 **Hamilton**, Mary Agnes. *British trade unions.* London: Oxford U.P., 1943. 31p. (Oxford pamphlets on home affairs H7.)

1206 **Kuczynski**, Jürgen. *British trade unionism: a short study course for scientific workers.* London: Association of Scientific Workers, 1943. 44p.

1207 **Parker**, John. 'Trade union difficulties in new areas.' Cole, G. D. H. *British trade unionism today: a survey . . .* London: Metheun, 1945. p. 241–8.
Earlier edition. 1939.

1208 **Wright**, Peter. *Working partners: a study of British trade unionism.* London: Current Affairs, 1945. 19p.

1209 **Sullivan**, Bernard. *Trade unions.* Manchester: R. P. Walsh, 1946. (Catholic Worker pamphlet.)

1210 **Barou**, Noi Isaakovich. *British trade unions.* London: Gollancz, 1947. xvi, 271p.
Also Left Book Club edition.

1211 **Jefferys**, James Bavington. *Trade unions in a Labour Britain.* London: Fabian Publications and Gollancz, 1947. 13p. (Discussion series 2.)

1212 **Navvy Mission Society**. *Trade unionism: whence and whither?* London, 1947. 14p.

1213 **Roberts**, Benjamin Charles. *Trade unions in the new era.* London: International Publishing Co., 1947. 42p.

1214 **Flanders**, Allan David. *British trade unionism.* London: Bureau of Current Affairs, 1948. 64p. (Background handbook.)

1215 **Laidler**, Harry Wellington. *Labor movements at work: British, Scandinavian, Australasian.* New York: League for Industrial Democracy, 1948. 23p.

1216 **Political and Economic Planning.** *British trade unionism: six studies by P.E.P.* London: P.E.P., 1948. 184p.

Contents: Trade union structure; The formal machinery of negotiation; The subjects of negotiation; The General Staff of labour; Relations on the job; Trade unions in post-war Britain.

Revised edition. 1955.

1217 **Political and Economic Planning.** 'Trade unions to-day.' *Planning*, xv, 286 (16 August 1948), 61–75.

1218 **Pridgeon**, Charles. *Opportunity for trade unionists.* Oxford: Catholic Social Guild, 1948. 162p.

1219 **Sturmthal**, Adolf Fox. 'National patterns of union behavior.' *J. Polit. Econ.*, LVI, 6 (December 1948), 515–26.

1220 **Cole**, George Douglas Howard. 'Trade unions and trade unionists in Britain today.' *Polit. Q.*, xx, 1 (January–March 1949), 64–74.

1221 **Laski**, Harold Joseph. *Trade unions in the new society.* New York: Viking P., 1949. x, 182p.

'The substance of this book derives from the Sidney Hillman lectures for 1949.'

English edition. London: Allen and Unwin, 1950. x, 182p.

1222 **Liberal Party.** Liberal Trade Union Commission. *Report.* London: Liberal Publication Department, 1949. 52p.

1223 **Phelps Brown**, Ernest Henry. 'Prospects of labour.' *Economica*, n.s., XVI, 61 (February 1949), 1–10.

'The substance of this paper was given as an Inaugural Lecture in the Chair of the Economics of Labour, at the London School of Economics, on 29th November, 1948 . . .'

1224 **Turner-Samuels**, Moss. *British trade unions.* London: Sampson Law, Marston, 1949. xii, 212p. (Living in Britain series.)

1225 **Collins**, Henry J. *Trade unions today.* London: Muller, 1950. 141p. (Man and society series.)

Intended for use by students in adult classes.

1226 **England**, Betty. *Trade union problems.* London: Labour Research Department, 1950. 127p.

1227 **Acton Society Trust**. *The future of the unions.* Claygate, Surrey: the Trust, 1951. 31p. (Studies in nationalised industry 8.)

1228 **Feather**, Victor. *Trade unions: true or false?* London: Batchworth P., 1951. 38p. (Background books.)

1229 **Lowe**, John. 'Trade unions and the future.' *Twentieth Century*, CXLIX, 887 (January 1951), 27–32.

1230 **Flanders**, Allan David. *Trade unions.* London: Hutchinson's University Library, 1952. 172p.

Second revised edition. 1957.

Third revised edition. 1960.

Fourth edition. 1963.

Fifth edition. 1965.

Sixth edition. 1965.

Seventh revised edition. 1968. 212p.

Also National Council of Labour Colleges editions, 1958, 1960, 1965, 1969.

1231 **Mikardo**, Ian. 'Trade unions in a full employment economy.' Crossman, R. H. S. (ed.). *New Fabian essays.* London: Turnstile P., 1952. p. 143–60.

1232 **Tracey**, Herbert. *Trade unionism: its origins, growth and role in modern society.* London: Labour Party, 1952. 31p. (Labour Party educational series 1.)

Foreword by Morgan Phillips.

1233 **British Institute of Management.** *Trade unions today: substance of three talks delivered to the Institute by Sir V. Tewson, T. Williamson, J. A. Birch.* London: B.I.M., 1953. 15p.

1234 **Cole**, George Douglas Howard. *An introduction to trade unionism.* London: Allen and Unwin, 1953. 324p.

A complete revision of *British trade unionism to-day.* 1939.

N.B. A different work, with the same title, by Cole, was published in 1918.

1235 **Cole**, George Douglas Howard. *Trade unions.* London: Casement Publications, 1953. 33p. (Casement booklet 11.)

1236 **Sturmthal**, Adolf Fox. *Unity and diversity in European labor: an introduction to contemporary labor movements.* Glencoe, Ill.: Free Press, 1953. 237p.

1237 **Lorwin**, Val R. 'Recent research on Western European labor movements.' Industrial Relations Research Association. *Proceedings of the seventh annual meeting, Detroit, 1954.* p. 69–80.

Discussion, p. 81–9.

1238 **O'Brien**, Tom. 'Trade unions and national prosperity.' *Natn. Prov. Bank Rev.*, 26 (May 1954), 1–9.

The author was President of the Trades Union Congress, 1953.

1239 **Tracey**. Herbert. *The British trade union movement.* Brussels: International Confederation of Free Trade Unions, 1954. 105p. (ICFTU monographs on national trade union movements 2.)

1240 **Conservative and Unionist Party.** Conservative Industrial Department. *Trade unions and industrial peace.* London: Conservative Political Centre, 1955. 27p. (Trade union series 9.)

Revised edition. 1964. (New trade union series 9.)

1241 **Political and Economic Planning.** *British trade unionism: five studies.* London: P.E.P., 1955. xi, 199p.

Revised edition of *British trade unionism: six studies*.

1242 **Round Table**. 'Trade unionism today: the responsibilities of power.' *Round Table*, 181 (December 1955), 27–37.

1243 **Wilkes**, Elijah. *Trade unions: a warning*. London: Routledge and Kegan Paul, 1955. 16p. (Passport to survival series 2.)

A warning to trade unions of the dangers of nationalisation.

1244 **Cole**, George Douglas Howard. *What is wrong with the trade unions?* London: Fabian Society, 1956. 28p. (Fabian tract 301.)

Based in part on a series of articles which appeared in *Tribune* early in 1956.

1245 **Pollock**, George. 'Employers and trade unions.' *Polit. Q.*, XXVII, 3 (July–September 1956), 237–49.

1246 **Roberts**, Benjamin Charles. 'Trade unions in the welfare state.' *Polit. Q.*, XXVII, 1 (January–March 1956), 6–18.

1247 **Wigham**, Eric Leonard. *Trade unions*. London: Oxford U.P., 1956. 277p. (Home university library of modern knowledge 229.)

New edition. 1969. 189p. (Opus 41.)

1248 **Allen**, Victor L. 'The trade unions.' *Twentieth Century*, CLXII, 968 (October 1957), 361–70.

'Powers within the state, IV.'

1249 **Ball**, Frank Norman. 'The trade unions.' *Ind. Law Rev.*, XI, 3 (January 1957), 126–40.

1250 **Jacobson**, Sydney and **Connor**, William. *Trade unions*. London: Daily Mirror Newspapers, 1957. 42p. (Spotlight series.)

1251 **Weiner**, H. E. *British trade unionism and nationalization, 1868–1945: the evolution of the nationalization policies of the British Trades Union Congress*. 1957. 554 leaves. (Ph.D. thesis, Columbia University.)

1252 **Balfour**, William Cambell. 'British unions: a cultural analysis.' *Relat. Ind.*, XIII, 3 (July 1958), 313–27.

1253 **Price**, John. *Functions of trade-unionism in relation to welfare policy*. The Hague: Van Keulen, 1958. 47p. (Institute of Social Studies. Publications on social change 9.)

Five lectures.

1254 **Sturmthal**, Adolf Fox. 'The labor movement abroad.' Chamberlain, Neil W., Pierson, Frank C. and Wolfson, Theresa (eds.). *A decade of industrial relations research, 1946–1956*. New York: Harper, 1958. p. 174–205.

1255 **Turner**, W. 'Trade unions in the United Kingdom.' *Indian J. Labour Econ.*, I, 1–2 (April–July 1958), 117–23.

A paper presented at the First All-India Labour Economics Conference held in Lucknow on January 6th, 7th and 8th, 1958.

1256 **Citrine**, Walter McLennan. 'Developments in British trade union policies.' Australian Institute of Political Science. *Trade unions in Australia*. Sydney: Angus and Robertson, 1959. p. 47–70.

Paper read at the 25th Summer School, Canberra, 1959.

1257 **Clements**, Richard. *Glory without power: a study of trade unionism in our present society*. London: Barker, 1959. 143p.

1258 **Copps**, John A. 'The union in British socialist thought.' *Sth. Econ. J.*, XXVI, 1 (July 1959), 50–7.

1259 **Roberts**, Benjamin Charles. *Trade unions in a free society*. London: Institute of Economic Affairs, 1959. 120p.

Second edition. *Trade unions in a free society: studies in the organisation of labour in Britain and the U.S.A.* London: Hutchinson for the Institute of Economic Affairs, 1962. 206p.

1260 **Bealey**, Frank William and **Parkinson**, Stephen. *Unions in prosperity*. London: Barrie and Rockliff for Institute of Economic Affairs, 1960. 55p. (Hobart papers 6.)

1261 **Cyriax**, George and **Oakeshott**, Robert. *The bargainers: a survey of modern trade unionism*. London: Faber, 1960. 228p.

1262 **Munby**, Denys Lawrence. *The workers and their organisations*. London: Industrial Christian Fellowship, 1960. 15p.

Reprinted with minor omissions, from *Christianity and economic problems*, London: Macmillan, 1956.

1263 **Williams**, Francis. *Journey into adventure: the story of the Workers' Travel Association*. London: Odhams P., 1960. 176p.

1264 **Alexander**, Kenneth and **Hughes**, John Dennis. *Trade unions in opposition*. London: Fabian Society, 1961. 37p. (Fabian tract 335. Socialism in the Sixties.)

1265 **Carron**, William J. 'The function of labour and the trade unions in industry and commerce.' *R. Soc. Arts J.*, CIX, 5056 (March 1961), 248–64.

Read to the Society, 14 December 1960.

The author was President of the Amalgamated Engineering Union.

1266 **Cuss**, Roger, **Gent**, Maurice and **Smith**, Trevor. *New unions for old*. London: Liberal Publication Department for New Orbits Publications Group, 1961. 48p. (Publications 6.)

1267 **Davison**, Robert Barry. *Trade unions: a practical approach*. London: Longmans, 1961. 2v.

1268 **Galenson**, Walter. 'The strength of unified trade unionism: Great Britain and Scandinavia.' *Trade union democracy in Western Europe*. Berkeley, Los Angeles: U. of California P., 1961. p. 42–86.

1269 **International Labour Office**. *The trade union situation in the United Kingdom*. Geneva: I.L.O., 1961. 123p.

1270 **Lipset**, Seymour Martin. 'Trade unions and social structure.' *Ind. Relat.*, I, 1 (October 1961), 75–89; I, 2 (February 1962), 89–110.

1271 **Wigham**, Eric Leonard. *What's wrong with the unions*. Harmondsworth: Penguin Books, 1961. 234p. (Penguin special S198.)

1272 **McCarthy**, William Edward John. *The future of the unions*. London: Fabian Society, 1962. 36p. (Fabian tract 339.)

1273 **Mikardo**, Ian. 'Present-day problems of Great Britain's labour movement.' Infield, H. F. (ed.). *Essays in Jewish sociology, labour and co-operation in memory of Dr. Noah Barou 1889–1955*. London, New York: T. Yoseloff, 1962. p. 125–35.

1274 **Carron**, *Sir* William. 'Trade unions in industry.' *Wisc. Rev.*, 496 (Summer 1963), 114–27.

1275 **Donoughue**, Bernard and **Alker**, Janet. 'Trade unions in a changing society.' *Planning*, XXIX, 472 (10 June 1963), 173–222.

1276 **Feather**, Victor. *The essence of trade unionism*. London: Bodley Head, 1963. 127p. (Background books.)

Also Chester Springs, Pa.: Dufour Editions, 1963. 127p.

1277 **McCarthy**, William Edward John. 'The challenge facing British unions.' *Ann. Am. Acad. Polit. Soc. Sci.*, CCCL (November 1963), 129–37.

1278 **Renshaw**, Patrick. 'Trade-unions in America and Britain.' *Q. Rev.*, CCCI, 638 (October 1963), 413–22.

1279 **Allen**, Victor L. 'Trade unions in contemporary capitalism.' *Social. Regist.* (1964), 157–74.

1280 **Hughes**, John Dennis. *Change in the trade unions*. London: Fabian Society, 1964. 39p. (Research series 244.)

1281 **Clegg**, Hugh Armstrong. *Change & the unions*. London: Neame, 1965. 16p. (Take home books.)

1282 **Flanders**, Allan David. 'Movement in unions?' *New Soc.*, V, 124 (11 February 1965), 15–17.

1283 **Jenkins**, Clive and **Mortimer**, James Edward. *British trade unions today*. Oxford, London: Pergamon P., 1965. vii, 125p. (Commonwealth and international library. Economics, commerce, industry, administration and management division.)

1284 **Marsh**, Arthur I. 'The unions' way forward.' *New Soc.*, VI, 153 (2 September 1965), 10–12.

1285 **Robertson**, Andrew. *The trade unions*. London: Hamilton, 1965. 122p. (Men and movements series.)

1286 **Coulter**, Ian. 'The trade unions.' Kaufman, G. (ed.). *The left: a symposium*. London: Bland, 1966.

1287 **Hughes**, John Dennis. 'British trade unionism in the sixties.' *Social. Regist.* (1966), 86–113.

1288 **Allen**, Victor L. 'The paradox of militancy.' Blackburn, R. and Cockburn, A. (eds.). *The incompatibles: trade union militancy and the consensus*. Harmondsworth: Penguin in association with *New Left Review*, 1967. p. 241–62.

Originally published as chapter VII of the author's *Militant trade unionism*, London, 1966, under the title 'The paradox of positive action'.

1289 **Anderson**, Perry. 'The limits and possibilities of trade union action.' Blackburn, R. and Cockburn, A. (eds.). *The incompatibles: trade union militancy and the consensus*. Harmondsworth: Penguin in association with *New Left Review*, 1967. p. 263–80.

1290 **Blackburn**, Robin and **Cockburn**, Alexander (eds.). *The incompatibles: trade union militancy and the consensus*. Harmondsworth: Penguin in association with *New Left Review*, 1967. 281p. (Penguin special.)

1291 **Evans**, Lloyd and **Pledger**, Philip J. (comps.). 'Working conditions and the labour movement.' *Contemporary sources and opinions in modern British history*. London, New York: F. Warne, 1967. Vol. 2. p. 1–85.

1292 **Fabian Society**. Group on Trade Unions. *The trade unions: on to 1980*. London: Fabian Society, 1967. 21p. (Tract 373.)

1293 **Huddleston**, John. 'Trade unions in a technological society.' *Contemp. Rev.*, CCXI, 1222 (November 1967), 251–9.

1294 **Jenkins**, Clive. 'We haven't got enough!' Blackburn, R. and Cockburn, A. (eds.). *The incompatibles: trade union militancy and the consensus*. Harmondsworth: Penguin in association with *New Left Review*, 1967. p. 228–38.

1295 **Jones**, Jack. 'Unions today and tomorrow.' Blackburn, R. and Cockburn, A. (eds.). *The incompatibles: trade union militancy and the consensus*. Harmondsworth: Penguin in association with *New Left Review*, 1967. p. 121–32.

1296 **Kassalow**, Everett M. *The development of Western labor movements: some comparative considerations*. Madison, Wis.: Industrial Relations Research Institute, Wisconsin University, 1967. p. 71–88. (Reprint series 62.)

Reprinted from Lester, R. A. (ed.). *Labor: readings on major issues*. New York: Random House, 1965.

1297 **Parker**, Stanley Robert. 'Industrial interest groups.' Parker, S. R., and others. *The sociology of industry*. London: Allen and Unwin, 1967. p. 126–37.

1298 **Phelps Brown**, Ernest Henry. *The trade union and the common weal: the second annual lecture under the 'Thank-offering to Britain Fund', 7 June 1967*. London: Oxford U.P. for the British Academy, 1967. 14p.

1299 **Reynaud**, Jean-Daniel. 'The role of trade unions in national political economies (developed countries of Europe).' Barkin, S., and others (eds.). *International labor*. New York, Evanston, London: Harper and Row, 1967. p. 33–61.

1300 **Rowthorn**, Bob. 'Unions and the economy.' Blackburn, R. and Cockburn, A. (eds.). *The incompatibles: trade union militancy and the consensus*. Harmondsworth: Penguin in association with *New Left Review*, 1967. p. 210–27.

1301 **Dawson**, Keith and **Wall**, Peter. *Trade unions*. London: Oxford U.P., 1968. 46p. (Society and industry in the 19th century: a documentary approach.)

1302 **Harman**, Nicholas. *Trade unions*. London: 'The Economist', 1968. 25p. ('The Economist' brief booklets 10.)

1303 **Nicholson**, M. 'The purposes and functions of trade unionism before and after independence.' University of London, Institute of Commonwealth Studies. *Collected seminar papers on labour unions and political organisations October 1966–March 1967*. London: the Institute, 1968. p. 12–27.

On the 'British model' of trade unionism in developing countries.

1304 **Organisation for Economic Co-operation and Development.** *The role of trade unions in housing: regional trade union seminar, Hamburg, 17th–19th January 1967. Final report*. Paris: O.E.C.D., 1968. 208p. (International seminars 1967–1.)

1305 **Daly**, Lawrence. 'Protest and disturbance in the trade union movement.' *Polit. Q.*, XL, 4 (October–December 1969), 447–53.

1306 **Gunter**, Ray. *The future of the trade unions*. London: Industrial Educational and Research Foundation, 1969. 8 leaves. (Seminar papers: The Company and its responsibilities.)

'Prepared for a seminar to be held on April 22nd, The Company and its responsibilities 1969.'

1307 **Higgs**, Phillip. 'Whither the trade unions? – a reply.' *Ind. Relat. Res. Bull.*, 2 (September 1969), 5–10.

A reply to the article by A. J. M. Sykes, *Ind. Relat. Res. Bull.*, 1 (June 1969), 5–12.

1308 **Hinton**, James. *Unions and strikes*. London, Sydney: Sheed and Ward, 1969. 64p. (Perspectives on work, welfare and society.)

1309 **Kassalow**, Everett M. *Trade unions and industrial relations: an international comparison*. New York: Random House, 1969. xvii, 333p.

1310 **Lane**, Peter. *Trade unions*. London: Batsford, 1969. 96p. (Past-into-present series.)

1311 **Smith**, Anthony. *The trade unions*. Edinburgh: Oliver and Boyd, 1969. 119p. (History topics series.)

1312 **Sykes**, Andrew James Macintyre. 'Whither the trade unions?' *Ind. Relat. Res. Bull.*, 1 (June 1969), 5–12.

1313 **Warner**, Malcolm. 'The big trade unions: militancy or maturity?' *New Soc.*, XIV, 376 (11 December 1969), 938–9.

1314 **Fay**, Stephen. *Measure for measure: reforming the trade unions*. London: Chatto and Windus; Knight, 1970. viii, 131p. (The reform series [2].)

1315 **Flanders**, Allan David. 'Trade unions and the force of tradition.' *Management and unions: the theory and reform of industrial relations*. London: Faber, 1970. p. 277–94.

'The Sixteenth Fawley Foundation Lecture given at the University of Southampton in November 1969 and published by the University', in 1969.

1316 **Flanders**, Allan David. 'Trade unions in the sixties.' *Management and unions: the theory and reform of industrial relations*. London: Faber, 1970. p. 13–23.

'A lecture to a Workers' Educational Association conference first published as an article in *Socialist Commentary*, August 1961.'

1317 **Flanders**, Allan David. 'What are trade unions for?' *Management and unions: the theory and reform of industrial relations*. London: Faber, 1970. p. 38–47.

'A shortened version of the Second Joe Madin Memorial Lecture given at Sheffield and first published as an article in *Socialist Commentary*, December 1968.'

1318 **Gard**, Elizabeth. *British trade unions*. London: Methuen, 1970. 96p. (Methuen's outlines.)

1319 **Paynter**, Will. *British trade unions and the problem of change*. London: Allen and Unwin, 1970. 172p.

1320 **Van Den Bergh**, Tony. *The trade unions: what are they?* Oxford: Pergamon, 1970. xvii, 261p. (The commonwealth and international library.)

1321 **Warner**, Malcolm. 'Towards trans-national trade unions?' *New Soc.*, XVI, 420 (15 October 1970), 670–1.

1322 **Warner**, Malcolm. 'Unions, integration and society.' *Ind. Relat. J.* (Summer 1970), 43–53.

1323 **Williamson**, Hugh. *The trade unions*. London: Heinemann Educational, 1970. viii, 134p. (Studies in the British economy 5.)

See also: 10; 12; 15; 22; 24; 27; 59; 8028; 9035; 9126; 12,781.

B. CHRONOLOGICAL STUDIES

This section does not attempt to cover the whole of radical history but only those aspects specifically concerned with trade unionism. For example, general works on Chartism are excluded.

1. General

This section contains general historical studies of trade unionism as opposed to general discussions and analyses which appear in Part Three, III, A. See also Part Five, I; and Part Five, IV, A.

1324 **Howell**, George. *The conflicts of capital and labour historically and economically considered, being a history . . . of the trade unions of Great Britain*. London, 1878.

'Second and revised edition, brought down to date.' London: Macmillan, 1890. xxxvi, 536p.

1325 **Rogers**, [Frederick?]. 'A century-and-a-half of English labour.' Co-operative Wholesale Society. *Annual and diary for the year 1885*. p. 327–51.

1326 **Burns**, John. *Trades unionism, past, present and future*. Rotherham, 1890. 9p.

1327 **Roundell**, Charles Savile. *The progress of the working classes during the reign of the Queen: 'A goodly record.'* Skipton: Edmondson, 1890. 50p.

1328 **Webb**, Sidney and **Webb**, Beatrice. *The history of trade unionism.* London: Longmans, 1894. xvi, 558p. bibliog.
Bibliography prepared by R. A. Peddie.
Second edition. 1896. xvi, 558p.
New edition. 1902. xxxiv, 558p. bibliog. chart. New introduction provides supplementary material.
New edition. 1911. lxvii, 558p. bibliog. chart. Includes new introductory chapter.
Revised edition, extended to 1920. 1920. xviii, 784p. The bibliography of the earlier editions is not included. Some copies of the 1920 edition were privately printed, December 1919.
Reissued 1926, 1950.
See also entries 146, 1365–6.

1329 **Dendy**, Helen. 'Dr. Brentano on English trade unionism.' *Econ. J.*, v, 19 (September 1895), 488–90.
Description of an article in *Archiv für Soziale Gesetzgebung und Statistik.*

1330 **Edwards**, Clement. *The tale of the toilers; or, an epitome of the labour movement.* London, 1895. 20p.

1331 **Humphrey**, A. W. *A history of labour representation.* London: Constable, 1912. xxi, 198p.

1332 **Cole**, George Douglas Howard. *The British labour movement: a syllabus for study circles.* London: University Socialist Federation, 1917. 18p.
Another edition. London: Labour Research Department, 1921. 30p. (Syllabus series 1.)
Reissued 1922. (Syllabus series 1.)

1333 **Craik**, William White. *A short history of the modern British working-class movement.* London: Plebs League, 1919. xi, 118p.
Third edition.

1334 **Fairchild**, Edwin Charles. *Labour and the Industrial Revolution.* London: Allen and Unwin, 1923. 222p.

1335 **Starr**, Mark. *Trade unionism, past and future.* London: The Plebs, 1923. 40p.
Revised edition. 1926. 40p.

1336 **Cole**, George Douglas Howard. *A short history of the British working class movement, 1789–1937.* London: Allen and Unwin.
Vol. 1. 1925, 1927, 1930.
Vol. 2. 1926, 1927.
Vol. 3. 1927, 1937.
In one volume. 1932, 1937.
...*1789–1947.* 1948.
1948 edition revised. 1952.

1337 **Postgate**, Raymond William. *A short history of the British workers.* London: Plebs League, 1926. 126p.

1338 **Perlman**, Selig. *A theory of the labor movement.* New York: Macmillan, 1928. xii, 321p.
Reprinted New York: Kelley, 1949.
Chap. IV. 'The British labor movement.'

1339 **Milne-Bailey**, Walter (ed.). *Trade union documents.* London: Bell, 1929. xxvii, 552p.

1340 **Rayner**, Robert Macey. *The story of trade unionism from the Combination Acts to the General Strike.* London: Longmans, 1929. ix, 277p.

1341 **Rothstein**, Theodore. *From Chartism to labourism: historical sketches of the English working class movement.* London: Martin Lawrence, 1929. vi, 365p. (Marxist library 2.)

1342 **Murphy**, John Thomas. *Preparing for power: a critical study of the history of the British working-class movement.* London: Cape, 1934. 290p.

1343 **Morgans**, Horace. *The teachings of Karl Marx: their influence on English labour organisations, 1850–1900.* 1936. (M.A. thesis, University of Wales, Swansea.)

1344 **Postgate**, Raymond William. *A pocket history of the British workers to 1914.* London: *Fact*, 1937. 98p. (Fact 5.)
Another edition. Tillicoultry: N.C.L.C. Publishing Society, 1943. 99p.
Third edition brought up to date. N.C.L.C. Publishing Co. 1964. 103p. (Plebs publications.)

1345 **Cole**, George Douglas Howard and **Postgate**, Raymond William. *The common people, 1746–1938.* London: Methuen, 1938. x, 671p.
Second edition, enlarged, brought up to date and partly rewritten. *The common people, 1746–1946.* London: Methuen, 1946. x, 742p.
Fourth edition. 1949. x, 742p.
A reduced photographic reprint of the edition of 1946. 1961.
Published in the United States as *The British common people, 1746–1938.* New York: Knopf, 1939. viii, 588, xxxiii p.
Second edition revised and enlarged. *The British people, 1746–1946.* 1947. x, 600, xxv p.
The British people, 1746–1946. New York: Barnes and Noble, 1961. x, 742p.

1346 **Hutt**, George Allen. *British trade-unionism: an outline history.* London: Lawrence and Wishart, 1941. 160p.
Second edition. 1942.
Third edition. 1945.
Fourth edition. 1952.
Fifth edition. 1962. 220p.

1347 **McConagha**, William Albert. *Development of the labor movement in Great Britain, France & Germany.* Chapel Hill, N.C.: U. of North Carolina P., 1942. ix, 199p.

1348 **Cole**, George Douglas Howard. *The British working-class movement: an outline study guide.* London: Fabian Publications and Gollancz, 1944. 24p. (Fabian special number 7.)
Revised edition. 1949. 32p.

1349 **Frey**, John Philip. *Craft unions of ancient and modern times.* Washington, 1945. xi, 120p.

1350 **Fay**, Charles Ryle. 'The spirit of association.' *Life and labour in the nineteenth century*... Cambridge: Cambridge U.P., 1947. p. 49–54.
Earlier editions. 1920, 1933, 1943.

1351 **Trades Union Congress.** *A short history of British trade unionism*. London: T.U.C., 1947. 31p. (A T.U.C. study pamphlet.)

1352 **Erickson**, Charlotte. 'The encouragement of emigration by British trade unions, 1850–1900.' *Populat. Studies*, III, 3 (December 1949), 248–73.

1353 **Hobsbawm**, Eric John Ernest. 'Trends in the British labor movement since 1850.' *Sci. Soc.*, XIII, 4 (Fall 1949), 289–312.

1354 **Hobsbawm**, Eric John Ernest. 'Economic fluctuations and some social movements since 1800.' *Econ. Hist. Rev.*, 2nd ser., v, 1 (1952), 1–25.

1355 **Conservative and Unionist Party**. Conservative Industrial Department. *The growth of the trade union movement*. London: Conservative Political Centre, 1953. 19p. (Trade Union Services series 1.)
Revised edition. 1963. 15p. (New trade union series 1.)

1356 **Bailey**, Jack. *Three movements – one purpose*. London: Co-operative Party, 1954. [15]p.
Trade unions, co-operative societies, Labour Party.

1357 **Williams**, Francis. *Magnificent journey: the rise of the trade unions*. London: Odhams P., 1954. 448p.

1358 **Clements**, Roger Victor. 'Trade unions and emigration, 1840–80.' *Populat. Studies*, IX, 2 (November 1955), 167–80.

1359 **Trades Union Congress.** *Two centuries of trade unionism*. London: T.U.C., 1955. 63p.

1360 **Pearce**, Brian Leonard. *Some past rank and file movements*. London, 1959. 40p.
Reprinted from *Labour Review*, April–May.

1361 **Briggs**, Asa and Saville, John (eds.). *Essays in labour history, in memory of G. D. H. Cole, 25 September 1889–14 January 1959*. London: Macmillan; New York: St Martin's P., 1960. viii, 364p.
Revised edition. 1967.

1362 **McCann**, W. P. *Trade unionist, co-operative and socialist organisations in relation to popular education, 1870–1902*. 1960. (Ph.D. thesis, University of Manchester.)

1363 **Bendix**, Reinhard. 'The lower classes and the "democratic revolution".' *Ind. Relat.*, I, 1 (October 1961), 91–116.

1364 **Rostan Romano**, Emilia. *From guilds to trade unions: a brief survey*. Torino: Giappichelli, 1961. 174p. (Corsi universitari.)

1365 **Allen**, Victor L. 'A methodological criticism of the Webbs as trade union historians.' *Soc. Study Labour Hist. Bull.*, 4 (Spring 1962), 4–6.
Abstract of a paper given at the 4th Conference of the Society for the Study of Labour History, 27 January 1962.

1366 **Clegg**, Hugh Armstrong. 'The Webbs as historians of trade unionism, 1874–1894.' *Soc. Study Labour Hist. Bull.*, 4 (Spring 1962), 8–9.
Abstract of a paper given at the 4th Conference of the Society for the Study of Labour History, 27 January 1962.

1367 **Cole**, George Douglas Howard. 'Phases of Labour's development in Great Britain, 1914–1958.' Infield, H. F. (ed.). *Essays in Jewish sociology, labour and co-operation in memory of Dr. Noah Barou 1889–1955*. London, New York: T. Yoseloff, 1962. p. 99–124.
Written in 1958.

1368 **Pattison**, George. *An outline of trade union history: an introduction for young people and others*. London: Barrie and Rockliff, 1962. 143p.

1369 **Cowden**, Morton H. 'Early Marxist views on British labor, 1837–1917.' *West. Polit. Q.* XVI, 1 (March 1963), 34–52.

1370 **Pelling**, Henry Mathison. *A history of British trade unionism*. London: Macmillan; New York: St Martin's P., 1963. xi, 287p.
Another edition. Harmondsworth: Penguin Books, 1963. 286p. (Pelican books A616.)

1371 **Thompson**, Edward Palmer. *The making of the English working class*. London: Gollancz, 1963. 848p.
American edition. New York: Vintage Books, 1966.
New edition. Harmondsworth: Penguin, 1968. 958p. (Pelican books.)

1372 **Hobsbawm**, Eric John Ernest. 'Economic fluctuations and some social movements since 1800.' *Labouring men: studies in the history of labour*. London: Weidenfeld and Nicolson, 1964. p. 126–57.
Based on a paper read before the annual meeting of the Economic History Society in April 1951.
First published in *Econ. Hist. Rev.*, 2nd ser., v, 1 (1952), 1–25.

1373 **Hobsbawm**, Eric John Ernest. 'Labour traditions.' *Labouring men: studies in the history of labour*. London: Weidenfeld and Nicolson, 1964. p. 371–85.

1374 **Hobsbawm**, Eric John Ernest. *Labouring men: studies in the history of labour*. London: Weidenfeld and Nicolson, 1964. viii, 401p.
Also Weidenfeld goldbacks 1968.

1375 **Hobsbawm**, Eric John Ernest. 'Trends in the British labour movement since 1850.' *Labouring men: studies in the history of labour*. London: Weidenfeld and Nicolson, 1964. p. 316–43.
First published in *Sci. Soc.*, XIII, 4 (Fall 1949), 289–312.

1376 **Williams**, D. J. *Strike or bargain? The story of trades unionism*. London: Blond Educational, 1964. 64p. (Today is history, 2.)

1377 **Mehta**, Ashok. 'Dynamics of the labour movement.' *Indian J. Labour Econ.*, IX, 1 (April 1966), 1–13.

'Presidential address delivered at the Ninth Annual Conference of the Indian Society of Labour Economics, B.H.U. Varanasi, Dec. 29–31, 1965.'

1378 **Thompson**, Edward Palmer. 'The making of the English working class.' Lorwin, V. R. (ed.). *Labor and working conditions in modern Europe*. New York: Macmillan; London: Collier-Macmillan, 1967. p. 31–50.

Reprinted from *The making of the English working class*. London: Gollancz, 1963. p. 189–207.

1379 **Buckley**, Ken. 'Emigration and the engineers, 1851–87.' *Labour Hist.*, 15 (November 1968), 31–9.

1380 **Kuczynski**, Jürgen. *The rise of the working class*. London: Weidenfeld and Nicolson, 1967 [i.e. 1968]. 253p. (World university library.)

Translated by C. T. A. Ray.

1381 **Barrow**, Logie. *A short history of the British labour movement*. London: Sheed and Ward, 1969. vii, 56p. (Perspectives on work, welfare and society.)

1382 **Hobley**, Leonard Frank. *The trade union story*. Glasgow: Blackie, 1969. [11], 116p. (Topics in modern history series.)

A school text book.

1383 **Lobban**, Robert Dalziel. *The trade unions: a short history*. London: Macmillan, 1969. 64p. (Sources of history series.)

1384 **Evans**, Lloyd. *British trade unionism, 1850–1914*. London: Arnold, 1970. 64p. (The archive series.)

1385 **Hobley**, Leonard Frank. *Working-class and democratic movements*. Glasgow: Blackie, 1970. 102p. (Topics in modern history series.)

For Certificate of Secondary Education students.

See also: 2; 13; 31; 33; 35–40; 46; 48; 51; 58; 60; 68; 123; 127; 133–4; 141; 144; 151–2; 157–8; 164–5; 168; 7669.

2. Pre-1880

In addition to general works relating to the pre-1880 period, this section also includes more specialised material on such subjects as the First International and Marx's influence on the trade union movement, and Luddism. General material on the Tolpuddle Martyrs is also included here, but that specifically relating to the Combination Laws and their repeal is classified in Part Seven, VII, B, 2. Material specifically concerned with the Grand National Consolidated Trades Union is included here, but general works on Robert Owen are classified in Part Five, V, B, 1. See also Part Three, III, H–I.

1386 **Howell**, George. 'The work of trade unions: a retrospective review.' *Contemp. Rev.*, XLIV (September 1883), 331–49.

Financial history of seven unions, 1876–1881.

1387 **Peel**, Frank. *The risings of the Luddites, Chartists and Plugdrawers*. Heckmondwike: Senior, 1888. 354p.

Second edition.

Fourth edition. London: Cass, 1968. 349p. With a new introduction by E. P. Thompson.

1388 **Hewins**, W. A. S. 'The origin of trade-unionism.' *Econ. Rev.*, V, 2 (April 1895), 200–20.

'...Remarks...mainly suggested by the first chapter . . . of Mr. and Mrs. Sidney Webb's *History of trade-unionism* . . . They are not intended as a criticism of that chapter so much as a slight contribution to the elucidation of an obscure subject.'

1389 **Ashley**, *Sir* William James. 'Journeymen's clubs.' *Polit. Sci. Q.*, XII (March 1897), 128–40.

Germany and England.

On work by B. Schoenlank and S. and B. Webb.

1390 **Ashley**, *Sir* William James. 'Journeymen's clubs.' *Surveys, historic and economic*. London: Longmans, Green, 1900. p. 249–62.

1391 **Balmforth**, Ramsden. *Some social and political pioneers of the nineteenth century*. London: Swan Sonnenschein, 1900. 232p.

Contents include: 'Lord Shaftesbury, and factory reform'; 'Thomas Carlyle and the "organisation of labour" '; 'The trade unionist movement'; 'The later co-operative movement'.

1392 **Committee Appointed to Erect a Monument to the Tolpuddle Martyrs**. *The Tolpuddle martyrs: a chapter in the early history of trade unionism and Village Methodism*. Weymouth, [1908?]. 11p.

1393 **Waddy**, J. T. *The story of 'the Tolpuddle martyrs'*. London, 1908. 8p.

1394 **Sociological Society**. 'Apprenticeship associations in London.' *Sociol. Rev.*, V, 3 (July 1912), 244–6.

1395 **Hurst**, Gerald B. 'The Dorchester labourers, 1834.' *Engl. Hist. Rev.*, XL, 157 (January 1925), 54–66.

1396 **Jones**, Idris. *Changes in theory and public opinion concerning the status and interests of a wage-earning class in Great Britain during the period 1600–1800*. 1928. (M.A. thesis, University of Wales, Cardiff.)

1397 **Stekloff**, G. M. *History of the First International*. London: Lawrence, 1928. xi, 463p.

Translated by Eden and Cedar Paul.

1398 **Kiddier**, William. *The old trade unions from unprinted records of the brushmakers*. London: Allen and Unwin, 1930. 245p.

Second edition. 1931. 245p.

1399 **Rattenbury**, Owen. *Flame of freedom: the romantic story of the Tolpuddle martyrs*. London: Epworth P., 1931. 196p.

Second edition. London: the author, 1933. 169p.

Reprinted, 1950 with 'An afterthought: the reliability of Loveless's diary', dated January 1950. p. 165–9.

1400 **Darvall**, Frank Ongley. *The Luddite disturbances and the machinery of order.* 1932–33. (Ph.D. thesis, University of London.)

1401 **Jones**, M. *Some organisations of some industrial employees in England in the early eighteenth century.* 1933. (M.A. thesis, University of Manchester.)

1402 **Walker**, W. Maitland. 'An impartial appreciation of the Tolpuddle martyrs.' *Dors. Nat. Hist. Archaeol. Soc. Proc.*, LV (1933), 47–76.

1403 **Citrine**, Walter McLennan. *The Tolpuddle martyrs: how the T.U.C. will commemorate the Dorsetshire labourers' centenary.* London: Trades Union Congress General Council, 1934. 14p.

1404 **Darvall**, Frank Ongley. *Popular disturbances and public order in Regency England, being an account of the Luddite and other disorders in England during the years 1811–1817, and of the attitude and activity of the authorities.* London: Oxford U.P., 1934. 363p.

Reprinted 1969, with a new introduction by Angus Macintyre. xix, 363p.

1405 **Firth**, Marjorie M. and **Hopkinson**, Arthur Wells. *The Tolpuddle martyrs.* London: M. Hopkinson, 1934. xiii, 140p.

1406 **Hammond**, John Lawrence Le Breton. 'The tragedy of Tolpuddle.' *Essays of the year, 1933–34.* London: Argonaut P., 1934. p. 253–62.

From the *Manchester Guardian.*

1407 **Hutt**, George Allen. *Class against class, 1834–1934: the Tolpuddle Martyrs – and what the General Council does not say.* London: Lawrence, 1934. 32p.

Cover title: *Tolpuddle and to-day.*

Criticises the T.U.C. publication *The book of the Martyrs of Tolpuddle*..., 1934.

1408 **Quinlan**, John. 'Tolpuddle and its moral: a retrospect of the trade union movement, 1799–1934.' *Month*, CLXIV, 844 (October 1934), 301–9.

1409 *The story of the Tolpuddle martyrs: centenary celebration, Dorchester, 1934.* 1934. 75p.

1410 **Trades Union Congress**. *The book of the Martyrs of Tolpuddle, 1834–1934.* London: T.U.C. General Council, 1934. xvi, 240p.

Contributions by W. M. Citrine, S. Cripps, H. J. Laski, J. R. Clynes, A. Henderson, G. D. H. Cole, H. V. Morton, H. L. Beales, with documentation.

1411 **Lozovsky**, Aleksandr. *Marx and the trade unions.* London: Lawrence, 1935. 188p.

Another edition. Calcutta: Radical Book Club, 1944. 173p.

Chap. IV. 'Marx and the trade union movement in England.' p. 49–62.

1412 **Cole**, George Douglas Howard. 'Some notes on British unionism in the third quarter of the nineteenth century.' *Int. Rev. for Soc. Hist.*, II (1937), 1–27.

Republished in E. M. Carus-Wilson (ed.). *Essays in economic history*, III, 1962.

1413 **Evatt**, Herbert Vere. *Injustice within the law: a study of the case of the Dorsetshire labourers.* Sydney: Law Book Co. of Australia, 1937. xv, 136p.

1414 **Cole**, George Douglas Howard. 'A study in British trade union history: attempts at "General Union", 1829–1834.' *Int. Rev. for Soc. Hist.*, IV (1939), 359–462.

Later published as *Attempts at general union: a study in British trade union history, 1818–1834.* London: Macmillan, 1953.

1415 **Jolliffe**, M. F. 'Fresh light on John Francis Bray, author of "Labour's wrongs and labour's remedy" [1839].' *Econ. Hist.*, III, 14 (February 1939), 240–4.

1416 **Jolliffe**, M. F. 'John Francis Bray.' *Int. Rev. for Soc. Hist.*, IV (1939), 1–38.

Author of *Labour's wrongs and labour's remedy*, 1839.

1417 **Jackson**, T. A. 'The Tolpuddle martyrs.' *Trials of British freedom, being some studies in the history of the fight for democratic freedom in Britain.* London: Lawrence and Wishart, 1940. p. 111–20.

1418 **Tuckwell**, Gertrude Mary. 'The first International Labour Association: the passing of the British Section.' *J. Comp. Legisl.*, 3rd ser., XXVIII, 3–4 (1946), 53–6.

1419 **Dunning**, Thomas. 'The reminiscences of Thomas Dunning (1813–1894) and the Nantwich Shoemakers' case of 1834.' *Lanc. Chesh. Antiq. Soc. Trans.*, LIX (1947), 85–130.

Edited with introduction and notes by W. H. Chaloner.

1420 **Grunwald Ivanyi**, Béla. *The working classes of Britain and Eastern European revolutions, 1848.* Frome and London: Butler and Tanner, 1948.

1421 **Jefferys**, James Bavington (ed.). *Labour's formative years, 1849–1879: extracts from contemporary sources.* London: Lawrence and Wishart, 1948. 203p. (History in the making. Nineteenth century 2.)

1422 **Morris**, Max (ed.). *From Cobbett to the Chartists, 1815–1848: extracts from contemporary sources.* London: Lawrence and Wishart, 1948. 257p. (History in the making. Nineteenth century 1.)

1423 **Aspinall**, Arthur (ed.). *The early English trade unions: documents from the Home Office papers in the Public Record Office.* London: Batchworth P., 1949. xxxi, 410p.

1424 **Wearmouth**, Robert Featherstone. *Some working-class movements of the nineteenth century.* London: Epworth P., 1948 [i.e. 1949]. xii, 338p.

1425 **Garbati**, Irving. 'British trade unionism in the mid-Victorian era.' *Univ. Tor. Q.*, **XX**, 1 (October 1950), 69–84.

1426 **Gardner**, C. W. *The attitude of the English people towards the introduction of labour-saving machinery during the Industrial Revolution.* 1950. 270p. (M.A. thesis, McGill University.)

1427 **Hobsbawm**, Eric John Ernest. 'The machine breakers.' *Past Pres.*, I (February 1952), 57–70.

Reprinted in the author's *Labouring men.* London: Weidenfeld and Nicolson, 1964.

1428 **McCready**, Herbert W. *Frederic Harrison and the British working-class movement, 1860–1875.* 1952. (Ph.D. dissertation, Harvard University.)

1429 **Morris**, D. C. *The history of the labour movement in England, 1825–1852: the problem of leadership and the articulation of demands.* 1952. (Ph.D. thesis, University of London.)

1430 **Cole**, George Douglas Howard. *Attempts at general union: a study in British trade union history, 1818–1834.* London: Macmillan, 1953. viii, 218p.

Published originally as 'A study in British trade union history: attempts at "General Union", 1829–1834.' *Int. Rev. for Soc. Hist.*, IV (1939), 359–462.

1431 **Mack**, Edward Clarence and **Armytage**, Walter Harry Green. *Thomas Hughes: the life of the author of Tom Brown's Schooldays.* London: Benn, 1952 [i.e. 1953]. 302p.

1432 **Hobsbawm**, Eric John Ernest. 'The labour aristocracy in 19th century Britain.' Saville, J. (ed.). *Democracy and the labour movement,...* London: Lawrence and Wishart, 1954. p. 201–39.

Reprinted in the author's *Labouring men.* London: Weidenfeld and Nicolson, 1964. p. 272–315.

1433 **Oliver**, W. H. *Organisations and ideas behind the efforts to achieve a general union of the working classes in England in the early 1830's.* 1954. 522 leaves. (D.Phil. thesis, University of Oxford.)

1434 **Harrison**, Royden J. *The activity and influence of the English positivists on labour movements, 1859–1885.* 1955. (D.Phil. thesis, University of Oxford.)

1435 **Coltham**, Stephen W. *George Potter and the Bee-Hive newspaper.* 1956. (D.Phil. thesis, University of Oxford.)

1436 **Communist Party of Great Britain.** Historians' Group. *Luddism in the period 1779–1830.* London: C.P.G.B., Historians' Group, 1956. 25p. (Our history pamphlets 2.)

1437 **Halévy**, Élie. *Thomas Hodgskin.* London: Benn, 1956. 197p.

Edited in translation with an introduction by A. J. Taylor.

1438 **Hozumi**, Fumio. 'Some notes on the Luddites.' *Kyoto Univ. Econ. Rev.*, XXVI, 2 (October 1956), 10–38.

1439 **Trades Union Congress.** *The story of the Dorchester labourers: a guide to the Old Crown Court, Dorchester and the village of Tolpuddle.* London: T.U.C. 1957. 16p.

Reprinted 1961.

1440 **Coats**, A. W. 'Changing attitude to labour in the mid-eighteenth century.' *Econ. Hist. Rev.*, 2nd ser., XI, I (August 1958), 35–51.

1441 **Larsen**, Egon. 'The secret oath: the Tolpuddle Martyrs.' *Men who fought for freedom.* London: Phoenix House; New York: Roy Publishers, 1958. p. 75–91.

1442 **Collins**, Henry J. *England and the First International, 1864–72.* 1959. (D.Phil. thesis, University of Oxford.)

1443 **Pole**, Jack Richon. *Abraham Lincoln and the working classes of Britain.* London: Commonwealth-American Current Affairs Unit, English Speaking Union, 1959. 36p.

1444 **Collins**, Henry J. 'The English branches of the First International.' Briggs, A. and Saville, J. (eds.). *Essays in labour history . . .* London: Macmillan; New York: St Martin's P., 1960. p. 242–75.

Revised edition. 1967.

1445 **Coltham**, Stephen W. 'The *Bee-Hive* newspaper: its origin and early struggles.' Briggs, A. and Saville, J. (eds.). *Essays in labour history . . .* London: Macmillan; New York: St Martin's P., 1960. p. 174–204.

Revised edition. 1967.

1446 **Harrison**, Royden J. 'Professor Beesly and the working-class movement.' Briggs, A. and Saville, J. (eds.). *Essays in labour history . . .* London: Macmillan; New York: St Martin's P., 1960. p. 205–41.

Revised edition. 1967.

1447 **Lean**, Garth. 'Reluctant revolutionaries: the Tolpuddle Martyrs.' *Brave men choose.* London: Blandford P., 1961. p. 70–86.

1448 **Cole**, George Douglas Howard. 'Some notes on British trade unionism in the third quarter of the nineteenth century.' Carus-Wilson, E. M. (ed.). *Essays in economic history.* Vol. 3. London: Arnold, 1962. p. 202–19.

Reprinted from *Int. Rev. for Soc. Hist.*, II (1937).

1449 **Collins**, Henry J. 'Karl Marx, the International and the British trade union movement.' *Sci. Soc.*, XXVI, 4 (Fall 1962), 400–21.

1450 **Kennedy**, William F. 'Lord Brougham, Charles Knight, and "*The rights of industry*".' *Economica*, n.s., XXIX, 113 (February 1962), 58–71.

1451 **Musson**, Albert Edward. 'The Webbs and their phasing of trade-union development between the 1830s and the 1860s.' *Soc. Study Labour Hist. Bull.*, 4 (Spring 1962), 6–8.

Abstract of a paper given at the 4th Conference of the Society for the Study of Labour History, 27 January 1962.

1452 **Communist Party of Great Britain.** Historians' Group. *Chartism and the trade unions.* London: C.P.G.B., Historians' Group, 1963. 17p. (Our history 31.)

1453 **Collins**, Henry J. 'The International and the British labour movement.' *Soc. Study Labour Hist. Bull.*, 9 (Autumn 1964), 24–39.
Discussion on this paper, *Bull.*, 10 (Spring 1965), 7–9.

1454 **Harrison**, Royden J. 'The British labour movement and the International in 1864.' *Social. Regist.* (1964), 293–308.

1455 **Hobsbawm**, Eric John Ernest. 'The labour aristocracy in nineteenth century Britain.' *Labouring men: studies in the history of labour.* London: Weidenfeld and Nicolson, 1964. p. 272–315.
First published in Saville, J. (ed.). *Democracy and the labour movement.* London: Lawrence and Wishart, 1954. p. 201–39.

1456 **Hobsbawm**, Eric John Ernest. 'The machine breakers.' *Labouring men: studies in the history of labour.* London: Weidenfeld and Nicolson, 1964. p. 5–22.
First published in *Past Pres.*, 1 (February 1952), 57–70.

1457 **Klugmann**, James. 'The First International.' *Marxism Today*, VIII, 11 (November 1964), 339–50.
'Extracts from a lecture in Commemoration of the Foundation of the International Working Men's Association, given at the Finsbury Town Hall on September 6th, 1964.'

1458 **Mahon**, John. 'Marx, Engels and the London workers.' *Marxism Today*, VIII, 9 (September 1964), 266–74.
'... based on the annual Marx Memorial Lecture given ... under the auspices of the Marx Memorial Library in March ...'

1459 **Oliver**, W. H. 'The Consolidated Trades' Union of 1834.' *Econ. Hist. Rev.*, 2nd ser., XVII, 1 (August 1964), 77–95.

1460 **Renshaw**, Patrick. 'The First International.' *Hist. Today*, XIV, 12 (December 1964), 863–9.

1461 **Coltham**, Stephen W. 'George Potter, the Junta, and the *Bee-Hive*.' *Int. Rev. of Soc. Hist.*, IX, 3 (1964), 391–432; X, 1 (1965), 23–65.

1462 **Rowe**, David J. *London Radicalism, 1829–1841, with special reference to the relationship of its middle and working class components.* 1964–65. (M.A. thesis, University of Southampton.)

1463 **Collins**, Henry J. and **Abramsky**, Chimen. *Karl Marx and the British labour movement: years of the First International.* London: Macmillan, 1965. xi, 356p.

1464 **Harrison**, Royden J. *Before the socialists: studies in labour and politics, 1861–1881.* London: Routledge and Kegan Paul; Toronto: Toronto U.P., 1965. xiii, 369p. (Studies in political history.)

1465 **Harrison**, Royden J. 'The setting.' *Before the socialists: studies in labour and politics, 1861–1881.* London: Routledge and Kegan Paul; Toronto: Toronto U.P., 1965. p. 1–39.

1466 **Soffer**, R. N. 'Attitudes and allegiances in the unskilled North, 1830–1850.' *Int. Rev. of Soc. Hist.*, X, 3 (1965), 429–54.

1467 **Oliver**, W. H. 'Tolpuddle martyrs and trade union oaths.' *Labour Hist.*, 10 (May 1966), 5–12.

1468 **Braunthal**, Julius. *History of the International.* London: Nelson.
1864–1914. Translated by Henry Collins and Kenneth Mitchell. 1966 [i.e. 1967]. xiii, 393p.
Originally published as *Geschichte der Internationale.* Vol. 1. Hanover: Dietz, 1961.
1914–1943. Translated by John Clark. 1967. xi, 596p. Originally published as *Geschichte der Internationale.* Vol. 2. Hanover: Dietz, 1963.

1469 **Coltham**, Stephen W. 'The British working-class press in 1867.' *Soc. Study Labour Hist. Bull.*, 15 (Autumn 1967), 4–5.
Deals mainly with the journals *Bee-Hive*, *Commonwealth*, *Working Man*, *International Courier* and *National Reformer*.
Abstract of a paper given at a conference of the Society for the Study of Labour History, Birkbeck College, London, 20 May 1967.
An abstract of the discussion following the paper appears on p. 5–6.

1470 **Hill**, Christopher. 'Pottage for freeborn Englishmen: attitudes to wage labour in the sixteenth and seventeenth centuries.' Feinstein, C. H. (ed.). *Socialism, capitalism and economic growth: essays presented to Maurice Dobb.* London: Cambridge U.P., 1967. p. 338–50.

1471 **McCord**, Norman. 'Tyneside discontents and Peterloo.' *Nth. Hist.*, II (1967), 91–111.

1472 **Frow**, Edmund and **Katanka**, Michael (eds.). *1868: year of the unions. A documentary survey.* Edgware, Mx.: Katanka, 1968. 184p.
Includes 'Main personalities and events'. p. 176–81.

1473 **McCord**, Norman and **Brewster**, David E. 'Some labour troubles of the 1790's in North East England.' *Int. Rev. of Soc. Hist.*, XIII, 3 (1968), 366–83.

1474 **Pelling**, Henry. 'The concept of the labour aristocracy.' *Popular politics and society in late Victorian Britain: essays.* London: Macmillan; New York: St Martin's P., 1968. p. 37–61.

1475 **Thompson**, Edward Palmer. 'English trade unionism and other labour movements before 1790.' *Soc. Study Labour Hist. Bull.*, 17 (Autumn 1968), 19–24.
Abstract of a paper given at a conference of the Society for the Study of Labour History, Birkbeck College, London, 3 May 1968.

1476 **Usherwood**, Stephen. 'The Tolpuddle Martyrs, 1834–37: a case of human rights.' *Hist. Today*, XVIII, 1 (January 1968), 14–21.

1477 **Williams**, Gwyn A. *Artisans and sans-culottes: popular movements in France and Britain* *during the French Revolution.* London: Arnold, 1968. vi, 128p.

1478 **Wyncoll**, Peter. 'The First International and working class activity in Nottingham, 1871–73.' *Marxism Today*, XII, 12 (December 1968), 372–9.

1479 **Brantlinger**, Patrick. 'The case against trade unions in early Victorian fiction.' *Vic. Studies*, XIII, 1 (September 1969), 37–52.

1480 **Berry**, J. *The Luddites in Yorkshire.* Lancaster: The Dalesman, 1970. 29p.

1481 **Fraser**, W. Hamish. 'Trade unionism.' Ward, J. T. (ed.). *Popular movements c. 1830–1850.* London: Macmillan, 1970. p. 95–115.

1482 **Hobsbawm**, Eric John Ernest. 'Lenin and the "aristocracy of labour".' *Marxism Today*, XIV, 7 (July 1970), 207–10.

1483 **Thomis**, Malcolm Ian. *The Luddites: machine-breaking in Regency England.* Newton Abbot: David and Charles, 1970. 196p. (Library of textile history.)

See also: 1595; 1616; 7601.

3. 1880–1913

In addition to general works relating to the period 1880–1913, this section also includes more specialised material on such subjects as the 'New Unionism', the 'Great Unrest', and William Collison and the National Free Labour Association. See also Part Three, III, D; and Part Five, IV, A.

1484 **Liberty and Property Defence League.** *William Collison, the apostle of free labour.* London: the League, n.d. 11p.
A biography of the founder of the National Free Labour Association, a strike-breaking organisation.

1485 **Harrison**, Frederic. 'The new trades-unionism.' *Nineteenth Century*, XXVI, 153 (November 1889), 712–32.
Reprinted as 'Socialist unionism' in the author's *National & social problems.* London: Macmillan, 1908. p. 421–39.

1486 **Daniell**, M. and **Nicol**, R. A. *The new trade unionism: its relation to the old and the conditions of its success.* Bristol, 1890. 20p.

1487 **Mann**, Tom. 'The development of the labour movement.' *Nineteenth Century*, XXVII, 159 (May 1890), 709–20.

1488 **Mann**, Tom and **Tillett**, Ben. *The new trades unionism: a reply to Mr. George Shipton.* London: Green and McAllan, 1890. 16p.
A reply to G. Shipton's article 'Trades unionism, the old and the new' in *Murray's Magazine.*

1489 **Crombie**, J. W. 'The ordeal of trade unionism.' *Westm. Rev.*, CXXXVI, 4 (October 1891), 353–9.

1490 **Herbert**, Auberon. 'The true line of deliverance.' Mackay, T. (ed.). *A plea for liberty: an argument against socialism . . .* London: Murray, 1891. p. 379–414.

1491 **Howell**, George. *Trade unionism: new and old.* London: Methuen, 1891. xv, 235p. (Social questions of today.)
Other editions. 1894, 1900.

1492 **Ransome**, James Stafford. *Master and man, versus the new unionism.* London: Wise and Freeman, 1891. 16p.
Two articles reprinted from *The Globe.*

1493 **Howell**, George. 'The labour platform: old style.' *New Rev.*, VI, 35 (April 1892), 472–83.
A reply to T. Mann and B. Tillett (February 1892).

1494 **Mann**, Tom and **Tillett**, Ben. 'The labour platform: new style.' *New Rev.*, VI, 33 (February 1892), 166–80.
T. Mann, p. 166–72.
B. Tillett, p. 173–80.

1495 **Massingham**, Henry William. 'The trend of trade unionism.' *Fortn. Rev.*, n.s., LII, 310 (October 1892), 450–7.

1496 **Leppington**, C. H. d'E. 'The teachings of the Labour Commission.' *Contemp. Rev.*, LXIV (September 1893), 388–404.
New unionism.

1497 **Mann**, Tom. 'The labour problem. II. The new unionism.' *New Rev.*, VIII, 46 (March 1893), 272–80.

1498 **Hall**, Leonard. *The old and new unionism.* Manchester, 1894. 15p.

1499 **Ludlow**, John M. 'The National Free Labour Association.' *Econ. Rev.*, V, 1 (January 1895), 110–18.

1500 **Morant**, A. C. *The crisis at Cardiff: a critical review of the present aspect of trade unionism in this country.* London, 1895. 7p.

1501 **Quarterly Review.** 'The methods of the new trade unionism.' *Q. Rev.*, CLXXX, 359 (January 1895), 138–59.
Review article.

1502 **Ritson**, G. *Free labour.* London, 1896. [4]p.

1503 **Smeetom**, Owd (*pseud.*) [i.e. William Broadhead]. *'Owd Smeetom': the Sheffield outrages.* Sheffield: D. Nicholl, 1896. 16p.
Second edition.

1504 **National Free Labour Association.** Executive Council. *Federation of non-unionists.* London, 1897. 8p.

1505 **Ritson**, G. *Speech delivered . . . at the fifth annual congress [of the National Free Labour Association]. . . 1897.* London, 1897. 15p.

1506 **Baylee**, J. Tyrrell. 'New unionism.' *Westm. Rev.*, CL, 4 (October 1898), 396–403.

1507 **M.**, J. C. *The National Free-Labour Association: its foundation, history, and work.* London: National Free-Labour Association, 1898. 96p.
Preface signed J.C.M.

1508 **Chapman**, Sydney John. 'Trade union federation.' *Econ. Rev.*, IX, 2 (April 1899), 241–4.

1509 **Home Office.** Departmental Committee on Shop Clubs. *Report to Her Majesty's Principal Secretary of State for the Home Department, with reference to complaints made by certain friendly societies that men are compelled by employers, as a condition of employment, to join shop clubs and to discontinue their membership of other benefit societies.* London: H.M.S.O., 1899. ix, 16p. (C. 9203.)
Chairman: Jesse Collings.

1510 **Collison**, William. *For industrial freedom: correspondence between the Royal Commission on Trade Disputes and Trade Combinations and the National Free Labour Association, together with the outlines of Mr. W. Collison's evidence.* 1904.

1511 **Harrison**, Frederic. 'Socialist unionism.' *National & social problems.* London: Macmillan, 1908. p. 421–39.
First published in vol. XXVI of *Nineteenth Century*, 1889, under the title 'The new trades-unionism.'

1512 **Hyndman**, Henry Mayers. 'Trade union unrest and the class war.' *Engl. Rev.*, VI, 23 (October 1910), 539–53.

1513 **MacDonald**, James Ramsay. 'The trade union unrest.' *Engl. Rev.*, VI, 24 (November 1910), 728–39.

1514 **Atherley-Jones**, Llewellyn Arthur. 'A servile war.' *Nineteenth Century*, LXX, 417 (November 1911), 928–41.

1515 **Barker**, J. Ellis. 'The labour revolt and its meaning.' *Nineteenth Century*, LXX, 415 (September 1911), 441–60.

1516 **Newlove**, John G. 'The unrest among workpeople.' *Econ. J.*, XXI, 83 (September 1911), 468–81.

1517 **Collison**, William. *The apostle of free labour: the life story of William Collison; founder and general secretary of the National Free Labour Association, told by himself.* London: Hurst and Blackett, 1913. xvi, 336p.

1518 **Barnes**, George Nicoll. 'Thirty years of the trade union movement.' Co-operative Wholesale Societies. *Annual.* 1914. p. 189–210.

1519 **Hutt**, George Allen. 'A forgotten campaign of "The Times" against trade unionism.' *Mod. Q.*, II, 1 (January 1939), 63–7.
Eleven articles published in 1901–2.
Based on the work of Paul Mantoux and Maurice Alfassa, published as *La crise du trade-unionisme*. Paris, Bibliothèque du Musée Social, 1903.

1520 **Hobsbawm**, Eric John Ernest (ed.). *Labour's turning point . . . 1880–1900: extracts from contemporary sources.* London: Lawrence and Wishart, 1948. xxvi, 166p. (History in the making. Nineteenth century 3.)

1521 **Hobsbawm**, Eric John Ernest. 'General labour unions in Britain, 1889–1914.' *Econ. Hist. Rev.*, 2nd ser., I, 2–3 (1949), 123–42.
Reprinted in the author's *Labouring men.* London: Weidenfeld and Nicolson, 1964. p. 179–203.

1522 **Cole**, George Douglas Howard and **Filson**, Alexander Warnock (eds.). *British working class movements: select documents, 1789–1875.* London: Macmillan, 1951. xxii, 628p.
Reissued. London: Macmillan; New York: St Martin's P., 1965.

1523 **Levine**, A. L. *Industrial change and its effects upon labour, 1900–1914.* 1954. (Ph.D. thesis, University of London.)

1524 **Sires**, Ronald V. 'Labor unrest in England, 1910–1914.' *J. Econ. Hist.*, XV, 3 (September 1955), 246–66.

1525 **Pelling**, Henry. 'The Knights of Labor in Britain, 1880–1901.' *Econ. Hist. Rev.*, 2nd ser., IX, 2 (December 1956), 313–31.

1526 **Clements**, Roger Victor. 'British trade unions and popular political economy, 1850–1875.' *Econ. Hist. Rev.*, 2nd ser., XIV, 1 (August 1961), 93–104.

1527 **Duffy**, A. E. P. 'New unionism in Britain, 1889–1890: a reappraisal.' *Econ. Hist. Rev.*, 2nd ser., XIV, 2 (December 1961), 306–19.

1528 **Williams**, L. J. 'The new unionism in South Wales, 1889–92.' *Welsh Hist. Rev.*, I, 4 (1963), 413–29.

1529 **Clegg**, Hugh Armstrong, **Fox**, Alan and **Thompson**, A. F. *A history of British trade unions since 1889.* Oxford: Clarendon P., 1964.
Vol. 1. 1889–1910. xi, 514p.

1530 **Hobsbawm**, Eric John Ernest. 'General labour unions in Britain, 1889–1914.' *Labouring men: studies in the history of labour.* London: Weidenfeld and Nicolson, 1964. p. 179–203.
First published in *Econ. Hist. Rev.*, 2nd ser., I, 2–3 (1949), 123–42.

1531 **Schofield**, J. *The labour movement and educational policy, 1900–1931.* 2v. 1964. (M.Ed. thesis, University of Manchester.)

1532 **Jones**, J. C. *The labour movement in relation to state secondary education, 1902–1924.* 1965–66. (M.Ed. thesis, University of Leicester.)

1533 **Hobsbawm**, Eric John Ernest. 'Thoughts on the "new trades unionism".' *Soc. Study Labour Hist. Bull.*, 13 (Autumn 1966), 14–15.
Abstract of a paper given at a joint meeting of the Society for the Study of Labour History with the French Institute of Social History and Social Movements, Birkbeck College, London, 16–17 April 1966.

1534 **Society for the Study of Labour History.** 'Report of the Anglo-French colloquium on trade unions and labour movements 1890–1914.' *Soc. Study Labour Hist. Bull.*, 13 (Autumn 1966), 13–20.
The report of a joint meeting of the Society with the French Institute of Social History and Social Movements, Birkbeck College, London, 16–17 April 1966.

1535 **Taplin**, E. L. *The origins and development of new unionism, 1870–1910.* 1966–67. (M.A. thesis, University of Liverpool.)

1536 **Fraser**, J. D. *The impact of the labour unrest, 1910–14, on the British labour movement.* 1967–68. (Ph.D. thesis, University of Leicester.)

1537 **Pelling**, Henry. 'The labour unrest, 1911–14.' *Popular politics and society in late Victorian Britain: essays.* London: Macmillan; New York: St Martin's P., 1968. p. 147–64.

See also: 9106.

4. 1914–1938

In addition to general works relating to the period 1914–1938, this section also includes more specialised material on the Triple Alliance. See also Part Three, III, F, 4; Part Three, III, G, 9; Part Three, III, I; Part Five, IV, B–C; Part Five, V, C; and Part Seven, IV, C, 1.

1538 **Coulton**, George Gordon. *Workers and war.* Cambridge: Bowes and Bowes, 1914. 23p.

1539 **Alden**, Percy. 'Labour unrest and the war.' *Contemp. Rev.*, CVIII (August 1915), 146–57.

1540 *The British labour movement and the war.* London: Harrison, 1915. 12p.

1541 **Cole**, George Douglas Howard and **Mellor**, William. *Trade unionism in war-time, being open letters to the labour movement.* London: 'Limit' Printing and Publishing Co., 1915. 14p. ('Herald' pamphlets 5.)

1542 **Edinburgh Review**. 'The workshops and the war.' *Edinb. Rev.*, CCXXII, 454 (October 1915), 248–72.

Review article.

1543 **Jones**, John Harry. 'Labour unrest and the war.' *Polit. Q.*, 6 (May 1915), 86–118.

1544 **Round Table**. 'The war and English life.' *Round Table*, 21 (December 1915), 56–85.

1545 **Carter**, George Reginald. 'The triple alliance of labour: its national and trade-union significance.' *Econ. J.*, XXVI, 103 (September 1916), 380–95.

1546 **Round Table**. 'Labour and reconstruction.' *Round Table*, 25 (December 1916), 67–90.

1547 **Carter**, George Reginald. *The significance and possibilities...of the triple alliance of industrial trade unionism.* Huddersfield, 1917. 23p.

Third edition.

1548 **Seddon**, James Andrew. *Why British labour supports the war.* London: L. U. Gill, [1917?]. 12p.

The author was a former President of both the National Amalgamated Union of Shop Assistants and the Trades Union Congress.

1549 **Shann**, George. 'Trade unionism after the war.' Code, G. B. (ed.). *War and the citizen: urgent questions of the day.* London: Hodder and Stoughton, 1917. p. 15–20.

Reprinted from the *Birmingham Street Children's Union Magazine.*

1550 **Webb**, Sidney. *The British Labour movement under war pressure.* Bologna, 1917. [16]p.

1551 **Cole**, George Douglas Howard. 'Recent developments in the British labor movement.' *Am. Econ. Rev.*, VIII, 3 (September 1918), 485–504.

1552 **Tead**, Ordway. 'The war's effects on English trade unions.' *J. Polit. Econ.*, XXVI, 2 (February 1918), 125–35.

1553 **Dewar**, George A. B. 'The great home problem of 1919. I. Impressions from the industrial North.' *Nineteenth Century*, LXXXV, 504 (February 1919), 205–25.

1554 **Kellogg**, Paul Underwood and **Gleason**, Arthur. *British labour and the war: reconstructors for a new world.* New York: Boni and Liveright, 1919. viii, 504p.

Appendix XIV. *Shop committees and labour boards*, by A. Gleason. Reprinted from *Survey*, May 1917.

1555 **Zimmern**, *Sir* Alfred Eckhard. 'The labour movement and the future of British industry.' *Nationality & government; with other war-time essays.* London: Chatto and Windus, 1919. p. 204–42.

From *Round Table*, June 1916.

1556 **Begbie,** Edward Harold. *The betrayal of labour: an open letter to the Rt. Hon. J. R. Clynes. By the author of 'The mirrors of Downing Street'.* London: Mills and Boon, 1921. 52p.

1557 **Bramley**, Fred. *Trade unions and the ex-service men: a reply to the critics.* London: Caledonian P., 1921. 20p. (Caledonian pamphlet 1.)

1558 **Gould**, Gerald. *The lesson of Black Friday: a note on trade union structure.* London: Labour Publishing Co.; Allen and Unwin, 1921. 39p.

15 April 1921.

1559 **International Labour Office**. 'The growth of trade unionism since 1913.' *Int. Labour Rev.*, III, 1–2 (July–August 1921), 78–109.

Brings up to date and extends the I.L.O. report *The growth of trade unionism during the ten years 1910–1919.* (Studies and reports, Ser. A, no. 17.)

Supplementary material given in *Int. Labour Rev.*, IV, 3 (December 1921), 53–6 (505–8).

1560 **Cole**, George Douglas Howard. *Trade unionism and munitions.* Oxford: Clarendon P., 1923. xvi, 251p. (Economic and social history of the war, British series.)

For the Carnegie Endowment for International Peace.

1561 **Webb**, Sidney. 'The British labour movement and the industrial depression.' *Int. Labour Rev.*, VII, 2–3 (February–March 1923), 209–29.

1562 **Irish Transport and General Workers' Union**. *The attempt to smash the Irish Transport and General Workers' Union: a report of the actions in the law courts, with an historical introduction, and appendix of unpublished documents from 1911 to 1923.* Dublin: National Executive Council, Irish Transport and General Workers' Union, 1924. xxxi, 170p.

1563 **Nearing**, Scott. *British labor bids for power: the historic Scarboro' conference of the Trades Union Congress.* New York: Social Science Publishers, 1926. 32p.

1564 **Trotsky**, Leon. 'Problems of the British labour movement.' *Communist Int.*, 22 [1926], 19–41.

'. . . a collection of fragments written at different times dating from the end of . . . [1925].'

1565 **Militant Trade Unionist.** *Trade unionists and the united front.* London: Militant Trade Unionist, 1933. 15p.

1566 **Brand**, Carl Fremont. 'British labor and the International during the Great War.' *J. Mod. Hist.*, VIII, 1 (March 1936), 40–63.

The Second Communist International.

1567 **Hutt**, George Allen. *The post-war history of the British working class.* London: Gollancz, 1937. 320p.

Also Left Book Club edition.

American edition. New York: Coward-McCann, 1938. xi, 274p.

1568 **Dobb**, Maurice Herbert. *Trade union experience and policy, 1914–1918: an outline.* London: Lawrence and Wishart, 1940. 32p.

1569 **Brand**, Carl Fremont. 'British labour and the International during the World War.' *British labour's rise to power.* Stanford, Calif.: Stanford U.P.; London: Oxford U.P., 1941. p. 165–98.

1570 **Brand**, Carl Fremont. 'British labour and the reconstruction of the International, 1919–1923.' *British labour's rise to power.* Stanford, Calif.: Stanford U.P.; London: Oxford U.P., 1941. p. 199–231.

1571 **Van Der Slice**, Austin. *International labor, diplomacy, and peace, 1914–1919.* Philadelphia: U. of Pennsylvania P.; London: Oxford U.P., 1941. xi, 408p.

Issued also as a Ph.D. thesis, University of Pennsylvania.

'The present study will confine its investigation to the labor movements of France, Great Britain, and the United States during the period of the war and the peace.'

1572 **Balfour**, William Campbell. 'British labour from the great depression to the Second World War.' International Institute of Social History. *Mouvement ouvriers et dépression économique de 1929 à 1939.* Assen: Van Gorcum, 1966. p. 234–44.

1573 **Pollard**, Sidney. 'The trade unions and the crisis of the early 1930's.' *NE. Group Study Labour Hist. Bull.*, 2 (October 1968), 8–9.

A paper read at Van Mildert College, University of Durham on 18 May 1968.

1574 **Pollard**, Sidney. 'Trade union reactions to the economic crisis.' *J. Contemp. Hist.*, IV, 4 (October 1969), 101–15.

See also: 238.

5. 1939–1970

See also Part Seven, IV, C, 2–3.

1575 **Price**, John. *Organised labour in the war.* Harmondsworth, New York: Allen Lane, 1940. 176p. (Penguin books. Penguin special 70.)

1576 **Tracey**, Herbert. *Trade unions, fight – for what?* London: Routledge, 1940. 222p.

1577 **Dimock**, Marshall E. 'Labor's part in war and reconstruction.' *Am. Polit. Sci Rev.*, XXXV, 2 (April 1941), 217–31.

1578 **Williams**, Francis. *Dynamic democracy: labour during the war.* London: Macmillan, 1941. 32p. (Macmillan war pamphlets 15.)

1579 **International Labour Office.** 'Trade union membership problems of transferred war workers in Great Britain.' *Int. Labour Rev.*, XLV, 2 (February 1942), 151–6.

1580 **Radcliffe**, J. V. 'Trade unions' part in Britain's war effort.' *Ann. Am. Acad. Polit. Soc. Sci.*, CCXXIV (November 1942), 117–23.

1581 **Halpern**, D. B. 'The trade union movement since the outbreak of war.' *Oxf. Univ. Inst. Statist. Bull.*, V, 14 (9 October 1943), 232–9.

1582 **Kuczynski**, Jürgen and **Heinemann**, Margot. *British workers in the war.* New York: International Publishers, 1943. 64p.

1583 **Worswick**, George David Norman. 'The T.U.C. and reconstruction.' *Oxf. Univ. Inst. Statist. Bull.*, VI, 16–17 (4 December 1944), 287–92.

On the T.U.C. statement *Interim report on reconstruction.*

1584 **Barou**, Noi Isaakovich. *Recent trends in British trade unions; and British Trade Union Congress' Interim report on post-war reconstruction: a summary.* New York: League of Industrial Democracy, 1945.

1585 **Price**, John. *British trade unions and the war.* London: Ministry of Information, 1945. 55p.

1586 **Wood**, T. N. *The changing character of British trade union practices and policies under the Labour government, 1945–1950.* 1950. 345p. (M.S. thesis, University of Illinois.)

1587 **Alexander**, Robert Jackson. *World labor today: highlights of trade unions on six continents, 1945–52.* New York: League for Industrial Democracy, 1952. 54p.

'This manuscript deals with the trade union movement in all important countries with the exception of the United States and Russia . . .'

1588 **Norman**, Clarence Henry. *The British worker in retreat, 1938–1952.* London: the author, 1952. 15p.

1589 **Warner**, Aaron W. *British trade unionism under a labor government, 1945–1951.* 1954. 309p. (Ph.D. thesis, Columbia University.)

1590 **Evans**, Eric Wyn. 'Trade unionism in the fifties.' *Westm. Bank Rev.* (August 1961), 16–24.

1591 **Carbery**, Thomas F. and **Kelly**, David M. *Progress to prosperity: an examination of the role of the unions in the post-devaluation period.* Glasgow: Scottish Council of Fabian Societies, 1968. 33p.

C. REGIONAL STUDIES

This section includes works which focus on a particular town, county, or region. Regional works relating to a specific industry are classified with that industry in Part Three, III, E. See also Part Three, III, G, 3.

1. England

1592 **Bryher**, Samson. *An account of the labour and socialist movement in Bristol.* Bristol: reprinted from and published by the *Bristol Labour Weekly*, 1929–31. 3 pts.

Part I. *Prior to 1888.*

Part II. *To the end of the XIXth century.*

Part III. *The XXth century.*

1593 **Armytage**, Walter Harry Green. 'Stuart Uttley and the file trade of Sheffield.' *Notes Quer.*, CXCIII, 13 (26 June 1948), 279–80.

1594 **Armytage**, Walter Harry Green. 'William Dronfield and the good name of the Sheffield workman in the 1860's.' *Notes Quer.*, CXCIII, 7 (3 April 1948), 145–8.

1595 **Patterson**, A. Temple. 'Luddism, Hampden Clubs, and trade unions in Leicestershire, 1816–17.' *Engl. Hist. Rev.*, LXIII, 247 (April 1948), 170–88.

1596 **Yates**, John A. *Pioneers to power.* Coventry: Coventry Labour Party, 1950. 124p.

A history of the working-class movement of Coventry.

1597 **Fox**, Alan. *Industrial relations in Birmingham and the Black Country, 1860–1914.* 1952. (B.Litt. thesis, University of Oxford.)

1598 **Crawshaw**, H. M. *Social and industrial movements in Sheffield, 1760–1830.* 1954. (M.A. thesis, University of Sheffield.)

1599 **Pollard**, Sidney. 'The ethics of the Sheffield outrages.' *Hunter Archaeol. Soc. Trans.*, VII, 3 (1954), 118–39.

1600 **Fox**, Alan. 'Industrial relations in nineteenth-century Birmingham.' *Oxf. Econ. Pap.*, n.s., VII, 1 (February 1955), 57–70.

1601 **Pollard**, Sidney. 'The trade unions.' Linton, D. L. (ed.). *Sheffield and its region: a scientific and historical survey.* Sheffield: Local Executive Committee for the British Association, 1956. p. 190–6.

1602 **Hastings**, R. P. *The labour movement in Birmingham, 1927–45.* 1959. (M.A. thesis, University of Birmingham.)

1603 **Pollard**, Sidney. *A history of labour in Sheffield.* Liverpool: Liverpool U.P., 1959. xix, 372p.

1604 **Salt**, John. 'Trades union farms in Sheffield.' *Notes Quer.*, n.s., VIII, 3 (March 1961), 82–3.

1605 **Neale**, R. S. *Economic conditions and working class movements in the City of Bath, 1800–1850.* 1962. (M.A. thesis, University of Bristol.)

1606 **Pollard**, Sidney. 'Aspects of the labour movement in Sheffield, 1880–1939.' *Soc. Study Labour Hist. Bull.*, 6 (Spring 1963), 11–12.

Abstract of a paper given at a conference of the Society for the Study of Labour History, Birkbeck College, London, 25 January 1963.

An abstract of the discussion on the paper appears on p. 12.

1607 **Barnsby**, George John. *The working class movement in the Black Country, 1815–1867.* 1964–65. (M.A. thesis, University of Birmingham.)

1608 **McDermott**, T. P. *Centuries of conflict: the story of the trade unionism on Tyneside.* Newcastle-upon-Tyne: Newcastle and District Trades Council, 1965. 36p.

1609 **Rose**, R. B. 'The origins of working-class radicalism in Birmingham.' *Labour Hist.*, 9 (November 1965), 6–14.

1610 **Barnsby**, George John. *The Dudley working class movement, 1750–1832.* Dudley, Worcs.: Dudley Public Libraries, Local History and Archives Department, 1966. 21 leaves. (Transcripts from the Dudley archives 7.)

1611 **Brown**, Raymond. *The labour movement in Hull, 1870–1900, with special reference to new unionism.* 1966. (M.Sc. Econ. thesis, University of Hull.)

1612 **Barnsby**, George John. *The Dudley working class movement, 1832–1860.* Dudley, Worcs.: Dudley Public Libraries, Local History and Archives Department, 1967. 48p. (Transcripts from the Dudley archives 8.)

1613 **Prothero**, I. J. *London working-class movements, 1825–1848.* 1967. (Ph.D. thesis, University of Cambridge.)

1614 **Foster**, John. 'Revolutionaries in Oldham.' *Marxism Today*, XII, 11 (November 1968), 335–43.

1615 **Golby**, J. M. 'Public order and private unrest: a study of the 1842 riots in Shropshire.' *Univ. Birm. Hist. J.*, XI, 2 (1968), 157–69.

1616 **Thomis**, Malcolm Ian. *Old Nottingham.* Newton Abbot: David and Charles, 1968.

Chap. XI. 'The Nottingham Luddites.'

Chap. XII. 'The trade union experiment of 1812–14.'

1617 **Brown**, D. *The labour movement in Wigan, 1874–1967.* 1968–69. (M.A. thesis, University of Liverpool.)

1618 **Atkinson**, Brian James. *The Bristol labour movement, 1868 to 1906.* 1969. vi, 449 leaves. (D.Phil. thesis, University of Oxford.)

1619 **Smethurst**, John, **Frow**, Edmund and **Frow**, Ruth. 'Frederick Engels and the English working class movement in Manchester, 1842–1844.' *Marxism Today*, XIV, 11 (November 1970), 340–6.

See also: 43; 76.

2. Ireland

1620 **Ryan**, William Patrick. *The labour revolt and Larkinism.* London: 'Daily Herald', 1913. 32p.

1621 **Macdonnell**, J. M. *The story of Irish labour.* London, [1919?]. 24p.

1622 **Ryan**, William Patrick. *The Irish labour movement from the 'twenties to our own day.* Dublin: Talbot P.; London: Fisher Unwin, 1919. vi, 266p. (Modern Ireland in the making.)

1623 **Good**, James Winder. *Irish unionism.* Dublin, London, 1920. vii, 240p. (Modern Ireland in the making.)

1624 **Clarkson**, Jesse Dunsmore. *Labour and nationalism in Ireland.* New York: Columbia University, 1925. 502p. (Studies in history, economics and public law, ed. by the Faculty of Political Science of Columbia University, vol. cxx, no. 266.)

Based on the author's Ph.D. dissertation of the same title, Columbia University, 1925.

1625 **Mortished**, R. J. P. 'Trade union organisation in Ireland.' *Statist. Soc. Inq. Soc. Ir. J.*, xv, 101 (October 1927), 213–28.

1626 **Crofts**, Ambrose M. *Workers of Ireland, which way?* Waterford: Aquinas Study Circle, 1935. 24p.

An appeal for the formation of Christian trade unions in Ireland.

1627 **Judge**, J. J. *Organisation of trade unions in the Republic of Ireland.* 1950–51. (M.A. thesis, National University of Ireland.)

1628 **Bleakley**, D. W. 'The Northern Ireland trade union movement.' *Statist. Soc. Inq. Soc. Ir. J.*, xx (1953–54), 156–69.

1629 **O'Mahony**, David P. *Trade unionism in Ireland: a preliminary report.* 1953–54. (Ph.D. thesis, National University of Ireland.)

1630 **Bleakley**, D. W. *Trade union beginnings in Belfast and district with special reference to the period 1881–1900 and to the work of the Belfast and District Trades' Council during that period.* 1955–56. (M.A. thesis, Queen's University, Belfast.)

1631 **Judge**, J. J. *The labour movement in the Republic of Ireland.* 1955–56. (Ph.D. thesis, National University of Ireland.)

1632 **Roberts**, Ruaidhri. 'Trade union organisation in Ireland.' *Statist. Soc. Inq. Soc. Ir. J.*, xx, 2 (1958–59), 93–110.

Discussion, p. 110–11.

1633 **Shillman**, Bernard J. *Trade unionism and trade disputes in Ireland.* Dublin: Dublin P., 1960. 67p.

1634 **Boyle**, J. W. *The rise of the Irish movement, 1888–1907.* 1960–61. (Ph.D. thesis, Trinity College, Dublin.)

1635 **Casey**, Sean. 'Irish trade unionim: achievements and new tasks.' *Christus Rex*, XVII, 4 (October–December 1963), 298–307.

1636 **Giblin**, P. J. *The origins and development of trade unionism in Ireland.* 1964–65. (Ph.D. thesis, National University of Ireland.)

1637 **Coughlan**, Anthony. *Trade unionism in Ireland today.* London: Connolly Publications, 1965. [8]p.

Reprinted from the *Irish Democrat*, April 1965.

1638 **Cain**, Leonard Francis. *The Irish labor movement under the Free State and the Republic.* 1966. xiii, 304 leaves. (Ph.D., thesis, Catholic University of America.)

1639 **Daura**, M. *Structural problems of Irish trade union movement.* 1968–69. (M.S.A. thesis, Trinity College, Dublin.)

See also: 2684.

3. Scotland

1640 **Johnston**, Thomas. *The history of the working classes in Scotland.* Glasgow: Forward Publishing Co., 1922. 408p.

1641 **Marwick**, William Hutton. 'Early trade unionism in Scotland.' *Econ. Hist. Rev.*, v, 2 (April 1935), 87–95.

1642 **Marwick**, William Hutton. 'The beginnings of the Scottish working class movement in the nineteenth century.' *Int. Rev. for Soc. Hist.*, III (1938), 1–24.

1643 **Johnston**, Thomas. 'Trade unionism in Scotland.' Cole, G. D. H. *British trade unionism today: a survey . . .* London: Methuen, 1945. p. 223–31.

Earlier edition. 1939.

1644 **Marwick**, William Hutton. *Labour in Scotland: a short history of the Scottish working class movement.* Glasgow: Scottish Secretariat, 1949.

1645 **Bell**, Joseph Denis Milburn. *The strength of trade unionism in Scotland.* Glasgow: McNaughton and Gowanlock, 1950. 48p. (University of Glasgow, Department of Economic and Social Research. Occasional papers 4.)

1646 **Bell**, Joseph Denis Milburn. 'Trade unions.' Cairncross, A. K. (ed.). *The Scottish economy: a statistical account of Scottish life.* London: Cambridge U.P., 1954. p. 280–96.

1647 **Buckley**, Kenneth Donald. *Trade unionism in Aberdeen, 1878 to 1900.* Edinburgh: Oliver and Boyd, 1955. xii, 201p. (Aberdeen University studies 135.)

1648 **Marwick**, William Hutton. 'Developments in the labour movement in Scotland since 1880.' *Soc. Study Labour Hist. Bull.*, 6 (Spring 1963), 8–9.

Abstract of a paper given at a conference of the Society for the Study of Labour History, Birkbeck College, London, 25 January 1963.

An abstract of the discussion on the paper appears on p. 10.

1649 **Marwick**, William Hutton. *A short history of labour in Scotland*. Edinburgh and London: W. and R. Chambers, 1967. 119p.

See also: 176; 8088.

4. Wales

1650 **Thomas**, *Sir* D. L. *Labour unions in Wales: their early struggle for existence*. Swansea, 1901. 32p.

1651 **Jones**, E. J. '"Scotch cattle" and early trade unionism in Wales.' *Econ. Hist.*, I, 3 (January 1928), 385–93.

1652 **Marquand**, Hilary Adair. 'Trade unionism in Wales.' Cole, G. D. H. *British trade unionism today: a survey* . . . London: Methuen, 1945. p. 232–40.

Earlier edition. 1939.

1653 **Davies**, David James. *The Tredegar Workmen's Hall, 1861–1951, with some general observations on the life of the period*. Tredegar: Tredegar Workmen's Institute Society, 1952. 111p.

1654 **Rogers**, Emlyn. 'Labour struggles in Flintshire, 1830–1850.' *Flints. Hist. Soc. Publs.*, XIV (1953–54), 47–71; XV (1945–55), 102–9.

1655 **Webb**, Harri. *Dic Penderyn and the Merthyr rising of 1831*. Swansea: Gwasg Penderyn, 1956. 16p.

1656 **Morgan**, Walter T. 'Chartism and industrial unrest in South Wales in 1842.' *Natn. Libr. Wales J.*, X, 1 (Summer 1957), 8–16.

1657 **Williams**, Gwyn A. 'The insurrection at Merthyr Tydfil in 1831.' *Hon. Soc. Cymm. Trans.* (1965), pt. 2, 222–43.

Includes section on Melbourne and the Welsh trade unions.

The Cecil-Williams Memorial Lecture, 1965.

1658 **Jones**, David J. V. 'The Merthyr riots of 1831.' *Welsh Hist. Rev.*, III, 2 (December 1966), 173–205.

1659 **Donovan**, P. W. *Unskilled labour unions in South Wales, 1889–1914*. 1968–69. (M.Phil. thesis, University of London.)

1660 **Jones**, David. 'The Merthyr riots of 1800: a study in attitudes.' *Board Celt. Studies Bull.*, XXIII, 2 (May 1969), 166–79.

D. GENERAL UNIONS

Most of the works in this section relate to the General and Municipal Workers' Union, the Transport and General Workers' Union, and their predecessors where their membership also was of a general nature. Although many other unions have increasingly acquired a 'general' nature, material relating to them is classified with the industry or occupational group in which most of their membership has usually been located. In particular, material relating to the Amalgamated Union of Engineering Workers, the Electrical Trades Union, and their predecessors are classified in Part Three, III, E, 3, d. Material relating to general white-collar and professional unions is contained in Part Three, III, E, 9, a. See also Part Three, III, B, 3; and Part Three, III, G. In particular, see Part Three, III, G, 8 for material on the leaders of general unions.

1661 **O'Keeffe**, T. J. *Rise and progress of the National Amalgamated Labourers' Union*. Cardiff, 1891.

1662 **Gas-Workers and General Labourers' Union.** *1904 Conference souvenir.*

1663 **National Union of General and Municipal Workers.** *Jubilee history*. 1929.

1664 **Transport and General Workers' Union.** *Official opening of Transport House, Smith Square, Westminster, London, S.W.1. . . May 15, 1929*. London, 1929. 47p.

1665 **Suthers**, Robert B. 'The National Union of General and Municipal Workers.' *Labour Mag.*, X, 3 (July 1931), 115–19.

1666 **Suthers**, Robert B. 'The Transport and General Workers' Union.' *Labour Mag.*, X, 5 (September 1931), 203–7.

1667 **National Union of General and Municipal Workers.** *Fifty years of the National Union of General and Municipal Workers*. 1939.

1668 'The Transport and General Workers' Union: the union and its background.' Gannett, F. E. and Catherwood, B. F. (eds.). *Industrial and labour relations in Great Britain: a symposium*. New York: the editors, 1939. p. 152–201.

1669 **Clynes**, John Robert. 'The general workers.' Cole, G. D. H. *British trade unionism today: a survey* . . . London: Methuen, 1945. p. 443–52.

Earlier edition. 1939.

1670 **Cameron**, Alice Mackenzie. *In pursuit of justice: the story of Hugh Lister and his friends in Hackney Wick*. London: S.C.M. Press, 1946. 189p.

Describes the organisation of a branch of the Transport and General Workers' Union in Hackney Wick.

1671 **National Union of General and Municipal Workers.** *Sixty years of the National Union of General and Municipal Workers, 1889–1949*. 1949. 97p.

1672 **Clegg**, Hugh Armstrong. *General union: a study of the National Union of General and Municipal Workers*. Oxford: Blackwell, 1954. xiv, 358p.

1673 **Edwards**, Huw Thomas. *It was my privilege*. Denbigh: Gee, 1957. viii, 90p.

A history of the Transport and General Workers' Union in North Wales.

1674 **Irish Transport and General Workers' Union.** *Fifty years of Liberty Hall: the Golden Jubilee of the Irish Transport and General Workers' Union, 1909–59.* Dublin: I.T.G.W.U., [1959?]. 94, [10]p.

1675 **Transport and General Workers' Union.** *Home study course.* London: the Union, 1962. 6v.
An account of the history and structure of the union.

1676 **Clegg**, Hugh Armstrong. *General union in a changing society: a short history of the National Union of General and Municipal Workers, 1889–1964.* Oxford: Blackwell, 1964. xi, 226p.

1677 **Hyman**, Richard. *The Workers' Union, 1898–1929.* 1968. (D.Phil. thesis, University of Oxford.)

See also: 1414; 1430; 1433; 2650; 2813.

E. STUDIES OF PARTICULAR OCCUPATIONS AND INDUSTRIES

Material relating to specific unions, with the exception of the general manual and white-collar unions (see Part Three, III, D; and Part Three, III, E, 9, a) is classified with that industry or occupational group in which most of their membership is located. See also Part III, G. In particular, see Part Three, III, G, 8 for material on the leaders of individual unions. See also Part Five, III; and Part Five, IV, E.

1. Agriculture, Forestry, and Fishing

1678 **Acland**, Arthur H. D. 'Land, labourers and association.' *Contemp. Rev.*, L (July 1886), 112–27.

1679 **Selley**, Ernest. *Village trade unions in two centuries.* London: Allen and Unwin; New York: Macmillan, 1919. 182p.

1680 **Agricultural and Industrial Union.** *The Agricultural and Industrial Union.* London: the Union, 1923. 7p.
A statement of its aims.
Also 1925 edition. 6p.

1681 **Duncan**, Joseph F. 'The Scottish agricultural labourer.' Jones, D. T., Duncan, J. F., and others. *Rural Scotland during the war.* London: Oxford U.P., 1926.

1682 **MacDougall**, J. D. 'Socialism among the Scottish fishermen before and after the war.' *Nineteenth Century*, CI, 604 (June 1927), 824–30.

1683 **Okeden**, W. H. Parry. 'Agricultural riots in Dorset in 1830.' *Dors. Nat. Hist. Archaeol. Soc. Proc.*, LII (1931), 75–95.

1684 **Suthers**, Robert B. 'National Union of Agricultural Workers.' *Labour Mag.*, X, 12 (April 1932), 547–51.

1685 **Gash**, N. *The unrest in rural England in 1830, with special reference to Berkshire.* 1934. (B.Litt. thesis, University of Oxford.)

1686 **Colson**, Alice. *The revolt of the Hampshire agricultural labourers.* 1937. (M.A. thesis, University of London.)

1687 **Pointing**, J. 'Trade unionism in agriculture.' Cole, G. D. H. *British trade unionism today: a survey . . .* London: Methuen, 1945. p. 433–42.
Earlier edition. 1939.

1688 **Fussell**, George Edwin. *From Tolpuddle to T.U.C.: a century of farm labourers' politics.* Slough: Windsor P., 1948. 150p.

1689 **Groves**, Reginald. 'The long journey home.' *Tribune*, 632 (18 February 1949), 11.
Kent and Sussex Agricultural Labourers' Union.

1690 **Groves**, Reginald. *Sharpen the sickle! The history of the Farm Workers' Union.* London: Porcupine P., 1949. 256p.

1691 **Evans**, Gwenllian. 'Farm servants' unions in Aberdeenshire from 1870–1900.' *Scott. Hist. Rev.*, XXXI, 1 (April 1952), 29–40.

1692 **Box**, Sidney. *The good old days: then and now.* Marden: the author, 1954. 110p.
An account of the development of the agricultural labour movement in Herefordshire.

1693 **Russell**, Rex C. (comp.). *The 'revolt of the field' in Lincolnshire: the origins and early history of farmworkers' trade unions.* Boston: Lincolnshire County Committee, National Union of Agricultural Workers, 1956. 168p.

1694 **Brown**, Arthur Frederick James. 'Working class movements in the countryside, 1790–1850.' *Amat. Hist.*, III, 2 (Winter 1956–57), 49–54.
In Essex and Suffolk.

1695 **Madden**, M. *The National Union of Agricultural Workers.* 1957. (B.Litt. thesis, University of Oxford.)

1696 **Dunbabin**, J. P. D. 'The "revolt of the field": the agricultural labourers' movement in the 1870s.' *Past Pres.*, 26 (November 1963), 68–97.
Comment by D. H. Aldcroft, 27 (April 1964), 109.
Reply by J. P. D. Dunbabin, 27 (April 1964), 110–13.

1697 **Mills**, F. D. 'The National Union of Agricultural Workers.' *J. Agric. Econ.*, XVI, 2 (December 1964), 230–52.
Discussion, p. 253–8.

1698 **Singleton**, F. 'Captain Swing in East Anglia.' *Soc. Study Labour Hist. Bull.*, 8 (Spring 1964), 13–15.

1699 **Mills**, F. D. *The National Union of Agricultural Workers.* 1964–65. (Ph.D. thesis, University of Reading.)

1700 **Peacock**, Alfred James. *Bread or blood: a study of the agrarian riots in East Anglia in 1816.* London: Gollancz, 1965. 191p.

1701 **Dutt**, M. *The agricultural labourers' revolt of 1830 in Kent, Surrey and Sussex.* 1966–1967. (Ph.D. thesis, University of London.)

1702 **Horn**, Pamela L. R. 'The farm workers, the dockers and Oxford University.' *Oxoniensia*, 32 (1967), 60–70.

1703 **Peacock**, Alfred James. 'The revolt of the field in East Anglia, 1872–1874.' *NE. Group Study Labour Hist. Bull.*, 1 (October 1967), 6–8.

A paper read on 3 February 1967 at Rutherford College of Technology.

1704 **Horn**, Pamela L. R. *Agricultural labourers' trade unionism in four Midland counties, 1860–1900.* 1967–68. (Ph.D. thesis, University of Leicester.)

1705 **Dunbabin**, J. P. D. 'The incidence and organization of agricultural trades unionism in the 1870's.' *Agric. Hist. Rev.*, XVI, 2 (1968), 114–41.

1706 **Peacock**, Alfred James. *The revolt in the fields in East Anglia.* London: Communist Party of Great Britain, Historians' Group, 1968. 37p. (Our history, 49–50.)

1707 **Hobsbawm**, Eric John Ernest and **Rudé**, George. *Captain Swing.* London: Lawrence and Wishart, 1969. 384p.

1708 **Brickell**, George Ernest. *The north-west Hampshire agricultural labourer, 1867–1875.* Andover: Andover Local Archives Committee, 1960. 18p. (Andover records 5.)

2. Mining and Quarrying

See also Part Three, III, G, 9.

1709 **Burt**, Thomas and **Crawford**, W. *To the miners of the United Kingdom.* Durham, 1883.

1710 **North Wales Quarrymen's Union.** *The struggle for the right of combination, 1896–97.* Carnarvon, 1897. 18p.

1711 **Wilson**, John. *A history of the Durham Miners' Association, 1870–1904.* Durham: Veitch, 1907. xv, 365p.

1712 **Harvey**, George. *Industrial unionism and the mining industry.* Pelaw-on-Tyne: the author, 1917. 222p.

1713 **Durham Miners' Association.** *Jubilee souvenir.* Durham, 1919. [16]p.

1714 **Webb**, Sidney. *The story of the Durham miners, 1662–1921.* London: Fabian Society; Labour Publishing Co., 1921. ix, 154p.

1715 **Griffiths**, Thomas Hughes. *The development of the South Wales anthracite coal area, with special reference to its industrial and labour organisations.* 1922. (M.A. thesis, University of Wales, Aberystwyth.)

1716 **Welbourne**, Edward. *The miners' unions of Northumberland and Durham.* Cambridge: Cambridge U.P., 1923. 321p.

1717 **Edwards**, Ness. *The history of the South Wales miners.* London: Labour Publishing Co., 1926. 122p.

1718 **MacDougall**, J. D. 'The Scottish coal-miner.' *Nineteenth Century*, CII, 610 (December 1927), 761–81.

1719 **Rogers**, Emlyn. *The history of trade unionism in the coal-mining industry of North Wales up to 1914.* 1928. (M.A. thesis, University of Wales, Bangor.)

1720 **Hall**, W. S. *A historical survey of Durham Colliery Mechanics' Association, 1879–1929.* Durham: Veitch, 1929. [vii], 126p.

1721 **Machin**, Frank. *Labour organization of miners of South Yorkshire from 1858 to 1914.* 1930. (B.Litt. thesis, University of Oxford.)

1722 **Ellis**, Gweirydd. *A history of the slate quarryman in Caernarvonshire in the nineteenth century.* 1931. (M.A. thesis, University of Wales, Bangor.)

1723 **Arnot**, Robert Page. 'The Miners' Federation of Great Britain: its history and organization.' Williams, W. H. (ed.). *The miner's two bob.* London: Lawrence, 1936. p. 78–93.

1724 **Edwards**, Ness. *History of the South Wales Miners' Federation. Vol. 1.* London: Lawrence and Wishart, 1938.

1725 **Ginzberg**, Eli. *Grass on the slag heaps: the story of the Welsh miners.* New York, London: Harper, 1942. xiv, 228p.

1726 **Edwards**, Ness. 'The miners' unions.' Cole, G. D. H. *British trade unionism today: a survey . . .* London: Methuen, 1945. p. 283–92.

Earlier edition. 1939.

1727 **Metcalfe**, G. H. *A history of the Durham Miners' Association, 1869–1915.* 1947. (M.A. thesis, University of Durham.)

1728 **Arnot**, Robert Page. *The miners: a history of the Miners' Federation of Great Britain, 1889–1910.* London: Allen and Unwin, 1949. 409p.

1729 **Baldwin**, George Benedict. 'The effect of nationalization on Britain's National Union of Mineworkers.' Industrial Relations Research Association. *Proceedings of the fifth annual meeting, December 1952.* p. 170–82.

Discussion, p. 183–9.

Reprinted as Massachusetts Institute of Technology Department of Economics and Social Science, *Publications in social science*, series 2, no. 38. Cambridge, Mass., 1952. 13p.

1730 **Arnot**, Robert Page. *The miners: years of struggle. A history of the Miners' Federation of Great Britain, from 1910 onwards.* London: Allen and Unwin, 1953. 567p.

1731 **Baldwin**, George Benedict. 'Structural reform in the British miners' union.' *Q.J. Econ.*, LXVII, 4 (November 1953), 576–97.

1732 **Youngson Brown**, A. J. 'Trade union policy in the Scots coalfields, 1855–1885.' *Econ. Hist. Rev.*, 2nd ser., VI, 1 (August 1953), 35–50.

1733 **Arnot**, Robert Page. *A history of the Scottish miners from the earliest times.* London: Allen and Unwin, 1955. xiv, 445p.

1734 **Griffin**, Alan Ramsay. *The miners of Nottinghamshire: a history of the Nottinghamshire Miners' Association (now the Notts. Area of the National Union of Mineworkers). Vol. 1. 1881 to 1914.* Nottingham: [National Union of Mineworkers, 1955]. xii, 212p.

'The basis of [the author's] B.A. dissertation.'

1735 **Taylor**, Arthur John. 'The Miners' Association of Great Britain and Ireland, 1842–48: a study in the problem of integration.' *Economica*, n.s., XXII, 85 (February 1955), 45–60.

1736 **Morgan**, John Edward. *A village workers council and what it accomplished; being a short history of the Lady Windsor Lodge, S.W.M.F.* Pontypridd: Celtic P., 1956. 75p.

South Wales Miners' Federation.

1737 **Machin**, Frank. *The Yorkshire miners: a history. Vol. 1.* Barnsley: National Union of Mineworkers (Yorkshire Area), 1958. xi, 496p.

1738 **Meyers**, Frederic. 'Nationalization, union structures, and wages policy in the British coal mining industry.' *Sth. Econ. J.*, XXIV (April 1958), 421–33.

1739 **Johnson**, W. H. *The North-East Miners' Union (Hepburn's Union) of 1831–2.* 1959. (M.A. thesis, University of Durham.)

1740 **Williams**, James Eccles. *The political, social and economic factors influencing the growth of trade union organisation amongst the Derbyshire coal miners, 1880–1944.* 1959. (Ph.D. thesis, University of Sheffield.)

1741 **McCormick**, Brian J. 'Managerial unionism in the coal industry.' *Br. J. Sociol.*, XI, 4 (December 1960), 356–69.

1742 **McCutcheon**, John Elliott. *A Wearside mining story, including an account of the sinking of Wearmouth Pit, Co. Durham, and the birth of the Durham Miners' Association at that colliery.* Seaham: the author, 1960. 101p.

1743 **Arnot**, Robert Page. *The miners in crisis and war: a history of the Miners' Federation of Great Britain, from 1930 onwards.* London: Allen and Unwin, 1961. 451p.

The third volume of the history of the M.F.G.B.

1744 **Evans**, Eric Wyn. *The miners of South Wales.* Cardiff: University of Wales P., 1961. ix, 274p.

1745 **Meyers**, Frederic. *European coal mining unions: structure and function.* Los Angeles: University of California, Institute of Industrial Relations, 1961. 161p. (Industrial relations monographs 7.)

'This is a case study. It deals with unions active in the coal mining industries of four countries: France, Belgium, West Germany, and Great Britain.'

1746 **Griffin**, Alan Ramsay. *The miners of Nottinghamshire, 1914–1944: a history of the Nottinghamshire miners' unions.* London: Allen and Unwin, 1962. 323p.

1747 **National Association of Colliery Overmen, Deputies and Shotfirers.** *Midland area, 1908–1962: a short history.* Hindley: J. R. Rudd for the Association, 1962.

1748 **Williams**, James Eccles. *The Derbyshire miners: a study in industrial and social history.* London: Allen and Unwin, 1962. 933p.

1749 **Williams**, James Eccles. 'Militancy among the British coalminers, 1890–1914.' *Soc. Study Labour Hist. Bull.*, 13 (Autumn 1966), 16.

Abstract of a paper given at a joint meeting of the Society for the Study of Labour History with the French Institute of Social History and Social Movements, Birkbeck College, London, 16–17 April 1966.

1750 **Arnot**, Robert Page. *South Wales miners. Glowyr De Cymru: a history of the South Wales Miners' Federation, 1898–1914.* London: Allen and Unwin, 1967. 390p.

1751 **Mason**, Antony. *The miners' unions of Northumberland and Durham, 1918–1931, with special reference to the General Strike of 1926.* 1967–68. (Ph.D. thesis, University of Hull.)

1752 **Smethurst**, John B. 'Ballads of the coalfields.' *Eccles Distr. Hist. Soc. Trans.* (1967–1968), 25–40.

1753 **Challinor**, Raymond and **Ripley**, Brian. *The Miners' Association: a trade union in the age of the Chartists.* London: Lawrence and Wishart, 1968. 266p.

1754 **Edelstein**, J. David. 'Countervailing powers and the political process in the British Mineworkers' Union.' *Int. J. Comp. Sociol.*, IX, 3–4 (September–December 1968), 255–88.

1755 **Gregory**, Roy George. *The miners and British politics, 1906–1914.* London: Oxford U.P., 1968. xi, 207p. (Oxford historical monographs.)

Based on the author's Ph.D. thesis *The miners and politics in England and Wales, 1906–14.* 1963.

1756 **Ravensdale**, J. R. 'The China Clay Labourers Union.' *Hist. Studies*, I, 1 (May 1968), 51–62.

1757 **Smethurst**, John B. 'Lancashire and the Miners' Association of Great Britain and Ireland.' *Eccles Distr. Hist. Soc. Trans.* (1968–69). 36p.

1758 **Allen**, Edward. *The Durham Miners' Association 1869–1969: 'a commemoration'.* [Durham?]: National Union of Mineworkers, Durham Area, 1969. 68p.

For private circulation.

1759 **Cartwright**, John Anthony. *A study in British syndicalism: the miners of South Wales 1906–1914.* 1969. (M.Sc. Econ. thesis, University of Wales Institute of Science and Technology.)

1760 **Garside**, W. Richard. *The Durham Miners' Association, 1919–1947.* 1969. (Ph.D. thesis, University of Leeds.)

1761 **Woodhouse**, M. G. *Rank-and-file movements amongst the miners of South Wales, 1910–26.* 1970. (D.Phil. thesis, University of Oxford.)

See also: 41; 61–2; 162; 2615; 2786; 3077.

3. Manufacturing Industries

a. FOOD, DRINK, AND TOBACCO

1762 **Swift**, John. *History of the Dublin bakers and others.* [Dublin?]: Irish Bakers, Confectionery and Allied Workers Union, 1948. 383p.

b. CHEMICALS AND ALLIED INDUSTRIES

1763 **Lerner**, Shirley Walowitz. 'The Chemical Workers' Union: a case study.' *Breakaway unions and the small trade union.* London: Allen and Unwin, 1961. p. 13–65.

c. IRON, STEEL, AND OTHER METALS

1764 **Cunninghame-Graham**, Robert Bontine. *The nail and chainmakers.* London, [1889?]. (Labour platform series.)

1765 **National Union of Stove-Grate Workers.** *Mr. Sanders and the Sheffield Iron Founders' Society.* [Rotherham], 1891. 11p.

1766 **Jones**, John Harry. 'Trade unionism in the tinplate industry.' British Association for the Advancement of Science. *Reports of meetings.* 1908. p. 793–4.

1767 **Jones**, John Harry. 'Trade unions in the tinplate industry.' *Econ. J.*, XIX, 74 (June 1909), 299–305.

1768 **Amalgamated Society of Coremakers of Great Britain and Ireland.** *Jubilee souvenir.* 1910.

1769 **Kelly**, Thomas Herbert. *Wages and labour organisation in the brass trades of Birmingham and district.* 1930. (Ph.D. thesis, University of Birmingham.)

1770 **Pugh**, *Sir* Arthur. 'Trade unionism in the iron and steel industry.' Cole, G. D. H. *British trade unionism today: a survey . . .* London: Methuen, 1945. p. 344–52.
Earlier edition. 1939.

1771 **Kidd**, A. T. *History of the tin-plate workers and sheet metal workers and braziers societies.* London: National Union of Sheet Metal Workers and Braziers, 1949.

1772 **Pugh**, *Sir* Arthur. *Men of steel: a chronicle of eighty-eight years of trade unionism in the British iron and steel industry, by one of them.* London: Iron and Steel Trades Confederation, 1951 [i.e. 1952]. xiv, 624p.
The author was a former General Secretary of the Confederation.

1773 **Owen**, Jack. *Ironmen: a short story of the history of the Union from 1878 to 1953, compiled from our records and other sources by the General Secretary.* Middlesbrough: National Union of Blastfurnacemen, Ore Miners, Coke Workers and Kindred Trades, [1953]. 48p.
Earlier edition. 1935.

1774 **Furth**, Hubert Jim and **Collins**, Henry. *The foundry workers: a trade union history.* Manchester: Amalgamated Union of Foundry Workers, 1959. xii, 348p.

1775 **National Union of Gold, Silver and Allied Trades**, *A short history of the National Union of Gold, Silver & Allied Trades to commemorate the fiftieth anniversary of the Union.* [Sheffield, 1961?] 24p.

1776 **Chadwick-Jones**, John K. 'The union branch in the steel industry: a socio-psychological interpretation.' *Occup. Psychol.*, XXXIX, 4 (October 1965), 261–70.

1777 **Howard**, Nicholas. 'A note on the *Ironworkers journal*, 1869–1916.' *Soc. Study Labour Hist. Bull.*, 13 (Autumn 1966), 42–43.

See also: 2668.

d. ENGINEERING AND SHIPBUILDING

See also Part Three, III, G, 9.

1778 **Anderson**, John. *Forty years' industrial progress.* London, 1891.
Amalgamated Society of Engineers.

1779 **Hammill**, Fred. *An address . . . at the first annual conference [of the National Vehicular Traffic Workers' Union].* 1892. 15p.

1780 **Amalgamated Society of Engineers.** *Jubilee souvenir, 1901.* London: Co-operative Printing Society, 1901. 125p.
History of the A.S.E. and its activities.

1781 **Cummings**, David Charles. *A historical survey of the Boiler Makers' and Iron and Steel Ship Builders' Society from August 1834 to August 1904.* Newcastle-on-Tyne: R. Robinson, 1905. 220p.

1782 **Rose**, Frank Herbert. *A call to war workers of the engineering and ship-building industries.* London: Hyman, Christy and Lilly, 1918. 20p.
The author was a member of the Amalgamated Society of Engineers.

1783 **Mosses**, William. *History of the United Pattern Makers' Association, 1872–1922.* London: U.P.A., 1922. 367p.
Souvenir edition.

1784 **Robinson**, Thomas Hoben. *The antecedents and beginnings of the Amalgamated Society of Engineers.* 1928. (B.Litt. thesis, University of Oxford.)

1785 **Suthers**, Robert B. 'Electrical Trades Union.' *Labour Mag.*, x, 1 (May 1931), 20–3.

1786 **Suthers**, Robert B. 'Amalgamated Engineering Union.' *Labour Mag.*, x, 10 (February 1932), 467–72.

1787 **National Union of Vehicle Builders.** *A hundred years of vehicle building, 1834–1934: centenary of the N.U.V.B.* Manchester: the Union, 1934. 120p.
By J. Nicholson.

1788 **Robinson**, Thomas Hoben. *The Amalgamated Society of Engineers, 1851–1892: a case study in welfare policy.* Chicago: privately printed, 1938. 34p.

Abstract of University of Chicago Ph.D. thesis, lithoprinted; 'private edition distributed by the University of Chicago Libraries.'

1789 **Electrical Trades Union**, *Souvenir of fifty years, 1889–1939*. 1939.

1790 **McLaine**, William. *The engineers' union. Book I. The millwrights and 'old mechanics'*. 1939. (Ph.D. thesis, University of London.)

1791 **Wild**, J. *1889–1939: fifty years of the Electrical Trades Union*. Manchester, 1939. 83p.

1792 **Chapman**, Dennis. 'The New Shipwright Building Company of Dundee, 1826 to 1831.' *Econ. Hist. Rev.*, x, 2 (November 1940), 148–51.

1793 **Bussey**, E. W. 'Organisations of the industry. XIII. Electrical Trades Union.' *Electl. Rev.*, cxxxv, 3486 (15 September 1944), 383–6.

1794 **Hannington**, Walter. *The rights of engineers*. London: Gollancz, 1944. 122p.

1795 **Miller**, G. D. 'Trade unionism in the engineering industry.' Cole, G. D. H. *British trade unionism today: a survey* . . . London: Methuen, 1945. p. 258–366.

Earlier edition. 1939.

1796 **Jefferys**, James Bavington. *The story of the engineers, 1800–1945*. London: Lawrence and Wishart, 1946.

1797 **Trory**, Ernie. *The sacred band: a contribution to the social history of Brighton*. Brighton: Crabtree P., 1946. 128p.

A historical account of the Brighton 1st Branch of the Amalgamated Engineering Union.

1798 **Schaffer**, Gordon. *Light and liberty: sixty years of the Electrical Trades Union*. Hayes, 1949. 94p.

1799 **Bending**, Harry (ed.). *Forty years: National Union of Scalemakers, 1909–1949*. London: the Union, [1950]. 32p.

The author was General Secretary of the Union.

1800 **Amalgamated Society of Engineers.** *Centenary souvenir*. 1951.

1801 **National Union of Vehicle Builders.** Glasgow Branch. *Souvenir brochure, 1846–1951*. Glasgow, 1951.

1802 **Electrical Trades Union.** *The story of the E.T.U.: the official history of the Electrical Trades Union*. Hayes, Kent: E.T.U., 1953. ix, 248p.

1803 **National Union of Vehicle Builders.** *A short history of the National Union of Vehicle Builders to commemorate the 125th anniversary of the Union, 1834–1959*. [Manchester, 1959?] 40p.

1804 **Bean**, R. 'Militancy, policy formation and membership opposition in the Electrical Trades Union, 1945–61.' *Polit. Q.*, vi, 2 (April–June 1965), 181–90.

1805 **Edelstein**, J. David. 'Democracy in a national union: the British AEU.' *Ind. Relat.*, iv, 3 (May 1965), 105–25.

1806 **Clarke**, J. F. 'The shipwrights.' *NE. Group Study Labour Hist. Bull.*, 1 (October 1967), 21–3.

Includes a guide to some of the Sunderland local history documents, which is followed by reprints of some of the documents, p. 23–40.

1807 **Lewis**, D. R. *The Electrical Trades Union and the growth of the electrical industry to 1926*. 1970. (D.Phil. thesis, University of Oxford.)

See also: 2047; 2066; 2074; 2778; 3083; 3114; 13,209.

e. TEXTILES

1808 **Chapman**, Sydney John. 'Some policies of the cotton spinners' trade unions.' *Econ. J.*, x, 40 (December 1900), 467–73.

1809 **Williamson**, Arthur. *50 years record . . . of the Hyde and District Operative Cotton Spinners Association*.

Reprinted from *North Cheshire Herald*, January 1906.

1810 **Turner**, *Sir* Ben. *A short account of the rise and progress of the Heavy Woollen District Branch of the General Union of Textile Workers*. 1917.

1811 **Turner**, *Sir* Ben. *A short history of the General Union of Textile Workers*. Heckmondwike, 1920. 195p.

1812 **Rowe**, John Wilkinson Foster. 'The ball warpers: the policy of their unions and its results.' *Economica*, ii, 4 (January 1922), 69–74.

1813 **Managers' and Overlookers' Society.** *Managers' and Overlookers' Society: centenary celebrations, 1827–1927*. Bradford: the Society, 1927.

1814 **Williamson**, Arthur. *The Hyde and District Operative Cotton Spinners' Association: historical sketch*. Hyde: H. Secker, 1929. 19p.

1815 **General Union of Associations of Loom Overlookers.** *Jubilee 1885–1935: a brief record of the Association's history*. Ashton (printed), [1935?]. 68p.

1816 **Amalgamated Association of Card, Blowing and Ring Room Operatives.** *After 50 years: Golden Jubilee Souvenir, 1886–1936*. Manchester: the Association, 1936. 48p.

1817 **Bradford and District Power-Loom Overlookers' Society.** *Centenary celebrations, 1844–1944: souvenir programme*. Bradford, [1944?]. [16]p.

1818 **Wadsworth**, Alfred Powell. 'The cotton trade unions.' Cole, G. D. H. *British trade unionism today: a survey*. London: Methuen, 1945. p. 386–95.

Earlier edition. 1939.

1819 **Chapman**, Dennis. 'The combination of hecklers in the East of Scotland, 1822 and 1827.' *Scott. Hist. Rev.*, xxvii, 2 (October 1948), 156–64.

'Hecklers prepared the flax for spinning . . .'

1820 **Minchington**, W. E. 'The beginnings of trade unionism in the Gloucestershire woollen industry.' *Bris. Glouc. Archaeol. Soc. Trans.*, LXX (1951), 126–41.

1821 **Thornton**, E. *Trade unionism and the cotton industry*. Manchester, 1953. 19p,

1822 **Cuthbert**, Norman H. *The Lace Makers' Society: a study of trade unionism in the British lace industry, 1760–1960*. Nottingham: Amalgamated Society of Operative Lace Makers and Auxiliary Workers, 1960. xiii, 293p.

1823 **Singleton**, F. 'The Saddleworth Union, 1827–30.' *Soc. Study Labour Hist. Bull.*, 5 (Autumn 1962), 33–6.

1824 **Turner**, Herbert Arthur. *Trade union growth, structure and policy: a comparative study of the cotton unions*. London: Allen and Unwin, 1962. 412p.

Based on the author's *Labour organisation in the cotton trade of Great Britain*. 1959. (Ph.D. thesis, University of Manchester.)

1825 **Cuthbert**, Norman H. *A study of trade unions in the British lace industry*. 1962–63. (Ph.D. thesis, University of Nottingham.)

1826 **Hustwick**, Wade. *The celebration of the fiftieth anniversary of the amalgamation*. Bradford: Managers' and Overlookers' Society, 1963. 20p.

1827 **Bolton and District Weavers' and Winders' Association**. *Centenary, 1965*. Bolton: printed by Tillotsons (Bolton) Limited, [1965?]. 18p.

Written by the Industrial Correspondents of the Bolton Evening News.

1828 **Hopwood**, Edwin. *The Lancashire weavers' story: a history of the Lancashire cotton industry and the Amalgamated Weavers' Association*. Manchester: the Association, 1969. [xiv], 199p.

f. CLOTHING AND FOOTWEAR

1829 **Schloss**, David Frederick. 'Trade unionism and sweating: trade organisations in the boot-making industry of East London and Hackney.' *Char. Orgn. Rev.*, v, 49 (January 1889), 7–15.

Based on an investigation made in connection with the inquiry of Charles Booth.

1830 **Galton**, Frank W. (ed.). *Select documents illustrating the history of trade unionism. I. The tailoring trade*. London: London School of Economics and Political Science, 1896. xcviii, 242p.

Reprinted. London: King, 1923.

Preface by S. Webb.

1831 **Unwin**, George. 'A seventeenth century trade union.' *Econ. J.*, x, 39 (September 1900), 394–403.

Journeymen Hatters of Great Britain and Ireland.

1832 **National Union of Boot and Shoe Operatives**. *Fifty years, being the history of the National Union of Boot & Shoe Operatives, 1874–1924*. London: N.U.B.S.O., 1924. 137p.

By E. L. Poulton.

1833 **Elsbury**, Sam and **Cohen**, Dave. *The Rego revolt: how the United Clothing Workers' Trade Union was formed*. London: Dorritt P., 1929. 31p.

1834 **Suthers**, Robert B. 'National Union of Boot and Shoe Operatives.' *Labour Mag.*, XI, 3 (July 1932), 112–16.

1835 **Allen**, Arthur C. and **Bartley**, L. J. *An epic of trade unionism; being an account of the Rushden and District Branch of the National Union of Boot and Shoe Operatives from its earliest days to the Raunds Strike in 1905*. Rushden: 'Rushden Echo', 1934. 47p.

Founded 1873.

1836 **Chester**, George. 'The boot and shoe operatives.' Cole, G. D. H. *British trade unionism today: a survey* . . . London: Methuen, 1945. p. 415–24.

Earlier edition. 1939.

1837 **Conley**, A. 'Trade unionism among garment workers.' Cole, G. D. H. *British trade unionism today: a survey* . . . London: Methuen, 1945. p. 405–14.

Earlier edition. 1939.

1838 *Ever since fig leaves came into fashion: tale of the Tailors' Union*. London, 1947. 6p.

1839 **Walton**, J. *The rise of trade unionism in Leicester with special reference to the hosiery workers' union*. 1952. (M.A. thesis, University of Sheffield.)

1840 **Lerner**, Shirley Walowitz. *The history of the United Clothing Workers' Union: a case study of social disorganisation*. 1956–57. (Ph.D. thesis, University of London.)

1841 **Fox**, Alan. *A history of the National Union of Boot and Shoe Operatives, 1874–1957*. Oxford: Blackwell, 1958. viii, 684p.

1842 **Helfgott**, Roy B. 'Minimum wages as a deterrent to union organization: experience in the British clothing industry.' *Current Econ. Comment*, XXI (May 1959), 47–58.

1843 **Helfgott**, Roy B. 'Trade unionism among the Jewish garment workers of Britain and the United States.' *Labor Hist.*, II, 2 (Spring 1961), 202–14.

1844 **Lerner**, Shirley Walowitz. 'The United Clothing Workers' Union: a case study.' *Breakaway unions and the small trade union*. London: Allen and Unwin, 1961. p. 85–143.

1845 **Stewart**, Margaret and **Hunter**, Leslie David Stevenson. *The needle is threaded: the history of an industry*. London: Heinemann; Newman Neame, 1964. 241p.

National Union of Tailors and Garment Workers.

g. BRICKS, POTTERY, GLASS, AND CEMENT

1846 **Warburton**, William Henry. *The progress of labour organisation in the pottery industry of Great Britain*. 1928. (B.Litt. thesis, University of Oxford.)

1847 **Warburton**, William Henry. *The history of trade union organisation in the North Staffordshire potteries.* London: Allen and Unwin, 1931. 288p.

1848 **Thomas**, John. 'Trade unionism in the Potteries.' Cole, G. D. H. *British trade unionism today: a survey* . . . London: Methuen, 1945. p. 425–32.
Earlier edition. 1939.

h. PAPER, PRINTING, AND PUBLISHING

1849 **London Society of Compositors.** *Proposed federation of the printing and paper trades.* 1886. 8p.

1850 **Typographical Association.** *The Typographical Association.* Manchester, 1892. [6]p.

1851 **Porritt**, Edward. 'Trade unionism and the evolution of the type-setting machine.' *J. Polit. Econ.*, II, 2 (March 1894), 292–7.

1852 **London Society of Compositors.** *Jubilee volume.* 1898.

1853 **Manchester Typographical Society.** *Centenary souvenir.* Manchester, 1898.

1854 **Typographical Association.** *A fifty years' record, 1849–99.* Manchester, 1899. xvi, 140p.

1855 **Scottish Typographical Association.** Executive Council. *Scottish Typographical Association: a fifty years' record, 1853–1903.* Glasgow, 1903. 114p.

1856 **Dibblee**, G. Binney. 'The printing trades and the crisis in British industry.' Commons, J. R. (ed.). *Trade unions and labor problems.* Boston, Mass.: Ginn, 1905. p. 289–303.
First published in *Econ. J.*, XII (1902), 1–12.
Reprinted. New York: Kelley, 1967.

1857 **Suthers**, Robert B. *The story of 'NATSOPA', 1889–1929.* London: National Society of Operative Printers and Assistants, [1929?]. 151p.

1858 **Sproat**, Thomas (comp.). *History and progress of the Amalgamated Society of Lithographic Printers and Auxiliaries of Great Britain and Ireland: a jubilee souvenir.* Manchester, 1930. 92p.

1859 **Suthers**, Robert B. 'London Society of Compositors.' *Labour Mag.*, XI, 7 (November 1932), 316–19.

1860 **Suthers**, Robert B. 'National Union of Operative Printers and Assistants.' *Labour Mag.*, XI, 4 (August 1932), 159–64.

1861 **Suthers**, Robert B. 'National Union of Printing, Bookbinding and Paper Workers.' *Labour Mag.*, XI, 6 (October 1932), 268–72.

1862 **Society of Lithographic Artists, Designers, Engravers and Process Workers.** *A record of fifty years, 1885–1935.* London, 1935. 32p.

1863 **National Society of Operative Printers and Assistants.** *Jubilee souvenir of Natsopa, 1889–1939.* 1939. 35p.

1864 **Taylor**, H. A. 'Through fifty years: an outline of the history of the Institute of Journalists.' *Journal*, XXVIII, 278 (January–March 1940), Supplement. 12p.

1865 **Mansfield**, Frederick John. *'Gentlemen, the Press!' Chronicles of a crusade: official history of the National Union of Journalists.* London: W. H. Allen, 1943. 579p.

1866 **Temple**, H. S. 'Trade unionism in the printing industry.' Cole, G. D. H. *British trade unionism today: a survey* . . . London: Methuen, 1945. p. 367–75.
Earlier edition. 1939.

1867 **Howe**, Ellic and **Waite**, Harold E. *The London Society of Compositors: a centenary history.* London: Cassell, 1948. xvi, 359p.

1868 **Rowles**, G. E. *The 'line' is on: a centenary souvenir of the London Society of Compositors, 1848–1948.* London: the Society, [1948?]. 116p.

1869 **Howe**, Ellic. *The London bookbinders, 1780–1806.* London: Dropmore P., 1950. ii, 182p.

1870 **Musson**, Albert Edward. *A history of trade unionism in the provincial printing industry during the nineteenth century.* 1950. (M.A. thesis, University of Manchester.)

1871 **Journalist.** 'Highlights of our union history.' *Journalist*, XXXIV, 3 (March 1951), 36; 5 (May 1951), 72; 6 (June 1951), 92; 8 (August 1951), 124; 10 (November 1951), 160.
National Union of Journalists.

1872 **Hollings**, W. H. *Circulation Representatives Branch of the N.U.P.B. & P.W.* London: the Branch, 1952.
Reprinted in the Branch Rule Book, 1957. p. 3–11.
National Union of Printing, Bookbinding and Paper Workers.

1873 **Howe**, Ellic and **Child**, John. *The Society of London Bookbinders, 1780–1951.* London: Sylvan P., 1952. 288p.

1874 **Gillespie**, Sarah C. *A hundred years of progress: the record of the Scottish Typographical Association, 1853 to 1952.* Glasgow: Maclehose for the Association, 1953. xv, 268p.

1875 **Coleman**, Donald Cuthbert. 'Combinations of capital and of labour in the English paper industry, 1789–1825.' *Economica*, n.s., XXI, 81 (February 1954), 32–53.

1876 **Gillespie**, Sarah C. *A hundred years of progress: the record of the Scottish Typographical Association, 1853–1952.* 1954. (Ph.D. thesis, University of Glasgow.)

1877 **Musson**, Albert Edward. *The Typographical Association: origins and history up to 1949.* London: Oxford U.P., 1954. viii, 550p.

1878 **Shane**, T. N. (*pseud.*) [i.e. Harry Augustus Hubbard Healey.] *Passed for press: a centenary history of the Association of Correctors of the Press.* London: Association of Correctors of the Press, 1954. 63p.

1879 **Typographical Association.** *The Typographical Association: origins and history up to 1949.* London: Oxford U.P., 1954. viii, 550p.

1880 **Howe,** Ellic. *The typecasters.* London: privately printed for presentation to the Monotype Casters' and Typefounders' Society by the Monotype Corporation Ltd., 1955. 38p.
Monotype Casters' and Typefounders' Society.

1881 **Richards,** J. H. *Social and economic aspects of combination in the printing trade before 1875.* 1956–57. (M.A. thesis, University of Liverpool.)

1882 **Bundock,** Clement James. *The National Union of Journalists: a jubilee history, 1907–1957.* Oxford: Oxford U.P., 1957. viii, 254p.

1883 **Association of Publishers' Educational Representatives.** *Diamond jubilee, 1898–1958* [brochure]. [Leicester? the Association, 1958?] 16p.

1884 **Collier,** J. 'Your Branch in focus: Manchester.' *Natsopa J.*, XLII, 487 (January 1958), 12–13, 19.

1885 **Bundock,** Clement James. *The story of the National Union of Printing, Bookbinding and Paper Workers.* Oxford: Oxford U.P., 1959. vii, 588p.

1886 **Hill,** G. D. 'Your Branch in focus: London Clerical.' *Natsopa J.*, XLIII, 499 (January 1959), 8–9, 21.

1887 **Sykes,** Andrew James Macintyre. 'Trade-union workshop organization in the printing industry: the chapel.' *Hum. Relat.*, XIII, 1 (February 1960), 49–65.

1888 **Sykes,** Andrew James Macintyre. 'Unity and restrictive practices in the British printing industry.' *Sociol. Rev.*, n.s., VIII, 2 (November 1960), 239–54.

1889 **Printing and Kindred Trades Federation.** *Sixty years of service, 1901–1961.* [1961?]

1890 **Smith,** Kenneth. *The Book Publishers' Representatives' Association: an appraisal.* n.p.: the Association, 1964. 4p.
'Originally prepared for the Dutch Publishers' Representatives' Association and printed in *De Vertegenwoordiger.*'
The author was Co-Trustee and Past President of the Association.

1891 **Moran,** James. *Natsopa seventy-five years: The National Society of Operative Printers and Assistants, 1889–1964.* London: Heinemann on behalf of Natsopa, 1964 [i.e. 1965]. ix, 160p.

See also: 2653; 3001; 3094; 13,162; 13,198.

i. OTHER MANUFACTURING

1892 **Amalgamated Protective Society of Female Brushmakers.** *Female Brushmakers' Amalgamated Society.* Glasgow: [the Society?], [190–]. [3]p.

4. Construction

See also Part Three, III, E, 3, d.

1893 **Hart,** Ernest Abraham. *The registration and regulation of plumbers: facts in support of the extension of the existing Statute law as to house drainage.* London: Smith, Elder, 1884. 19p.
Reprinted from *The Sanitary Record.*

1894 **Dew,** George. 'The Amalgamated Society of Carpenters, by "A London Carpenter".' *Char. Orgn. Rev.*, II, 22 (15 October 1886), 349–53.

1895 **Allison,** John. *How to elevate the status of plumbers.* Manchester: John Heywood, 1892. 8p.

1896 **Select Committee on the Plumbers' Registration Bill.** *Report, proceedings, appendix and index.* London: H.M.S.O., 1892. (H.C. 140.)
Special report in the following session with the proceedings. 1893–94. (H.C. 347.)
Report in a subsequent Session, with the proceedings. 1897. (H.C. 208.)

1897 **Chandler,** F. *History of the Amalgamated Society of Carpenters and Joiners, 1860–1910.* 1910.

1898 **Postgate,** Raymond William. *The builders' history.* London: National Federation of Building Trades Operatives, 1923. xxx, 487p.

1899 **Telling,** A. H. [Onlooker *pseud.*]. *'Hitherto': the story of an Association.* 1930.
National Association of Plasterers.

1900 **Suthers,** Robert B. 'The Amalgamated Union of Building Trade Workers of Great Britain and Ireland.' *Labour Mag.*, x, 4 (August 1931), 150–3.

1901 **Suthers,** Robert B. 'The Plumbers, Glaziers, and Domestic Engineers' Union.' *Labour Mag.*, XI, 1 (May 1932), 19–23.

1902 **Hicks,** G. *The Operative Stone Masons' centenary.* 1932–33. 15p.

1903 **Cox,** Herbert Arthur (comp.). *'These stones': the story of 'The Builder' and of other builders.* London: *The Builder*, 1937. 236p.
A history of the author's family, including an account of the periodical *The Builder.*
With contributions by Arthur Frederick Cox and Edward Webster Cox.
Printed for private circulation.

1904 **Higenbottam,** Samuel. *Our Society's history.* Manchester: Amalgamated Society of Woodworkers, 1939. 348p.

1905 **Coppock,** Richard and **Heumann,** Harry. 'Trade unionism in the building industry.' Cole, G. D. H. *British trade unionism today: a survey*... London: Methuen, 1945. p. 327–37.
Earlier edition. 1939.

1906 **Heumann,** Harry. '[History of the National Federation of Construction Unions.]' *Oper. Bldr.* (1947–1956).
In serial form.

1907 **Amalgamated Union of Building Trade Workers.** *The building workers' struggle: centenary souvenir.* London: the Union, 1948. 36p.
Drawings by Philip Mendoza.

1908 **New Builders Leader.** *18 years of struggle: the history of the 'New Builders Leader'.* London: *New Builders Leader*, 1953. 24p.

1909 **Baird**, George. *History of the Scottish Painters' Society.* [1959.]
Part published by the Society, part typescript.

1910 **Connelly**, T. J. *The woodworkers, 1860–1960.* London: Amalgamated Society of Woodworkers, 1960. vii, 120p.

1911 **Newman**, James Robert. *The N.A.O.P. heritage: a short historical review of the growth and development of the National Association of Operative Plasterers, 1860–1960.* Wembley, Mx.: National Association of Operative Plasterers, 1960. viii, 180p.

1912 **Hilton**, William Samuel. *Foes to tyranny: a history of the Amalgamated Union of Building Trade Workers.* London: Amalgamated Union of Building Trade Workers, 1963. 301p.

1913 **Emerson**, J. R. 'A brief history of the Association.' *Supervisor*, I, 1 (January 1965), 3, 5.
The Sussex Association of Builders Foremen and Clerks of Works.

1914 **French**, John Oliver. *Plumbers in unity: history of the Plumbing Trades Union 1865–1965.* London: P.T.U., 1965. xi, 172p.

5. Gas, Electricity, and Water

See also Part Three, III, D; and Part Three, III, E, 3, d.

1915 **Palmer**, Arthur. *How we began: a short history of the Association.* Chertsey, Surrey: Electrical Power Engineers' Association, n.d.

1916 **Metropolitan Water Board Staff Association.** *Aquarius*, XLIV, 7 (July 1955).
Golden jubilee issue of the Association's journal.

1917 **Institution of Water Engineers.** 'The Institution of Water Engineers: sixty years history.' *Instn. Wat. Engrs. J.*, x, 7 (November 1956), 509–14.
Reprinted from *Contract Journal*, LXXVIII, 4029 (1956).

1918 **Hobsbawm**, Eric John Ernest. 'British gasworkers 1873–1914.' *Labouring men: studies in the history of labour.* London: Weidenfeld and Nicolson, 1964. p. 158–78.

6. Transport and Communications

See also Part Three, III, D.

a. GENERAL

1919 **Jones**, Arthur Creech. 'Transport and trade unionism.' Cole, G. D. H. *British trade unionism today: a survey . . .* London: Methuen, 1945. p. 310–24.
Earlier edition. 1939.

1920 **Phillips**, G. A. *The National Transport Workers' Federation, 1910–27.* 1969. (D.Phil. thesis, University of Oxford.)

b. RAILWAYS AND LONDON TRANSPORT

See also Part Three, III, G, 9; and Part Seven, VII, B, 2 for material on the Taff Vale case.

1921 **Vincent**, Charles Bassett. *An authentic history of railway trade unionism.* Derby: printed by H. Mee, 1902. 66p.
Reprinted. Derby: Mrs C. E. S. Hallam, 1963.

1922 **Standard.** *The railway position with regard to labour questions.* London, 1907. 8p.
'Extract from the *Standard*, June 13, 1907.'

1923 **Amalgamated Society of Railway Servants.** *Souvenir history, published on the occasion of the opening of the new offices, Unity House, Euston Road, N.W., September 17th 1910.* London, 1910. 147p.

1924 **Cole**, George Douglas Howard and **Arnot**, Robert Page. *Trade unionism on the railways: its history and problems.* London: Fabian Research Department; Allen and Unwin, 1917. 147p. (Trade union series 2.)

1925 **Raynes**, John R. *Engines and men: the history of the Associated Society of Locomotive Engineers and Firemen. A survey of organisation of railway locomotive men.* Leeds: Goodall and Suddick, 1921. xv, 302p.

1926 **Alcock**, George W. *Fifty years of railway trade unionism.* London: Co-operative Printing Society, 1922. xvi, 631p.

1927 **Higginson**, P. R. *A suggested basis for the discussion of one union for railway workers.* London, 1924. 19p.

1928 **National Union of Railwaymen.** Edinburgh No. 1 Branch. *Jubilee souvenir, 1876–1926.* Edinburgh, 1926. 46p.

1929 **Railway Clerks' Association.** *The Railway Clerks' Association and its path of progress, 1897–1928.* London: the Association, 1928.
Written by A. G. Walkden.

1930 **Suthers**, Robert B. 'Associated Society of Locomotive Engineers and Firemen.' *Labour Mag.*, x, 7 (November 1931), 320–4.

1931 **Suthers**, Robert B. 'The National Union of Railwaymen.' *Labour Mag.*, x, 6 (October 1931), 268–72.

1932 **Suthers**, Robert B. 'The Railway Clerks' Association.' *Labour Mag.*, x, 8 (December 1931), 338–42.

1933 **National Union of Railwaymen.** *Silver Jubilee Souvenir. General Secretary's report to the Annual General Meeting, Southport, July 1938.* London, 1938. 136p.
p. 1–22, historical account of railway trade unionism.

1934 **National Union of Railwaymen.** *What trade unionism has done for railwaymen and other transport workers: N.U.R. silver jubilee.* 1938.

1935 **Dalley**, Fred W. 'Trade unionism on the railways.' Cole, G. D. H. *British trade unionism today: a survey* . . . London: Methuen, 1945. p. 297–306.
Earlier edition. 1939.

1936 **Griffith**, Wyn. *Fifty years of trade union endeavour*. London: Railway Clerks' Association, 1947. 16p.

1937 **McKillop**, Norman. *The lighted flame: a history of the Associated Society of Locomotive Engineers and Firemen*. London: Nelson, 1950. xiii, 402p.

1938 **Transport Salaried Staff Journal**. 'Highlights of R.C.A. history.' *Transp. Sal. Staff J.*, XLVIII, 567 (May 1951), 192–3; 568 (June 1951), 231–3; 570 (August 1951), 336–8; 571 (September 1951), 388–9; 572 (October 1951), 421–2; 574 (December 1951), 504–5; XLIX, 575 (January 1952), 6–7.
On the Railway Clerks' Association.

1939 **Bagwell**, Philip Sidney. 'Early attempts at national organization of the railwaymen, 1865–1867.' *J. Transp. Hist.*, III, 2 (November 1957), 94–102.

1940 **Gupta**, P. S. *The history of the Amalgamated Society of Railway Servants, 1871–1913*. 1960. vii, 537 leaves. (D.Phil. thesis, University of Oxford.)

1941 **Cox**, E. S. 'The history of the Institution of Locomotive Engineers: the ten years to the golden jubilee.' *Instn. Loco. Engrs. J.*, L, 6 (1960/1), 682–6.

1942 **Holcroft**, H. 'The history of the Institution of Locomotive Engineers: the first forty years.' *Instn. Loco. Engrs. J.*, L, 6 (1960/1), 662–82.

1943 **Bagwell**, Philip Sidney. *National Union of Railwaymen golden jubilee souvenir 1913–1963*. 1963.

1944 **Bagwell**, Philip Sidney. *The railwaymen: the history of the National Union of Railwaymen*. London: Allen and Unwin, 1963. 725p.

1945 **National Union of Railwaymen**. Glasgow and West of Scotland District Council. *Fifty years of struggle, 1913–1963: jubilee souvenir*. Glasgow, 1963. 36p.

1946 **Gupta**, P. S. 'Railway trade unionism in Britain, c. 1880–1900.' *Econ. Hist. Rev.*, 2nd ser., XIX (April 1966), 124–53.
Based on part of the author's thesis, *The history of the Amalgamated Society of Railway Servants, 1871–1913*, Oxford, D.Phil., 1960.

See also: 56; 69; 13,232.

c. ROAD

1947 **Lyon**, Hugh. *The History of the Scottish Horse and Motormen's Association, 1898–1919*. 1919.

1948 **Tuckett**, Angela. *The Scottish carter: the history of the Scottish Horse and Motormen's Association, 1898–1964*. London: Allen and Unwin, 1967. 448p.

d. SEA

1949 **McGeogh**, Alexander. *Labour in the merchant service, 1850–1920*. 1921. 260p. (M. Com. thesis, University of Birmingham.)

1950 **Suthers**, Robert B. 'The National Union of Seamen.' *Labour Mag.*, X, 2 (June 1931), 77–81.

1951 **Mercantile Marine Service Association.** *Annual report: centenary edition, 1857–1957*. Liverpool: C. Birchall and Sons, 1957.

e. PORT AND INLAND WATER

1952 **Tillett**, Ben. *Dock, Wharf, Riverside, and General Workers' Union: a brief history of the dockers' union, commemorating the 1889 dockers' strike*. London: Twentieth Century P., 1910. 47p.

1953 **Turner**, Edward Raymond. 'The keelmen of Newcastle.' *Am. Hist. Rev.*, XXI, 3 (April 1916), 542–5.

1954 **Transport and General Workers' Union.** *The growth of the trade union idea and spirit among the staffs of the Port of London*. London: T.G.W.U., 1923. 51p.
Edited by A. Creech Jones.

1955 **Fewster**, J. M. 'Keelmen of Tyneside in the eighteenth century.' *Durham Univ. J.*, L, 1 (December 1957), 24–33; 2 (March 1958), 66–75; 3 (June 1958), 111–23.

1956 **Mogridge**, Basil. 'Militancy and inter-union rivalries in British shipping, 1911–1929.' *Int. Rev. of Soc. Hist.*, VI, 3 (1961), 375–412.

1957 **Fewster**, J. M. 'The last struggles of the Tyneside keelmen.' *Durham Univ. J.*, LV, 1 (December 1962), 5–15.

1958 **Hobsbawm**, Eric John Ernest. 'National unions on the waterside.' *Labouring men; studies in the history of labour*. London: Weidenfeld and Nicolson, 1964. p. 204–30.

1959 **National Union of Seamen.** *The story of the seamen: a short history of the National Union of Seamen*. London: the Union, 1964. 48p.
'First published as a series of articles in *The Seaman*. . .'

1960 **Lovell**, John C. *Trade unionism in the Port of London, 1870–1914*. 1965–66. (Ph.D. thesis, University of London.)

1961 **Lane**, A. D. 'The officials on shore.' *New Soc.*, IX, 241 (11 May 1967), 688–90.
Merchant Navy and Airline Officers' Association.

1962 **Rowe**, David J. 'The keelmen.' *NE. Group Study Labour Hist. Bull.*, 1 (October 1967), 19–20.
A brief description followed by a select list of printed sources and manuscript sources.

1963 **Lovell**, John C. *Stevedores and dockers: a study of trade unionism in the Port of London, 1870–1914*. London: Macmillan, 1969. 270p.

1964 **Rowe**, David J. 'The decline of the Tyneside keelmen in the nineteenth century.' *Nth. Hist.*, IV (1969), 111–31.

1965 **Rowe**, David J. 'The keelmen of Tyneside.' *Hist. Today*, XIX, 4 (April 1969), 248–54.

See also: 1702; 2770.

f. AIR

1966 **Brown**. David Byron. *The history of the Guild of Air Pilots and Air Navigators 1929–1964*. London: Guild of Air Pilots and Air Navigators.
Vol. 1. 1967. x, 105p.

g. POSTAL SERVICES AND TELECOMMUNICATIONS

1967 **Postmen's Federation.** *The Postmen's Federation: report of the mass meeting of postmen ... on Thursday, the 25th March, 1897, to protest against the findings of the Interdepartmental Committee on Post Office Establishments.* London: printed for private circulation, 1897. 56p.

1968 **Swift**, Henry G. *A history of postal agitation from fifty years ago till the present day, including a few forgotten pages in the wider 'history of our own times'.* London: C. Arthur Pearson, 1900. 310p.
New and revised edition. Vol. 1. Manchester, London: Percy, 1929.
No more published.

1969 **Hall**, C. E. *Thirty years of agitation being a short account of the origin, work and progress of the Postal Telegraph Clerks' Association.* Liverpool: the Association, 1902.

1970 **Neale**, W. *The history of the National Federation of Sub-Postmasters, 1897–1913.* Bristol: Burleigh P., 1917.

1971 **Union of Post Office Workers.** *How we began: postal trade unionism, 1870–1920.* London: the Union, 1920. 39p.
Written by J. M. Chalmers.
Also later editions. 1956, 1960.

1972 **Smith**, L. M. *Some aspects of staff organisation in the postal service with special reference to (a) the general history and development of the movement since 1895; (b) the struggle for official recognition; (c) the efforts to secure full civil rights; and (d) the working of Whitleyism.* 1931. (B.Litt. thesis, University of Oxford.)

1973 **Suthers**, Robert B. 'Union of Post Office Workers.' *Labour Mag.*, XI, 2 (June 1932), 64–8.

1974 **Andrews**, Francis. 'Trade unionism in the Post Office.' Cole, G. D. H. *British trade unionism today: a survey* ... London: Methuen, 1945. p. 491–500.
Earlier edition. 1939.

1975 **Coward**, D. J. W. 'The civil service staff movement. IV. The Post Office Engineering Union.' *Whit. Bull.*, XXVII, 10 (October 1947), 158–9.

1976 **Geddes**, C. J. 'The civil service staff movement. III. The Union of Post Office Workers.' *Whit. Bull.*, XXVII, 9 (September 1947), 142–3.

1977 **Hodgson**, E. P. 'The civil service staff movement. II. The Federation of Post Office Supervising Officers.' *Whit. Bull.*, XXVII, 7 (July 1947), 104–5.

1978 **Committee on Post Office (Departmental Classes) Recognition.** *Report.* London: H.M.S.O., 1952. 24p. (Cmd. 8470.)
Chairman: Lord Terrington.

1979 **Read**, A. J. 'An anniversary.' *Review*, XXII, 11 (November 1960), 220–3.
Society of Telecommunication Engineers.

1980 **Taylor**, H. M. 'An anniversary.' *Review*, XXII, 10 (October 1960), 201–5.
Society of Telecommunication Engineers.

1981 **Baker**, E. C. 'An anniversary.' *Review*, XXIII, 9 (September 1961), 199–202.
Society of Telecommunication Engineers.

1982 **Fagg**, R. L. 'A decade of conflict.' *Review*, XXIII, 11 (November 1961), 258–61.
Society of Telecommunication Engineers.

1983 **Lerner**, Shirley Walowitz. 'Fission and fusion in the Post Office Engineering Union: a case study.' *Breakaway unions and the small trade union.* London: Allen and Unwin, 1961. p. 144–86.

1984 **Whittaker**, W. N. 'An anniversary.' *Review*, XXIII, 10 (October 1961), 229–30.
Society of Telecommunication Engineers.

1985 **Williams**, Rosalie A. 'An anniversary.' *Review*, XXIII, 12 (December 1961), 284–5.
Society of Telecommunication Engineers.

1986 **Association of Head Postmasters.** 'Looking back.' *Notes* (December 1962), 96–9.

1987 **Golding**, John. *75 years: a short history of the Post Office Engineering Union.* Northampton: Belmont P. for the Union, 1962. 65p.

1988 **Seaton**, S. A. R. 'The civil service staff movement. I. The Association of Post Office Controlling Staffs.' *Whit. Bull.*, XLIII, 4 (April 1963), 53–5.

1989 **Smith**, Ron. 'The civil service staff movement. III. The Union of Post Office Workers.' *Whit. Bull.*, XLIII, 6 (June 1963), 86–7.

1990 **Glynn**, J. K. 'The civil service staff movement. XII. The Post Office shared seat.' *Whit. Bull.*, XLIV, 4 (April 1964), 56–7.

1991 **Smith**, Charles. 'The civil service staff movement. XI. The Post Office Engineering Union.' *Whit. Bull.*, XLIV, 3 (March 1964), 44–6.

1992 **Brown**, Kenneth. 'Sub-postmasters: private traders and trade unionists.' *Br. J. Ind. Relat.*, III, 1 (March 1965), 31–45.

7. Distributive Trades

See also Part Five, V, B.

1993 **Hewitt**, A. *The Amalgamated Union of Co-operative Employés.* Manchester, [*c.* 1900]. 16p.

1994 **Russell**, Charles Edward Bellyse and **Campagnac**, Ernest Trafford. 'The organization of costermongers and street-vendors in Manchester.' *Econ. Rev.*, x, 2 (April 1900), 188–95.
Description of the Manchester and District Costermongers' and Street-vendors' Trade-protection Society.

1995 **Anderson**, W. C. *Servitude of the shop, and its abolition.* London: National Union of Shop Assistants, 1906.

1996 **Hallsworth**, *Sir* Joseph and **Mercer**, Thomas William. *The need for trade-unionism in the co-operative movement.* Manchester, 1909. 8p.

1997 **Amalgamated Union of Cooperative Employés.** *The Amalgamated Union of Co-operative Employés: why it has withdrawn from the Trades Union Congress.* Manchester: Co-operative Newspaper Society, 1915. 12p.
By A. Hewitt.

1998 **Suthers**, Robert B. 'National Amalgamated Union of Shop Assistants, Warehousemen and Clerks.' *Labour Mag.*, x, 11 (March 1932), 512–16.

1999 **Hann**, Maurice. 'The struggle for organisation among shop workers.' Cole, G. D. H. *British trade unionism today: a survey* . . . London: Methuen, 1945. p. 453–62.
Earlier edition. 1939.

2000 **Wilkinson**, Ellen. 'Trade unionism in the co-operative movement.' Cole, G. D. H. *British trade unionism today: a survey*. . . London: Methuen, 1945. p. 463–73.
Earlier edition. 1939.

2001 **Hoffmann**, P. C. *They also serve: the story of the shopworker.* London: Porcupine P., 1949.

2002 **Hancox**, T. W. (ed.). *Seventy years, 1883–1953.* London: United Commercial Travellers' Association, 1953, vii, 95p.
History of the Association.

2003 **Knight**, Robert E. L. 'Unionism among retail clerks in postwar Britain.' *Ind. Labor Relat. Rev.*, xiv, 4 (July 1961), 515–27.

2004 **Osahon**, N. *Trade union militancy in retailing (a study of members' attitude to their trade union).* 1968–9. (M.Sc. thesis, University of Salford.)

8. Insurance, Banking, and Finance

2005 **O'Connor**, J. Desmond (comp.). *The Royal Liver Agents' and Employees' Union, 1890–1930: why it was formed, what it has achieved.* Royal Liver Workers' Journal. Supplement, October 1931. [iv], 138p.
Edited by J. P. Hutchings.

2006 **Bank Officers' Guild**. *The Bank Officers' Guild: its origin, policy and achievements.* London: the Guild, 1933. 10p.
Another edition. 1940.

2007 **Chartered Insurance Institute.** [Historical notes, etc.] London: the Institute, 1934. 38p.
Prepared to commemorate the opening of the new hall and offices of the Institute.

2008 **Oliver**, Alfred. *Our business: the story of the National Pearl Federation, 1920–40.* London: the Federation, 1940. 154p.

2009 **Ridley**, Wynter. 'Professional people.' *Bankers' Mag.*, CLXXIV, 1305 (December 1952), 467–71.

2010 **Federation of Insurance Staff Associations.** *Federation of Insurance Staff Associations: the formation, benefits and activities.* London: the Federation, 1953.

2011 **National Union of Bank Employees.** *Down the years with NUBE.* London: the Union, 1953.

2012 **Cockerell**, Hugh Anthony Lewis. *Sixty years of the Chartered Insurance Institute, 1897–1957.* London: Chartered Insurance Institute, 1957. 92p.

2013 **Allen**, Victor L. and **Williams**, Sheila. 'The growth of trade unionism in banking.' *Manchr. Sch.*, XXVIII, 3 (September 1960), 299–381.
England and Wales only.

2014 **Bankers' Magazine**. 'The Cameron Inquiry.' *Bankers' Mag.*, CXCV, 1431 (June 1963), 447–60; CXCVI, 1432 (July 1963), 19–24.

2015 **Ministry of Labour**. *Report of the inquiry by the Honourable Lord Cameron, into the complaint made by the National Union of Bank Employees on 12th March 1962 to the Committee on Freedom of Association of the International Labour Organisation.* London: H.M.S.O., 1963. (Cmnd. 2202.)

2016 **Bankers' Magazine**. 'The Cameron Report.' *Bankers' Mag.*, CXCVII (January 1964), 11–17.

2017 **A Special Correspondent.** 'Representing the staffs.' *Banker*, CXIV, 455 (January 1964), 30–6.

2018 **Blackburn**, Robert Martin. *Union character and social class: a study of white-collar unionism.* London: Batsford, 1967. 304p. (Foundations of modern society.)
Based on the author's *Unionisation and union character in banking*. 1965. (Ph.D. thesis, University of Liverpool.)

2019 **Robinson**, Olive. 'Representation of the white-collar worker: the bank staff associations in Britain.' *Br. J. Ind. Relat.*, VII, 1 (March 1969), 19–41.

9. Professional and Scientific Services

In addition to including works on white-collar and professional unions, this section also includes material on the process of professionalisation and the status of professions.

a. GENERAL WHITE-COLLAR AND PROFESSIONAL

2020 **National Union of Clerks**. *The Clerks' Union: its object, methods, and conditions of membership.* London, [1890?].

2021 **Spencer**, Herbert. 'Professional institutions. I. Professions in general.' *Contemp. Rev.*, LXVII (May 1895), 721–4.

The first of a series of articles eventually to form chapters of Part VII of *The principles of sociology* – 'Professional institutions.'

2022 **Spencer**, Herbert. 'Professional institutions. II. Physician and surgeon.' *Contemp. Rev.*, LXVII (June 1895), 898–908.

2023 **Spencer**, Herbert. 'Professional institutions. III. Dancer and musician.' *Contemp. Rev.*, LXVIII (July 1895), 114–24.

2024 **Spencer**, Herbert. 'Professional institutions. IV. Orator and poet, actor and dramatist.' *Contemp. Rev.*, LXVIII (August 1895), 228–40.

2025 **Spencer**, Herbert. 'Professional institutions. V. Biographer, historian and man of letters.' *Contemp. Rev.*, LXVIII (September 1895), 395–403.

2026 **Spencer**, Herbert. 'Professional institutions. VI. Men of science and philosophers.' *Contemp. Rev.*, LXVIII (October 1895), 538–47.

2027 **Spencer**, Herbert. 'Professional institutions. VII. Judge and lawyer.' *Contemp. Rev.*, LXVIII (November 1895), 688–96.

2028 **Spencer**, Herbert. 'Professional institutions. VIII. Teacher.' *Contemp. Rev.*, LXVIII (December 1895), 853–61.

2029 **Spencer**, Herbert. 'Professional institutions. IX. Architect.' *Contemp. Rev.*, LXIX (January 1896), 100–5.

2030 **Spencer**, Herbert. 'Professional institutions. X. Sculptor.' *Contemp. Rev.*, LXIX (February 1896), 285–91.

2031 **Spencer**, Herbert. 'Professional institutions. XI. Painter.' *Contemp. Rev.*, LXIX (March 1896), 391–8.

2032 **Spencer**, Herbert. 'Professional institutions. XII. The evolution of the professions.' *Contemp. Rev.*, LXIX (April 1896), 547–53.

2033 **Read**, Walter J. *The clerks' charter*. London: National Union of Clerks, 1910.

2034 **Howes**, A. B. *Trades unionism for professions*. London, 1913. 79p.

2035 **Professional Classes War Relief Council**. *Professional Classes War Relief Council*. London, [1916]. 28p.

2036 **Hayward**, Frank Herbert. *Professionalism and originality: with an appendix of suggestions bearing on professional, administrative, and educational topics*. London: Allen and Unwin, 1917. xv, 260p.

2037 **Webb**, Sidney and **Webb**, Beatrice. 'Professional associations.' *New States.*, IX, 211 (21 April 1917), Supplement; IX, 212 (28 April 1917), Supplement. 48p. altogether.

A draft of the 4th report of the Fabian Research Department, investigation on 'The control of industry'.

Contents:

Introduction.

Chap. I. 'Professional organization among lawyers.'

Chap. II. 'Professional organization among medical men.'

Chap. III. 'Professional organization among teachers.'

Chap. IV. 'Professional organization among the technicians of industry.'

Chap. V. 'Professional associations in literature and the fine arts', by G. B. Shaw.

Chap. VI. 'Professional organization among the technicians of the office.'

Chap. VII. 'Professional organization among the manipulators of men.'

Chap. VIII. 'The success of professional organizations; with its shortcomings and limitations.'

Chap. IX. 'Conclusions.'

2038 **Lloyd**, James Henry and **Scouller**, R. E. *Trade unionism for clerks*. London: Palmer and Hayward, 1919. 31p.

With introductions by J. R. Clynes and G. Bernard Shaw.

2039 *Report of a Court of Inquiry into the position of foremen as regards trade union membership.* London: H.M.S.O., 1920. (Cmd. 990.)

2040 **Griffiths**, Ben. *Reflections on the organisation of brain workers*. London: Clerical and Administrative Workers' Confederation. 1921.

2041 **Oudegeest**, J. *Commercial, clerical and technical employees and professional workers in the trade union movement*. 1927. 8p.

2042 **Smit**, G. J. A. *Salaried employees, civil servants, and professional workers in the trade union movement*. 1927. 9p.

2043 **Thomson**, George Walker. 'Professional workers and organisation.' *Sociol. Rev.*, XIX, 3 (July 1927), 208–17.

2044 **Carr-Saunders**, *Sir* Alexander Morris. *Professions: their organization and place in society*. Oxford: Clarendon P., 1928. 31p.

The Herbert Spencer lecture, 1928.

2045 **National Federation of Professional Workers**. *The non-manual point of view: a note on the work of the National Federation of Professional Workers*. London, 1932. 3p.

2046 **Carr-Saunders**, *Sir* Alexander Morris and **Wilson**, Paul Alexander. *The professions*. Oxford: Clarendon P., 1933. vii, 536p.

Reprinted. London: Cass, 1964. viii, 536p.

2047 **Association of Engineering and Shipbuilding Draughtsmen**. *Short history of the Association of Engineering and Shipbuilding Draughtsmen, 1913 to 1934*. London: Draughtsmen Publishing Co., 1934. 63p.

Goes back beyond 1913.

Written by George W. Thomson.

2048 **Klingender**, Francis Donald. *The black-coated worker in London*. 1934. (Ph.D. thesis. University of London.)

2049 **Marshall**, T. H. 'The recent history of professionalism in relation to social structure and social policy.' *Can. J. Econ. Polit. Sci.*, v, 3 (August 1939), 325–40.

Reprinted in T. H. Marshall. *Citizenship*

and social class and other essays. London: Cambridge U.P., 1950.

2050 **Thomson**, George Walker. 'Organisation among non-manual workers.' Cole, G. D. H. *British trade unionism today: a survey*...London: Methuen, 1945. p. 474–82.
Earlier edition. 1939.

2051 **Lloyd**, Dennis. 'The disciplinary powers of professional bodies.' *Mod. Law Rev.*, XIII, 3 (July 1950), 281–306.

2052 **Fremlin**, Reinet. 'Scientists and the T.U. movement.' *Sci. Wkr.*, VII, 2 (March 1952), 15–18; 4 (July 1952), 15–18.

2053 **Hughes**, Edward. 'The professions in the eighteenth century.' *Inst. Hist. Res. Bull.*, XXV, 71 (May 1952), 29–30.
Summary of a paper given at the Anglo-American Conference of Historians, 1951.

2054 **Lewis**, Roy and **Maude**, Angus Edmund Upton. *Professional people*. London: Phoenix House, 1952. vii, 284p.

2055 **Lloyd**, Dennis. 'Judicial review of expulsion by a domestic tribunal.' *Mod. Law Rev.*, XV, 4 (October 1952), 413–24.

2056 **Hughes**, Fred. *By hand and brain: the story of the Clerical and Administrative Workers' Union*. London: Lawrence and Wishart, for the C. and A.W.U., 1953. 150p.

2057 **Williams**, Alan E. 'The foreman's story: an ASSET history.' *ASSET* (November 1953), 12–14; (January 1954), 4–6; (March–April 1954), 12–14; (January–February 1955), 8–9, 22.

2058 **Kelsall**, Roger Keith. 'Self-recruitment in four professions.' Glass, D. V. (ed.). *Social mobility in Britain*. London: Routledge and Kegan Paul, 1954. p. 308–20.

2059 **Pickard**, Ormonde George. 'Clerical workers and the trade unions.' *Br. Mgmt. Rev.*, XIII, 2 (April 1955), 102–20.

2060 **Pickard**, Ormonde George. *The office worker: a study in labour economics and organization*. 1955. (Ph.D. thesis, University of London.)

2061 **Conference on the Concept of Professional Status**, London, 1957. *The proceedings of a conference arranged by the College of Preceptors in Church House, Westminster, London, S.W.1, on Saturday, March 9th, 1957*. London: College of Preceptors, 1957. 64p.

2062 **Wooster**, W. A. 'Twenty-five years of the AScW.' *A.Sc.W. J.*, III, 5 (September 1957), 3–5.
Association of Scientific Workers.

2063 **Grant**, Andrew. *Socialism and the middle classes*. London: Lawrence and Wishart, 1958. 171p.
Chaps. III, V, VI. White collar workers.

2064 **Lockwood**, David. *The blackcoated worker: a study in class consciousness*. London: Allen and Unwin, 1958. 224p. (Studies in society.)
Second edition. 1966. (University books 48.) Paperback.
'... incorporates the substance of a thesis which was approved by the University of London for the award of the degree of Doctor of Philosophy.'

2065 **Hines**, Jennifer S. 'Professional bodies in the United Kingdom.' *Publ. Adm.*, XXXVII, 2 (Summer 1959), 165–78.

2066 **Mortimer**, James Edward. *A history of the Association of Engineering and Shipbuilding Draughtsmen*. London: Association of Engineering and Shipbuilding Draughtsmen, 1960. xi, 489p.

2067 **Miller**, J. Gareth. *An examination of the disciplinary powers of professional bodies in those professions which are now regulated by statute*. 1960–61. (LL.M. thesis, University of Wales, Aberystwyth.)

2068 **Wootton**, Graham. 'Parties in union government: the AESD.' *Polit. Studies*, IX, 2 (June 1961), 141–56.
Association of Engineering and Shipbuilding Draughtsmen.

2069 **Miller**, J. Gareth. 'The disciplinary jurisdiction of professional tribunals.' *Mod. Law Rev.*, XXV, 5 (September 1962), 531–43.

2070 **Millerson**, Geoffrey L. *The development, nature and role of the qualifying professional association in England and Wales*. 1962–63. (Ph.D. thesis, University of London.)

2071 **Jenkins**, Clive. 'Gaffers' men are organizing.' *New Soc.*, 35 (30 May 1963), 9–10.

2072 **Kassalow**, Everett M. 'White-collar unionism in Western Europe.' *Mon. Labor Rev.*, LXXXVI, 7 (July 1963), 765–71; 8 (August 1963), 889–96.

2073 **A Special Correspondent**. 'Ancillary services – competing with the professions?' *Banker*, CXIII, 452 (October 1963), 690–6.

2074 **Wootton**, Graham. 'A technicians' trade union.' *New Soc.*, II, 40 (4 July 1963), 13–15.
Draughtsmen's and Allied Technicians' Association.

2075 **Millerson**, Geoffrey L. 'Dilemmas of professionalism.' *New Soc.*, III, 88 (4 June 1964), 15–16.

2076 **Millerson**, Geoffrey L. *The qualifying associations: a study in professionalization*. London: Routledge and Kegan Paul, 1964. xiii, 306p. (International library of sociology and social reconstruction.)

2077 **Paton**, George E. C. 'Managerial trade unionism in Britain.' *Sci. Bus.*, II, 7 (November 1964), 263–8.

2078 **Phillipson**, Charles Michael. *A study of the attitudes towards and participation in trade union activities of selected groups of non-manual workers*. 1964. (M.A. thesis, University of Nottingham.)

2079 **Sykes**, Andrew James Macintyre. 'The problem of clerical trade unionism.' *Sci. Bus.*, II, 6 (August 1964), 176–83.

2080 **Blackburn**, Robert Martin and **Prandy**, Kenneth. 'White-collar unionization: a conceptual framework.' *Br. J. Sociol.*, XVI, 2 (June 1965), 111–22.

2081 **Prandy**, Kenneth. 'Professional organization in Great Britain.' *Ind. Relat.*, v, 1 (October 1965), 67–79.

2082 **Sykes**, Andrew James Macintyre. 'Some differences in the attitudes of clerical and of manual workers.' *Sociol. Rev.*, n.s., xiii, 3 (November 1965), 297–310.

In a Scottish company, towards promotion, trade unionism, and their company and management.

2083 **Bain**, George Sayers. 'The growth of white-collar unionism in Great Britain.' *Br. J. Ind. Relat.*, iv, 3 (November 1966), 304–35.

2084 **Lees**, Dennis Samuel. *Economic consequences of the professions*. London: Institute of Economic Affairs, 1966. iv, 48p. (Research monographs 2.)

2085 **Raison**, Timothy. 'In defence of the professions.' *New Soc.*, viii, 203 (18 August 1966), 262–4.

2086 **Reader**, William Joseph. *Professional men: the rise of the professional classes in nineteenth-century England*. London: Weidenfeld and Nicolson, 1966. 248p.

2087 **Routh**, Guy. 'White-collar unions in the United Kingdom.' Sturmthal, A. (ed.). *White-collar trade unions: contemporary developments in industrialized societies*. Urbana, Ill., London: U. of Illinois P., 1966. p. 165–204.

2088 **Bain**, George Sayers. *Trade union growth and recognition, with special reference to white-collar unions in private industry*. London: H.M.S.O., 1967. xi, 116p. (Royal Commission on Trade Unions and Employers' Associations. Research papers 6.)

2089 **Halmos**, Paul. 'The personal service society.' *Br. J. Sociol.*, xviii, 1 (March 1967), 13–28.

2090 **Murphy**, Keith. 'The technicians' unions.' *New Soc.*, ix, 227 (2 February 1967), 159–61.

2091 **Organisation of Employers' Federations and Employers in Developing Countries.** *Supervisory staff and trade union membership*. London: the Federation, 1967. 32p. (Occasional paper.)

Appendix C. *Current practice in the U.K.*
Also Appendix J. 1968. 4p.

2092 **Bain**, George Sayers. *The growth of non-manual workers' unions in manufacturing industries in Great Britain since 1948*. 1968. (D.Phil. thesis, University of Oxford.)

2093 **Fraser**, Charles A. *The future of the profession*. Edinburgh: Law Society of Scotland, 1968. 19p.

Law Society of Scotland, Study Weekend, St Andrews, 1968.

2094 **Freeman**, Roger. *Professional practice: a policy for the professions*. London: Bow Publications, 1968. 44p. (Bow Group pamphlets.)

2095 **Charlton**, K. 'The professions in sixteenth-century England.' *Univ. Birm. Hist. J.*, xii, 1 (1969), 20–41.

Medicine, law, teaching.

2096 **Hickson,** D. J. and **Thomas**, M. W. 'Professionalization in Britain: a preliminary measurement.' *Sociology*, iii, 1 (January 1969), 37–53.

2097 **Imam**, F. B. *Supervisory associations: a study of outside organizations and foremen's reasons for joining them with particular reference to North-West England*. 1969. (M.Sc. dissertation, Department of Management Sciences, University of Manchester Institute of Science and Technology.)

2098 **Bain**, George Sayers. *The growth of white-collar unionism*. Oxford: Clarendon P., 1970. xvi, 233p.

2099 **Harries-Jenkins**, G. 'Professionals in organizations.' Jackson, J. A. (ed.). *Professions and professionalization*. London: Cambridge U.P., 1970. p. 53–107.

2100 **Jackson**, John Archer. 'Professions and professionalization – editorial introduction.' *Professions and professionalization*. London: Cambridge U.P., 1970. p. 3–15.

2101 **Monopolies Commission.** *A report on the general effect on the public interest of certain restrictive practices so far as they prevail in relation to the supply of professional services*. London: H.M.S.O., 1970. 2 parts. (Cmnd. 4463, 4463-I.)

Part 1. *The report.*
Part 2. *The appendices.*

2102 **Olesen**, Virginia and **Whittaker**, Elvi W. 'Critical notes on sociological studies of professional socialization.' Jackson, J. A. (ed.). *Professions and professionalization*. London: Cambridge U.P., 1970. p. 181–221.

2103 **Turner**, C. and **Hodge**, M. N. 'Occupations and professions.' Jackson, J. A. (ed.). *Professions and professionalization*. London: Cambridge U.P., 1970. p. 19–50.

See also: 30; 49; 1954; 3438; 9684; 9892.

b. ACCOUNTANCY

2104 **Worthington**, Beresford. *Professional accountants: an historical sketch*. London: Gee, 1895. 127p.

2105 **Brown**, Richard. 'England and Ireland.' *A history of accounting and accountants*. Edinburgh, London: Jack, 1905. p. 232–52.

Incorporating notes by T. A. Onions and James Martin.

Reprinted. London: Cass, 1959.

2106 **Brown**, Richard. 'The position and prospect.' *A history of accounting and accountants*. Edinburgh, London: Jack, 1905. p. 334–40.

Reprinted. London: Cass, 1959.

2107 **Brown**, Richard. 'Scotland before the Charters.' *A history of accounting and accountants*. Edinburgh, London: Jack, 1905. p. 181–220.

Incorporating notes by Alexander Sloan.
Reprinted. London: Cass, 1959.

2108 **Brown**, Richard. 'Scottish chartered accountants.' *A history of accounting and accountants*. Edinburgh, London: Jack, 1905. p. 203–31.
Incorporating notes by Alexander Sloan.
Reprinted. London: Cass, 1959.

2109 **Patrick**, Joseph. 'Development of the profession.' Brown, R. (ed.). *A history of accounting and accountants*. Edinburgh, London: Jack, 1905. p. 314–33.
Reprinted. London: Cass, 1959.

2110 **Crew**, Albert. *The profession of an accountant: characteristics, etiquette, registration, recognition, and some notes on the legal profession*. London: Gee, 1925. viii, 117p.

2111 **Board of Trade.** Departmental Committee on the Registration of Accountants. *Report*. London: H.M.S.O., 1930. 22p. (Cmd. 3645.)
Minutes of evidence, etc. 1930.
Chairman: Lord Goschen.

2112 **Association of Certified and Corporate Accountants.** *Fifty years: the story of the Association of Certified and Corporate Accountants, 1904–54*. London: the Association, 1954. ix, 70p.

2113 **Institute of Chartered Accountants of Scotland.** *A history of the chartered accountants of Scotland from the earliest times to 1954*. Edinburgh: the Institute, 1954. 183p.

2114 **Osbourn**, F. C. and **Bell**, R. T. *Fifty years*. London, 1954. 70p.
Association of Certified and Corporate Accountants.

2115 **Alban**, *Sir* Frederick John. *Socialisation in Great Britain and its effects on the accountancy profession*. London: Society of Incorporated Accountants and Auditors, 1955. 49p. ('Reprint' series 12.)
A reprint of a paper presented at the Annual Meeting of the American Institute of Accountants held in Chicago in September 1948.

2116 **Robinson**, Howard Waterhouse. *A history of accountants in Ireland*. 1963–64. (Ph.D. thesis, Trinity College, Dublin.)
Published Dublin, Institute of Chartered Accountants in Ireland, 1964. xii, 485p.

2117 **Association of Certified and Corporate Accountants.** *The accountancy profession in the United Kingdom*. 1966. 28p.

2118 **Institute of Book-Keepers.** *Golden jubilee*. London: the Institute, 1966. 28p.
Written by D. W. Bradley.

2119 **Accountant's Magazine.** 'Since 1954.' *Acctnt. Mag.*, LXXII, 746 (August 1968), 427–32.
Institute of Chartered Accountants of Scotland.

2120 **Accountant's Magazine.** 'Institute services for members. 7. The professional body in action.' *Acctnt. Mag.*, LXXIII, 753 (March 1969), 167–9.
Institute of Chartered Accountants of Scotland.

2121 **Hastings**, A. and **Hinings**, C. R. 'Role relations and value adaptation: a study of the professional accountant in industry.' *Sociology*, IV, 3 (September 1970), 353–66.

c. ARCHITECTURE

2122 **Society of Architects Journal.** 'After twenty-five years.' *Soc. Archit. J.*, n.s., II, 17 (March 1909), 174–9.
On 'the inception, rise and progress of the Society'.
Reprinted from the *Building News*, 12 February 1909.

2123 **Butler**, Charles McArthur. 'The Society of Architects, 1884–1913.' *Soc. Archit. J.*, n.s. VII, 77 (March 1914), 184–95.

2124 **Briggs**, Martin S. 'The architect in history: his training, status and work.' *R. Inst. Br. Archit. J.*, 3rd ser., XXXII, 18 (15 August 1925), 571–84; 19 (19 September 1925), 604–13; 20 (17 October 1925), 630–9.

2125 **Butler**, Charles McArthur. *The Society of Architects*. London: Royal Institute of British Architects, 1926. 94p.
A history.

2126 **Select Committee on the Architects (Registration) Bill.** *Special report, proceedings, minutes of evidence, appendices, index*. London: H.M.S.O., 1927. xiv, 239p. (H.C. 105.)
Chairman: Sir Clement Kinloch-Cooke.

2127 **Watson**, William Ernest. *Professional conduct and practice*. London: Royal Institute of British Architects, 1929. 26p.
'Extracted from the *R.I.B.A. Journal*.'

2128 **Gotch**, John Alfred (ed.). *The growth and work of the Royal Institute of British Architects, 1834–1934*. London: Royal Institute of British Architects, 1934. ix, 187p.

2129 **Summerson**, *Sir* John Newenham. *The Architectural Association, 1847–1947*. London: Pleiades Books, 1947. viii, 53p.

2130 **Kaye**, Barrington Laurence Burnett. *The development of the architectural profession in Great Britain, 1800–1945*. 1951–52. (Ph.D. thesis, London School of Economics.)

2131 **Kaye**, Barrington Laurence Burnett. *The development of the architectural profession in England: a sociological study*. London: Allen and Unwin, 1960. 223p.

2132 'RIAS.' *RIBA J.* (July 1963), 270–2.
Royal Incorporation of Architects of Scotland.

2133 **Higgin**, Gurth. 'The architect as professional.' *RIBA J.*, LXXI, 4 (April 1964), 139–45.

2134 **Webb**, Sidney. 'The functions of an architectural society.' *RIBA J.*, LXXI, 4 (April 1964), 145–8.
Shortened version of a paper originally delivered at an informal conference held at the R.I.B.A. on 22 November 1917.

2135 **Official Architecture and Planning.** 'Association of Official Architects.' *Off. Archit. Plann.* (July 1965), 915.

2136 **Mullin**, Stephen. 'What architects and the RIBA do.' *New Soc.*, XI, 297 (6 June 1968), 828–9.

2137 **Fricker**, L. J. 'Forty years a-growing.' *J. Inst. Lands. Archit.*, 86 (May 1969), 8–15.

d. EDUCATION

i. *Primary and Secondary*

2138 **Graves**, John J. *National Union of Elementary Teachers: an address* . . . London: J. Hughes, 1881. 20p.

2139 **Shirreff**, Emily Anne Eliza. *Kindergarten teachers and their qualifications.* London: W. Rice, 1885.
The annual address delivered before the Froebel Society, 1885.

2140 **Storr**, Francis. *The registration of teachers.* London: W. Rice, 1887. 27p.
'with an appendix containing the Registration Bill of 1881.'

2141 **Milligan**, James. *Is teaching a profession? Inaugural address delivered to Glasgow Branch of Educational Institute of Scotland.* Glasgow: Bryce, 1889. 23p.

2142 **Select Committee on Teachers' Registration and Organisation Bill.** *Special report, with the proceedings, evidence, appendix and index.* London: H.M.S.O., 1890–1. (H.C. 335.)

2143 **Storr**, Francis. 'Registration and status of teachers.' International Congress of Women, London, 1899. *Transactions. Vol. II. Women in education.* London: T. Fisher Unwin, 1900. p. 140–6.
Discussion, p. 146–7.

2144 **Webb**, Beatrice. 'English teachers and their professional organisation.' *New States.*, v, 129 (25 September 1915), Supplement, 24p.; v, 130 (2 October 1915), Supplement, 24p.
Report prepared for the Fabian Research Department.

2145 **Webb**, Sidney. *The teacher in politics.* London: Fabian Society, 1918. 15p. (Fabian tract 187.)

2146 **London Head Teachers' Association.** *The future of the London Head Teachers' Association.* London, 1919.

2147 **National Union of Teachers.** *National Union of Teachers war record, 1914–1919: a short account of duty and work accomplished during the war.* London: N.U.T., 1920. 207p.

2148 **Thompson**, Donna Fay. *Professional solidarity among the teachers of England.* New York: Columbia U.P., 1927. 338p. (Studies in history, economics and public law 288.)
'. . . an outline of the history of the National Union of Teachers.'

2149 **National Union of Teachers.** *N.U.T. Diamond Jubilee, Bournemouth, 1930. Conference souvenir.* 1930. 104p.

2150 **Van Camp**, R. *The National Union of Teachers in England: its history and present status.* 1935. (Ph.D. thesis, Western Reserve University, Cleveland, Ohio.)

2151 **Hughes**, G. W. *The social and economic status of the elementary school teacher in England and Wales, 1833–1870.* 1936. (M.Ed. thesis, University of Manchester.)

2152 **London Head Teachers' Association.** *The London Head Teachers' Association, 1888–1938: jubilee book.* London: London U.P., 1938. 143p.
Articles by various contributors recording progress.

2153 **University of Oxford.** Nuffield College. *The teaching profession today and to-morrow: a statement.* London: Oxford U.P., 1944. 48p.
Made by members of the education subcommittee of Nuffield College.

2154 **Hill**, William Wills. 'Teachers' organisations.' Cole, G. D. H. *British trade unionism today:* a survey . . . London: Methuen, 1945. p. 501–9.
Earlier edition. 1939.

2155 **Belford**, Alexander J. *Educational Institute of Scotland: centenary handbook.* Edinburgh: the Institute, 1946.

2156 **National Association of Head Teachers.** *The first fifty years: jubilee volume of the National Association of Head Teachers.* London: U. of London P., 1947. xvi, 219p.
Contributions by various authors.

2157 **Simpson**, Alexander B. *The Educational Institute of Scotland, 1847–1947.* Edinburgh: the Institute, 1947.
A summary of the book by A. J. Belford.

2158 **Baron**, George. *The secondary schoolmaster, 1895–1914: a study of the qualifications, conditions of employment and professional associations of masters in English secondary schools.* 1952–53. (Ph.D. thesis, University of London.)

2159 **Tropp**, Asher. 'The changing status of the teacher in England and Wales.' *Yr. Bk. Educ.* (1953), 143–70.

2160 **Tropp**, Asher. 'The first teachers' associations.' *Schoolmaster*, CLXIV, 2317 (25 December 1953), 803, 813.
The General Associated Body of Church Schoolmasters of England and Wales, and the United Association of Schoolmasters.

2161 **Williams**, Reginald Arthur. *The development of professional status among the elementary school teachers under the School Board for London, 1870–1904.* 1953. (M.A. thesis, University of London.)

2162 **Tropp**, Asher. *Elementary schoolteachers as a professional group, 1800 to the present day.* 1953–54. (Ph.D. thesis, University of London.)

2163 **Massey**, F. L. *The registration of teachers in England and Wales from 1846–1899, with special reference to the development of common interest and professional independence.* 1956–57. (M.A. thesis, University of London.)

2164 **Picker**, J. M. *The part played by teachers and teachers' associations in the administration of education at the local level: a study of authorities in the North West.* 1956–57. (M.A. thesis, University of Manchester.)

2165 **Tropp**, Asher. *The school teachers: the growth of the teaching profession in England and Wales from 1800 to the present day.* London: Heinemann, 1957. viii, 286p. (Kingswood social history series.)

2166 **National Association of Inspectors of Schools and Educational Organisers.** *A history of the National Association of Inspectors of Schools and Educational Organisers, 1919–1959.* Bristol: the Association, 1959.
A reprint of a history of the Association by J. B. Chapman, R. E. Sopwith and Dr Jagger, first published in 1946, with a fifteen-page addendum.

2167 **Baron**, George and **Tropp**, Asher. 'Teachers in England and America.' Halsey, A. H., Floud, J. and Anderson, C. A. (eds.). *Education, economy, and society: a reader in the sociology of education.* New York: Free Press; London: Collier-Macmillan, 1961. p. 545–57.
'Published for the first time in this volume.'

2168 **Incorporated Association of Assistant Masters in Secondary Schools.** *Seventy years of progress.* London: the Association, 1961.

2169 **Edmonds**, Edward L. *The school inspector.* London: Routledge and Kegan Paul; New York: Humanities P., 1962. x, 202p. (International library of sociology and social reconstruction.)

2170 **Evans**, Raymond. *The 'image' of the teacher in the national press.* 1962. (M.A. thesis, University of Manchester.)

2171 **Roy**, Walter. *The National Union of Teachers: a study of the political process within an association of professional workers.* 1963. (Ph.D. thesis, University of London.)

2172 **Scottish Education Department.** *The teaching profession in Scotland: arrangements for the award and withdrawal of certificates of competency to teach. Report of the Committee appointed by the Secretary of State for Scotland.* Edinburgh: H.M.S.O., 1963. (Cmnd. 2066.)
Chairman: Lord Wheatley.

2173 **National Association of Schoolmasters.** *Building for the future.* Hemel Hempstead, Herts.: the Association, 1964.

2174 **Rée**, Harry. 'Teaching: a profession?' *New Soc.*, VI, 159 (14 October 1965), 16–17.

2175 **Manzer**, Ronald Alexander. *Teachers and politics: a study of the role of the National Union of Teachers in making education policy in England and Wales, 1944 to 1964.* 1965–66. (Dissertation, Harvard University.)

2176 **Corbett**, Anne. 'Teachers: how professional?' *New Soc.*, VIII, 222 (29 December 1966), 977–8. (Society at work.)

2177 **Roach**, John Peter Charles. *The teaching profession: some reflections on a century of development; inaugural lecture delivered 23 February, 1966.* Sheffield: Sheffield University, 1966. 22p.

2178 **Roy**, Walter. *The teachers' union: aspects of policy and organisation in the National Union of Teachers, 1950–1966.* London: Schoolmaster Publishing, 1968. xv, 183p.

2179 **Morton**, Bernard (ed.). *Action, 1919–1969: a record of the growth of the National Association of Schoolmasters.* Hemel Hempstead: Educare, 1969. 30p.
Published for the Golden Jubilee of the Association.
The author was President of the Association from 1948 to 1949.

2180 **New Schoolmaster**. Golden jubilee issue, XLVI, 4 (April–May 1969).
National Association of Schoolmasters.

2181 **O'Connell**, Thomas James. *History of the Irish National Teachers' Organisation, 1868–1968.* Dublin: Irish National Teachers' Organisation, 1969. xvi, 491p.
Wrapper title: *100 years of progress.*

2182 **Percival**, Alicia Constance. *The origins of the Headmasters' Conference.* London: Murray, 1969. 98p.

2183 **Thomasson**, Raymond. 'Home rule for teachers?' *New Soc.*, XIV, 365 (25 September 1969), 476–7.
On the General Teaching Council in Scotland.

2184 **Bourne**, Richard and **MacArthur**, Brian. *The struggle for education, 1870–1970: a pictorial history of popular education and the National Union of Teachers.* London: Schoolmaster Publishing, 1970. 128p.

2185 **Coates**, R. D. *Organizations representing school teachers, as interest groups within the educational system of England and Wales.* 1970. (D.Phil. thesis, University of Oxford.)

2186 **Gretton**, John. 'Cloth cap and gown.' *New Soc.*, XV, 400 (28 May 1970), 909–10.

2187 **Inglis**, W. B. 'The General Teaching Council for Scotland.' *Br. J. Educ. Studies*, XVIII, 1 (1 February 1970), 56–68.

2188 **Leggatt**, T. 'Teaching as a profession.' Jackson, J. A. (ed.). *Professions and professionalization.* London: Cambridge U.P., 1970. p. 155–77.

2189 **Manzer**, Ronald Alexander. *Teachers and politics: the role of the National Union of Teachers in the making of national educational policy in England and Wales since 1944.* Manchester: Manchester U.P., 1970. xi, 164p.

2190 **Scottish Secondary Teachers' Association.** *The history of the SSTA.* Edinburgh: the Association, 1970. 4p.
Reprinted.

2191 **Myers**, John Douglas. *Scottish teachers and educational policy, 1803–1872: attitudes and influence.* 1970–71. (Ph.D. thesis, University of Edinburgh.)

See also: 2678.

ii. *Higher*

2192 **Laurie**, R. Douglas. 'The Association of University Teachers: historical sketch.' *Univ. Bull.*, I, 1 (January 1922), 6–8.

2193 **Evans**, A. E., **Wilson**, J. and **Ing**, W. *The Association of Teachers in Technical Institutions: the first half century, 1904–1954*. London: the Association, 1954. 64p.

2194 **Mitchell**, K. *The A.T.T.I.: its origins and growth*. 1963. (Dissertation, Bolton Technical Teachers Training College.)

Association of Teachers in Technical Institutions.

2195 **Bolam**, T. R. 'The Scottish Association of University Teachers.' *Br. Univ. A.* (1964), 77–87.

2196 **Mitchell**, K. 'Early years of the A.T.T.I.' *Tech. J.*, n.s., II, 1 (October 1964), 21, 23–4.

2197 **Perkin**, Harold J. 'Manchester and the origins of the A.U.T.' *Br. Univ. A.* (1964), 88–91.

2198 **Roberts**, Kenneth Owen. *The emergence of the teachers in technical institutions as a distinct group within the teaching profession in England*. 1968. (M.Phil. thesis, University of London.)

2199 **Pearsall**, D. S. *The Association of Teachers in Technical Institutions: a study of its development and organisation*. 1969. (M.A. dissertation, University of Warwick.)

2200 **Perkin**, Harold J. *Key profession: the history of the Association of University Teachers*. London: Routledge and Kegan Paul, 1969. 268p.

2201 **Trow**, Martin and **Halsey**, A. H. 'British academics and the professorship.' *Sociology*, III, 3 (September 1969), 321–39.

e. LEGAL SERVICES

2202 **Battersby**, T. S. Frank. 'Amalgamation: being some considerations on proposed changes in the relations of the legal professions in Ireland.' *Statist. Soc. Inq. Soc. Ir. J.*, IX, 64 (July 1886), 30–46.

2203 **Sawyer**, Frederick Ernest. *A history of solicitors and attorneys: a paper*... London: Spottiswoode, 1887. 22p.

2204 **Clarke**, *Sir* Edward George. *The future of the legal profession: an address*... London: Stevens and Haynes, 1888. 11p.

2205 **Lawson**, William. 'The fusion of the two branches of the legal profession.' *Statist. Soc. Inq. Soc. Ir. J.*, IX, 72 (August 1892), 632–6.

2206 **Murphy**, Joseph John. 'A suggestion for the fusion of the two branches of the legal profession.' *Statist. Soc. Inq. Soc. Ir. J.*, IX, 72 (August 1892), 613–16.

2207 **Treasury.** Commissioners appointed . . . to inquire into the matter at issue between the Irish Benchers and the Incorporated Law Society of Ireland regarding the allocation of part of the Stamp Duty on Indentures of Solicitors' Apprentices in Ireland. *Reports*. 1892. (H.C. 217 – Sess. 1.)

2208 **Christian**, Edmund Brown Viney. *A short history of solicitors*. London: Reeves and Turner, 1896. xiv, 255p.

2209 **Henderson**, John Alexander (ed.). *History of the Society of Advocates in Aberdeen*. Aberdeen: New Spalding Club, 1912. xxiv, 504p.

2210 **Barron**, Edward Evelyn (comp.). *A short account of the founding and formation of the Law Association*. London: Harrison, 1921. 28p.

Compiled from the minutes of the Association for its first centenary.

2211 **Gamble**, Charles. *Solicitors in Ireland, 1607–1921: the Incorporated Law Society's work*. Dublin, London: Maunsel and Roberts, 1921. 71p.

2212 **Christian**, Edmund Brown Viney. *Solicitors: an outline of their history*. London: Stevens, 1925. 166p.

2213 **Barron**, Edward Evelyn (comp.). *A short history of the Law Association from its foundation in 1817 to 1938*. London: Law Association, 1938. 40p.

Compiled from the minutes of the Association.

A new edition of *A short account of the founding and formation of the Law Association*.

2214 **Joint Committee on the Solicitors' Bill (HL)**. *Report*. London: H.M.S.O., 1939. xiii, 121p.

Chairman: Lord Wright.

On the examination of solicitors' accounts.

2215 **Society of Advocates in Aberdeen.** *Supplementary history of the Society of Advocates in Aberdeen, 1912–1938*. Aberdeen: Society of Advocates, 1939. [vii], 205p.

2216 **Grant**, *Sir* Francis James (ed.). *The Faculty of Advocates in Scotland, 1532–1943*. Edinburgh: Skinner, 1944. iv, 228p. (Indices and calendars of records issued by the Scottish Record Society, pt. 145.)

Also issued as *Publications*, vol. LXXVI.

2217 **Gower**, L. C. B. 'The future of the English legal profession.' *Mod. Law Rev.*, IX, 3 (October 1946), 211–34.

2218 **Secretary of the Law Society**. 'The professional discipline of solicitors.' *Publ. Adm.*, XXV, 1 (Spring 1947), 21–8.

2219 **Watkins**, Ernest Shilston. *The Law Society, 1939–1945*. London, 1947. 89p.

2220 **Lund**, Thomas G. 'The professional discipline of solicitors.' Pollard, R. S. W. (ed.). *Administrative tribunals at work*. London: Stevens, 1950. p. 118–30.

'This essay deals with what is called in the introduction "a domestic tribunal".'

2221 **Ives**, E. W. *Some aspects of the legal profession in the late fifteenth and early sixteenth centuries*. 1954–55. (Ph.D. thesis, University of London.)

2222 **Robson**, R. *The English attorney in the eighteenth century*. 1956–57. (Ph.D. thesis, University of Cambridge.)

2223 **Gower**, L. C. B. and **Price**, Leolin. 'The profession and practice of the law in England and America.' *Mod. Law Rev.*, XX, 4 (July 1957), 317–46.

2224 **Ives**, E. W. 'The reputation of the common lawyers in English society, 1450–1550.' *Univ. Birm. Hist. J.*, VII, 2 (1960), 130–61.

2225 **Lucas**, Paul. 'Blackstone and the reform of the legal profession.' *Engl. Hist. Rev.*, LXXVII, 304 (July 1962), 456–89.

2226 **National Association of Justices' Clerks' Assistants.** *Twenty-five years.* Hastings: the Association, 1963. 35p.

2227 **Ghai**, Yash and **McAuslan**, Patrick. 'Is the law a closed shop?' *New Soc.*, III, 78 (26 March 1964), 11–12.

2228 **Whiteside**, James. *The Justices' Clerks' Society.* Wigan: the Society, 1964. 57p.

2229 **Wilson**, N. *The sociology of a profession: the Faculty of Advocates.* 1964–65. (Ph.D. thesis, University of Edinburgh.)

2230 **Zander**, Michael. 'Reforming the English legal profession.' *Polit. Q.*, XXXVII, 1 (January–March 1966), 33–45.

2231 **Harris**, H. R. *The legal profession in England and Wales: a study of lawyers, with special reference to solicitors, barristers, and the higher judiciary.* 1966–67. (Ph.D. thesis, University of Reading.)

2232 **Zander**, Michael. *Lawyers and the public interest: a study in restrictive practices.* London: Weidenfeld and Nicolson for the London School of Economics and Political Science, 1968. xi, 342p.

2233 **Baker**, J. H. 'Counsellors and barristers: an historical study.' *Camb. Law J.*, XXVII, 2 (November 1969), 205–29.

f. LIBRARIANS

2234 **Tedder**, Henry Richard. *Librarianship as a profession: a paper read . . . Sept. 1882.* London: Chiswick P., 1884. 30p.

2235 **Campbell**, Francis Bunbury Fitz-Gerald. *Remarks addressed to the members of the Library Assistants' Association, September 18, 1895.* London: Chiswick P., 1895. 23p.

2236 **Thorne**, W. Benson. 'The Library Assistants' Association: an outline of its development and work.' *Librn. Bk. World*, XI, 4 (November 1911), 124–7; 5 (December 1911), 163–6; 6 (January 1912), 207–11.

2237 **Guppy**, Henry. *Seventy-five years.* London: Library Association, 1926. 24p. (Presidential address 1926.)

2238 **Pacy**, F. *The Library Association: early days. A retrospect, by the Hon. Secretary.* London: Library Association, 1927. 24p.

2239 **Minto**, John. 'The Library Association.' *A history of the public library movement in Great Britain and Ireland.* London: Allen and Unwin; the Library Association, 1932. p. 162–207.

2240 **Gillett**, J. T. 'Where we stand today.' *Libr. Assist.*, XXVIII, 5 (September–October 1945), 80–3.
Association of Assistant Librarians.

2241 **Jones**, Gurner P. '1919–1930.' *Libr. Assist.*, XXXVIII, 5 (September–October 1945), 76–80.
Association of Assistant Librarians.

2242 **Sayers**, W. C. Berwick. 'The later days.' *Libr. Assist.*, XXXVIII, 5 (September–October 1945), 73–6.
Association of Assistant Librarians.

2243 **Thorne**, W. Benson. 'The early days.' *Libr. Assist.*, XXXVIII, 5 (September–October 1945), 70–3.
Association of Assistant Librarians.

2244 **Savage**, Ernest A. 'Movements and men of the past in the Association.' *Libr. Ass. Rec.*, LII, 9 (September 1950), 321–9.

2245 **Stewart**, James D. 'The last twenty years and the Association.' *Libr. Ass. Rec.*, LII, 9 (September 1950), 338–45.

2246 **Macleod**, Robert Duncan. 'The Anglo-American Library Associations.' *Libr. Ass. Rec.*, LIII, 11 (November 1951), 362–4.

2247 **Munford**, William Arthur. 'The Library Association.' *Penny rate: aspects of British public library history, 1850–1950.* London: Library Association, 1951. p. 122–31.

2248 **Association of Assistant Librarians.** 'Special issue, 1895–1955.' *Assist. Librar.*, XLVIII, 4 (April 1955).
Jubilee issue.

2249 **Macleod**, Robert Duncan. *The Anglo-American Library Associations: an historical note on the beginnings.* London: Library Association, 1958. 15p. (Library Association pamphlet 19.)

2250 **Haslam**, D. D. 'The fighting fifties: an informal review of the Association's activities during 1950–59.' *Libr. Ass. Rec.*, LXII, 1 (January 1960), 2–10.

2251 **Munford**, William Arthur. 'The Library Association in the twentieth century: selected aspects.' Foskett, D. J. and Palmer, B. I. (eds.). *The Sayers memorial volume: essays in librarianship in memory of William Charles Berwick Sayers.* London: Library Association, 1961. p. 26–47.

2252 **Piper**, Alfred Cecil. *Association of Assistant Librarians, Sussex Division, 1912–1962.* Lewes: Association of Assistant Librarians, Sussex Division, 1963 [i.e. 1964]. 12p.

2253 **Munford**, W. A. (ed.). *Annals of the Library Association, 1877–1960.* London: Library Association, 1965. 128p.

2254 **Palmer**, Bernard Ira. *From little acorns: the library profession in Britain.* Bombay: Asia Publishing House, 1965. 176p. (Ranganathan series in library science. Sarada Ranganathan lectures 1965.)
Chapter on Library Association, p. 141–64.

2255 **Hunt**, K. G. *The Association of Metropolitan Chief Librarians*. London: Library Association, 1967. 37p. (Library Association pamphlet 29.)

2256 **Haslam**, D. D. 'The Library Association.' Vollans, R. F. (ed.). *Libraries for the people: international studies in librarianship in honour of Lionel R. McColvin*. London: Library Association, 1968. p. 53–73.

g. MEDICAL SERVICES

See also Part Three, III, E, 11, a and c.

i. *Doctors*

2257 **Laffan**, Thomas. *The medical profession in the three kingdoms in 1879*. Dublin: Fannin, 1879. viii, 218p.
'The essay to which was awarded the Carmichael Prize.'
Also *The medical profession in the three kingdoms in 1887*. 1888. viii, 385p. 'The essay to which was awarded...the Carmichael Prize ...1887.'

2258 **Select Committee on the Medical Act (1858) Amendment Bills, and the Medical Appointments Qualifications Bill.** *Special report, with the proceedings, evidence, appendix, and notes*. London: H.M.S.O., 1880. (H.C. 121.)

2259 **Flinn**, David Edgar. *I. Unqualified medical practitioners*. Second edition. *II. The system of unqualified medical assistants in England, and the use and abuse of their services*. Dublin: Fannin, 1882. 24p.

2260 **Royal College of Physicians of Edinburgh.** *Historical sketch and laws of the Royal College of Physicians of Edinburgh, from its institution to August, 1882*. Edinburgh: printed for the Royal College of Physicians, 1882. 182p.
Earlier edition. 1867. 170p.
Later edition.... *to 1925*. 1925. 288p.

2261 **Royal Commissioners Appointed to Inquire into the Grant of Medical Degrees.** *Report; with evidence, appendices, and index*. London: H.M.S.O., 1882. (C. 3259.)

2262 **Foster**, Balthazar Walter, Baron Ilkeston. *The political powerlessness of the medical profession: its causes and its remedies*. London: Churchill, 1883. 19p.
Printed in Birmingham.

2263 **Gamgee**, Joseph Sampson. *On representative government in the British Medical Association*. Birmingham, 1883. 8p.

2264 **Hickman**, William. *Pleas for the establishment of a Royal College of Medicine by the amalgamation of the Royal Colleges of Physicians and Surgeons of England*. London: J. Martin, 1885. 19p.
'Reprinted from the medical journals.'

2265 **Cameron**, *Sir* Charles Alexander. *History of the Royal College of Surgeons in Ireland and of the Irish Schools of Medicine, including numerous biographical sketches, also a medical bibliography*. Dublin: Fannin, 1886. x, 759p.
Second edition, revised and enlarged. 1916. xiii, 882p.

2266 **Erichsen**, *Sir* John Eric. *The Member, the Fellow and the Franchise* [in the Royal College of Surgeons]. London: H. K. Lewis, 1886. 16p.

2267 *The medical profession and its morality*. London: Pewtress, 1886. 42p.
Reprinted, with additions, from *Modern Review*, April 1881.

2268 **Ormsby**, *Sir* Lambert Hepenstal. *The social, scientific and political influence of the medical profession in the year 1886: an address*. Dublin: J. Atkinson, 1886. 41p.

2269 **Leyland**, John. *Contemporary medical men and their professional work*. Leicester: Offices of the *Provincial Medical Journal*, 1888. 2 v.

2270 **Rivington**, Walter. *The medical profession of the United Kingdom: the essay to which was awarded the first Carmichael Prize . . . 1887*. Dublin: Fannin, 1888. 1200p.

2271 **Du Styrap**, J. *The young practitioner*. London, 1890. 278p.

2272 **Snell**, Simeon. *A history of the medical societies of Sheffield*. Sheffield: Parkins, 1890. 74p.

2273 **Hart**, Ernest Abraham. *The professors, the public and the code: an address delivered . . . before the third general meeting of the Pan-American Medical Congress, Washington, Sept. 7, 1893*. London: Smith, Elder, 1893. 16p.

2274 **Bailey**, James Blake. 'The medical societies of London.' *Br. Med. J.* (6 July 1895), 24–6, 100–3.

2275 **Du Styrap**, J. *Code of medical ethics*. London, 1895. 103p.

2276 **Turner**, Percival. *Guide to the medical profession*. London: Baillière, 1895. viii, 159p.
'With a chapter on lady-doctors by Miss F. M. Strutt-Cavell.'

2277 **Duncan**, Alexander. *Memorials of the Faculty of Physicians and Surgeons of Glasgow, 1599–1850, with a sketch of the rise and progress of the Glasgow Medical School and of the medical profession in the West of Scotland*. Glasgow: J. Maclehose, 1896. xiii, 307p.

2278 **West**, Charles. *The profession of medicine, its study and practice, its duty and rewards*. London: Kegan Paul, 1896. x, 115p.
Earlier edition. . . . *an address*. 1850.

2279 **Sprigge**, *Sir* Samuel Squire. *The life and times of Thomas Wakley*. London: Longmans, 1897. xix, 509p.

2280 **Ritchie**, Robert Peel. *The early days of the Royall Colledge of Phisitians, Edinburgh: the extended oration of the Harveian Society, Edinburgh, delivered at the 114th festival*. Edinburgh: G. P. Johnston, 1899. xvi, 313p.

2281 **Royal College of Surgeons.** *Souvenir of*

the centenary of the Royal College of Surgeons of England, 1800–1900. London: Ballantyne, 1900. 32p.

2282 **Moore,** *Sir* Norman and **Paget**, Stephen. *The Royal Medical and Chirurgical Society of London: centenary, 1805–1905*. Aberdeen, 1905. 337p.

2283 **House of Lords**. Select Committee on the Prohibition of Medical Practice by Companies Bill (H.L.) and the Dental Companies (Restriction of Practice) Bill (H.L.). *Report, proceedings, minutes of evidence, appendix*. London: H.M.S.O., 1907. viii, 94p.

2284 **Medical Council**. *Report as to the practice of medicine and surgery by unqualified persons in the United Kingdom*. London: H.M.S.O., 1910. 86p. (Cd. 5322.)

2285 **Webb**, Sidney and **Webb**, Beatrice. *The state and the doctor*. London: Longmans, 1910. xiii, 276p.

2286 **Royal Society of Medicine**. *Royal Society of Medicine: record of the events and work which led to the formation of that Society by the amalgamation of the leading medical societies of London with the Royal Medical and Chirurgical Society*. London, 1914.

Extracts from the *Medico-Chirurgical Transactions*, 1905–7.

2287 **Dawson**, Bertrand Edward, Viscount Dawson of Penn. *The nation's welfare: the future of the medical profession*. London: Cassell, 1918. 40p.

The Cavendish Lectures delivered before the West London Medico-Chirurgical Society.

2288 **Cox**, Alfred. 'The medical profession and health insurance in Great Britain.' *Int. Labour Rev.*, XI, 5 (May 1925), 632–58.

The author was Medical Secretary, British Medical Association.

2289 **Cresswell**, Clarendon Hyde. *The Royal College of Surgeons of Edinburgh: historical notes from 1505 to 1905*. Edinburgh: Royal College of Surgeons of Edinburgh, 1926. xv, 315p.

2290 **King**, Norman Carew. *The General Medical Council: memorandum as to the constitution, functions, and procedure*. London: General Council of Medical Education, 1926. 14p.

2291 **Rowlette**, Robert J. 'The relation of the medical profession to the public.' *Statist. Soc. Inq. Soc. Ir. J.*, XVI, 102 (October 1938), 68–86.

2292 **Little**, Ernest Muirhead. *History of the British Medical Association, 1832–1932*. London: British Medical Association, 1932. 342p.

2293 **Clendening**, Logan. *Behind the doctor*. London: Heinemann, 1933. xxi, 458p.

A history of the medical profession.

Printed in Norwood, Mass.

'With illustrations from contemporary sources, portraits, photographs . . .'

2294 **Medical Officers of Schools Association.** *A record of fifty years' work, 1884–1934*. Hereford: G. Creasey, 1934. 137p.

2295 **Woolf**, Albert Edward Mortimer. *British medical societies: their early history and development, the Hunterian Society*. London, 1936. 16p.

Reprinted from *The Medical Press and Circular*.

2296 **Barclay-Smith**, E. *The first fifty years of the Anatomical Society of Great Britain & Ireland: a retrospect*. London: printed by John Roberts P., [1937]. 48p., 3 plates.

2297 **Power**, *Sir* D'Arcy (ed.). *British medical societies*. London: Medical Press and Circular, 1939. xvi, 311p.

2298 **Cawadias**, A. P. 'The Royal College of Physicians of London, on the occasion of its recent bombing.' *R. Soc. Med. Proc.*, XXXIV, 12 (October 1941), 811–22.

A sketch of the history.

2299 **Hill**, Charles. 'The B.M.A. and the medical services.' *Hlth. Soc. Welf.* (1944–45), 52–7.

2300 **Brook**, Charles Wortham. *Battling surgeon*. Glasgow: Strickland P., 1945. 176p.

A life of Thomas Wakley.

2301 **British Medical Journal**. 'The B.M.A. and trade union law: a factual statement.' *Br. Med. J.* (21 September 1946), Supplement, 83–4.

2302 **British Medical Association**. 'Report by Council on the constitutional position of the Association.' *Br. Med. J.* (26 February 1949), Supplement, 95–100.

2303 **Pridham**, J. A. 'Whither the B.M.A.?' *Br. Med. J.* (25 March 1950), Supplement, 99–100.

2304 **A Special Correspondent**. 'Fifty years of the B.M.A.' *Br. Med. J.* (7 January 1950), Supplement, 1–4.

2305 **Hamilton**, Bernice. 'The medical professions in the eighteenth century.' *Econ. Hist. Rev.*, 2nd ser. IV, 2 (1951), 141–69.

2306 **Hill**, A. Bradford. 'The doctor's day and pay: some sampling inquiries into the pre-war status.' *R. Statist. Soc. J.*, Ser. A, CXIV, 1 (1951), 1–34.

The inaugural address of the President, delivered to the Royal Statistical Society, 22 November 1950.

2307 **Smith**, Bernice Margaret. *Some aspects of the rise of the medical profession in the eighteenth century as a factor in the growth of the professional middle classes*. 1951. (Ph.D. thesis, London School of Economics.)

2308 **Brand**, Jeanne L. *The British medical profession and state intervention in public health, 1870–1911*. 1953–4. (Ph.D. thesis, University of London.)

2309 **Willcocks**, Arthur John. *Interest groups and the National Health Service Act, 1946*. 1953–4. (Ph.D. thesis, University of Birmingham.)

2310 **Davidson**, Maurice. *The Royal Society of Medicine: the realization of an ideal, 1805–1955*. London: Royal Society of Medicine, 1955. 201p.

2311 **Eckstein**, Harry Horace. 'The politics of the British Medical Association.' *Polit. Q.*, XXVI, 4 (October–December 1955), 345–59.

2312 **Pyke-Lees**, Walter. *Centenary of the General Medical Council, 1858–1958: the history and present work of the Council.* London: General Medical Council, 1958. 31p.

2313 **McMenemey**, William Henry. *The life and times of Sir Charles Hastings, founder of the British Medical Association.* Edinburgh, London: Livingstone, 1959. xii, 516p.

2314 **Vaughan**, Paul. *Doctors' commons: a short history of the British Medical Association.* London: Heinemann, 1959. xvii, 254p.

2315 **Dukes**, Cuthbert E. 'London medical societies in the eighteenth century.' *R. Soc. Med. Proc.*, LIII (1960), 699–706.
Section of the History of Medicine, President's Address.

2316 **Eckstein**, Harry Horace. *Pressure group politics: the case of the British Medical Association.* London: Allen and Unwin, 1960. 168p.

2317 **McMenemey**, William Henry. 'The influence of medical societies on the development of medical practice in nineteenth-century Britain.' Poynter, F. N. L. (ed.). *The evolution of medical practice in Britain.* London: Pitman, 1961. p. 67–79.

2318 **Vaughan**, Paul. 'The experiment at Worcester: the growth of the British Medical Association.' *Med. J. Aust.* XLIX, (1962), 759–64.

2319 **Jenkins**, Peter. *Bevan's fight with the B.M.A.: Labour and nationalisation.* Sissons, M. and French, P. (eds.). *Age of austerity.* London: Hodder and Stoughton, 1963. p. 231–54.

2320 **Widdess**, John David Henry. *A history of the Royal College of Physicians of Ireland, 1654–1963.* Edinburgh, London: Livingstone, 1963. xii, 255p.

2321 **Widdess**, John David Henry. *History of the Royal College of Surgeons and the Royal College of Physicians in Ireland.* 1963–4. (Litt.D. thesis, Trinity College, Dublin.)

2322 **Clark**, *Sir* George Norman. *A history of the Royal College of Physicians of London.* Oxford: Clarendon P., for the Royal College of Physicians.
Vol. 1. *1518–1688.* 1964. xxiii, 425p.

2323 **Brand**, Jeanne L. *Doctors and the state: the British medical profession and government action in public health, 1870–1912.* Baltimore: Johns Hopkins P., 1965. xiii, 307p.

2324 **Bullough**, V. L. *The development of medicine as a profession: the contribution of the medieval university to modern medicine.* Basel: Kargei; New York: Hafner Publishing Co., 1966. 125p.

2325 **McMenemey**, William Henry. 'Charles Hastings, 1794–1866: founder of the British Medical Association.' *Br. Med. J.* (16 April 1966), 937–42.

2326 **Bolaria**, Bhopinder Singh. *Professionalism among American and English physicians.* 1966–67. (Dissertation, Washington State University.)

2327 **Lapping**, Anne. 'Our brown doctors.' *New Soc.*, XIV, 357 (31 July 1969), 161–2.

2328 **Freidson**, Eliot. *Profession of medicine: a study of the sociology of applied knowledge.* New York: Dodd, Mead and Co., 1970. xxi, 409p.

2329 **Medical Officer**. 'Professional associations of the community health services: the Health Council Ltd.' *Med. Offr.*, CXXIV, 1 (3 July 1970), 13–16.

2330 **Royal College of Surgeons**. *Brief history of the College and its constitution.* London: the College, 1970. 4p.
Written by R. S. Johnson-Gilbert, the Secretary.

2331 **A Special Correspondent**. 'The General Medical Council.' *Br. Med. J.* (7 February 1970), Supplement, 42–3.

2332 **World Medicine**. 'Apathy or disenchantment.' *Wld. Med.*, v, 8 (13 January 1970), 7–8.

ii. *Dentists*

2333 **School Dentists' Society**. *The School Dentists' Society: its objects and aims.* Watford: W. Michael, 1913. 116p.
Second edition.

2334 **Departmental Committee on the Acceptance by the Board of Education of Dental Certificates from Unregistered Practitioners.** *Report.* London: H.M.S.O., 1914. 8p. (Cd. 7538.)

2335 **Departmental Committee to Inquire into the Extent and Gravity of the Evils of Dental Practice by Persons not Qualified under the Dentists Act, 1878.** *Report.* London: H.M.S.O., 1919. 57p. (Cmd. 33.)
Chairman: Sir Francis Dyke Acland.

2336 **Wood**, *Sir* Howard Kingsley. *Dental registration, being a practical guide to the new Dentists Act.* London: Baillière, 1921. vii, 128p.

2337 **Lindsay**, Lilian. 'The London dentist of the eighteenth century.' *R. Soc. Med. Proc.*, XX (1926–27), 355–66.

2338 **British Dental Association**. *The jubilee book of the British Dental Association.* London: Bale and Danielsson, 1930. 145p.

2339 **Inter-Departmental Committee on Dentistry**. *Interim report.* London: H.M.S.O., 1944. 25p. (Cmd. 6565.)
Final report. 1946. 60p. (Cmd. 6727.)
Chairman: Lord Teviot.

2340 **Denture Service Association**. *The case for the Denture Repair Service.* London, 1947. 14p.

2341 **British Dental Association**. *The British Dental Association.* London: the Association, 1952.

2342 **British Dental Journal**. 'Birth of the Association.' *Br. Dent. J.*, XCVI, 5 (2 March 1954), 120.
British Dental Association.

2343 **British Dental Journal.** '1880–1955.' *Br. Dent. J.*, XCIX, 1 (5 July 1955), 17–18.
British Dental Association.

2344 **Lindsay**, Lilian. '75 years of annual meetings.' *Br. Dent. J.*, XCIX, 1 (5 July 1955), 4–10.
British Dental Association.

2345 **Woods**, A. R. *The Western Counties branch of the British Dental Association.* Bristol: John Wright, 1958.

2346 **Campbell**, J. Menzies. 'A backward glance.' *Br. Dent. J.*, CXII, 5 (20 March 1962), 231–2.
British Dental Association.

2347 **King**, Christina. 'The history of the dental hygienist in the United Kingdom.' *Dent. Hlth.*, I, 1 (January–March 1962), 22–3.

2348 **British Association of Oral Surgeons.** [History of the Association.] *Br. J. Oral Surg.*, I, 1 (July 1963), 1–7.

iii. *Nurses*

See also Part Three, III, E, 9, g, iv.

2349 **Lückes**, Eva C. E. *What will trained nurses gain by joining the British Nurse's Association?* London: Churchill, 1889. 16p.

2350 **Select Committee on Registration of Nurses.** *Report, proceedings, minutes of evidence, appendices.* London: H.M.S.O., 1904. viii, 107p. (H.C. 281.)
Index. 1904. (H.C. 281–Ind.)
Report . . . 1905. xiv, 234p. (H.C. 263.)
Chairman: H. J. Tennant.

2351 **Queen Victoria's Jubilee Institute for Nurses.** [History and organisation, etc.] London, 1913. 37p.

2352 **Falkiner**, N. M. 'The nurse and the state.' *Statist. Soc. Inq. Soc. Ir. J.*, XIV, 98 (October 1920), 29–43.
Discussion, p. 43–60.

2353 **Royal College of Nursing.** *The College of Nursing and Cowdray Club.* London: the College, [1927?].

2354 **Royal College of Nursing.** *The College of Nursing: its history and progress.* London: the College, [193–].

2355 **Seymer**, Lucy Ridgely. *A general history of nursing.* London: Faber, 1932. xi, 307p.
Second edition. 1949. xii, 332p.
Third edition. 1954. xii, 332p.

2356 **Maddox**, H. 'The work and status of mental nurses.' *Sociol. Rev.*, n.s., II 2 (December 1954), 195–208.

2357 **Abel-Smith**, Brian. *A history of the nursing profession.* London: Heinemann, 1960. xiv, 285p. (Kingswood books on social history.)

2358 **Pavey**, Agnes Elizabeth. *The story of the growth of nursing as an art, a vocation, and a profession.* London: Faber, 1960. xvi, 515p.
Fifth edition.

2359 **Spectator.** 'Nursing organizations. 1. The past.' *Nurs. Times*, LVI, 9 (26 February 1960), 241–2.

2360 **Spectator.** 'Nursing organizations. 2. The future?' *Nurs. Times*, LVI, 10 (4 March 1960), 279–80.

2361 **Royal College of Nursing.** *The Royal College of Nursing: a retrospect.* London: the College, 1961.

2362 **Central Council for District Nursing in London.** *History of the Central Council for District Nursing in London, 1914–1966.* London: the Council, 1966. 15p.

2363 **Lancaster**, Arnold. *A study of professional values and attitudes among registered nurses.* 1966–67. (M.Sc. thesis, University of Edinburgh.)

2364 **Bowman**, Gerald. *The lamp and the book: the story of the RCN, 1916–1966.* London: Queen Anne P., 1967. 206p.
Royal College of Nursing.

iv. *Other*

2365 **Departmental Committee to Consider the Working of the Midwives Act, 1902.** Vol. I. *Report, appendices.* London: H.M.S.O., 1909. iv, 51p. (Cd. 4822.)
Vol. II. *Minutes of evidence, index.* 1909. (Cd. 4823.)
Chairman: A. W. FitzRoy.

2366 **Departmental Committee on Public Veterinary Services.** *Report.* London: H.M.S.O., 1913. 15p. (Cd. 6575.)
Evidence, appendices, index. 1913. (Cd. 6652.)

2367 **Brierly**, Emma. *In the beginning.* London. 34p.
'Reproduced from *Nursing notes*, September, 1924.'
With an appreciation of the author by Lilian A. Maule.
The author was Editor of *Nursing Notes.*
Midwives' Institute.

2368 **Departmental Committee on the Optical Practitioners (Registration) Bill, 1927.** *Report.* London: H.M.S.O., 1927. 27p. (Cmd. 2999.)
Chairman: F. B. Merriman.

2369 **Mental Hospital and Institutional Workers' Union.** *The history of the Mental Hospital and Institutional Workers' Union from infancy to its 21st year.* Manchester: the Union, 1931. 132p.

2370 **Select Committee on Registration and Regulation of Osteopaths Bill.** *Report.* London: H.M.S.O., 1935. xx, 490p. (H.L. 29, 130.)
Chairman: Lord Amulree.

2371 **Clark**, C. A. *The National Association of Clerks to Insurance Committees: its constitution and activities, 1913 to 1945.* London: Society of Clerks of Executive Councils (National Health Service), 1945. 18p.
The author was Secretary of the Association.

2372 **Wicksteed**, Jane Honora. *The growth of a profession, being the history of the Chartered Society of Physiotherapy, 1894–1945*. London: Arnold, 1948. 212p.

2373 **Hospital**. 'The Institute of Hospital Administrators: the first fifty years, 1902–1952.' *Hospital*, XLVIII, 5 (May 1952), 285–321.

2374 **Walker**, Arnold, and others. *Historical review of British obstetrics and gynaecology 1860–1950*. London and Edinburgh: Livingstone, 1954.
p. 334–6. Midwives' Institute.

2375 **Evans**, Sybil M. 'To thy heritage be true.' *Physiotherapy*, XLI, 10 (October 1955), 302–7.
Chartered Society of Physiotherapy.

2376 **Gerard**, A. T. 'The work of the General Optical Council in their first year.' *Optician*, CXXXVIII, 3587 (1 January 1960), 590–3.

2377 **Jepson**, W. J. *Fifty years of progress*. Banstead: Confederation of Health Service Employees, 1960.

2378 **Strachan**, A. E. 'Diamond jubilee of the Ulster Chemists' Association.' *Chem. Drugg*. (23 September 1961), 351–4.

2379 **Walk**, Alexander and **Walker**, D. Lindsay. 'Gloucester and the beginnings of the R.M.P.A.' *J. Ment. Sci*., CVII, 449 (July 1961), 603–32.
Royal Medico-Psychological Association.

2380 **Dagnall**, J. C. 'Fiftieth anniversary of the first British chiropodial society: the National Society of Chiropodists, 1913.' *J. Soc. Chirop*., XVIII, 2 (February 1963), 40–9.

2381 **Dowling**, W. C. *The Ladies Sanitary Association and the origins of the health visiting service*. 1963. (M.A. thesis, University of London.)

2382 **Barnes**, N. H. *An analysis of the nature and function of professions and of the growth and development of professional status among some medical auxiliary groups*. 1963–64. (M.A. thesis, University of Nottingham.)

2383 **Crellin**, John K. 'Early organisation in British hospital pharmacy.' *J. Hosp. Pharm*. (February 1964), 28–9.

2384 **Institute of Hospital Administration**. *Hospitals year book 1965*. London: the Institute, 1964.
p. 507–47. Short histories of all unions in the medical field.

2385 **National Institute of Medical Herbalists Ltd.** *1864–1964: a brief history and outline of the foundation of the National Institute of Medical Herbalists Ltd*. [London?: the Institute, 1964.] 8p.
Members are all practitioners of botanic medicine.

2386 **Society of Hospital Laundry Managers**. *History of the Society of Hospital Laundry Managers*. London: the Society, 1964. 22p.
For members only.

2387 **Macmillan**, Allan. *A profile of the Scottish National Committee of Ophthalmic Opticians*. Edinburgh, 1966. 20p.

2388 **Weller**, M. F. 'Seventy years on: inaugural lecture at the annual conference of the Health Visitors' Association, held in Folkestone in October 1966.' *Int. J. Nurs. Studies*, IV, 3 (August 1967), 233–43.

2389 **Martin**, E. Margaret. *An analysis of the role of the professions supplementary to medicine*. 1967–68. (Ph.D. thesis, University of Nottingham.)

2390 **Bellamy**, Joyce Margaret (comp.). *A hundred years of pharmacy in Hull*. Hull: Hull University Department of Economics and Commerce, 1968. 19p.
Published in commemoration of the Hull Chemists' Association, 1868–1968.

2391 **Adams**, F. R. 'From association to union: professional organization of asylum attendants, 1869–1919.' *Br. J. Sociol*., XX, 1 (March 1969), 11–26.

2392 **Martin**, E. Margaret. *Colleagues or competitors? a study of the role of five of the professions supplementary to medicine*. London: Bell, 1969. 103p. (Occasional papers on social administration 31.)

2393 **Scottish Pharmaceutical Federation**. *Fifty years of the Scottish Pharmaceutical Federation, 1919–1969*. Glasgow: the Federation, 1969. 12p.

2394 **Young**, Patricia. 'A short history of the Chartered Society of Physiotherapy.' *Physiotherapy*, LV, 7 (July 1969), 271–8.

2395 **Young**, Patricia. 'The structure and functions of the Chartered Society of Physiotherapy.' *Physiotherapy*, LV, 7 (July 1969), 281–90.

2396 **Moodie**, Ian. *50 years of history*. London, 1970. 77p.
Society of Radiographers.

h. PROFESSIONAL SCIENTISTS AND ENGINEERS

2397 **Adamson**, James. 'The Institute of Marine Engineers.' *Inst. Mar. Engrs. Trans*., XXVIII (1916–17), 109–14.

2398 **Pilcher**, Richard Bertram. *The profession of chemistry*. London: Constable, 1919. xiv, 199p.
Revised edition. London: Institute of Chemistry, 1927. x, 94p.
Third edition. Institute of Chemistry, 1935. viii, 104p.
Fourth edition. Institute of Chemistry, 1938. xii, 108p.

2399 **Institution of Chemical Engineers**. 'The history of the formation of the Institution of Chemical Engineers.' *Instn. Chem. Engrs. Trans*., I (1923), vii–x.

2400 **Chapman**, Alfred Chaston. *The growth of the profession of chemistry during the past half-century, 1877–1927*. London: Royal Institute of Chemistry, 1927. 23p.

2401 **Institution of Civil Engineers**. *A brief history of the Institution of Civil Engineers, with an account of the charter centenary celebration, June 1928*. London: the Institution, 1928. 95p.

2402 **Dyer**, Bernard. *The Society of Public Analysts and Other Analytical Chemists: some reminiscences of its first fifty years*. Cambridge: Heffer, 1932. viii, 278p.

With *A review of its activities* by C. Ainsworth Mitchell.

2403 **Association of Consulting Engineers**. *History of the formation of the Association of Consulting Engineers Incorporated*. London: the Association, 1936. 7p.

2404 **Dean**, A. C. (ed.). *Some episodes in the Manchester Association of Engineers: a series of extracts from the early minute books of the Association*. Manchester: Manchester Association of Engineers, 1938. 144p.

2405 **Donkin**, Sydney B. 'The Society of Civil Engineers (Smeatonians).' *Newc. Soc. Trans. for 1936–37*, XVII (1938), 51–71.

Founded 1771.

2406 **Appleyard**, Rollo. *The history of the Institution of Electrical Engineers, 1871–1931*. London: Institution of Electrical Engineers, 1939. 342p.

2407 **Association of Supervising Electrical Engineers**. 'Silver jubilee.' *Electl. Superv.* (March 1939), 229–46.

2408 **Hoover**, Theodore Jesse and **Fish**, John Charles Lounsbury. *The engineering profession*. Stanford, Calif.: Stanford U.P.; London: Oxford U.P., 1941. xii, 441p.

2409 **Smith**, Edgar C. 'An early marine engineering institution.' *Engineering*, CLI, 2 (4 April 1941), 275–6.

Institution of Marine Engineers, 1876–79.

2410 **Parsons**, Robert Hodson. *A history of the Institution of Mechanical Engineers, 1847–1947: centenary memorial volume*. London: Institution of Mechanical Engineers, 1947. xi, 299p.

2411 **Pendred**, Loughnan St. Lawrence. *British engineering societies*. London: Longmans, Green, for the British Council, 1947. vii, 38p. (Science in Britain.)

2412 **Howard**, W. R. 'Presidential address, 1954.' *Trans. Soc. Engrs.* (March 1954), 9–26.

Centenary address read before the Society of Engineers (Inc.) on 1 February 1954.

2413 **McFarlane**, B. A. *The chartered engineer: a study of the recruitment, qualification, conditions of employment and professional associations of chartered civil, electrical and mechanical engineers in Great Britain*. 1960. (Ph.D. thesis, University of London.)

2414 **Association of Public Analysts**. *A hundred years of public analysts, 1860–1960*. London: the Association, 1961. 23p.

2415 **Curling**, Bernard Charles. *History of the Institute of Marine Engineers*. London: printed by Eyre and Spottiswoode, 1961. [xii], 242p.

2416 **Braunholtz**, Walter Theodore Karl. *The first hundred years, 1863–1963*. London: Institution of Gas Engineers, 1963. 336p.

2417 **Prandy**, Kenneth. *Professional employees: a study of qualified scientists and engineers*. 1963. (Ph.D. thesis, University of Liverpool.)

2418 **Association of Supervising Electrical Engineers**. 'Golden jubilee.' *Electl. Superv.* (January 1964), 2–3.

2419 **Prandy**, Kenneth. *Professional employees: a study of scientists and engineers*. London: Faber, 1965. 197p. (Society today and tomorrow.)

2420 **Gerstle**, J. E. and **Hutton**, S. P. *Engineers: the anatomy of a profession*. London: Tavistock, 1966. 229p.

2421 **Millard**, Patricia. 'A history of the Society of Environmental Engineers.' *Envir. Engng.*, 23 (November 1966), 17–19.

2422 **Pym**, Denis. 'Technology, effectiveness and predisposition towards work-changes among mechanical engineers.' *J. Mgmt. Studies*, III, 3 (October 1966), 304–11.

2423 **Orr**, J. G. 'A study of engineering responsibility levels in the United Kingdom.' Organization for Economic Co-operation and Development. *Policy Conference on Highly Qualified Manpower, Paris 26th–28th September 1966*. Paris: O.E.C.D., 1967. p. 211–26.

'The object of the study is to establish criteria for the definition of professional engineering work. . .'

2424 **Rolt**, Lionel Thomas Caswall. *The mechanicals: progress of a profession*. London: Heinemann, 1967. xii, 163p.

Published on behalf of the Institution of Mechanical Engineers.

2425 **Box**, G. A. *Student chemists and professional values*. 1967–68. (Ph.D. thesis, University of London.)

2426 **Moon**, J. A. *The ethical attitudes of chartered mechanical engineers and their relationship to formal education*. 1967–68. (M.Litt. thesis, University of Lancaster.)

2427 **King**, Michael D. 'Science and the professional dilemma.' Gould, J. (ed.). *Penguin social sciences survey 1968*. Harmondsworth: Penguin, 1968. p. 34–73.

2428 **Caplen**, Rowland. 'A short history of the Institution of Engineering Inspection.' *Qual. Engr.* XXXIII, 2 (March–April 1969), 5–20.

2429 **Morton**, R. A. *The Biochemical Society: its history and activities, 1911–1969*. London: Biochemical Society, 1969. 160p.

2430 **Cohen**, L. and **Derrick**, T. 'Occupational values and stereotypes in a group of engineers.' *Br. J. Ind. Relat.*, VIII, 1 (March 1970), 100–4.

'Research note.'

2431 **Holt**, B. W. G. 'Social aspects in the emergence of chemistry as an exact science: the British chemical profession.' *Br. J. Sociol.*, XXI, 2 (June 1970), 181–99.
'Revision of a chapter in a Ph.D. thesis, *The Chemical Profession in Great Britain: a study of recruitment, training, careers and organisation*, London.'

i. SOCIAL WORKERS

2432 **C.**, O. 'The Federation of Professional Social Workers.' *Char. Orgn. Rev.*, n.s., XLVIII, 286 (October 1920), 98–100.

2433 **Institute of Medical Social Workers**. *Almoner*, VI, 8 (November 1953), 343–81.
Golden jubilee number.

2434 **Bell**, Enid Hester Chataway Moberly. *The story of hospital almoners: the birth of a profession*. London: Faber, 1961. 160p.

2435 **Bochel**, Dorothy. 'A brief history of N.A.P.O.' *Probation*, X, 3 (September 1962), 33–6; 4 (December 1962), 53–5.
National Association of Probation Officers.

2436 **Dawtry**, F. *Souvenir programme for jubilee conference*. London: National Association of Probation Officers, 1962.

2437 **Parr**, Thomas John. *The role and professional identity of youth leaders in statutory and voluntary organisations*. 1969. (M.Ed. thesis, University of Manchester.)

j. OTHER

2438 **Tarn**, Arthur Wyndham. *The educational work of the Institute of Actuaries*. Berlin: Mittler and Sohn, 1906.
From the Proceedings of the fifth International Congress of Actuaries.

2439 **Rogers**, Julian C. 'The Surveyors' Institution: a forty years' retrospect.' *Survey. Instn. Trans.*, XLII (1909–10), 303–62.

2440 **Oakley**, *Sir* John Hubert. 'The fifty years' history and work of the Institution.' *Survey. Instn. Trans.*, LI (1918–19), 1–38.
Presidential address, Surveyors' Institution, 11 November 1918.

2441 **Higham**, Charles Daniel. *Notes as to The Actuaries' Club, The Institute of Actuaries, The Institute of Actuaries' Club and The Life Offices' Association, especially with regard to their early history*. London: privately printed, 1929. 20p.
Signed C. D. H.

2442 **Newbolt**, F. *History of the Royal Society of Painter-Etchers and Engravers, 1880–1930*. 1930. (Publications 9.)

2443 **Chartered Surveyors' Institution**. *The chartered surveyor, his training and his work*. London: the Institution, 1932. 27p.

2444 **Select Committee on Auctioneers', House Agents' and Valuers' Licences**. *Report*. London: H.M.S.O., 1935. x, 100p. (H.L. 97, 134.)
Chairman: Lord Mersey.

2445 **Byng**, E. S. 'Administration – a profession.' *Hum. Factor*, X, 11 (November 1936), 381–92.
'Part of a paper read before Section F (Economic Science and Statistics) of the British Association Meeting at Blackpool, September 1936.'

2446 **Crew**, Albert. *The profession of a secretary: secretarial problems, the charter and bye-laws of the CIS*. Cambridge: Heffer, 1942. x, 85p.
Chartered Institute of Secretaries.

2447 **Pear**, Tom Hatherley. 'The social status of the psychologist and its effect upon his work.' *Sociol. Rev.*, XXXIV, 1–2 (January–April 1942), 68–81.

2448 **Royal Institution of Chartered Surveyors**. 'The Royal Institution of Chartered Surveyors.' *R. Instn. Chart. Survey. J.*, XXVI, 1 (July 1946), 3–10.

2449 **Killick**, Alexander H. 'The Institution – quo vadit?' *R. Instn. Chart. Survey. Trans.*, LXXIX, 1 (1946–7), 18–36.

2450 **Simmonds**, Reginald Claud. *The Institute of Actuaries, 1848–1948: an account of the Institute of Actuaries during its first one hundred years*. Cambridge: Cambridge U.P., 1948. xi, 318p.

2451 **Clapham**, Anthony. 'A short history of the surveyor's profession.' *R. Instn. Chart. Survey. Trans.*, LXXXII, 1 (1949–50), 16–54.

2452 **Watson**, John A. F. 'The spirit of a profession.' *R. Instn. Chart. Survey. Trans.*, LXXXII, 1 (1949–50), 3–15.
Presidential address.

2453 **Committee on the Qualifications of Planners**. *Report*. London: H.M.S.O., 1950. vi, 85p. (Cmd. 8059.)
Chairman: Sir George Schuster.

2454 **Elias**, Norbert. 'Studies in the genesis of the naval profession. I.' *Br. J. Sociol.*, I, 4 (December 1950), 291–309.
'This is the first of three studies in the origins and the early development of the career of naval officers in England.'

2455 **Chartered Institute of Secretaries**. *The Chartered Institute of Secretaries 1891–1951: a review of sixty years*. London: the Institute, 1951. x, 206p.

2456 **Chapman**, F. T. 'The implications of membership of a professional body: education.' *Br. Mgmt. Rev.*, XII, 3 (April 1954), 151–60.
With special reference to the Institute of Industrial Administration.

2457 **Meigh**, Edward. 'The implications of membership of a professional body.' *Br. Mgmt. Rev.*, XII, 3 (April 1954), 126–40.
With special reference to the Institute of Industrial Administration.

2458 **Roberts**, Arthur. 'The implications of membership of a professional body: sociological and industrial.' *Br. Mgmt. Rev.*, XII, 3 (April 1954), 141–50.
With special reference to the Institute of Industrial Administration.

2459 **Rose**, Thomas Gerald. *A history of the Institute of Industrial Administration, 1919–1951.* London: the Institute, 1954. ix, 204p.
In 1951 the Institute merged with the British Institute of Management.

2460 **Tyrell-Evans**, H. G. *The Quantity Surveyors' Committee, 1904–1954.* [1954?]

2461 **Bird**, William Henry. *A history of the Institute of Brewing.* London: Institute of Brewing, 1955. ix, 139p.

2462 **Davidson**, Andrew Rutherford. *The history of the Faculty of Actuaries in Scotland, 1856–1956.* Edinburgh, 1956. xviii, 272p.

2463 **Urwick**, Lyndall Fownes. *Is management a profession?* London: Urwick, Orr, 1958. 27p.

2464 **Lumby**, Agatha. 'IMA 1938–1959.' *I.M.A. Journal* (June 1959), 148–50.
Institutional Management Association.
Reprinted in *I.M.A. Journal*, XIV, 5 (May 1963), 149–51.

2465 **Turpin**, W. H. 'How the IMA was founded.' *I.M.A. Journal* (June 1959), 151–2.
Institutional Management Association.

2466 **Menzler**, Frederick August Andrew. *The first fifty years, 1910–1960.* London, 1960. 166p.
Institute of Actuaries Students' Society.

2467 **Woolgar**, M. J. *The development of the Anglican and Roman Catholic clergy as a profession since the middle of the eighteenth century.* 1960–61. (Ph.D. thesis, University of Leicester.)

2468 **Steinberg**, Hannah (ed.). *The British Psychological Society, 1901–1961.* London, 1961. 63p.

2469 **Prescott**, R. B. *An examination of some trends towards making business administration in manufacturing industry a profession.* 1961–62. (M.A. (Econ.) thesis, University of Sheffield.)

2470 **Phillips**, C. J. 'The time has come, the Walrus said, to talk of many things . . .' *Chart. Survey.*, Scottish Supplement (July 1962), iii.
History of quantity surveyors in Scotland.

2471 **Razzell**, P. E. 'Social origins of officers in the Indian and British home army.' *Br. J. Sociol.*, XIV, 3 (September 1963), 248–60.

2472 **Bonham-Carter**, Victor. *80 years ago: the Society of Authors, 1884–1964.* London: the Society, 1964. 12p.

2473 **Engineer Surveyors' Association.** *Jubilee 1914–1964.* Manchester: the Association, 1964.

2474 **The Times**. *Supplement on the actuary's profession, to mark the occasion of the Seventeenth International Congress of Actuaries meeting in London and Edinburgh.* June 1964.

2475 **Thompson**, Francis Michael Longstreth. *Chartered surveyors: the growth of a profession.* London: Routledge and Kegan Paul, 1968. xvi, 400p.

2476 **Hudson**, Derek. *Professionalism among art specialists.* Leicester: School of Education, Leicester University, 1968–9. [67]p.

2477 **Turnbull**, Audrey. 'Teachers and teaching: the Institute of Choreology.' *Dance & Dancers*, XX, 10 (October 1969), 52, 54; XX, 11 (November 1969), 52–6.

2478 **Chapman**, D. H. *The Chartered Auctioneers' and Estate Agents' Institute: a short history.* London: the Institute, 1970. viii, 103p.

2479 **Coats**, A. W. and **Coats**, S. E. 'The social composition of the Royal Economic Society and the beginnings of the British economics "profession", 1890–1915.' *Br. J. Sociol.*, XXI, 1 (March 1970), 75–85.

10. Miscellaneous Services

a. DOMESTIC SERVICE

2480 **Papworth**, Lucy Wyatt. 'The Association of Trained Charwomen.' *Char. Orgn. Rev.*, n.s., XIV, 81 (September 1903), 156–8.
Describes aims and work of the Association.

2481 **Ministry of Labour Gazette**. 'The National Institute of Houseworkers.' *Minist. Labour Gaz.*, LIV, 10 (October 1951), 387–9.

b. ENTERTAINMENT

2482 **Chadfield**, Edward. *National musical associations: their duties to music, to musicians and to the people. An address delivered at the meeting of the Music Teachers' National Association of America, held in Philadelphia, July, 1889.* Derby: Incorporated Society of Musicians, 1890. 15p.

2483 **Williams**, J. B. 'Playing to live.' *Labour Mag.*, I, 7 (November 1922), 315–17.
Musicians' Union.
The author was General Secretary of the Union.

2484 **Teale**, E. S. 'The story of the Amalgamated Musicians' Union. *Musicians' J.* (April 1929); (July 1929); (October 1929); (January 1930).

2485 **Scholes**, Percy Alfred. 'The Musicians' Company: a curious question.' *Mon. Music. Rec.*, LXII, 741 (November 1932), 195–6.

2486 **Wall**, A. M. 'Trade unionism on the stage: the rise of British Equity.' *Labour Mag.*, XI, 5 (September 1932), 213–15.

2487 **Knott**, Thomas. 'The Royal Society of Musicians.' *Music. Times*, LXXIX, 1143 (May 1938), 342–3.

2488 **Scholes**, Percy Alfred. 'The Musicians' Company: a curious question.' *Mon. Music. Rec.*, LXXI, 828 (July–August 1941), 128–31.
Date of the seventeenth-century charter.

2489 **Elvin**, George H. 'Trade unionism in the British film industry.' *The Penguin film review, 3.* London, New York: Penguin Books, 1947. p. 42–8.

2490 **Association of Broadcasting Staff.** *BBC Staff Ass. Bull.*, 23 (May 1950).
Tenth anniversary number.

2491 **Imperial Society of Teachers of Dancing Incorporated.** *The Imperial Society.* London: the Society, 1960. 32p.

2492 **Gray**, Dulcie and **Denison**, Michael. 'Equity.' *The actor and his world.* London: Gollancz, 1964. Chap. VI.

2493 **Budd**, Sidney. 'How we laid the foundations.' *ABS Bull.*, 139 (May 1965), 104–5.
Association of Broadcasting Staff.

2494 **Bush**, Alan and **Bush**, Nancy. '21 years of the Composers' Guild.' *Composer*, 16 (July 1965), 22–3.

2495 **Fletcher**, H. L. 'The beginnings of staff representation in the BBC.' *ABS Bull.*, 139 (May 1965), 101–3.

2496 **Incorporated Society of Musicians.** *Introduction to the Incorporated Society of Musicians.* London: the Society, 1956. 20p.

See also: 13,200–1; 13,203.

11. Public Administration

See also Part Three, III, E, 2; Part Three, III, E, 3, c; Part Three, III, E, 5; Part Three, III, E, 6; and Part Three, III, E, 9.

a. GENERAL

2497 **National Association of Local Government Officers.** *The constitution, objects and influence of the National Association of Local Government Officers.* London, 1914. 12p.

2498 **Hill**, Levi Clement. *The fight for superannuation.* London: National Association of Local Government Officers, 1938. 39p. (NALGO histories [1].)
A record of the work of NALGO.

2499 **Hill**, Levi Clement. *Compensation on abolition of office.* London: National Association of Local Government Officers, [1939]. 62p. (NALGO histories 2.)

2500 **National Union of Public Employees.** *Souvenir, 1934–1939, Union's five year expansion plan.* Brighton, 1939.

2501 **Hill**, Levi Clement. *The recruitment, training and education of local government officers.* London: National Association of Local Government Officers, [1940]. 56p. (NALGO histories 3.)

2502 **Roberts**, Bryn. *The battle for Britain's county workers.* London: National Union of Public Employees, 1941. 44p.

2503 **National and Local Government Officers' Association.** *Publ. Service* (October 1955). 30p.
Golden jubilee issue.

2504 **Indian Institute of Public Administration.** *Staff councils and associations in the U.K. and India.* New Delhi: the Institute, 1960. vi, 53p.

2505 **British Council Staff Association.** 'How it all began.' *News Br. Coun. Staff Ass.*, 1 (October 1962), 4; 2 (April 1963), 4; 3 (October 1963), 4; 4 (April 1964), 4; 5 (October 1964), 4; 6 (April 1965), 4; 7 (October 1965), 4; 8 (April 1966), 4.

2506 **Volker**, D. 'NALGO'S affiliation to the T.U.C.' *Br. J. Ind. Relat.*, IV, 1 (March 1966), 59–76.

2507 **Spoor**, Alec. *White-collar union: sixty years of Nalgo.* London: Heinemann, 1967. xi, 625p.

b. NATIONAL GOVERNMENT

Works relating to the National Association of Local Government Officers and the National Union of Public Employees are classified at Part Three, III, E, 11, a.

2508 **Kidd**, Benjamin. 'The civil service as a profession.' *Nineteenth Century*, XX, 116 (October 1886), 491–502.

2509 **Brown**, William John. *The Civil Service Clerical Association: its history, its achievements and its plans for the future.* [London: the Union, 1925.] 128p.

2510 **Bowen**, J. W. 'Trade unionism in the civil service.' *Publ. Adm.*, XV, 4 (October 1937), 419–32.
'Lecture delivered to the Institute of Public Administration, London, March, 1937.'

2511 **Brown**, William John. 'Civil service trade unionism.' Cole, G. D. H. *British trade unionism today: a survey* ... London: Methuen, 1945. p. 483–90.
Earlier edition. 1939.

2512 **Bentley**, R. 'The civil service staff movement. V. The Association of H.M. Inspectors of Taxes (A.I.T.).' *Whit. Bull.*, XXVII, 11 (November 1947), 172–3.

2513 **Carvell**, G. V. 'The civil service staff movement. I. The Civil Service Union.' *Whit. Bull.*, XXVII, 6 (June 1947), 84–5.

2514 **Herbert**, L. A. C. 'The civil service staff movement. VI. The Institution of Professional Civil Servants.' *Whit. Bull.*, XXVII, 12 (December 1947), 188–9.

2515 **Broom**, A. J. 'The civil service staff movement. VIII. The Society of Civil Servants.' *Whit. Bull.*, XXVIII, 2 (February 1948), 20–2.

2516 **Brown**, A. J. 'The civil service staff movement. XIII. Inland Revenue Staff Federation.' *Whit. Bull.*, XXVIII, 7 (July 1948), 102–4.

2517 **Buck**, E. E. 'Civil service staff movement. X. Customs and Excise Group of Departmental Associations.' *Whit. Bull.*, XXVIII, 4 (April 1948), 54–6.

2518 **Crook**, *Lord*. 'The civil service staff movement. XIV. Ministry of Labour Staff Association.' *Whit. Bull.*, XXVIII, 8 (August 1948), 116–17.

2519 **Ladd**, F. C. 'The civil service staff movement. VII. The Federation of Civil Service Professional and Technical Staffs.' *Whit. Bull.*, XXVIII, 1 (January 1948), 4–5.

2520 **Palmer**, George G. 'The civil service staff movement. IX. The Association of Officers of the Ministry of Labour.' *Whit. Bull.*, XXVIII, 3 (March 1948), 36–7.

2521 **White**, L. C. 'Civil service staff movement. XI. The Civil Service Alliance.' *Whit. Bull.*, XXVIII, 5 (May 1948), 68–70.

2522 **White**, L. C. 'The civil service staff movement. XII. The Civil Service Clerical Association.' *Whit. Bull.*, XXVIII, 6 (June 1948), 84–7.

2523 **Turner-Samuels**, Moss. 'The civil service.' *British trade unions*. London: Sampson Low, Marston, 1949. p. 167–77.

2524 **Le Fevre**, R. H. 'Diamond jubilee.' *Taxes*, XXXV, 5 (May 1952), 211–13.
Account of the Inland Revenue Staff Federation.

2525 **Beard**, Arthur. 'The birth of a Section.' *Red Tape*, XLII, 501 (August 1953), 385–7, 400; 502 (September 1953), 415–16.
History of the Admiralty Section of the Civil Service Clerical Association.
Reprinted from *Admiralty Section News*.

2526 **Newman**, Bernard. *Yours for action*. London: Jenkins, 1953. viii, 196p.
A work to commemorate the fiftieth anniversary of the Civil Service Clerical Association and its activities.

2527 **Humphreys**, Betty Vance. *The development of clerical trade unions in the British civil service*. 1954. (Ph.D. thesis, University of London.)

2528 **Cagan**, Leo D. *Civil service unions: a comparative study of American and British experience until 1951*. 1957. 256 leaves. (Ph.D. thesis, University of Chicago.)

2529 **Society of Technical Civil Servants.** *Right Angle* (April 1957).
Golden jubilee issue.

2530 **Humphreys**, Betty Vance. *Clerical unions in the civil service*. Oxford: Blackwell and Mott, 1958. xv, 254p.

2531 **Haswell**, Wilfred J. 'The Federation.' *J. H.M. Cust. Exc.* (August 1959), 108–9; (September 1959), 120–1; (October 1959), 132–3; (November 1959), 163–4, 168–9; (December 1959), 195–7; (January 1960), 231–3.

2532 **Brown**, A. J. 'Forty years hard.' *Taxes*, XLV, 9 (September 1962), 423–6.
By the editor of *Taxes*, 1922–62.
Journal of the Inland Revenue Staff Federation.

2533 **Houghton**, Douglas. 'Dear Mr. Editor.' *Taxes*, XLV, 9 (September 1962), 429–32.
An account of *Taxes*, the journal of the Inland Revenue Staff Federation, and the work of its editor, A. J. Brown, over forty years.

2534 **Ministry of Labour Staff Association.** *Civ. Serv. Argus*, XXXVIII, 5 (May 1962).
Golden jubilee issue.

2535 **Taxes.** '1892–1962: a short history of the IRSF.' *Taxes*, XLV, 9 (September 1962), 427–8.

2536 **Taxes.** 'The first ten years: *Tax Clerks' Journal* into *Taxes*.' *Taxes*, XLV, 9 (September 1962), 419–22.
Sums up the first decade of the journal, 1912–22.

2537 **Haswell**, Wilfred J. 'The civil service staff movement. IV. The Customs and Excise Group of Departmental Associations.' *Whit. Bull.*, XLIII, 7 (July 1963), 101–2.

2538 **Hewlett**, Edward. 'The Institution.' *St. Ser.*, XLIII, 2 (February 1963), 40–5, 56–7.
History of the Institution of Professional Civil Servants. Based on a lecture given at the 13th Herbert Memorial School, October 1962.

2539 **Morawetz**, L. 'The civil service staff movement. II. The Association of H.M. Inspectors of Taxes (A.I.T.).' *Whit. Bull.*, XLIII, 5 (May 1963), 74–5.

2540 **Tindall**, John L. 'The civil service staff movement. VIII. The Ministry of Labour Staff Association.' *Whit. Bull.*, XLIII, 11 (December 1963), 172–3.
Reprinted in *Civil Service Argus*, XL, 2 (February 1964), 23–4.

2541 **Vickers**, J. O. N. 'The civil service staff movement. V. Civil Service Union.' *Whit. Bull.*, XLIII, 8 (August 1963), 126.

2542 **Williams**, Leslie. 'The civil service staff movement. VII. The Society of Civil Servants.' *Whit. Bull.*, XLIII, 10 (November 1963), 152–4.

2543 **Wines**, L. A. 'The civil service staff movement. VI. Civil Service Clerical Association.' *Whit. Bull.*, XLIII, 9 (September–October 1963), 138–9.

2544 **Brown**, A. J. 'The civil service staff movement. XIII. Inland Revenue Staff Federation.' *Whit. Bull.*, XLIV, 5 (May 1964), 75–7.

2545 **Cooper**, Cyril. 'The civil service staff movement. IX. The Federation of Civil Service Professional and Technical Staffs.' *Whit. Bull.*, XLIV, 1 (January 1964), 8–9.

2546 **Kear**, G. F. 'The civil service staff movement. XV. Association of First Division Civil Servants.' *Whit. Bull.*, XLIV, 7 (July 1964), 111–13.

2547 **Walker**, G. A. 'The civil service staff movement. X. The Institution of Professional Civil Servants.' *Whit. Bull.*, XLIV, 2 (February 1964), 24–5.

2548 **Walsh**, N. 'The civil service staff movement. XIV. County Court Officers' Association.' *Whit. Bull.*, XLIV, 6 (June 1964), 94–5.
Reprinted in *County Court Officer* (23 October 1964), 344–5.

2549 **Armstrong**, *Sir* William. 'Whitleyism in the civil service.' *Whit. Bull.*, XLIX, 9 (September–October 1969), 136–9; 10 (November 1969), 151–5.
A lecture given on 3 July 1969 to commemorate fifty years of Whitleyism.

2550 **Canning**, N. J. H. 'The Customs & Excise Launch Service Association.' *Portcullis* (April 1969), 5.

2551 **Houghton**, Douglas. 'Whitley jubilee: the first 20 years, 1920–1940.' *Whit. Bull.*, XLIX, 6 (June 1969), 84–9.
Written for the golden jubilee year of civil service Whitleyism.

2552 **Jones**, T. R. 'The war years and after.' *Whit. Bull.*, XLIX, 7 (July 1969), 100–6.
Account of Whitleyism in the civil service written for the golden jubilee year.

2553 **Stack**, Frieda. 'Civil service associations and the Whitley Report of 1917.' *Polit. Q.*, XL, 3 (July–September 1969), 283–95.

2554 **Armstrong**, *Sir* William. *Professionals and professionalism in the civil service: an address prepared for the Oration at the London School of Economics and Political Science, 4 December, 1969.* London: London School of Economics and Political Science, 1970. 19p.

See also: 13,245

c. LOCAL GOVERNMENT

Works relating to the National Association of Local Government Officers and the National Union of Public Employees are classified at Part Three, III, E, 11, a.

2555 **Alexander**, Hugh. *The Association of Public Sanitary Inspectors: inaugural address.* London, 1887. 25p.

2556 **Alexander**, Hugh. *The status of sanitary inspectors: an address.* London: the Association of Public Sanitary Inspectors of Great Britain, 1889.

2557 **Lovegrove**, Henry. *Some account of the District Surveyors' Association of London.* Beckenham: T. W. Thornton, 1906. 24p.

2558 **Martyn**, Edith How. *Administrative and clerical staffs in the local government service of England and Wales.* 1922. i, 85 leaves. (M.Sc. (Econ.) thesis, University of London.)

2559 **Bent**, Frederick Timothy. *British municipal trade unions: policies, practices, relation to Whitleyism and influence on local government.* 1954. 465p. (Ph.D. thesis, University of Chicago.)

2560 **Barton**. Terence Charles. *A history of the Manchester Municipal Officers' Guild (branch of the National and Local Government Officers' Association), 1906–1956.* Manchester: Manchester Municipal Officers' Guild, 1956. vii, 61p.

2561 **Smith**, H. R. H. 'Our Society.' *Soc. Clerks Urb. Distr. Coun. Off. J.* (May 1956), 66–8.
Society of Clerks of Urban District Councils. The journal is confidential to members.

2562 **London County Council Staff Association**. *Progress report, 1909–1959: the first fifty years in the history of the London County Council Staff Association.* London: the Association, 1959. 128p.
By C. D. Andrews and G. C. Burger.

2563 **Curry**, Tom H. 'A brief history of the U.P.O.A.' *Publ. Offr.*, I, 2 (Spring 1960), 3–5.
Ulster Public Officers' Association.

2564 **Institute of Municipal Treasurers and Accountants.** *The Institute of Municipal Treasurers and Accountants: a short history, 1885–1960.* London: the Institute, 1960. vii, 166p.
By T. L. Poynton.

2565 **Stephens**, *Sir* Leon Edgar (comp.). *The clerks of the counties, 1360–1960.* Warwick: Society of Clerks of the Peace of Counties and of Clerks of County Councils, 1961. xvi, 274p.

2566 **City of Birmingham Municipal Officers' Guild.** *Golden jubilee, 1914–1964.* Birmingham: the Guild, 1964.

2567 **Association of Registrars of Scotland.** *One hundred and first annual report and financial statement including souvenir programme of events to mark the centenary (1865–1965) of the Association.* Edinburgh: the Association, 1965.

2568 **Mann**, L. R. M. 'Reflections on reaching our majority.' *ALGES Bull.*, V, 7 (February 1968), 1.
Association of Local Government Engineers and Surveyors.

d. POLICE, PRISON OFFICERS, AND FIREMEN

2569 **Prison Officers' Association.** *A short history of the Association and a copy of the rules and constitution.* London: the Association, 1948.
Revised edition. 1959.

2570 **Turner-Samuels**, Moss. 'The police.' *British trade unions.* London: Sampson Low, Marston, 1949. p. 178–85.

2571 **Radford**, Frederick Henry. *'Fetch the engine . . .': the official history of the Fire Brigades' Union.* London: the Union, 1951. 192p.

2572 **Home Office**. *Police representative organisations and negotiating machinery: report of the Committee of the Police Council.* London: H.M.S.O., 1952. 36p.
Chairman: S. J. Baker.

2573 **Scottish Home Department**. *Police representative organisations and negotiating machinery: report of the Scottish Police Council Committee.* Edinburgh: H.M.S.O., 1952. 26p.
Chairman: F. O. Stewart.

2574 **Allen**, Victor L. 'The National Union of Police and Prison Officers.' *Econ. Hist. Rev.*, 2nd ser., XI, 1 (August 1958), 133–43.

2575 **Judge**, Anthony. *The first fifty years: the story of the Police Federation.* London: Police Federation, 1968. 140p.

F. STUDIES OF PARTICULAR GROUPS

1. Immigrants

See also Part Six, II, E, 2.

2576 **Radin**, Beryl. 'Coloured workers and British trade unions.' *Race*, VIII, 2 (October 1966), 157–73.

2577 **John**, DeWitt. *Indian workers' associations in Britain.* London: Oxford U.P. for Institute of Race Relations, 1969. xi, 194p. (Survey of race relations in Britain.)

2578 **Allen**, Sheila and **Bornat**, Joanna. *Unions and immigrant workers: how they seem to each other.* London: Runnymede Industrial Unit, 1970. 5p. (Industrial education series A1.)
Edited and summarised for Runnymede Industrial Unit by Robert Whymant.

2579 **Harrison**, Robert M. *Union policy and workplace practice: a black worker alleges discrimination.* London: Runnymede Industrial Unit, 1970. 8p. (Industrial education series A3.)

2. Jews

See also Part Six, II, E, 2.

2580 **Elman**, Peter. 'The beginnings of the Jewish trade union movement in England.' *Jew. Hist. Soc. Engl. Trans.*, XVII (1951–52), 53–62.

2581 **Hebrew University of Jerusalem.** [Project on the Jewish labour movement: labour unions in England, 1886–90.] 1967. 84p.
Contains facsimile reprints of the rules of five London unions.

See also: 1843; 10,085.

3. Women

See also Part Six, II, C, 4; Part Six, III, F; and Part Six, IV, A, 4, b.

2582 **Black**, Clementina. 'The organisation of working women.' *Fortn. Rev.*, n.s., XLVI, 275 (November 1889), 695–704.

2583 **Dilke**, *Lady* Emilia Frances Strong. 'Benefit societies and trades unions for women.' *Fortn. Rev.*, n.s., XLV, 270 (June 1889), 852–6.

2584 **Dilke**, *Lady* Emilia Frances Strong. 'The seamy side of trades unionism for women.' *New Rev.*, II, 12 (May 1890), 418–22.

2585 **Dilke**, *Lady* Emilia Frances Strong. 'Trades unionism for women.' *New Rev.*, II, 8 (January 1890), 43–53.

2586 **Abraham**, H. 'Trade unionism among women in Ireland.' *Dublin Rev.*, CIX (July 1891), 41–8.

2587 **Dilke**, *Lady* Emilia Frances Strong and **Routledge**, Florence. 'Trades unionism among women.' *Fortn. Rev.*, n.s., XLIX, 293 (May 1891), 741–50.

2588 **Dilke**, *Lady* Emilia Frances Strong. 'Trades-unions for women.' *N. Am. Rev.*, CLIII, 2 (August 1891), 227–39.

2589 **Morgan-Browne**, H. 'A new union for women.' *Westm. Rev.*, CXXXVIII, 5 (November 1892), 528–35.

2590 **Talbot**, M. S. *A plea for women's trade unions.* Clifton, 1892. 12p.

2591 **Holyoake**, Emilie A. 'The capacity of women for industrial union.' *Westm. Rev.*, CXXXIX, 2 (February 1893), 164–8.

2592 **March-Phillipps**, Evelyn. 'The progress of women's trades unions.' *Fortn. Rev.*, n.s., LIV, 319 (July 1893), 92–104.

2593 **Pattison**, Emilia Frances Strong. *Benefit societies and trades unions for women.* London: Chapman and Hall, 1893. 7p.
Reprinted from *Fortnightly Review.*

2594 **Pattison**, Emilia Frances Strong and **Routledge**, Florence. *Trades unionism among women.* London: Women's Trades Union League, 1893. 12p.
Reprinted from *Fortnightly Review.*
I. By Lady Dilke.
II. By Florence Routledge.

2595 **Holyoake**, Emilie A. *Capacity of women for trade organisation.* London: Women's Trade Union League Office, 1894. 7p.
From the *Westminster Review.*

2596 **Holyoake**, Emilie A. 'The need of organisation among women.' Galton, F. W. (ed.). *Workers on their industries.* London: Sonnenschein, 1895 [i.e. 1894]. p. 201–11.
The author was Secretary of the Women's Trade Union League.

2597 **Brodie**, *Mrs.* Marland. 'Women's trades unions in Great Britain and Ireland.' International Congress of Women, London, 1899. *Transactions. Vol. VI. Women in industrial life.* London: T. Fisher Unwin, 1900. p. 178–86.
Discussion, p. 186–8.

2598 **Association of Trade Union Officials.** *Women as trade unionists.* London, [1902?]. 15p. ([Pamphlet] 3.)

2599 **National Council of Women of Great Britain.** *What is the National Union of Women Workers?* London, 1906. [4]p.

2600 **Macarthur**, Mary R. 'Trade unions.' *Women in industry from seven points of view.* London: Duckworth, 1908. p. 61–83.
Title in Contents: 'Trade unionism.'

2601 **Macarthur**, Mary R. 'The women trade-unionists' point of view.' Phillips, M. (ed.). *Women and the Labour Party, by various women writers.* London: Headley Bros., 1919. p. 18–28.

2602 **Drake**, Barbara. *Women in trade unions.* London: Labour Research Department; Allen and Unwin, 1921. 244p. (Trade union series 6.)

2603 **Bennett**, Louie. 'With Irish women workers.' *Irish Econ.*, VII, 4 (August 1922), 294–301.

2604 **Hamilton**, Mary Agnes. *Women at work: a brief introduction to trade unionism for women.* London: Routledge, 1941. ix, 188p.

2605 **Boone**, Gladys. *The women's trade union leagues in Great Britain and the United States of America.* New York: Columbia U.P.; London: P. S. King and Son, 1942. 283p. (Columbia University studies in history, economics and public law 489.)
A thesis.

2606 **Drake**, Barbara. 'Women in trade unions.' Cole, G. D. H. *British trade unionism today: a survey*... London: Methuen, 1945. p. 249–61.
Earlier edition. 1939.

2607 **National Council of Women of Great Britain.** *Women in council: the jubilee book of the National Council of Women of Great Britain.* London: Oxford U.P., 1945. viii, 115p.
Edited by H. Pearl Adam.
Central Conference of Women Workers, 1892–93.
Central Conference Council of the National Union of Women Workers, 1894.
National Union of Women Workers of Great Britain and Ireland, 1895–1918.
National Council of Women of Great Britain and Ireland, 1918–24.
National Council of Women of Great Britain, 1924– .

2608 **Turner-Samuels**, Moss. 'Women in trade unions.' *British trade unions.* London: Sampson Low, Marston, 1949. p. 186–96.

2609 **Trades Union Congress.** *Women in the trade union movement.* London: T.U.C., 1955. 99p.

2610 **Potter**, Allen. 'The Equal Pay Campaign Committee: a case-study of a pressure group.' *Polit. Studies*, V, 1 (February 1957), 49–64.

2611 **Neale**, R. S. 'Working-class women and women's suffrage.' *Labour Hist.*, 12 (May 1967), 16–34.

2612 **Frow**, Edmund and **Frow**, Ruth. 'Women in the early radical and labour movement.' *Marxism Today*, XII, 4 (April 1968), 105–12.
'Written as a tribute to the work of Marian Ramelson.'

2613 **Blackman**, Janet. 'The campaign for women's rights, 1968.' *Trade Un. Regist.* (1969), 60–7.

See also: 77.

4. The Unemployed

See also Part Three, III, B, 4; Part Six, II, D; Part Six, IV, A, 4, d; and Part Seven, IX, B, 1.

2614 **Hannington**, Walter. *The insurgents in London, being a history of the great national hunger march to London, which commenced on October 17th, 1922, and continued until the end of February, 1923.* National Unemployed Workers' Committee Movement, 1923. 32p.

2615 **Hannington**, Walter. *The march of the miners: how we smashed the opposition.* National Unemployed Workers' Committee Movement, 1928. 33p.

2616 **Hannington**, Walter. *Our march against the starvation government: an account of the Scottish unemployed march to Edinburgh, September, 1928.* National Unemployed Workers' Committee Movement, 1928. 19p.

2617 **Hannington**, Walter. *The story of the national hunger march to London, January 22–March 4, 1929.* National Unemployed Workers' Committee Movement, 1929. 71p.

2618 **Hannington**, Walter. *Achievements of the hunger march of 1930 against the Labour government.* National Unemployed Workers' Committee Movement, 1930. 15p.

2619 **Hannington**, Walter. *Unemployed struggles, 1919–1936: my life and struggles amongst the unemployed.* London: Lawrence and Wishart, 1936. xii, 328p.

2620 **Hannington**, Walter. *A short history of the unemployed.* London: Gollancz, 1938. 94p. (New people's library 15.)
Also Left Book Club edition.

2621 **Hannington**, Walter. *Black coffins and the unemployed.* London: *Fact*, 1939. 96p. (Fact: a monograph a month 26.)

2622 **Hannington**, Walter. *Fascist danger and the unemployed.* London: Speedee Press Services, 1939. 16p.

2623 **Hannington**, Walter. 'The unemployed.' Cole, G. D. H. *British trade unionism today: a survey*... London: Methuen, 1945. p. 153–62.
Earlier edition. 1939.

2624 **Irvine**, R. J. *Unemployed labour as a pressure group in Great Britain, 1919–1939.* 1951. (B.Litt. thesis, University of Oxford.)

2625 **Hannington**, Walter. *Never on our knees.* London: Lawrence and Wishart, 1967. 367p.

See also: 3172.

5. Other

2626 **Wray**, J. V. C. 'Trade unions and young workers in Great Britain.' *Int. Labour Rev.*, LXXV, 4 (April 1957), 304–18.

2627 **Rhodes**, Frank Arthur. *The National Union of Students, 1922–1967.* 1968. 434p. (M.Ed. thesis, University of Manchester.)

2628 **Tarbuck**, Ken. 'Students and trade unions.' *Trade Un. Regist.* (1969), 101–5.

G. GROWTH, STRUCTURE, GOVERNMENT, AND ADMINISTRATION

See also Part Seven, VII, B, 3.

1. General

Material on the powers of professional bodies to discipline their members is classified at Part Three, III, E, 9. See also Part Three, III, A.

2629 **Webb**, Sidney and **Webb**, Beatrice. 'Primitive democracy in British trade-unionism.' *Polit. Sci. Q.*, XI, 3 (September 1896), 397–432.
Title on contents page, and running title, is 'Trade-union democracy'.

2630 **Webb**, Sidney and **Webb**, Beatrice. 'Representative institutions in British trade-unionism.' *Polit. Sci. Q.*, XI, 4 (December 1896), 640–71.
Title on contents page, and running title, is 'Trade-union democracy'.

2631 **Webb**, Sidney and **Webb**, Beatrice. *Industrial democracy*. London: Longmans, 1897. 2v.
Second edition. 1898. In 1 vol.
New edition. 1902. lxi, 929p.
Reissue. London: printed by the authors for the trade unionists of the United Kingdom, 1911.
New edition, with new introduction. Longmans, 1920. xxxix, 899p.

2632 **Hollander**, J. H. A study of trade unionism.' *Polit. Sci. Q.*, XIII, 4 (December 1898), 694–704.
On *Industrial democracy* by S. and B. Webb.

2633 **Young**, Robert. 'The daily routine in a trade union office.' *Econ. J.*, XVI, 63 (September 1906), 440–2.

2634 **Slesser**, *Sir* Henry Herman. *Trade unionism*. London: Methuen, 1913. vii, 168p.
Second edition, revised. 1921. viii, 136p.

2635 **Bell**, *Sir* Hugh. 'Trade union regulations: the employer's point of view.' Gardner, L. (ed.). *The hope for society: essays on 'Social reconstruction after the war', by various writers*. London: Bell, 1917. p. 62–83.

2636 **Carlyle**, Alexander James. 'Trade union regulations from the trade union point of view.' Gardner, L. (ed.). *The hope for society: essays on 'Social reconstruction after the war', by various writers*. London: Bell, 1917. p. 84–100.

2637 **Independent Labour Party**. Industrial Policy Committee. *The organised worker: problems of trade union structure and policy*. London: I.L.P., 1927. 29p.

2638 **Petch**, Arthur William. *Trade union administration*. London, 1929. 23p.

2639 **General Federation of Trade Unions**. *Report on the causes of failure to increase trade union membership*. London, 1932. 16p.

2640 **Gray**, A. J. *The transferable vote in trade union elections*. London, 1935. 12p.

2641 **General Federation of Trade Unions**. Management Committee. *Report on trade union organisation*. London, 1937. 16p.

2642 **Hilton**, John. 'The British trade union at work.' Gannett, F. E. and Catherwood, B. F. (eds.). *Industrial and labour relations in Great Britain: a symposium*. New York: the editors, 1939. p. 89–100.
Reprinted from the *Atlantic Monthly*.

2643 **Tracey**, Herbert. 'British trade union organisation and methods.' Gannett, F. E. and Catherwood, B. F. (eds.). *Industrial and labour relations in Great Britain: a symposium*. New York: the editors, 1939. p. 296–330.

2644 **Davis**, Horace B. 'The theory of union growth.' *Q. J. Econ.*, LV, 4 (August 1941), 611–37.

2645 **Trades Union Congress**. *Interim report on trade union structure and closer unity*. London: T.U.C., [1944]. 36p.

2646 **Political and Economic Planning**. 'Inside the unions.' *Planning*, 249 (10 May 1946), 1–16.

2647 **Trades Union Congress**. *Trade union structure and closer unity: final report*. London: T.U.C., 1947. 77p.

2648 **Bell**, Joseph Denis Milburn. *Industrial unionism: a critical analysis*. Glasgow: McNaughton and Gowanlock, 1949. 28p. (University of Glasgow. Department of Social and Economic Research. Occasional papers 2.)

2649 **Goldstein**, Joseph. *Apathy and the democratic process in the government of a British trade union*. 1950. (Ph.D. thesis, University of London.)

2650 **Goldstein**, Joseph. *The government of British trade unions: a study of apathy and the democratic process in the Transport and General Workers' Union*. London: Allen and Unwin, 1952. 300p.
American edition. *The government of a British union*. Glencoe, Ill.: Free P.

2651 **Allen**, Victor Leonard. *A study of power in trade unions in Great Britain*. 1953–54. (Ph.D. thesis, University of London.)

2652 **Alexander**, Kenneth John Wilson. 'Economic research by the trade unions.' *Yorks. Bull. Econ. Soc. Res.*, VI, 1 (February 1954), 85–90.

2653 **Alexander**, Kenneth John Wilson. 'Membership participation in a printing trade union.' *Sociol. Rev.*, n.s., II, 2 (December 1954), 161–8.
Scottish Typographical Association.

2654 **Allen**, Victor Leonard. *Power in trade unions: a study of their organization in Great Britain*. London: Longmans, Green, 1954. xi, 323p.

2655 **Bell**, Joseph Denis Milburn. 'Stability of membership in trade unions.' *Scott. J. Polit. Econ.*, I, 1 (March 1954), 49–74.

2656 **Bell**, Joseph Denis Milburn. 'Trade unions.' Flanders, A. and Clegg, H. A. (eds.). *The system of industrial relations in Great Britain. . .* Oxford: Blackwell, 1954. p. 128–96.

2657 **Conservative and Unionist Party**. Conservative Industrial Department. *Trade union organization*. London: Conservative Political Centre, 1954.
Revised edition. 1963. 10p. (New trade union series 3.)

2658 **Independent Labour Party**. National Industrial Committee. *The changing structure of trade unions: an inquiry*. London: I.L.P., 1954. 25p.

2659 **Mitra**, A. 'The British trade union movement: a statistical analysis.' *Indian Econ. J.*, III, 1 (July 1955), 1–17.

2660 **Roberts**, Benjamin Charles. *Trade union government and administration in Great Britain.* London: London School of Economics and Political Science; Bell, 1956. viii, 570p.

2661 **Turner**, Herbert Arthur. 'Trade union organization.' *Polit. Q.*, XXVII, 1 (January–March 1956), 57–70.

2662 **Birch**, Alan. 'Structure of the British trade union movement.' *Manchr. Statist. Soc. Trans.* (1956–57), 25p.

2663 **Corfield**, Alan John. 'How the unions are developing their communication systems.' Chisholm, C. (ed.). *Communication in industry.* London: Business Publications in association with Batsford, 1957. p. 218–38.

2664 **Stephenson**, Thomas Edward. 'The changing role of local democracy: the trade union branch and its members.' *Sociol. Rev.*, n.s., V, 1 (July 1957), 27–42.

2665 **Turner**, Nigel. 'The preservation of democracy in the British trade unions.' *Cah. Bruges*, VIII, 3–4 (1958), 74–86.

2666 **Magrath**, C. Peter. 'Democracy in overalls: the futile quest for union democracy.' *Ind. Labor Relat. Rev.*, XII, 4 (July 1959), 503–25.

Includes 'a critical tour of the major literature on the problem of union democracy . . .' by such writers as V. L. Allen, Goldstein, Barbash and Lipset, Trow and Coleman.

2667 **Jones**, T. K. *The effect of large scale technological development and industrial expansion upon the local organisation of a trade union.* 1959–60. (M.A. thesis, University of Wales.)

2668 **Parsons**, C. J. *Workplace and union: a study of the relation between workshop and union-member involvement in two trade union branches of a large steelworks.* 1959–60. (M.A. thesis, Liverpool University.)

2669 **Sykes**, Andrew James Macintyre. 'The approaching crisis in the trade unions.' *Q. Rev.*, CCXCVIII, 626 (October 1960), 383–95.

2670 **Cyriax**, George. 'How to make trade unions more responsible.' *Polit. Q.*, XXXII, 4 (October–December 1961), 319–27.

2671 **Lerner**, Shirley Walowitz. *Breakaway unions and the small trade union.* London: Allen and Unwin, 1961. 210p.

2672 **Hindell**, Keith. 'Trade union membership.' *Planning*, XXVIII, 463 (2 July 1962), 153–200.

2673 **Lerner**, Shirley Walowitz. 'The future organisation and structure of trade unions.' Roberts, B. C. (ed.). *Industrial relations: contemporary problems and perspectives.* London: Methuen, 1962. p. 83–107.

2674 **Routh**, Guy. 'Future trade union membership.' Roberts, B. C. (ed.). *Industrial relations: contemporary problems and perspectives.* London: Methuen, 1962. p. 62–82.

2675 **Donoughue**, Bernard, **Oakley**, Alan and **Alker**, Janet. 'The structure and organisation of British trade unions.' *Planning*, XXIX, 477 (2 December 1963), 433–84.

2676 **Selvin**, David F. 'Communications in trade unions: a study of union journals.' *Br. J. Ind. Relat.*, I, 1 (February 1963), 73–93.

2677 **Mortimer**, James Edward. 'The structure of the trade union movement.' *Social. Regist.* (1964), 175–91.

2678 **Roy**, Walter. 'Membership participation in the National Union of Teachers.' *Br. J. Ind. Relat.*, II, 2 (July 1964), 189–208.

2679 **Turner**, Herbert Arthur. 'British trade union structure: a new approach?' *Br. J. Ind. Relat.*, II, 2 (July 1964), 165–81.

2680 **Rideout**, Roger William. 'The content of trade union disciplinary rules.' *Br. J. Ind. Relat.*, III, 2 (July 1965), 153–63.

2681 **Summers**, Clyde W. 'Internal relations between trade unions and their members.' *Int. Labour Rev.*, XCI, 3 (March 1965), 175–90.

2682 **Rideout**, Roger William. 'The content of trade union rules regulating admission.' *Br. J. Ind. Relat.*, IV, 1 (March 1966), 77–89.

2683 **Rideout**, Roger William. 'Responsible self-government in British trade unions.' *Br. J. Ind. Relat.*, V, 1 (March 1967), 74–86.

2684 **Dignam**, J. J. *Organisational structure of trade unions and the trade union movement in Ireland.* 1967–69. (M.S.A. thesis, Trinity College, Dublin.)

2685 **Hughes**, John Dennis. *Trade union structure and government.* London: H.M.S.O., 1967–68. 2 pts. (Royal Commission on Trade Unions and Employers' Associations. Research papers 5.)

Part 1. *Structure and development.*

Part 2. *Membership participation and trade union government.*

2686 **Lerner**, Shirley Walowitz. 'The effect of technological change on the structure of British trade unions.' Roberts, B. C. (ed.). *Industrial relations: contemporary issues*. . . London: Macmillan; New York: St Martin's P., 1968. p. 172–9.

2687 **Martin**, Roderick. 'Union democracy: an explanatory framework.' *Sociology*, II, 2 (May 1968), 205–20.

2688 **Turner**, Herbert Arthur. 'Trade union organization.' McCormick, B. J. and Smith, E. O. (eds.). *The labour market: selected readings.* Harmondsworth: Penguin, 1968. p. 105–19.

Reprinted from *Pol. Q.*, XXV, (1955), 57–70.

2689 **Edelstein**, J. David, **Warner**, Malcolm and **Cooke**, W. F. 'The pattern of opposition in British and American unions.' *Sociology*, IV, 2 (May 1970), 145–63.

'The major objective here is to convey an overall picture of the extent of electoral opposition for top posts in trade unions in Britain and the United States.'

2690 **Fletcher**, Richard. 'Trade union democracy: structural factors.' *Trade Un. Regist.* (1970), 73–85.

2691 **Hughes**, John. 'Giant firms and British trade unions' response.' *Trade Un. Regist.* (1970), 62–72.

2692 **Warner**, Malcolm. 'Organizational background and "union parliamentarianism": an examination of British and American cases.' *J. Ind. Relat.*, XII, 2 (July 1970), 205–17.

See also: 1754; 1776; 1804–5; 1824; 2068; 2311; 2316; 9606.

2. Federations

a. TRADES UNION CONGRESS

2693 **Dundee Courier**. *The Trades Union Congress.* Dundee, 1889. [vi], 82p.

2694 **Woods**, Samuel. *The Trades Union Congress at Newcastle: a review and criticism.* Wigan, 1891.

2695 **Threlfall**, T. R. 'The Trades Union Congress, and the rocks ahead.' *Nineteenth Century*, XXXII, 188 (October 1892), 614–21.

2696 **Chapman**, Sydney John. 'The Trade Unions Congress and federation.' *Econ. J.*, IX, 33 (March 1899), 80–5.

2697 **Durand**, E. Dana. 'The British Trade-union Congress of 1902.' *Q.J. Econ.*, XVII (November 1902), 181–4.

2698 **Davis**, William John. *The British Trades Union Congress: history and recollections.* London: Co-operative Printing Society, 1910, 1916. 2v.

2699 **International Labour Organisation**. *Annual meeting of the British Trades Union Congress, 1920.* Geneva: I.L.O., 1920. 12p. (Studies and reports, series A, 3.)

2700 **Bramley**, Fred. 'The Trades Union Congress.' Hogue, R. W. (ed.). *British labour speaks.* New York: Boni and Liveright, 1924. p. 71–91.
The title at the head of the chapter is 'The industrial and political structure of the British trade union movement.'

2701 **Trades Union Congress**. *The General Council of the T.U.C., its powers, funds and work.* London: T.U.C. General Council, [1926]. 12p. (Trades unionism in action 2.)

2702 **Citrine**, Walter McLennan. *Trades Union Congress campaign for freedom.* London, 1928. 39p.

2703 **Trades Union Congress**. *Sixty years of trade unionism, 1868–1928: souvenir of the sixtieth Trades Union Congress.* London: T.U.C., 1928. 84p.

2704 **Trades Union Congress**. *Seventy years of trade unionism, 1868–1938.* London: T.U.C., 1938. 362p.

2705 **Citrine**, Walter McLennan. *The T.U.C. in war-time: an informal record of three months progress.* London: Trades Union Congress, 1939–45. 10 pts.

2706 **Elvin**, Herbert H. 'The Trades Union Congress.' Cole, G. D. H. *British trade unionism today: a survey...* London: Methuen, 1945. p. 175–83.
Earlier edition. 1939.

2707 **Roberts**, Bryn. *At the T.U.C.: resolutions, speeches, comments.* 1947. [viii], 344p.
Printed by Leicester Co-operative Printing Society.

2708 **Conservative and Unionist Party**. Conservative Industrial Department. *Trade unions and the T.U.C.* London: Conservative Political Centre, 1954. 15p. (Trade union services series 4.)
Revised edition. 1963. 13p. (New trade union series 4.)

2709 **Musson**, Albert Edward. *The Congress of 1868: the origins and establishment of the Trades Union Congress.* London: T.U.C., 1955. 48p.
Revised edition. 1968.

2710 **Trades Union Congress**. *The T.U.C. and communism.* London: T.U.C., 1955. 11p.

2711 **Harrison**, Royden J. ' "Practical, capable men".' *New Reas.*, 6 (Autumn 1958), 105–19.
A review of B. C. Roberts, *The Trades Union Congress, 1868–1921.*

2712 **Roberts**, Benjamin Charles. *The Trades Union Congress, 1868–1921.* London: Allen and Unwin, 1958. 408p.

2713 **Allen**, Victor Leonard. 'The re-organisation of the Trades Union Congress, 1918–1927.' *Br. J. Sociol.*, XI, 1 (March 1960), 24–43.

2714 **Roberts**, Bryn. *The price of T.U.C. leadership.* London: Allen and Unwin, 1961. 148p.

2715 **Martin**, Ross M. 'The authority of trade union centres: the Australian Council of Trade Unions and the British Trades Union Congress.' *J. Ind. Relat.*, IV, 1 (April 1962), 1–19.

2716 **Allen**, Victor Leonard. 'The centenary of the British Trades Union Congress, 1868–1968.' *Social. Regist.* (1968), 231–52.

2717 **Birch**, Lionel (ed.). *The history of the T.U.C., 1868–1968: a pictorial survey of a social revolution.* London: Trades Union Congress, 1968. 161p. (chiefly illus.)

2718 **Lovell**, John Christopher and **Roberts**, Benjamin Charles. *A short history of the T.U.C.* London: Macmillan, 1968. 200p.

2719 **National Book League**. *T.U.C. centenary, 1868–1968: books reflecting the social changes of the last century.* London: the League, 1968. 62p.

2720 **Hughes**, John Dennis. *The T.U.C.: a plan for the 1970's.* London: Fabian Society, 1969. 36p. (Fabian tract 397.)

See also: 1193; 1251; 11,140.

b. IRISH CONGRESS OF TRADE UNIONS

2721 **Roberts**, Ruaidhri. *Structure and functions of the Irish Congress of Trade Unions.* [Dublin?]: I.C.T.U., 1966. 14 leaves.

2722 **Sams**, K. I. 'The creation of the Irish Congress of Trade Unions.' *J. Ind. Relat.*, VIII, 1 (March 1966), 68–78.

2723 **Sams**, K. I. 'The Appeals Board of the Irish Congress of Trade Unions.' *Br. J. Ind. Relat.*, VI, 2 (July 1968), 204–19.

c. SCOTTISH TRADES UNION CONGRESS

2724 **Scottish Trades Union Congress.** *50 years of progress: the building of the STUC, 1897–1947.* Glasgow, 1947. 40p.

d. OTHER

2725 **Edwards**, Clement. 'Labour federations.' *Econ. J.*, III, 10 (June 1893), 205–17; III, 11 (September 1893), 408–24.

' "Federation" . . . is used to signify that kind of organization in which a number of separate unions become mutually attached, on the basis of each retaining its distinct and independent identity with full autonomy in matters of an internal character, while at the same time subjecting itself to one common control for certain limited and clearly defined purposes.'

2726 **King**, P. J. and **Blatchford**, Robert. *Trades federation.* London, 1897. 35p. (Clarion pamphlet 17.)

2727 **King**, P. J. *Federation in a nutshell.* London, 1898. 24p. (Clarion pamphlet 28.)

2728 **King**, P. J. *Good and bad federation.* London, 1898. 31p. (Clarion pamphlet 24.)

2729 **Burke**, William Maxwell. *History and functions of central labor unions.* New York: Macmillan; London: King, 1899. 125p. (Studies in history, economics and public law, vol. 12, no. 1.)

Reprinted. New York: A.M.S. Press, 1968. xi, 125p.

2730 **King**, P. J. and **Blatchford**, Robert. *The federation of trade unions.* London, 1899. 31p.

2731 **General Federation of Trade Unions.** *Jubilee souvenir, 1899–1949.* London: G.F.T.U., 1949. 71p.

3. Trades Councils

2732 **Richards**, Cicely. *A history of trades councils from 1860 to 1875.* London: Labour Research Department, 1920. 36p.

Introduction by G. D. H. Cole.

2733 **Dalley**, William Arthur. *An historical sketch of the Birmingham Trades Council, 1886–1926.* Birmingham: printed for Birmingham Trades Council, 1927. 36p.

2734 **Purcell**, Albert Arthur. *The trades councils and local working-class movement.* Manchester, 1930. 15p.

2735 **Yarwood**, J. *Newcastle and District Trades Council: a retrospect and explanation.* 1932.

2736 **Huddersfield Trades Council.** *Jubilee souvenir, 1885–1935.* 1935.

2737 **London Trades Council.** *A short history of the London Trades Council, by a delegate.* London: the Council, 1935. 160p.

2738 **Cambridge Trades Council and Labour Party.** *Silver jubilee, 1912–1937.* 1937.

2739 **Northampton Trades Council.** *Golden jubilee, 1888–1938.* 1938.

2740 **Diack**, William. *History of the Trades Council and the trade union movement in Aberdeen.* Aberdeen: Trades Council, 1939. xv, 260p.

2741 **North Staffordshire Trades Council.** *Jubilee souvenir, 1892–1942.* 1942.

2742 **Hamling**, W. *A short history of the Liverpool Trades' Council, 1848–1948.* Liverpool: [the Council?, 1948.]

2743 **Brighton Trades Council.** *The history of sixty years, 1890–1950.* Brighton: Brighton Trades Council, 1950. 19p.

2744 **Heanor Trades Council.** *Thirty memorable years.* 1950.

2745 **Tate**, George Kenneth. *The London Trades Council, 1860–1950: a history.* London: Lawrence and Wishart, 1950. viii, 160p.

2746 **Belfast and District Trade Union Council.** *Short history, 1881–1951.* 1952.

2747 **Hall**, P. P. *History of Blackpool Trades Council.* 1951.

2748 **Rawtenstall Borough Trades Council.** *50th anniversary, 1902–1952.* 1952.

Mimeographed.

2749 **Williams**, H. B. *History of Plymouth and District Trades Council, 1892–1952.* 1952.

2750 **Bather**, L. *A history of Manchester and Salford Trades Council.* 1956. (Ph.D. thesis, University of Manchester.)

2751 **Grant**, Betty. 'Trades councils, 1860–1914.' *Amat. Hist.*, III, 4 (Summer 1957), 160–5.

2752 **McShane**, Harry. *Glasgow and District Trades Council centenary brochure, 1858–1958.* Glasgow: the Council, 1958. 41p.

2753 **Pollard**, Sidney, **Medelson**, J., **Owen**, W. and **Thorne**, V. *Sheffield Trades and Labour Council, 1858–1958.* Sheffield: the Council, 1958. 105p.

2754 **Maddock**, S. *The Liverpool Trades Council and politics, 1878–1918.* 1958–59. (M.A. thesis, University of Liverpool.)

2755 **Peterborough Trades Council.** *Diamond jubilee, 1899–1959.* 1959.

2756 **Bather**, L. 'Manchester and Salford Trades Council from 1880.' *Soc. Study Labour Hist. Bull.*, 6 (Spring 1963), 13–16.

Abstract of a paper given at a conference of the Society for the Study of Labour History, Birkbeck College, London, 25 January 1963.

An abstract of the discussion on the paper appears on p. 16.

2757 **Barnsby**, George. *The origins of the Wolverhampton Trades Council.* Wolverhampton: Wolverhampton Trades Council, 1965. 17p.

2758 **Corbett**, John. *The Birmingham Trades Council, 1866–1966.* London: Lawrence and Wishart, 1966. 192p.

2759 **Fraser**, W. Hamish. 'Scottish trades councils in the nineteenth century.' *Soc. Study Labour Hist. Bull.*, 14 (Spring 1967), 11.

Abstract of a paper given at a meeting of the Scottish Committee of the Society for the Study of Labour History, Dundee, January 1967.

2760 **Saville**, John. 'Trade councils and the labour movement to 1900.' *Soc. Study Labour Hist. Bull.*, 14 (Spring 1967), 29–34.

A review article based on J. Corbett. *The Birmingham Trades Council 1866–1966.* London: Lawrence and Wishart, 1966; and R. Brown. *The labour movement in Hull, 1870–1900.* 1966. (M.Sc. thesis, University of Hull.)

2761 **Fraser**, W. Hamish. *Trades councils in England and Scotland, 1858–1897.* 1967–68. (D.Phil. thesis, University of Sussex.)

2762 **McDougall**, Ian (ed.). *The minutes of Edinburgh Trades Council, 1859–1878.* Edinburgh: Scottish History Society, 1968.

2763 **Bullock**, Paul Scott. *Role and power of the Birmingham Trades Council in Birmingham city politics.* 1970. [iv], 73p. (M.Soc. Sc. thesis, University of Birmingham.)

2764 **Clinton**, Alan. 'Trade councils during the First World War.' *Int. Rev. of Soc. Hist.*, xv, 2 (1970), 202–34.

4. Mergers and Amalgamations

2765 **Willis**, Jack. *The case for amalgamation.* London: Bowman, [19—?]. 15p.

2766 **Conference on the Question of the Amalgamation of Trade Unions in the Distributive Industry**, London, 1911. *Amalgamation of trade unions in the distributive industry.* Manchester, 1911. 22p.

2767 **Gillespie**, H. J. *Industrial unionism or amalgamation versus federation as the future form of trade union organisation.* London, [1913?]. 22 leaves.

2768 **Webb**, Sidney. 'The process of amalgamation in British trade unionism.' *Int. Labour Rev.*, I, 1 (January 1921), 45–60.

2769 **Hart**, P. E. and **Phelps Brown**, Ernest Henry. 'The sizes of trade unions: a study in the laws of aggregation.' *Econ. J.*, LXVII, 265 (March 1957), 1–15.

2770 **Estey**, Martin S. 'Trends in concentration of union membership, 1897–1962.' *Q. J. Econ.*, LXXX, 3 (August 1966), 343–60.

2771 **Smith**, E. Owen. 'The trend in trade union amalgamation.' *Lough. J. Soc. Studies*, 3 (June 1967), 17–19.

'Why should trade unions amalgamate? A comment', by A. A. I. Wedderburn, 4 (November 1967), 35–8. 'A reply', by E. O. Smith, 6 (November 1968), 26–30.

5. Inter-Union Relations

2772 **Gillespie**, H. J. *Demarcation.* London, [1913?]. 12 leaves.

2773 **Davies**, S. Clement. 'Trade union rivalry and the Bridlington Agreement.' *Br. J. Adm. Law*, I, 3 (December 1954), 97–101.

2774 **Boyfield**, Ray. 'T.U.C. machinery for disputes between unions.' *Br. J. Adm. Law*, II, 2 (September 1955), 56–60.

2775 **Gamser**, Howard G. 'Interunion disputes in Great Britain and the United States.' *Ind. Labor Relat. Rev.*, IX, 1 (October 1955), 3–23.

2776 **Hunter**, William. *Hands off the 'blue union'. 1. Democracy on the docks.* London: New Park Publications, 1958. 24p. (Labour Review. Pamphlets.)

2777 **Lerner**, Shirley Walowitz. 'The T.U.C. jurisdictional dispute settlement, 1924–1957.' *Manchr. Sch.*, XXVI, 3 (September 1958), 222–40.

Reprinted in a slightly revised form in the author's *Breakaway unions and the small trade union.* London: Allen and Unwin, 1961. p. 66–81.

2778 **Oakley**, Peter Allan. *Demarcation and amalgamation: a study of union antagonism between the shipwrights and boilermakers in the Cammell Laird shipyard, Birkenhead, 1959–1965.* 1968. 262p. (M.A. (Econ.) thesis, University of Manchester.)

6. Finances and Benefits

See also Part Three, II; and Part Seven, IX, B.

2779 **Howell**, George. 'The financial condition of trades unions.' *Nineteenth Century*, XII, 68 (October 1882), 481–501.

2780 **Howell**, George. 'The provident side of trades unionism.' *New Rev.*, V, 31 (December 1891), 546–58.

2781 **Webb**, Sidney and **Webb**, Beatrice. 'Are trade unions benefit societies?' *Econ. Rev.*, VI, 4 (October 1896), 441–55.

2782 **Wood**, George Henry. 'Trade union expenditure on unemployed benefits since 1860.' *R. Statist. Soc. J.*, LXIII, 1 (March 1900), 81–92.

2783 **Hartley**, Edwin Leach. 'Trade union expenditure on unemployed benefit.' *R. Statist. Soc. J.*, LXVII, 1 (March 1904), 52–71.

With discussion, p. 72–80.

Read before the Society, 16 February 1904.

2784 **Mitchell**, Isaac H. 'Trade unions and thrift.' *Char. Orgn. Rev.*, n.s., XXII, 128 (August 1907), 113–27.

Describes the financial and benefit activities of trade unions.

2785 **Lynch**, Joseph. *Business methods and accountancy in trade unions.* London: Labour Publishing Co., 1922. 183p.

2786 **Oxberry**, John. *Gateshead District Aged Mineworkers' Homes: the birth of the movement.* Felling: R. Heslop, 1924. 35p.

2787 **Ward**, A. E. and **Sweetingham**, C. R. *Trade union accounting and financial administration.* London: Pitman, 1937. ix, 126p.

2788 **Beales**, Hugh Lancelot. 'Trade union finance.' Cole, G. D. H. *British trade unionism today: a survey*...London: Methuen, 1945. p. 195–205.
Earlier edition. 1939.

2789 **Hutt**, Rosemary. 'Trade unions as friendly societies, 1912–1952.' *Yorks. Bull. Econ. Soc. Res.*, VII, 1 (March 1955), 69–87.

2790 **Transport and General Workers Union.** *The law and you: a manual on a vital trade union service.* London: T.G.W.U., 1956. 112p.

2791 **Marsh**, Arthur I. and **Cope**, Peter. 'The anatomy of trade union benefits in the 1960's.' *Ind. Relat. J.* (Summer 1970), 4–18.

See also: 3101.

7. Closed Shop and Check-Off

See also Part Seven, VII, B, 3.

2792 **Post**, Louis Freeland. *The open shop and the closed shop.* London: Land Values Publication Department, [c. 1905]. 32p.

2793 **Thomas**, Philip Sydney. *An outline of the activities of some trade unions of South Wales, with reference to the question of compulsory membership.* 1920. (M.A. thesis, University of Wales, Aberystwyth.)

2794 **Trades Union Congress**. *The closed shop.* London: T.U.C., 1946. 7p.

2795 **Toner**, Jerome L. *The closed shop in Great Britain.* Washington: Labor's Non-Partisan League, [1947?]. 18p.

2796 **Wigham**, Wilfred S. *The closed shop.* London: Independent Labour Party, 1947. 11p.

2797 **Allen**, Victor Leonard. 'Some economic aspects of compulsory trade unionism.' *Oxf. Econ. Pap.*, n.s., VI, 1 (February 1954), 69–81.

2798 **McKelvey**, Jean Trepp. 'The "closed shop" controversy in postwar Britain.' *Ind. Labor Relat. Rev.*, VII, 4 (July 1954), 550–74.

2799 **Berkowitz**, Monroe. ' "Economic aspects of compulsory trade unionism": a note.' *Oxf. Econ. Pap.*, n.s., VII, 2 (June 1955), 221–5.

2800 **McCarthy**, William Edward John. *The closed shop in British trade unions.* 1961–62. (D.Phil. thesis, University of Oxford.)

2801 **McCarthy**, William Edward John. *The closed shop in Britain.* Oxford: Blackwell, 1964. xii, 294p.

2802 **Fox**, Alan. 'The closed shop.' *New Soc.*, VI, 168 (16 December 1965), 6–8.

2803 **Organisation of Employers' Federations and Employers in Developing Countries.** *Deduction of union dues by the employer (check-off).* London: the Federation, 1967. 36p. (Occasional paper.)
Reprinted.
Also *Appendix 8.* 2p.

2804 **Marsh**, Arthur I. and **Staples**, J. W. 'Check-off agreements in Britain: a study of their growth and functions.' Royal Commission on Trade Unions and Employers' Associations. *Three studies in collective bargaining.* London: H.M.S.O., 1968. p. 45–64. (Research papers 8.)

2805 **Cordova**, Efrén. 'The check-off system: a comparative study.' *Int. Labour Rev.*, XCIX, 5 (May 1969), 463–91.

8. Leadership and Leaders

This section does not include works on Labour politicians unless they were also prominent in the trade union movement.

a. LEADERSHIP

2806 **Watson**, William Foster. 'Trade union officialism as a career.' *Engl. Rev.*, XLVI, 1 (January 1938), 50–8.

2807 **Robson**, Norman S. *Politics or power? The tragedy of trade union leadership.* London: Liberal Publication Department, 1932. 36p.

2808 **Allen**, Victor Leonard. 'The ethics of trade union leaders.' *Br. J. Sociol.*, VII, 4 (December 1956), 314–36.

2809 **Head**, Philip James. *The status, functions and policy of the trade union official, 1870–1930.* 1956. (M.Litt. thesis, University of Cambridge.)

2810 **Mack**, John A. 'Trade union leadership.' *Polit. Q.*, XXVII, 1 (January–March 1956), 71–81.

2811 **Clegg**, Hugh Armstrong, **Killick**, Anthony John and **Adams**, Rex. *Trade union officers: a study of full-time officers, branch secretaries, and shop stewards in British trade unions.* Oxford: Blackwell; Cambridge, Mass.: Harvard U.P., 1961. 273p.

2812 **Jenkins**, Peter. 'Unions: what makes the leaders tick?' *New Soc.*, 3 (18 October 1962), 9–12.

2813 **Corfield**, Tony. *Collective leadership for the Transport & General Workers' Union.* Sidcup: Ron Brierly, 1968. 30p.

2814 **Bonnar**, Robert. 'Negotiating at the top.' Fraser, R. (ed.). *Work, volume 2: twenty personal accounts.* Harmondsworth: Penguin, 1969. p. 330–45.
The author served on the executive committee of the N.U.R. for a three-year period, 1964–6.

b. BIOGRAPHIES, AUTOBIOGRAPHIES, AND MEMOIRS

i. *Collections*

2815 **Hallam**, William (ed.). *Miners' leaders: thirty portraits and biographical sketches.* London: Bemrose, 1894. xv, 118p.

2816 **Phillips**, Elizabeth. *A history of the pioneers of the Welsh coalfield*. Cardiff: *Western Mail*, 1925. viii, 261p.

2817 **Cole**, Margaret Isabel. *Makers of the labour movement*. London: Longmans, Green, 1948. xv, 319p.

2818 **Murphy**, John Thomas. *Labour's big three: a biographical study of Clement Attlee, Herbert Morrison and Ernest Bevin*. London: Bodley Head, 1948. 266p.

2819 **Fagan**, Hyman. *Unsheathed sword: episodes in English history*. London: Lawrence and Wishart.

Part 1. Commoners of England. 1958. 136p.

Part 2. Champions of the workers. 1959. 108p.

2820 **Boyle**, J. W. (ed.). *Leaders and workers*. Cork: Mercier P. for Radio Éireann, 1965. 95p. (Thomas Davis lectures.)

'Nine lectures . . . broadcast during the winter of 1961.' Contents: 'William Thompson and the socialist tradition', by P. Lynch; 'John Doherty', by A. Boyd; Fergus O'Connor and J. Bronterre O'Brien', by A. Briggs; 'James Fintan Lalor', by T. P. O'Neill; 'Michael Davitt', by T. W. Moody; 'William Walker', by J. W. Boyle; 'James Connolly', by D. Ryan; 'Jim Larkin', by J. Plunket; 'The sum of things', by J. W. Boyle.

2821 **Evans**, Jack Naunton. *Great figures in the labour movement*. Oxford, London: Pergamon P., 1966. viii, 176p. (Commonwealth and international library. History division.)

ii. *Individual Leaders*

1. *A–B*

2822 **Davidson**, John Morrison. 'Joseph Arch.' *Eminent radicals in and out of Parliament*. London: Stewart, 1880. p. 158–67.

Originally published in the *Weekly Dispatch*.

2823 **Davidson**, John Morrison. 'Thomas Burt.' *Eminent radicals in and out of Parliament*. London: Stewart, 1880. p. 95–104.

Originally published in the *Weekly Dispatch*.

2824 **Arch**, Joseph. *Joseph Arch: the story of his life, told by himself and edited with a preface by the Countess of Warwick*. London: Hutchinson, 1898. xx, 412p.

New edition. *The autobiography of Joseph Arch*. Edited by John Gerard O'Leary. London: MacGibbon and Kee, 1966. 147p. (Fitzroy editions.)

2825 **Stead**, William Thomas. 'How Joseph Arch was driven from the state church.' *Contemp. Rev.*, LXXIII (January 1898), 71–83.

2826 **Donald**, Robert. 'Mr. John Burns, the workman-minister.' *Nineteenth Century*, LIX, 348 (February 1906), 191–204.

2827 **Grubb**, Arthur Page. *From candle factory to British Cabinet: the life story of the Right Hon. John Burns, P.C., M.P.* London: E. Dalton, 1908. 313p.

2828 **Meech**, Thomas Cox. *From mine to ministry: the life and times of the Right Hon. Thomas Burt, M.P.* Darlington: North of England Newspaper Co., 1908. 118, iv p.

2829 **Watson**, Aaron. *A great labour leader: being a life of the Right Hon. Thomas Burt, M.P.* London: Brown, Langham, 1908. xv, 312p.

2830 **Burgess**, Joseph. *John Burns: the rise and progress of a Right Honourable*. Glasgow: Reformers' Bookstall, 1911. xxi, 201p.

2831 **Humphrey**, A. W. *Robert Applegarth: trade unionist, educationist, reformer*. Manchester: National Labour P., 1913. xv, 328p.

2832 **Grigg**, Joseph W. *The workers' resolve: an interview with W. A. Appleton*. London: Fisher Unwin, 1917. 8p.

2833 **Barnes**, George Nicholl. *From workshop to War Cabinet*. London: H. Jenkins, 1924 [i.e. 1923]. xiii, 315p.

An autobiography.

2834 **Burt**, Thomas. *Thomas Burt, pitman and privy councillor: an autobiography*. London: Fisher Unwin, 1924. 319p.

With supplementary chapters by Aaron Watson.

2835 **Hamilton**, Mary Agnes. *Margaret Bondfield*. London: Parsons, 1924. 191p.

2836 **Skom**, Ruth. *William J. Brown, trade unionist M.P.: a biography*. 1931. 155 leaves. (A.M. thesis, University of Chicago.)

Civil Service Clerical Association.

2837 **Postgate**, Raymond William. 'Robert Applegarth, 1834–1924.' Brown, A. Barratt (ed.). *Great democrats*. London: Nicholson and Watson, 1934. p. 15–25.

2838 **Warwick**, Frances Evelyn. 'Joseph Arch, 1826–1919.' Brown, A. Barratt (ed.). *Great democrats*. London: Nicholson and Watson, 1934. p. 29–38.

2839 **Bower**, Fred. *Rolling stonemason: an autobiography*. London: Cape, 1936. 256p.

2840 **Bell**, Thomas. *Pioneering days*. London: Lawrence and Wishart, 1941. 316p.

Reminiscences.

2841 **Brown**, William John. *So far—*. London: Allen and Unwin, 1943. 295p.

An autobiography.

Civil service unionism.

2842 **Cole**, George Douglas Howard. *John Burns*. London: Gollancz; Fabian Society, 1943. 36p. (Fabian biographical series 14.)

2843 **Evans**, *Sir* Trevor M. *Bevin*. London: Allen and Unwin, 1946. 231p.

2844 **Cole**, Margaret Isabel. 'Robert Applegarth, 1834–1924.' *Makers of the labour movement*. London: Longmans, Green, 1948. p. 145–64.

2845 **Bondfield**, Margaret Grace. *A life's work*. London: Hutchinson, 1949. 368p.

An autobiography.

2846 **Kent**, William Richard Gladstone. *John Burns; labour's lost leader: a biography.* London: Williams and Norgate, 1950. xv, 389p.

2847 **Williams**, Francis. *Ernest Bevin: portrait of a great Englishman.* London: Hutchinson, 1952. ii, 288p.

2848 **Evans**, Eric Wyn. *William Abraham, 1842–1922.* 1954. (M.A. thesis, University of Wales.)
See also 2928.

2849 **Fox**, Richard Michael. *Louie Bennett: her life and times.* Dublin: Talbot P., 1958. 123p.
Irish Women Workers' Union.

2850 **Bullock**, Alan Louis Charles. *The life and times of Ernest Bevin.* London: Heinemann, 1960, 1967.
Vol. 1. Trade union leader, 1881–1940.
Vol. 2. Ministry of Labour, 1940–1945. 1967.

2851 **Ashby**, Mabel K. *Joseph Ashby of Tysoe, 1859–1919: a study of English village life.* Cambridge: Cambridge U.P., 1961. xiv, 303p.

2852 **Nethercot**, Arthur Hobart. *The first five lives of Annie Besant.* London: Hart-Davis, 1961. 435p.
The last four lives of Annie Besant. 1963. 483p.

2853 **Briggs**, Asa. 'Robert Applegarth and the trade-unions.' Briggs, A. *Victorian people: a reassessment of persons and themes, 1851–67.* rev. ed. Chicago: U. of Chicago P., 1970. p. 168–96.
Earlier editions. 1954, 1955, 1965.

2. *C–D*

2854 **Chapman**, Joseph. *1899. Joseph Chapman, Alford, labourer, aged 77, the working man's friend: the story of his life told by himself with other writings.* 1899. 16p.

2855 **Haw**, George. *From workhouse to Westminster: life of Will Crooks, M.P.* London: Cassell, 1907. xx, 306p.
Another edition. 1911. xx, 312p.
Another edition. *The life story of Will Crooks, M.P.* 1917. xx, 328p.

2856 **Dalley**, William Arthur. *The life story of W. J. Davis, J.P. The industrial problem. Achievements and triumphs of conciliation.* Birmingham: Birmingham Printers, 1914. 402p.

2857 **George**, Edward. *From mill boy to Minister: an intimate account of the life of the Rt. Hon. J. R. Clynes, M.P.* London: Fisher Unwin, 1918. 119p.

2858 **Alcock**, George W. *The life of John H. Dobson, ex-organiser, National Union of Railwaymen.* London: King's Cross Publishing Co., 1921. 79p.

2859 **Ryan**, Desmond. *James Connolly: his life, work & writings.* Dublin: Talbot P.; London: Labour Publishing Co., 1924. x, 142p.

2860 **Strachey**, John. 'Who A. J. Cook is.' *Social. Rev.*, n.s., 8 (September 1926), 8–14.
Brief life-story of A. J. Cook with an account of his views on trade unionism and the labour movement.

2861 **O'Brien**, Nora Connolly. *Portrait of a rebel father.* London: Rich and Cowan; Dublin: Talbot P., 1935. 327p.
Portrait of James Connolly.

2862 **Citrine**, Walter McLennan. *I search for truth in Russia.* London: Routledge, 1936. x, 368p.
Popular edition, revised. 1938. x, 420p.

2863 **Clynes**, John Robert. *Memoirs.* London: Hutchinson. 2v.
Vol. 1. *1869–1924.* 1937. 351p.
Vol. 2. *1924–1937.* 1938. 299p.

2864 **Citrine**, Walter McLennan. *My Finnish diary.* Harmondsworth, New York: Penguin Books, 1940. 192p. (Penguin special 56.)

2865 **Citrine**, Walter McLennan. *My American diary.* London: Routledge, 1941. x, 353p.

2866 **Davies**, Noelle. *Connolly of Ireland: patriot and socialist.* Caernarfon: Swyddfa'r Blaid, 1946. 59p.

2867 **Fox**, Richard Michael. *James Connolly: the forerunner.* Tralee: Kerryman, 1946. 252p.

2868 **Clunie**, James. *Labour is my faith: the autobiography of a house painter.* Dunfermline: the author, 1954. 95p.
The author was a member of the Executive of the Scottish Painters' Society for 18 years.

2869 **Allen**, Victor Leonard. *Trade union leadership, based on a study of Arthur Deakin.* London: Longmans, Green, 1957. xiii, 336p.

2870 **Clunie**, James. *The voice of labour: the autobiography of a house painter.* Dunfermline: the author, 1958. 168p.

2871 **Cousins**, Frank. 'Frank Cousins "Face to face": interview with John Freeman on B.B.C. television.' *Listener*, LXVI, 1700 (26 October 1961), 637–41.

2872 **Greaves**, C. Desmond. *The life and times of James Connolly.* London: Lawrence and Wishart, 1961. 363p.

2873 **Citrine**, Walter McLennan, Baron Citrine. *Men and work: an autobiography.* London: Hutchinson, 1964. 384p.

2874 **Quine**, William Greenhalgh. *A. J. Cook: miners' leader in the General Strike.* 1964. iii, 122p. (M.A. thesis, University of Manchester.)

2875 **Torode**, John A. 'Cannon in front of them.' *New Soc.*, IV, 102 (10 September 1964), 19–20.

2876 **Clunie**, James. *Literature of labour: the autobiography of a house painter.* Dunfermline, 1966. 192p.

2877 **Citrine**, Walter McLennan, Baron Citrine. *Two careers.* London: Hutchinson, 1967. 384p.
Volume 1 of this autobiography published as *Men and work*, 1964.

2878 **Harris**, U. *Conversations.* London: Hodder and Stoughton, 1967.
Lord Citrine, p. 11–25.

2879 **Sinclair**, Betty. 'James Connolly, trade unionist.' *Marxism Today*, XII, 6 (June 1968), 177–83.
On the centenary of Connolly's birth.

2880 **Stewart**, Margaret. *Frank Cousins: a study.* London: Hutchinson, 1968. xiv, 210p.

2881 **Dash**, Jack. *Good morning, brothers!* London: Lawrence and Wishart, 1969. 190p.
Another edition. London: Mayflower, 1970. 175p.

2882 **Goodman**, Geoffrey. *Brother Frank: the man and the union.* London: Panther, 1969. 128p. (chiefly illus., facsims., ports.)
Frank Cousins.

3. *E–H*

2883 **Glasier**, John Bruce. *J. Keir Hardie: a memorial.* Manchester, London: National Labour Press, [c. 1915]. 85p.

2884 **Glasier**, John Bruce. *Keir Hardie: the man and his message.* London: Independent Labour Party, 1919. 11p.
An abridgement of *J. Keir Hardie: a memorial.*

2885 **Stewart**, William. *J. Keir Hardie: a biography.* London: Independent Labour Party, 1921. xxvi, 387p.
Issued for the Keir Hardie Memorial Committee.

2886 **Edwards**, *Sir* George. *From crow-scaring to Westminster: an autobiography.* London: Labour Publishing Co., 1922. 240p.
Agricultural unionism.

2887 **Gallacher**, William. *Willie Gallacher's story: the Clyde in wartime.* Glasgow: Collet's Bookshop, 1922. 32p.
'The material contained in this pamphlet is also to be found in Gallacher's book *Revolt on the Clyde.*' (Chamberlin.)

2888 **Lowe**, David. *From pit to parliament: the story of the early life of James Keir Hardie.* London: Labour Publishing Co., 1923. 207p.

2889 **Hodges**, Frank. *My adventures as a labour leader.* London: Newnes, 1925. vi, 185p.
The author was General Secretary of the Miners' Federation of Great Britain from 1918 to 1924, the first full-time occupant of that post.

2890 **Gosling**, Harry. *Up and down stream.* London: Methuen, 1927. 246p.
An autobiography.

2891 **Stewart**, William. *The making of an agitator; or, the early days of Keir Hardie.* London: I.L.P. Publication Department, 1929. 15p.
Chap. I of *J. Keir Hardie: a biography.*

2892 **Hodge**, John. *Workman's cottage to Windsor Castle.* London: Sampson Low, 1931. xi, 376p.
Autobiography.

2893 **Fyfe**, Henry Hamilton. *Keir Hardie.* London: Duckworth, 1935. 141p. (Great lives series 57.)

2894 **Gallacher**, William. *Revolt on the Clyde: an autobiography.* London: Lawrence and Wishart, 1936. xiv, 301p.
New edition. 1949. ix, 301p.

2895 **Hughes**, Emrys. *Keir Hardie: some memories.* London: Francis Johnson, 1939. 16p.

2896 **Maxton**, James. *Keir Hardie: prophet and pioneer.* London: Francis Johnson, 1939. 15p.
'Reprinted from *The post Victorians.*'

2897 **Cole**, George Douglas Howard. *James Keir Hardie.* London: Gollancz; Fabian Society, 1941. 34p. (Fabian biographical series 12.)

2898 **Gallacher**, William. *The rolling of the thunder.* London: Lawrence and Wishart, 1947. 229p.
A continuation of the author's autobiography.

2899 **Hughes**, Emrys. *Keir Hardie.* London: Lincolns-Prager, 1950. 79p.

2900 **Gallacher**, William. '*Rise like lions.*' London: Lawrence and Wishart, 1951. 253p.
Memoirs.

2901 **Wearmouth**, Robert Featherstone. 'George Edwards: the product and leader of the agricultural labourers.' *Lond. Q. Hol. Rev.*, 6 ser., XXI, 1 (January 1952), 40–3.

2902 **Cockburn**, John. *The hungry heart: a romantic biography of James Keir Hardie.* London: Jarrolds, 1956. 286p.

2903 **Hardy**, George. *Those stormy years: memories of the fight for freedom on five continents.* London: Lawrence and Wishart, 1956. 256p.

2904 **Hughes**, Emrys. *Keir Hardie.* London: Allen and Unwin, 1956. 248p.

2905 **Keir Hardie**, James. *Selected writings of Keir Hardie.* 1957. (Vanguard pamphlets 7.)
Commentary by D. Sparkes.

2906 **Horner**, Arthur Lewis. *Incorrigible rebel.* London: MacGibbon and Kee, 1960. 234p.
Miners' leader.

2907 **Connole**, Nellie. *Leaven of life: the story of George Henry Fletcher.* London: Lawrence and Wishart, 1961. ix, 211p.

2908 **Lean**, Garth. 'The damnedest aristocrat: Keir Hardie.' *Brave men choose.* London: Blandford P., 1961. p. 161–84.

2909 **Seaborne**, Malcolm and **Isham**, Gyles. 'A Victorian schoolmaster: John James Graves, 1832–1903, Master of Lamport and Hanging Houghton Endowed School and first President of the National Union of Teachers.' *Northamps. Past Pres.*, IV, 1 (1966), 3–12; 2 (1967), 107–19.

2910 **Church**, Roy A. and **Chapman**, Stanley D. 'Gravener Henson and the making of the English working class.' Jones, E. L. and Mingay, G. E. (eds.). *Land, labour and population in the Industrial Revolution: essays presented to J. D. Chambers.* London: Arnold, 1967. p. 131–61.
Midlands labour leader, 1785–1852, in the hosiery industry.

2911 **Morgan**, Kenneth Owen. *Keir Hardie.* London: Oxford U.P., 1967. 64p. (Clarendon biographies.)

2912 **Craik**, William White. *Sydney Hill and the National Union of Public Employees.* London: Allen and Unwin, 1968. 119p.

2913 **Horn**, Pamela L. R. 'Christopher Holloway: an Oxfordshire trade union leader.' *Oxoniensia*, 33 (1968), 125–36.

2914 **Reid**, Fred. 'Keir Hardie's biographers.' *Soc. Study Labour Hist. Bull.*, 16 (Spring 1968), 30–33.
Review article.

2915 **Reid**, Fred. *The early life and political development of James Keir Hardie, 1856–92.* 1969. (D.Phil. thesis, University of Oxford.)

2916 **Gould**, Tony. 'A union man.' *New Soc.*, xv, 381 (15 January 1970), 85–7.
Personal account by an official of the hosiery workers' union.

4. *I–O*

2917 **Operative Bricklayers' Society**. Greenwich Branch. *A short biographical sketch of Bro. John Jeffery, Secretary of Greenwich Branch.* London, 1906. 8p.

2918 **Mann**, Tom. *Tom Mann's memoirs.* London: Labour Publishing Co., 1923. 334p.
Another edition. London: MacGibbon and Kee, 1967. xiv, 278p. (Fitzroy edition.) Preface by Ken Coates.

2919 **Soutter**, F. W. 'Memories of George Odger.' *Nineteenth Century*, XCIV, 562 (December 1923), 898–907.

2920 **Lawson**, John James, Baron Lawson. *A man's life.* London: Hodder and Stoughton, 1932. 288p.
An autobiography of a miners' leader.
New edition. 1944. 191p.
Edited and abridged. London: U. of London P., 1951. 192p. (Pathfinder library.)

2921 **Lawson**, John James, Baron Lawson. *Peter Lee.* London: Hodder and Stoughton, 1936. 316p.
Another edition. London: Epworth P., 1949. viii, 216p.

2922 **Torr**, Dona. *Tom Mann.* London: Lawrence and Wishart, 1936. 48p.
Second edition, with an introduction by Harry Pollitt. 1944. 48p.

2923 **Murphy**, John Thomas. *New horizons.* London: John Lane, 1941. 352p.
An autobiography.

2924 **Eastwood**, George Granville. *George Isaacs: printer, trade union leader, cabinet minister.* London: Odhams, 1952. 223p.

2925 **Torr**, Dona. *Tom Mann and his times. Vol. 1. 1856–1890.* London: Lawrence and Wishart, 1956.

2926 **Fox**, Richard Michael. *Jim Larkin: the rise of the underman.* London: Lawrence and Wishart, 1957. 183p.
American edition. *Jim Larkin, Irish labor leader.* New York: International Publishers, 1957. 183p.

2927 **Larkin**, Emmet J. *James Larkin and the Irish labour movement, 1876–1914.* 1957. 464p. (Ph.D. thesis, Columbia University.)

2928 **Evans**, Eric Wyn. *Mabon; William Abraham 1842–1922: a study in trade union leadership.* Cardiff: U. of Wales P., 1959. xii, 115p.
See also 2848.

2929 **Thompson**, Edward Palmer. 'Homage to Tom Maguire.' Briggs, A. and Saville, J. (eds.). *Essays in labour history . . .* London: Macmillan; New York: St Martin's P., 1960. p. 276–316.
Revised edition. 1967.

2930 **Larkin**, Emmet J. *James Larkin: Irish labour leader, 1876–1947.* London: Routledge and Kegan Paul, 1965. xviii, 334p.
Also published Cambridge, Mass.: M.I.T. Press, 1965. 'An outgrowth of the author's thesis, Columbia University, issued in microfilm form in 1957 under the title: *James Larkin and the Irish labour movement, 1876–1914.*'
Another edition. London: New English Library, 1968. xiv, 306p. (Mentor books.)

2931 **Moffat**, Abe. *My life with the miners.* London: Lawrence and Wishart, 1965. 324p.

2932 **Wolfe**, B. D. *Strange communists I have known.* London: Allen and Unwin, 1966.
James Larkin, p. 52–71.

2933 **Challinor**, Raymond. *Alexander Macdonald and the miners.* London: Central Books, 1968. 34p. (Communist Party. 'Our history' pamphlets 48.)

2934 **Sichel**, J. R. *The political thought of Tom Mann, 1856–1941.* 1968–69. (M.Sc. thesis, University of Bristol.)

2935 **Lawther**, *Sir* William. 'An interview with Sir William Lawther.' *Soc. Study Labour Hist. Bull.*, 19 (Autumn 1969), 14–21.
Interview by J. F. Clarke, Secretary of the North Eastern Group of the Society for the Study of Labour History, 7 March 1968.

5. *P–S*

2936 *Mr. John Potter, J.P.* [Maidstone, 1893.] 9p.
Reprinted from *The Kent Times and Chronicle and Maidstone Advertiser*, 12 January 1893.
Local leader of paper workers.

2937 **Rogers**, Frederick. *Labour, life and literature: some memories of sixty years.* London: Smith, Elder, 1913. xii, 334p.
The author was Secretary of the National Committee of Organised Labour.

2938 **Postgate**, Raymond William. 'Mr. Smith: the Rev. J. E. Smith.' *Out of the past: some revolutionary sketches.* London: Labour Publishing Co., 1922. p. 97–106.
Grand National Consolidated Trades Union.

2939 **Smillie**, Robert. *My life for labour*. London: Mills and Boon, 1924. 310p.

The author was President of the Miners' Federation of Great Britain.

2940 **Reilly**, Sarah A. *I walk with the king: the life story of John Edward Reilly*. London: Epworth P., 1931.

2941 **Sexton**, *Sir* James. *Sir James Sexton, agitator: the life of the dockers' M.P. An autobiography*. London: Faber, 1936. 300p.

2942 **Lawson**, John James. *The man in the cap: the life of Herbert Smith*. London: Methuen, 1941. xi, 263p.

Miners' leader.

2943 **Ap Nicholas**, Islwyn. *Dic Penderyn, Welsh rebel and martyr*. London: Foyle's Welsh P., 1945. 61p.

2944 **Peacock**, William Arthur. *Yours fraternally*. London: Pendulum Publications; Maclean's Printing Works, 1945. 126p.

Autobiographical reminiscences.

2945 **Sage**, Josiah. *The memoirs of Josiah Sage, concerning Joseph Arch and the pioneering days of trade unionism among the agricultural workers*. London: Lawrence and Wishart, 1951. 63p.

2946 **Roberts**, Bryn. *Topical comments*. London: National Union of Public Employees, 1952. xi, 119p.

Collected articles and lectures.

2947 **Williams**, J. Roose. *The life and work of William John Parry, Bethesda, with particular reference to his trade union activities among the slate quarrymen of North Wales*. 1953. (M.A. thesis, University of Wales.)

2948 **Craik**, William White. *Bryn Roberts and the National Union of Public Employees*. London: Allen and Unwin, 1955. 238p.

2949 **Roberts**, Bryn. *As I see it*. [London?]: National Union of Public Employees, 1957. 142p.

Collected articles and speeches.

2950 **Rocker**, Rudolph. *The London years*. London: Robert Anscombe for the Rudolph Rocker Book Committee, 1956 [i.e. 1957]. 360p.

Translated by Joseph Leftwich.

An abridgement of the memoirs of Rudolph Rocker.

2951 **Peacock**, Alfred James. 'Joseph Robinson.' *Soc. Study Labour Hist. Bull.*, 5 (Autumn 1962), 36–8.

Secretary of E. Counties Labour Federation.

2952 **Williams**, J. Roose. '"Quarryman's champion": the life and activities of William John Parry of Coetmor.' *Caern. Hist. Soc. Trans.*, XXIII, (1962), 92–115; XXIV (1963), 217–38; XXV (1964), 81–116; XXVI (1965), 107–56; XXVII (1966), 149–91.

2953 **Fishman**, W. J. 'Rudolph Rocker: anarchist missionary, 1873–1958.' *Hist. Today*, XVI, 1 (January 1966), 45–52.

2954 **Perrins**, Wesley. 'An interview with Wesley Perrins.' *Soc. Study Lab. Hist. Bull.*, 21 (Autumn 1970), 16–24.

An abridged transcript of the interview of W. Perrins by Eric Taylor, recorded on 22 and 30 June 1970.

6. *T–Z*

2955 **Wilson**, John. *Autobiography of Ald. John Wilson, J.P., M.O.* Durham: *Durham Chronicle*, 1909. 110p.

Reprinted from the *Durham Chronicle*.

2956 **Wilson**, John. *Memories of a labour leader: the autobiography of John Wilson, J.P., M.P.* London: Fisher Unwin, 1910. xvi, 300p.

With an introduction by the Dean of Durham and an appreciation by the Bishop of Durham.

2957 **Moir Bussey**, J. F. *From engine cleaner to Privy Councillor: a biographical sketch of the Rt. Hon. J. H. Thomas, M.P. . . .* London: Co-operative Printing Society, 1917. 147p.

Thomas was General Secretary of the National Union of Railwaymen from 1918 to 1924.

Full title on cover. Title page has *From E.C. to P.C. . . .*

2958 **Thorne**, Will. *My life's battles*. London: Newnes, 1925. 221p.

2959 **Wilson**, Joseph Havelock. *My stormy voyage through life*. London: Co-operative Printing Society, 1925.

2960 **Turner**, *Sir* Ben. *About myself, 1863–1930*. London: Cayme P., 1930. 368p.

One of the trade union leaders in the textile industry in Yorkshire.

2961 **White**, James Robert. *Misfit: an autobiography*. London, Toronto: Cape, 1930. 351p.

2962 **Tillett**, Ben. *Memories and reflections*. London: J. Long, 1931. 286p.

2963 **Wright**, William. *From chimney-boy to councillor: the story of my life*. Medstead: Azania P., 1931. 54p.

2964 **Phillpott**, Henry Roy Stewart. *The Right Hon. J. H. Thomas: impressions of a remarkable career*. London: Sampson Low, 1932. vii, 214p.

Railway unionism.

2965 **Fuller**, Basil. *The life story of the Rt. Hon. J. H. Thomas, a statesman of the people*. London: Stanley Paul, 1933. 251p.

Railway unionism.

2966 **Thomas**, James Henry. *My story*. London: Hutchinson, 1937. 311p.

National Union of Railwaymen.

2967 **Tupper**, Edward. *Seamen's torch: the life story of Captain Edward Tupper, National Union of Seamen*. London: Hutchinson, 1938. 320p.

Written with the assistance of Ernest F. Charles.

2968 **Tillett**, Ben. *Ben Tillett: fighter and pioneer*. London: Blandford P., 1943. 14p.

Selected speeches, edited by George **Light**.

2969 **Blackburn**, Fred. *George Tomlinson*. London: Heinemann, 1954. v, 210p.

2970 **Blaxland**, William Gregory. *J. H. Thomas: a life for unity*. London: Muller, 1964. 303p.

2971 **Waddington-Feather**, John. 'Sir Ben Turner, 1863–1942.' *Yorks. Dial. Soc. Trans.*, XII, pt. 69 (1969), 14–20.

2972 **Yergin**, Dan. 'New man.' *New Soc.*, XVI, 417 (24 September 1970), 529–30.
About Rodney Tucker, an ex-Draughtsmen's and Allied Technicians' Association national youth committee secretary.

9. Shop Stewards and Workshop Organisation

See also Part Three, III, B, 4; Part Three, III, G, 1; and Part Five, II. Material on the more informal aspects of work group organisation is classified at Part Two, I.

2973 **Murphy**, John Thomas. *The workers' committee: an outline of its principles and structure*. Sheffield: Sheffield Workers' Committee, 1917. 15p.

2974 **Gallacher**, William and **Campbell**, John Ross. *Direct action: an account of workshop and social organisation*. Glasgow: Scottish Workers' Committee, 1919. 30p. (Pamphlet 1.)

2975 **Ellery**, George. 'The British shop steward movement.' Bloomfield, D. (ed.). *Selected articles on modern industrial movements*. London: Pitman, 1920. p. 103–8.
From *The Voice of Labor I* (30 August 1919), 13–14.

2976 **Gleason**, Arthur. 'The shop stewards and their significance.' Bloomfield, D. (ed.). *Selected articles on modern industrial movements*. London: Pitman, 1920. p. 87–102.
From *Survey*, XLI (4 January 1919), 417–22.
Reprinted in *British labor and the war*, by P. U. Kellogg and Arthur Gleason. New York: Boni and Liveright, 1919.

2977 **Goodrich**, Carter Lyman. *The frontier of control: a study in British workshop politics*. London: Bell, 1920. xvi, 277p.
Also New York: Harcourt, Brace and Howe, 1920.
Ph.D. thesis, University of Chicago.

2978 **Murphy**, John Thomas. 'The shop stewards and workers' committee movement.' Gleason, A. *What the workers want: a study of British labor*. London: Allen and Unwin, 1920. p. 184–200.

2979 **Murphy**, John Thomas. 'Their ideas.' Gleason, A. *What the workers want: a study of British labor*. London: Allen and Unwin, 1920. p. 201–11.
Ideas behind the shop stewards' movement.

2980 **Sullivan**, James W. 'The passing of the British shop steward movement.' Bloomfield, D. (ed.). *Selected articles on modern industrial movements*. London: Pitman, 1920. p. 108–13.
From *National Civic Federation Review*, IV (30 August 1919), 3–4.
'This article represents the attitude of organized labor in the United States – Ed.'

2981 **Walsh**, Tom. *What is this shop stewards movement? A survey with diagrams*. London: National Federation of Shop Stewards (Building Industry), 1920. 8p.

2982 **Wrong**, E. M. 'Some tendencies in industry. I. The shop stewards' movement.' Muscio, B. (ed.). *Lectures on industrial administration*. London: Pitman, 1920. p. 33–9.

2983 **Cole**, George Douglas Howard. *Workshop organization*. Oxford: Clarendon P. for the Carnegie Endowment for International Peace, 1923. xvi, 186p. (Economic and social history of the war, British series.)

2984 **Hannington**, Walter. *Industrial history in war time, including a record of the shop stewards' movement*. London: Lawrence and Wishart, 1940. 119p. (Marxist text book series.)

2985 **Anarchist Federation**. *Equity: the struggle in the factory; history of a Royal Ordnance factory*. Glasgow: the Federation, 1945. 22p.

2986 **Warner**, Aaron W. 'The role of the union in the shop in Britain.' Industrial Relations Research Association. *Proceedings of the eighth annual meeting, New York City, December 28–30, 1955*. p. 234–48.

2987 **Neal**, Leonard Francis. 'The changing role of the shop steward.' Chisholm, C. (ed.). *Communication in industry*. London: Business Publications in association with Batsford, 1957. p. 239–52.

2988 **Pribićević**, Branko. *The demand for 'workers' control' in the coal mining, engineering and railway industries, 1910–1922*. 1957. (D.Phil. thesis, University of Oxford.)

2989 **Zweig**, Ferdynand. 'Two profiles: the shop-steward and the foreman.' *Occup. Psychol.*, XXXI, 1 (January 1957), 47–54.

2990 **Pribićević**, Branko. *The shop stewards' movement and workers' control, 1910–1922*. Oxford: Blackwell, 1959. xii, 179p.

2991 **Moore**, William. *Sheffield shop stewards, 1916–1918*. London: History Group of the Communist Party, 1960. 18p. (Our history 18.)

2992 **Sykes**, Andrew James Macintyre. 'The shop steward's place in industry.' *Q. Rev.*, CCXCVIII, 623 (January 1960), 8–16.

2993 **Clegg**, Hugh Armstrong. 'Unions: the shop floor leaders.' *New Soc.*, 3 (18 October 1962), 13–14.

2994 **Flanders**, Allan David. 'The importance of shop stewards.' *New Soc.*, 20 (14 February 1963), 13–14.

2995 **Marsh**, Arthur I. and **Coker**, E. E. 'Shop steward organization in the engineering industry.' *Br. J. Ind. Relat.*, I, 2 (June 1963), 170–90.

2996 **Goodwin**, Dennis. 'Shop stewards: past, present and future.' *Marxism Today*, VIII, 4 (April 1964), 109–15.

'Discussion contribution', by Hugh Wyper, 6 (June 1964), 185–7.

'Discussion', by J. V. Gibb, 8 (August 1964), 258–9.

2997 **Hinton**, James Sebastian. 'The shop stewards' movement in the first world war.' *Soc. Study Labour Hist. Bull.*, 13 (Autumn 1966), 4–5.

Abstract of a paper given at the Conference of the Society for the Study of Labour History, 4 June 1966, Birkbeck College, London.

An abstract of the discussion on this paper is given p. 5–7.

2998 **Lerner**, Shirley Walowitz and **Bescoby**, John. 'Shop steward combine committees in the British engineering industry.' *Br. J. Ind. Relat.*, IV, 2 (July 1966), 154–64.

2999 **McCarthy**, William Edward John. *The role of shop stewards in British industrial relations: a survey of existing information and research.* London: H.M.S.O., 1966. vi, 81p. (Royal Commission on Trade Unions and Employers' Associations. Research papers 1.)

3000 **Monaghan**, William. 'The shop steward in British industry.' *Co-existence*, III, 1 (January 1966), 75–86.

3001 **Sykes**, Andrew James Macintyre. 'The cohesion of a trade union workshop organization.' *Sociology*, 1, 2 (May 1967), 141–63.

The Printing Chapel.

3002 **Burrow**, T. W., **Somerton**, M. F., **Whittingham**, T. G. and **Williams**, N. *Shop stewards and industrial relations*, Nottingham: U. of Nottingham, Department of Adult Education; Workers' Educational Association, East Midland District, 1968. 98p.

3003 **Eldridge**, John E. T. 'The shop steward's role: a comment on the North East of England.' *Industrial disputes: essays in the sociology of industrial relations.* London: Routledge and Kegan Paul; New York: Humanities P., 1968. Appendix D. p. 259–63.

'... reprinted from *Voice of North East Industry* (September 1966) where it appeared under the title, "The vital role of the North East Shop Steward".'

3004 **McCarthy**, William Edward John and **Parker**, Stanley Robert. *Shop stewards and workshop relations: the results of a study undertaken by the Government Social Survey for the Royal Commission on Trade Unions [and] Employers' Associations.* London: H.M.S.O., 1968. viii, 158p. (Research papers 10.)

3005 **McCarthy**, William Edward John. 'Shop stewards at work.' *New Soc.*, XI, 291 (25 April 1968), 593–5.

3006 **Parker**, Stanley Robert and **Bynner**, J. M. *Correlational analysis of data obtained from a survey of shop stewards: a comparison of McQuitty cluster analysis, factor analysis and principal component analysis.* [1968.] 14p. (Social Survey methodological paper m. 137.)

3007 **Hinton**, James Sebastian. *Rank and file militancy in the British engineering industry, 1914–1918.* 1968–69. (Ph.D. thesis, University of London.)

3008 **Biggs**, Ken. 'Coventry and the shop stewards' movement, 1917.' *Marxism Today*, XIII, 1 (January 1969), 14–23.

Comment by Frank Jackson, 5 (May 1969), 159–60.

3009 **Goodman**, J. F. B. and **Whittingham**, T. G. *Shop stewards in British industry.* New York, Maidenhead: McGraw-Hill, 1969. xiv, 256p.

3010 **Higgs**, Phillip. 'The convenor.' Fraser, R. (ed.). *Work, volume 2: twenty personal accounts.* Harmondsworth: Penguin, 1969. p. 109–29.

First published in *New Left Review*, 48 (March–April 1968), 27–40.

3011 **Kendall**, Walter. *The revolutionary movement in Britain 1900–21: the origins of British communism.* London: Weidenfeld and Nicolson, 1969. xii, 453p.

Includes chapters on the Shop Stewards Movement, and Guild Socialism.

3012 **Frow**, Ruth and **Frow**, Edmund. 'The shop stewards movement during and after the First World War, 1914–1920: a bibliography.' *Marx Meml. Libr. Q. Bull.*, 54 (April–June 1970), 15–18; 55 (July–September 1970), 12–15.

3013 **MacFarlane**, James. 'Shipboard union representation in the British merchant navy.' *Int. Rev. of Soc. Hist.*, XV, 1 (1970), 1–18.

3014 **Parker**, Stanley Robert and **Bynner**, J. M. 'Correlational analysis of data obtained from a survey of shop stewards: a comparison of McQuitty elementary linkage analysis, factor analysis and principal component analysis.' *Hum. Relat.*, XXIII, 4 (August 1970), 345–59.

See also: 1360; 1761; 2668; 3217; 3219–20; 8073; 8195; 12,238; 12,785.

H. POLITICAL ACTION AND THE LABOUR PARTY

This section generally excludes works on the Labour Party which are not concerned with the relationship between it and the trade union movement. See also Part Three, III, A–B; Part Five, V; and Part Seven, VII, B, 4.

3015 **Binning**, Thomas. *Organised labour: the duty of the trades' unions in relation to socialism.* London: Socialist League, 1887. p. 83–96. (Socialist platform 5.)

Continuing pagination throughout series to no. 5.

3016 **Burt**, Thomas, **Champion**, Henry Hyde, **Keir Hardie**, James and **Woods**, Sam. 'Mr. Chamberlain's programme.' *Nineteenth Century*, XXXII, 190 (December 1892), 864–98.
T. Burt, 864–74.
H. H. Champion, 875–82.
J. Keir Hardie, 883–90.
S. Woods, 891–8.

3017 **Smart**, H. Russell. *Trade unionism and politics*. Manchester, 1893.

3018 **Beever**, J. H. *An appeal to trades unionists for political action*. Halifax, 1894. 16p.

3019 **Hammill**, Fred. 'Labour representation.' *Fortn. Rev.*, n.s., LV, 328 (April 1894), 546–56.
Description of various bodies and movements including trade unions, strikes and lock-outs, unemployment, political societies, all leading towards labour representation.

3020 **Threlfall**, T. R. 'The political future of "labour".' *Nineteenth Century*, XXXV, 204 (February 1894), 203–16.

3021 **Tillett**, Ben. *Trades unionism and socialism*. Manchester, 1894. 16p. (Clarion pamphlet 16.)

3022 **Wicks**, Frederick. 'The insignificance of the trades union vote.' *Nineteenth Century*, XXXV, 206 (April 1894), 602–17.

3023 **Mavor**, James. 'Labor and politics in England.' *Polit. Sci. Q.*, X, 3 (September 1895), 486–517.

3024 **Diack**, William. 'Radicalism and labour: a programme and policy.' *Westm. Rev.*, CLIV, 2 (August 1900), 131–42.

3025 **Lees-Smith**, Hastings Bernard. 'The latest chapter in the history of trade unionism.' *Econ. J.*, XIV, 55 (September 1904), 469–73.
'Old' and 'New' unionism and the Labour Representation Committee.
Letter, by J. M. Ludlow, 56 (December 1904), 649–50, headed 'Trade unionism and individualistic radicals'.
Comments by H. B. Lees-Smith, p. 650–1.

3026 **Gill**, A. H. 'The organisation of labour as a political force.' *Manchr. Statist. Soc. Trans.* (1904–5), 81–91.

3027 **Kelly**, Edmond. *A practical programme for workingmen*. London: Swan Sonnenschein, 1906. xiii, 227p.

3028 **Bibby**, Frederick. *Trades unionists and socialism: an address to liberals and conservatives*. Manchester: *Manchester Courier*, 1907. 15p.

3029 **Rose**, Frank Herbert. *The coming force: the labour movement*. Salford: Independent Labour Party, 1909. x, 125p.

3030 **Wilson**, J. B. *The socialist plot to capture the trade unions*. London, 1910. 12p.

3031 **Marriott**, John Arthur Ransome. 'Syndicalism and socialism.' *Nineteenth Century*, LXXII, 429 (November 1912), 913–29.

3032 **Lacey**, *Canon* T. A. 'Political basis of trade unionism.' *Nineteenth Century*, LXXXVIII, 521 (July 1920), 136–43.

3033 **Read**, Conyers. 'The political progress of the English workingman.' *J. Polit. Econ.*, XXVIII, 6 (June 1920), 505–17; 7 (July 1920), 601–18.

3034 **Green**, Walford D. 'The labour crisis. II. Party and the State.' *Nineteenth Century*, LXXXIX, 531 (May 1921), 780–7.

3035 **Attlee**, Clement Richard. *Socialism for trade unionists*. London, 1922. 11p.

3036 **Lord**, *Sir* Walter Greaves. *Trade unions & political levies: a speech . . . in the House of Commons on March 14th, 1924 . . .* London: National Unionist Association, 1924. 47p. ([Publication] 2312.)

3037 **Brand**, Carl Fremont. 'The conversion of the British trade-unions to political action.' *Am. Hist. Rev.*, XXX, 2 (January 1925), 251–70.

3038 **Hutchinson**, Keith. *Labour in politics*. London: Labour Publishing Co., 1925. 127p.

3039 **Mallalieu**, William C. *The influence of British labor upon politics and legislation, 1875–1900*. 1925. (Ph.D. dissertation, Johns Hopkins University.)

3040 **Stone**, F. G. 'The Labour Party and the trade unions.' *Nineteenth Century*, XCVII, 577 (March 1925), 309–25.

3041 **Tracey**, Herbert (ed.). *The book of the Labour Party: its history, growth, policy, and leaders*. London: Caxton Publishing Co., 1925. 3v.
Vol. 1 includes a history of the labour movement leading to the formation of the Labour Party.
Vols. 1, 2, 3 cover Labour Party policy.
Vol. 3 gives brief biographies of labour leaders.

3042 **Gillespie**, Frances Elma. *Labor and politics in England, 1850–67*. Durham, N.C.: Duke University, 1927. vi, 319p.
Reprinted. London: Cass; New York: Octagon Books, 1966. vi, 319p.

3043 **Lamb**, W. K. *British labour and Parliament, 1867–1893*. 1933–34. (Ph.D. thesis, University of London.)

3044 **Braatoy**, B. E. *Labour and war: the theory of labour action to prevent war*. 1934. (Ph.D. thesis, University of London.)

3045 **Cole**, George Douglas Howard. 'The arrival of labour in politics.' Taylor, G. R. S. (ed.). *Great events in history*. London: Cassell, 1934. p. 707–72.
'. . . a discussion of the rise and significance of the Labour movement both in Great Britain and as an international manifestation of the developing capitalist system.'

3046 **Good**, Dorothy M. *Economic and political origins of the Labour Party from 1884 to 1906*. 1936. (Ph.D. thesis, University of London.)

3047 **Neumann**, Franz. *European trade unionism and politics*. New York: League for Industrial Democracy, 1936. 61p. (Pamphlet series.)

3048 **Strachey**, Evelyn John St. Loe. *What are we to do?* London: Gollancz, 1938. 398p.
A study of the labour movement.
Also published New York: Random House, 1938.

3049 **Drinkwater**, Thomas Leonard. *History of the trades unions and the Labour Party in Liverpool, 1911–1926.* 1940. (B.A. thesis, University of Liverpool.)

3050 **Brand**, Carl Fremont. 'British labour and the wartime coalitions.' *British labour's rise to power.* Stanford, Calif.: Stanford U.P.; London: Oxford U.P., 1941. p. 28–54.

3051 **Brand**, Carl Fremont. 'The British Labour Party and the Communists.' *British labour's rise to power.* Stanford, Calif.: Stanford U.P.; London: Oxford U.P., 1941. p. 232–86.

3052 **Brand**, Carl Fremont. 'The conversion of the British trade unions to political action.' *British labour's rise to power.* Stanford, Calif.: Stanford U.P.; London: Oxford U.P., 1941. p. 3–27.

3053 **Cole**, George Douglas Howard. *British working class politics, 1832–1914.* London: Routledge, 1941. viii, 320p.
Also Labour Book Service edition.
Sequel: *A history of the Labour Party from 1914.* London: Routledge and Kegan Paul, 1948.

3054 **Miller**, John. *The rise of labor representation in Parliament.* 1942. (Ph.D. thesis, University of Iowa.)

3055 **Gee**, Thomas. *Politics and the trade unions.* London: Signpost P., 1945. 19p. (Signpost booklets.)
Author was a trade unionist, of Rugby.

3056 **Reid**, John Hotchkiss Stewart. *British labor and social politics to 1914.* 1946. 348p. (Ph.D. thesis, University of Toronto.)

3057 **Cole**, Margaret. 'British trade unions and the Labour Government.' *Ind. Labor Relat. Rev.*, I, 4 (July 1948), 573–9.

3058 **Flexner**, Jean Atherton. 'British labor under the Labor government. Part II. Position and role of trade unions.' *Mon. Labor Rev.*, LXVII, 4 (October 1948), 366–72.

3059 **Tracey**, Herbert (ed.). *The British Labour Party: its history, growth, policy and leaders.* London: Caxton Publishing Co., 1948. 3v.
Vol. 1. History.
Vol. 2. Policy.
Vol. 3. Biographies.

3060 **Williams**, Francis. *Fifty years' march: the rise of the Labour Party.* London: Odhams P., 1949. 383p.

3061 **Pelling**, Henry Mathison. *Origins and early history of the Independent Labour Party, 1880–1900.* 1951. (Ph.D. thesis, University of Cambridge.)

3062 **Mowat**, Charles Loch. 'The history of the Labour Party: the Coles, the Webbs, and some others.' *J. Mod. Hist.*, XXIII (June 1951), 146–53.

3063 **Briggs**, Asa. 'Industry and politics in early nineteenth century Keighley.' *Brad. Antiq.*, IX, n.s., VII (1952), 305–17.

3064 **Crowley**, D. W. *The origins of the revolt of the British labour movement from Liberalism, 1875–1906.* 1952. (Ph.D. thesis, University of London.)

3065 **Cole**, George Douglas Howard. 'The Labour Party and the trade unions.' *Polit. Q.*, XXIV, 1 (January–March 1953), 18–27.

3066 **Roberts**, Benjamin Charles. 'Trade unions and party politics.' *Camb. J.*, VI, 7 (April 1953), 387–402.

3067 **Conservative and Unionist Party.** Conservative Industrial Department. *Trade unions and politics.* London: Conservative Political Centre, 1954. 23p. (Trade union services series 6.)
Revised edition. 1963. 18p. (New trade union series 6.)

3068 **Pelling**, Henry Mathison. *The origins of the Labour Party, 1880–1900.* London: Macmillan, 1954. ix, 257p.
Second edition. Oxford: Clarendon P., 1965. ix, 256p.

3069 **Hennessy**, B. 'Trade unions and the British Labor Party.' *Am. Polit. Sci. Rev.*, XLIX, 4 (December 1955), 1050–66.

3070 **Pelling**, Henry Mathison. 'The American economy and the foundation of the British Labour Party.' *Econ. Hist. Rev.*, 2nd ser., VIII, 1 (August 1955), 1–17.

3071 **Reid**, John Hotchkiss Stewart. *The origins of the British Labour Party.* Minneapolis: U. of Minnesota P., 1955. [xiv], 258p.

3072 **Duffy**, A. E. P. *The growth of trade unionism in England from 1867–1906 in its political aspects.* 1956. (Ph.D. thesis, University of London.)

3073 **Jacobson**, Sydney and **Connor**, William. 'The trade unions and Parliament.' *Parl. Aff.*, IX, 4 (Autumn 1956), 470–7.
'This article first appeared in a Spotlight pamphlet by Sydney Jacobson and William Connor, published by The Daily Mirror Newspapers Ltd.'

3074 **McCready**, Herbert W. 'British labour's lobby, 1867–75.' *Can. J. Econ. Polit. Sci.*, XXII, 2 (May 1956), 141–60.

3075 **Morton**, Arthur Leslie and **Tate,** George Kenneth. *The British Labour movement, 1770–1920: a history.* London: Lawrence and Wishart, 1956. 313p.
American edition. *The British Labor movement, 1770–1920: a political history.* New York: International Publishers, 1957. 313p.

3076 **Bealey**, Frank. 'The Northern weavers, independent labour representation and Clitheroe, 1902.' *Manchr. Sch.*, XXV, 1 (January 1957), 26–60.

3077 **Williams**, James Eccles. 'The political activities of a trade union, 1906–1914.' *Int. Rev. of Soc. Hist.*, II, 1 (1957), 1–21.
Derbyshire Miners' Association.

3078 **Harrison**, Martin. *The political activities of British trade unions, 1945–1954.* 1957–58. (D.Phil. thesis, University of Oxford.)

3079 **Bealey**, Frank William and **Pelling**, Henry Mathison. *Labour and politics, 1900–1906: a history of the Labour Representation Committee.* London: Macmillan, 1958. xi, 313p.

3080 **Finer**, S. E. 'The anonymous empire.' *Polit. Studies*, VI, 1 (February 1958), 16–32.
'This article is the final chapter of a short book entitled *Anonymous Empire: a Study of the Lobby in Great Britain . . .*'

3081 **Hennessy**, B. 'Left and right in British labor: Bevanism and the trade unions.' *Soc. Sci.*, XXXIII, 2 (April 1958), 73–80.

3082 **Melitz**, Jack. 'The trade unions and Fabian socialism.' *Ind. Labor Relat. Rev.*, XII, 4 (July 1959), 554–67.

3083 **Newell**, P. M. *The political activities of a trade union: the Electrical Trades Union, 1944–1956.* 1959. (M.A. thesis, University of Manchester.)

3084 **Shanks,** Michael. 'Politics and the trade unionist.' *Polit. Q.*, XXX, 1 (January–March 1959), 44–53.

3085 **Cyriax**, George. 'Labour and the unions.' *Polit. Q.*, XXXI, 3 (July–September 1960), 324–32.

3086 **Harrison**, Martin. *Trade unions and the Labour Party since 1945.* London: Allen and Unwin, 1960. 360p.
American edition. Detroit: Wayne State University, 1960. 360p.

3087 **Flanders**, Allan David. *Trade unions and politics.* London: London Trades Council, 1961. 16p.
1860–1960 Centenary Lecture.
Reprinted in a shortened version in the author's *Management and unions.* London: Faber, 1970. p. 24–37.

3088 **O'Higgins**, Rachel. 'Irish trade unions and politics, 1830–50.' *Hist. J.*, IV, 2 (1961), 208–17.

3089 **Duffy**, A. E. P. 'Differing policies and personal rivalries in the origins of the Independent Labour Party.' *Vic. Studies*, VI, 1 (September 1962), 43–65.

3090 **Pickles**, William. 'Trade unions in the political climate.' Roberts, B. C. (ed.). *Industrial relations: contemporary problems and perspectives.* London: Methuen, 1962. p. 28–61.

3091 **Gregory**, Roy George. *The miners and politics in England and Wales, 1906–14.* 1963. 2v. (D.Phil. thesis, University of Oxford.)
Published as *The miners and British politics, 1906–1914.* London: Oxford U.P., 1968.

3092 **Thompson**, P. R. *London working-class politics and the formation of the London Labour Party 1885–1914.* 1963–64. (D.Phil. thesis, University of Oxford.)

3093 **Middlemas**, R. K. *The Clydesiders: a left wing struggle for parliamentary power.* London: Hutchinson, 1965.

3094 **Sykes**, Andrew James Macintyre. 'Attitudes to political affiliation in a printing trade union.' *Scott. J. Polit. Econ.*, XII, 2 (June 1965) 161–79.
The Scottish Typographical Association.

3095 **Cyriax**, George. 'Trade unions under a Labour government.' *Natn. Prov. Bank Rev.*, 75 (August 1966), 9–14.

3096 **Muller**, William Dale. *The parliamentary activity of trade union MPs, 1959–1964.* 1966. (Ph.D. thesis, University of Florida.)

3097 **Wanczycki**, Jan K. 'Union dues and political contributions; Great Britain, United States, Canada: a comparison.' *Relat. Ind.*, XXI, 2 (April 1966), 143–209.

3098 **Read**, A. G. 'Trade unions and politics in Britain.' Shri Ram Centre for Industrial Relations. Third National Seminar on Industrial Relations in a Developing Economy, September 20–23, 1967, Chandigarh. *Trade unions and politics in India.* [New Delhi]: the Centre, 1967. Vol. 1. leaves 23–32.
Mimeographed.
The author was First Secretary (Labour), British High Commission, New Delhi.

3099 **Pelling**, Henry. 'Labour and the downfall of Liberalism.' *Popular politics and society in late Victorian Britain: essays.* London: Macmillan; New York: St Martin's P., 1968. p. 101–20.

3100 **Pelling**, Henry. 'Then and now: popular attitudes since 1945.' *Popular politics and society in late Victorian Britain: essays.* London: Macmillan; New York: St Martin's P., 1968. p. 165–79.

3101 **Heidenheimer**, Arnold J. 'Trade unions, benefit systems and party mobilization styles: "horizontal" influences on the British Labour and German Social Democratic parties.' *Comp. Polit.*, I, 3 (April 1969), 313–42.

3102 **Flanders**, Allan David. 'Trade unions and politics.' *Management and unions: the theory and reform of industrial relations.* London: Faber, 1970. p. 24–37.
'A shortened version of the London Trades Council 1860–1960 Centenary Lecture in January 1961.'

See also: 1356; 1589; 9876.

I. TRADE UNIONISM AND COMMUNISM

This section generally excludes works on Communism which are not specifically concerned with the relationship between it and the trade union movement. See also Part Three, III, A–B; and Part Five, V.

3103 **Watson**, William Foster. *Watson's reply: a complete answer to the charges of espionage levelled against W. F. Watson and an exposure of the espionage system.* London: the author, 1920. 86p.

3104 **Citrine**, Walter McLennan. *Democracy or disruption? an examination of communist influences in the trade unions.* London: T.U.C. Publicity Department, 1928. 29p.

3105 **National Minority Movement.** *What is this National Minority Movement?* London, 1928. 16p.

3106 **Mahon**, John Augustus. *Trade unionism and communism.* London, 1936. 16p.

3107 **Citrine**, Walter McLennan. *Citrine & others v. Pountney: full summary with extracts from verbatim evidence . . .* London: Modern Books, 1940. 47p.

The *Daily Worker* libel case.

3108 **Citrine**, Walter McLennan, and others. *Union leaders vindicated: a full account of the libel action brought by Sir Walter Citrine . . . against the proprietor of the Daily Worker.* London: T.U.C. Publicity Department, 1940. 109p.

3109 **Horner**, Arthur Lewis. *Trade unions and communism.* London: Trinity Trust, 1948. 11p.

Reprinted, with additions, from *Labour Monthly*.

3110 **Darke**, Bob. *The communist technique in Britain.* London: Penguin Books, 1952. 159p. (Penguin special.)

3111 **Conservative and Unionist Party.** Conservative Industrial Department. *Trade unions and communism.* London: Conservative Political Centre, 1954. 23p. (Trade union service series 7.)

Revised edition. 1964. 26p. (New trade union series 8.)

3112 **Wyatt**, Woodrow Lyle. *The peril in our midst.* London: Phoenix House, 1956. 70p.

3113 **Hart**, Finlay. *The Communist Party and the trade unions.* London: Communist Party, 1958. 24p.

3114 **Byrne**, John Thomas and **Chapple**, Francis Joseph. *All those in favour? An account of the High Court action against the Electrical Trades Union and its officers for ballot-rigging in the election of union officials. Byrne & Chapple v. Foulkes & others, 1961, prepared from the official court transcript by C. H. Rolph . . .* London: Deutsch, 1962. 255p.

3115 **Bottomley**, Arthur George. *The use and abuse of trade unions.* London: Ampersand Books, 1963. 89p.

3116 **Martin**, Roderick. *The National Minority Movement: a study in the organisation of trade union militancy in the inter-war period.* 1964–65. (D.Phil. thesis, University of Oxford.)

3117 **Economic League.** *The agitators: extremist activities in British industry.* London: the League, 1968. 68p.

3118 **Martin**, Roderick. 'The National Minority Movement.' *Soc. Study Labour Hist. Bull.*, 17 (Autumn 1968), 2–4.

Abstract of a paper given at a Conference of the Society for the Study of Labour History, Birkbeck College, London, 3 May 1968.

An abstract of the discussion which followed the paper appears on p. 4–6.

3119 **Martin**, Roderick. *Communism and the British trade unions, 1924–1933: a study of the National Minority Movement.* Oxford: Clarendon P., 1969. xii, 209p.

See also: 1343; 2710.

J. TRADE UNIONISM AND RELIGION

3120 **Richardson**, R. 'Primitive methodism: its influence on the working classes.' *Prim. Method. Q. Rev.*, xxv (1883), 261–73.

3121 **Orr**, Emily C. *Our working men: an attempt to reach them.* London: Christian Knowledge Society, 1886. 239p.

3122 **Fischer**, Ernest. *The ethics of labour: a lecture.* London: Christian Knowledge Society, 1891. 32p.

3123 **Guild of St Matthew.** *The church and 'labour day', Sunday, May 1st, 1892.* London, 1892. 8p.

3124 **Holland**, Henry Scott. 'What attitude should the Church adopt towards the aims and methods of labour combinations?' *Econ. Rev.*, II, 4 (October 1892), 441–51.

3125 **Snow**, Terence Benedict. *Christian aspects of the labour question.* London: Catholic Truth Society, 1894. 32p.

3126 **Wilson**, James Maurice. *The ethical basis of the labour movement: an address . . . to the Labour Church and Independent Labour Party . . . Bolton . . . Dec. 16, 1894.* London: Christian Knowledge Society, 1894. 20p.

3127 **Wilson**, James Maurice. *The labour problem and Christ's teaching: an address to men . . . in the Parish Church, Rochdale, on . . . May 5, 1895.* [1895?]

3128 **Wilson**, James Maurice. *The religious aspect of the labour movement in England: an address to men . . . in Rochdale Parish Church . . . January 6, 1895.* London: Christian Knowledge Society, 1895. 23p.

3129 **Andrews**, Charles Freer. *The relation of Christianity to the conflict between capital and labour.* London: Methuen, 1896. 142p. (Burney prize essay, 1894.)

3130 **Snow**, Terence Benedict. *The church and labour: four lectures.* London: Catholic Truth Society, 1896. 44p.

3131 **Orr**, Emily C. *Our working boys: suggestions for their teachers.* London: Christian Knowledge Society, 1900. 128p.

3132 **Jones**, Ebenezer Griffith. *The economics of Jesus; or work and wages in the kingdom of God. A study of the money parables.* London: J. Clarke, 1905. 128p.

3133 **Haw**, George (ed.). *Christianity and the working classes.* London, New York: Macmillan, 1906. 257p.

Contributors: G. W. Kitchin, Will Crooks, R. F. Horton, Canon Barnett, Arthur Henderson, Silas K. Hocking, Bramwell Booth, George Lansbury, Ensor Walters, T. Edmund Harvey, J. G. Adderley.

3134 **Paxton**, Thomas. *Practical Christianity and labour.* Birmingham: T. Paxton, 1909. 91p.

3135 **Thompson**, C. Bertrand. *The churches and the wage earners: a study of the cause and cure of their separation.* London: Fisher Unwin, 1909. xiii, 229p.

3136 **Ward**, William. *Religion and labour.* London: 'Gazette' Office, 1909. 188p. (Talks to toilers 2.)

3137 **Muir**, William. *Christianity and labour.* London: Hodder and Stoughton, 1910. xxiii, 316p.

3138 **Bray**, Reginald Arthur. *Labour and the churches.* London: Constable, 1912. 111p. (Modern religious problems.)

3139 **Evans**, Idris. *Christian Socialism, its rise and development, its economic and social results, and its relation to other working-class movements.* 1912. (M.A. thesis, University of Wales, Aberystwyth.)

3140 **Green**, T. C. E. *The rights of capital and labour and the duty of the church.* Clifton: Baker, 1914. 60p.

3141 **Cohen**, Chapman. *Christianity and slavery, with a chapter on Christianity and the labour movement.* London: Pioneer P., 1918. 95p.

3142 **Barnes**, George Nicoll, and others. *The religion in the labour movement.* London: Holborn P., 1919. 200p.

International Conference on Labour and Religion, London, 1919.

Contributors: G. N. Barnes, Einar Li, A. Henderson, and others.

3143 **Cunningham**, William, Archdeacon of Ely. *Personal ideals and social principles: some comments on the Report of the Archbishops' Committee on Christianity and Industrial Problems.* London: Society for Promoting Christian Knowledge, 1919. 40p.

3144 **Ryan**, John Augustine and **Husslein**, Joseph (eds.). *The Church and labor.* London, 1920. xvii, 305p. (Social action series 1.)

Printed in U.S.A.

Documents issued by Papal and other authorities, with contributions by the editors.

3145 **Kennedy**, Geoffrey Anketell Studdert. *Democracy and the dog collar: the relations between organised religion and organised labour.* London: Hodder and Stoughton, 1921. xii, 248p.

3146 **Armstrong**, Walter Henry. *Christianity and trade unionism.* London: Epworth P., 1922. 16p.

3147 **Andrews**, Charles Freer. *Christ and labour.* London: Student Christian Movement, 1923. 183p.

3148 **Bampton**, Joseph M. *Christianity and reconstruction: the labour question.* London: Sands, 1923. vii, 176p.

3149 **Britton**, James Nimmo. *Religion and industry.* London: Kingsgate P., 1926. 19p.

3150 **Skelhorn**, Samuel. *Labour & religion.* London: Drane's, 1926. 96p.

3151 **Church of England**. Archbishops' Committee on Christianity and Industrial Problems. *Christianity and industrial problems.* London: Society for Promoting Christian Knowledge, 1927. xxiii, 221p.

3152 **Goad**, J. Newcombe. *Labour and religion: or, the making of men.* London: Morgan and Scott, 1927. xiv, 245p.

3153 **Kenyon**, Ruth. *Does the Church stand for a living wage?* Letchworth: League of the Kingdom of God, 1927. 19p. (New series, pamphlet 1.)

3154 **Watson**, *Sir* Angus. *The quest for the Kingdom of God in industry.* London: Independent P., 1928. 20p.

3155 **Demant**, Vigo Auguste. *The miners' distress and the coal problem: an outline for Christian thought and action.* London: Student Christian Movement P., 1929. 96p.

Submitted to the Christian Social Council by its Research Committee.

3156 **Ingram**, Archibald Kenneth. *The Sunday mass and the industrial problem.* London: Society of SS. Peter and Paul, 1929. 23p.

3157 **Reckitt**, Maurice Benington. *Christian cooperative thought & action in relation to industry.* London: Society of SS. Peter and Paul, 1929. 23p.

3158 **Wearmouth**, Robert Featherstone. *Methodism and the working classes of England, 1800–1850.* 1935. (Ph.D. thesis, University of London.)

3159 **Wearmouth**, Robert Featherstone. *Methodism and the working-class movements of England, 1800–1850.* London: Epworth P., 1937. 289p.

3160 **Council for the Investigation of Vatican Influence and Censorship.** *Memorandum on the penetration of the trades unions by Roman Catholic guilds.* London, 1938. 7p.

3161 **Walsh**, Robert Patrick. *Catholics and trade unions.* Manchester: Catholic Worker, 1944.

3162 **Wearmouth**, Robert Featherstone. *Methodism and the common people of the eighteenth century.* London: Epworth P., 1945. 276p.

3163 **British Council of Churches**. *Christian responsibility in industry: some vital questions, with an introductory statement for discussion.* London: the Council, 1950. 20p.

3164 **Industrial Christian Fellowship**. *The Christian doctrine of work.* London: the Fellowship, 1950. 15p.

3165 **Wearmouth**, Robert Featherstone. *Methodism and the struggle of the working classes, 1850–1900.* Leicester: Backus, 1954. xv, 269p.

3166 **Inglis**, Kenneth S. *English churches and the working-classes, 1880–1900, with an introductory survey of tendencies earlier in the century.* 1956. (D.Phil. thesis, University of Oxford.)

3167 **Wearmouth**, Robert Featherstone. *The social and political influence of methodism in the twentieth century.* London: Epworth P., 1957. xiii, 265p.

3168 **Weller**, T. *The influence of Nonconformity on the wage-earning population of Nottingham in the 19th century.* 1957. (M.A. thesis, University of Nottingham.)

3169 **Wearmouth**, Robert Featherstone. *Methodism and the trade unions.* London: Epworth P., 1959. 78p. (Wesley historical lecture 25.)

3170 **Mayor**, Stephen Harold. *The relations between organised religion and the English working-class movements, 1850–1914.* 1960. ix, 711p. (Ph.D. thesis, University of Manchester.)

3171 **Todd**, John Murray. 'The worker priests.' *Work: Christian thought and practice; a symposium.* London: Darton, Longman and Todd; Baltimore, Md.: Helicon P., 1960. p. 113–19.

3172 **Barnes**, R. 'The late Canon Donaldson and the Leicester unemployed march of 1905: a note on the interrelation of religion and politics in a midland town.' *Soc. Study Labour Hist. Bull.*, 5 (Autumn 1962), 16–17.

3173 **Hopkinson**, Alfred Stephan. *God at work: the working world and the kingdom of God.* London: Hodder and Stoughton, 1962. 126p.

3174 **Saint**, J. G. *The influence of the non-conformist religions on the character of the British labour movement.* 1962. 182p. (M.A. thesis, McGill University.)

3175 **Inglis**, Kenneth S. *Churches and the working-classes in Victorian England.* London: Routledge and Kegan Paul; Toronto: U. of Toronto P., 1963. viii, 350p. (Studies in social history.)

3176 **Mayor**, Stephen Harold. *The churches and the labour movement.* London: Independent P., 1967. 414p.

3177 **Pelling**, Henry. 'Popular attitudes to religion.' *Popular politics and society in late Victorian Britain: essays.* London: Macmillan; New York: St Martin's P., 1968. p. 19–36.

3178 **Moore**, Robert. 'Methodism and the working classes in Durham.' *NE. Group Study Labour Hist. Bull.*, 3 (October 1969), 7–9.

Summary of a paper read to the Group, 17 May 1969.

3179 **Evans**, Hilary Anne. *Religion and the working classes in mid-nineteenth century England.* 1970. (M.Phil. (Arts) thesis, University of London.)

K. TRADE UNIONISM AND INTERNATIONAL AFFAIRS

See also Part Three, III, B. In particular, see Part Three, III, B, 2 for works on the First International.

3180 **Stockton**, Frank T. 'Agreements between American and European molders' unions.' *J. Polit. Econ.*, XXIV, 3 (March 1916), 284–98.

3181 **Klingberg**, Frank J. 'Harriet Beecher Stowe and social reform in England.' *Am. Hist. Rev.*, XLIII, 3 (April 1938), 542–52.

Anti-slavery and labour movements.

3182 **Brand**, Carl Fremont. 'The attitude of British labour toward President Wilson during the peace conference.' *British labour's rise to power.* Stanford, Calif.: Stanford U.P.; London: Oxford U.P., 1941. p. 150–64.

3183 **Brand**, Carl Fremont. 'The reaction of British labour to the policies of President Wilson during the World War.' *British labour's rise to power.* Stanford, Calif.: Stanford U.P.; London: Oxford U.P., 1941. p. 121–49.

3184 **Brand**, Carl Fremont. 'The war aims and peace programs of British labour, 1914–1918.' *British labour's rise to power.* Stanford, Calif.: Stanford U.P.; London: Oxford U.P., 1941. p. 55–120.

3185 **Davies**, Ernest. 'Anglo-American trade union co-operation.' *Polit. Q.*, XIV, 1 (January–March 1943), 60–70.

3186 **Greenleaf**, Richard. 'British labor against American slavery.' *Sci. Soc.*, XVII, 1 (Winter 1953), 42–58.

3187 **Graubard**, Stephen Richards. *British labour and the Russian revolution, 1917–1924.* Cambridge, Mass.: Harvard U.P.; London: Oxford U.P., 1956. 305p. (Harvard historical monographs 30.)

3188 **Pelling**, Henry. 'America and the British "labour unrest".' *America and the British Left: from Bright to Bevan.* London: Black, 1956. p. 89–107.

3189 **Harrison**, Royden J. 'British labour and the Confederacy: a note on the Southern sympathies of some British working class journals and leaders during the American Civil War.' *Int. Rev. of Soc. Hist.*, II, 1 (1957), 78–105.

3190 **Harrison**, Royden J. 'British labor and American slavery.' *Sci. Soc.*, XXV, 4 (December 1961), 291–319.

3191 **Beever**, R. Colin. 'Trade unions and the Common Market.' *Planning*, XXVIII, 461 (1 May 1962), 73–109.

3192 **Beever**, R. Colin. 'Trade union rethinking.' *J. Common Mkt. Studies*, II, 2 (November 1963), 140–54.

'The purpose of this contribution is to show the trend of trade union thought in Britain concerning economic integration with Europe over the period 1956–62. It is based mainly on the records of the Trades Union Congress...'

3193 **Davies**, D. I. 'The politics of the TUC's colonial policy.' *Polit. Q.*, XXXV, 1 (January–March 1964), 23–34.

3194 **Harrison**, Royden J. 'British labour and American slavery.' *Before the socialists: studies in labour and politics, 1861–1881.* London: Routledge and Kegan Paul; Toronto: U. of Toronto P., 1965. p. 40–77.

3195 **Pelling**, Henry. 'British labour and British imperialism.' *Popular politics and society in late Victorian Britain: essays*. London: Macmillan; New York: St Martin's P., 1968. p. 82–100.

3196 **Neufeld**, Maurice F. 'Realms of thought and organized labor in the age of Jackson.' *Labor Hist.*, x, 1 (Winter 1969), 5–43.

L. TRADE UNION EDUCATION

This section is concerned with the education of trade unionists by trade unions or other organisations. It is not concerned with workers' education more broadly defined or with adult education. Hence material relating to such bodies as the Workers' Educational Association has generally been excluded. Material on the wider aspects of worker education is listed in T. Kelly (ed.), *A Select Bibliography of Adult Education in Britain* (2nd edition; London: National Institute of Adult Education for Universities Council for Adult Education, 1962).

3197 **Sinclair**, William. 'Oxford's labour college: its aims and results.' *Westm. Rev.*, CLXV, 6 (June 1906), 630–8.

3198 **Workers' Educational Association.** *The Workers' Educational Association considered in relation to working class organisation.* London: W.E.A., [1911]. 20p.

3199 **Atkins**, Edward (ed.). *The Vaughan Working Men's College, Leicester, 1862–1912.* London, 1912. 154p.

3200 **International Labour Office.** 'Workers' education in Great Britain.' *Int. Labour Rev.*, IV, 2 (November 1921), 153–70 (365–82).

3201 **Senturia**, Joseph J. 'The Trades Union Congress and workers' education.' *Am. Econ. Rev.*, XX, 4 (December 1930), 673–84.

3202 **Nicholson**, John H. 'Workers' education in Great Britain.' *Int. Labour Rev.*, XXIX, 5 (May 1934), 656–74.

3203 **Pugh**, *Sir* Arthur. *The W.E.A. and the trade union movement.* London: Workers' Educational Association, 1957. 7p.
'The substance of a speech.'

3204 **Hyde**, Christina. 'Training workers' representatives.' *Occup. Psychol.*, XIX, 2 (April 1945), 93–6.

3205 **British Institute of Management.** *Training of trades union officials.* London: B.I.M., 1949. 30p. (Conference series, 8.)
Paper by E. P. Harries, with discussion.

3206 **Elvin**, Lionel. 'Ruskin College, 1899–1949.' *Adult Educ.*, XXI, 4 (June 1949), 189–93.

3207 **Millar**, J. P. M. 'Forty years of independent working-class education.' *Adult Educ.*, XXI, 4 (June 1949), 210–15.
On the founding and work of the National Council of Labour Colleges.

3208 **Chester**, Theodore Edward. 'Education for trade union members: some approaches and suggestions.' *Adult Educ.*, XXV, 1 (Summer 1952), 20–29.
Description of three experiments.

3209 **Bayliss**, Frederick Joseph. 'The future of trade union education.' *Adult Educ.*, XXXII, 2 (Autumn 1959), 109–15.
A discussion of *Trade union education with special reference to the pilot areas: a report for the Workers' Educational Association*, by H. A. Clegg and Rex Adams.

3210 **Clegg**, Hugh Armstrong and **Adams**, Rex. *Trade union education with special reference to the pilot areas: a report for the Workers' Educational Association.* London: W.E.A., 1959. 102p.

3211 **Jenkins**, W. E. 'Intermediate courses for trade unionists: problems of organization.' *Adult Educ.*, XXXII, 4 (1960), 293–6.

3212 **Hopkins**, P. G. M. 'Labour education in Britain.' *Adult Educ.*, XXXVIII, 1 (May 1965), 15–20.
'This article deals with education aimed at adults primarily in their functions as workers and particularly as organised workers.'

3213 **Thornton**, A. H. and **Bayliss**, Frederick Joseph. *Adult education and the industrial community.* London: National Institute of Adult Education, 1965. 50p.

3214 **Banks**, Robert Frederick. 'Labor education's new role in Britain.' *Ind. Relat.*, V, 2 (February 1966), 67–82.

3215 **Robinson**, James W. 'British and American workers' education.' *J. Ind. Relat.*, X, 1 (March 1968), 64–70.

3216 **Corfield**, Alan John. *Epoch in workers' education: a history of the Workers' Educational Trade Union Committee.* London: Workers' Educational Association, 1969. 272p.

3217 **Jordan**, Iain. *Shop steward training: the case for day release.* Edinburgh: Workers' Educational Association (South-East Scotland District), 1969. 8 leaves.

3218 **Park**, Trevor. 'Trade union education.' *Trade Un. Regist.* (1969), 96–100.

3219 **Robinson**, T. R. 'Shop steward training: palliative or panacea?' *Ind. Relat. Res. Bull.*, 1 (June 1969), 13–18.

3220 **Carr**, Peter. 'Shop steward courses in technical colleges. *Ind. Tutor*, I, 2 (March 1970), 16–19.

3221 **Roberts**, John Hywel. *The National Council of Labour Colleges: an experiment in workers' education.* 1970–71. (M.Sc. thesis, University of Edinburgh.)

See also: 25.

PART FOUR

EMPLOYERS AND THEIR ORGANISATION

I. EMPLOYERS' ASSOCIATIONS

This section includes material on those employers' associations which perform industrial relations functions. Works relating to employers' associations which are exclusively concerned with 'trade' matters are generally excluded. See also Part Three, I; and Part Seven, VII, C.

3222 **Midland Master Printers' Alliance.** *Organisation in the printing industry.* Birmingham: the Alliance, n.d. 16p.

A 'short account of the Midland Master Printers' Alliance, its work and organisation'.

3223 **Newspaper Society.** *Objects and activities of the Newspaper Society.* [London: the Society], n.d. 8p.

Written by W. G. Ridd, a former Director of the Society.

3224 **Chapman**, Sydney John. 'An historical sketch of masters' associations in the cotton industry.' *Manchr. Statist. Soc. Trans.* (1900–1901), 65–84.

3225 **National Association of Master Bakers, Confectioners and Caterers.** *21 years' history of the N.A.* London, 1908. 130p.

3226 **Robertson**, William Alexander. *Combination among railway companies.* London: London School of Economics and Political Science, 1912. 105p. (Studies in economics and political science 26.)

3227 **Hilton**, John. *Memorandum on combines and trade organisations.* London: Garton Foundation, [1916? 17]. 138p.

3228 **Geoghegan**, J. E. 'Farmers' associations.' *Bett. Bus.*, III, 2 (February 1918), 110–18.

In Ireland.

3229 **Newbold**, J. T. Walton. *Solidarity amongst the shipowners.* Glasgow: Reformers' Bookstall, 1918. 16p.

3230 **Birmingham Jewellers' and Silversmiths' Association.** *A record of the Association's work from its commencement in 1887 to its reorganization in 1919, together with some notes on the jewellery, silver & allied trades in Birmingham from 1649.* Birmingham: the Association, 1919. 61p.

By F. H. Sanders.

3231 **Hilton**, John. *A study of trade organisations and combinations in the United Kingdom.* London: Harrison, 1919. 138p.

Prepared for the Committee on Trusts.

3232 **Engineering and Allied Employers' National Federation.** *Thirty years of industrial conciliation.* London: the Federation, 1927. 115p.

3233 **Bordoli**, Ernest. *The story of the Northampton Town Boot Manufacturers' Association.* Northampton: the Association, 1929.

3234 **National Confederation of Employers' Organisations.** *A short description of its work.* London: the Confederation, [1931].

3235 **British Electrical and Allied Manufacturers' Association.** *Twenty-one years: a review of the progress and achievements of the BEAMA.* London, 1933. 59p.

3236 **Laurie**, A. Dyson and **Wilson**, E. J. *1913–1934: a short record of the first twenty-one years of the Sevenoaks Branch, National Farmers' Union.* Sevenoaks: Caxton and Holmesdale P., 1934. 56p.

3237 **Coke Oven Managers' Association.** *The history of coke making and of the Coke Oven Managers' Association.* Cambridge: Heffer, 1936. vii, 139p.

Contents:

The history of coke making, edited by R. A. Mott.

The Coke Oven Managers' Association: the first twenty-one years, edited by G. J. Greenfield.

3238 **Newspaper Society.** *The Newspaper Society, 1836 to 1936: a centenary retrospect.* Birmingham: Silk and Terry, 1936. 71p.

3239 **Birmingham Jewellers' and Silversmiths' Association.** *Record of the work of the Birmingham Jewellers and Silversmiths Association from 1887 to 1937, together with a brief survey of the rise and development of the jewellery, silver and allied trades in Birmingham from 1524.* Birmingham: privately printed, 1937. 55p.

3240 **Davies**, William Tudor. *Trade associations and industrial co-ordination.* London: Machinery Users' Association; Pitman, 1938. xiii, 117p.

Third edition. 1946. ix, 150p.

3241 **Sutcliffe**, Charles E., **Brierley**, J. A. and **Howarth**, F. (comps.). *The story of the Foot-*

ball League, 1888–1938. Preston: Football League, 1938. 300p.
Second edition. 1939.

3242 **Richardson**, John Henry. 'Employers' organisations in Great Britain.' Gannett, F. E. and Catherwood, B. F. (eds.). *Industrial and labour relations in Great Britain: a symposium*. New York: the editors, 1939. p. 139–51.
'Based upon the chapter on "Employers' Organisations" in the author's book on "Industrial Relations in Great Britain" published by the International Labour Office, Geneva, 1938.'

3243 **Federation of British Industries**. *Twenty-five years, 1916–1941*. London: F.B.I., 1941.

3244 **Levy**, Hermann Joachim. *Retail trade associations: a new form of monopolist organisation in Britain. A report to the Fabian Society*. London: Kegan Paul, 1942. x, 265p. (International library of sociology and social reconstruction.)

3245 **Political and Economic Planning**. 'British trade associations.' *Planning*, 221 (12 May 1944), 1–24.

3246 **Corp**, W. G. *Fifty years: a history of the Booksellers' Association*. Oxford: Blackwell, 1945. 64p.

3247 **Dixey**, Charles J. *The Music Publishers' Association Ltd.: 1881–1944*. London, 1945. 8p.

3248 **Political and Economic Planning**. 'Trade associations and government.' *Planning*, 240 (5 October 1945), 1–20.

3249 **Newspaper Society**. *Yesterday, today, tomorrow*. York, London: Herald Printers, 1948. 53p.

3250 **Calico Printers' Association Ltd**. *Fifty years of calico printing: a jubilee history of the C.P.A.* Manchester: the Association, 1949. 64p.

3251 **Turner-Samuels**, Moss. 'Employers' associations.' *British trade unions*. London: Sampson Low, Marston, 1949. p. 197–207.

3252 **Howe**, Ellic. *The British Federation of Master Printers, 1900–1950*. London: the Federation, 1950. xxv, 248p.

3253 **Powell**, Leslie Hughes. *The Shipping Federation: a history of the first sixty years, 1890–1950*. London: Shipping Federation, 1950. 149p.

3254 **Sessions**, Dorothy Mary. *The Federation of Master Printers: how it began*. London: William Sessions, 1950. xv, 370p.

3255 **Shone**, R. M. 'The Iron and Steel Federation.' Milward, G. E. (ed.). *Large-scale organisation: a first-hand account of the day-to-day organisation and management of large industrial undertakings and public services*. London: Macdonald and Evans for the Institute of Public Administration, 1950. p. 16–33.

3256 **Puységur**, Guy J. 'Employers' associations in Europe and North America.' *Int. Labour Rev.*, LXIII, 5 (May 1951), 507–36.

3257 **Dunlop**, J. M. *The British Fisheries Society, 1786–1893*. 1951–52. (Ph.D. thesis, University of Edinburgh.)

3258 **Manchester, Salford and District Building Trades Employers' Association**. *Fifty years: a brief history of the Manchester, Salford & District Building Trades Employers' Association*. Manchester: the Association, 1952. 76p.
Compiled by James Denver.

3259 **Weir**, William. *The first hundred years, 1851–1951: a sketch of the history of the Glasgow Pawnbrokers' Association*. Glasgow, 1952. 95p.

3260 **Baker**, Arthur. *The Employers' Federation of Papermakers and Boardmakers: a brief history*. [printed for private circulation], 1953. 20p.
The author was President of the Federation.

3261 **Burton**, Kenneth J. *The British Employers' Confederation*. Geneva: Centre d'Études Industrielles, 1953.

3262 **Clegg**, Hugh Armstrong. 'Employers.' Flanders, A. and Clegg, H. A. (eds.). *The system of industrial relations in Great Britain*. Oxford: Blackwell, 1954. p. 197–251.

3263 **Federation of British Industries**. *The Federation of British Industries: a paper*. London: F.B.I., 1954.
By Sir Norman Kipping.

3264 **Glasgow and West of Scotland Master Slaters' Association**. *The first seventy-five years, 1873–1948*. Glasgow: the Association, 1954. 71p.
Written by Robert McGill.

3265 **National Association of Goldsmiths**. *Diamond jubilee N.A.G. year book*. Watford: Edson (Printers) Ltd., 1954. 96p.

3266 **Political and Economic Planning**. 'Industrial trade associations.' *Planning*, XXI, 383 (25 July 1955), 121–39.

3267 **Finer**, S. E. 'The Federation of British Industries.' *Polit. Studies*, IV, 1 (February 1956), 61–84.

3268 **Brewers' Guardian**. 'The A.B.T.A. golden jubilee.' *Brew. Guard.*, LXXXVI, 2 (1 February 1957), 61–70.
Allied Brewery Traders' Association.

3269 **Cocoa, Chocolate and Confectionery Alliance Ltd**. *Golden jubilee, 1901–1951*. London: the Alliance, 1957. 40p.

3270 **Crampton**, John Alvah. *The National Farmers Union: a study in the resolution of ideology and practice*. 1957–58. (Dissertation, University of California, Berkeley.)

3271 **Jackson**, A. J. *Official history of the National Federation of Meat Traders' Associations (Inc.)*. Plymouth, [1958?]. 343p.

3272 **Powell**, Leslie Hughes. *A hundred years on: history of the Liverpool Steamship Owners' Association, 1858–1958*. Liverpool: Liverpool Steam Ship Owners' Association, 1958. 84p.

3273 **Self**, Peter and **Storing**, Herbert. 'The farmers and the state.' *Polit. Q.*, XXIX, 1 (January–March 1958), 17–27.

Discusses the activities of the National Farmers' Union.

3274 **Tivey**, Leonard and **Wohlgemuth**, Ernest. 'Trade associations as interest groups.' *Polit. Q.*, XXIX, 1 (January–March 1958), 59–71.

3275 **Allen**, George. 'The National Farmers' Union as a pressure group.' *Contemp. Rev.* (May 1959), 257–68; (June 1959), 321–9.

'A comment' by Peter Self, p. 329–34.

3276 **British Employers' Confederation.** *The British Employers' Confederation: its structure and work.* London: B.E.C., 1959. 16p.

3277 **Engineering and Allied Employers' National Federation.** *Looking at industrial relations.* London: the Federation, 1959. 47p.

3278 **Federation of British Industries.** *Some co-operative activities of trade associations: addresses given at a meeting on 7 July 1959.* London: F.B.I., 1959. v, 25p.

3279 **Higgin**, G. W. *Communications in the National Farmers' Union.* London: National Farmers' Union, 1959. 29p.

3280 **Varley**, Donald Emerson. *A history of the Midland Counties Lace Manufacturers' Association, 1915–1958.* Long Eaton: Lace Productions, 1959. xi, 212p.

3281 **Wholesale Clothing Manufacturers' Federation of Great Britain.** *Golden jubilee, 50th annual report, 1959–1960.* London: the Federation, 1960. 32p.

3282 **Bolton Master Cotton Spinners' Association.** *Bolton Master Cotton Spinners' Association, 1861–1961: centenary commemoration. A brief history of the Association and the development of the cotton spinning industry in Bolton and District.* Bolton: the Association, 1961. 16p.

Written by Thomas B. Boothman, Secretary of the Association.

3283 **Hurry**, F. D. 'A brief outline of the history and objects of the N.A.F.D.' *Fun. Dir.* (January 1961).

Subsequently issued as a reprint, and later revised.

3284 **Pratt Boorman**, H. R. *The Newspaper Society's 125 years of progress.* Maidstone: *Kent Messenger*, 1961. 190p.

3285 **Spring**, David and **Crosby**, Travis L. 'George Webb Hall and the Agricultural Association.' *J. Br. Studies*, II, 1 (November 1962), 115–31.

3286 **Venning**, L. B. *The Federation of Master Builders: 21st anniversary.* London: F.M.B., 1962. 16p.

3287 **British Paper and Board Makers' Association, Employers' Federation of Papermakers and Boardmakers** and **British Paper and Board Industry Research Association.** *Central organisations of the British paper and board making industry.* 1963. 35p. (B.P.B.M.A. pamphlet 6.)

3288 **Holmes**, Richard A. 'The National Farmers' Union and the British negotiations for membership in the European Economic Community.' *Res. Publ.*, v, 3 (1963), 276–87.

3289 **Institute of Burial and Cremation Administration.** *50 years of progress: golden jubilee, 1913–1963.* The Institute, 1963. 60p.

3290 **National Farmers' Union of Scotland.** *Farming Leader*, jubilee issue (October 1963).

3291 **Sharpe**, Ivan (comp.). *The Football League jubilee book, 1938–1963.* London: Stanley Paul, 1963. xii, 304p.

'Embracing an abridged version of *The Story of the Football League*', by C. E. Sutcliffe and others.

3292 **Shirt, Collar and Tie Manufacturers' Federation.** *Golden jubilee report, 1913–1963.* London, 1963. 28p.

The annual report for 1963.

3293 **Benson**, *Sir* Henry and **Brown**, *Sir* Sam. *Report on the formation of a national industrial organisation.* London: National Association of British Manufacturers, Federation of British Industries and British Employers' Confederation. 1964. [8], 61, [33]p.

The result of an enquiry which led to the formation of the Confederation of British Industry.

3294 **Corsetry Manufacturers Association.** *Golden jubilee report, 1914–1964.* London: the Association, 1964. 24p.

Report by H. F. Hill, Chairman, and M. K. Reid, Secretary.

3295 [**Lovesy**, A. N.] *History of Ulster Launderers' Association, extracted from minute books, 1914–1964.* [Belfast: the Association, 1964.] 24p.

The author was Secretary of the Association.

3296 **Fairfield**, Victor. 'The Allied Brewery Traders' Association.' *Brew. J.*, Centenary issue (1965), 251–2.

3297 **Hunter**, G. A. 'The history of the Coke Oven Managers' Association.' Coke Oven Managers' Association. *Papers to be presented at the jubilee conference.* 1965. p. 1–8.

Reprinted in the *Year Book of the Coke Oven Managers' Association, 1966.* p. 15.

3298 **Dawson**, H. I. *Agricultural interest groups in Canada and Great Britain.* 1966. (B.Litt. thesis, University of Oxford.)

3299 **Longworth**, J. E. *Oldham Master Cotton Spinners' Association Ltd.: centenary year.* Oldham: the Association, 1966. 43p.

3300 **Manufacturers' Association.** *Golden jubilee report, 1916–1966.* London: the Association, 1966. 32p.

3301 **National Federation of Building Trades Employers.** Liverpool Region. *Centenary programme.* Liverpool: the Federation, 1966. 22p.

By H. Langford.

3302 **Tripp**, Basil H. *The Joint Iron Council, 1945–1966: the origins and history of the Council and its constituents, the Council of Iron Producers and the Council of Ironfoundry Associations.* London: Allen and Unwin, 1966. 138p.

3303 **United Kingdom Textile Manufacturers' Association.** *The centenary of the United Kingdom Textile Manufacturers' Association, 1866–1966.* Manchester: the Association, 1966. 36p.
Written by George B. Fielding.

3304 **Catchpole**, W. L. and **Elverston**, E. *B.I.A. fifty: 1917–1967; fifty years of the British Insurance Association.* Stockport: P. H. Press, 1967. 85p.

3305 **Caterers' Association of Great Britain.** Caterers' Association Bulletin, 584 (June 1967), 13–22.
Jubilee issue – 50 years.

3306 **Corporation of Insurance Brokers.** *The CIB: what it is and how it works.* London: the Corporation, 1967. [iv], 16p.

3307 **Dobson**, Jack. 'Vehicle Builders & Repairers Association: what it is and what it does.' *Mot. Trad.* (28 June 1967), 605.

3308 **Fox**, Alan. 'The combinations of masters.' *New Soc.*, IX, 230 (23 February 1967), 268–70.

3309 **McCarthy**, William Edward John. 'A survey of employers' association officials.' Royal Commission on Trade Unions and Employers' Associations. *Employers' associations: the results of two studies.* London: H.M.S.O., 1967. p. 82–121. (Research papers 7.)

3310 **Munns**, V. G. 'The functions and organisation of employers' associations in selected industries.' Royal Commission on Trade Unions and Employers' Associations. *Employers' associations: the results of two studies.* London: H.M.S.O., 1967. p. 1–81. (Research papers 7.)

3311 **National Economic Development Office.** *Trade associations in the distributive trades.* London: N.E.D.O., 1967.

3312 **Rule**, Leonard and **Rider**, Dennis. *The flame of the lamp.* London: Glass Manufacturers' Federation for the British Lampblown Scientific Glassware Manufacturers' Association, 1967. 16p.
First published in *Glass*, 1967.

3313 **Bramley**, D. A. (ed.). 'The B.O.G.F.E.M.A. story.' *Oil Gas Fir.*, II, 5 (January 1968), 14–16.
British Oil and Gas Firing Equipment Manufacturers Association.

3314 **Engineering Employers' West of England Association.** *Engineering Employers' West of England Association.* Bristol: the Association, [1968?]. 16p.
Constitution in pocket at end.

3315 **Horn**, Pamela L. R. 'Farmers' Defence Associations in Oxfordshire, 1872–1874.' *Hist. Studies*, I, 1 (May 1968), 63–70.

3316 **Ovington**, C. E. *The first sixty years: a history of the Corporation of Insurance Brokers, 1906–1966.* London: the Corporation, 1968. 93p.
The author was Secretary of the Corporation from 1932 to 1964.

3317 **Sidney**, Elizabeth. *The Industrial Society, 1918–1968.* London: Industrial Society, 1968. ix, 51p.

3318 **Bugler**, Jeremy. 'Bosses unite.' *New Soc.*, XIV, 355 (17 July 1969), 85–6.
Confederation of British Industry.

3319 **Federation of Civil Engineering Contractors.** *Golden jubilee, 1919–1969.* London: the Federation, 1969. 15p.

3320 **Meldrum**, A. J. 'The story of the Scottish Grocers' Federation, 1918–1968.' *Scottish grocery trade handbook.* Edinburgh: Scottish Federation of Grocers' and Provision Merchants' Association, 1969. Section 3. 52p.

3321 **Reclamation Industries Review.** British Scrap Federation, 50th Anniversary. *The Review*, 1969. 40p.

3322 **Wilmot**, R. T. D. 'The BIA past and present.' *Review* (16 May 1969).
The author was Secretary General of the British Insurance Association.

3323 **Crawford**, T. S. *A history of the umbrella.* Newton Abbot: David and Charles, 1970. 220p.
p. 196–198. National Federation of Umbrella Manufacturers and the Federation of Umbrella Industries.

3324 **Kingsford**, Reginald John Lethbridge. *The Publishers' Association, 1896–1946.* London: Cambridge U.P., 1970. x, 228p.

3325 **National Federation of Building Trades Employers.** Eastern Region. *Fifty years of service: a booklet issued to commemorate the golden jubilee of the Eastern Federation of Building Trades Employers.* Cambridge: N.F.B.T.E., Eastern Region, 1970. 15p.

See also: 1186; 1875.

II. PERSONNEL MANAGEMENT

A. GENERAL

This section includes general works on the development of personnel administration as an explicit management function; business leadership; and ideologies of employers, particularly those aspects which relate to the management of employees. Such technical aspects of personnel management as interviewing, selection, and testing techniques have generally been excluded; these are covered by Carole Faubert, *Personnel Management: A Bibliography* (London: Institute of Personnel Management, 1968). More general works on manpower planning at firm and industry level have been classified at Part Six, II, B. Business histories have generally been excluded except where, as in the case of Quaker firms, they have been particularly important in the development of personnel management. Similarly, general material relating to the experiments at the Glacier Metal Company is included here. Some of the general works in Part One, IV; Part Three, III, A; Part Five, I; and Part Five, IV, A also contain material on employer attitudes towards labour. See also Part Five, V, A–B for employer views on joint consultation and industrial democracy. Material on William Collison and the National Free Labour Association is classified at Part Three, III, B, 3. Material on managers' attitudes to work and behaviour at work is included in Part Two. See also Part Six, IV, C.

3326 **Bruce**, Alexander Balmain. *The life of William Denny, shipbuilder, Dumbarton.* London: Hodder and Stoughton, 1888. xvi, 479p.
Second edition revised. 1889. xvi, 479p.
Includes his attitudes as an employer, adoption of piecework system, etc.

3327 **Meath**, *Earl of.* 'A model factory.' *Nineteenth Century*, XXIII, 134 (April 1888), 536–40.

3328 **Brocklebank**, M. Petrena. 'A visit to Port Sunlight.' *Econ. Rev.*, VIII, 4 (October 1898), 524–8.

3329 **Greenwood**, Edgar. *The employed, with observations by employers.* London: Scott, Greenwood, 1903. 48p.

3330 **Shadwell**, Arthur. *Industrial efficiency: a comparative study of industrial life in England, Germany and America.* London: Longmans, 1906. 2v.
New edition. 1909. xx, 720p.

3331 **Dale**, J. A. 'Bournville.' *Econ. Rev.*, XVII, 1 (January 1907), 13–27.

3332 **George**, Walter Lionel. *Labour and housing at Port Sunlight.* London: Alston Rivers, 1909. xi, 210p.

3333 **Cadbury**, Edward. *Experiments in industrial organisation.* London, New York: Longmans, Green, 1921. xxi, 296p.
'In the following pages an account is given of the organization of a large factory', the cocoa and chocolate works of Cadbury Brothers, Bournville. (Intro.)

3334 **Cadbury**, Edward. 'Some principles of industrial organization: the case for and against scientific management.' *Sociol. Rev.*, VII, 2 (April 1914), 99–117.
Criticises American scientific management.
Describes own methods at Bournville.
Contributions by other writers in relation to the paper follow:
J. A. Hobson, p. 117–18.
G. D. H. Cole, p. 119–20.
W. Hazell, p. 120–1.
C. G. Renold, p. 122–4.
W. H. Jackson, p. 124–5.
Reply from F. W. Taylor, VII, 3 (July 1914), 266–9.
'The case for scientific management' by C. Bertrand Thompson, VII, 4 (October 1914), 315–27.
E. Cadbury's reply, p. 327–31.

3335 **Ashley**, William James. 'The task of the welfare supervisor.' *Econ. J.*, XXVI, 104 (December 1916), 448–58.

3336 **Lever**, William Hesketh, Baron Leverhulme. *Girls and boys; Harmonizing capital and labour; and Industrial administration: three addresses.* Port Sunlight: Lever Bros., 1916. 36p.

3337 **Daniels**, George W. 'Employers and property.' Furniss, H. Sanderson (ed.). *The industrial outlook.* London: Chatto and Windus, 1917. p. 22–60.

3338 **Joint Social Studies Committee**. *A report upon the selection and training of welfare supervisors in factories and workshops.* London: King, 1917. 8p.

3339 **Rowntree**, Benjamin Seebohm. 'Towards industrial efficiency.' *Nineteenth Century*, LXXXI, 480 (February 1917), 399–412.

3340 **Webb**, Sidney. *The works manager today: an address.* London: Longmans, Green, 1917. v, 162p.

3341 **Deeley**, William Joseph. *Labour difficulties and suggested solutions: a manual for technical students, cashiers, foremen, departmental or works managers and employers.* Manchester: Sherratt and Hughes, 1918. viii, 175p.

3342 **Fisher**, Boyd. *Industrial loyalty: its value, its creation, its preservation. A discussion . . . showing the costliness of the present method and the remedies for it.* London: Routledge, 1918. 79p.
Previously issued under the title *How to reduce labour turnover.*

3343 **Lever**, William Hesketh, Baron Leverhulme. *The six-hour day & other industrial questions.* London: Allen and Unwin, 1918. xv, 331p.
Second edition. 1919. xv, 344p.
Edited by Stanley Unwin.

3344 **Proud**, Emily Dorothea. *Welfare work, employer's experiments for improving working conditions in factories.* London: Bell, 1918. xx, 363p. (London School of Economics. Studies 49.)
Based on the author's D.Sc.(Econ.) thesis, University of London, 1916.

3345 **Simon**, E. D. 'Labour from the employers' point of view.' *Contemp. Rev.*, CXIII (May 1918), 551–8.
A lecture given at the London School of Economics.

3346 **Denning**, Arthur du Pré. *Scientific factory management.* London: Nisbet, 1919. xii, 211p.
Including personnel management.

3347 **Ioteyko**, Josefa. *The science of labour and its organisation.* London: Routledge, 1919. viii, 199p.

3348 **Rowntree**, Benjamin Seebohm. *The human needs of labour.* London: Nelson, 1919. 168p.
New edition, revised and re-written. London: Longmans, 1937. 162p.

3349 **Collis**, Edgar Leigh. 'The practice of industrial welfare and health.' Muscio, B. (ed.). *Lectures on industrial administration.* London: Pitman, 1920. p. 200–31.

3350 **Lever**, William Hesketh, Baron Leverhulme.

Capital and capitalism. Port Sunlight: Lever Bros., 1920. 14p.

An address.

3351 **Lever**, William Hesketh, Baron Leverhulme. *The six-hour shift and industrial efficiency.* New York: Holt, 1920. viii, 265p.

'An abridged and rearranged edition of the author's *Six-hour day*, with an introduction by Henry R. Seager.'

Preparation of this edition by Frank Tannenbaum.

3352 **Rowntree**, Benjamin Seebohm. 'My dream of a factory.' Gleason, A. *What the workers want: a study of British labor.* London: Allen and Unwin, 1920. p. 306–16.

3353 **Rowntree**, Benjamin Seebohm. 'Social obligations of industry to labour.' Berriman, A. E., and others. *Industrial administration: a series of lectures.* Manchester: Manchester U.P.; London: Longmans, Green, 1920. p. 1–21.

Also published separately by Manchester College of Technology, 1919.

3354 **Stelling**, A. Robert. 'Taylor's principles in modern British management.' Muscio, B. (ed.). *Lectures on industrial administration.* London: Pitman, 1920. p. 56–78.

3355 **Voysey**, E. B. 'The human element in industry.' Manchester University. *Labour and industry: a series of lectures.* Manchester: Manchester U.P.; London: Longmans, 1920. p. 113–29.

'A lecture given on Tuesday, November 18, 1919.'

3356 **Hyde**, Robert Robertson. *The boy, in industry and leisure.* London: Bell, 1921. xxviii, 281p. (Social service library 2.)

3357 **Kelly**, Eleanor T. and **Haskins**, M. L. 'Foundations of industrial welfare.' *Economica*, 1, 2 (May 1921), 116–31.

3358 **Kerr**, Constance Ursula. *Guide to industrial welfare work.* Manchester: Co-operative Press Agency, 1921. 82p.

3359 **Mackworth**, Margaret Haig, Viscountess Rhondda, and others. *D. A. Thomas, Viscount Rhondda, by his daughter and others.* London: Longmans, Green, 1921. ix, 335p.

Chapters on the coal industry contributed by David Evans; chapter on D. A. Thomas's philosophy by Harold Begbie.

3360 **Rowntree**, Benjamin Seebohm. *The human factor in business.* London: Longmans, 1921. ix, 176p.

A description of the methods employed in the Cocoa Works, York.

Second edition. 1925. xii, 188p.

Third edition. 1938. xx, 244p.

3361 **Society of Friends**. *Industry for service: report of conference, 1921.* 1921. 32p.

3362 **Marston**, *Sir* Charles. *The teachings of experience applied to labour and capital.* London: League of Truth and Freedom, 1922. 28p.

Fourth edition.

3363 **Newcomb**, Elizabeth D. 'Industrial welfare work in Great Britain.' *Int. Labour Rev.*, v, 4 (April 1922), 553–71.

3364 **Gardiner**, Alfred George. *Life of George Cadbury.* London: Cassell, 1923. ix, 324p.

3365 **Sheldon**, Oliver. *The philosophy of management.* London: Pitman, 1923. xvi, 296p.

3366 **Lee**, John. *The principles of industrial welfare.* London: Pitman, 1924. ix, 93p.

3367 **Turner**, James. *Service versus disservice: the national need.* Manchester: Sherratt and Hughes, 1924. 50p.

3368 **Hammersley**, Samuel Schofield. *Industrial leadership.* London: Simpkin, Marshall, 1925. viii, 238p.

3369 **Kelly**, Eleanor T. (ed.). *Welfare work in industry.* London: Pitman, 1925. vii, 119p.

'By members of the Institute of Industrial Welfare Workers.'

3370 **National Movement Towards a Christian Order of Industry and Commerce.** *The control of industry: papers . . . Balliol College, Oxford, January 9th to 12th, 1925.* [York?]: the Movement, [1925?]. 71p. (Christian order of industry series 6.)

Papers by A. P. M. Fleming and E. E. Wilson, H. G. Jenkins, John Lee, C. H. Northcott, Will Reason, H. G. Tanner, L. Urwick.

3371 **Cadbury Brothers**. *Social organization at small factories: an account of experience at the branch factories of Cadbury Brothers Ltd.* Bournville: Publications Dept., [1927?]. 56p.

3372 **Lever**, William Hulme, Viscount Leverhulme. *Viscount Leverhulme.* London: Allen and Unwin, 1927. 325p.

Biography of William Hesketh Lever.

3373 **Wood**, Henry George. 'George Cadbury, 1839–1922.' Martin, H. (ed.). *Christian social reformers of the nineteenth century.* London: Student Christian Movement, 1927. p. 183–203.

3374 **Macara**, *Sir* Charles Wright and **Kerr**, Philip Henry. *Pulling together in the industrial world.* Manchester: Sherratt and Hughes, 1928. 57p.

3375 **National Institute of Industrial Psychology**. 'The attitude of employers towards the Institute's investigations: a symposium.' *Natn. Inst. Ind. Psychol. J.*, IV, 2 (April 1928), 98–112.

An account of proceedings of, and a summary of papers read at, a meeting held on March 8th, 1928.

3376 **Society of Friends**. Conference of Quaker Employers. *Quakerism and industry, 1928, being the full record of a conference of employers, members of the Society of Friends, held at Woodbrooke, Birmingham, April, 1928, together with the report issued by the Conference.* London, 1928. 97p.

3377 **Davies**, John Percival. *The politics of a*

socialist employer. Skipton-in-Craven: Maurice Webb, 1929. 149p.

3378 **Miles**, George Herbert. *Lecture on 'The human factor in industry'*. Johannesburg: Hortors, 1929. 16p.

3379 **Personnel Administration**. *The personnel function in British industry*. London, [193–?]. 23p.

3380 **Metcalf**, Henry Clayton (ed.). *Business leadership*. London: Pitman, 1931. x, 375p.

By various authors.

3381 **Rowntree**, Benjamin Seebohm. 'Some industrial problems of to-day.' *Natn. Inst. Ind. Psychol. J.*, v, 7 (July 1931), 370–5.

'An address delivered at an evening meeting arranged by the Women's Committee . . . on February 18, 1931.'

3382 **Williams**, Iolo Aneurin. *The firm of Cadbury, 1831–1931*. London: Constable, 1931. ix, 295p.

3383 **Casson**, Herbert Newton. *The art of handling people*. London: *Efficiency Magazine*, 1932. 146p.

Second edition. 1937. 146p.

3384 **Lee**, Christopher A. 'The employer's point of view. IV. Efficiency and personal leadership.' *Hum. Factor*, vii, 11 (November 1933), 401–6.

3385 **Macgregor**, A. E. *The technique of loyalty*. London: *Efficiency Magazine*, 1933. 30p. (Up-to-date bulletins for business men 40.)

3386 **Montague Burton Ltd**. *Ideals in industry; being the impressions of social students and visitors to the Montague Burton workshops*. Leeds: Montague Burton, 1933. 139p.

Edited by Stewart Wilkinson.

Third edition. London, 1936. 312p.

3387 **Moorrees**, V. and **Northcott**, Clarence Hunter. 'Industrial psychology at Rowntree's cocoa works.' *Hum. Factor*, vii, 5 (May 1933), 159–68.

Two papers read at the meeting of the British Association for the Advancement of Science, York, 1932.

3388 **Pope**, A. C. R. 'The employer's point of view. III. The management of lads in industry.' *Hum. Factor*, vii, 10 (October 1933), 341–6.

3389 **Watson**, William Foster. 'The worker's point of view. XVIII. Stray thoughts on works management.' *Hum. Factor*, viii, 9 (September 1934), 312–22.

3390 **Young**, Arthur Primrose. *Industrial leadership*. Manchester, 1934. 32p.

3391 **Holland**, Robert Wolstenholme (ed.). *Business organization and personnel: a course in commerce and business practice*. London: Pitman, 1935. viii, 362p.

3392 **Hyde**, Robert Robertson. *Industrial welfare*. Loughborough: Association of Teachers in Technical Institutions, 1936. 3p. (Miscellaneous pamphlets.)

Paper read at the Summer Meeting of ATTI.

3393 **Whitehead**, Thomas North. *Leadership in a free society: a study in human relations based on an analysis of present-day industrial civilization*. London: Oxford U.P., 1936. xv, 266p.

3394 **Stewart**, Alan F. 'Industrial psychology and personnel management.' *Hum. Factor*, xi, 9 (September 1937), 305–9.

3395 **Casson**, Herbert Newton. *Getting value for salaries and wages: the new technique of employership*. London: *Efficiency Magazine*, 1938. 174p.

3396 **National Institute of Industrial Psychology**. 'Some recent developments in the psychology of personnel management in Great Britain.' *Seventh International Management Congress, Washington, D.C., September 19th to September 23rd 1938. Personnel-General Management pages, part I*. Baltimore, Md.: Waverly P., 1938. p. 84–6.

3397 **Raistrick**, Arthur. *Two centuries of industrial welfare: the London (Quaker) Lead Company, 1692–1905. The social policy and work of the 'Governor and Company for smelting down lead with pit coal and sea coal', mainly in Alston Moor and the Pennines*. London: Friends' Historical Society, 1938. 152p. (Friends' Historical Society Journal. Supplement 19.)

3398 **Shepard**, Jean L. *Human nature at work*. London: Pitman, 1938. xi, 219p.

3399 **Society of Friends.** *Quakerism and industry 1938, being the papers read at a conference of employers, members of the Society of Friends, held at Woodbrooke, Birmingham, 22nd–25th April, 1938, together with a report of the conference*. London: Friends' Book Centre, 1938. 124p.

Published for the Quaker Employers' Conference.

3400 **Woodward**, A. G. *Personnel management*. London: *Efficiency Magazine*, 1938. 162p.

3401 **Fenelon**, Kevin Gerard. *Management and labour*. London: Methuen, 1939. 276p.

Based on lectures delivered at the Manchester College of Technology.

3402 **Emden**, Paul Herman. *Quakers in commerce: a record of business achievement*. London: Sampson Low, 1940. xiii, 273p.

3403 **Industrial Welfare Society**. *Elements of industrial welfare and personnel management*. London: the Society, 1940. 19p.

3404 **Bournville Village Trust**. *When we build again: a study based on research into conditions of living and working in Birmingham*. London: Allen and Unwin, 1941. xii, 138p.

3405 **Bournville Village Trust.** *Sixty years of planning: the Bournville experiment*. Bournville, 1942. 48p.

Reissued. 1948.

3406 **Roberts**, R. Lloyd. *The human problems of management*. London: Institute of Labour Management, 1942. 16p.

Revised edition.

3407 **Locke**, Henry William. *Fundamentals of personnel management*. London: Institute of Labour Management, 1943. 20p.

Also 1951. 18p.

3408 **Moxon**, Gerald Richard. *Functions of a personnel department.* London: Institute of Labour Management, 1943. 27p.
Third edition, completely revised and rewritten. Institute of Personnel Management, 1951. 36p.

3409 **Poulton**, Gerald and **Brook**, Francis H. C. *Personnel management: defining the scope of a personnel organisation.* London: P.W.S. (Industry), 1943. 47p.

3410 **Urwick**, Lyndall Fownes. *Personnel management in relation to factory organization.* London: Institute of Labour Management, 1943. 27p.

3411 **Industrial Welfare Society.** *Personnel records.* London: the Society, 1944. 24p.
Second edition revised. 1948. 23p.

3412 **Lawe**, Frank Walsham. *Staff management.* London: Institute of Labour Management, 1944. 28p.

3413 **Moxon**, Gerald Richard. 'The growth of personnel management in Great Britain during the war.' *Int. Labour Rev.*, L, 6 (December 1944), 709–35.
Reprinted. London: Institute of Labour Management, 1945. 32p.

3414 **Puckey**, *Sir* Walter Charles. *What is this management?* London: Chapman and Hall, 1944. viii, 281p.

3415 **Roberts**, R. Lloyd. *The human problems of management.* London: Institute of Personnel Management, 1944. 20p.

3416 **Hyde**, Robert Robertson. 'The development and scope of industrial welfare work.' *Hlth. Soc. Welf.* (1944–45), 108–19.
The author was Director of the Industrial Welfare Society.

3417 **Moxon**, Gerald Richard. *The growth of personnel management in Great Britain during the war, 1939–1945.* London: Institute of Labour Management, 1945. 32p.
Reprinted from the *International Labour Review.*

3418 **Northcott**, Clarence Hunter. *Personnel management: its management scope and practice.* London: Pitman, 1945. x, 239p.
Reissued: 1947.
Second edition. 1950. viii, 336p.
Third edition. *Personnel management: principles and practice.* 1955. vii, 427p.
Third edition, revised and reprinted. 1958. vii, 428p.
Fourth edition. 1960. vii, 421p.

3419 **Bartlett**, *Sir* Charles. 'An employer's view of the future of industrial relations.' *Occup. Psychol.*, XX, 3 (July 1946), 119–24.
An address delivered on the occasion of the Institute's 25th anniversary on February 11th, 1946.

3420 **Davis**, Norah M. *Human problems in industry.* London: Nicholson and Watson, 1946. 127p. (The new democracy.)

3421 **Industrial Welfare Society.** *Outline of industrial welfare and personnel management.* London: the Society, 1946. 24p.
Second edition.

3422 **Renold**, *Sir* Charles Garonne. *The employer and the social fabric.* Manchester: Manchester Municipal College of Technology, Department of Industrial Administration, 1946. 28p. (Series of monographs on higher management 4.)

3423 **Hauser**, P. B. 'Welfare in industry.' *Hlth. Soc. Welf.* (1947), 80–2.

3424 **Moxon**, Gerald Richard. *An approach to personnel management.* Manchester: Manchester Municipal College of Technology, Department of Industrial Administration, 1947. 23p. (Series of monographs on higher management 9.)

3425 **Parmenter**, Raymond. *Human relations in industry.* London: Bureau of Current Affairs, 1948. 16p. (Current Affairs 67.)

3426 **Political and Economic Planning.** *The human factor in industry.* London: P.E.P., 1948. 35p.

3427 **British Institute of Management.** *Management in private enterprise and nationalized industry.* London: B.I.M., 1949. p. 15–22. (Conference series 2.)
By Sir Miles Thomas.
Speech given at the 53rd Oxford Management Conference, Cliftonville, May 5–8, 1949.

3428 **British Institute of Management.** *Working together: an introduction to personnel management.* London: B.I.M., 1949. 24p. (Personnel management series 2.)

3429 **Courtauld**, Samuel. *Ideals and industry: war-time papers.* Cambridge: Cambridge U.P., 1949. xvii, 133p.
Contents include 'Some industrial relationships'; 'Further thoughts on industrial relationships'; 'Employer-employee relationships'; 'An industrialist's view of labour management'; 'Co-operation in industry'.

3430 **Renold**, *Sir* Charles Garonne. *The nature of management.* London: British Institute of Management, 1949. 15p. (Occasional papers 2.)
An address.

3431 **Thomas**, F. J. Blayney (ed.). *Welfare in industry.* London: Caxton Publishing Co., 1949. xi, 590p.
Contents. 1. 'How welfare began: historical survey and appreciation', by W. H. Watkinson. 2. 'Make-up of the industrial welfare officer', by the editor. 3. 'Plan for a welfare department', by H. A. Goddard. 4. 'Social and other "liaisons" ', by A. T. Carr. 5. 'Background information', by E. J. Macdonald. 6. 'Recruitment and induction', by H. A. Goddard. 7. 'Education and training', by J. Clark. 8. 'Films and visual aids in training and welfare', by R. N. Paterson. 9. 'Putting the worker in the picture: the house magazine', by P. C. Vigor. 10.

'Industrial health', by G. F. Keatinge. 11. 'Industrial hygiene', by W. J. S. Graham. 12. 'Industrial catering', by H. C. J. Kelley. 13. 'Industrial accident prevention', by C. Fenna. 14. 'Colour's aid to welfare', by R. F. Wilson. 15. 'Industry's call for light', by R. Freeth.

3432 **Tredgold**, Roger Francis. *Human relations in modern industry.* London: Duckworth, 1949. 192p. (Social science studies.)

Second and revised edition. 1963. 192p.

Reprinted. London: Methuen, 1965. 192p. (University paperbacks 133.)

3433 **Whitehead**, Archibald Charles. *Practical management and works relations.* Manchester: Emmott, 1949. 138p. ('Mechanical world' monographs 54.)

3434 **Bland**, F. A. 'Personnel management in England.' *Publ. Adm.* (Sydney), n.s., IX, 1 (March 1950), 187–99.

3435 **Neden**, W. J. 'Personnel management in the Ministry of Labour, I.' *Publ. Adm.* XXVII, 4 (Winter 1950), 263–9.

3436 **Swindin**, C. A. 'Personnel management in the Ministry of Labour.' *Publ. Adm.*, XXVII, 4 (Winter 1950), 269–74.

3437 **Willmott**, Francis Benedict. *A philosophy of production.* London: C. Johnson, 1950. 173p.

3438 **Crichton**, Anne Olivia Janet. *An examination of trends towards professionalism in the personnel function of management.* 1950–51. (M.A. thesis, University of Liverpool.)

3439 **Jaques**, Elliott. *The changing culture of a factory.* London: Tavistock Publications, 1951. xvii, 341p.

Sub-title on dust jacket only: *A study of authority and participation in an industrial setting.*

Report of a three-year study carried out by the Tavistock Institute of Human Relations in collaboration with the Glacier Metal Company.

3440 **Montague Burton Ltd**. *Ideals in industry, being the story of Montague Burton Ltd., 1900–1950.* Leeds: Montague Burton, 1951. xxviii, 481p.

Golden jubilee issue, compiled and edited by Ronald Redmayne.

3441 **Northcott**, Clarence Hunter. *The personnel aspects of management.* London: Institute of Personnel Management, 1951. 60p. (Occasional paper 1.)

Three lectures.

3442 **Northcott**, Clarence Hunter. *Policy and leadership in personnel management.* Manchester: Manchester Municipal College of Technology, Department of Industrial Administration, 1951. 60p. (Series of monographs on higher management 24.)

3443 **Petch**, G. A. 'A mid-Victorian employer on factory management.' *Bus. Hist. Soc. Bull.*, XXV, 4 (December 1951), 257–60.

On W. & R. Chambers, printers, Edinburgh.

Mainly reproduces a letter to *The British Workman and Friend of the Sons of Toil*, 1859.

3444 **Richards**, R. A. 'Some aspects of personnel management in the British Civil Service.' *Publ. Adm.* (Sydney), n.s., X, 1 (March 1951), 368–97.

Covers primarily the Post Office.

3445 **Schuster**, *Sir* George Ernest. *Christianity and human relations in industry.* London: Epworth P., 1951. 128p.

The Beckly Social Service Lecture.

3446 **Willmott**, Francis Benedict. *The human touch in industry.* London: Saint Catherine P., 1951. 220p.

3447 **Brook**, Francis H. C. *Personnel management and welfare.* London: Burke, 1952. 287p.

3448 **Forsaith**, John William. *The factory manager and the young employee.* London: the author, 1952. 27p. (Institute of Printing Management lectures 4.)

Private circulation.

3449 **Menzies**, Isabel Edgar Punton and **Anstey**, Edgar. *Staff reporting.* London: Allen and Unwin for the Institute of Public Administration, 1951 [i.e. 1952]. 95p.

3450 **Micklem**, Philip Arthur. *The human factor in industry.* London: Industrial Christian Fellowship, 1952. 7p.

3451 **Ministry of Labour and National Service.** *Human relations in industry: report of a conference arranged by the Ministry of Labour and National Service, and held at the Institution of Civil Engineers, London, S.W.1, on 18th, 19th and 20th March, 1952.* London: H.M.S.O., 1952. vi, 128p.

Chairman: Sir Guildhaume Myrddin-Evans.

3452 **Scott**, Jerome Fentress and **Lynton**, Rolf Paul. *Three studies in management.* London: Routledge and Kegan Paul, 1952. x, 220p.

3453 **Brown**, Wilfred Banks Duncan. *Some problems of a factory: an analysis of industrial institutions.* London: Institute of Personnel Management, 1953. 20p. (Occasional paper 2.)

'An analysis of the problems of the Glacier Metal Company Ltd.'

3454 **Kendall**, Maurice George. *Statistics and personnel management.* London: Institute of Personnel Management, 1953. 16p. (Occasional paper 3.)

3455 **Warriar**, R. N. *Personnel administration in the British coal mining industry with particular reference to conditions in the North Western coalfields.* 1953. (M.Sc. Tech., University of Manchester.)

3456 **Willmott**, Francis Benedict. *The time for decision: an industrialist looks at life.* London: Saint Catherine P., 1953. xi, 202p.

3457 **Bakke**, Edward Wight. *The impact of human relations on production.* London: Industrial Co-partnership Association, 1954.

3458 **Clark**, Harold Watton. 'The contribution of the personnel manager.' Ling, T. M. (ed.). *Mental health and human relations in* *industry*. London: H. K. Lewis, 1954. p. 141–60.

3459 **Fogarty**, Michael Patrick. *Human relations in industry*. Oxford: Catholic Social Guild, 1954. 104p. (C.S.G. year book 45.)

3460 **Ling**, Thomas Mortimer (ed.). *Mental health and human relations in industry*. London: H. K. Lewis, 1954. xix, 265p.

3461 **Rimmer**, N. C. 'Implications for management.' Ling, T. M. (ed.). *Mental health and human relations in industry*. London: H. K. Lewis, 1954. p. 249–56.

3462 **Rowntree and Co. Ltd.** *B. Seebohm Rowntree, C.H., Ll.D., D.H.L., R.St.O.O., 1871–1954: a tribute to the life and work of B.S.R.* York: Rowntree, 1954. 36p.

3463 **Coulter**, *pseud.* [i.e. Hugh William Fordham]. *Techniques or men?* London: Institute of Personnel Management, 1955. 11p. (Occasional paper 6.)

Originally published in *Personnel Management*, December 1954.

3464 **Heller**, Frank Alexander (ed.). *New developments in industrial leadership in Great Britain, the United States, Germany and France*. London: Polytechnic Management Association, 1955. 75p. (New development series 1.)

'Surveying the British scene', by J. A. C. Brown, p. 10–28.

3465 **Higham**, T. M. 'Thirty years of psychology in an industrial firm.' *Occup. Psychol.*, XXIX, 4 (October 1955), 232–9.

A paper read at the 1955 annual conference of the British Psychological Society.

In the firm of Rowntree's.

3466 **Hopkins**, Richard Robert. *A handbook of industrial welfare*. London: Pitman, 1955. vi, 258p.

3467 **Taylor**, Arthur John. 'The Third Marquis of Londonderry and the North-Eastern coal trade.' *Durham Univ. J.*, XLVIII, 1 (December 1955), 21–7.

3468 **Bendix**, Reinhard. *Work and authority in industry: ideologies of management in the course of industrialization*. New York: Wiley; London: Chapman and Hall, 1956. xxx, 466p. (California University, Institute of Industrial Relations. Research program series.)

3469 **Birmingham College of Technology.** *The technology of human relations as applied to the human aspects of management*. Birmingham: the College, 1956. 37p.

3470 **Forman**, Michael Bertram. *The personnel function of management*. London: Institute of Personnel Management, 1956. 11p. (Occasional papers 9.)

3471 **Jackson**, Fred and **Fraser**, John Munro. *The personnel department*. London: Pitman, 1956. iv, 60p. (Supervisors guides 5.)

3472 **Marsh**, Henry John. *An introduction to human relations at work*. London: Industrial Welfare Society, 1956. 15p.

Second edition.

3473 **Rogers**, T. G. P. 'Recent advances in personnel management.' *Polit. Q.*, XXVII, 3 (July–September 1956), 260–9.

3474 **Rothman**, Stanley. 'Entrepreneurial behaviour and political consensus in England and France.' *Explor. Entrepren. Hist.*, VIII, 3 (February 1956), 167–71.

3475 **Adams**, William Wheen Scovell. 'Leverhulme.' *Edwardian portraits*. London: Secker and Warburg, 1957. p. 147–73.

3476 **Bendix**, Reinhard. 'A study of managerial ideologies.' *Econ. Rev. Cult. Change*, v, 2 (January 1957), 118–28.

3477 **Collingridge**, Jean Mary and **Ritchie**, Mary. *Personnel management in the small firm*. London: Institute of Personnel Management, 1957. 55p.

3478 **Cooper**, Andrew R. 'The human relations aspect of management.' Thomson, D. C. (ed.). *Management, labour and community*. London: Pitman, 1957. p. 8–17.

3479 **Hunter**, Guy. *The role of the personnel officer: a group review*. London: Institute of Personnel Management, 1957. 21p. (Occasional papers 12.)

3480 **Krugel**, S. W. *Certain aspects of industrial welfare and personnel management in selected undertakings in Scotland, with special reference to Fife and Dundee*. 1957. (Ph.D. thesis, University of St Andrews.)

3481 **Morris**, A. (ed.). *Human relations in industry*. Manchester: North Western District Joint Advisory Council for the Electricity Supply Industry, [1957?]. 99p.

'A series of six evening lectures.'

Contributors: Asa Briggs, Sir Charles G. Renold, Edwin Fletcher, A. R. Cooper, the Very Rev. H. A. Jones, T. E. Daniel.

3482 **O'Kelly**, F. F. 'Personnel administration.' *Administration*, v, 3 (Autumn 1957), 139–48.

At the Electricity Supply Board, Republic of Ireland.

3483 **Department of Scientific and Industrial Research**. *Management and technology*. London: H.M.S.O., 1958. (Problems and progress in industry 3.)

By J. Woodward.

3484 **Hardwicke**, Thomas Hydes. *Management of man*. London: the author, 1958. 254p.

3485 **Ministry of Labour and National Service** and **Central Office of Information.** *Positive employment policies: examples of management practice contributing to good relations in industry*. London: H.M.S.O., 1958. 40p.

3486 **Office Management Association.** *Trends in personnel practice: a summary of answers given by 54 large office employers in the County of London to questions affecting nearly 40,000 office workers*. London: the Association, 1958. 21p.

3487 **Organisation of Employers' Federations and Employers in Developing Countries.** *Managerial functions and collective bargaining*. London: the Federation, 1958. 8p. (Occasional paper.)

3488 **Robens**, Alfred. *Enlightened management and*

peace in industry. London: Industrial Co-Partnership Association, 1958. 20p.

3489 **Ross**, Norman Scott. 'Organized labour and management. Part II. The United Kingdom.' Hugh-Jones, E. M. (ed.). *Human relations and modern management*. Amsterdam: North-Holland Publ. Co., 1958. p. 100–32.

3490 **Vernon**, Anne. *A Quaker business man: the life of Joseph Rowntree, 1836–1925*. London: Allen and Unwin, 1958. 207p.

3491 **Barling**, Elizabeth. *Staff management*. London: Institute of Personnel Management, 1959. 46p. (Broadsheets.)

3492 **Beer**, Stafford and **Revans**, Reginald William. *Operational research and personnel management*. London: Institute of Personnel Management, 1959. 25p. (Occasional papers 14.)

Part 1 by S. Beer.

Part 2 by R. W. Revans.

3493 **Urwick**, Lyndall Fownes. *Personnel management in perspective: suggestions on the correct place of personnel activities in business organization*. London: Institute of Personnel Management, 1959. 23p. (Occasional paper 13.)

3494 **McGivering**, Ian C. *Personnel management in large manufacturing firms in Liverpool*. 1959–60. (M.A. thesis, University of Liverpool.)

3495 **Waring**, A. B. *People and productivity: a practical guide for administrators*. Birmingham: Joseph Lucas Limited, [1959? 60]. 95p.

The author was Chairman of Joseph Lucas (Industries) Ltd.

This book 'is about the contribution that good human relations can make to productivity . . . deals with subjects which bear on the attitude of workpeople to their supervisors and vice versa, and of both to their jobs; the subjects have been culled from addresses . . .'

3496 **Brown**, Wilfred Banks Duncan. *Exploration in management: a description of the Glacier Metal Company's concepts and methods of organisation and management*. London: Heinemann, 1960. xxii, 326p.

New York: Wiley, 1961.

Exploration in management. Harmondsworth: Penguin, 1965. 344p. (Pelican books.) With a foreword by Michael Shanks.

3497 **Fraser**, John Munro. *Human relations in a fully employed democracy*. London: Pitman, 1960. viii, 352p.

3498 **McGivering**, Ian C., **Matthews**, D. G. J. and **Scott**, William Henry. *Management in Britain: a general characterization*. Liverpool: Liverpool U.P., 1960. viii, 157p. (Social research series.)

3499 **Personnel Management and Methods.** *Personnel management in practice*. London: Shaw Publishing Co., 1960. 76p.

Edited by W. L. Edwards.

New edition. 1962. 76p.

3500 **Anstey**, Edgar. *Staff reporting and staff development*. London: Allen and Unwin for the Royal Institute of Public Administration, 1961. 96p.

Another edition. 1969. 96p. (Studies in management 6.)

3501 **Brown**, *Sir* William Robson. *Management and society*. London: Pitman, 1961. ix, 84p.

Based on public addresses and speeches.

3502 **Durham**, William. *Personnel records, forms and procedures*. London: Industrial Welfare Society, 1961. v, 85p.

Revised edition. 1966.

3503 **Heller**, Frank Alexander. 'An evaluation of the personnel management function.' *J. Ind. Relat.*, III, 1 (April 1961), 32–43.

3504 **Hunter**, Guy. *Studies in management*. London: U. of London P., 1961. 158p.

3505 **McKendrick**, Neil. 'Josiah Wedgwood and factory discipline.' *Hist. J.*, IV, 1 (1961), 30–55.

'. . . a revised and slightly extended version of a paper given to the Cambridge Historical Society, on 24 November 1959. . .'

3506 **Crichton**, Anne. *Personnel management and working groups*. London: Institute of Personnel Management, 1962. 62p.

3507 **Jacques**, John. *Personnel—the challenge of the 1960's: an address to the Co-operative Education Convention, 1962*. Loughborough: Co-operative Union Education Department, 1962. 14p.

3508 **Smith**, Peter B. *A survey of research into attitude and behaviour changes resulting from human relations training*. Leeds: Leeds University, Department of Economics and Commerce, Industrial Management Division, 1962. 14p.

3509 **Aris**, Stephen. 'Is the sack a myth?' *New Soc.*, II, 62 (5 December 1963), 17–18.

3510 **Edwards**, *Sir* Ronald Stanley. *Human values and human problems in electricity supply*. London: Electricity Council, 1963. 24p.

Address given by the author at the Summer School of the Industrial Co-partnership Association on 13 July 1963 in Oxford.

The author was Chairman of the Electricity Council from 1962 to 1968.

3511 **Personnel Management and Methods.** *Personnel management handbook*. London: Business Publications, 1963. 84p.

Third edition. Edited by Howard Griffiths.

Previous edition, 1962, published as *Personnel management in practice*.

3512 **Belford**, John A. 'Centralized policy direction of the industrial relations function in an international company.' Industrial Relations Research Association. *Proceedings of the seventeenth annual meeting, Chicago, Illinois, December 28 and 29, 1964*. p. 74–80.

Discussion, p. 87–95.

3513 **Bosticco**, Isabel Lucy Mary. *Modern personnel management*. London: Business Publications, 1964. ix, 244p.

3514 **Buzzard**, Richard Bethune and **Radforth**, John Leslie. *Statistical records about people a* *work*. London: National Institute of Industrial Psychology, 1964. 22p. (Reports 16.)

3515 **Child**, John. 'Quaker employers and industrial relations.' *Sociol. Rev.*, n.s., XII, 3 (November 1964), 293–315.

3516 **Edwards**, Maldwyn Lloyd. *Management and men in industry*. London: Epworth P., 1964. 9p. (Beckly pamphlets, sixth series 6.)

3517 **Lupton**, Tom. *Industrial behaviour and personnel management*. London: Institute of Personnel Management, 1964. 43p. (Industrial relations series.)

3518 **Woodward**, Joan. *Industrial behaviour: can it be studied scientifically?* London: Institution of Production Engineers, 1964. 12p.

3519 **Woodward**, Joan. 'Industrial behaviour: is there a science?' *New Soc.*, IV, 106 (8 October 1964), 11–14.

Based on the 1964 E. W. Hancock Paper to the Institution of Production Engineers.

3520 **Singh**, B. P. *Impact of the size of organisation on the personnel management function: a comparative study of personnel departments in some British and Indian industrial firms*. 1964–65. (Ph.D. thesis, University of Nottingham.)

3521 **Garnett**, John. *Targets for leaders in industry*. London: Industrial Welfare Society, 1965. iv, 34p.

3522 **Hacon**, Richard Jeffery. *Conflict and human relations training*. Oxford, London: Pergamon, 1965. ix, 118p. (Commonwealth and international library. Economics, commerce, industry administration and management division.)

3523 **Industrial Welfare Society**. *A guide to employment practices*. London: the Society, 1965. 41p. (Notes for managers 8.)

Compiled by Janet B. Marcham and other I.W.S. staff.

3524 **Rice**, Albert Kenneth. *Learning for leadership: interpersonal and intergroup relations*. London: Tavistock Publications, 1965. xii, 200p.

3525 **Woodward**, Joan. *Industrial organisation: theory and practice*. London: Oxford U.P., 1965.

3526 **Chen**, Phoebe Shu-Heng. *A comparison of English and American organization for central personnel management*. 1965–66. (Dissertation, University of Chicago.)

3527 **Kelly**, Joe. *A critical evaluation of the Glacier system of management*. 1965–66. (Ph.D. thesis, University of Strathclyde.)

3528 **Bedford**. Management Services. *Reshaping for our future: personnel management in Bedford Corporation, its organisation, control and execution*. Bedford: the Corporation, 1966. [36] leaves.

3529 **Crichton**, Anne and **Collins**, Raymond G. 'Personnel specialists: a count by employers. A report on a survey made in South Wales in 1964.' *Br. J. Ind. Relat.*, IV, 2 (July 1966), 137–53.

3530 **Flanders**, Allan David. 'The internal social responsibilities of industry.' *Br. J. Ind. Relat.*, IV, 1 (March 1966), 1–21.

3531 **Fox**, Alan. 'From welfare to organisation.' *New Soc.*, VII, 193 (9 June 1966), 14–15. (Trends in personnel management 1.)

3532 **Fox**, Alan. 'Managerial ideology and labour relations.' *Br. J. Ind. Relat.*, IV, 3 (November 1966), 366–78.

3533 **Haire**, Mason, **Ghiselli**, Edwin E. and **Porter**, Lyman W. *Managerial thinking: an international study*. New York, London: Wiley, 1966. viii, 298p. (California University Institute of Industrial Relations. Research program series.)

3534 **K.**, K. M. 'Work: the manager.' *New Left Rev.*, 39 (September–October 1966), 17–24.

Personal account of management in the steel industry.

3535 **Stewart**, Rosemary. 'The socio-cultural setting of management in the United Kingdom.' *Int. Labour Rev.*, XCIV, 2 (August 1966), 108–31.

A paper submitted to a meeting of experts convened by the I.L.O. in November 1965.

3536 **Thornton**, A. P. *The habit of authority: paternalism in British history*. London: Allen and Unwin, 1966.

3537 **Wille**, Edgar. *The computer in personnel work*. London: Institute of Personnel Management, 1966. 55p.

3538 **Child**, John. *British management, thought and education – their interpretation of industrial relationships*. 1966–67. (Ph.D. thesis, University of Cambridge.)

3539 **Fereday**, R. P. *The career of Richard Smith (1783–1868), manager of Lord Dudley's mines and ironworks*. 1966–67. (M.A. thesis, University of Kent.)

3540 **Child**, John. 'Industrial management.' Parker, S. R., and others. *The sociology of industry*. London: Allen and Unwin, 1967. p. 85–98.

3541 **Fogarty**, Michael Patrick. 'British management: an uneasy legitimacy.' *Columb. J. Wld. Bus.*, II, 4 (July–August 1967), 57–64.

3542 **Greater London Council**. *Management & personnel services in the Greater London Council*. London: G.L.C., 1967. 31p. (Publications 82.)

3543 **Henderson**, Joan. *The effective use of people*. London: Industrial Society, 1967. 36p.

3544 **Kenny**, Ivor. 'Industrial relations: management's role.' *Christus Rex*. XXI, 4 (October–December 1967), 343–57.

3545 **Martin**, Alec Owen. *Welfare at work*. London: Batsford, 1967. 293p. (Modern management.)

3546 **Niven**, Mary Margaret. *Personnel management 1913–63: the growth of personnel management and the development of the Institute*. London: Institute of Personnel Management, 1967. 168p.

3547 **Shearer**, John C. 'Industrial relations of American corporations abroad.' Parkin, S., and others (eds.). *International labor*. New

York, Evanston, London: Harper and Row, 1967. p. 109–31.

3548 **Burns**, Tom and **Stalker**, G. M. 'Leadership and executive subordination.' Dubin, R. *Human relations in administration, with readings*. 3rd ed. Englewood Cliffs, N.J.: Prentice-Hall, 1968. p. 400–5.

From Burns, T. and Stalker, G. M. *The management of innovation*. London: Tavistock Publications, 1966. p. 211–20.

3549 **Child**, John. 'British management thought as a case study within the sociology of knowledge.' *Sociol. Rev.*, n.s., XVI, 2 (July 1968), 217–39.

Part of the substance of Chapter 7, 'Assessment: British management thought as a body of knowledge', in the author's *British management thought*, 1969.

3550 **Crichton**, Anne. *Personnel management in context*. London: Batsford, 1968. 360p. (Modern management series.)

3551 **Cuming**, Maurice William. *The theory and practice of personnel management*. London: Heinemann, 1968. ix, 325p. (Studies in management.)

3552 **Deverell**, Cyril Spencer. *Personnel management: human relations in industry*. London: Gee, 1968. vii, 263p.

3553 **Dodds**, D. A. *People and the new factory: a check list*. London: Institute of Personnel Management, 1968. 16p.

3554 **Flanders**, Allan David. *Can managers be taught industrial relations? Speech delivered at Management Education Review Conference, June 18, 1968*. London: Palantype Organisation for British Institute of Management, 1968. 61p.

3555 **Hyde**, *Sir* Robert Robertson. *Industry was my parish; being the autobiography of Robert R. Hyde, K.B.E., M.V.O.* London: Industrial Society, 1968. xii, 143p.

Founder of the Industrial Society.

3556 **Kelly**, Joe. *Is scientific management possible? A critical examination of Glacier's theory of organisation*. London: Faber, 1968. 332p.

3557 **Moreby**, David Henry. *Personnel management in merchant ships*. Oxford, London: Pergamon P., 1968. vii, 239p. (Commonwealth and international library. Navigation and nautical courses division.)

3558 **Murphy**, Patrick. 'Personnel management.' *Administration*, XVI, 4 (Winter 1968), 392–9.

In Coras Iompair Eireann, the national transport authority.

3559 **Rodgers**, Winston. *Practical statistics for personnel management*. London: Industrial and Commercial Techniques Ltd., 1968. 54p.

3560 **Williams**, Michael R. *Human relations*. London: Longmans, 1967 [i.e. 1968]. xiii, 77p. (Supervisory series 4.)

A National Extension College course prepared in collaboration with the Institute of Supervisory Management.

3561 **Willings**, David Richard. *The human element in management*. London: Batsford, 1968. 224p. (Modern management series.)

3562 **Nichols**, W. A. T. *Ownership, control and ideology*. 1968–69. (M.A. thesis, University of Hull.)

3563 **Roberts**, C. J. *A study of managerial motivations and satisfactions*. 1968–69. (M.Phil. thesis, University of London.)

3564 **Anthony**, Peter and **Crichton**, Anne. *Industrial relations and the personnel specialists*. London: Batsford, 1969. 302p. (Foundations of modern society.)

3565 **British Institute of Management**. *What managers read*. London: B.I.M., 1969. 19p. (Occasional paper, new series, OPN 3.)

3566 **Child**, John. *British management thought: a critical analysis*. London: Allen and Unwin, 1969. 272p. (Studies in management 5.)

3567 **Fox**, Alan. 'Management's frame of reference.' Flanders, A. (ed.). *Collective bargaining: selected readings*. Harmondsworth: Penguin Books, 1969. p. 390–409.

Excerpt from *Industrial sociology and industrial relations*. Royal Commission on Trade Unions and Employers' Associations research papers, 3. London: H.M.S.O., 1966. Part 1, p. 2–14.

3568 **Grant**, Jeanne Valerie and **Smith**, G. J. *Personnel administration and industrial relations*. Harlow: Longmans, 1969. x, 337p. (Management study series.)

3569 **Holroyd**, Geoffrey. *Managing people: how to get the best from your staff*. Rugby: Mantec Publications, 1969. 37p.

3570 **Howells**, George William. *Human aspects of management*. London: Heinemann in association with the Institute of Supervisory Management, 1969. xii, 124p. (The supervisor's bookshelf.)

3571 **Industrial Society**. *Design of personnel systems and records*. London: Gower P., 1969. ix, 133p.

3572 **Kenny**, Ivor. 'Management's role in industrial relations.' Irish Management Institute. *Industrial democracy: a symposium*. Dublin: the Institute, 1969. p. 11–24.

The author was Director of the Irish Management Institute.

3573 **Light**, Horace Robert. *The business executive: principles of management and human relations, and guide to personal efficiency in business*. 1969. viii, 152p.

Second edition.

3574 **Mullins**, Patrick. 'The challenge of industrial relations.' Irish Management Institute. *Industrial democracy: a symposium*. Dublin: the Institute, 1969. p. 41–8.

The author was Assistant Personnel Manager, Aer Lingus – Irish.

3575 **Nichols**, Theo. *Ownership control and ideology: an enquiry into certain aspects of modern business ideology*. London: Allen and Unwin, 1969. 272p. (Studies in management 8.)

3576 **Thompson**, *Sir* Geoffrey. 'The Devlin

report: the personnel problems.' *Administration*, XVII, 4 (Winter 1969), 390–9.
'Address delivered to members of the Institute of Public Administration on 3rd February, 1970.'

3577 **Torrington**, Derek. *Successful personnel management*. London: Staples P., 1969. 163p.

3578 **Woodward**, Joan. 'Management and technology.' Burns, T. (ed.). *Industrial man*. Harmondsworth: Penguin, 1969. p. 196–231.
Excerpt from *Management and technology*. London: H.M.S.O., 1958. p. 4–40.

3579 **Barber**, David. *The practice of personnel management*. London: Institute of Personnel Management, 1970. 46p.

3580 **Bendix**, Reinhard. 'The contribution of Elton Mayo to managerial ideology.' Worsley, P. (ed.). *Modern sociology: introductory readings*. Harmondsworth: Penguin, 1970. p. 232–4.
Abridged from R. Bendix. *Work and authority in industry*. New York: Harper and Row, 1963. p. 311–18. First published in 1956.

3581 **Biggs**, Norman. *The changing nature of industrial responsibility: foundation lecture given by Mr. Norman Biggs, chairman of Esso Petroleum Ltd., on the occasion of the fiftieth anniversary of the founding of the Department of Management Sciences*. Manchester: U.M.I.S.T., 1970. 8p.

3582 **British Association for Commercial and Industrial Education**. *Bacie case studies*. London: B.A.C.I.E., 1970. 141p.

3583 **Cameron**, Matthew Archibald. *Management and men: the missing factor*. Pinner: Grosvenor Books, 1970. 23p.

3584 **Collingridge**, Jean Mary and **Ritchie**, Mary. *Personnel management: problems of the smaller firm*. London: Institute of Personnel Management, 1970. 42p.

3585 **Davey**, Douglas Mackenzie, **Rockingham Gill**, D., and **McDonnell**, P. *Attitude surveys in industry*. London: Institute of Personnel Management, 1970. 62p. (Information report, new series 3.)

3586 **Denny**, Elizabeth. *Signposts to staff management: a brief guide for managers of small business*. London: Institute of Personnel Management, 1970. 62p. (Practical handbooks 2.)

3587 **Flanders**, Allan David. 'The internal social responsibilities of industry.' *Management and unions: the theory and reform of industrial relations*. London: Faber, 1970. p. 129–53.
'A revised version of a paper presented to an International Seminar jointly convened at New Delhi in March 1965 by the India International Centre and the Gandhian Institute of Studies. The original paper is included in *Social Responsibilities of Business*, Maraktalas Bombay, 1966, and the revised paper appeared as an article in the *British Journal of Industrial Relations*, March 1966.'

3588 **Flunder**, D. J. 'The management of human resources.' Robertson, D. J. and Hunter, L. C. *Labour market issues of the 1970s*. Edinburgh: Oliver and Boyd for the Scottish Economic Society, 1970. p. 179–87.
First appeared in the June 1970 issue of the *Scottish Journal of Political Economy*.

3589 **Gretton**, John. 'The dock bosses.' *New Soc.*, XVI, 408 (23 July 1970), 141–2.

3590 **Grunfeld**, Cyril. 'American management in the United Kingdom.' Kamin, A. (ed.). *Western European labor and the American corporation*. Washington, D.C.: Bureau of National Affairs, 1970. p. 467–71.

3591 **Hughes**, Ernest William. *Human relations in management*. Oxford: Pergamon, 1970. ix, 234p. (Commonwealth and international library. Social administration, training economics and production division.)

3592 **McCartney**, J. B. 'The U.S. corporation in Ireland.' Kamin, A. (ed.). *Western European labor and the American corporation*. Washington, D.C.: Bureau of National Affairs, 1970. p. 475–83.

3593 **Robens**, Alfred, Baron Robens of Woldingham. *Human engineering*. London: Cape, 1970. 186p.

3594 **Symposium on the Management of Staff in General Practice**, Radcliffe Infirmary, 1969. *Report of a symposium on the Management of Staff in General Practice, held at the New Medical Lecture Theatre, the Radcliffe Infirmary, University of Oxford, 20 April 1969*. London: Royal College of General Practitioners, 1970. iii, 48p. (*Journal of the Royal College of General Practitioners*, XIX, 95, supplement 3.)

3595 **Walsh**, William. *Industrial relations and communications*. London: Gee, 1970. xi, 215p. (Gee's supervisory management studies 1.)

3596 **Woodward**, Joan (ed.). *Industrial organization: behaviour and control*. London: Oxford U.P., 1970. xiii, 262p.

3597 **Anderson**, Ian Robert. *A study of a firm's labour problem: its causes, effects and some attempted solutions*. 1970–71. (M.Sc. thesis, University of Edinburgh.)

See also: 63; 3763; 3965; 7737; 7739–41; 7744; 8823–4; 9222.

B. COMMUNICATIONS IN INDUSTRY

This section includes the literature dealing with communications as an aspect of personnel management. The literature is primarily normative in nature and is generally concerned with arguing the need for better communications in industry and pointing out how this can be achieved. Much of the basic sociological and psychological research listed in Part Two also contains material on communications in industry.

3598 **Cook**, P. H. 'An examination of the notion of communication in industry.' *Occup. Psychol.*, XXV, 1 (January 1951), 1–14.

3599 **Scott**, Jerome Fentress and **Lynton**, Rolf Paul. *Maintaining flexibility of communication in the changing circumstances of an old industry.* London: British Institute of Management, 1951.

3600 **Acton Society Trust.** *The worker's point of view: a discussion of 'reporting back' based on a study in a coalfield.* London: the Trust, 1952. 32p. (Studies in nationalised industry series 11.)

3601 **Burns**, Tom. 'The directions of activity and communication in a departmental executive group: a quantitative study in a British engineering factory with a self-recording technique.' *Hum. Relat.*, VII, 1 (February 1954), 73–97.

'. . . to provide information about the way in which individuals at executive level spent their time, about their field of interaction; and about the distribution of work within a departmental executive group.'

3602 **Chisholm**, Cecil (ed.). *Communication in industry.* London: Business Publications, 1955. 284p.

Revised edition. 1957. xi, 314p.

3603 **Coates**, R. H. *Effective communication in industry.* London: British Institute of Management, 1956. 4p.

National Conference, Harrogate, 1956.

3604 **British Institute of Management.** *Presenting financial information to employees.* London: B.I.M., 1957. ix, 110p. (Personnel management series 8.)

3605 **British Productivity Council.** *Communications in industry.* London: the Council, 1960. 16p.

Productivity, men and methods conference, London, 1960.

3606 **Humble**, J. W. *Communications within and without the industry.* London: British Institute of Management, 1960. 6p.

Midlands management conference, Leamington Spa, 1960.

3607 **Ministry of Labour**, Personnel Management Advisory Branch, **British Institute of Management** and **Institute of Personnel Management**. Joint Conference on the Challenge of Economic and Technical Change: Human Problems of Management, Buxton, 1960. [Papers.] 1960.

Communications: the underlying principles, by A. C. Leyton. 3p.

Communications: a case study, by J. H. Kean. 5p.

3608 **Tunley**, A. E. *Developing and maintaining communications.* London: British Institute of Management, 1960. 14p.

Northern management conference, Southport, 1960.

3609 **Cooper**, R. E. 'Internal communications and employee information.' Wells, M. J. (ed.). *Information and its dissemination: report of the Summer Meeting of the Institute of Petroleum held at Harrogate 7 to 10 June, 1961.* London: Institute of Petroleum, 1961. p. 75–92.

3610 **Eccles**, *Sir* J. *Communication and the responsibility of the chief executive.* London: British Institute of Management, 1961. 16p.

One-day conference on communications in industry and commerce, London, 1961.

3611 **Moonman**, Eric. *Communications in industry and commerce.* London: British Institute of Management, 1961. 7p.

One-day conference on communications in industry and commerce, London, 1961.

3612 **Moonman**, Eric. *Training methods for improved communications.* London: British Institute of Management, 1961. 2p.

One-day conference on communications, Newport, 1961.

3613 **Department of Scientific and Industrial Research.** *The problem of communication: proceedings of a conference on science and industry, Swansea, 1961.* London: H.M.S.O., 1962. 113p.

Chairman: Sir Maynard Jenour.

3614 **Industrial Welfare Society.** *Keeping in touch with retired employees.* London: the Society, 1962. 15p. (Survey 96.)

3615 **Chappell**, Ronald Thomas and **Read**, Walter Leonard. *A textbook of business communications.* London: Macdonald and Evans, 1963. x, 195p.

3616 **Higgin**, Gurth and **Jessop**, Neil. *Communications in the building industry.* London: National Consultative Committee of Architects, Quantity Surveyors and Builders; Tavistock Institute of Human Relations, 1963.

Second edition. London: Tavistock Publications, 1965. 125p.

3617 **Humble**, J. W. *Communications: the neglected skill.* London: British Institute of Management, 1963. 7p.

3618 **Ivens**, Michael William. *The practice of industrial communication.* London: Business Publications, 1963. xiii, 332p.

3619 **Kean**, J. H. *Communications in the smaller business.* London: British Institute of Management, 1963. 4p.

3620 **Ministry of Health.** Standing Medical Advisory Committee and Central Health Services Council. Standing Nursing Advisory Committee. Joint Committee. *Communication between doctors, nurses and patients: an aspect of human relations in the hospital service.* London: H.M.S.O., 1963. 20p.

3621 **Ministry of Labour.** *People at work: a report on communications in industry.* London: H.M.S.O., 1963. 39p.

3622 **Deverell**, Cyril Spencer. *The techniques of communication in business.* London: Gee, 1964. 214p.

3623 **Garnett**, John. *The manager's responsibility for communication.* London: Industrial Society, 1964. 34p.

Third edition. 1970. (Notes for managers 2.)

3624 **Lomax**, Eric Sutherland. *A survey of the*

influence of human factors on the effectiveness of communication in management and administration. Edinburgh: E. S. Lomax Ltd., 1964. 12 leaves.

Reproduced from typewriting.

Second edition. 1964.

3625 **Cohen**, John, **Cooper**, Peter and **Thorne**, Paul. 'A note on communication in a factory.' *Occup. Psychol.*, XXXIX, 1 (January 1965), 25–30.

3626 **Little**, Peter. *Communication in business.* London: Longmans, 1965. x, 259p.

3627 **Revans**, Reginald William. 'Managers, men and the art of listening.' *New Soc.*, V, 123 (4 February 1965), 13–15.

3628 **Barlow**, Kenneth Graham Ireland. *A study of aspects of communication in the Central Electricity Generating Board North Western Region, with special reference to human relations and interpersonal aspects of communication and control.* 1966. 2v. (Ph.D. thesis, University of Manchester.)

3629 **Barry**, W. A. *Problems of organisation and communication in a growing company.* 1966. (Ashridge Management College research project. Third interim report.)

3630 **Mackechnie**, G. N. *Communications in large scale organisations, with special reference to adaptability to policy changes in the field of industrial relations.* 1966. (M.Sc. Tech. thesis, University of Manchester.)

3631 **Tavistock Institute of Human Relations.** *Interdependence and uncertainty: a study of the building industry. Digest of a report from the Tavistock Institute to the Building Industry Communication Research Project.* London: Tavistock Publications, 1966. 83p.

Edited by Charles Crichton.

3632 **Harlow**, E. and **Compton**, H. *Practical communication.* London: Longmans, 1967. 160p.

3633 **Docherty**, P. H. G. *A study of communication in an office situation.* 1967–68. (M.Phil. thesis, University of London.)

3634 **Peirce**, M. A. *A comparative study of management-worker communications.* 1967–68. (M.Sc. thesis, University College, Dublin.)

3635 **Burns**, Tom. 'Authority and communications to subordinates.' Dubin, R. *Human relations in administration, with readings.* 3rd ed. Englewood Cliffs, N.J.: Prentice-Hall, 1968. p. 330–2.

From 'The direction of activity and communication in a departmental executive group.' *Hum. Relat.*, VII, 73–97.

3636 **Leyton**, A. C. *The art of communication: communication in industry.* London: Pitman, 1968. ix, 214p.

3637 **McLeod**, Elizabeth. *Producing an employee handbook.* London: Industrial Society, 1968. 20p.

3638 **Sikka**, S. K. *An assessment of managerial communications. An examination of factory attitudes and opinions: the application of statistical and other quantitative methods to the study of management communications.* 1969. (Ph.D. thesis, University of Manchester Institute of Science and Technology, Department of Management Sciences.)

3639 **Spence**, Alexander Clarence. *Management communication: its process and practice.* London: Macmillan, 1969. 211p.

3640 **Lillico**, Thomas Michael. *A study of some aspects of managerial communication.* 1969–70. (Ph.D. thesis, University of Edinburgh.)

3641 **Irvine**, A. S. *Improving industrial communication: a basic guide for line managers.* London: Industrial Society and Gower P., 1970. 319p.

3642 **Moonman**, Eric. *Communication in an expanding organization: a case study in action research.* London: Tavistock Publications, 1970. vii, 182p.

3643 **Robinson**, T. R. 'Persuasion and perception: how to increase the efficacy of intra-firm communications.' *Ind. Relat. Res. Bull.*, 3 (February 1970), 10–18.

C. SUPERVISION OF EMPLOYEES

See also Part Six, II, B, 2, b; and Part Six, II, B, 3, b, iii.

3644 *Lecture conference for works directors, managers, foremen, and forewomen.* York, [etc.], 1921–26. 13v.

Papers of conferences held in different parts of the country, Birmingham, Oxford, etc.

3645 **Watson**, William Foster. 'The worker's point of view. XII. The human factor in foremen.' *Hum. Factor*, VII, 2 (February 1933), 62–7.

Reprinted in *The worker's point of view: a symposium.* London: Woolf, 1933. p. 38–46.

3646 **Gillespie**, James J. *Training in foremanship and management.* London: Pitman, 1934. xiii, 171p.

Second edition. 1937. xv, 179p.

Third edition. 1941. xv, 179p.

Fourth edition. 1943. xii, 179p.

Fifth edition. 1948. xv, 206p.

3647 **An Industrial Designer**. 'The worker's point of view. XXVII. Too many cooks.' *Hum. Factor*, X, 3 (March 1936), 114–18.

3648 **Burnham**, Thomas Hall. *Modern foremanship* ... London: Pitman, 1937. xi, 175p.

3649 **Watson**, John Munro. *The deputy and the coal face: a lecture* . . . Nottingham, 1937. 27p. (National Association of Colliery Deputies. Lectures.)

3650 **Davis**, H. McFarland. *Introduction to foremanship.* Birmingham: Institute of Industrial Administration, 1942.

3651 **Morton**, Frederick John Burns. *The new foremanship.* London: Chapman and Hall, 1943. xii, 253p.

Second edition, revised. 1946, 1949. 2v.

3652 **Hovey**, Robert Baldwin. *The foreman's guide, for the foreman, the forewoman, the manager,*

the student. London: Pitman, 1945. viii, 63p.
Second edition. 1946. x, 65p.

3653 **Davis**, H. McFarland (ed.). *Introduction to foremanship*. London: Macdonald and Evans, 1946. viii, 200p.
Written for the Institute of Industrial Administration.

3654 **Radcliffe**, R. A. C. *Leadership on the shop floor*. London: Management Research Groups, 1947. 12p.
Given as an address to the National Conference of the Association of Supervisors' Discussion Groups.

3655 **Birmingham Central Technical College**. Students' Union. Industrial Administration Group. *A code of management practice relating to the status of the foreman*. Birmingham: the Industrial Administration Group, 1948. 19p.
Published by the Group on behalf of its members and on behalf of the Institute of Industrial Supervisors.

3656 **Brierley**, John Paul. *Management, men and morale, being the substance of an address on 'The responsibilities of a supervisor'*. Port Sunlight: Lever Bros., 1949. 19p.

3657 **British Institute of Management**. *Supervisor's residential training*. London: B.I.M., 1949. 32p. (Conference series 4.)
Paper by W. F. F. Scott, with discussion.

3658 **Morton**, Frederick John Burns. *The supervisor and the specialists: result of an enquiry*. Birmingham: Institute of Industrial Supervisors, 1950. 20p.

3659 **Morton**, Frederick John Burns. *Foremanship: a textbook*. London: Chapman and Hall, 1951. xii, 316p.

3660 **National Institute of Industrial Psychology**. *The foreman: a study of supervision in British industry, undertaken by the National Institute of Industrial Psychology and sponsored by the Human Factors Panel of the Committee on Industrial Productivity*. London: Staples P., 1951. 158p.

3661 **Fraser**, John Munro. *Leadership in the factory*. London: Pitman, 1953. iv, 59p. (Supervisor's guides 1.)

3662 **Fraser**, John Munro. *Understanding other people: the five-fold grading method*. London: Pitman, 1953. v, 58p. (Supervisor's guides 3.)

3663 **Morton**, Frederick John Burns. *The foreman and methods improvement*. Birmingham: Institute of Industrial Supervisors, 1953. 15p.

3664 **National Institute of Industrial Psychology**. *Two studies in supervison*. London: N.H.P., 1953. 59p. (Reports 10.)
Messrs. Exe & Co., by Elizabeth Livingstone.
Supervision in a cotton spinning firm, by John D. Handyside.

3665 **Stanes**, D. F. *The employment of women in supervisory and managerial positions in the cotton, clothing, biscuit, and cocoa, chocolate and sugar confectionery industries in England, with a historical introduction from 1900*. 1954–55. (M.Sc. (Econ.) thesis, University of London.)

3666 **Tatlow**, Ann Elizabeth. *The foreman: the man and his role. A study of industrial foremanship in the light of the general principles of analytical psychology*. 1954–55. (Ph.D. thesis, University of London.)

3667 **National Institute of Industrial Psychology**. *The place of the foreman in management: seven case studies undertaken by the National Institute of Industrial Psychology*. London: Staples P., 1957. 143p.
By David S. C. Williams and P. McDonnell.

3668 **Mather**, J. D. *A comparative sociological study of foremen in two engineering factories in North-West England*. 1959. (M.A. (Econ.) thesis, University of Manchester.)

3669 **Gloag**, Joseph. *Management on the factory floor*. London: Pitman, 1961. v, 138p.

3670 **Revans**, Reginald William. *The measurement of supervisory attitudes*. Manchester: Manchester Statistical Society, 1961. 32p. (Papers.)

3671 **Sykes**, Andrew James Macintyre. 'The effect of a supervisory training course in changing supervisors' perceptions and expectations of the role of management.' *Hum. Relat.*, xv, 3 (August 1962), 227–43.

3672 **Department of Scientific and Industrial Research**. *The supervisor and his job*. London: H.M.S.O., 1963. (Problems of progress in industry 13.)
By K. E. Thurley and A. C. Hamblin.

3673 **Evans**, M. G. *Supervisory attitudes: a case study from the packaging industry, with an evaluation of the method used*. 1963. (M.Sc. Tech. thesis, University of Manchester.)

3674 **Fraser**, John Munro and **Bridges**, John Mackay. *The industrial supervisor*. London: Business Publications. 1964. vii, 239p.
Part 1. *Fulfilling his role in industry*, by J. Munro Fraser.
Part 2. *Solving his workaday problems*, by J. M. Bridges.

3675 **Henderson**, Joan. *Being a supervisor in a factory*. London: Industrial Welfare Society, 1964. 17p. (Notes for managers 5.)

3676 **Henderson**, Joan and **Marcham**, Janet B. *Being a supervisor in an office*. London: Industrial Society, 1964. 16p. (Notes for managers 7.)

3677 **Henderson**, Joan and **Marcham**, Janet B. *Being a supervisor in retail distribution*. London: Industrial Society, 1964. 16p. (Notes for managers 6.)

3678 **Wylie**, Thomas. *Group exercises in industrial relations*. Birmingham: Institute of Industrial Supervisors, 1964. 68p.

3679 **Reynaud**, C. B. *The work of a building site manager*. 1964–65. (M.Sc. thesis, University of Birmingham.)

3680 **Hamblin**, Anthony Crandell, **Thurley**, Keith E. and **Voon**, Dolores. *Essential facts on the British foreman.* Birmingham: Institute of Industrial Supervisors, 1965. 71p.

3681 **Hopper**, Earl. 'Some effects of supervisory style: a sociological analysis.' *Br. J. Sociol.*, XVI, 3 (September 1965), 189–205.
'This study is based on a replication, in an English factory and under controlled structural conditions, of an American laboratory investigation of some effects of supervisory styles.'

3682 **Henson**, Basil Howard. *The Certificate in Supervisory Studies: a new approach to foremanship and supervisory education.* London: Association of Technical Institutions, 1966. 14p.

3683 **Thurley**, Keith E. 'Changing technology and the supervisor.' Stieber, J. (ed.). *Employment problems of automation and advanced technology: an international perspective.* London: Macmillan; New York: St Martin's P., 1966. p. 334–53.
Discussion, p. 364–7.

3684 **White**, James Richard Henry. *The modern supervisor.* London: Macdonald, 1965 [i.e. 1966]. 159p.

3685 **Compton**, H. and **Bennett**, W. *Communications in supervisory management.* London: Nelson, 1967. 128p.

3686 **Dickinson**, Arthur William. *Industrial relations in supervisory management.* London: Nelson, 1967. viii, 128p. (Studies in supervisory management.)

3687 **Fraser**, John Munro. *Principles and practice of supervisory management.* London: Nelson, 1967. viii, 120p. (Studies in supervisory management.)

3688 **Peters**, David Alexander. *Principles of supervision.* London: Longmans, 1967. ix, 85p. (Supervisory series 1.)
A National Extension College course prepared in collaboration with the Institute of Supervisory Management.

3689 **Turner**, Patricia. *The personnel function and the role of supervisors: a study based on three firms.* 1967. 148 leaves. (M.Sc. thesis, University of London.)

3690 **Barnes**, Robert Johnson. *Principles and practice of supervision.* London: Heinemann in association with the Institute of Supervisory Management, 1968. 89p. (Supervisor's bookshelf.)

3691 **Industrial Society**. *Changes in supervisory structure.* London: the Society, 1968. 28p. (Information survey and report series 149.)

3692 **Norton**, Kenneth Alfred and **Fraser**, John Munro. *Engineering aspects of supervisory management.* London: Nelson, 1968. viii, 144p. (Studies in supervisory management.)

3693 **Peters**, David Alexander. *The principles and practice of supervision.* Oxford, London: Pergamon, 1967 [i.e. 1968]. v, 89p. (Commonwealth and international library. Supervisory studies.)

3694 **Donovan**, A. *Some determinants of effective supervision in Irish industry.* 1968–69. (Ph.D. thesis, National University of Ireland.)

3695 **Brown**, Alice. 'The forelady.' Fraser, R. (ed.). *Work, volume 2: twenty personal accounts.* Harmondsworth: Penguin, 1969. p. 298–310.

3696 **Fletcher**, Colin. 'Men in the middle: a reformulation of the thesis.' *Sociol. Rev.*, n.s., XVII, 3 (November 1969), 341–54.
'This paper is a modification of a thesis submitted in September 1967 as part of the course for the Diploma in Industrial Administration at the University of Liverpool.'

3697 **Foster**, Charles. 'The foreman's tale.' *New Soc.*, XIV, 355 (17 July 1969), 89–90.

3698 **Harding**, H. A. *Introduction to foremanship.* London: Macdonald and Evans, 1969. xii, 258p.
Second edition.
Previous edition edited by H. McFarland Davis, 1942.

3699 **King-Scott**, Peter. *Industrial supervision.* London: Pitman, 1969. viii, 176p.

See also: 7777.

PART FIVE

LABOUR–MANAGEMENT RELATIONS

I. GENERAL

This section contains works concerned with general aspects of the relationship between workers and employers as distinct from works on the industrial relations system in general, which are to be found in Part One, IV. Also included here is general material on Whitleyism and national bargaining. See also Part Three, III, A; Part Three, III, B, 1; Part Five, IV, A; Part Five, V, A; and Part Seven, I and VIII.

3700 **Williams**, J. Herbert. *Notes on labour, compiled from an original manuscript*. London: E. Stanford, 1891. 2v.

3701 **Webb**, Sidney and **Webb**, Beatrice. 'The method of collective bargaining.' *Econ. J.*, vi, 21 (March 1896), 1–29.

3702 **Cree**, Thomas S. *Evils of collective bargaining in trade unions*. Glasgow: Bell and Bain, 1898. 29p.
Second edition.
'A paper read to the Civic Society of Glasgow on Thursday, 20th January, 1898.'

3703 **Board of Trade**. *Report on collective agreements between employers and workpeople in the United Kingdom*. London: Darling for H.M.S.O., 1910. xxxviii, 504p. (Cd. 5366.)
Report submitted by G. R. Askwith.
'The report discusses the chief subjects dealt with in agreements. The bulk of the volume is composed of detailed examples of agreements in force in the major industries.' (Ford.)

3704 **Industrial Council**. *Report on enquiry into industrial agreements*. London: H.M.S.O., 1913. 22p. (Cd. 6952.)
Minutes of evidence. xiii, 665p. (Cd. 6953.)
Chairman: G. Askwith.

3705 **United States**. *Report of the Industrial Council of the British Board of Trade on its inquiry into industrial agreements*. 1913. 41p.

3706 **Athenæum**. *The politics of industry: an examination of the Whitley Report*. London: *The Athenæum*, 1917. 15p.
Reprinted from *The Athenæum*.
On 3709.

3707 **Bristol Association for Industrial Reconstruction**. *Memorandum . . . on the interim report on joint standing industrial councils issued by the Reconstruction Committee*. Bristol, 1917. 8p.
On the Whitley report.

3708 **Ministry of Labour**. *Industrial Councils: the Whitley Report together with the letter of the Minister of Labour explaining the government's view of its proposals*. London: H.M.S.O., 1917. 16p. (Industrial reports 1.)

3709 **Reconstruction Committee**. Sub-Committee on Relations between Employers and Employed. *Interim report on joint standing industrial councils*. London: H.M.S.O., 1917. 8p. (Cd. 8606.)
Chairman: J. H. Whitley.

3710 **Benn**, *Sir* Ernest John Pickstone. *Trade parliaments and their work*. London: Nisbet, 1918. 91p.

3711 **Industrial Reconstruction Council**. *Reconstruction handbook for students and speakers*. London: Nisbet, 1918. 46p.
A handbook for speakers advocating the Whitley Councils.

3712 **Industrial Reconstruction Council**. *Trade parliaments: why they should be formed and how to form one in your trade*. London: the Council, 1918. 12p.

3713 **Ministry of Labour**. *Industrial Councils and Trade Boards: joint memorandum of the Minister of Reconstruction and the Minister of Labour, explaining the Government's view of the proposals of the Second Whitley Report, together with the text of the report*. London: H.M.S.O., 1918. 16p. (Industrial reports 3.)

3714 **Ministry of Labour**. *Works committees: report of an enquiry made by the Ministry of Labour*. London: H.M.S.O., 1918. ii, 146p. (Industrial reports 2.)

3715 **Ministry of Labour**. *Works committees: suggestions as to the constitution and functions of works committees*. London, 1918. 4p.

3716 **Ministry of Reconstruction**. Committee on Relations between Employers and Employed. *Memorandum on industrial councils and trade boards*. London: H.M.S.O., 1918. 4p. (Cd. 9085.)

3717 **Ministry of Reconstruction.** Committee on Relations between Employers and Employed. *Second report on joint standing industrial councils.* London: H.M.S.O., 1918. 7p. (Cd. 9002.)

Second report of the 'Whitley Committee'.

3718 **Ministry of Reconstruction.** Committee on Relations between Employers and Employed. *Supplementary report on works committees.* London: H.M.S.O., 1918. 4p. (Cd. 9001.)

Third report of the 'Whitley Committee'.

3719 **Ministry of Reconstruction.** Committee on Relations between Employers and Employed. *Report on conciliation and arbitration (in substitution of Cd. 9081).* London: H.M.S.O., 1918. 5p. (Cd. 9099.)

'Apparently the same as Cd. 9081, which omitted Carter's name as signee of report.' (Ford.)

Fourth report of the 'Whitley Committee'.

3720 **Ministry of Reconstruction.** Committee on Relations between Employers and Employed. *Final report.* London: H.M.S.O., 1918. 4p. (Cd. 9153.)

Final report of the 'Whitley Committee' which summed up those that preceded it.

3721 **Murphy**, John Thomas. *Compromise or independence? An examination of the Whitley Report, with a plea for the rejection of the proposals for Joint Standing Industrial Councils.* Sheffield: Sheffield Workers' Committee, 1918. 12p.

3722 **National Guilds League.** Vigilance Committee on After-War Problems. *Notes for trade unionists in connection with the adoption by the war cabinet of the . . . Whitley report.* London, 1918. 8p.

3723 **Bloomfield**, Meyer. *Management and men: a record of new steps in industrial relations.* New York: Century, 1919. xv, 591p.

'The main text of this book is made up of articles written for the *Saturday evening post.*' (Pref.)

The Whitley Report together with a letter of the Minister of Labour explaining the government's view of its proposals, p. 297–465.

London edition (T. F. Unwin) has title: *The new labour movement in Great Britain: management and men.*

3724 **Holme**, J. B. *The British scheme for self-government of industry and its counterpart in New South Wales.* London, 1919. 2v.

3725 **Ministry of Labour.** *Suggestions as to the constitution and functions of a joint industrial council.* London, 1919. 4p.

3726 **Ministry of Reconstruction.** *Industrial councils: the Whitley scheme.* London: H.M.S.O., 1919. 14p. (Reconstruction problems 18.)

3727 **Sub-Committee of the Inter-Departmental Committee on the Application of the Whitley Report to Government Establishments.** *Report on the application of the Whitley Report to the administrative departments of the Civil Service.* London: H.M.S.O., 1919. 10p. (Cmd. 9.)

Reprinted 1925.

3728 **United States.** Bureau of Industrial Research. *The industrial council plan in Great Britain: reprints of the Report of the Whitley Committee on Relations between Employers and Employed of the Ministry of Reconstruction and of related documents.* Washington, D.C.: B.I.R., 1919. 132p.

3729 **United States.** Bureau of Labor Statistics. *Joint Industrial Councils in Great Britain: reports of Committee on Relations between Employers and Employed, and other official documents.* Washington, D.C.: U.S.G.P.O., 1919. 207p. (Bulletin 255.)

3730 **Watts**, Sidney Maurice (ed.). *The industrial future in the light of the brotherhood ideal.* London: Allen and Unwin, 1919. 64p.

Short papers by John Clifford, G. J. Wardle, Lord Leverhulme, A. Lyle Samuel, A. Maude Royden, Frank Hodges, J. A. Seddon, S. Maurice Watts given at a series of meetings at the Whitefield's Men's Meeting.

3731 **Wethered**, Ernest Handel Cossham. *The place of conciliation and arbitration in the 'Whitley' scheme of industrial self-government.* London, 1919. 11p.

3732 **Whitley**, John Henry, and others. *Making a new world: report of speeches.* London, 1919. 10p.

3733 **Whitley**, John Henry. *Whitley councils: what they are, and what they are doing.* London, [1919?]. 28p.

3734 **Wolfe**, Albert Benedict. *Works committees and joint industrial councils: a report.* Philadelphia: United States Shipping Board Emergency Fleet Corporation, Industrial Relations Division, 1919. 254p.

3735 **Cole**, George Douglas Howard. 'The industrial councils of Great Britain.' Bloomfield, D. (ed.). *Selected articles on modern industrial movements.* London: Pitman, 1920. p. 231–41.

From *Dial*, LXVI (22 February 1919), 171–3.

3736 **Garton Foundation.** 'Joint industrial councils and trade boards.' Bloomfield, D. (ed.). *Selected articles on modern industrial movements.* London: Pitman, 1920. p. 223–35.

From the Foundation's report, *Memorandum on the industrial situation after the war.* Revised edition. London, 1919.

3737 **Johnston**, Thomas Bertram. 'Industrial councils and their possibilities.' Berriman, A. E., and others. *Industrial administration: a series of lectures.* Manchester: Manchester U.P.; London: Longmans, Green, 1920. p. 133–59.

3738 **Johnston**, Thomas Bertram. *Industrial councils and their possibilities*. Manchester, 1920. 25p.

3739 **Ministry of Labour**. 'Functions and constitution of district councils and of works committees.' Bloomfield, D. (ed.). *Selected articles on modern industrial movements*. London: Pitman, 1920. p. 213–23.

From *Industrial reports*, 4. 1919.

3740 **Ministry of Labour**. *Industrial councils: suggestions as to the constitution and functions of a national joint industrial council, of district councils of national joint industrial councils, and of works committees in industries in which national joint industrial councils are established*. London: H.M.S.O., 1920. 32p. (Industrial reports 4. Revised.)

First published 1919.

3741 **Ministry of Reconstruction**. 'The Whitley scheme.' Bloomfield, D. (ed.). *Selected articles on modern industrial movements*. London: Pitman, 1920. p. 199–213.

Originally published by the Ministry as *Reconstruction problems, pamphlet no. 18*, 1919.

3742 **Renold**, Charles Garonne. 'Workshop committees.' Bloomfield, D. (ed.). *Selected articles on modern industrial movements*. London: Pitman, 1920. p. 177–99.

From *Survey*, XLI, Sec. 1 (5 October 1918).

3743 **Whitley**, John Henry. 'Works committees and industrial councils: their beginnings and possibilities.' Manchester University. *Labour and industry: a series of lectures*. Manchester: Manchester U.P.; London: Longmans, 1920. p. 1–25.

3744 **International Labour Office**. 'Joint industrial councils in Great Britain.' *Int. Labour Rev.*, LV, 3 (December 1921), 111–26 (563–78).

3745 **Trades Union Congress** and **Labour Party**. *Industrial negotiations and agreements*. London: T.U.C. and Labour Party, 1922. 76p.

3746 **Liddall**, M. E. *Experiments in the maintenance of industrial peace*. 1923. (B.A. thesis, University of Bristol.)

3747 **Ministry of Labour**. *Report on the establishment and progress of Joint Industrial Councils set up in accordance with the recommendations of the Committee on the Relations of Employers and Employed, 1917–1922*. London: H.M.S.O., 1923. 231p.

3748 **Reid**, M. L. *Works councils: do they offer a solution for the present day industrial problem?* 1923. i, 107p. (M.A. thesis, University of British Columbia.)

3749 **Hewes**, Amy. 'The changing structure of the bargaining unit of labor.' *Q. J. Econ.*, XXXIX, 4 (August 1925), 612–34.

England, p. 614–18.

3750 **Nutting**, A. Forde. *Employer and employed: a treatise*. London: Stockwell, 1928. 16p.

3751 *Goodwill in industry, from a new angle: a symposium by five practical men*. London: London General Press, [1929]. 59p.

Five prize essays submitted to a competition held by the Glasgow and West of Scotland Association of Foremen Engineers and Draughtsmen on 'Goodwill in industry'. The essays are by: J. G. Pearce, Robert Allan, J. Williamson, John Butler, Alan Andrews.

3752 **Pugh**, *Sir* Arthur. *Wage fixing: a lecture . . . delivered at Ruskin College, Oxford, July 1929*. (Trades Union Congress. Summer School. Pamphlets 3.)

3753 **Seymour**, John Barton. *The Whitley Councils scheme*. London: King, 1932. viii, 253p.

3754 **Wethered**, Ernest Handel Cossham. *Collective agreements*. London: Gee, 1933. 27p. ('Accountant' lecture series 16.)

3755 **Ministry of Labour**. *Report on collective agreements between employers and workpeople in Great Britain and Northern Ireland. Vol. 1. Mining and quarrying industries, engineering, shipbuilding, iron and steel and other metal industries, building, woodworking and allied industries*. London: H.M.S.O., 1934. xxxiv, 454p.

'This volume is the first of the series . . . It is proposed to deal in subsequent volumes with other groups of industries.' (p. iv.)

No more published?

3756 **Thomas**, Philip Sydney. *Industrial relations: a short study of the relations between employers and employed in Swansea and neighbourhood, from about 1800 to recent times*. Swansea: University of Wales P., 1940. 125p.

3757 **Industrial Welfare Society**. *Works councils and committees*. London, 1941. 40p.

Other editions. 1947, 1952.

3758 **Cole**, George Douglas Howard. *The impact of current economic changes on industrial relations and on the demand for labour*. London, Southampton: Camelot P. (printed), 1944. 20p.

A lecture given before the 47th 'Oxford' Management Conference held in London in May, 1944, and reprinted from vol. v, no. 2 of *British Management Review*.

3759 **Ministry of Labour and National Service**. National Joint Advisory Council. *Statement on the economic considerations affecting relations between employers and workers*. London: H.M.S.O., 1947. 9p. (Cmd. 7018.)

3760 **Political and Economic Planning**. 'Framework of collective bargaining.' *Planning*, XIV, 272 (3 October 1947), 101–19.

3761 **Evans**, Lincoln. 'Union–management relations.' Tracey, H. (ed.). *The British Labour Party: its history, growth, policy, and leaders*. London: Caxton Publishing Co., 1948. Vol. 2. p. 84–94.

3762 **Ball**, Frank Norman. 'An industrial relations policy.' *Ind. Law Rev.*, III, 4 (April 1949), 268–72.

3763 **Jaques**, Elliott. 'Studies in the social development of an industrial community

(The Glacier Project). I. Collaborative group methods in a wage negotiation situation.' *Hum. Relat.*, III, 3 (August 1950), 223–49.

3764 **Somervell**, Hubert. *Industrial peace in our time*. London: Allen and Unwin, 1950. 224p.

Introduction by Elton Mayo.

3765 **Kirkaldy**, Harold Stewart. 'Industrial relations in Great Britain: a survey of post-war developments.' *Int. Labour Rev.*, LXVIII, 6 (December 1953), 468–92.

3766 **Flanders**, Allan David. 'Collective bargaining.' Flanders, A. and Clegg, H. A. (eds.). *The system of industrial relations in Great Britain* . . . Oxford: Blackwell, 1954. p. 252–322.

3767 **Conservative and Unionist Party**. Conservative Industrial Department. *Trade unions and employers*. London: Conservative Political Centre, 1955. 20p. (Trade union series 10.)

Revised edition. 1964. 15p. (New trade union series 10.)

3768 **Edinburgh Junior Chamber of Commerce and Manufacturers**. *Report on relations between employers and employees*. Edinburgh, 1955.

3769 **Rogow**, Arnold Austin. 'Labor relations under the British Labor government.' *Am. J. Econ. Sociol.*, XIV, 4 (July 1955), 357–76.

3770 **Jensen**, Vernon Horton. 'Notes on the beginnings of collective bargaining.' *Ind. Labor Relat. Rev.*, IX, 2 (January 1956), 225–34.

3771 **Roberts**, Benjamin Charles. 'Employers and industrial relations in Britain and America.' *Polit. Q.*, XXVII, 3 (July–September 1956), 324–39.

3772 **Routh**, Guy. 'The structure of collective bargaining.' *Polit. Q.*, XXVII, 1 (January–March 1956), 44–56.

3773 **Blair-Cunynghame**, J. O. 'Management and trade unions.' Thomson, D. C. (ed.). *Management, labour and community*. London: Pitman, 1957. p. 91–103.

3774 **Flanders**, Allan David. 'Great Britain.' Sturmthal, A. (ed.). *Contemporary collective bargaining in seven countries*. Ithaca, N.Y.: Institute of International Industrial and Labor Relations, Cornell University, 1957. p. 1–52.

3775 **Fletcher**, Edwin. 'Trade unions and management.' Thomson, D. C. (ed.). *Management, labour and community*. London: Pitman, 1957. p. 104–16.

3776 **Lester**, Richard A. 'Reflections on collective bargaining in Britain and Sweden.' *Ind. Labor Relat. Rev.*, X, 3 (April 1957), 375–401.

3777 **Sturmthal**, Adolf. 'An essay on comparative collective bargaining.' Sturmthal, A. (ed.). *Contemporary collective bargaining in seven countries*. Ithaca, N.Y.: Institute of International Industrial and Labor Relations, Cornell University, 1957. p. 308–71.

3778 **Institute of Directors**. *Understanding labour relations*. London: the Institute, 1958. 37p.

3779 **Shanks**, Michael. 'New phase in wage bargaining.' *Banker*, CVIII, 386 (March 1958), 150–5.

3780 **International Labour Office**. *An account of an Asian Bipartite Study Tour on Labour Management Relations to the United Kingdom and Federal Republic of Germany, 6 September–8 November 1958*. Geneva: I.L.O., 1959. 205p. (Labour–management relations series 6.)

Also published as *Report on a labour management relations study tour, 1 September–22 November 1958*. 1959. iii, 205p. (ILO/TAP/AFE/R. 7.)

3781 **Sykes**, Andrew James Macintyre. 'The pattern of industrial relations.' *Q. Rev.*, CCXCVII, 622 (October 1959), 432–43.

3782 **Chivers**, Colin. 'The pattern of collective bargaining.' Roberts, B. C. (ed.). *Industrial relations: contemporary problems and perspectives*. London: Methuen, 1962. p. 108–38.

3783 **Genders**, John Elton and **Urwin**, Noel John. *Wages and salaries*. London: Institute of Personnel Management, 1962. 63p.

3784 **Yuill**, Bruce F. *Union management relations*. 1962. (Ph.D. thesis, University of Glasgow.)

3785 **Forsythe**, E. J. 'Collective bargaining in Western Europe.' *Labour Law J.*, XIV, 11 (November 1963), 919–34.

3786 **Swift**, B. M. 'The duration of wage negotiations, 1950–58.' *R. Statist. Soc. J.*, Ser. A, CXXVI, 2 (1963), 300–14.

3787 **Topham**, Tony. 'The implication of "package deals" in British collective bargaining.' *Int. Social. J.*, I, 5–6 (September–December 1964), 520–41.

3788 **Anthony**, Peter. 'Mutual interest?' *New Soc.*, VII, 179 (3 March 1966), 15–16. (Society at work.)

3789 **Allen**, A. J. *Management and men: a study in industrial relations*. London: Hallam P., 1967. 65p. (Quarterly survey of business opinion.)

3790 **Mitchell**, David. *Fuller employment: some thoughts on restrictive practices, strikes, and the status of the employee*. London: Aims of Industry, 1967. 21p. (Publication 12A.)

3791 **Derber**, Milton. 'Collective bargaining in Great Britain and the United States.' *Q. Rev. Econ. Bus.*, VIII, 4 (Winter 1968), 55–66.

3792 **Flanders**, Allan David. 'Collective bargaining: a theoretical analysis.' *Br. J. Ind. Relat.*, VI, 1 (March 1968), 1–26.

'A paper entitled "Bargaining theory under modern capitalism", presented to the First World Congress of the International Industrial Relations Association held at Geneva in September 1967.'

Then published as 'Bargaining theory: the classical model reconsidered.' Roberts, B. C. (ed.). *Industrial relations: contemporary issues* . . . London: Macmillan; New York: St Martin's P., 1968, p. 3–33, and later as 'Collective bargaining: a theoretical analysis.' Flanders, A. *Management and unions: the theory and reform of industrial relations*. London: Faber, 1970. p. 213–40.

An excerpt was published as 'The nature of collective bargaining.' Flanders, A. (ed.). *Collective bargaining: selected readings*. Harmondsworth: Penguin Books, 1969. p. 11–41.

3793 **Flanders**, Allan David (ed.). *Collective bargaining: selected readings*. Harmondsworth: Penguin Books, 1969. 431p. (Penguin modern management, readings; Penguin education.)

3794 **Fox**, Alan and **Flanders**, Allan David. 'The reform of collective bargaining: from Donovan to Durkheim.' *Br. J. Ind. Relat.*, VII, 2 (July 1969), 151–80.

Reprinted as 'Collective bargaining: from Donovan to Durkheim.' Flanders, A. *Management and unions: the theory and reform of industrial relations*. London: Faber, 1970. p. 241–76.

3795 **Jenkins**, W. E. 'The parties to negotiation.' McCarthy, W. E. J. (ed.). *Industrial relations in Britain: a guide for management and unions*. London: Lyon, Grant and Green, 1969. p. 29–51.

3796 **Thomas**, Griffith Bowen. 'The national system of negotiations.' McCarthy, W. E. J. (ed.). *Industrial relations in Britain: a guide for management and unions*. London: Lyon, Grant and Green, 1969. p. 105–26.

3797 **Brown**, William Arthur. *Collective bargaining in transition: report of a conference at Ditchley Park, 14–17 November 1969*. Enstone: Ditchley Foundation, 1970. 22p. (Ditchley paper 25.)

3798 **Charles**, R. F. *National consultation and co-operation between trade unionists and employers in Britain 1911–39*. 1970. (D.Phil. thesis, University of Oxford.)

3799 **Fairweather**, Owen. 'Western European labor movements and collective bargaining – an institutional framework.' Kamin, A. (ed.). *Western European labor and the American Corporation*. Washington, D.C.: Bureau of National Affairs, 1970. p. 69–92.

United Kingdom, p. 71–4.

3800 **Morley**, Ian E. and **Stephenson**, Geoffrey M. 'Strength of case, communication systems, and the outcomes of simulated negotiations: some social psychological aspects of bargaining.' *Ind. Relat. J.* (Summer 1970), 19–29.

See also: 17; 20; 23; 5354; 12,888.

II. PLANT AND PRODUCTIVITY BARGAINING AND LABOUR UTILISATION

The more sociological and psychological literature on restriction of output is classified at Part Two, I, II and IV. The literature on the relationship between effort and remuneration is classified at Part Six, III, G. See also Part Three, III, G, 9; Part Six, II, B; and Part Six, II, D, 3.

3801 **Edwards**, Clement. 'Do trade unions limit output?' *Contemp. Rev.*, LXXXI (January 1902), 113–28.

3802 **Brassey**, Thomas, Earl Brassey. *The comparative efficiency of English and foreign labour*. London: Longmans, 1904. 15p.

Address to the Manchester Chamber of Commerce.

3803 **Richardson**, *Sir* Alexander. *The man power of the nation: suggestions as to industrial efficiency for employers and workers*. London: *Engineering*, 1916. 111p.

Reprinted from *Engineering*.

3804 **Ellinger**, B. *Productivity of labour, after the war*. [Manchester?], 1917. 24p.

3805 **Board of Trade.** Coal Mines Department. *Address by the Controller of Coal Mines to a conference of delegates of the Miners' Federation of Great Britain at Southport, on the 20th August, 1918*. London: Merritt and Hatcher, 1918. 8p.

3806 **Brownlie**, J. T. and **Grimshaw**, H. A. *The trade unions and output*. Birmingham, Oxford: Council of Ruskin College, 1920. 70p. (Re-organisation of industry series vii.)

Papers, with a report of the discussions.

The workers' interest in output, by J. T. Brownlie.

The influence of the distribution of wealth upon output, by H. A. Grimshaw.

3807 **Watson**, William Foster. *Should the workers increase output? A reply to the paper read by Mr. J. T. Brownlie . . . at the Ruskin College Conference . . . 1920*. London: E. London Workers' Committee, 1920. 19p.

J. T. Brownlie's paper *The gate to more*.

3808 **Corser**, Haden. 'Trade unions and efficiency, in local government.' *Publ. Adm.*, VI, 2 (April 1928), 133–41.

'Discussed at the Institute of Public Administration Winter Conference, March, 1928.'

3809 **Pugh**, Arthur. 'Trade unions and efficiency, in industry.' *Publ. Adm.*, VI, 2 (April 1928), 147–61.

'Discussed at the Institute of Public Administration Winter Conference, March, 1928.'

3810 **Ramsay**, Alexander. 'Trade unions and efficiency, in industry and commerce.' *Publ. Adm.*, VI, 2 (April 1928), 142–6.

'Discussed at the Institute of Public Administration Winter Conference, March 1928.'

3811 **Stuart-Bunning**, G. H. 'Trade unions and efficiency, in the Civil Service.' *Publ. Adm.*, VI, 2 (April 1928), 120–5.

'Discussed at the Institute of Public Administration Winter Conference, March 1928.'

3812 **Wiltshire**, F. H. C. 'Trade unions and efficiency, in local government.' *Publ. Adm.*, VI, 2 (April 1928), 126–32.

'Discussed at the Institute of Public Administration Winter Conference, March 1928.'

3813 **Good**, E. T. and **Hunter**, G. B. *Trade union restrictions: their effects on trade, labour, employment, wages, and cost of living*. 1932. 8p.

3814 **Katin**, Louis. 'The worker's point of view. VI. Craft-distinction in the factory.' *Hum. Factor*, VI, 8 (August 1932), 302–5.

Reprinted in *The worker's point of view: a symposium*. London: Hogarth P., 1933. p. 137–42.

3815 **Watson**, William Foster. 'The worker's point of view. XVII. Whose job is it?' *Hum. Factor*, VIII, 4 (April 1934), 136–45.

3816 **Hilton**, John, and others (eds.). *Are trade unions obstructive? An impartial inquiry*. London: Gollancz, 1935. 349p.

Under the joint editorship of J. Hilton, J. J. Mallon, S. Mavor, B. S. Rowntree, Sir A. Salter, F. D. Stuart, assisted by V. M. S. Heigham.

A series of industry reports.

3817 **Gardiner**, Glenn Lion. *When foreman and steward bargain*. New York, London: McGraw-Hill, 1945. viii, 194p. (McGraw-Hill industrial organisation and management series.)

3818 **Cole**, George Douglas Howard. 'Trade unions, workers and production.' *Polit. Q.*, XVIII (July–September 1947), 250–60.

3819 **Zweig**, Ferdynand. *Productivity and trade unions*. Oxford: Blackwell, 1951. 240p.

3820 **Ord**, Lewis Craven. *Industrial frustration: commonsense for trade unionists*. London: Mayflower Publishing Co., 1953. xi, 178p.

3821 **Crawford**, J. *The attitude of trade unions towards modern management methods*. London: British Institute of Management, 1954.

3822 **Crawford**, J. *The trade union attitude to research and productive efficiency*. London: Institution of Production Engineers, 1954.

3823 **Gintz**, H. *Effects of technological change on labour in selected sections of the iron and steel industries in Great Britain, the United States and Germany, 1901–1939*. 1954. (Ph.D. thesis, University of London.)

3824 **Conservative and Unionist Party**. Conservative Industrial Department. *Trade unions and productivity*. London: Conservative Political Centre, 1955. 15p. (Trade union series 11.)

3825 **Gray**, Ailsa Patricia. 'Afterthoughts on Fawley.' *Occup. Psychol.*, XXIX, 2 (April 1955), 117–24.

A paper read to the Industrial Section of the British Psychological Society, 14 July 1954.

See also entry 4014.

3826 **Hugh-Jones**, E. M. 'Industrial productivity: the lessons of Fawley.' *J. Ind. Econ.*, III, 3 (July 1955), 173–83.

3827 **Roberts**, Cecil. *Attempts to increase co-operative shop productivity*. 1955. (M.Com. thesis, University of Birmingham.)

3828 **Harle**, R. 'The role of trade unions in increasing productivity.' *Polit. Q.*, XXVII, 1 (January–March 1956), 93–100.

3829 **F. R. Bentley Company**. *The Rucker plan*. London: F. R. Bentley Company, 1957. 27p.

'A new approach to higher productivity and increased labour co-operation.'

Based on the research of Allen W. Rucker.

3830 **Balfour**, William Campbell. *Productivity and the worker*. 1958. (M.A. thesis, University of Wales.)

3831 **F. R. Bentley Company**. *People, productivity, progress: a proved British approach to higher productivity and increased labour co-operation*. London, 1958. 19p.

3832 **Melman**, Seymour. *Decision-making and productivity*. Oxford: Blackwell, 1958. xii, 260p.

Based on a detailed study of the Standard Motor Company, Coventry, between 1950 and 1953.

3833 **Ministry of Labour and National Service**. *Practices impeding the full and efficient use of manpower: report of an inquiry undertaken by the National Joint Advisory Council*. London: H.M.S.O., 1959. 15p.

3834 **Martell**, Edward and **Butler**, Ewan. *The murder of the News Chronicle and the Star, killed by trade union restrictive practices, October 17, 1960*. London: C. Johnson, 1960. 112p.

3835 **Hickson**, D. J. *A case-study of restriction of output and associated issues of payment and work study*. 1961. (M.Sc. Tech. thesis, University of Manchester.)

3836 **Seear**, Nancy. 'Relationships at factory level.' Roberts, B. C. (ed.). *Industrial relations: contemporary problems and perspectives*. London: Methuen, 1962. p. 139–65.

3837 **Marsh**, Arthur I. *Managers and shop stewards*. London: Institute of Personnel Management, 1963. 40p. (Occasional papers. Industrial relations series.)

3838 **Flanders**, Allan David. *The Fawley productivity agreements: a case study of management and collective bargaining*. London: Faber, 1964. 360p. (Society today and tomorrow.)

Second edition. 1966. 360p.

Also paperback edition 1966, 265p., which lacks illustrations and the five appendices. See author's note p. 12.

3839 **Flanders**, Allan David. 'The lessons of Fawley.' *New Soc.*, III, 83 (30 April 1964), 16–19; III, 84 (7 May 1964), 12–15.

Extract from the author's *The Fawley productivity agreements*.

3840 **Hunter**, Laurence Colvin. 'Productivity agreements.' *Scott. J. Polit. Econ.*, XI, 3 (November 1964), 260–86.

Review article, mainly devoted to a discussion of *The Fawley productivity agreements*, by A. Flanders.

3841 **Lerner**, Shirley Walowitz. 'Factory agreements and national bargaining in the British engineering industry.' *Int. Labour Rev.*, LXXXIX, 1 (January 1964), 1–18.

3842 **McCormick**, Brian J. 'Trade union reaction to technological change in the construction industry.' *Yorks. Bull. Econ. Soc. Res.*, XVI, 1 (May 1964), 15–30.

3843 **Robertson**, Andrew. 'Technological change, management and labour.' *Polit. Q.*, XXXV, 2 (April–June 1964), 171–81.

3844 **Torode**, John A. 'Restrictive practices.' *New Soc.*, IV, 114 (3 December 1964), 13–14.

3845 **Cannon**, Leslie. 'The trade union attitude to technological change.' British Productivity Council. *Automation and its implications.* London, 1965. p. 34–40.

3846 **Eldridge**, John E. T. 'Plant bargaining in steel: North East case studies.' *Sociol. Rev.*, n.s., XIII, 2 (July 1965), 131–48.

3847 **Turner**, Herbert Arthur. 'The contribution of workers to productivity growth.' Robinson, E. A. G. (ed.). *Problems in economic development: proceedings of a Conference held by the International Economic Association.* London: Macmillan; New York: St Martin's P., 1965. p. 336–44.

Discussion, p. 344–9.

3848 **Bugler**, Jeremy. 'Along the road from Fawley.' *New Soc.*, VII, 184 (7 April 1966), 5–7.

3849 **Flanders**, Allan David. 'The problems of consent for change: the Fawley refinery case.' Stieber, J. (ed.). *Employment problems of automation and advanced technology: an international perspective.* London: Macmillan; New York: St Martin's P., 1966. p. 394–409.

Discussion, p. 410–11.

3850 **Fox**, Alan. 'Productivity bargaining.' *New Soc.*, VIII, 208 (22 September 1966), p. 446–8.

3851 **Ivens**, Michael and **Broadway**, Frank (eds.). *Case studies in human relations productivity and organization.* London: Business Publications, 1966. xxxii, 380p.

3852 **Jones**, Ken and **Golding**, John. *Productivity bargaining.* London: Fabian Society, 1966. 39p. (Research series 257.)

3853 **McKersie**, Robert B. *A behavioural analysis of productivity bargaining.* 1966. 25p.

A lecture given at the London School of Economics and Political Science, March 1966.

3854 **McKersie**, Robert B. *Productivity bargaining: deliverance or delusion?* London: Institute of Personnel Management, 1966.

3855 **Ministry of Labour**, and others. *The efficient use of manpower: a management responsibility. Conference papers, Stratford-upon-Avon, March 1966.* London: the Ministry, 1966. 53p.

3856 **Ross**, Norman Scott. *Workshop bargaining: a new approach.* London: Fabian Society, 1966. 29p. (Fabian tract 366.)

3857 **Smith**, John Harold. *Social and technical efficiency: an inaugural lecture delivered at the University on 15th March, 1966.* Southampton: University of Southampton, 1966. 20p.

3858 **Trades Union Congress**. *Productivity bargaining.* London: T.U.C., 1966. 16p.

3859 **Bucklow**, Maxine. 'A note on the Fawley agreements.' *J. Ind. Relat.*, IX, 1 (March 1967), 72–5.

A discussion of the work of Allan Flanders.

3860 **Confederation of British Industry**. *Productivity: joint initiative by the CBI and TUC.* London: C.B.I., 1967.

3861 **Fisher**, Patrick. *Pay and productivity.* Oxford, London: Pergamon P., 1967. 19p. (Take home books; Productivity progress series.)

3862 **Industrial Society**. *Productivity agreements: the processes of negotiating and communicating.* London: the Society, 1967. 56p. (Information survey and report series 141.)

3863 **Jones**, Glyn and **Barnes**, Michael. *Britain on borrowed time.* Harmondsworth: Penguin, 1967. 352p. (Pelican originals.)

3864 **Jones**, Gwynn. *Productivity bargaining: its place in the British system of industrial relations.* Hove: Editype, 1967. 39p. (Editype mini-book 13.)

3865 **Lincoln**, John Abraham. *The restrictive society: a report on restrictive practices.* London: Allen and Unwin, 1967. 262p.

3866 **McCullough**, Ellen. 'Productivity agreements and the structure of collective bargaining.' *Br. J. Ind. Relat.* V, 1 (March 1967), 28–39.

3867 **Ministry of Labour**. *Efficient use of manpower: report of a study group composed of directors and senior managers of well known firms in the Midlands.* London: H.M.S.O., 1967. 19p.

Chairman: A. J. Nicol.

3868 **Ministry of Labour**, and others. *Management and manpower utilization: conference papers, Southport, February 1967.* London: the Ministry, 1967. 53p.

3869 **Ministry of Labour**, and others. *Management and manpower utilization: conference papers, Stratford-upon-Avon, March 1967.* London: the Ministry, 1967. 118p.

3870 **National Board for Prices and Incomes.** *Productivity agreements.* London: H.M.S.O., 1967. vi, 77p. (Report 36. Cmnd. 3311.)

3871 **National Board for Prices and Incomes.** *Productivity agreements in the bus industry.* London: H.M.S.O., 1967. (Report 50. Cmd. 3498.)

3872 **Organisation for Economic Co-operation and Development**. *The British 'productivity agreements': some reflections based on a case study by N. Cooper.* Paris: O.E.C.D., 1967. 15p.

3873 **Roberts**, Geoffrey. *Demarcation rules in shipbuilding and shiprepairing.* London: Cambridge U.P., 1967. 45p. (University of Cambridge, Department of Applied Economics. Occasional papers 14.)

3874 **Royal Commission on Trade Unions and Employers' Associations.**

1. *Productivity bargaining.* 2. *Restrictive prac-*

tices. London: H.M.S.O., 1967. vi, 67p. (Research papers 4.)

3875 **Ryder**, M. S. 'Collective bargaining for greater productivity: some factors in the American labour relations system possibly generating greater productivity.' *Br. J. Ind. Relat.*, v, 2 (July 1967), 190–7.

3876 **Schultz**, George P. and **McKersie**, Robert B. 'Stimulating productivity: choices, problems and shares.' *Br. J. Ind. Relat.*, v, 1 (March 1967), 1–18.

3877 **Topham**, Tony. 'New types of bargaining.' Blackburn, R. and Cockburn, A. (eds.). *The incompatibles: trade union militancy and the consensus.* Harmondsworth: Penguin in association with *New Left Review*, 1967. p. 133–59.

3878 **Banerjee**, R. N. 'The psycho-economic concept of incentive and the perspective of collective bargaining.' *Indian J. Labour Econ.*, x, 4 (January 1968), C-55–C-63.

3879 **Barratt Brown**, Michael. *Opening the books.* Nottingham: Institute for Workers' Control, 1968. [15]p. (Pamphlet series 4.)

3880 **Bayhylle**, J. E. *Productivity improvements in the office.* London: Engineering Employers' Federation, 1968. 83p.

3881 **Confederation of British Industry**. *Productivity bargaining.* London: C.B.I., 1968. 17p.

3882 **Economic Development Committee for the Rubber Industry**. *Plant bargaining: a report on negotiation and plant bargaining in the rubber industry.* London: National Economic Development Office, 1968. [5], 19p.

3883 **Einzig**, Paul. *The case against unearned wage increases.* London: Aims of Industry, 1968. 10p. (Studies 21.)

3884 **Engineering Employers' Federation**. *Productivity bargaining and the engineering industry.* London: E.E.F., 1968. [4], 60p. (Federation research papers 1.)

By E. J. Robertson.

3885 **Fielding**, Francis James. *Towards a high wage, high productivity economy.* London: Economic Research Council, 1968. i, 14p.

3886 **Fox**, Alan. 'Labour utilization and industrial relations.' Pym, D. (ed.). *Industrial society: social sciences in management.* Harmondsworth: Penguin, 1968. p. 41–64.

3887 **Government Social Survey**. *Workplace industrial relations.* London: H.M.S.O., 1968. ix, 215p. (SS402.)

'An enquiry undertaken for the Royal Commission on Trade Unions and Employers' Associations in 1966.'

3888 **Institute of Personnel Management**. Industrial Relations Committee. *The realities of productivity bargaining: Industrial Relations Committee report* . . . London: I.P.M., 1968. 46p. (Industrial relations series.)

Edited by Marjorie Harris.

3889 **McKersie**, Robert B. 'The significance of productivity bargaining in Great Britain.' Roberts, B. C. (ed.). *Industrial relations: contemporary issues* . . . London: Macmillan; New York: St Martin's P., 1968. p. 220–33.

3890 **National Board for Prices and Incomes.** *Electricity supply industry: national guidelines covering productivity payments.* London: H.M.S.O., 1968. (Report 79. Cmnd. 3726.)

3891 **National Board for Prices and Incomes.** *Productivity agreements in the road haulage industry.* London: H.M.S.O., 1968. (Report 94. Cmnd. 3847.)

3892 **Ulman**, Lloyd. 'Collective bargaining and industrial efficiency.' Caves, R. E. (ed.). *Britain's economic prospects.* Washington: Brookings Institution; London: Allen and Unwin, 1968. p. 324–80.

3893 **Alexander**, D. C. (ed.). *A productivity bargaining symposium.* London: Engineering Employers' Federation, 1969. 109p.

'. . . an edited version of the papers delivered at a Conference held on the 29th, 30th and 31st January, 1968, at the Engineering Employers' Federation, Broadway House, London.'

3894 **Alexander**, Kenneth John Wilson. *Productivity bargaining and the reform of industrial relations.* London: Industrial and Commercial Techniques, 1969. 73 leaves.

3895 **Behrend**, Hilde, **Knowles**, Ann and **Davies**, Jean. ' "Have you heard the phrase 'productivity agreements'?" Findings from two national sample surveys.' *Scott. J. Polit. Econ.*, xvi, 3 (October 1969), 256–70.

3896 **Beinum**, Hans van. 'Industrial relations on the shop floor.' Irish Management Institute. *Industrial democracy: a symposium.* Dublin: the Institute, 1969. p. 25–40.

3897 **Bodington**, Stephen. 'Trade unionists and computers.' *Trade Un. Regist.* (1969), 139–146.

3898 **Clegg**, Hugh Armstrong. 'The substance of productivity agreements.' Flanders, A. (ed.). *Collective bargaining: selected readings.* Harmondsworth: Penguin Books, 1969. p. 352–65.

Excerpts from National Board for Prices and Incomes, Report 36. *Productivity agreements.* London: H.M.S.O., 1967. p. 1–10.

3899 **Coker**, E. E. 'Local negotiations.' McCarthy, W. E. J. (ed.). *Industrial relations in Britain: a guide for management and unions.* London: Lyon, Grant and Green, 1969. p. 129–51.

3900 **Desai**, Ashok V. 'Productivity and managerial responsibility.' *Indian J. Ind. Relat.*, iv, 3 (January 1969), 322–32.

3901 **Engineering Employers' Federation**. *Productivity improvements in the office.* London: the Federation, 1969. (Research paper 2.)

3902 **Fisher**, Pat. *Representing the union: a guide to trade union productivity bargaining.* London: British Broadcasting Corporation, 1969. 48p.

'This booklet corresponds broadly with the television series "Representing the Union" . . . it has been prepared by a working party consisting of Pat Fisher and

Roy Jackson of the T.U.C. and Tony Matthews, producer of the television series.'

3903 **Flanders**, Allan David. 'Restrictive practices and productivity bargaining.' Flanders, A. (ed.). *Collective bargaining: selected readings.* Harmondsworth: Penguin Books, 1969. p. 333–51.

Excerpts from *The Fawley productivity agreements.* London: Faber, 1964. p. 230–48.

3904 **Gottschalk**, Andrew W. and **Towers**, B. *Productivity bargaining: a case study and simulation exercise.* Nottingham: Nottingham University, Department of Adult Education, 1969. 3 pts.

Part 1. *The company: background to the negotiations.*

Part 2. *The management.*

Part 3. *The trade unions.*

3905 **Hall**, P. G. 'Productivity planning and bargaining.' Lamble, J. H. (ed.). *Men, machines and the social sciences.* Bristol: Bath U.P., 1969. p. 54–71.

Includes discussion.

3906 **Lerner**, Shirley Walowitz, **Cable**, John Reginald and **Gupta**, S. (eds.). *Workshop wage determination.* Oxford: Pergamon P., 1969. x, 294p. (Commonwealth and international library. Industrial relations division.)

Based on research by a team from the Economics Department of the University of Manchester.

Contents:

1. Problems, methods, and approaches.
2. The engineering industry. Appendix, by T. Lupton.
3. The chemical industry, by P. Verma.
4. Soap: a case study.
5. The baking industry, by K. G. Knight.
6. Conclusions.

General appendix: the British system of industrial relations.

3907 **McCarthy**, William Edward John. 'Shop stewards' bargaining in Britain.' Flanders, A. (ed.). *Collective bargaining: selected readings.* Harmondsworth: Penguin Books, 1969. p. 286–314.

Excerpts from *The role of shop stewards in British industrial relations.* Royal Commission on Trade Unions and Employers' Associations. Research papers, 1. London: H.M.S.O., 1966. p. 19–36.

3908 **National Board for Prices and Incomes.** *Productivity agreements.* London: H.M.S.O., 1969. (Report 123. Cmnd. 4136.)

3909 **North**, Dick Trevor Brooke and **Buckingham**, Graeme L. *Productivity agreements and wage systems.* London: Gower P., 1969. xvii, 262p.

3910 **Searle-Barnes**, Robert Griffiths. *Pay and productivity bargaining: a study of the effect of national wage agreements in the Nottinghamshire coalfield.* Manchester: Manchester U.P., 1969. xxv, 190p.

3911 **Stettner**, Nora. *Productivity bargaining and industrial change.* Oxford: Pergamon for the Foundation on Automation and Employment Ltd., 1969. xi, 185p. (Commonwealth and international library of science and technology. Engineering and liberal studies.)

3912 **Topham**, Tony, 'Productivity bargaining.' *Trade Un. Regist.* (1969), 68–95.

3913 **Burrow**, T. W. 'Productivity bargaining and the economy.' Towers, B. and Whittingham, T. G. *The new bargainers: a symposium on productivity bargaining.* Nottingham: U. of Nottingham, Department of Adult Education, 1970. p. 123–40.

3914 **Cliff**, Tony. *The employers' offensive: productivity deals and how to fight them.* London: Pluto Press, 1970. 234p.

Second impression, with minor corrections. 1970.

3915 **Collins**, Ray. 'Trends in productivity bargaining.' *Trade Un. Regist.* (1970), 86–108.

3916 **Daniel**, William Wentworth. 'Beyond the wage-work bargain: a review of productivity bargaining with two case studies of workers' evaluations of agreements.' *PEP Broad.* XXXVI, 519 (July 1970), IV, 99p.

3917 **Ditchley Foundation.** *Labour-management relations and productivity: report of a conference at Ditchley Park, 10th–13th March 1967.* Enstone: Ditchley Foundation, 1970. 70p. (Ditchley papers 10.)

3918 **Flanders**, Allan David. 'The Fawley experiment.' *Management and unions: the theory and reform of industrial relations.* London: Faber, 1970. p. 51–65.

'A paper read to a residential course for managers at Cambridge and published as an article in *Industrial Welfare*, October 1963.'

3919 **Flanders**, Allan David. 'Labor-management relations and the democratic challenge.' Kamin, A. (ed.). *Western European labor and the American corporation.* Washington, D.C.: Bureau of National Affairs, 1970. p. 487–501.

3920 **Flanders**, Allan David. 'Productivity bargaining prospects.' *Management and unions: the theory and reform of industrial relations.* London: Faber, 1970. p. 66–71.

'First published as an article entitled "The Case for the Package Deal" in *The Times*, 9 July 1968.'

3921 **Fleeman**, R. K. and **Thompson**, A. G. *Productivity bargaining: a practical guide.* London: Butterworth, 1970. 140p.

3922 **Gottschalk**, Andrew W. and **Mee**, L. G. 'The process of plant productivity bargaining.' Towers, B. and Whittingham, T. G. (eds.). *The new bargainers: a symposium on productivity bargaining.* Nottingham: U. of Nottingham, Department of Adult Education, 1970. p. 91–115.

3923 **Gottschalk**, Andrew W. 'Productivity bargaining and the industrial relations system.' Towers, B. and Whittingham, T. G. (eds.). *The new bargainers: a symposium on productivity bargaining.* Nottingham: U. of Nottingham, Department of Adult Education, 1970. p. 116–22.

3924 **Hill**, Thomas Michael. *A case study approach to a productivity agreement.* 1970. (M.Sc. thesis, Department of Management Sciences, U.M.I.S.T.)

3925 **Mee**, L. G. and **Gottschalk**, Andrew W. 'The effects on managers and the management function.' Towers, B. and Whittingham, T. G. (eds.). *The new bargainers: a symposium on productivity bargaining.* Nottingham: U. of Nottingham, Department of Adult Education, 1970. p. 82–90.

3926 **Ramelson**, Bert. *Productivity agreements: an exposure of the latest and greatest swindle on the wages front.* London: Communist Party of Great Britain, 1970. 24p.

3927 **Roberts**, Benjamin Charles and **Gennard**, John. 'Trends in plant and company bargaining.' Robertson, D. J. and Hunter, L. C. *Labour market issues of the 1970s.* Edinburgh: Oliver and Boyd for the Scottish Economic Society, 1970. p. 31–50.
First appeared in the June 1970 issue of the *Scottish Journal of Political Economy.*

3928 **Smith**, Ian George. *Productivity measurement in productivity agreements.* 1970. (M.Sc. Econ. thesis, University of Wales, Cardiff.)

3929 **Somerton**, Michael F. 'The effects of productivity bargaining on trade unions and their members.' Towers, B. and Whittingham, T. G. (eds.). *The new bargainers: a symposium on productivity bargaining.* Nottingham: U. of Nottingham, Department of Adult Education, 1970. p. 42–56.

3930 **Towers**, B. 'The development of productivity bargaining.' Towers, B. and Whittingham, T. G. (eds.). *The new bargainers: a symposium on productivity bargaining.* Nottingham: U. of Nottingham, Department of Adult Education, 1970. p. 28–41.

3931 **Towers**, B. and **Whittingham**, T. G. (eds.). *The new bargainers: a symposium on productivity bargaining.* Nottingham: U. of Nottingham, Department of Adult Education, 1970. 197p.
'Introduction' and 'Conclusions and perspectives', by the editors.

3932 **Towers**, B. 'Productivity and productivity bargaining.' Towers, B. and Whittingham T. G. (eds.). *The new bargainers: a symposium on productivity bargaining.* Nottingham: U. of Nottingham, Department of Adult Education, 1970. p. 15–27.

3933 **Wearne**, S. H. (ed.). *Management and productivity of engineering site manpower: proceedings of a symposium, 24th April 1970.* Manchester: University of Manchester Institute of Science and Technology, 1970. 68p.

3934 **Whittingham**, T. G. 'The effects of productivity bargaining on full-time officials.' Towers, B. and Whittingham, T. G. (eds.). *The new bargainers: a symposium on productivity bargaining.* Nottingham: U. of Nottingham, Department of Adult Education, 1970. p. 57–69.

3935 **Whittingham**, T. G. 'The effects of productivity bargaining on shop stewards.' Towers, B. and Whittingham, T. G. (eds.). *The new bargainers: a symposium on productivity bargaining.* Nottingham: U. of Nottingham, Department of Adult Education, 1970. p. 70–81.

3936 **Williams**, N. 'Productivity bargaining and the firm.' Towers, B. and Whittingham, T. G. (eds.). *The new bargainers: a symposium on productivity bargaining.* Nottingham: U. of Nottingham, Department of Adult Education, 1970. p. 141–57.

See also: 42; 54; 8049; 8073; 8195; 12,823.

III. COLLECTIVE BARGAINING IN PARTICULAR OCCUPATIONS AND INDUSTRIES

See also Part Three, III, E; Part Five, IV, E; Part Five, V, A; Part Six, III, E; and Part Six, IV, A, 3.

A. AGRICULTURE, FORESTRY, AND FISHING

3937 **Houston**, George. 'Labour relations in Scottish agriculture before 1870.' *Agric. Hist. Rev.*, VI, 1 (1958), 27–41.

3938 **Sheahan**, A. D. 'Labour relations.' *Administration*, VII, 1 (Spring 1959), 25–31.
At Bord na Mona.

3939 **Commission on Industrial Relations**. *W. Stevenson & Sons, Suttons Cornwall, Ltd.* London: H.M.S.O., 1969. vi, 7p. (Report 2. Cmnd. 4248.)

3940 **Hodson**, D. and **Merridew**, J. N. *Labour relations in farming.* Newcastle-upon-Tyne: Agricultural Adjustment Unit, Department of Agricultural Economics, Newcastle University, 1970. 24p.

B. COAL MINING

3941 **Colliery Guardian**. *The South Wales wages agreement.* London, 1910. 31p.

3942 **Bowie**, James Alexander. 'The British coal agreement.' *J. Polit. Econ.*, XXXII, 2 (April 1924), 236–49; 4 (August 1924), 393–415.
1921 agreement.

3943 **Richardson**, John Henry. 'Industrial relations in the British coal mining industry.'

J. Leeds Univ. Min. Soc., 11 (September 1932), 11–15.

3944 **Baldwin**, George Benedict. *Industrial relations in the British coal industry.* 1952. (Ph.D. thesis, Massachusetts Institute of Technology.)

3945 **Lee**, William Alexander. *Thirty years in coal, 1917–1947: a review of the coal mining industry under private enterprise.* London: Mining Association of Great Britain, 1954. 256p.
The author was Chairman of the Mining Association of Great Britain.
Appendices reproduce documents.

3946 **Baldwin**, George Benedict. *Beyond nationalization: the labor problems of British coal.* Cambridge, Mass.: Harvard U.P.; London: Oxford U.P., 1955. xxiv, 324p. (Wertheim Fellowship publications.)

3947 **Evans**, Eric Wyn. *A history of industrial relations in the South Wales coal industry to 1912.* 1955. (Ph.D. thesis, University of Wales, Aberystwyth.)

3948 **Paynter**, William Henry. *Outlook for mining.* London: Communist Party, 1958. 16p.
Introduction by Arthur Horner.

3949 **Anthony-Jones**, W. J. *Labour relations in the South Wales coal mining industry, 1926–1939.* 1959. (Ph.D. thesis, University of Wales, Aberystwyth.)

3950 **Morris**, J. H. and **Williams**, L. J. 'The South Wales sliding scale, 1876–1879: an experiment in industrial relations.' *Manchr. Sch.*, XXVIII, 2 (May 1960), 161–76.

3951 **Scott**, William Henry, **Mumford**, Enid, **McGivering**, Ian C. and **Kirkby**, J. M. *Coal and conflict: a study of industrial relations at collieries.* Liverpool: Liverpool U.P., 1963. 214p. (Social research series.)

3952 **Griffin**, Alan Ramsay. *The development of industrial relations in the Nottinghamshire coalfield.* 1963–64. (Ph.D. thesis, University of Nottingham.)

3953 **Jencks**, Clinton Edward. 'British coal: labor relations since nationalization.' *Ind. Relat.*, VI, 1 (October 1966), 95–110.

3954 **Hepworth**, R., and others. 'The effects of technological change in the Yorkshire coalfield, 1960–1965.' *Econ. Studies*, IV, 1–2 (October 1969), 221–37.
By R. Hepworth, A. Kelly, A. Stokoe, S. Williams, J. Weaver, M. Welsh, B. J. McCormick.

See also: 41; 61; 3910.

C. MANUFACTURING INDUSTRIES

1. Food, Drink, and Tobacco

3955 **Society of Friends.** Committee on War and the Social Order. *Industrial relations in the cocoa, chocolate and sugar confectionery industry.* London, 1928.
Reprinted from *The Friend.*

3956 **Green**, L. H. 'Labour problems in the British flour milling industry: an experiment in the ordering of industrial relations.' Gannett, F. E. and Catherwood, B. F. (eds.). *Industrial and labour relations in Great Britain: a symposium.* New York: the editors, 1939. p. 120–38.
Author was secretary of the Flour Milling Employers' Federation, and of the National Joint Industrial Council for the Flour Milling Industry.

3957 **Banks**, Robert Frederick. *Labour relations in the baking industry in England and Wales since 1860, with special reference to the impact of technical and economic change on union administration and bargaining procedure.* 1965. (Ph.D. thesis, University of London.)

See also: 3906.

2. Chemical and Allied Industries

Material on productivity bargaining at the Esso Fawley refinery is classified at Part Five, II.

3958 **Verma**, Pramod Chandra. *Labour relations and industrial organisation in the British chemical industry.* 1966. 473p. (Ph.D. thesis, University of Manchester.)

3959 **Commission on Industrial Relations.** *The Associated Octel Company Limited.* London: H.M.S.O., 1969. vi, 9p. (Report 1. Cmnd. 4246.)

3960 **Commission on Industrial Relations.** *Brock's Fireworks Limited.* London: H.M.S.O., 1970. iv, 12p. (Report 7. Cmnd. 4325.)

See also: 3906.

3. Iron, Steel, and Other Metals

3961 **Jones**, Edward Haydn. *A study of industrial relations in the British tinplate industry, 1874–1939.* 1940. (M.A. thesis, University of Wales, Aberystwyth.)

3962 **Wigham**, Eric Leonard. *The steel industry's labour record.* London: British Iron and Steel Federation, 1958. 5p. (Steel today series.)

3963 **Thomas**, Brenda M. *Labour relations in steel: a comparative analysis of Great Britain and the U.S.A.* 1961–62. (M.A. thesis, University of Liverpool.)

3964 **Pride**, Emrys. 'The steelman in industrial relations.' *Hon. Soc. Cymm. Trans.* (1964), pt. 1, 130–40.

3965 **Brown**, Wilfred Banks Duncan. 'Negotiation between managers and representatives.' Brown, W. B. D. and Jaques, E. *Glacier Project papers: some essays on organization and management from the Glacier Project research.* London: Heinemann, 1965. p. 196–214.

3966 **Balfour**, William Campbell. 'Union-management relations in the steel industry from the great depression to the Second World War.' International Institute of Social History. *Mouvements ouvriers et dépression économique de 1929 à 1939.* Assen: Van Gorcum, 1966. p. 245–61.

3967 **Smith**, E. Owen. 'Some of the labour problems of the British Steel Corporation.' *Lough. J. Soc. Studies*, 4 (November 1967), 17–34.

3968 **Eldridge**, John E. T. 'Industrial relations in the North East iron and steel industry.' *Industrial disputes: essays in the sociology of industrial relations*. London: Routledge and Kegan Paul; New York: Humanities P., 1968. p. 155–205.

Some of the material in this essay was previously published in 'Plant bargaining in steel: North East case studies.' *Sociol. Rev.*, XIII, 2 (July 1965).

See also: 3823; 3846.

4. Engineering and Shipbuilding

3969 **Richmond**, J. R. *Some aspects of labour and its claims in the engineering industry*. Glasgow, 1916. 27p.

3970 **Elbourne**, Edward T. *The story of Ponders End shell works: its labour problems and their solution*. 1918. 12p.

3971 **Labour Research Department**. *Labour & capital in the engineering trades*. London: Labour Publishing Co., 1922. 48p. (Studies of capital and labour I.)

3972 **Shuman**, H. E. *Local and district collective agreements in the British engineering industry*. 1952. (B.Litt. thesis, University of Oxford.)

3973 **Tatlow**, Ann. 'The underlying issues of the 1949–50 engineering wage claim.' *Manchr. Sch.*, XXI, 3 (September 1953), 258–70.

3974 **Derber**, Milton. 'Labor relations in British metalworking.' *Mon. Labor Rev.*, LXXVIII, 4 (April 1955), 403–9.

Reprinted in *University of Illinois Bulletin*, LII, 64 (1955).

3975 **Derber**, Milton. *Labor–management relations at the plant level under industry-wide bargaining: a study of the engineering (metal-working) industry in Birmingham, England*. Chicago: University of Illinois, Institute of Labor and Industrial Relations, 1955. 130p.

3976 **Ranet**, B. McL. 'Labour relations in the royal dockyards in 1739.' *Mar. Mirror*, XLVII, 4 (November 1961), 281–91.

3977 **Derber**, Milton. 'Adjustment problems of a long-established industrial relations system: an appraisal of British engineering 1954–1961.' *Q. Rev. Econ. Bus.*, III, 4 (Winter 1963), 37–48.

3978 **Marsh**, Arthur I. and **Jones**, R. S. 'Engineering *Procedure* and Central Conference at York in 1959: a factual analysis.' *Br. J. Ind. Relat.*, II, 2 (July 1964), 228–50.

3979 **Marsh**, Arthur I. *Industrial relations in engineering*. Oxford, London: Pergamon P., 1965. xxiii, 362p. (Commonwealth and international library. Economics, commerce, industry, administration and management division.)

3980 **Cameron**, G. C. 'The Fairfields affair.' *New Soc.*, VII, 172 (13 January 1966), 15–17. (Society at work.)

3981 **Marsh**, Arthur I. (ed.). *A collection of teaching documents and case studies: industrial relations in engineering*. Oxford, London: Pergamon P., 1966. v, 143p. (Commonwealth and international library. Social administration, training, economics and production division.)

With model answers '. . . for use with my book "Industrial relations in engineering" '. (Introduction.)

3982 **Clarke**, J. F. *Labour relationships in engineering and shipbuilding on the North East coast in the second half of the nineteenth century*. 1966–67. (M.A. thesis, University of Newcastle-upon-Tyne.)

3983 **Clack**, Garfield. *Industrial relations in a British car factory*. London: Cambridge U.P., 1967. 100p. (University of Cambridge, Department of Applied Economics. Occasional paper 9.)

3984 **Turner**, Herbert Arthur, **Clack**, Garfield and **Roberts**, Geoffrey. *Labour relations in the motor industry: a study of industrial unrest and an international comparison*. London: Allen and Unwin, 1967. 365p.

3985 **Paulden**, Sydney Maurice and **Hawkins**, Bill. *Whatever happened at Fairfields?* London: Gower P., 1969. x, 214p.

Fairfields (Glasgow) Ltd.

3986 **Smith**, Peter. 'The engineering settlement: an analysis of the new Long Term Agreement and the emergence of productivity bargaining in the engineering industry.' *Trade Un. Regist.* (1969), 150–70.

3987 **Thomas**, Ron (ed.). *An exercise in redeployment: the report of a trade union study group*. Oxford: Pergamon, 1969. xiii, 266p. (Commonwealth and international library.)

In the aircraft industry.

3988 **Alexander**, Kenneth John Wilson and **Jenkins**, C. L. *Fairfields: a study of industrial change*. London: Allen Lane, 1970. 286p.

Fairfield Shipbuilding and Engineering Company.

3989 **Commission on Industrial Relations**. *Armstrong Patents Company Limited*. London: H.M.S.O., 1970. iv, 28p. (Report 13. Cmnd. 4541.)

3990 **Commission on Industrial Relations**. *BSR Limited*. London: H.M.S.O., 1970. vi, 25p. (Report 5. Cmnd. 4274.)

3991 **Commission on Industrial Relations**. *Birmingham Aluminium Casting (1903) Company Limited, Dartmouth Auto Castings Limited, Midland Motor Cylinder Company Limited*. London: H.M.S.O., 1970. iv, 38p. (Report 4. Cmnd. 4264.)

3992 **Commission on Industrial Relations**. *Frederick Parker Limited*. London: H.M.S.O., 1970. iv, 19p. (Report 8. Cmnd. 4374.)

3993 **Commission on Industrial Relations**.

Hoover Limited. London: H.M.S.O., 1970. iv, 56p. (Report 11. Cmnd. 4537.)

3994 **Commission on Industrial Relations.** *The International Harvester Company of Great Britain, Limited*. London: H.M.S.O., 1970. iv, 39p. (Report 10. Cmnd. 4469.)

3995 **Copp**, Robert. 'Negotiating a new wage structure at Ford of Britain.' Kamin, A. (ed.). *Western European labor and the American corporation*. Washington, D.C.: Bureau of National Affairs, 1970. p. 109–18.

3996 **Somerton**, Michael F. 'The proposals for changes in the engineering procedural agreement.' *Trade Un. Regist.* (1970), 205–12.

See also: 3832; 3841; 3873; 3884; 3906.

5. Textiles

3997 **Wiggins**, W. M. 'Survey of industrial relations in the cotton industry of Great Britain.' Gannett, F. E. and Catherwood, B. F. (eds.). *Industrial and labour relations in Great Britain: a symposium*. New York: the editors, 1939. p. 214–40.

Author was President of the Federation of Master Cotton Spinners' Associations.

3998 **Hankinson**, J. A. *An examination of the historical and present structure of industry and industrial relationships in the cotton textiles and men's tailoring industries, to determine the reasons for the variations in the respective current bargaining methods*. 1957–58. (M.A. thesis, University of Liverpool.)

6. Clothing and Footwear

3999 **Colvin**, G. R. 'Industrial organisation: the arrangements for negotiations between employers and operatives in the boot and shoe manufacturing industry of Great Britain.' Gannett, F. E. and Catherwood, B. F. (eds.). *Industrial and labour relations in Great Britain: a symposium*. New York: the editors, 1939. p. 202–13.

Author was Secretary of the Incorporated Federated Associations of Boot and Shoe Manufacturers of Great Britain and Ireland.

4000 **Helfgott**, Roy B. *Trade-unionism and collective bargaining in the British clothing industry*. 1956–57. (Thesis, New School for Social Research.)

4001 **Helfgott**, Roy B. 'Union-management co-operation in the British clothing industry.' *Labor Law J.*, x, 5 (May 1959), 309–15.

4002 **Robinson**, Olive. 'Labour problems in the clothing industry.' *Cloth. Inst. J.*, x, 4 (Summer 1962), 287–99.

7. Pottery, Timber, and Furniture

4003 **Staffordshire Sentinel.** *National Council of the pottery industry*. Hanley, [1918?]. 12p.

4004 **Robertson**, Norman. *A study of the development of labour relations in the British furniture trade*. 1955. (B.Litt. thesis, University of Oxford.)

4005 **Commission on Industrial Relations.** *Elliotts of Newbury Limited*. London: H.M.S.O., 1970. iv, 19p. (Report 6. Cmnd. 4311.)

8. Paper, Printing, and Publishing

4006 **Dibblee**, G. Binney. 'The printing trades and the crisis in British industry.' *Econ. J.*, XII, 45 (March 1902), 1–14.

Includes discussion of articles in *The Times* headed 'The crisis in British industry', no. VIII, 27 December 1901.

4007 **Child**, John. *History of industrial relations in the British printing industry*. 1954. (D.Phil. thesis, University of Oxford.)

4008 **Holroyde**, Francis James. *The challenge to the printing industry*. London: Printing Trades Alliance, 1956. 30p.

A series of articles reprinted from *Alliance Record*.

4009 **Strick**, H. C. *British newspaper journalism, 1900–1956: a study in industrial relations*. 1957. (Ph.D. thesis, University of London.)

4010 **Child**, John. *Industrial relations in the British printing industry: the quest for security*. London: Allen and Unwin, 1967. 387p.

4011 **Sadler**, Philip. 'Sociological aspects of skill.' *Br. J. Ind. Relat.*, VIII, 1 (March 1970) 22–31.

Skill, technical change and industrial relations in printing.

See also: 3834.

D. CONSTRUCTION

4012 **Garton Foundation.** *The Industrial Council for the Building Industry*. London: Harrison, 1919. 153p.

4013 **Sparkes**, Malcolm. 'The team spirit in industry.' *Engl. Rev.*, XXX (February 1920), 153–8.

'The work of the Building Trades Parliament of Great Britain.'

4014 **Gray**, Ailsa Patricia and **Abrams**, Mark Alexander. *Construction of Esso refinery, Fawley: a study in organization*. London: British Institute of Management, 1954. 39p. (Occasional papers 6.)

See also: 3825–6.

4015 **Elliott**, John. 'The building-site imbroglio.' *New Soc.*, IX, 246 (15 June 1967), 880–1. (Society at work.)

4016 **Economic Development Committee for Building.** *Employers and unions in building: structure of employers' organisations in the building industry and of trade unions in the construction industry as a whole*. London: National Economic Development Office, 1968. 16p.

4017 **Hilton**, William Samuel. *Industrial relations*

in construction. Oxford: Pergamon, 1968. xii, 243p. (Commonwealth and international library. Industrial relations division.)

See also: 3842; 3933; 8307.

E. GAS, ELECTRICITY, AND WATER

4018 **Williamson**, T. 'Trade unionism and negotiating machinery in the gas industry of Great Britain.' Gannett, F. E. and Catherwood, B. F. (eds.). *Industrial and labour relations in Great Britain: a symposium*. New York: the editors, 1939. p. 101–19.

Author was National Industrial Officer of the National Union of General and Municipal Workers.

4019 **Taft**, Cynthia H. *Collective bargaining in the electricity supply industry*. 1951. (M.Sc. (Econ.) thesis, University of London.)

4020 **Thompson**, A. E. *Industrial relations in the fuel and power industries with special reference to selected undertakings in Midlothian*. 1952–53. (Ph.D. thesis, University of Edinburgh.)

4021 **Edwards**, *Sir* Ronald Stanley. *An experiment in industrial relations: the electricity supply industry's status agreement for industrial staff*. London: Electricity Council, 1967. 38p.

The author was Chairman of the Electricity Council from 1962 to 1968.

4022 **Roberts**, R. D. V. 'The status agreement for industrial staff in electricity supply.' *Br. J. Ind. Relat.*, v, 1 (March 1967), 48–62.

4023 **Eire**. Department of Labour. Committee on Industrial Relations in the Electricity Supply Board. *Interim report*. 1968. (V.2)

Final report. 1969. (V.2/1)

4024 **National Joint Industrial Council for the Waterworks Undertakings Industry**. *One-day jubilee conference souvenir programme . . . Wednesday, 23rd July, 1969*. [London: the Council, 1969.] 22p.

Includes 'Historical background'.

See also: 3890.

F. TRANSPORT AND COMMUNICATIONS

1. General

4025 **International Labour Office**. *Studies on industrial relations. I. Siemens Works; Lens Mining Company; London Traffic Combine; State Mines of the Saar Basin; Bata Boot and Shoe Factory*. Geneva: I.L.O., 1930. xii, 263p.

4026 **Gilbert**, Frank. *Transport staff relations: machinery of negotiation, joint consultation, training and education*. London: Pitman, 1951. xii, 260p.

4027 **Fitzpayne**, E. R. L. 'The problem of wages.' *Inst. Transp. J.*, xxviii, 3 (March 1959), 67–86.

2. Railways and London Transport

4028 **Farrer**, Thomas Cecil. 'Some English railway problems of the next decade.' *Econ. J.*, i, 2 (June 1891), 351–9.

4029 **Great Western Railway**. *Memorandum in regard to management*. London: Great Western Railway, 1920. 30p. (Great Western pamphlets 3.)

4030 **Labour Research Department**. *Labour and capital on the railways*. London: Labour Publishing Co., 1923. 64p. (Studies in labour and capital, IV)

4031 **Railway Clerks' Association**. *The London Passenger Transport Act, 1933: a summary of its main provisions with special articles on the negotiation machinery established to deal with salaries, wages and conditions of service . . .; also, particulars of the personnel of the new Board with terms and conditions of appointment and a two-page map of the Transport Board area*. London, 1933. 13p.

Reprinted from *Railway Service Journal*, June and July 1933.

4032 **London Passenger Transport Board**. *Scheme for establishment of staff councils, etc*. London, 1934. 20p.

4033 **Clegg**, Hugh Armstrong. *Labour relations in London Transport*. Oxford: Blackwell, 1950. viii, 188p.

4034 **Pickstock**, Frank. *British railways: the human problem*. London: Fabian Publications; Gollancz, 1950. 36p. (Fabian research series 142.)

4035 **Halverson**, G. C. *Development of labour relations in the British railways since 1860*. 1952. (Ph.D. thesis, University of London.)

4036 **Kingsford**, P. W. 'Labour relations on the railways, 1835–1875.' *J. Transp. Hist.*, i, 2 (November 1953), 65–81.

4037 **Williams**, Clifford Glyn. *The process of negotiation in the railway industry under nationalisation*. 1958. (M.A. thesis, University of Manchester.)

4038 **McLeod**, Charles. *All change: railway industrial relations in the sixties*. London: Gower P., 1970. xviii, 222p. (A Gower Press special study.)

See also: 4041; 8343.

3. Road

4039 **Johnston**, G. A. and **Spates**, T. G. 'Industrial relations in the London Traffic Combine.' *Int. Labour Rev.*, xxi, 4 (April 1930), 494–518; 5 (May 1930), 613–42.

4040 **Jackson**, T. E. A. K. *Industrial relations in road transport*. 1946. (Ph.D. thesis, University of Manchester.)

4041 **Tan-Sim-Hont**. *Industrial relations in nationalised road and rail transport with particular reference to road haulage*. 1953–54. (M.A. thesis, University of Bristol.)

See also: 3871; 3891.

4. Sea

4042 **National Maritime Board.** *Report on the work of the National Maritime Board, 1917–1919.* London: H.M.S.O., 1920. 42p. (Cmd. 545.)

4043 **Powell**, L. H. 'Industrial relations in the British shipping industry.' *Int. Labour Rev.*, LXV, 6 (June 1952), 681–702.

'Mr. Powell, of the Chamber of Shipping of the United Kingdom, is the author of *The Shipping Federation: a history of the first sixty years*, published in 1950 to commemorate the "diamond jubilee" of the Federation.'

4044 **Gretton**, John. 'Put 'em in the scuppers?' *New Soc.*, XV, 385 (12 February 1970), 255–8.

4045 **MacFarlane**, James. ' "Our seamen": a study of labour relations in the British Merchant Navy.' *Trade Un. Regist.* (1970), 137–52.

5. Air

4046 **Blain**, Alexander Nicholas John. *Industrial relations in the United Kingdom airlines: a study of pilots and managements.* 1970. (Ph.D. (Econ.) thesis, University of London.)

G. DISTRIBUTIVE TRADES

4047 **Carr**, Rutter. *The relationship which ought to exist between cooperative store committees and employés . . .* Manchester, [1892?]. 12p.

4048 **Miller**, Glenn W. *Labor policies of consumers' cooperatives in Great Britain and the United States.* 1940. (Thesis, University of Illinois.)

4049 **Bennett**, K. 'Labour relations in the co-operative movement.' Barou, N. (ed.). *The co-operative movement in Labour Britain.* London: Gollancz, 1948. p. 74–85.

4050 **Tizard**, J. *Industrial relations in the British co-operative movement.* 1949. (B.Litt. thesis, University of Oxford.)

See also: 3827.

H. INSURANCE, BANKING, AND FINANCE

4051 **Davies**, D. O. 'Bank clerks are our business.' *Bankers' Mag.*, CXCVII (May 1964), 336–41.

4052 **Robinson**, Olive. 'White-collar bargaining: a case study in the private sector.' *Scott. J. Polit. Econ.*, XIV, 3 (November 1967), 256–74.

4053 **Commission on Industrial Relations.** *General Accident Fire and Life Assurance Corporation Limited.* London: H.M.S.O., 1969. vi, 11p. (Report 2. Cmnd. 4247.)

I. PROFESSIONAL AND SCIENTIFIC SERVICES

4054 **Ross**, E. H. *Health work for Whitley Councils.* London, 1919. 13p.

4055 **Speller**, Sidney Reginald. 'Whitleyism: the formation and work of the Administrative and Clerical Staffs Council of the Whitley Councils for the Health Services.' *Hospital*, XLVII, 12 (December 1951), 867–75.

4056 **Sofer**, Cyril. 'Reactions to administrative change: a study of staff relations in three British hospitals.' *Hum. Relat.*, VIII, 3 (August 1955), 291–316.

4057 **Picton**, Glyn. 'Whitley Councils in the Health Services.' *Publ. Adm.*, XXXV, 4 (Winter 1957), 359–71.

4058 **Barnes**, S. E. *Individual, local, and national bargaining for teachers in England and Wales: a study of the period 1858–1944.* 1959. (Ph.D. thesis, University of London.)

4059 **National Association of Hospital Management Committee Group Secretaries.** Manchester Regional Branch. *Co-ordination of the work of Whitley Councils for the Health Services: paper by a working party.* Lancaster, 1962.

4060 **Brennan**, T. *Staff relations in secondary schools.* 1962–63. (M.Ed. thesis, University of Leeds.)

4061 **Gill**, H. S. *Industrial relations in the United Kingdom Atomic Energy Authority.* 1967–68. (Ph.D. thesis, University of Bradford.)

4062 **Jenkins**, G. C. 'The Whitley Councils and salary negotiations.' *Chiropodist*, XXIV, 9 (September 1969), 338–46.

4063 **Commission on Industrial Relations** *Medical Research Council.* London: H.M.S.O., 1970. iv, 30p. (Report 12. Cmnd. 4531.)

4064 **Scottish Secondary Teachers' Association.** *History of the salaries negotiations, 1969–70.* Edinburgh: S.S.T.A., 1970. 18p.

J. PUBLIC ADMINISTRATION

General material on Whitleyism is classified at Part Five, I.

1. General

4065 **Collins**, *Sir* W. J. *Conciliation, arbitration and 'Whitleyism' applied to the public services.* 1919. 12p.

4066 **Political and Economic Planning**. 'Whitley Councils.' *Planning*, VII, 151 (11 July 1939), 1–14.

4067 **Day**, A. J. T. 'The principles of Whitleyism.' *Publ. Adm.*, XXVL, 4 (Winter 1948), 234–49.

The author was asked to advise on the establishment of Whitleyism in the Ceylon Public Service. This article is composed of extracts from his report (Ceylon Sessional Paper XX – 1947).

4068 **Public Services International.** *Negotiating rights of public servants, and, The right to strike in the public service.* London: P.S.I., 1966. 132p.

Contains the text of two lectures: 'Negotiating rights of public servants', by Folke Schmidt, and 'The right to strike in the public service', by Marc Somerhausen.

4069 **Kassalow**, Everett M. 'Public employee bargaining in Europe: what lessons for the United States?' Industrial Relations Research Association. *Proceedings of the twenty-first annual winter meeting, December 29–30, 1968, Chicago, Illinois.* p. 48–58.
Discussion, p. 59–69.

4070 **Johnston**, Thomas L. 'Public sector and white collar bargaining.' Robertson, D. J. and Hunter, L. C. *Labour market issues of the 1970s.* Edinburgh: Oliver and Boyd for the Scottish Economic Society, 1970. p. 51–67.
First appeared in the June 1970 issue of the *Scottish Journal of Political Economy.*

See also: 10,024.

2. National Government

4071 **Inter-Departmental Committee on the Application of the Whitley Report to Government Establishments.** Sub-Committee. *Report on the application of the Whitley Report to the administrative departments of the Civil Service.* London: H.M.S.O., 1919. 10p. (Cmd. 9.)

4072 *Report of the National Provisional Joint Committee on the Application of the Whitley Report to the administrative departments of the Civil Service.* London: H.M.S.O., 1919. 8p. (Cmd. 198.)

4073 **Brown**, William John. *Whitleyism on its trial: a critical examination of the first year's working of the Whitley system in the Civil Service.* London: W. J. Brown, 1921. 20p.

4074 **Macrae-Gibson**, J. H. *The Whitley system in the Civil Service.* London: Fabian Society, 1922. 47p.

4075 **Stuart-Bunning**, G. H. 'Whitley Councils in the Civil Service.' *J. Publ. Adm.*, II, 2 (April 1924), 172–83.
A lecture delivered at the London School of Economics on 14 February 1924 under the auspices of the Institute of Public Administration.

4076 **Houghton**, A. L. N. D. 'Collective bargaining in the Civil Service.' *Publ. Adm.*, XI, 1 (January 1933), 86–97.
'Paper to be discussed at the Northern Regional Groups' Conference at Leeds, February, 1933.'
The author was General Secretary, Association of Officers of Taxes.

4077 **White**, Leonard Dupee. *Whitley Councils in the British Civil Service: a study in conciliation and arbitration.* Chicago: U. of Chicago P., 1933. xvii, 357p. (Social science studies 25.)

4078 **Birkett**, F. G. 'Whitleyism in the Central Government Service.' *Publ. Adm.*, XIV, 2 (April 1936), 169–80.
'Discussed at the Northern Winter Conference, Institute of Public Administration, February/March 1936.'

4079 **Gladden**, Edgar Norman. *Civil Service staff relationships.* London: Hodge, 1943. xi, 184p. (Administrative research series.)

4080 **Treasury**. *Staff relations in the Civil Service.* London: H.M.S.O., 1949.
Later editions. 1955, 1958, 1965.

4081 **Callaghan**, Leonard James. *Whitleyism: a study of joint consultation in the Civil Service.* London: Fabian Publications, Gollancz, 1953. 40p. (Fabian research series 159.)

4082 **Muttalib**, M. A. *On the Whitley Councils in the British Civil Service.* 1960. 385 leaves. (Ph.D. thesis, University of London.)

4083 **Hayward**, Richard A. *Whitley Councils in the United Kingdom Civil Service: a study in staff relations.* London: Civil Service National Whitley Council (Staff Side), 1963.
A paper read at the Symposium organised by l'Institut International des Sciences Administratives, Brussels, June 1963.

4084 **Williams**, Leslie. 'The role of the Staff Side in Civil Service reform.' *Publ. Adm.*, XLVII, 3 (Autumn 1969), 281–7.

See also: 3811.

3. Local Government

4085 **Association of Municipal Corporations**. *Industrial councils.* London: the Association, 1918. 20p.

4086 **Gee**, J. *Whitley Councils in relation to the local government service.* London: London County Council Staff Association, 1922. 50p. (Pamphlet 5.)
The author was Chairman of the London District Council for Local Authorities' Administrative, Technical and Clerical Services.

4087 **Bishop**, Edward. 'Present position of collective bargaining in the local government services.' *Publ. Adm.*, XI, 1 (January 1933), 79–85.
'Paper to be discussed at the Northern Regional Groups' Conference at Leeds, February, 1933.'
The author was Employers' Secretary, Lancashire and Cheshire Provincial Council for Officers of Local Authorities, and Labour Officer of Manchester Corporation.

4088 **Simey**, Thomas Spensley. 'Whitleyism in the local government service: the next fifteen years.' *Publ. Adm.*, XIV, 2 (April 1936), 181–7.
'Discussed at the Northern Winter Conference, Institute of Public Administration, February/March 1936.'

4089 **Chamberlin**, H. C. 'Municipal wage regulation – how the Joint Industrial Council System works.' *Publ. Adm.*, XVI, 1 (January 1938), 73–85.
'A Paper delivered at a Meeting of the

Institute of Public Administration, Birmingham and West Midlands Regional Group.'

4090 **Keast**, Horace. 'Local authority joint negotiation machinery.' *Ind. Law Rev.*, II, 1 (June 1947), 9–11.

4091 **Keast**, Horace. 'Local authority negotiating machinery: voluntary and statutory.' *Ind. Law Rev.*, IV, 2 (October 1949), 96–102.

4092 **Jackson**, Margery W. *The development of the North Western Provincial Whitley Council for the administration, professional, technical and clerical services of local authorities 1921–50.* 1950–51. (M.A. thesis, University of Manchester.)

4093 **McIntosh**, Marjorie. 'The negotiation of wages and conditions for local authority employees in England and Wales.' *Publ. Adm.*, XXXIII, 2 (Summer 1955), 149–62; 3 (Autumn 1955), 307–23; 4 (Winter 1955), 401–17.

4094 **Kramer**, L. 'Reflections on Whitleyism in English local government.' *Publ. Adm.*, XXXVI, 1 (Spring 1958), 47–69.

4095 **Simmons**, Michael John. *Industrial relations in a new local authority.* 1970. (Dip. in Pub. Admin., University of London.)

See also: 3808; 3812.

4. Nationalised Industries

See also Part Five, III, B; Part Five, III, C, 3; Part Five, III, E; Part Five, III, F; and Part Five, III, I.

4096 **Clegg**, Hugh Armstrong. *Labour in nationalized industry.* London: Fabian Publications, 1950. 40p. (Fabian research series 141.)

4097 **Cole**, George Douglas Howard. 'Labour and staff problems under nationalisation.' *Polit. Q.*, XXI, 2 (April–June 1950), 160–70.

4098 **Louw**, M. H. H. 'Labour unions and the management of public enterprises.' *S. Afr. J. Econ.*, XIX (September 1951), 241–7.

4099 **Cole**, George Douglas Howard. 'Labour and staff problems under nationalization.' Robson, W. A. (ed.). *Problems of nationalized industry.* London: Allen and Unwin, 1952.

4100 **Keane**, J. J. 'Industrial relations machinery in British nationalized industries.' *Asian Labour*, II, 4 (March 1952), 81–115.

4101 **Buckingham**, Walter S. 'Collective bargaining in British nationalized industries.' *Labor Law J.*, IV, 9 (September 1953), 618–23.

4102 **Hobson**, Oscar R. 'Report on nationalization. III. Labour relations.' *Banker*, C, 329 (June 1953), 332–8.

4103 **Chester**, Theodore Edward and **Clegg**, Hugh Armstrong. 'Nationalization and the problem of communication.' *Br. Mgmt. Rev.*, XII, 5 (October 1954), 307–16.

4104 **Spero**, Sterling Denhard. *Labor relations in British nationalized industry.* New York: New York U.P., 1955. 86p.

4105 **Baldwin**, George Benedict. 'Nationalization in Britain: a sobering decade.' *Ann. Am. Acad. Polit. Soc. Sci.*, CCCX (March 1957), 39–54.

4106 **Dempsey**, J. F. 'Labour relations in state-sponsored organisations.' *Administration*, X, 1 (Spring 1962), 29–35.

'A talk by the General Manager of Aer Lingus, Irish International Airlines at a week-end seminar of the Liberty Study Group of the Irish Transport and General Workers' Union at Greystones, Co. Wicklow, on 26th January, 1962.'

4107 **Hanson**, A. H. (ed.). 'Industrial relations.' *Nationalization: a book of readings.* London: Allen and Unwin for the Royal Institute of Public Administration, 1963. p. 371–421.

4108 **Huddleston**, John. 'Sociological aspects of employment in the nationalised industries.' *Lough. J. Soc. Studies*, 6 (November 1968), 16–25.

IV. INDUSTRIAL CONFLICT

See also Part Five, I. Many of the works in Part Three, III, A–F also contain material on industrial conflict. Material on conciliation and arbitration by the state is listed in Part Seven, VIII, C. Works on private conciliation and arbitration are listed here. The law relating to industrial conflict is in Part Seven, VIII, B–C.

A. GENERAL

Some of the general works in Part One, IV also contain material on industrial conflict. See also Part Seven, VIII, C.

4109 **Samuel**, J. Rhys. *Stop the strikes: the use and abuse of trades unionism.* n.d. 103p.

4110 **Bevan**, G. Phillips. 'The strikes of the past ten years.' *R. Statist. Soc. J.*, XLII, 1 (March 1880), 35–54.

Discussion, p. 55–64.

'Read before the Statistical Society, 20 January 1880.'

4111 **Howell**, George. *Conciliation and arbitration in trade disputes.* London, 1880. 24p.

4112 *Some thoughts on strikes, free trade, and protection.* London: Stanesby, 1880. 14p.

4113 **M.**, J. *No more strikes. By a Journeyman Tailor.* London: H. Robinson, 1883. 7p.

4114 **Stephen**, James Fitzjames. 'On the suppression of boycotting.' *Nineteenth Century*, XX, 118 (December 1886), 765–84.

4115 **Howell**, George. 'Great strikes: their origin, cost and results.' Co-operative Wholesale Societies. *Annual for 1889.* p. 266–311.

4116 **Boulton**, S. B. 'Labour disputes and the Chamber of Commerce.' *Nineteenth Century*, XXVII, 160 (June 1890), 987–1000.

Includes the description of a scheme put

forward by the London Chamber of Commerce.

4117 **Price**, Langford Lovell Frederick Rice. 'The position and prospects of industrial conciliation.' *R. Statist. Soc. J.*, LIII, 3 (September 1890), 420–49.
With discussion, p. 450–9.
'Read before the Royal Statistical Society, 20th May, 1890.'

4118 **Price**, Langford Lovell Frederick Rice. 'The relations between industrial conciliation and social reform.' *R. Statist. Soc. J.*, LIII, 2 (June 1890), 290–302.
'A paper read before Section F of the British Association for the Advancement of Science at Newcastle-upon-Tyne, September, 1889.'

4119 **Robarts**, N. F. *Strikes and lock-outs.* London: Whittingham, 1890. 20p.

4120 **Tustin**, Frank. *The great war between capital and labour and how to emancipate the working classes within twelve months.* London: Thos. Williams, 1890. 8p.

4121 **Watson**, R. Spence. 'The peaceable settlement of labour disputes.' *Contemp. Rev.*, LVII (May 1890), 730–41.

4122 **Samuelson**, James. *Boards of conciliation and arbitration for the settlement of labour disputes.* London: Kegan Paul, Trench, Trübner, 1891. 32p.

4123 **Schloss**, David Frederick. 'The road to social peace.' *Fortn. Rev.*, n.s., XLIX, 290 (February 1891), 245–58.

4124 **Vincent**, Edmund. 'The discontent of the working-classes.' Mackay, T. (ed.). *A plea for liberty: an argument against socialism.* London: Murray, 1891. p. 201–23.
Revised edition. 1892.

4125 **Derfel**, Robert Jones. *Socialism: what it is, and what it teaches; a paper read at the Literary & Debating Society, Winsford, February 9th, 1892. Strikes: a talk between a trade unionist and a socialist.* Manchester: the author, 1892. 18p.

4126 **H.**, R. H. 'Strikes and lock-outs in 1890.' *R. Statist. Soc. J.*, LV, 1 (March 1892), 127–32.
Condensed from the report of J. Burnett, Labour Correspondent to the Board of Trade.

4127 **Samuelson**, James. *Boards of conciliation in labour disputes: a short address to the artizans and labourers of Liverpool.* Liverpool: Rockliff, 1892.

4128 **Cunliffe**, John W. 'Modern industrial warfare.' *Westm. Rev.*, CXL, 2 (August 1893), 109–14.

4129 **Sladen**, L. B. 'The London Conciliation Board.' *Econ. Rev.*, III, 2 (April 1893), 252–60.

4130 **Fogg**, William. 'Strikes and economic fallacies.' *Manchr. Statist. Soc. Trans.* (1893–94), 1–42.

4131 **Jeans**, James Stephen. *Conciliation and arbitration in labour disputes: a historical sketch and brief statement of the present position of the question at home and abroad.* London: Crosby Lockwood, 1894. xiv, 194p.

4132 **Kenny**, P. D. *How to prevent strikes: applied economics.* Manchester: J. Heywood, 1894. 76p.

4133 **Newcastle Daily Leader**. *Conciliation in trade disputes.* Newcastle-upon-Tyne, 1894. 34p.

4134 **Cunningham**, William, Archdeacon of Ely. *Strikes: an address delivered during the recent great strike at Leicester, England.* Boston: Diocesan House, 1895. 8p. (Publications of the Church Social Union. Series B, no. 5.)

4135 **Johnston**, Alexander W. *Strikes, labour questions and other economic difficulties: a short treatise of political economy.* London: Bliss, 1895. 128p.

4136 **Ransome**, James Stafford. *Modern labour: a review of the labour question.* London: Eyre and Spottiswoode, 1895. viii, 159p.

4137 **Nicholson**, Joseph Shield. 'Strikes and a living wage.' *Strikes and social problems.* London: Black, 1896. p. 1–21.
First published in *North British Economist.*

4138 **Aves**, Ernest. 'Some recent labour disputes.' *Econ. J.*, VII, 25 (March 1897), 124–31.

4139 **Shaxby**, W. J. *The case against picketing.* London: Liberty Review Publishing Co., 1897. 86p.
Second edition. 1897. viii, 86p.
Fourth edition 'with a statement of public opinion and a draft bill'. 1900.

4140 **Bosanquet**, Helen. 'The lines of industrial conflict.' *The standard of life and other studies.* London, New York: Macmillan, 1898. p. 102–13.

4141 **Fry**, *Sir* Edward. 'Conciliation and arbitration in trade disputes.' *Law Mag. Law Rev.*, (November 1898).

4142 **Price**, Langford Lovell Frederick Rice. 'Industrial conciliation – a retrospect.' *Econ. J.*, VIII, 32 (December 1898), 461–73.
'A Paper read before Section F of the British Association at Bristol, September, 1898.'

4143 **Dale**, *Sir* David. *Thirty years' experience of industrial conciliation & arbitration.* London: Labour Association, 1899. 8p.
Read at the Leeds Industrial Conference, 4 March 1899.

4144 **Cree**, Thomas S. *Business men and modern economics: a paper...* Glasgow: Bell and Bain, 1903. 26p.

4145 **Johnston**, Ruddiman. *The new industrialism: how the antagonisms between capital and labour may be made to disappear.* London: Simpkin, Marshall, 1903. 32p.

4146 **Gilman**, Nicolas Paine. *Methods of industrial peace.* Boston, New York: Houghton, Mifflin; London: Macmillan, 1904. x, 436p.

4147 **Knoop**, Douglas. *Industrial conciliation and arbitration.* London: King, 1905. xxiv, 241p.

4148 **Pigou**, Arthur Cecil. *Principles & methods of industrial peace.* London: Macmillan, 1905. xx, 240p.

4149 **Board of Trade**. Labour Department. *Rules of voluntary conciliation and arbitration boards and joint committees. Report, appendices.* 1907 [i.e. 1908]. xxv, 298p. (Cd. 3788.)
Second report. 1910. xxx, 334p.

4150 **Johnson**, Arthur Graham. *Industrial peace.* Bath: Harding and Curtis, 1907. 20p.

4151 **Furness**, Christopher, Baron Furness. *Industrial peace and industrial efficiency: proposals submitted . . . to a conference of trades-union representatives.* West Hartlepool: A. Salton, 1908. 40p.

4152 **Amery**, Leopold Charles Maurice Stennett, and others (eds.). *Papers on unrest among the working classes, read to a few Unionist Members of Parliament at Oxford, 19–23 Oct. 1911.* London: private circulation, 1911. 77p.

4153 **Kitson**, Arthur. *An open letter to the Right Hon. David Lloyd-George, M.P., Chancellor of the Exchequer, on the causes of strikes and bank failures.* London: Dent, 1911. 76p.

4154 **Lilly**, W. S. 'The philosophy of strikes.' *Nineteenth Century*, LXX, 416 (October 1911), 627–42.

4155 **London Chamber of Commerce.** *Report of the special committee on trade disputes as adopted by the council of the Chamber on November 30th, 1911.* London, 1911. 10p.

4156 **Reeves**, William Pember. *How to end strikes.* London, 1911. [9]p.

4157 **Association of British Chambers of Commerce**. *Industrial unrest . . .* London, 1912. 18p.

4158 **Cox**, Harold. *Labour unrest.* London, 1912. 16p.

4159 **Cunningham**, William, Archdeacon of Ely. *The causes of labour unrest, and the remedies for it: the draft of a report.* London: Murray, 1912. 29p.

4160 **Eddie**, F. M. *Co-operation and labour uprisings.* London, 1912. 15p.

4161 **Harding**, S. 'Some recent strikes.' *Dublin Rev.*, CLI (July 1912), 141–54.

4162 **Henderson**, Fred. *The labour unrest: what it is and what it portends.* London: Jarrold, 1912. 174p.

4163 **Hobson**, John Atkinson. *Industrial unrest: an address.* London: Political Committee of the National Liberal Club, 1912. 15p.

4164 **Macaulay**, J. *Effects of trade disputes.* Newport, 1912. 24p.

4165 **Watney**, Charles and **Little**, James A. *Industrial warfare: the aims and claims of capital and labour.* London: Murray, 1912. x, 353p.

4166 **Wells**, Herbert George. *The labour unrest.* London, 1912. 32p.

4167 **Williams**, Marshall Bruce. *Military and industrial war and the science of organization.* London: Association of Standardised Knowledge, 1921. 16p.

4168 **Ablett**, N. *Local autonomy versus centralisation in regard to the making of war and peace.* London, [1913?]. 10 leaves.

4169 **Booth**, Charles. *Industrial unrest and trade union policy.* London: Macmillan, 1913. 32p.

4170 **Healy**, T. M. *Dublin strikes, 1913: facts regarding the labour disputes contained in speech . . .* Dublin, 1913. 31p.

4171 **Inter-Denominational Conference of Social Service Unions.** *Industrial unrest and the living wage.* London, 1913. 182p.

4172 **St Stephen's Club.** *'Industrial unrest': report of an address delivered by N. Craig . . . 1913.* 1913. 47p.

4173 **Hills**, John Waller, **Ashley**, William James and **Woods**, Maurice. *Industrial unrest: a practical solution.* London: Unionist Social Reform Committee, 1914. viii, 39p.

4174 **Political Quarterly**. 'The Dublin labour dispute.' *Polit. Q.*, 1 (February 1914), 25–40.

4175 **Wright**, Arnold. *Disturbed Dublin: the story of the great strike of 1913–14, with a description of the industries of the Irish capital.* London: Longmans, Green, 1914. xii, 337p.
The strike was called by the Irish Transport and General Workers' Union.

4176 **Toogood**, George Edson. *Labour unrest: wartime thoughts on a national danger.* London: A. Brown, 1915. 78p.

4177 **Thomas**, Griffith Bowen. *The workers' grievances and the remedy.* Cardigan: M. M. and W. R. Thomas, 1916. 12p.

4178 **British Constitution Association**. *Industrial unrest: the reports of the Commissioners (July 1917).* London: King, 1917. 39p.
'Collated and epitomised by Sir W. Chance.'

4179 **Commission of Enquiry into Industrial Unrest**. *Summary of the reports of the Commission by the Right Honourable G. N. Barnes, M.P.* London: H.M.S.O., 1917. 8p. (Cd. 8696.)

4180 **Commission of Enquiry into Industrial Unrest**. No. 1 Division. *Report of the Commissioners for the North-Eastern area.* London: H.M.S.O., 1917. 12p. (Cd. 8662.)

4181 **Commission of Enquiry into Industrial Unrest**. No. 2 Division. *Report of the Commissioners for the North-Western area, including a supplemental report on the Barrow-in-Furness district.* London: H.M.S.O., 1917. 36p. (Cd. 8663.)

4182 **Commission of Enquiry into Industrial Unrest**. No. 3 Division. *Report of the Commissioners for the Yorkshire and East Midlands area.* London: H.M.S.O., 1917. 7p. (Cd. 8664.)

4183 **Commission of Enquiry into Industrial Unrest**. No. 4 Division. *Report of the Commissioners for the West Midlands area.* London: H.M.S.O., 1917. 12p. (Cd. 8665.)

4184 **Commission of Enquiry into Industrial Unrest**. No. 5 Division. *Report of the Commissioners for the London and South-Eastern area.* London: H.M.S.O., 1917. 8p. (Cd. 8666.)

4185 **Commission of Enquiry into Industrial Unrest**. No. 6 Division. *Report of the Commissioners for the South-Western area*. London: H.M.S.O., 1917. 6p. (Cd. 8667.)

4186 **Commission of Enquiry into Industrial Unrest**. No. 7 Division. *Report of the Commissioners for Wales, including Monmouthshire*. London: H.M.S.O., 1917. 50p. (Cd. 8668.)

4187 **Commission of Enquiry into Industrial Unrest**. No. 8 Division. *Report of the Commissioners for Scotland*. London: H.M.S.O., 1917. 15p. (Cd. 8669.)

4188 **Foxwell**, Herbert Somerton. 'The nature of the industrial struggle.' *Econ. J.*, XXVII, 107 (September 1917), 315–29.

'The first of two lectures delivered at the Royal Institution on April 19 and 26, 1917.'

4189 **Ramsay**, *Sir* Alexander. *Terms of industrial peace*. London: Constable, 1917. xi, 144p.

4190 **Richardson**, H. M. 'Capital and labour after the war.' Co-operative Wholesale Societies. *Annual for 1917*. p. 257–75.

4191 **Thorp**, Joseph Peter (ed.). *The other war; being chapters . . . on some causes of class misunderstanding*. London: Allen and Unwin, 1917. ii, 107p.

By John Hilton, P. H. Kerr, Alec Loveday, Harold Mess and Joseph Thorp.

I. 'The other war and the two nations', by Joseph Thorp.
II. 'Labour and industry', by P. H. Kerr.
III. 'Common fallacies', by Alec Loveday.
IV. 'The two nations', by H. A. Mess.
V. 'Industrial reconstruction', by John Hilton.

4192 **Engineer**. 'Strikes and the striker: a practical criticism.' *Natn. Rev.*, LXX, 420 (February 1918), 703–13.

4193 **Holmes**, H. V. *An infantryman on strikes: an appeal to the workers of Great Britain*. London: Wyman, 1918. 20p.

4194 **Maclean**, John. *The war after the war in the light of the elements of working-class economics*. Glasgow: J. Maclean, 1918. 16p.

4195 **Thomas**, W. H. *A memorandum on the industrial unrest*. London, 1918. 14p.

4196 **Argus**. *The vital principle of business*. London: British Commonwealth Union, 1919. 16p.

Attacks the labour manifesto *Causes and remedies for labour unrest*.

4197 **Carnegie**, D. *The promotion of co-operation between employers and employed*. London, 1919. 25p.

4198 **Johnston**, Thomas Bertram. *Industrial peace: capital, labour, and consumer: a basis of co-operation*. Bristol: Arrowsmith, 1919. 21p.

A paper delivered before the British Association.

4199 *Labour unrest: the debate in the House of Lords, February and March, 1919*. London: W. H. Smith, 1919. 84p.

4200 **Lever**, William Hesketh, Baron Leverhulme. *Prevention of strikes: a contribution to the volume . . . entitled 'Labour and capital after the war'*. Port Sunlight: Lever Bros., 1919. 30p.

4201 **Macassey**, *Sir* Lynden. 'Economic fallacy in industry.' *Edinb. Rev.*, CCXXIX, 468 (April 1919), 326–44.

4202 **Macassey**, *Sir* Lynden. 'More economic fallacy in industry.' *Edinb. Rev.*, CCXXX, 470 (October 1919), 387–506.

4203 **North London Manufacturers' Association**. *Industrial unrest . . . being the report of a joint committee of employers and employed . . .* London, 1919. 37p.

4204 *The real cause of strikes and how to prevent them*. London: *The Field* and *Queen*, 1919. 7p.

4205 **Wilson**, Thomas. 'Notes on labour unrest.' *Econ. J.*, XXIX, 115 (September 1919), 367–72.

The author was Secretary of the Edinburgh Bakers' and Confectioners' Union.

4206 **Baillie**, James Black. 'Industrial unrest: some causes and remedies.' Manchester University. *Labour and industry: a series of lectures*. Manchester: Manchester U.P.; London: Longmans, 1920. p. 83–112.

'A lecture given on Tuesday, November 11, 1919.'

4207 **Cole**, George Douglas Howard. *Chaos and order in industry*. London: Methuen; New York: Frederick A. Stokes, 1920. viii, 292p. (Library of social studies.)

Appendices: I. Memorandum on the causes of and remedies for labour unrest, submitted to the National Industrial Conference by the trade-union representatives. II. The Miners' Bill, select provisions.

4208 **Crotch**, William Walter. *Industrial anarchy – and the way out*. London: Hutchinson, 1920. vii, 132p.

4209 **Gould**, Gerald. *The coming revolution in Great Britain*. London: W. Collins, 1920. xiv, 281p.

4210 **Macara**, *Sir* Charles Wright. *The Industrial Council: the methods of procedure and application to the settlement of labour disputes*. London, 1920. 16p.

Reprinted from *The Financial Review of Reviews*.

4211 **Macassey**, *Sir* Lynden. 'Discontent in industry.' *Edinb. Rev.*, CCXXXI, 472 (April 1920), 393–408.

Review article.

4212 **Major**, Mark Bonaventura F. *The ethics of strikes*. London, [1920?]. 7p.

4213 **Mellor**, William. *Direct action*. London: Leonard Parsons, 1920. 157p. (New era series 8.)

4214 **Myers**, Charles Samuel. 'Industrial overstrain and unrest.' Muscio, B. (ed.). *Lectures on industrial administration*. London: Pitman, 1920. p. 172–84.

4215 **National Party**. Industrial Committee. *Report . . . on industrial unrest and labour policy*. London, 1920. 16p.

4216 **Parsons**, E. *Industrial unrest: profiteering and food prices.* Ripley: G. C. Brittain, 1920. 23p.

4217 **Webb**, Sidney. *The root of labour unrest: an address to employers and managers.* London: Fabian Society, 1920. 15p. (Fabian tract 196.)

'An Address to a representative private gathering of Employers, Managers and Foremen in 1919; reproduced as delivered with bibliographical footnotes added.'

4218 **Clow**, William Maccallum. *The quest of industrial peace.* London, New York: Hodder and Stoughton, 1921. xi, 300p.

4219 **Macara**, *Sir* Charles Wright. 'Bringing capital and labour together.' *Recollections.* London: Cassell, 1921. p. 165–78.

4220 **Barnard**, W. E. and **Grout**, A. *How to prevent strikes.* London, [after 1921]. 14p.

4221 **Paterson**, Arthur. *The weapon of the strike.* London: Hodder and Stoughton, 1922. 291p.

4222 **Rowntree**, Benjamin Seebohm. *Industrial unrest: a way out.* London: Longmans, 1922. 48p.

Another edition. New York: G. H. Doran, 1922. 29p. (Christianity and industry 8.)

4223 **Turner**, James. *Production and fair profits: the key to industrial peace.* Manchester: Sherratt and Hughes, 1922. 242p.

4224 **Miles**, T. B. *Industrial unrest: its cause and suggested cure.* London: Heath Cranton, 1923. 96p.

4225 **Guedalla**, Philip. *A council of industry.* London: *Daily News*, 1924. 28p. ('The new way' series 11.)

4226 **Industrial Peace**. [The strike.] Oxford, [1924?]. 8 pts. (Pamphlets, series B, 1–8.)

4227 **Labour Publications Department**. *Labour and industrial peace.* London, 1924. 15p.

4228 **Rowntree**, Benjamin Seebohm. 'Industrial unrest.' Hogue, R. W. (ed.). *British labour speaks.* New York: Boni and Liveright, 1924. p. 93–107.

4229 **Thomson**, David Cleghorn. *Towards industrial peace: an address.* Edinburgh, London: Oliver and Boyd, 1924. 31p.

4230 **Milner**, Alfred, Viscount Milner. 'Towards peace in industry.' *Questions of the hour.* London: Nelson, 1925. p. 53–108.

First edition. Hodder and Stoughton, 1923.

4231 **Association of British Chambers of Commerce**. *Industrial unrest.* London, 1926. 8p.

4232 **Atherley-Jones**, Llewellyn Arthur. 'Labour disputes.' *Fortn. Rev.*, n.s., CXX, 720 (December 1926), 757–67.

4233 **Corbett**, James. 'The necessity for compromise.' *Fortn. Rev.*, n.s., CXX, 716 (August 1926), 248–58.

4234 **Gore**, Charles, Bishop. *Strikes and locks-out* [sic]: *the way out.* London: King, 1926. 16p. (Present day papers 1.)

4235 **Kerr**, Philip Henry. *The industrial dilemma.* London: *Daily News*, 1926. 48p. ('The new way' series 14.)

4236 **Ogilvie**, *Sir* Frederick Wolff. *Industrial conflict.* London: H. Milford, 1926. 39p.

4237 **Wildridge**, O. *A peaceful revolution: the gateway to a greater Britain.* London, 1926. 48p.

4238 **Blane**, Gilbert Gordon. *Peace in industry: a practical system.* Nairn: *Nairnshire Telegraph*, 1927. 4p.

4239 **Freedom Association**. *Memorandum: trade disputes and trade unions.* London, 1927. 6p.

4240 **Garnett**, James Clerk Maxwell. *Conciliation.* London: King, 1927. 16p. (Present day papers 7.)

4241 **Hobson**, John Atkinson. *The conditions of industrial peace.* London: Allen and Unwin, 1927. 123p.

Also New York: Macmillan, 1927.

4242 **National Citizens' Union**. Edinburgh Branch. *The maintenance of strikers or persons locked out and their dependents.* Edinburgh, 1927. 8p.

4243 **Snowden**, Philip. *The way to industrial peace.* 1927. 40p. (John Clifford lecture for 1927.)

4244 **Wood**, Henry George. *What about industrial peace?* London: King, 1927. 16p. (Present day papers 9.)

4245 **Price**, Langford Lovell Frederick Rice. 'Industrial peace: its present position and its future prospects in England.' *Scientia* (February 1929), 105–14.

4246 **Wicksteed**, Charles. *Bygone days and now: a plea for co-operation between labour, brains, and capital.* London: Williams and Norgate, 1929. 160p.

4247 **Hicks**, John Richard. 'The early history of industrial conciliation in England.' *Economica*, x, 28 (March 1930), 25–39.

4248 **Rowland**, *Sir* John Thomas Podger. *Should labour co-operate with capital?* London: London General P., 1930. 19p.

Based on an address.

4249 **Lloyd George**, David. 'Problems of labour unrest.' *War memoirs.* London: Nicholson and Watson, 1934. Vol. IV. Chap. LIX. p. 1925–63.

New edition. London: Odhams, 1938. Vol. 2. Chap. LIX. p. 1141–63.

4250 **Turner**, A. 'Theory of industrial disputes.' *Rev. Econ. Studies*, I, 2 (February 1934), 154–6.

4251 **Walser**, Frank. *The art of conference.* London: Pitman, 1934. x, 305p.

4252 **Watson**, William Foster. 'The worker's point of view. XXIII. Strikes and the human factor.' *Hum. Factor*, IX, 4 (April 1935), 150–7.

4253 **Chang**, Ducksoo. *British methods of industrial peace: a study of democracy in relation to labor disputes.* New York: Columbia U.P.; London: King, 1936. 332p. (Columbia University Faculty of Political Science. Studies in history, economics and public law 425.)

Also Ph.D. thesis, Columbia University.

4254 **Beloff**, Max. *Public order and popular disturbances in England, 1689–1714.* 1937. (B.Litt. thesis, University of Oxford.)

4255 **Raphael**, Winifred. 'Grievances – their ascertainment and alleviation.' *Hum. Factor*, XI, 3 (March 1937), 91–6.

4256 **Daly**, Michael and **Atkinson**, Enid. 'A regional analysis of strikes, 1921–1936.' *Sociol. Rev.*, XXXII, 3–4 (July–October 1940), 216–23.

4257 **Braithwaite**, Constance. *Are strikes a pacifist method?* London: *Peace News*, 1944. 11p.

4258 **Gomberg**, Eugene L. 'Strikes and lockouts in Great Britain.' *Q. J. Econ.*, LIX, 1 (November 1944), 92–106.

4259 **James**, H. E. O. and **Tenen**, Cora. 'Grievances and their displacement.' *Occup. Psychol.*, XX, 4 (October 1946), 181–7.

4260 **Knowles**, Kenneth Guy Jack Charles. 'Strikes and their changing economic context.' *Oxf. Univ. Inst. Statist. Bull.*, IX, 9 (September 1947), 285*b*–306.

4261 **Rogers**, Douglas. *Strikes and the Labour government.* London: Independent Labour Party, 1947. 11p.

4262 **Registry of Friendly Societies.** *Reports of selected disputes referred to the Registrar of Friendly Societies under the Building Societies Acts, Friendly Societies Acts, Trade Union Acts, Post Office, Trustee and Municipal Savings Banks Acts, 1938–1949.* London: H.M.S.O., 1950. ix, 260p.

4263 **British Council of Churches.** *Strikes and lockouts.* London, 1951. 16p.

4264 **Knowles**, Kenneth Guy Jack Charles. *Strikes: a study in industrial conflict, with special reference to British experience between 1911 and 1947.* Oxford: Blackwell; New York: Philosophical Library, 1952. xiv, 330p. (Oxford University Institute of Statistics. Monograph 3.)

4265 **Giblin**, P. J. *The strike weapon in Irish unionism.* 1952–53. (M.A. thesis, National University of Ireland.)

4266 **Hopkins**, Sheila V. 'Industrial stoppages and their economic significance.' *Oxf. Econ. Pap.*, n.s., V, 2 (June 1953), 209–20.

4267 **Isaac**, D. G. D. *A study of popular disturbances in Great Britain, 1715–54.* 1953. (Ph.D. thesis, University of Edinburgh.)

4268 **Kahn-Freund**, Otto. 'Intergroup conflicts and their settlement.' *Br. J. Sociol.*, V, 3 (September 1954), 193–227.

Excerpts reprinted in Flanders, A. (ed.). *Collective bargaining: selected readings.* Harmondsworth: Penguin Books, 1969. p. 59–85.

4269 **Knowles**, Kenneth Guy Jack Charles. '"Strike-proneness" and its determinants.' *Am. J. Sociol.*, LX, 3 (November 1954), 213–29.

Reprinted in Galenson, W. and Lipset, S. M. (eds.). *Labor and trade unionism: an interdisciplinary reader.* New York, London: Wiley, 1960. p. 301–18.

Paper presented to the Second Congress of the International Sociological Association, Liège, Belgium, August, 1953.

4270 **Richmond**, Anthony Henry. 'Conflict and authority in industry.' *Occup. Psychol.*, XXVIII, 1 (January 1954), 24–33.

4271 **Chester**, Theodore Edward. 'In search of industrial peace.' *Distr. Bank Rev.*, 115 (September 1955), 1–19.

4272 **Richardson**, John Henry. 'Causes and significance of recent industrial disputes.' *Westm. Bank Rev.* (August 1955), 5–10.

4273 **Clegg**, Hugh Armstrong. 'Strikes'. *Polit. Q.*, XXVII, 1 (January–March 1956), 31–43.

4274 **Rose**, Arthur Gordon. 'The Plug Riots of 1842 in Lancashire and Cheshire.' *Lanc. Chesh. Antiq. Soc. Trans.*, LXVII (1957), 75–112.

4275 **Kelsall**, E. P. 'A theoretical setting for the study and treatment of strikes.' *Occup. Psychol.*, XXXII, 1 (January 1958), 1–20.

4276 **McCarthy**, William Edward John. 'The reasons given for striking: an analysis of official statistics, 1945–1957.' *Oxf. Inst. Statist. Bull.*, XXI, 1 (February 1959), 17–29.

4277 **Bird**, A. D. *A sociological analysis of management-worker conflict in industry.* 1960. (M.A. (Econ.) thesis, University of Manchester.)

4278 **Colyer**, William Thomas. *Strikes – and the remedy.* London: People's League for the Defence of Freedom, 1960. 40p.

4279 **Paterson**, Thomas Thomson. *Glasgow Limited: a case-study in industrial war and peace.* Cambridge: Cambridge U.P., 1960. x, 243p. (Social and economic studies 7.)

4280 **Gratch**, Alan S. 'Grievance settlement machinery in England.' *Labor Law J.*, XII, 9 (September 1961), 861–70.

4281 **Kovarsky**, Irving. 'The jurisdictional dispute in England.' *Labor Law J.*, XII, 3 (March 1961), 217–35.

4282 **Institute of Industrial Supervisors.** *Management responsibilities and the avoidance of industrial disputes.* Birmingham: the Institute, 1962. 55p.

4283 **Welton**, Harry. *The unnecessary conflict: a commonsense view of industrial relations.* London, Dunmow: Pall Mall P., 1962. 107p.

4284 **Daly**, George F. A. *Factors involved in industrial harmony.* 1962–63. (M.Econ.Sc. thesis, National University of Ireland.)

4285 **Choudhri**, S. U. R. *The British worker's attitude towards industrial unrest.* 1963. (M.Sc. Tech. thesis, University of Manchester.)

4286 **Fogarty**, Michael Patrick. *Working together: a commentary on the Marlow Declaration.* Oxford: Catholic Social Guild, 1963. 15p.

With the text of the Marlow Declaration.

4287 **Lerner**, Shirley Walowitz. 'Strikes.' *Distr. Bank Rev.*, 146 (June 1963), 29–36.

4288 **Lupton**, Tom. 'Industrial conflict.' *New Soc.*, II, 59 (14 November 1963), 11–13.

4289 **Turner**, Herbert Arthur. *The trend of strikes: an inaugural lecture.* Leeds: Leeds U.P., 1963. 22p. (Leeds University. Inaugural lectures, 1963.)

4290 **Allen**, Victor Leonard. 'The origins of industrial conciliation and arbitration.' *Int. Rev. of Soc. Hist.*, IX, 2 (1964), 237–54.
Originally read to a meeting of the Labour History Group in Leeds on 9 October 1963.

4291 **Eldridge**, John E. T. and **Cameron**, G. C. 'Unofficial strikes: some objections considered.' *Br. J. Sociol.*, XV, 1 (March 1964), 19–37.

4292 **Nevin**, Donald (ed.). *1913: Jim Larkin and the Dublin lock-out*. Dublin: Workers' Union of Ireland, 1964. 124p.

4293 **Richter**, D. C. *Public order and popular disturbances in Great Britain, 1865–1914*. 1965. (Ph.D. thesis, Maryland University.)

4294 **Jones**, David J. V. *Popular disturbances in Wales, 1792–1832*. 1965–66. (Ph.D. thesis, University of Wales, Aberystwyth.)

4295 **Badger**, Alfred Bowen (ed.). *Investing in people: the Marlow idea*. London: Bles, 1966. 96p.
Contents: 'An employer's view', by Lord Robens; 'A trade unionist's view', by Lord Cooper; 'A churchman's view', by A. Stephan Hopkinson; 'An educationalist's view', by R. S. Peters.
On the 'Marlow Declaration' on industry.

4296 **Barker**, Colin. *Involvement in strikes: some recent case-studies*. 1966. 69p. (M.A. thesis, University of Manchester.)

4297 **Eldridge**, John E. T. 'Are any strikes "wildcat"?' *New Soc.*, VII, 181 (17 March 1966), 15–16. (Society at work.)

4298 **Galambos**, P. and **Evans**, Eric Wyn. 'Work-stoppages in the United Kingdom, 1951–1964: a quantitative study.' *Oxf. Univ. Inst. Econ. Statist. Bull.*, XXVIII, 1 (February 1966), 33–57.
With comment by K. G. J. C. Knowles, p. 59–62.
Reply (November 1966), 283–4.

4299 **Marsh**, Arthur I. *Disputes procedures in British industry*. London: H.M.S.O., 1966. x, 27p. (Royal Commission on Trade Unions and Employers' Associations. Research papers 2, part 1.)

4300 **Frayn**, Michael. 'A perfect strike.' Blackburn, R. and Cockburn, A. (eds.). *The incompatibles: trade union militancy and the consensus*. Harmondsworth: Penguin in association with *New Left Review*, 1967. p. 160–6.
First published in the *Observer*.

4301 **Goodman**, J. F. B. 'Strikes in the United Kingdom: recent statistics and trends.' *Int. Labour Rev.*, XCV, 5 (May 1967), 465–81.

4302 **Marsh**, Peter. *Anatomy of a strike: unions, employers and Punjabi workers in a Southall factory*. London: Institute of Race Relations, 1967. vi [i.e. x], 119p. (Special series.)

4303 **Williams**, Shirley. 'Industrial conflict reconsidered.' *Christus Rex.*, XXI, 4 (October–December 1967) 333–7.

4304 **Confederation of British Industry** and **Trades Union Congress**. *Investigation of strikes: report by CBI & TUC*. London: T.U.C., C.B.I., 1968. 68p.

4305 **Eldridge**, John E. T. 'Explanations of strikes: a critical review.' *Industrial disputes: essays in the sociology of industrial relations*. London: Routledge and Kegan Paul; New York: Humanities P., 1968. p. 12–67.

4306 **Eldridge**, John E. T. *Industrial disputes: essays in the sociology of industrial relations*. London: Routledge and Kegan Paul; New York: Humanities P., 1968, x, 277p. (International library of sociology and social reconstruction.)

4307 **Eldridge**, John E. T. and **Cameron**, G. C. 'Unofficial strikes: some objections considered.' Eldridge, J. E. T. *Industrial disputes: essays in the sociology of industrial relations*. London: Routledge and Kegan Paul; New York: Humanities P., 1968. p. 68–90.
First published, in slightly altered form, in *British Journal of Sociology*, XV, 1 (March 1964).

4308 **Fairweather**, Owen. 'A comparison of British and American grievance handling.' Rehmus, C. M. (ed.). *Developments in American and foreign arbitration: proceedings of the 21st annual meeting, National Academy of Arbitrators, Cleveland, Ohio, January 30–February 2, 1968*. Washington, D.C.: Bureau of National Affairs, 1968. p. 1–18.

4309 **Marlow Association**. *Industry and the individual*. London: Marlow Association, 1968. [14]p. (Marlow discussion papers 3.)
Includes: M. Ivens, 'A management view'; and General and Municipal Workers' Union, 'A trade union view'.

4310 **Marsh**, Arthur I. and **McCarthy**, William Edward John. *Disputes procedures in Britain*. London: H.M.S.O., 1968. xvi, 121p. (Royal Commission on Trade Unions and Employers' Associations. Research papers 2, part 2.)

4311 **Mulvey**, Charles. 'Unemployment and the incidence of strikes in the Republic of Ireland 1942–1966.' *J. Econ. Studies*, III, 2 (July 1968), 73–84.

4312 **Porter**, Jeffrey H. *Industrial conciliation and arbitration, 1860–1914*. 1968. (Ph.D. thesis, University of Leeds.)

4313 **Dooley**, K. P. *An analysis of industrial conflict*. 1968–69. (M.S.A. thesis, Trinity College, Dublin.)

4314 **Aaron**, Benjamin (ed.). *Dispute settlement procedures in five Western European countries*. Los Angeles: Institute of Industrial Relations, University of California, 1969. 90p.
Papers by Xavier Blanc-Jouvan, Thilo Ramm, Gino Giugni, Folke Schmidt, K. W. Wedderburn.
Based on talks originally made at a conference held at the University of California at Los Angeles, 11 November 1967.

4315 **Roberts**, Paul. *Industry: conflict or co-*

operation? London: Marlow Association, 1969. 14p. (Marlow discussion paper 4.)

4316 **Ross**, Norman Scott. *Constructive conflict: an essay on employer-employee relations in contemporary Britain.* Edinburgh: Oliver and Boyd, 1969. vii, 98p.

4317 **Trades Union Congress**. *Disputes procedure.* London: T.U.C., 1969. 12p.

Sets out the procedures that unions will be expected to follow.

4318 **Turner**, Herbert Arthur. *Is Britain really strike-prone? a review of the incidence, character and costs of industrial conflict.* London: Cambridge U.P., 1969. 48p. (University of Cambridge. Department of Applied Economics. Occasional papers 20.)

4319 **Vidler**, D. *Model procedural agreements.* London: Industrial Society, 1969.

4320 **Wedderburn**, Kenneth William and **Davies**, P. L. *Employment grievances and disputes procedures in Britain.* Berkeley, Los Angeles, London: U. of California P., 1969. xvi, 301p.

4321 **Aims of Industry**. *The road to ruin.* London: Aims of Industry, 1970. 8p.

On strikes.

4322 **Blumler**, Jay G. and **Ewbank**, Alison J. 'Trade unionists, the mass media and unofficial strikes.' *Br. J. Ind. Relat.*, VIII, 1 (March 1970), 32–54.

4323 **Buchanan**, R. T. and **Gray**, R. B. 'Some evidence in support of a power theory of conflict.' *Br. J. Ind. Relat.*, VIII, 1 (March 1970), 85–93.

4324 **Confederation of British Industry**. *Disputes procedures for the avoidance and settlement of disputes arising at the place of work.* London: C.B.I., 1970. 29p.

4325 **McCarthy**, William Edward John. 'The nature of Britain's strike problem: a reassessment of arguments in the Donovan Report and a reply to H. A. Turner.' *Br. J. Ind. Relat.*, VIII, 2 (July 1970), 224–36.

4326 **Pencavel**, John H. 'An investigation into industrial strike activity in Britain.' *Economica*, n.s., XXXVII, 147 (August 1970), 239–56.

4327 **Porter**, Jeffrey H. 'Wage bargaining under conciliation agreements, 1860–1914.' *Econ. Hist. Rev.*, 2nd ser., XXIII, 3 (December 1970), 460–75.

4328 **Silkin**, Samuel C. 'American investments and European cultures: conflict and cooperation.' Kamin, A. (ed.). *Western European labour and the American corporation.* Washington, D.C.: Bureau of National Affairs, 1970. p. 441–54.

4329 **Thomson**, Andrew William John. 'Disputes procedures.' Robertson D. J. and Hunter, L. C. *Labour market issues of the 1970s.* Edinburgh: Oliver and Boyd for the Scottish Economic Society, 1970. p. 69–87.

First appeared in the June 1970 issue of the *Scottish Journal of Political Economy.*

See also: 1308; 1376; 4799; 7048; 7894.

B. GENERAL STRIKES

4330 **D.** *The general strike; or, Scaring the capitalists.* Aberdeen: James Leatham, 1890. 14p.

Reprinted from *The Commonweal.*

4331 **Barton**, A. *The universal strike: why it is needed and how it is possible.* Sheffield, [1911 ?]. 16p.

4332 **Chart**, D. A. 'The "general strike" as a labour weapon.' *Statist. Soc. Inq. Soc. Ir. J.*, XII, 92 (December 1912), 559–68.

4333 **Carpenter**, Niles. 'William Benbow and the origin of the general strike.' *Q. J. Econ.*, XXXV, 3 (May 1921), 491–9.

4334 **Atkinson**, Meredith. 'The general strike in history.' *Nineteenth Century*, XCIX, 592 (June 1926), 795–804.

4335 **Plummer**, Alfred. 'The general strike during one hundred years.' *Econ. Hist.*, I, 2 (May 1927), 184–204.

4336 **Plummer**, Alfred. *The general strike during one hundred years.* 1927. (M.Sc. (Econ.) thesis, University of London.)

4337 **Crook**, Wilfrid Harris. *The general strike: a study of labor's tragic weapon in theory and practice.* Chapel Hill, N.C.: U. of North Carolina P., 1931. xvi, 650p. (University of North Carolina social study series.)

4338 **Rüter**, A. J. C. (ed.). 'William Benbow's *Grand national holiday and congress of the productive classes.*' *Int. Rev. for Soc. Hist.*, I (1936), 217–56.

Introduction, facsimile text and notes.

4339 **Brown**, Tom. *The social general strike.* London: A.F.B., 1948. 14p.

4340 **Poels**, J. A. *Law and history of the general strike.* 1952. (B.Litt. thesis, University of Oxford.)

See also: 5178.

C. THE GENERAL STRIKE, 1926

See also Part Three, III, B, 4.

4341 **All-Russian Council of Trade Unions**. *Red money: a statement of the facts relating to the money raised in Russia during the General Strike and mining lock-out in Britain.* London: Labour Research Department, 1926. 90p.

Translated by Eden and Cedar Paul.

Foreword by A. J. Cook.

4342 **Anglo-Russian Parliamentary Committee**. *Some documents concerning the campaign against the help rendered by the Russian workers to British strikers.* London, 1926. 34p.

4343 **Arnot**, Robert Page. *The General Strike, May 1926: its origin & history.* London: Labour Research Department, 1926. viii, 245p.

4344 **Benn**, *Sir* Ernest John Pickstone. *If I were a labour leader.* London: Benn; New York: Scribner, 1926. 154p.

4345 **Branford**, Victor Verasis (ed.). *The coal crisis and the future: a study of social disorders and their treatment.* London: Leplay House P., Williams and Norgate, 1926. 111, xlvi p. (Making of the future.)

By P. Abercrombie, V. Branford, C. Desch, P. Geddes, C. W. Saleeby and E. Kilburn Scott.

4346 **Britannicus** (*pseud.*). *The policy adopted to produce the present decay and suspension of the coal industry: its purpose – to bring about revolution.* Letchworth: G. W. Wardman, 1926. 20p.

4347 **Brockway**, Archibald Fenner. 'A diary of the great strike.' *Social. Rev.*, n.s., 5 (June 1926), 9–18.

In London and Manchester.

4348 **Burns**, Emile. *The General Strike, May 1926: trades councils in action.* London: Labour Research Department, 1926. 191p.

4349 **Cook**, Arthur James. *The nine days: the story of the General Strike told by the miners' secretary.* London: Co-operative Printing Society, 1926. 24p.

4350 **'Curio'**. 'The General Strike and the Conservative leadership.' *Fortn. Rev.*, n.s., CXIX, 714 (June 1926), 730–40.

4351 **Dollan**, P. J. 'The strike of the Clyde.' *Social. Rev.*, n.s., 5 (June 1926), 19–26.

4352 **Dutt**, Rajani Palme. 'The first British general strike.' *Communist Int.*, 21 [1926], 3–36.

4353 **Fyfe**, Henry Hamilton. *Behind the scenes of the Great Strike.* London: Labour Publishing Co., 1926. 88p.

4354 **Glasgow**, George. *General strikes and road transport; being an account of the road transport organisation prepared by the British Government to meet national emergencies, with a detailed description of its use in the emergency of May 1926.* London: Bles, 1926. 151p.

4355 **Horner**, Arthur Lewis. *Coal: the next round.* London: Workers' Publications, 1926. 17p.

4356 **Labour Research Department.** *The coal shortage: why the miners will win.* London, 1926. 16p. (Labour white papers 24.)

4357 **London and District Economic League.** *The lesson of the General Strike: its origins, object and consequences.* London, [1926?]. 8p.

4358 **Lorwin**, Lewis Levitzki. *The British strike and international labor.* Washington, 1926. 11p.

From *The Journal of Electrical Workers and Operators.*

4359 **Macassey**, *Sir* Lynden. '"Sedition, privy conspiracy, and rebellion."' *Q. Rev.*, CCXLVII, 489 (July 1926), 120–39.

General Strike and previous trade union strike policy.

4360 **MacDonald**, James Ramsay. 'The outlook.' *Social. Rev.*, n.s., 5 (June 1926), 1–8.

4361 **Martin**, Basil Kingsley. *The British public and the General Strike.* London: Woolf, 1926. 127p.

4362 **Morgan**, Alfred. 'The coal problem as seen by a colliery official.' *Econ. J.*, XXXVI, 144 (December 1926), 563–76.

4363 **Murphy**, John Thomas. *The political meaning of the Great Strike.* 1926.

4364 **National Institute of Industrial Psychology.** 'The Institute and the coal dispute.' *Nat. Inst. Ind. Psychol. J.*, III, 3 (July 1926), 121–3.

'The part played by the Institute in the General Strike and some fundamental causes of the dispute between the coal owners and the miners are indicated.'

4365 **Pepper**, John. *The General Strike and the general betrayal.* Chicago: Workers (Communist) Party of America, 1926. 100p.

4366 **Petrovskii**, David Aleksandrovich. *The General Council and the General Strike: an analysis of the General Council's report on the strike, by A. J. Bennet* [pseud.]. London: Communist Party of Great Britain, 1926. 21p.

4367 **Price**, M. Phillips. 'The General Strike, and a labour majority: industrial or political action; an historical analysis.' *Social. Rev.*, n.s., 6 (July 1926), 9–15.

4368 **Robertson**, Dennis Holme. 'A narrative of the General Strike of 1926.' *Econ. J.*, XXXVI, 143 (September 1926), 375–93.

4369 **Schmidt**, P. J. 'The effect of the strike on the Continent.' *Social. Rev.*, n.s., 6 (July 1926), 16–21.

The author was head of the Publications and Research Department of the Netherlands Federation of Trade Unions.

4370 **Simon**, John Allsebrook, Viscount Simon, *Three speeches on the General Strike.* London: Macmillan, 1926. xxvi, 96p.

'With an introduction, diary of events and appendices.'

4371 **The Times.** *Strike nights in Printing House Square: an episode in the history of The Times.* London: printed for private circulation, 1926. 47p.

4372 **Wells**, Gabriel. *The great English strike: its three lessons.* Garden City, N.Y.: Doubleday, Page, 1926. 10p.

4373 **Yorkshire Conservative Newspaper Co. Ltd.** *The Yorkshire Post and the General Strike.* Leeds, 1926. 42p.

4374 **Nearing**, Scott. *The British General Strike: an economic interpretation of its background and its significance.* New York: Vanguard P., 1927. xxi, 186p.

Introduction by Ellen Wilkinson.

4375 **Phillips**, Marion. *Women and the miners' lock-out: the story of the Women's Committee for the Relief of the Miners' Wives and Children.* London: Labour Publishing Co., 1927. 94p.

4376 **Postgate**, Raymond William, **Wilkinson**, Ellen and **Horrabin**, J. F. *A workers' history of the Great Strike.* London: Plebs League, 1927. 110p.

4377 **Wynne**, William H. 'The British coal

strike and after.' *J. Polit. Econ.*, xxxv, 3 (June 1927), 364–89.

4378 **Crook**, Wilfred Harris. 'Social security and the General Strike.' *Polit. Sci. Q.*, XLIX, 3 (September 1934), 411–20.

4379 **Dobrée**, Bonamy. 'The General Strike, 1926.' *English revolts*. London: Joseph, 1937. p. 163–97.

4380 **Brown**, Tom. *The British General Strike*. London: Freedom P., 1943. 17p.

Reprinted from *War Commentary*, November–December 1942.

Another edition published by the Anarchist Federation, 1948.

Another edition published by Direct Action, 1962.

4381 **Keeton**, G. W. 'The General Strike and afterwards.' *Ind. Law Rev.*, I, 4 (September 1946), 119–26.

4382 **Murray**, John. *The General Strike of 1926: a history*. London: Lawrence and Wishart, 1951. 208p.

Foreword by William Gallacher.

4383 **Thomson**, L. D. *The relations between government and the trade unions in the General Strike of May 1926*. 1951. (Ph.D. thesis, University of London.)

4384 **Clegg**, Hugh Armstrong. 'Some consequences of the General Strike.' *Manchr. Statist. Soc. Trans.* (1953–54), 29p.

4385 **Symons**, Julian. *The General Strike: a historical portrait*. London: Cresset P., 1957. xi, 259p.

4386 **Crook**, Wilfred Harris. *Communism and the General Strike*. Hamden, Conn.: Shoe String P., 1960. xiii, 483p.

4387 **Shefftz**, Melvin Charles. *British labour, the General Strike, and the Constitution, 1910–1927*. 1961–62. (Dissertation, Harvard University.)

4388 **Mowat**, Charles Loch. 'Dead centre: the General Strike and after, 1925–1929.' *Britain between the wars, 1918–1940*. London: Methuen, 1962. Chap. VI. p. 284–352.

Reprinted. First published 1955.

4389 **Hyman**, Richard. *Oxford workers in the Great Strike*. Oxford: Centre for Socialist Education, Oxford Branch, 1966. 8p.

4390 **Hughes**, Michael. *Cartoons from the General Strike*. London: Evelyn, Adams and Mackay, 1968. 72p.

4391 **Communist Party of Great Britain.** History Group. *The General Strike: a project for group research and tape-recording*. London: C.P.G.B. (History Group), 1969. 7p.

4392 **Communist Party of Great Britain.** History Group. 'The General Strike of 1926.' *Soc. Study Labour Hist. Bull.*, 18 (Spring 1969), 5–7.

Report of a meeting held in Manchester on 5 October 1968 'to discuss the group's project to tape record interviews with veterans of the 1926 General Strike'.

4393 **Klugmann**, James. *History of the Communist Party of Great Britain: formation and early years*. London: Lawrence and Wishart, 1969.

Vol. 1. *1919–1924*.

Vol. 2. *1925–1927, the General Strike*.

4394 **Mason**, Antony. 'The government and the General Strike, 1926.' *Int. Rev. of Soc. Hist.*, XIV, 1 (1969), 1–21.

4395 **Mason**, Anthony. 'The local press and the General Strike: an example from the North East.' *Durham Univ. J.*, LXI, 3 (June 1969), 147–51.

4396 **Mowat**, Charles Loch. *The General Strike, 1926*. London: Arnold, 1969. 64p. (Archive series.)

4397 **Feeney**, J. '[Extracts from a speech on the General Strike in Teesside.]' *NE. Group Study Labour Hist. Bull.*, 4 (November 1970), 22–4.

J. Feeney was a member of the first strike committee set up in Middlesbrough in 1926. He spoke to the Group's meeting, 13 June 1970, Teesside.

4398 **Leonard**, J. W. '*The North Eastern Daily Gazette* and the General Strike.' *NE. Group Study Labour Hist. Bull.*, 4 (November 1970), 19–22.

Summary of a paper given at the Group's half-day school on 'The General Strike in the North East', 13 June 1970, Teesside.

4399 **Mason**, Antony. 'The General Strike.' *Soc. Study Labour Hist. Bull.*, 20 (Spring 1970), 45–9.

Review article.

4400 **Mason**, Antony. 'The General Strike on Teesside.' *NE. Group Study Labour Hist. Bull.*, 4 (November 1970), 17–19.

Summary of a paper given at the Group's half-day school on 'The General Strike in the North East', 13 June 1970, Teesside.

4401 **Millar**, J. P. M. 'The 1926 General Strike and the N.C.L.C.' *Soc. Study Labour Hist. Bull.*, 20 (Spring 1970), 41–5.

N.C.L.C. – National Council of Labour Colleges.

4402 **Short**, George. 'The General Strike and class struggles in the North-East, 1925–28.' *Marxism Today*, XIV, 10 (October 1970), 306–15.

4403 **Stephenson**, James. 'A comment [on the General Strike in the North East].' *NE. Group Study Labour Hist. Bull.*, 4 (November 1970), 25–32.

A record of an interview with John Adamson. J. Stephenson was Secretary of the Rowlands Gill Miners' Lodge during the 1926 strike.

See also: 71; 73; 13,292.

D. INTERNATIONAL COMPARISONS

See also Part Five, IV, A.

4404 **Lowes-Dickinson**, *Sir* Arthur. 'Publicity in industrial accounts with a comparison of English and American methods.' *R. Statist.*

Soc. J., LXXXVII, 3 (May 1924), 391–419.
Discussion, p. 420–32.
'Read before the Royal Statistical Society, April 15, 1924.'

4405 **Riches**, E. J. 'International comparisons of the time lost through industrial disputes.' *Econ. Rec.*, IX, 17 (December 1933), 226–34.

4406 **Spielmans**, John V. 'Strike profiles.' *J. Polit. Econ.*, LII, 4 (December 1944), 319–39.

4407 **Forchheimer**, K. 'Some international aspects of the strike movement.' *Oxf. Univ. Inst. Statist. Bull.*, X, 1 (January 1948), 9–24; X, 9 (September 1948), 294–304.

4408 **Woodbury**, Robert Morse. 'The incidence of industrial disputes: rates of time-loss, 1927–1947.' *Int. Labour Rev.*, LX, 5 (November 1949), 451–66.

4409 **Ross**, Arthur Max and **Irwin**, Donald. 'Strike experience in five countries, 1927–1947: an interpretation.' *Ind. Labor Relat. Rev.*, IV, 3 (April 1951), 323–42.
See also comments on this article by Adolf Sturmthal, VI, 3 (April 1953), 391–4, and a rejoinder by Arthur M. Ross, 395–8.

4410 **Sturmthal**, Adolf. 'Some comments on "Strike experience in five countries".' *Ind. Labor Relat. Rev.*, VI, 3 (April 1953), 391–4.
For original article by Arthur M. Ross and Donald Irwin see IV, 3 (April 1951), 323–42; and for a rejoinder by A. M. Ross, VI, 3 (April 1953), 391–4.

4411 **Kerr**, Clark and **Siegel**, A. 'The inter-industry propensity to strike: an international comparison.' Kornhauser, A., Dubin, R. and Ross, A. (eds.). *Industrial conflict*. New York: McGraw-Hill, 1954. p. 189–204.
An excerpt was reprinted in Flanders, A. (ed.). *Collective bargaining: selected readings*. Harmondsworth: Penguin, 1969. p. 138–60.
Also in Kerr, C. *Labor and management in industrial society*. New York: Doubleday, 1964. p. 105–47.

4412 **International Labour Office**. 'Industrial disputes, 1937–54.' *Int. Labour Rev.*, LXXII, 1 (July 1955), 78–91.

4413 **International Labour Office**. 'The incidence of industrial disputes by industry.' *Int. Labour Rev.*, LXXIV, 3 (September 1956), 290–302.

4414 **International Labour Office**. 'Incidence and duration of industrial disputes.' *Int. Labour Rev.*, LXXVII, 5 (May 1958), 455–68.

4415 **Ross**, Arthur Max. 'Changing patterns of industrial conflict.' Industrial Relations Research Association. *Proceedings of the twelfth annual meeting, Washington, D.C., 1959*. p. 146–69.
Discussion, 170–8.
Reprinted in Flanders, A. (ed.). *Collective bargaining: selected readings*. Harmondsworth: Penguin Books, 1969. p. 161–90.

4416 **Ross**, Arthur Max and **Hartman**, Paul T. *Changing patterns of industrial conflict*. New York, London: Wiley, 1960. x, 220p. (University of California. Institute of Industrial Relations. Research program.)

4417 **Shanmuga Sundram**, V. 'Analysis of strikes.' *Indian J. Labour Econ.*, III, 4 (January 1961), 274–84.

4418 **Oxnam**, D. W. 'International comparisons of industrial conflict: an appraisal.' *J. Ind. Relat.*, VII, 2 (July 1965), 149–63.

4419 **Stieber**, Jack. 'Unauthorized strikes under the American and British industrial relations systems.' *Br. J. Ind. Relat.*, VI, 2 (July 1968), 232–8.

4420 **Garbarino**, Joseph W. 'Managing conflict in industrial relations: U.S. experience and current issues in Britain.' *Br. J. Ind. Relat.*, VII, 3 (November 1969), 317–35.

See also: 4495.

E. PARTICULAR OCCUPATIONS AND INDUSTRIES

See also Part Three, III, E; Part Five, III; Part Five, IV, C; Part Six, III, E; Part Six, IV, A, 3; and Part Seven, VIII, C.

1. Agriculture, Forestry, and Fishing

4421 **Ministry of Labour**. *Report by a Court of Inquiry concerning the dispute in the Hull fishing industry, 1935*. London: H.M.S.O., 1935. 9p. (Cmd. 4917.)
Chairman: Sir James Baillie.

4422 **Ministry of Labour and National Service**. *Report of a Court of Inquiry into the circumstances and causes of the stoppage of work in the trawler fishing industry*. London: H.M.S.O., 1946. 15p. (Cmnd. 6882.)
Chairman: Sir John Forster.

4423 **Allan**, D. G. C. *Agrarian discontent under the early Stuarts and during the last decade of Elizabeth*. 1950. xiii, iv [203] leaves. (M.Sc. thesis, University of London.)

4424 **Duncan**, P. 'Conflict and co-operation among trawlermen.' *Br. J. Ind. Relat.*, I, 3 (October 1963), 331–47.

4425 **Horn**, Pamela L. R. 'The Evenley strike in 1867.' *Northamps. Past Pres.*, IV, 1 (1966), 47–50.

4426 **Mulvey**, Charles. *Report of inquiry into strikes in Bord na Móna, in November 1967 and February/March 1968*. Dublin: Stationery Office, [1969]. 83p. (Prl. 548.)
Conducted at the request of the Minister for Labour, Eire.

2. Mining and Quarrying

See also Part Five, IV, C.

4427 **Durham Coal Owners' Association**. *Silksworth strike, 1890–91*. Newcastle-upon-Tyne, 1891. 32p.

4428 **Beesly**, Edward Spencer. 'The coal strike.' *Pos. Rev.*, I, 11 (November 1893), 197–205.

4429 **Edwards**, Clement. 'The lock-out in the

coal trade.' *Econ. J.*, III, 12 (December 1893), 650–7.

4430 **Green**, Charles Alfred Howell, Archbishop of Wales. 'The South Wales coal strike.' *Econ. Rev.*, III, 4 (October 1893), 556–62.

4431 **Jeans**, James Stephen. 'The coal crisis and the paralysis of British industry.' *Nineteenth Century*, XXXIV, 201 (November 1893), 791–801.

4432 **Nash**, Vaughan. 'The lockout in the coal trade.' *Fortn. Rev.*, n.s., LIV, 323 (November 1893), 604–15.
Discussion of events.

4433 **Olivier**, Sydney. 'The miners' battle – and after.' *Contemp. Rev.*, LXIV (November 1893), 749–64.

4434 **Percy**, Cornelius McLeod. 'The coal dispute of 1893: its history, policy, and warnings.' *Econ. J.*, III, 12 (December 1893), 644–9.

4435 **Woods**, Sam. 'The coal war.' *New Rev.*, IX, 52 (September 1893), 225–35.

4436 **Departmental Committee Appointed to Inquire into the Disturbances at Featherstone, on the 7th September 1893.** *Report*. London: H.M.S.O., 1893–94. (C. 7234.)
Evidence and appendices. (C. 7234-I.)

4437 **Bainbridge**, Emerson. 'The coal strike of 1893.' *Contemp. Rev.*, LXV (January 1894), 1–15.

4438 **Chadburn**, James. 'The coal war. II. Lancashire.' *Econ. Rev.*, IV, 1 (January 1894), 80–6.

4439 **Ellis**, Thomas Ratcliffe. *Miners' wages dispute, 1893*. London, 1894. 70p.

4440 **Grier**, R. M. 'The coal war. I. Cannock Chase.' *Econ. Rev.*, IV, 1 (January 1894), 68–79.

4441 **Longe**, F. D. 'The coal strike and a "minimum" wage.' *Econ. J.*, IV, 13 (March 1894), 25–35.

4442 **Munro**, Joseph Edwin Crawford. 'Some economic aspects of the coal dispute, 1893.' *Econ. J.*, IV, 13 (March 1894), 14–24.

4443 **Fothergill**, Samuel. 'Trades union tactics in relation to law and order: the colliery strikes of 1892 and 1893.' *Westm. Rev.*, CXLIX, 1 (January 1898), 82–93.

4444 **An Onlooker**. 'Strike of colliers in South Wales.' *Westm. Rev.*, CL, 3 (September 1898), 297–300.

4445 **Parry**, W. J. *The Penrhyn lock-out, 1900–1901: statement and appeal*. London, 1901. 184p.

4446 **Terrett**, J. J. *The Rt. Hon. H. H. Asquith, M.P., and the Featherstone massacre*. London, 1906. 23p.

4447 **Colliery Guardian**. *The threatened national strike in the coal trade*. London: Colliery Guardian Co., 1911. (Coal trade pamphlets, 1–4, 6, 8–10.)
'Reprinted from the *Colliery Guardian*.'

4448 **Evans**, David. *Labour strife in the South Wales coalfield, 1910–11: a historical and critical record of the Mid-Rhondda, Aberdare Valley, and other strikes*. Cardiff: Educational Publishing Co., 1911. vii, 257p.

4449 **Home Office**. *Colliery strike disturbances in South Wales: correspondence and report, November 1910*. London: H.M.S.O., 1911. 54p. (Cd. 5568.)

4450 **Robertson**, Dennis Holme. 'A narrative of the coal strike.' *Econ. J.*, XXII, 87 (September 1912), 365–87.

4451 **Smillie**, Robert. 'The coal crisis, 1912.' Co-operative Wholesale Societies. *Annual for 1913*. p. 248–68.

4452 **Carter**, George Reginald. 'The coal strike in South Wales.' *Econ. J.*, XXV, 99 (September 1915), 453–65.

4453 **Carter**, George Reginald. 'The sequel of the Welsh coal strike and its significance.' *Econ. J.*, XXV, 100 (December 1915), 521–31.
Sequel to article in September 1915.

4454 **Renwick**, W. H. 'The coal industry under war conditions.' *Nineteenth Century*, LXXVIII, 462 (August 1915), 413–28.
An account of the South Wales coal strike of 1915 and of the reports of various committees on conditions within the coal industry.

4455 **Hodges**, Frank. *The case for the miner*. London, 1920. 4p.

4456 **International Labour Office**. *The British government and the Miners' Federation of Great Britain*. Geneva: I.L.O., 1920. 34p. (Studies and reports, series A, 5.)
Report of a conference held 9 September 1920, between the President of the Board of Trade, Sir Robert Horne, and the officers of the Miners' Federation.

4457 **International Labour Office**. *The British government and the Miners' Federation of Great Britain. The conference between the government and the Triple Industrial Alliance*. Geneva: I.L.O., 1920. 44p. (Studies and reports, series A, 10.)

4458 **International Labour Office**. *The miners' strike in Great Britain*. Geneva: I.L.O., 1920. 28p. (Studies and reports, series A, 13.)

4459 **McCurdy**, Charles Albert. *What do the miners want?* London: Harrison, 1920. 11p.

4460 **Triple Industrial Alliance**. *Facts about the coal dispute*. London, 1920. 10p.

4461 **Hewlett**, Maurice. 'The labour crisis. III. Some misgivings.' *Nineteenth Century*, LXXXIX, 531 (May 1921), 788–93.

4462 **Livesey**, W. *The mining crisis: its history and meaning to all workers*. London: Simpkin, Marshall, 1921. vi, 89p.
Second edition. 1922. vi, 89p.
The author was Chief Clerk to the Miners' Federation.

4463 **Macara**, *Sir* Charles Wright. 'The coal crisis of 1921.' *Recollections*. London: Cassell, 1921. p. 242–54.

Reprinted. Manchester: Sherratt and Hughes, 1926. 16p.

4464 **Osborn**, E. B. 'The labour crisis. I. The coal strike.' *Nineteenth Century*, LXXXIX, 531 (May 1921), 766–79.

4465 **Rose**, Frank Herbert. *Stop the strike! A plea for industrial peace.* London: St Catherine P., 1921. 39p.

4466 **Ritchie**, A. 'The struggle in Scottish coalfields.' *Communist Rev.*, II, 6 (April 1922), 414–22.

4467 **Thomas**, John. 'The present and future prospects of the South Wales miners.' *Communist Rev.*, II, 3 (January 1922), 206–24.

4468 **Ministry of Labour**. *Report by a Court of Inquiry concerning the coal mining industry dispute, 1925.* London: H.M.S.O., 1925. 28p. (Cmd. 2478.)
Chairman: H. P. Macmillan.

4469 **Wakinshaw**, William Holmes. *The solution of the coal problem.* Newcastle-upon-Tyne: A. Reid, 1925. 12p.

4470 **Fidler**, J. W. *The mining trouble: some suggestions to secure a solution.* London: Stockwell, 1926. 24p.

4471 **Gifford**, Dick. *Why this bother about coal?* London: Keystone P., 1926. 8p.

4472 **Labour Research Department**. *The coal crisis: facts from the Samuel Commission, 1925–26.* London: L.R.D., 1926. 79p. (Studies in labour and capital IX.)

4473 **Ashton**, Thomas. *Three big strikes in the coal industry.* Manchester: Miners' Federation of Great Britain, [1927?]. 3v.

4474 **Lubin**, Isador and **Everett**, Helen. *The British coal dilemma.* London: Allen and Unwin, 1927. xii, 370p. (Investigations in industry and labor.)
Also New York: Macmillan, 1927.
Printed in U.S.A.

4475 **Vernon**, Francis Lawrence William Venables, Baron Vernon. *Coal & industry: the way to peace.* London: Benn, 1927. 40p.

4476 **Eastman**, Mack. 'The European coal crisis, 1926–1927.' *Int. Labour Rev.*, XVII, 2 (February 1928), 157–78.

4477 **Raynes**, John R. *Coal and its conflicts: a brief record of the disputes between capital & labour in the coal mining industry of Great Britain.* London: Benn, 1928. 342p.

4478 **Cole**, George Douglas Howard. 'The problem of the mines.' *Polit. Q.*, I, 1 (January 1930), 38–69.

4479 **Mitchell**, J. H. 'The worker's point of view. VII. The personal element in the British coal industry.' *Hum. Factor*, VI, 9 (September 1932), 321–31.
Reprinted in *The worker's point of view: a symposium.* London: Woolf, 1933. p. 49–65.

4480 **Slater**, Montagu. *Stay down miner.* London: Lawrence, 1936. 81p. (Reportage books 1.)
Story of the Nine Mile Point, Monmouthshire, colliery dispute and strike, 1935.

4481 **Kidd**, Ronald. *The Harworth colliery strike: a report to the Executive Committee of the National Council for Civil Liberties, by the Secretary of the Council.* London: National Council for Civil Liberties, 1937. 15p.

4482 **Ministry of Labour and National Service**. *Report by a Court of Inquiry concerning a dispute between the Clerical and Administrative Workers' Union and certain colliery companies in South Wales and Monmouthshire.* London: H.M.S.O., 1943. 8p. (Cmd. 6493.)
Chairman: Charles Doughty.

4483 **Evans**, Brinley. *A history of the trade disputes and the formation and operation of the several sliding scale agreements in the South Wales coal trade, 1870 to 1903, with special reference to the work of Sir William Thomas Lewis, First Baron Merthyr of Senghenydd.* 1944. (M.A. thesis, University of Wales, Cardiff.)

4484 **Parsons**, Owen Henry. 'Conciliation machinery. I. Coal.' *Ind. Law Rev.*, I, 10 (March 1947), 318–22.

4485 **Ministry of Labour and National Service**. *Report of an Inquiry into a dispute between the National Coal Board and the National Union of Colliery Winding Enginemen.* London: H.M.S.O., 1948. 14p. (H.C. 47.)
Chairman: Sir John Forster.

4486 **Paterson**, Thomas Thomson and **Willett**, F. J. 'Unofficial strike.' *Sociol. Rev.*, XLIII, 4 (1951), 57–94.
Detailed sociological description and analysis of a strike at a Scottish colliery.

4487 **Bevan-Evans**, M. 'The Mold riot of 1831: a note.' *Flints. Hist. Soc. Publs.*, XIII (1952–53), 72–6.
A colliers' riot.

4488 **Wellisz**, Stanislas. 'Strikes in coal-mining.' *Br. J. Sociol.*, IV, 4 (December 1953), 346–66.
'The purpose of this paper is to analyse the overt causes of strikes in coal-mining and to probe into some of the factors underlying the disputes.'

4489 **Saxena**, S. K. *Nationalisation and industrial conflict: example of British coalmining.* The Hague: Nijhoff, 1955. viii, 185p.

4490 **Jones**, W. Hugh. 'A strike at Talargoch lead mine one hundred years ago.' *Flints. Hist. Soc. Publs.*, XVI (1956), 22–30.

4491 **Rimlinger**, Gaston Victor. *Labor protest in British, American, and German coal mining prior to 1914.* 1956–57. (Thesis, University of California, Berkeley.)

4492 **McCord**, Norman. 'The murder of Nicolas Fairles.' *S. Shields Archaeol. Hist. Soc. Pap.*, I, 6 (January–December 1958), 12–19.

4493 **Slaughter**, Clifford. 'The strike of Yorkshire mineworkers in May, 1955.' *Sociol. Rev.*, n.s., VI, 2 (December 1958), 241–59.

4494 **Goldthorpe**, John H. 'Technical organization as a factor in supervisor-worker conflict: some preliminary observations on a study made in the mining industry.' *Br. J. Sociol.*, X, 3 (September 1959), 213–30.

4495 **Rimlinger**, Gaston Victor. 'International

differences in the strike propensity of coal miners: experience in four countries.' *Ind. Labor Relat. Rev.*, XII, 3 (April 1959), 389–405.

4496 **Rimlinger**, Gaston Victor. 'The legitimation of protest: a comparative study in labour history.' *Comp. Studies Soc. Hist.*, II, 3 (April 1960), 329–43.

'... Analyses the British and German coal miners' struggles to overcome opposition to their endeavours to rise from traditional submission to the employer to some sort of partnership in industrial government.'

4497 **Hopkins**, T. N. *The operation of the National Reference Tribunal in the coal industry since 1943*. 1961–62. (M.A. thesis, University of Wales, Aberystwyth.)

4498 **Scott**, William Henry. 'Conflict in coal-mines.' *New Soc.*, 4 (25 October 1962), 23–4.

Represents one aspect of the book *Coal and conflict*, by W. H. Scott, E. Mumford, I. McGivering and J. M. Kirby.

4499 **Chaloner**, William Henry. 'The British miners and the coal industry between the wars.' *Hist. Today*, XIV, 6 (June 1964), 418–26.

Discussion, 505–6, 581.

4500 **Ministry of Labour**. *Report of the Committee of Investigation appointed by the Minister of Labour on December 31, 1963 to inquire into the difference existing in the Yorkshire area of the coalmining industry involving members of the Yorkshire Winding Enginemen's Association and members of the National Union of Mineworkers employed by the National Coal Board, and the National Coal Board.* London: H.M.S.O., 1964. 38p.

Chairman: R. Wilson.

4501 **Ministry of Labour**. *Report of an inquiry into the difference in the South Wales coalfield.* London: H.M.S.O., 1965. 35p.

Chairman: J. G. Picton.

4502 **Smethurst**, John B. 'Strikes and strike-breakers in the Worsley coal field.' *Eccles Distr. Hist. Soc. Trans.* (1966–67), 24p.

4503 **Best**, Geoffrey Francis Andrew. *Bishop Westcott and the miners.* London: Cambridge U.P., 1967. 40p. (Bishop Westcott memorial lecture 1966.)

4504 **McCormick**, Brian J. 'Strikes in the Yorkshire coalfield, 1947–1963.' *Econ. Studies*, IV, 1–2 (October 1969), 171–97.

'An earlier form of this paper was read at the Northern Economists' Conference in Sheffield on 19th November 1966 and to a seminar in the Department of Economics at the University of Strathclyde, 4th March, 1967.'

4505 **Oldham**, Jim, and others. 'The miners' strike.' *Trade Un. Regist.* (1970), 129–36.

For the most part reproduces the document prepared by the Yorkshire strike leaders, October 1970.

See also: 13,279; 13,281; 13,285.

3. Manufacturing Industries

a. FOOD, DRINK, AND TOBACCO

4506 **Black**, Clementina. 'The chocolate-makers' strike.' *Fortn. Rev.*, n.s., XLVIII, 284 (August 1890), 305–314.

4507 **Co-operative Union**. *Report of inquiry made by the Scottish section of the Co-operative Union, into certain charges made against Co-operative Societies in Scotland in regard to the treatment of their bakers; the said charges being made by the Operative Bakers of Scotland Federal Union.* Manchester, 1891.

b. IRON, STEEL, AND OTHER METALS

4508 **Iron Trades Employers' Association**. *The strike at Bolton: letters to the 'Times'.* London, 1887. 32p.

4509 **Odber**, A. J. 'The origins of industrial peace: the manufactured iron trade of the North of England.' *Oxf. Econ. Pap.*, n.s., III, 12 (June 1951), 202–20.

An account of the establishment in 1869 of the Board of Conciliation and Arbitration for the Manufactured Iron Trade of the North of England.

4510 **Ministry of Labour and National Service**. *Report of a court of inquiry into the causes and circumstances of a dispute between the Iron and Steel Trades Employers' Association and the National Joint Trade Unions' Craftsmen's Iron and Steel Committee.* London: H.M.S.O., 1956. 22p. (Cmd. 9843.)

Chairman: Sir John Stewart.

4511 **Eldridge**, John E. T. 'Redundancy conflict in an isolated steel community.' *J. Mgmt. Studies*, III, 3 (October 1966), 285–303.

Consett Iron Co.

4512 **Ministry of Labour**. *Report by Mr A. J. Scamp of a Court of Inquiry into the causes and circumstances of the dispute at Birmingham Aluminium Castings Limited involving members of the Transport and General Workers' Union and the National Society of Metal Mechanics.* London: H.M.S.O., 1967. 8p. (Cmnd. 3201.)

4513 **Ministry of Labour**. *Report of a Court of Inquiry into the causes and circumstances of a dispute at the Tube Works of Stewarts and Lloyds Limited at Corby.* London: H.M.S.O., 1967. 19p. (Cmnd. 3260.)

Chairman: Sir G. Honeyman.

4514 **Ministry of Labour**. *Report of an inquiry into a dispute between the Steel Company of Wales and the Amalgamated Union of Building Trade Workers.* London: H.M.S.O., 1967. 17p.

Chairman: D. J. Robertson.

4515 **Department of Employment and Productivity**. *Report of a Court of Inquiry under Sir Jack Scamp into a dispute concerning wage* *structure proposals for time workers employed at Pressed Steel Fisher Limited, Cowley.* London: H.M.S.O., 1968. 23p. (Cmnd. 3688.)

4516 **Eldridge**, John E. T. 'Redundancy conflict in an isolated steel community.' *Industrial steel disputes: essays in the sociology of industrial relations.* London: Routledge and Kegan Paul; New York: Humanities P., 1968. p. 206–28.

First published in slightly altered form, in *Journal of Management Studies*, III, 3 (October 1966).

4517 *Report of a Court of Inquiry under Lord Pearson into the dispute between the British Steel Corporation and certain of their employees.* London: H.M.S.O., 1968. 47p. (Cmnd. 3754.)

4518 **Department of Employment and Productivity**. *Report of a Court of Inquiry under Professor D. J. Robertson into a dispute at the Port Talbot works of the British Steel Corporation.* London: H.M.S.O., 1969. 25p. (Cmnd. 4147.)

4519 **Porter**, Jeffrey H. 'David Dale and conciliation in the Northern manufactured iron trade 1869–1914.' *Nth. Hist.*, v (1970), 157–71.

c. ENGINEERING AND SHIPBUILDING

See also Part Five, IV, C.

4520 *River Thames barge builders' strike, from April 12th to September 13th, 1890.* London, 1890. 31p.

4521 **Harris**, T. *A plea for the striking nail-makers of Bromsgrove and district.* Manchester, 1891. 16p.

4522 **Aves**, Ernest. 'Labour notes: the dispute in the engineering trade, etc.' *Econ. J.*, VII, 28 (December 1897), 623–30.

4523 **Engineering**. *The engineers' strike: a series of articles reprinted from 'Engineering', September 24th to November 12th, 1897.* London: Offices of *Engineering*, 1897. 50p.

4524 **Amalgamated Society of Engineers**. *Notes on the engineering trade lock-out 1897–8, with list of contributions.* London: A.S.E., 1898. 166p.

4525 **Aves**, Ernest. 'The dispute in the engineering trades.' *Econ. J.*, VIII, 29 (March 1898), 115–24.

4526 **Hirst**, Francis W. 'The policy of the engineers.' *Econ. J.*, VIII, 29 (March 1898), 124–7.

4527 **Hurd**, Archibald S. 'The navy and the engineering dispute.' *Nineteenth Century*, XLIII, 253 (March 1898), 366–70.

4528 **Hurd**, Archibald S. 'The retardation of the navy by the engineers' strike.' *Nineteenth Century*, XLV, 265 (March 1899), 477–85.

4529 **Birmingham Association of Mechanical Engineers**. *The prevention of strikes and lock-outs.* Birmingham, 1902. 22p.

4530 **Muir**, W. Errol. 'The engineers and the war.' *Engl. Rev.*, XXI (August 1915), 78–88.

4531 **Labour Party**. *Report of the Special Committee appointed by the Labour Party to inquire into the report upon the circumstances which resulted in the deportation in March, 1916, of David Kirkwood and other workmen employed in munition factories in the Clyde district.* London, 1916. 63p.

4532 **Bremner**, David Alexander. *The pathology of industrial unrest, with some special reference to the engineering industry.* London, 1920. 7p.

4533 **Ministry of Labour**. *Report by a Court of Inquiry concerning the electrical trades dispute, Penistone.* London: H.M.S.O., 1920. 4p. (Cmd. 990.)

4534 **Ministry of Labour**. *Report by a Court of Inquiry concerning the engineering trades dispute, 1922.* London: H.M.S.O., 1922. 27p. (Cmd. 1653.)

By Sir William W. Mackenzie.

4535 **Shadwell**, Arthur. *The engineering industry and the crisis of 1922.* London: Murray, 1922. vi, 90p.

4536 **Daniels**, George W. 'A "turn-out" of Bolton machine-makers in 1831.' *Econ. Hist.*, I, 4 (January 1929), 591–602.

4537 **Daniels**, George W. 'The organisation of a "turn-out" of Bolton machine-makers in 1831.' *Econ. Hist.*, II, 5 (January 1930), 111–16.

4538 **Glasgow and West of Scotland Association of Foremen Engineers and Draughtsmen**. *Paths to peace in industry.* Glasgow, 1930. 42p.

4539 **Ministry of Labour and National Service**. *Report by a Court of Inquiry in the matter of a trade dispute apprehended at Briggs Motor Bodies, Ltd., Dagenham.* London: H.M.S.O., 1941. 6p. (Cmd. 6284.)

Chairman: Charles Doughty.

4540 **Ministry of Labour and National Service**. *Report by a Court of Inquiry into a dispute between Trent Guns and Cartridges, Limited, Grimsby and the National Union of General and Municipal Workers.* London: H.M.S.O., 1941. 10p. (Cmd. 6300.)

Chairman: Charles Doughty.

4541 **Ministry of Labour and National Service**. *Report by a Court of Inquiry concerning a dispute at an engineering undertaking in Scotland.* London: H.M.S.O., 1943. 19p. (Cmd. 6474.)

Chairman: John L. Wark.

4542 **Ministry of Labour and National Service**. *Report of a Court of Inquiry into the causes of industrial unrest in the wire and wire rope industry.* London: H.M.S.O., 1947. 15p. (Cmd. 7097.)

Chairman: Charles Doughty.

4543 **Ministry of Labour and National Service**. *Shipbuilding and shiprepairing industry: report by a Court of Inquiry into the difference that has arisen between the Shipbuilding Employers' Federation and the Confederation of Shipbuilding*

and Engineering Unions on the trade union claim for a 40-hour week of five days. London: H.M.S.O., 1947. 14p. (Cmd. 7036.)
Chairman: Sir John Forster.

4544 **Ministry of Labour and National Service.** *Report of a Court of Inquiry appointed to inquire into a dispute between the Engineering and Allied Employers' National Federation and the Confederation of Shipbuilding and Engineering Unions.* London: H.M.S.O., 1948. 14p. (Cmd. 7511.)
Chairman: Sir John Forster.

4545 **Turner**, Herbert Arthur. 'The Crossley strike.' *Manchr. Sch.*, XVIII, 3 (September 1950), 179–216.
'Analysis of a strike of 1,000 engineering workers at Crossley motor works in February 1950, owing to the dismissal of certain workers.'

4546 **Ministry of Labour and National Service.** *Report of a Court of Inquiry into the dispute between the Austin Motor Company, Limited and certain workpeople, members of the National Union of Vehicle Builders.* London: H.M.S.O., 1953. 28p. (Cmd. 8839.)

4547 **Ministry of Labour and National Service.** *Report of a Court of Inquiry into a dispute between employers who are members of the Engineering and Allied Employers' National Federation and workmen who are members of trade unions affiliated to the Confederation of Shipbuilding and Engineering Unions.* London: H.M.S.O., 1954. 48p. (Cmd. 9084.)
Chairman: Lord Justice Morris.
Also report relating to Shipbuilding Employers' Federation. (Cmd. 9085.)

4548 **Ball**, Frank Norman. 'The B.M.C. dispute.' *Ind. Law Rev.*, XI, 1 (July 1956), 1–5.

4549 **Clarke**, Ronald Oliver. 'The dispute in the British engineering industry, 1897–98: an evaluation.' *Economica*, n.s., XXIV, 94 (May 1957), 128–37.

4550 **Clegg**, Hugh Armstrong and **Adams**, Rex. *The employers' challenge: a study of the national shipbuilding and engineering disputes of 1957.* Oxford: Blackwell, 1957. 179p.

4551 **Ministry of Labour and National Service.** *Report of a Court of Inquiry into a dispute between employers who are members of the Engineering and Allied Employers' National Federation and workmen who are members of trade unions affiliated to the Confederation of Shipbuilding and Engineering Unions.* London: H.M.S.O., 1957. 24p. (Cmnd. 159.)
Chairman: D. T. Jack.

4552 **Ministry of Labour and National Service.** *Report of a Court of Inquiry into a dispute between employers who are members of the Shipbuilding Employers' Federation and workmen who are members of trade unions affiliated to the Confederation of Shipbuilding and Engineering Unions.* London: H.M.S.O., 1957. 28p. (Cmnd. 160.)
Chairman: D. T. Jack.

4553 **Ministry of Labour and National Service.** *Report of a Court of Inquiry into the causes and circumstances of a dispute at Briggs Motor Bodies, Limited, Dagenham, existing between the Ford Motor Company Limited and members of the trade unions represented on the trade union side of the Ford National Joint Negotiating Committee.* London: H.M.S.O., 1957. 36p. (Cmnd. 131.)

4554 **Bescoby**, John and **Turner**, Herbert Arthur. 'An analysis of post-war labour disputes in the British car-manufacturing firms.' *Manchr. Sch.*, XXIX, 2 (May 1961), 133–160.

4555 **Shea**, R. A. *A general analysis and case study of unofficial strikes in the manual-worker section of the British engineering industry.* 1961. (M.Sc. (Econ.) thesis, University of London.)

4556 **Turner**, Herbert Arthur and **Bescoby**, John. 'Strikes, redundancy and the demand cycle in the motor car industry.' *Oxf. Univ. Inst. Statist. Bull.*, XXIII, 2 (May 1961), 179–85.

4557 **Aris**, Stephen. 'Behind the Ford troubles.' *New Soc.*, VII (15 November 1962), 9–10.
'*New Society* special report.'

4558 **Frow**, Eddie. 'The engineers' strike of 1852.' *Marxism Today*, VII, 4 (April 1963), 118–21.

4559 **Ministry of Labour.** *Report of a Court of Inquiry into the causes and circumstances of a dispute between the Ford Motor Company, Limited, Dagenham and members of the trade unions represented on the Trade Union side of the Ford National Joint Negotiating Committee.* London: H.M.S.O., 1963. 58p. (Cmnd. 1999.)
By D. T. Jack.

4560 **Cameron**, G. C. 'Post-war strikes in the North-East shipbuilding and ship-repairing industry, 1946–1961.' *Br. J. Ind. Relat.*, II, 1 (March 1964), 1–22.

4561 **Knowles**, Kenneth Guy Jack Charles and **Robinson**, Derek. 'Some concepts relevant to the consideration of the engineering wage settlement of November 1963.' *Oxf. Univ. Inst. Statist. Bull.*, XXVI, 2 (May 1964), 93–111.

4562 **Ministry of Labour.** *Report of a Court of Inquiry into a dispute between employers who are members of the Shipbuilding Employers' Federation and workmen who are members of the Draughtsmen's and Allied Technicians' Association.* London: H.M.S.O., 1965. 25p. (Cmnd. 2704.)
Chairman: E. H. Phelps Brown.

4563 **Ministry of Labour.** Motor Industry Joint Labour Council. *Report by Mr A. J. Scamp, J.P., on the activities of the Council.* London: H.M.S.O., 1966. 16p.

4564 **Beynon**, Huw. 'A wildcat strike.' *New Soc.*, XII, 310 (5 September 1968), 336–7.
At Fords.

4565 **Department of Employment and Productivity.** *Report of a Court of Inquiry under*

Sir Jack Scamp into a dispute concerning sewing machinists employed by the Ford Motor Company Limited. London: H.M.S.O., 1968. 50p. (Cmnd. 3749.)

4566 **Department of Employment and Productivity.** *Report of the Court of Inquiry under Professor D. J. Robertson into a dispute at Rootes Motors, Limited, Linwood, Scotland.* London: H.M.S.O., 1968. 43p. (Cmnd. 3692.)

4567 **Eldridge**, John E. T. 'The demarcation dispute in the shipbuilding industry: a study in the sociology of conflict.' *Industrial disputes: essays in the sociology of industrial relations.* London: Routledge and Kegan Paul; New York: Humanities P., 1968. p. 91–125.

4568 *Report of a Court of Inquiry under Professor D. J. Robertson into a dispute at the Bromborough, Cheshire, plant of Girling Limited.* London: H.M.S.O., 1968. 20p. (Cmnd. 3855.)

4569 **Bugler**, Jeremy. 'The Ford fight.' *New Soc.*, XIII, 337 (13 March 1969), 393–4.

4570 **Bugler**, Jeremy. 'Leyland deflowered.' *New Soc.*, XIII, 350 (12 June 1969), 905–6.

4571 **Burgess**, Keith. 'Technological change and the 1852 lock-out in the British engineering industry.' *Int. Rev. of Soc. Hist.*, XIV, 2 (1969), 215–36.

4572 **Department of Employment and Productivity.** *Report of a Court of Inquiry under Sir Jack Scamp into a dispute at Vickers Limited, Barrow-in-Furness.* London: H.M.S.O., 1969. 36p. (Cmnd. 3984.)

4573 **Eire**. Department of Labour. *Dispute between F.U.E. and maintenance craft unions: report of inquiry by Con Murphy.* Dublin: Stationery Office, 1969. 43p.

F.U.E. = Federated Union of Employers.

4574 **Newens**, Stan and **Adams**, Charles. 'The G.E.C./A.E.I. takeover and the fight against redundancy at Harlow.' *Trade Un. Regist.* (1969), 171–4.

4575 *Report of a Court of Inquiry under Professor John C. Wood, L.L.M., into a dispute at the Woodend Avenue, Liverpool, plant of Standard-Triumph (Liverpool) Limited.* London: H.M.S.O., 1969. 11p. (Cmnd. 4220.)

4576 **Chadwick**, Graham. ' "The big flame": an account of the events at the Liverpool factories of G.E.C.–E.E.' *Trade Un. Regist.* (1970), 178–97.

4577 **Gretton**, John. 'The GKN-Sankey strike.' *New Soc.*, XVI, 416 (17 September 1970), 498–9.

4578 **Silberman**, Freddy. 'The 1969 Ford's strike.' *Trade Un. Regist.* (1970), 213–28.

d. TEXTILES

4579 **Helm**, Elijah. 'The recent wages dispute in the Lancashire cotton-spinning industry.' *Econ. J.*, III, 10 (June 1893), 342–5.

4580 **Conciliation Scheme Committee.** *Conciliation in the cotton trade: report of negotiations, 1899–1900, and press comments.* Manchester, 1901. 52p.

4581 **Price**, Langford Lovell Frederic Rice. 'Conciliation in the cotton trade.' *Econ. J.*, XI, 42 (June 1901), 235–44.

An account and discussion of *Conciliation in the cotton trade: report of negotiations, 1899–1900, and press comments.* 1901.

4582 **Macara**, *Sir* Charles Wright. 'Strikes.' *Recollections.* London: Cassell, 1921. p. 10–29.

Cotton spinning industry.

4583 **Ministry of Labour.** *Report by a Court of Inquiry concerning the matters in dispute regarding wages in the Northern counties wool textile industry.* London: H.M.S.O., 1930. 32p. (Cmd. 3505.)

Chairman: H. P. Macmillan.

4584 **Ministry of Labour and National Service.** *Report by a Court of Inquiry into the wages and hours of work in the woolcombing section of the wool textile industry in Yorkshire.* London: H.M.S.O., 1944. 28p. (Cmd. 6499.)

Chairman: Sir Harold Morris.

4585 **Burley**, K. H. 'A note on a labour dispute in early eighteenth-century Colchester.' *Inst. Hist. Res. Bull.*, XXIX, 80 (November 1956), 220–30.

Textile workers, 1715.

4586 **McShane**, Harry (comp.). *Calton weavers' memorial, 1787: the first recorded industrial strike in the history of Glasgow.* Glasgow, [1957?]. 12p.

4587 **Carnall**, Geoffrey. 'Dickens, Mrs. Gaskell and the Preston strike.' *Vic. Studies*, VIII, 1 (September 1964), 31–48.

4588 **Foot**, Paul. *The strike at Courtaulds, Preston, 24 May to 12 June 1965.* London: Institute of Race Relations, 1965. [15]p.

Supplement to *Institute of Race Relations Newsletter*, July 1965.

4589 **Porter**, Jeffrey H. 'Industrial peace in the cotton trade 1875–1913.' *Yorks. Bull. Econ. Soc. Res.*, XIX, 1 (May 1967), 49–61.

4590 **Jenkins**, Mick. 'Cotton struggle, 1929–1932: the fight against the More Loans System.' *Marxism Today*, XIII, 2 (February 1969), 51–8.

e. CLOTHING AND FOOTWEAR

4591 **Davidson**, John Morrison. 'Anthony John Mundella.' *Eminent Radicals in and out of Parliament.* London: Stewart, 1880. p. 125–33.

Originally published in the *Weekly Dispatch.*

4592 **Holmes**, J. *The strike in the Hinckley hosiery trade.* Leicester, 1891. 8p.

4593 **Hoffman**, W. B. 'The late boot war.' *Econ. J.*, V, 18 (June 1895), 264–9.

4594 **Armytage**, Walter Harry Green. 'A. J. Mundella and the hosiery industry.' *Econ. Hist. Rev.*, XVIII, 1–2 (1948), 91–9.

4595 **Brunner**, Elizabeth. 'The origins of industrial peace: the case of the British boot and shoe industry.' *Oxf. Econ. Pap.*, n.s., I, 2 (June 1949), 247–59.

4596 **Armytage**, Walter Harry Green. *A. J. Mundella, 1825–1897: the Liberal background to the labour movement.* London: Benn, 1951. 386p.

4597 **Church**, Roy. 'Technological change and the Hosiery Board of Conciliation and Arbitration 1860–1884.' *Yorks. Bull. Econ. Soc. Res.*, XV, I (May 1963), 52–60.

4598 **Porter**, Jeffrey H. 'The Northampton Arbitration Board and the shoe industry dispute of 1887.' *Northamps. Past Pres.*, IV, 3 (1968), 149–54.

4599 **Swan**, J. M. 'A sequel to the shoe industry dispute of 1887.' *Northamps. Past Pres.*, IV, 4 (1969), 247–8.
Sequel to article by J. H. Porter, IV, 3.

4600 **Roche**, Jim. 'The Leeds clothing strike.' *Trade Un. Regist.* (1970), 162–72.

f. BRICKS, POTTERY, GLASS, AND CEMENT

4601 **Brownfield**, Arthur. *The lock-out: a potters' guild proposal.* Hanley: New Press Printing Co., 1892. 39p.

4602 **Y.** 'The arbitration in the china and earthenware trade.' *Econ. J.*, XII, 45 (March 1902), 129–32.

4603 **Barker**, Colin. *The Pilkington strike.* [London: International Socialists, 1970.] 24p. (Socialist Worker pamphlet.)

4604 *Report of a Court of Inquiry under Professor John C. Wood, LL.M., into a dispute between Pilkington Bros. Ltd. (and subsidiaries of that company) and certain of their employees.* London: H.M.S.O., 1970. 28p.

g. TIMBER AND FURNITURE

4605 *The bedstead workers' great strike.* [Birmingham?], 1889. 6p.

4606 **Smith**, W. *Fifty to one: who is to win? The big Bedstead Manufacturers' Association, or the little maker?* London, 1895. 55p.

h. PAPER, PRINTING, AND PUBLISHING

4607 **Ministry of Labour and National Service.** *Report of a Court of Inquiry into the nature and circumstances of a dispute between the British Federation of Master Printers and the Printing and Kindred Trades Federation.* London: H.M.S.O., 1946. 24p. (Cmd. 6912.)
Chairman: William Gorman.

4608 **Ministry of Labour and National Service.** *Report of a Court of Inquiry into the causes and circumstances of a dispute between the London Master Printers' Association and the London Society of Compositors.* London: H.M.S.O., 1950. (Cmd. 8074.)
Chairman: J. L. Brierly.

4609 **Ministry of Labour and National Service.** *Report of a Court of Inquiry into a dispute between D. C. Thomson and Company Limited and certain workpeople, members of the National Society of Operative Printers and Assistants.* London: H.M.S.O., 1952. 47p. (Cmd. 8607.)

4610 **Ministry of Labour and National Service.** *Report of a Court of Inquiry into an apprehended dispute affecting the National Society of Operative Printers and Assistants, the Printing Machine Managers Trade Society, Associated Newspapers Limited, and the Newspaper Proprietors Association.* London: H.M.S.O., 1953. 28p. (Cmd. 8931).
Dispute arising from the transfer of the production of the *Daily Sketch* to the offices of the *News of the World.*

4611 **Ministry of Labour and National Service.** *Report of a Court of Inquiry into a dispute between members of the Newspaper Proprietors' Association and members of the Amalgamated Engineering Union and the Electrical Trades Union.* London: H.M.S.O., 1955. 12p. (Cmd. 9439.)

4612 **Ministry of Labour and National Service.** *Report of a Court of Inquiry into the causes and circumstances of disputes between the London Master Printers' Association and the London Typographical Society and the Association of the Correctors of the Press.* London: H.M.S.O., 1956. 19p. (Cmd. 9717.)

4613 **Ministry of Labour.** *Report of a Court of Inquiry into the problems caused by the introduction of web-offset machines in the printing industry, and the problems arising from the introduction of other modern printing techniques and the arrangements which should be adopted within the industry for dealing with them.* London: H.M.S.O., 1967. 92p. (Cmnd. 3184.)
Chairman: Lord Cameron.

4614 **Gennard**, John. *Major post-war disputes in the printing industry.* 1968. 346p. (M.A. (Econ.) thesis, University of Manchester.)

See also: 13,296.

4. Construction

4615 **Ministry of Labour.** *Report by a Court of Inquiry concerning the dispute in the building industry, 1924.* London: H.M.S.O., 1924. 26p. (Cmd. 2192.)
Chairman: Lord Buckmaster.

4616 **Ministry of Labour.** *Report by a Court of Inquiry concerning disputes between plasterers and joiners in Scotland.* London: H.M.S.O., 1937. 13p. (Cmd. 5554.)
Chairman: Alexander Gray.

4617 **Parsons**, Owen Henry. 'Conciliation machinery. 2. Building.' *Ind. Law Rev.*, I, 11 (April 1947), 335–7.

4618 **Ministry of Labour.** *Report of a Court of Inquiry into trade disputes at the Barbican and Horseferry Road construction sites in London.* London: H.M.S.O., 1967. 92p. (Cmnd. 3396.)
Chairman: Lord Cameron.

4619 **Department of Employment and Productivity.** *Report of the Committee of Inquiry under Professor E. H. Phelps Brown into certain matters concerning labour in building and civil engineering.* London: H.M.S.O., 1968. 192p. (Cmnd. 3714.)
Research supplement. v, 75p. (Cmnd. 3714-I.)

4620 **Eldridge**, John E. T. and **Roberts**, Geoffrey. 'An official dispute in the constructional engineering industry.' Eldridge, J. E. T. *Industrial disputes: essays in the sociology of industrial relations.* London: Routledge and Kegan Paul; New York: Humanities P., 1968. p. 126–54.

5. Gas, Electricity, and Water

4621 **Labour Association for Promoting Co-operative Production Based on the Co-partnership of the Workers.** *Brief account of the Labour Association's action in the South metropolitan gas strike.* London, 1889. 7p.

4622 **Ministry of Labour and National Service.** *Report of a Court of Inquiry into the causes and circumstances of a dispute between the Electrical Trades Union and the London Electricity Board.* London: H.M.S.O., 1951. 15p. (Cmd. 8232.)

4623 **Ministry of Labour and National Service.** *Report of a Court of Inquiry into a dispute between the National Federated Electrical Association and the Electrical Trades Union.* London: H.M.S.O., 1953. 24p. (Cmd. 8968.)

4624 **Ministry of Labour.** *Report of a Court of Inquiry into the causes and circumstances of a dispute between the parties represented on the National Joint Industrial Council for the Electricity Supply Industry.* London: H.M.S.O., 1964. 54p. (Cmnd. 2361.)
Chairman: Sir Colin Pearson.

4625 *Report of a Court of Enquiry under Professor A. D. Campbell into a dispute between the parties represented on the National Joint Board for the Electricity Supply Industry.* London: H.M.S.O., 1970. 35p. (Cmnd. 4410.)

See also: 4751.

6. Transport and Communications

See also Part Five, IV, C.

a. GENERAL

4626 **Hikins**, H. R. 'The Liverpool general transport strike, 1911.' *Hist. Soc. Lanc. Chesh. Trans.*, CXIII (1961), 169–95.

b. RAILWAYS

4627 **Liberty and Property Defence League.** *Trade-unionism and free labour: speeches in the House of Lords by the Earl of Wemyss, Earl Fortescue, Lord Bramwell.* London: Hansard Publishing Union, 1891. 11p.
'The Scottish railway strike. On the question of protection for unionists and non-unionists who are willing to work.' (Ottley).

4628 **Mavor**, James. 'The Scottish railway strike.' *Econ. J.*, I, 1 (March 1891), 204–18.

4629 **Mavor**, James. *The Scottish railway strike, 1891: a history and criticism.* Edinburgh: W. Brown, 1891. 66p.

4630 **Maxwell**, Herbert. 'The Scottish railway strike.' *Nineteenth Century*, XXIX, 168 (February 1891), 238–50.

4631 **Croker**, Edward J. O'B. *Retrospective lessons on railway strikes, United Kingdom.* London: Simpkin, Marshall, Hamilton, Kent; Cork: Guy, 1898. vi, 205p.

4632 *The cause and cure of railway labor disputes; to railway shareholders and the men who earn the dividends. By an experienced railwayman.* London: Simpkin, Marshall, 1902. 16p.

4633 *Report to the Board of Trade upon matters connected with the establishment and working of railway conciliation boards, set up in accordance with the agreement of 6th November 1907.* London: H.M.S.O., 1909. (Cd. 4534.)

4634 *Railway strike (employment of military): correspondence between Home Office and local authorities.* London: H.M.S.O., 1911. 40p. (H.C. 323.)

4635 **Royal Commission on the Working of the Railway Conciliation and Arbitration Scheme of 1907.** *Report.* 1911. 24p. (Cd. 5922.)
Evidence, appendices, index. vii, 788p. (Cd. 6014.)
Chairman: D. Harrel.

4636 **Shann**, Montague Churchill. *The lesson of the railway strike; or, The true method of co-partnership between labour and capital, particularly in the coming motor industry.* London, 1911. 7p.

4637 **Stephenson**, W. Tetley. 'The Railway Conciliation Scheme, 1907, and the report of the Royal Commission thereon.' *Econ. J.*, XXI, 84 (December 1911), 503–12.
'The major portion of this article was written prior to the appearance of the report of the Royal Commission.'

4638 **Taylor**, Graham. *The English railway strike and its revolutionary bearings.* Chicago, 1911. 15p. (City Club bulletin, vol. 4, no. 19.)
Paper read 11 October 1911.
Also appeared in *Survey*, 7 (October), under the title 'England's revolutionary strike'.

4639 **Railway News.** 'Railway conciliation boards.' *Jubilee of the* Railway News, *1864–1914.* London: *Railway News*, 1914. p. 191.

4640 **Henderson**, Hubert Douglas. 'The railway strike.' *Econ. J.*, XXIX, 116 (December 1919), 451–9.

4641 **Labour Research Department.** *Report from the Labour Research Department to the*

National Union of Railwaymen on publicity work undertaken in connection with the recent strike. London: L.R.D., 1919. 8p.

Special supplement to monthly circular of the Labour Research Department.

4642 **Montagu**, *Lord.* 'On the footplate.' *Nineteenth Century*, LXXXVI, 513 (November 1919), 851–8.

Experiences during late railway strike as a volunteer.

4643 **National Transport Workers' Federation.** *Railway dispute, 1919: report to the labour movement.* London, 1919. 14p.

4644 **Saldanha**, C. N. *An inner view of the railway strike, by a student of nature.* London: H. Deane, 1919. 8p.

4645 **Sellers**, Edith. 'Among strikers' womenfolk.' *Nineteenth Century*, LXXXV, 507 (May 1919), 971–80.

4646 **Thatcher**, A. J. *The 1919 railway strike and the settlement of January, 1920.* Manchester, 1920. 8p.

4647 **Lloyd George**, David. *The Prime Minister states the case for the nation, replying to a deputation representing the National Union of Railwaymen and the Transport Workers Federation at a conference held at No. 10, Downing Street, on Thursday, April 14th, 1921.* London: H.M.S.O., 1921. 15p.

4648 **Associated Society of Locomotive Engineers and Firemen.** *Locomotive journal.* Special strike issue (February 1924). London, 1924. 94p.

'The full history of the first official national railway strike of locomotivemen, Jan. 20–29, 1924.'

4649 **Ministry of Labour.** *Report by a Court of Inquiry concerning railway shopmen – Gt. Northern Section of the London and North Eastern Railway.* London: H.M.S.O., 1924. 11p. (Cmd. 2113.)

Chairman: Holman Gregory.

4650 **Ministry of Labour.** *Report by a Court of Inquiry concerning railway shopmen – Gt. Central Section of the London and North Eastern Railway.* London: H.M.S.O., 1926. 12p. (Cmd. 2583.)

Chairman: Holman Gregory.

4651 **Ministry of Labour and National Service.** *Report of a Court of Inquiry into applications by the trade unions representing the employees of the railway companies for improvements in wages and reductions in weekly hours of work.* London: H.M.S.O., 1947. 31p. (Cmd. 7161.)

Chairman: C. W. Guillebaud.

4652 **Ministry of Labour and National Service.** *Report of a Board of Conciliation appointed by the Minister of Labour and National Service to assist in the consideration of certain problems relating to wages and conditions of service of railway shopmen with a view to promoting a settlement.* London: H.M.S.O., 1949.

Chairman: John Forster.

4653 **Ministry of Labour and National Service.** *Report of a Court of Inquiry into applications for an improvement in wages and salaries made to the Railway Executive by the National Union of Railwaymen, the Associated Society of Locomotive Engineers and Firemen, and the Railway Clerks' Association.* London: H.M.S.O., 1951. v, 70p. (Cmd. 8154.)

4654 **Ministry of Labour and National Service.** Court of Inquiry into a Dispute between the British Transport Commission and the National Union of Railwaymen. *Interim report.* London: H.M.S.O., 1955. 7p. (Cmd. 9352.)

Final report. London: H.M.S.O., 1955. 28p. (Cmd. 9372.)

Chairman: John Cameron.

4655 **Roberts**, Benjamin Charles. 'Wages on the railways.' *Polit. Q.*, XXVI, 2 (April–June 1955), 117–27.

On the Cameron Report on the wage dispute.

4656 **Ministry of Labour.** *Report of a Court of Inquiry under Mr A. J. Scamp into the issues arising in negotiations between the British Railways Board, the Associated Society of Locomotive Engineers and Firemen and the National Union of Railwaymen.* London: H.M.S.O., 1965. 31p. (Cmnd. 2779.)

4657 **Brooker**, R. P. 'The British rail strike of 1887.' *Labour Hist.*, 11 (November 1966), 54–61.

'Documents . . . taken from a series of articles which appeared in the *Railway magazine* (London) during the period 1912–14, under the title *Leaves from the log of a locomotive engineer*. The author . . . was . . . Robert Weatherburn . . . [who] held a senior position [on the staff of the Midland Railway Company] at the time of the railwaymen's strike . . .'

4658 **McCarthy**, William Edward John. 'How silly a dispute?' *New Soc.*, X, 271 (7 December 1967), 817–18.

4659 **Ministry of Labour.** *Report of a Court of Inquiry under Professor D. J. Robertson into a dispute between the British Railways Board and the National Union of Railwaymen concerning guards and shunters.* London: H.M.S.O., 1967. 40p. (Cmnd. 3426.)

4660 **Hudson**, Kenneth. *Working to rule: railway workshop rules; a study of industrial discipline.* Bath: Adams and Dart, 1970. 115p.

c. ROAD

4661 **Carter**, J. 'The transport workers' strike in London.' *Econ. Rev.*, XXII, 4 (October 1912), 436–41.

An account of events, reproducing relevant documents.

4662 **Tillett**, Ben. *History of the London Transport workers' strike, 1911.* London: National

Transport Workers' Federation, 1912. xii, 71p.

4663 **Ministry of Labour**. *Report by a Court of Inquiry concerning the dispute in the tramway industry*. London: H.M.S.O., 1921. 9p. (H.C. 37.)
Chairman: Sir David Harrel.

4664 **Ministry of Labour**. *Interim report by a Court of Inquiry concerning the stoppage of the London tramway and omnibus services, 1924*. London: H.M.S.O., 1924. 5p. (Cmd. 2087.)
Report. 1924. 28p. (Cmd. 2101.)
Chairman: Sir Arthur Colefax.

4665 **Davies**, Ernest. 'The London bus strike and the public corporation'. *Polit. Q.*, VIII, 3 (July–September 1937), 379–91.

4666 **Marsh**, F. *Busmen on strike*. London, 1937. 72p.

4667 **Ministry of Labour**. *Interim report by a Court of Inquiry concerning the stoppage of the London Central Omnibus Services, 1937*. London: H.M.S.O., 1937. 6p. (Cmd. 5454.)
Report. 1937. 24p. (Cmd. 5464.)
Chairman: John Forster.

4668 **Ministry of Labour and National Service**. *Report by a Court of Inquiry into a difference between the two sides of the National Council for the Omnibus Industry on the trade union application for a national wages and conditions agreement*. London: H.M.S.O., 1946. 19p. (Cmd. 6796.)
Chairman: Sir John Forster.

4669 **Ministry of Labour and National Service**. *Report by a Court of Inquiry into the differences which have arisen between the two sides of the National Joint Industrial Council for the Road Haulage Industry on the trade union claim*. London: H.M.S.O., 1947. 10p. (Cmd. 7025.)
Chairman: Lord Terrington.

4670 **Ministry of Labour and National Service**. *Report of a Court of Enquiry into a dispute between employers represented by the Employer's side and trade unions represented by the Trade Union Side of the National Council for the Omnibus Industry*. London: H.M.S.O., 1954. 18p. (Cmd. 9093.)
Chairman: H. G. Hanbury.

4671 **Frow**, Edmund and **Hikins**, H. R. 'The Liverpool central transport strike of 1911.' *Marxism Today*, VIII, 3 (March 1964), 78–86.

4672 **Solidarity**. *Glasgow busmen in action*. London: B. Potter, 1964. 20p. (Solidarity. Pamphlets 17.)
1964 bus strike.

4673 **Ministry of Labour**. *Report of the Committee of Inquiry into the causes and circumstances of the difference existing between the two sides of the National Council for the Omnibus Industry*. London: H.M.S.O., 1965.
Chairman: Sir Roy Wilson.

4674 **Ministry of Labour**. *Report by Mr A. J. Scamp of a Court of Inquiry into the causes and circumstances of the dispute between employers in membership of the Longbridge Group of Delivery Agents and their employees*. London: H.M.S.O., 1966. 23p. (Cmnd. 2905.)

4675 **Ministry of Labour**. *Report by Mr A. J. Scamp of a Court of Inquiry into the causes and circumstances of the dispute between Motor Vehicle Collections Ltd. and Avon Car Transporters Ltd., both of Solihull, on the one hand and their respective employees on the other hand*. London: H.M.S.O., 1966. 16p.

d. SEA

4676 **Abraham**, W. H. 'The Hull strike.' *Econ. Rev.*, III, 3 (July 1893), 357–63.

4677 **Edwards**, Clement. 'The Hull shipping dispute.' *Econ. J.*, III, 10 (June 1893), 345–51.

4678 **Boulton**, S. B. 'A typical instance of conciliation.' *Econ. J.*, IV, 16 (December 1894), 713–15.
The Victoria Steamboat Company dispute.
The author was Chairman of the London Labour Conciliation and Arbitration Board.

4679 **Hood**, W. H. *The blight of insubordination: the Lascar question and rights and wrongs of the British shipmaster*. London, Liverpool: Spottiswoode, 1903. 103p.
'Including the Mercantile Marine Committee Report.'

4680 **Rose**, R. Barrie. 'A Liverpool sailor's strike in the eighteenth century.' *Lanc. Chesh. Antiq. Soc. Trans.*, LXVIII (1960), 85–92.
1775 strike.

4681 **Doxey**, John Martyn. *The seamen's strikes of 1960: an examination of recent industrial relations in the merchant shipping industry*. 1961. x, 218p. (M.A. (Econ.) thesis, University of Manchester.)

4682 **Bugler**, Jeremy. 'A sea of troubles.' *New Soc.*, VII, 189 (12 May 1966), 5–6.

4683 **Foulser**, George. *Unholy alliance; the 1966 seamen's strike: an analysis*. London: Syndicalist Workers' Federation, 1966. 16p. (Direct action pamphlets 10.)

4684 **Foot**, Paul. 'The seamen's struggle.' Blackburn, R. and Cockburn, A. (eds.). *The incompatibles: trade union militancy and the consensus*. Harmondsworth: Penguin in association with *New Left Review*, 1967. p. 169–209.
1966 strike.

4685 **Nolan**, Michael. *Lessons of the 1966 seamen's strike*. London: Socialist Labour League, 1967. [24]p. (Socialist Labour League. Pamphlets.)

4686 **McCord**, Norman. 'The seamen's strike of 1815 in north-east England.' *Econ. Hist. Rev.*, 2nd ser., XXI, 1 (April 1968), 127–43.

e. PORT AND INLAND WATER

4687 **London and St Katherine Docks Company**. *Report of an address on the late labour* *strike* . . . London, 1889. 74p.

4688 **Manning**, Henry Edward, Cardinal, and **Burns**, John. 'The great strike.' *New Rev.*, I, 5 (October 1889), 410–22.
Dock strike, 1889.
Cardinal Manning, p. 410–11.
J. Burns. p. 410–22.

4689 **Smee**, Alfred Hutchinson. *The great strike and its lesson: labour, capital and investment, being six articles* . . . Carshalton: W. Pile, 1889. 16p.

4690 **Smith**, *Sir* Hubert Llewellyn and **Nash**, Vaughan. *The story of the dockers' strike.* London: Fisher Unwin, 1889. 190p.

4691 **The Times**. 'Public sympathy v. political economy.' *R. Statist. Soc. J.*, LII, 4 (December 1889), 595–604.
Three articles from *The Times*, September–October 1889, on the dock strike.

4692 **Champion**, Henry Hyde. *The great dock strike in London, August, 1889.* London: Swan Sonnenschein, 1890. 30p.

4693 **Adderley**, James G. 'Some results of the great dock strike.' *Econ. Rev.*, II, 2 (April 1892), 202–13.

4694 *Report on certain disturbances at Rotherhithe on 11th June, 1912, and the conduct of the police in connection therewith.* London: H.M.S.O., 1912. 6p. (Cd. 6367.)
By Chester Jones.

4695 *Report on the present disputes affecting transport workers in the Port of London and on the Medway, with minutes of evidence.* London: H.M.S.O., 1912. 50p. (Cd. 6229.)

4696 **Spender**, Harold. 'The London port strike.' *Contemp. Rev.*, CII (August 1912), 173–82.

4697 **Leslie**, S. 'Cardinal Manning & the London strike of 1889.' *Dublin Rev.*, CLXVII (October 1920), 219–31.

4698 **Ministry of Labour**. *Report by a Court of Inquiry concerning the dock labour dispute, 1924.* London: H.M.S.O., 1924. 4p. (Cmd. 2056.)
Chairman: Holman Gregory.

4699 **Ministry of Labour**. *Report by a Court of Inquiry concerning the threatened stoppage of work at the coal exporting ports of Great Britain, 1924.* London: H.M.S.O., 1924. 12p. (Cmd. 2149.)
Chairman: Lord Anderson.

4700 **Ministry of Labour and National Service**. *London docks dispute, March 1945: report of Committee of Enquiry.* London: H.M.S.O., 1945.
Chairman: Lord Ammon.

4701 **Ministry of Labour and National Service**. *Port transport industry: report of a Committee of Investigation on a difference between employers and workpeople regarding the national minimum wage and the pieceworkers' minimum guarantee.* London: H.M.S.O., 1945. 5p.
Chairman: Mr Justice Evershed.

4702 **Ministry of Labour and National Service**. *Review of the British docks strikes, 1949.* London: H.M.S.O., 1949. 47p. (Cmd. 7851.)

4703 **Knowles**, Kenneth Guy Jack Charles. 'The post-war dock strikes (in Britain).' *Polit. Q.*, XXII, 3 (July–September 1951), 266–90.

4704 **Ministry of Labour and National Service**. *Report on certain aspects of the Manchester (Salford) dock strike, April–June, 1951.* London: H.M.S.O., 1951. 32p. (Cmd. 8375.)

4705 **Ministry of Labour and National Service**. *Unofficial stoppages in the London Docks: report of a Committee of Enquiry.* London: H.M.S.O., 1951. iv, 44p. (Cmd. 8236.)
Chairman: Sir Frederick Leggett.

4706 **McKelvey**, Jean Trepp. *Dock labor disputes in Great Britain: a study in the persistence of unrest.* Ithaca, N.Y.: Cornell University, New York State School of Industrial and Labor Relations, 1953. vi, 61p. (Bulletin 23.)

4707 **Ministry of Labour and National Service**. *Interim report of a Court of Inquiry into a dispute in the London Docks.* London: H.M.S.O., 1954. 8p. (Cmd. 9302.)
Final report of a Court of Enquiry into a dispute in London Docks. 1954. (Cmd. 9310.)
Chairman: Sir F. R. Evershed.

4708 **Ministry of Labour and National Service**. *Report of a Court of Inquiry into a dispute between employers who are members of the employers' side and workpeople who are represented on the workpeople's side of the National Joint Council for the Port Transport Industry.* London: H.M.S.O., 1958. 20p. (Cmnd. 510.)

4709 **Ministry of Labour**. Committee to consider the Difficulties which have Arisen in the Port of London concerning Ocean Shipowners' Tally Clerks. *Ocean shipowners' tally clerks: report.* London: H.M.S.O., 1960. 17p.
Chairman: Hugh Lloyd-Williams.

4710 **Stafford**, Ann, (*pseud.*) [i.e. Ann Pedlar]. *A match to fire the Thames.* London: Hodder and Stoughton, 1961. 219p.
Match girls' strike, 1888.
Dock strike, 1889.

4711 **Ministry of Labour**. *Report of an inquiry by Mr A. D. Flanders into the causes and circumstances of a difference over the appointment of dock foremen at Southampton Docks.* London: H.M.S.O., 1964. 26p.

4712 **Oram**, Robert Bruce. 'The great strike of 1889: the fight for the "dockers' tanner".' *Hist. Today*, XIV, 8 (August 1964), 532–41.

4713 **Saffin**, N. W. 'The portrait of Cardinal Manning in Ballarat Trades Hall.' *Labour Hist.*, 8 (May 1965), 6–9.

4714 **Ministry of Labour**. *Report by Mr. Allan Flanders of a Committee of Investigation into the Bristol and Avonmouth Docks dispute.* London: H.M.S.O., 1966. 24p.

4715 **Ministry of Labour**. *Report by Mr. H. A. Clegg of a Court of Inquiry into a dispute concerning the operation of fork lift trucks at the Albert Edward Dock, North Shields.* London: H.M.S.O., 1966. 30p. (Cmnd. 3061.)

4716 **Ministry of Labour**. *Report of a Court of Inquiry into the causes and circumstances of a strike by members of the National Amalgamated*

Stevedores and Dockers in the Port of London, and into practices relevant thereto. London: H.M.S.O., 1966. 37p. (Cmnd. 3146.)
Chairman: Sir Roy Wilson.

4717 **Sams**, K. I. 'The Devlin Committee and unrest in the British ports.' *J. Ind. Relat.*, LX, 1 (March 1967), 65–71.

4718 **Northcote**, Catherine. *A docker goes on strike.* London: Oxford U.P., 1968. 32p. (People of the past, series G: the nineteenth century 6.)
For children.

4719 **Rowe**, David J. 'The strikes of the Tyneside keelmen in 1809 and 1819.' *Int. Rev. of Soc. Hist.*, XIII, 1 (1968), 58–75.

4720 **Pattison**, George. 'The coopers' strike at the West India Dock, 1821.' *Mar. Mirror*, LV, 2 (May 1969), 163–84.

4721 **Department of Employment and Productivity.** *Report of a Committee of Inquiry into the difference between Newlyn Pier and Harbour Commissioners and the Transport and General Workers Union over the reinstatement of former employees.* London: H.M.S.O., 1970. 11p.
Chairman: Professor Walter Hagenbuch.

4722 **Department of Employment and Productivity.** *Report of a Court of Inquiry under the Rt. Hon. the Lord Pearson into a dispute between the parties represented on the National Joint Council for the Transport Industry.* London: H.M.S.O., 1970. 28p. (Cmnd. 4429.)

f. AIR

4723 **Ministry of Labour and National Service.** *Report of a Court of Inquiry into the causes and circumstances of a dispute between the British Overseas Airways Corporation and the Merchant Navy and Airline Officers' Association.* London: H.M.S.O., 1957. 20p. (Cmnd. 105).

4724 **Ministry of Labour and National Service.** *Report of a Court of Inquiry into the causes and circumstances of a dispute at London Airport existing between employers and unions represented on the National Joint Council for Civil Air Transport.* London: H.M.S.O., 1958. 42p. (Cmnd. 608.)

4725 **Ministry of Labour.** *Report of a Court of Inquiry under Mr A. J. Scamp into the dispute between the British Air Line Pilots Association and the National Joint Council for Civil Air Transport.* London: H.M.S.O., 1967. 32p. (Cmnd. 3428.)

4726 **Ministry of Labour.** *Report of a Court of Inquiry under Lord Pearson into the dispute between the British Overseas Airways Corporation and the British Air Line Pilots Association.* London: H.M.S.O., 1968. 45p. (Cmnd. 3551.)

4727 **Department of Employment and Productivity** and **Board of Trade.** Committee of Inquiry into the Disruption of Operations and Industrial Relations at Heathrow (London) Airport. *First report.* London: H.M.S.O., 1970. 24p. (Cmnd. 4405.)
Final report. 1970. 37p. (Cmnd. 4449.)
Chairman: Professor D. J. Robertson.

g. POSTAL SERVICES AND TELECOMMUNICATIONS

4728 **Schneider**, B. V. H. 'The British post office strike of 1964.' Ocheltree, K. (ed.). *Government labor relations in transition.* Chicago: Public Personnel Association, [1965?]. p. 27–33.

4729 *Report of a Court of Inquiry by Mr. E. T. C. Grint, C.B.E., into a dispute at the British Broadcasting Corporation.* London: H.M.S.O., 1969. 28p. (Cmnd. 4240.)

7. Distribution

4730 **Ministry of Labour.** *Report by a Court of Inquiry concerning the dispute at Covent Garden and the threatened stoppage of work at the ports and elsewhere arising therefrom.* London: H.M.S.O., 1924. 39p. (Cmd. 2244.)
Chairman: John A. Compston.

4731 **Ministry of Labour and National Service.** *Report by a Court of Inquiry set up to inquire whether there are any causes of industrial unrest amongst the workers concerned likely to affect the future smooth and efficient running of Smithfield Market.* London: H.M.S.O., 1946. 16p. (Cmd. 6932.)
Chairman: Sir John Forster.

4732 **Constable**, Harry. *The lessons of the Covent Garden defeat.* London: Peter Fryer, 1957. 11p.
On the strikes at Covent Garden and the Port of London, 1957.

4733 **Ministry of Labour and National Service.** *Report of the Committee of Inquiry appointed by the Minister of Labour and National Service to inquire whether there are any causes of industrial unrest arising from the present arrangements for the delivery, handling and distribution of meat in Smithfield Market.* London: H.M.S.O., 1958. 40p.
Chairman: R. M. Wilson.

4734 **Ministry of Labour** and **Ministry of Agriculture, Fisheries and Food.** *Report of the Committee of Inquiry into the dispute at the Spitalfields, Borough, Stratford, Brentford and King's Cross Markets.* London: H.M.S.O., 1964. 23p.
Chairman: D. T. Jack.

8. Professional and Scientific Services

4735 **Thompson**, A. Hamilton. 'Note on clerical strikes.' *Thores. Soc. Publs.*, XXVIII, 3 (1926), 236–7.
'. . . the rebellion of the canons of Beverley against Archbishop Alexander Nevill's at-

tempt to exercise his ordinary jurisdiction as visitor of their church in 1381, which was an infringement upon their liberties.'

4736 **Barlow**, Graham. 'Some latent influences in a pay claim: an examination of a white-collar dispute.' *Br. J. Ind. Relat.*, VII, 2 (July 1969), 200–10.

4737 **Department of Employment and Productivity** and **Department of Education and Science.** *Report of the Committee of Inquiry into the dispute between the Durham Local Education Authority and the National Association of Schoolmasters.* London: H.M.S.O., 1969. 43p. (Cmnd. 4152.)
Chairman: W. E. J. McCarthy.

4738 **Griffiths**, Toni. *The teachers' strike.* London: National Union of Teachers, 1970. 29p.

4739 **Margerison**, C. J. and **Elliott**, C. K. 'A predictive study of the development in teacher militancy.' *Br. J. Ind. Relat.*, VIII, 3 (November 1970), 408–17.

4740 **Price**, Peter. 'The teachers' strike.' *Trade Un. Regist.* (1970), 173–7.

9. Miscellaneous Services

4741 **Industrial Law Review.** 'Reflections on the hotel strike.' *Ind. Law Rev.*, I, 7 (December 1946), 203–7.

4742 **Ministry of Labour and National Service.** *Report of a Court of Inquiry into the causes and circumstances of a dispute between the Savoy Hotel Limited and members of the National Union of General and Municipal Workers.* London: H.M.S.O., 1947. 45p. (Cmd. 7266.)
Chairman: Sir John Forster.

4743 **Ministry of Labour and National Service.** *Report of the Independent Committee appointed by the Minister of Labour and National Service to make an award on a question which has arisen between the British Broadcasting Corporation and the Musicians' Union concerning minimum fees for casual studio broadcasts and to examine and make recommendations on certain other questions.* London: H.M.S.O., 1949.
Chairman: Sir John Forster.

4744 **Ministry of Labour and National Service.** *Report of a Committee of Investigation into a difference regarding the terms and conditions of Association Football players.* London: H.M.S.O., 1952. 20p.

4745 **Ministry of Labour.** *Report of a Committee of Investigation into a difference between the Film Artistes' Association and the Film Production Association of Great Britain over the operation of the employment agency for crowd artistes known as Central Castings Limited.* London: H.M.S.O., 1967. iii, 16p.

10. Public Administration

a. NATIONAL GOVERNMENT

4746 **Edwards**. Kenneth. *The mutiny at Invergordon.* London: Putnam, 1937. xvi, 425p.

4747 **Home Office.** *Carlisle and District State Management Scheme: inquiry into certain allegations made by the Civil Service Union.* London: H.M.S.O., 1957. (Cmnd. 168.)
Report by C. S. S. Burt.

4748 **Frankels**, S. J. 'Arbitration in the British Civil Service.' *Publ. Adm.*, XXVIII, 3 (Autumn 1960), 197–211.

4749 **Hughes**, H. D. 'The settlement of disputes in the public service.' *Publ. Adm.*, XLVI, 1 (Spring 1968), 45–61.
Based on a paper delivered at the 18th Congress of the Public Services International, Paris, October 1967.

4750 **Divine**, David. *Mutiny at Invergordon.* London: Macdonald, 1970. 259p.

b. LOCAL GOVERNMENT AND THE POLICE

4751 **Laughlin**, A. C. 'The strike in the municipal gasworks at Glasgow.' *Econ. Rev.*, X, 2 (April 1900), 237–9.

4752 **Clynes**, John Robert. *The broken bargain in the Leeds Corporation men's strike.* Oldham, 1914. 15p.

4753 **Greenwood**, Arthur. 'The Leeds municipal strike.' *Econ. J.*, XXIV, 93 (March 1914), 138–45.
Followed by M. E. Sadler's note, 146–52.

4754 **Macgregor**, D. H. 'Municipal wage disputes.' *Econ. Rev.*, XXIV, 2 (April 1914), 145–52.

4755 *Report of special committee on the strike of municipal workmen, December 11th, 1913 to January 13th, 1914.* Leeds, 1914. 148p.

4756 **Hart**, J. M. 'The growth of representative machinery and police strikes.' *The British police.* London: Allen and Unwin, 1951. p. 39–43.
One section of chapter II: 'Historical background: to 1919'.

4757 **Reynolds**, Gerald William and **Judge**, Anthony. *The night the police went on strike.* London: Weidenfeld and Nicolson, 1968. 246p.

c. NATIONALISED INDUSTRIES

See also Part Five, IV, E, 2; Part Five, IV, E, 3, b; and Part Five, IV, E, 5–6.

4758 **Heilbroner**, Robert Louis. 'Labor unrest in the British nationalized sector.' *Soc. Res.*, XIX, 1 (March 1952), 61–78.
Observations gathered during a visit to England during the spring of 1951.

4759 **Chester**, Theodore Edward. 'Industrial conflicts in British nationalized industries.' Kornhauser, A., Dubin, R. and Ross, A. M. (eds.). *Industrial conflict.* New York, London: McGraw-Hill, 1954. p. 454–66.

V. JOINT CONSULTATION, INDUSTRIAL DEMOCRACY, AND WORKERS' CONTROL

See also Part Three, III, H–I.

A. GENERAL

Works on syndicalism are included in this section. See also Part Three, III, G, 9; and Part Five, I.

4760 **Zueblin**, Charles. 'Industrial democracy.' *J. Polit. Econ.*, VII, 2 (March 1899), 182–203.

4761 **Vivian**, Henry H. *Industrial democracy.* London, [1903?]. 8p.

4762 **Allen**, E. J. B. *Revolutionary unionism!* London: Industrialist League, 1909. 23p. (Industrialist library 1.)

4763 **Fabian Society**. Committee of Inquiry on the Control of Industry. *Memorandum by the chairman, Mrs Sidney Webb.* Letchworth, [*c.* 1910]. 11p.

4764 **Boyd-Carpenter**, William Boyd. *Syndicalism, being four addresses.* Blackburn: Standard P., 1912. 46p.

4765 **Harley**, John Hunter. *Syndicalism.* London, Edinburgh: Jack; New York: Dodge, 1912. 94p. (The people's books 80.)

4766 **Jenkinson**, A. J. 'Reflections on a pamphlet entitled "The miners' next step".' *Econ. Rev.*, XXII, 3 (July 1912), 302–12.

'The full title of the pamphlet is *The Miners' Next Step, being a suggested scheme for the Reorganization of the Federation*, issued by the Unofficial Reform Committee. It was printed at Tonypandy this year, but suppressed on the eve of publication.'

4767 **Lewis**, Arthur D. *Syndicalism and the general strike: an explanation.* Boston, Mass.: Small, Maynard, 1912. 320p.

English edition. London, Leipsic: Fisher Unwin, 1912.

Chapter VI. 'England.' p. 171–214.

4768 **McCartney**, W. *Syndicalism.* London, [1912]. 18p.

4769 **MacDonald**, James Ramsay. *Syndicalism: a critical examination.* London: Constable, 1912. vi, 74p.

4770 *The miners' next step, being a suggested scheme for the reorganisation of the Federation, issued by the Unofficial Reform Committee.* Tonypandy: R. Davies (printed), 1912. 31p.

4771 **Webb**, Sidney and **Webb**, Beatrice. *The labour unrest and the control of industry.* Letchworth, 1912. [8]p.

4772 **Webb**, Sidney and **Webb**, Beatrice. *What syndicalism means: an examination of the origin and motives of the movement with an analysis of its proposals for the control of industry.* London: National Committee for the Prevention of Destitution, 1912. 20p.

Published as a supplement to *The Crusade*, August 1912.

4773 **Cole**, George Douglas Howard. *Syndicalism: what validity does our enquiry show it to possess? Its influence on English trade unionism and the Labour Party.* London, [1913?]. 12 leaves.

4774 **Mann**, Tom. *From single tax to syndicalism.* London: Guy Bowman, 1913. xv, 112p.

4775 **Snowden**, Philip. *Socialism and syndicalism.* London, Glasgow: Collins Clear-Type P., 1913. 262p. (The nation's library.)

4776 **Tridon**, André. *The new unionism: a clear statement of the philosophy and practice of syndicalism.* New York: Huebsch, 1913. 198p.

4777 **Kirkaldy**, Adam Willis. *Economics and syndicalism.* Cambridge: Cambridge U.P., 1914. xii, 140p. (Cambridge manuals of science and literature.)

4778 **Mann**, Tom and **Lewis**, Arthur M. *Debate between Tom Mann and Arthur M. Lewis at the Garrick Theatre. Chicago, Illinois, Sunday, November 16, 1913.* Chicago: Kerr, 1914. 77p.

'Resolved, that economic organization is sufficient and political action unnecessary to the emancipation of the working class.' Affirmed by Tom Mann, denied by Arthur M. Lewis.

4779 **Wilshire**, Henry Gaylord. *Syndicalism: what it is.* London: Twentieth Century P., 1914. 8p.

4780 **Democritus**. *Before and after.* London: British Workers' League, 1916. 16p.

By Victor Fisher.

4781 **Macara**, *Sir* Charles Wright. *The Industrial Council and the mobilisation of the nation's industries.* London, 1916. 18p.

4782 **Fisher**, Victor. *The British Workers' League: a statement of our ideals and aims.* London: British Workers' League, 1917. 8p.

4783 **Fisher**, Victor. *Labour and democracy.* London: British Workers' League, 1917. 16p.

4784 **Gallacher**, William and **Paton**, John. *Towards industrial democracy: a memorandum on workshop control.* Paisley, [1917].

4785 **Gleason**, Arthur. *Inside the British Isles.* New York: Century Co., 1917. 434p.

Chapter II. Labour.

4786 **Renold**, *Sir* Charles Garonne. *Workshop committees: suggested lines of development.* Manchester, 1917. 34p.

Revised edition. London: Pitman, 1921. 48p. Reprinted from the Report of the British Association Sub-Committee on Industrial Unrest.

4787 **Sparkes**, Malcolm. *A memorandum on industrial self-government, with a draft scheme for a Builders' National Industrial Parliament.* London: Garton Foundation (Harrison and Sons), 1917. 28p.

4788 **Sladen**, Douglas (ed.). *Cosmos: a scheme for industrial co-operation between capital and labour.* [London, 1918.] 31p.

4789 **Stanton**, G. *The story of an industrial democracy, 1896–1917.* Leicester, 1918. 59p.

4790 **Benn**, *Sir* Ernest John Pickstone. *The industrial awakening*. London, 1919. 11p.

4791 **Cole**, George Douglas Howard. *Workers' control in industry*. London: Independent Labour Party, 1919. 15p. (Pamphlet 25.)

4792 **Hodges**, Frank. *Workers' control in the coal mining industry*. London: Mines for the Nation Campaign Committee, [1919]. 8p.

4793 **Humphrey**, G. H. *Workmen as directors*. London, 1919. 16p.

4794 **Husslein**, Joseph Casper. *Democratic industry: a practical study in social history*. New York: P. J. Kenedy, 1919. ix, 362p.

4795 *The miners' case for nationalisation: facts v. fairy tales* . . . Manchester: National Labour P., 1919. 15p.

4796 **Scott**, John Waugh. *Syndicalism and philosophical realism: a study in the correlation of contemporary social tendencies*. London: Black, 1919. 215p.

4797 **South Wales Socialist Society**. *Industrial democracy for miners: a plan for the democratic control of the mining industry*. Glasgow: the Society, 1919. 32p.

4798 **Zimmern**, *Sir* Alfred Eckhard. 'The control of industry after the war.' *Nationality & government; with other war-time essays*. London: Chatto and Windus, 1919. p. 252–77.

'A Paper read at a Conference of working-class organisations convened at Oxford, under the auspices of Ruskin College, on July 21–23, 1916.'

4799 **Cole**, George Douglas Howard. *Chaos and order in industry*. London: Methuen, 1920. viii, 292p.

On workers' control in industry.

In certain parts of the book have been incorporated articles which previously appeared in periodicals.

Contents:

I. 'The cause of strikes.'
II. 'Motives in industry.'
III. 'The reconstruction of profiteering.'
IV. 'The guild solution.'
V. 'Coal.'
VI. 'Railways.'
VII. ' "Encroaching control" *versus* "industrial peace".'
VIII. 'Engineering and shipbuilding.'
IX. 'Cotton and building.'
X. 'Distribution and the consumer.'
XI. 'The finance of industry.'
XII. 'The real class struggle.'

Appendices. I. 'Memorandum on the causes of and remedies for labour unrest, submitted to the National Industrial Conference by the trade union representatives.' II. 'The Miners' Bill – select provisions.'

4800 **Cole**, George Douglas Howard. 'Democracy in industry: a plea for industrial self-government.' Manchester University. *Labour and industry: a series of lectures*. Manchester: Manchester U.P.; London: Longmans, 1920. p. 59–81.

'A lecture delivered on Tuesday, November 4, 1919.'

4801 **Cramp**, C. T. 'Self-government by railwaymen.' Gleason, A. *What the workers want: a study of British labor*. London: Allen and Unwin, 1920. p. 212–14.

The author was President of the National Union of Railwaymen.

4802 **Hodges**, Frank. 'Workers' control.' Gleason, A. *What the workers want: a study of British labor*. London: Allen and Unwin, 1920. p. 169–83.

The author was Secretary of the Miners' Federation of Great Britain.

4803 **Marriott**, *Sir* John Arthur Ransome. *Syndicalism: economic and political*. London: Duckworth, 1920. 64p.

4804 **Meeker**, Royal. 'Employees' representation in management of industry.' *Am. Econ. Rev.*, x, 1 (March 1920), Supplements, 89–102.

4805 **Smillie**, Robert. 'The England the workers want – when – how.' Gleason, A. *What the workers want: a study of British labor*. London: Allen and Unwin, 1920. p. 215–21.

4806 **Stavenhagen**, C. H. *Labour's final weapon: 'industrial unionism'*. London: National Labour P., [1920?]. 40p.

4807 **Tawney**, Richard Henry. 'Recent thought on the government of industry.' Manchester University. *Labour and industry: a series of lectures*. Manchester: Manchester U.P.; London: Longmans, 1920. p. 191–212.

4808 **Cadbury Brothers**. *A works council in being: an account of the scheme in operation at Bournville Works*. Bournville: Bournville Works Publication Department, 1921. 16p.

Third revised impression. 1924. 19p.

4809 **Cole**, George Douglas Howard. *Workers' control series, 1–5*. London: National Guilds League, 1921. 5 pts.

Reprinted from the author's *Chaos and order in industry*. London: Methuen, 1920.

4810 **Thomas**, James Henry. *The red light on the railways*. London: Cassell, 1921. 143p.

4811 **Hobson**, John Atkinson. *Incentives in the new industrial order*. London: Parsons, 1922. 160p. (New era series 15.)

4812 **London District Committee of Workers' Councils**. *The workers' council, being an explanation of the aims and objects of workers' councils*. London: the Committee, 1922. [6]p. ([Pamphlets] 1.)

4813 **Flexner**, J. 'Some aspects of workers' control in industry.' *Economica*, III, 7 (January 1923), 67–82.

4814 **Elvin**, Herbert H. 'Labour's advancing ideals.' Hogue, R. W. (ed.). *British labour speaks*. New York: Boni and Liveright, 1924. p. 213–38.

4815 **Harty**, Frank. *A plan of industrial democracy*. [London? 1924?]. 7p.

4816 **Cole**, George Douglas Howard. 'Principles of industrial reconstruction.' Tracey, H.

(ed.). *The book of the Labour Party: its history, growth, policy, and leaders.* London: Caxton Publishing Co., 1925. Vol. 1. p. 265–79.

4817 **Harty**, Frank and **Valder**, Harry. *Wanted!! A practical solution to Britain's industrial problem: a contribution from New Zealand.* London: Mowbray, 1926. 32p.
Third edition. 1927.

4818 **Cheyney**, Edward Potts. 'The trend toward industrial democracy.' *Ann. Am. Acad. Polit. Soc. Sci.*, xc (July 1930), 1–9.

4819 **Cole**, George Douglas Howard. *Modern theories and forms of industrial organisation.* London: Gollancz, 1932. 159p. (Outline series.)
Also published in Rose, W. (ed.). *An outline of modern knowledge.* New York: Putnam, 1931. p. 663–700.

4820 **Clay**, Harold. *Workers' control.* London: Socialist League, 1933. 9p. (Forum lecture series 8.)

4821 **Clay**, Harold. 'Workers' control.' Addison, C., and others. *Problems of a socialist government.* London: Gollancz, 1933. p. 209–28.
The author was a member of the Transport and General Workers' Union.

4822 **Cole**, George Douglas Howard and **Mellor**, William (eds.). *Workers' control and self-government in industry.* London, 1933. 19p.
Memorandum prepared in 1933.
One of the signatories was G. D. H. Cole.
Reprinted by the Union of Post Office Workers [1943?].

4823 **Trades Union Congress**. *Workers' control.* London, 1933. 16p.

4824 **Macmillan**, H. *A reply to the* Economist *article on self-government for industry.* London, 1935. 4p.

4825 **Clynes**, John Robert. *Workers' control of industry.* 1936. 12p.

4826 **Political and Economic Planning**. 'Partners in industry.' *Planning*, v, 103 (13 July 1937), 1–15.

4827 **Rocker**, Rudolph. *Anarcho-syndicalism.* London: Secker and Warburg, 1938. 158p.

4828 **Wolman**, Leo. 'Industrial democracy.' Warren, R. B., Wolman, L. and Clay, H. *The state in society: a series of public lectures delivered under the auspices of McGill University, Montreal, January 23, 1939 – February 10, 1939.* London, New York: Oxford U.P., 1940. p. 90–103.

4829 **Brown**, Tom. *Trade unionism or syndicalism?* London: Freedom P., 1941. 29p.
Revised and enlarged edition. 1942. 23p.

4830 **International Labour Office**. 'Recent developments in joint production machinery in Great Britain.' *Int. Labour Rev.*, xlvi, 3 (September 1942), 284–98.

4831 **Political and Economic Planning**. 'Production committees.' *Planning*, 189 (26 May 1942), 1–16.

4832 **Populus**, (*pseud.*). *Take over the war industries!* London: Fabian Society Socialist Propaganda Committee, 1942. 23p. (Pamphlet 1.)

4833 **International Labour Office**. *Joint production committees in Great Britain.* Montreal: I.L.O., 1943. lv, 74p. (Studies and reports, series A, 42.)

4834 **Walpole**, George Stanley. *Joint consultation at all levels: a plea for a National Industrial Council elected on a democratic basis.* London, 1943. 15p.

4835 **Price**, John. *Democracy in industry: the problem of workers' control.* London: Workers' Educational Association, 1944. 56p. (W.E.A. study outlines.)

4836 **Riegelman**, Carol. *British joint production machinery.* Montreal: International Labour Office, 1944. v, 273p. (I.L.O. studies and reports, series A (industrial relations) 43.)
Expands and supplements: International Labour Office. *Joint production committees in Great Britain.* (Studies and reports, series A, 42.)

4837 **Walpole**, George Stanley. *Management and men: a study of the theory and practice of joint consultation at all levels.* London: Cape, 1944. 200p.

4838 **Walpole**, George Stanley. *Techniques of successful joint consultation.* London, 1944. 15p.

4839 **Watchurst**, J. L. and B., E. (*pseud.*). *Total efficiency through democracy.* Warrington, 1944. 19p.

4840 **International Labour Office**. 'Wartime methods of labour–management consultation in the United States and Great Britain.' *Int. Labour Rev.*, lii, 4 (October 1945), 309–34.
This article 'forms the concluding chapter of a study about to be published by the I.L.O. on *Labour-management collaboration in the United States*'.

4841 **McCartney**, W. *The French cooks' syndicate.* London, 1945. 30p.

4842 **Andrews**, George Francis Victor. *Jack and his master: an introduction to democracy in industry.* London: Socialist Book Centre, 1946. 32p.

4843 **Dahl**, Robert A. 'Workers' control of industry and the British Labor Party.' *Am. Polit. Sci. Rev.*, xli, 5 (October 1947), 875–900.

4844 **Reaveley**, Constance and **Winnington**, John. *Democracy and industry.* London: Chatto and Windus, 1947. x, 165p.

4845 **Association of Supervisory Staffs, Executives and Technicians** and **Fabian Society**. *Management by consent: a report by a research group appointed jointly by A.S.S.E.T. and the Fabian Society.* London: A.S.S.E.T., Fabian Publications, Gollancz, 1948. 29p. (Research series 125.)

4846 **Industrial Welfare Society**. *Joint consultation: a symposium.* London, 1948. 75p.

4847 **Labour Party**. *Industrial democracy.* London:

Labour Party, 1948. 15p. (Towards tomorrow 1.)

4848 **Ministry of Labour and National Service.** *Joint consultation, training within industry, works information and personnel management: report of conference held on September 15, 1948.* London: H.M.S.O., 1948.

4849 **British Institute of Management.** *Financial information and joint consultation.* London: B.I.M., 1949. 28p. (Conference series 10.)
Paper by G. Chelioti, with discussion.

4850 **Chalmers,** J. M., **Mikardo,** Ian and **Cole,** George Douglas Howard. *Consultation or joint management? A contribution to the discussion of industrial democracy.* London: Fabian Publications, Gollancz, 1949. 28p. (Fabian tract 277.)

4851 **Citrine,** Walter McLennan, Baron Citrine. *Joint consultation in industry: address, with replies to questions, by Lord Citrine, at a conference of chairmen and secretaries of works committees held at Buxton, March, 1949.* [London?]: British Electricity Authority, [1949?]. 36p.

4852 **Clay,** Harold. *Industrial democracy: its development and significance to the individual.* London: Oxford U.P., 1949. 18p. (Barnett House papers 30.)

4853 **International Labour Office.** 'Labour-management co-operation in the undertaking: recent surveys in France, the United States and Canada.' *Int. Labour Rev.*, LIX, 2 (February 1949), 192–205.

4854 **White,** Eirene. *Worker's control?* London: Fabian Publications, Gollancz, 1949. 29p. ('The challenge of 1950.' 'Challenge' series 4.)
Also published as *Fabian tract* 271.
Revised edition. 1951.

4855 **Brown,** William Robson and **Howell-Everson,** N. A. *Industrial democracy at work: a factual survey.* London: Pitman, 1950. xii, 104p.

4856 **Burdick,** E. L. *Syndicalism and industrial unionism in England until 1918.* 1950. (D.Phil. thesis, University of Oxford.)

4857 **Cadbury Brothers.** *A works council in action: an account of the scheme in operation at Bournville Works.* Bournville: Cadbury Bros., 1950. 48p.

4858 **Graves,** H. C. H. *Joint consultation at all levels in a small company: a case history.* London: British Institute of Management, 1950. 26p. (Winter proceedings 10.)

4859 **Institute of Personnel Management.** *Joint consultation: a practical approach.* London: the Institute, 1950. 47p.

4860 **Ministry of Labour.** *Joint consultation in industry.* London: H.M.S.O., 1950. 100p.

4861 **National Amalgamated Union of Life Assurance Workers.** *Memorandum on workers' control in insurance as a public service.* Manchester: Assurance Agents' Press, 1950. 12p.

4862 **Renold,** *Sir* Charles Garonne. *Joint consultation over thirty years: a case study.* London: Allen and Unwin, 1950. 195p.

4863 **Roper,** Joseph Igal. *Joint consultation and responsibility in modern industry.* London: Workers' Educational Association, 1950. 72p. (W.E.A. study outlines 19.)

4864 **Scott,** William Henry. *Joint consultation in a Liverpool manufacturing firm: a case study in human relations in industry.* Liverpool: U.P. of Liverpool, 1950. vi, 81p.
Preface by H. Mason Bibby.
Title page headed: University of Liverpool, Department of Social Science.

4865 **Simmons,** J. C. *Employee participation in industrial management in Great Britain.* 1950. (M.Sc.(Econ.) thesis, University of London.)

4866 **Cadbury Brothers.** *Bournville Works Youths' Committee.* Bournville, 1951. 16p.

4867 **Clegg,** Hugh Armstrong. *Industrial democracy and nationalization: a study prepared for the Fabian Society.* Oxford: Blackwell, 1951. viii, 147p.

4868 **Latham,** *Lord. Staff information and joint consultation: an address . . . on 20th November, 1951.* London: London Transport Executive, 1951. 7p.

4869 **Sansom,** Philip. *Syndicalism: the workers' next step.* London: Freedom P., 1951. 48p.
First published in *Freedom*, May–August 1951.

4870 **Tatlow,** Ann. 'Joint consultation in nine firms.' *Yorks. Bull. Econ. Soc. Res.*, III, 1 (February 1951), 37–55.

4871 **Turner-Samuels,** Moss and **Turner-Samuels,** David Jessel. *Industrial negotiation and arbitration, including matters relating to joint workshop and industrial collaboration and joint consultation.* London: Solicitors' Law Stationery Society, 1951. xxxii, 532p.

4872 **Veness,** Thelma. 'The human problems of building industry: joint consultation on building sites.' *Occup. Psychol.*, XXV, 2 (April 1951), 131–41.

4873 **Scott,** William Henry. *Joint consultation in industry: a sociological appraisal. A study of human relations in three Merseyside firms.* 1951–52. (Ph.D. thesis, University of Liverpool.)

4874 **Acton Society Trust.** *The framework of joint consultation.* London: the Trust, 1952. 35p. (Studies in nationalised industry series 10.)

4875 **Bannister,** D. *Workers' control in the modern world.* Leicester, 1952. 8p.

4876 **Lawther,** *Sir* William. *Can industrial democracy survive?* Leicester, 1952. 14p.

4877 **National Institute of Industrial Psychology.** *Joint consultation in British industry: a report of an inquiry undertaken by the National Institute of Industrial Psychology, sponsored by the Human Factors Panel of the Committee on Industrial Productivity.* London: Staples P., 1952. 276p.

4878 **Reckitt,** Maurice Benington. *Industry and democracy: the problem of workers' control; an* *historical outline*. London: League for Workers' Control, 1952. 16p.

4879 **Schuster**, *Sir* George Ernest. 'Self-government in industry.' Ministry of Labour and National Service. *The worker in industry: a series of ten centenary lectures delivered during Festival of Britain year*. London: H.M.S.O., 1952. p. 68–79.

4880 **Scott**, William Henry. *Industrial leadership and joint consultation: a study of human relations in three Merseyside firms*. Liverpool: U.P. of Liverpool, 1952. xii, 207p. (Social research series.)

4881 **Birmingham College of Technology**. Department of Industrial Administration. *The working of joint consultation*. 1953. 40p.

4882 **Campbell**, H. 'Some effects of joint consultation on the status and role of the supervisor.' *Occup. Psychol.*, XXVII, 4 (October 1953), 200–6.

4883 **Ostergaard**, G. N. *Public ownership in Great Britain: a study in the origin and development of socialist ideas concerning the control and administration of publicly-owned industries and services*. 1953. (D.Phil. thesis, University of Oxford.)

4884 **Sturmthal**, Adolf Fox. 'Nationalization and workers' control in Britain and France.' *J. Polit. Econ.*, LXI, 1 (February 1953), 43–79.

'This paper, part of a series of studies of nationalized enterprises in France and Great Britain, deals with the evolution of policy, first, on the issue of the nationalization of industry and, second, on workers' participation in the management of nationalized enterprises.'

4885 **Clegg**, Hugh Armstrong and **Chester**, Theodore Edward. 'Joint consultation.' Flanders, A. and Clegg, H. A. *The system of industrial relations in Great Britain* . . . Oxford: Blackwell, 1954. p. 323–64.

4886 **International Confederation of Free Trade Unions.** *Workers' participation in industry*. Brussels: I.C.F.T.U., 1954. 116p.

4887 **Wheelwright**, E. L. 'Joint consultation in Britain.' *Publ. Adm.* (Sydney), n.s., XIII, 4 (December 1954), 236–50.

Based on an address delivered to the New South Wales Regional Group of the Royal Institute of Public Administration, 4 March 1954.

4888 **Ridley**, F. F. *Syndicalism and the revolt against reason*. 1954–55. (Ph.D. thesis, University of London.)

4889 **Brown**, Tom. *What's wrong with the unions: a syndicalist answer*. London: Syndicalist Workers Federation, 1955. 16p. ('Direct action' pamphlets 1.)

4890 **Ditz**, Gerhard William. *Joint consultation in the British coal industry*. 1955. 492p. (Ph.D. thesis, Columbia University.)

4891 **Newman**, Jeremiah. *Co-responsibility in industry: social justice in labour-management relations*. Dublin: Gill, 1955. xxiii, 187p.

Preface by Michael P. Fogarty.

4892 **Scott**, William Henry. *Industrial democracy: a revaluation*. Liverpool: Liverpool U.P., 1955. 40p. (University of Liverpool, Department of Social Science. Occasional papers 2.)

4893 **Banks**, N. D. 'Joint consultation and negotiation.' *Ind. Law Rev.*, XI, 2 (October 1956), 59–66.

4894 **British Transport Commission**. *Making joint consultation work*. [London?]: the Commission, 1956. 15p.

4895 **Organisation for European Economic Co-operation.** European Productivity Agency. Trade Union Research and Information Service. *Productivity through joint consultation, based on a study in a British engine works*. Paris: O.E.E.C., 1956. 12p. (Project 175. Union studies 4.)

By F. E. Chappell.

4896 **Progressive League**. Occupational Democracy Group. *Democracy in our working lives: a report*. London: Progressive League, 1956. 47p.

4897 **Ross**, Norman Scott. 'Joint consultation and workers' control.' *Polit. Q.*, XXVII, 1 (January–March 1956), 82–92.

4898 **McKinlay**, H. *Formal joint consultation: a study of the Works Council Scheme in a chemical factory*. 1957. (B.Litt. thesis, University of Glasgow.)

4899 **Masefield**, Peter. 'Making joint consultation work.' Chisholm, C. (ed.). *Communication in industry*. London: Business Publications in association with Batsford, 1957. p. 203–17.

4900 **Roberts**, R. D. V. 'Joint consultation.' Thomson, D. C. (ed.). *Management, labour and community*. London: Pitman, 1957. p. 117–31.

4901 **Shell**, Kurt L. 'Industrial democracy and the British labor movement.' *Polit. Sci. Q.*, LXXII, 4 (December 1957), 515–39.

4902 **Brown**, Tom. *Nationalisation and the new boss class*. London: Syndicalist Workers Federation, 1958. 15p. ('Direct action' pamphlets 3.)

4903 **Roberts**, R. D. V. and **Sallis**, Howard. 'Labor-management co-operative committees in Britain's electricity supply industry.' *Ind. Labor Relat. Rev.*, XII, 1 (October 1958), 86–103.

4904 **Chester**, Theodore Edward and **Forsythe**, Gordon. '[Worker participation in management]: Great Britain.' *Indian J. Labour Econ.*, II, 2–3 (July–October 1959), 141–51.

4905 **De Schweinitz**, Karl. 'Industrialization, labor controls, and democracy.' *Econ. Dev. Cult. Change*, VII, 4 (July 1959), 385–404.

4906 **Fuerstenberg**, Friedrich. 'The dynamics of joint consultation.' *Br. J. Sociol.*, X, 3 (September 1959), 204–12.

4907 **Organisation for European Economic Co-operation.** European Productivity

Agency. *Joint consultation in practice: a survey in British industry.* Paris: O.E.E.C., 1959. 43p. (Industrial version 1.)

4908 **Roberts**, R. D. V. and **Sallis**, Howard. 'Joint consultation in the electricity supply industry, 1949–59.' *Publ. Adm.*, XXXVII, 2 (Summer 1959), 115–33.

4909 **Syndicalist Workers' Federation.** *Workers' control.* London: the Federation, 1959. 17p. ('Direct action' pamphlets 4.)

4910 **Broadley**, O. *The colliery consultative committee.* 1959–60. (M.A. thesis, University of Liverpool.)

4911 **Stewart**, F. G. *Consultative councils in the nationalised gas and electricity industries.* 1959–60. (M.A. thesis, University of Liverpool.)

4912 **Weinberg**, R. L. '*Workers' control': a study in British socialist thought.* 1959–60. (Ph.D. thesis, University of London.)

4913 **Clegg**, Hugh Armstrong. *A new approach to industrial democracy.* Oxford: Blackwell, 1960. 140p.

'Published under the auspices of the Congress for Cultural Freedom.'

4914 **Harrison**, Royden J. 'Retreat from industrial democracy.' *New Left Rev.*, 4 (July–August 1960), 32–8.

With reference to H. A. Clegg. *A new approach to industrial democracy.* Oxford: Blackwell, 1960.

4915 **Woodcock**, George. 'Trades unions and managers.' Todd, J. M. (ed.). *Work: Christian thought and practice; a symposium.* London: Darton, Longman and Todd; Baltimore: Helicon P., 1960. p. 145–52.

4916 **Butt**, Denis. 'Workers' control.' *New Left Rev.*, 10 (July–August 1961), 24–33.

4917 **Organisation of Employers' Federations and Employers in Developing Countries.** *Joint consultation at national level.* London: the Federation, [1961?]. (Occasional paper.)

4918 **Richards**, C. G. and **Sallis**, Howard. 'The joint consultative committee and the working groups: a power station experiment.' *Publ. Adm.*, XXXIX, 4 (Winter 1961), 361–7.

4919 **Davies**, David Lloyd. *Formal consultation in practice.* London: Industrial Welfare Society, 1962. 35p.

4920 **Fogarty**, Michael Patrick. *Opportunity knocks: plan for partnership.* London: Liberal Publications Department, 1962. 35p. (New directions series 4.)

4921 **International Labour Office.** *Consultation and co-operation between employers and workers at the level of the enterprise: outline of the regulations in force in 11 European countries.* Geneva: I.L.O., 1962. 79p. (L.M.R. 13.)

Report drawn up in collaboration with O.E.C.D.

4922 **Livermore**, John (ed.). *Controlling interest: participation and power in industry.* London: New Orbits Group, 1962. 45p. (Publications 8.)

4923 **Scottish Education Department.** *Appointment of teachers to Education Committees: report of the Working Party on the appointment of teachers in the employment of education authorities in Scotland to the education committees of the authorities.* Edinburgh: H.M.S.O., 1962.

Chairman: H. H. Donnelly.

4924 **Scottish Education Department.** *Consultation on educational matters: report of the Working Party on consultation between the teachers' associations and the Scottish Education Department on educational matters.* Edinburgh: H.M.S.O., 1962.

Chairman: Dr J. Craigie.

4925 **Rees**, W. D. *The practical functions of joint consultation considered historically and in the light of some recent experiences in South Wales.* 1962–63. (M.Sc. thesis, University of London.)

4926 **Banks**, Joseph Ambrose. *Industrial participation: theory and practice; a case study.* Liverpool: Liverpool U.P., 1963. 150p. (Social research series.)

4927 **Palmer**, R. G. and **Jolliffe**, B. R. 'Participate, by order.' *New Soc.*, II, 59 (14 November 1963), 21–2. (Work & business.)

4928 **Taylor**, J. K. L. *Attitudes and methods of communication and consultation between employers and workers at individual firm level.* Paris: Organisation for Economic Cooperation and Development, 1963. 122p.

International Joint Seminar, London, 26 February–2 March 1962.

4929 *Workers' control in the mining industry.* 1963. 25p.

Outcome of a series of discussions by a group of students at Ruskin College, Oxford, spread over the autumn, winter and spring months of 1962/63.

4930 **Barlow**, Kenneth Graham Ireland. *Participative management: a study of permissiveness in managerial control.* 1964. (M.Sc. Tech. thesis, University of Manchester.)

4931 **Clark**, Laurence Walter. *On political and economic democracy.* Rickmansworth: Veracity Ventures, 1964. 24p. (Interim papers 1.)

4932 **Das**, Nabagopal. *Experiments in industrial democracy.* London, New York: Asia Publishing House, 1964. vii, 175p.

4933 **Derber**, Milton. 'Labor participation in management: some impressions of experience in the metal working industries of Britain, Israel, and the United States.' Industrial Relations Research Association. *Proceedings of the seventeenth annual meeting, Chicago, Illinois, December 28 and 29, 1964.* p. 261–9.

Also published as Illinois University, Institute of Labor and Industrial Relations, *Reprint series*, 154, Urbana, 1965. 9p.

4934 **Greaves**, Harold Richard Goring. *Democratic participation and public enterprise.*

London: Athlone P., 1964. 27p. (Hobhouse Memorial Trust lectures 34.)

Delivered on 25 May 1964 at University College London.

4935 **Ross**, Norman Scott. *The democratic firm.* London: Fabian Society, 1964. 34p. (Fabian research series 242.)

4936 **Sturmthal**, Adolf Fox. 'Industrial democracy in the affluent society.' Industrial Relations Research Association. *Proceedings of the seventeenth annual meeting, Chicago, Illinois, December 28 and 29, 1964.* p. 270–9.

4937 **Thornton**, Merle. 'Alienation and socialism, [Part 1].' *Labour Hist.*, 7 (November 1964), 34–44.

4938 **Topham**, Anthony. 'Shop stewards and workers' control.' *New Left Rev.*, 25 (May–June 1964), 3–16.

4939 **Van De Vall**, Mark. 'The workers' councils in Western Europe: aims and results.' Industrial Relations Research Association. *Proceedings of the seventeenth annual meeting, Chicago, Illinois, December 28 and 29, 1964.* p. 280–91.

4940 **Miles**, A. W. *Staff consultation in the hospital service.* 1964–65. (M.A. thesis, University of Leeds.)

4941 **Ashwell**, Jack. *Four steps for progress: the operation of a municipal transport system with workers' control.* Hull: *Humberside Voice*, 1965. 18p.

Second edition. Nottingham: Institute for Workers' Control, 1969. 32p. (Pamphlet series 13.)

4942 **Coates**, Ken. 'Democracy and workers' control.' Anderson, P. and Blackburn, R. (eds.). *Towards socialism.* London: Fontana, 1965. p. 291–316.

4943 **Henderson**, Joan. *Effective joint consultation.* London: Industrial Welfare Society, 1965. 24p. (Notes for managers 9.)

4944 **Ross**, Norman Scott. 'Workers' participation and control.' *Sci. Bus.*, II, 8 (February 1965), 352–9.

4945 **Sallis**, Howard. 'Joint consultation and meetings of primary working groups in power stations.' *Br. J. Ind. Relat.*, III, 3 (November 1965), 326–44.

4946 **Thornton**, Merle. 'Alienation and socialism. Part 2. Worker satisfaction and worker control.' *Labour Hist.*, 8 (May 1965), 10–18.

Includes a discussion of H. A. Clegg. *A new approach to industrial democracy.* Oxford: Blackwell, 1960.

4947 **Layden**, D. J. *Joint consultation – its role in industrial relations.* 1965–66. (M.S.A. dissertation, Trinity College, Dublin.)

4948 **Confederation of British Industry**. *Communication and consultation: report of a working party.* London: C.B.I., 1966. [16]p.

4949 **De Schweinitz**, Dorothea. *Labor–management consultation in the factory: the experience of Sweden, England, and the Federal Republic of Germany.* Honolulu: University of Hawaii, Industrial Relations Center, 1966. ix, 128p. (Occasional publications 55.)

4950 **Marsh**, Arthur I. 'Joint consultation revived?' *New Soc.*, VII, 194 (16 June 1966), 14–15. (Trends in personnel management 2.)

4951 **Paterson**, Janis. *Establishing joint consultation: a study of conflicting interests.* London, Edinburgh: Nelson, 1966. v, 23p. (Bradford exercises in management 2.)

4952 **Thorsrud**, Einar and **Emery**, Frederick Edmund. 'Industrial conflict and "industrial democracy".' Lawrence, J. R. (ed.). *Operational research and the social sciences.* London: Tavistock Publications, 1966. Chap. XXXII. p. 439–48.

4953 **Coates**, Ken and **Topham**, Tony. *Participation or control?* London: Bertrand Russell Centre for Social Research, 1967. 19p. (Pamphlet series 1.)

Reprinted from *Tribune* and *Voice of the Unions.*

4954 **Emery**, Frederick Edmund. 'The democratisation of the workplace.' *Manp. Appl. Psychol.*, I, 2 (Autumn 1967), 118–29.

4955 **Graham**, George. 'Labour participation in management: a study of the National Coal Board.' *Polit. Q.*, XXXVIII, 2 (April–June 1967), 184–99.

4956 **International Institute for Labour Studies**. 'Workers' participation in management.' *Int. Inst. Labour Studies Bull.*, 2 (February 1967), 64–125.

I. 'A fruitful field for enquiry', by Robert W. Cox, p. 64–7.

II. 'The concept and its implementation', by Kenneth F. Walker and L. Greyfié de Bellecombe, p. 67–100.

III. 'A research project', p. 101–25.

4957 **Irish National Productivity Committee**. *Joint consultation in industry.* Dublin: I.N.P.C., 1967. 131p.

4958 **Labour Party**. *Industrial democracy: a discussion document presented by the National Executive Committee for discussion at the sixth national conference of the Labour Party Young Socialists.* 1967. 15p.

4959 **Labour Party**. Working Party on Industrial Democracy. *Report.* London: Labour Party, 1967. 63p.

Chairman: J. L. Jones.

4960 **Layton**, Christopher. 'The search for industrial democracy.' *Listener*, 77 (23 February 1967), 247–9.

4961 **Nightingale**, H. *Report on workers' participation in management.* London: British Institute of Management, 1967. 141p.

4962 **Political and Economic Planning**. *Joint consultation: a survey of the chocolate and sugar confectionery industry.* London: National Economic Development Office, [1967]. 45p.

Survey carried out for P.E.P. by Val Schur.

4963 **Spiro**, Herbert J. 'Comparative analysis of

worker participation in decision making.' *Politico*, XXXII, 4 (December 1967), 777–85.

4964 **Barratt Brown**, Michael. 'The search for workers' control.' *New Soc.*, XI, 289 (11 April 1968), 526–7.

4965 **Blumberg**, Paul. *Industrial democracy: the sociology of participation.* London: Constable; New York: Schocken Books, 1968. viii, 278p. (Sociology and social welfare series.)

4966 **British Institute of Management**. *Industrial democracy: some implications for management; an exploratory study.* London: B.I.M., 1968. 52p. (Occasional papers, new series, OPN 1.)

4967 **Coates**, Ken (ed.). *Can the workers run industry?* London: Sphere Books in association with the Institute for Workers' Control, 1968. 254p.

4968 **Coates**, Ken and **Topham**, Tony (eds.). *Industrial democracy in Great Britain: a book of readings and witnesses for workers' control.* London: MacGibbon and Kee, 1968. xxxvi, 431p.

Revised edition. *Workers' control: a book of readings and witnesses for workers' control.* London: Panther, 1970. xl, 464p.

4969 **Coates**, Ken and **Topham**, Tony. 'Participation or control?' Coates, K. (ed.). *Can the workers run industry?* London: Sphere Books in association with the Institute for Workers' Control, 1968. p. 227–52.

4970 **Edmonds**, John. 'The worker.' Lapping, B. and Radice, G. (eds.). *More power to the people: Young Fabian essays on democracy in Britain.* London: Longmans, 1968. p. 34–56.

4971 **Goodman**, Geoffrey. *Industrial democracy.* Oxford: Pergamon, 1968. 22p. (Productivity progress.)

4972 **Harrison**, Bob. 'The motor industry.' Coates, K. (ed.). *Can the workers run industry?* London: Sphere Books in association with the Institute of Workers' Control, 1968. p. 141–6.

4973 **Hay**, William Ferris, and others. *Industrial democracy for miners.* Nottingham: Institute for Workers' Control, 1968. 3p., 15 leaves, 5 plates. (Archives in trade union history and theory, series 1, no. 6.)

4974 **Hodges,** Frank, **Miners' Federation of Great Britain** and **Sankey Commission**. *Nationalisation of the mines.* Nottingham: Institute for Workers' Control, 1968. 10p., [25] leaves. (Archives in trade union history and theory, series 1, no. 5.)

4975 **Hughes**, John. 'Democracy and planning: Britain 1968.' Coates, K. (ed.). *Can the workers run industry?* London: Sphere Books in association with the Institute for Workers' Control, 1968. p. 75–85.

4976 **Industrial Educational and Research Foundation**. *Worker representation on company boards: an edited discussion.* London: the Foundation, 1968. 43p. (Discussion paper 2.)

4977 **Jaques**, Elliott. *Employee participation and managerial authority: one practical basis for resolving the growing crisis in industrial relations.* London: Brunel University, School of Social Sciences, 1968. 12p.

4978 **Labour Party**. *Industrial democracy: a statement by the National Executive Committee to the Annual Conference of the Labour Party.* London: Labour Party, 1968. 4p.

4979 **Mikardo**, Ian. 'The scope and limits of legislation.' Coates, K. (ed.). *Can the workers run industry?* London: Sphere Books in association with the Institute for Workers' Control, 1968. p. 89–95.

4980 **Ramelson**, Bert. 'Workers' control? Possibilities and limitations.' *Marxism Today*, XII, 10 (October 1968), 296–303.

'Discussion contributions', by Tony Topham and Ken Coates, XIII, 1 (January 1969), 24–8, and by Charlie Swain, 29–30.

4981 **Richman**, Geoffrey. 'The National Health Service.' Coates, K. (ed.). *Can the workers run industry?* London: Sphere Books in association with the Institute for Workers' Control, 1968. p. 131–40.

4982 **Roberts**, Ernie. 'Workers' control and the trade unions.' Coates, K. (ed.). *Can the workers run industry?* London: Sphere Books in association with the Institute for Workers' Control, 1968. p. 96–103.

The author was Assistant General Secretary of the Amalgamated Engineering Union.

4983 **Rooney**, Alan. 'The aircraft industry.' Coates, K. (ed.). *Can the workers run industry?* London: Sphere Books in association with the Institute for Workers' Control, 1968. p. 181–216.

4984 **Sawtell**, Roger. *Sharing our industrial future? A study of employee participation sponsored by William Temple College, Rugby.* London: Industrial Society, 1968. viii, 64p.

4985 **Scanlon**, Hugh. *The way forward for workers' control.* Nottingham: Institute for Workers' Control, 1968. [11]p. (Pamphlet series 1.)

'Contains the text of a speech . . . to the sixth Conference on Workers' Control . . . on March 30–31st 1968 at Nottingham University.' (Foreword.)

4986 **Sheffield Steel Group**. 'Nationalised steel.' Coates, K. (ed.). *Can the workers run industry?* London: Sphere Books in association with the Institute for Workers' Control, 1968. p. 147–56.

4987 **Sherratt**, Eric. 'The fuel industry.' Coates, K. (ed.). *Can the workers run industry?* London: Sphere Books in association with the Institute for Workers' Control, 1968. p. 119–30.

4988 **Topham**, Tony. 'The dockers.' Coates, K. (ed.). *Can the workers run industry?* London: Sphere Books in association with the Institute for Workers' Control, 1968. p. 157–80.

4989 **Topham**, Tony. *Productivity bargaining and workers' control.* Nottingham: Institute for Workers' Control, 1968. [13]p. (Pamphlet series 2.)

4990 **Topham**, Tony (ed.). *Report of the 5th National Conference on Workers' Control and Industrial Democracy held at Transport House, Coventry on June 10th and 11th 1967.* Hull: Centre for Socialist Education, 1968. 162p.

4991 **Walker**, Kenneth Frederick. 'Conceptual framework and scope of national studies [in workers' participation in management].' *Int. Inst. Labour Studies Bull.*, 5 (November 1968), 138–52.

4992 **Poole**, M. J. F. *A power approach to worker' participation in decision making.* 1968–69. (Ph.D. thesis, University of Sheffield.)

4993 **Barratt Brown**, Michael and **Coates**, Ken. *The 'big flame'; and, What is the I.W.C.?* Nottingham: Institute for Workers' Control, 1969. [10]p. (Pamphlet series 14.)

4994 **Batson**, R. W., **Bird**, W. J., **Clarke**, Ronald Oliver, **Harris**, L. G., **Tuck**, G. R. and **Willmott**, P. *How far is it possible in practice to carry workers' participation in company decisions? Reports of the discussion of six study groups.* London: Co-partnership, 1969.

4995 **Chadwick**, Graham. 'Steelworkers' control and redundancy.' *Trade Un. Regist.* (1969), 175–84.

4996 **Clegg**, Ian. *Industrial democracy.* London: Sheed and Ward, 1969. 61p. (Perspective on work, welfare and society.)

4997 **Coates**, Ken and **Williams**, Wyn (eds.). *How and why industry must be democratized: papers submitted to the Workers' Control Conference, Nottingham, March 30–31st, 1968.* Nottingham: Institute for Workers' Control, 1969. 222p.

4998 **Coates**, Ken and **Topham**, Tony. *The Labour Party's plans for industrial democracy.* Nottingham: Institute for Workers' Control, 1969. 9p. (Pamphlet series 5.)

4999 **Cuffe**, Charles R. 'Who makes the final decision?' Irish Management Institute. *Industrial democracy: a symposium.* Dublin: the Institute, 1969. p. 97–103.

The author was Director General of the Federated Union of Employers.

5000 **Emery**, Frederick Edmund, **Thorsrud**, Einar and **Trist**, Eric Lansdowne. *Form and content in industrial democracy: some experiences from Norway and other European countries.* London: Tavistock; Assen: Van Gorcum, 1969. xi, 116p. (Technology and democratic society.)

Originally published as *Industrielt demokrati.* Oslo: Oslo University Press, 1964.

5001 **Fitzgerald**, Garret. 'Shareholders, management and workers.' Irish Management Institute. *Industrial democracy: a symposium.* Dublin: the Institute, 1969. p. 116–20.

5002 **Fogarty**, Michael. 'Power to disrupt, ability to contribute.' Irish Management Institute. *Industrial democracy: a symposium.* Dublin: the Institute, 1969. p. 64–73.

5003 **Geddes**, *Sir* Reay. *Industry and worker participation.* London: Industrial Educational and Research Foundation, 1969. 10 leaves. (The company and its responsibilities.)

5004 **Gray**, E. J. 'Build, not destroy.' Irish Management Institute. *Industrial democracy: a symposium.* Dublin: the Institute, 1969. p. 90–3.

The author was Director General of the Federation of Irish Industries.

5005 **Heath**, R. H. 'The National Power-Loading Agreement in the coal industry and some aspects of workers' control.' *Trade Un. Regist.* (1969), 185–200.

5006 **Hillery**, Patrick J. 'Experiment, experience and evolution.' Irish Management Institute. *Industrial democracy: a symposium.* Dublin: the Institute, 1969. p. 110–15.

The author was Fianna Fáil Minister for Labour.

5007 **Hull and London Port Workers' Control Groups**. *The dockers' next step.* Nottingham: Institute for Workers' Control, 1969. [26]p. (Institute for Workers' Control. Pamphlet series 12.)

New revised edition.

5008 **Industrial Educational and Research Foundation**. *Worker representation on company boards: an edited discussion.* London: the Foundation, [1969?]. 43p. (Discussion paper 2.)

5009 **Institute for Workers' Control**. *Industrial democracy and national fuel policy.* Nottingham: Institute for Workers' Control, 1969. [13]p. (Pamphlet series 8.)

5010 **Irish Management Institute**. *Industrial democracy: a symposium.* Dublin: the Institute, 1969. 148p.

Chapters 1 to 6, 8, 11 and 14 appeared originally in *Management.*

5011 **Johnston**, Thomas L. *Industrial democracy revisited.* Glasgow: Institution of Engineers and Shipbuilders in Scotland, 1969. 38p.

Third Marlow (Scotland) Lecture.

Reprinted from the *Transactions* of the Institution, 1968.

5012 **Jones**, Bill and **Cosgrove**, Frank. 'A paper on workers' control within the road passenger industry.' *Trade Un. Regist.* (1969), 223–31.

5013 **King**, Charles D. and **Van de Vall**, Mark. 'Dimensions of workers' participation in managerial decision making.' Industrial Relations Research Association. *Proceedings of the twenty-second annual meeting, 1969.* p. 164–77.

Discussions, p. 200–7.

5014 **MacNeill**, Hugh. 'Participation at the workplace.' Irish Management Institute. *Industrial democracy: a symposium.* Dublin: the Institute, 1969. p. 127–34.

The author was Group Personnel Manager, Cement Limited.

5015 **Miles**, A. W. and **Smith**, Duncan. *Joint*

consultation: defeat or opportunity. A survey of joint consultation in the health service. London: King Edward's Hospital Fund for London, 1969. 80 leaves.

5016 **O'Leary**, Michael. 'Alienation.' Irish Management Institute. *Industrial democracy: a symposium.* Dublin: the Institute, 1969. p. 104–9.

5017 **O'Rourke**, J. J. 'A case study of joint consultation.' Irish Management Institute. *Industrial democracy: a symposium.* Dublin: the Institute, 1969. p. 56–63.

In the Waterford Glass Company.

The author was Waterford Secretary/Organiser of the Amalgamated Transport and General Workers' Union.

5018 **Roberts**, Ruaidhri. 'Unithink.' Irish Management Institute. *Industrial democracy: a symposium.* Dublin: the Institute, 1969. p. 94–6.

The author was General Secretary of the Irish Congress of Trade Unions.

5019 **Sheffield Steel Workers' Group**. *Steel workers next step.* Nottingham: Institute for Workers' Control, 1969. [8]p. (Pamphlet series 7.)

5020 **Turner**, Denys. 'Work and personal values.' Irish Management Institute. *Industrial democracy: a symposium.* Dublin: the Institute, 1969. p. 121–6.

5021 **Anthony**, Peter David. *Joint consultation: its meaning and purpose in a nationalized industry.* 1970. (M.Sc. Econ. thesis, University of Wales, Cardiff.)

5022 **Coates**, Ken and **Topham**, Tony (eds.). *Workers' control: a book of readings and witnesses for workers' control.* London: Panther, 1970. xl, 464p. (Panther modern society.)

Revised edition.

Previous edition published as *Industrial democracy in Great Britain.* London: MacGibbon and Kee, 1968. xxxvi, 431p.

5023 **Derber**, Milton. 'Crosscurrents in workers' participation.' *Ind. Relat.*, IX, 2 (February 1970), 123–36.

Part of a symposium on *Workers' participation in management: an international comparison.*

5024 **Jones**, D. D. 'Industrial democracy.' *Ind. Relat. Res. Bull.*, 4 (September 1970), 17–21.

5025 **McGregor**, Peter and **Lishman**, Gordon. *Participation in a competitive economy.* London: Liberal Publication Department, 1970. 24p. (Liberal focus 3.)

5026 **Scanlon**, Hugh. 'Workers' control and the threat of the international combines.' *Trade Un. Regist.* (1970), 45–52.

5027 **Strauss**, George and **Rosenstein**, Eliezer. 'Workers' participation: a critical view.' *Ind. Relat.*, IX, 2 (February 1970), 197–214.

Part of a symposium on *Workers' participation in management: an international comparison.*

5028 **Topham**, Tony. 'The Ports Bill, joint control and rationalization.' *Trade Un. Regist.* (1970), 153–61.

5029 **Walker**, Kenneth Frederick. *Industrial democracy: fantasy, fiction or fact?* London: Times Newspapers, 1970. 36p. ('The Times' management lecture 1970.)

See also: 9; 10; 67; 5410.

B. CO-OPERATIVE PRODUCTION, CO-PARTNERSHIP, AND PROFIT-SHARING

Some of the general works in Part Four, II, A also contain material on employers' attitudes towards co-partnership and industrial democracy. See also Part Five, III, G.

1. Owenism

Those works primarily concerned with Owen's role in the Grand National Consolidated Trades Union are classified in Part Three, III, B, 2.

5030 **Jones**, Lloyd. *The life, times and labours of Robert Owen.* London: Labour Association, 1889.

Volume 1 only published.

With a short notice of the author by William Cairns Jones.

Another edition. London: Swan Sonnenschein, 1890. 2 v. in 1. Edited by W. C. Jones.

Later editions. 1895, 1900, 1905, 1912, 1919.

5031 **Holyoake**, George Jacob. *Robert Owen Co-operative Memorial at Newtown: the unveiling ceremony on July 13th 1902; address.* Manchester: Co-operative Union, 1902. 19p.

Reprinted from the *Co-operative News.*

5032 **Holyoake**, George Jacob. *Robert Owen, the precursor of social progress: in justification of the Newtown Memorial.* Manchester: Co-operative Union, 1902. 22p.

5033 **Brown**, William Henry. *Robert Owen.* London: C. W. Daniel; Leicester: Leicester Co-operative Printing Society, [1903?]. 16p. (Pioneer biographies of social reformers 4.)

5034 **Podmore**, Frank. *Robert Owen: a biography.* London: Hutchinson, 1906. 2v.

5035 **Davies**, R. E. *The life of Robert Owen, philanthropist and social reformer: an appreciation.* London: Robert Sutton, 1907. 57p. (Historical character studies.)

5036 **Sadler**, *Sir* Michael Ernest. *Owen, Lovett, Maurice, and Toynbee.* London, Manchester: Sherratt and Hughes, 1907. 12p.

Reprinted from *University Review*, July 1907.

5037 **Clayton**, Joseph. *Robert Owen, pioneer of social reforms.* London: Fifield, 1908. 67p. (Social reformers series 1.)

5038 **Cullen**, Alexander. *Adventures in socialism: New Lanark establishment and Orbiston community.* Glasgow: John Smith; London: Black, 1910. xvi, 330p.

5039 **Hutchins**, B. Leigh. *Robert Owen: social*

reformer. London: Fabian Society, 1912. 24p. (Fabian tract 166. Biographical series 2.)

5040 **Joad**, Cyril Edwin Mitchison. *Robert Owen, idealist*. London: Fabian Society, 1917. 32p. (Fabian tract 182. Biographical series 7.)

5041 **McCabe**, Joseph. *Robert Owen*. London: Watts, 1920. viii, 120p. (Life-stories of famous men.)
'Issued for the Rationalist Press Association, Limited.'

5042 **Podmore**, Frank. *Robert Owen*. London: Allen and Unwin, 1923. xiii, 688p.

5043 **Boales**, Hugh Lancelot. 'The Industrial Revolution and Robert Owen.' *Highway*, XVII, 4 (Autumn 1925), 159–63.
Review article.

5044 **Cole**, George Douglas Howard. *Robert Owen*. London: Benn, 1925. 267p. (Curiosities in politics 1.)
Second edition. *The life of Robert Owen*. 1930.

5045 **Greening**, Edward Owen. *Memories of Robert Owen and the co-operative pioneers: two lectures*. Manchester: Co-operative Union, 1925. 18p.

5046 **Johnson**, Dorothy Catherine. 'Robert Owen, 1771–1858.' *Pioneers of reform*. London: Methuen, 1929. p. 55–80.

5047 **Lloyd**, Eynon. *Robert Owen and social legislation*. 1932. (M.A. thesis, University of Wales, Aberystwyth.)

5048 **Gotô**, Shigeru. *Robert Owen, 1771–1858: a new biographical study. Vol. II. A supplement to Volume One, with special reference to the various Robert Owen collections in England, Wales and Scotland*. Osaka: Osaka University of Commerce, 1934. x, 220, 18p. (Studies from the Osaka University of Commerce 3.)
Notes, etc. in Japanese.

5049 **Rennard**, Thomas Ambler. *Robert Owen*. Exeter: A. Wheaton, 1937. 47p. (Makers of history 18.)

5050 **Fraser**, Elizabeth Margaret. 'Robert Owen in Manchester, 1787–1800.' *Mem. Proc. Manchr. Lit. Phil. Soc.*, LXXXII (1937–38), 29–41.

5051 **Wallas**, Graham. 'Robert Owen.' *Men and ideas: essays*. London: Allen and Unwin, 1940. p. 65–74.
'First published in the *Sociological Review*, January 1910, under the title "The Beginning of Modern Socialism".'

5052 **Desai**, Raman K. *Robert Owen and our times*. Bombay, [1940–58?].

5053 **Fay**, Charles Ryle. 'Robert Owen.' *Life and labour in the nineteenth century* . . . Cambridge: Cambridge U.P., 1947. p. 55–65.
Earlier editions. 1920, 1933, 1943.

5054 **Cole**, Margaret Isabel. 'Robert Owen, 1771–1858.' *Makers of the labour movement*. London: Longmans, Green, 1948. p. 62–85.

5055 **Davies**, *Sir* Alfred T. (ed.). *Robert Owen, 1771–1858: pioneer social reformer and philanthropist*. Glynceiriog: Ceiriog Memorial Institute, 1948. 84p.
Another edition. Manchester: Co-operative Wholesale Society, 1948.

5056 **McCabe**, Joseph. *The life story of Robert Owen*. Girard, Kan.: Haldeman-Julius Publications, 1948. 58p.

5057 **Morton**, Frederick John Burns. *Teamwork in industry*. London: Chapman and Hall, 1948. xii, 273p.

5058 **Harvey**, Rowland H. *Robert Owen: social idealist*. Berkeley, Los Angeles: U. of California P., 1949. vi, 269p. (University of California publications in history 38.)

5059 **Cole**, Margaret Isabel. *Robert Owen of New Lanark*. London: Batchworth P., 1953. vii, 231p.

5060 **Oliver**, W. H. 'Robert Owen and the English working-class movements.' *Hist. Today*, VIII, 11 (November 1958), 787–96.

5061 **Briggs**, Asa. *Robert Owen in retrospect*. Loughborough: Education Department, Co-operative Union, 1959. p. 3–16. (Co-operative College papers 6.)
A lecture, published with one by Sidney Pollard on *Dr. William King of Ipswich: a co-operative pioneer*. p. 17–33.

5062 **Thomas**, Brinley. 'Robert Owen of Newtown, 1771–1858.' *Hon. Soc. Cymm. Trans.* (1960), 18–35.

5063 **Morton**, Arthur Leslie. *The life and ideas of Robert Owen*. London: Lawrence and Wishart, 1962. 187p.
Part 1. 'Owen's life and work.'
Part 2. 'Selected writings.'

5064 **Pride**, Emrys. 'Work study and Robert Owen.' *Hon. Soc. Cymm. Trans.* (1967), pt. 1, 92–9.

5065 **Harrison**, John Fletcher Clews. 'The Owenite socialist movement in Britain and the United States.' *Labor Hist.*, IX, 3 (Fall 1968), 323–37.
'A version of this article was read as a paper at the annual meeting of the American Historical Association in New York on December 28, 1966.'

5066 **Turner**, David Anthony. *The educational influence of Robert Owen in England, with particular reference to the infant schools directly developed from the New Lanark pattern between 1819–1939*. 1968–69. (M.Phil. thesis, University of London.)

5067 **Harrison**, John Fletcher Clews. *Robert Owen and the Owenites in Britain and America: the quest for the new moral world*. London: Routledge and Kegan Paul, 1969. xi, 392p.

See also: 7; 32.

2. Other

5068 **Gray**, J. C. *The future of productive co-operation: a plea for unity*. Manchester: Co-operative Union, [188–?]. 8p.

5069 **Rafferty**, M. *Capital and labour united; or, The true position of the working classes resulting in abundance of work and wealth for all.* Birmingham, 1881. ii, 28p.

5070 **Taylor**, Sedley. 'On profit-sharing between capital and labour.' *Manchr. Statist. Soc. Trans.* (1882–83), 65–92.

5071 **Aylett**, G. H. *Building and co-operation.* London, 1884. 13p.

5072 **Simcox**, Edith. 'Eight years of co-operative shirtmaking.' *Nineteenth Century*, XV, 88 (June 1884), 1037–54.

5073 **Taylor**, Sedley. *Profit-sharing between capital and labour: six essays; to which is added a memorandum on the industrial partnership at the Whitwood Collieries (1865–1874), by Archibald Briggs and...H. G. Briggs, together with remarks on the memorandum by S. Taylor.* London: Kegan Paul, 1884. xiii, 170p.

5074 **Westminster Review**. 'Co-operation or spoliation.' *Westm. Rev.*, n.s., LXV, 2 (April 1884), 430–50.

5075 **Greening**, Edward Owen. 'Profit-sharing and co-operative production.' Industrial Remuneration Conference. *The report of the proceedings and papers.* London: Cassell, 1885. p. 304–11.
Discussion, p. 323–35.

5076 **Neale**, Edward Vansittart. *The Labour Association for Promoting Co-operative Production based on the co-partnership of the workers: its principles, objects and methods.* London: Central Office, 1885. 12p.

5077 **Westminster Review**. 'Industrial co-operation.' *Westm. Rev.*, n.s., LXVIII, 136 (October 1885), 309–40.
Review article.

5078 **Slatter**, Henry. 'Co-operative production.' Co-operative Wholesale Society. *Annual and diary for the year 1886.* p. 188–94.

5079 **Swallow**, William. *Co-operative production: a paper read...at the Congress held at Plymouth, Whitsuntide, 1886.* Manchester: Central Co-operative Board, 1886. 12p.

5080 **Donisthorpe**, Wordsworth. *Labour capitalization.* London: Liberty and Property Defence League, 1887. 218p.

5081 **Gray**, J. C. *Co-operative production in Great Britain.* Manchester: Central Co-operative Board, 1887. 14p.
Reprinted from *Age of Steel*, January 1887.

5082 **Hughes**, Thomas. *Co-operative production: an address delivered . . . at the annual Co-operative Congress, held at Carlisle, May, 1887.* Manchester: Central Co-operative Board, 1887. 12p.

5083 **Powell**, G. M. 'Profit sharing, historically and theoretically considered.' *J. Am. Soc. Sci. Ass.*, 23 (November 1887), 48–67.

5084 **Copland**, Elijah. *Ought productive works to be carried on as departments of the wholesale societies? If so, under what conditions? A paper.* Manchester: Central Co-operative Board, 1888. 12p.

5085 **Gray**, J. C. *Co-operative production: a paper read . . . at the Congress held at Plymouth, Whitsuntide, 1888.* Manchester: Central Co-operative Board, 1888. 16p.

5086 **Quirk**, G. E. *What should be the true relations between a wholesale distributive society and productive societies whose work it may sell? A paper read . . . at the Congress held at Dewsbury, Whitsuntide, 1888.* Manchester: Central Co-operative Board, 1888. 8p.

5087 **Bowyear**, Henry. *Industrial and social co-operation: its aims, methods, and organisation.* Manchester: Central Co-operative Board, 1889. 15p.

5088 **Greenwood**, Joseph. *The story of the formation of the Hebden Bridge Fustian Manufacturing Society.* Manchester: Central Co-operative Board, 1889. 23p.
The author was manager of the Society.

5089 **Schloss**, David Frederick. *Co-operators at work: an account of the Leicester Co-operative Boot and Shoe Manufacturing Society, Ltd.* London, 1889. 10p.

5090 **Schloss**, David Frederick. 'The labour problem.' *Fortn. Rev.*, n.s., XLVI, 274 (October 1889), 437–47.
On profit-sharing.

5091 **Cummings**, Edward. 'Co-operative production in France and England.' *Q. J. Econ.*, IV, (July 1890), 357–86.

5092 **Nicholson**, Joseph Shield. 'Profit-sharing.' *Contemp. Rev.*, LVII (January 1890), 64–77.

5093 **Schloss**, David Frederick. 'Industrial co-operation.' *Contemp. Rev.*, LVII (April 1890), 552–68.

5094 **Schloss**, David Frederick. 'Profit-sharing.' *Char. Orgn. Rev.*, VI, 61 (January 1890), 10–16.

5095 *Report to the Board of Trade on profit-sharing.* London: H.M.S.O., 1890–1. (C. 6267.)
1894. (C. 7458.)
1895. (C. 7848.)

5096 **Arnold**, John. *The best means of bringing co-operation and trade unions into closer union.* Manchester: Co-operative Union, 1891. 8p.

5097 **Kinley**, David. 'Recent progress of profit-sharing abroad.' *Q. J. Econ.*, V (July 1891), 497–503.

5098 **Rawson**, Henry Gilbert. *Profit-sharing precedents, with notes.* London: Stevens, 1891. xii, 192p.

5099 **Schloss**, David Frederick. 'The increase in industrial remuneration under profit-sharing.' *Econ. J.*, I, 2 (June 1891), 292–303.

5100 **Deans**, James. *The best method of consolidating and federating existing productive effort.* Manchester: Co-operative Union, 1892. 11p.
Paper read at the Twenty-fourth annual congress of Co-operative Societies held at Rochdale, June 1892.

5101 **Jones**, Benjamin. 'Co-operation and profit-sharing.' *Econ. J.*, II, 8 (December 1892), 616–28.

Reply to Price, L. L. 'Profit-sharing and co-operative production.' *Econ. J.*, II (September 1892), 442–62.

5102 **Labour Association for Promoting Co-operative Production Based on the Co-partnership of the Workers.** *Eight years work.* London, 1892. 8p.

5103 **Nash**, Rosalind. *Cooperative production and the needs of labour.* 1892. 8p.

5104 **Price**, Langford Lovell Frederick Rice. 'Profit-sharing and co-operative production.' *Econ. J.*, II, 7 (September 1892), 442–62.

5105 **Tutt**, W. G. *The marriage of trade unionists and co-operators.* Manchester, 1892. 12p.

5106 **Webb**, Beatrice. *The relationship between co-operation and trade unionism: paper.* Manchester: Co-operative Union, 1892. 16p.

5107 **Bushill**, Thomas William. *Profit-sharing and the labour question.* London: Methuen, 1893. 262p.

Thomas Bushill and Sons, Coventry.

5108 **Maxwell**, *Sir* William. *The relation of employés to the co-operative movement.* Manchester: Co-operative Union, 1893. 14p.

Paper read May 1893.

5109 **Snell**, W. E. 'Co-operators and profit-sharing.' *Econ. Rev.*, III, 2 (April 1893), 201–11.

5110 **Chappell**, Alfred. *Labour studies for master and man: the co-operation of labour.* London: Co-operative Printing Society, 1894. 23p.

5111 *Historical sketches of our productive societies.* Leicester, 1894. 52p.

5112 **Jones**, Benjamin. *Co-operative production.* Oxford: Clarendon P., 1894. 2v.

5113 **Labour Association for Promoting Co-operative Production**. *The co-partnership of labour.* London, 1894. 17p.

5114 **Vivian**, Henry H. and **Williams**, Aneurin. 'The co-partnership of labour.' *Econ. Rev.*, IV, 3 (July 1894), 297–317.

5115 **Webb**, Catherine. *Should co-operative employés understand the principles of the movement, and if so, how are they to be taught?* Manchester: Co-operative Union, 1894. 24p.

5116 **Board of Trade**. *Report on 'gain-sharing' and certain other systems of bonus on production.* London: Eyre and Spottiswoode for H.M.S.O., 1895. 132p. (C. 7848.)

Prepared by D. F. Schloss of the Labour Department as a supplement to his *Report on profit-sharing.*

5117 **Coal Mining Committee on Cooperative Collieries.** *Report.* Glasgow, 1895. 11p.

5118 **Halstead**, Robert. *Cooperative production viewed in the light of some first principles.* London, 1895. 8p.

5119 **Hobson**, John Atkinson. *Co-operative labour upon the land, and other papers: the report of a conference upon 'Land, co-operation and the unemployed' held at Holborn Town Hall in October, 1894.* London: Swan Sonnenschein, 1895. xv, 140p.

5120 **Ludlow**, John M. 'Co-operative production in the British Isles.' *Atl. Mon.*, LXXV, 447 (January 1895), 96–102.

5121 **Ludlow**, John M. 'Some words on the ethics of co-operative production.' *Atl. Mon.*, LXXV, 449 (March 1895), 383–8.

5122 **Wolff**, Henry William. 'Co-operative production.' *Econ. Rev.*, V, 1 (January 1895), 19–38.

5123 **Labour Association for Promoting Co-operative Production.** *Co-operative workshops in Great Britain, 1896.* London, 1896. 57p.

5124 **Nicholson**, Joseph Shield. 'Profit-sharing.' *Strikes and social problems.* London: Black, 1896. p. 45–69.

First published in *Contemporary Review*, January 1890.

5125 **Pratt**, Hodgson. *The marriage of labour and capital.* London: Labour Association, 1896. 8p.

An address delivered at the opening of the annual exhibition of co-operative productions held at the Crystal Palace, 18 August, 1896.

5126 **Vivian**, Henry H. 'A novel attempt at co-operative production in the building trades.' *Econ. J.*, VI, 22 (June 1896), 270–2.

General Builders, Limited.

5127 **Burton**, Francis G. 'The advantages of co-operative over municipal and state management of production and distribution.' Co-operative Wholesale Societies. *Annual for 1897.* p. 303–30.

5128 **Johnston**, J. *Trade unionism and co-operation.* Manchester, 1897. 12p.

5129 **Vivian,** Henry H. *How cooperative production may be successfully applied to the building trades.* London, 1897. 8p.

5130 **Blandford**, Thomas. *Co-operative workshops in Great Britain, 1898.* London: Labour Association, 1898. 54p.

5131 **Blandford**, Thomas and **Newell**, G. *History of the Leicester Co-operative Hosiery Manufacturing Society Ltd.* Leicester, 1898. 116p.

5132 **Brassey**, Thomas, Earl Brassey. *Co-operative and profit sharing industries, with remarks on trades unions.* Melbourne, 1898. 24p.

5133 **Lloyd**, Henry Demarest. *Labor co-partnership: notes of a visit to co-operative workshops, factories and farms in Great Britain and Ireland.* New York, London: Harper, 1898. 351p.

5134 **Vivian**, Henry H. *Partnership of capital and labour as a solution of the conflict between them.* London: Labour Association, 1898. 12p.

5135 **Bonar**, James. *Labour co-partnership.* London: Labour Association, 1899. 12p.

Read at the Leeds Industrial Conference, March 4th, 1899.

5136 **Brassey**, Thomas, Earl Brassey. *Can labour co-operation furnish a satisfactory solution of industrial problems?* London, 1899. 8p.

5137 **Campsie**, J. *Glimpses of co-operative land,*

including an account of the largest bakery in the world. Glasgow, 1899. 63p.

5138 **Monroe**, Paul. 'Profit-sharing and co-operation.' *Am. J. Sociol.*, IV, 5 (March 1899), 593–602; 6 (May 1899), 788–806.

Part 1. Theory. Part 2. Great Britain, etc.

5139 **Shuddick**, R. 'Co-operative workshops.' *Westm. Rev.*, CLII, 3 (September 1899), 266–70.

5140 **Vivian**, Henry H. *Co-operative stores and labour co-partnership*. London, 1899. 8p.

5141 **Williams**, Aneurin. *Suggested scheme for establishing co-partnership between an unregistered private business and its employees*. London, [19–?]. [4]p.

5142 **Williams**, Aneurin. *A better way: some facts and suggestions as to introducing the partnership of labour with capital into established business*. London, [19–?]. 12p.

5143 **Ashley**, William James. 'Co-operative production in England.' *Surveys, historic and economic*. London: Longmans, Green, 1900. p. 399–404.

'A letter from London, dated August 15, 1899, printed in the *Nation*, no. 1785, September 1899.'

5144 **Chesterton**, C. E. *Co-operative production: an outline of the principles sought to be applied to the granite industry*. London, [c. 1900?]. 8p.

5145 **Greenwood**, William. 'Fifty years of British industry from the workman's point of view.' *Econ. Rev.*, X, 3 (July 1900), 323–32.

On co-operative production at Hebden Bridge Fustian Society.

5146 **Halstead**, Robert. *Variations of wages in some labour co-partnership workshops, with some comparisons with non-co-operative industries*. London, 1900. 16p.

5147 **Phillips**, Lawrence. 'Two profit-sharing concerns.' *Econ. Rev.*, X, 2 (April 1900), 239–41.

1. Messrs. William Thomson & Sons, Woollen and Worsted Cloth Mills, Huddersfield. 2. Messrs. Clarke, Nickolls & Coombs, Ltd., Confectionery Works, Hackney Wick.

5148 **Vivian**, Henry H. 'Co-operative production.' *International Congress of Women, London, 1899, Transactions. Vol. VI. Women in industrial life*. London: T. Fisher Unwin, 1900. p. 231–5.

Discussion, p. 235–7.

5149 **Board of Trade**. *Workmen's co-operative societies in the United Kingdom*. 1901. xlviii, 252p. (Cd. 698.)

By J. J. Dent.

Also *Industrial and agricultural co-operative societies in the United Kingdom*. 1912. lv, 273p. (Cd. 6045.) Revises and extends Cd. 698.

5150 **Kitchin**, G. W. *The relation of trade unions to co-operation*. London, [1901?]. 8p.

5151 **Lever**, William Hesketh. 'Prosperity-sharing: a rejoinder.' *Econ. Rev.*, XI, 3 (July 1901), 316–21.

5152 **Lever**, William Hesketh. 'Prosperity-sharing *versus* profit-sharing in relation to workshop management.' *Econ. Rev.*, XI, 1 (January 1901), 47–64.

5153 **Livesey**, George. 'Profit-sharing: a vindication.' *Econ. Rev.*, XI, 4 (October 1901), 410–21.

5154 **Williams**, Aneurin and **Vivian**, Henry H. 'Recent progress of labour co-partnership.' *Econ. Rev.*, XI, 2 (April 1901), 201–17.

5155 **Mathieson**, George. 'Some aspects of profit-sharing.' *Econ. Rev.*, XII, 1 (January 1902), 35–42.

On Clarke, Nickolls & Coombs, Ltd., the author's own firm.

5156 **Vivian**, Henry H. *Co-operation and trade unionism*. London, [1902?]. 8p.

5157 **Webb**, Beatrice. 'The relationship between co-operation and trade unionism.' Webb, S. and Webb, B. *Problems of modern industry*. 2nd ed. London, New York, Bombay: Longmans, Green, 1902. p. 192–208.

'A paper read at a conference of Trade Union Officials and Co-operators, Tynemouth, 15th August 1892.'

5158 **Livesey**, George. 'Industrial partnership and the prevention of distress.' *Char. Orgn. Rev.*, n.s., XIII, 77 (May 1903), 229–38.

With details of profit-sharing or industrial partnership adopted by gas companies.

5159 **Macrosty**, Henry W. 'Productive co-operation: its principles and methods.' Co-operative Wholesale Societies. *Annual for 1903*. p. 161–92.

5160 **Middleton**, M. W. 'Profit-sharing experiments.' *Econ. Rev.*, XIII, 2 (April 1903), 213–15.

Charter United Gas Company and Thomson's woollen factory, Huddersfield.

5161 **Williams**, Aneurin. *History and present position of labour co-partnership*. London, 1903. 8p.

5162 **Williams**, Aneurin. *Labour co-partnership: its theory and practice*. London: Labour Co-partnership Association, 1903. 8p.

5163 **Davies**, Margaret Llewelyn. *The Women's Co-operative Guild, 1883–1904*. Kirkby Lonsdale: Women's Co-operative Guild, 1904. 170p.

5164 **Industrial Co-partnership Association**. *Industrial democracy*. London, [1904?]. 8p.

5165 **Jones**, Thomas. *Profit-sharing in relation to other methods of remunerating labour*. Edinburgh: Blackwood, 1904. 31p.

Reprinted from the *Accountants' Magazine*, 1904.

5166 **Livesey**, George. 'Industrial partnership and the prevention of distress.' Loch, C. S. (ed.). *Methods of social advance: short studies in social practice by various authors*. London, New York: Macmillan, 1904. p. 107–17.

5167 **Vivian**, Henry H. *The labour co-partnership movement in Great Britain*. London, 1904. 10p.

5168 **Bisset**, George. *Is co-operation capable of solving the industrial problem?* Manchester: Co-operative Union, 1905. 23p.

5169 **Quarterly Review**. 'Profit-sharing and co-partnership.' *Q. Rev.*, CCII, 402 (January 1905), 61–87.
Review article.

5170 **Williams**, Aneurin. 'Twenty years of co-partnership.' *Econ. Rev.*, XV, 1 (January 1905), 15–27.

5171 **Williams**, Aneurin. *Twenty-one years' work for co-partnership*. 1905. 12p.

5172 **Vivian**, Henry H. 'Co-partnership.' *Lpool. Econ. Statist. Soc. Trans.* (1905–6), 41–54.

5173 **Halstead**, Robert. *Co-partnership and the store movement*. London, [1907?]. 11p.

5174 **Williams**, Aneurin. *Labour co-partnership and the aspirations of labour*. London, 1907. 11p.

5175 **Fels**, Joseph and **Orr**, John. 'The remedy for unemployment.' *Social. Rev.*, II, 8 (October 1908), 589–97.

5176 **Cooper**, *Sir* William Earnshaw. *Britain for the Briton: co-operative working of agriculture and other industries a necessity. An earnest appeal for land, industrial, economic and other vital reforms.* London: Smith, Elder, 1909. xix, 390p.

5177 **Edinburgh Review**. 'The principles and practice of labour co-partnership.' *Edinb. Rev.*, CCIX, 428 (April 1909), 308–33.
Review article.

5178 **Molloy**, Bernard C. 'A general strike: its consequences and a remedy.' *Nineteenth Century*, LXVII, 395 (January 1910), 37–47.
On co-partnership.

5179 **Jackson**, Edward. *A study in democracy: rise and progress of industrial democracy in Bristol*. 1911.

5180 **London Municipal Society**. Department of Social Economics. *Co-operation, distributive and productive: co-operative production compared with production under private employers*. London, 1911. 12p. (Monographs 10.)
Second edition. 1911. 12p.

5181 **Worley**, J. J. *The Women's Co-operative Guild and the co-partnership movement*. London, [1911?]. 7p.

5182 **Board of Trade**. *Report on profit-sharing and labour co-partnership in the United Kingdom*. London: H.M.S.O., 1912. 160p. (Cd. 6496.)
By D. F. Schloss and G. S. Barnes.
1914. (Cd. 7283.)
1920. (Cmd. 544.)

5183 **Carpenter**, Charles C. *Co-partnership in industry*. London: Co-partnership Publishers, 1912. 28p.
With an appendix comprising chronological notes on British profit sharing and co-partnership, 1829–1912, by W. T. Layton.

5184 **Clarke**, E. Dillon. *Housing the workers: a criticism of co-partnership housing and a housing policy for trade unions*. London, 1912. 38p.

5185 **Fay**, Charles Ryle. 'Co-partnership in industry.' *Econ. J.*, XXII, 88 (December 1912), 529–41.
'A paper read before the Economic Section of the British Association, 1912.'

5186 **Halstead**, Robert. *Co-partnership and modern labour troubles*. London, [1912?]. 11p.

5187 **Lever**, William Hesketh, Baron Leverhulme. *Co-partnership*. Port Sunlight: Lever Bros., 1912. 24p.
An address to members of the Agricultural and Horticultural Association, 13 June 1912.

5188 **Lever**, William Hesketh, Baron Leverhulme. *Co-partnership and efficiency*. Port Sunlight: Lever Bros., 1912. 15p.
An address delivered in the Mason College of Birmingham University.

5189 **May**, H. J. *The relation of co-operation to other working-class movements*. Manchester, 1912. 16p.

5190 **Stocks**, J. L. 'Profit sharing in operation.' *Econ. Rev.*, XXII, 3 (July 1912), 313–17.
An account of the scheme at Messrs. J., T. and J. Taylor Ltd., woollen manufacturers, of Batley.

5191 **Taylor**, Theodore Cooke. 'Profit sharing and labor co-partnership.' *Contemp. Rev.* CL (May 1912), 625–34.

5192 **Ashley**, William James. 'Profit sharing.' *Q. Rev.*, CCXIX, 437 (October 1913), 509–30.
Review article.

5193 **Carpenter**, Charles C. *Are trades unionism and co-partnership incompatible?* London, 1913. 12p.

5194 **Fay**, Charles Ryle. *Co-partnership in industry*. Cambridge: Cambridge U.P., 1913. 146p. (Cambridge manuals of science and literature.)

5195 **Furniss**, H. Sanderson. 'Co-partnership and labour unrest.' *Econ. Rev.*, XXIII (January 1913), 61–72.
The case for the trade unions against co-partnership.

5196 **Lester-Garland**, L. V. 'Co-partnership and labour.' *Econ. Rev.*, XXIII, 2 (April 1913), 150–7.
A reply to H. Sanderson Furniss (January 1913).

5197 **Pease**, Edward Reynolds. *Profit-sharing and co-partnership: a fraud & a failure?* London: Fabian Society, 1913. 16p. (Fabian tract 170.)

5198 **Smith**, James Carmichael. 'The theory of equitable profit-sharing.' *Westm. Rev.*, CLXXX, 5 (November 1913), 492–512.

5199 **Williams**, Aneurin. *Co-partnership and profit-sharing*. London: Williams and Norgate, Thornton Butterworth; New York: Holt, 1913. 256p. (Home university library of modern knowledge.)

5200 **Woolf**, Leonard Sidney. *The control of industry by co-operators and trade unionists*. London, [1913?]. 16p.

5201 **Gregory**, Theodore. 'Labour co-partnership and labour unrest.' *Manchr. Statist. Soc. Trans.* (1913–14), 1–28.

5202 **Mann**, Amos. *Democracy in industry: story of 21 years' work of the Leicester Anchor Boot and Shoe Production Society Ltd.* 1914.

5203 **Price**, Langford Lovell Frederick Rice. *Co-operation and co-partnership.* London, Glasgow: Collins' Clear-Type P., 1914. 264p. (The nation's library.)

5204 **Vivian**, Henry H. *Co-partnership in practice.* London, 1914. 19p.

5205 **Webb**, Sidney and **Webb**, Beatrice. 'Co-operative production and profit sharing.' *New States.*, II, 45 (14 February 1914), Supplement. 31p.

Draft of the first report of the Committee of the Fabian Research Department, submitted by S. and B. Webb.

5206 **Greening**, Edward Owen. *A policy of conciliation for co-operators: how to reconcile the interests, ideals & work of agricultural, productive and distributive societies.* London: Palmer, Sutton, 1915. 7p.

5207 **Woolf**, Leonard Sidney. *The control of industry by the people.* London: Women's Co-operative Guild, 1915. 16p.

5208 **Better Business**. 'The relation of producer to consumer in co-operation.' *Bett. Bus.*, I, 2 (January 1916), 174–80.

5209 **Paul**, Alexander. *Lessons of war and co-partnership: an address to the Co-partnership in War Time Committee . . . May 1st, 1916.* Port Sunlight: Lever Bros., 1916. 20p.

5210 **Women's Co-operative Guild**. *Women's Co-operative Guild 1895 to 1916: a review of twenty-one years' work.* London: the Guild, 1916. 12p.

5211 **Downie**, John. 'The relation of the producer and the consumer in the co-operative movement.' *Bett. Bus.*, II, 3 (May 1917), 226–39.

5212 **Foster**, Thomas. *Masters & men: a new co-partnership.* London: Headley Bros., 1917. 9p.

5213 **Labour Co-partnership Association.** *Co-partnership after the war.* London: the Association, 1917. 16p.

Another edition. 1920. 16p.

5214 **Piercy**, William. 'The control of industry by producers and consumers.' Furniss, H. Sanderson (ed.). *The industrial outlook.* London: Chatto and Windus, 1917. p. 170–206.

5215 *Trade unionists and co-operators: basis of joint action by the Trades Union Congress Parliamentary Committee and the central board of the Co-operative Union.* [1917?] 6p.

5216 **Button**, Howard. *Notes on principles of profit-sharing and labour co-partnership.* London: Boyle and Watchurst, 1918. 18p.

5217 **Mather**, William. 'Ways to industrial peace. I. The capital of labour: a suggestion for the engineering trades.' *Nineteenth Century*, LXXXIII, 492 (February 1918), 437–42.

5218 **O'Brien**, Cruise and **O'Brien**, D. C. 'Co-operative production.' *Bett. Bus.*, III, 4 (August 1918), 352–62; IV, 2 (February 1919), 133–45; IV, 4 (August 1919), 290–6; V, 4 (August 1920), 265–79; *Irish Econ.*, VII, 2 (February 1922), 131–7; VIII, 2 (April 1923), 156–63.

5219 **Priestley**, Neville. 'Co-partnership *versus* labour unrest.' *Nineteenth Century*, LXXXIII, 495 (May 1918), 948–65.

5220 **Woolf**, Leonard Sidney. *Co-operation & the future of industry.* London: Allen and Unwin, 1918. 141p.

5221 **Barker**, J. Ellis. 'Labour unrest: its causes and its permanent cure.' *Nineteenth Century*, LXXXV, 508 (June 1919), 1146–64.

On profit-sharing.

5222 **Bowerman**, C. W. *Some industrial problems.* London, 1919. 11p.

5223 **Carter**, C. K. 'The great home problem of 1919. II. An employee co-partner on co-partnership.' *Nineteenth Century*, LXXXV, 504 (February 1919), 227–31.

On the gas industry.

5224 **Cecil**, Robert, *Lord* and **Clynes**, John Robert. *Speeches on profit-sharing and labour co-partnership.* London, 1919. 24p.

5225 **Clarke, Nickolls and Coombs**. *The proof of the pudding: being some notes on co-partnership and profit-sharing in general and on the particular experiences thereof in the works of Clarke, Nickolls & Coombs.* London: Clarke, Nickolls and Coombs, 1919. 43p.

5226 **Constructional Co-partners**. *Security for capital: an experiment in industrial method.* Chepstow, 1919. 15p.

5227 **Cooke**, Howard E. T. *How capital and labour can share equally in net profits.* [Montreal: H. E. T. Cooke, 1919.] 7p.

5228 **Davies**, Margaret Llewelyn, **Enfield**, A. Honora and **Harris**, Lilian. *Co-operation and labour unrest.* Manchester: Co-operative Union, 1919. 8p.

5229 **Dewar**, George A. B. 'The decay of the wage system.' *Nineteenth Century*, LXXXV, 506 (April 1919), 659–70.

5230 **Labour Co-partnership Association.** *Experiments in profit-sharing and co-partnership.* Birmingham, 1919.

5231 **South Suburban Gas Company**. *A development of co-partnership.* London, 1919. 16p.

5232 **United Advisory Council of Co-operators and Trade Unionists**. *Trade unionism and co-operation: the union of forces.* London, 1919. 8p.

5233 **Coote**, Colin R. 'Is industrial peace possible?' *Nineteenth Century*, LXXXVIII, 523 (September 1920), 450–61.

On co-partnership.

5234 **Hall**, Fred. *The history of the Co-operative Printing Society, 1869–1919, being a record of fifty years' progress and achievement.* Manchester: Co-operative Printing Society, 1920. 352p.

5235 **Trombert**, Albert. *Profit-sharing: a general study of the system as in actual operation.* London: King, 1920. 94p.

Translated from the French.

5236 **Greening**, Edward Owen. *A democratic co-partnership*. Leicester, 1921. 121p.

5237 **Halstead**, Robert. *The producer's place in society*. Manchester, 1921. 48p.

5238 **International Labour Office.** 'Profit-sharing and labour co-partnership in Great Britain.' *Int. Labour Rev.*, IV, 1 (October 1921), 114–26.

5239 **Pease**, Edward Reynolds. *Profit-sharing and co-partnership*. London: Labour Party, 1921. 12p.

5240 **Bowie**, James Alexander. 'Profit-sharing and co-partnership, including a study of the recent coal settlement.' *Econ. J.*, XXXII, 128 (December 1922), 466–76.

5241 **Bowie**, James Alexander. *Sharing profits with employees: a critical study of methods in the light of present conditions*. London: Pitman, 1922. ix, 222p. (Pitman's industrial administration series.)

Second edition. 1923. x, 254p.

5242 **Coffey**, D. 'Industrial co-operative production in Ireland.' *Sociol. Rev.*, XIV, 4 (October 1922), 310–14.

5243 **Lever**, William Hesketh. *Co-partnership: laying the three ghosts, unemployment, sickness, death. Speech* . . . Port Sunlight: Lever Bros., 1922. 16p.

5244 **Manchester Guardian Commercial.** *Practical profit sharing: a survey of existing schemes*. Manchester, 1922. 67p. ('M.G. Commercial' handbooks 2.)

'Reprinted from the *Manchester Guardian Commercial*. With an introduction by Seebohm Rowntree.'

5245 **Potter**, W. Charles. *The National Co-operative Men's Guild*. Manchester: Co-operative Union, 1922. 18p.

New and revised edition. 1926. 18p.

5246 **Bowie**, James Alexander. *Sharing profits with employees: a critical study of methods in the light of present conditions*. 1923. (D.Litt. thesis, University of Aberdeen.)

5247 **Greening**, Edward Owen. *A pioneer co-partnership, being the history of the Leicester Co-operative Boot and Shoe Manufacturing Society*. Leicester: the Society, 1923. xviii, 192p.

5248 **Harris**, Lilian. *The position of employees in the co-operative movement*. London: Fabian Society, 1923. 32p. (Fabian tract 204.)

5249 **Bramley**, Fred. *Why trade-unionists should be co-operators*. Manchester: Co-operative Union, 1924. 9p.

5250 **Gilchrist**, Robert Niven. *The payment of wages and profit-sharing. With a chapter on Indian conditions*. Calcutta: University of Calcutta, 1924. 422p.

5251 **Kidd**, James. *Unity in industry*. London: Murray, 1924. 160p.

5252 **Kettering Clothing Manufacturing Co-operative Society.** *The story of a successful experiment in co-partnership*. Kettering, 1925. 24p.

5253 **Askwith**, Mark Ernest. *Profit-sharing: an aid to trade revival . . . with . . . a special chapter on the coal-mining industry*. London: Duncan Scott, 1926. 119p.

5254 **Hazell**, Walter Howard. 'Profit sharing and share purchase for employees.' *Q. Rev.*, CCXLVI, 487 (January 1926), 49–59.

5255 **Atkinson**, Henry. *Co-operative production: the Priestman-Atkinson system*. London: Benn, 1927. 214p.

5256 **Carpenter**, Charles C. *Industrial co-partnership*. London: Labour Co-Partnership Association, 1927. vi, 115p.

Fourth edition of *Co-partnership in industry*.

5257 **Hazell**, Walter Howard. *Labour and capital in alliance*. London: Murray, 1927. xii, 116p.

5258 **Mundy**, Ernest William. *Profit-sharing and co-partnership: an introduction*. London: Labour Co-Partnership Association, 1927. 31p.

Second edition. 1928. 31p.

Third edition. 1931. 31p.

5259 **Hovey**, Robert Baldwin. *Co-partnership and income tax: notes on co-partnership schemes with special reference to an income tax concession*. Sandbach, Glasgow: Hopol, 1928. 13p.

5260 **Raffety**, Frank Walter. *Partnership in industry*. London: Cape, 1928. 160p.

5261 **Worley**, J. J. *The producers' theory of co-operation and its relation to the development of co-operation*. Leicester, 1928. 11p.

5262 **Mercer**, Thomas William. *Servants of democracy: reflections on co-operative employment and co-operative employees*. Manchester, 1929. 24p.

5263 **Palmer**, Robert Alexander, Baron Rusholme. *Employment in co-operative service: a paper* . . . Manchester, 1931. 15p. (Better service series.)

5264 **Gregg**, Frances. 'The resistance of employees to co-partnership schemes.' *Hum. Factor*, VI, 6 (June 1932), 222–7.

5265 **Sladen**, Norman St. Barbe. *Ark; or, A new industrial era*. London: Williams and Norgate, 1932. 78p.

5266 **Palmer**, Robert Alexander, Baron Rusholme. *What does co-operative employment mean to you?* Manchester, 1933. 14p. (Better service series.)

Third edition.

5267 **Steed**, Henry Wickham. *A way to social peace*. London: Allen and Unwin, 1934. 148p.

Halley Stewart lecture 1933.

5268 **Urwick**, Lyndall Fownes. 'Co-partnership and control.' *Hum. Factor*, VIII, 11 (November 1934), 385–6.

'Part of an address on *Co-partnership and management* delivered to the Annual Congress of the Industrial Co-partnership Association at Somerville College, Oxford, July 22, 1934.'

5269 **Brown**, William Henry. *The trek of men: history, programme and policy, rules and standing* *orders of the N.C.M.G.* Manchester: National Co-operative Men's Guild, 1937. 24p.

5270 **Hughes**, John Henry. *Ark: an economic citizenship.* London: Ark Industrial Association of Great Britain, 1937. 100p.

A manifesto of the Ark Industrial Association of Great Britain.

5271 **Brown**, William Henry. *Co-operative understanding, being the jubilee story of the 'Holyoake' Boot and Shoe.* Leicester: Co-operative Productive Federation, 1938. 28p.

5272 **Goddard**, H. A. 'Profit-sharing and the amenities of the Nuffield factories.' Gannett, F. E. and Catherwood, B. F. (eds.). *Industrial and labour relations in Great Britain: a symposium.* New York: the editors, 1939. p. 265–9.

5273 **Ramage**, John. 'Profit-sharing and co-partnership in Great Britain.' Gannett, F. E. and Catherwood, B. F. (eds.). *Industrial and labour relations in Great Britain: a symposium.* New York: the editors, 1939. p. 243–64.

Author was Secretary of the Industrial Co-partnership Association of Great Britain.

5274 **Smith**, Joseph Henry. 'Some considerations affecting the operation of profit-sharing schemes in farming.' University College of Wales, Aberystwyth. Department of Agricultural Economics. *Welsh Studies in agricultural economics.* 1945. p. 67–70.

Reprinted from the *Welsh Journal of Agriculture*, Vol. XVIII.

5275 **Afford**, H. *The co-operative employee: his place in the movement.* London: London Co-operative Society, Education Committee, 1946. 15p. (Co-operative discussion group outlines 5.)

5276 **Cole**, George Douglas Howard. *Co-operation, labour and socialism.* Leicester: Co-operative Co-partnership Propaganda Committee, 1946. 15 leaves.

6th Blandford memorial lecture.

5277 **Conservative Research Department.** *Co-partnership today: a survey of profit-sharing and co-partnership schemes in industry.* London: Conservative Political Centre, 1946. 46p. bibliog.

By Geoffrey D. M. Block.

Published without the author's name.

Reissued in 1955 with a new preface and amended bibliography. 44p.

5278 **Dymond**, W. R. *The movement for labour–management co-operation in industry.* 1946. 313p. (M.A. thesis, Toronto University.)

5279 **Hunt**, S. C. *Industrial co-partnership: the labour–capital ideal.* Topsham: Co-Partnership Printing and Publishing Association, [1946?]. 32p.

5280 **National Union of Conservative and Constitutional Associations.** Advisory Committee on Policy and Political Education. *Co-partnership to-day: a survey of profit-sharing and co-partnership schemes in industry.* London, 1946. 48p.

5281 **Australia.** Department of Labour and National Service. *Profit-sharing: a study of the results of overseas experience.* Industrial Welfare Division, Department of Labour and National Service, 1947.

5282 **Co-operative Co-partnership Propaganda Committee.** *The trade unions and co-operative co-partnership.* Leicester, 1947. 12p.

5283 **Holden**, A. S. *The co-partnership of the South Metropolitan Gas Company.* London, 1947. 8p.

5284 **Hemstock**, Arthur. 'Co-operative co-partnership production in Great Britain.' *Ann. Collect. Econ.*, XIX, 1 (January–March 1948), 43–51.

5285 **Hemstock**, Arthur. 'Industrial co-operatives.' Barou, N. (ed.). *The co-operative movement in Labour Britain.* London: Gollancz, 1948. p. 64–73.

5286 **Lewis**, John Spedan. *Partnership for all.* London: Kerr-Cross Publishing Co., 1948. xviii, 532p.

On the John Lewis Partnership.

A reissue, with an additional appendix. 1948. xx, 536p. The foreword bears the date 1952.

5287 **Hope**, Charles Graham. 'Teamwork and ownership in industry.' *Nineteenth Century*, CXLVI (December 1949), 376–84.

5288 **Dalal**, K. L. 'Profit-sharing: the experience of foreign countries.' *Indian J. Econ.*, XXXI, 1 (July 1950), 1–15.

5289 **Narasimhan**, P. S. 'Profit-sharing: a review.' *Int. Labour Rev.*, LXII, 6 (December 1950), 469–99.

5290 **Perkins**, Alfred Richard. *The principles and organisation of workers' co-operative productive societies.* Leicester: Co-operative Co-Partnership Propaganda Committee, 1952. 16p.

Second edition, revised. 1955. 16p.

5291 **Scott**, Lawrence Prestwich. *Education for co-operation in industry: copy of a paper given by L. P. Scott at the one-day conference in the Engineers' Club Manchester, Wednesday, March 22, 1950.* London: British Association for Commercial and Industrial Education, 1952. 12p.

5292 **Richards**, Edith Ryley. *Shoemenders: a study of goodwill in industry.* London: Allen and Unwin, 1953. 92p.

5293 **Lane**, P. J. *Distribution and classification of co-operative societies in Ireland.* 1953–54. (M.A. thesis, National University of Ireland.)

5294 **Lewis**, John Spedan. *Fairer shares: a possible advance in civilisation and perhaps the only alternative to communism.* London: Staples P., 1954. ix, 244p.

5295 **Harper**, John Charles. *Profit-sharing in practice and law.* London: Sweet and Maxwell, 1955. xxiv, 368p.

5296 **Hughes**, John Henry. *Ark: the solution of the industrial problem.* London: Ark Industrial

Association of Great Britain, 1955. 22p.
Revised and reprinted. 1957. 28p.

5297 **Perkins**, Alfred Richard. 'The co-operative co-partnership productive societies of Great Britain.' *Ann. Collect. Econ.*, XXVI, 5 (November–December 1955), 357–76.

5298 **Reddish**, *Sir* Halford Walter Lupton. *This is industrial partnership.* London: Staples P., 1955. 34p.

5299 **Wallace**, William. *Co-partnership re-examined.* London: Industrial Co-Partnership Association, [1955]. 64p.

5300 **Bader**, Ernest. *From profit sharing to common ownership: a practical example of growth from the old to the new.* Wollaston: Scott Bader Commonwealth, 1956. 38p.

5301 **Ball**, Frank Norman. 'The present trouble.' *Ind. Law Rev.*, XI, 4 (April 1957), 194–204.
On profit-sharing.

5302 **Banks**, N. D. 'Industrial co-partnership.' *Ind. Law Rev.*, XI, 4 (April 1957), 214–23.

5303 **Beck**, George Andrew, Bishop of Salford. *Towards industrial co-operation.* Oxford: Catholic Social Guild, 1957. 16p.

5304 **Cole**, George Douglas Howard. *The case for industrial partnership.* London: Macmillan, 1957. v, 121p.

5305 **Co-operative Party**. *Co-operation for trade unionists.* London, 1957. [13]p.

5306 **Wallace**, William. *Partnership in industry.* London: Industrial Co-Partnership Association, 1957. 14p.
An address.

5307 **Copeman**, George Henry. *The challenge of employee shareholding: how to close the gap between capital and labour.* London: Business Publications, Batsford, 1958. viii, 200p.

5308 **Daw**, John Ward. *Partnership and the ideal workman.* London: Industrial Co-Partnership Association, 1958. [8]p.

5309 **Lewis**, John Spedan. *Inflation's cause and cure.* London: Museum P., 1958. 36p.
On the John Lewis Partnership.

5310 **Payne**, Harry Herbert. *Team work in industry.* London: Industrial Co-Partnership Association, 1958. 23p.
Profit-sharing at Harry H. Payne Ltd., Birmingham.

5311 **Wade**, Donald William, Baron Wade. *Towards a nation of owners: a challenge answered.* London: Liberal Publications Department, 1958. 40p.

5312 **Wainwright**, Richard. *Own as you earn.* London: Liberal Publications Department, 1958. 27p.

5313 **Birch**, *Sir* John Alan. *Industrial relations in co-operative employment.* Leicester: Co-operative Co-Partnership Propaganda Committee, 1959. 17p. (19th Blandford memorial lecture.)
The author was General Secretary of the Union of Shop, Distributive and Allied Workers.

5314 **Wallace**, William. *Prescription for partnership: a study of industrial relations.* London: Pitman, 1959. xvi, 228p.

5315 **Brolly**, M. H. 'Profit sharing.' *Occup. Psychol.*, XXXIV, 2 (April 1960), 86–108.

5316 **Goyder**, George. *The responsible company.* Oxford: Blackwell, 1961. x, 192p.

5317 **Blount**, Patrick Clavell. *Ideas into action: a plea and a plan for teamwork.* London: Clair P., 1962. 178p.

5318 **Tyson**, R. E. *The Sun Mill Company Ltd.: a study in democratic investment, 1858–1959.* 1962. (M.A. thesis, University of Manchester.)

5319 **Derrick**, Paul. 'Is co-ownership the answer?' *New Soc.*, 31 (2 May 1963), 11–13.

5320 **British Institute of Management.** *Survey of share of production plans.* London: B.I.M., 1965. 12p.

5321 **Hanson**, C. G. 'Profit-sharing schemes in Great Britain.' *J. Mgmt. Studies*, II, 3 (October 1965), 331–50.

5322 **Wilken**, Folkert. *The liberation of work: the elimination of strikes & strife in industry through associative organization of enterprise.* Madison, Wis.: Center for the Study of Productivity Motivation, School of Commerce, University of Wisconsin, [1965?6]. iii, 87p.
A translation of *Die Befreiung der Arbeit.* Freiburg i.Br.: 'Die Kommenden', 1965.
Printed by the Center 'for limited distribution to educators and publishers in the United States with the permission of the author'.
'Some chapters at the end of the book have been omitted as they deal mainly with specific German situations.'
A complete translation published London: Routledge and Kegan Paul, 1969. 109p.

5323 **Wallace**, William. 'Profit-sharing schemes in Great Britain: a comment.' *J. Mgmt. Studies*, III, 1 (February 1966), 122–3.
Followed by C. G. Hanson's reply.

5324 **Acton Society Trust** and **Naylor**, Guy. *Sharing the profits; an inquiry into the habits, attitudes and problems of employees' shareholding schemes: the text of two studies made for the Wider Share Ownership Council, one by the Acton Trust Society and the other by Guy Naylor.* London: Garnstone P., 1968. xxii, 129p.

5325 **Blum**, Fred Herman. *Work and community: the Scott Bader Commonwealth and the quest for a new social order.* London: Routledge and Kegan Paul, 1968. xviii, 392p. (New Era Centre publications.)

5326 **Flanders**, Allan David, **Pomeranz**, Ruth and **Woodward**, Joan. *Experiment in industrial democracy: a study of the John Lewis Partnership.* London: Faber, 1968. 261p. (Society today and tomorrow.)

5327 **Liberal Party.** Industrial Partnership Committee. *Partners at work.* London: Liberal Publication Dept., 1968. 40p. (Liberal Party reports.)

5328 **Daly**, George F. A. 'Is there a case for profit sharing?' Irish Management Institute. *Industrial democracy: a symposium.* Dublin: the Institute, 1969. p. 74–89.

5329 **Derrick**, Paul and **Phipps**, John Francis (eds.). *Co-ownership, co-operation and control: an industrial objective.* London: Longmans, 1969. 184p. (Management studies series.)

5330 **Farrow**, Nigel. 'The John Lewis Partnership. 1. The profit in worker-ownership.' Derrick, P. and Phipps, J.-F. (eds.). *Co-ownership, co-operation and control* . . . London: Longmans, 1969. p. 83–91.
Reprinted from *Business*, 1964.

5331 **Farrow**, Nigel. 'The Scott Bader Commonwealth Ltd.' Derrick, P. and Phipps, J.-F. (eds.). *Co-ownership, co-operation, and control* . . . London: Longmans, 1969. p. 95–100.
Reprinted from *Business*, January 1965.

5332 **John Lewis Partnership**. 'The John Lewis Partnership. 2. The partnership system and how it works.' Derrick, P. and Phipps, J.-F. (eds.). *Co-ownership, co-operation and control* . . . London: Longmans, 1969. p. 91–4.
'Information provided by the John Lewis Partnership.'

5333 **McAlpine**, Tom. 'Factories for peace. 1. Rowen Engineering Ltd., Glasgow.' Derrick, P. and Phipps, J.-F. (eds.). *Co-ownership, co-operation and control* . . . London: Longmans, 1969. p. 104–6.
The author was Manager of the firm.

5334 **Maxwell**, J. F. 'Company law reform – moral justification.' Derrick, P. and Phipps, J-F. (eds.). *Co-ownership, co-operation and control* . . . London: Longmans, 1969. p. 123–78.
Condensed from 'Should Christians press for revision of company law.' *University of Detroit Law Journal*, XL, 1, October 1962.
The author was Director, Catholic Social Guild, Southwark.

5335 **Prince**, Rod. 'Factories for peace. 2. Onllwyn, South Wales.' Derrick, P. and Phipps, J.-F. (eds.). *Co-ownership, co-operation and control* . . . London: Longmans, 1969. p. 106–8.

5336 **Spreckley**, David. 'Landsman's (Co-ownership) Ltd.' Derrick, P. and Phipps, J.-F. (eds.). *Co-ownership, co-operation and control* . . . London: Longmans, 1969. p. 100–4.
The author was Managing Director of the firm.

5337 **Turner**, Graham. *Business in Britain.* London: Eyre and Spottiswoode, 1969. 451p.
The John Lewis Partnership is discussed in the section on retail trade.

See also: 29; 283; 1146; 1356; 1362; 1391; 7106; 7958.

C. GUILD SOCIALISM

See also Part Three, III, B, 4.

5338 **National Guilds League**. *National guilds or Whitley Councils? Being a reprint, with a new introduction, of two pamphlets, entitled:- 'Observations on the Whitley Report', and 'Notes for trade unionists on the Whitley Report'.* London: the League, n.d. 20p.

5339 **Wilkinson**, R. E. *How to start a local guild.* London: C. W. Daniel, n.d. 48p.

5340 **Cobden-Sanderson**, Thomas James. *Ecce mundus: industrial ideals, and the book beautiful.* London: Hammersmith Publishing Society, 1902. [34]p.

5341 **Penty**, Arthur Joseph. *The restoration of the gild system.* London: Swan Sonnenschein, 1906. ix, 103p.

5342 **Cole**, George Douglas Howard. *The world of labour: a discussion of the present and future of trade unionism.* London: Bell, 1913. vii, 443p.
Second and revised edition. 1915. ix, 443p.
Third edition. 1917.
Fourth edition. 1919.
Fourth edition, reprinted. London: Macmillan, 1928. xli, 443p.

5343 **Hobson**, Samuel George. *National guilds: an inquiry into the wages system and the way out.* London: Bell, 1914. viii, 370p.
Edited by A. R. Orage.
Most of the material appeared in *The New Age*, during 1912 and 1913, before the book was first published in 1914.
Third edition. 1919. viii, 370p.

5344 **National Guilds League**. *The guild idea: an appeal to the public.* London: Victoria House Printing Co. for the League, [1915]. 19p. (Pamphlets 2.)
Second edition. The League, [1918?].

5345 **National Guilds League**. *National guilds: an appeal to trade economists.* London: Victoria House Printing Co. for the League, [1915]. 20p. (Pamphlets 1.)
Second edition. The League, [1917]. 16p.
Third edition. 1920. 16p.

5346 **National Guilds League**. *Towards a miners' guild.* London: Victoria House Printing Co. for the League, [1915? 16]. 15p. (Pamphlets 3.)

5347 **Cole**, George Douglas Howard. *Self-government in industry.* London: Bell, 1917. x, 329p.
Reprinted. 1918, 1919.
Third edition. 1918. x, 329p.
Fourth edition, revised. 1919. x, 283p.
Fifth edition, revised. 1920.
Another edition. 1928. x, 283p.

5348 **Hobson**, Samuel George. *Guild principles in war and peace.* London: Bell, 1917. viii, 176p.
A collection of essays.
Introductory essay by A. R. Orage.

5349 **Penty**, Arthur Joseph. *Old worlds for new: a study of the post-industrial state.* London: Allen and Unwin, 1917. 186p.

5350 **National Guilds League**. *A short statement of the principles and objects of the National Guilds League.* London: the League, [1917? 18]. 8p.

5351 **National Guilds League**. *Towards a national railway guild*. London: Victoria House Printing Co. for the League, [1917? 18]. 16p. (Pamphlets 4.)

5352 **Cole**, George Douglas Howard and **Mellor**, William. *The meaning of industrial freedom*. London: Allen and Unwin, 1918. 44p.

5353 **Goldwell**, Francis. *Guild socialism: a criticism of the national guild theory*. London: Catholic Social Guild, 1918. 48p.

5354 **National Guilds League**. *National guilds or Whitley Councils?* London: the League, 1918. 20p.

5355 **Reckitt**, Maurice Benington and **Bechofer**, C. E. *The meaning of national guilds*. London: C. Palmer and Hayward, 1918. xvi, 452p.

Second revised edition. London: Palmer, 1920. xvi, 291p.

Also New York: Macmillan, 1920.

5356 **Richardson**, H. M. 'National guilds: the new trade unionism.' Co-operative Wholesale Societies. *Annual, 1918*. p. 283–8.

5357 **Wilkinson**, R. E. *How to start a local guild*. London: C. W. Daniel, 1918. 48p.

5358 **Middleton**, George. 'Self government in industry.' *Manchr. Statist. Soc. Trans.* (1918–1919), 43–54.

5359 **Cole**, George Douglas Howard. *National guilds and the Coal Commission*. London: National Guilds League, 1919. 16p.

Summary of evidence submitted to the Commission by G. D. H. Cole.

Reprinted from *New Age*.

5360 **Cole**, George Douglas Howard. 'National guilds and the state.' *Social. Rev.*, XVI, 88 (January–March 1919), 22–30.

5361 **Gould**, Frederick James. *Labour's unrest and labour's future: brief notes on Comte, Marx, Orage, national guilds, and the social outlook*. London: Watts, 1919. 16p.

5362 **Penty**, Arthur Joseph. *Guilds and the social crisis*. London: Allen and Unwin, 1919. 103p.

5363 **Taylor**, George Robert Stirling. *The guild state: its principles and possibilities*. London: Allen and Unwin, 1919. 153p.

5364 **Bull**, Paul Bertie. *Gild socialism*. [Mirfield: Community of the Resurrection?], [*c.* 1920]. 8p.

5365 **Cole**, George Douglas Howard. *Guild socialism*. London: Fabian Society, 1920. 20p. (Fabian tract 192.)

First published as *Guild socialism. Fabian Society lecture . . . November 7th, 1919*. Supplement to *New Commonwealth*, 6 (21 November 1919).

5366 **Cole**, George Douglas Howard. *Guild socialism re-stated*. London: Parsons, 1920. 224p.

Reprinted as a 'Special W.E.A. cheap edition'. 1921.

5367 **Cole**, George Douglas Howard. 'National guilds movement in Great Britain.' Bloomfield, D. (ed.). *Selected articles on modern industrial movements*. London: Pitman, 1920. p. 158–67.

5368 **Cole**, George Douglas Howard. 'Reviving the guild idea.' Bloomfield, D. (ed.). *Selected articles on modern industrial movements*. London: Pitman, 1920. p. 153–8.

From *Living Age*, 302 (26 July 1919), 214–17.

5369 **Cole**, George Douglas Howard. *Social theory*. London: Methuen, 1920. v, 219p. (Library of social studies.)

Second edition, revised. 1921. vii, 219p.

Third edition. 1923. vii, 220p.

5370 **Hobson**, Samuel George. *Guilds of house-builders*. London, [1920?]. 4p.

5371 **Hobson**, Samuel George. *National guilds and the state*. London: Bell, 1920. xix, 406p.

5372 **Penty**, Arthur Joseph. *A guildsman's interpretation of history*. London: Allen and Unwin, 1920. 327p.

5373 **Reynard**, Hélène. 'The guild socialists.' *Econ. J.*, XXX, 119 (September 1920), 321–30.

5374 **Taylor**, George Robert Stirling. 'The guild state.' *Nineteenth Century*, LXXXVII, 515 (January 1920), 177–86.

5375 **Withers**, Hartley. *The case for capitalism*. London: Everlersh Nash, 1920. 255p.

Also New York: Dutton, 1920.

Chaps. IX–X are on Guild Socialism.

Another edition. 1925. 277p.

5376 **Besant**, Annie. *The guild system as a substitute for trade unionism: a paper read before the Political Section of the 1921 Club, Madras, on November 2nd, 1921*. Madras: National Home Rule League, 1921. 17, ixp. (Pamphlets 20.)

5377 **Cole**, George Douglas Howard. *Capitalist speculation and workers' control in the textile industries*. London: Labour Publishing Co. for the National Guilds League, 1921. 23p. (Workers' control series 5.)

Reprinted from the author's *Chaos and order in industry*.

5378 **Cole**, George Douglas Howard. *Guild socialism: a plan for economic democracy*. New York: Frederick A. Stokes, 1921. vii, 202p.

5379 **Cole**, George Douglas Howard. *Unemployment and industrial maintenance*. London: Labour Publishing Co. for the National Guilds League, 1921. 16p.

5380 **Cole**, George Douglas Howard. *Workers' control for railwaymen*. London: Labour Publishing Co. for the National Guilds League, 1921. 23p. (Workers' control series 3.)

Reprinted from the author's *Chaos and order in industry*.

5381 **Cole**, George Douglas Howard. *Workers' control in engineering and shipbuilding: a plan for collective contract*. London: Labour Publishing Co. for the National Guilds League, 1921. 14p. (Workers' control series 4.)

Reprinted from the author's *Chaos and order in industry*.

5382 **Cole**, George Douglas Howard. *Workers' control in the distributive industry: a plan for co-operative employees and shop workers.* London: Labour Publishing Co. for the National Guilds League, [1921]. 25p. (Workers' control series 2.)

Reprinted from the author's *Chaos and order in industry.*

5383 **Cole**, George Douglas Howard. *Workers' control in the mining industry.* London: Labour Publishing Co. for the National Guilds League, 1921. 27p. (Workers' control series 1.)

Reprinted from the author's *Chaos and order in industry.*

5384 **Cole**, Margaret Isabel. *The control of industry.* London: Labour Publishing Co., 1921. 12p. (Labour booklets 4.)

5385 **Cox**, Garfield V. 'The English building guilds: an experiment in industrial self-government.' *J. Polit. Econ.*, XXIX, 10 (December 1921), 777–90.

5386 **Lloyd**, James Henry. *Guilds and the salary earner.* London: Labour Publishing Co. for the National Guilds League, 1921. 15p.

5387 **Ludlam**, H. E. B. *Industrial democracy and the printing industry.* Coventry: the author, 1921. 15p.

5388 **Milne-Bailey**, Walter. *Towards a postal guild.* London: Labour Publishing Co. for the National Guilds League, 1921. 12p.

5389 **National Guilds League.** *Education and the guild idea.* London: Labour Publishing Co. for the League, 1921. 19p.

5390 **National Guilds League.** *The policy of guild socialism: a statement prepared and issued in accordance with the instructions of the Annual Conference of the National Guilds League.* London: Labour Publishing Co. for the League, 1921. 23p.

5391 **Penty**, Arthur Joseph. *Guilds, trade and agriculture.* London: Allen and Unwin, 1921. 127p.

5392 **Selley**, Ernest. 'An inquiry into the working of the building guilds.' *Gdn. Cities Tn. Plann.*, XI, 6 (June 1921), 134–42.

5393 **Carpenter**, Niles. *Guild socialism: an historical and critical analysis.* New York, London: Appleton, 1922. xv, 350p.

5394 **Cole**, George Douglas Howard. 'The guild movement in Great Britain.' *Int. Labour Rev.*, VI, 2 (August 1922), 185–99.

5395 **Hewes**, Amy. 'Guild socialism: a two years' test.' *Am. Econ. Rev.*, XII, 2 (June 1922), 209–37.

5396 **Joslyn**, Carl S. 'The British building guilds: a critical survey of two years' work.' *Q. J. Econ.*, XXXVII, 1 (November 1922), 75–133.

'...the substance of an investigation undertaken by the author for Professor Graham Wallas during the academic year 1921–22.'

5397 **Penty**, Arthur Joseph. *Post-industrialism.* London: Allen and Unwin, 1922. 157p.

5398 **Cole**, George Douglas Howard. 'The guild movement in Great Britain.' An appendix to Por, O. *Guilds and co-operatives in Italy.* London: Labour Publishing Co., 1923. p. 167–93.

5399 **Fordham**, Montague. *Agriculture and the guild system, containing a practical proposal providing a democratic economic basis for the reconstruction of British agriculture and rural life.* London: King, 1923. 24p.

'Issued by the National Guilds League.'

5400 **Joslyn**, Carl S. 'A catastrophe in the British building guilds.' *Q. J. Econ.*, XXXVII, 3 (May 1923), 523–34.

5401 **Mortished**, R. J. P. 'Irish labour and the guild idea.' *Irish Econ.*, VIII, 2 (April 1923), 119–33.

5402 **Cole**, George Douglas Howard. 'Guild socialism'. Hogue, R. W. (ed.). *British labour speaks.* New York: Boni and Liveright, 1924. p. 239–66.

5403 **Cole**, George Douglas Howard. 'The meaning of guild socialism.' *Theosophist* (June 1929), 225–32.

5404 **Penty**, Arthur Joseph. *Means and ends.* London: Faber, 1932. 116p.

5405 **Hobson**, Samuel George. *Pilgrim to the left: memoirs of a modern revolutionist.* London: Arnold, 1938. 303p.

5406 **Kenyon**, Ruth, 'Christian corporatism: a new guild system for industry.' Wilson, H. A., Bishop of Chelmsford, and others. *Towards a Christian order.* London: Eyre and Spottiswoode, 1942. p. 157–76.

5407 **Clegg**, Hugh Armstrong. 'Guild socialism in the Post Office.' *Publ. Adm.*, XVIII, 2 (Summer 1950), 129–33.

Review article on *Consultation or joint management*, by J. M. Chalmers, Ian Mikardo and G. D. H. Cole. (Fabian tract 277.)

5408 **Schapiro**, J. Salwyn. *Movements of social dissent in modern Europe.* Princeton, London: Van Nostrand, 1962. 189p.

Includes short readings on guild socialism.

5409 **Glass**, Stanley Thomas. *The political theory of the British Guild Socialists.* 1963. (B.Litt. thesis, University of Oxford.)

5410 **Kramer**, Daniel Caleb. *G. D. H. Cole, guild socialism, and workers' control of industry.* 1963–64. (Dissertation, University of Pennsylvania.)

5411 **Carpenter**, Luther Pirie. *G. D. H. Cole: an intellectual biography.* 1966. 406 leaves. (Ph.D. thesis, Harvard University.)

5412 **Glass**, Stanley Thomas. *The responsible society: the ideas of the English guild socialist.* London: Longmans, 1966. 79p. (Monographs in politics.)

5413 **Haggar**, George Salem. *The political and social thought of G. D. H. Cole.* 1966–67. (Dissertation, Columbia University.)

See also: 44; 3011; 4799.

D. OTHER SCHEMES

5414 **Bushill**, Thomas William. 'The proposed Industrial Union of Employers and Employed: an employer's view.' *Econ. Rev.*, IV, 2 (April 1894), 195–207.

5415 **Industrial Conference**, 1894. *Report of proceedings at the preliminary Industrial Conference held in London, March 16th, 1894. With a description of the proposed Industrial Union of Employers & Employed.* London: Methuen, 1894. 72p.

5416 **Industrial Union of Employers and Employed.** *The proposed Industrial Union of Employers and Employed.* [Coventry?], 1895. 3 pts.

5417 **Ludlow**, John M. 'The Industrial Union of Employers and Employed.' *Econ. Rev.*, V, 4 (October 1895), 549–56.

5418 **Smith**, Edward James. *The New Trades Combination Movement: its principles, methods and progress as explained by E. J. Smith in a series of articles recently published in the 'Birmingham Daily Post'.* Birmingham: Cornish, 1895. 42p.

Another edition. London: Rivingtons, 1899. xxiv, 96p. With introduction by J. Carter.

5419 **Bosanquet**, Helen. 'The lines of industrial conflict.' *Econ. J.*, VII, 28 (December 1897), 503–10.

On the New Trades' Combination Movement started by E. J. Smith.

5420 **Smith**, Edward James. 'The New Trades Combination Movement.' *Econ. Rev.*, VIII, 2 (April 1898), 145–79.

By one of the founders of the movement.

5421 **Smith**, Edward James. 'Foreign competition in relation to the New Trades Combination Movement.' *Econ. Rev.*, IX, 1 (January 1899), 1–19.

5422 **Smith**, Edward James. *The New Trades Combination Movement: its principles, methods, and progress.* London: Rivingtons, 1899. xxiv, 96p.

A collection of articles previously published in *Economic Review*.

5423 **Smith**, Edward James. 'The New Trades Combination Scheme and the interests of the consumer.' *Econ. Rev.*, IX, 3 (July 1899), 351–60.

5424 **Smith**, Edward James. 'The workman's side of the New Trades Combination Scheme.' *Econ. Rev.*, IX, 2 (April 1899), 221–34.

5425 **Ashley**, William James. 'Mr Smith's New Trades Combination.' *Surveys, historic and economic.* London: Longmans, Green, 1900. p. 394–8.

5426 **Smith**, Edward James. 'Some recent criticism on the New Trades Combination Movement.' *Econ. Rev.*, X, 2 (April 1900), 145–63.

5427 **National Federation of Employers' Associations and Trade Unions.** *The national industrial association to create and cement between employer and employee a feeling of common interest.* London, 1901. 5p.

5428 **National Federation of Employers' Associations and Trade Unions.** *The proposed National Federation of Employers' Associations and Trades Unions to create and cement between employer and employee a feeling of common interest.* London, 1901. 54p.

5429 **National Federation of Employers' Associations and Trade Unions.** *The national industrial association to promote and maintain between employer and employee a feeling of common interest.* London, 1903. 21p.

5430 **Smith**, Edward James. 'The present position of the Trades Combination Movement.' *Econ. Rev.*, XIII, 2 (April 1903), 178–87.

5431 **Industrial League and Council for the Improvement of Relations Between Employer and Employed.** [Objects of the Industrial League explained in a series of speeches delivered...on July 20th, 1917.] London, 1917. 20p.

5432 **Duberry**, Harry. *The National Alliance of Employers and Employed: its origin, objects and ideals.* London: National Alliance of Employers and Employed, 1918. 8p.

The author was General Secretary of the Federation of Post Office Associates.

5433 **Industrial League and Council for the Improvement of Relations Between Employer and Employed.** *The Industrial League.* London, 1918. [8]p.

5434 **National Alliance of Employers and Employed.** *A suggested scheme of industrial reorganization.* London: the Alliance, 1918. 4p.

5435 **Industrial League and Council for the Improvement of Relations Between Employer and Employed.** *The Industrial League and Council.* London, [1919?]. 16p. ([Pamphlet] 5.)

5436 **MacCarthy**, Maud. *The temple of labour: four lectures on the plan beautiful in relation to modern industrialism.* London: Theosophical Publishing House, 1926. 130p.

On a scheme of Workers' Guilds and Labour Temples.

5437 **Penty**, Arthur Joseph. *Communism and the alternative.* London: Student Christian P., 1933. 128p.

PART SIX

THE LABOUR FORCE, LABOUR MARKETS, AND CONDITIONS OF EMPLOYMENT

The literature in this part of the bibliography has been particularly difficult to classify as most of it deals with more than one subject. The most general literature has been classified in Part Six, I; Part Six, III, A; and Part Six, IV, A, 1, and these sections should be consulted in conjunction with each other. But there is also considerable overlap with sections Part Six, III, C–F, and Part Six, IV, A, 3–4, and hence these sections should be consulted together.

I. GENERAL

This section contains general works dealing with more than one aspect of the labour market. In particular, it includes general works which are primarily concerned with analysing the interrelationships between such factors as unemployment, wages, and prices. But material on wages and prices which is primarily of a descriptive nature is classified at Part Six, III, A, and C–E. See also Part Six, II, B, 1; Part Six, II, C, 1; Part Six, II, D, 1; Part Six, III, A; and Part Six, IV, A, 1.

5438 **Hutchinson**, James G. 'Progress and wages: a workman's view.' *Nineteenth Century*, XVI, 92 (October 1884), 630–8.

5439 **Jones**, Lloyd. 'Profits of industry and the workers.' Industrial Remuneration Conference. *The report of the proceedings and papers* . . . London: Cassell, 1885. p. 23–41.
Discussion, p. 62–83.

5440 **Marshall**, Alfred. 'How far do remediable causes influence prejudicially (a) the continuity of employment, (b) the rates of wages?' Industrial Remuneration Conference. *The report of the proceedings and papers* . . . London: Cassell, 1885. p. 173–99.
Discussion, p. 208–14.

5441 **Mawdsley**, J. 'Rates of wages and combination.' Industrial Remuneration Conference. *The report of the proceedings and papers* . . . London: Cassell, 1885. p. 156–64.
Discussion, p. 164–72.

5442 **Owen**, W. 'The unionist view of possible remedies for prejudicial influences on rates of wages and continuity of employment.' Industrial Remuneration Conference. *The report of the proceedings and papers* . . . London: Cassell, 1885. p. 149–56.
Discussion, p. 164–72.

5443 **Paterson**, Emma A. 'Continuity of employment and rates of wages.' Industrial Remuneration Conference. *The report of the proceedings and papers* . . . London: Cassell, 1885. p. 199–207.
Discussion, p. 208–14.

5444 **Philip**, Alexander. *The function of labour in the production of wealth*. Edinburgh, London: Blackwood, 1890. 134p.

5445 **Mallock**, William Hurrell. *Labour as an agent in the production of national wealth*. London, [1894?]. 23p.

5446 **Dietzel**, H. 'Free trade and the labour market.' *Econ. J.*, XV, 57 (March 1905), 1–11.

5447 **Beveridge**, William Henry. 'The organisation of the labour market.' *Lpool. Econ. Statist. Soc. Trans.* (1908–9), 19–30.

5448 **Mitchell**, Andrew Ackworth. 'The influence of trades unions on wages.' *Edinb. Rev.*, CCXVIII, 445 (July 1913), 64–81.

5449 **Leppington**, C. H. d'E. 'The demand for labour as shown by rates of wages offered by employers.' *Econ. J.*, XXVI, 104 (December 1916), 533–6.

5450 **Martin**, Edgar Walford. *Food, wages, and economy to-day and to-morrow: a paper* . . . Birmingham: Cornish, 1916. 16p.

5451 **Snowden**, Philip. *Wages and prices: an inquiry into the wages system and the relation of wages and prices*. London: Faith P., 1920. vii, 124p.

5452 **Cable**, Boyd (*pseud.*) [i.e. Ernest Andrew Ewart]. *Labour and profits*. London: Jarrolds, 1925. 96p. (Library of capitalism 3.)

5453 **Clay**, Henry. 'Unemployment and wage rates.' *Econ. J.*, XXXVIII, 149 (March 1928), 1–15.

5454 **Dobb**, Maurice Herbert. *Wages*. London: Nisbet; Cambridge: Cambridge U.P.; New York: Harcourt, Brace, 1928. ix, 169p. (Cambridge economic handbooks 6.)

New edition, rewritten and reset. 1938. x, 205p.

New edition, revised and reset. 1946. xvi, 222p.

New edition, revised and reset. 1956. xv, 201p.

5455 **Schwartz**, George Leopold. *Output, employment and wages in industry in the United Kingdom, 1924*. London: London and Cambridge Economic Service, 1928. 14p. (Special memorandum 26.)

5456 **Beard**, Gilbert. *Employment and labour costs; or, How Lancashire is losing her trade*. Manchester: Sherratt and Hughes, 1931. 111p.

5457 **Thomas**, Brinley. *Studies in labour supply and labour costs*. 1931–32. (Ph.D. thesis, University of London.)

5458 **Stamp**, *Sir* Josiah. 'The influence of the price level on the higher incomes.' *R. Statist. Soc. J.*, XCIX, 4 (1936), 627–60.

Discussion, p. 661–73.

'Read before the Royal Statistical Society, May 19th, 1936.'

5459 **Kuczynski**, Jürgen. 'A comedy of errors with a serious ending, or Mr. Hicks' theory of wages.' *New frontiers in wage theory: Keynes, Robinson, Hicks, Rueff*. London: Lawrence and Wishart, 1937. p. 38–47.

5460 **Kuczynski**, Jürgen. '"Increasing real wages a cause of depression and unemployment": remarks on the theory of Mr. J. Rueff.' *New frontiers in wage theory: Keynes, Robinson, Hicks, Rueff*. London: Lawrence and Wishart, 1937. p. 3–12.

5461 **Kuczynski**, Jürgen. *New fashions in wage theory: Keynes, Robinson, Hicks, Reuff*. London: Lawrence and Wishart; New York: International Publishers, 1937. viii, 99p.

'This collection of studies is in a sense a companion volume to my *Labour conditions in Western Europe, 1820–1935*' (preface).

5462 **Kuczynski**, Jürgen. 'Providing an "absolutely new and perfectly fitting" theory for anti-working-class dictators: Mr. Keynes and Mrs. Robinson.' *New frontiers in wage theory: Keynes, Robinson, Hicks, Rueff*. London: Lawrence and Wishart, 1937. p. 13–37.

5463 **Schwartz**, George Leopold and **Rhodes**, E. C. *Output, employment and wages in the United Kingdom, 1924, 1930, 1935*. London: London and Cambridge Economic Service, 1938. 35p. (Special memorandum 47.)

5464 **Kalecki**, Michael. 'Employment, wage-bill and cash circulation.' *Oxf. Univ. Inst. Statist. Bull.*, IV, 3 (21 February 1942), 67–70.

5465 **Richardson**, John Henry. 'Labour's part in Britain's economic recovery.' *Westm. Bank Rev.* (May 1949), 1–8.

5466 **Sargant Florence**, Philip. *Labour*. London: Hutchinson, 1949. 230p. (Hutchinson's university library 25.)

5467 **Groves**, P. S. *Two studies in the influence of wages on changes in labour forces*. 1950–51. (Ph.D. thesis, University of Cambridge.)

5468 **Peacock**, Alan Turner and **Ryan**, W. J. L. 'Wage claims and the pace of inflation, 1948–51.' *Econ. J.*, LXIII, 250 (June 1953), 385–92.

5469 **Organisation for European Economic Co-operation.** Manpower Committee. *Trend of the labour market in Europe in recent years*. Paris: O.E.E.C., 1955. 54p.

'Stencilled.'

'Ireland', p. 28–9.

'United Kingdom', p. 42–5.

5470 **Banker.** 'Raising wages without inflation.' *Banker*, CVI, 360 (January 1956), 11–16.

5471 **Byrne**, James J. 'Prices, wages and the cost of living.' *J. Inst. Bankers Ir.*, LVIII, 3 (July 1956), 171–82.

5472 **Clark**, Colin. 'An international comparison of "overemployment" trends in money wages.' *Oxf. Econ. Pap.*, n.s., IX, 2 (June 1957), 178–89.

5473 **Phelps Brown**, Ernest Henry and **Hopkins**, Sheila V. 'Wage-rates and prices: evidence for population pressure in the sixteenth century.' *Economica*, n.s., XXIV, 96 (November 1957), 289–306.

5474 **Roberts**, Benjamin Charles. 'Trade union behaviour and wage determination in Great Britain.' Dunlop, J. T. (ed.). *The theory of wage determination: proceedings of a conference held by the International Economic Association*. London: Macmillan; New York: St Martin's P., 1957. p. 107–22.

Discussion of paper, p. 384–91.

5475 **Shackle**, G. L. S. 'The nature of the bargaining process.' Dunlop, J. T. (ed.). *The theory of wage determination: proceedings of a conference held by the International Economic Association*. London: Macmillan; New York: St Martin's P., 1957. p. 292–314.

Discussion of paper, p. 355–9.

5476 **Dow**, J. C. R. and **Dicks-Mireaux**, L. A. 'The excess demand for labour: a study of conditions in Great Britain, 1946–56.' *Oxf. Econ. Pap.*, n.s., X, 1 (February 1958), 1–33.

5477 **Lydall**, Harold French. 'Inflation and the earnings gap.' *Oxf. Univ. Inst. Statist. Bull.*, XX, 3 (August 1958), 285–304.

Reprinted in McCormick, B. J. and Smith, E. O. (eds.). *The labour market: selected readings*. Harmondsworth: Penguin, 1968. p. 320–46.

5478 **Parkinson**, J. R. 'Wage stability and employment.' *Scott. J. Polit. Econ.*, v, 2 (June 1958), 85–98.
Comment by Harry G. Johnson, p. 149–53.

5479 **Phillips**, A. W. 'The relation between unemployment and the rate of change of money wage rates in the United Kingdom, 1861–1957.' *Economica*, n.s., xxv, 100 (November 1958), 283–99.
Reprinted in Mueller, M. G. (ed.). *Readings in macroeconomics*. New York: Holt, Rinehart and Winston, 1966. p. 245–56.

5480 **Campbell**, John Ross. *Some economic illusions in the labour movement*. London: Lawrence and Wishart, 1959. 67p. (Socialism today series 2.)

5481 **Dicks-Mireaux**, L. A. and **Dow**, J. C. R. 'The determinants of wage inflation: United Kingdom 1946–1956.' *R. Statist. Soc. J.*, Series A, cxxii, 2 (1959), 145–74.
With discussion, p. 174–84.
'Read before the Royal Statistical Society, December 18th, 1958.'

5482 **Klein**, L. R. and **Ball**, R. J. 'Some econometrics of the determination of absolute prices and wages.' *Econ. J.*, lxix, 275 (September 1959), 465–82.
'The present paper arises out of work being done by the authors on the construction of an econometric model of the United Kingdom economy as a whole.'

5483 **Knowles**, Kenneth Guy Jack Charles and **Winsten**, C. B. 'Can the level of unemployment explain changes in wages?' *Oxf. Univ. Inst. Statist. Bull.*, xxi, 2 (May 1959), 113–20.

5484 **Leiserson**, Mark Whittlesey. *A brief interpretive survey of wage-price problems in Europe*. Washington, D.C.: U.S.G.P.O., 1959. p. 31–86. (U.S. Congress. Joint Economic Committee. Study of employment, growth, and price levels. Study paper 11.)

5485 **Routh**, Guy. 'The relation between unemployment and the rate of change of money wage rates: a comment.' *Economica*, n.s., xxvi, 104 (November 1959), 299–315.
On the article by A. W. Phillips, November 1958.

5486 **Turner**, Herbert Arthur. 'Employment fluctuations, labour supply and bargaining power.' *Manchr. Sch.*, xxvii, 2 (May 1959), 175–202.

5487 **Lipsey**, Richard G. 'The relation between unemployment and the rate of change of money wage rates in the United Kingdom, 1862–1957: a further analysis.' *Economica*, xxvii, 105 (February 1960), 1–31.
On A. W. Phillips' article, November 1958.
Reprinted in American Economic Association. *Readings in business cycles*. London: Allen and Unwin, 1966. p. 456–87.

5488 **Palmer**, Gladys L. 'Contrasts in labor market behavior in Northern Europe and the United States.' *Ind. Labor. Relat. Rev.*, xiii, 4 (July 1960), 519–32.

5489 **Turner**, Herbert Arthur. 'Employment fluctuations, productivity and cost-inflation in manufacturing industry.' *Int. Labour Rev.*, lxxxi, 5 (May 1960), 379–402.

5490 **Dicks-Mireaux**, L. A. 'The interrelationship between cost and price changes, 1946–1959: a study of inflation in post-war Britain.' *Oxf. Econ. Pap.*, n.s., xiii, 3 (October 1961), 267–92.

5491 **Lipsey**, Richard G. and **Steuer**, M. D. 'The relation between profits and wage rates.' *Economica*, n.s., xxviii, 110 (May 1961), 137–55.

5492 **Robertson**, Donald James. *The economics of wages and the distribution of income*. London: Macmillan; New York: St Martin's P., 1961. xii, 242p.

5493 **Robertson**, Donald James. *A market for labour*. London: Barrie and Rockliff for the Institute of Economic Affairs, 1961. 46p. (Hobart papers 12.)

5494 **Evans**, Eric Wyn. 'Trade unions and the post-war inflation.' *Inst. Bankers J.*, lxxxiii, 5 (October 1962), 295–305.

5495 **Evans**, Eric Wyn. 'Wage theory and the post-war labour market.' *Natn. Prov. Bank Rev.*, 57 (February 1962), 13–16.

5496 **Griffin**, K. B. 'A note on wages, price and unemployment.' *Oxf. Univ. Inst. Statist. Bull.*, xxiv, 3 (August 1962), 379–85.

5497 **Knowles**, Kenneth Guy Jack Charles. 'Wages and productivity.' Worswick, G. D. N. and Ady, P. H. (eds.). *The British economy in the nineteen-fifties*. Oxford: Clarendon P., 1962. p. 502–36.

5498 **Steuer**, M. D. 'Economic policy and union activity.' Roberts, B. C. (ed.). *Industrial relations: contemporary problems and perspectives*. London: Methuen, 1962. p. 227–57.

5499 **Streeten**, P. 'Wages, prices and productivity.' *Kyklos*, xv, 4 (1962), 723–31.

5500 **Bowen**, William G. and **Berry**, R. Albert. 'Unemployment conditions and movements of the money wage level.' *Rev. Econ. Statist.*, xlv, 2 (May 1963), 163–72.

5501 **United States**. Congress. House Committee on Education and Labor. *Comparative wage costs and trade advantage: the European Economic Community, Great Britain, and the United States*. Washington, D.C.: U.S.G.P.O., 1963. vi, 103p.
88th Congress, 1st session.

5502 **Aaronovitch**, Sam. *Economics for trade unionists: the wages system*. London: Lawrence and Wishart, 1964. 98p.

5503 **Hines**, A. G. 'Trade unions and wage inflation in the United Kingdom, 1893–1961.' *Rev. Econ. Studies*, xxxi, 88 (October 1964), 221–52.

5504 **Hobsbawm**, Eric John Ernest. 'The nineteenth century London labour market.' Glass, R., and others. *London: aspects of change.* London: MacGibbon and Kee, 1964. (Centre for Urban Studies. Reports 3.)

5505 **Knowles**, Kenneth Guy Jack Charles. 'Wage structure and productivity in Great Britain.' Dunlop, J. T. and Diatchenko, V. P. (eds.). *Labor productivity.* New York: McGraw-Hill, 1964. p. 249–60.

5506 **Sargan**, J. D. 'Wages and prices in the United Kingdom: a study in econometric methodology.' Hart, P. E., Mills, G. and Whitaker, J. K. (eds.). *Econometric analysis for national economic planning: proceedings of the sixteenth symposium of the Colston Research Society held in the University of Bristol, April 6th–9th, 1964.* London: Butterworths, 1964. p. 25–54.

Discussion, p. 55–63.

5507 **Cowling**, Keith and **Metcalf**, David. 'An analysis of the determinants of wage inflation in agriculture.' *Manchr. Sch.*, XXXIII, 2 (May 1965), 179–204.

5508 **Eagly**, Robert V. 'Market power as an intervening mechanism in Phillips curve analysis.' *Economica*, XXXII, 125 (February 1965), 48–64.

5509 **Knowles**, Kenneth Guy Jack Charles. 'Wages and productivity in Great Britain.' Robinson, E. A. G. (ed.). *Problems in economic development: proceedings of a conference held by the International Economic Association.* London: Macmillan; New York: St Martin's P., 1965. p. 320–2.

Discussion, p. 323–8.

5510 **Pollard**, Sidney. 'Trade unions and the labour market, 1870–1914.' *Yorks. Bull. Econ. Soc. Res.*, XVII, 1 (May 1965), 98–112.

5511 **Routh**, Guy. *Occupation and pay in Great Britain 1906–60.* London: Cambridge U.P., 1965. xi, 185p. (National Institute of Economic and Social Research. Economic and social studies 24.)

5512 **Conference on Manpower Policy and Employment Trends**, 1965, London. *Manpower policy and employment trends.* London: Bell for the London School of Economics and Political Science, 1966. 137p.

Edited by B. C. Roberts and J. H. Smith.

5513 **Cowling**, Keith. *The determinants of wage inflation in Ireland.* Dublin: Economic Research Institute, 1966. 20p. (Paper 31.)

5514 **Cowling**, Keith and **Metcalf**, David. 'Determinants of wage inflation in Scottish agriculture, 1948–63.' *Manchr. Sch.*, XXXIV, 2 (May 1966), 189–95.

5515 **Crossley**, John Rodney. 'Collective bargaining, wage-structure and the labour market in the United Kingdom.' Hugh-Jones, E. M. (ed.). *Wage structure in theory and practice: three studies.* Amsterdam: North-Holland Publishing Co., 1966. p. 157–235.

5516 **Hunter**, Laurence Colvin. 'The regional labour market.' *The Lothians regional survey and plan. Vol. 1. Economic and social aspects.* Edinburgh: H.M.S.O., 1966. p. 92–104.

5517 **Kuska**, Edward A. 'The simple analytics of the Phillips curve.' *Economica*, n.s., XXXIII, 132 (November 1966), 462–7.

5518 **Pullen**, M. J. 'Unemployment and regional income per head.' *Manchr. Sch.*, XXXIV, 1 (January 1966), 15–40.

5519 **Corry**, Bernard and **Laidler**, David. 'The Phillips relation: a theoretical explanation.' *Economica*, n.s., XXXIV, 134 (May 1967), 189–97.

Comment by John Vanderkamp, n.s., XXXV, 138 (May 1968), 179–83.

Reply, p. 184.

5520 **Cowling**, Keith and **Metcalf**, David. 'Wage-unemployment relationships: a regional analysis for the UK, 1960–65.' *Oxf. Univ. Inst. Econ. Statist. Bull.*, XXIX, 1 (February 1967), 31–9.

5521 **Phelps**, Edmund S. 'Phillips curves expectations of inflation and optimal unemployment over time.' *Economica*, n.s., XXXIV, 135 (August 1967), 254–81.

Comment by John Williamson, n.s., XXXV, 139 (August 1968), 283–7.

Reply, p. 288–96.

5522 **Stoney**, Peter John Milton. *A survey of econometric studies of the wage-price mechanism in the United Kingdom.* 1967. 92p. (M.A. thesis, University of Manchester.)

5523 **Jones**, R. M. *The dynamics of a labour market.* 1967–68. (M.A. thesis, University of Wales, Swansea.)

5524 **Grime**, E. K. and **Starkie**, D. N. M. 'New jobs for old: an impact study of a new factory in Furness.' *Reg. Studies*, II, 1 (September 1968), 57–67.

5525 **Hines**, A. G. 'Trade unions and wage inflation in the United Kingdom, 1893–1961.' McCormick, B. J. and Smith, E. O. (eds.). *The labour market: selected readings.* Harmondsworth: Penguin, 1968. p. 284–319.

Excerpt from an article of the same title in *Rev. Econ. Stud.*, XXXI, 88 (October 1964), 221–5.

5526 **Hines**, A. G. 'Unemployment and the rate of change of money wage rates in the United Kingdom, 1862–1963: a reappraisal.' *Rev. Econ. Statist.*, L, 1 (February 1968), 60–7.

5527 **McCormick**, Brian J. and **Smith**, E. Owen (eds.). *The labour market: selected readings.* Harmondsworth: Penguin, 1968. 393p. (Penguin modern economics. Penguin education X55.)

5528 **Oliver**, F. F. 'Maladjustment and excess demand in the labour market, 1960–1966.' *Br. J. Ind. Relat.*, VI, 3 (November 1968), 376–80.

5529 **Robinson**, Derek. *Wage drift, fringe benefits and manpower distribution: a study of employer practices in a full employment labour market.* Paris: Organisation for Economic Co-operation and Development, 1968. 178p. (Labour mobility 7.)

5530 **Turner**, Herbert Arthur. 'Inflation and wage differentials in Great Britain.' McCormick, B. J. and Smith, E. O. (eds.). *The labour market: selected readings.* Harmondsworth: Penguin, 1968. p. 228–42.

Reprinted from J. T. Dunlop (ed.). *The theory of wage determination.* London: Macmillan, 1957. p. 123–35.

5531 **Archibald**, G. C. 'Wage-price dynamics, inflation, and unemployment: the Phillips curve and the distribution of unemployment.' *Am. Econ. Rev.*, LIX, 2 (May 1969), 124–34.

5532 **Deakin**, Brian Measures and **Seward**, Thelma. *Productivity in transport: a study of employment, capital, output, productivity and technical change.* London: Cambridge U.P., 1969. 248p. (University of Cambridge. Department of Applied Economics. Occasional paper 17.)

5533 **Hines**, A. G. 'Wage inflation in the United Kingdom 1948–62: a disaggregated study.' *Econ. J.*, LXXIX, 313 (March 1969), 66–89.

5534 **Hunter**, Laurence Colvin and **Robertson**, Donald James. *Economics of wages and labour.* London: Macmillan, 1969. 544p.

5535 **Sloane**, Peter J. 'The labour market in professional football.' *Br. J. Ind. Relat.*, VII, 2 (July 1969), 181–99.

5536 **Thirlwall**, A. P. 'Demand disequilibrium in the labour market and wage rate inflation in the United Kingdom.' *Yorks. Bull. Econ. Soc. Res.*, XXI, 1 (May 1969), 66–76.

5537 **Bowers**, J. K. and **Webb**, A. E. 'The change in the relationship between unemployment and earnings increases: a review of some possible explanations.' *Natn. Inst. Econ. Rev.*, 54 (November 1970), 44–63.

5538 **Garbarino**, Joseph W. 'British and American labor market trends: a case of convergence?' Robertson, D. J. and Hunter, L. C. (eds.). *Labour market issues of the 1970s.* Edinburgh: Oliver and Boyd for the Scottish Economic Society, 1970. p. 203–20.

First appeared in the June 1970 issue of the *Scottish Journal of Political Economy.*

5539 **Goodman**, J. F. B. 'The definition and analysis of local labour markets: some empirical problems.' *Br. J. Ind. Relat.*, VIII, 2 (July 1970), 179–96.

5540 **Habakkuk**, H. J. 'The economic effects of labour scarcity.' Saul, S. B. (ed.). *Technological change: the United States and Britain in the nineteenth century.* London: Methuen, 1970. p. 23–76.

Abstracted from *American and British technology in the nineteenth century*, by H. J. Habakkuk, Cambridge U.P., 1962.

5541 **Holmes**, James M. and **Smyth**, David J. 'The relation between unemployment and excess demand for labour: an examination of the theory of the Phillips curve.' *Economica*, n.s., XXXVII, 147 (August 1970), 311–15.

5542 **Jackson**, Joseph Michael. *Wages and labour economics.* Maidenhead: McGraw-Hill, 1970. vii, 244p.

5543 **Rees**, Albert. 'The Phillips curve as a menu for policy choice.' *Economica*, n.s., XXXVII, 147 (August 1970), 227–38.

5544 **Robertson**, Donald James and **Hunter**, Laurence Colvin. 'The emerging issues.' Robertson, D. J. and Hunter, L. C. (eds.). *Labour market issues of the 1970s.* Edinburgh: Oliver and Boyd for the Scottish Economic Society, 1970. p. 1–9.

First appeared in the June 1970 issue of the *Scottish Journal of Political Economy.*

5545 **Robertson**, Donald James and **Hunter**, Laurence Colvin (eds.). *Labour market issues of the 1970s.* Edinburgh: Oliver and Boyd for the Scottish Economic Society, 1970. viii, 223p.

'These papers were first printed in *Scottish Journal of Political Economy*, Vol. XVII, No. 2, June 1970 . . .'

5546 **Robertson** E. J. 'Local labour markets and plant wage structures: an introduction.' Robinson, D. (ed.). *Local labour markets and wage structures.* London: Gower P., 1970. p. 15–27.

5547 **Robinson**, Derek. 'External and internal labour markets.' Robinson, D. (ed.). *Local labour markets and wage structures.* London: Gower P., 1970. p. 28–67.

5548 **Robinson**, Derek (ed.). *Local labour markets and wage structures.* London: Gower P., 1970. 296p. (A Gower Press special study.)

5549 **Robinson**, Derek. 'Practical conclusions.' Robinson, D. (ed.). *Local labour markets and wage structures.* London: Gower P., 1970. p. 261–85.

5550 **Robinson**, Derek and **Conboy**, William Morgan. 'Wage structures and internal labour markets.' Robinson, D. (ed.). *Local labour markets and wage structures.* London: Gower P., 1970. p. 215–60.

5551 **Shearer**, John C. 'Manpower environments confronting American firms in Western Europe.' Kamin, A. (ed.). *Western European labor and the American corporation.* Washington, D.C.: Bureau of National Affairs, 1970. p. 377–93.

5552 **Stamp**, Maxwell. 'Trade unions and inflation.' *Moor. Wall Street* (Autumn 1970), 5–18.

5553 **Thirlwall**, A. P. 'Regional Phillips curves.' *Oxf. Univ. Inst. Econ. Statist. Bull.*, XXXII, 1 (February 1970), 19–32.

5554 **Vernon**, Keith. *An econometric study of wage and price inflation in the United Kingdom for the post-war period.* 1970. (Ph.D. (Econ.) thesis, University of London.)

5555 **Wilkinson**, Roy Keith and **Rainnie**, G. F. 'Industrial structure, unemployment and earnings: a study of three sub-regions in Yorkshire and Humberside.' *Yorks. Bull. Econ. Soc. Res.*, XXII, 2 (November 1970), 101–22.

See also: 103; 111; 153; 175; 303.

II. THE LABOUR FORCE

A. ENTRY INTO EMPLOYMENT

Some of the general works in Part Two, I contain material on attitudes towards choice of occupation and problems arising on entry into employment. See also Part Six, II, C, 5.

1. General

This section contains general references on the problems arising in the transition from school to work. More specific material on vocational choice is contained in Part Six, II, A, 2. See also Part Seven, IV, D, 1–2.

5556 **Watson**, John. *Our boys and girls and what to do with them.* London: Ward, Lock, Bowden, 1892. viii, 173p.

Chapters by various writers including Sir George Baden-Powell, Sir Herbert Maxwell, Clementina Black, on professions.

5557 **Gibb**, Spencer James. 'The choice of employment for boys.' *Econ. Rev.*, XIV, 4 (October 1904), 436–48.

5558 **D'Aeth**, Frederic George. 'Enquiry into the methods of obtaining employment in Liverpool.' *Lpool. Econ. Statist. Soc. Trans.* (1906–7), 29–60.

5559 **Knight**, H. V. *How to get employment.* London, 1910. 16p.

5560 **Bloomfield**, Meyer. *The school and the start in life: a study of the relation between school and employment in England, Scotland, and Germany.* Washington, D.C.: U.S.G.P.O., 1914. 146p. (U.S. Bureau of Education. Bulletin, 1914, no. 4. Whole no. 575.)

5561 **Burt**, Cyril. 'Vocational diagnosis in industry and at school.' Musico, B. (ed.). *Lectures on industrial administration.* London: Pitman, 1920. p. 79–120.

5562 **Marshall**, M. E. *The adolescent in industry.* Cardiff, 1922. 23p.

5563 **Lewis**, Evan Llewelyn. *The children of the unskilled: an economic and social study.* London: King, 1924. xxii, 109p.

The substance of a D.Phil. thesis, University of Glasgow.

'The inquiry was conducted with a view to determining the supply of skilled labour that might be recruited from the ranks of unskilled workmen's children.'

5564 **Board of Education** and **Ministry of Labour**. Committee on Education and Industry (England and Wales). *Report.* London: H.M.S.O., 1926. 115p.

Chairman: Sir Dougal Orme Malcolm.

Second part. Report. 1928. 79p.

5565 **Committee on Education and Industry in Scotland.** *First report.* Edinburgh: H.M.S.O., 1927. 32p.

Chairman: Lord Salvesen.

5566 **Political and Economic Planning.** *The entrance to industry: a survey of points of contact between education and industry in Great Britain, together with proposals for raising the school leaving age.* London: P.E.P., 1935. 56p.

5567 **Ministry of Labour and National Service.** *Problems of post-war entry of juveniles into employment: memorandum prepared by the London Regional Advisory Committee for Juvenile Employment.* London: H.M.S.O., 1942. 10p.

5568 **Ministry of Labour and National Service.** Juvenile Employment Service. *The young worker.* London: H.M.S.O., 1944. (Pamphlet 1.)

5569 **Slater**, Patrick. 'The economics of vocational selection.' *Occup. Psychol.*, XX, 1 (January 1946), 12–23.

5570 **Ministry of Education.** Central Advisory Council for Education (England). *School and life: a first enquiry into the transition from school to independent life.* London: H.M.S.O., 1947. 115p.

5571 **Tenen**, Cora. *Psychological aspects of the change from school to work.* 1948. 2v. (Ph.D. thesis, University of Manchester.)

5572 **Whitehead**, Edward. 'The transition from school to work.' Thomson, D. C. (ed.). *Training worker citizens . . .* London: Macdonald and Evans, 1949. p. 1–14.

5573 **Turrent**, E. R. *A study of the problems of adjustment of boys from a secondary modern school to their employment and further education.* 1958–59. (M. Ed. thesis, University of Nottingham.)

5574 **Smurthwaite**, Ronald. *Welcome, stranger: hints to school leavers on going to work.* London: British Association for Commercial and Industrial Education, 1960. 18p.

5575 **Lloyd**, C. 'Education, training and employment of young people.' *Progress*, XLVIII, 269 (May 1961), 138–43.

5576 **Pepperell**, Elizabeth M. *Transition from school to work.* London: Industrial Welfare Society, 1962. 12p.

5577 **Rodger**, Alec. *Occupational versatility and planned procrastination: an inaugural lecture delivered at Birkbeck College, 16th October, 1961.* London: Birkbeck College, 1962. 15p.

5578 **Veness**, Thelma. *School leavers: their aspirations and expectations.* London: Methuen, 1962. xxv, 252p.

5579 **Keil**, E. Theresa, **Riddell**, David S. and **Tipton**, Colin B. 'The entry of school leavers into employment.' *Br. J. Ind. Relat.*, I, 3 (October 1963), 408–11.

5580 **Avent**, Catherine and **Fried**, Eleanor L. *Starting work.* London: Parrish, 1965. 139p.

5581 **Maizels**, Joan. 'The entry of school leavers into employment.' *Br. J. Ind. Relat.*, III, 1 (March 1965), 77–89.

5582 **Pepperell**, Elizabeth M. *What do they expect from work?* London: Industrial Welfare Society, 1965. 16p. (Transition from school to work series.)

5583 **Ashton**, G. L. *Socialisation into the work role: a study of apprentices.* 1965–66. (M.A. thesis, University of Leicester.)

5584 **Roberts**, Kenneth. *The entry into employment: a study of the development of the careers and job attitudes of adolescents in a London suburb.* 1965–66. (M.Sc. dissertation, University of London.)

5585 **Ainscough**, Roy. 'Visits to industry: collaboration between a sixth former and a technical college at Worcester.' *Voc. Asp.*, XVIII, 41 (Autumn 1966), 236–40.

5586 **Cambridge University Balance Group.** *Students and industry: essays by members of the Cambridge Balance Group.* Cambridge: Heffer, 1966. 56p.

'The essays in this small book are the result of a competition organized by the Cambridge University Balance Group in which members were invited to comment on the ways in which a Cambridge education prepared them for a career in industry.'

5587 **Carter**, Michael Percy. *Into work.* Harmondsworth: Penguin, 1966. 240p. (Pelican books.)

5588 **Keil**, E. Teresa, **Riddell**, David S. and **Green**, B. S. R. 'Youth and work: problems and perspectives.' *Sociol. Rev.*, n.s., XIV, 2 (July 1966), 117–37.

5589 **Mapes**, Roy Ernest, **Cooper**, B. and **McQuail**, Denis. 'School-leavers' hopes.' *New Soc.*, VII, 171 (6 January 1966), 13–14.

5590 **Smurthwaite**, Ronald and **Udall**, Rita. *Starting work.* London: Batsford, 1966. 128p. (Career books.)

5591 **Jones**, Esmor. *From school to work.* Oxford, London: Pergamon P., 1967. [15]p. (Take home books.)

5592 **McFadyen**, Edward. *Young people at work.* Oxford, London: Pergamon P., 1968. 22p. (Productivity progress.)

5593 **Princeton Manpower Symposium**, 4th, Princeton University, 1968. *The transition from school to work: a report based on the Princeton Manpower Symposium, May 9–10, 1968, organized by U.S. Dept. of Health, Education and Welfare, National Manpower Policy Task Force and the Woodrow Wilson School and the Industrial Relations Section of Princeton University.* Princeton, N. J.: Princeton University, Industrial Relations Section, 1968. viii, 282p. (Research report series 111.)

5594 **Venables**, Ethel. *Leaving school and starting work.* Oxford, London: Pergamon, 1968. viii, 71p. (Commonwealth and international library. Problems and progress in development.)

5595 **Smithers**, Alan 'Occupational aspirations and expectations of engineering students on sandwich courses.' *Br. J. Ind. Relat.*, VII, 3 (November 1969), 414–22.

'Research note.'

5596 **Carter**, Michael Percy. *A sociological study of the adjustment to employment of a sample of secondary modern school leavers in an industrial city.* 1969–70. (Ph.D. thesis, University of Edinburgh.)

5597 **Gretton**, John. 'Degrees of idleness.' *New Soc.*, XV, 402 (11 June 1970), 985–6.

5598 **Keil**, E. Theresa, **Riddell**, David S. and **Green**, B. S. R. 'Entry into the occupational system.' Butterworth, E. and Weir, D. (eds.). *The sociology of modern Britain: an introductory reader.* London: Fontana/Collins, 1970. p. 160–3.

Reprinted from 'Youth and work: problems and perspectives.' *Sociological Review*, n.s., XIV, 2 (July 1966), 117–37.

5599 **Maizels**, Joan. *Adolescent needs and the transition from school to work.* London: Athlone P., 1970. xvi, 354p.

See also: 6270.

2. Vocational Choice

See also Part Seven, IV, D, 1.

5600 **Chapman**, Sydney John and **Abbott**, W. 'The tendency of children to enter their fathers' trades.' *R. Statist. Soc. J.*, LXXVI, 6 (May 1913), 599–604.

5601 **National Institute of Industrial Psychology.** 'Choosing a career.' *Natn. Inst. Ind. Psychol. J.*, IV, 3 (July 1928), 132–43.

Proceedings and summaries of papers read at a meeting held on 18 May 1928.

Papers read by F. M. Earle and A. Macrae.

5602 **Valentine**, C. W. and **Ritchie**, F. M. 'An inquiry as to reasons for the choice of occupation among secondary school pupils.' *Natn. Inst. Ind. Psychol. J.*, IV, 4 (October 1928), 211–23.

Reproduced in an abridged form from *The Forum of Education.*

5603 **Valentine**, C. W. 'An inquiry into reasons for the choice of occupation among technical school pupils.' *Hum. Factor*, VII, 10 (October 1933), 347–53.

5604 **Bowley**, Arthur Lyon. 'The occupations of fathers and of their children.' *Economica*, n.s., II, 8 (November 1935), 400–7.

Material collected for the *New Survey of London Life and Labour.*

5605 **Williams**, Gertrude. 'A study in the industrial career of secondary school boys.' *Sociol. Rev.*, XXX, 4 (October 1938), 400–13.
Based on an enquiry into the industrial history of boys who left a certain secondary school during the years 1931–6.

5606 **Mercer**, Edith O. 'Some occupational attitudes of girls.' *Occup. Psychol.*, XIV, 1 (January 1940), 14–25.

5607 **Lingwood**, Joan. 'The vocational information possessed by secondary school girls.' *Occup. Psychol.*, XV, 4 (October 1941), 185–98.

5608 **Social Survey**. *The attitudes of women towards nursing: an inquiry made by the Regional Organisation of the Social Survey for Campaigns Division of the Ministry of Information.* 1943. 51p. (Regional S. 5.)
By Kathleen Box assisted by Enid Croft-White.

5609 **Crichton**, Ruth M. 'A study of the occupational histories of juveniles in Edinburgh, 1943–1945.' *Sociol. Rev.*, XXXVII, 1–4 (January–October 1945), 10–27.

5610 **Greenwell**, E. G. 'Unrest and changes in juvenile employment.' *Occup. Psychol.*, XIX, 1 (January 1945), 35–8.

5611 **Knight**, Rex. 'The reluctance to teach.' *Occup. Psychol.*, XIX, 2 (April 1945), 53–60. (Essays presented to Dr Myers, XXIII.)
'Based on the writer's Presidential Address delivered to the Scottish Branch of the British Psychological Society on 6th November, 1943.'

5612 **Evans**, Kathleen M. *A study of attitude towards teaching as a career.* 1946. (M.A. thesis, University of London.)

5613 **Champ**, Joan M. *A study of the attitude of women (student teachers and former teachers) towards teaching as a career.* 1948. (M.A. thesis, University of London.)

5614 **Jahoda**, Gustav. 'Adolescent attitudes to starting work.' *Occup. Psychol.*, XXIII, 3 (July 1949), 184–8.

5615 **Wilkins**, Leslie T. 'Incentives and the young male worker in England, with some notes on ranking methodology.' *Int. J. Opin. Att. Res.*, IV (1950), 541–62.
Incentives which determine entry into a particular occupation or firm.

5616 **Macfarlane**, Jean C. *A study of the choice of careers in a group of adolescent pupils.* 1950–51. (M.A. thesis, University of London, Institute of Education.)

5617 **Ginzberg**, Eli, **Ginsburg**, Sol W., **Axelrad**, Sidney and **Herma**, John L. *Occupational choice: an approach to a general theory.* New York: Columbia U.P., 1951. viii, 271p.

5618 **Jahoda**, Gustav. *A study of the chief social determinants of occupational choice in secondary modern school leavers, with special reference to social class factors and the level of social aspiration.* 1951–52. (Ph.D. thesis, University of London.)

5619 **Perry**, J. A. *An enquiry into the circumstances and influences which condition a student's choice of training as a primary or secondary school teacher.* 1951–52. (M.A. thesis, University of London.)

5620 **Wilson**, Mary Dixon. *Realism in vocational choice: a study of the vocational preferences of secondary modern school children, aged thirteen to fifteen, with special reference to their intelligence.* 1951–52. (Ph.D. thesis, University of London.)

5621 **Jahoda**, Gustav. 'Job attitudes and job choice among secondary modern school leavers.' *Occup. Psychol.*, XXVI, 3 (July 1952), 125–40; 4 (October 1952), 206–24.
'Based on a thesis submitted for the degree of Ph.D. in the University of London.'

5622 **Stone**, M. W. *An investigation into the vocational preferences of children. The significance and relationship of the following factors to the determined preferences will also be considered: (a) age and sex; (b) intelligence and achievement; (c) parental occupation and choice.* 1952–53. (M.A. thesis, University of Wales.)

5623 **Sykes**, Emily G. 'School and work.' *Sociol. Rev.*, n.s., I, 1 (July 1953), 29–47.

5624 **Wilson**, Mary Dixon. 'The vocational preference of secondary modern school children.' *Br. J. Educ. Psychol.*, XXIII (1953), 97–113, 163–79.

5625 **Dyson**, T. W. *A study of the changes of occupational choice of secondary schoolboys.* 1953–54. (M.Ed. thesis, University of Nottingham.)

5626 **Thompson**, Walter Gerald. *Vocational preferences of approved school boys.* 1954–55. (M.A. thesis, University of London.)

5627 **McGuffin**, S. J. *An investigation into the factors influencing the choice of career by boys in two Belfast grammar schools.* 1955–56. (M.Sc. thesis, Queen's University, Belfast.)

5628 **Chown**, Sheila M. *The formation of occupational choices by grammar school children.* 1956–57. (Ph.D. thesis, University of Liverpool.)

5629 **Stephens**, M. M. *Vocational preferences of secondary modern school girls in a London suburb.* 1956–57. (M.A. thesis, University of London.)

5630 **Chown**, Sheila M. 'The formation of occupational choice among grammar school pupils.' *Occup. Psychol.*, XXXII, 3 (July 1958), 171–82.

5631 **Rowlands**, R. G. *Some sociological and psychological factors affecting the choice of scientific careers by grammar school boys.* 1958–59. (Ph.D. thesis, University of London.)

5632 **Basu**, C. K. *A study of occupational information possessed by secondary modern schoolboys of school-leaving age.* 1959–60. (M.A. thesis, University of London.)

5633 **Pheasant**, J. H. *The influence of the school organisation and curriculum on the choice of examination subjects and careers made by G.C.E. candidates.* 1959–60. (Ph.D. thesis, University of London.)

5634 **Allison**, A. R. *An investigation into the occupational preferences and dislikes of primary and secondary school children.* 1960–61. (M.Sc. thesis, University of London.)

5635 **Brown**, W. G. *Job characteristics: a comparative study of the judgments of youth employment officers and secondary modern school children.* 1960–61. (M.Sc. thesis, University of London.)

5636 **Nelson**, D. M. *A study of the stability of occupational preferences in fourteen-year-old secondary modern school boys and girls.* 1960–61. (M.A. thesis, University of London.)

5637 **Bramah**, John Albert. *An enquiry into the choice of occupation among pupils aged eleven to sixteen in certain secondary modern schools.* 1961. 410, [10], clxiii leaves. (M.Ed. thesis, University of Manchester.)

5638 **Richards**, N. D. *An empirical study of the prestige of selected occupations.* 1961–62. (M.A. thesis, University of Nottingham.)

5639 **Gordon**, Wolfgang. *A comparative study of the occupational stereotypes of secondary school leavers and first year apprentices.* 1963–64. (M.A. thesis, University of London.)

5640 **Hill**, Graham B. 'Choice of career by grammar school boys.' *Occup. Psychol.*, XXXIX, 4 (October 1965), 279–87.

5641 **Nisbet**, J. D. and **Grant**, Wilma. 'Vocational intentions and decisions of Aberdeen arts graduates.' *Occup. Psychol.*, XXXIX, 3 (July 1965), 215–19.

5642 **Department of Education and Science.** *Scientists and engineers and their choice of jobs 1956–59: report on a survey sponsored by the Department and undertaken by the Government Social Survey to discover the factors affecting recruitment of scientists and engineers in all branches of the government service, and more generally those influencing the choice between the several kinds of jobs which a scientist or engineer might take up.* London: H.M.S.O., [1966?]. 129p. [Social Survey S.S. 334.]

By D. Sheppard.

5643 **Mathew**, W. M. 'The origins and occupations of Glasgow students 1740–1839.' *Past Pres.*, 33 (April 1966), 74–94.

Based on information contained in the Matriculum Albums of the University of Glasgow.

5644 **Social Survey**. *Undergraduates' attitudes to school teaching as a career: a survey carried out among English and Welsh university students in November 1963 for the Department of Education and Science.* 1966. 267p. (S.S. 354.)

By Roma Morton-Williams, Stewart Finch and Chris Poll.

5645 **Maizels**, Joan. 'Changes in employment among school leavers: a sample study of one cohort of secondary modern boys.' *Br. J. Ind. Relat.*, v, 2 (July 1967), 211–21.

5646 **Musgrave**, P. W. 'Towards a sociological theory of occupational choice.' *Sociol. Rev.*, n.s., XV, 1 (March 1967), 33–46.

Reply, by Julienne Ford and Steven Box, based on British data, XV, 3 (November 1967), 287–99.

'A critique', by M. A. Coulson, E. T. Keil, D. S. Riddell, and J. S. Struthers, p. 301–9.

'A note', by P. W. Musgrave, XVI, 1 (March 1968), 93–7.

5647 **Swinhoe**, K. 'Factors affecting career choice among full-time students in a college of commerce.' *Voc. Asp.*, XIX, 43 (Summer 1967), 139–54.

5648 **Butler**, John Richard. *Occupational choice: a review of the literature with special reference to science and technology.* London: H.M.S.O., 1968. v, 25p. (Science policy studies 2.)

5649 **Government Social Survey**. *Young school leavers: report of an enquiry carried out for the Schools Council. Enquiry 1.* London: H.M.S.O., 1968. 396p.

By Roma Morton-Williams, and others.

5650 **Last**, John M. and **Stanley**, Gillian R. 'Career preference of young British doctors.' *Br. J. Med. Educ.*, II, 2 (June 1968), 137–55.

5651 **Roberts**, K. 'The entry into employment: an approach towards a general theory.' *Sociol. Rev.*, n.s., XVI, 2 (June 1968), 165–84.

5652 **Smithers**, Alan. 'Some characteristics of business students in a technological university. II. Occupational values.' *Occup. Psychol.*, XLII, 4 (October 1968), 231–8.

5653 **White**, Stephanie. 'The process of occupational choice.' *Br. J. Ind. Relat.*, VI, 2 (July 1968), 166–84.

5654 **Brown**, W. G. *Factors influencing a graduate's choice of occupation.* 1968–69. (Ph.D. thesis, University of Aston.)

5655 **Weale**, D. A. H. *Reasons given by sixth form boys for choosing a scientific career and an enquiry into factors which may have influenced their choice.* 1968–69. (M.A. thesis, University of Wales, Cardiff.)

5656 **Hayes**, John. 'Occupational choice and the perception of occupational roles.' *Occup. Psychol.*, XLIII, 1 (January 1969), 15–22.

'This paper was presented at the conference "Into Work" organised by the National Foundation for Educational Research, Wolverhampton, 18–20 July 1968.'

5657 **Starkey**, Hubert Farrell. *Factors influencing occupational choice among secondary modern school leavers.* 1969. 210p. (M.Ed. thesis, University of Manchester.)

5658 **Williams**, Roger. 'Industry as a career: what students think.' *New Soc.*, XV, 391 (26 March 1970), 516–18.

See also: 6962.

B. MANPOWER PLANNING AT FIRM AND INDUSTRY LEVEL

This section includes material dealing with manpower planning by employers; material on the government as employer in this context is also classified here. Material on the state as a regulator of manpower for the economy as a whole is classified at Part Seven, IV. Material dealing with redundancy in particular firms is classified at Part Six, II, D. See also Part Four, II, A.

1. General

See also Part Five, II; Part Six, II, B, 2; Part Six, II, E, 4; and Part Six, II, E, 5.

5659 **Treasury**. Committee Appointed to Enquire into the Organisation and Staffing of Government Offices. London: H.M.S.O.
Interim report. 1918. 8p. (Cd. 9074.)
Second interim report. 1918. 2p. (Cd. 9219.)
Third interim report. 1918. 26p. (Cd. 9220.)
Fourth interim report. 1919. 12p. (Cmd. 61.)

5660 **Treasury**. National Whitley Council. Joint Committee (Reorganisation Committee). *Organisation, etc. of the Civil Service: report*. London: H.M.S.O., 1920. 12p.
Chairman: Malcolm G. Ramsay.
Reprinted. 1933.
Final report. 1921. 13p.

5661 **Treasury**. National Whitley Council. Joint Committee (Reorganisation Committee). Sub-Committee on Temporary Staffs. *Report*. London: H.M.S.O., 1920. 3p.
Chairman: Sir Robert Russell Scott.

5662 **Dunkerley**, R. *Management of office staffs (industrial establishments)*. London, 1927. 17p.

5663 **Marsh**, W. W. *Management of office staffs (government departments)*. London, 1927. 16p.

5664 **Rodger**, Alec. 'The effective use of manpower.' *Br. Mgmt. Rev.*, XIII, 4 (October 1955), 229–48.

5665 **Rodger**, Alec. 'The effective use of manpower: address.' *Advmt. Sci.*, XII, 46 (September 1955), 237–49.

5666 **Lewis**, R. W. *Methodology of manpower projection*. 1962–63. (M.Sc. thesis, University of London.)

5667 **British Association for Commercial and Industrial Education**. *Economic growth and manpower: papers presented at the BACIE spring conference held at the Federation of British Industries, London, S.W.1*. London: B.A.C.I.E., 1963. 55p.

5668 **Seear**, Beatrice Nancy and **Thurley**, Keith E. 'Problems of employee recruitment to a factory in a rural area.' *Br. J. Ind. Relat.*, I, 2 (June 1963), 241–59.

5669 **Mumford**, Enid. *Living with a computer*. London: Institute of Personnel Management, 1964. 43p.

5670 **Fox**, Alan. *The Milton plan: an exercise in manpower planning and the transfer of production*. London: Institute of Personnel Management, 1965. 66p. (Occasional papers.)

5671 **Moser**, C. A. and **Redfern**, P. 'Education and manpower: some current research.' Berners-Lee, C. M. (ed.). *Models for decision*. London: English Universities P., 1965. p. 71–83.
Describes two projects going on in the Unit for Economic and Statistical Studies on Higher Education, London School of Economics, one a study of manpower needs, the second concerning a model of the educational system.

5672 **Mumford**, Enid. 'Clerks and computers: a study of the introduction of technical change.' *J. Mgmt. Studies*, II, 2 (May 1965), 138–52.

5673 **Organisation for Economic Co-operation and Development**. *Report by the Norwegian joint team which visited the United Kingdom from 5th–10th October, 1964, to study manpower adjustment techniques for technological change*. Paris: O.E.C.D., 1965. 23p. (Programme for employers and unions, national missions, 1964, report 8.)

5674 **Young**, Andrew. 'Models for planning recruitment and promotion of staff.' *Br. J. Ind. Relat.*, III, 3 (November 1965), 301–10.
Originally presented as a paper to a conference, at Imperial College, London in April 1965, organized by the Industrial Applications Section of the Royal Statistical Society.

5675 **Armstrong**, D. *Manpower planning: occupations and talent*. London: Tavistock Institute, 1966. (Document T.924.)

5676 **Gray**, Daniel Hale. *Manpower planning: an approach to the problem*. London: Institute of Personnel Management, 1966. 54p.

5677 **Hall**, Michael. 'Productive manpower planning.' *New Soc.*, VIII, 199 (21 July 1966), 88–90. (Trends in personnel management 7.)

5678 **McBeath**, Maurice Gordon. *Organization and manpower planning*. London: Business Publications, 1966. xiii, 298p.
Second edition. 1969. ix, 262p.

5679 **Roberts**, Benjamin Charles. 'Social change.' British Automation Conference, 1965. *Report of the meeting at Eastbourne, 7–10 November, 1965*. London: Institution of Production Engineers, 1966. p. 41–7.

5680 **Rogers**, T. G. P. *Manpower planning: paper presented at the British Institute of Management's national conference, March 1966*. London: B.I.M., 1966. 5p.

5681 **Barkin**, Solomon. *Technical change and manpower planning: co-ordination at enterprise level*. Paris: Organisation for Economic Co-operation and Development, 1967. 292p.

5682 **Blaug**, Mark, **Peston**, Maurice H. and **Ziderman**, Adrian. *The utilization of educated manpower in industry: a preliminary report*. London: Oliver and Boyd, 1967. ix, 103p. (London University. London School of Economics and Political Science, Unit for Economic and Statistical Studies on Higher Education. Reports 2.)

5683 **British Petroleum**. *Manpower planning in the British Petroleum Company*. London, Paris: B.P., 1967.

5684 **Hunter**, Laurence Colvin. *Manpower and productivity*. Oxford: Pergamon P., 1967. 19p. (Take home books; Productivity progress.)
'. . . provides a background setting to a series of booklets which will investigate in detail more specific problems and cases concerned with labour and productivity.'

5685 **Institute of Personnel Management.** The Edinburgh Group. *Perspectives in manpower planning*. London: the Institute, 1967. 93p.

5686 **Ministry of Labour.** Study Group of the Efficient Use of Manpower. *Efficient use of manpower: report of a Study Group composed of directors and senior managers of well-known firms in the Midlands*. London: H.M.S.O., 1967. iv, 20p.
Chairman: A. J. Nicol.

5687 **National Economic Development Office.** *Better use of labour in the firm*. London: N.E.D.O., 1967. [20]p.

5688 **Organisation for Economic Co-operation and Development.** Manpower and Social Affairs Directorate. Social Affairs Division. *Technical change and manpower planning: co-ordination at enterprise level; a series of national case studies*. Paris: O.E.C.D., 1967. 287p. (Industrial relations aspects of manpower policy 4.)

5689 **Redfern**, P. *Input-output analysis and its application to education and manpower planning*. London: H.M.S.O., 1967. 10p. 4 folding sheets of tables. (Treasury. C.A.S. occasional paper 5.)

5690 **Smith**, Anthony Robert. 'Manpower planning in management.' *Manp. Appl. Psychol.*, I, 2 (Autumn 1967), 102–11.

5691 **Smith**, Anthony Robert. 'Manpower planning in management of the Royal Navy.' *J. Mgmt. Studies*, IV, 2 (May 1967), 127–39.

5692 **Butters**, S. J. *Technical change, manpower policy and organisation in the furniture industry of metropolitan England*. 1967–68. (M.A. thesis, University of Sussex.)

5693 **Jackson**, Peter. *A manpower planning survey in the British Transport Docks Board and some implications of its findings*. 1967–68. (M.Phil. thesis, University of London.)

5694 **British Iron and Steel Research Association.** *Manpower and investment expenditure*. London: B.I.S.R.A., Inter-Group Laboratories of the British Steel Corporation, 1968. (Report OR/17/68.)

5695 **Department of Employment and Productivity.** *Company manpower planning*. London: H.M.S.O., 1968. 54p. (Manpower papers 1.)

5696 **Gascoigne**, I. M. 'Manpower forecasting at the enterprise level: a case study.' *Br. J. Ind. Relat.*, VI, 1 (March 1968), 94–106.

5697 **Lynch**, James John. *Making manpower effective*. London: Pan Books. (Management and marketing series; Pan piper.)
Part 1. 1968. 173p.
Part 2. 1971.

5698 **Mumford**, Enid and **Ward**, Tom B. 'Computer people and their impact.' *New Soc.*, XII, 313 (26 September 1968), 443–5.
Adapted from part of the authors' book *Computers: planning for people*.

5699 **Mumford**, Enid and **Ward**, Tom B. *Computers: planning for people*. London: Batsford, 1968. 176p. (Modern management series.)

5700 **Wedderburn**, Dorothy. *Enterprise planning for change: co-ordination of manpower and technical planning*. Paris: Organisation for Economic Co-operation and Development, 1968. 137p. (Industrial relations aspects of manpower policy 5.)

5701 **Richardson**, V. A. *The problems of manpower and educational planning: analysis and appraisal of techniques, illustrated by some empirical models*. 1968–69. (Ph.D. thesis, University of Manchester.)

5702 'Manpower planning in the British Petroleum Company.' Wilson, N. A. B. (ed.). *Manpower research*. London: English Universities P., 1969. p. 41–66.
Contents: 'Introduction', by H. S. Mullaly; 'The socio-economic environment in the 1980's', by V. Brijatoff; 'Manpower planning in the British Petroleum Company', by E. S. M. Chadwick; 'Summary and conclusions', by H. S. Mullaly; 'Comment', by J. A. A. Van Doorn.

5703 **Mumford**, Enid. *Computers, planning and personnel management*. London: Institute of Personnel Management, 1969. 55p.

5704 **Bryant**, D. T. and **Pollard**, J. de B. 'Manpower planning: a review of current practice.' Heald, G. (ed.). *Approaches to the study of organizational behaviour*. London: Tavistock Publications, 1970.

5705 **Civil Service Department.** Civil Service College. *Some statistical techniques in manpower planning*. London: H.M.S.O., 1970. 43p. (C.A.S. occasional paper 15.)
By D. J. Bartholomew, P. L. Ashdown, J. A. Rowntree and R. W. Morgan.
Edited by A. R. Smith.

5706 **Davidmann**, Manfred. *Salary administration and manpower planning*. London: Social Organisation Ltd, 1970. 17 leaves.

5707 **Newton**, Dudley. 'What planning manpower means.' *Mgmt. Today* (July 1970), 81–83, 144.

5708 **Sharp**, Evelyn, Baroness Sharp. *Transport planning: the men for the job; a report to the Minister of Transport*. London: H.M.S.O., 1970. v, 138p.

See also: 57; 72.

2. Recruitment, Selection, and Placement

This section includes the general literature dealing with the problems of recruiting, selecting, and placing staff in industry. The more specialist literature dealing exclusively with the techniques of recruitment, selection, and placement has generally been excluded. It is extremely difficult to separate the literature dealing with managerial training from that concerned with the recruitment, selection, and placement of managers, and hence the literature pertaining to the latter subjects has been classified at Part Six, II, B, 3, b, iii. See also Part Six, II, B, 3.

a. GENERAL

5709 **Chapman**, Sydney John and **Shimmin**, Arnold N. 'Industrial recruiting and the displacement of labour.' *Manchr. Statist. Soc. Trans.* (1913–14), 93–147.

5710 **Bottomley**, Cyril. 'The recruitment of juvenile labour in Warrington.' *Manchr. Statist. Soc. Trans.* (1930–31), 129–55.

5711 **Watson**, William Foster. 'The worker's point of view. IX. Hiring and firing.' *Hum. Factor*, VI, 11 (November 1932), 423–7.

5712 **Political and Economic Planning**. 'The entrance to industry.' *Planning*, I, 22 (13 March 1934), 3–15.

5713 **British Management Review**. 'The manager today: recruitment, training and duties.' *Br. Mgmt. Rev.*, II, 4 (October–December 1937). 180p.

A special issue of *British Management Review*.

5714 **Social Survey**. *Women and industry: an inquiry into the problem of recruiting women to industry carried out for the Ministry of Labour and National Service.* 1948. 43p. (N.S. 104.)

By Geoffrey Thomas.

5715 **Institute of Personnel Management**. *Selection and placement.* London: I.P.M., 1949. 52p.

Also 1955 edition.

5716 **Institute of Personnel Management**. *Induction: introducing industry to the individual.* London: I.P.M., 1950. 26p.

5717 **Acton Society Trust**. *Problems of promotion policy.* Claygate: the Trust, 1951. 20p. (Studies in nationalised industry 3.)

5718 **Roskill**, O. W. and Co. (Reports), Ltd. *Methods of recruitment and selection of personnel in industry and commerce.* London: Roskill, 1951. 67 leaves.

Looseleaf.

5719 **Cunnison**, James. 'Youth and recruitment to industry.' Cairncross, A. K. (ed.). *The Scottish economy: a statistical account of Scottish life.* London: Cambridge U.P., 1954. p. 266–79.

This is the title given on the Contents page. The title at the head of the chapter is 'Recruitment and training of young workers for industry and commerce.'

5720 **Federation of British Industries**. *Public school and grammar school boys in industry.* London: F.B.I., 1954. 12p.

5721 **Wilson**, V. W. 'The importance of selection and allied procedures.' Ling, T. M. (ed.). *Mental health and human relations in industry.* London: H. K. Lewis, 1954. p. 83–103.

5722 **Smith**, G. W. *Problems of recruitment and selection.* London: British Institute of Management, 1955. 6p.

Conference on Retail Distribution, Eastbourne, 1955.

5723 **Federation of British Industries**. *Report of the conference on industry and the public and grammar schools, organised by the Federation of British Industries, the Headmasters' Conference and the Incorporated Association of Head Masters, and held at Ashorne Hill, Leamington Spa, Warwickshire, 11–13 November 1955.* London: F.B.I., 1956. vii, 52p.

5724 **Higham**, T. M. *Selecting the right man for the job: a review of modern procedures.* London: British Institute of Management, 1957. 6p.

Northern Management Conference 1957.

5725 **British Association for Commercial and Industrial Education**. *The recruitment and training of university graduates: report of Bacie Control Group No. 2, Ashridge, 7–10 June, 1960.* London: B.A.C.I.E., 1960. 36p.

5726 **British Institute of Management**. *Selection of staff: proceedings of a conference held at the Connaught Rooms, London, W.C.2 on 29 November 1960.* London: B.I.M., 1961. 47p.

5727 **Federation of British Industries**. *Invest in the future: report of a conference organised by the Federation of British Industries and held at the Palace Hotel, Buxton, from 26 to 28 September, 1960.* London: F.B.I., 1961. 60p.

5728 **Carter**, C. F. 'The economic use of brains.' *Econ. J.*, LXXII, 285 (March 1962), 1–11.

5729 **Durman**, L. F. *The selection, training and management of staff.* London: Institute of Chartered Accountants in England and Wales, 1966. 42p.

5730 **Van Gelder**, Roy. *Induction.* London: Industrial Society, 1967. 48p.

5731 **Denerley**, Ronald Alfred and **Plumbley**, P. R. *Recruitment and selection in a full-employment economy.* London: Institute of Personnel Management, 1968. 132p.

5732 **Isbister**, William. *Performance and progress in working life: a study.* Oxford, [etc.]: Pergamon, 1968. viii, 135p. (Commonwealth and international library. Social administration, training, economics and production division.)

5733 **Bacon**, Curtiss. *Selecting, appraising and motivating employees . . .* London: Industrial Education International Ltd, [1969?]. 58p.

5734 **Monk**, D. M. 'The social survey in manpower research.' Wilson, N. A. B. (ed.). *Manpower research.* London: English Universities P., 1969. p. 234–40.

5735 **Purkiss**, C. J. 'Approaches to recruitment, training and redeployment planning in an industry.' Wilson, N. A. B. (ed.). *Manpower research*. London: English Universities P., 1969. p. 67–78.
On the British iron and steel industry.

5736 **Marks**, Winifred Rose. *Induction – acclimatizing people to work*. London: Institute of Personnel Management, 1970. 43p. (Practical handbooks 3.)

5737 **Ungerson**, Bernard (ed.). *Recruitment handbook*. London: Gower P., 1970. xviii, 285p.
Contents: 1. 'Introduction: the scientific method of selection', by B. Ungerson; 2. 'Internal selection and manpower planning', by A. Lovering; 3. 'Writing the job specification', by R. A. Denerley; 4. 'Choosing the method of recruitment', by T. Higham; 5. 'Job advertising', by K. G. Fordham; 6. 'Application forms', by B. Edwards; 7. 'Physical testing', by D. Malcolm; 8. 'Intelligence and aptitude testing', by A. C. Pendlebury; 9. 'Personality assessment', by K. M. Miller; 10. 'Testing trade skills', by G. Jessup; 11. 'Interviewing techniques', by A. Rodger; 12. 'Deciding the appointment', by L. Holman; 13. 'Operative staff', by D. Torrington; 14. 'Sales staff', by T. S. Duxfield; 15. 'Technological staff', by H. Stuart; 16. 'Recruitment of graduates at the universities', by J. S. Gough; 17. 'Management trainees in retailing', by J. F. Jenkins; 18. 'Retail staff', by J. J. Mooney; 19. 'Manpower and selection policy in the financial sector', by P. H. Lynch; 20. 'Banking: management trainees', by R. L. Hopps.

b. PARTICULAR OCCUPATIONS AND INDUSTRIES

5738 **Yoxall**, J. H. and **Ainslie**, W. L. 'British seamen for British ships.' *Nineteenth Century*, XLV, 263 (January 1899), 39–45.

5739 **Chapman**, Sydney John and **Marquis**, F. J. 'The recruiting of the employing classes from the ranks of the wage-earners in the cotton industry.' *R. Statist. Soc. J.*, LXXV, 3 (February 1912), 293–306.
Discussion, p. 307–13.
'Read before the Royal Statistical Society, January 16, 1912.'

5740 **Royal Commission on the Civil Service.** 1912–16. [6 reports and 7 vols. of evidence and appendices.] (Cd. 6209, 6210, 6534, 6535, 6739, 6740, 7338, 7339, 7340, 7748, 7749, 7832, 8130.)
Chairman: Lord MacDonnell.
On making of appointments and promotion.

5741 **Martyn**, Edith How. 'The methods of appointment of administrative and clerical staffs in the local government service of England and Wales.' *Economica*, II, 4 (January 1922), 51–68.

5742 **Leathes**, *Sir* Stanley. 'The qualifications, recruitment and training of public servants.' *J. Publ. Adm.*, I (1923), 343–60.
Discussion, p. 360–2.
A paper discussed at the Summer Conference of the Institute of Public Administration, 31 July 1923.

5743 **Northern Ireland**. *Report of the Departmental Committee on Civil Service Re-Grading*. Belfast: H.M.S.O., 1930. 72p. (Cmd. 116.)

5744 **Houghton**, A. L. N. D. 'Recruitment and training of public officials.' *Publ. Adm.*, IX, 3 (July 1931), 248–62.
'Paper to be discussed at the Summer Conference of the Institute of Public Administration, July, 1931.'
The author was General Secretary, Association of Officers of Taxes.

5745 **Waldegrave**, A. J. 'Annual reports on efficiency and qualification for promotion.' *Publ. Adm.*, IX, 3 (July 1931), 293–300.
'Paper to be discussed at the Summer Conference of the Institute of Public Administration, July, 1931.' Procedure recommended for the Civil Service by the Whitley Committee.

5746 **National Institute of Industrial Psychology**. 'The Institute's evidence to the Royal Commission on the Civil Service.' *Hum. Factor*, VI, 6 (June 1932), 209–15.

5747 **Johnson**, Thomas. *Labour recruitment and training in the coal mining industry in the county of Durham since 1926*. 1936. 113 leaves. (M.Com. thesis, University of Durham.)

5748 **Lidbury**, C. 'Personnel problems of banking.' *Br. Mgmt. Rev.*, II (July–September 1937), 54–77.

5749 **Houghton**, A. L. N. D. 'Assessment of qualifications for promotion in the British Civil Service.' International Management Congress, 7th, Washington, D.C., 19–23 September 1938. *Administration papers*. Baltimore, Md.: Waverly P., 1938. p. 136–9.

5750 **Ministry of Fuel and Power**. Committee on the Recruitment of Juveniles in the Coal-Mining Industry. *First report*. London: H.M.S.O., 1942. 20p.
Chairman: Sir John Forster.
Supplemental report. 1943. 2p.

5751 **Box**, Kathleen and **Croft-White**, Enid. *Recruitment to nursing: an inquiry into the attitudes of student nurses to their profession with special reference to the present recruiting campaign*. [London], 1943. i, 38p. (Wartime Social Survey, Regional S.7.)
'Carried out by the Wartime Social Survey for Campaigns Division of the Ministry of Information.'

5752 **Clarke**, Joan Simeon. 'The staff problem.' Robson, W. A. (ed.). *Social security*. London: Allen and Unwin for the Fabian Society, 1943. p. 373–394.

Second edition. 1945.
Third edition. 1948.
On recruitment for a new Ministry of Social Security.

5753 **Ministry of Works and Planning.** Central Council for Works and Buildings. Education Committee. *Report.* 1943. 56p.
Chairman: E. D. Simon.
Government statement. 1943. 6p. (Cmd. 6428.)

5754 **King Edward's Hospital Fund for London.** *Nursing staff: considerations on standards of staffing.* London, 1945. 26p.

5755 **Stone,** Valerie C. 'An investigation into the allocation of labour in a filling factory.' *Occup. Psychol.*, XIX, 1 (January 1945), 6–14.

5756 **Barclay,** James. *Why no nurses? The nursing recruitment problem, its history, terms and solution.* London: Faber, 1946. 176p.

5757 **Ockleberry,** W. *A comparative study of the methods of selecting professional personnel for the public services of the United States, Great Britain and Canada.* 1946. 130p. (M.A. thesis, University of Chicago.)

5758 **Scottish Education Department.** Scottish Youth Advisory Committee. *The recruitment and training of youth leaders and organisers: report.* London: H.M.S.O., 1946. 39p.
Chairman: J. Keith.

5759 **Social Survey.** *Recruitment to the Civil Service: an inquiry made . . . for H.M. Treasury.* 1946. 48p. (New series 80.)
By Kathleen Box.

5760 **Ministry of Health, Department of Health for Scotland** and **Ministry of Labour and National Service.** *Report of the Working Party on the recruitment and training of nurses.* London: H.M.S.O., 1947. v, 122p.
Chairman: R. S. Wood.
Minority report, by John Cohen. 1948. vi, 78p.

5761 **Northern Ireland.** Ministry of Education. Committee on the Recruitment and Training of Teachers. *Report.* Belfast, 1947. viii, 87p. (Cmd. 254.)

5762 **Political and Economic Planning.** 'Recruiting civil servants.' *Planning*, XIII, 266 (23 May 1947), 1–19.

5763 **Another Banking Correspondent.** 'Staffing the clearing banks. II. Case for a two-tier system.' *Banker*, LXXXVI, 269 (June 1948), 191–6.

5764 **Another Banking Correspondent.** 'Staffing the clearing banks. IV. The role of the training centres.' *Banker*, LXXXVII, 272 (September 1948), 159–68.

5765 **A Special Banking Correspondent.** 'Staffing the clearing banks. I. The problem posed.' *Banker*, LXXXVI, 267 (April 1948), 19–29.

5766 **A Third Banking Correspondent.** 'Staffing the clearing banks. III. Formulating a new policy.' *Banker*, LXXXVII, 270 (July 1948), 25–31.

5767 **Tonkyn,** John. 'Staffiing the clearing banks. V. A personal rejoinder.' *Banking*, LXXXVIII, 274 (November 1948), 96–100.
The author was Assistant General Manager, Barclays Bank.

5768 **Ministry of Civil Aviation.** *Report of the Committee on Recruitment, Training and Licensing of Personnel for Civil Aviation and memorandum by the Minister of Civil Aviation.* London: H.M.S.O., 1949. (Cmd. 7746.)

5769 **Ministry of Education.** *Report of the Committee on Recruitment, Training and Conditions of Service of Youth Leaders and Community Centre Wardens.* London: H.M.S.O., 1949. iv, 16p.
Chairman: E. J. W. Jackson.

5770 **Ministry of Works.** *Recruitment of masons: special report of the Building Apprenticeship and Training Council.* London: H.M.S.O., 1949.
Chairman: Sir George Gater.

5771 **Social Survey.** *Recruitment to agriculture: an inquiry for the Ministry of Labour into the attitudes held towards the agricultural industry and how far these were or were not likely to affect recruitment.* 1949. 26p. (N.S. 116.)
By B. M. Osborne.

5772 **Thomas,** Geoffrey. *Public opinion in Lancashire cotton towns.* [London]: Central Office of Information, [1949?]. ii, 32p. (Social Survey. N.S. 127.)
'An inquiry carried out for the Ministry of Labour and National Service in July and August, 1948.'
A further survey was carried out in November 1949 and published as report 147.
On attempts to improve recruitment.

5773 **Hobson,** Oscar R. 'The bank staff problem.' *Banker*, XCV, 296 (September 1950), 158–62.

5774 **Medical Research Council.** Building Research Unit. 'The human problems of the building industry: guidance, selection and training.' *Occup. Psychol.*, XXIV, 2 (April 1950), 96–104.

5775 **Thomas,** Geoffrey. *The recruitment of hospital nursing staff by advertisement: an inquiry carried out for the Ministry of Labour and National Service in April 1949.* [London]: Central Office of Information, [1950?]. 19p. (Social Survey report N.S. 137.)

5776 **Ministry of Education.** National Advisory Council on the Training and Supply of Teachers. *Second report, on the recruitment and training of youth leaders and community centre wardens.* London: H.M.S.O., 1951.

5777 **Ministry of Labour and National Service.** *Report of the Committee on Recruitment and Training for the Youth Employment Service.* London: H.M.S.O., 1951.
Chairman: Lord Piercy.

5778 **Western,** J. R. *The recruitment of the land forces in Great Britain, 1793–9.* 1952–53. (Ph.D. thesis, University of Edinburgh.)

5779 **Ministry of Health**. *Report of the Working Party on the Recruitment, Training and Qualification of Sanitary Inspectors*. London: H.M.S.O., 1953. vi, 145p.
Chairman: Sir John Maude.

5780 **National Joint Council for Local Authorities' Administrative, Professional and Clerical Services**. *Recruiting of university graduates*. London: the Council, 1953. 5p.

5781 **Taylor**, Roy. *Manning the Royal Navy: the reform of the recruiting system, 1847–1861*. 1953–54. (M.A. thesis, University of London.)

5782 **Davies**, Delwyn Griffith. *The problem of recruitment, education and training in the water industry*. London: British Waterworks Association, 1954. 18p.
Public Works and Municipal Services Congress, London, 1954.

5783 **Helsby**, L. N. 'Recruitment to the Civil Service.' *Polit. Q.*, xxv, 4 (October–December 1954), 324–35.

5784 **Kelsall**, Roger Keith. *Higher civil servants in Britain from 1870 to the present day*. London: Routledge and Kegan Paul, 1955. xvi, 233p. (International library of sociology and social reconstruction.)

5785 **Macdonald**, E. M. *A survey of certain therapeutic services, their development and interrelationship and their place in the social framework. Examination of the effect of these factors on recruitment, selection and training of personnel*. 1955. (B.Litt. thesis, University of Oxford.)

5786 **Mathúna**, S. O. 'The Christian Brothers and the Civil Service.' *Administration*, III, 2–3 (Summer–Autumn 1955), 69–74.
On the results of a survey in Ireland to determine what proportion of staff in certain grades had been educated at Christian Brothers schools.

5787 **Office of the Lord President of the Council**. Advisory Council on Scientific Policy. Committee on Scientific Manpower. *Report on the recruitment of scientists and engineers by the engineering industry*. London: H.M.S.O., 1955. 31p.
Chairman: Sir Solly Zuckerman.

5788 **Robinson**, Kenneth. 'Selection and the social background of the Administrative Class.' *Publ. Adm.*, XXXIII, 4 (Winter 1955), 383–8.
On *Higher Civil Servants in Britain from 1870 to the present day*, by R. K. Kelsall. Routledge and Kegan Paul, 1955.
'Rejoinder', by R. K. Kelsall, XXXIV, 2 (Summer 1956), 169–71.
'A further comment', by K. Robinson, 172–4.

5789 **Barrington**, T. J. 'Selection in the civil service.' *Administration*, IV, 3 (Autumn 1956), 56–79.
'A paper read to the Discussion Group of the Association of Higher Civil Servants in December, 1955.'

5790 **Ministry of Health** and **Department of Health for Scotland**. *Report of the Committee on Recruitment to the Dental Profession*. London: H.M.S.O., 1956. 62p. (Cmd. 9861.)

5791 **Northern Ireland**. *The staffing of technical schools*. Belfast: H.M.S.O., 1956. 23p. (Cmd. 356.)

5792 **Smith**, John Harold. 'The rise of a bureaucracy.' International Sociological Association. *Transactions of the third world congress of sociology . . . 1956*. Vol. 2. London: the Association, 1956. p. 56–70.
Road haulage industry.

5793 **Walters**, A. D. *Qualifications of training college students: an investigation into the value of various types of information in the selection of training college students and an estimate of the validity of certain college results*. 1956–57. (M.A. thesis, University of Liverpool.)

5794 **Civil Service Commission**. *Recruitment to the administrative class of the home Civil Service and the senior branch of the foreign service: statement of government policy and report by the Civil Service Commission*. London: H.M.S.O., 1957. 32p. (Cmnd. 232.)

5795 **Institute of Municipal Treasurers and Accountants**. Weekend Conference, Oxford, 22nd–24th March, 1957. *The finance officer in local and public authorities: recruitment, training and functions*. London: the Institute, 1957. 106p.

5796 **Lewis**, David W. P. 'Selection of candidates to the Administrative Class of the British Civil Service: a study of methods and their relation to the aims of public administration and the educational system.' *Cah. Bruges*, VII, 2 (1957), 4–23.

5797 **Farnworth**, M. *A study of the psychological aspects of the recruitment of nurses*. 1957–58. (Ph.D. thesis, University of London.)

5798 **Pepperell**, Elizabeth M. *Office staff: selection, supervision, training*. London: Industrial Welfare Society, 1959. 51p.

5799 **White**, H. C. *Recruitment, training and development of the sales force*. London: British Institute of Management, 1959. 10p.
Northern Management Conference, Southport, 1959.

5800 **Scorer**, E. R. *A study of the recruitment and success in training of scientific assistants in a large research establishment*. 1959–60. (M.A. thesis, University of London.)

5801 **Woods**, S. *Recruitment and training for advertising*. London: Institute of Practitioners in Advertising, 1960. 12p.

5802 **British Institute of Management**. *Survey of methods of selecting and training salesmen*. London: B.I.M., 1961. 13p.

5803 **British Iron and Steel Federation**. *Report on the recruitment and training of technicians*. London: the Federation, 1961. 22p.

5804 **International Association of Universities**. *The staffing of higher education: some European situations*. Paris: I.A.U., 1961. 169p.

Covers Austria, France, Germany, Italy, the Netherlands, Norway, Poland, Switzerland and the U.K.

5805 **British Medical Association**. *Recruitment to the medical profession: the report of a special committee*. London: B.M.A., 1962. 128p.

5806 **Department of Technical Co-operation**. *Recruitment for service overseas: future policy*. London: H.M.S.O., 1962. 30p. (Cmnd. 1740.)

5807 **Engineering and Allied Employers' National Federation**. *Recruitment and training of young persons in the engineering industry: analysis of survey carried out in October 1961 and comparison with the position in March 1958*. London: the Federation, 1962. 22p.

5808 **Insurance Institute of London**. Advanced Study Group 167. *The problems arising in the recruitment of staff with special reference to mechanisation: report*. London: the Institute, 1962. 45p.

5809 **Council of Europe**. European Committee on Crime Problems. *The status, recruitment and training of penitentiary staff*. Strasbourg: C. of E., 1963.

5810 **Crichton**, Anne Olivia Janet. *Report on a survey: administrative and clerical staffs in hospitals in Wales, 1960–1961*. Cardiff: Welsh Hospital Board, Welsh Staff Advisory Committee, 1963. 74p.

Survey for planning recruitment and training.

5811 **Hanson**, A. H. (ed.). 'Personnel.' *Nationalization: a book of readings*. London: Allen and Unwin for the Royal Institute of Public Administration, 1963. p. 176–208.

5812 **Ministry of Health**. *Report of the Committee of Inquiry into the Recruitment, Training and Promotion of Administrative and Clerical Staff in the Hospital Service*. London: H.M.S.O., 1963. 64p.

Chairman: Sir Stephen Lycett Green.

5813 **Monsky**, Selma F. *Staffing of local authority residential homes for children: an inquiry carried out November 1961–January 1962 for the Home Office*. [London]: Central Office of Information, 1963. iv, 165, [124]p.

5814 **Association of Hospital Treasurers**. Oxford Branch. *An enquiry into the methods of keeping staff records with a view to establishment control: report prepared by the Oxford Branch*. Swansea: the Association, 1964. 18p.

5815 **Barker**, Paul. 'Redbrick. I. The career.' *New Soc.*, III, 84 (7 May 1964), 9–11.

5816 **Barker**, Paul. 'Redbrick. II. The hierarchy.' *New Soc.*, III, 85 (14 May 1964), 12–14.

5817 **Ministry of Agriculture, Fisheries and Food**. *Report of the Departmental Committee of Inquiry into Recruitment for the Veterinary Profession*. London: H.M.S.O., 1964. (Cmnd. 2430.)

Chairman: Duke of Northumberland.

5818 **Shaw**, Colin. 'How BBC 2 was staffed.' *New Soc.*, III, 81 (16 April 1964), 12–13.

5819 **Marsh**, David Charles and **Willcocks**, Arthur John. *Focus on nurse recruitment: a snapshot from the provinces*. London: Oxford U.P. for the Nuffield Provincial Hospitals Trust, 1965. vi, 50p.

5820 **Marsh**, David Charles and **Willcocks**, Arthur John. 'Why don't we recruit more nurses?' *New Soc.*, v, 144 (1 July 1965), 6–8.

5821 **Paige**, Deborah C. and **Jones**, Kit. 'Health and welfare.' Beckerman, W., and others. *The British economy in 1975*. Cambridge: Cambridge U.P., 1965. p. 404–57.

Includes '5. Requirements in 1975: staff.'

5822 **Welch**, E. W. 'Staff structures in banking.' *Bankers' Mag.*, CXCIX (May 1965), 363–6.

5823 **Wood**, S. 'A simple arithmetical approach to career planning and recruitment.' *Br. J. Ind. Relat.*, III, 3 (November 1965), 292–300.

Originally presented as a paper to a conference, at Imperial College, London in April 1965, organized by the Industrial Applications Section of the Royal Statistical Society.

In the Civil Serivce.

5824 **Scottish Education Department**. *Future recruitment and training of teachers for further education in Scotland: report by the Standing Committee on the Supply and Training of Teachers for Further Education*. Edinburgh: H.M.S.O., 1966. 40p.

5825 **Smith**, Trevor. *Town and county hall: problems of recruitment and training*. London: Acton Society Trust, 1966. 52p.

5826 **Watson**, Edward Thomas Ronald. *The inter-departmental mobility of senior civil servants*. 1966. 123p. (M.A.(Econ.) thesis, University of Manchester.)

5827 **Allen**, Bryan. 'Choosing head teachers.' *New Soc.*, IX, 226 (26 January 1967), 129–30. 'Society at work.'

5828 **Corbett**, Anne. 'Teachers on probation.' *New Soc.*, IX, 229 (16 February 1967), 236–7. 'Society at work.'

5829 **Council of Europe**. European Committee on Crime Problems. *The status, selection and training of basic grade custodial prison staff*. Strasbourg: C. of E., 1967.

Second report of sub-committee no. VI of the E.C.C.P.

5830 **Coxon**, Anthony P. M. 'Patterns of occupational recruitment: the Anglican ministry.' *Sociology*, I, 1 (January 1967), 73–9.

5831 **Dodd**, C. H. 'Recruitment to the Administrative Class, 1960–1964.' *Publ. Adm.*, XLV, 1 (Spring 1967), 55–80.

The first part of a study undertaken jointly by the author and J. F. Pickering.

5832 **Hindle**, R. 'Bank staffing policy and systems developments.' *Bankers' Mag.*, CCIV (September 1967), 113–17.

5833 **Home Office**. Working Party on the Recruitment of People with Higher Educational Qualifications into the Police Service. *Report*. London: H.M.S.O., 1967. 31p.

Chairman: Dick Taverne.

5834 **Martin**, Michael and **Wild**, Ray. 'The five-day ward.' *New Soc.*, IX, 247 (22 June 1967), 920–1. (Society at work.)
Impact on recruitment.

5835 **National Council of Social Service.** *Caring for people: staffing residential homes; the report of the Committee of Enquiry set up by the National Council of Social Service.* London: Allen and Unwin, 1967. 222p. (National Institute for Social Work Training Publications 11.)
Chairman: Gertrude Williams.

5836 **Pickering**, J. F. 'Recruitment to the Administrative Class, 1960–64. Part 2.' *Publ. Adm.*, XLV, 2 (Summer 1967), 169–99.
First part prepared by C. H. Dodd.

5837 **Szreter**, R. 'A note on the staffing of the public schools, 1939–1964.' *Br. J. Sociol.*, XVIII, 2 (June 1967), 187–90.
'Research note.'

5838 **O'Connor**, T. P. *The higher Civil Service in Ireland: its role, recruitment and training.* 1967–68. (M.Litt. thesis, Trinity College, Dublin.)

5839 **Blackburn**, Robert Martin, 'The bank clerks.' *New Soc.*, XII, 305 (1 August 1968), 156–7.

5840 **Dutton**, Ann. *Factors affecting recruitment of nurse tutors: a survey carried out on behalf of the King's Fund and the RCN.* London: King Edward's Hospital Fund for London, 1968. [9], 79 leaves.

5841 **Government Social Survey**. *Operatives in the building industry.* London: H.M.S.O., 1968. iii, 72p. (SS 371.)
By Geoffrey Thomas.
'An enquiry carried out for the Building Research Station of the Ministry of Public Building and Works.'

5842 **Mapes**, Roy. 'Promotion in static hierarchies.' *J. Mgmt. Studies*, V, 3 (October 1968), 380–7.
Civil Service.

5843 **Smith**, Anthony Robert. 'Defence manpower studies.' *Operat. Res. Q.*, XIX, 3 (September 1968), 257–73.
A paper presented to the Operational Research Society Conference at Exeter in September 1967.
Describes the Defence Manpower Studies Unit and its work.

5844 **Stokes**, D. J. *A study of selection, training and performance of operators in a mass production company.* 1968–69. (M.Sc. thesis, University of Birmingham.)

5845 **Council of Europe**. European Committee on Crime Problems. *The status, selection and training of governing grades of staff of penal establishments.* Strasbourg: C. of E., 1969.

5846 **Crichton**, Anne Olivia Janet. *Aspects of staffing in the hospital service in England and Wales: professionalism and management, 1946–68.* 1969. (Ph.D. thesis, University of Wales, Cardiff.)

5847 **MacGuire**, Jillian. *Threshold to nursing: a review of the literature on recruitment to and withdrawal from nurse training programmes in the United Kingdom.* London: Bell, 1969. 271p. (Occasional papers on social administration 30.)

5848 **Baldamus**, Wilhelm. 'The assessment of academic competence.' *New Soc.*, XVI, 405 (2 July 1970), 14–15.

5849 **Gaffney**, Seamus. 'Recruitment to the Irish Civil Service.' *Administration*, XVIII, 2 (Summer 1970), 159–73.
Reprinted from *The Irish Banking Review*, March 1969.

5850 **Rogers**, T. G. P. and **Williams**, Peter. *The recruitment and training of graduates.* London: Institute of Personnel Management, 1970. 58p.

See also: 9876; 9947; 9953; 10,024.

3. Industrial Training and Retraining

This section includes works dealing with training provided by private employers or by the state in its role as an employer. Many popular management and professional journals also contain material on training, but it has not been included here. Works dealing with industrial training provided by the state for society as a whole are classified at Part Seven, IV, E. It is very difficult to separate material on the training of the disabled from that on other employment problems they face, and hence it has been excluded from this section and classified at Part Six, II, C, 7. Material on education as contrasted to industrial training has generally been excluded but material relating to the provision of education for working children is classified at Part Six, IV, A, 4, c, iii. See also Part Three, III, L; and Part Six, II, B, 2. Many of the references classified in Part Six, II, C, 3–6 also contain material on training.

a. APPRENTICESHIP

See also Part Three, I; and Part Six, II, B, 3, b, i–ii.

5851 **Bird**, S. G. *The apprentice question.* London, 1881. 14p.

5852 **Solly**, Henry. *Apprenticeship: what it is and what it should be.* London, 1882. 4p.

5853 **Cunynghame**, Henry. 'Technical education, with reference to the apprenticeship system.' *R. Soc. Arts J.*, XXXIII, 1692 (24 April 1885), 627–32.
Discussion, p. 632–6.
Paper read at a meeting of the Society of Arts, 22 April 1885.

5854 **Wright**, Thomas. 'Our craftsmen.' *Nineteenth Century*, XX, 116 (October 1886), 530–552.
The author was a journeyman engineer.

5855 **Inglis**, J. *The apprentice question.* Glasgow, 1894. 12p.

5856 *Report on an investigation of the Fishing Apprenticeship System.* 1894. (C. 7576.)
By A. D. Berrington and J. S. Davy.

5857 **Sanger**, C. P. 'The fair number of apprentices in a trade.' *Econ. J.*, v, 20 (December 1895), 616–36.

5858 **Erskine-Risk**, J. 'Apprenticeship indentures from Stockleigh English parish chest.' *Devon. Ass. Advmt. Sci. Lit. Art. Rep. Trans.*, XXXIII (1901), 484–94.

5859 **Bradby**, M. K. and **Durham**, F. H. 'Apprenticeship.' *Char. Orgn. Rev.*, n.s., XIII, 78 (June 1903), 302–13.

5860 **Bradby**, M. K. and **Durham**, F. H. 'Apprenticeship in relation to the unemployed.' Loch, C. S. (ed.). *Methods of social advance: short studies in social practice by various authors.* London, New York: Macmillan, 1904. p. 118–30.

5861 **London County Council**. Education Committee. *The apprenticeship question: report of the section of the Education Committee appointed to consider the question of apprenticeships.* London: L.C.C., 1906. 43p. (L.C.C. [Publication] 925.)

5862 **Jevons**, H. Winifred. 'Apprenticeship and skilled employment committees; with an account of the work of the Cambridge boys' employment registry, by Eglantyne Jebb.' Sadler, M. E. (ed.). *Continuation schools in England & elsewhere: their place in the educational system of an industrial state.* Manchester: Manchester U.P., 1907. p. 454–71.

5863 **Parsons**, James. 'Skilled employment committees.' *Char. Orgn. Rev.*, n.s., XXII, 127 (July 1907), 19–35.
Paper read at the Annual Conference of Charity Organisation and Kindred Societies, Norwich, 1907.
Discussion, p. 36–40.
Describes a scheme in operation for placing children in employment as apprentices.

5864 **Gibbon**, Ioan Gwilym. 'The industrial future of boys and girls. I. Skilled Employment & Apprenticeship Committees in England.' *Progress Civic Soc. Ind.*, III, 3 (July 1908), 165–75.

5865 **Bray**, Reginald Arthur. 'The apprenticeship question.' *Econ. J.*, XIX, 75 (September 1909), 404–15.

5866 **Bray**, Reginald Arthur. *Boy labour and apprenticeship.* London: Constable, 1911. xi, 248p.

5867 *Apprenticeship vs. conscription.* Herne Bay: Stanbrook, 1912. 13p.
By Robert Cecil Turle Evans?

5868 **Dunlop**, Olive Jocelyn. *English apprenticeship & child labour: a history.* London, Leipsic: Fisher Unwin; New York: Macmillan, 1912. 390p.
With a supplementary section on the modern problem of juvenile labour, by O. Jocelyn Dunlop and Richard D. Denman.
Based on the author's D.Sc.(Econ.) thesis, University of London.

5869 **Jackson**, Cyril. 'Apprenticeship and the training of the workman.' *Edinb. Rev.*, CCVXI, 442 (October 1912), 411–27.
Review article.

5870 **Scott**, Jonathan French. *Historical essays on apprenticeship and vocational education.* Ann Arbor, Mich.: Ann Arbor P., 1914. 96p.
The author's Ph.D. thesis, University of Wisconsin, 1913.

5871 **Longden**, Frederick. *Apprenticeship in iron-moulding: a comparison of conditions in English and Belgian foundries.* London: Hodgson Pratt Memorial, 1915. 57p.

5872 **Fleming**, *Sir* Arthur Percy Morris and **Pearce**, J. G. *The principles of apprentice training with special reference to the engineering industry.* London: Longmans, 1916. xiii, 202p.

5873 **Fleming**, *Sir* Arthur Percy Morris. *Training of apprentices.* London, 1916. 12p.

5874 **Moore**, R. C. *The industrial training and education of apprentices.* 1921. (M.Ed. thesis, University of Manchester.)

5875 **Thomson**, George Walker. *Apprenticeship in modern industry.* London: National Guilds League, 1923. 14p.

5876 **National Federation of Merchant Tailors**. *Schemes for dilution of labour.* London, 1924. 23p.

5877 **Twemlow**, J. A. 'Manx notes from Tudor Liverpool. 2. A sixteenth century Manx apprentice at Liverpool.' *Isle Man Nat. Hist. Antiq. Soc. Proc.*, n.s., II, 3 (1924), 253.
Note from Liverpool municipal records.

5878 **Jenkinson**, Hilary. 'List of Bedfordshire apprentices, 1711–1720.' *Bedford. Hist. Rec. Soc. Octavo Publs.*, IX (1925), 147–76.
With introduction.

5879 **Derry**, T. K. *The enforcement of a seven years' apprenticeship under the Statute of Artificers.* 1930–31. (D.Phil. thesis, University of Oxford.)

5880 **Gay**, Margaret Randolph. 'Aspects of Elizabethan apprenticeship.' *Facts and factors in economic history: articles by former students of Edwin Francis Gay.* Cambridge, Mass.: Harvard U.P., 1932. p. 134–63.

5881 **Knoop**, Douglas and **Jones**, Gwilym Peredur. 'Masons and apprenticeship in mediaeval England.' *Econ. Hist. Rev.*, III, 3 (April 1932), 346–66.

5882 **Butler**, Raymond Renard. *Paper read at the summer meeting . . . 1934 . . . on Apprenticeship and the Irish Apprenticeship Act.* Loughborough: Association of Technical Institutions, 1934. 19p. (Miscellaneous pamphlets.)

5883 **An Apprentice**. 'The worker's point of view. XXII. Too much drudgery.' *Hum. Factor*, IX, 3 (March 1935), 109–14.
Apprenticeship in printing.

5884 **Thomson**, George Walker. 'Technical education in Scotland.' *Hum. Factor*, IX, 1 (January 1935), 21–9.

'Extracts from a paper delivered at a joint meeting of Sections F and L (Economic and Educational Service) of the British Association Meeting in Aberdeen, September 1934.'

5885 **Benham**, *Sir* William Gurney. 'Apprenticeship in ancient times: a "writing school" and a "grammar school".' *Essex Rev.*, XLVII, 185 (January 1938), 19–21.

On a Colchester indenture of apprenticeship, 1522, with mention of the Royal Grammar School and *Scola Scripturalis*.

5886 **Walker**, W. F. 'A Hull apprenticeship indenture for 1647 for service in Maryland.' *E. Rid. Antiq. Soc. Trans.*, XXIX, 6 (1940–8).

5887 **Beloff**, Max. 'A London apprentice's notebook, 1703–5.' *History*, n.s., XXVII, 105 (June 1942), 38–45.

5888 **Cole**, George Douglas Howard. 'The reorganisation of apprenticeship in the building industry of Great Britain.' *Int. Labour Rev.*, XLVIII, 2 (August 1943), 174–200.

5889 **Twyman**, Frank. *Apprenticeship for a skilled trade*. London: C. Griffin, 1944. vi, 70p.

'With an appendix: Apprentices and the law, by Henry Newcome Knight.'

5890 **Northern Ireland**. Ministry of Education. *Training of apprentices: report of the joint committee appointed by the Minister of Education*. Belfast, 1945. 20p.

5891 **Ministry of Fuel and Power**. *Report of the Departmental Committee on Apprenticeship for Coal Face Workers*. London: H.M.S.O., 1947. 18p.

Chairman: W. Foster.

5892 **McLaine**, William. *New views on apprenticeship*. London: Staples P., 1948. 198p.

Printed in Leyden.

5893 **Evans**, Kenneth R. 'Training through apprenticeship.' Thomson, D. C. (ed.). *Training worker citizens*. London: Macdonald and Evans, 1949. p. 37–47.

5894 **Ministry of Works**. *Building apprenticeship: recruiting and training. Special report of the Building Apprenticeship and Training Council*. London: H.M.S.O., 1949.

Chairman: Sir George Gater.

5895 **Briggs**, W. J. 'Records of an apprenticeship charity, 1685–1753.' *Derby. Archaeol. Nat. Hist. Soc. J.*, LXXIV (1954), 43–61.

German Pole Apprenticeship Charity, Derbyshire.

5896 **Carr**, Harry. *The mason and the burgh: an examination of the Edinburgh Register of Apprentices and the Burgess Rolls*. London: Quatuori Coronati Lodge, no. 2076, 1954. 84p.

5897 **Davies**, Margaret Gay. *The enforcement of English apprenticeship: a study in applied mercantilism, 1563–1642*. Cambridge, Mass.: Harvard U.P., 1956. x, 319p. (Harvard economic studies 97.)

5898 **Industrial Welfare Society**. *Trends in apprenticeship training*. London: the Society, 1957. 27p.

5899 **Williams**, Gertrude, *Lady*. *Recruitment to skilled trades*. London: Routledge and Kegan Paul; New York: Humanities P., 1957. vii, 216p. (International library of sociology and social reconstruction.)

5900 **Beverstock**, Albert George. *Modern apprenticeship*. London: Classic Publications, 1958. xiii, 89p.

5901 **Harman**, Harold. *Commercial apprenticeship*. London: Pitman, 1958. ix, 94p.

5902 **Williams**, Gertrude, *Lady*. *Training for skill*. London: Fabian Society, 1959. 28p. (Research series 205.)

5903 **Croft**, Margaret. *Apprenticeship and the 'bulge'*. London: Fabian Society, 1960. 20p. (Research series 216.)

The increased numbers of school leavers between the years 1956 and 1964.

5904 **Liepmann**, Kate K. *Apprenticeship: an enquiry into its adequacy under modern conditions*. London: Routledge and Kegan Paul, 1960. x, 204p. (International library of sociology and social reconstruction.)

5905 **Dale**, Christabel (ed.). *Wiltshire apprentices and their masters, 1710–1760*. Devizes: Wiltshire Archaeological and Natural History Society, Records Branch, 1961. xvi, 224p. ([Publications] 17.)

5906 **Williams**, Philip Clive. *The industrious apprentice*. 1961–62. (M.A. thesis, University of Wales, Cardiff.)

5907 **Industrial Welfare Society**. *Apprentice training for the sixties*. London: the Society, 1962. 28p.

5908 **Moffat**, Andrew. *The transition from school to work: what is apprenticeship?* London: Industrial Welfare Society, 1962. 16p.

5909 **Oakley**, Charles Allen (ed.). *Commercial apprenticeships*. London: U. of London P., 1962. 112p.

By Ernest Tonkinson, Raymond E. Thomas and R. G. Magnus-Hannaford.

5910 **Beveridge**, Andrew. *Apprenticeship now: notes on the training of young entrants to industry*. London: Chapman and Hall, 1963. 168p.

5911 **McDonald**, J. G. 'Apprenticeship schools: an example.' *Christus Rex*, XVII, 1 (January–March 1963), 66–71.

5912 **Siklos**, Theodore. *Partnership incorporated: an account of a joint effort to solve the problems of apprentice training*. London: City and Guilds of London Institute, 1963. 40p.

5913 **Sterland**, Ernest George and **Crawford**, Samuel. *Apprentice training*. London: Institute of Personnel Management, 1963. 60p.

5914 **Williams**, Gertrude, *Lady*. *Apprenticeship in Europe: the lesson for Britain*. London: Chapman and Hall, 1963. ix, 208p.

5915 **Lee**, D. J. *A study of apprentice training*. 1963–64. (Ph.D. thesis, University of Birmingham.)

5916 **Fisher**, Norman George. *Apprenticeship: an address given by Mr Norman Fisher, M.A. to the . . . Annual Convention . . . 1963.* Leeds: Yorkshire Council for Further Education, 1964. 11p. (Pamphlet 64.)

5917 **Welchman**, Christopher. *A London apprentice.* London: Oxford U.P., 1964. 32p. (People of the past series.)

5918 **Bloor**, T. *Trade union job-control through apprenticeship training: the case of the printing industry.* 1965. (M.A.(Econ.) thesis, University of Manchester.)

5919 **Howden**, H. A. *The training of craftsmen with particular reference to the building and engineering industries in the Manchester area.* 1965. (M.Ed. thesis, University of Manchester.)

5920 **Marsh**, Henry John. *Notes for an apprentice finishing his time.* London: Industrial Welfare Society, 1965. 8p.

5921 **Williams**, Gertrude, *Lady. From Dick Whittington to Act of Parliament.* London: Neame, 1965. [16]p. (Take home books.)

5922 **Butler**, Angela and **Grabe**, Sven. *European apprenticeship: effects of educational, social and technical development on apprentice training practices in eight countries.* Geneva: CIRF [International Vocational Training Information and Research Centre], 1966. [277]p. (CIRF monographs, vol. 1, no. 2.)

Report prepared for the Manpower Administration, Office of Manpower, Automation and Training, U.S. Department of Labor.

Photocopy of typescript. Springfield, Va.: Clearinghouse for Federal Scientific and Technical Information, 1968.

Each leaf represents two pages of the original.

5923 **Garlick**, Vera Frances Mabel. *Out of work: the apprentice looks at his job.* London: Longmans, 1966. 62p.

5924 **International Labour Office**. *European apprenticeship.* Geneva: I.L.O., 1966, 276p. (CIRF monographs, vol. 1, no. 2.)

5925 **Wild**, B. M. *A survey of apprentice recruitment, selection and training for the printing industry in the Manchester and Salford area.* 1966. (M.Sc. thesis, University of Manchester.)

5926 **Diggle**, Margaret. 'An apprentice of the 1880s.' *Voc. Asp.*, XIX, 44 (Autumn 1967), 195–202.

5927 **Wardle**, David. 'Education in Nottingham in the age of apprenticeship, 1500–1800.' *Thoro. Soc. Trans.*, LXXI (1967), 36–54.

'Apprenticeship', p. 36–41.

5928 **Livingstone**, D. A. *The costing of craft apprenticeship in the engineering industry.* 1967–68. (M.Sc. thesis, University of Strathclyde.)

5929 **Lyon**, J. *Engineering apprenticeships in the Bolton area (1900–1940).* 1967–68. (M.Ed. thesis, University of Manchester.)

5930 **McPherson**, D. *Training for skill: an investigation into the problems of training for skill, particularly at craft level, and an appraisal of the significance of the findings in relation to social and economic efficiency.* 1968–69. (Ph.D. thesis, University of Edinburgh.)

5931 **Engineering Industry Training Board**. *Dual-role craftsmen.* Watford: the Board, 1970. [15]p. (Booklet SP1.)

5932 **Williams**, Jill Christine. *Apprentices and operatives: a study of the facilities for training and guidance available to the 15 and 16 year old school leaver in Wales.* 1970. (M.Sc. Econ. thesis, University of Wales, Cardiff.)

See also: 5583; 6950; 7086; 11,394; 12,092; 12,108; 12,124; 12,174; 12,649.

b. TRAINING AND DEVELOPMENT

i. *General*

5933 **Bosanquet**, Helen. 'The education of women.' *The standard of life, and other studies.* London, New York: Macmillan, 1898. p. 136–56.

5934 **Bosanquet**, Helen. 'The industrial training of women.' *The standard of life, and other studies.* London, New York: Macmillan, 1898. p. 157–73.

5935 **Bosanquet**, Helen. *The industrial training of women.* London, 1899. 19p.

5936 **Black**, Clementina. 'Trade schools for girls in London.' *Econ. J.*, XVI, 63 (September 1906), 449–54.

5937 **Millis**, C. T. 'Trade schools for boys and girls: their economic value and their place in a national system of education.' Sadler, M. E. (ed.). *Continuation schools in England & elsewhere: their place in the educational system of an industrial and commercial state.* Manchester: Manchester U.P., 1907. p. 401–26.

'Part of this chapter was read as a paper at the meeting of the British Association (Section L) at Leicester, August, 1907.'

5938 **Sadler**, Michael Ernest and **Beard**, Mary S. 'Certain trade schools and pre-apprenticeship schools in England: a brief review of their aims and courses of study.' Sadler, M. E. (ed.). *Continuation schools in England & elsewhere: their place in the educational system of an industrial and commercial state.* Manchester: Manchester U.P., 1907. p. 427–53.

5939 **Winslow**, Charles Henry. *Report on the relations of European industrial schools to labor.* Boston: Wright and Potter, 1908. 22p. (Massachusetts Commission on Industrial Education. Bulletin 10.)

5940 **Durham**, F. H. 'The industrial training of women workers.' National Conference on the Prevention of Destitution. *Report of the proceedings . . . 1911.* London: King, 1911. p. 290–9.

Discussion, p. 299–307.

5941 **Rowntree**, Benjamin Seebohm and **Lasker**, Bruno. 'The training of unemployed youths.' *Bull. Trim. Ass. Int. Lutte Chôm.*, II, 1–2 (Janvier–Juin 1912), 170–6.

5942 **Brereton**, Cloudesley. 'Co-operation between the school and the employer.' *Contemp. Rev.*, cv (February 1914), 227–35.

5943 **Dearle**, Norman Burrell. *Industrial training, with special reference to the conditions prevailing in London*. London: King, 1914. xiii, 596p. (Studies in economics and political science.)
Also D.Sc.(Econ.) thesis, University of London, 1915.

5944 **Pelham**, Herbert Sidney. *The training of a working boy*. London: Macmillan, 1914. xv, 165p.

5945 **Boag**, Harold. 'Human capital and the cost of the war.' *R. Statist. Soc. J.*, LXXIX, 1 (January 1916), 7–17.

5946 **Berriman**, A. E. 'Education as a function of management.' Berriman, A. E., and others. *Industrial administration: a series of lectures*. Manchester: Manchester U.P.; London: Longmans, Green, 1920. p. 49–77.

5947 **Goldstone**, F. W. 'Labour and continued education.' Manchester University. *Labour and industry: a series of lectures*. Manchester: Manchester U.P.; London: Longmans, 1920 p. 131–46.
'A lecture given on Tuesday, December 9, 1919.'

5948 **Thomas**, Emrys. *A scheme of industrial and technical education with special reference to rural areas*. 1920. (M.A. thesis, University of Wales, Bangor.)

5949 **Trainees' National Guild**. *Report . . . on the training schemes, and submitted to the Minister of Labour*. 1922. 16p.

5950 **Abbott**, Albert. 'Recent trends in education for industry and commerce in Great Britain.' *Int. Labour Rev.*, XXXII, 2 (August 1935), 176–94.

5951 **Frankel**, H. 'Professional training of women.' *Oxf. Univ. Inst. Statist. Bull.*, IV, 10 (18 July 1942), 205–7.

5952 **Institute of Labour Management**. *Training for industrial employment*. London, [1946?]. 65p.

5953 **International Labour Office**. *Vocational training of adults in the United Kingdom*. Geneva: I.L.O., 1948. vi, 88p. (Monographs on vocational training and retraining in different countries 1.)

5954 **Forrester**, *Lord*. 'Education in industry and the rôle of the industrial architect.' Thomson, D. C. (ed.). *Training worker citizens*. London: Macdonald and Evans, 1949. p. 179–89.

5955 **Graely**, J. W. 'Training the young worker.' Thomson, D. C. (ed.). *Training worker citizens*. London: Macdonald and Evans, 1949. p. 15–36.

5956 **Oxford Conference on the Education of the Young Worker**. [Report of the first [-sixth] conference held at Oxford in 1948 [-1956] under the auspices of the University Department of Education.] London: Heinemann, 1949 [- 1957].
Second–Third published for the King George's Jubilee Trust by the Oxford University Press.

5957 **Revans**, Reginald William. 'The County College: its significance to industry.' Thomson, D. C. (ed.). *Training worker citizens*. London: Macdonald and Evans, 1949. p. 83–97.

5958 **Richards**, G. O. 'Memorandum on "day release".' *Ind. Law Rev.*, III, 3 (January 1949), 214–19.

5959 **Seear**, Beatrice Nancy and **Shaw**, Anne. 'Training and education for girls in industry.' Thomson, D. C. (ed.). *Training worker citizens*. London: Macdonald and Evans, 1949. p. 49–62.

5960 **Thomson**, David Cleghorn (ed.). *Training worker citizens: an exposition by experts of some modern educational methods designed to equip youth for the service of industry and the state*. London: Macdonald and Evans, 1949. xvi, 255p.

5961 **Tickner**, Frederick James. *Modern staff training: a survey of training needs and methods of today*. London: U. of London P., 1952. 159p.

5962 **Roy**, A. 'Selection and training.' *Br. Mgmt. Rev.*, XI, 3 (April 1953), 25–37.

5963 **Barker**, R. McC. *An evaluation of certain training methods with specific reference to juveniles entering industry*. 1953–54. (M.A. thesis, University of Leeds.)

5964 **Jones**, F. *A survey of some of the problems of vocational education in part-time day release classes*. 1953–54. (M.Ed. thesis, University of Nottingham.)

5965 **Newton**, L. S. *The prediction of success in training of trade operatives*. 1954. (M.Ed. thesis, University of Manchester.)

5966 **Seymour**, William Douglas. *Industrial training for manual operations*. London: Pitman, 1954. xi, 203p.

5967 **Cole**, George Douglas Howard. 'General education and vocational training in Great Britain.' *Int. Labour Rev.*, LXXII, 2–3 (August–September 1955), 164–86.

5968 **Wellens**, John. *Education & training in industry*. Manchester: Columbine P., 1955. x, 142p.
Includes one chapter on the graduate in industry.

5969 **National Institute of Industrial Psychology**. *Training factory workers: a report on a survey of the training of semi-skilled and unskilled workers in the United Kingdom carried out under Project 179 of the European Productivity Agency by the National Institute of Industrial Psychology*. London: Staples P., 1956. 127p.

5970 **Seymour**, William Douglas. *Training for manual operations: the technology of human relations*. Birmingham: Industrial Administration Group, College of Technology, 1956.

5971 **Dalvi**, M. A. *Commercial education in England during 1851–1902: an institutional study*. 1956–57. (Ph.D. thesis, University of London.)

5972 **Frisby**, A. A. *Selection for technical education.* 1956–57. (M.A. thesis, University of Birmingham.)

5973 **Davies**, Arfor Tegla. *Industrial training: an introduction.* London: Institute of Personnel Management, 1956 [i.e. 1957]. 40p. (Broadsheet.)

5974 **Organisation for European Economic Co-operation.** European Productivity Agency. *The training of workers within the factory: survey of industrial in-plant training programmes in seven European countries.* Paris: O.E.E.C., 1957. 90p. (Project 179.)
Report prepared by the National Institute of Industrial Psychology.

5975 **Ministry of Labour and National Service.** *Training for skill: recruitment and training of young workers in industry. Report by a Sub-committee of the National Joint Advisory Council.* London: H.M.S.O., 1958. vi, 36p.
Chairman: Robert Carr.

5976 **Eagleson**, D. E. *Employment and training of girls leaving Belfast primary, secondary intermediate, and grammar schools in relation to the educational system and the employment services.* 1958–59. (Ph.D. thesis, Queen's University, Belfast.)

5977 **Karim**, A. A. A. *Training in industry.* 1958–59. (M.A. thesis, University of Leeds.)

5978 **Harrison**, Cyril A. *BACIE and its forebears: a fortieth anniversary review.* London: British Association for Commercial and Industrial Education, 1959. 12p.

5979 **Le Mare**, M. W. *Girl entrants to industry, with special reference to the training of girls aged fifteen to eighteen years, for semi-skilled work in selected firms.* 1959. (B.Litt. thesis, University of Oxford.)

5980 **Ministry of Education.** *Report of the Advisory Committee on Further Education for Commerce.* London: H.M.S.O., 1959. 34p.

5981 **Seymour**, William Douglas. *Operator training in industry.* London: Institute of Personnel Management, 1959. 52p.

5982 **Silberston**, Dorothy Marion. *Youth in a technical age: a study of day release.* London: Parrish, 1959. 228p.

5983 **Rolls**, I. F. *Present trends in part-time day release schemes in further education.* 1959–60. (M.A. thesis, University of London.)

5984 **Council of Europe.** Partial Agreement [in the social and public health field]. Social Committee. *Polyvalent vocational training.* Strasbourg: C. of E., [196–?].

5985 **Department of Scientific and Industrial Research.** *Training made easier: review of four recent studies.* London: H.M.S.O., 1960. 32p. (Problems of progress in industry 6.)

5986 **Ministry of Labour.** Personnel Management Advisory Service. *Examples of operative training schemes in industry.* London: the Advisory Service, 1960. 14p.

5987 **Organisation for Economic Co-operation and Development.** European Productivity Agency. *Accelerated vocational training for unskilled and semi-skilled manpower.* Paris: O.E.C.D., 1960. 492p.
'Great Britain', p. 275–311.

5988 **Percival**, R. *A study of some determinants of the response of approved school boys to vocational training.* 1960–61. (M.A. thesis, University of London.)

5989 **Taylor**, Ernest A. *A critical examination of the post-war education problems within industry.* 1960–61. (Ph.D. thesis, University of Leicester.)

5990 **British Association for Commercial and Industrial Education.** *New routes to further education: papers presented at the BACIE Spring conference, Senate House, University of London, 19 April 1961.* London: B.A.C.I.E., 1961. 31p.

5991 **Venables**, *Sir* Percy Frederick Ronald and **Williams**, William John. *The smaller firm and technical education.* London: Parrish, 1961. 223p.

5992 **British Association for Commercial and Industrial Education.** *Industrial training – whose responsibility? Papers presented at the BACIE Spring Conference, Federation of British Industries, 21 Tothill St., London, S.W.1, 10th May 1962.* London: B.A.C.I.E., 1962. vii, 32p.

5993 **Old**, Charles Leslie. *The role of the industrial education officer.* London: Association of Technical Institutions, 1962. 14p.

5994 **Women's Group on Public Welfare.** *The education and training of girls: a study.* London: National Council of Social Service, 1962. 122p.

5995 **Association of Teachers in Technical Institutions.** *Development of day release: evidence submitted to the Henniker-Heaton Committee.* London: A.T.T.I., 1963. 12p.

5996 **Department of Scientific and Industrial Research.** *Teaching machines and their use in industry.* London: H.M.S.O., 1963. 30p. (Problems of progress in industry 14.)
By H. Kay, J. Annett and M. E. Sime.

5997 **Griffin**, Joseph. 'Education and industry.' *Christus Rex*, XVII, 1 (January 1963), 17–33.

5998 **Wellens**, John. *The training revolution: from shop-floor to board-room.* London: Evans, 1963. 136p.

5999 **City and Guilds of London Institute.** *Further education for craftsmen.* London: the Institute, 1964. 36p.

6000 **Department of Education and Science.** Committee on Day Release. *Day release: the report of a Committee set up by the Minister of Education.* London: H.M.S.O., 1964. 48p.
Chairman: C. Henniker-Heaton.

6001 **Department of Scientific and Industrial Research.** *How research can help training.* London: H.M.S.O., 1964. 20p. (Problems of progress in industry 16.)
By H. M. Clay.

6002 **Department of Scientific and Industrial Research.** *Research in relation to operator training.* London: H.M.S.O., 1964. 20p.
By H. M. Clay.

6003 **Department of Scientific and Industrial Research.** *Training the adult worker.* London: H.M.S.O., 1964. 44p. (Problems of progress in industry 15.)
By Eunice Belbin.

6004 **Industrial Society.** *Methods of training your staff.* London: the Society, 1964. 21p.

6005 **Central Committee of Study Groups.** *The training of young people in industry: summary of an investigation by the study groups based on H.R.H. the Duke of Edinburgh's Commonwealth Study Conferences.* London: Industrial Welfare Society.
[Summary of reports from Great Britain.] 1965. xii, 57p.
Summary of reports from the Commonwealth, 1965. ii, 21p.
By James H. Downie.

6006 **Holding**, Dennis Harry. *Principles of training.* Oxford, London: Pergamon P., 1965. xvi, 156p. (Commonwealth and international library. Psychology division.)

6007 **Industrial Society.** *The training of young people in industry.* London: the Society, 1965. 57p.

6008 **Institute of Personnel Management.** *Costing the training function.* London: I.P.M., 1965. 20p.

6009 **Allsop**, Kathleen. *A new deal for young workers?* London: Hodder and Stoughton in association with Hilary Rubinstein, 1966. 127p. (Zenith books.)

6010 **Casey**, Patrick John. *Getting into training.* London: Neame, 1966. 16p. (Take home books.)

6011 **Lee**, D. J. 'Industrial training and social class.' *Sociol. Rev.*, n.s., XIV, 3 (November 1966), 269–86.
'. . . recent thinking in the study of bureaucracy is used to analyse current patterns of industrial training in Britain and their impact upon social stratification.'

6012 **Ministry of Labour.** Central Training Council. Commercial and Clerical Training Committee. *Training for commerce and the office: a report.* London: H.M.S.O., 1966. viii, 139p.
Chairman: Sir Joseph Hunt.

6013 **National Federation of Business and Professional Women's Clubs of Great Britain.** *The changing pattern: report on the training of the older woman.* London, 1966. 24p.

6014 **Nesbitt-Hawkes**, *Sir* Ronald (ed.). *The training of youth in industry.* Oxford, London: Pergamon P. (Commonwealth and international library. Social administration, training economics and production division.)
Vol. 1. *Engineering.* 1966. viii, 235p.

6015 **Robertson**, Keith B. 'Training for a purpose.' *New Soc.*, VII, 196 (30 June 1966), 12–13. (Trends in personnel management 4.)

6016 **Smith**, Peter B. and **Moscow**, David. 'After the T-group is over.' *New Soc.*, VIII, 222 (29 December 1966), 972–4.

6017 **Estimates Committee of the House of Commons.** *Ninth report: manpower training for industry.* London: H.M.S.O., 1967.

6018 **Grégoire**, Roger. *Vocational education.* Paris: Organisation for Economic Co-operation and Development, 1967. 138p.

6019 **Tickner**, Frederick James. *Training in modern society: an international review of training practices and procedures in government and industry.* Albany, N.Y.: Graduate School of Public Affairs, State University of New York at Albany, 1967.

6020 **Avent**, Catherine. 'The second-class sex?' Hutchings, D. (ed.). *Education for industry: Symposium on the Integration of Further Education and Industrial Training.* London: Longmans, 1968. p. 60–8.

6021 **Belbin**, Raymond Meredith. 'New possibilities in the retraining of older workers.' Wright, H. B. (ed.). *Solving the problems of retirement.* London: Institute of Directors, 1968. p. 74–82.

6022 **Belbin**, Eunice and **Belbin**, Raymond Meredith. 'Retraining and the older worker.' Pym, D. (ed.). *Industrial society: social sciences in management.* Harmondsworth: Penguin, 1968. p. 152–67.

6023 **Dicker**, E. V. 'The purpose of training.' Hutchings, D. (ed.). *Education for industry: Symposium on the Integration of Further Education and Industrial Training.* London: Longmans, 1968. p. 29–36.

6024 **Holding**, Dennis Harry. 'Training for skill.' Pym, D. (ed.). *Industrial society: social sciences in management.* Harmondsworth: Penguin, 1968. p. 134–51.

6025 **Hutchings**, Donald (ed.). *Education for industry: Symposium on the Integration of Further Education and Industrial Training.* London: Longmans, 1968. xv, 128p.

6026 **Jessup**, F. W. 'The new opportunity.' Hutchings, D. (ed.). *Education for industry: Symposium on the Integration of Further Education and Industrial Training.* London: Longmans, 1968. p. 1–10.

6027 **Kennedy**, Finola. 'Industrial training and further education of young people.' *Administration*, XVI, 2 (Summer 1968), 160–6.

6028 **King**, S. D. M. *Training within the organization: a study of company policy and procedures for the systematic training of operators and supervisors.* London: Tavistock Publications in association with Social Science Paperbacks, 1968. xxii, 274p.

6029 **Lauwerys**, J. A. and **Scanlon**, D. G. *Education within industry.* London: Evans, 1968. xvi, 382p.

6030 **MacLennan**, Alex. 'The technical teachers.' Hutchings, D. (ed.). *Education for industry: Symposium on the Integration of Further Education and Industrial Training.* London: Longmans, 1968. p. 98–108.

6031 **Page**, Graham Terry. 'What is a training officer?' Hutchings, D. (ed.). *Education for industry: Symposium on the Integration of Further Education and Industrial Training.* London: Longmans, 1968. p. 90–7.

6032 **Peterson**, A. D. C. 'The immediate problem.' Hutchings, D. (ed.). *Education for Industry: Symposium on the Integration of Further Education and Industrial Training.* London: Longmans, 1968. p. 109–14.

6033 **Tilley**, K. 'A technology of training.' Pym, D. (ed.). *Industrial society: social sciences in management.* Harmondsworth: Penguin, 1968. p. 111–33.

6034 **Tovell**, W. A. 'After school: what next?' Hutchings, D. (ed.). *Education for industry: Symposium on the Integration of Further Education and Industrial Training.* London: Longmans, 1968. p. 45–50.

6035 **Watson**, Leonard E. 'Retraining the older worker.' Hutchings, D. (ed.). *Education for industry: Symposium on the Integration of Further Education and Industrial Training.* London: Longmans, 1968. p. 80–9.

6036 **Weedall**, A. 'The problem of the unskilled.' Hutchings, D. (ed.). *Education for industry: Symposium on the Integration of Further Education and Industrial Training.* London: Longmans, 1968. p. 51–9.

6037 **Peers**, S. *The education and training of the professional and commercial worker in the Greater Dortmund and South Lancashire areas.* 1968–69. (M.Ed. thesis, University of Manchester.)

6038 **Belbin**, Raymond Meredith. *The discovery method: an international experiment in retraining.* Paris: Organisation for Economic Co-operation and Development, 1969. 85p. (Employment of older workers 6.)
'The United Kingdom project', p. 39–52.

6039 **Board of Trade**. *Exports and the industrial training of people from overseas: report of a working party.* London: H.M.S.O., 1969. iv, 57p.

6040 **Singer**, E. J. *Training in industry and commerce.* London: Institute of Personnel Management, 1969. 66p. (Training series.)

6041 **Smith**, C. Selby. 'Benefits to British employers from post-secondary education.' *R. Statist. Soc. J.*, Ser. A, CXXXII, 3 (1969), 408–17.

6042 **Smith**, Duncan. *Productivity & training: a review of an urgent problem.* London: King Edward's Hospital Fund, 1969. 66 leaves.

6043 **Talbot**, J. R. and **Ellis**, C. D. *Analysis and costing of company training.* London: Gower P., 1969. 176p.

6044 **Thomas**, Brinley, **Moxham**, John and **Jones**, J. A. G. 'A cost-benefit analysis of industrial training.' *Br. J. Ind. Relat.*, VII, 2 (July 1969), 231–64.

6045 **Turner**, Barry Trevor. *The organisation and management of company training.* London: Industrial and Commercial Techniques, 1969. 120 leaves.

6046 **Ziderman**, Adrian. 'Costs and benefits of adult retraining in the U.K.' *Economica*, n.s., XXXVI, 144 (November 1969), 363–76.

6047 **Association of Teachers in Technical Institutions**. *Education, training and employment of women and girls.* London: A.T.T.I., 1970. 11p.

6048 **Council of Europe**. Partial Agreement [in the social and public health field]. Social Committee. *Selection and training of supervisors, especially in small and medium-sized firms.* Strasbourg: C. of E., 1970.

6049 **Department of Employment**. *Cost-benefit aspects of manpower retraining.* London: H.M.S.O., 1970. 40p. (Manpower papers 2.)

6050 **Finnigan**, John. *Industrial training management.* London: Business Books, 1970. x, 166p.

6051 **Oatey**, Michael. 'The economics of training with respect to the firm.' *Br. J. Ind. Relat.*, VIII, 1 (March 1970), 1–21.
'The article is a revised version of a Master's paper submitted in May 1967 to the Department of Educational Policy Studies of the University of Wisconsin.'

6052 **Pratt**, John. 'What about the workers?' *New Soc.*, XV, 391 (26 March 1970), 520–1. (Society at work.)
On day release.

6053 **Seear**, Nancy. 'Education and vocational training in schools of various levels.' Organisation for Economic Co-operation and Development. *Employment of women: Regional Trade Union Seminar, Paris, 26th–29th November 1968. Final Report.* Paris: O.E.C.D., 1970. p. 113–129.

See also: 26; 28; 66; 6270; 7773; 11,892; 14,240.

ii. *Particular Occupations and Industries*

6054 **Cooper**, A. J. 'The training of teachers.' International Congress of Women, London, 1899. *Transactions. Vol. II. Women in education.* London: T. Fisher Unwin, 1900. p. 174–80.

6055 **Pycroft**, Ella. 'The training of teachers of domestic economy.' International Congress of Women, London, 1899. *Transactions. Vol. II. Women in education.* London: T. Fisher Unwin, 1900. p. 191–4.

6056 **London County Council**. Education Department. *Training and employment of boys in the building trades in London: report by education officer submitting a report by Mr. J. C. Smail, organizer of trade schools for boys, on the training and employment of boys in the building trades in London.* London: L.C.C., 1914. 26p.

6057 **Departmental Committee on the Training, Appointment and Payment of Probation Officers**. *Report.* London: H.M.S.O., 1922. 32p. (Cmd. 1601.)
Chairman: Sir John Baird.

6058 **Ferguson**, Reginald William. *Education in the factory: an account of the educational schemes & facilities at Cadbury Brothers Ltd., Bournville Works.* Bournville: Publication Department, 1924. 68p.

6059 **Departmental Committee on the Training of Teachers for Public Elementary Schools.** *Report.* London: H.M.S.O., 1925. 195p. (Cmd. 2409.)
Chairman: Lord Burnham.

6060 **Jones**, L. G. E. *The training of teachers in England and Wales: a critical survey.* 1926. (Ph.D. thesis, University of London.)

6061 **Board of Education.** Departmental Committee on the Training of Rural Teachers. *Report.* London: H.M.S.O., 1929. 121p.
Chairman: J. Q. Lamb.

6062 **Ministry of Health.** Departmental Committee on Training and Employment of Midwives. *Report.* London: H.M.S.O., 1929. 96p.
Chairman: Sir Robert Bolam.

6063 **Association for Education in Industry and Commerce.** *Report on the training of manual workers in the engineering industry.* Birmingham, 1930. 99p.

6064 **Pick**, Frank. *Education for the railway service: a new standard of efficiency.* London: *Modern Transport*, 1930. 7p.
Reprinted in *Modern Transport*, 8 and 15 November 1930.
Presidential address, L.S.E. Railway Students' Association, 30 October 1930.

6065 **Fitch**, Miriam G. *The history of the training of teachers for secondary schools in England (approx. 1846–1930).* 1930–31. (M.A. thesis, University of London.)

6066 **Pendleton**, Dorothy S. *Staff training in department stores.* London: *Efficiency Magazine*, 1932. 204p.

6067 **Ministry of Health.** Departmental Committee on Qualifications, Recruitment, Training and Promotion of Local Government Officers. *Report.* London: H.M.S.O., 1934. 91p.
Chairman: William Henry Hadow.

6068 **Ault**, O. E. *The relation of certain problems to the training of teachers in the United States, Ontario, France, Scotland and Germany.* 1935. 334p. (Ph.D. thesis, University of Edinburgh.)

6069 **Scottish Education Department.** Advisory Council. *Training of women primary school teachers: report.* Edinburgh: H.M.S.O., 1935. 6p.
Chairman: John Brown Clark.

6070 **Walker**, Harvey. *Training public employees in Great Britain.* New York, London: McGraw-Hill, 1935. xi, 213p. (Commission of inquiry on public service personnel. Monograph 6.)

6071 **Scottish Departmental Committee on the Training of Nurses.** *Report.* Edinburgh: H.M.S.O., 1936. 58p. (Cmd. 5093.)
Chairman: A. C. Black.

6072 **Clark**, Harold Watton. *Personnel in retail distribution, with special reference to the training of juvenile employees.* 1937. 137p. (M.Com. thesis, University of Birmingham.)

6073 **Cadbury Brothers.** *Education in industry: a survey of schemes for the recruitment, training and for the education of the employees of Cadbury Brothers Ltd.* Bournville: Publication Department, 1938. 86p.

6074 **Cole**, George Douglas Howard. *Training and recruitment for the building industry.* 1941. 27p.
A memorandum prepared for the Ministry of Works and Buildings by G. D. H. Cole on behalf of the Nuffield College Reconstruction Survey.

6075 **Committee on the Training of Civil Servants.** *Report.* London: H.M.S.O., 1944. 34p. (Cmd. 6525.)
Chairman: R. Assheton.

6076 **Abd**, E. F. Nabib. *Recent changes in the structure and training of labour in the British engineering industry.* 1945. (Ph.D. thesis, University of Manchester.)

6077 **Cotton Board.** Recruitment and Training Department. *Education and training for cotton and rayon industry: papers and discussions at a conference in Manchester in September 1946.* Manchester, 1946. 160p.

6078 **Younghusband**, Eileen Louise. *Report on the employment and training of social workers.* Dunfermline: Carnegie United Kingdom Trust, 1947. viii, 180p.

6079 **Martin**, Loveday. *Into the breach: the emergency training scheme for teachers.* London: Turnstile P., 1949. ix, 65p.

6080 **Pickard**, Ormonde George. 'Clerical trade unions and education for office work.' *Voc. Asp.* (1949), 101–11.

6081 **Pickard**, Ormonde George. 'Office work and education, 1848–1948.' *Voc. Asp.* (1949), 221–43.

6082 **Taylor**, Evelyn. 'Training for the retail distributive trade.' Thomson, D. C. (ed.). *Training worker citizens.* London: Macdonald and Evans, 1949. p. 63–72.

6083 **Acton Society Trust.** *Training and promotion in nationalised industry.* London: Allen and Unwin, Acton Society Trust, 1951. 138p.

6084 **Herzberg**, Else. *Some principles of training, applied to the retail trade.* London: Institute of Personnel Management, 1955. 23p.

6085 **Northern Ireland.** *Technical education for the textile industry: report of the Committee appointed by the Minister of Education and the Minister of Commerce.* Belfast: H.M.S.O., 1955. 15p. (Cmd. 329.)

6086 **Ellis**, J. R. *Training for medicine.* 1955–56. (M.D. thesis, University of Cambridge.)

6087 **British Institute of Management.** *Sales training in industry.* London: B.I.M., 1957. 40p.

6088 **Polding**, M. E. *The male clerk in industry.* 1957–58. (M.A. thesis, University of Liverpool.)

6089 **Headrick**, T. 'The town clerk: his training and career.' *Publ. Adm.*, XXXVI, 3 (Autumn 1958), 231–48.

6090 **Brent**, E. J. *The training, recruitment and conditions of service of the London elementary schoolteacher, 1919–1939.* 1958–59. (M.A. thesis, University of London.)

6091 **Dale**, John Rodney. *The clerk in industry.* 1958–59. (M.A. thesis, University of Liverpool.)

Published Liverpool: Liverpool U.P., 1962. 118p.

6092 **Magnus-Hannaford**, R. G. *Education and training for distribution.* Paris: Organisation for European Economic Co-operation, 1959. 149p.

6093 **Industrial Welfare Society.** *Training for the sales force: summaries of current sales training schemes.* London: the Society, 1960. 43p. (Inf. summary 69.)

6094 **Sheppard**, D. *Formal training in agriculture.* [London]: Central Office of Information, 1960. 108p. (Social Survey SS 283.)

Attitudes of farmers and farm workers towards young men who have had formal training.

6095 **Hamer**, J. W. *A critical survey of the technical training of 'part-time release' engineering apprentices.* 1960–61. (M.Sc. thesis, University of London.)

6096 **Institution of Mechanical Engineers.** *The education and training of professional mechanical engineers.* London: the Institution, 1961.

6097 **Ministry of Education.** *The future pattern of the education and training of teachers: eighth report of the National Advisory Council on the Training and Supply of Teachers.* London: H.M.S.O., 1962. viii, 34p.

6098 **Ministry of Health** and **Scottish Home and Health Department.** *Report of the Study Group on the Work, Grading, Training and Qualifications of Hospital Engineers.* London: H.M.S.O., 1962.

Chairman: Major-General Sir Leslie Tyler.

6099 **Sheppard**, D. *The views of farmers, farm workers and ex-students on the value of formal training for farming.* 9p. (Government Social Survey report G. 62.)

Reprinted from *Agricultural Progress*, XXXVII, 1962.

6100 **Belbin**, Eunice and **Sergean**, Robert. *Training in the clothing industry: a study of recruitment, training and education.* London: Twentieth Century P., 1963. 199p.

Summary, by Margaret Stewart, also available: *Why train? A summary of a report on training in the clothing industry.* 25p.

6101 **Institution of Mechanical Engineers.** Committee on Practical Training. *The practical training of professional mechanical engineers.* London: the Institution, 1963.

6102 **King Edward's Hospital Fund for London.** Working Party on the Training of Domestic Administrators. *Report.* London: the Fund, 1963. viii, 20p.

6103 **King Edward's Hospital Fund for London.** Working Party on the Training of Head Porters. *Report.* London: the Fund, 1963. vi, 17p.

6104 **Brent**, E. J. *The training, recruitment and conditions of service of the London senior (elementary) secondary modern school teacher, 1939–1961.* 1963–64. (Ph.D. thesis, University of London.)

6105 **Musgrave**, P. W. *Technical change, the labour force and education in the British and German iron and steel industries from 1860.* 1963–64. (Ph.D. thesis, University of London.)

6106 **Gunn**, I. A. 'Vocational training for the British merchant navy.' *Int. Labour Rev.*, LXXXIX, 2 (February 1964), 166–80.

6107 **Institution of Mechanical Engineers.** Education and Training Group, and Administration and Engineering Production Group. *Engineering education and career patterns: a conference.* London: I.M.E., 1964. vi, 95p. (Proceedings 1963–4, vol. 178, part 3F.)

6108 **Organisation for Economic Co-operation and Development.** Directorate for Scientific Affairs. *Training of technicians in Ireland.* Paris: O.E.C.D., 1964. 112p. (O.E.C.D. reviews of national policies for science and education.)

6109 **Women's Employment Federation** and **National Council of Social Service.** *Training and employment in social work.* London, 1964. 34p.

6110 **Ghazi**, G. *The training and supply of teachers in England and Iran, with special reference to primary school education.* 1965. (M.A. thesis, University of Exeter.)

6111 **Department of Education and Science** and **Ministry of Technology.** Committee on Manpower Resources for Science and Technology. *Education and training requirements for the electrical and mechanical manufacturing industries.* London: H.M.S.O., 1966. v, 34p.

First report of the Working Group on Engineering Training and the Requirements of Industry.

Chairman: G. S. Bosworth.

6112 **General Dental Council.** *Final report on the experimental scheme for the training and employment of dental auxiliaries.* London: the Council, 1966. 100p.

6113 **Ministry of Labour.** Central Training Council. *The selection and training of instructors.* London: H.M.S.O., 1966. 7p.

6114 **Musgrave**, P. W. 'The growth in the demand for training in the iron and steel industry, 1945–1964.' *Voc. Asp.*, XVIII, 39 (Spring 1966), 10–16.

6115 **National Dock Labour Board.** *Training of dock workers: Great Britain.* London: Review P., 1966. 15p.

6116 **Parry,** J. P. 'The Russell Report: the supply and training of teachers for further education.' *Voc. Asp.*, XVIII, 41 (Autumn 1966), 157–63.

On the Report of the Standing Sub-Committee on Teachers for Further Education of the National Advisory Council on the Training and Supply of Teachers, 1966.

6117 **Pickering,** Sally. 'The late starters.' *New Soc.*, VII, 173 (20 January 1966), 17, 19. (Society at work.)

Training mature women to be teachers.

6118 **Reynolds,** O. Walter and **Baker,** John. *A time to train: an account of experience gained by RTB at its Spencer works.* Oxford: Pergamon P., 1966. xiii, 246p. (Commonwealth and international library. Social administration, training, economics and production division.)

Richard Thomas and Baldwins Ltd.

6119 **Taylor,** Nancy. *Selecting and training the training officer.* London: Institute of Personnel Management, 1966. 90p. (Training series.)

6120 **Briscoe,** R. *An examination of the training problem of a 'voluntary' chain of retail food distributors.* 1967. (M.Sc. thesis, University of Manchester.)

6121 **Council of Europe.** *Social workers: role, training and status.* Strasbourg: C. of E., 1967.

6122 **Dodd,** Bernard. 'A study in adult retraining: the gas man.' *Occup. Psychol.*, XLI, 2–3 (April–June 1967), 143–53.

6123 **Engineering Employers' Federation.** Lancashire and Cheshire Region. *Report of the clerical and commercial training working party of the Regional Training Committee.* 1967. 20p.

6124 **Kahan,** Barbara. 'What Williams didn't cover.' *New Soc.*, IX, 244 (1 June 1967), 801. (Society at work.)

Training, pay and conditions of staff in residential institutions.

6125 **Zucker,** Elizabeth and **Smith,** Duncan. 'Rethinking medical social work.' *New Soc.*, IX, 235 (30 March 1967), 462–3. (Society at work.)

6126 **Rains,** C. E. *The professional training of primary teachers in physical education.* 1968–69. (M.Ed. thesis, University of Leicester.)

6127 **Rees,** L. M. *A critical examination of teacher training in Wales, 1846–1898.* 1968–69. (Ph.D. thesis, University of Wales, Bangor.)

6128 **British Iron and Steel Research Association.** *Forecasting and planning training loads in the steel industry.* London: B.I.S.R.A., Inter-Group Laboratories of the British Steel Corporation, 1969. (Report OR/47/68 and appendices.)

6129 **Confederation of British Industry.** Research and Technology Committee. *Technicians in research and development: report of a working party.* London: C.B.I., 1969. vi, 44p.

6130 **Jeffries,** Anthony Arthur and **Duxfield,** T. S. *Management and training of technical salesmen.* London: Gower P., 1969. xi, 178p.

6131 **Joint Committee of Industrial Training Boards.** *The training of system analysts (commercial): report prepared and presented to the Department of Employment and Productivity.* London: H.M.S.O., 1969. 23p.

6132 **Organisation for Economic Co-operation and Development.** Directorate for Scientific Affairs. *Training, recruitment and utilisation of teachers: country case studies, primary and secondary education, France, Ireland.* Paris: O.E.C.D., 1969. 493p.

6133 **Organisation for Economic Co-operation and Development.** Directorate for Scientific Affairs. *Training, recruitment and utilisation of teachers: country case studies, primary and secondary education, Germany, Belgique, United Kingdom.* Paris: O.E.C.D., 1969. 312p.

'Section Belgique' in French.

6134 **Baker,** C. J. *The recruitment, training and development of graduates in the administrative grades of the local government service.* 1970. (Dip. in Pub. Admin., University of London.)

6135 **Lowe,** Robert Graham. *Training in the Civil Service.* 1970. (Dip. in Pub. Admin., University of London.)

6136 **Ministry of Technology.** Working Group on Engineering Training and the Requirements of Industry. *Graduate training in manufacturing technology.* London: H.M.S.O., 1970. 36p.

Chairman: Dr G. S. Bosworth.

6137 **Watson,** Peter. 'Becoming a policeman.' *New Soc.*, XV, 400 (28 May 1970), 921–2.

See also: 5856; 5871–2; 5881; 5883; 5918–19; 5925; 5928–9; 6153; 6204; 6219; 9876; 9892; 9947; 9953.

iii. *Supervisors and Managers*

In addition to containing material on the training of supervisors and managers, this section includes literature dealing with their recruitment, selection, placement, performance and appraisal, and career development. See also Part Four, II, C; and Part Six, II, B, 2.

6138 **Heath,** St George. 'Training for factory administration.' Berriman, A. E., and others. *Industrial administration: a series of lectures.* Manchester: Manchester U.P.; London: Longmans, Green, 1920. p. 161–84.

6139 **Sankey,** H. R. *Training for administration in industry: the work of the Institute and its aspirations.* London: Institute of Industrial Administration, 1922. 15p.

6140 **Robinson,** George Allen. *An experiment in management education.* Loughborough: Association of Technical Institutions, 1933. 31p. (Miscellaneous pamphlets.)

Paper read at the Summer Meeting, 1933.

6141 **Perkins**, F. H. 'Training within industry for supervisors.' Thomson, D. C. (ed.). *Training worker citizens.* London: Macdonald and Evans, 1949. p. 73–81.

6142 **Satow**, Graham F. 'Training the supervising grades as a link between management and men.' Thomson, D. C. (ed.). *Training worker citizens.* London: Macdonald and Evans, 1949. p. 99–108.

6143 **International Labour Office.** *Supervisory training in European countries.* Geneva: I.L.O., 1950. 18p.

6144 **Rule**, A. M. B. and **Bramley**, D. H. *Training in supervision and management.* Birmingham: Birmingham College of Technology, 1950. 16p.

6145 **British Institute of Management.** *Foremanship training in technical colleges: report of a BIM sub-committee.* London: B.I.M., 1951. 36p.

6146 **Castle**, Peter F. C. 'The evaluation of human relations training for supervisors.' *Occup. Psychol.*, XXVI, 4 (October 1952), 191–205.

6147 **Castle**, Peter F. C. *An attempt to establish a criterion of the effectiveness of training courses for supervisors.* 1952–53. (Ph.D. thesis, University of London.)

6148 **Federation of British Industries.** *Education and training for management.* London: F.B.I., 1953.

6149 **Scott**, William Henry and **McGivering**, Ian C. 'Some impressions of human relations training for supervisors.' *Occup. Psychol.*, XXVII, 3 (July 1953), 137–51.

6150 **Ministry of Labour and National Service.** *Report of Committee of Inquiry on the Training of Supervisors.* London: H.M.S.O., 1954. 56p.

Chairman: P. H. St John Wilson.

6151 **British Institute of Management.** *The recruitment and training of men intended for management positions.* London: B.I.M., 1955. 70p.

6152 **Copeman**, George Henry. *Leaders of British industry: a study of the careers of more than a thousand public company directors.* London: Gee, 1955. 173p.

6153 **Royal Institute of Public Administration.** *Training managers in the public services.* London: Allen and Unwin, 1955. 84p.

By F. Bray and others.

A symposium derived from a series of lectures organised by the Royal Institute of Public Administration in 1954.

6154 **Silberston**, Aubrey. *Education and training for industrial management: a critical survey.* London: Management Publications, 1955. vii, 101p.

6155 **Ungerson**, Bernard. *Selection of executives.* London: British Institute of Management, 1955. 1p.

B.I.M. Scottish conference, 1955.

6156 **Acton Society Trust.** *Management succession: the recruitment, selection, training and promotion of managers.* London: the Trust, 1956. 139p.

Report by Rosemary Stewart, Nancy Joy, Paul Duncan-Jones.

Research planned and supervised by T. E. Chester.

6157 **Grabe**, Sven and **Silberer**, Paul. *Selection and training of foremen in Europe.* Paris: Organisation for European Economic Co-operation, European Productivity Agency, 1956. vii, 170p. (Project 234.)

'United Kingdom', p. 136–48.

6158 **Handyside**, John Duncan. *An experiment with supervisory training.* London: National Institute of Industrial Psychology, 1956. 48p. (Report 12.)

6159 **Organisation for European Economic Co-operation.** European Productivity Agency. *Training facilities in the field of human relations. 4. Report on the United Kingdom.* Paris: O.E.E.C., 1956. 86p. (Project 178.)

By S. D. M. King, revised with additional material, by V. M. Clarke.

6160 **Stewart**, Rosemary G. and **Duncan-Jones**, Paul. 'Educational background and career history of British managers, with some American comparisons.' *Explor. Entrepren. Hist.*, IX, 2 (December 1956), 61–71.

6161 **Urwick**, Lyndall Fownes. *Management studies and training for management.* London: Institute of Industrial Administration, 1956. 15p.

6162 **British Institute of Management.** *Company executive development schemes.* London: B.I.M., 1957. 164p.

6163 **Fraser**, John Munro. 'Training management students in human relations.' Thomson, D. C. (ed.). *Management, labour and community.* London: Pitman, 1957. p. 205–221.

6164 **Sidney**, Elizabeth and **Brown**, Margaret. 'A new method of training in human relations.' Thomson, D. C. (ed.). *Management, labour and community.* London: Pitman, 1957. p. 176–91.

6165 **Clements**, Roger Victor. *Managers: a study of their careers in industry.* London: Allen and Unwin, 1958. 200p.

6166 **Sofer**, Cyril and **Hutton**, Geoffrey. *New ways in management training: a technical college develops its service to industry.* London: Tavistock Publications, 1958. xii, 127p.

On the work of the Department of Management and Production Engineering, Acton Technical College.

6167 **Urwick**, Lyndall Fownes. *16 questions about the selection and training of managers.* London: Urwick, Orr, 1958. 35p.

6168 **Garforth**, Frederick Ivor de la Poer. *Management development: a systematic approach to the provision of supervisors and managers.* London: Institute of Personnel Management, 1959. 72p.

6169 **Roff**, Harry Eastman. *Selection of senior staff.* London: British Institute of Management, 1959. 3p.

B.I.M. National Conference, 1959.

6170 **Ungerson**, Bernard. *Selection of senior staff.* London: British Institute of Management, 1959.
B.I.M. National Conference, 1959.

6171 **British Institute of Management.** *Management of development schemes: interim report.* London: B.I.M., 1960. 76p.

6172 **British Productivity Council.** *Training of supervisors.* London: the Council, 1960. 20p.
Productivity, men and methods conference.

6173 **Armstrong**, John Reginald. *Supervisory training.* London: Institute of Personnel Management, 1961. 51p.

6174 **British Association for Commercial and Industrial Education.** *Management training and development.* London: B.A.C.I.E., 1961.

6175 **Eldridge**, John E. T. and **Jones**, F. C. *The selection and training of supervisors in the Black Country.* Stafford: Staffordshire College of Commerce, 1961. 59p.

6176 **Federation of British Industries.** *Stocktaking on management education: a report of a conference at the FBI, April 1961.* London: F.B.I., 1961. 81p.

6177 **Humblet**, J. E. 'A comparative study of management in three European countries: preliminary findings.' *Sociol. Rev.*, n.s., IX, 3 (November 1961), 351–60.

6178 **Acton Society Trust.** *Training managers.* London: the Trust, 1962. 87p.
By Michael Argyle and Trevor Smith with M. J. Kirton.

6179 **British Institute of Management.** *New trends in management training and succession.* London: B.I.M., 1962. 35p.

6180 **Doulton**, Joan and **Hay**, David. *Managerial and professional staff grading.* London: Allen and Unwin for the Royal Institute of Public Administration, 1962. 141p. (Studies in management 7.)
Second edition. 1969. 141p.

6181 **Ministry of Labour.** *Report of the Committee on the Selection and Training of Supervisors.* London: H.M.S.O., 1962. 36p.
Chairman: D. C. Barnes.

6182 **Ministry of Labour** and **Central Office of Information.** *Supervisory training pays.* London: H.M.S.O., 1962. 9p.

6183 **Lake**, J. R. *A follow-up study of managerial appointments.* 1962–63. (Ph.D. thesis, University of London.)

6184 **British Institute of Management.** *Management training and developing in retailing: a symposium.* London: B.I.M., 1963. 53p.

6185 **Federation of British Industries.** *Management education and training needs of industry.* London: F.B.I., 1963. 27p.

6186 **Organisation for Economic Co-operation and Development.** *Evaluation of supervisory and management training methods: co-ordination of research.* Paris: O.E.C.D., 1963. 159p.
Contributions by G. M. Stalker and K.E. Thurley for the United Kingdom.

6187 **Rogers**, Kenn. *Managers: personality and performance.* London: Tavistock Publications, 1963. vii, 184p.

6188 **Federation of British Industries, British Institute of Management** and **Foundation for Management Education.** *Management education and the British business schools: report on the 1964 appeal and statement of future policy.* London: F.B.I., 1964. 11p.

6189 **Harris**, Peter and **Thurley**, Keith E. *The future of supervisory training in the Thurrock area.* [London]: Mercury Publications, 1964. 35p.

6190 **King**, D. *Training within the organisation: a study of company policy and procedures for the systematic training of operators and supervisors.* London: Tavistock, 1964.

6191 **Ministry of Labour.** *Selection and training of supervisors: progress report.* London: H.M.S.O., 1964. 29p.
Chairman: A. S. Marre.

6192 **British Association for Commercial and Industrial Education.** *Clarifying objectives in supervisory training.* London: B.A.C.I.E., 1965. 5p.

6193 **British Institute of Management.** *Making management development effective.* London: B.I.M., 1965. 35p.

6194 **Clark**, David George. *An inquiry into the social and educational backgrounds and career patterns of a sample of managers in private and public industry in the Northwest of England.* 1965. (M.Sc. Tech. thesis, University of Manchester.)

6195 **Koontz**, H. *Requirements for basic and professional formal education for scientific management.* London: British Institute of Management, 1965. 32p.

6196 **Mortensen**, Vivika. *Training your supervisors.* London: Industrial Society, 1965. 20p. (Notes for managers 1.)
Revised edition.
Previous edition. 1963.

6197 **National Economic Development Office.** *Management, recruitment and development.* London: H.M.S.O., 1965. iv, 63p.

6198 **Pollard**, Sidney. *The genesis of modern management: a study of the industrial revolution in Great Britain.* London: Arnold, 1965. 328p.

6199 **Smith**, Barbara Mary Dimond. *Education for management: its conception and implementation in the Faculty of Commerce at Birmingham.* Birmingham: University of Birmingham, Faculty of Commerce and Social Science, 1965. 57p. (Occasional paper 5.)

6200 **Association of Teachers of Management.** *Policies for management education.* Oxford: Blackwell, 1966. v, 57p. (Occasional paper 3.)
Edited by Arthur Henderson.

6201 **Clark**, David George. *The industrial manager: his background and career pattern.* London: Business Publications, 1966. ix, 205p. (Business books.)

6202 **Foster**, G. 'Making managers: executives on the grid.' *Mgmt. Today* (April 1966), 3–8.

6203 **Ministry of Labour.** Central Training Council. *Supervisory training: a new approach for management.* London: H.M.S.O., 1966. viii, 60p.

By J. P. de C. Meade and F. W. Greig.

6204 **Musgrave**, P. W. 'The educational profiles of management in two British iron and steel companies with some comparisons, national and international.' *Br. J. Ind. Relat.*, IV, 2 (July 1966), 201–11.

6205 **British Association for Commercial and Industrial Education.** *A guide to the training of office supervisors.* London: B.A.C.I.E., 1967. 28p.

6206 **McClelland**, W. Grigor. 'Career patterns and organizational needs.' *J. Mgmt. Studies*, IV, 1 (February 1967), 56–70.

'Based on a public lecture at the University of Newcastle-upon-Tyne, March 1965.'

Reprinted in Hacon, R. J. (ed.): *Organisational necessities and individual needs.* Oxford: Blackwell, 1968. p. 19–33.

6207 **Ministry of Labour.** Central Training Council. Management Training and Development Committee. *An approach to the training and development of managers.* London: H.M.S.O., 1967. vii, 16p.

Chairman: Sir J. Hunt.

6208 **Rapoport**, Robert Norman. *Career patterns and Henley: a research note.* Henley: Administrative Staff College, 1967. 1p.

6209 **Roberts**, Tom John. *Developing effective managers.* London: Institute of Personnel Management, 1967. 63p. (Training series.)

6210 **Adair**, John. *Training for leadership.* London: Macdonald, 1968. 158p.

6211 **Bernstein**, Lesley (ed.). *Management development.* London: Business Books, 1968. x, 188p. (Management in action; 'Business management' books.)

6212 **Engineering Employers' Federation.** Lancashire and Cheshire Region. *Report of working party on management training and development.* 1968. 36p.

6213 **Jenkins**, David. *Supervisory selection and training in manufacturing industry.* London: Staples P., 1968. 77p.

6214 **Mosson**, T. M. and **Clark**, David George. 'Some inter-industry comparisons of the backgrounds and careers of managers.' *Br. J. Ind. Relat.*, VI, 2 (July 1968), 220–31.

6215 **Warr**, Peter Bryan and **Bird**, Michael W. *Identifying supervisory training needs.* London: H.M.S.O., 1968. v, 22p. (Training information paper 2.)

6216 **Beahan**, Patrick Henry, **Pontefract**, F. and **Upton**, M. J. G. *Three case studies in management and supervisory training.* London: British Association for Commercial and Industrial Education, 1969. 21p.

6217 **McClelland**, W. Grigor. 'Executive development and manpower planning.' Farrow, N. (ed.). *Progress of management research.* Harmondsworth: Penguin, 1969. p. 85–91.

6218 **Ministry of Labour.** Central Training Council. Management Training and Development Committee. *Training and development of managers: further proposals; report.* London: H.M.S.O., 1969. vii, 50p.

Chairman: Sir John Hunt.

6219 **Turner**, Barry Trevor. *Management training for engineers.* London: Business Books, 1969. xviii, 401p.

6220 **Rapoport**, Robert Norman. *Mid-career development: research perspectives on a developmental community for senior administrators.* London: Tavistock Publications, 1970. xiii, 290p.

With contributions by M. B. Brodie and E. A. Life.

6221 **Sofer**, Cyril. *Men in mid-career: a study of British managers and technical specialists.* London: Cambridge U.P., 1970. xxii, 376p. (Cambridge studies in sociology 4.)

6222 **Warr**, Peter Bryan, **Bird**, Michael W. and **Rackham**, Neil. *Evaluation of management training: a practical framework, with cases, for evaluating training needs and results.* London: Gower P., 1970. 111p. (Gower Press special study.)

See also: 6837; 7761.

C. THE LEVEL AND STRUCTURE OF EMPLOYMENT

The literature on employment and unemployment overlaps considerably. Hence this section should be consulted in conjunction with Part Six, II, D; Part Six, IV, A, 4, d; and Part Seven, IV, A–C.

1. General

In addition to containing general works on the level and structure of employment, this section includes general references on such topics as labour supply; the relationship between employment, output, and productivity; and models for forecasting employment. See also Part Six, II, D, 1.

6223 **Booth**, Charles. *Occupations of the people: England, Scotland, Ireland, 1841–81, being a restatement of the figures given in the census returns.* London: Stanford, 1886. 85p.

Extract from a paper read before the Statistical Society.

6224 **Booth**, Charles. 'Occupations of the people of the United Kingdom, 1801–81.' *R. Statist. Soc. J.*, XLIX, 2 (June 1886), 314–435.

Discussion, p. 436–44.

Read before the Society, 18 May 1886.

6225 **B.**, J. L. 'Englishmen in the world of labour.' Co-operative Wholesale Societies. *Annual for 1887* p. 270–303.
Includes statistics of distribution of occupations, unemployed, etc.

6226 **Nicholson**, Joseph Shield. 'The living capital of the United Kingdom.' *Econ. J.*, I (March 1891), 95–107.
Reprinted in Unesco. *Readings in the economics of education.* Paris, 1969. p. 227–34.

6227 **Welton**, Thomas A. 'On forty years' industrial changes in England and Wales.' *Manchr. Statist. Soc. Trans.* (1897–98), 153–243.
On occupations as described in the Census of Population.

6228 **Welton**, Thomas A. 'On the 1891 Census of Occupations of males in England and Wales, so far as relates to the large towns and to the counties after the exclusion of such towns.' *Manchr. Statist. Soc. Trans.* (1897–98), 245–66.

6229 **Welton**, Thomas A 'Memorandum on primary occupations in the principal English towns in 1901.' *R. Statist. Soc. J.*, LXVI, 2 (June 1903), 360–5.

6230 **Spencer**, M. G. and **Falk**, Herman John. *Employment pictures from the Census.* London: King, 1906. xi, 101p.

6231 **Welton**, Thomas A. 'Occupations in England and Wales, 1881 and 1901.' *R. Statist. Soc. J.*, LXXIII. 2 (February 1910) 164–6.

6232 **Bowley**, *Sir* Arthur Lyon. 'Rural population in England and Wales: a study of the changes of density, occupations, and ages.' *R. Statist., Soc. J.*, LXXVII, 6 (May 1914), 597–645.
Discussion, p. 646–52.
Read before the Society, 21 April 1914.

6233 **Welton**, Thomas A. 'Occupations of the people of England and Wales in 1911, from the point of view of industrial developments.' *Manchr. Statist. Soc. Trans.* (1914–15), 47–170.

6234 **Bowley**, *Sir* Arthur Lyon. *The war and employment.* London: Oxford U.P., 1915. 21p. (Oxford pamphlets, 1914–1915.)
'... the substance of a lecture delivered at the London School of Economics, February 15, 1915.'

6235 **Jones**, David Caradog. 'Some notes on the Census of Occupations for England and Wales.' *R. Statist. Soc. J.*, LXXVIII, 1 (January 1915), 55–78.
With discussion, p. 78–81.
'Read before the Royal Statistical Society, December 15, 1914.'

6236 **Welton**, Thomas A. 'Occupations of the people, England and Wales, 1911: memorandum as to merchants and clerks.' *R. Statist. Soc. J.*, LXXIX, 1 (January 1916), 55–60.

6237 **Bowley**, *Sir* Arthur Lyon. *Estimates of the working population of certain countries in 1931 and 1941, submitted to the Preparatory Committee for the International Economic Conference, 1927.* Geneva: League of Nations, 1926. 19p.

6238 **Bowley**, *Sir* Arthur Lyon. *Numbers occupied in the industries of England and Wales, 1911 and 1921.* London: Executive Committee of London and Cambridge Economic Service, 1926. 18p. (Special memorandum 17A.)

6239 **Bowley**, *Sir* Arthur Lyon. *Occupational changes in Great Britain, 1911 and 1921.* London: Executive Committee of London and Cambridge Economic Service, 1926. 24p. (Special memorandum 17.)

6240 **Political and Economic Planning**. 'Employment analysed.' *Planning*, II, 34 (25 September 1934), 3–13.

6241 **Tawney**, A. J. and **Tawney**, Richard Henry. 'An occupational census of the seventeenth century.' *Econ. Hist. Rev.*, v, 1 (October 1934), 25–64.
Source: a reprint of a Muster Roll for Gloucestershire.

6242 **Snow**, E. C. 'The limits of industrial employment. II. The influence of growth of population on the development of industry.' *R. Statist. Soc. J.*, XCVIII, 2 (1935), 239–73.
Discussion, p. 273–92.
'Read before the Royal Statistical Society, January 15th, 1935.'

6243 **George**, R. F. 'A sample investigation of the 1931 Population Census with reference to earners and non-earners.' *R. Statist. Soc. J.*, XCIX, 1 (1936), 147–61.
'A paper read to the Study Group, December 10th, 1935.'

6244 **Watson**, William Foster. 'The worker's point of view. XXVI. Is there a shortage of skilled craftsmen?' *Hum. Factor*, x, 1 (January 1936), 29–33.

6245 **Makower**, H. and **Robinson**, H. W. 'Labour potential in war-time.' *Econ. J.*, XLIX, 196 (December 1939), 656–62.

6246 **Political and Economic Planning**. 'Industrial man-power.' *Planning*, VII, 155 (21 November 1939), 1–14.

6247 **Bowley**, *Sir* Arthur Lyon. 'Changes in occupation and in employment, 1932 to 1938 and 1938 to 1939.' *Lond. Camb. Econ. Serv. Bull.*, XVIII, 1 (January 1940), 9–13.
Confined to occupations which come under the General Insurance Scheme.

6248 **Dearle**, Norman Burrell. *The labour cost of the world war to Britain, 1914–22: a statistical analysis.* New Haven: Yale U.P., 1940. ix, 260p. (Carnegie Endowment for International Peace. Supplementary vol.)

6249 **Jones**, John Harry. 'The Report of the Royal Commission on the Distribution of the Industrial Population.' *R. Statist. Soc. J.*, CIII, 3 (1940), 323–30.
Discussion, p. 330–43.

6250 **Owen**, Arthur David Kemp and **Little**, Neil. *The labour situation in Great Britain: a survey, May–October 1940.* Montreal: International Labour Office, 1940. 56p. (Studies and reports, Series B, no. 34.)

6251 **Political and Economic Planning.** 'Industrial man-power 2.' *Planning*, 167 (7 May 1940), 1–13.

6252 **Royal Commission on the Geographical Distribution of the Industrial Population.** *Report.* London: H.M.S.O., 1940. x, 320p. (Cmd. 6153.)
Chairman: Sir Montague Barlow.
Minutes of evidence. 1937–39.

6253 **Kalecki,** Michael. 'War-time changes in employment and the wage bill.' *Oxf. Univ. Inst. Statist. Bull.*, III, 13 (20 September 1941), 294–8.

6254 **Political and Economic Planning.** 'Man and woman power.' *Planning*, 175 (12 August 1941), 1–15.

6255 **Curtis,** C. R. *A statistical investigation of post-war industrial trends, with particular reference to employment, mechanisation and output.* 1942. (Ph.D. thesis, University of London.)

6256 **Kalecki,** Michael. 'Employment in the United Kingdom during and after the transition period.' *Oxf. Univ. Inst. Statist. Bull.*, VI, 16–17 (4 December 1944), 265–87.

6257 **Norris,** Alec. *Why we are short of coal and man power.* Mansfield: A. Norris, 1944. 12p.

6258 **Barna,** Tibor. 'A manpower budget for 1950.' *Lond. Camb. Econ. Serv. Bull.*, XXIII, 4 (October 1945), 85–90.

6259 **Burchardt,** F. A. 'Manpower in the reconversion period in U.S.A. and U.K.' *Oxf. Univ. Inst. Statist. Bull.*, VII, 17 (15 December 1945), 303–5.

6260 **Forchheimer,** K. 'War-time changes in industrial employment.' *Oxf. Univ. Inst. Statist. Bull.*, VII, 16 (24 November 1945), 269–78.

6261 **Frankel,** H. 'The industrial distribution of the population in Great Britain in July 1939.' *R. Statist. Soc. J.*, CVIII, 3–4 (1945), 392–422.
Discussion, p. 422–30.
'Read before the Royal Statistical Society, May 29th, 1945.'

6262 **Jewkes,** John. 'The shortage of labour.' *Distr. Bank Rev*, 80 (December 1946), 3–8.

6263 **Political and Economic Planning.** 'Britain's need for brain-power.' *Planning*, 259 (6 December 1946), 1–19.

6264 **Saunders,** Christopher Thomas. 'Manpower distribution 1939–1945: some international comparisons.' *Manchr. Sch.*, XIV, 2 (May 1946), 1–39.
U.K., U.S., Canada, Australia and New Zealand.
Originally read before the Manchester Statistical Society on 20 February 1946, and published in *Manchr. Statist. Soc. Trans.* (1945–46). Revised and brought up to date.

6265 **Barna,** Tibor. 'Manpower during 1946 and the coming months.' *Lond. Camb Econ. Serv. Bull.*, XXV, 1 (10 February 1947), 8–12.

6266 **Baudewyns,** J. J. J. *The determinants of the level of employment.* 1947. (B.Litt. thesis, University of Oxford.)

6267 **Williams,** Gertrude, *Lady. Men, women and jobs.* London: Bureau of Current Affairs, 1947. 20p. (Current affairs 39.)

6268 **Economics Committee.** *Present population trends and economic implications.* London: H.M.S.O., 1950.

6269 **Pigou,** Arthur Cecil. 'Over-employment.' *Economica*, n.s., XVII, 66 (May 1950), 211–14.
'This enquiry was suggested by the first chapter of Professor Ohlin's *The Problem of Employment Stabilization*, where over-employment is discussed, but in a quite different way.'
Reprinted in the author's *Essays in economics.* London: Macmillan, 1952. p. 108–12.

6270 **Political and Economic Planning.** *Manpower: a series of studies of the composition and distribution of Britain's labour-force.* London: P.E.P., 1951. ix, 102p.
Contents: I. The size of the labour-force. II. Distribution of the labour-force. III. Employment of women. IV. Entry into employment. V. Education and training of wage-earners.

6271 **Brayshaw,** Shipley Neave. *Employment and production: a new approach.* London: Industrial and Social Order Council of the Religious Society of Friends, 1952. 42p.

6272 **House,** John William. *Population structure and employment conditions.* [London]: North Tyne Survey Committee, [1952?]. 56p.

6273 **Leser,** Conrad Emanuel Victor. 'Men and women in industry.' *Econ. J.*, LXII, 246 (June 1952), 326–44.

6274 **Long,** Clarence D. *The labor force in war and transition: four countries.* New York: National Bureau of Economic Research, 1952. 61p. (Occasional paper 36.)

6275 **Piercy,** W., 1st Baron Piercy. 'The nation's youth and manpower needs.' Ministry of Labour and National Service. *The worker in industry: a series of ten centenary lectures delivered during Festival of Britain Year.* London: H.M.S.O., 1952. p. 1–7.

6276 **Wilson,** Thomas. 'Manpower.' Worswick, G. D. N. and Ady, P. H. (eds.). *The British economy 1945–1950.* Oxford: Clarendon P., 1952. p. 224–52.

6277 **Bellamy,** Joyce. 'A note on occupation statistics in British censuses.' *Populat. Studies*, VI, 3 (March 1953), 306–8.
Draws attention to omissions in *Guides to official sources.* No. 2. *Census reports of Great Britain, 1801–1931.* London: H.M.S.O., 1951.

6278 **Ince,** *Sir* Godfrey Herbert. 'The re-distribution of man-power in Great Britain following the Second Great War.' *Manchr. Statist. Soc. Trans.* (1953–54). 36p.

6279 **Weber,** B. 'Post-war trends in industrial output, employment and productivity: an international comparison.' *Scott. J. Polit. Econ.*, II, 2 (June 1955), 166–76.

6280 **Richardson**, I. M. *Age and occupation: a socio-medical study of 698 men.* 1955–56. (Ph.D. thesis, University of Aberdeen.)

6281 **Citrine**, Walter McLennan, Baron Citrine. 'The varying pattern of industry: a general survey.' *His Royal Highness The Duke of Edinburgh's Study Conference on the Human Problems of Industrial Communities . . .* London: Oxford U.P., 1957. Vol. I. *Report and proceedings.* p. 55–77.

6282 **Bellerby**, G. R. 'The distribution of manpower in agriculture and industry, 1851–1951.' *Farm Econ.*, IX, 1 (1958), 1–11.

6283 **Cairncross**, A. K. 'Production and employment in Scotland.' *Scott. J. Polit. Econ.*, V, 3 (October 1958), 249–53.

6284 **Musgrove**, Frank. 'Middle-class education and employment in the nineteenth century.' *Econ. Hist. Rev.*, 2nd ser., XII, 1 (August 1959), 99–111.

6285 **Robertson**, Donald James. 'A note on the composition of the working population.' *Scott. J. Polit. Econ.*, VI, 2 (June 1959), 153–60.

6286 **Musgrove**, Frank. 'Middle-class education and employment in the nineteenth century: a rejoinder.' *Econ. Hist. Rev.*, 2nd ser., XIV, 2 (December 1961), 320–9.
A reply to H. J. Perkin.

6287 **Perkin**, Harold J. 'Middle-class education and employment in the nineteenth century: a critical note.' *Econ. Hist. Rev.*, 2nd ser., XIV, 1 (August 1961), 122–30.
On the article by F. Musgrove, 1959.

6288 **Phillips**, A. W. 'A simple model of employment, money and prices in a growing economy.' *Economica*, n.s., XXVIII, 112 (November 1961), 360–70.

6289 **Robertson**, Isobel M. L. 'The occupational structure and distribution of rural population in England and Wales.' *Scott. Geogr. Mag.* LXXVII, 3 (December 1961), 165–79.

6290 **Shepherd**, J. R. 'Labour supplies: trends and prospects.' *Natn. Inst. Econ. Rev.*, 16 (July 1961), 17–23.

6291 **Nove**, Alec. 'Occupational patterns in the U.S.S.R. and Great Britain: some comparisons and contrasts.' *Manchr. Statist. Soc. Trans.* (1961–62). 23p.
Also printed separately in *Papers* of the Manchester Statistical Society.

6292 **Phillips**, A. W. 'Employment, inflation and growth.' *Economica*, XXIX, 113 (February 1962), 1–16.
'Inaugural lecture given at the London School of Economics and Political Science on 28th November, 1961.'

6293 **Wilkinson**, Roy Keith. 'Differences in earnings and changes in the distribution of manpower in the U.K., 1948–57.' *Yorks. Bull. Econ. Soc. Res.*, XIV, 1 (May 1962), 46–57.

6294 **Brown**, A., **Stone**, R., **Pyatt**, G. and **Leicester**, Colin. *Economic growth and manpower.* London: British Association for Commercial and Industrial Education, 1963.

6295 **Hunter**, Laurence Colvin. 'Cyclical variations in the labour supply: British experience, 1951–1960.' *Oxf. Econ. Pap.*, XV, 2 (July 1963), 140–53.

6296 **Musgrove**, Frank. *The migratory elite.* London: Heinemann, 1963. v, 185p. (Heinemann books on sociology.)

6297 **Peacock**, Alan Turner. 'Economic growth and the demand for qualified manpower.' *Distr. Bank Rev.*, 146 (June 1963), 3–18.

6298 **Brown**, A., **Leicester**, Colin and **Pyatt**, G. 'Output, manpower and industrial skills in the UK, 1948–1970.' Vaisey, J. (ed.). *The residual factor and economic growth.* Paris: O.E.C.D., 1964. p. 240–60.

6299 **Buxton**, N. K. and **MacKay**, Donald Iain. 'Comparability of Ministry of Labour statistics of employment, 1923–64.' *Br. J. Ind. Relat.*, II, 3 (November 1964), 418–23.

6300 **Eire**. National Industrial Economic Council. *Report on manpower.* Dublin: Stationery Office, 1964.

6301 **Farrag**, Abdelmegid M. 'The occupational structure of the labour force: patterns and trends in selected countries.' *Populat. Studies*, LVIII, 1 (July 1964), 17–34.

6302 **Ministry of Labour**. Manpower Research Unit. *The pattern of the future.* London: H.M.S.O., 1964. 52p. (Manpower studies 1.)

6303 **Kacser**, P. M. H. *An investigation into the possibility of projecting the occupational deployment of the labour force in England and Wales.* 1964–65. (Ph.D. thesis, University of London.)

6304 **Beckerman**, Wilfred. 'The future growth of national product.' Beckerman, W., and others. *The British economy in 1975.* Cambridge: Cambridge U.P., 1965. p. 73–103.
Contents:
1. Total population.
2. Population of working age.
3. The active labour force.
4. Working hours and holidays.
5. The development of gross national product, 1960–1975.

6305 **Beckerman**, Wilfred. 'The pattern of growth of output, employment and productivity, 1960 to 1975.' Beckerman, W., and others. *The British economy in 1975.* Cambridge: Cambridge U.P., 1965. p. 201–34.
Contents:
1. Summary of procedure.
2. The projection of output by industry.
3. The projection of productivity and employment by industry.

6306 **Burn**, Duncan, **Seale**, John Richard and **Ratcliff**, A. R. N. *Lessons from central forecasting: three essays on the techniques and fallibility of statistical measurement and projection in steel, doctors and social insurance.* London: Institute of Economic Affairs, 1965. 62p. (Eaton papers 6.)

6307 **Marshall**, T. H. 'The population problem during the industrial revolution: a note on the present state of the controversy.' Glass, D. V. and Eversley, D. E. C. (eds.). *Population in history: essays in historical demography.* Chicago: Aldine Publishing Co.; London: Arnold, 1965. p. 247–68.

Reprinted from *Economic History*, vol. 1, no. 4, 1929. (Supplement to the *Economic Journal*.)

6308 **Organisation for Economic Co-operation and Development.** *Active manpower policy: International Management Seminar, Brussels, 14th – 17th April 1964. Final report.* Paris: O.E.C.D., Manpower and Social Affairs Directorate, Social Affairs Division, 1965. 166p. (International seminars 1964–1.)

6309 **Crossley**, John Rodney. 'Essential statistics for manpower forecasting.' Roberts, B. C. and Smith J. R. (eds.). *Manpower policy and employment trends.* London: Bell for the London School of Economics and Political Science, 1966. p. 25–34.

6310 **Crossley**, John Rodney. 'Forecasting manpower demand and supply.' Roberts, B. C. and Smith, J. R. (eds.). *Manpower policy and employment trends.* London: Bell for the London School of Economics and Political Science, 1966. p. 15–24.

6311 **Freeman**, Christopher A. 'Research, technical change and manpower forecasting.' Roberts, B. C. and Smith, J. R. (eds.). *Manpower policy and employment trends.* London: Bell for the London School of Economics and Political Science, 1966. p. 47–62.

6312 **Layard**, P. R. G. and **Saigal**, J. C. 'Educational and occupational characteristics of manpower: an international comparison.' *Br. J. Ind. Relat.*, IV, 2 (July 1966), 222–66.

6313 **Layard**, P. R. G. 'Manpower needs and the planning of higher education.' Roberts, B. C. and Smith, J. R. (eds.). *Manpower policy and employment trends.* London: Bell for the London School of Economics and Political Science, 1966. p. 63–88.

6314 **Organisation for Economic Co-operation and Development.** *Manpower aspects of automation and technical change: European conference, Zurich, 1st–4th February 1966. Final report.* Paris: O.E.C.D., Manpower and Social Affairs Directorate, Social Affairs Division, 1966. 138p. (International seminars 1966–1.)

Also *Supplement to the final report.* 1966. vi, 438p.

6315 **Roberts**, Benjamin Charles and **Smith**, J. R. (eds.). *Manpower policy and employment trends.* London: Bell for the London School of Economics and Political Science, 1966. 137p.

6316 **Routh**, Gerald Guy Cumming. 'The changing pattern of employment since 1900.' Roberts, B. C. and Smith, J. R. (eds.). *Manpower policy and employment trends.* London: Bell for the London School of Economics and Political Science, 1966. p. 35–46.

6317 **St Cyr**, Eric Baldwin Anderson. *The cyclical behaviour of employment and factor income shares in British manufacturing industry, 1955–1964.* 1966. 304p. (Ph.D. thesis, University of Manchester.)

6318 **Stieber**, Jack. 'Manpower adjustments to automation and technological change in Western Europe.' *Technology and the American economy.* Washington, D.C.: National Commission on Technology, Automation, and Economic Progress, 1966. Appendix III. p. 41–125.

Also, reprinted by Michigan State University, School of Labor and Industrial Relations.

A condensed version appeared in Bowen, H. R. and Mangum, G. L. (eds.). *Automation and economic progress.* Englewood Cliffs, N.J.: Prentice-Hall, 1966. p. 159–67.

6319 **Blaug**, Mark, **Peston**, Maurice H. and **Ziderman**, Adrian. 'The utilisation of qualified manpower in industry.' Organisation for Economic Co-operation and Development. *Policy Conference on Highly Qualified Manpower, Paris 26th–28th September 1966.* Paris: O.E.C.D., 1967. p. 227–87.

Based on research at the Unit for Economic and Statistical Studies on Higher Education, London School of Economics and Political Science.

6320 **Galambos**, P. 'Activity rates of the population of Great Britain, 1951–1964: an analysis by regions and age-groups.' *Scott. J. Polit. Econ.*, XIV, 1 (February 1967), 48–69.

6321 **Jones**, Lyndon Hamer and **Dart**, G. *Manpower.* Hove: Editype, 1967. 38p. (Editype minibook 8.)

6322 **Kindleberger**, Charles Poor. *Europe's postwar growth: the role of labour supply.* Cambridge, Mass.: Harvard U.P.; London: Oxford U.P., 1967. xiii, 270p.

Chapter IV. 'The slow growers with limited supplies of labor: Scandinavia, Belgium, and the United Kingdom.'

6323 **Knight**, Rose. 'Changes in the occupational structure of the working population.' *R. Statist. Soc. J.*, Ser. A, CXXX, 3 (1967), 408–22.

6324 **Davies**, Glyn. 'Labour supply shortages: causes, consequences and cures?' *J. Econ. Studies*, III, 1 (March 1968), 25–53.

6325 **Ministry of Labour.** Manpower Research Unit. *Occupational changes, 1951–61.* London: H.M.S.O., 1967 [i.e. 1968]. 34p. (Manpower studies 6.)

6326 **Smith**, J. M. 'Age and occupation: an examination of 1961 census data.' *Occup. Psychol.*, XLII, 2–3 (April–July 1968), 133–8.

6327 **Zeisel**, Joseph Samuel. *The structure of employment at full employment in Great Britain and the United States.* Washington, D.C., 1968. vii, 169 leaves. (Ph.D. thesis, The American University.)

6328 **Durcan**, J. W. *On the short-run elasticity of the labour supply with respect to employment.* 1968–69. (M.Sc. thesis, University of Bristol.)

6329 **Gowler**, Dan. 'Determinants of the supply of labour to the firm.' *J. Mgmt. Studies*, VI, 1 (February 1969), 73–95.

6330 **International Labour Office.** *Manpower aspects of recent economic development in Europe.* Geneva: I.L.O., 1969. iv, 175p.

6331 **Flanders**, Allan David. 'Hidden manpower resources.' Kamin, A. (ed.). *Western European labor and the American corporation.* Washington, D.C.: Bureau of National Affairs, 1970. p. 419–22.

6332 **Hunter**, Laurence Colvin. 'Some problems in the theory of labour supply.' *Scott. J. Polit. Econ.*, XVII, 1 (February 1970), 39–59.

6333 **Livesey**, F. 'The composition of employment in branch factories.' *Oxf. Econ. Pap.*, n.s., XXII, 3 (November 1970), 420–36.

See also: 93; 7782; 8021; 8126.

2. Regional Distribution of Employment

For the purposes of this section Wales, Scotland, and Ireland are treated as regions, and material on employment in these areas is generally classified here. See also Part Six, II, D, 5; Part Six, II, E, 4; Part Six, III, D; and Part Seven, IV, D, 3.

6334 **Mearns**, Andrew. *London and its teeming toilers. Who they are and how they live. Facts and figures suggested by recent statistics of the census and charities commission.* London: Warren Hall and Lovitt, 1885. vii, 65p.

6335 **Scott**, Frederick. 'The condition and occupations of the people of Manchester and Salford.' *Manchr. Statist. Soc. Trans.* (1888–89), 93–116.

6336 **O'Donoghue**, David James. *The geographical distribution of Irish ability.* Dublin: O'Donoghue, 1906. xvii, 333p.

6337 **Moore**, S. C. 'The industrial evolution of a manufacturing village.' *Econ. J.*, XXI, 84 (December 1911), 613–24.
Hebden Bridge, Yorkshire.

6338 **Bureau of Social Research for Tyneside.** *Occupations and industries of Tyneside.* Newcastle-upon-Tyne, 1926. 8p. (Tyneside papers 4.)

6339 **Ford**, T. *Work and wealth in a modern port: an economic survey of Southampton.* London, 1934. 217p.

6340 **Jones**, David Caradog. *Merseyside: trade and employment.* Liverpool: U.P. of Liverpool, 1935. 39p. (New Merseyside series 1.)

6341 **Ackroyd**, E. and **Plummer**, A. 'Industry.' Barnett House, Oxford. Survey Committee. *A survey of the social services in the Oxford district.* Vol. 1. London: Oxford U.P., 1938. p. 71–98.

6342 **Marshak**, J. 'Occupations.' Barnett House, Oxford. Survey Committee. *A survey of the social services in the Oxford district.* Vol. 1. London: Oxford U.P., 1938. p. 63–70.

6343 **McGuinness**, T. W. 'Changes of population in West Cornwall with the rise and decline of mining.' *R. Corn. Polytech. Soc. Rep.*, IX, 4 (1940), 22–95.

6344 **Richards**, Mary Ann. *A study of statistics of population and occupations in the counties, urban and rural districts of Wales, 1901–31.* 1942. (M.Sc. thesis, University of Wales, Aberystywth.)

6345 **McGuinness**, T. W. 'Occupational changes in Cornwall (over a period of c. 100 years).' *R. Corn. Polytech. Soc. Rep.*, XI, 2 (1943), 78–107.

6346 **McGuinness**, T. W. *Population changes in Cornwall in relation to economic resources.* 1944. (Ph.D., thesis, University of London.)

6347 **Political and Economic Planning.** 'Location of employment.' *Planning*, 224 (25 August 1944), 1–16.

6348 **Shenfield**, A. and **Sargant Florence**, Philip. 'Labour for the war industries: the experience of Coventry.' *Rev. Econ. Studies*, XII, 1 (1944–45), 31–49.

6349 **Topping**, James Frederick. *A survey of industrial trends in employment in the West Riding of Yorkshire since 1921.* 1946. (M.Comm. thesis, University of Leeds.)

6350 **Buckatzsch**, E. J. 'Occupations in the parish registers of Sheffield, 1655–1719.' *Econ. Hist. Rev.*, 2nd ser., I, 2–3 (1949), 145–50.

6351 **Leser**, Conrad Emanuel Victor. 'Changes in level and diversity of employment in regions of Great Britain, 1939–47.' *Econ. J.*, LIX, 235 (September 1949), 326–42.

6352 **Gribbin**, T. K. 'The population and employment of Kingston-upon-Hull and the Humberside area, 1921–48.' *Yorks. Bull. Econ. Soc. Res.*, II, 2 (July 1950), 129–54.

6353 **Leser**, Conrad Emanuel Victor. *Some aspects of the industrial structure of Scotland: an analysis of the industrial distribution of insured persons in Scotland, parts of Scotland and regions of England and Wales in 1947.* Glasgow: Jackson, 1951. 52p. (University of Glasgow. Department of Social and Economic Research. Occasional papers 5.)

6354 **Bellamy**, Joyce. 'Occupations in Kingston upon Hull, 1841–1948.' *Yorks. Bull. Econ. Soc. Res.*, IV, 1 (January 1952), 33–50.

6355 **Leser**, Conrad Emanuel Victor. 'Manpower.' Cairncross, A. K. (ed.). *The Scottish economy: a statistical account of Scottish life.* London: Cambridge U.P., 1954. p. 35–45.

6356 **Newholm**, R. E. *A geographical study of the occupations and regional function of Carlisle.* 1954–55. (Ph.D. thesis, University of Durham.)

6357 **Evans**, T. R. *A study of some social effects of recent changes in the employment structure of the Kidwelly district.* 1957–58. (M.A. thesis, University of Wales.)

6358 **Johnson**, B. L. C. 'The distribution of factory population in the West Midlands conurbation.' *Inst. Br. Geogr. Publs.*, XXV, (1958), 209–23.

6359 **University of Exeter**. Research Group. *Working and living in Exeter*. Exeter: Exeter University, 1958. v, 90p.

6360 **Birmingham Area Study Group**. *Changes in employment opportunity: a report by the Birmingham Area Study Group based on H.R.H. The Duke of Edinburgh's Study Conference 1956*. London: Central Committee of Study Groups, 1961. 47p.

6361 **McKay**, William Machoven and **Stagg**, M. B. *South-west Northumberland: recent trends in rural population and employment, with a policy for the future*. Newcastle-upon-Tyne: Northumberland Rural Community Council, 1961. 22p.

'Summarised from theses by W. Mc. McKay, M. B. Stagg, edited by the Northumberland Rural Community Council.'

6362 **Dunning**, John Harry. *Economic planning and town expansion: a case study of Basingstoke*. Southampton: Workers' Educational Association (Southern District), 1963. 168p.

6363 **Ministry of Housing and Local Government**. *London: employment; housing; land*. London: H.M.S.O., 1963. (Cmnd. 1952.)

6364 **Northern Ireland Government Information Service**. *Changes in the structure of employment in Northern Ireland since 1949*. Belfast, 1963. 8 leaves. (Facts and figures 3.)

6365 **Garmany**, J. W. 'A survey of manpower: Londonderry, Coleraine, Limavady and Strabane – a case study.' *Statist. Soc. Inq. Soc. Ir. J.*, XXI, 2 (1963–64), 55–66.

6366 **Davies**, H. W. E. and **Hagger**, D. F. 'Aspects of the geography of employment.' Manners, G. (ed.). *South Wales in the sixties: studies in industrial geography*. Oxford: Pergamon, 1964. p. 129–59.

6367 **Evans**, Eric Wyn and **Hartley**, Keith. *Employment and unemployment in the Hull region, 1951–1968*. Hull: University of Hull, Department of Economics, 1964. 91p.

6368 **Alexander**, Kenneth John Wilson and **Alpine**, R. L. W. *Regional problems of recruitment of technical manpower in the electronics industry*. London: Electronics Economic Development Committee, Manpower Working Group, 1965.

6369 **Chambers**, Jonathan David. 'Three essays on the population and economy of the Midlands.' Glass, D. V. and Eversley, D. E. C. (eds.). *Population in history: essays in historical demography*. Chicago: Aldine Publishing Co.; London: Arnold, 1965. p. 308–53.

1. 'Enclosure and labour supply in the Industrial Revolution.' Reprinted from *Economic History Review*, 2nd ser., vol. 5, 1953, p. 319–43.

2. 'The course of population change.' Reprinted from 'The Vale of Trent 1670–1800: a regional study of economic change' in *Economic History Review*, supplement 3, 1957.

3. 'Population change in a provincial town: Nottingham, 1700–1800.' Reprinted from *Studies in the Industrial Revolution: essays presented to T. S. Ashton*, edited by L. S. Pressnell, London, 1960.

6370 **Houston**, George. 'Farm labour in Scotland 1800–1850.' *Soc. Study Labour Hist. Bull.*, 11 (Autumn 1965), 10–12.

Discussion, p. 12–13.

A paper given at the annual meeting of the Scottish Committee of the Society for the Study of Labour History, 23 May 1965.

6371 **Smith**, D. M. 'Recent changes in the regional pattern of British industry.' *Tijdschr. Econ. Soc. Geogr.*, LVI, 4 (July–August 1965), 133–45.

'The differential growth pattern from 1951 to 1961 in terms of employment.' (Townroe.)

6372 **Symes**, David Gilyard. *The population resources of the Connemara Gaeltacht: an analysis of the employment potential; a memorandum to the Board of Gaeltarra Eireann*. Hull: Hull University, Department of Geography, 1965. 2 parts.

1. Connemara. 37p. (Miscellaneous series 1.)

2. County Donegal. 23p. (Miscellaneous series 2.)

6373 **Brook**, F. *Industry and employment in West Northumberland*. 1965–66. (M.A. thesis, University of Newcastle-upon-Tyne.)

6374 **Baker**, Terence J. *Regional employment patterns in the Republic of Ireland*. Dublin: Economic Research Institute, 1966. 34p. (Paper 32.)

6375 **Diamond**, D. R. 'Aspects of commercial employment.' *The Lothians regional survey and plan. Vol. 1. Economic and social aspects*. Edinburgh: H.M.S.O., 1966. p. 82–91.

6376 **Ó hEideáin**, E. M. 'Galway Labour Survey.' *Administration*, XIV, 1 (Spring 1966), 20–3.

6377 **Orr**, S. C. 'Industry and employment.' *The Lothians regional survey and plan*. Vol. 1. *Economic and social aspects*. Edinburgh: H.M.S.O., 1966. p. 49–64.

6378 **Pound**, J. F. 'The social and trade structure of Norwich 1525–1575.' *Past Pres.*, 34 (July 1966), 48–69.

6379 **Thomas**, Spencer. 'The agricultural labour force in some south-west Carmarthenshire parishes in the mid-nineteenth century.' *Welsh Hist. Rev.*, III, 1 (June 1966), 63–73.

6380 **Wilson**, Gail Graham. *Social and economic statistics of North East England: sub-regional and local authority statistics on population, housing, rateable values and employment*. Durham: University of Durham, 1966. iii, 216p.

6381 **Lee**, R. L. *Manpower needs on Tyneside, 1965–70*. 1966–67. (M.Sc. thesis, University of Salford.)

6382 **Davies**, Glyn. 'Regional unemployment, labour availability, and redeployment.' *Oxf. Econ. Pap.*, n.s., XIX, 1 (March 1967), 59–74.

'Regional labour reserves: a comment', by D. I. MacKay. n.s., XX, 1 (March 1968), 109–21.

6383 **Evans**, Alan W. 'Myths about employment in Central London.' *J. Transp. Econ. Policy*, I, 2 (May 1967), 214–25.

6384 **Northern Ireland Economic Council.** *Manpower: an appraisal of the position 1964–70.* Belfast: H.M.S.O., 1967. 42p.

6385 **Rimmer**, W. Gordon. 'The industrial profile of Leeds, 1740–1840.' *Thores. Soc. Publs.*, L, 2 (1967), 130–57.

6386 **Rimmer**, W. Gordon. 'Occupations in Leeds, 1841–1951.' *Thores. Soc. Publs.*, L, 2 (1967), 158–79.

6387 **Steed**, Guy P. F. 'Locational changes: a "shift and share" analysis of Northern Ireland's manufacturing-mix, 1950–64.' *Tijschr. Econ. Soc. Geogr.*, LVIII, 5 (September–October 1967), 265–70.

'Relating local growth patterns with national trends.' (Townroe.)

6388 **Beath**, J. A. *A study of the economies of selected rural areas of England and Scotland, with particular reference to the use of the local employment multiplier.* 1967–68. (M.Phil. thesis, University of London.)

6389 **Davidson**, R. N. *Aspects of the distribution of employment in Glasgow: a locational analysis of employee/area relationships.* 1968. 3v. (Ph.D. thesis, University of Glasgow.)

6390 **MacKay**, Donald Iain. 'Industrial structure and regional growth: a methodological problem.' *Scott. J. Polit. Econ.*, XV, 2 (June 1968), 129–43.

'Industrial structure and regional economic growth: a comment', by P. M. Townroe. XVI, 1 (February 1969), 95–8.

'A further comment.' XVI, 1 (February 1969), 99–101, in reply to P. M. Townroe.

6391 **Spence**, N. A. 'A multifactor uniform regionalization of British counties on the basis of employment data for 1961.' *Reg. Studies*, II, 1 (September 1968), 87–104.

6392 **Tulpule**, A. H. *The distribution of employment in a big conurbation – the Greater London.* 1968. (B.Litt. thesis, University of Oxford.)

6393 **Tulpule**, A. H. 'Towards an integrated model of distribution of service employment in the non-central areas of Greater London.' *Oxf. Univ. Inst. Econ. Statist. Bull.*, XXX, 3 (August 1968), 207–29.

6394 **Walsh**, Brendan M. *Some Irish population problems reconsidered.* Dublin: Social and Economic Research Institute, 1968. 36p. (Paper 42.)

6395 **Warren**, K. 'Iron and steel in North East England: the regional implications of development in a basic industry.' *Older Industrial Areas Conference*, Regional Studies Association, March 1968. p. 14.

6396 **Walker**, R. G. *Population and employment in the London and Glasgow new towns, 1951–64.* 1968–69. (Ph.D. thesis, University of Birmingham.)

6397 **Brown**, Arthur Frederick James. *Essex at work, 1700–1815.* Chelmsford: Essex County Council, 1969. 183p. (Essex Record Office. Publications 49.)

6398 **Cambridge**. City. Department of Architecture and Planning. *Industry & employment: a report on Cambridge & the surrounding area.* Cambridge: the Department, 1969. 38 leaves.

6399 **Hughes**, Garth Owen. *The prospective trends in the industrial and occupational pattern of the population of Wales.* 1969. (M.A. thesis, University of Wales, Aberystwyth.)

6400 **Wabe**, J. S. 'Labour force participation rates in the London metropolitan region.' *R. Statist. Soc. J.*, Ser. A, CXXXII, 2 (1969), 245–64.

6401 **Wexford Junior Chamber**. Manpower Survey Committee. *Manpower survey report On Wexford. Part 1.* Wexford: Wexford Junior Chamber, 1969. 19p.

Chairman: Edward Culleton.

6402 **Barratt Brown**, Michael. 'The concept of employment opportunities with special reference to Yorkshire and Humberside.' *Yorks. Bull. Econ. Soc. Res.*, XXII, 2 (November 1970), 65–100.

6403 **Burt**, Roger (ed.). *Industry and society in the South-West.* Exeter: University of Exeter, 1970. 110p. (Exeter papers in economic history 3.)

'. . . papers . . . given at two seminars on the industrial and social history of the south-west held at Dartington Hall, Totnes on 4 and 5 May 1968 and the 22 and 23 February 1969.' (Intro.)

6404 **Craig**, J., **Evans**, Eric Wyn, **Showler**, Brian and **Hamilton**, A. 'Humberside: employment, unemployment and migration – the evolution of industrial structure, 1951–1966.' *Yorks. Bull. Econ. Soc. Res.*, XXII, 2 (November 1970), 123–42.

6405 **Cunningham**, N. J. 'The pattern of Merseyside employment 1949–66.' Lawton, R. and Cunningham, C. M. (eds.). *Merseyside: social and economic studies.* London: Longman, 1970. p. 149–201.

6406 **Davidson**, R. N. 'The pattern of employment densities in Glasgow.' *Urb. Studies*, VII, 1 (February 1970), 69–75.

6407 **Eire**. Department of Labour. *Manpower in an industrial growth centre.* 1970. (V. 9.)

6408 **Law**, C. M. 'Employment growth and regional policy in North-west England.' *Reg. Studies*, IV, 3 (October 1970), 359–66.

6409 **Alexander**, Edward. *Employment, prices, output and expenditure in Scotland: a comparative study.* 1970–71. (M.Sc. thesis, University of Edinburgh.)

See also: 94; 6283; 6414; 6417; 6423; 6425; 6431; 6435–8; 6440; 6442–3; 6454–5; 6463; 6468; 6499;

6504; 6511; 6515; 6528–9; 6531; 6534; 6589–90; 6594; 6597–8; 6622; 6641; 6653; 6659; 6702; 6705; 6734; 6754; 6824; 6854; 6871; 6878–9; 6890–2; 6900; 6902; 6905; 6907; 6945; 6951; 6960; 6965–7; 7308; 8102.

3. Occupational and Industrial Distribution of Employment

See also Part Six, II, B, 2, b; Part Six, II, B, 3, b, ii–iii; Part Six, II, D, 6; and Part Seven, IV, D, 4.

a. AGRICULTURE, FORESTRY, AND FISHING

6410 **Ogle**, William. 'The alleged depopulation of the rural districts of England.' *R. Statist. Soc. J.*, LII, 2 (June 1889), 205–32.
With discussion, p. 232–240.
Read before the Society, 19 March 1889.

6411 **Moore**, Harold Edward. *Back to the land.* London: Methuen, 1893. xv, 216p. (Social questions of to-day.)

6412 **Bear**, William E. 'Our agricultural population.' *Econ. J.*, IV, 14 (June 1894), 317–31.

6413 *Report on the decline in the agricultural population of Great Britain, 1881–1906.* London: H.M.S.O., 1906. 146p. (Cd. 3273.)
By R. H. Rew.

6414 **Turnbull**, Robert E. 'Labourers and the land: Yorkshire.' British Association for the Advancement of Science. *Reports of meetings.* 1906. p. 654–5.

6415 **Eversley**, G. Shaw-Lefevre, *Lord.* 'The decline in number of agricultural labourers in Great Britain.' *R. Statist. Soc. J.*, LXX, 2 (June 1907), 267–306.
Discussion, p. 307–19.

6416 **Smith**, Will C. 'Back to the land.' *Econ. J.*, XVIII, 70 (June 1908), 242–53.

6417 **Hughes**, Evan. *The changes in the numbers of agricultural labourers and in their wages and efficiency during the past fifty years, and the causes of these changes, with special reference to Wales.* 1909. (M.A. thesis, University of Wales, Aberystwyth.)

6418 **Clapham**, J. H. 'The growth of an agrarian proletariat, 1688–1832: a statistical note.' *Camb. Hist. J.*, I, 1 (1923), 92–5.

6419 **King**, J. S. *Seasonal distribution of employment in agriculture.* London, 1925. 9p.

6420 **Senior**, W. H. *An account of 'An investigation into the labour force employed on farms'.* 1929. (M.Sc. thesis, University of Reading.)

6421 **Kirkpatrick**, W. H. *The seasonal distribution of farm labour requirements.* Cambridge, 1930. iv, 44p.

6422 **Maxton**, John P. 'Man power in agriculture.' *Manchr. Statist Soc. Trans.* (1939–40). 19p.

6423 **Smith**, Joseph Henry. 'The labour requirements of the ploughing-up campaign in Wales.' University College of Wales, Aberystwyth, Department of Agricultural Economics. *Welsh studies in agricultural economics.* 1940. p. 17–26.
Reprinted from the *Welsh Journal of Agriculture*, vol. XVI, 1940.

6424 **Committee on the Supply of Crews for Trawlers.** *Report.* 1943.
Chairman: A. Gray.
The report was not published, but communicated to owners' associations and men's unions.
Summary in Ministry of Agriculture and Fisheries. *Fisheries in war time.* 1946. p. 51–2.

6425 **University of Aberdeen.** North of Scotland College of Agriculture. Agricultural Economics Department. *Agricultural labour in North-East Scotland.* Aberdeen, 1946. 21 leaves. (Economic reports 4.)
Mimeographed.

6426 **Wilson**, M. A. *The composition and recruitment of the agricultural labour force and their bearing on future supply.* 1949. (B.Litt. thesis, University of Oxford.)

6427 **Hirsch**, Guenther Paul Hermann. 'Migration from the land in England and Wales.' *Farm Econ.*, VI, 9 (1951), 270–80.

6428 **University of Cambridge.** School of Agriculture. Farm Economics Branch. *Labour use in agriculture: a comparative study of conditions in certain areas in the United States and the United Kingdom.* Cambridge: School of Agriculture, [1951?]. 56p. (Report 36.)

6429 **King**, Howard Frederick. *Age and work in agriculture.* 1953–54. (M.Sc. thesis, University of Cambridge.)

6430 **Hirsch**, Guenther Paul Hermann. 'Land and labour.' *Westm. Bank Rev.* (August 1955), 10–12.
Causes of the decline in the number of agricultural workers.

6431 **Beilby**, O. J. 'Regional changes in agricultural employment.' Department of Agriculture for Scotland. *Scottish agricultural economics: some studies of current economic conditions in Scottish farming.* Vol. VII. Edinburgh: H.M.S.O., 1956. p. 37–40.

6432 **Cowie**, William John Gavin and **Giles**, Anthony Kent. *An inquiry into reasons for 'the drift from the land'.* Bristol: University of Bristol, Department of Economics (Agricultural Economics), 1957. p. 69–113. (Selected papers in agricultural economics, vol. V, no. 3.)

6433 **Hughes**, John Dennis. 'A note on the decline in numbers of farmworkers in Great Britain.' *Farm Econ.*, VIII, 9 (1957), 34–9.

6434 **Saville**, John. *Rural depopulation in England and Wales, 1851–1951.* London: Routledge and Kegan Paul, 1957. xvi, 253p. (International library of sociology and social reconstruction.)
One of the 'Dartington Hall studies in rural sociology'.

6435 **Hendry**, G. F. and **McEwan**, L. V. 'The changing labour situation.' Department of Agriculture for Scotland. *Scottish agricultural economics: some studies of current economic conditions in Scottish farming*. Vol. x. Edinburgh: H.M.S.O., 1960. p. 36–8.

6436 **Beilby**, O. J. 'Scotland's farm population.' Department of Agriculture and Fisheries for Scotland. *Scottish agricultural economics: some studies of current economic conditions in Scottish farming*. Vol. xi. Edinburgh: H.M.S.O., 1961. p. 39–40.

6437 **Sheppard**, June A. 'East Yorkshire's agricultural labour force in the mid-nineteenth century.' *Agric. Hist. Rev.*, ix, 1 (1961), 43–54.

6438 **Arends**, A. W. *Forestry Commission employment and housing in Wales*. 1962–63. (Ph.D. thesis, University of London.)

6439 **Home Office**. *Demand for agricultural graduates: report of an Interdepartmental Committee*. London: H.M.S.O., 1964. 54p. (Cmnd. 2419.)
Chairman: C. I. C. Bosanquet.

6440 **McIntosh**, F. 'Changes in the structure of the Scottish farm labour force since 1951.' Department of Agriculture and Fisheries for Scotland. *Scottish agricultural economics: some studies of current economic conditions in Scottish farming*. Vol. xvii. Edinburgh: H.M.S.O., 1967. p. 57–67.

6441 **Black**, Michael. 'Agricultural labour in an expanding economy.' *J. Agric. Econ.*, xix, 1 (January 1968), 59–76.
Discussion on paper, p. 71–6.

6442 **Dunn**, J. M. 'The age structure of Scottish farm workers.' Department of Agriculture and Fisheries for Scotland. *Scottish agricultural economics: some studies of current economic conditions in Scottish farming*. Vol. xviii. Edinburgh: H.M.S.O., 1968. p. 133–7.

6443 **Rathore**, A. H. *The role of agricultural labour in the depopulation trends in rural Scotland (1945–63)*. 1968–69. (B.Litt. thesis, University of Glasgow.)

6444 **Ministry of Agriculture, Fisheries and Food**. *The changing structure of the agricultural labour force in England and Wales: numbers of workers, hours and earnings, 1945–1965*. London: the Ministry, 1969. vi, 99p.

6445 **National Economic Development Office**. *Agricultural manpower: proceedings of a symposium held by the Agriculture EDC at Hulme Hall, Manchester University, December 1968*. London: N.E.D.O., 1970. v, 50p.

See also: 6282; 6370; 6379; 6728; 6732; 6736; 6751; 6754; 6761–2; 6884; 6899; 6908; 6959.

b. MINING, MANUFACTURING, AND CONSTRUCTION

6446 **Lynch**, J. 'Skilled and unskilled labour in the shipbuilding trade.' Industrial Remuneration Conference. *The report of the proceedings and papers*. London: Cassell, 1885. p. 114–18.
Discussion, p. 119–36.

6447 **United States**. Bureau of Labor. *Coal mine labor in Europe*. Washington, D.C.: Govt. Print. Off., 1905. 547p. (Twelfth special report of the Commissioner of Labor.)
58th Congress, 3rd session, House, Doc. 301.
'A compilation of statistics and other matter bearing upon coal-mine labor in the leading coal and lignite producing countries of Europe, namely, Austria, Belgium, France, Germany, and Great Britain.'

6448 **Committee Appointed to Consider the Position of the Engineering Trades After the War**. *Report*. London: H.M.S.O., 1918. (Cd. 9073.)

6449 **Departmental Committee Appointed to Consider the Position of the Iron and Steel Trades after the War**. *Report*. London: H.M.S.O., 1918. (Cd. 9071.)

6450 **Departmental Committee Appointed to Consider the Position of the Textile Trades after the War**. *Report*. London: H.M.S.O., 1918. (Cd. 9070.)

6451 **Departmental Committee on the Post-War Position of the Sulphuric Acid and Fertiliser Trades**. *Report*. London: H.M.S.O., 1918. (Cd. 8994.)
Complete edition. 1919. (Cmd. 23.)

6452 **International Labour Office**. 'Employment in the British building trade.' *Int. Labour Rev.*, ii, 1 (March [i.e. April] 1921), 48–55.

6453 **National House Building Committee**. *Report on the present position in the building industry with regard to the carrying out of a full housing programme, having particular reference to the means of providing an adequate supply of labour and materials*. London: H.M.S.O., 1924. (Cmd. 2104.)

6454 **Bureau of Social Research for Tyneside**. *Employment and unemployment at the shipyards*. Newcastle-upon-Tyne, 1926. 12p. (Tyneside papers 6.)

6455 **Shimmin**, Arnold N. 'Distribution of employment in the wool textile industry of the West Riding of Yorkshire.' *R. Statist. Soc. J.*, lxxxix, 1 (January 1926), 96–118.
Discussion, p. 120–8.
'Read before the Royal Historical Society, at a meeting held at the University of Leeds, on December 16, 1925.'

6456 **Allen**, R. G. D. and **Thomas**, Brinley. 'The supply of engineering labour under boom conditions.' *Econ. J.*, xlix, 194 (June 1939), 259–75.

6457 **Political and Economic Planning**. 'Labour in engineering.' *Planning*, vi, 140 (7 February 1939), 1–14.

6458 **Political and Economic Planning**. 'Labour in the building industry.' *Planning*, 212 (28 September 1943), 1–20.

6459 **Moos**, S. 'The age structure of building labour.' *Oxf. Univ. Inst. Statist. Bull.*, VI, 3 (26 February 1944), 39–44.

6460 **Streat**, *Sir* Edward Raymond. *Manpower shortage and economies in labour utilisation: text of address . . . delivered at a special meeting of members of the Manchester Chamber of Commerce on Tuesday, 28th May, 1946.* Manchester: Manchester Chamber of Commerce, [1946]. 20p.

The author was Chairman of the Cotton Board.

6461 **Ministry of Works**. *Brickmaking*. London: H.M.S.O., 1947.

1. The getting of clay with special reference to labour requirements. 21p.

2. Labour involved in the making and firing of common bricks and a summary of the total labour requirements of brickmaking. 60p.

6462 **Ross**, Norman Scott. 'Employment in shipbuilding and ship-repairing in Great Britain.' *R. Statist. Soc. J.*, Ser. A, CXV, 4 (1952), 524–33.

6463 **Lancashire and Merseyside Industrial Development Association**. *The Lancashire coalfield: a survey of employment prospects.* Manchester: the Association, 1953. 19p. (Research memorandum 3.)

6464 **Garrett**, J. L. *The aircraft industry with special reference to its location and labour supply.* 1955. (B.Litt. thesis, University of Oxford.)

6465 **Maddison**, A. 'Output, employment, and productivity in British manufacturing in the last half century.' *Oxf. Univ. Inst. Statist. Bull.*, XVII, 4 (November 1955), 363–86.

6466 **Black**, W. *Employment in the linen industry.* 1955–56. (Ph.D. thesis, Queen's University, Belfast.)

6467 **Murrell**, K. F. H., **Griew**, S. and **Tucker**, W. A. 'Age structure in the engineering industry.' *Occup. Psychol.*, XXXI, 3 (July 1957), 150–68.

6468 **Murrell**, K. F. H. and **Griew**, S. 'Age structure in the engineering industry: a study of regional effects.' *Occup. Psychol.*, XXXII, 2 (April 1958), 86–8.

6469 **Odber**, A. J. and **Eldridge**, John E. T. 'Shrinkage in industry.' *New Soc.*, 16 (17 January 1963), 9–11.

6470 **Galambos**, P. 'On the growth of the employment of non-manual workers in the British manufacturing industries 1948–1962.' *Oxf. Univ. Inst. Statist. Bull.*, XXVI, 4 (November 1964), 369–87.

6471 **Brechling**, Frank P. R. 'The relationship between output and employment in British manufacturing industries.' *Rev. Econ. Studies*, XXXII, 91 (July 1965), 187–216. [Errata] 92 (October 1965), 346.

6472 **Ministry of Labour**. Manpower Research Unit. *The construction industry.* London: H.M.S.O., 1965. 50p. (Manpower studies 3.)

6473 **Ministry of Labour**. Manpower Research Unit. *The metal industries: a study of occupational trends in the metal manufacturing and metal using industries.* London: H.M.S.O., 1965. 98p. (Manpower studies 2.)

6474 **Ball**, R. J. and **St Cyr**, Eric Baldwin Anderson. 'Short term employment functions in British manufacturing industry.' *Rev. Econ. Studies*, XXXIII, 3 (July 1966), 179–207.

6475 **Maton**, J. M. 'Manufacturing output, employment and new building. Regional analysis, 1948–1958.' *Board of Trade J.* (28 January 1966). Supplement. 16p.

6476 **Brechling**, Frank and **O'Brien**, Peter. 'Short-run employment functions in manufacturing industries: an international comparison.' *Rev. Econ. Statist.*, XLIX, 3 (August 1967), 277–87.

6477 **Economic Development Committee for Hosiery and Knitwear**. *Progress report on manpower.* London: National Economic Development Committee, 1967. 8p.

6478 **Economic Development Committee for the Chemical Industry**. *Manpower in the chemical industry: a comparison of British and American practices.* London: H.M.S.O., 1967. v, 62p.

6479 **Freeman**, Christopher A. 'Situation of manpower in the electronics sector working for the aircraft industry.' Organisation for Economic Co-operation and Development. *Geographical and occupational mobility of workers in the aircraft and electronics industries: Regional Trade Union Seminar, Paris 21st–22nd September 1966. Final report.* Paris: O.E.C.D., 1967. p. 89–109.

6480 **Holt**, O. Vesey. 'Situation of manpower in the aerospace industries in Europe.' Organisation for Economic Co-operation and Development. *Geographical and occupational mobility of workers in the aircraft and electronics industries: Regional Trade Union Seminar, Paris, 21st–22nd September, 1966. Final report.* Paris: O.E.C.D., 1967. p. 51–88.

6481 **Hunter**, Laurence Colvin. *Problems of labour supply in shipbuilding.* Glasgow: Institution of Engineers and Shipbuilders in Scotland, 1967. 73–110p.

Second Marlow (Scotland) Lecture.

Reprinted from the Transactions of the Institution, 1966.

6482 **Ministry of Labour**. Manpower Research Unit. *Electronics.* London: H.M.S.O., 1967. 74p. (Manpower studies 5.)

6483 **Walton**, F. T. 'Manufacturing employment, growth and labour supply.' *Scott. J. Polit Econ.*, XIV, 1 (February 1967), 30–47.

6484 **Daly**, Lawrence. 'A future for the miners.' *Trade Un. Regist.* (1969), 53–9.

6485 **Economic Development Committee for the Chemical Industry**. *Manpower and communications.* London: the Committee, 1969. [6]p.

6486 **Kelly**, David M. 'Contraction of the coal industry: some aspects of the effects on manpower.' *Econ. Studies*, IV, 1–2 (October 1969), 199–220.

6487 **Department of Employment.** *Printing and publishing.* London: H.M.S.O., 1970. 116p. (Manpower paper 9.)

6488 **National Economic Development Office.** *Labour losses in the electronics industry.* London: N.E.D.O., 1970.

6489 **National Economic Development Office.** *Qualified manpower in the electronics industry: a preliminary report.* London: N.E.D.O., 1970.

See also: 6306; 6317; 6337; 6343; 6368; 6395; 6690; 6748; 6750; 6764; 6779; 6781; 6803; 6902; 6930; 6934; 6936; 6938; 8166; 8254–5.

c. TRANSPORT AND DISTRIBUTION

6490 *Return of the number of persons employed by each of the railway companies of the United Kingdom on 31st March 1884 (classified according to the nature of the work performed by them), etc.* 1884. (H.C. 242.)

6491 *Report on the supply of British seamen, the number of foreigners serving on board British merchant ships, and the reasons given for their employment; and on crimping and other matters bearing on those subjects.* London: H.M.S.O., 1886. (C. 4709.)

6492 **Booth**, Charles. *Dock and wharf labour, 1891–2.* London: G. Philip, 1892.
Folding charts, with explanatory text.

6493 **Departmental Committee Appointed to Inquire into the Manning of British Merchant Ships.**
Vol. I. *Report.* London: H.M.S.O., 1896. (C. 8127.)
Vol. II. *Minutes of evidence and appendices.* (C. 8128.)
Vol. III. *Digest of evidence and index.* (C. 8129.)

6494 **Departmental Committee Appointed to Consider the Position of the Shipping and Shipbuilding Industries After the War.** *Report.* London: H.M.S.O., 1918. (Cd. 9092.)

6495 **International Labour Office.** 'Census of British seamen in 1930.' *Int. Labour Rev.*, XXV, 2 (February 1932), 251–4.
A comparison of the figures for 1930 given in a supplement to the *Board of Trade Journal*, 30 July 1931 and those for 1929 in *Industrial and Labour Information*, XXXV, 10 (8 September 1930), p. 325–7.

6496 **Davis**, Ralph. 'Seamen's sixpences: an index of commercial activity, 1697–1828.' *Economica*, n.s., XXIII, 92 (November 1956), 328–43.
On the use of the records of the sixpence per month which was collected from merchant seamen for the maintenance of Greenwich Hospital for disabled seamen.

6497 **Department of Employment and Productivity.** *Food retailing.* London: H.M.S.O., 1968. 56p. (Manpower studies 8.)

6498 **Road Transport Industry Training Board.** *Manpower in the road transport industry.* Wembley: the Board, 1969. 76p.

6499 **Cunningham**, Catherine M. 'The dock industry on Merseyside.' Lawton, R. and Cunningham, C. M. (eds.). *Merseyside: social and economic studies.* London: Longman, 1970. p. 235–57.

See also: 6881; 6939.

d. WHITE-COLLAR AND PROFESSIONAL

i. *Teachers*

6500 **Departmental Committee on the Pupil-Teacher System.**
Vol. I. *Report.* London: H.M.S.O., 1898. (C. 8761.)
Vol. II. *Evidence and index.* (C. 8762.)

6501 **Ministry of Education.** *Report of the Committee appointed by the President of the Board of Education to consider the supply, recruitment and training of teachers and youth leaders.* London: H.M.S.O., 1944. 176p.
Chairman: Sir Arnold McNair.

6502 **Scottish Education Department.** Advisory Council on Education in Scotland. *Reports on the supply, recruitment and training of teachers in the period immediately following the war.* Edinburgh: H.M.S.O., 1944. 56p. (Cmd. 6501.)
Chairman: W. H. Fyfe.

6503 **Ministry of Education.** National Advisory Council on the Training and Supply of Teachers. *First report covering the period July 1949 to February 1951.* London: H.M.S.O., 1951.

6504 **Scottish Education Department.** Departmental Committee on Numbers of Teachers Required for Service in Scotland. *Supply of teachers: first report.* Edinburgh: H.M.S.O., 1951. 20p. (Cmd. 8123.)
Second report. 1953. (Cmd. 8721.)
Third report. 1957. (Cmnd. 196.)
Fourth report. 1962. (Cmnd. 1601.)
Chairman: T. Grainger-Stewart.

6505 **Flemming**, *Sir* Gilbert Nicolson. *The supply of teachers as a national task: address delivered to a meeting of members and officials of local education authorities, Scarborough Conference, Easter 1952.* London: National Union of Teachers, 1952. 16p.

6506 **Ministry of Education.** National Advisory Council on the Training and Supply of Teachers. *Graduate teachers of mathematics and science: a report.* London: H.M.S.O., 1953. iv, 12p.
Chairman: Sir Philip Morris.

6507 **Political and Economic Planning.** 'Schools under pressure. I. The shortage of teachers.' *Planning*, XIX, 358 (14 December 1953), 265–80.

6508 **Committee on the Shortage of Science Teachers.** *The shortage of science teachers: report of an independent committee set up by resolution of the conference convened by the Federation of British Industries in January, 1954.* London: F.B.I., 1954. viii, 23p.

6509 **Ministry of Education.** National Advisory Council on the Training and Supply of Teachers. *Training and supply of teachers of handicapped pupils: fourth report of the National Advisory Council on the Training and Supply of Teachers.* London: H.M.S.O., 1954. 46p.
Chairman: Sir Philip Morris.

6510 **University of Nottingham.** Senate. *The shortage of graduate teachers of mathematics and science: a memorandum.* Nottingham: Nottingham University [private circulation], 1954. 10p.

6511 **Scottish Education Department.** Committee on the Supply of Teachers of Mathematics and Science in Scotland. *Report.* Edinburgh: H.M.S.O., 1955. 40p. (Cmd. 9419.)
Chairman: Sir Edward Appleton.

6512 **Ministry of Education.** *Supply and training of teachers for technical colleges: report of Special Committee appointed in September 1956 by the Minister of Education.* London: H.M.S.O., 1957.
Chairman: W. Jackson.

6513 **Dixon,** John Leslie. *Wanted – one hundred thousand teachers: an examination of the problem of staffing the schools.* London: National Association of Labour Teachers, 1958. [16]p.

6514 **Ministry of Education.** National Advisory Council on the Training and Supply of Teachers. *The supply of teachers in the 1960's: correspondence between the Chairman of the National Advisory Council on the Training and Supply of Teachers and the Minister of Education, July, 1958.* London: H.M.S.O., 1958. 11p.

6515 **Scottish Education Department.** Advisory Council on Education in Scotland. Special Committee on Measures to Improve the Supply of Teachers in Scotland. *Report.* Edinburgh: H.M.S.O., 1958. 56p. (Cmnd. 644.)
Interim report. 1957. (Cmnd. 202.)
Chairman: T. M. Knox.

6516 **Russell,** Edward Lionel. *The crucial factor: the supply and training of teachers, 1960–1970.* London: National Union of Teachers, 1960. 10p.

6517 **Ministry of Education.** National Advisory Council on the Training and Supply of Teachers. *Teachers for further education: report of an Advisory Sub-Committee.* London: H.M.S.O., 1961.
Chairman: E. L. Russell.

6518 **Ministry of Education.** National Advisory Council on the Training and Supply of Teachers. *Demand and supply of teachers, 1960–1980.* London: H.M.S.O., 1962.
Seventh report of the Council.
Chairman: J. S. Fulton.

6519 **Burgess,** Tyrrell. 'How many teachers do we need?' *New Soc.,* 15 (10 January 1963), 9–11.

6520 **Pile,** William Dennis. *Some problems of teacher supply: an address to a meeting of members and officials of Education Committees at the Annual Conference, Margate 1963.* London: National Union of Teachers, 1963. 15p.

6521 **Association of Teachers in Technical Institutions.** *The planning of teacher supply: a policy statement.* London: A.T.T.I., 1964. 8p.

6522 **Burgess,** Tyrrell. 'Not enough teachers.' *New Soc.,* III, 77 (19 March 1964), 11–13. (Non-issues 2.)

6523 **Association of University Teachers.** University Statistics Committee. *Future staffing possibilities in university departments of economics, French and mathematics.* London: A.U.T., 1965. 8p.

6524 **Carruthers,** James Pirrie. *The teacher shortage: a report for the Council of Educational Advance.* London: Council for Educational Advance, 1965. 16p.

6525 **Department of Education and Science.** *The demand for and supply of teachers, 1963–1986: 9th report of the National Advisory Council on the Training and Supply of Teachers.* London: H.M.S.O., 1965. 98p.
Chairman: A. L. C. Bullock.

6526 **Parris,** J. J. *The supply and utilization of part-time teachers, and their place in the profession.* 1965. (M.Ed. thesis, University of Manchester.)

6527 **Department of Education and Science.** National Advisory Council on the Training and Supply of Teachers. Standing Sub-Committee on Teachers for Further Education. *Supply and training of teachers for further education: report.* London: H.M.S.O., 1966. 36p.

6528 **Scottish Education Department.** Committee on Measures to Secure a More Equitable Distribution of Teachers in Scotland. *Measures to secure a more equitable distribution of teachers in Scotland.* Edinburgh: H.M.S.O., 1966. 31p.
Chairman: Dame Jean Roberts.

6529 **General Teaching Council for Scotland.** Committee on the Supply of Teachers. *Report of the Committee on the Supply of Teachers, with a note of the Council's reaction.* Edinburgh: the Council, 1969. 24 leaves.

6530 **Royal Society.** *The shortage of mathematics and science teachers in schools: report of a working party appointed by the Royal Society and the Council of Engineering Institutions in 1967, which was joined by representatives of the Council of Science and Technology Institutes in 1969.* London: Royal Society, 1969. 18p.

6531 **Scottish Education Department.** *Staffing of secondary schools in Scotland.* Edinburgh: H.M.S.O., 1969. 48p.

6532 **Ahamad**, Billy. 'A post mortem on teacher supply forecasts.' *Higher Educ. Rev.*, II, 3 (Summer 1970), 21–40.

6533 **Armitage**, Peter. 'So when do we get the teachers?' *Higher Educ. Rev.*, II, 3 (Summer 1970), 41–7.

6534 **Headmasters' Association of Scotland.** *Crisis and opportunity: the staffing shortage in Scottish secondary schools.* Edinburgh: Scottish Academic P., 1970. 23p.

See also: 6716; 6800; 6830; 6835; 6856; 6864–5.

ii. *Scientists and Engineers*

6535 *Scientific man-power: report of a Committee appointed by the Lord President of the Council.* London: H.M.S.O., 1946. 26p. (Cmd. 6824.)
Chairman: Sir Alan Barlow.

6536 **Ministry of Labour and National Service.** Technical and Scientific Register. Chemists' Sub-Committee. *Present and future supply and demand for persons with professional qualifications in chemistry.* London: H.M.S.O., 1949. 23p.
Chairman: Lord Hankey.

6537 **Ministry of Labour and National Service.** Technical and Scientific Register. Engineering Sub-Committee. Electrical Engineering Panel. *Present and future supply and demand for persons with professional qualifications in electrical engineering.* London: H.M.S.O., 1949. 20p.
Chairman: Sir Arthur P. M. Fleming.

6538 **Ministry of Labour and National Service.** Technical and Scientific Register. Geologists' Sub-Committee. *Present and future supply and demand for persons with professional qualifications in geology.* London: H.M.S.O., 1949. 14p.
Chairman: Sir Clement Jones.

6539 **Ministry of Labour and National Service.** Technical and Scientific Register. Physicists' Sub-Committee. *Present and future supply and demand for persons with professional qualifications in physics.* London: H.M.S.O., 1949. 29p.
Chairman: Lord Hankey.

6540 **Ministry of Labour and National Service.** Technical and Scientific Register. Biologists' and Agriculturalists' Sub-Committee. *Present and future supply and demand for persons with professional qualifications in biology, agriculture and related sciences.* London: H.M.S.O., 1950. 23p.
Chairman: Sir Edward Salisbury.

6541 **Ministry of Labour and National Service.** Technical and Scientific Register. Building and Civil Engineers' Sub-Committee. Building and Quantity Surveyors' Panel. *Present and future supply and demand for persons with professional qualifications in building and quantity surveying.* London: H.M.S.O., 1950. 19p.
Chairman: A. H. Killick.

6542 **Ministry of Labour and National Service.** Technical and Scientific Register. Chemical Engineers' Sub-Committee. *Present and future supply and demand for persons with professional qualifications in chemical engineering.* London: H.M.S.O., 1950. 22p.
Chairman: A. M. Tyndall.

6543 **Ministry of Labour and National Service.** Technical and Scientific Register. Engineering Sub-Committee. Civil Engineers' Panel. *Present and future supply and demand for persons with professional qualifications in civil engineering.* London: H.M.S.O., 1950. 17p.
Chairman: Sir Roger Hetherington.

6544 **Ministry of Labour and National Service.** Technical and Scientific Register. Engineering Sub-Committee. Mechanical Engineers' Panel. *Present and future supply and demand for persons with professional qualifications in mechanical engineering.* London: H.M.S.O., 1950. 19p.
Chairman: Sir William A. Stanier.

6545 **Ministry of Labour and National Service.** Technical and Scientific Register. Metallurgists' Sub-Committee. *Present and future supply and demand for persons with professional qualifications in metallurgy.* London: H.M.S.O., 1951. 14p.
Chairman: Sir William Griffiths.

6546 **Social Survey.** *Scientific manpower.* [London]: Central Office of Information, [1952?]. v, 26p. (S.S. 190.)
'The inquiry was carried out for the D.S.I.R. to give some indication of the occupations taken up by science graduates after graduation, and of the reasons why particular occupations are chosen. The inquiry was based upon a postal questionnaire sent to over 900 graduates, November 1951–January 1952.'

6547 **Organisation for European Economic Co-operation.** Manpower Committee. *Shortages and surpluses of highly qualified scientists and engineers in Western Europe.* Paris: O.E.E.C., 1955. 156p.

6548 **Office of the Lord President of the Council** and **Ministry of Labour and National Service.** Advisory Council on Scientific Policy. Committee on Scientific Manpower. *Scientific and engineering manpower in Great Britain: a report on the number and distribution of scientists and engineers now employed in Great Britain, and a study of the likely trend in the future demand for scientific and engineering manpower.* London: H.M.S.O., 1956. 28p.

6549 **Carter**, C. F. and **Williams**, Bruce Rodda. *Industry and technical progress: factors governing the speed of application of science.* London: Oxford U.P., 1957.

Chap. IX. 'Trained men and women.' p. 87–108.

6550 **Organisation for European Economic Co-operation.** Manpower Committee. *The problem of scientific and technical manpower in Western Europe, Canada and the United States.* Paris: O.E.E.C., 1957. 220p.
'Ireland', p. 119–24.
'United Kingdom', p. 181–93.

6551 **McCrensky**, Edward. *Scientific manpower in Europe: a comparative study of scientific manpower in the public service of Great Britain and selected European countries.* London: Pergamon P., 1958. ix, 188p.

6552 **Rudd**, Ernest. *Scientific research and technical development in British industries: a study of manpower and expenditure.* 1958. (Ph.D. thesis, University of London.)

6553 **Alexander**, Joyce. *Scientific manpower.* London: Hilger and Watts, 1959. viii, 135p.

6554 **Carter**, C. F. and **Williams**, Bruce Rodda. *Science in industry: policy for progress.* London: Oxford U.P., 1959.
Chap. XI. 'Some aspects of educational policy.' p. 122–35.
Proposals for relieving shortages of scientists.

6555 **Fort**, Richard. 'Scientific and engineering manpower survey.' *Planning*, XXV, 430 (19 January 1959), 3–27.
Revised and up-to-date statement.
Originally written in 1957 for the Scientific and Technical Committee set up by the NATO Parliamentarians' Conference.

6556 **Office of the Lord President of the Council and Minister for Science.** Advisory Council on Scientific Policy. Committee on Scientific Manpower. *Scientific and engineering manpower in Great Britain, 1959.* London: H.M.S.O., 1959. vi, 49p. (Cmnd. 902.)
Chairman: Sir Solly Zuckerman.
The second report.

6557 **Jewkes**, John. 'How much science?' *Econ. J.*, LXX, 277 (March 1960), 1–16.

6558 **Payne**, George Louis. *Britain's scientific and technological manpower.* Stanford, Calif.: Stanford U.P.; London: Oxford U.P., 1960. xiii, 466p.
Prepared for the President's Committee on Scientists and Engineers.

6559 **Pike**, R. M. *The growth of scientific institutions and employment of natural science graduates in Britain, 1900–1960.* 1960–61. (M.Sc.(Econ). thesis, University of London.)

6560 **Office of the Lord President of the Council and Minister for Science.** Advisory Council on Scientific Policy. Committee on Scientific Manpower. *The long-term demand for scientific manpower.* London: H.M.S.O., 1961. ix, 26p. (Cmnd. 1490.)
Chairman: Sir Solly Zuckerman.

6561 **Jackson**, Willis. *Scientific, technological and technical manpower.* Southampton: University of Southampton, 1963. 23p. (Fawley Foundation lectures 10.)

6562 **Office of the Lord President of the Council and Minister for Science.** Advisory Council on Scientific Policy. Committee on Scientific Manpower. *Scientific and technological manpower in Great Britain, 1962.* London: H.M.S.O., 1963. 59p. (Cmnd. 2146.)
Chairman: Sir Solly Zuckerman.
The third report.

6563 **Organisation for Economic Co-operation and Development.** *Resources of scientific and technical personnel in the OECD area: statistical report of the Third International Survey on the Demand for and Supply of Scientific and Technical Personnel.* Paris: O.E.C.D., 1963. 293p.

6564 **Department of Education and Science** and **Ministry of Technology.** Committee on Manpower Resources for Science and Technology. *A review of the scope and problems of scientific and technological manpower policy.* London: H.M.S.O., 1965. ii, 17p. (Cmnd. 2800.)
Chairman: Sir Willis Jackson.

6565 **Department of Education and Science** and **Ministry of Technology.** Committee on Manpower Resources for Science and Technology. *Interim report of the working group on manpower parameters for scientific growth.* London: H.M.S.O., 1966. 38p. (Cmnd. 3102.)
Chairman: M. M. Swann.

6566 **Department of Education and Science** and **Ministry of Technology.** Committee on Manpower Resources for Science and Technology. *Report on the 1965 triennial manpower survey of engineers, technologists, scientists and technical supporting staff.* London: H.M.S.O., 1966. vii, 64p. (Cmnd. 3103.)
Chairman: Sir Willis Jackson.

6567 **Millar**, I. A. 'The scientist in industry.' *New Soc.*, VIII, 197 (7 July 1966), 17–18. (Trends in personnel management 5.)

6568 **Ministry of Technology** and **Council of Engineering Institutions.** *Survey of professional engineers, 1966.* London: H.M.S.O., 1967. 44p.

6569 **Spence**, G. J. 'The growth and co-ordination of scientific and technical manpower studies in the United Kingdom.' Organisation for Economic Co-operation and Development. *Policy Conference on Highly Qualified Manpower, Paris 26th–28th September 1966.* Paris: O.E.C.D., 1967. p. 333–40.

6570 **Council for Scientific Policy.** *Enquiry into the flow of candidates in science and technology into higher education.* London: H.M.S.O., 1968. 180p. (Cmnd. 3541.)
Chairman: Dr F. S. Dainton.

6571 **Department of Education and Science** and **Ministry of Technology.** Committee on Manpower Resources for Science and Technology. *The flow into employment of*

scientists, engineers and technologists: report of the working group on manpower for scientific growth. London: H.M.S.O., 1968. viii, 186p. (Cmnd. 3670.)
Chairman: Michael Swann.

6572 **Jackson**, Willis, Baron Jackson of Burnley. *The problems of engineering and scientific manpower and their implications for national policy.* London: Council of Engineering Institutions, [1968?]. (Graham Clark lecture, 1968.)

6573 **Walters**, Gerald and **Cotgrove**, Stephen (eds.). *Scientists in British industry.* Bath: Bath U.P., 1967 [i.e. 1968]. viii, 123p.
Reproduced from typewriting.
Contents: 1. 'Science and industry: an introductory survey of the problems', by S. Cotgrove and A. Cherns. 2. 'The education of industrial scientists', by M. L. Burstall. 3. 'The recruitment and selection of scientists', by G. F. Thomason. 4. 'The employment of scientists in industry', by W. Thain. 5. 'The creativity and productivity of industrial scientists', by S. Cotgrove. 6. 'The career problems of middle-aged industrial scientists', by S. Box.

6574 **Paton**, George E. C. *The sociological aspects of the growth of technician occupations in British industry.* 1968–69. (M.A. thesis, University of Nottingham.)

6575 **Pym**, Denis. 'Education and employment opportunities of engineers.' *Br. J. Ind. Relat.*, VII, 1 (March 1969), 42–51.

6576 **Richardson**, V. A. 'Measurement of demand for professional engineers.' *Br. J. Ind. Relat.*, VII, 1 (Marsh 1969), 52–70.

6577 **Jackson**, Willis, Baron Jackson of Burnley. *Manpower for engineering and technology: a review of what has happened over the last fifty years and what lies ahead.* London: British Association for Commercial and Industrial Education, 1970. 14p. (1st annual Willis Jackson lecture, 13 November 1969.)

6578 **Ministry of Technology** and **Council of Science and Technology Institutes**. *The survey of professional scientists 1968.* London: H.M.S.O., 1970. 41p. (Studies in technological manpower 2.)

See also: 6811.

iii. *Medical*

6579 **James**, Prosser. 'Men as nurses.' *Westm. Rev.*, CXLVII, 3 (March 1897), 309–10.
On the Hamilton Association for Providing Trained Male Nurses.

6580 **Departmental Committee on the Nursing of the Sick Poor in Workhouses.** *Report.* London: H.M.S.O., 1902.
Part I. *Report.* 41p. (Cd. 1366.)
Part II. *Minutes of evidence.* (Cd. 1367.)
Chairman: J. G. Lawson.

6581 **Ministry of Health** and **Board of Education.** Inter-Departmental Committee on Nursing Services. *Report.* London: H.M.S.O.' 1939. 93p.
Chairman: Lord Athlone.

6582 **Ministry of Health, Scottish Office** and **Ministry of Labour and National Service.** *Staffing the hospitals: an urgent national need.* London: H.M.S.O., 1945.

6583 **Ministry of Health, Department of Health for Scotland** and **Ministry of Labour and National Service.** *Report of the working party on midwives.* London: H.M.S.O., 1949.
Chairman: M. D. Stocks.

6584 **Ministry of Health** and **Department of Health for Scotland.** *Report of the committee to consider the future numbers of medical practitioners and the appropriate intake of medical students.* London: H.M.S.O., 1957.
Chairman: Sir Henry Willink.

6585 **Ministry of Health.** *Report on the grading structure of administrative and clerical staff in the hospital service.* London: H.M.S.O., 1957.
By Sir Noel Hall.

6586 **Ministry of Health** and **Department of Health for Scotland.** Joint Working Party on the Medical Staffing Structure in the Hospital Service. *Report.* London: H.M.S.O., 1961. v, 89p.
Chairman: Professor Sir Robert Platt.

6587 **Bennett**, B. A. 'Part-time nursing employment in Great Britain.' *Int. Labour Rev.*, LXXXV, 4 (April 1962), 347–56.

6588 **Seale**, John Richard. *The supply of doctors and the future of the British medical profession.* London: Fellowship for Freedom in Medicine, 1962. 13p.
Private circulation.

6589 **Scottish Home and Health Department.** Committee on Medical Staffing Structure in Scottish Hospitals. *Medical staffing structure in Scottish hospitals: report.* Edinburgh: H.M.S.O., 1964. 79p.
Chairman: J. H. Wright.

6590 **Scottish Home and Health Department.** Scottish Health Services Council. *Staffing of the midwifery services in Scotland: report by the Committee of the Council.* Edinburgh: H.M.S.O., 1965.
Chairman: Mrs. J. Wolrige-Gordon.

6591 **Association of British Pharmaceutical Industry.** Office of Health Economics. *Medical manpower.* London: O.H.E., 1966. 32p. (Publications 20.)

6592 **Donald**, Brian Louis. *Manpower for hospitals: a study of problems in some West European countries.* London: Institute of Hospital Administrators, 1966. 51p.

6593 **Forsyth**, Gordon. 'Solving the general practice crisis.' *New Soc.*, VII, 181 (17 March 1966), 10–13. (Reshaping social policy 3.)

6594 **Last**, John M. 'Regional distribution of general practitioners and consultants in the National Health Service.' *Br. Med. J.* (24 June 1967), 796–9.

6595 **Peacock**, Alan and **Shannon**, Robin. 'The new doctor's dilemma.' *Lloyds Bank Rev.*, n.s., 87 (January 1968), 26–38.

6596 **Rose**, June. 'Bedside men.' *New Soc.*, XII, 306 (8 August 1968), 196–7.

6597 **Brown**, R. G. S. 'The supply of general practitioners to East Yorkshire.' *Yorks. Bull. Econ. Soc. Res.*, XXII, 2 (November 1970), 164–79.

6598 **Scottish Home and Health Department.** Scottish Health Services Council. *The staffing of mental deficiency hospitals: report of a Sub-Committee constituted jointly by the Standing Medical Advisory Committee and the Standing Nursing and Midwifery Advisory Committee.* Edinburgh: H.M.S.O., 1970. 60p.
Chairman: Professor I. R. C. Batchelor.

See also: 6306; 6672–3; 6678; 6681; 6686; 6688; 6757; 6797; 6849; 6861; 6868.

iv. *Other*

6599 **National Union of Students.** *Graduate employment: a report of the 1937 congress and the preparatory investigation.* London, 1937. 93p.

6600 **International Labour Office.** 'Higher appointments in Great Britain.' *Int. Labour Rev.*, LI, 5 (May 1945), 612–20.

6601 **Dunsheath**, Percy. *The graduate in industry.* London: Hutchinson's Scientific and Technical Publications, 1948. x, 276p.

6602 **Ministry of Labour and National Service.** Technical and Scientific Register. Architects' Sub-Committee. *Present and future supply and demand for persons with professional qualifications in architecture.* London: H.M.S.O., 1949. 19p.
Chairman: T. E. Scott.

6603 **Ministry of Labour and National Service.** Technical and Scientific Register. Building and Civil Engineering Sub-Committee. Surveyors' Panel (Valuation and Estate Management). *Present and future supply and demand for persons with professional qualifications in valuation and estate management.* London: H.M.S.O., 1950. 19p.
Chairman: G. A. Coombe.

6604 **Federation of British Industries.** *Report of the conference on the university graduate in industry held at the University of Bristol, 29th November 1950.* London: F.B.I., 1951.

6605 **Younghusband**, Eileen Louise. *Social work in Britain: a supplementary report on the employment and training of social workers.* Dunfermline: Carnegie United Kingdom Trust, 1951. viii, 256p.

6606 **Banks**, Joseph Ambrose. 'The employment of sociologists: graduates, 1952 and 1953.' *Br. J. Sociol.*, V, 2 (June 1954), 161–2.

6607 **Collins**, Anthea. *Non-specialist graduates in industry.* London: Bow Group, 1955. 24p. (Bow Group pamphlets.)

6608 **Political and Economic Planning.** 'Graduates' jobs.' *Planning*, XXI, 387 (24 October 1955), 193–207.

6609 **Banks**, Joseph Ambrose and **Banks**, Olive Lucy. 'Employment of sociology and anthropology graduates 1952 and 1954.' *Br. J. Sociol.*, VII, 1 (March 1956), 46–51.

6610 **Kahn**, Hilda Renate. 'Economic graduates in the labour market.' *Scott. J. Polit. Econ.*, III, 2 (June 1956), 165–7.
Results of an inquiry among Economics graduates of Glasgow University.

6611 **Political and Economic Planning.** *Graduate employment: a sample survey, September, 1956.* London: P.E.P., Allen and Unwin, 1956. xiii, 300p.

6612 **Brown**, James Douglas and **Harbison**, Frederick Harris. *High-talent manpower for science and industry: an appraisal of policy at home and abroad.* Princeton, N.J.: Princeton University, Department of Economics and Sociology, Industrial Relations Section, 1957. 98p. (Research report series 95.)

6613 **Political and Economic Planning.** *Graduates in industry.* London: P.E.P., Allen and Unwin, 1957. xxii, 261p.

6614 **Watt**, D. E. R. *Scotsmen at universities between 1340 and 1410 and their subsequent careers: a study of the contribution of graduates to the public life of their country.* 1957–58. (D.Phil. thesis, University of Oxford.)

6615 **Banks**, Joseph Ambrose. 'Employment of sociology and anthropology graduates: final report.' *Br. J. Sociol.*, IX, 3 (September 1958), 271–83.

6616 **Gales**, Kathleen. 'A survey of Fellows.' *R. Statist. Soc. J.*, Ser. A, CXXI, 4 (1958), 438–57; CXXII, 3 (1959), 348–72.
Enquiry on the utilisation of statistical methods.
Part of questionnaire included questions on age, salary, qualifications and employment and was sent to Fellows of the Royal Statistical Society and of the Association of Incorporated Statisticians.

6617 **Royal Statistical Society.** 'Report of the Committee on the Supply of and Demand for Statisticians.' *R. Statist. Soc. J.*, Ser. A, CXXII, 1 (1959), 47–67.
Discussion, p. 68–76.
Chairman of the Committee: Prof. E. S. Pearson.

6618 **Working Party on Social Workers in the Local Authority Health and Welfare Services.** *Report.* London: H.M.S.O., 1959.
Chairman: E. L. Younghusband.

6619 **Morris**, R. N. *The occupations of commerce graduates.* Birmingham: University of Birmingham, Faculty of Commerce and Social Science, 1962. 24p. (Occasional paper 2.)
Mimeographed.

6620 **Craig**, Christine. *The employment of Cambridge graduates.* Cambridge: Cambridge U.P., 1963. xi, 102p.

6621 **Holland**, D. G. 'Costs, productivities, and the employment of salaried staff.' *Oxf. Univ. Inst. Econ. Statist. Bull.*, xxv, 3 (August 1963), 127–64.

6622 **Scottish Home and Health Department.** Scottish Advisory Council on Child Care: *Staffing of local authority children's departments: a report.* Edinburgh: H.M.S.O., 1963.
Chairman: Baroness Elliot of Harwood.

6623 **Rodgers**, Barbara Noel. *Careers of social science graduates: a follow-up study of those completing social science courses at British universities in 1950, 1955 and 1960.* Welwyn: Codicote P. for the Social Administration Research Trust, 1964. 75p. (Occasional papers on social administration 11.)

6624 **Ardewer**, E. and **Ardewer**, S. 'A directory study of social anthropologists.' *Br. J. Sociol.*, xvi, 4 (December 1965), 295–314.

6625 **Curtis**, Helene and **Howell**, Catherine. *Part-time social work: a study of opportunities for the employment of trained social workers.* London: National Council of Social Service, 1965. 118p.

6626 **Davies**, J. G. W. 'Graduates and industry: why the gulf?' *New Soc.*, v, 143 (24 June 1965), 12–15.

6627 **Younghusband**, Eileen Louise. 'A comparative view of manpower problems: the British approach.' *Int. Soc. Wk.*, ix, 1 (1966), 1–4.
On the shortage of social workers.

6628 **Gales**, Kathleen and **Wright**, Reginald Charles. *A survey of manpower demand forecasts for the social services.* London: National Council of Social Service, [1967?]. 95p.

6629 **Pym**, Denis. '"Technical" change and the misuse of professional manpower: some studies and observations.' *Occup. Psychol.*, xli, 1 (January 1967), 1–16.
'This article is based on a paper read to a Conference on Technological Change, in June, 1966, sponsored by the British Sociological Association, the British Psychological Society and the Institute of Personnel Management.'

6630 **British Institute of Management.** *The employment of graduates.* London: B.I.M., 1968. (Information summary 132.)

6631 **Department of Education and Science.** *The employment of highly specialised graduates: a comparative study in the UK and the USA.* London: H.M.S.O., 1968.

6632 **Department of Education and Science.** Library Advisory Council (England) and Library Advisory Council (Wales). *Report on the supply and training of librarians.* London: H.M.S.O., 1968. viii, 64p.
Chairman: F. W. Jessup.

6633 **McCarthy**, M. C. *The employment of highly specialised graduates: a comparative study in the United Kingdom and the United States of America.* London: H.M.S.O., 1968. viii, 36p. (Science policy studies 3.)

6634 **Pym**, Denis. 'The misuse of professional manpower.' *Industrial society: social sciences in management.* Harmondsworth: Penguin, 1968. p. 82–106.

6635 **Rudd**, Ernest and **Hatch**, Stephen. *Graduate study and after.* London: Weidenfeld and Nicolson, 1968. 229p.

6636 **Stanic**, Vladimir and **Pym**, Denis. *Brains down the drain: the misuse of highly-qualified manpower.* London: Anbar Publications, 1968. 39p. (Anbar monographs 12.)

6637 **Abbott**, Joan. *Employment of sociology and anthropology graduates 1966–67: a report of research surveys conducted for the British Sociological Association, Sociology Teachers' Section.* London: British Sociological Association, 1969. 88p.

6638 **Waugh**, M. 'The changing distribution of professional and managerial manpower in England and Wales between 1961 and 1966.' *Reg. Studies*, iii, 2 (September 1969), 157–69.

See also: 6694–5; 6697–9; 6703; 6818; 6831; 6842; 6850–1; 6855; 6860; 6874.

e. PUBLIC ADMINISTRATION

6639 **Committees Appointed to Investigate the Staffing and Methods of Work of the Ministry of Labour, the Ministry of Agriculture and Fisheries, and the Royal Commission on Sugar Supplies.** *Reports.* London: H.M.S.O., 1920. (Cmd. 1069.)

6640 **Committees Appointed to Investigate the Staffing and Methods of Work of the Board of Trade, Department of Overseas Trade, and the National Savings Committee.** *Reports.* London: H.M.S.O., 1921. (Cmd. 1461.)

6641 **Scottish Home Department.** Scottish Local Government Manpower Committee. *First report.* Edinburgh: H.M.S.O., 1950. 28p. (Cmd. 7951.)
Second report. 1952. 38p. (Cmd. 8658.)
Chairman: D. Muline.

6642 **Treasury.** Local Government Manpower Committee. *First report.* London: H.M.S.O., 1950. 30p. (Cmd. 7870.)
Chairman: P. D. Proctor.
Second report. 1951. 54p. (Cmd. 8421.)
Chairman: E. W. Playfair.

6643 **Abramovitz**, Moses and **Eliasberg**, Vera F. 'The trend of public employment in Great Britain and the United States.' *Am. Econ. Rev.*, xliii, 2 (May 1953), 203–15.

6644 **Abramovitz**, Moses and **Eliasberg**, Vera F. *The growth of public employment in Great Britain.* Princeton, N.J.: Princeton U.P.; London: Oxford U.P., 1957. xiii, 151p. (National Bureau of Economic Research. General series 60.)

6645 **Peacock**, Alan Turner and **Johnston**, Thomas L. 'The government as an employer.' *Westm. Bank Rev.* (August 1958), 6–10.

6646 **Ministry of Housing and Local Government.** *London Government Staff Commission (1963–1965): report presented to the Minister of Housing and Local Government.* London: H.M.S.O., 1966. 76p.
Chairman: Sir H. Emmerson.

6647 **Home Office.** Police Advisory Board. *Police manpower, equipment and efficiency.* London: H.M.S.O., 1967. vii, 150p.

6648 **Ministry of Housing and Local Government.** Committee on the Staffing of Local Government. *Staffing of local government: report of the committee.* London: H.M.S.O., 1967. xix, 272p.
Chairman: G. Mallaby.

6649 **Morton,** Jane. 'The direct-labour row.' *New Soc.*, IX, 228 (9 February 1967), 201–2. (Society at work.)

6650 **Rendel,** Margherita. *Graduate administrators in local education authorities.* London: University of London Institute of Education and Appointments Board, 1968. 43p.

6651 **Knox,** Francis. *The growth of central government manpower.* London: Aims of Industry, 1969. 12p. (Aims of Industry. Study 21.)

6652 **Martin,** John Powell and **Wilson,** Gail. *The police: a study in manpower; the evolution of the service in England and Wales, 1829–1965.* London: Heinemann Educational, 1969. ix, 296p. (Cambridge studies in criminology 24; Heinemann library of criminology and penal reform.)

6653 **Royal Commission on Local Government in Scotland.** Intelligence Unit. *Manpower surveys; the ratio of councillors to electors in the different types of local authorities in Scotland. Percentage polls and contested seats.* Edinburgh: H.M.S.O., 1969. 42p. (Research studies 3.)

See also: 6675; 6715; 6726; 6737; 6770–1; 6775; 6838.

f. OTHER

6654 **Justice.** *Solution of the domestic servant problem.* North Shields: Camden P., 1910.

6655 **Committee on Clerical and Commercial Employment.** *Report.* London: H.M.S.O., 1915. (Cd. 8110.)
Chairman: Cecil Harmsworth.

6656 **Ministry of Reconstruction.** Women's Advisory Committee. *Report on the domestic service problem, together with reports by sub-committees on training, machinery of distribution, organisation and conditions.* London: H.M.S.O., 1919. 36p. (Cmd. 67.)
Chairman: Lady G. Emmott.

6657 **Ministry of Labour.** Committee on the Supply of Female Domestic Servants. *Report.* London: H.M.S.O., 1923. 53p.
Chairman: E. M. Wood.

6658 **Mills,** Ernestine. *The domestic problem, past, present and future.* London: Castle, 1925. 117p.

6659 **Parker.** H. J. H. 'The independent worker and the small family business: a study of their importance on Merseyside.' *R. Statist. Soc. J.*, XCV, 3 (1932), 531–45.
Based on material collected and analysed in the course of the Merseyside social survey.

6660 **Committee on Man-power in Banking and Allied Businesses, in Ordinary Insurance, and Industrial Assurance.** *Report.* London: H.M.S.O., 1942. 23p. (Cmd. 6402.)
Chairman: Lord Kennet.

6661 **Labour Party.** National Conference of Labour Women. *Reports on population problems and post-war organisation of private domestic employment.* London, 1945. 18p.
Prepared by Standing Joint Committee of Working Women's Organisations.

6662 **Ministry of Labour and National Service.** *Report on post-war organisation of private domestic employment.* London: H.M.S.O., 1945. 26p. (Cmd. 6650.)
By Violet Markham and Florence Hancock.

6663 **Bugler,** Jeremy. 'The new nightwatchmen.' *New Soc.*, VI, 166 (2 December 1965), 5–6.

6664 **Torode,** John A. 'Keeping a secretary.' *New Soc.*, V, 138 (20 May 1965), 5–6.

6665 **Economic Development Committee for Hotels and Catering.** *Your manpower: a practical guide to the manpower statistics of the hotel and catering industry.* London: H.M.S.O., 1967. v, 53p.
Chairman: Sir W. Swallow.
Supplement. National Economic Development Office, 1969.

6666 **Employment Agents Federation of Great Britain.** *Office employment: the effects of the freeze.* London, 1967. 15p. (Study one.)

6667 **Organisation for Economic Co-operation and Development.** Manpower and Social Affairs Directorate. Social Affairs Division. *Manpower problems in the service sector.* Paris: O.E.C.D., 1967. 121p. (International seminars, 1966. No. 2.)
Also *Background report.* 2v.

6668 **Richardson,** Sheila Janice. '*The servant question*': *a study of the domestic labour market 1851–1917.* 1967. (M.Phil. thesis, University of London.)

6669 **Bugler,** Jeremy. 'Temps take over.' *New Soc.*, XII, 302 (11 July 1968), 41–2.

6670 **Ministry of Labour.** *Growth of office employment.* London: H.M.S.O., 1968. 88p. (Manpower studies 7.)

6671 **Economic Development Committee for Motor Vehicle Distribution and Repair.** *Demand for garage workshop services and labour to 1980.* London: National Economic Development Office, 1970. 26p.

4. Female Employment

See also Part Three, III, F, 3; Part Six, II, B, 3, b, i; Part Six, II, D, 7; Part Six, III, F; Part Six, IV, A, 4, b; Part Seven, IV, C; Part Seven, V, B, 2, b; and Part Seven, VI, E.

6672 **Jex-Blake**, Sophia. *Medical women: two essays. I. Medicine as a profession for women. II. Medical education of women.* Edinburgh: Oliphant, 1872. 162p.
Second edition. Edinburgh: Oliphant, Anderson and Ferrier, 1886. 2v.

6673 **Bolton**, Henry Carrington. *The early practice of medicine by women.* London, 1881. 16p.
Reprinted from the *Journal of Science.*

6674 **Huth**, Alfred Henry. *The employment of women.* London: Sampson, Low, 1882. 40p.

6675 **Manners**, Janetta, Duchess of Rutland. *Employment of women in the public service.* Edinburgh: Blackwood, 1882. 54p.
Reprinted from *Quarterly Review.*

6676 **Kingsbury**, Elizabeth. *Work for women.* London: Bickers, 1884. 186p.

6677 **Hadland**, Selina. *Occupations of women other than teaching: a paper.* London: Alexander and Shepheard, 1886. 14p.

6678 **Wilson**, Robert. *Æsculapia victrix.* London: Chapman and Hall, 1886. 32p.
Reprinted from the *Fortnightly Review.*

6679 **Pfeiffer**, Emily Jane. *Women and work: an essay.* London: Trübner, 1888 [i.e. 1887]. 186p.

6680 **Twining**, Louisa. *Women's work, official and unofficial.* [1887?] 11p.
Reprinted from *The National Review,* July 1887.

6681 **Blackwell**, Elizabeth. *The influence of women in the profession of medicine: address given at the opening of the Winter Session of the London School of Medicine for Women.* London: Bell, 1889. 32p.

6682 **Westminster Review**. 'Work and women.' *Westm. Rev.*, CXXI, 3 (March 1889), 270–9.

6683 **Karsland**, Vera. *Women and their work.* London: Sampson Low, 1891. xi, 166p.
An account of different occupations open to women.

6684 **Bulley**, Agnes Amy and **Whitley**, Margaret. *Women's work.* London: Methuen, 1894. xiii, 172p. (Social questions of to-day 13.)

6685 **Collet**, Clara Elizabeth. *Report by Miss Collet on the statistics of employment of women and girls.* London: Eyre and Spottiswoode for H.M.S.O., 1894. vii, 152p. (C. 7564.)

6686 **Blackwell**, Elizabeth. *Pioneer work in opening the medical profession to women: autobiographical sketches.* London: Longmans, 1895. ix, 265p.
Another edition. Introduction by M. G. Fawcett. London: Dent, 1914. xix, 236p. (Everyman's library.)

6687 **Collet,** Clara Elizabeth. 'Statistics of employment of women and girls.' *R. Statist. Soc. J.*, LVIII, 3 (September 1895), 518–28.
Extracts from Board of Trade report, 1894. (C. 7564.)

6688 **Ford**, Isabella O. *Women as factory inspectors and certifying surgeons.* Manchester: Women's Co-operative Guild, [1895?]. 8p. (Investigation papers 4.)

6689 **Collet**, Clara Elizabeth. 'The collection and utilisation of official statistics bearing on the extent and effects of the industrial employment of women.' *R. Statist. Soc. J.*, LXI, 2 (June 1898), 219–60.
With discussion, p. 261–70.
'Read before the Royal Statistical Society, 15th March, 1898.'

6690 **Collet**, Clara Elizabeth. *Report by Miss Collet on changes in the employment of women and girls in industrial centres. Part 1. Flax and jute centres.* London: Eyre and Spottiswoode for H.M.S.O., 1898. vi, 113p. (C.8794.)

6691 **Philipps**, Leonora. *A dictionary of employment open to women, with details of wages, hours.* London: Women's Institute, 1898. vi, 152p.
Assisted by M. Edwardes, J. Tuckey, and E. Dixon.

6692 **Crawford**, Floyd Wardlaw. *Some aspects of the political and economic problems of woman in English society, 1884–1901.* [19—.] 701p. (Ph.D. thesis, New York University.)

6693 **Women's Co-operative Guild**. *Replacement of men by women.* London: the Guild, [19—.] 11p.

6694 **Byles**, W. P. 'The work of women inspectors.' International Congress of Women, London, 1899. *Transactions. Vol. III. Women in professions, I.* London: T. Fisher Unwin, 1900. p. 95–101.
Discussion, p. 108–14.

6695 **Hurlbatt**, Ethel. 'Professions open to women.' International Congress of Women, London, 1899. *Transactions. Vol. III. Women in professions, I.* London: T. Fisher Unwin, 1900. p. 30–3.

6696 **International Congress of Women**, London, 1899. *Women in industrial life: the transactions of the Industrial and Legislative Section.* London: T. Fisher Unwin, 1900. xii, 252p.
Vol. VI of the Transactions.

6697 **International Congress of Women**, London, 1899. *Women in professions, being the Professional Section.* London: T. Fisher Unwin, 1900. 2v.
Vols. III and IV of the Transactions.

6698 **Miller**, *Mrs* Fenwick. 'The effect upon domestic life of the entry of women into professions.' International Congress of Women, London, 1899. *Transactions. Vol. III. Women in professions, I.* London: T. Fisher Unwin, 1900. p. 38–44.
Discussion, p. 44–6.

6699 **Smith**, Lucy Toulmin. 'Women and their future in library work: discussion.' International Congress of Women, London, 1899. *Transactions. Vol. IV. Women in professions, II.* London: T. Fisher Unwin, 1900. p. 224–8.
Followed by contribution by B. L. Dyer. p. 228–9.

6700 **Lyttelton**, *Hon.* Mary Kathleen. *Women and their work.* London: Methuen, 1901. 152p.

6701 **Hutchins**, B. Leigh. 'A note on the distribution of women in occupations.' *R. Statist. Soc. J.*, LXVII, 3 (September 1904), 479–90.

6702 **Spencer**, A. *Women's industries in Liverpool.* London: Williams and Norgate, 1904. 64p.

6703 **Woman Sanitary Inspectors' Association.** *Woman's place in sanitary administration: a paper read November 25th, 1904 to which is appended a short report of the discussion thereon, by T. O. Dudfield.* London: Adlard, 1904. 18p.

6704 **Wood**, George Henry. 'An outline of the history of the employment of women and children in industry.' Co-operative Wholesale Societies. *Annual, 1904.* p. 209–38.

6705 *Home industries of women in London, 1906.* London, 1906. 45p.

6706 **Zimmern**, A. *Unpaid professions for women.* London, 1906. 86p.

6707 **Central Bureau for the Employment of Women.** *Women as inspectors.* London, 1907. 20p.

6708 *Woman in industry from seven points of view.* London: Duckworth, 1908. xiv, 217p.

6709 **Campbell**, R. J. *Some economic aspects of the women's suffrage movement.* London, 1909. 12p.
Second edition.

6710 **Fabian Society.** Fabian Women's Group. *A summary of six papers and discussions upon the disabilities of women as workers.* London: the Group, 1909. 24p.
Issued for private circulation only.
Writers: Emma Brooke, Constance Long, Ernestine Mills, Mrs Gallichan (G. Gasquoine Hartley), Millicent Mawby, Ethel Benthoun.

6711 **Hutchins**, B. Leigh. *Statistics of women's life and employment.* London: printed for private circulation, 1909. 43p.
Reprinted from *Journal of the Royal Statistical Society*, vol. LXXII.

6712 **Fabian Society.** Fabian Women's Group. *Summary of eight papers and discussions upon the disabilities of mothers as workers.* [London]: the Group, 1910. 32p.
Issued for private circulation only.
Writers: Mrs Pember Reeves, Ethel Vaughan Sawyer, Mrs Spence Weiss, Mrs Bartrick Baker, Mrs Stanbury, Mrs S. K. Ratcliffe, B. L. Hutchins, Mrs O'Brien Harris.

6713 **Williams**, Constance and **Jones**, Thomas. *Some industries employing women paupers.* London: H.M.S.O., 1910. (Cd. 5200.)
Supplement to the *Report . . . on the effect of outdoor relief on wages and the conditions of employment*, Royal Commission on the Poor Laws and Relief of Distress.

6714 **Bird**, M. Mostyn. *Woman at work: a study of the different ways of earning a living open to women.* London: Chapman and Hall, 1911. 257p.

6715 **Brownlow**, Jane M. E. *Women's work in local government, England and Wales.* London: D. Nutt, 1911. 219p.

6716 **Grant**, Clara Ellen. *Married women in our schools.* London, 1911. 31p.

6717 **Hutchins**, B. Leigh. *The working life of women.* London: Fabian Society, 1911. 14p. (Fabian tract 157. Fabian Women's Group series 1.)

6718 **Shreiner**, Olive. *Woman and labour.* London, Leipsic: Fisher Unwin, 1911. 282p.

6719 **Mackirdy**, Olive Christian. *A year and a day.* London: Hutchinson, 1912. xiii, 333p.
Records of investigations into the employment of women.

6720 **Hutchins**, B. Leigh. *Conflicting ideals: two sides of the woman's question.* London: T. Murby, 1913. vii, 83p.
Popular edition. *Conflicting ideals of woman's work.* 1916. vii, 83p.

6721 **Davies**, M. *Employments for women.* Cardiff, [*c.* 1914?]. 31p.

6722 **Low**, B. *Some considerations concerning women in the labour market.* London, 1914. 32p.

6723 **Papworth**, Lucy Wyatt and **Zimmern**, Dorothy M. *The occupations of women . . . summary tables.* London, 1914. 41p.

6724 **Central Committee on Women's Employment.** *Interim report.* London: H.M.S.O., 1915. 42p. (Cd. 7848).
Chairman: Lady Crewe.

6725 **Hutchins**, B. Leigh. *Women in modern industry.* London: Bell, 1915. xix, 315p.
With a chapter 'Women's wages in the wage census of 1906' by J. J. Mallon.

6726 **Maynard**, Edith L. *Women in the public health service.* London: Scientific P., 1915. 128p.

6727 **Smith**, Ellen. *Wage-earning women and their dependants.* London: Fabian Society, 1915. 36p.
Written on behalf of the Executive Committee of the Fabian Women's Group.

6728 **Wilkins**, Louisa. *The work of educated women in horticulture and agriculture.* London: J. Truscott, 1915. ii, 43p.
Reprinted from the *Journal of the Board of Agriculture.*

6729 **Scott**, Emma. 'Woman's work.' *Plym. Instn. Devon. Corn. Nat. Hist. Soc. A. Rep. Trans.*, XVI (1915–22), 123–39.

6730 **Caine**, *Sir* Thomas Henry Hall. *Our girls: their work for the war.* London: Hutchinson, 1916. 127p.

6731 **Churchill**, Jenny Spencer, Lady Randolph Churchill (ed.). *Women's war work.* London: Pearson, 1916. 159p.

6732 **Greig**, G. A. *Women's work on the land.* London: Jarrold, 1916. 48p.

6733 **MacLean**, Annie Marion. *Women workers and society.* London: C. F. Cazenovey, 1916. 135p. (National social science series.)

6734 **Manchester, Salford, and District Women's War Interests Committee.** *Women in the labour market, Manchester and district, during the war.* Manchester, 1916. 29p.

6735 **Standing Joint Committee of Industrial Women's Organisations.** *The position of women after the war.* London, [1916?]. 20p.

6736 **Wolseley**, Frances Garnet, Viscountess Wolseley. *Women and the land.* London: Chatto and Windus, 1916. xi, 229p.

6737 **Zimmern**, Dorothy M. *The Civil Service and women.* London, 1916. [25]p.

6738 **Abbott**, Edith. 'The war and women's work in England.' *J. Polit. Econ.*, xxv, 7 (July 1917), 641–78.

6739 **Atherton**, Gertrude Franklin. *The living present.* London: Murray, 1917. xvi, 304p.
Comparing *French women in war time* and *Feminism in peace and war.*

6740 **Bondfield**, Margaret Grace. 'The position of women in industry.' Gardner, L. (ed.). *The hope for society: essays on 'Social reconstruction after the war', by various writers.* London: Bell, 1917. p. 123–40.

6741 **Fawcett**, Millicent Garrett. 'The position of women in economic life.' Dawson, W. H. (ed.). *After-war problems.* London: Allen and Unwin, 1917. p. 191–215.

6742 **Hutchins**, B. Leigh. *Women in industry after the war.* London: Athenaeum, 1917. 28p. (Social reconstruction pamphlets III.)

6743 'The increase in women's employment during the war.' Gollancz, V. (ed.). *The making of women: Oxford essays in feminism.* London: Allen and Unwin; New York: Macmillan, 1917. Appendix B. p. 215–17.

6744 **McLaren**, Barbara, *Hon. Mrs* Francis McLaren. *Women of the war.* London: Hodder and Stoughton, 1917. xii, 148p.
Introduction by H. H. Asquith.

6745 **Usborne**, H. M. (ed.). *Women's work in war time: a handbook of employments.* London: T. Werner Laurie, 1917. 174p.

6746 **Andrews**, Irene Osgood. *Economic effects of the war upon women and children in Great Britain.* New York: Oxford U.P., 1918. x, 190p. (Carnegie Endowment for International Peace. Preliminary economic studies of the war 4.)

6747 **Bristol Association for Industrial Reconstruction.** *Report of a conference . . . 16th and 17th March, 1918, on the position of women in industry after the war.* Bristol: the Association, 1918. 23p.

6748 **Drake**, Barbara. *Women in the engineering trades.* London: Labour Research Department, 1918. 143p. (Trade union series 3.)

6749 **Harriman**, *Mrs* J. Borden. 'How England meets her labor.' *Ann. Am. Acad. Polit. Soc. Sci.*, LXXVIII (July 1918), 80–5.

6750 **Yates**, L. K. *The women's part: a record of munition work.* New York: Doran, 1917; London: Hodder and Slaughter, 1918. 64p.

6751 **Board of Agriculture.** Sub-Committee on Employment of Women in Agriculture in England and Wales. *Report.* London: H.M.S.O., 1919. 121p.
Chairman: L. Wilkins.

6752 **Bondfield,** Margaret Grace. 'Women as domestic workers.' Phillips, M. (ed.). *Women and the Labour Party, by various women writers.* London: Headley Bros., 1919. p. 66–73.

6753 *Increased employment of women during the war in the United Kingdom.* London: H.M.S.O., 1919. 16p. (Cmd. 9164.)

6754 **Board of Agriculture for Scotland.** Committee on Women in Agriculture in Scotland. *Report.* Edinburgh: H.M.S.O., 1920. 115p.
Chairman: A. Douglas.

6755 **Lind-af-Hageby**, Emelie Augusta Louise. *Unbounded gratitude! Women's right to work.* London: Women's Freedom League, 1920. 11p.

6756 **Rowntree**, Benjamin Seebohm and **Stuart**, Frank D. *The responsibility of women workers for dependants.* Oxford: Clarendon P., 1921. 68p.

6757 **Martindale**, Louisa, the younger. *The woman doctor and her future.* London: Mills and Boon, 1922. 196p.

6758 **Cox**, Ethel Emily (ed.). *Girls' work in trade and industry.* London: Pitman, 1923. x, 162p.

6759 **Tickner**, Frederick Windham. *Women in English economic history.* London, Toronto: Dent, 1923. xii, 236p.

6760 **Upcott**, J. M. *Women house property managers.* St Albans: Building News, 1925. 36p.

6761 **Pinchbeck**, Ivy. *The work of women in agriculture in the late eighteenth and early nineteenth centuries, and the influence of the agrarian revolution thereon.* 1927. (M.A. thesis, University of London.)

6762 **Wilkins**, Louisa. *The training and employment of educated women in horticulture and agriculture.* London: Women's Farm and Garden Association, 1927. 43p.
Reprinted from the *Journal of the Board of Agriculture*, 1915. Revised and brought up-to-date.

6763 **Brittain**, Vera Mary. *Women's work in modern England.* London: Noel Douglas, 1928. ix, 222p.

6764 **Dale**, Marian K. *Women in the textile industries and trade of 18th century England.* 1928. (M.A. thesis, University of London.)

6765 **Neff**, Wanda Fraiken. *Victorian working women: an historical and literary study of women in British industries and professions 1832–1850.* New York: Columbia U.P., 1929. 288p.
Ph.D. thesis, Columbia University, 1929. Printed in Great Britain.
Another issue. London: Allen and Unwin, 1929. Without the author's Vita.
Reprinted with a new bibliographical note. London: Cass, 1966. 288p.

6766 **Pinchbeck**, Ivy. *Women workers and the Industrial Revolution, 1750–1850.* London: Routledge, 1930. x, 342p. (Studies in economic and social history.)

Based on the author's Ph.D. thesis, of the same title, University of London, 1929–30.

Reprinted with a new preface by the author. London: Cass, 1969.

Also New York: Kelley, 1969. (Reprints of economic classics.)

6767 *A study of the factors which have operated in the past and are operating now to determine the distribution of women in industry.* London: H.M.S.O., 1930. 33p. (Cmd. 3508.)

6768 **Angus**, Eliza Y. *The higher education and employment of women in the 20th century.* 1930–31. (M.A. thesis, University of London.)

6769 **Anthony**, Sylvia. *Women's place in industry and home.* London: Routledge, 1932. xi, 243p.

6770 **Evans**, Dorothy Elizabeth. *Women and the Civil Service: a history of the development of the employment of women in the Civil Service, and a guide to present day opportunities.* London: Pitman, 1934. xiii, 165p.

6771 **Hutchins**, Grace. *Women who work.* London: Lawrence, 1934. 285p.

6772 **London and National Society for Women's Service.** *Memorandum on the increasing employment of women.* London, 1935. [4]p.

6773 **Interdepartmental Committee on the Admission of Women to the Diplomatic and Consular Services.** *Report, and government statement.* London: H.M.S.O., 1936. 38p. (Cmd. 5166.)

Chairman: Sir Claud Schuster.

6774 **Standing Joint Committee of Industrial Women's Organisations.** *Women in offices.* London, 1936. 17p.

6775 **Martindale**, Hilda. *Women servants of the state, 1870–1938: a history of women in the Civil Service.* London: Allen and Unwin, 1938. 218p.

6776 **Scott**, Peggy. *British women in war.* London: Hutchinson, 1940. 324p.

6777 **Burton**, Elaine Frances, Baroness Burton of Coventry. *What of the women? A study of women in wartime.* London: Muller, 1941. 224p.

6778 **Cox**, Mary Désirée. *British women at war.* London: Murray Pilot P., 1941. 71p.

Part of the 'Britain at war series'.

6779 **Haslett**, *Dame* Caroline. *Women in war-time engineering.* London: Women's Engineering Society, 1941. 33p.

Presidential address, 27 September 1941.

6780 **Frankel**, H. 'The employment of married women.' *Oxf. Univ. Inst. Statist. Bull.*, IV, 9 (27 June 1942), 183–5.

6781 **Haslett**, *Dame* Caroline. *Munitions girl: a handbook for the women of the industrial army.* London: English Universities P., 1942. 92p.

6782 **London Women's Parliament.** *Woman power.* London, 1942. 24p.

6783 **Stafford**, Ann. *Army without banners.* London: Collins, 1942. 192p.

6784 **Thomson**, Joan. *Women in industry.* London: Lawrence and Wishart, 1942. 39p. (Marx House syllabus 10.)

6785 **Goldsmith**, Margaret Leland. *Women at war.* London: Drummond, 1943. 224p.

6786 **Priestley**, John Boynton. *British women go to war.* London: Collins, 1943. 59p.

With 49 colour photographs by P. G. Hennell.

6787 **Williams-Ellis**, Mary Anabel Nassau. *Women in war factories.* London: Gollancz, 1943. 95p.

6788 **Menzies**, Hilda. 'Effects of the whole-time employment of mothers in industry.' *Occup. Psychol.*, XVIII, 2 (April 1944), 76–85.

6789 **Wartime Social Survey.** *Women at work: the attitudes of working women toward post-war employment and some related problems. An inquiry made for the Office of the Ministry of Reconstruction.* 1944. 37p. (Regional I. 3.)

By Geoffrey Thomas.

6790 **Ministry of Labour.** *Women in industry.* London: H.M.S.O., 1945. 252p.

6791 **Williams**, Gertrude, *Lady. Women and work.* London: Nicholson and Watson, 1945. 128p. (The new democracy.)

6792 **Goldsmith**, Margaret Leland. *Women and the future.* London: Drummond, 1946. 137p.

6793 **International Labour Office.** *The war and women's employment: the experience of the United Kingdom and the United States.* Montreal: I.L.O., 1946. vii, 287p. (Studies and reports, new series 1.)

6794 **Political and Economic Planning.** 'Mothers in jobs.' *Planning*, 254 (23 August 1946), 1–15.

6795 **Keast**, Horace. 'Married women in established employment.' *Ind. Law Rev.*, II, 6 (November 1947), 161–3.

6796 **Woolfitt**, Susan. *Idle women.* London: Benn, 1947. 223p.

On the work of women volunteers on inland waterways of England during the war.

6797 **Eaton**, Maude S. *Domestic workers in hospitals: a field of women's employment.* 1948. (Ph.D. thesis, University of London.)

6798 **Political and Economic Planning.** 'Employment of women.' *Planning*, XV, 285 (23 July 1948), 37–60.

6799 **Douie**, Vera. *Daughters of Britain.* Oxford: the author, 1949. 159p.

An account of the work of British women during the Second World War.

6800 **Ministry of Education.** *Report of the Working Party on the Supply of Women Teachers.* London: H.M.S.O., 1949. iv, 19p.

Chairman: Sir Martin P. Roseveare.

6801 **Associated Country Women of the World.** *Report on part-time work of countrywomen.* London: Associated Country Women of the World, 1953. 47p.

6802 **Dunning**, John Harry. 'Employment for women in the development areas 1939–51.' *Manchr. Sch.*, XXI, 3 (September 1953), 271–7.

6803 **Hewitt**, Margaret. *The effect of married women's employment in the cotton textile districts on the organisation and structure of the home in Lancashire, 1840–1880.* 1953. (Ph.D. thesis, University of London.)

6804 **Harris**, Evelyn Marjorie. *Married women in industry.* London: Institute of Personnel Management, 1954. 30p. (Occasional papers 4.)

Revised 1960.

6805 **Political and Economic Planning**. 'Graduate wives.' *Planning*, xx, 361 (5 April 1954), 21–44.

'The results of an enquiry initiated and organised by Mrs. Judith Hubback . . . have been made available to PEP for this broadsheet.'

6806 **Political and Economic Planning**. 'Graduate wives' tales.' *Planning*, xx, 365 (31 May 1954), 117–32.

A selection of letters from correspondence which arose as a result of the publication of *Planning* 361.

6807 **International Labour Office**. 'The employment of older women.' *Int. Labour Rev.*, LXXII, 1 (July 1955), 61–77.

6808 **Leser**, Conrad Emanuel Victor. 'The supply of women for gainful work in Britain.' *Populat. Studies*, IX, 2 (November 1955), 142–7.

6809 **Davidoff**, Leonore. *The employment of married women in England, 1850–1950.* 1956. (M.A. thesis, University of London.)

6810 **Myrdal**, Alva and **Klein**, Viola. *Women's two roles: home and work.* London: Routledge and Kegan Paul, 1956. xiii, 208p. (International library of sociology and social reconstruction.)

Extensively revised and reset. 1967. 236p.

Second edition, revised and reset. 1968. xvii, 213p.

6811 **British Productivity Council**. North London Productivity Committee. *Britain's need for women technologists.* London, 1957. 30p.

6812 **International Labour Office**. 'Part-time employment for women with family responsibilities.' *Int. Labour Rev.*, LXXV, 6 (June 1957), 543–53.

A summary of the studies undertaken for a meeting convened by the I.L.O. to advise on further action.

6813 **Hewitt**, Margaret. *Wives & mothers in Victorian industry.* London: Rockliff, 1958. x, 245p.

6814 **Kelsall**, Roger Keith and **Mitchell**, Sheila. 'Married women and employment in England and Wales.' *Populat. Studies*, XIII, 1 (July 1959), 19–33.

6815 **Department of Scientific and Industrial Research**. *Woman, wife and worker.* London H.M.S.O., 1960. 31p. (Problems of progress in industry 10.)

By the Social Science Department, London School of Economics and Political Science.

6816 **Klein**, Viola. 'Married women in employment.' *Int. J. Comp. Sociol.*, I, 2 (September 1960), 254–61.

'An earlier version of this paper was read at the Annual Conference of the British Sociological Association in 1960.'

6817 **Klein**, Viola. *Working wives: a survey of facts and opinions concerning the gainful employment of married women in Britain, carried out in co-operation with Mass Observation, Ltd.* London: Institute of Personnel Management, 1960. 63p. (Occasional papers 15.)

6818 **Coxhead**, Eileen Elizabeth. *Women in the professions.* London: Longmans, Green for British Council, 1961. [6], 37p.

6819 **Klein**, Viola. *Employing married women.* London: Institute of Personnel Management, 1961. 51p.

A 'sequel to *Working wives*'.

6820 **Smith**, John H. 'Managers and married women workers.' *Br. J. Sociol.*, XII, 1 (March 1961), 12–22.

'A paper read to a one-day conference of the British Sociological Association on "Married Women and Employment" at Bedford College, London, on 26th March, 1960.'

6821 **Stewart**, C. M. 'Future trends in the employment of married women.' *Br. J. Sociol.*, XII, 1 (March 1961), 1–11.

'A paper read to a one-day conference of the British Sociological Association on "Married Women and Employment" at Bedford College, London, on 26th March, 1960.'

6822 **Broughton**, Margaret E. 'Children with mothers at work.' *R. Inst. Publ. Hlth. Hyg. J.*, XXV, 5 (May 1962), 107–14; 6 (June 1962), 131–45.

6823 **Clark**, Frederick Le Gros. *Woman, work and age: to study the employment of working women throughout their middle lives.* London: Nuffield Foundation, 1962. 111p.

6824 **Collver**, Andrew and **Langlois**, Eleanor. 'The female labor force in metropolitan areas: an international comparison.' *Econ. Dev. Cult. Change*, x, 4 (July 1962), 367–85.

6825 **Holcombe**, Lee. *Middle-class working women in England, 1850–1914.* 1962. (Ph.D. dissertation, Columbia University.)

6826 **James**, Edward. 'Women at work in twentieth century Britain: the changing structure of female employment.' *Manchr. Sch.*, XXX, 3 (September 1962), 283–99.

6827 **Jephcott**, Agnes Pearl, **Seear**, Nancy and **Smith**, John H. *Married women working.* London: Allen and Unwin, 1962. 208p.

'Under the direction of Professor Richard Titmuss.'

6828 **Seear**, Nancy. 'Womanpower needs a policy.' *New Soc.*, 9 (29 November 1962), 14–16.

6829 **Beckerman**, Wilfred and **Sutherland**, Jane. 'Married women at work in 1972.' *Natn. Inst. Econ. Rev.*, 23 (February 1963), 56–60.

6830 **Ministry of Education.** *Women and teaching: report on an independent Nuffield Survey following-up a large national sample of women who entered teaching in England and Wales at various dates pre-war and post-war.* London: H.M.S.O., 1963. iii, 59p.
By R. K. Kelsall.

6831 **Rodgers**, Barbara Noel. *A follow-up study of social administration students of Manchester University, 1940–60: their further training and subsequent careers with particular reference to the contribution made by the married woman to social work.* Manchester: Manchester U.P., 1963. viii, 44p.

6832 **Thompson**, Barbara and **Finlayson**, Angela. 'Married women who work in early motherhood.' *Br. J. Sociol.*, XIV, 2 (June 1963), 150–68.
On an inquiry in Aberdeen.

6833 **Yudkin**, Simon and **Holme**, Anthea. *Working mothers and their children: a study for the Council for Children's Welfare.* London: Joseph, 1963. 199p.

6834 **Yudkin**, Simon and **Holme**, Anthea. 'Working mothers' children.' *New Soc.*, 24 (14 March 1963), 9–11.
'This article summarizes the main conclusions of the authors' book, *Working mothers and their children* . . .'

6835 **British Federation of University Women.** Working Party on the Crowther Report. *Women graduates and the teaching profession: report of a working party of the British Federation of University Women.* Manchester: Manchester U.P., 1964. 68p.
Edited by Mildred Collins.

6836 **Brock**, John. 'Women in responsible jobs in industry.' *Car. Res. Advis. Centre J.*, I, 2 (Autumn 1964), 12–15.
Results of a study based at the London School of Economics 'to enquire into the factors affecting the employment of women in responsible positions in industry'.

6837 **Brown**, R. K., **Kirkby**, J. M. and **Taylor**, K. F. 'The employment of married women and the supervisory role.' *Br. J. Ind. Relat.*, II, 1 (March 1964). 23–41.

6838 **McKenna**, Anne T. 'Women in public administration.' *Administration*, XII, 1 (Spring 1964), 61–6.

6839 **Pearson**, Sylvia. *Mothers at work.* London: Epworth P., 1964. 10p. (Beckly Social Service Trust. Beckly pamphlets, 6th series, 4.)

6840 **Seear**, Nancy, **Roberts**, Veronica and **Brock**, John. *A career for women in industry?* London: Oliver and Boyd for the London School of Economics and Political Science, 1964. 93p.

6841 **Women's Employment Federation.** *Women want to work: some notes on prospects, training and finding work for the older woman with a good educational background.* London: the Federation, 1964. 44p.

6842 **British Broadcasting Corporation.** *Women and work; for returners and latecomers to the professions: a symposium based on the Home Service broadcasts 'Women and work' in the first series of 'A second start' (October 1964–March 1965) produced by Shirley Franklin.* London: B.B.C., 1965. 159p.

6843 **Klein**, Viola. *Britain's married women workers.* London: Routledge and Kegan Paul; New York: Humanities P., 1965. xiv, 166p. (International library of sociology and social reconstruction.)

6844 **Stott**, D. H. 'Do working mothers' children suffer?' *New Soc.*, VI, 151 (19 August 1965), 8–9.

6845 **Williams**, Gertrude, *Lady. The changing pattern of women's employment.* Liverpool: Liverpool U.P., 1965. 16p. (Eleanor Rathbone memorial lecture 15, 1964.)

6846 **Arregger**, Constance E. (ed.). *Graduate women at work: a study by a working party of the British Federation of University Women.* Newcastle-upon-Tyne: Oriel P., 1966. xvii, 156p.

6847 **Fabian Society.** A Study Group. *Womanpower.* London: Fabian Society, 1966. 27p. (Young Fabian pamphlet 11.)

6848 **International Federation of University Women.** *The position of the woman graduate today: a survey, 1956–1965.* London: I.F.U.W., 1966. 32p.
By Germaine Cyfer-Diderich.
English translation by Marianne Welter.
Also available in French.

6849 **Jefferys**, Margot and **Elliott**, Patricia M. *Women in medicine: the results of an inquiry conducted by the Medical Practitioners' Union in 1962–63.* London: Office of Health Economics, 1966. 47p.

6850 **Junior Chamber of Commerce for London.** *Women executives, their training and careers: a survey by the Junior Chamber of Commerce for London on behalf of the Commercial Education Department of the London Chamber of Commerce.* London: London Chamber of Commerce, 1966. 36p.

6851 **Klein**, Viola. 'The demand for professional womanpower.' *Br. J. Sociol.*, XVII, 2 (June 1966), 183–97.

6852 **MacCarthy**, Fiona. *Work for married women.* London: Conservative Political Centre, 1966. 18p. (Conservative new techniques 3.)

6853 **Seear**, Nancy. 'The future employment of women.' Roberts, B. C. and Smith, J. R. (eds.). *Manpower policy and employment trends.* London: Bell for the London School of Economics and Political Science, 1966. p. 98–110.

6854 **Taylor**, Jim. 'Estimating labour reserves: a study on the Furness sub-region.' *Manchr. Sch.*, XXXIV, 2 (May 1966), 197–209.

6855 **Ward**, Patricia Layzell. *Women and librarianship: an investigation into certain problems of library staffing*. London: Library Association, 1966. 59p. (Pamphlet 25.)

6856 **Sommerkorn**, I. *On the position of women in the university teaching profession in England: an ivterview study of 100 women university teachers*. 1966–67. (Ph.D. thesis, University of London.)

6857 **Confederation of British Industry**. *Employing women: the employers' view*. London: C.B.I., 1967. 32p.

6858 **Gundrey**, Elizabeth. *Jobs for mothers*. London: Hodder and Stoughton in association with Hilary Rubinstein, 1967. 159p. (Zenith books.)

6859 **Meade**, E. M. 'The employment of married women.' *Three Banks Rev.*, 74 (June 1967) 3–15.

6860 **Political and Economic Planning**. *Women and top jobs: an interim report*. London: P.E.P., 1967. 81p.

An interim report of a study being carried on by P.E.P. with the collaboration of the Tavistock Institute, by Michael P. Fogarty, Rhona Rapoport and Robert Rapoport.

Final report. *Women in top jobs: four studies in achievement*. 1971. 328p.

6861 **Ramsden**, Gertrude A. and **Skeet**, Muriel H. *Marriage and nursing: a survey of state registered and enrolled nurses*. London: Dan Mason Nursing Research Committee, 1967. 113p. (Reports 5.)

6862 **Williams**, Gertrude, *Lady*. *The marriage rate and women's employment: the Fawcett lecture 1966–67, 3rd November 1966*. London: Bedford College, 1967. 17p.

6863 **Hogg**, S. *The employment of women in Great Britain, 1891–1921*. 1967–68. (D.Phil. thesis, University of Oxford.)

6864 **Norris**, A. *The wastage of married women teachers: a social survey*. 1967–68. (M.Sc. thesis, University of Salford.)

6865 **Wenban**, J. E. A. *The employment of married women in teaching in primary and secondary schools in England and Wales, 1956–1966*. 1967–68. (M.Ed. thesis, University of Leeds.)

6866 **Government Social Survey**. *A survey of women's employment*. London: H.M.S.O., 1968. 2v. (SS 379.)

By Audrey Hunt.

A survey carried out on behalf of the Ministry of Labour in 1965.

Vol. 1. Report.

Vol. 2. Tables.

6867 **Rendel**, Margherita, and others. *Equality for women*. London: Fabian Society, 1968. 43p. (Research series 268.)

'Employment', p. 7–20.

6868 **Stanley**, Gillian R. and **Last**, John M. 'Careers of young medical women.' *Br. J. Med. Educ.*, II, 3 (September 1968), 204–9 .

6869 **Taylor**, Jim. 'Hidden female labour reserves.' *Reg. Studies*, II, 2 (November 1968), 221–31.

6870 **Taylor**, Jim. 'Hidden female labour reserves and the older industrial areas.' *Older Industrial Areas Conference*, Regional Studies Association, March, 1968. 22p.

6871 **Davies**, R. G. *Aspects of married-female employment in Cray Valley industry, Bromley borough*. 1968–69. (M.A. thesis, University of Sussex.)

6872 **Cooper**, Beryl and **Howe**, Geoffrey. *Opportunity for women*. London: Conservative Political Centre, 1969. 28p.

6873 **Pinder**, Pauline. 'Women at work.' *PEP Broadsheet*, XXXV, 512 (May 1969), i–iv, 523–654.

6874 **Williams**, Pat. *Working wonders: the success story of wives engaged in professional work part-time*. London: Hodder and Stoughton, 1969. 126p.

Based on materials compiled and edited by Joan Wheeler-Bennett, and other members of the Women's Information and Study Centre.

6875 **Fawcett Society**. *Half a whole: women's complementary role in work and society: report of the Fawcett Society 1969 conference at Queen Mary Hall, Y.W.C.A. Club, Great Russell Street, London, W.C.1. on Saturday, 3rd May*. London: Fawcett Society, 1970. 24p.

6876 **Francis**, Madeleine. 'Classified sex.' *New Soc.*, XVI, 419 (8 October 1970), 632–3. (Society at work.)

6877 **Klein**, Viola. 'Synchronisation and harmonisation of working hours with the opening and closing of social services, administrative offices, etc.' Organisation for Economic Co-operation and Development. *Employment of women: Regional Trade Union Seminar, Paris, 26th–29th November 1968; final report*. Paris: O.E.C.D., 1970. p. 239–53.

6878 **Murphy**, Florence. 'Ireland.' Organisation for Economic Co-operation and Development. *Employment of women: Regional Trade Union Seminar, Paris, 26th–29th November 1968; final report*. Paris: O.E.C.D., 1970. p. 319–49.

See also: 8; 6270; 6906; 6910; 6947; 6950; 7538.

5. Youth Employment

See also Part Six, II, A; Part Six, II, D, 7; Part Six, IV, A, 4, c; Part Seven, IV, D, 2, b; and Part Seven, V, B, 2, a.

6879 **Campagnac**, Ernest Trafford and **Russell**, Charles Edward Bellyse. *The school training and early employment of Lancashire children*. London, 1903. iii, 39p. (Board of Education. Special reports on educational subjects. Supplement to vol. 8.)

6880 **McMillan**, Margaret. *The economic aspects of child labour and education*. London: P. S. King, [1905?]. 16p. (National Liberal Club Political and Economic Circle. Transactions, vol. v, part 9.)

6881 **Board of Trade**. Departmental Committee appointed to inquire into the Supply and Training of Boy Seamen for the Mercantile Marine.
Vol. I. *Report*. London: H.M.S.O., 1907. iii, 8p. (Cd. 3722.)
Vol. II. *Minutes of evidence, appendices, analysis and index*. 1908. (Cd. 3723.)
Chairman: H. E. Kearley.

6882 **Leeds Education Committee**. *Employment of children: report on children attending school full time and working out of school hours*. 1910. 7p.

6883 **Tawney**, Richard Henry. 'The present position of opinion as to the labour of adolescents.' National Conference on the Prevention of Destitution. *Report of the proceedings . . . 1912*. London: King, 1912. p. 241–5.
Discussion, p. 260–5.

6884 *Agricultural employment of children*. 1914–16. (Cd. 7803, 7881, 7932.)
Also 1916. (Cd. 8202, 8302, 8171.)
Returns.

6885 **Macartney**, Douglas Halliday. *Boy labour: organisation of youth*. London, 1916. 16p.

6886 **Rochester**, Anna. *Child labor in warring countries: a brief review of foreign reports*. Washington, D.C.: Government Printing Office, 1917. 75p. (U.S. Children's Bureau. Publication 27. Industrial series 4.)

6887 **Ministry of Labour**. *Report on an enquiry into the personal circumstances and industrial history of 3,331 boys and 2,701 girls registered for employment at Employment Exchanges and Juvenile Employment Bureaux, June and July 1925*. London: H.M.S.O., 1926. 80p.

6888 **International Association for Social Progress**. British Section. *Report on the raising of the school age and its relation to employment and unemployment*. London, 1928. 18p.

6889 **Ministry of Labour**. *Memorandum on the shortage, surplus and redistribution of juvenile labour during the years 1928 to 1933*. London: H.M.S.O., 1929. 16p. (Cmd. 3327.)

6890 **Winterbottom**, Allan. *An enquiry into the employment of juveniles in Lancashire*. Manchester, 1932. 23p. (University of Manchester, Department of Economics and Commerce, Research Section. Pamphlet 1.)

6891 **Winterbottom**, Allan. 'An enquiry into the employment of juveniles in Lancashire.' *Manchr. Sch.*, III, 1 (1932), 29–47.

6892 **Owen**, Arthur David Kemp. *A survey of juvenile employment and welfare in Sheffield*. Sheffield: Sheffield Social Survey Committee, 1933. 48p. (Survey pamphlet 6.)

6893 **Rowlinson**, E. G. *Juvenile employment and the lengthening of school life*. London, 1934. 8p.

6894 **Tawney**, Richard Henry. *Juvenile employment and education*. London: Oxford U.P., 1934. 20p. (Barnett House papers 17.)

6895 **Political and Economic Planning**. 'The declining importance of boy and girl labour.' *Planning*, 60 (22 October 1935), 14–16.

6896 **Political and Economic Planning**. 'Employment and the School Age Bill.' *Planning*, 65 (31 December 1935), 11–12.

6897 **Eire**. Inter-Departmental Committee on the Raising of the School-Leaving Age. *Report*. 1936. (R.58/1.)

6898 **Jewkes**, John and **Jewkes**, Sylvia. *The juvenile labour market*. London: Gollancz, 1938. 175p.
Also Left Book Club edition.

6899 **Easterbrook**, Laurence Frank. *Youth and the land*. London: Longmans for the British Council, 1944. 31p. (Britain advances 21.)

6900 **British Association for Commercial and Industrial Education**. *The young worker in industry and commerce, with special reference to Scotland*. London: B.A.C.I.E., 1945. 52p.

6901 **Thomas**, Maurice Walton. *Young people in industry, 1750–1945*. London: Nelson, 1945. v, 183p. (Charter for youth series 7.)

6902 **Scarf**, I. W. *The employment of juveniles and young persons (14–18) in the West Riding wool textiles industry, with some reference to the effect of the raising of the school-leaving age and release for part-time further education*. 1947. (B.Litt. thesis, University of Oxford.)

6903 **Godson**, R. 'The industrial distribution of juvenile labour.' *Oxf. Univ. Inst. Statist. Bull.*, XI, 11 (November 1949), 337–56.

6904 **Godson**, R. 'Juvenile labour supply.' *Oxf. Univ. Inst. Statist. Bull.*, XI, 2–3 (February–March 1949), 21–34.

6905 **Godson**, R. 'The regional distribution of juvenile labour.' *Oxf. Univ. Inst. Statist. Bull.*, XI, 9 (September 1949), 269–78.

6906 **Jephcott**, Agnes Pearl. *Studies of employed adolescent girls in relation to their development and social background*. 1949. 3v. (M.A. thesis, University of Wales, Aberystwyth.)

6907 **Godson**, R. 'Juvenile labour in Oxford.' *Oxf. Univ. Inst. Statist. Bull.*, XII, 11 (November 1950), 315–25.

6908 **Carter**, Jean and **Hirsch**, Guenther Paul Hermann. *Juvenile labour in agriculture: report of an enquiry*. Oxford: University of Oxford, Institute for Research in Agricultural Economics, 1952. 34p.

6909 **International Labour Office**. 'The influx of young people into the employment market in Western and Northern Europe.' *Int. Labour Rev.*, LXXV, 4 (April 1957), 335–53.

6910 **Jephcott**, Agnes Pearl. '"Going out to work": a note on the adolescent girl in Britain.' *His Royal Highness The Duke of Edinburgh's Study Conference on the Human Problems of Industrial Communities . . .* London: Oxford U.P., 1957. Vol. II. *Background papers*. p. 21–7.

6911 **Marsh**, Henry John. *Youth and industrial society.* London: Clarke Hall Fellowship, 1957. 24p. (Clarke Hall lecture 17.)

6912 **Occupational Psychology**. 'Young people at work: some statistics.' *Occup. Psychol.*, XXXII, 3 (July 1958), 133–52.

'The purpose of this paper is to provide statistics about the world of employment for those giving vocational advice to young people about to leave school.'

6913 **Rodger**, Alec. 'Fifteen plus: another problem.' *Occup. Psychol.*, XXXIV, 1 (January 1960), 55–60.

A paper read to Section J (Psychology) of the British Association, York, 3 September 1959.

6914 **Ministry of Labour**. Central Youth Employment Executive. *Interim report of the National Youth Employment Council on the employment and training of young people, April 1959–October 1961.* London: H.M.S.O., 1961. 21p.

Chairman: Lord Coleraine.

6915 **Carter**, Michael Percy. *Home, school and work: a study of the education and employment of young people in Britain.* Oxford: Pergamon, 1962. xi, 340p. (International series of monographs on social and behavioural sciences 1.)

6916 **Carter**, Michael Percy. *Education, employment and leisure: a study of 'ordinary' young people.* Oxford: Pergamon; New York: Macmillan, 1963. 170p. (Commonwealth and international library of science, technology, engineering and liberal studies 171.)

'An abridgement of *Home, school and work*, 1962.'

6917 **Leicester**, Colin. 'Economic growth and the school leaver.' *Car. Res. Advis. Centre J.*, I, 1 (Summer 1964), 9–15.

See criticism by Gareth Jones, 'The needs of industry.' I, 2 (Autumn 1964), 7–11.

6918 **Department of Education and Science**. Schools Council. *Raising the school leaving age.* London: H.M.S.O., 1965. v, 34p. (Working papers 2.)

6919 **Hanson**, William John. *Youth employment.* London: Longmans, 1965. vi, 57p. (Our community at work 10.)

6920 **Goddard**, A. D. *Youth employment and the socio-economic environment.* 1965–66. (M.A. thesis, University of Liverpool.)

6921 **Roberts**, K. 'The incidence and effects of spare-time employment amongst schoolchildren.' *Voc. Asp.*, XIX, 43 (Summer 1967), 129–36.

'This article is based on a thesis submitted to the University of London for the degree of M.Sc. (Econ.).'

6922 **Associated Lancashire Schools Examining Board**. *C.S.E. 1967 and after.* Manchester: the Board, 1969. 17p. (Report 4.)

6923 **Keene**, Nancy Beatrice. *The employment of young workers.* London: Batsford, 1969. 237p. (Modern management series.)

See also: 6950–1; 6960; 6962; 7671; 7676.

6. Employment of Older Workers

See also Part Six, II, D, 7; Part Six, IV, C, 5; and Part Seven, IX, B, 4.

6924 **Social Survey**. *The employment of older persons: an inquiry carried out in mid 1945 for the Industrial Health Research Board of the Medical Research Council.* 1947. 73p. (N.S. 60/2.)

By Geoffrey Thomas.

6925 **Social Survey**. *Older people and their employment.* [195–.] vi, 36; iii, 21p. (Report nos. 150/1 and 150/2.)

By Geoffrey Thomas and Barbara Osborne.

Part 1. *The older worker and his attitudes to employment.*

Part 2. *The policy of employers: an inquiry made by the Social Survey in April 1950 for the Ministry of Labour and National Service.*

6926 **Belbin**, Raymond Meredith. *A study of the employment of older people in industry.* 1951–52. (Ph.D. thesis, University of Cambridge.)

6927 **Belbin**, Raymond Meredith. 'Difficulties of older people in industry.' *Occup. Psychol.*, XXVII, 4 (October 1953), 177–90.

6928 **Ministry of Labour and National Service**. National Advisory Committee on the Employment of Older Men and Women. *Age and employment.* London: Central Office of Information, 1953. [12]p.

6929 **Ministry of Labour and National Service**. National Advisory Committee on the Employment of Older Men and Women.

First report. London: H.M.S.O., 1953. 24p. (Cmd. 8963.)

Second report. 1955. (Cmd. 9628.)

Chairman: H. Watkinson.

6930 **Clark**, Frederick le Gros. *The later working life in the building industry: a study of 320 aging maintenance workers.* London: Nuffield Foundation, 1954. 21p.

6931 **Moss**, John. 'The employment of older men and women.' *Fortnightly*, o.s., CLXXXI, n.s., CLXXV (January 1954), 8–14.

The author was a member of the National Advisory Committee on the Employment of Older Men and Women and chairman of the National Old People's Welfare Committee.

6932 **Moss**, Louis. *Older people and their employment: commentary on a sample survey made in Britain in 1950.* 9p. [Government Social Survey G. 50.]

'Paper read at the Third International Gerontology Congress in London on 20 July 1954.'

6933 **Clark**, Frederick Le Gros and **Dunne**, Agnes C. *Ageing in industry: an inquiry, based on figures derived from census reports, into the problem of ageing under the conditions of modern industry.* London: Nuffield Foundation, 1955. x, 146p.

Another edition. New York: Philosophical Library, 1956. x, 146p.

6934 **Clark**, Frederick Le Gros. *Ageing men in the labour force: the problems of organising older workers in the building industry.* London: Nuffield Foundation, 1955. 18p.

Third report on the later working life in the building industry.

6935 **Clark**, Frederick Le Gros and **Dunne**, Agnes C. *New jobs for old workers: an examination of the statistical evidence for the provision of alternative occupations: (first report on alternative work in later life).* London: Nuffield Foundation, [1955]. 19p.

6936 **Clark**, Frederick Le Gros. *The working fitness of older men: a study of men over sixty in the building industry. Second report on the later working life in the building industry.* [London: Nuffield Foundation, 1955?] 40p.

6937 **Rainsbury**, John Philip. *There's life in the old dog yet*... Darlaston: Rubery, Owen, 1955. iv, 45p.

An account of the 'Sons of Rest' workshop scheme of Rubery, Owen and Co. for the employment of men of pensionable age.

6938 **Clark**, Frederick Le Gros. *Ageing on the factory floor; the production of domestic furniture: an inquiry made through works records and work descriptions into the prospects of ageing men within a mechanised industry.* London: Nuffield Foundation, 1957. 35p. (Studies of ageing within the conditions of modern industry.)

6939 **Clark**, Frederick Le Gros. *Bus workers in their later lives: a study of the employment of 300 drivers and conductors from the age of 60 onwards.* London: Nuffield Foundation, 1957. 26p. (Studies of ageing within the conditions of modern industry.)

6940 **Clark**, Frederick Le Gros. *Age and the working lives of men: an attempt to reduce the statistical evidence to its practical shape.* London: Nuffield Foundation, 1959. 67p. (Studies of ageing within the conditions of modern industry.)

6941 **Ministry of Labour and National Service**. *The length of working life of males in Great Britain.* London: H.M.S.O., 1959. 24p. (Studies in official statistics 4.)

6942 **Clark**, Frederick Le Gros. *Growing old in a mechanized world: the human problem of a technical revolution.* London: Nuffield Foundation, 1960. 145p. (Studies of ageing within the conditions of modern industry.)

6943 **Department of Scientific and Industrial Research**. *The older worker and his job.* London: H.M.S.O., 1960. 20p. (Problems of progress in industry 7.)

By H. M. Clay.

6944 **National Old People's Welfare Council**. *Employment and workshops for the elderly.* London: National Council of Social Service for the National Old People's Welfare Council, 1961. 16p.

Another edition. 1963. 24p.

6945 **Nuffield Foundation**. *Workers nearing retirement: studies based upon interviews with older employees in the industrial town of Slough.* London: Nuffield Foundation, 1963. vii, 53p.

6946 **Snellgrove**, Douglas Roseberry. *Elderly employed: a report on elderly people who are in employment.* Luton: White Crescent P., 1963. 72p.

6947 **National Corporation for the Care of Old People**. *Not too old at sixty: an experiment in the employment of women of pensionable age by the Over Forty Association for Women.* London: the Corporation, 1964. 20p.

6948 **Clark**, Frederick Le Gros. *Work, age and leisure: causes and consequences of the shortened working life.* London: Joseph, 1966. 152p. (Michael Joseph books on live issues.)

6949 **Hackett**, Anne-Marie. 'Flexibility of retirement age in the United Kingdom.' Organisation for Economic Co-operation and Development. *Flexibility of retirement age.* Paris: O.E.C.D., 1970. p. 51–92.

See also: 11,875.

7. Employment of the Disabled

See also Part Seven, IV, E, 3; and Part Seven, IX, B, 3.

6950 **Charity Organisation Review**. 'The industrial training of invalid children.' *Char. Orgn. Rev.*, n.s., XVI, 92 (August 1904), 81–96.

Papers read at the Guildhall Conference on Invalid Children, 7–8 June 1904.

I. The work of the Potteries Cripples' Guild, by the Duchess of Sutherland, p. 81–5.

II. The apprenticeship of crippled children, by M. K. Bradby, p. 85–92.

III. Fine Needlework Association for Invalid Women and Girls, by Miss Tancred, p. 93–6.

6951 **McMurtrie**, Douglas Crawford. *Industrial training in Edinburgh for crippled boys and girls.* New York, 1916. 8p.

Reprinted from the *Journal of the Missouri State Medical Association.*

6952 **Amar**, Jules. *The physiology of industrial organisation and the re-employment of the disabled.* London: Library P., 1918. xxv, 371p.

Edited by A. F. Stanley Kent.

Translated by Bernard Miall from *Organisation physiologique du travail.* Paris, 1917. 2 pt. (L'orientation professionelle. Supplement.)

6953 **Camus**, Jean. *Physical and occupational re-education of the maimed.* London: Baillière, 1918. xi, 195p.

With the collaboration of A. Nyns and others. Authorized translation by W. F. Castle.

With articles on British institutions.

6954 **Purse**, Ben. *The blind in industry: fifty years of work and wages.* London: Edson, 1925. viii, 109p.

6955 **National Institute for the Blind**. 'The N.I.I.P. and the National Institute for the Blind.' *Natn. Inst. Ind. Psychol. J.*, IV, 7 (July 1929), 389–90.

Reprint of memorandum on the problem of blind employment circulated to the Conference of Workshops for the Blind.

6956 **Wagg**, Henry John. *A chronological survey of work for the blind . . . from the earliest records up to the year 1930*. London: Pitman, 1932. xii, 235p.

Assisted by Mary G. Thomas.

Supplement, 1931–1951. Compiled by M. G. Thomas. 1953. vii, 88p.

6957 **Levy**, Hermann Joachim. *Back to work? The case of the partially disabled worker*. London: Gollancz, Fabian Society, 1941. 24p. (Fabian Society. Research series 56.)

6958 **Mental After-Care Association**. *Employable or unemployable? Report on pioneer experimental work covering period Feb. 6, 1939–Aug. 1, 1940*. London: the Association, 1941. 33p.

By Kathleen F. Laurie.

6959 **Foulds**, Graham. 'The mental defective and agriculture.' *Occup. Psychol.*, XVIII, 3 (July 1944), 142–7.

6960 **MacPhail**, A. N. *A survey of the experience of young persons registered, under the Disabled Persons (Employment) Act, at the labour exchanges in the city of Glasgow*. 1950–51. (M.D. thesis, University of Glasgow.)

6961 **Davies**, Muriel Llewella Owen. *'Home work' with a difference: the report of a survey of remunerated 'home work' for tuberculous patients, based on personal investigation and actual cases*. London: National Association for the Prevention of Tuberculosis, 1951. 76p.

6962 **Duncan**, William. 'The vocational guidance and employment of handicapped and disabled young people.' *Occup. Psychol.*, XXV, 1 (January 1951), 56–63.

6963 **Ministry of Labour and National Service**. Working Party on the Employment of Blind Persons. *Report*. London: H.M.S.O., 1951. iv, 72p.

Chairman: W. Taylor.

6964 **Arthur**, John. *Through movement to life: the economic employment of the disabled*. London: Chapman and Hall, 1952. 93p.

The author was Life Governor of the Isobel Cripps Centre.

6965 **Medical Research Council**. *Employment problems of disabled youth in Glasgow*. London: H.M.S.O., 1952. vi, 66p. (Memorandum 28.)

By T. Ferguson, A. N. MacPhail and Margaret I. McVean.

6966 **Pearson**, A. M. *The employment of disabled persons in a Liverpool manufacturing firm*. 1952–53. (M.A. thesis, University of Liverpool.)

6967 **Central Council for the Care of Cripples**. *Some notes on sheltered workshops and home industries for the seriously disabled in South East England*. London: the Council, 1954. 31p.

6968 **Weiner**, M. *An investigation into psychological factors affecting the employability of defectives under statutory supervision*. 1954–55. (Ph.D. thesis, University of London.)

6969 **Williams**, I. S. *A follow-up study of 200 men and women one year after a course of industrial rehabilitation*. 1957–58. (Ph.D. thesis, University of London.)

6970 **National Spastics Society**. Employment Committee. *After school what?* London: the Society, 1959. 9p.

6971 **Ferguson**, Thomas and **Kerr**, Agnes W. *Handicapped youth: a report on the employment problems of handicapped young people in Glasgow*. London: Oxford U.P. for the Nuffield Foundation, 1960. vi, 141p.

6972 **Ministry of Labour**. Working Party on Workshops for the Blind. *Report*. London: H.M.S.O., 1962. xi, 143p.

Chairman: J. G. Stewart.

6973 **Ingram**, Thomas Theodore Scott, **Jameson**, Stella, **Errington**, Jane and **Mitchell**, R. G. *Living with cerebral palsy: a study of school leavers suffering from cerebral palsy in Eastern Scotland*. London: Spastics Society, Medical Education and Information Unit in association with Heinemann Medical Books, 1964. 106p. (Clinics in developmental medicine series 14.)

6974 **Hartmann**, P. G. *The assessment of changes in attitude during industrial rehabilitation*. 1967–68. (M.Sc. thesis, University of Durham.)

6975 **Rotary Club of Manchester North**. *Report on handicapped and disabled persons*. Cheadle Hulme: Manchester North Rotary Club, 1968. 24 leaves.

6976 **Greaves**, Mary. *Work and disability: some aspects of the employment of disabled persons in Great Britain*. London: British Council for Rehabilitation of the Disabled, 1969. 109p.

D. THE LEVEL AND STRUCTURE OF UNEMPLOYMENT

The literature on employment and unemployment overlaps considerably. Hence this section should be consulted in conjunction with Part Six, II, C; Part Six, IV, A, 4, d; and Part Seven, IV, A–C. See also Part Three, III, F, 4; and Part Seven, IX, B, 1.

1. General

This section contains general works on the level and structure of unemployment. In particular, it contains works which are concerned with the causes and consequences of, and cures for, unemployment. But that literature which is primarily concerned with the consequences as they affect the conditions of the unemployed worker are classified at Part Six, IV, A, 4, d. And that literature which describes solutions which primarily involve action by the state are classified at Part Seven, IV, B. See also Part Six, II, C, 1; and Part Six, IV, A, 1.

6977 **Edie**, Henry. *The charter of the people; or, the regeneration of a great nation.* London: the author, 1885. viii, 80p.

6978 **Smyth**, J. W. *The true reason why you are out of work.* London: W. King and Sell, 1885. 12p.

A lecture, reprinted from *Paper and Print*, 1879.

6979 **Williams**, H. *Depression of trade and want of employment: a search after a sound basis of political economy.* London: Cull, 1885. 56p.

6980 **Foxwell**, Herbert Somerton. 'Irregularity of employment and fluctuations of prices.' Oliphant, J. (ed.). *The claims of labour: a course of lectures delivered in Scotland in the summer of 1886, on various aspects of the labour problem.* Edinburgh: Co-operative Printing Co., 1886. p. 186–275.

6981 **Mills**, Herbert V. *Poverty and the state; or, work for the unemployed: an enquiry into the causes . . . of enforced idleness.* London: Kegan Paul, 1886. 382p.

6982 **Hake**, Alfred Egmont. *The unemployed problem solved.* London: Hatchards, 1888. 32p.

6983 **Southern**, James W. *The unemployed: an examination of some of the causes and remedies of poverty.* Manchester: J. Heywood, 1888. 24p.

Reprinted from the *Manchester Guardian.*

6984 **Bourne**, H. Clarence. 'The unemployed.' *Mac. Mag.*, LXVII, 398 (December 1892), 81–90.

6985 **Samuels**, H. B. *What's to be done? The unemployed question considered.* London, 1892. 8p.

6986 **Barnett**, Samuel Augustus. 'The unemployed.' *Fortn. Rev.*, n.s., LIV, 324 (December 1893), 741–9.

6987 **Dendy**, Helen. 'The industrial residuum.' *Econ. J.*, III, 12 (December 1893), 600–16.

'Read at the Economic Club, 10th January 1893.'

6988 **Macdonald**, J. A. Murray. 'The problem of the unemployed.' *New Rev.*, IX, 55 (December 1893), 561–76.

6989 **Campbell**, D. *The unemployed problem: the socialist solution.* London: Twentieth Century P., 1894. 16p.

6990 **Drage**, Geoffrey. *The unemployed.* London: Macmillan, 1894. xiv, 277p.

6991 **Hammill**, Fred. *Out of work: the problem of the unemployed.* Newcastle-on-Tyne, 1894. 18p.

6992 **Shuttleworth**, H. C. 'The Christian Church and the problem of poverty.' Reid, A. (ed.). *Vox clamantium: the gospel of the people, by writers, preachers & workers.* London: A. D. Innes, 1894. p. 6–46.

6993 **Hobson**, John Atkinson. 'The economic cause of unemployment.' *Contemp. Rev.*, LXVII (May 1895), 744–60.

6994 **Loch**, Charles Stewart. 'Manufacturing a new pauperism.' *Nineteenth Century*, XXXVII, 118 (April 1895), 697–708.

6995 **Mann**, Tom. *The programme of the I.L.P. and the unemployed.* London: *Clarion* Newspaper, 1895. 16p. (*Clarion* pamphlet 6.)

6996 **Martin**, A. J. *The remedy for unemployment.* London, 1895. 15p.

6997 **Smart**, H. Russell. *The right to work.* Manchester: Labour Press Society, 1895. 16p. (Manchester labour library.)

6998 **Whitehead**, R. R. *The unemployed.* 1895. (Arrows of the dawn 1.)

6999 **Hobson**, John Atkinson. 'The problem of the unemployed.' Co-operative Wholesale Societies. *Annual for 1896.* p. 351–73.

7000 **Hobson**, John Atkinson. *The problem of the unemployed: an enquiry and an economic policy.* London: Methuen, 1896. xvi, 163p. (Social questions of to-day, vol. 19.)

7001 **Oldham**, C. H. 'The fluctuating character of modern employment.' *Statist. Soc. Inq. Soc. Ir. J.*, x, 76 (August 1896), 128–35.

7002 **Withy**, Edward. 'Daylight on the land question: lack of employment, its cause and its cure.' *Westm. Rev.*, CXLV, 2 (February 1896), 123–35.

7003 **Greville**, Frances Evelyn, Countess of Warwick. *Unemployment.* London, [190–?]. 16p.

7004 **Jones**, Edward David. *Economic crises.* New York: Macmillan, 1900. 251p.

7005 **Alden**, Percy (ed.). *Extracts from various Commissions, etc. . . .* [on] *the problem of the unemployed . . . Guildhall Conference, 27th and 28th February.* 1903.

7006 **Barnett**, Samuel Augustus. 'The unemployed and the unemployable.' *Econ. Rev.*, XIII, 4 (October 1903), 385–94.

7007 **Alden**, Percy. *The unemployed problem.* London: Friends' Social Union, 1904.

7008 **Alden**, Percy. 'The unemployed problem.' Co-operative Wholesale Societies. *Annual.* 1904. p. 163–84.

7009 **Higgs**, Mary. *How to deal with the unemployed.* London: S. C. Brown, Langham, 1904. xii, 202p.

7010 **Keir Hardie**, James. *The unemployed problem, with some suggestions for solving it.* London: Independent Labour Party, 1904. 16p.

7011 **Paton**, John Brown. *The unemployable and the unemployed.* London, 1904. 26, ivp.

New edition. London: J. Clarke, 1906. 64p. (Social questions of the day 1.)

7012 **Wood**, William. *Problem of unemployment.* Newcastle-on-Tyne, 1904.

7013 **Alden**, *Sir* Percy. *The unemployed: a national question.* London: King, 1905. viii, 199p.

Second edition. 1905. viii, 199p.

7014 **Carryer**, A. Percy. 'Protection and the unemployed.' *Westm. Rev.*, CLXIV, 1 (July 1905), 7–13.

7015 **Cox**, Harold. *Protection and employment; being a paper read at Liverpool to the New Century Society.* London: Fisher Unwin, 1905. 31p.

7016 **Critolaos** (*pseud.*). *The unemployed: cause and cure by one of them.* London: Elliot Stock. 1905. 16p.

7017 **Crooks**, William. *An address on the unemployed problem.* London: Political Committee of the National Liberal Club, 1905. 14p.

7018 **Eltzbacher**, O. 'Unemployment and the "Moloch of free trade".' *Nineteenth Century*, LVIII, 346 (December 1905), 884–9.

7019 **General Federation of Trade Unions.** *Report on unemployment.* 1905.

7020 **Keir Hardie**, James. 'Dealing with the unemployed: a hint from the past.' *Nineteenth Century*, LVII, 335 (January 1905), 46–60.

7021 **Masterman**, C. F. G. 'The problem of the unemployed.' *Indep. Rev.*, IV, 16 (January 1905), 553–71.

7022 **Mitchell**, Isaac H. 'Organised labour and the unemployed problem.' *Nineteenth Century*, LVIII, 341 (July 1905), 116–26.

7023 **Quarterly Review.** 'The unemployed.' *Q. Rev.*, CCII, 403 (April 1905), 624–45.
Review article.

7024 *The unemployed: cause and cure, by one of them.* London: Elliot Stock, 1905. 16p.
By Critolaos.

7025 **Christian Social Union.** *Unemployment.* Oxford, 1906. (Leaflet 45.)

7026 **Gooch**, G. P. 'The unemployed.' *Contemp. Rev.*, LXXXIX (March 1906), 406–17.

7027 **Greville**, Frances Evelyn, Countess of Warwick. *Unemployment: its causes and consequences.* [1906?] 16p.

7028 **Hatch**, *Sir* Ernest Frederick George. *A reproach to civilization: a treatise on the problem of the unemployed, and some suggestions for a possible solution.* London: Waterlow, 1906. 110p.

7029 **Kaspary**, Joachim. *The permanent settlement of the unemployed question.* London: Humanitarian Publishing Society, 1906. 19p.

7030 **Masterman**, C. F. G. 'The unemployed.' *Contemp. Rev.*, LXXXIX (January 1906), 106–20.

7031 **Millbourne**, A. *The first rung: an attempt to deal with the poverty problem.* 1906.

7032 **Suthers**, Robert B. *My right to work.* London: Clarion P., 1906. 143p.

7033 **Beveridge**, William Henry. 'The problem of the unemployed.' Sociological Society. *Sociological papers*, vol. 3. London, New York: Macmillan, 1907. p. 323–31.
Discussion, p. 332–41.

7034 **Kelly**, Edmond. *The unemployables.* London: King, 1907. vii, 60p.

7035 **Lansbury**, George. 'Unemployment. II.' *Econ. Rev.*, XVII, 3 (July 1907), 299–308.

7036 **Major**, Mark Bonaventura F. *Unemployment and the gold reserve.* Croydon: *Croydon Guardian*, [1907?]. 24p.
Reprinted from the *Croydon Guardian* of October and November 1907.

7037 **Propert**, P. S. G. 'The problem of unemployment.' *Westm. Rev.*, CLXVIII, 2 (August 1907), 193–200.
'Read at the Oxford Conference of the British Constitutional Association, July 12th, 1907.'

7038 **Alden**, *Sir* Percy. 'The causes of unemployment.'. *Method. Times*, XXIV, 1208 (20 February 1908), 148.
'The remedies for unemployment.' XXIV, 1209 (27 February 1908), 168.

7039 **Alden**, *Sir* Percy and **Hayward**, Edward Ernest. *The unemployable and the unemployed.* 1908. (Social service series 4.)
Second edition, revised. London: Headley Bros., 1910. 159p.

7040 **Bailey**, George W. 'The right to work.' *Westm. Rev.*, CLXX, 6 (December 1908), 618–28.

7041 **Bailward**, William Amyas. 'The problem of the unemployed.' *Char. Orgn. Rev.*, n.s., XXIV, 139 (July 1908), 16–30.
Paper read at the Annual Conference of Charity Organisation and Kindred Societies, Blackburn, 1908.
Discussion, p. 30–9.

7042 **Baldwinson**, P. H. *Unemployment: its causes, and suggestions for its cure.* New Wortley, [*c.* 1908]. 16p.

7043 **Barnes**, George Nicoll. *The problem of the unemployed.* London: Independent Labour Party, 1908. 16p.

7044 **Beveridge**, William Henry. 'Unemployment and its cure: the first step.' *Contemp. Rev.*, XCIII (April 1908), 385–98.

7045 **Cooper**, *Sir* R. A. *Unemployment: its cause and remedy.* [1908?] 8p.

7046 **Davies**, H. L. *What can I do for the unemployed? A criticism and a suggestion.* London: Land Values Publication Department, 1908. 20p.

7047 **Fels**, Joseph and **Orr**, John. *The remedy for unemployment.* Glasgow: Land Valuation Publication Department, 1908. 10p.
Reprinted from *Socialist Review.*
Another issue. Glasgow: 'Land Values' Publication Department, 1908.

7048 **Forrester**, J. *Cure for unemployment, strikes and lock-outs.* Shrewsbury: Brown and Brinnand, 1908.

7049 **Frewen**, Moreton. *The problem of the unemployed and the crisis in Eastern exchange: some recent correspondence.* London, Aylesbury: Hazell and Watson, 1908. 47p.

7050 **General Federation of Trade Unions.** Management Committee. *Unemployment report.* 1908.

7051 **Howgrave**, Walter. 'A sociological view of unemployment.' *Westm. Rev.*, CLXIX, 4 (April 1908), 376–87.

7052 **Lee**, Alice. 'On the manner in which the percentage of employed workmen in this country is related to the import of articles wholly or mainly manufactured.' *Econ. J.*, XVIII, 69 (March 1908), 96–101.

7053 **Malthusian League.** *Unemployment.* London, 1908. 8p.

7054 **Money**, Leo George Chiozza. 'The extent of British unemployment.' *International*, I, 3 (February 1908), 179–86.

7055 **Money**, Leo George Chiozza. 'Some notes on unemployment.' *International*, IV, 13 (December 1908), 49–59.

7056 **Newbie Liberal Committee.** *The remedy for unemployment.* Annan, [*c.* 1908]. 52p.

7057 **Orr**, John. *Unemployment: its causes and their removal.* Glasgow: 'Land Values' Publication Department, 1908. 23p.
Published for the United Committee for the Taxation of Land Values.

7058 **Raine**, G. E. *Present-day socialism and the problem of the unemployed: a criticism of the platform proposals of the moderate socialists, together with some suggestions for a constructive scheme of reform.* London: E. Nash, 1908. x, 207p.

7059 **Snowden**, Philip. 'The unemployed problem.' *Social. Rev.*, I, 1 (March 1908), 67–74.

7060 **Tariff Commission.** *Unemployment.* London, 1908. 4p. (Memoranda 37.)

7061 **Barker**, J. Ellis. *Tariff reform, and how it will help to remedy the unemployment problem.* London: Women's Unionist and Tariff Reform Association, 1909. 16p.

7062 **Barnes**, George Nicoll. *The unemployed problem.* London: Independent Labour Party, 1909. 12p.

7063 **Beveridge**, William Henry. *Unemployment: a problem of industry.* London: Longmans, 1909. xvi, 317p.
Third edition. 1912. xvi, 405p.

7064 **Cox**, Harold. *The right to work.* [London?]: Liberty and Property Defence League, 1909.
Reprinted, with additions, from the *Quarterly Review*, January 1908.

7065 **Free Lance.** *The unemployed: a solution and a suggestion.* Liverpool: P.P. Press, 1909. 56p.

7066 **Jevons**, H. Stanley. 'The causes of unemployment. I. Defects in elementary education.' *Contemp. Rev.*, XCV (May 1909), 548–65.

7067 **Jevons**, H. Stanley. 'The causes of unemployment. II. Trade unionism and oversupply of skilled labour.' *Contemp. Rev.*, XCVI (July 1909), 67–89.

7068 **Jevons**, H. Stanley. 'The causes of unemployment. III. Trade fluctuations and solar activity.' *Contemp. Rev.*, XCVI (August 1909), 165–89.

7069 **Lansbury**, George. 'Unemployment: the next step.' Crooks, W., and others. *Social ideals: papers on social subjects.* London: R. Culley, 1909. p. 27–42.
'Address delivered . . . at the Leysian Mission Men's Meeting.'

7070 **Lightbody**, W. M. 'The problem of unskilled labour.' *Econ. Rev.*, XIX, 4 (October 1909), 423–31.

7071 **Lightbody**, W. M. 'The root problem of unemployment.' *Econ. Rev.*, XIX, 2 (April 1909), 158–64.

7072 **Loch**, Charles Stewart. 'Present-day want of employment.' *Char. Orgn. Rev.*, n.s., XXVI, 151 (July 1909), 78–94.
Paper read at the Annual Conference of Charity Organisation and Kindred Societies, Malvern and Worcester, 1909.
Discussion, p. 94–98.

7073 **Paton**, John Brown. *Present remedies for unemployment.* London, 1909. 28p.

7074 **Sheild**, A. M. *Unemployment and the unemployed.* London, 1909. 31p.

7075 **Smith**, Thomas. *A solution of the unemployed problem.* London, 1909. 16p.

7076 **Vivian**, Henry H. *Notes on the problem of unemployment.* [Liverpool], 1909. 16p.

7077 **Wallace**, Alfred Russel. *The remedy for unemployment.* London, 1909. 23p. (Pass on pamphlets 8.)

7078 **Webb**, Sidney. 'The problem of unemployment in the United Kingdom, with a remedy by organization and training.' *Ann. Am. Acad. Polit. Soc. Sci.*, XXXIII, 2 (March 1909), 420–39.

7079 **Christian Social Union.** *Report on unemployment.* Oxford, 1910. 15p.

7080 **An Economist.** *Effects of tariffs on unemployment, by an economist.* London, 1910. 35p.

7081 **Jevons**, H. Stanley. *The causes of unemployment.* London, 1910. 77p.

7082 **A Prizeman of the Institute of Bankers.** *Unemployment and the wage fund, by a prizeman of the Institute of Bankers.* Manchester, [*c.* 1910]. 16p.

7083 **Smith**, E. H. *Free trade, employment, unemployment.* London, 1910. 27p.

7084 **Whetham**, *Sir* William Cecil Dampier. *Eugenics and unemployment: a lecture delivered in Trinity College, Cambridge . . . January 24th, 1910.* Cambridge: Bowes and Bowes, 1910. 19p.

7085 **Chapman**, Sydney John. 'The problem of unemployment.' *Lpool. Econ. Statist. Soc. Trans.* (1910/11–1911/12), 33–9.

7086 **Lupton**, W. *In the gloom of unemployment and a way out through modern apprenticeships . . .* Birmingham, 1911. 24p.

7087 **Mallock**, William Hurrell. 'The facts at the back of unemployment.' *Nineteenth Century*, LXIX, 412 (June 1911), 1104–23.

7088 **Melrose**, C. J. *Protection and unemployment: a pamphlet for the man in the street.* London: F. H. Melrose, 1911. 40p.

7089 **Molesworth**, *Sir* Guilford Lindsey. *How socialism causes poverty and unemployment.* Bexley: the author, [1911?]. [4]p.

7090 **Mond**, *Sir* Alfred. 'The presidential address.' National Conference on the Prevention of Destitution. *Report of the proceedings . . . 1911.* London: King, 1911. p. 379–93.
At the Unemployment Section.

7091 **Mond**, *Sir* Alfred. 'The problem of unemployment.' *Engl. Rev.*, IX, 33 (August 1911), 145–66.
'Presidential Address delivered at the Unemployment Section of the National Conference on the Prevention of Destitution

at Caxton Hall, Westminster, on the 30th May, 1911.'

7092 **Scott**, Alexander. 'Physical unfitness as a cause of unemployment.' National Conference on the Prevention of Destitution. *Report of the proceedings . . . 1911*. London: King, 1911. p. 466–72.

Discussion, p. 472–81.

7093 **Smith**, A. *Surplus labour: a lecture . . .* [Manchester], 1911. 14p.

7094 **A Dental Surgeon**. *Unemployment and diseases caused by decay and loss of teeth*. London: W. Dawson, 1912. 22p.

7095 **Webb**, Sidney. 'The presidential address [of the Unemployment and Industrial Regulation Section].' National Conference on the Prevention of Destitution. *Report of the proceedings...1912*. London: King, 1912. p. 391–401.

7096 **Lubbock**, Nora. *Patriotism and unemployment*. London: W. H. Smith, 1913. 12p.

7097 **Pigou**, Arthur Cecil. *Unemployment*. London: Williams and Norgate, Thornton Butterworth; New York: Holt, 1914. 256p. (Home university library of modern knowledge.)

7098 **Rowntree**, Benjamin Seebohm. *The way to industrial peace and the problem of unemployment*. London, Leipsic: Fisher Unwin, 1914. vi, 182p.

7099 **Money**, *Sir* Leo George Chiozza. 'The war and British trade and employment.' Co-operative Wholesale Societies. *Annual, 1916*. p. 461–78.

7100 **Harvey**, A. Gordon. 'Unemployment and protection.' *Common Sense* (January 1917), 5–6; (13 January 1917), 20.

7101 **Kettering Trades Council**. *An urgent problem: unemployment in relation to the control of industry*. Kettering, 1917. 8p.

7102 **Mills**, Frederick Cecil. *Contemporary theories of unemployment and of unemployment relief*. New York, 1917. 179p. (Ph.D. thesis, Columbia University.)

Published also as Studies in history, economics and public law, edited by the Faculty of Political Science of Columbia University, vol. LXXIX, no. 1, whole no. 183.

7103 **Vago**, Alfred Ernest. *A better England: work for all; a problem and its solution*. London: Drane's, 1918. 30p.

7104 **Alden**, Percy. 'Unemployment.' Manchester University. *Labour and industry: a series of lectures*... Manchester: Manchester U.P.; London: Longmans, 1920. p. 27–57.

'A lecture delivered on Tuesday, October 21, 1919.'

7105 **Cole**, George Douglas Howard. *Unemployment and industrial maintenance*. London: Labour Publishing Co. for National Guilds League, 1921. 16p.

7106 **Hall**, Fred. *Co-operation and the problem of unemployment*. Manchester, 1921. 15p.

7107 **Harris**, W. *Unemployment: its cause and cure*. 1921. 15p.

7108 **Kitson**, Arthur. *Unemployment: the cause and a remedy*. London: Palmer, 1921. 95p.

7109 *Only effective solution of land, housing and unemployment problems*. London, [1921?]. 14p.

7110 **Verinder**, Frederick. *Is there a cure for unemployment?* London: English League for the Taxation of Land Values, 1921. 16p.

7111 **Abrahamson**, H. S. *Unemployment: a contribution to the discussion*. Wolverhampton: Whitehead, 1922. 47p.

7112 **Economic Study Group**. *Worklessness*. London, [*c*. 1922]. 4p.

7113 **Hobson**, John Atkinson. *The economics of unemployment*. London: Allen and Unwin, 1922. 157p.

Revised edition. 1931. 152p.

7114 **Johnston**, Thomas Bertram. *Unemployment and the gold standard*. Weston-super-Mare, 1922. 40p.

7115 **Macgregor**, D. H. 'British aspects of unemployment.' *J. Polit. Econ.*, XXX, 6 (December 1922), 725–49.

7116 **McKenna**, R. 'The problem of unemployment.' *Mon. Rev. Lond. Joint City Midl. Bank* (31 January 1922), 1–5.

7117 **Pell**, Charles Edward. *The riddle of unemployment and its solution*. London: Palmer, 1922. 217p.

7118 **Pethwick-Lawrence**, Frederick William. *Unemployment*. London: Oxford U.P., 1922. 64p. (The world of to-day.)

7119 **Randall**, James Alfred. *The only effective solution of land, housing and unemployment problems*. London: Blackmore, 1922. 15p.

7120 **Rowntree**, Benjamin Seebohm. 'Unemployment and its alleviation.' *Ann. Am. Acad. Polit. Soc. Sci.*, C (March 1922), 95–102.

7121 **Appleton**, William Archibald. *Unemployment: a study of causes, palliatives and remedies*. London: Hodder and Stoughton, 1923. 157p.

7122 **Astor**, *Hon.* John Jacob. *The third winter of unemployment: the report of an enquiry*. London: King, 1923. viii, 350p.

By J. J. Astor and others.

Other authors: A. L. Bowley, Henry Clay, Robert Grant, W. T. Layton, P. J. Pybus, B. Seebohm Rowntree, George Schuster, F. D. Stuart.

7123 **Bellerby**, John Rotherford. *Control of credit as a remedy for unemployment*. London: International Association on Unemployment, 1923. 120p.

Printed in Geneva.

7124 **Beveridge**, *Sir* William Henry. 'Population and unemployment.' *Econ. J.*, XXXIII, 132 (December 1923), 447–75.

'Presidential Address to Section F of the British Association, Liverpool, 1923.'

Also published in the British Association's *Reports of meetings*, 1923, p. 138–61.

Keynes, J. M. 'A reply to Sir William Beveridge.' 476–86.

7125 **Cole**, George Douglas Howard. *Out of work: an introduction to the study of unemployment.* London: Labour Publishing Co., 1923. 96p.

7126 **Crewdson**, Roger Bevan. *Our unemployment problem.* London: Economic Publishing Co., 1923. 124p.

7127 **Hickson**, Gerrard H. *Employment for all: a practical solution of the unemployment problem.* London: Hicksonia Publishing Co., 1923. 7p.

7128 **McCurdy**, Charles Albert. *Protection or common sense: a radical programme for unemployment.* London: Hodder and Stoughton, 1923. 92p.

'The greater part of this book appeared in the columns of the *Daily Chronicle.*'

7129 **National Movement Towards a Christian Order of Industry and Commerce.** *Oxford Conference, New College, Oxford, July 20th to 23rd, 1923 [on unemployment]: papers.* [York?]: the Movement, [1923?]. 78p. (Christian order of industry series 3.)

Papers by John Hilton, Ernest Mahaim, John A. Todd, Dr Gillett, Clarence H. Northcott, Joseph L. Cohen.

7130 **Robertson**, *Sir* Dennis Holme. *The ebb and flow of unemployment.* London, 1923. 23p. ('The new way' series 6.)

7131 **Astor**, *Hon.* John Jacob, and others. *Is unemployment inevitable? An analysis and a forecast.* London: Macmillan, 1924. viii, 388p.

'A continuation of the investigation embodied in *The third winter of unemployment.*'

A series of papers by members of a Committee of J. J. Astor and others under the chairmanship of W. T. Layton.

7132 **Conservative Labour**. *Trade recovery and relief of unemployment.* London: Health Cranton, 1924. 88p.

7133 **Hambling**, *Sir* Herbert. 'The unemployment problem: inaugural address of the President.' *Inst. Bankers J.*, XLV, 9 (December 1924), 484–95.

7134 **Hook**, Alfred. *Unemployment: its cause and cure.* London: Labour Publishing Co., 1924. 217p.

7135 **International Labour Office**. *Unemployment in its national and international aspects.* Geneva: I.L.O., 1924. 227p. (Studies and reports. Series C, 9.)

Report of a conference organised by the League of Nations Union of Great Britain.

7136 **Kemp**, John. *Unemployment as affecting the British Isles, together with some ideas regarding the social system there and elsewhere.* New York: the author, 1924. 48p.

7137 **National Unionist Association**. *Fighting notes against unemployment.* London, [1924?]. [93]p.

7138 **Rowntree**, Benjamin Seebohm. *The unemployment problem: some practical steps towards its solution.* York: National Movement Towards a Christian Order of Industry and Commerce, 1924. 23p. (Christian order of industry series 2.)

Reprinted from *The Times.*

7139 **Wakinshaw**, William Holmes. *The solution of unemployment; or, the postulates and implications of the social credit theorem of Major C. H. Douglas.* Newcastle-upon-Tyne: A. Reid, 1924. viii, 289p.

7140 **Brown**, H. F. *Unemployment: a way out; memorandum.* Chester: S. G. Mason, 1925. 19p.

The author was Vice-President of the Chester Council of Social Welfare.

7141 **Cole**, George Douglas Howard. *Unemployment: a study syllabus...* London: Labour Research Department, 1925. 31p. (Syllabus series 8.)

Second edition.

7142 **Dawe**, Joseph. *'The workman's charter': work for all.* London, 1925. 44p.

Joseph Dawe's Pure and True Literature Bureau.

7143 **Geary**, Frank. *Land tenure and unemployment.* London: Allen and Unwin, 1925. 256p.

Reprinted. New York: Kelley, 1969. 256p. (Reprints of economic classics.)

7144 **Griffin**, H. W. *A new gospel for industry: an alternative to Sir Alfred Mond's employment scheme.* London: Simpkin, Marshall, 1925. 48p.

7145 **Mond**, Alfred Moritz, Baron Melchett. *Liberalism and modern industrial problems: a paper . . . trade, currency, industry and unemployment. A speech . . .* Llanelly: J. Davies, 1925. 40p.

7146 **Mond**, Alfred Moritz, Baron Melchett. *The remedy for unemployment.* Llanelly: South Wales P., 1925. 20p.

7147 **Petter**, *Sir* Ernest Willoughby. *The disease of unemployment and the cure.* London: Hutchinson, 1925. 63p.

7148 **Radford**, E. A. *Unemployment: a suggested remedy.* London, 1925. 12p.

7149 **Scott**, John Waugh. *Unemployment: a suggested policy.* London: Black, 1925. 63p.

7150 **Smith**, Sam. *Unemployment under capitalism.* London: Independent Labour Party, 1925. 30p. (I.L.P. study courses 10.)

7151 **Somerville**, A. P. *The remedy for unemployment.* Glasgow, 1925. 31p.

7152 **Wells**, Gabriel. *The inwardness of unemployment.* London: Elkin Matthews, 1925. 12p.

7153 **Batten**, Edward. *National economics for Britain's day of need: the solution of the unemployment problem.* London: Pitman, 1926. xi, 217p.

7154 **Cook**, Ernest Hampden. *Unemployment – its causes and its cure: an address.* Printed for private circulation, 1926. 8p.

7155 **Parsons**, Gerald O. *Income tax in relation to unemployment: an address.* London: Witherby, 1926. 27p.

'Second impression in extenso.'

7156 **Glasgow Chamber of Commerce.** *Report by Directors in answer to questions asked of them by the Management Committee of the General Federation of Trade Unions in pursuance of an investigation by them into the causes of and the possible remedies for unemployment.* Glasgow, 1927.

7157 **Pigou**, Arthur Cecil. 'Wage policy and unemployment.' *Econ. J.*, XXXVII, 147 (September 1927), 355–68.
Erratum (December 1927), 688.

7158 **Appleton**, William Archibald. *Unemployment: its cause and cure; an enquiry authorised by the General Federation of Trades Unions, summarised by W. A. Appleton.* London: P. Allan, 1928. x, 182p.

7159 **Fleck**, Robert. *The tragedy of the weekly slump.* Glasgow: Pilot P., 1928.

7160 **Hartley**, E. L. *Money and unemployment.* Preston, 1928. 24p.

7161 **Rowntree**, Benjamin Seebohm. *Economic conditions in industry.* [1928?] 10p.

7162 **Wedgwood**, Josiah Clement, Baron Wedgwood. *The truth about unemployment.* London: English League for the Taxation of Land Values, 1928. 11p.

7163 **Bibby**, John Pye. *Unemployment: an analysis and suggested solution.* London: King, 1929. viii, 136p.

7164 **Bibby**, Joseph. *Capitalism, socialism & unemployment.* Liverpool: J. Bibby and Sons, 1929. 32p.

7165 **Clay**, *Sir* Henry. *The post-war unemployment problem.* London: Macmillan, 1929. x, 208p.

7166 **Holsinger**, Frederic E. *The mystery of the trade depression: an analysis of the collapse of production and employment under the capitalist system, with the outline of a plan for the economic re-organization of human society.* London: King, 1929. xxxix, 360p.
Second edition. London: the author, 1932. xlii, 360p.

7167 **Hunt**, *Sir* John. *Burdening the tax-payer: de-rating exposed. Unemployment: the vital national problem.* London: H. L. Angold, 1929. 63p.

7168 **Kenyon**, Ruth. *Unemployment.* London: Society for Promoting Christian Knowledge, 1929. 8p. (Major issues of the day 3.)

7169 **Lawson**, Francis Malcolm. *'Equal distribution': the only permanent cure for unemployment.* Littlehampton: F. M. Lawson, 1929. 27p.

7170 **Martin**, Percival William. *Unemployment and purchasing power.* London: King, 1929. vii, 85p.

7171 **Pickering**, J. *The cause and cure of unemployment.* Easingwold: J. Pickering, 1929. 15p.

7172 **Randall**, James Alfred. *The only effective solution of un-employment: the alternative to 'working for wages'.* Wimbledon: J. A. Randall, 1929.

7173 **Robson**, Norman S. *Unemployment: an examination of the causes of and possible remedies for, the prevailing depression in industry.* London: Simpkin, Marshall, 1929. 27p.

7174 **Snow**, E. C. 'The limits of industrial employment.' *R. Statist. Soc. J.*, XCII, 3 (1929), 323–57.
With discussion, p. 358–73.
'Read before the Royal Statistical Society, March 19, 1929.'

7175 **Thomas**, *Sir* William Beach. *Out of the national pigeon holes.* London: British Portland Cement Association, [1929?]. 26p.

7176 **White**, James Dundas. *The ABC of plenty: employment.* London: C. W. Daniel, 1929. 30p.

7177 **Enock**, Charles Reginald. *The remedy for unemployment: an 'auxiliary industrial system'.* Petersfield: privately printed, [1929–30]. 8p.

7178 **Benn**, *Sir* Ernest John Pickstone. *Unemployment and work.* London: Faber, 1930. 43p. (Criterion miscellany 22.)

7179 **Beveridge**, *Sir* William Henry. *Unemployment: a problem of industry, 1909 and 1930.* London: Longmans, 1930. xxvii, 514p.

7180 **Boden**, John Francis Worsley. *Birth control: a key to unemployment and a way to married happiness.* London: N. Douglas, 1930. 8p.

7181 **Cannan**, Edwin. 'The problem of unemployment.' *Econ. J.*, XL, 157 (March 1930), 45–55.
On *The post-war unemployment problem*, by H. Clay.
Reply by H. Clay, *Econ. J.*, XL, 158 (June 1930), 331–5.

7182 **Cass**, W. G. Linn. 'Unemployment and hope.' *Nature*, CXXV, 3146 (15 February 1930), 225–8.
Reply, with rejoinder, CXXV, 3149 (8 March 1930), 345–6.

7183 **Collier**, A. W. *Equality of opportunity; or, unemployment and its consequences.* London, [*c.* 1930?]. 37p.

7184 **Emmerson**, Harold Corti. 'An analysis of the unemployed.' *Publ. Adm.*, VIII, 1 (January 1930), 86–96.

7185 **Hobson**, John Atkinson. *Rationalisation and unemployment: an economic dilemma.* London: Allen and Unwin, 1930. 126p.

7186 **Large**, Thomas. *How to end unemployment.* London: Bale, 1930. x, 48p.

7187 **Roberts**, E. R. B. *British railways and unemployment: how British railways can solve our greatest national problem.* London: Industrial Transport Publications, 1930. 65p.

7188 **Rural Reconstruction Association.** *Unemployment, with special relation to trade and agriculture.* London, 1930. 16p.

7189 **Tuke**, J. E. *Unemployment.* London, [*c.* 1930?]. 10p.

7190 **Ashley**, J. G. *Can unemployment be cured?* Bristol: St Stephen's P., 1931. 10p.

7191 **Beveridge**, *Sir* William Henry. *Causes and cures of unemployment.* London: Longmans, 19731. op.

7192 **Davies**, Rhys John. 'Problems of unemployment. Are women taking men's jobs?' *Polit. Q.*, II, 1 (January 1931), 126–30.

7193 *Decaying industries; unemployment: a few guide posts.* London: H. Howes, 1931.

7194 **Demant**, Vigo Auguste. *This unemployment: disaster or opportunity? An argument in economic philosophy submitted to the Christian Social Council by its Research Committee.* London: Student Christian Movement Press, 1931. 157p.

7195 **Elias**, S. *One reply to the Royal Commission on Unemployment.* London, 1931. 15p.

7196 **Knoop**, Douglas. *The riddle of unemployment.* London: Macmillan, 1931. viii, 192p.
Based on a series of lectures given to an Advanced Tutorial Class on Unemployment.

7197 **Meriam**, R. S. 'Unemployment: its literature and its problems.' *Q.J. Econ.*, XLVI, 3 (November 1931), 158–86.
Review article of books published in U.S. and U.K.

7198 **Piatnitsky**, O. *Unemployment, and the tasks of the communists.* London: Modern Books, 1931. 41p.

7199 **Schunemann**, Julius. *Unemployment: its causes, effect, and a complete plan for its cure, in Europe and beyond.* London: J. Schunemann, 1931. 16p.

7200 **Trouton**, Rupert. *Unemployment: its causes and their remedies.* London: Woolf, 1931. 51p. (Day to day pamphlets 2.)

7201 **Wallis**, Percy and **Redfern**, Arthur. *The road to prosperity. Unemployment: its cause and cure.* London: J. Lane, 1931. xii, 124p.

7202 **Meredith**, James Creed. 'Separate markets for unemployed.' *Statist. Soc. Inq. Soc. Ir. J.*, LXXXV (1931–32), 35–56.

7203 **Benham**, Frederic C. 'Fluctuations in unemployment in Great Britain.' *International unemployment: a study of fluctuations in employment and unemployment in several countries 1910–1930, contributed to the World Social Economic Congress, Amsterdam, August 1931.* The Hague: International Industrial Relations Institute, 1932. p. 229–78.

7204 **Hopkins**, Lewis Egerton. *Unemployment and the £.* London: L. E. Hopkins, 1932. 20p.

7205 **Maxwell**, Denis Wellesley. *The principal cause of unemployment: a simple explanation of our defective money system.* London: Williams and Norgate, 1932. 273p.

7206 **Slater**, Gilbert. *Currency credit and the unemployment crisis.* London: Fabian Society, 1932. 15p. (Fabian tract 239.)

7207 **Brayshaw**, Shipley Neave. *Unemployment and plenty.* London: Allen and Unwin, 1933. 146p. (Swarthmore lecture 1933.)

7208 **Engineering and Allied Employers' National Federation.** *Unemployment: its realities and problems.* London: the Federation, 1933. vi, 94p.

7209 **Gill**, Arthur Eric Rowton. *Unemployment.* London: Faber, 1933. 32p.

7210 **Jacob**, Claud P. G. *Economic salvation: a treatise on unemployment, taxation, debt. The cause and a remedy.* London: Butterworth, 1933. 141p.

7211 **Mais**, Stuart Petre Brodie. *S.O.S.: talks on unemployment.* London, New York: Putnam, 1933. xxvii, 377p.

7212 **Mond**, H. *The economics of unemployment.* London, 1933. 6p.

7213 **Pigou**, Arthur Cecil. *The theory of unemployment.* London: Macmillan, 1933. xxv, 319p.
New impression. London: Cass, 1968.

7214 **Swaffield**, D. E. *Work for a million unemployed.* London: Universal Publications, 1933. 36p.

7215 **Whitehead**, George. *Unemployment: causes and remedies.* London: Bale, 1933. vi, 434p.

7216 **Fielding**, *Sir* Charles William. *Permanent prosperity for Britain and profitable work for all unemployed.* Billingshurst: C. Tiller, 1934. 12p.

7217 **Pointing**, Horace B. (ed.). *'Unemployment is beating us?' Is it our concern? A series of letters.* London: London Young Friends' Group, 1934. 47p.

7218 **Shadforth**, William. *Unemployment banished for ever!* London, 1934. 8p.

7219 **Blackwell**, Philip Henry. *Some notes on unemployment.* London: Gee, 1935. 43p. (*The Accountant* lecture series 19.)

7220 **Morton**, Nelson Whitman. *Occupational abilities: a study of unemployed men.* Toronto: Oxford U.P., 1935. xxvi, 279p. (McGill social research series 3.)

7221 **Mulligan**, James. *Get them work: an old man's dream of coming good.* London: Barber, 1935. 33p.

7222 **Royal Institute of International Affairs.** *Unemployment: an international problem.* London: Oxford U.P., 1935. viii, 496p.

7223 **Colyer**, William Thomas. *An outline history of unemployment.* London: N.C.L.C. Publishing Society, 1936. 79p.

7224 **Hutchinson**, *Sir* Herbert John. *Facts of unemployment.* London: Industrial Christian Fellowship, 1936. 15p.

7225 **Keynes**, John Maynard, Baron Keynes. *The general theory of employment, interest and money.* London: Macmillan, 1936. xii, 403p.

7226 **Beveridge**, *Sir* William Henry. *An analysis of unemployment.* Washington, D.C., 1937. 50p. (U.S. Social Security Board. Bureau of Research and Statistics. Reprint series 6.)

7227 **Bowden**, Witt. 'Surplus labor and the social wage in Great Britain.' *Am. Econ. Rev.*, XXVII, 1 (March 1937), 31–44.

7228 **Brayshaw**, Shipley Neave. *The total abolition of unemployment.* London: Allen and Unwin, 1937. 47p.
An address given to a conference of the Society of Friends.

7229 **Council of Action for Peace and Reconstruction.** *Is there no hope for the unemployed? The Council of Action's answer.* London, 1937. 11p.

7230 **Galloway**, Janet. 'Neurasthenia and unemployment: an analysis of 52 cases.' Blacker, C. P. (ed.). *A social problem group?* London: Oxford U.P., 1937. p. 162–219.

7231 **Kuczynski**, Jürgen. 'Death and unemployment.' *New frontiers in wage theory: Keynes, Robinson, Hicks, Rueff.* London: Lawrence and Wishart, 1937. p. 86–93.

7232 **Marsh**, Leonard Charles. *Health and unemployment: some studies of their relationships.* London: Oxford U.P., 1938. xxv, 243p. (McGill social research series 7.)

Printed in Canada.

In collaboration with A. Grant Fleming and C. F. Blackler.

7233 **Meade**, James Edward. *Consumers' credits and unemployment.* London: Oxford U.P., 1938. vii, 115p.

Chapter IV. 'A practical scheme for Great Britain.'

7234 **Pool**, Arthur George. *Wage policy in relation to industrial fluctuations.* London: Macmillan, 1938. xiii, 305p.

The author's Ph.D. thesis, University of London, 1939.

7235 **Robinson**, H. W. 'Employment and unemployment.' British Association. Economic Science and Statistics Section. *Britain in recovery.* London: Pitman, 1938. p. 85–104

7236 **Beveridge**, William Henry. 'Unemployment in the trade cycle.' *Econ. J.*, XLIV, 193 (March 1939), 52–65.

7237 **Crisp**, Dorothy. *Unemployment: its cause and cure.* London: *National Review*, 1939. 65p.

The first part of *England mightier yet.*

7238 **McGregor**, Alexander Grant. *Unemployment and the rationing complex.* London: Pitman, 1940. 32p.

7239 **Northern Ireland.** *Interim report of the Select Committee of the House of Commons on Unemployment.* Belfast: H.M.S.O., 1940. 6p. (H.C. 515.)

Second interim report and special report. 1941. 6p. (H.C. 520.)

First and second interim reports and a special report . . . with proceedings of the Committee, appendices and minutes of evidence. 1941. 422p. (H.C. 537.)

Final report . . . with proceedings of the Committee and minutes of evidence. 1942. 99p. (H.C. 552.)

7240 **Singer**, Hans Wolfgang. *Unemployment and the unemployed.* London: King, 1940. x, 152p.

7241 **Pigou**, Arthur Cecil. *Employment and equilibrium: a theoretical discussion.* London: Macmillan, 1941. xi, 283p.

Second, revised edition. 1949. x, 283p.

7242 **Smallpeice**, *Sir* Basil. *Freedom from fear and want: a study of the unemployment problem.* Potters Bar: Gee; London: City Library, 1942. 47p.

'A series of five articles reprinted from *The Accountant.*'

7243 **Lever Brothers and Unilever.** *The problem of unemployment.* London, 1943. 38p.

Another edition. London: Harrap, 1943. 38p.

7244 **Balogh**, Thomas. 'The international aspects of full employment.' Oxford University. Institute of Statistics. *The economics of full employment.* Oxford: Blackwell, 1944. p. 126–80.

7245 **Burchardt**, F. A. 'The causes of unemployment.' Oxford University. Institute of Statistics. *The economics of full employment.* Oxford: Blackwell, 1944. p. 1–38.

7246 **Edgeworth**, Kenneth Essex. *Unemployment can be cured.* Dublin: Eason and Son, 1944. 157p.

7247 **Clay**, *Sir* Henry. *War and unemployment.* London: Oxford U.P., 1945. 16p. (Barnett House papers 28.)

Sidney Ball lecture 1945.

7248 **Collier**, Aubrey. *Why unemployment?* Canterbury: J. A. Jennings, 1945. 148p.

7249 **Political and Economic Planning.** 'Transatlantic employment outlook.' *Planning*, 237 (13 July 1945), 1–16.

7250 **Shipley**, E. T. *Unemployment in Canada, Great Britain and the United States.* 1946. 149p. (M.A. thesis, Acadia University.)

7251 **Kamakura**, N. 'Involuntary unemployment explained by over-determinateness.' *Kyoto Univ. Econ. Rev.*, XXIII, 2 (October 1953), 20–9.

7252 **Kuzminov**, I. 'The unemployment problem in Great Britain.' *Int. Aff.*, 9 (September 1956), 47–60.

7253 **Acton Society Trust.** *Redundancy: a survey of problems and practices.* London: the Trust, 1958–59. 2 parts.

1. Introductory study based on research by J. S. Hutchinson and N. Wansbrough directed by R. Stewart. 56p.

2. Three studies on redundant workers, based on work by J. S. Hutchinson and G. A. Cass, edited by Honor Croome, directed by R. Stewart. 40p.

7254 **Ackerman**, Paul. *Unemployment: the problem of industrial nations.* Montreal, 1959. 75p.

Rearranged edition. *Unemployment, its cause and cure: the problem of industrial nations.* 1962. 2v.

7255 **National Institute Economic Review.** 'Employment and unemployment.' *Natn. Inst. Econ. Rev.*, 2 (March 1959), 12–15.

7256 **Hancock**, Keith J. 'Unemployment, and the economists in the 1920's.' *Economica*, XXVII, 108 (November 1960), 305–21.

7257 **Miernyk**, William H. 'Foreign experience with structural unemployment and its remedies.' *Studies in unemployment.* Washington, D.C.: U.S.G.P.O., 1960. p. 411–32.

7258 **Organisation of Employers' Federations and Employers in Developing Countries.** *Redundancy.* London: the Federation, 1961. (Occasional paper.)

Revised edition. [1964?] 51p.

7259 **Aris**, Stephen. 'Softening the sack.' *New Soc.*, 1 (4 October 1962), 8–10.

'A *New Society* special report.'

7260 **Goodman**, Geoffrey. *Redundancy in the affluent society*. London: Fabian Society, 1962. 37p. (Fabian tract 340. Socialism in the sixties.)

7261 **Hunter**, Laurence Colvin. 'Unemployment in a full employment society.' *Scott. J. Polit. Econ.*, x, 3 (November 1963), 289–304.

7262 **Nicol**, B. N. 'Tackling redundancy.' *New Soc.*, iv, 113 (26 November 1964), 16–18.
A case study.

7263 **Stewart**, Iain. *Problem of redundancy*. London: Newman Neame Take Home Books, 1964. 14p.

7264 **Kahn**, Hilda Renate. *Repercussions of redundancy: a local survey*. London: Allen and Unwin, 1964 [i.e. 1965]. 267p.

7265 **Robertson**, Donald James. 'Redundancy.' Reid, G. L. and Robertson, D. J. (eds.). *Fringe benefits, labour costs and social security*. London: Allen and Unwin, 1965. p. 246–72.

7266 **Evans**, Eric Wyn. 'Economic growth and unemployment.' *Inst. Bankers J.*, LXXXVII, 1 (February 1966), 27–36.

7267 **Staniland**, Alan Charles. *Patterns of redundancy: a psychological study*. Cambridge: Cambridge U.P., 1966. viii, 216p.

7268 **Shimizu**, K. *Unemployment and vacancies unfilled*. 1966–67. (M.Soc.Sc. dissertation, University of Birmingham.)

7269 **Sant**, M. E. C. 'Unemployment and industrial structure in Great Britain.' *Reg. Studies*, I, 1 (May 1967), 83–91.

7270 **Fowler**, Ronald Frederick. *Duration of unemployment on the register of wholly unemployed*. London: H.M.S.O., 1968. ii, 37p. (Studies in official statistics, research series, 1.)

7271 **Matthews**, R. C. O. 'Why has Britain had full employment since the war?' *Econ. J.*, LXXVIII, 311 (September 1968), 555–69.
'A revised version of a University of London Special Lecture delivered at University College London on February 1, 1968.'
Comment by G. B. Stafford, LXXX, 317 (March 1970), 165–72.
Reply, p. 173–6.

7272 **Sinfield**, Adrian. *The long-term unemployed: a comparative survey*. Paris: Organisation for Economic Co-operation and Development, 1968. 98p. (Employment of special groups 4.)

7273 **Wedderburn**, Dorothy. 'Redundancy.' Pym, D. (ed.). *Industrial society: social sciences in management*. Harmondsworth: Penguin, 1968. p. 65–81.

7274 **Seglow**, P. E. J. *Redundancy and factory social structure*. 1968–69. (M.A. thesis, University of Leicester.)

7275 **Whitaker**, T. K. 'Productivity and full employment.' *Administration*, XVII, 1 (Spring 1969), 11–22.
'Address given at the Annual General Meeting of the College of Industrial Relations, Dublin, 25 March 1969.'

7276 **Doughty**, George. 'Mergers and redundancy: a study of the Industrial Reorganization Corporation.' *Trade Un. Regist.* (1970), 53–61.

7277 **Martin**, Roderick and **Fryer**, Robert H. 'Management and redundancy: an analysis of planned organizational change.' *Br. J. Ind. Relat.*, VIII, 1 (March 1970), 69–84.

7278 **Pillay**, Celia. *Survey of redundancy: technical sampling report*. [1970.] 37p. (Social Survey M.150. New sampling series 2.)

7279 **Showler**, Brian. 'Who are the unemployed?' *New Soc.*, XVI, 408 (23 July 1970), 146–8. (Out of work, 1.)

See also: 6; 11; 14; 7507; 7706; 7782; 12,960.

2. Types and Measurement

7280 **Hobson**, John Atkinson. 'Meaning and measure of unemployment.' *Contemp. Rev.*, LXVII (March 1895), 415–32.

7281 **Willoughby**, William Franklin. 'The measurement of unemployment: a statistical study.' *Yale Rev.*, o.s., x (August 1901), 188–202; x (November 1901), 268–97.

7282 **Mercer**, Alexander. 'Board of Trade unemployed returns.' *Char. Orgn. Rev.*, n.s., XXII, 131 (November 1907), 303–8.
Discusses the nature and limits of figures taken from the returns.
Correspondence. (January 1908), 50.
Reply by author. (February 1908), 111–12.

7283 **Mercer**, Alexander. 'Unemployment. I.' *Econ. Rev.*, XVII, 2 (April 1907), 167–76.
Interpretation of statistics with reference to Board of Trade returns.

7284 **Webb**, Augustus D. 'Statistics of unemployment, with special reference to seasonal unemployment.' National Conference on the Prevention of Destitution. *Report of the proceedings . . . 1911*. London: King, 1911. p. 541–7.
Discussion, p. 542–50.

7285 **Bowley**, Arthur Lyon. 'The measurement of employment: an experiment.' *R. Statist. Soc. J.*, LXXV, 8 (July 1912), 791–822.
With discussion, p. 822–9.

7286 **Gibbon**, Ioan Gwilym. 'Report [on statistics of unemployment available for the United Kingdom].' *Q.J. Int. Ass. Unempl.*, III, 2 (April–June 1913), 481–503.

7287 **Dearle**, Norman Burrell. *English statistics of unemployment*. 1915. (D.Sc. (Econ.) thesis, University of London.)

7288 **Bradford**, E. S. 'Methods used in measuring unemployment.' *J. Am. Statist. Ass.*, XVII (December 1921), 983–94.

7289 **Hilton**, John. 'Statistics of unemployment derived from the working of the Unemployment Insurance Acts.' *R. Statist. Soc. J.*, LXXXVI, 2 (March 1923), 154–93.
With discussion, p. 194–205.
'Read before the Royal Statistical Society, February 20, 1923.'

7290 **Hilton**, John. 'Enquiry by sample: an experiment and its results.' *R. Statist. Soc. J.*, LXXXVII, 4 (July 1924), 544–61.
With discussion, p. 562–70.
'Read before the Royal Statistical Society, June 17, 1924.'
The author was Director of Statistics, Ministry of Labour.

7291 **Jones**, David Caradog. 'Some statistics concerning occupational invalidity: economic, mental and moral.' *R. Statist. Soc. J.*, LXXXIX, 4 (July 1926), 680–702.

7292 *Memorandum on the influence of legislative and administrative changes on the official unemployment statistics.* London: H.M.S.O., 1926. 9p. (Cmd. 2601.)

7293 **Hilton**, John. 'Some further enquiries by sample.' *R. Statist. Soc. J.*, XCI, 4 (1928), 519–30.
Discussion, p. 531–40.
'Read before the Royal Statistical Society, June 19, 1928.'

7294 **Hill**, Arthur Cheney Clifton. 'Employment statistics as measures of unemployment.' *J. Am. Statist. Ass.*, XXVI (June 1931), 184–7.

7295 **Dale**, J. A. 'The interpretation of the statistics of unemployment.' *R. Statist. Soc. J.*, XCVII, 1 (1934), 85–101.
Discussion, p. 101–13.
'Read before the Royal Statistical Society on December 19th, 1933.'

7296 **Saunders**, Christopher Thomas. 'The importance of seasonal variations in employment in the United Kingdom.' *Econ. J.*, XLV, 178 (June 1935), 269–79.

7297 **Saunders**, Christopher Thomas. *Seasonal variations in employment.* London: Longmans, 1936. xii, 311p.

7298 **Beveridge**, *Sir* William Henry. 'An analysis of unemployment.' *Economica*, n.s., III, 12 (November 1936), 357–86; IV, 13 (February 1937), 1–17; IV, 14 (May 1937), 168–83.

7299 **Brew**, E. 'The "out of work" enquiry of 1931.' *Manchr. Sch.*, X, 1 (1939), 50–4.
Comparison of results obtained by 'out of work' enquiry of Census of Population and Ministry of Labour.

7300 **Dessauer-Meinhardt**, Marie. 'Monthly unemployment records, 1854–1892.' *Economica*, n.s., VII, 27 (August 1940), 322–6.

7301 **Dessauer-Meinhardt**, Marie. 'Unemployment records, 1848–59.' *Econ. Hist. Rev.*, X, 1 (February 1940), 38–43.

7302 **Frankel**, H. 'Quantitative and qualitative full employment.' *Oxf. Univ. Inst. Statist. Bull.*, III, 15 (1 November 1941), 342–6.

7303 **Morgan**, Edward Victor. 'What is "full employment"?' *Banker*, XCIX, 319 (August 1952), 76–82.

7304 **Turner**, Herbert Arthur. 'Measuring unemployment.' *R. Statist. Soc. J.*, Ser. A, CXVIII, 1 (1955), 28–50.

7305 **Galenson**, Walter and **Zellner**, Arnold. 'International comparison of unemployment rates.' *Measurement and behavior of unemployment: a conference of the Universities-National Bureau Committee for Economic Research.* Princeton: Princeton U.P., 1957. p. 439–583.

7306 **Bailey**, Donald. 'Note on British unemployment statistics.' *Appl. Statist.*, IX, 1 (March 1960), 51–9.

7307 **Shelton**, William C. and **Neef**, Arthur F. 'Foreign job vacancy statistics, programs.' National Bureau of Economic Research. *The measurement and interpretation of job vacancies.* New York: N.B.E.R., 1966. p. 145–71.

7308 **Showler**, Brian. *An analysis of the characteristics of adult unemployment in the sub-region of Humberside since 1951.* 1969. (M.Sc. Econ. thesis, University of Hull.)

7309 **Thirlwall**, A. P. 'Types of unemployment, with special reference to "non demand-deficient" unemployment in Great Britain.' *Scott. J. Polit. Econ.*, XVI, 1 (February 1969), 20–49.

3. Unemployment and Technological Change

See also Part Two, IV; Part Five, II; and see Part Three, III, B, 2 for material on the Luddites.

7310 **Mongredien**, Augustus. *On the displacement of labour and capital: a neglected chapter in political economy.* London: Cassell, Petter and Galpin, 1886. 36p. (Cobden Club pamphlet.)

7311 **Samuelson**, James. *Labour-saving machinery: an essay on the effect of mechanical appliances in the displacement of manual labour in various industries.* London: Kegan Paul, 1893. xi, 94p.

7312 **Hazell**, Walter Howard. 'Labour-saving machinery and employment.' *Nineteenth Century*, XCIV, 559 (September 1923), 454–61.

7313 **Gregory**, *Sir* Theodore Emanuel Gugenheim. 'Rationalisation and technological unemployment.' *Econ. J.*, XL, 160 (December 1930), 551–67.

7314 **Lester**, A. M. 'The problem of technological unemployment.' *Hum. Factor*, VIII, 5 (May 1934), 180–7.

7315 **Durbin**, E. F. M. 'The economist's view.' Williams, H. (ed.). *Man and the machine.* London: Routledge, 1935. p. 158–95.

7316 **Henniker-Heaton**, C. 'Machines and manpower in spinning.' *Banker*, XC, 280 (May 1949), 115–20.
The author was Director of the Federation of Master Cotton Spinners' Associations.

7317 **British Productivity Council**. *Productivity and redundancy.* London: the Council, 1956. 16p. (Action pamphlets 6.)

7318 **Aris**, Stephen. 'Machines or people?' *New Soc.*, 32 (9 May 1963), 15–16.

7319 **Ministry of Labour**. Manpower Research Unit. *Computers in offices.* London: H.M.S.O., 1965. 63p. (Manpower studies 4.)

7320 **Robertson**, Donald James. 'Economic effects of technological change.' *Scott. J. Polit. Econ.*, XII, 2 (June 1965), 180–94.
'A shortened version of a paper presented to the Second International Conference on Automation and Technological Progress organised by the Metal Industry Trade Union, Germany, March, 1965.'

7321 **Conference on Employment Problems of Automation and Advanced Technology**, Geneva, 1964. *Employment problems of automation and advanced technology: an international perspective; proceedings of a conference held at Geneva by the International Institute for Labour Studies, 19–24 July 1964.* London: Macmillan; New York: St Martin's P., 1966. xvii, 479p. (International Institute for Labour Studies. Publications.)
Edited and introduced by Jack Stieber.

7322 **Holmberg**, Per. 'The relationship between full employment and technological change in Western Europe.' Stieber, J. (ed.). *Employment problems of automation and advanced technology: an international perspective.* London: Macmillan; New York: St Martin's P., 1966. p. 162–81.

7323 **Evans**, *Sir* Trevor and **Stewart**, Margaret. *Pathway to tomorrow: the impact of automation on people; a survey of the International Conference on Automation, Full Employment and a Balanced Economy at Rome in June 1967.* London: Newman Neame for the Foundation on Automation and Employment Limited of Great Britain and the American Foundation on Automation and Employment, 1967. viii, 123p.

7324 **Malik**, Rex. 'Employment and the computer.' *Westm. Bank Rev.* (August 1967), 32–42.
Discusses some of the manpower implications of computer systems, in a British context.

7325 **Paukert**, Felix. 'Technological change and the level of employment in Western Europe.' *Br. J. Ind. Relat.*, VI, 2 (July 1968), 139–55.

7326 **Hunter**, Laurence Colvin, **Reid**, Graham Livingstone and **Boddy**, David. *Labour problems of technological change.* London: Allen and Unwin, 1970. 363p. (University of Glasgow social and economic studies. New series 18.)

4. Chronological Studies

This section contains works which are primarily concerned with describing or explaining the level and structure of unemployment prevailing in a specific period or the changes in these levels over time. Chronological studies with a primarily regional focus are classified at Part Six, II, D, 5; those with a primarily industrial or occupational focus at Part Six, II, D, 6; and those relating to particular aspects and groups are classified at Part Six, II, D, 7.

7327 **Board of Trade**. *State of employment in the United Kingdom in October 1914. Report, appendices.* London: H.M.S.O., 1914. 41p. (Cd. 7703.)
By H. Llewellyn-Smith.
Report in December 1914. 1915. 10p. (Cd. 7755.)
Report in February 1915. 1915. 19p. (Cd. 7850.)

7328 **Pigou**, Arthur Cecil. 'Unemployment and the great slump.' *Essays in applied economics.* London: King, 1923.
Revised edition. 1924. p. 34–40.
From the *Contemporary Review*, December 1921.

7329 **Clay**, *Sir* Henry. 'The course of employment since the war.' *Manchr. Statist. Soc. Trans.* (1928–29), 1–27.
Followed by discussion, i–xii.

7330 **Clark**, Colin Grant. 'A graphical analysis of the unemployment position, 1920–1928.' *R. Statist. Soc. J.*, XCII, 1 (1929), 74–99.
Frances Wood Memorial Prize Essay.

7331 **Clay**, *Sir* Henry. *The post-war unemployment problem.* London: Macmillan, 1929. x, 208p.

7332 **Griffith**, Ernest S. 'New analysis of unemployment.' *Sociol Rev.*, XXII, 2 (April 1930), 119–27.

7333 **Gayer**, A. D. *Unemployment in British industries, 1815–1850.* 1930–31. (D.Phil. thesis, University of Oxford.)

7334 **Clay**, *Sir* Henry. 'British unemployment and the world depression.' *Lloyds Bank Rev.*, n.s., III, 34 (December 1932), 514–29.

7335 **International Industrial Relations Institute**. *International unemployment: a study of fluctuations in employment and unemployment in several countries, 1910–1930.* The Hague, New York: the Institute, 1932. iii, 496p.
Contributed to the World Social Economic Congress, Amsterdam, August 1931.
Editor: M. L. Fleddérus.

7336 **Allen**, R. G. D. 'The unemployment situation at the outbreak of war.' *R. Statist. Soc. J.*, CIII, 2 (1940), 191–207.
Discussion, p. 207–17.

7337 **International Labour Office**. 'The impact of war on long-term unemployment in Great Britain.' *Int. Labour Rev.*, XLV, 1 (January 1942), 44–63.
Appendix, XLV, 3 (March 1942), 297–301.

7338 **Reubens**, Beatrice G. 'Unemployment in war-time Britain.' *Q. J. Econ.*, LIX, 2 (February 1945), 206–36.

7339 **Beck**, G. M. A. *A survey of British employment and unemployment, 1927–45.* Oxford: Oxford University Institute of Statistics, 1951. v, 87p.

7340 **Leser**, Conrad Emanuel Victor. 'Variations in unemployment rates.' *Oxf. Univ. Inst. Statist. Bull.*, XIII, 1 (January 1951), 23–31.

7341 **United Nations**. *Problems of unemployment and inflation 1950 and 1951.* New York: U.N., 1951. 173p. (ST/ECA/12.)

An analysis of replies by governments to questionnaires with selected replies from U.K. and others.

7342 **Carney**, James Joseph. *Institutional change and the level of employment: a study of British unemployment, 1918–1929.* Coral Gables, Fla.: U. of Miami P., 1956. vi, 129p. (University of Miami publications in economics 1.)

7343 **Hancock**, Keith J. *The problem of unemployment in the United Kingdom, 1919–1929.* 1959. (Ph.D. thesis, University of London.)

7344 **Kalachek**, Edward and **Westebbe**, Richard. 'Rates of unemployment in Great Britain and the United States, 1950–1960.' *Rev. Econ. Statist.*, XLIII, 4 (November 1961), 340–50.

7345 **Gillion**, C. and **Black**, I. 'Some characteristics of unemployment.' *Nat. Inst. Econ. Rev.*, 37 (August 1966), 33–8.

Analysis of figures during the preceding 10–15 years.

7346 **O'Boyle**, Lenore. 'The problem of an excess of educated men in Western Europe, 1800–1850.' *J. Mod. Hist.*, XLII, 4 (December 1970), 471–95.

England, Germany, France.

See also: 7542.

5. Regional Studies

See also Part Six, II, C, 2; and Part Seven, IV, D, 3.

a. COMPARATIVE

7347 **Ministry of Labour.** *Investigations into the industrial conditions in certain depressed areas.* London: H.M.S.O., 1934. 240p. (Cmd. 4728.)

I. Cumberland and Haltwhistle. (By J. C. C. Davidson.)

II. Durham and Tyneside. (By D. Euan Wallace.)

III. South Wales and Monmouthshire. (By Sir Wyndham Portal.)

IV. Scotland. (By Sir A. Rose.)

7348 **Greenwood**, Harry Powys. *Employment and the depressed areas.* London: Routledge, 1936. xiii, 167p.

7349 **Hannington**, Walter. *The problem of the distressed areas.* London: Gollancz, 1937. 286p.

Also Left Book Club edition.

7350 **Champernowne**, D. G. 'The uneven distribution of unemployment in the United Kingdom, 1929–36.' *Rev. Econ. Studies*, V, 2 (February 1938), 93–106; VI, 2 (February 1939), 111–26.

7351 **Singer**, Hans Wolfgang. 'The process of unemployment in the depressed areas (1935–1938).' *Rev. Econ. Studies*, VI, 3 (June 1939), 177–88.

7352 **Singer**, Hans Wolfgang. 'Regional labour markets and the process of unemployment.' *Rev. Econ. Studies*, VII, 1 (October 1939), 42–58.

7353 **Sykes**, Joseph L. 'Some results of distribution of industry policy.' *Manchr. Sch.*, XXIII, 1 (January 1955), 1–21.

7354 **Dunning**, John Harry. 'The development areas: a further note.' *Manchr. Sch.*, XXIV, 1 (January 1956), 77–92.

'The purpose of this note is to provide elementary statistical information about some of the employment and industrial trends referred to in' the article by J. Sykes, January 1955.

7355 **Sykes**, Joseph L. 'Local unemployment.' *Three Banks Rev.*, 39 (September 1958), 20–32.

7356 **Sykes**, Joseph L. 'Employment and unemployment in regions and the development areas.' *Scott. J. Polit. Econ.*, VI, 3 (November 1959), 193–210.

'Changes in employment 1949–57, and differences between areas.' (Townroe.)

7357 **Federation of British Industries.** *The regional problem: a study of the areas of high unemployment.* London: F.B.I., 1963. 7p.

7358 **Hunter**, Laurence Colvin. 'Employment and unemployment in Great Britain: some regional considerations.' *Manchr. Sch.*, XXXI, 1 (January 1963), 21–38.

7359 **Shinton**, D. A. *Post-war regional unemployment and development.* 1965. (M.A. thesis, University of Exeter.)

7360 **Thirlwall**, A. P. 'Regional unemployment as a cyclical phenomenon.' *Scott. J. Polit. Econ.*, XIII, 2 (June 1966), 205–19.

7361 **Brechling**, Frank P. R. 'Trends and cycles in British regional unemployment.' *Oxf. Econ. Pap.*, n.s., XIX, 1 (March 1967), 1–21.

7362 **Davies**, Glyn. 'Regional unemployment, labour availability, and redeployment.' *Oxf. Econ. Pap.*, n.s., XIX, 1 (March 1967), 59–74.

7363 **Tandon**, B. B. 'The regional problem of unemployment.' *Indian J. Labour Econ.*, X, 3 (October 1967), 209–15.

7364 **Stilwell**, F. J. B. 'The regional distribution of concealed unemployment.' *Urb. Studies*, VII, 2 (June 1970), 209–14.

See also: 8077.

b. PARTICULAR REGIONS

7365 **Clerke**, E. M. 'The labour market of East London.' *Dublin Rev.*, CV (October 1889), 386–406.

7366 **Leeds Trades and Labour Council** and **Leeds Independent Labour Party.** Joint Committee. *The unemployed: a discussion of the causes of and remedies for scarcity of employment with special reference to Leeds.* Leeds, [189–?]. 16p.

7367 **Liverpool Labour Conference**. *Report of the Executive Committee, with recommendations for giving work to the unemployed*. Liverpool, 1893.

7368 **London County Council**. *Lack of employment in London*. London, 1903. 50p.

7369 **Woolwich (Borough)**. *Report of Conference . . . to consider the present and probable future lack of employment in the Borough*. 1903.

7370 **Camberwell (Borough)**. *Report of the... Unemployed Central Committee*. 1904.

7371 **Islington (Borough)**. *The unemployed: report of Conference*. 1904.

7372 **Leeds Fabian Society**. *Leeds and the unemployed*. 1905. 10p. (Tract 1.)

7373 **Metropolitan Borough of Hackney**. *Report of the joint committee of borough councillors and guardians of a census of unemployed for the borough of Hackney, 1904–1905*. London, 1905. 16p.

7374 **Woolwich Pioneer**. *The unemployed last winter: London, Woolwich*. 1905.

Reprinted from the *Woolwich Pioneer*.

7375 **Alington**, Charles W. 'Aspects of unemployment in West Ham.' *Econ. Rev.*, XVI, 1 (January 1906), 56–67.

7376 **Loch**, Charles Stewart. 'The problem of the unemployed.' *Char. Orgn. Rev.*, n.s., XX, 119 (November 1906), 239–64.

'Paper read at the Congress of the Institut International de Sociologie, held in London July 3–6, 1906.'

Mainly London.

7377 **Chapman**, *Sir* Sydney John and **Hallsworth**, Harry Mainwaring. *Unemployment: the results of an investigation made in Lancashire and an examination of the Report of the Poor Law Commission*. Manchester: U. of Manchester, 1909. xii, 164p. (Publications. Economic series 12.)

7378 **Birchall**, E. V. 'The conditions of distress: an investigation of 4000 Birmingham cases.' *Econ. Rev.*, XX, 1 (January 1910), 25–40.

From records of the City of Birmingham Aid Society.

7379 **Heath**, J. St. George. 'The war and unemployment among skilled men in London.' *Polit. Q.*, 5 (February 1915), 69–81.

7380 **Toynbee Hall**. *Unemployment in East London: the report of a survey made from Toynbee Hall*. London: King, 1922. 63p.

7381 **Eason**, J. C. M. 'Unemployment: its causes and their remedies.' *Statist. Soc. Inq. Soc. Tr. J.*, XV, 101 (October 1927), 229–38.

Mainly Ireland.

7382 **Hanham**, F. G. *Report of enquiry into casual labour in the Merseyside area*. Liverpool: H. Young, 1930. xiii, 190p.

7383 **Owen**, Arthur David Kemp. *A report on unemployment in Sheffield*. Sheffield: Sheffield Social Survey Committee, 1932. 74p. (Survey pamphlet 4.)

7384 **Evans**, Richard. *Unemployment in Hull*. Hull, 1933. 31p.

7385 **Pallister**, Minnie. 'Transforming a devastated town.' *Millg. M.* (February 1933), 267–9.

On Brynmawr.

7386 **Brynmawr**, Brecknockshire. Brynmawr Community Study Council. *Brynmawr: a study of a distressed area*. London: Allenson, 1934. xi, 246p.

Based on the results of the social survey carried out by the Brynmawr Community Study Council by Hilda Jennings.

7387 **New Statesman and Nation**. *What's wrong with South Wales?* London: *New Statesman and Nation*, 1935. 23p.

7388 **Sharp**, Thomas Wilfrid. *A derelict area: a study of the South-West Durham coalfield*. London: Woolf, 1935. 49p. (Day to day pamphlets 25.)

7389 **Oakley**, Charles Allen. 'Some psychological problems of a depressed area.' *Hum. Factor*, X, 11 (November 1936), 393–404.

'A paper read before Section J (Psychology) of the British Association Meeting at Blackpool, September 1936.'

7390 **Richardson**, John Henry. *Industrial employment and unemployment in West Yorkshire: a statistical review of recent trends*. London: Allen and Unwin, 1936. 142p.

7391 **Findlay**, Ronald Macdonald. *Scotland at the crossroads: self help or state aid*. Edinburgh: W. Bishop, 1937. vii, 135p.

7392 **Hall**, R. L. 'Unemployment.' Barnett House, Oxford. Survey Committee. *A survey of the social services in the Oxford district*. Vol. 1. London: Oxford U.P., 1938. p. 99–109.

7393 **Northern Ireland**. *Reports from the Select Committee on Unemployment in Northern Ireland*. 1941–42. 2 pts.

7394 **Cuthbert**, Norman. 'The employment problem in Northern Ireland.' *Banker*, XCIX, 320 (September 1952), 175–80.

7395 **Political and Economic Planning**. 'Social security and unemployment in Lancashire.' *Planning*, XIX, 349 (1 December 1952), 113–36.

7396 **Scottish Council (Development and Industry)**. *Report of the Committee on Unemployment in Aberdeen and District*. Edinburgh, 1952. 27p.

7397 **Sykes**, Joseph L. 'Remedies for cyclical unemployment in the north-east.' *Manchr. Sch.*, XX, 1 (January 1952), 85–102.

7398 **Rose**, Arthur Gordon. *The older unemployed man in Hull*. Hull: University College, Department of Social Studies, 1953. 38p.

Reproduced from typescript.

7399 **Smyth**, R. L. 'Male unemployment problems in large ports and urban areas with special reference to Kingston-upon-Hull.' *Yorks. Bull. Econ. Soc. Res.*, V, 2 (August 1953), 155–78.

7400 **Collinge**, H. *The problem of unemployment on Merseyside*. 1953–54. (M.A. thesis, University of Liverpool.)

7401 **Morgan**, Edward Victor. 'How serious is Welsh unemployment?' *Banker*, CVIII, 378 (April 1958), 252–6.

7402 **Robson**, Peter. 'Ulster's unemployment problem.' *Banker*, CVIII, 391 (August 1958), 529–33.

7403 **Awbery**, S. L. *Self-help and unemployment in Gwynedd*. 1961–62. (M.A. thesis, University of Wales, Aberystwyth.)

7404 **Aris**, Stephen. 'Struggles of a dying town.' *New Soc.*, 18 (31 January 1963), 9–10.

7405 **Black**, R. D. Collison. 'Employment prospects in Northern Ireland.' *Christus Rex*, XVIII, 4 (October–December 1964), 258–66.

7406 **Eire**. Committee on Industrial Organisation. *Fifth interim report: certain aspects of redundancy*. 1964. (I. 109/22.)

7407 **Smith**, Louis P. F. 'Employment prospects in the Republic of Ireland.' *Christus Rex*, XVIII, 4 (October–December 1964), 246–57.

7408 **Lancashire and Merseyside Industrial Development Association**. *The problems of seasonal employment and labour supply in the coastal towns of Lancashire*. Manchester: the Association, 1965. 32p.

7409 **Salt**, John. *A consideration of some post-war unemployment problems in the Merseyside and Manchester conurbations*. 1966–67. (Ph.D. thesis, University of Liverpool.)

7410 **Barr**, John. 'Whitehaven waits for work.' *New Soc.*, x, 253 (3 August 1967), 157–8.
'Society at work.'

7411 **Salt**, John. 'The impact of the Ford and Vauxhall plants on the employment situation of Merseyside, 1962–1965.' *Tijdschr. Econ. Soc. Geogr.*, LVIII, 5 (September–October 1967), 255–64.

7412 **Steane**, J. M. 'The poor in Rothwell, 1750–1840.' *Northamps. Past Pres.*, IV, 3 (1968), 143–8.
Particularly the unemployed.

7413 **Showler**, Brian. *An analysis of the characteristics of adult unemployment in the sub-region of Humberside since 1951*. 1969. (M.Sc. Econ. thesis, University of Hull.)

7414 **Cunningham**, N. J. 'Unemployment on Merseyside, 1957–67.' Lawton, R. and Cunningham, C. M. (eds.). *Merseyside: social and economic studies*. London: Longman, 1970. p. 202–34.

7415 **Geary**, R. C. and **Hughes**, J. G. *Certain aspects of non-agricultural unemployment in Ireland*. Dublin: Economic and Social Research Institute, 1970. 33p. (Paper 52.)

7416 **Gittus**, Elizabeth. 'A study of the unemployed of Merseyside.' Lawton, R. and Cunningham, C. M. (eds.). *Merseyside: social and economic studies*. London: Longman, 1970. p. 324–73.

7417 **Stedman Jones**, G. *Some social consequences of the casual labour problem in London 1860–90, with particular reference to the East End*. 1970. (D.Phil. thesis, University of Oxford.)

See also: 4516; 7419; 7421; 7444–5; 7447–9; 7460; 7462–3; 7466–7; 7470; 7472; 7474–5.

6. Occupational and Industrial Studies

See also Part Six, II, C, 3; and Part Seven, IV, D, 4.

7418 **Fielden**, John C. 'On the employment of surplus labour, more especially during periods of commercial depression.' *Manchr. Statist. Soc. Trans.* (1881–82), 141–58.
Mainly cotton trade.

7419 **Dearle**, Norman Burrell. *Problems of unemployment in the London building trades*. London: Dent, 1908. xix, 203p. (A Toynbee Trust essay.)

7420 **Popplewell**, Frank. 'Seasonal fluctuations in employment in the gas industry.' *R. Statist. Soc. J.*, LXXIV, 7 (June 1911), 693–730.
Discussion, p. 730–4.

7421 **Dearle**, Norman Burrell. *Problems of unemployment in the London building trades*. 1915. (D.Sc. (Econ.) thesis, University of London.)

7422 **Mess**, Henry Adolphus. *Casual labour at the docks*. London: Bell, 1916. 147p. (Ratan Tata Foundation. Publications.)

7423 **International Labour Office**. 'Seasonal unemployment in the clothing industries.' *Int. Labour Rev.*, XVIII, 1 (July 1928), 1–28; 2 (August 1928), 184–201.

7424 **Campbell**, C. Douglas. 'Cyclical fluctuations in the railway industry.' *Manchr. Statist. Soc. Trans.* (1929–30).
1870–1928, with particular reference to unemployment figures.

7425 **Jewkes**, John and **Winterbottom**, Allan. 'Unrecorded unemployment in the cotton industry.' *Econ. J.*, XLI, 164 (December 1931), 639–46.

7426 **Railway Clerks' Association**. *The case for safeguarding railway employment. Submitted by A. G. Walkden to the Railway Pool Committee*. London, 1932. 119p.

7427 **Railway Clerks' Association.** *Railway pooling proposals and joint working arrangements . . . Employees' case for safeguards as submitted to the Railway Pool Committee, October 31–November 2, 1932. (Mr A. G. Walkden examined by Sir William Jowitt.)* London, 1932. 63p.

7428 **Liberal Women's Unemployment Enquiry Group.** *Report: Section 1. Agricultural employment; Section 2. 'Black-coated' unemployment; Section 3. The means test*. London, 1934. 18p.

7429 **Gash**, N. 'Rural unemployment, 1815–34.' *Econ. Hist. Rev.*, VI, 1 (October 1935), 90–3.

7430 **Kotschnig**, Walter Maria. *Unemployment in the learned professions: an international study of occupational and educational planning*. London: Oxford U.P., 1937. xi, 347p.

7431 **Gray**, Edward Mayall. 'Under-employment in cotton weaving: a recent wages census.' *Manchr. Sch.*, x, 1 (1939), 62–76.

7432 **Turner**, Herbert Arthur. 'Unemployment in textiles: a note and some conclusions.' *Oxf. Univ. Inst. Statist. Bull.*, xv, 8 (August 1953), 295–306.

7433 **Jenkins**, Clive. *Jets and jobs: disarmament and the workers.* London: Union of Democratic Control, 1960. 16p.

7434 **Naylor**, Rachel. 'Redundancy in cotton.' *New Soc.*, 25 (21 March 1963), 10–13.

7435 **Cook**, Pauline Lesley. 'Contraction in the workshops.' *New Soc.*, iv, 95 (23 July 1964), 12–14.

7436 **Cook**, Pauline Lesley. *Railway workshops: the problems of contraction.* Cambridge: Cambridge U.P., 1964. viii, 92p. (University of Cambridge. Department of Applied Economics. Occasional paper 2.)

'The planning of contraction and redundancy, 1962–7.' p. 71–88.

7437 **Wedderburn**, Dorothy. 'White collar redundancy.' *New Soc.*, iii, 75 (5 March 1964), 16–17.

'Welfare & work.'

'This article discusses some of the material from the author's *White-collar redundancy: a case study.*'

7438 **Wedderburn**, Dorothy. *White-collar redundancy: a case study.* Cambridge: Cambridge U.P., 1964. vii, 56p. (University of Cambridge. Department of Applied Economics. Occasional papers 1.)

7439 **United Nations Association.** Working Party on Disarmament and Jobs. *Disarmament and jobs.* London: U.N.A., 1965. 30p.

7440 **Wedderburn**, Dorothy. *Redundancy and the railwaymen.* Cambridge: Cambridge U.P., 1965. 239p. (University of Cambridge. Department of Applied Economics. Occasional papers 4.)

7441 **Wedderburn**, Dorothy. 'Redundant railwaymen.' *New Soc.*, vi, 145 (8 July 1965), 12–14.

Based on the author's *Redundancy and the railwaymen.*

7442 **Smith**, A. D. *Redundancy practices in four industries: a comparison of structural redundancy practices in the railway, steel, cotton textiles and telecommunications industries of the United States and the United Kingdom.* Paris: Organisation for Economic Co-operation and Development, 1966. 129p. (Industrial relations aspects of manpower policy 3.)

7443 **Barratt Brown**, Michael. 'What will the miners do now?' *New Soc.*, x, 269 (23 November 1967), 734–6.

7444 **House**, John William and **Knight**, Elizabeth Mary. *Pit closure & the community: report to the Ministry of Labour.* Newcastle-upon-Tyne: University of Newcastle-upon-Tyne (Department of Geography), 1967. [6], 144p. (Papers on migration and mobility in Northern England 5.)

7445 **Sams**, K. I. and **Simpson**, J. V. 'A case study of a shipbuilding redundancy in Northern Ireland.' *Scott. J. Polit. Econ.*, xv, 3 (November 1968), 267–82.

7446 **Shenfield**, Barbara E. 'Security of employment: a study in the construction industry.' *Planning*, xxxiv, 505 (November 1968). iv, 66p.

7447 **Elliott**, B. J. *The social and economic effects of unemployment in the coal and steel industries of Sheffield between 1925 and 1935.* 1968–69. (M.A. thesis, University of Sheffield.)

7448 **Snaith**, W. 'The adjustment of the labour force on the Durham coalfield: a study of redundancy.' *Econ. Studies*, iv, 1–2 (October 1969), 239–52.

7449 **Department of Employment and Productivity.** *Ryhope: a pit closes. A study in redeployment.* London: H.M.S.O., 1970. 148p.

See also: 4556; 4574; 4995; 7316; 7388; 7674.

7. Studies of Particular Aspects and Groups

This section includes works which discuss unemployment in relation to age and sex, as well as those dealing with juvenile unemployment, executive unemployment, and unemployment among women.

7450 **Committee on Civil Employment of Ex-soldiers and Sailors.** *Report, appendices.* London: H.M.S.O., 1906. 73p. (Cd. 2991.)

Minutes of evidence, etc. 1906. (Cd. 2992.)

Chairman: E. W. D. Ward.

7451 **Kittermaster**, D. B. 'Unemployment and boy labour.' *St. George*, x, 37 (January 1907), 1–10.

7452 **National Conference on the Unemployment of Women Dependent on Their Own Earnings.** *Report.* London, 1907. 39p.

7453 **Hamilton**, C. J. 'Unemployment in relation to age and accident.' National Conference on the Prevention of Destitution. *Report of the proceedings . . . 1911.* London: King, 1911. p. 460–6.

Discussion, p. 472–81.

7454 **Morrison**, G. B. 'Age and unemployment.' *R. Statist. Soc. J.*, lxxiv, 8 (July 1911), 863–8.

7455 **Tawney**, Jeanette. 'Women and unemployment.' *Econ. J.*, xxi, 81 (March 1911), 131–9.

7456 **Greenwood**, Arthur and **Kettlewell**, John E. 'Some statistics of juvenile employment and unemployment.' *R. Statist. Soc. J.*, lxxv, 7 (June 1912), 744–53.

7457 **Fabian Society.** Women's Group Executive. *The war, women, and unemployment.* London: Fabian Society, 1915. 28p. (Fabian tract 178. Fabian Women's Group series 5.)

7458 **Morley**, Felix. 'The incidence of unemployment by age and sex.' *Econ. J.*, XXXII, 128 (December 1922), 477–88.

7459 **Griffin**, J. R. 'Unemployment. II. The ex-Service man.' *Nineteenth Century*, XCV (April 1924), 523–9.

7460 **Allen**, Edward. 'Unemployment amongst boys in Sheffield.' *Economica*, V, 14 (June 1925), 180–90.

7461 **Eagar**, Waldo McGillycuddy and **Secretan**, Hubert Arthur. *Unemployment among boys*. London, Toronto: Dent, 1925. xii, 164p.
With an introduction by H. A. L. Fisher.

7462 **Roker**, Peter and **Scott**, H. Crawford. 'Juvenile unemployment in West Ham.' *Economica*, VI, 16 (March 1926), 58–77.

7463 **Roker**, Peter. *I. Juvenile unemployment in West Ham. II. The making of a casual*. London, 1927. 2 pts.

7464 **Hughes**, D. E. R. 'A comparative study of unemployed and employed boys.' *Sociol. Rev.*, XX, 4 (October 1928), 310–21.

7465 **Diepenhorst**, Isaac Nicolaas Theodoor. *Juvenile unemployment and how to deal with it*. Amsterdam: Drukkerij Holland, 1931. 296, iii p.

7466 **Bevington**, Sheila Macfarlane. *Factors in occupational maladjustment: a comparative study of the careers of employed and unemployed lads in a typical London district*. 1932–33. (Ph.D. thesis, University of London.)

7467 **Bevington**, Sheila Macfarlane. *Occupational misfits: a comparative study of North London boys employed and unemployed*. London: Allen and Unwin, 1933. 102p.

7468 **Jewkes**, John and **Winterbottom**, Allan. *Juvenile unemployment*. London: Allen and Unwin, 1933. 159p.
Manchester University, Department of Economics and Commerce, Research Section.

7469 **Save the Children Fund**. Unemployment Enquiry Committee. *Unemployment and the child: being the report of an enquiry . . . into the effects of unemployment on the children of the unemployed and on unemployed young workers of Great Britain*. London: Longmans, Green, 1933. 136p.

7470 **Sheffield Social Survey Committee**. *A survey of juvenile employment and welfare in Sheffield*. Sheffield: the Committee, 1933. 48p. (Survey pamphlets 6.)

7471 **Tawney**, Richard Henry. *The school-leaving age and juvenile unemployment*. London: Workers' Educational Association, 1934. 31p.

7472 **Meara**, Gwyn. *Juvenile unemployment in the South Wales industrial region: an economic and statistical enquiry, with special reference to* (*a*) *the incidence of juvenile unemployment in certain industries and districts of the region;* (*b*) *the remedies proposed; and* (*c*) *the work of ameliorative agencies among the juvenile unemployed*. 1935. (Ph.D. thesis, University of Wales, Cardiff.)

7473 **Tait**, D. Christie. 'Unemployment of young people in Great Britain.' *Int. Labour Rev.*, XXXI, 2 (February 1935), 166–89.

7474 **Meara**, Gwynne. *Juvenile unemployment in South Wales*. Cardiff: Gwasg Prifysgol Cymru, 1936. 141p.
A thesis.

7475 **Lush**, Archibald James. *The young adult, being a report prepared in cooperation with young men in Cardiff, Newport and Pontypridd, under the auspices of the Carnegie United Kingdom Trust*. Cardiff: University of Wales Press for South Wales and Monmouthshire Council of Social Service, 1941. vi, 89p.

7476 **Eire**. Commission on Youth Unemployment, 1951. [Report.] 1952. (R.82.)

7477 **Martin**, John Powell. *Offenders as employees: an enquiry by the Cambridge Institute of Criminology*. London: Macmillan; New York: St Martin's P., 1962. xiii, 178p. (Cambridge studies in criminology 16.)

7478 **Bugler**, Jeremy. 'The redundant boss.' *New Soc.*, XIII, 342 (17 April 1969), 585–6.

7479 **Institute of Personnel Management**. *Executive redundancy and obsolescence*. London: I.P.M., 1970. 69p. (Information reports. New series 5.)
Prepared by C. Howard.

7480 **Smyth**, David J. and **Lowe**, Peter D. 'The vestibule to the occupational ladder and unemployment: some econometric evidence on United Kingdom structural unemployment.' *Ind. Labor Relat. Rev.*, XXIII, 4 (July 1970), 561–5.

See also: 10,312; 10,362; 10,381; 10,384.

E. LABOUR MOBILITY

1. General

In addition to including literature which covers more than one aspect of labour mobility, this section contains works dealing with the movement of labour between countries. Literature on the movement of labour into the United Kingdom is classified at Part Six, II, E, 2, and that on the movement of labour from the United Kingdom is classified at Part Six, II, E, 3.

7481 **Economic Advisory Council**. Committee on Empire Migration. *Report*. London: H.M.S.O., 1932. 90p. (Cmd. 4075.)
Chairman: Lord Astor.

7482 **Robinson**, H. W. *Labour mobility: its measurement and causes*. 1939. (D.Phil. thesis, University of Oxford.)

7483 **Rostowski**, Roman. *A study of the economics of international migration 1820–1914*. 1942–43. (Ph.D. thesis, University of Edinburgh.)

7484 **Isaac**, J. *Economics of migration*. 1943. (Ph.D. thesis, University of London.)

7485 **Moxon**, H. F. *Labour mobility in Great Britain: an examination of the extent, character, and motives of movements of labour, with special reference to the period since 1945.* 1951. (B.Litt thesis, University of Oxford.)

7486 **Social Survey**. *Labour mobility in Great Britain 1945–1949.* [1953.] 80p. (Report 134.)
By Geoffrey Thomas.
'An inquiry carried out for the Ministry of Labour and National Service.'

7487 **Thomas**, Geoffrey. 'The mobility of labour in Great Britain.' *Occup. Psychol.*, XXVII, 4 (October 1953), 215–20.
A paper read at a meeting of the Industrial Section of the British Psychological Society, London, 7 July 1953.

7488 **Lannes**, Xavier. 'International mobility of manpower in Western Europe.' *Int. Labour Rev.*, LXXIII, 1 (January 1956), 1–24; 2 (February 1956), 135–51.

7489 **Thomas**, Brinley. 'International movements of capital and labour since 1945.' *Int. Labour Rev.*, LXXIV, 3 (September 1956), 225–38.

7490 **Political and Economic Planning**. 'Britain and Commonwealth migration.' *Planning*, XXIII, 409 (15 April 1957), 69–83.

7491 **Robinson**, E. 'The international exchange of men and machines, 1750–1800, as seen in the business records of Matthew Boulton.' *Bus. Hist.*, I, 1 (December 1958), 3–15.

7492 **Levens**, G. E. *A study of the occupational and social mobility of 'white-collar criminals' after their discharge from prison.* 1963–64. (M.Sc. thesis, University of London.)

7493 **Organisation for Economic Co-operation and Development**. International Joint Seminar on Geographical and Occupational Mobility of Manpower, Castelfusano, 19th to 22nd November, 1963. *Final report.* Paris: O.E.C.D., Manpower and Social Affairs Directorate, Social Affairs Division, 1964. 213p. (International seminars 1963—3.)

7494 **Elliott**, C. K. *International labour mobility and age: a study of job change among factory workers over thirty years of age.* 1964–65. (Ph.D. thesis, University of Liverpool.)

7495 **Organisation for Economic Co-operation and Development**. *Wages and labour mobility: a report by a group of independent experts on the relation between changes in wage differentials and the pattern of employment with a foreword on the implications of the study for incomes policy by Pieter de Wolff.* Paris: O.E.C.D., 1965. 258p.
Supplement 1. *Abstracts of selected articles.*
Supplement 2. *Statistical data.* 1967. 159p.

7496 **Government Social Survey**. *Labour mobility in Great Britain, 1953–63.* London: H.M.S.O., 1966. 138p. (SS. 333.)
By Amelia I. Harris assisted by Rosemary Clausen.
'An enquiry undertaken for the Ministry of Labour and National Service in 1963.'
Reissued 1968.

7497 **Smith**, John Harold. 'The analysis of labour mobility.' Roberts, B. C. and Smith, J. R. (eds.). *Manpower policy and employment trends.* London: Bell for the London School of Economics and Political Science, 1966. p. 89–97.

7498 **Smith**, John Harold. 'Labour mobility in advanced technological societies.' Stieber, J. (ed.). *Employment problems of automation and advanced technology: an international perspective.* London: Macmillan; New York: St Martin's P., 1966. p. 278–94.
Discussion, p. 294–7.

7499 **Parker**, Stanley Robert. 'The labour force and mobility.' Parker, S. R., and others. *The sociology of industry.* London: Allen and Unwin, 1967. p. 138–46.

7500 **Reid**, Graham Livingstone and **Hunter**, Laurence Colvin. 'Integration and labor mobility.' Barkin, S., and others (eds.). *International labor.* New York, Evanston, London: Harper and Row, 1967. p. 175–201.

7501 **Thomas**, Brinley. 'The international circulation of human capital.' *Minerva*, V, 4 (Summer 1967), 479–506.

7502 **Adams**, Walter (ed.). *The brain drain.* New York: Macmillan; London: Collier-Macmillan, 1968. xiii, 273p.
Papers presented at an international conference held at Lausanne, Switzerland, August 1967.

7503 **Hunter**, Laurence Colvin. 'Income structure and labour mobility.' Roberts, B. C. (ed.). *Industrial relations: contemporary issues . . .* London: Macmillan; New York: St Martin's P., 1968. p. 305–20.

7504 **Beijer**, G. 'Brain drain as a burden, a stimulus, and a challenge to European integration.' Bechhofer, F. (ed.). *Population growth and the brain drain.* Edinburgh: Edinburgh U.P., 1969. p. 3–30.
'Comments', by R. Illsley, p. 57–62.
'General discussion', p. 63–71.

7505 **Fleming**, Donald Harnish and **Bailyn**, Bernard (eds.). *The intellectual migration: Europe and America, 1930–1960.* Cambridge, Mass.: Belknap P. of Harvard U.P., 1969. 748p.

7506 **Last**, John M. 'International mobility in the medical profession.' Bechhofer, F. (ed.). *Population growth and the brain drain.* Edinburgh: Edinburgh U.P., 1969. p. 31–42.
'Comments', by R. Illsley, p. 57–62.
'General discussion', p. 63–71.

7507 **Daniel**, William Wentworth. 'Strategies for displaced employees.' *PEP Broad.*, XXXV, 517 (January 1970), iv, 85p.

7508 **Oldham**, C. H. G. *International migration of talent from and to the less-developed countries: report of a conference at Ditchley Park, 16–19*

February 1968. Enstone: Ditchley Foundation, 1970. 29p. (Ditchley paper 13.)
See also: 74; 11,399.

2. Immigration

This section includes works dealing with immigrants and the process of immigration. The emphasis is on the employment aspects of these subjects, and material relating to the non-work aspects of race relations has generally been excluded. See also Part Three, III, F, 1–2.

7509 **White**, Arnold. 'The invasion of pauper foreigners.' *Nineteenth Century*, XXIII, 133 (March 1888), 414–22.

7510 **Jeyes**, S. H. 'Foreign pauper immigration.' *Fortn. Rev.*, n.s., L, 295 (July 1891), 13–24.

7511 **Dunraven**, *Earl of*. 'The invasion of destitute aliens.' *Nineteenth Century*, XXXI, 184 (June 1892), 985–1000.

7512 **Wilkins**, William Henry. *The alien invasion*. London: Methuen, 1892. xii, 192p.

7513 **Hourwich**, Isaac A. 'The Jewish laborer in London.' *J. Polit. Econ.*, XIII, 1 (December 1904), 89–98.
Review of *Die jüdischen Arbeiter in London*, by Georg Halpern. München: Brentano und Lotz, 1903. 84p.

7514 **Samuel**, Herbert. 'Immigration.' *Econ. J.*, XV, 59 (September 1905), 317–39.

7515 **Landa**, M. J. 'The economic aspect of alien labour.' *Econ. Rev.*, XVI, 1 (January 1906), 43–55.

7516 **McLauchlan**, Francis. '"Polish labour" in the Scottish mines, from the miner's point of view.' *Econ. J.*, XVII, 66 (June 1907), 287–9.

7517 **Departmental Committee on Belgian Refugees.** *First report, appendices*. London: H.M.S.O., 1914. iv, 62p. (Cd. 7750.)
Minutes of evidence, etc. 1915. (Cd. 7779.)
Chairman: E. Hatch.

7518 **Salway**, Cyril Claude. *Refugees and industry*. London: Williams and Norgate, 1942. 23p.

7519 **Watson**, Arnold R. *West Indian workers in Britain*. London: Hodder and Stoughton, 1942. 24p.

7520 **International Labour Office**. 'The transfer of Irish workers to Great Britain.' *Int. Labour Rev.*, XLVIII, 3 (September 1943), 338–42.

7521 **Political and Economic Planning**. 'Refugees in Britain.' *Planning*, 216 (14 January 1944), 1–11.
A modified version also published as a pamphlet under the title *Are refugees an asset?*

7522 **Cohen**, Israel. *The economic value of refugees*. Letchworth: Garden City P., 1945. 7p.
Reprinted from *Contemporary Review*.

7523 **Political and Economic Planning**. 'British immigration policy.' *Planning*, XIV, 268 (4 July 1947), 17–36.

7524 **Richmond**, Anthony Henry. 'Relation between skill and adjustment of a group of West Indian Negro workers in England.' *Occup. Psychol.*, XXV, 3 (July 1951), 153–65.
Part of a wider enquiry at the time being prepared for publication.

7525 **Stadulis**, Elizabeth. 'The resettlement of displaced persons in the United Kingdom.' *Populat. Studies*, V, 3 (March 1952), 207–37.
'This study is an attempt to survey broadly some of the principles and results of the labour schemes, launched by the British Government after 1946, to bring to the United Kingdom a large and mixed group of refugees.'

7526 **Watson**, W. 'British and foreign immigrant miners in Fife.' *Manchr. Sch.*, XX, 2 (May 1952), 203–11.

7527 **Banton**, Michael. 'The economic and social position of Negro immigrants in Britain.' *Sociol. Rev.*, n.s., I, 2 (December 1953), 43–62.

7528 **Bülbring**, Maud. 'Post-war refugees in Great Britain.' *Populat. Studies*, VIII, 2 (November 1954), 99–112.

7529 **Hecht**, Joseph Jean. *Continental and colonial servants in eighteenth-century England*. Northampton, Mass.: Smith College, 1954. iv, 61p. (Studies in history 40.)

7530 **Richmond**, Anthony Henry. *Colour prejudice in Britain: a study of West Indian workers in Liverpool, 1941–1951*. London: Routledge and Kegan Paul, 1954. xi, 184p. (International library of sociology and social reconstruction.)

7531 **International Labour Office**. 'Post-war migration of West Indians to Great Britain.' *Int. Labour Rev.*, LXXIV, 2 (August 1956), 193–209.

7532 **Reid**, Janet. 'Employment of Negroes in Manchester.' *Sociol. Rev.*, n.s., IV, 2 (December 1956), 199–211.

7533 **Stephens**, Leslie. *Employment of coloured workers in the Birmingham area: report of an enquiry initiated by the Birmingham Christian Social Council and undertaken by the Race Relations Group of Fircroft College, Birmingham*. London: Institute of Personnel Management, 1956. 30p. (Occasional paper 10.)

7534 **Eggington**, Joyce. *They seek a living*. London: Hutchinson, 1957. 192p.
On West Indian emigration to Britain.

7535 **Tannahill**, John Allan. *European volunteer workers in Britain*. Manchester: Manchester U.P., 1958. x, 143p.

7536 **Desai**, R. H. *The social organisation of Indian migrant labour in the United Kingdom, with special reference to the Midlands*. 1959–60. (M.A. thesis, University of London.)

7537 **Aurora**, G. S. *Indian workers in England: a sociological and historical survey*. 1960. (M.Sc. (Econ.) thesis, University of London.)

7538 **Hendon Overseas Friendship Association**. *Foreign girls in Hendon*. London: the Association, 1961. 80p.

A survey by Sheila Williams and F. D. Flower.

7539 **Desai**, R. H. *Some aspects of social relations between Indian immigrants in the United Kingdom and the host society, with particular reference to economic activities.* 1961–62. (Ph.D. thesis, University of London.)

7540 **Chadwick-Jones**, John K. 'Inter-group attitudes: a stage in attitude formation.' *Br. J. Sociol.*, XIII, 1 (March 1962), 57–63.

'Research note.'

Attitudes towards Italian workers near Swansea both in the community and in a factory.

7541 **Ministry of Labour.** *Commonwealth Immigrants Act, 1962: notice to prospective employers.* London: H.M.S.O., 1962. 2p.

7542 **Davison**, Robert Barry. 'Immigration and unemployment in the United Kingdom, 1955–1962.' *Br. J. Ind. Relat.*, I, 1 (February 1963), 43–61.

7543 **Economist Intelligence Unit.** *The employment of immigrants.* London: E.I.U., 1963. 16p. (Studies on immigration from the Commonwealth 4.)

7544 **Nottingham Council of Social Service.** Commonwealth Citizens Consultative Committee. *Report on a survey of West Indians at work.* Nottingham: N.C.S.S., 1963. 36p.

7545 **Bayliss**, Frederick Joseph and **Coates**, J. B. 'West Indians at work.' *New Soc.*, IV, 92 (2 July 1964), 14–15.

7546 **Chadwick-Jones**, John K. 'The acceptance and socialization of immigrant workers in the steel industry.' *Sociol. Rev.*, n.s., XII, 2 (July 1964), 169–83.

7547 **Home Office.** *'Au pair' in Britain.* London: Central Office of Information, 1964. 28p.

7548 **Industrial Welfare Society.** *Employment of immigrants: a review.* London: I.W.S., 1964. 5p.

7549 **Israel**, W. H. *Colour and community: a study of coloured immigrants and race relations in an industrial town.* Slough: Council of Social Service, 1964. vi, 127p. tables.

7550 **Ng**, K. C. *Chinese restaurant workers in London.* 1964. (M.A. thesis, London School of Economics.)

7551 **Bayliss**, Frederick Joseph and **Coates**, J. B. 'West Indians at work in Nottingham.' *Race*, VII, 2 (October 1965), 157–66.

7552 **Chadwick-Jones**, John K. 'Italian workers in a British factory: a study of informal selection and training.' *Race*, VI, 3 (January 1965), 191–8.

7553 **Joshi**, S. *Coloured immigrants in industry in Birmingham.* 1965. (M.A. dissertation, University of Bradford.)

7554 **Torode**, John A. 'Race moves in on the unions.' *New Soc.*, V, 12 (17 June 1965), 5–7.

7555 **Fossick**, S. *Factors affecting the distribution of coloured immigrants in industry in Birmingham.* 1965–66. (M.Soc.Sc. thesis, University of Birmingham.)

7556 **Brittan**, E. *Some aspects of the life of coloured immigrants in Walsall: a sociological analysis of housing and employment.* 1966. (Dissertation for B.A. degree, University of Bradford.)

7557 **Jackson**, J. A. 'Irish immigrants and English labour.' *Soc. Study Labour Hist. Bull.*, 12 (Spring 1966), 5–6.

Abstract of a paper given at a conference of the Society for the Study of Labour History, November 1965.

Discussion, p. 6–9.

7558 **Lerner**, Shirley. 'The impact of the Jewish immigration of 1880–1914 on the London clothing industry and trade unions.' *Soc. Study Labour Hist. Bull.*, 12 (Spring 1966), 12–14.

Abstract of a paper given at a conference of the Society for the Study of Labour History, November 1965.

Discussion, p. 14–15.

7559 **Stokes**, A. J. *Immigrant workers in Sheffield.* Sheffield: the author, 1966. 4p. tables.

7560 **Thomas**, Brinley. *The economics of the immigration white paper.* London: Institute of Race Relations, 1966. 6p.

Paper presented at R.A.I./I.R.R. Conference, London, April 1966.

7561 **Wright**, Peter L. *The coloured worker in British industry with special reference to the Midlands and North of England.* 1966. (Ph.D. thesis, University of Edinburgh.)

7562 **Conference on Racial Equality in Employment**, London, February 1967. *Report.* London: National Committee for Commonwealth Immigrants, 1967. 107p.

7563 **Hattingh**, Ivan. *Race relations and the engineering industry.* London: Engineering Employers' Federation, 1967. 10p.

7564 **Hepple**, Bob. *Business and employment.* London: Institute of Race Relations, 1967. 12p.

Paper presented to second Race Relations Conference, London, September 1967.

7565 **Hepple**, Bob. *The position of coloured workers in British industry.* London: National Committee for Commonwealth Immigrants, 1967. 51p.

Paper prepared for the Conference on Racial Equality in Employment, London, February 1967.

7566 **Keighley Junior Chamber of Commerce.** *Immigration project: prospects for school-leavers in Keighley.* Keighley: K.J.C.C., 1967. 9p.

7567 **Lester**, Anthony and **Deakin**, Nicholas (eds.). *Policies for racial equality.* London: Fabian Society, 1967. 40p. (Research series 262.)

'Employment 1', by Jack Jones, p. 15–17.

'Employment 2', by Bob Hepple, p. 18–21.

7568 **Patterson**, Sheila. 'A hardening colour bar? 2. The jobs.' *New Soc.*, IX, 233 (16 March 1967), 380–2.

7569 **Peach**, G. C. K. 'West Indians as a replacement population in England and Wales.' *Soc. Econ. Studies*, XVI (September 1967), 289–94.

7570 **West Indian Standing Conference.** London Region. *The unsquare deal: London's bus colour bar.* London: W.I.S.C., 1967. 6p.

7571 **Buckman**, J. *The economic and social history of alien immigrants to Leeds, 1880–1914.* 1967–68. (Ph.D. thesis, University of Strathclyde.)

7572 **Choo**, N. K. *The Chinese in London.* London: Oxford U.P., 1968. ix, 92p.

7573 **Cohen**, B. G. and **Jenner**, P. J. 'The employment of immigrants: a case study within the wool industry.' *Race*, x, 1 (July 1968), 41–56.

7574 **Council of Europe.** *Social services for migrant workers.* Strasbourg: C. of E., 1968.

7575 **Daniel**, William Wentworth. *Racial discrimination in England.* Harmondsworth: Penguin Books, 1968. 251, 18p. (Penguin special S257.)

Based on the P.E.P. report *Racial discrimination in Britain.*

7576 **Hepple**, Bob. 'Ethnic minorities at work.' *Race*, x, 1 (July 1968), 17–30.

7577 **Hepple**, Bob. *Race, jobs and the law in Britain.* London: Allen Lane, 1968. 255p.

7578 **Kushnick**, Louis. *The role of management: nondiscrimination or affirmative action?* London: Industrial, Educational and Research Foundation, 1968. 20p. (Occasional paper 4.)

7579 **Mishan**, E. J. and **Needleman**, L. 'Immigration: long-run economic effects.' *Lloyds Bank Rev.*, n.s., 87 (January 1968), 15–25.

7580 **Mishan**, E. J. and **Needleman**, L. 'Immigration: some long-term economic consequences.' *Econ. Int.*, XXI, 2 (Maggio 1968), 281–300; XXI, 3 (Agosto 1968), 515–24.

7581 **Patterson**, Sheila. 'Immigrants and employment.' *Polit. Q.*, XXXIX, 1 (January–March 1968), 54–69.

Based on a study in Croydon.

7582 **Patterson**, Sheila. *Immigrants in industry.* London: Oxford U.P. for the Institute of Race Relations, 1968. xix, 425p.

7583 **Wright**, Peter L. *The coloured worker in British industry, with special reference to the Midlands and North of England.* London, New York: Oxford U.P., 1968. xvii, 245p.

7584 **McPherson**, Klim and **Gaitskell**, Julia. *Immigrants and employment: two case studies in East London and in Croydon.* London: Institute of Race Relations, 1969. viii, 96p. (Special series.)

Distributed by Research Publications.

7585 **Meth**, Monty. *Here to stay: a study of good practices in the employment of coloured workers.* London: Runnymede Trust, 1969. 19p.

7586 **Beetham**, David. *Transport and turbans: a comparable study in local politics.* London: Oxford U.P. for the Institute of Race Relations, 1970. 86p.

7587 **Confederation of British Industry.** *Race relations in employment: advice to employers.* London: C.B.I., 1970. 14p.

7588 **Cousins**, Frank. 'Race relations in employment in the United Kingdom.' *Int. Labour Rev.*, CII, 1 (July 1970), 1–13.

The author was Chairman of the Community Relations Commission.

7589 **Home Office.** *Problems of coloured school leavers: observations on the Report of the Select Committee on Race Relations and Immigration.* London: H.M.S.O., 1970. 16p. (Cmnd. 4268.)

7590 **Rees**, Tom B. *Immigrant workers: where they live, their industries, jobs and trade union membership.* London: Runnymede Industrial Unit, 1970. 10 leaves. (Background notes. Information paper B4.)

7591 **Rees**, Tom B. 'Managers against integration.' *New Soc.*, xv, 381 (15 January 1970), 95–6.

7592 **Robertson**, Mary F. 'Doing business in ignorance.' *New Soc.*, xv, 402 (11 June 1970), 995–6.

7593 **Thakur**, Manab. *Industry as seen by immigrant workers: a summary of research findings from a textile mill.* London: Runnymede Industrial Unit, 1970. 8p. (Industrial education series A2.)

Edited for Runnymede Industrial Unit by Robert Whymant.

See also: 9796; 11,025; 12,214; 14,729.

3. Emigration

See also Part Six, II, E, 1; and Part Six, IV, A, 4, d.

7594 **Aspdin**, James. *'Our boys': what shall we do with them? Or, emigration the real solution of the problem.* Manchester: J. Heywood, 1890. 32p.

Second edition.

7595 **Baylee**, J. Tyrrell. 'Pauper emigration.' *Char. Orgn. Rev.*, x, 117 (October 1894), 496–507.

7596 **Jones**, E. Alfred. 'The enticement of Scottish artificers to Russia and Denmark in 1784 and 1786.' *Scott. Hist. Rev.*, XVIII, 3 (April 1921), 233–4.

Notes from documents in the Public Records Office, London.

7597 **Political and Economic Planning.** 'People for the Commonwealth.' *Planning*, 226 (13 October 1944), 1–15.

See also 'Note', *Planning*, 238 (17 August 1945), 19–20.

7598 **Law**, D. T. S. *Emigration and the flight from the land, 1901–51.* 1952–53. (M.A. thesis, National University of Ireland.)

7599 **Berthoff**, Rowland Tappan. *British immigrants in industrial America, 1750–1950.* Cambridge, Mass.: Harvard U.P., 1953. ix, 296p.

7600 **Shepperson**, Wilbur Stanley. 'Industrial emigration in early Victorian Britain.' *J. Econ. Hist.*, XIII, 2 (Spring 1953), 179–92.

7601 **Clements**, Roger Victor. *English trade unions and the problem of emigration, 1840–1880.* 1954. (B.Litt. thesis, University of Oxford.)

7602 **Meenan**, James. 'Some features of Irish emigration.' *Int. Labour Rev.*, LXIX, 2 (February 1954), 126–39.

7603 **Thomas**, Brinley. *Migration and economic growth: a study of Great Britain and the Atlantic economy.* Cambridge: Cambridge U.P., 1954. xxv, 362p. (National Institute of Economic and Social Research. Economic and social studies 12.)

7604 **Eire**. Commission on Emigration. *Commission on emigration and other population problems.* Dublin: Stationery Office, 1955. xii, 417p.

7605 **Richardson**, Alan. *British emigrants to Australia: a study of some psycho-social differences between emigrant and non-emigrant skilled manual workers.* 1956. (Ph.D. thesis, University of London.)

7606 **Shepperson**, Wilbur Stanley. *British emigration to North America: projects and opinions in the early Victorian period.* Oxford: Blackwell, 1957. xvi, 302p.

Chap. III. 'Labour: emigration a palliative for problems.' p. 76–114.

7607 **Yearley**, Clifton K. *Britons in American labor: a history of the influence of the United Kingdom immigrants on American labor, 1820–1914.* Baltimore: Johns Hopkins P., 1957. 332p. (Johns Hopkins University. Studies in historical and political science, series 75, no. 1.)

7608 **Davison**, R. H. 'Medical emigration to North America.' *Br. Med. J.* (17 March 1962), 786–7.

7609 **Seale**, John Richard. 'Medical emigration from Britain, 1930–1961.' *Br. Med. J.* (17 March 1962), 782–6.

7610 **Lawless**, D. J. *Motivation for migration to Canada: studies of applicants in London, Cologne and Dublin.* 1962–63. (M.A. thesis, University of London.)

7611 **Appleyard**, R. T. 'The effect of unemployment on immigration to Australia.' *Econ. Rec.*, XXXIX, 85 (March 1963), 65–80.

7612 **Duncan**, Ross. 'Case studies in emigration: Cornwall, Gloucestershire and New South Wales, 1877–1886.' *Econ. Hist. Rev.*, 2nd ser., XVI, 2 (December 1963), 272–89.

7613 **Last**, John M. 'Migration of British doctors to Australia.' *Br. Med. J.* (21 September 1963), 744–5.

A letter giving figures of migration collected during a study of medical manpower in Australia.

7614 **Royal Society**. *Emigration of scientists from the United Kingdom: report of a committee appointed by the Council of the Royal Society.* London: Royal Society, 1963. 32p.

Summarised in *Minerva*, 1, 3 (Spring 1963), 358–62.

'Illustrative materials from the public discussion preceding the report of the Royal Society and of that which followed it, accompany the summary', p. 344–57, 363–80.

7615 **Women's Migration and Overseas Appointments Society**. *New horizons: a hundred years of women's migration.* London: H.M.S.O., 1963. 181p.

7616 **Wilson**, James A. *The depletion of national resources of human talent in the United Kingdom: a special aspect of migration to North America, 1952–64.* 1964–65. (Ph.D. thesis, Queen's University, Belfast.)

7617 **Barr**, John. 'Is the brain drain gaining pace?' *New Soc.*, VI, 154 (9 September 1965), 5–7.

7618 **Lawless**, D. J. 'The emigration of British graduates to Canada.' *Occup. Psychol.*, XXXIX, 2 (April 1965), 115–21.

7619 **Seale**, John Richard. 'Medical emigration: a study in the inadequacy of official statistics.' Burn, D., Seale, J. R. and Ratcliff, A. R. N. *Lessons from central forecasting.* London: Institute of Economic Affairs, 1965. p. 27–39.

7620 **Seale**, John Richard. 'Medical emigration from Great Britain and Ireland since 1962.' *Br. Med. J.* (3 September 1966), 576–8.

7621 **Wilson**, James A. 'The emigration of British scientists.' *Minerva*, V, 1 (Autumn 1966), 20–9.

7622 **Department of Education and Science** and **Ministry of Technology**. Committee on Manpower Resources for Science and Technology. *The brain drain: report of the Working Group on Migration.* London: H.M.S.O., 1967. viii, 125p. (Cmnd. 3417.)

Chairman: F. E. Jones.

7623 **Mishan**, E. J. 'The brain drain: why worry so much?' *New Soc.*, X, 266 (2 November 1967), 619–22.

7624 **Sutherland**, *Sir* Gordon. 'The brain drain.' *Polit. Q.*, XXXVIII, 1 (January–March 1967), 51–61.

7625 **Chorafas**, Dimitris N. *The knowledge revolution: an analysis of the international brain market and the challenge to Europe.* London: Allen and Unwin, 1968. 142p.

7626 **Lynn**, Richard. *The Irish brain drain.* Dublin: Economic and Social Research Institute, 1968. viii, 20p. (Paper 43.)

7627 **Bechhofer**, Frank (ed.). *Population growth and the brain drain.* Edinburgh: Edinburgh U.P., 1969. xvi, 236p.

Papers presented at a seminar held in Edinburgh, 1967.

7628 **MacKay**, Donald Iain. *Geographical mobility and the brain drain: a case study of Aberdeen University graduates, 1860–1960.* London: Allen and Unwin, 1969. 216p.

See also: 1352; 1358; 1379; 9239.

4. Internal Migration

This section includes works dealing with inter-regional or inter-industrial migration of labour within the United Kingdom. The literature which emphasises the movement of labour into and out of particular firms is classified at Part Six, II, E, 5. See also Part Six, II, C, 2; Part Seven, IV, D; and Part Seven, IV, E.

7629 **Registrar General for Ireland**. *Report . . . showing the result of the inquiries as to the diminution in the number of migratory labourers from Ireland visiting certain districts in Great Britain.* 1884. (H.C. 218.)

7630 **Smith**, *Sir* Hubert Llewellyn. *Modern changes in the mobility of labour, especially between trade and trade: a report to the Toynbee Trustees.* London: Froude, 1891. 23p.

7631 **Jeans**, James Stephen. 'On the recent movement of labour in different countries in reference to wages, hours of work, and efficiency.' *R. Statist. Soc. J.*, LV, 4 (December 1892), 620–51.

Discussion, p. 651–7.

'Read before the Royal Statistical Society, 17th May, 1892.'

7632 **Heath**, J. St. George. 'Underemployment and the mobility of labour.' *Econ. J.*, XXI, 82 (June 1911), 202–11.

7633 **Bowley**, Arthur Lyon. 'Wages and the mobility of labour.' *Econ. J.*, XXII, 85 (March 1912), 46–52.

'The gist of this article was read at the Portsmouth meeting of the British Association.'

7634 **Redford**, Arthur. *Labour migration in England, 1800–50.* Manchester: U. of Manchester, 1926. xvi, 174p. (Economic history series 3.)

Second edition, edited and revised by W. H. Chaloner. 1964. xx, 209p.

7635 **Hammond**, John Lawrence Le Breton. 'Historical revisions. XLII. The movement of population during the Industrial Revolution.' *History*, n.s., XII, 46 (July 1927), 146–8.

7636 **Jewkes**, John and **Campion**, H. 'The mobility of labour in the cotton industry.' *Econ. J.*, XXXVIII, 149 (March 1928), 135–7.

7637 **Robertson**, C. J. 'The mobility of labour in Liverpool industry.' *Sociol. Rev.*, XX, 3 (July 1928), 233–45.

7638 **Allen**, G. C. 'Labour transference and the unemployment problem.' *Econ. J.*, XL, 158 (June 1930), 242–8.

7639 **Thomas**, Brinley. 'The migration of labour into the Glamorganshire coalfield (1861–1911).' *Economica*, X, 30 (November 1930), 275–94.

7640 **Saunders**, Christopher Thomas. 'A study of occupational mobility.' *Econ. J.*, XLI, 162 (June 1931), 227–40.

Merseyside.

7641 **Thomas**, Brinley. 'Labour mobility in the South Wales and Monmouthshire coal mining industry, 1920–30.' *Econ. J.*, XLI, 162 (June 1931), 216–26.

7642 **Davison**, Ernest. *The mobility of labour in the North East coast area.* 1932. 84 leaves. (M.Com. thesis, University of Durham.)

7643 **Smith**, Edmond Lorrain. *Go East for a farm: a study in rural migration.* Oxford: University of Oxford Institute for Research in Agricultural Economics, 1932. 54p.

7644 **Hare**, Anthony Edward Christian. *Labour migration: a study of the mobility of labour.* 1932–33. (Ph.D. thesis, University of London.)

7645 **Jewkes**, John. 'The mobility of labour and the localisation of industry.' *Manchr. Statist. Soc. Trans.* (1932–33), 109–40.

7646 **Dawes**, H. 'Labour mobility in the steel industry.' *Econ. J.*, XLIV, 173 (March 1934), 84–94.

7647 **Morgan**, William Glyndwr. *The mobility of labour in the principal industries of Somersetshire, 1923–1933.* 1934. (M.A. thesis, University of Wales, Bangor.)

7648 **Thomas**, Brinley. 'The movement of labour into South-East England, 1920–32.' *Economica*, n.s., I, 2 (May 1934), 220–41.

'The substance of this article was read as a contribution to a symposium on the Location of Industries before Section F of the British Association in September 1932.'

7649 **Owen**, Arthur David Kemp. 'The social consequences of industrial transference.' *Sociol. Rev.*, XXIX, 4 (October 1937), 331–54.

'A reply', by Michael Daly, XXX, 3 (July 1938), 236–61.

'A rejoinder', by A. D. K. Owen, XXX, 4 (October 1938), 414–20.

7650 **Thomas**, Brinley. 'The influx of labour into London and the South East, 1920–36.' *Economica*, n.s., IV, 15 (August 1937), 323–36.

7651 **Howell**, Emrys Jones. *Movements of mining population in the anthracite area of South Wales.* 1938. (M.Sc. thesis, University of Wales, Swansea.)

7652 **Makower**, H., **Marschak**, J. and **Robinson**, H. W. 'Studies in mobility of labour: a tentative statistical measure.' *Oxf. Econ. Pap.*, I (October 1938), 83–123.

7653 **Marschak**, J. 'Industrial immigration.' Barnett House, Oxford. Survey Committee. *A survey of the social services in the Oxford district.* Vol. I. London: Oxford U.P., 1938. p. 50–62.

7654 **Thomas**, Brinley. 'The influx of labour into the Midlands, 1920–37.' *Economica*, n.s., V, 20 (November 1938), 410–34.

7655 **Daniel**, Goronwy H. 'Labour migration and age composition.' *Sociol. Rev.*, XXXI, 3 (July 1939), 281–308.

Differentials in movement from Wales to Oxford in the 1930s shown in unemployment insurance records.

7656 **Daniel**, Goronwy H. 'Labour migration and fertility.' *Sociol. Rev.*, XXXI, 4 (October 1939), 370–400.

7657 **Daniel**, Goronwy H. *Sample analyses of migration into the Oxford district.* 1939. (D.Phil. thesis, University of Oxford.)

7658 **Lamb**, V. M. *Migration in Great Britain since 1927, with special reference to the industrial population.* 1939. (B.Litt. thesis, University of Oxford.)

7659 **Makower**, H., **Marschak**, J. and **Robinson**, H. W. 'Studies in mobility of labour: analysis for Great Britain.' *Oxf. Econ. Pap.*, 2 (May 1939), 70–97; 4 (September 1940), 39–62.

7660 **Daniel**, Goronwy H. 'Some factors affecting the movement of labour.' *Oxf. Econ. Pap.*, 3 (March 1940), 144–79.

7661 **Attlee**, Margaret M. *Mobility of labour: a consideration of the question of industrial transference.* Oxford: Catholic Social Guild; London: Sword of the Spirit, 1944. 40p.

7662 **Gillespie**, Sarah C. and **Rothschild**, K. W. 'Migration and the distributive trades.' *Rev. Econ. Studies*, XIII, 2 (1946), 81–3.

7663 **Political and Economic Planning**. 'Manpower movements.' *Planning*, XIV, 276 (2 January 1948), 185–208.

7664 **Cairncross**, A. K. 'Internal migration in Victorian England.' *Manchr. Sch.*, XVII, 1 (January 1949), 67–87.

7665 **Crosland**, C. A. R. 'The movement of labour in 1948.' *Oxf. Univ. Inst. Statist. Bull.*, XI, 5 (May 1949), 117–26; XI, 7–8 (July–August 1949), 194–212.

7666 **Hagenbuch**, Walter. 'The mobility of labour.' *Distr. Bank Rev.*, 89 (March 1949), 12–19.

7667 **North-East Development Association** and **Northern Industrial Group**. *Migration: a study of movement of population and its effect on the North-East.* Newcastle-upon-Tyne, 1950. 22p.

Part of a wider study of the employment prospects of the region.

7668 **Thomas**, Brinley. 'Labour mobility, migration policy and the standard of living.' *Three Banks Rev.*, 5 (March 1950), 3–20.

7669 **Hobsbawm**, Eric John Ernest. 'The tramping artisan.' *Econ. Hist. Rev.*, 2nd ser., III, 3 (1951), 299–320.

Reprinted in the author's *Labouring men: studies in the history of labour.* London: Weidenfeld and Nicolson, 1964. p. 34–63.

7670 **Parsons**, E. C. *The geographical and industrial mobility of the labour force in Great Britain between 1924 and 1935.* 1951. (B.Litt, thesis, University of Oxford.)

7671 **House**, John William. *Migration and employment among school children and young adults 1931–1950.* [London]: North Tyne Survey Committee, [1952]. 56p.

7672 **Gallagher**, S. R. *The flight from the land.* 1952–53. (M.A. thesis, National University of Ireland.)

7673 **Chambers**, Jonathan David. 'Enclosure and labour supply in the Industrial Revolution.' *Econ. Hist. Rev.*, 2nd ser., V, 3 (1953), 319–43.

7674 **Heughan**, Hazel Elizabeth. *Pit closures at Shotts and the migration of miners.* Edinburgh: University of Edinburgh, Social Sciences Research Centre, 1953. 120p. (Monograph 1.)

Limited edition.

7675 **Long**, Joyce R. and **Bowyer**, Irene M. 'The influence of earnings on the mobility of labour.' *Yorks. Bull. Econ. Soc. Res.*, V, 1 (February 1953), 81–7.

7676 **House**, John William. *Migration and employment among school children and young adults, 1931–1950.* [London]: North Tyne Survey Committee, 1954. 56p.

7677 **Jefferys**, Margot and **Moss**, Winifred. *Mobility in the labour market: employment changes in Battersea and Dagenham.* London: Routledge and Kegan Paul, 1954. ix, 160p. (International library of sociology and social reconstruction.)

Preface by B. Wootton.

7678 **White**, P. N. 'Some aspects of urban development by colliery companies, 1919–1939.' *Manchr. Sch.*, XXIII, 3 (September 1955), 269–80.

7679 **Hartshorn**, J. E. 'How mobile is the economy?' *Banker*, CVI, 369 (October 1956), 611–18.

7680 **Williams**, Moelwyn I. 'Seasonal migrations of Cardiganshire harvest gangs to the Vale of Glamorgan in the nineteenth century.' *Ceredigion*, III, 2 (1957), 156–60.

7681 **Osborne**, R. H. 'The drift South in Britain continues.' *Tijdschr. Econ. Soc. Geogr.*, LI, 11 (November 1960), 286–9.

7682 **El Rayah**, M. E. M. *The internal migration of labour in Ireland, 1841–1911.* 1960–61. (M.A. thesis, Queen's University, Belfast.)

7683 **Taylor**, Percy. *A study of planned urban and rural industrial settlements and communities in the United Kingdom during the nineteenth century.* 1960–61. (Ph.D. thesis, University of Durham, Newcastle Division.)

7684 **Nalson**, John Spencer. *The mobility of farm families in an upland area of North East Staffordshire: a study of the locational and social origins of the farm population and its movements within and between agriculture and other occupations.* 1962. (Ph.D. thesis, University of Manchester.)

7685 **Routh**, Guy. 'Immobility of labour.' *New Soc.*, 11 (13 December 1962), 9–10.

7686 **Oliver**, F. R. 'Inter-regional migration and unemployment, 1951–61.' *R. Statist. Soc. J.*, Ser. A, CXXVII, 1 (1964), 42–69.

With discussion, p. 70–5.

Read before the Society, 18 December 1963.

7687 **Routh**, Guy. 'Geographical mobility of manpower.' Organisation for Economic Co-operation and Development. *International Joint Seminar on Geographical and Occupational Mobility of Manpower, Castelfusano, 19th to 22nd November 1963. Final report.* Paris: O.E.C.D., 1964. p. 121–46.

7688 **Bugler**, Jeremy. 'The Geordies come to Yorkshire.' *New Soc.*, VI, 148 (29 July 1965), 14–15.

7689 **Clegg**, Hugh Armstrong. 'Mobility of labour.' *Natn. Prov. Bank Rev.*, 70 (May 1965), 9–13.

7690 **North Regional Planning Committee.** *Inter-regional migration of employees 1951–1964: regional variations in earnings in selected industries, January 1965.* 1965.
Based on Ministry of Labour data.

7691 **Oliver**, F. R. 'A year-by-year analysis of inter-regional migration, 1951–1961.' *R. Statist. Soc. J.*, Ser. A, CXXVIII, 2 (1965), 285–7.

7692 **Wignall**, E. H. 'The migrant miners.' *New Soc.*, VI, 148 (29 July 1965), 13–14.

7693 **Breakell**, T. A. 'United Kingdom: sources or causes of change in location, size and nature of manpower requirements in the electronic sector working for the aircraft industry.' Organisation for Economic Co-operation and Development. *Geographical and occupational mobility of workers in the aircraft and electronics industries: regional trade union seminar, Paris, 21st–22nd September, 1966. Supplement to the final report.* Paris: O.E.C.D., 1966. p. 111–22.

7694 **Davies**, Wayne K. D. 'Latent migration potential and space preferences.' *Prof. Geogr.*, XVIII, 5 (September 1966), 300–4.

7695 **Elliott**, C. K. 'Age and internal labour mobility of semi-skilled workers.' *Occup. Psychol.*, XL, 4 (October 1966), 227–36.

7696 **Kahn**, Hilda Renate. 'Labour mobility: some critical reflections.' *Distr. Bank. Rev.*, 157 (March 1966), 47–64.

7697 **Scanlon**, Hugh. 'Aircraft industry: United Kingdom.' Organisation for Economic Co-operation and Development. *Geographical and occupational mobility of workers in the aircraft and electronics industries: regional trade union seminar, Paris, 21st–22nd September, 1966. Supplement to the final report.* Paris: O.E.C.D., 1966. p. 67–89.

7698 **Organisation for Economic Co-operation and Development.** *Geographical and occupational mobility of workers in the aircraft and electronics industries: regional trade union seminar, Paris, 21st–22nd September 1966. Final report.* Paris: O.E.C.D., 1967. 122p. (International seminars 1966–3.)
Supplement. 1966. 195p.

7699 **Taylor**, R. C. *Implications of migrations from the Durham coalfield: an anthropological study.* 1966–67. (Ph.D. thesis, University of Durham.)

7700 **Hunter**, Laurence Colvin. 'Income structure and mobility.' *Br. J. Ind. Relat.*, V, 3 (November 1967), 386–98.

7701 **Smith**, J. M. 'Age and re-employment: a regional study of external mobility.' *Occup. Psychol.*, XLI, 4 (October 1967), 239–43.

7702 **Wabe**, J. S. 'Dispersal of employment and the journey to work: a case study.' *J. Transp. Econ. Policy*, I, 3 (September 1967), 345–61.
'A study of one firm with 600 employees moving from Victoria to Epsom.' (Townroe.)

7703 **Whitby**, M. C. 'Labour mobility and training in agriculture.' *Westm. Bank Rev.* (August 1967), 43–57.

7704 **Rickerd**, P. E. *Mobility between the administrative elite and outside employment: a study of the British Civil Service against the background of French experience.* 1967–68. (Ph.D. thesis, University of London.)

7705 **Cowling**, Keith and **Metcalf**, David. 'Labour transfer from agriculture: a regional analysis.' *Manchr. Sch.*, XXXVI, 1 (March 1968), 27–48.

7706 **Gabor**, Dennis, and others. *Redundancy or redeployment: economic and social implications.* London: Marlow Foundation, 1968. [8]p. (Marlow papers 2.)

7707 **Hollingsworth**, T. H. 'Internal migration statistics from the Central Register for Scotland of the National Health Service.' *R. Statist. Soc. J.*, Ser. A, CXXXI, 3 (1968), 340–80.
Discussion, p. 380–3.
'Read before the Royal Statistical Society on Friday, April 26th, 1968.'

7708 **House**, John William, and others. *Mobility of the northern business manager: report to the Ministry of Labour.* Newcastle-upon-Tyne: U. of Newcastle-upon-Tyne, Department of Geography, 1968. [141]p. (Papers on migration and mobility in northern England 8.)

7709 **House**, John William and **Thomas**, Angela Dorothy. *Northern graduates of '64: brain-drain or brainbank? Report to the Department of Employment and Productivity.* Newcastle-upon-Tyne: U. of Newcastle-upon-Tyne, Department of Geography, 1968. 26p. (Papers on migration and mobility in northern England 9.)

7710 **Hunter**, Laurence Colvin and **Reid**, Graham Livingstone. *Urban worker mobility.* Paris: Organisation for Economic Co-operation and Development, 1968. 215p. (Labour mobility 5.)

7711 **Jansen**, Clifford J. *Social aspects of internal migration: research report.* Bath: Bath U.P., 1968. 216, 13, [12]p.

7712 **Knight**, Elizabeth Mary. *Men leaving mining: West Cumberland 1966–'67; report to the Ministry of Labour.* Newcastle-upon-Tyne: University of Newcastle-upon-Tyne, Department of Geography, 1968. 40p. (Papers on migration and mobility in northern England 6.)

7713 **Nalson**, John Spencer. *Mobility of farm families: a study of occupational and residential mobility in an upland area of England.* Manchester: Manchester U.P.; Nedlands: U. of Western Australia P., 1968. xvi, 299p.

7714 **Hughes**, B. T. *Teacher mobility in South Gloucestershire*. 1968–69. (M.Ed. thesis, University of Bristol.)

7715 **Carey**, Susan Jane. *Relocation of office staff: a study of the reactions of office staff decentralised to Ashford*. London: Location of Offices Bureau, 1969. 64p. (Research paper 4.)

7716 **Cullingworth**, John Barry. *Housing and labour mobility: a preliminary report*. Paris: Organisation for Economic Co-operation and Development, 1969. 73p. (Labour mobility 6.)

7717 **Gasson**, Ruth. *Occupational immobility of small farmers: a study of the reasons why small farmers do not give up farming*. Cambridge: Cambridge University, Department of Land Economy (Farm Economics Branch), 1969. 44p. (Occasional paper 13.)

7718 **Lind**, Harold. 'Internal migration in Britain.' Jackson, J. A. *Migration*. Cambridge: Cambridge U.P., 1969. (Sociological studies 2.) p. 74–98.

Labour migration in economic theory; a model for Britain, 1951–66.

7719 **Mitchell**, Daniel Jesse Brody. 'Some aspects of labour mobility and recent policy in Britain.' *Br. J. Ind. Relat.*, VII, 3 (November 1969), 353–67.

'Much of the material presented here is drawn from a section of Chapter Four of the author's doctoral thesis, *Incomes policy, costs and the balance of payments: the cases of Britain and Australia*, Department of Economics, Massachusetts Institute of Technology, 1968.'

7720 **Cunningham**, Catherine M. 'Labour mobility on the Liverpool docks.' Lawton, R. and Cunningham, C. M. (eds.). *Merseyside: social and economic studies*. London: Longman, 1970. p. 294–323.

See also: 8016; 14,117.

5. Labour Turnover

This section includes works dealing with the movement of labour into and out of particular firms. The literature which emphasises the inter-regional and inter-industrial migration of labour within the United Kingdom is classified at Part Six, II, E, 4. See also Part Two, III; and Part Seven, IV, D, 2.

7721 *Reports from certain foreign and colonial ports respecting the desertion of seamen from British ships*. London: H.M.S.O., 1899. (C.9265.)

7722 *Reports from certain foreign and colonial ports respecting the desertion of seamen from British ships*. London: H.M.S.O., 1909. 26p. (Cd. 4568.)

7723 **Medical Research Council.** Industrial Fatigue Research Board. *A statistical study of labour turnover in munition and other factories*. London, 1921. 92p. (Report 13. General series 4.)

By G. M. Broughton, E. M. Newbold and E. C. Allen.

7724 **National Institute of Industrial Psychology**. 'An inquiry into labour turnover.' *Nat. Inst. Ind. Psychol. J.*, I, 3 (July 1922), 103–7.

'Conducted on behalf of the N.I.I.P.'

7725 **Raphael**, Winifred, **Hearnshaw**, L. S., **Medd**, R. T. and **Fraser**, John H. Munro. 'Report on an inquiry into labour turnover in the London district.' *Occup. Psychol.*, XII, 3 (Summer 1938), 196–214.

7726 **Raphael**, Winifred, **White**, I. H. B., **Hearnshaw**, L. S. and **Fraser**, John H. Munro. 'An inquiry into labour turnover in the Leeds district.' *Occup. Psychol.*, XII, 4 (Autumn 1938), 257–70.

7727 **British Institute of Management**. *Labour turnover*. London: B.I.M., [1949?]. 12p. (Personnel management series 1.)

7728 **James**, Robert. 'Human waste: an analysis of labour turnover in industry.' *Econ. J.*, LIX, 233 (March 1949), 118–23.

7729 **Furness**, H. J. *The cost of labour turnover*. London: Institute of Cost and Works Accountants, 1950. 21p.

7730 **Rice**, Albert Kenneth, **Hill**, John Michael Meath and **Trist**, Eric Lansdowne. 'The representation of labour turnover as a social process: studies in the social development of an industrial community. (The Glacier Project, II.)' *Hum. Relat.*, III, 4 (November 1950), 349–72.

7731 **Terry**, Neville Vernon. *The foreman and labour turnover*. Birmingham: Institute of Industrial Supervisors, 1950. 16p.

7732 **Baldamus**, Wilhelm. 'Type of work and motivation.' *Br. J. Sociol.*, II, 1 (March 1951), 44–58.

7733 **Cook**, P. H. 'Labour turnover as a measure of control.' *Cost Acc.*, XXIX, 8 (January 1951), 258–65.

7734 **Greystoke**, J. R., **Birks**, G. W. and **Murphy**, T. 'Surveying labour in the Sheffield region.' *Yorks. Bull. Econ. Soc. Res.*, III, 2 (July 1951), 83–101.

7735 **Hill**, John Michael Meath. 'A consideration of labour turnover as the resultant of a quasi-stationary process, with a case illustration. (The Glacier Project, IV.)' *Hum. Relat.*, IV, 3 (August 1951), 255–64.

7736 **Long**, Joyce R. *Labour turnover under full employment*. Birmingham: Research Board, Faculty of Commerce and Social Science, University of Birmingham, 1951. 134p. (University of Birmingham. Studies in economics and society. Monograph A2.)

7737 **Rice**, Albert Kenneth. 'An examination of the boundaries of part-institutions: an illustrative study of departmental labour turnover in industry. (The Glacier Project, VI.)' *Hum. Relat.*, IV, 4 (November 1951), 393–400.

7738 **Pearce**, Frank Thomas. *The financial effects of labour turnover under full employment.* 1951–52. (Ph.D. thesis, University of Birmingham.)

7739 **Rice**, Albert Kenneth and **Trist**, Eric Lansdowne. 'Institutional and sub-institutional determinants of change in labour turnover. (The Glacier Project, VIII.)' *Hum. Relat.*, v, 4 (November 1952), 347–71.

7740 **Rice**, Albert Kenneth. *New approach to labour turnover: a case study.* London: British Institute of Management, 1952. 29p.

7741 **Rice**, Albert Kenneth. 'The relative independence of sub-institutions as illustrated by departmental labour turnover. (The Glacier Project, VII.)' *Hum. Relat.*, v, 1 (February 1952), 83–90.

7742 **Behrend**, Hilde M. 'A note on labour turnover and the individual factory.' *J. Ind. Econ.*, II, 1 (November 1953), 58–64.

7743 **Hill**, John Michael Meath. 'A note on labour turnover in an iron and steel works.' *Hum. Relat.*, VI, 1 (February 1953), 79–87.

7744 **Rice**, Albert Kenneth. 'An approach to problems of labour turnover: a case study.' *Br. Mgmt. Rev.*, XI, 2 (January 1953), 19–47.

An account of part of the work of the Glacier Project.

7745 **Worthington**, D. B. *Labour turnover and individual instability: a study of job-changing.* 1953–54. (M.A. thesis, University of Liverpool.)

7746 **Pearce**, Frank Thomas. *Financial effects of labour turnover.* Birmingham: Research Board, Faculty of Commerce and Social Science, University of Birmingham, 1954. iv, 228p. (University of Birmingham. Studies in economics and society. Monograph A4.)

Limited edition.

Reproduced from typescript.

7747 **Robertson**, Donald James. 'Labour turnover in the Clyde shipbuilding industry.' *Scott. J. Polit. Econ.*, I, 1 (March 1954), 9–32.

7748 **Silcock**, H. 'The phenomenon of labour turnover.' *R. Statist. Soc. J.*, Ser. A, CXVII, 4 (1954), 429–40.

7749 **Behrend**, Hilde M. 'Normative factors in the supply of labour.' *Manchr. Sch.*, XXIII, 1 (January 1955), 62–76.

Comparison of labour turnover of some grammar school teachers with that of factory workers.

7750 **Lane**, K. F. and **Andrew**, J. E. 'A method of labour turnover analysis.' *R. Statist. Soc. J.*, Ser. A, CXVIII, 3 (1955), 296–314.

A survey of the United Steel Companies Ltd.

Discussion, p. 314–23.

'Read before the Royal Statistical Society, April 20th, 1955.'

7751 **Silcock**, H. 'The recording and measurement of labour turnover.' *Pers. Mgmt.*, XXXVII, 232 (June 1955), 71–8.

7752 **Hutt**, Rosemary. 'Labour turnover and daily travel to work in the Leeds clothing industry.' *Yorks. Bull. Econ. Soc. Res.*, VIII, 1 (June 1956), 49–59.

7753 **Monmouth Technical College**. *A report based on a survey of labour turnover in the administrative county of Monmouthshire.* Crumlin: the College, 1958. 90p.

7754 **Edwards**, Bernard. *The problems of labour turnover.* 1958–59. (M.Litt. thesis, University of Durham.)

7755 **Bartholomew**, D. J. 'Note on the measurement and prediction of labour turnover.' *R. Statist. Soc. J.*, Ser. A, CXXII, 2 (1959), 232–9.

7756 **British Institute of Management**. *The cost of labour turnover.* London: B.I.M., 1959. 79p. (Personnel management series 9.)

7757 **Crookes**, T. G. and **French**, J. G. 'Intelligence and wastage of student mental nurses.' *Occup. Psychol.*, XXXV, 3 (July 1961), 149–54.

7758 **Hill**, Thomas Peter. 'Wages and labour turnover.' *Oxf. Univ. Inst. Statist. Bull.*, XXIV, 2 (May 1962), 185–233.

Coal mining, 1954.

7759 **Bucklow**, Maxine. 'Labour turnover: a reassessment.' *J. Ind. Relat.*, v, 1 (April 1963), 29–37.

7760 **Bryant**, D. T. 'A survey of the development of manpower planning policies.' *Br. J. Ind. Relat.*, III, 3 (November 1965), 279–90.

Originally presented as a paper to a conference, at Imperial College, London in April 1965, organized by the Industrial Applications Section of the Royal Statistical Society.

7761 **Evans**, M. G. 'Supervisors' attitudes and departmental performance.' *J. Mgmt. Studies*, II, 2 (May 1965), 174–90.

Research carried out in fulfilment of the degree of Master of Technical Science of the University of Manchester.

7762 **Institute of Pharmacy Management**. *Relationship of floorspace, staff and turnover in retail pharmacy.* Hatch End: the Institute, 1966. 13p. (Pharmacy management studies 1.)

By H. W. Tomski.

7763 **Gasson**, L. M. *A study of factors contributing to labour turnover among male psychiatric nurses.* 1966–67. (M.Sc. thesis, University of London.)

7764 **Downs**, Sylvia. 'Labour turnover in two public service organisations.' *Occup. Psychol.*, XLI, 2–3 (April–July 1967), 137–42.

7765 **Economic Development Committee for the Clothing Industry**. *Labour turnover.* London: National Economic Development Office, 1967. 18p. (Occasional papers 1.)

7766 **Economic Development Committee for Food Manufacturing**. *A study of labour turnover.* London: National Economic Development Office, 1968. 45p.

By J. M. M. Hill.

7767 **Economic Development Committee for the Rubber Industry**. *Costing your labour turnover*. London: National Economic Development Office, 1968. [4], 20p.

7768 **Burgoyne**, J. G. *A study of some determinants of labour turnover in retail selling*. 1968–69. (M.Phil. thesis, University of London.)

7769 **Bowey**, A. M. 'Labour stability curves and a labour stability index.' *Br. J. Ind. Relat.*, VII, 1 (March 1969), 71–83.

7770 **Economic Development Committee for Motor Vehicle Distribution and Repair**. *Labour utilisation and turnover survey: report of an E.D.C. working party*. London: National Economic Development Office, 1969. 11p.

7771 **Jones**, R. M. 'A case study in labour mobility.' *Manchr. Sch.*, XXXVII, 2 (June 1969), 169–74.

At the Swansea plant of the Ford Motor Company.

7772 **McIntosh**, F. 'A survey of workers leaving Scottish farms.' Department of Agriculture and Fisheries for Scotland. *Scottish agricultural economics: some studies of current economic conditions in Scottish farming*. Vol. XIX. Edinburgh: H.M.S.O., 1969. p. 191–7.

7773 **Newsham**, Dorothy Battersby. *The challenge of change to the adult trainee: a study of labour turnover during and following training of middle-aged men and women for new skills*. London: H.M.S.O., 1969. v, 39p. (Department of Employment and Productivity. Training information paper 3.)

7774 **Samuel**, Peter James. *Labour turnover? Towards a solution*. London: Institute of Personnel Management, 1969. 55p.

7775 **Tavistock Institute of Human Relations**. *Staff turnover*. London: H.M.S.O., 1969. vii, 60p.

Report for the Economic Development Committee for Hotels and Catering.

7776 **Turpin**, David Arthur Roderick. *Personnel practices, work systems and conditions, and early labour turnover: a comparative study in the motor industry*. 1969–70. (M.Sc. thesis, University of Edinburgh.)

7777 **Argyle**, Michael, **Gardner**, Godfrey and **Cioffi**, Frank. 'Supervisory methods related to productivity, absenteeism and labour turnover.' Vroom, V. H. and Deci, E. L. (eds.). *Management and motivation: selected readings*. Harmondsworth: Penguin, 1970. p. 170–91.

Abridged from the authors' article of the same title in *Human Relations*, XI (1958), 23–40.

7778 **Bibby**, John. 'A model to control for the biasing effects of differential wastage.' *Br. J. Ind. Relat.*, VIII, 3 (November 1970), 418–20.

'Research note.'

7779 **Cunningham**, N. J. 'Labour turnover on the Liverpool docks, 1960–65.' Lawton, R. and Cunningham, C. M. (eds.). *Merseyside: social and economic studies*. London: Longman, 1970. p. 258–93.

7780 **Hyman**, Richard. 'Economic motivation and labour stability.' *Br. J. Ind. Relat.*, VIII, 2 (July 1970), 159–78.

7781 **MacKay**, Donald Iain. 'Wages and labour turnover.' Robinson, D. (ed.). *Local labour markets and wage structures*. London: Gower P., 1970. p. 68–99.

7782 **Moreton**, P. W. T. *Labour turnover and its relationship to levels of employment and unemployment in some sectors of British manufacturing industry since 1948*. 1970. (Ph.D. thesis, University of Hull.)

7783 **Wild**, Ray and **Ridgeway**, C. C. 'A note on and a study of the "floating population" explanation of labour turnover.' *Br. J. Ind. Relat.*, VIII, 3 (November 1970), 420–2.

'Research note.'

6. Private Labour Exchanges

See also Part Seven, IV, D, 2.

7784 **Beveridge**, William Henry. 'A seventeenth-century labour exchange.' *Econ. J.*, XXIV, 95 (September 1914), 371–6.

Correction, XXIV, 96 (December 1914), 635–6.

In London and Paris.

7785 **Belasco**, Philip S. 'Note on the labour exchange idea in the seventeenth century.' *Econ. Hist.*, I, 2 (May 1927), 275–9.

7786 **University of Cambridge**. *Report of the Appointments Board on twenty-five years' work ended 27th February 1927*. Cambridge: Cambridge U.P., 1927. 21p.

7787 **Norman**, Frank A. and **Lee**, L. Gordon. 'A further note on labour exchanges in the seventeenth century.' *Econ. Hist.*, I, 3 (January 1928), 299–404.

7788 **George**, Mary Dorothy. 'The early history of registry offices: the beginnings of advertisement.' *Econ. Hist.*, I, 4 (January 1929), 570–90.

Includes a description of the Universal Register Office in the eighteenth century which acted as an employment agency.

7789 **Ministry of Labour and National Service**. Catering Wages Commission. *Employment agencies serving the catering industry*. London: H.M.S.O., 1947. 11p.

7790 **University Grants Committee**. *University Appointments Boards: a report by the Rt. Hon. the Lord Heyworth*. London: H.M.S.O., 1964. xii, 127p.

7791 **Employment Agents Federation of Great Britain**. *Employment agencies: part of Britain's modern business life; facts and figures*. London: the Federation, 1966. [20]p.

III. WAGES AND THE DISTRIBUTION OF INCOME

This section contains material which is primarily concerned with wages and salaries as opposed to other conditions of employment. Material relating to both wages and hours is generally classified here and is cross-referenced from Part Six, IV, B. See also the general note to Part Six. See also Part Seven, VI.

A. GENERAL

See also Part Six, I; and Part Six, IV, A, 1.

7792 **Fawcett**, Henry. *Labour and wages: chapters reprinted from the 'Manual of political economy'*. London: Macmillan, 1884. xii, 76p.

7793 **Jeans**, James Stephen. 'On the comparative efficiency and earnings of labour at home and abroad.' *R. Statist. Soc. J.*, XLVII, 4 (December 1884), 614–55.
With discussion, p. 656–65.
Read before the Society, 16 December 1884.

7794 **Toynbee**, Arnold. 'Wages and natural law.' *Lectures on the Industrial Revolution in England: popular addresses, notes and other fragments*. London: Rivingtons, 1884. p. 155–77.
'A lecture given at the Mechanics' Institute, Bradford, in January 1880, and repeated in part at Firth College, Sheffield, in February 1882.'
Later editions. 1887; London: Longmans, 1908; New York: Kelley, 1969.

7795 **Bell**, I. Lowthian. 'On the existing modes of distribution of the products of industry in the chemical works, collieries, ironstone mines, and blast furnaces in the North-East of England.' Industrial Remuneration Conference. *The report of the proceedings and papers*. London: Cassell, 1885. p. 137–49.
Discussion, p. 164–72.

7796 **Cunningham**, William, Archdeacon of Ely. *The Industrial Remuneration Conference*. Aberdeen, 1885. 12p.
'A paper read at Section F of the British Association, 16 September, 1885.'

7797 **Hutchinson**, James G. 'Labour and its reward.' Industrial Remuneration Conference. *The report of the proceedings and papers*. London: Cassell, 1885. p. 46–62.
Discussion, p. 62–83.

7798 **Industrial Remuneration Conference**, London, 1885. *The report of the proceedings and papers read in Prince's Hall, Picadilly under the presidency of the Right Hon. Sir Charles W. Dilke . . . on the 28th, 29th, and 30th January 1885*. London: Cassell, 1885. xxiv, 528p.
Reprinted. New York: Kelley, 1968. 44, xxiv, 528p. (Reprints of economic classics.) With an introduction, *The background of the Industrial Remuneration Conference of 1885*, by John Saville.

7799 **Levi**, Leone. *Wages and earnings of the working classes: report to Sir Arthur Bass, M.P.* London: Murray, 1885. vii, 151p.

7800 **Marshall**, Alfred. 'Theories and facts about wages.' Co-operative Wholesale Society. *Annual and diary for the year 1885*. p. 379–88.

7801 **Rimington**, G. D. *The labourer's hire*. Carlisle, [1885?]. 11p.

7802 **Giffen**, Robert. 'Recent changes in prices, and incomes compared.' *R. Statist. Soc. J.*, LI, 4 (December 1888), 713–805.
With discussion, p. 806–15.

7803 **Minton**, Francis. *Capital and wages*. London: Kegan Paul, 1888. xxiv, 441p.

7804 **Giffen**, Robert. 'The gross and the net gain of rising wages.' *Contemp. Rev.*, LVI (December 1889), 830–43.

7805 *High wages; respectfully dedicated to the working men of the United Kingdom*. Dundee: W. Kidd; London: Simpkin, Marshall, 1889. 72p.

7806 **Edinburgh Review**. 'The wages of labour.' *Edinb. Rev.*, CLXXI, 349 (January 1890), 208–33.
Review article.

7807 **Nicholson**, Joseph Shield. 'The living capital of the United Kingdom.' *Econ. J.*, I, 1 (March 1891), 95–107.

7808 **Playfair**, Lyon, Baron Playfair. *On the wages and hours of labour: speech*. London: Cassell, 1891. 16p.

7809 **Nicholson**, Joseph Shield. *The effects of machinery on wages*. London: Sonnenschein, 1892. x, 143p.
Cambridge Cobden prize essay for 1877.
New and revised edition.
Originally published Cambridge, 1878.

7810 **Schloss**, David Frederick. 'The basis of industrial remuneration.' *Econ. J.*, II, 8 (December 1892), 608–15.

7811 **Hobson**, John Atkinson. 'The economy of high wages.' *Contemp. Rev.*, LXIV (December 1893), 811–27.

7812 **Brentano**, Lujo. *Hours and wages in relation to production*. London: Swan Sonnenschein, 1894. viii, 143p.
Translated from the German by Mrs William Arnold.

7813 **Economic Journal**. 'A living wage.' *Econ. J.*, IV, 14 (June 1894), 365–8.
A survey of recently published articles on the subject.

7814 **Hamilton**, *Lord* George Francis. 'Ocean highways: their bearing on the food and wages of Great Britain.' *R. Statist. Soc. J.*, LVII, 1 (March 1894), 104–27.
Discussion, p. 128–35.
'Read before the Royal Statistical Society, 20th February, 1894.'

7815 **Levy**, Joseph Hiam. *The economics of labour remuneration: a lecture.* London: King, 1894. 16p.

7816 **Smart**, William. *A living wage.* [Glasgow, 1894.] 19p.

Philosophical Society of Glasgow, Presidential address to the Economic Science Section. Reprinted from the Proceedings, 1893–94.

7817 **Board of Trade.** Labour Department. [Wages and hours of labour.] London: H.M.S.O.

Part I. *Changes in the rates of wages and hours of labour in the United Kingdom.* 1894. lxxxviii, 222p. (C. 7567.)

Followed by annual reports up to 1914–16.

Part II. *Standard piece rates of wages.* 1894. xvi, 232p. (C. 7567 – I.)

Part III. *Standard time rates of wages.* 1894. 278p. (C. 7567 – II.)

Standard piece rates of wages and sliding scales in the United Kingdom: report. 1900. xxv, 308p. (Cd. 144.)

In continuation of C. 7567 – I.

Standard time rates of wages in the United Kingdom. 1900. xii, 210p. (Cd. 317.)

In continuation of C. 7567 – II.

Five succeeding reports between 1900 and 1914.

7818 **Halstead**, Robert. 'Some thoughts of a workman concerning the plea for a living wage.' *Econ. Rev.*, V, 3 (July 1895), 350–69.

7819 **Webb**, Sidney and **Webb**, Beatrice. 'The standard rate.' *Econ. J.*, VI, 23 (September 1896), 356–88.

7820 **Blunt**, Herbert W. 'English wages and foreign competition.' *Econ. Rev.*, IX, 2 (April 1899), 156–73.

7821 **Hobson**, John Atkinson. 'Protection as a working-class policy. II. Protection and wages.' Massingham, H. W. (ed.). *Labour and protection: a series of studies.* London: Fisher Unwin, 1903. p. 68–92.

7822 **Chapman**, *Sir* Sydney John. *Some aspects of the theory of wages in relation to practice.* London, 1905. [20]p.

7823 **Dawbarn**, Climenson Yelverton Charles. *Principles of employment.* Liverpool, 1905. 68p.

7824 **Keeble**, Samuel Edward. *Christianity and our wages system.* London: C. H. Kelly, 1907. 30p. (Social tracts for the times 3.)

7825 **Snow**, Terence Benedict. *Fair treatment for honest work.* London, 1908. 16p.

7826 **Keeble**, Samuel Edward. 'Christianity and our wages system.' Crooks, W., and others. *Social ideals: papers on social subjects.* London: R. Culley, 1909. p. 55–82.

7827 **Board of Trade.** *Earnings and hours of labour of workpeople of the United Kingdom.* London: H.M.S.O.

I. *Textile trades in 1906: report, appendices.* 1909. lxxiv, 250p. (Cd. 4545.)

II. *Clothing trades in 1906: report, appendices.* 1909. lxvi, 237p. (Cd. 4844.)

III. *Building and woodworking trades in 1906: report, appendices.* 1910. xl, 188p. (Cd. 5086.)

IV. *Public utility services in 1906: report, appendices.* 1910. xxviii, 194p. (Cd. 5196.)

V. *Agriculture in 1907: report, appendices.* 1910. xxvi, 58p. (Cd. 5460.)

VI. *Metal, engineering and shipbuilding trades in 1906: report, appendices.* 1911. lii, 200p. (Cd. 5814.)

VII. *Railway service in 1907: report, appendices.* 1912. xxix, 258p. (Cd. 6053.)

VIII. *Paper, printing, etc., trades; pottery, brick, glass and chemical trades; food, drink and tobacco trades; and miscellaneous trades, in 1906: report, appendices.* 1913. xxxv, 298p. (Cd. 6556.)

By G. R. Askwith.

7828 **Leppington**, C. H. d'E. 'Is there an upward limit to wages?' *Char. Orgn. Rev.*, n.s., XXX, 177 (September 1911), 190–201.

7829 **Wilkins**, William George. *Labourers' wages and how to raise them.* London, 1911. 124p.

7830 **Carlyle**, Alexander James. *Wages.* London: Mowbray, 1912. xi, 125p. (Christian Social Union handbooks.)

7831 **Money**, *Sir* Leo George Chiozza. 'A brief statement of the case for high wages.' *Things that matter: papers upon subjects which are, or ought to be, under discussion.* London: Methuen, 1912. p. 37–49.

7832 **Mackay**, Thomas. 'The wages and savings of working men.' *The dangers of democracy: studies in the economic questions of the day.* London: Murray, 1913. p. 116–55.

First published in the *Quarterly Review.*

7833 **Milligan**, George. 'The living wage.' Wright, T. and Milligan, G. *Practical social reform.* London: Catholic Truth Society, 1913. p. 14–28.

A paper read at the National Catholic Congress at Norwich, August 5, 1912.

Also included in *Catholic Social Guild pamphlets. Third series.* London: Catholic Truth Society, 1914.

7834 **Oyler**, P. *Wealth for the worker.* London: C. W. Daniel, 1914. 44p.

7835 **Ryan**, John Augustine. *The living wage.* London: Catholic Truth Society, 1914. 24p.

Also included in *Catholic Social Guild pamphlets. Third series.* London: Catholic Truth Society, 1914.

7836 **Bunting**, John Howard. *War and wages.* London: Garton Foundation, [1917]. xvi, 103p.

7837 **Mackmurdo**, Arthur Heygate. *What should fix your pay? or, the apportioning of a nation's wealth to each according to his rank.* London: P. S. King, 1917. 35p.

7838 **Mallock**, William Hurrell. *Capital, war and wages: three questions in outline.* London: Blackie, 1918. vii, 86p.

7839 **Milner**, E. Mabel and **Milner**, Dennis. *Scheme for a state bonus: a rational method of solving the social problem.* London: Simpkin, Marshall, 1918. 16p.

7840 **Swann**, Frederic. *Work and wages: a fair exchange.* London: P. B. Beddow, 1918. 16p.

7841 **Hichens**, William Lionel. *The wage problem in industry.* London, 1919. 8p.

7842 **Stafford**, John. *The wages problem and the money power.* London: Independent Labour Party, 1919. 31p.

7843 **Lyons**, Vyvyan Ashleigh. *Wages and empire.* London: Longmans, 1920. 96p.

7844 **Macassey**, Lynden. 'The national wage position.' *Nineteenth Century*, LXXXVIII, 525 (November 1920), 760–73.

7845 **Macfie**, Robert Andrew Scott. *Work, wages and salaries.* Liverpool: *Daily Post* Printers, 1920. [8]p.

Reprinted from *Liverpool Echo.*

7846 *Talks with workers on wealth, wages and production.* London: Pitman, 1920. viii, 124p.

7847 **Bell**, *Sir* Hugh. *High wages: their cause and effect.* London: National Association of Merchants and Manufacturers, 1921. 20p.

7848 **Drysdale**, Charles Vickery. *Wages and the cost of living.* London: Malthusian League, 1921. 48p.

7849 **Graham**, William. *The wages of labour.* London: Cassell, 1921. 165p. (Cassell's social economics series.)

Revised edition. 1924. 163p.

7850 **United States**. National Industrial Conference Board. *Wages in Great Britain, France and Germany.* New York: Century, 1921. vii, 110p. (Research report 40.)

7851 **Eire**. Dáil Éireann. *Report of Committee on Salaries and Allowances.* 1922. (T. 2.)

Another report. 1923. (T. 8.)

7852 **Richardson**, H. Y. *A lecture on wealth and work.* Newcastle-upon-Tyne: A. Reid, 1922. 20p. (Industrial life: a series of booklets.)

7853 **National Movement Towards a Christian Order of Industry and Commerce.** *Cambridge Conference, January 12th to 15th, 1923* [on the wages problem]: *papers.* [York?]: the Movement [1923?]. 62p. (Christian order of industry series 1.)

A conference for employers. Papers by Sydney W. Pascall, J. H. Jones, J. W. Madeley, Henry Atkinson, Theodore C. Taylor, T. R. Glover.

7854 **Pigou**, Arthur Cecil. 'Eugenics and some wage problems.' *Essays in applied economics.* London: King, 1923.

Revised edition. 1924. p. 80–91.

The Galton Lecture, also published in *Eugenics Review*, April 1923.

7855 **Clay**, Henry. 'The post-war wages problem.' *Econ. J.*, XXXIV, 133 (March 1924), 1–15.

'Paper read before Section F of the British Association at Liverpool, September, 1923.'

7856 **Fisher**, Allan George Barnard. *Some problems of wages and their regulation in Great Britain since 1918.* 1924. (Ph.D. thesis, University of London.)

7857 **Hunter**, George Burton. *The industrial and trade depression in Great Britain: the cause and the way out.* Wallsend, 1925. 16p.

7858 **Milnes**, Nora. *The economics of wages and labour.* London: King, 1926. vii, 197p.

7859 **Robbins**, Lionel Charles, Baron Robbins of Clare Market. *Wages: an introductory analysis of the wage system under modern capitalism.* London: Jarrolds, 1926. 94p.

7860 **Simon**, E. D. 'Wages and industrial peace.' *Manchr. Statist. Soc. Trans.* (1927–28), 79–104.

Followed by a discussion, p. i–x.

7861 **Renold**, Charles Garonne. 'The nature and present position of skill in industry.' *Econ. J.*, XXXVIII, 152 (December 1928), 593–604.

Figures from Hans Renold Ltd., Manchester.

7862 **Rowe**, John Wilkinson Foster. *Wages in practice and theory.* London: Routledge, 1928. x, 277p. (Studies in economics and political science 94.)

Reissued. Routledge and Kegan Paul, 1969. x, 277p.

7863 **Wedgwood**. Josiah Clement, Baron Wedgwood. *Work and wages: the root of the matter.* London: English League for the Taxation of Land Values, 1929. 8p.

7864 **Keynes**, John Maynard. 'The question of high wages.' *Polit. Q.*, I, 1 (January 1930), 110–24.

7865 **Harris**, C. 'Wages.' *Nineteenth Century*, CX, 658 (December 1931), 703–16.

7866 **Hunter**, *Sir* George Burton. *Wages and purchasing power.* Newcastle-upon-Tyne: Easey and Best, 1931. 7p.

7867 **International Association for Social Progress**. British Section. *Report . . . on the policy of high wages.* London: the Association, 1931. 66p.

Presented to Fourth General Assembly, Paris, October 1931.

Chairman of the High Wages Committee: S. Sanders.

7868 **Whiteford**, James Forbes. *Cost reduction or wages reduction?* London: *Efficiency Magazine*, 1931. 32p. (Up-to-date bulletins for business men 17.)

7869 **M'Devitt**, Philip. *The labourer and his hire: short studies in financial policy.* Edinburgh, London: Hodge, 1932. 66p.

7870 **McGregor**, Alexander Grant. *Raise wages!* London: London General Press, 1932. 60p.

7871 **United States**. Social Science Research Council. *International wage comparisons: documents arising out of conferences held at the International Labour Office in Jan. 1929, and May 1930, convened by the Social Science Research Council of New York; with* '*Report on the existing wage and cost of living material in Canada, France, Germany, Italy, the United Kingdom, and the United States*', *by John Jewkes.* Manchester: Manchester U.P., 1932. 262p.

Edited by J. W. Nixon and Henry Clay.

7872 **Edelberg**, V. G. *Wages and capitalist production.* 1935. (Ph.D. thesis, University of London.)

7873 **Asher**, Percy Henry. *Studies in the theories of wage rates.* 1935–36. (M.Sc. thesis, University of Cambridge.)

7874 **Jones**, W. D. *Problems of wage and wage regulation.* 1936. (M.A. thesis, University of London.)

Noted as 'lost' in printed list of London University theses.

7875 **Ralph**, James A. A. *The wage-system and some of its critics.* London: J. Clarke, 1937. 234p.

7876 **Kuczynski**, Jürgen. *Hunger and work: statistical studies.* New York: International Publishers, 1938. xii, 132p.

English edition. London: Lawrence and Wishart, 1938.

Contents: I. The cost of living. II. Wage statistics in Great Britain. III. Wages and cost of living in industry and agriculture. IV. Seven lean years. [1931–37.]

7877 **McGregor**, Alexander Grant. *Right wages: the index which determines the wages best for both capital and labour; the reforms required in wage, banking and exchange practice.* London: Pitman, 1938. xi, 316p.

7878 **Bowley**, Arthur Lyon. 'Earnings and prices, 1904, 1914, 1937–8.' *Rev. Econ. Studies*, VIII, 3 (June 1941), 129–42.

7879 **Nicholson**, John Leonard. 'Wages and prices.' *Oxf. Univ. Inst. Statist. Bull.*, IV, 17 (12 December 1942), 319–25.

7880 **Grey**, J. *Your money and your life.* Burnley, 1943. 39p.

7881 **Liberal Party Organisation.** *Remuneration of the worker: the report of the Liberal Remuneration of the Worker Sub-Committee.* London, 1943. 23p.

7882 **Northcott**, Clarence Hunter. *Wages: a chapter from a forthcoming book on labour management, its scope and practice.* London: Institute of Labour Management, 1943. 31p.

7883 **McGregor**, Alexander Grant. *Prosperity, wages and free enterprise.* London: Pitman, 1944. 119p.

7884 **Political and Economic Planning.** 'Wages and the cost of living index.' *Planning*, 220 (14 April 1944), 1–17.

7885 **McGregor**, Alexander Grant. *Labour's opportunity: the road to live and let live.* London: Pitman, 1945. 54p.

7886 **Rothschild**, K. W. 'Wages and risk-bearing.' *Oxf. Univ. Inst. Statist. Bull.*, VII, 11–12 (1 September 1945), 193–8.

7887 **McGregor**, Alexander Grant. *End wages conflict: 'prosperity wages' the great need.* London: Williams, Lea, 1947. 11p.

7888 **Bruce**, Donald William Trevor. *Our pay packets: should they be real or fictitious?* London: Labour Party, 1948. 15p.

7889 **Thorneycroft**, George Edward Peter. *Design for wages.* London: Design for Freedom, 1948. 21p.

7890 **Williams**, Gertrude, *Lady. The pay packet.* London: Bureau of Current Affairs, 1949. 19p. (Current affairs 92.)

7891 **Aller**, C. C. *Wage determination under full employment with particular reference to Great Britain.* 1950. (B.Litt. thesis, University of Oxford.)

7892 **Dennison**, S. R. 'Wages in full employment.' *Lloyds Bank Rev.*, n.s., 16 (April 1950), 18–37.

7893 **Morgan**, Edward Victor. 'First principles on wages.' *Banker*, CIII, 346 (November 1954), 299–303.

7894 **Roberts**, Benjamin Charles. 'Industrial unrest and the wage problem.' *Polit. Q.*, XXV, 2 (April–June 1954), 144–54.

7895 **Robertson**, *Sir* Dennis Holme. *Wages.* London: Athlone P., 1954. 18p. (Stamp memorial lecture 1954.)

7896 **Schreiner**, Johan. 'Wages and prices in England in the later Middle Ages.' *Scand. Econ. Hist. Rev.*, II, 2 (1954), 61–73.

7897 **Lydall**, Harold French. *British incomes and savings.* Oxford: Blackwell, 1955. xvi, 274p. (Oxford University, Institute of Statistics. Monographs 5.)

7898 **Political and Economic Planning.** 'New writing on wages.' *Planning*, XXI, 390 (12 December 1955), 245–60; 391 (12 December 1955), 261–75.

'This broadsheet looks at *The Great Inflation 1939–51* by A. J. Brown, *The social foundations of wage policy*, by . . . Barbara Wootton, and *The theory of wages*, by K. W. Rothschild. Its companion issue completes the survey with *Wages policy under full employment*, a symposium by four Swedish economists, edited by Ralph Turvey, *The economic foundation of wage policy*, an address by . . . J. R. Hicks to the British Association in 1955, and studies of wages policies by . . . E. H. Phelps Brown and B. C. Roberts in *Lloyds Bank Review*, and by J. Driscoll in a Bow Group pamphlet.'

7899 **Wootton**, Barbara Frances, Baroness Wootton of Abinger. *The social foundations of wage policy: a study of contemporary British wage and salary structure.* London: Allen and Unwin, 1955. 200p.

Second edition. 1962. 200p.

Second edition, second impression. 1964. (Unwin university books.)

7900 **Amphlett**, E. M. 'Employers' wage policy.' *Polit. Q.*, XXVII, 3 (July–September 1956), 293–302.

7901 **Hicks**, John Richard. 'The instability of wages.' *Three Banks Rev.*, 31 (September 1956), 3–19.

7902 **Kahn**, Hilda Renate. 'The element of "accident" in the national salary structure.' *Manchr. Sch.*, XXIV, 2 (May 1956), 180–96.

7903 **Labour Research Department.** *Wages questions.* London: L.R.D. Publications, 1956. 16p.

7904 **Williams**, Gertrude, *Lady*. 'The myth of "fair" wages.' *Econ. J.*, LXVI, 264 (December 1956), 621–34.

7905 **Roberts**, Benjamin Charles. 'Towards a rational wages structure.' *Lloyds Bank Rev.*, n.s., 44 (April 1957), 1–13.

7906 **Williams**, Gertrude, *Lady*. 'Wages in the post war world.' *Westm. Bank. Rev.* (May 1957), 5–8.

7907 **Proctor**, Theodore. 'Elusive conceptions of wages.' *Distr. Bank Rev.*, 126 (June 1958), 3–17.

7908 **Fogarty**, Michael Patrick. 'The just wage.' *Contemp. Rev.* (August–September 1959), 65–73.

'A comment', by Nancy Seear, p. 73–6.

7909 **International Labour Office**. *Labour costs in European industry*. Geneva: I.L.O., 1959. 170p. (Studies and reports, new series 52.)

7910 **Mayer**, Henry. 'Prestige and wages.' *J. Ind. Relat.*, I, 2 (October 1959), 126–9.

7911 **Reddaway**, W. B. 'Wage flexibility and the distribution of labour.' *Lloyds Bank Rev.*, n.s., 54 (October 1959), 32–48.

7912 **Behrend**, Hilde M. 'Some aspects of company wage policy.' *J. Ind. Econ.*, VIII, 2 (March 1960), 122–32.

7913 **Robertson**, Donald James. 'The determinants of wage structure.' *Scott. J. Polit. Econ.*, VII, 1 (February 1960), 1–13.

Based on a paper read to the Economics Society of King's College, Newcastle in November 1958.

7914 **Clegg**, Hugh Armstrong. 'The scope of fair wage comparisons.' *J. Ind. Econ.*, IX, 3 (July 1961), 199–214.

A paper read to Liverpool Economic and Statistical Society on 11 January 1961.

7915 **Fogarty**, Michael Patrick. *The just wage*. London: Chapman, 1961. 309p.

7916 **Jackson**, Joseph Michael. 'Wages, social income and the family.' *Manchr. Sch.*, XXIX, 1 (January 1961), 95–106.

7917 **Wootton**, Barbara Frances, Baroness Wootton of Abinger. *Remuneration in a welfare state*. Liverpool: Liverpool U.P., 1961. 17p. (Eleanor Rathbone memorial lectures 11.)

7918 **Powell**, V. G. E. *An examination of wages in the light of modern management techniques*. 1962. 2v. (Ph.D. thesis, University of Manchester.)

7919 **Fogarty**, Michael Patrick. 'Portrait of a pay structure.' Meij, J. L. (ed.). *Internal wage structure*. Amsterdam: North-Holland Publishing Co., 1963. p. 1–114.

7920 **Marsh**, David Charles. 'What are people worth?' *New Soc.*, 29 (18 April 1963), 12–13.

7921 **Behrend**, Hilde M. 'Price and income images and inflation.' *Scott. J. Polit. Econ.*, XI, 2 (June 1964), 84–103.

Comment by H. M. Begg and J. A. Stewart, XV, 1 (February 1968), 84–96.

Rejoinder by H. Behrend, p. 97–100.

7922 **Hobsbawm**, Eric John Ernest. 'Custom, wages and work-load in nineteenth-century industry.' *Labouring men: studies in the history of labour*. London: Weidenfeld and Nicolson, 1964. p. 344–70.

7923 **Blaug**, Mark. 'The rate of return on investment in education in Great Britain.' *Manchr. Sch.*, XXXIII, 3 (September 1965), 205–51.

'Appendix: Estimate of the rate of return to education in Great Britain', by D. Henderson-Stewart, p. 252–61.

7924 **Layton**, David. *Wages – fog or facts? A case for independent collection and analysis of information on incomes*. London: Institute of Economic Affairs, 1965. 38p. (Eaton papers 7.)

7925 **O'Mahony**, David. *Economic aspects of industrial relations*. Dublin: Economic Research Institute, 1965. 49p. (Paper 24.)

7926 **Shenfield**, Barbara E. 'The low wage problem.' *New Soc.*, VIII, 201 (4 August 1966), 189–91.

7927 **Taira**, Koji. 'The relation between wages and income from self-employment: estimates and international comparisons.' *Manchr. Sch.*, XXXIV, 2 (May 1966), 159–77.

7928 **Marquand**, Judith. 'Which are the lower paid workers?' *Br. J. Ind. Relat.*, V, 3 (November 1967), 359–74.

7929 **Baldwin**, Raymond Whittier. 'Fair pay.' *Manchr. Statist. Soc. Trans.* (1967–68). 18p.

7930 **Edmonds**, John and **Radice**, Giles. *Low pay*. London: Fabian Society, 1968. 20p. (Research series 270.)

7931 **Gough**, I. and **Stark**, Thomas. 'Low incomes in the United Kingdom, 1954, 1959 and 1963.' *Manchr. Sch.*, XXXVI, 2 (June 1968), 173–84.

7932 **Lipsey**, Richard G. 'Can there be a valid theory of wages?' McCormick, B. J. and Smith, E. O. (eds.). *The labour market: selected readings*. Harmondsworth: Penguin, 1968. p. 269–83.

Reprinted from *Advancement of Science*, XIX (1962), 105–12.

7933 **Social Research Development**. *Appropriate pay*. London: S.R.D., 1968. 10 leaves.

7934 **Stamford**, John. *Pay day simplified*. Oxford, London: Pergamon, 1968. 24p. (Productivity progress.)

7935 **Coates**, Ken and **Silburn**, Richard. 'Poverty, low-pay, and trade union action.' *Trade Un. Regist.* (1969), 106–23.

7936 **Gittus**, Elizabeth. 'Income.' Stacey, M. (ed.). *Comparability in social research*. London: Heinemann, 1969. p. 65–93.

Published for the British Sociological Association and the Social Science Research Council.

7937 **Hughes**, John. 'A note on low pay.' *Trade Un. Regist.* (1969), 133–8.

7938 **Organisation for Economic Co-operation and Development**. *Low income groups and methods of dealing with their problems: papers for a trade union seminar*. Paris: O.E.C.D., 1969. 295p. (International seminars 1965, 3.)

7939 **Behrend**, Hilde M., **Knowles**, Ann and **Davies**, Jean. *Views on pay increases, fringe benefits and low pay: findings from a national sample survey*. Dublin: Economic and Social Research Institute, 1970. 84p. (Papers 56.)

7940 **Henle**, Peter. 'Trends in labor compensation: United States and Western Europe.' Kamin, A. (ed.). *Western European labor and the American corporation*. Washington, D.C.: Bureau of National Affairs, 1970. p. 307–24.

7941 **MacKay**, Donald. 'Internal wage structures.' Robinson, D. (ed.). *Local labour markets and wage structures*. London: Gower P., 1970. p. 127–67.

7942 **Reid**, Graham Livingstone. 'Wages and labour costs.' Robertson, D. J. and Hunter, L. C. *Labour market issues of the 1970s*. Edinburgh: Oliver and Boyd for the Scottish Economic Society, 1970. p. 115–31.

First appeared in the June 1970 issue of the *Scottish Journal of Political Economy*.

7943 **Smith**, C. Selby. 'Costs and benefits in further education: some evidence from a pilot study.' *Econ. J.*, LXXX, 319 (September 1970), 583–604.

7944 **Trades Union Congress**. *Low pay: a T.U.C. General Council discussion document based on the report of a working party of T.U.C. staff and trade union research officers*. London: T.U.C., 1970. 57p.

7945 **National Board for Prices and Incomes**. *General problems of low pay*. London: H.M.S.O., 1971. (Report 169. Cmnd. 4648.)

See also: 5146; 6253; 6621; 7082; 7157; 7234; 7495; 7503; 7780–1; 8859; 11,961; 11,965.

B. DEFINITIONS AND MEASUREMENT

7946 **Mavor**, James. *The wage statistics and wage theories: a paper read before the Economic Section of the British Association at Bath, September, 1888*. Edinburgh: W. Brown, 1888. 17p.

7947 **Bullock**, C. J. 'Contributions to the history of wage statistics.' *J. Am. Statist. Ass.*, VI (March 1899), 187–218.

7948 **Edgeworth**, Francis Ysidro and **Bowley**, Arthur Lyon. 'Methods of representing statistics of wages and other groups not fulfilling the normal law of error.' *R. Statist. Soc. J.*, LXV, 2 (June 1902), 325–54.

7949 **Keynes**, John Maynard. '[Note on the Board of Trade index-numbers for rents, prices and wages.]' *Econ. J.*, XVIII, 71 (September 1908), 472–3.

Comment by G. Udny Yule, December 1908, 653–5.

Reply by J. M. Keynes, 655–7.

7950 **Bowley**, Arthur Lyon. 'A suggestion for the international comparison of wages by the use of the median.' *R. Statist. Soc. J.*, LXXII, 4 (December 1909), 718–21.

'Read before the Twelfth Congress of the International Statistical Institute at Paris, July 1909.'

7951 **Grier**, Lynda. 'The meaning of wages.' *Econ. J.*, XXXV, 140 (December 1925), 519–35.

'Presidential Address before Section F of the British Association, Southampton, 1925.'

7952 **Phelps Brown**, Ernest Henry. 'Real wages: a note.' *Econ. J.*, LVIII, 232 (December 1948), 599–600.

7953 **Knowles**, Kenneth Guy Jack Charles and **Hill**, Thomas Peter. 'On the difficulties of measuring wage differentials.' *Oxf. Univ. Inst. Statist. Bull.*, XVI, 11–12 (November–December 1954), 393–409.

7954 **Straw**, K. H. 'The savings surveys and official sources: a reconciliation of estimates of personal income.' *Oxf. Univ. Inst. Statist. Bull.*, XVII, 3 (August 1955), 283–302.

7955 **Kahn**, Hilda Renate. 'The distinction between wages and salaries.' *Scott. J. Polit. Econ.*, III, 2 (June 1956), 126–45.

7956 **Bechhofer**, Frank. 'Occupations.' Stacey, M. (ed.). *Comparability in social research*. London: Heinemann, 1969. p. 94–122.

Published for the British Sociological Association and the Social Science Research Council.

See also: 3.

C. CHRONOLOGICAL STUDIES

This section contains works which are primarily concerned with describing or explaining the level of wages prevailing in a specific period or the changes in these levels over time. Chronological studies with a primarily regional focus are classified in Part Six, III, D and those with a primarily industrial or occupational focus in Part Six, III, E; those relating to women's wages are classified in Part Six, III, F. Some of the works on trade unionism in Part Three, III, B also contain material on wages and salaries.

7957 *Returns of wages published between 1830 and 1886*. London: H.M.S.O., 1887. 437p. (C. 5172.)

7958 *Reports from select committees and other reports on wages, government contracts and on profit sharing, with proceedings, minutes of evidence, appendices and indices, 1890–97*. Shannon: Irish U.P., 1970. 1088p. (British parliamentary papers, industrial relations, 22.)

Reports made to the Board of Trade.

Facsimile reprint of first editions, London, H.M.S.O., 1891–97.

7959 *Reports on the wages of manual labourers and domestic servants and on wages and the cost of production, with appendices, index and tables, 1890–99*. Shannon: Irish U.P., 1970. 798p. (British parliamentary papers, industrial relations, 21.)

Reports made to the Board of Trade. Facsimile reprints of first editions, London, H.M.S.O., 1891–99.

7960 *Report on the wages of the manual labour classes in the United Kingdom, with tables of the average rate of wages and hours of labour of persons employed in several of the principal trades in 1886 and 1891*. London: H.M.S.O., 1893–4. (C. 6889.)

7961 **Bowley**, Arthur Lyon. 'Changes in average wages (nominal and real) in the United Kingdom between 1860 and 1891.' *R. Statist. Soc. J.*, LVIII, 2 (June 1895), 223–78.

With discussion, 279–85.

'Read before the Royal Statistical Society, 19th March, 1895.'

7962 **Bowley**, Arthur Lyon. 'Comparison of the rates of increase of wages in the United States and in Great Britain, 1860–1891.' *Econ. J.*, v, 19 (September 1895), 369–83.

'Read before Section F of the British Association, September 12th, 1895.'

7963 **Bowley**, Arthur Lyon. 'Comparison of the changes in wages in France, the United States, and the United Kingdom, from 1840 to 1891.' *Econ. J.*, VIII, 32 (December 1898), 474–89.

'A Paper read before Section F, British Association, Bristol, 1898.'

7964 **Bowley**, Arthur Lyon. 'Wages in the United States and Europe.' *Econ. J.*, IX, 33 (March 1899), 136–40.

Comparison of figures given in the *Bulletin of the Department of Labor*, Washington, no. 18, September 1898 with those estimated by the author for the December 1898 number of the *Economic Journal*.

7965 **Wood**, George Henry. 'The course of average wages between 1790 and 1860.' *Econ. J.*, IX, 36 (December 1899), 588–92.

'Read to British Association, Section F, at Dover, September 19, 1899.

7966 **Bowley**, *Sir* Arthur Lyon. *Wages in the United Kingdom in the nineteenth century: notes for the use of students of social and economic questions*. Cambridge: Cambridge U.P., 1900. vi, 148p.

7967 **Wood**, George Henry. 'A glance at wages and prices since the Industrial Revolution.' Co-operative Wholesale Societies. *Annual for 1901*. p. 244–68.

7968 **Wood**, George Henry. 'Stationary wage-rates.' *Econ. J.*, XI, 42 (June 1901), 151–6.

Nineteenth century, by trade, place, etc.

7969 **Board of Trade**. *Cost of living in German towns: report of an enquiry by the Board of Trade into working class rents, housing and retail prices, together with the rates of wages in certain occupations in the principal industrial towns of the German Empire*. London: Darling, 1908. lxi, 548p. (Cd. 4032.)

'With . . . a comparison of conditions in Germany and the United Kingdom.'

7970 **Board of Trade**. *Cost of living of the working classes: report of an enquiry by the Board of Trade into working class rents, housing and retail prices together with the standard rates of wages prevailing in certain occupations in the principal industrial towns of the United Kingdom. With an introductory memorandum*. London: Darling for H.M.S.O., 1908. liii, 616p. (Cd. 3864.)

7971 **Board of Trade**. *Cost of living in French towns: report of an enquiry by the Board of Trade into working class rents, housing and retail prices, together with the rates of wages in certain occupations in the principal industrial towns of France*. London: Darling, 1909. liv, 430p. (Cd. 4512.)

'With . . . a comparison of conditions in France and the United Kingdom.'

7972 **Wood**, George Henry. 'Real wages and the standard of comfort since 1850.' *R. Statist. Soc. J.*, LXXII, 1 (March 1909), 91–103.

Reprinted in Carus-Wilson, E. M. (ed.). *Essays in economic history*. Vol. 3. London: Arnold, 1962. p. 132–43.

7973 **Board of Trade**. *Cost of living in Belgian towns: report of an enquiry by the Board of Trade into working class rents, housing and retail prices, together with the rates of wages in certain occupations in the principal industrial towns of Belgium*. London: Darling, 1910. xli, 218p. (Cd. 5065.)

'With . . . a comparison of conditions in Belgium and the United Kingdom.'

7974 **Board of Trade**. *Cost of living in American towns: report of an enquiry by the Board of Trade into working class rents, housing and retail prices, together with the rates of wages in certain occupations in the principal industrial towns of the United States of America*. London: Darling, 1911. xcii, 533p. (Cd. 5609.)

'With . . . a comparison of conditions in the United States and the United Kingdom.'

7975 **London Municipal Society**. Department of Social Economics. *The growth of wages in amount and purchasing power since the middle of the nineteenth century*. London, 1911. 8p. (Monographs 13.)

7976 **Bickerdike**, C. F. 'International comparisons of labour conditions.' *Manchr. Statist. Soc. Trans.* (1911–12), 61–83.

On the Board of Trade inquiries on the United Kingdom, Germany, France, Belgium and the United States.

7977 **Money**, *Sir* Leo George Chiozza. 'The course of British wages.' Co-operative Wholesale Societies. *Annual for 1912*. p. 213–29.

7978 **Money**, *Sir* Leo George Chiozza. 'The recent fall in real wages.' *Things that matter: papers upon subjects which are, or ought to be, under discussion*. London: Methuen, 1912. p. 1–36.

7979 **Board of Trade.** *Cost of living of the working classes: report of an enquiry by the Board of Trade into working-class rents and retail prices together with the rates of wages in certain occupations in industrial towns of the United Kingdom in 1912.* London: Darling, 1913. lxiii, 398p. (Cd. 6955.)

In continuation of a similar report, 1905 (Cd. 3864).

7980 **Bowley,** *Sir* Arthur Lyon. *Prices & earnings in time of war.* London: Oxford U.P., 1915. 23p. (Oxford pamphlets, 1914–1915.)

7981 **Bowley,** *Sir* Arthur Lyon. *Prices and wages in the United Kingdom, 1914–1920.* Oxford: Clarendon P., 1921. xx, 228p. (Economic and social history of the war. British series.)

7982 **Wallis,** Percy and **Wallis,** Albert. *Prices and wages: an investigation of the dynamic forces in social economics.* London: King, 1921. xii, 456p.

7983 **Labour Research Department.** *Wages, prices and profits: a report.* London: L.R.D., 1922. 110p.

Preface by Sidney Webb.

7984 **Pigou,** Arthur Cecil. 'Prices and wages from 1896–1914.' *Econ. J.*, XXXIII, 130 (June 1923), 163–71.

Reprinted in Pigou, A. C. *Essays in applied economics.* London: King, 1923. Revised edition. 1924. p. 70–9.

7985 **Bowley,** *Sir* Arthur Lyon. *A new index number of wages.* London: London and Cambridge Economic Service, 1929. 7p. (Special memorandum 28.)

7986 **Gilboy,** Elizabeth Waterman. 'Wages in eighteenth-century England.' *J. Econ. Bus. Hist.*, II, 4 (August 1930), 603–29.

7987 **Stephens,** G. H. A. *Wage-rates: 1750–1800.* 1931. (B.Litt. thesis, University of Oxford.)

7988 **Clark,** Colin Grant. *The national income, 1924–1931.* London: Macmillan, 1932. x, 167p.

Chap. V. 'Wages.'

7989 **Clapham,** J. H. 'Work and wages.' Young, G. M. (ed.). *Early Victorian England, 1830–1865.* Vol. 1. London: Oxford U.P., 1934. p. 1–76.

7990 **Gilboy,** Elizabeth Waterman. *Wages in eighteenth century England.* Cambridge, Mass.: Harvard U.P., 1934. xxix, 297p. (Harvard economic studies XLV.)

'This study . . . began as a thesis for the doctor's degree at Radcliffe College [1929] . . . The whole study has been revised and many parts of it rewritten.'

Reprinted. New York: Russell and Russell, 1969. xxix, 297p.

7991 **Ramsbottom,** E. C. 'The course of wage rates in the United Kingdom, 1921–1934.' *R. Statist. Soc. J.*, XCVIII, 4 (1935), 639–73.

Discussion, p. 674–94.

7992 **Gilboy,** Elizabeth Waterman. 'The cost of living and real wages in eighteenth century England.' *Rev. Econ. Statist.*, XVIII, 3 (August 1936), 134–43.

7993 **Sargant Florence,** P. 'An index of working class purchasing power for Great Britain, 1929–35.' *J. Polit. Econ.*, XLIV, 5 (October 1936), 687–90.

7994 **Tucker,** R. S. 'Real wages of artisans in London, 1729–1935.' *J. Am. Statist. Ass.*, XXXI (March 1936), 73–84.

7995 **Bowley,** *Sir* Arthur Lyon. *Wages and income in the United Kingdom since 1860.* Cambridge: Cambridge U.P., 1937. xix, 151p.

7996 **Kuczynski,** Jürgen. *Labour conditions in Western Europe, 1820 to 1935.* London: Lawrence and Wishart, 1937. vii, 118p.

American edition. New York: International Publishers, [1937?]. Printed in Great Britain.

Primarily wages.

7997 **Dunlop,** John Thomas. 'The movement of real and money wage rates.' *Econ. J.*, XLVIII, 191 (September 1938), 413–34.

7998 **Ramsbottom,** E. C. 'The course of wage rates in the United Kingdom, 1934–1937.' *R. Statist. Soc. J.*, CI, 1 (1938), 202–4.

7999 **Tarshis,** Lorie. 'Real wages in the United States and Great Britain.' *Can. J. Econ. Polit. Sci.*, IV, 3 (August 1938), 362–76.

8000 **Dunlop,** John Thomas. 'Trends in the "rigidity" of English wage rates.' *Rev. Econ. Studies*, VI, 3 (June 1939), 189–99.

8001 **Keynes,** John Maynard. 'Relative movements of real wages and output.' *Econ. J.*, XLIX, 193 (March 1939), 34–51.

8002 **Ramsbottom,** E. C. 'Wage rates in the United Kingdom in 1938.' *R. Statist. Soc. J.*, CII, 2 (1939), 289–91.

8003 **Richardson,** John Henry. 'Real wage movements.' *Econ. J.*, XLIX (September 1939), 425–41.

8004 **Rostow,** W. W. 'Investment and real wages, 1873–86.' *Econ. Hist. Rev.*, IX, 2 (May 1939), 144–59.

8005 **Bowley,** *Sir* Arthur Lyon. 'Earnings, 1938 and 1940.' *Oxf. Univ. Inst. Statist. Bull.*, II, 11 (December 1940), 14–15.

8006 **Campion,** H. 'Changes in wage rates and earnings in 1939–1940: report of an enquiry conducted by the National Institute of Economic and Social Research.' *Econ. J.*, L, 198–9 (June–September 1940), 189–94.

8007 **Marley,** Joan G. and **Campion,** H. 'Changes in salaries in Great Britain, 1924–1939.' *R. Statist. Soc. J.*, CIII, 4 (1940), 524–33.

8008 **Ruggles,** Richard F. 'The relative movements of real and money wage rates.' *Q. J. Econ.*, LV, 1 (November 1940), 130–49.

Reply, by J. T. Dunlop, 4 (August 1941), 683–91.

Further comment, by L. Tarshis, 691–7.

Rejoinder, by R. F. Ruggles, 697–700.

8009 **Nicholson,** John Leonard. 'The trend of wages.' *Oxf. Univ. Inst. Statist. Bull.*, III, 11 (9 August 1941), 242–6.

8010 **Labour Research Department**. *Wages in 1942*. London: L.R.D., 1942. 20p. (Facts and figures for trade unionists.)

8011 **Brandis**, Buford. 'British prices and wage rates: 1939–1941.' *Q. J. Econ.*, LVII, 4 (August 1943), 543–64.

8012 **Nicholson**, John Leonard. 'Earnings in January 1943.' *Oxf. Univ. Inst. Statist. Bull.*, V, 12 (28 August 1943), 193–5.

8013 **Nicholson**, John Leonard. 'Earnings of work-people in 1938 and 1942.' *Oxf. Univ. Inst. Statist. Bull.*, V, 2 (30 January 1943), 31–5.

8014 **Nicholson**, John Leonard. 'Earnings and hours of labour.' *Oxf. Univ. Inst. Statist. Bull.*, VI, 7 (20 May 1944), 107–13.

8015 **Nicholson**, John Leonard. 'Wages during the war.' *Oxf. Univ. Inst. Statist. Bull.*, VI, 14 (14 October 1944), 232–5.

8016 **Nicholson**, John Leonard. 'Earnings, hours and mobility of labour.' *Oxf. Univ. Inst. Statist. Bull.*, VIII, 5 (May 1946), 146–63.

8017 **Flexner**, Jean Atherton. 'Great Britain: wage trends and policies, 1938–47.' *Mon. Labor Rev.*, LXV, 3 (September 1947), 285–92.

8018 **London and Cambridge Economic Service**. *Wages, earnings and hours of work, 1914–1947, United Kingdom*. London: the Service, 1947. 16p. (Special memoranda 50.)

By A. L. Bowley.

8019 **Flexner**, Jean Atherton. 'British labor under the Labor government. Part I. Economic position of labor: levels of national income, 1938 and 1947, workers' gains in earnings and working conditions.' *Mon. Labor Rev.*, LXVII, 2 (August 1948), 117–22.

8020 **Ainsworth**, Ralph B. 'Earnings and working hours of manual wage-earners in the United Kingdom in October, 1938.' *R. Statist. Soc. J.*, Ser. A, CXII, 1 (1949), 35–58.

Discussion, p. 58–66.

8021 **Mason**, W. H. *An analysis of wage-rates in Britain in relation to employment levels since 1920*. 1949. (M.Sc.(Econ.) thesis, University of London.)

8022 **Phelps Brown**, Ernest Henry. 'Wage levels after two wars.' *Westm. Bank Rev.* (November 1949), 1–7.

8023 **Phelps Brown**, Ernest Henry and **Hopkins**, Sheila V. 'The course of wage-rates in five countries, 1860–1939.' *Oxf. Econ. Pap.*, n.s., II, 2 (June 1950), 226–96.

France, Germany, Sweden, U.K., U.S.A.

8024 **Seers**, Dudley George. 'The levelling of incomes.' *Oxf. Univ. Inst. Statist. Bull.*, XII, 10 (October 1950), 271–98.

8025 **Knowles**, Kenneth Guy Jack Charles and **Robertson**, Donald James. 'Differences between the wages of skilled and unskilled workers, 1880–1950.' *Oxf. Univ. Inst. Statist. Bull.*, XIII, 4 (April 1951), 109–27.

8026 **Queensland Bureau of Industry**. 'The trend of real income in Great Britain.' *Rev. Econ. Prog.*, III, 7–8 (July–August 1951). 8p.

'Replacing and bringing up to date pp. 62–68, "Conditions of economic progress". Second Edition.'

8027 **Bowley**, Arthur Lyon. 'Index-numbers of wage-rates and cost of living.' *R. Statist. Soc. J.*, Ser. A, CXV, 4 (1952), 500–6.

8028 **Turner**, Herbert Arthur. 'Trade unions, differentials and the levelling of wages.' *Manchr. Sch.*, XX, 3 (September 1952), 227–82.

8029 **Chapman**, Agatha Louisa and **Knight**, Rose. *Wages and salaries in the United Kingdom, 1920–1938*. Cambridge: Cambridge U.P., 1953. xiv, 253p. (Studies in the national income and expenditure of the United Kingdom 5.)

8030 **Leak**, H. 'The industrial wages bill and earnings of operatives in 1935 and 1948.' *R. Statist. Soc. J.*, Ser. A, CXVI, 3 (1953), 275–82.

8031 **Penrice**, G. 'Earnings and wage rates, 1948–55.' *Lond. and Camb. Econ. Bull.*, n.s., 16 (December 1955), xi.

8032 **Schulz**, T. 'The means of subsistence: income from earnings and from assistance, 1935–53.' *Oxf. Univ. Inst. Statist. Bull.*, XVII, 1 (February 1955), 215–38.

8033 **Reynolds**, Lloyd George and **Taft**, Cynthia H. *The evolution of wage structure*. New Haven: Yale U.P., 1956. xii, 398p. (Yale studies in economics 6.)

With a section by Robert M. Macdonald. 'Great Britain', p. 251–85.

8034 **Turner**, Herbert Arthur. 'Wages: industry rates, workplace rates and the wage-drift.' *Manchr. Sch.*, XXIV, 2 (May 1956), 95–123.

'Some of this essay's material was first presented in a paper, "Social determinants of wages" to the 1955 meeting of the British Association for the Advancement of Science.'

8035 **Mansfield**, Edwin. 'A note on skill wage differentials in Britain, 1948–54.' *Rev. Econ. Statist.*, XXXIX, 3 (August 1957), 348–51.

8036 **Phelps Brown**, Ernest Henry. 'The long-term movement of real wages.' Dunlop, J. T. (ed.). *The theory of wage determination: proceedings of a conference held by the International Economic Association*. London: Macmillan; New York: St Martin's P., 1957. p. 48–65.

Discussion of paper, p. 346–51.

8037 **Robertson**, Donald James. 'Incomes in the U.K. and Scotland in 1949–50 and 1954–55: change and contrast.' *Scott. J. Polit. Econ.*, IV, 3 (October 1957), 230–4.

8038 **Rottier**, G. 'The evolution of wage differentials: a study of British data.' Dunlop, J. T. (ed.). *The theory of wage determination: proceedings of a conference held by the International Economic Association*. London: Macmillan; New York: St Martin's P., 1957. p. 238–50.

Discussion of paper, p. 366–72.

8039 **Butler**, E. B. 'Wages and salaries in the expenditure of county boroughs – 1951/2 and 1955/6.' *Accting. Res.*, IX, 4 (October 1958), 324–37.

8040 **O'Brien**, P. K. 'British incomes and property in the early nineteenth century.' *Econ. Hist. Rev.*, 2nd ser., XII, 2 (December 1959), 255–67.

8041 **Marquand**, Judith. 'Earnings-drift in the United Kingdom, 1948–57.' *Oxf. Econ. Pap.*, n.s., XII, 1 (February 1960), 77–104.

8042 **Turner**, Herbert Arthur. 'Wages, productivity and the level of employment: more on the "wage drift".' *Manchr. Sch.*, XXVIII, 1 (January 1960), 89–123.

8043 **Brenner**, Y. *Prices and wages in England, 1450–1550.* 1961. (M.A. thesis, University of London.)

8044 **Crossley**, John Rodney. 'Weekly and hourly wage rates since 1948.' *Lond. Camb. Econ. Bull.*, n.s., 39 (September 1961), viii–x.

8045 **Knowles**, Kenneth Guy Jack Charles and **Thorne**, E. M. F. 'Wage rounds, 1948–1959.' *Oxf. Univ. Inst. Statist. Bull.*, XXIII, 1 (February 1961), 1–26.

8046 **Phelps Brown**, Ernest Henry and **Hopkins**, Sheila V. 'Seven centuries of wages and prices: some earlier estimates.' *Economica*, n.s., XXVIII, 109 (February 1961), 30–36.

8047 **Robinson**, Derek. 'Wage-rate differentials over time.' *Oxf. Univ. Inst. Statist. Bull.*, XXIII, 4 (November 1961), 367–78.

8048 **Ball**, R. J. 'The prediction of wage-rate changes in the United Kingdom economy, 1957–60.' *Econ. J.*, LXXII, 285 (March 1962), 27–44.

8049 **Lerner**, Shirley Walowitz and **Marquand**, Judith. 'Workshop bargaining, wage drift and productivity in the British engineering industry.' *Manchr. Sch.*, XXX, 1 (January 1962), 15–60.

8050 **Phelps Brown**, Ernest Henry and **Browne**, Margaret H. 'Earnings in industries of the United Kingdom, 1948–59.' *Econ. J.*, LXXII, 287 (September 1962), 517–49.

8051 **Phelps Brown**, Ernest Henry. 'Wage drift.' *Economica*, n.s., XXIX, 116 (November 1962), 339–56.

8052 **Schulz**, T. 'Income, family structure, and food expenditure before and after the war.' *Oxf. Univ. Inst. Statist. Bull.*, XXIV, 4 (November 1962), 447–68.

8053 **Turner**, Herbert Arthur. 'The disappearing drift (or, in defence of Turner).' *Manchr. Sch.*, XXXII, 2 (May 1964), 155–96.

8054 **Lerner**, Shirley Walowitz. 'Wage drift, wage fixing and drift statistics.' *Manchr. Sch.*, XXXIII, 2 (May 1965), 155–77.

8055 **Svenska Arbetsgivareföreningen**. *Wage trends 1958–1963 and some labour-market institutions in ten countries.* Stockholm, 1965. 43 leaves.

8056 **Lomax**, K. S. 'Wages, prices, profits, and inflation.' *Manchr. Statist. Soc. Trans.* (1965–66). 22p.

8057 **Presland**, G. J. *Personal income from work and property, with particular reference to the United Kingdom during the period 1951–61.* 1965–66. (M.A. thesis, University of Liverpool.)

8058 **Layton**, David. *Incomes data: panorama, April 1965 to July 1966.* London: Hallam P., 1966. 62p.

8059 **Marquand**, Judith. *Wage drift: origins, measurement and behaviour; based on a lecture delivered at the Woolwich Polytechnic 11th May 1967.* London: Woolwich Polytechnic (Department of Economics and Business Studies), 1967. 31p. (Woolwich economic papers 14.)

8060 **Rosenberg**, Nathan. 'Anglo-American wage differences in the 1820's.' *J. Econ. Hist.*, XXVII, 2 (June 1967), 221–9.

8061 **Turner**, Herbert Arthur. 'That damned drift: a note on the Turner–Lerner controversy.' *Manchr. Sch.*, XXXV, 1 (January 1967), 83–6.
Reply, by S. W. Lerner, p. 87.
Turner's 'Envoi', p. 88.

8062 **Argy**, V. International comparisons of rates of change in earnings.' *Oxf. Econ. Pap.*, n.s., XX, 2 (July 1968), 218–29.

8063 **Department of Employment and Productivity**. *Labour costs in Great Britain in 1964.* London: H.M.S.O., 1968. 22p.

8064 **Gillion**, C. 'Wage rates, earnings and wage drift.' *Nat. Inst. Econ. Rev.*, 46 (November 1968), 52–67.

8065 **Phelps Brown**, Ernest Henry and **Browne**, Margaret H. *A century of pay: the course of pay and production in France, Germany, Sweden, the United Kingdom, and the United States of America, 1860–1960.* London: Macmillan, 1968. 476p.
Also New York: St Martin's P., 1969.

8066 **Olaloye**, A. O. *Wage drift in British manufacturing industries, 1956–1968.* 1968–69. (M.Sc. thesis, University of Bristol.)

8067 **Rondeau**, Claude. *The autonomous influence of the institutional determinants of the movements of money wages in the United Kingdom, 1862–1938.* 1969. (Ph.D. (Econ.) thesis, University of London.)

8068 **Adams**, Donald R. 'Some evidence on English and American wage rates, 1790–1830.' *J. Econ. Hist.*, XXX, 3 (September 1970), 499–520.

See also: 6293.

D. REGIONAL STUDIES

This section includes works with a primarily geographical orientation. Works comparing two or more regions are classified at Part Six, III, D, 1, while those dealing with a particular region are classified at Part Six, III, D, 2. Works comparing the United Kingdom as a whole with other countries are classified at Part Six, III, C. Many of the industrial and occupational studies in Part Six, III, E refer to a specific town or region. Some of the works on trade unionism in Part Three, III, C also contain material on wages and salaries.

1. Comparative

8069 **Pethick-Lawrence**, Frederick William. *Local variations in wages*. London: Longmans, Green, 1899. viii, 90p. (London School of Economics and Political Science. Studies in economics and political science [6].)

8070 **Deane**, Phyllis. 'Regional variations in United Kingdom incomes from employment, 1948.' *R. Statist. Soc. J.*, Ser. A, CXVI, 2 (1953), 123–35.
Discussion, p. 135–9.
'Read before the Royal Statistical Society, January 28th, 1953.'

8071 **Leser**, Conrad Emanuel Victor. 'Earnings in British regions in 1948.' *Scott. J. Polit. Econ.*, I, 3 (October 1954), 268–72.

8072 **Huggins**, H. D. 'Regional differentials in wages: some considerations.' *Soc. Econ. Studies*, IV, 3 (September 1955), 206–15.

8073 **Lerner**, Shirley Walowitz and **Marquand**, Judith. 'Regional variations in earnings, demand for labour and shop stewards' combine committees in the British engineering industry.' *Manchr. Sch.*, XXXI, 3 (September 1963), 261–96.

8074 **Holmans**, A. E. 'Inter-regional differences in levels of income: are there "two nations" or one?' Wilson, T. (ed.). *Papers on regional development*. Oxford: Blackwell, 1965. p. 1–19.
Supplementary volume to *Journal of Industrial Economics*.

8075 **Coates**, Bryan E. and **Rawstron**, Eric M. 'Regional variations in incomes.' *Westm. Bank Rev.* (February 1966), 28–46.

8076 **Sheail**, J. *The regional distribution of wealth in England as indicated in the 1524/5 lay subsidy returns*. 1967–68. (Ph.D. thesis, University of London.)

8077 **Harris**, C. P. and **Thirlwall**, A. P. 'Inter-regional variations in cyclical sensitivity to unemployment in the UK 1949–1964.' *Oxf. Univ. Inst. Econ. Statist. Bull.*, XXX, 1 (February 1968), 55–66.

See also: 7631; 7633; 7675; 7690; 7700; 9002.

2. Particular Regions

8078 **Price**, Langford Lovell Frederic Rice. *Industrial peace, its advantages, methods, and difficulties: a report of an inquiry made for the Toynbee trustees*. London, New York: Macmillan, 1887. xxxi, 127p.
'Reprinted (with additions) from a paper entitled "Sliding scales and other methods of wage-arrangement in the north of England"... read before The Statistical Society of London on 21st December, 1886, and inserted in the Journal of the Society for March, 1887.'

8079 **Price**, Langford Lovell Frederic Rice. 'Sliding scales and other methods of wage-arrangement in the north of England.' *R. Statist. Soc. J.*, L, 1 (March 1887), 5–74.
With discussion, p. 75–85.
Read before the Society, 21 December, 1886.

8080 **Hutchins**, B. Leigh. 'Notes towards the history of London wages.' *Econ. J.*, IX, 36 (December 1899), 599–605; X, 37 (March 1900), 103–4.

8081 **Wood**, George Henry. 'Notes on the history of Sheffield wages.' British Association for the Advancement of Science. *Reports of meetings*, 1910. p. 690–1.

8082 **Wood**, Frances. 'The course of real wages in London, 1900–12.' *R. Statist. Soc. J.*, LXXVII, 1 (December 1913), 1–55.
With discussion, p. 56–68.
Read before the Society, 18 November 1913.

8083 **Peat**, H. 'Economic welfare and family responsibility.' *Economica*, VI, 18 (November 1926), 269–84.
Data relating to the village of Stanley, County Durham.

8084 **Jones**, David Caradog. 'Data relating to rents and incomes in a sample of overcrowded families in Liverpool.' *R. Statist. Soc. J.*, XCIII, 4 (1930), 561–8.

8085 **Jones**, Annie Beatrice. *Some contributions to a study of work, wages and prices in Wales in the sixteenth century*. 1933. (M.A. thesis, University of Wales, Aberystwyth.)

8086 **Kelsall**, Roger Keith. 'The general trend of real wages in the north of England during the eighteenth century.' *Yorks. Archaeol. J.*, XXXIII, 129 (1936), 49–56.

8087 **Willan**, T. S. 'Some Bedfordshire and Huntingdonshire wage rates, 1697–1730.' *Engl. Hist. Rev.*, LXI, 240 (May 1946), 244–9.

8088 **Evans**, Gwenllian. *Trade unionism and the wage level in Aberdeen, from 1870–1920*. 1951. (Ph.D. thesis, University of Aberdeen.)

8089 **Lydall**, Harold French. 'Personal incomes in Oxford.' *Oxf. Univ. Inst. Statist. Bull.*, XIII, 11–12 (November–December 1951), 379–400.

8090 **Lydall**, Harold French. 'A pilot survey of incomes and savings.' *Oxf. Univ. Inst. Statist. Bull.*, XIII, 9 (September 1951), 257–93.
A general description of the purpose, methods and general findings of the survey, which was made in Oxford.

8091 **Campbell**, A. D. 'Income.' Cairncross, A. K. (ed.). *The Scottish economy: a statistical account of Scottish life*. London: Cambridge U.P., 1954. p. 46–64.

8092 **Pollard**, Sidney. 'Wages and earnings in the Sheffield trades, 1851–1914.' *Yorks. Bull. Econ. Soc. Res.*, VI, 1 (February 1954), 49–64.

8093 **Robertson**, Donald James. 'Wages.' Cairncross, A. K. (ed.). *The Scottish economy: a statistical account of Scottish life.* London: Cambridge U.P., 1954. p. 149–69.

8094 **Beveridge**, *Lord.* 'Westminster wages in the manorial era.' *Econ. Hist. Rev.*, 2nd ser., VIII, 1 (August 1955), 18–35.

8095 **Campbell**, A. D. 'Changes in Scottish incomes, 1924–1949.' *Econ. J.*, LXV, 258 (June 1955), 225–40.

8096 **Pollard**, Sidney. 'Real earnings in Sheffield, 1851–1914.' *Yorks. Bull. Econ. Soc. Res.*, IX, 1 (May 1957), 54–62.

8097 **Glasscock**, R. E. *The distribution of lay wealth in south-east England in the early fourteenth century.* 1962–63. (Ph.D. thesis, University of London.)

8098 **Attwood**, E. A. and **Geary**, R. C. *Irish county incomes in 1960.* Dublin: Economic Research Institute, 1963. 8p. (Paper 16.)

8099 **Nevin**, Edward Thomas. *Wages in Ireland, 1946–62.* Dublin: Economic Research Institute, 1963. 23p. (Paper 12.)

8100 **Law,** David. 'Work and wage patterns in Northern Ireland.' *Christus Rex*, XVIII, 2 (April–June 1964), 107–13.

8101 **Nevin**, Edward Thomas. 'Work and wage patterns in Ireland.' *Christus Rex*, XVIII, 2 (April–June 1964), 100–6.

8102 **O'Herlihy**, C. St J. *A statistical study of wages, prices and employment in the Irish manufacturing sector.* Dublin: Economic Research Institute, 1966. 41p. (Paper 29.)

8103 **Armstrong**, Eric George Abbott. 'Birmingham and some of its low-paid workers.' *Manchr. Sch.*, XXXVI, 4 (December 1968), 365–82.

8104 **Knowles**, Kenneth Guy Jack Charles and **Robinson**, Derek. 'Wage movements in Coventry.' *Oxf. Univ. Inst. Econ. Statist. Bull.*, XXXI, 1 (February 1969), 1–21; XXXI, 2 (May 1969), 145–52.

8105 **Loschky**, David J. and **Krier**, Donald F. 'Income and family size in three eighteenth-century Lancashire parishes: a reconstitution study.' *J. Econ. Hist.*, XXIX, 3 (September 1969), 429–48.

8106 **Ross**, Micéal. *Personal income by counties.* Dublin: Social and Economic Research Institute, 1969. 11p. (Paper 49.)

See also: 5504; 5513–14; 5524; 5555; 8037; 8128; 8131–2; 8141; 8146–7; 8149–50; 8152; 8154–7; 8169–70; 8178; 8240–1; 8258; 8262; 8298–9; 8313; 8332; 8355–8; 8361; 8370; 8411; 8460; 8465; 8467; 8470–2; 8494; 8496; 8498; 8500; 8506–8; 8530; 8539; 8544–5; 8551–3; 8556; 8559; 8561–2; 8625; 8661; 8868; 12,947; 12,961; 12,974; 12,988; 13,012; 13,017; 13,046–8.

E. OCCUPATIONAL AND INDUSTRIAL STUDIES

This section includes works with a primarily industrial or occupational orientation. Works comparing two or more industries or occupations are classified at Part Six, III, E, 1, while those dealing with a particular industry or occupation are classified at Part Six, III, E, 2–12. Some of the works on trade unionism in Part Three, III, D–E, on collective bargaining in Part Five, III, and on industrial conflict in Part Five, IV, E also contain material on wages and salaries. See also Part Six, IV, A, 3.

1. Comparative

8107 **Board of Trade**. *Report . . . on the relation of wages in certain industries to the cost of production.* London: H.M.S.O., 1890–1. (C. 6535.)

By T. H. Elliott.

8108 **London Municipal Society**. Department of Social Economics. *Digest of official statistics: earnings of adult males in certain principal industries.* London, 1912. 12p. (Monographs 19.)

8109 **Rowe**, John Wilkinson Foster. *Changes of wage rates in certain industries during the last 30–40 years, and in particular, the relations between changes in rates and changes in earnings, and their causes.* 1923. 4 pts. (M.Sc. (Econ.) thesis, University of London.)

8110 **Rowe**, John Wilkinson Foster. 'Wage disparities in British industries.' *Economica*, IV, 10 (February 1924), 82–8.

8111 **Bowley**, Arthur Lyon. 'Relative wages and earnings in different occupations.' *Oxf. Univ. Inst. Statist. Bull.*, III, 17 (13 December 1941), 383–9; IV, 1 (10 January 1942), 1–4.

8112 **Heinemann**, Margot. *Wages front.* London: Lawrence and Wishart, 1947. xii, 256p.

Prepared for the Labour Research Department.

8113 **Haddy**, Pamela Mary. *Changes in British interindustry earnings structure under full employment.* 1955. ix, 106 leaves. (M.S. thesis, Cornell University.)

8114 **Bellerby**, John Rotherford. *Agriculture and industry relative income.* London: Macmillan; New York: St Martin's P., 1956. xii, 369p.

Written in association with G. R. Allen and others.

Chapter XIV. 'Relative wages.' p. 225–46.

8115 **Haddy**, Pamela Mary and **Tolles**, N. Arnold. 'British and American changes in interindustry wage structure under full employment.' *Rev. Econ. Statist.*, XXXIX, 4 (November 1957), 408–14.

8116 **Devons**, Ely and **Ogley**, R. C. 'An index of wage rates by industries.' *Manchr. Sch.*, XXVI, 2 (May 1958), 77–115.

8117 **Haddy**, Pamela Mary and **Currell**, Melville E. 'British inter-industrial earnings differentials, 1924–55.' *Econ. J.*, LXVIII, 269 (March 1958), 104–11.

8118 **Crossley**, John Rodney. 'A monthly index of wage-rates by industries.' *Manchr. Sch.*, XXVII, 2 (May 1959), 211–19.

January 1955–December 1958.

8119 **Crossley**, John Rodney. 'A monthly index of wage-rates by industries.' *Manchr. Sch.*, XXVII, 3 (September 1959), 325–31.
January 1958–May 1959.

8120 **Crossley**, John Rodney. 'An index of wage-rates by industries.' *Manchr. Sch.*, XXVIII, 2 (May 1960), 207–13.

8121 **Crossley**, John Rodney. 'A monthly index of wage-rates by industries.' *Manchr. Sch.*, XXVIII, 1 (January 1960), 73–87.
January 1956–December 1957; January–August 1959.

8122 **Robertson**, Donald James. *Factory wage structures and national agreements*. Cambridge: Cambridge U.P., 1960. xi, 260p. (Glasgow University, Department of Social and Economic Research. Social and economic studies 5.)

8123 **Devons**, Ely and **Crossley**, John Rodney. *The 'Guardian' wage indexes: a series of indexes of wage rates in British industry since 1948, weekly and hourly, together with indexes of average earnings*. Manchester: *The Guardian*, 1962. 24p.

8124 **Shapiro**, J. C. *Inter-industry wage determination: the post-war United Kingdom experience*. 1965–66. (Ph.D. thesis, University of London.)

8125 **Devons**, Ely, **Crossley**, John Rodney and **Maunder**, W. F. 'Wage rate indexes by industry 1948–1965.' *Economica*, n.s., XXXV, 140 (November 1968), 392–423.

8126 **Reddaway**, W. B. 'Wage flexibility and the distribution of labour.' McCormick, B. J. and Smith, E. O. *The labour market: selected readings*. Harmondsworth: Penguin, 1968. p. 181–99.
Reprinted from *Lloyds' Bank Rev.*, LIV (1959), 32–48.

8127 **Papola**, T. S. and **Bharadwaj**, V. P. 'Dynamics of industrial wage structure: an inter-country analysis.' *Econ. J.*, LXXX, 317 (March 1970), 72–90.

2. Agriculture, Forestry, and Fishing

8128 **Barrington**, Richard M. 'The prices of some agricultural produce and the cost of farm labour for the past fifty years.' *Statist. Soc. Inq. Soc. Ir. J.*, IX, 65 (February 1887), 137–53.

8129 **Reade**, Compton. 'The equity of the rural wage-rate.' *Westm. Rev.*, CXXXVIII, 1 (July 1892), 57–64.

8130 **Bowley**, Arthur Lyon. 'The statistics of wages in the United Kingdom during the last hundred years. Part I. Agricultural wages.' *R. Statist. Soc. J.*, LXI, 4 (December 1898), 702–22.

8131 **Bowley**, Arthur Lyon. 'The statistics of wages in the United Kingdom during the last hundred years. Part II. Agricultural wages: Scotland.' *R. Statist. Soc. J.*, LXII, 1 (March 1899), 140–50.

8132 **Bowley**, Arthur Lyon. 'The statistics of wages in the United Kingdom during the last hundred years. Part III. Agricultural wages: Ireland.' *R. Statist. Soc. J.*, LXII, 2 (June 1899), 395–404.

8133 **Bowley**, Arthur Lyon. 'The statistics of wages in the United Kingdom during the last hundred years. Part IV. Agricultural wages: earnings and general averages.' *R. Statist. Soc. J.*, LXII, 3 (September 1899), 555–70.

8134 **Board of Trade**. Labour Department. *Earnings of agricultural labourers: report by Mr. Wilson Fox on the wages and earnings of agricultural labourers in the United Kingdom, with statistical tables and charts*. London: Eyre and Spottiswoode for H.M.S.O., 1900. x, 296p. (Cd. 346.)

8135 **Fox**, Arthur Wilson. 'Agricultural wages in England and Wales during the last fifty years.' *R. Statist. Soc. J.*, LXVI, 2 (June 1903), 273–348.
Discussion, p. 349–59.
'Read before the Royal Statistical Society, 21st April, 1903.'
Notes on the above paper, by A. L. Bowley, LXVI, 3 (September 1903), 598–601.

8136 **Board of Trade**. Labour Department. *Earnings of agricultural labourers: second report by Mr. Wilson Fox on the wages, earnings and conditions of employment of agricultural labourers in the United Kingdom, with statistical tables and charts*. London: Darling for H.M.S.O., 1905. xii, 263p. (Cd. 2376.)

8137 **Nicholson**, Joseph Shield. *The relations of rents, wages, and profits in agriculture, and their bearing on rural depopulation*. London: Swan Sonnenschein, 1906. viii, 176p.

8138 **Wilson**, James. 'Agricultural wages in England and in India.' *Econ. J.*, XXI, 82 (June 1911), 292–4.

8139 **Country Landowners' Association**. *The earnings of agricultural labourers in each county of England and Wales for the year 1912–1913*. London, 1913. 20p.

8140 **Central Land and Housing Council**. *The Liberal land and housing policy. 4. The agricultural labourer and his wage*. London, 1914. 47p.

8141 **Clark**, Joseph. 'Agricultural wages in Lincolnshire.' *Econ. Rev.*, XXIV, 2 (April 1914), 190–6.

8142 **Lennard**, Reginald. *Economic notes on English agricultural wages*. London: Macmillan, 1914. xi, 154p.

8143 **Money**, *Sir* Leo George Chiozza. 'The rural wage.' *The future of work, and other essays*. London: Fisher Unwin, 1914. p. 137–73.

8144 **Rew**, R. Henry. 'The land. II. The agricultural wage.' *Nineteenth Century*, XC, 536 (October 1921), 583–97.

8145 **International Labour Office**. 'Labour cost in agriculture in England and in Illinois.' *Int. Labour Rev.*, XVII, 2 (February 1928), 240–53.

8146 **Gilboy**, Elizabeth Waterman. 'Labour at Thornborough: an eighteenth-century estate.' *Econ. Hist. Rev.*, III, 3 (April 1932), 388–98.

A study of agricultural wages from the estate accounts, 1749–73.

8147 **Robo**, Etienne. 'Wages and prices in the Hundred of Farnham in the thirteenth century.' *Econ. Hist.*, III, 9 (January 1934), 26–34.

'Sources: the Pipe Rolls of the Bishopric of Winchester for Farnham Manor, 1208 to 1300.'

8148 **Carslaw**, R. McG. and **Graves**, P. E. 'The labour bill and output on arable farms.' *R. Statist. Soc. J.*, XCVIII, 4 (1935), 601–22.

Discussion, p. 623–37.

'Read before the Royal Statistical Society, May 21st, 1935.'

8149 **Beveridge**, *Sir* William Henry. 'Wages in the Winchester manors.' *Econ. Hist. Rev.*, VII, 1 (November 1936), 22–43.

8150 **Kelsall**, Roger Keith. 'Wages of northern farm labourers in mid-eighteenth century.' *Econ. Hist. Rev.*, VIII, 1 (November 1937), 80–1.

8151 **Thompson**, R. J. 'The agricultural labour bill in England and Wales.' *R. Statist. Soc. J.*, C, 4 (1937), 607–24.

8152 **Smith**, Joseph Henry. *Changes in farm costs of regular hired labour in Wales during 1939–40.*

Changes in farm costs of hired labour during 1940–41, by J. H. Smith and W. J. Thomas.

1941–2 – 1944–45, by J. H. Smith.

1945–6, *1946–7*, by A. Dorothy Hooper. Aberystwyth, [1940–48]. 6 parts. (University College of Wales. Agricultural Economics Department. Studies and Reports.)

Reproduced from typewriting.

8153 **Eccles**, *Sir* David McAdam. *Wages on the farm.* London: Signpost P., 1945. 47p. (Signpost booklets on post-war problems 20.)

8154 **Smith**, Joseph Henry. 'Changes of wages and costs of labour on farms in Wales, 1939–43.' University College of Wales, Aberystwyth. Department of Agricultural Economics. *Welsh studies in agricultural economics*, 1945. p. 53–9.

Reprinted from the *Welsh Journal of Agriculture*, vol. XVIII.

8155 **Molland**, R. and **Evans**, Gwenllian. 'Scottish farm wages from 1870 to 1900.' *R. Statist. Soc. J.*, Ser. A, CXIII, 2 (1950), 220–7.

8156 **Houston**, George. 'Farm wages in central Scotland from 1814–1870.' *R. Statist. Soc. J.*, Ser. A, CXVIII, 2 (1955), 224–8.

8157 **Mackenzie**, A. M. 'Variations in earnings of Scottish farm workers.' Department of Agriculture for Scotland. *Scottish agricultural economics: some studies of current economic conditions in Scottish farming.* Vol. VII. Edinburgh: H.M.S.O., 1956. p. 33–6.

8158 **Organisation for Economic Co-operation and Development.** *Low incomes in agriculture: problems and policies.* Paris: O.E.C.D., 1964. 515p.

8159 **Metcalfe**, David. *The determinants of the earning gap in agriculture: England and Wales, 1948–63.* 1965. 49p. (M.A. thesis, University of Manchester.)

8160 **National Board for Prices and Incomes.** *Pay of workers in agriculture in England and Wales.* London: H.M.S.O., 1967. 20p. (Report 25. Cmnd. 3199.)

8161 **National Board for Prices and Incomes.** *Pay of workers in agriculture in England and Wales.* London: H.M.S.O., 1969. vi, 14p. (Report 101. Cmnd. 3911.)

See also: 5507; 5514; 7827; 8114; 8759; 8801; 12,915; 12,955; 12,968; 12,978; 12,989.

3. Mining and Quarrying

8162 **Munro**, Joseph Edwin Crawford. *Sliding scales in the coal industry: a paper . . .* Manchester: J. Heywood, 1885. 55p.

8163 **Munro**, Joseph Edwin Crawford. 'Sliding scales in the coal and iron industries from 1885 to 1889.' *Manchr. Statist. Soc. Trans.* (1889–90), 119–71.

8164 *Return of rates of wages in mines and quarries in the United Kingdom, with report thereon.* London: H.M.S.O., 1890–1. (C. 6455.)

8165 **Munro**, Joseph Edwin Crawford. 'The probable effects of an eight hours day on the production of coal and the wages of miners.' *Econ. J.*, I, 2 (June 1891), 241–61.

8166 **Hooker**, Reginald H. 'On the relation between wages and the numbers employed in the coal mining industry.' *R. Statist. Soc. J.*, LVII, 4 (December 1894), 627–42; 4 unnumbered leaves of diagrams.

'Read before Section F of the British Association, Oxford, 1894.'

8167 **Smart**, William. *Miners' wages and the sliding scale.* Glasgow: J. Maclehose, 1894. 34p.

8168 **Ashley**, *Sir* William James. *The adjustment of wages: a study in the coal and iron industries of Great Britain and America.* London: Longmans, 1903. xx, 362p.

'Eight lectures . . . delivered on the Dunkin Foundation at Manchester College, Oxford, during the first three months of the present year [1903].'

8169 **Gibson**, Finlay A. *Statistical calculations* [of earnings in South Wales collieries], *showing the new 1915 standard rates at 1879 standard, 1877 standard and anthracite collieries . . .* Cardiff: *Western Mail*, 1915. 20 leaves.

8170 **Bowley**, Arthur Lyon and **Hogg**, Margaret Hope. 'Wages and production in a Durham colliery.' *Economica*, III, 9 (November 1923), 229–35.

8171 **Rowe**, John Wilkinson Foster. *Wages in the coal industry*. London: King, 1923. viii, 174p. (Studies in economics and political science 68.)

8172 **Ministry of Labour.** *Report by a Court of Inquiry concerning the wages position in the coal mining industry*. London: H.M.S.O., 1924. 18p. (Cmd. 2129.)
Chairman: Lord Buckmaster.

8173 **Bowie**, James Alexander. 'A new method of wage adjustment in the light of the recent history of wage methods in the British coal industry.' *Econ. J.*, XXXVII, 147 (September 1927), 384–94.

8174 **Mitchell**, J. H. 'The worker's point of view. IV. Wages in the mining industry.' *Hum. Factor*, VI, 6 (June 1932), 216–21.
Reprinted in *The worker's point of view: a symposium*. London: Hogarth P., 1933. p. 66–73.

8175 **Williams**, W. H. 'The miners' case.' Williams, W. H. (ed.). *The miner's two bob*. London: Lawrence, 1936. p. 1–26.

8176 *Coal Mines Guaranteed Wage Levy: explanatory memorandum*. London: H.M.S.O., 1941. 4p. (Cmd. 6278.)

8177 **Ministry of Labour and National Service.** Board of Investigation on the Coal-Mining Industry.
1. *Report into the immediate wages issue*. 1942. 8p.
2. *Output bonus. Supplemental report*. 1942. 4p.
3. *Machinery for determining wages and conditions of employment*. 1943. 16p.
4. *Fourth and final report*. 1943. 22p.
Chairman: Lord Greene.

8178 **Scott**, Hylton. 'Colliers' wages in Shropshire, 1830–1850.' *Shrops. Archaeol. Soc. Trans.*, LIII (1949–50), 1–22.

8179 **Alexander**, Kenneth John Wilson. 'Wages in coal-mining since nationalization.' *Oxf. Econ. Pap.*, n.s., VIII, 2 (June 1956), 164–80.

8180 **Sales**, W. H. and **Davies**, J. L. 'Introducing a new wage structure into coal mining.' *Oxf. Univ. Inst. Statist. Bull.*, XIX, 3 (August 1957), 201–24.

8181 **Taylor**, Arthur John. 'The sub-contract system in the British coal industry.' Pressnell, L. S. (ed.). *Studies in the Industrial Revolution*. London: U. of London, Athlone P., 1960. p. 215–35.

8182 **Hill**, Thomas Peter and **Knowles**, Kenneth Guy Jack Charles. 'Wages in coal mining.' *Oxf. Univ. Inst. Statist. Bull.*, XXIII, 2 (May 1961), 135–51.

8183 **National Board for Prices and Incomes.** *Coal prices*. London: H.M.S.O., 1966. iv, 20p. (Report 12. Cmnd. 2919.)

8184 **Nuttall**, T. *Changes in the wage structure of the coal industry since nationalisation*. 1966–67. (M.A. thesis, University of Leeds.)

8185 **Barratt Brown**, Michael. 'Determinants of the structure and level of wages in the coal-mining industry since 1956.' *Oxf. Univ. Inst. Econ. Statist. Bull.*, XXIX, 2 (May 1967), 139–70.

8186 **National Board for Prices and Incomes.** *Coal prices*. London: H.M.S.O., 1969. vi, 14p. (Report 124. Cmnd. 4149.)

8187 **National Board for Prices and Incomes.** *Coal prices: first report*. London: H.M.S.O., 1970. vi, 7p. (Report 138. Cmnd. 4255.)

8188 **National Board for Prices and Incomes.** *Coal prices: second report*. London: H.M.S.O., 1970. vi, 97p. (Report 153. Cmnd. 4455.)
Supplement 1. 1971. vii, 49p. (Report 153 (Supplement 1). Cmnd. 4455-I.)
Supplement 2. 1971. 132p. (Report 153 (Supplement 2). Cmnd. 4455-II.)

See also: 7758; 7795; 8211; 12,921–2; 12,928.

4. Manufacturing Industries

a. FOOD, DRINK, AND TOBACCO

8189 **National Board for Prices and Incomes.** *Prices of bread and flour*. London: H.M.S.O., 1965. iv, 20p. (Report 3. Cmnd. 2760.)

8190 **National Board for Prices and Incomes.** *Costs, prices & profits in the brewing industry*. London: H.M.S.O., 1966. vi, 15p. (Report 13. Cmnd. 2965.)

8191 **National Board for Prices and Incomes.** *Wages in the bakery industry*. London: H.M.S.O., 1966. iv, 11p. (Report 9 (Interim). Cmnd. 2878.)

8192 **National Board for Prices and Incomes.** *Wages in the bakery industry*. London: H.M.S.O., 1966. iv, 27p. (Report 17. Cmnd. 3019.)

8193 **National Board for Prices and Incomes.** *Costs and prices of the chocolate and sugar confectionery industry*. London: H.M.S.O., 1968. v, 27p. (Report 75. Cmnd. 3694.)

8194 **National Board for Prices and Incomes.** *Flour prices*. London: H.M.S.O., 1968. v, 5p. (Report 53. Cmnd. 3522.)

8195 **Knight**, Kenneth George. *Operatives' wages and work group behaviour in the baking industry of England and Wales: two case studies*. 1969. (M.A.(Econ.) thesis, University of Manchester.)

8196 **National Board for Prices and Incomes.** *Beer prices*. London: H.M.S.O., 1969. vii, 45p. (Report 136. Cmnd. 4227.)

8197 **National Board for Prices and Incomes.** *Bread prices and pay in baking*. London: H.M.S.O., 1970. v, 7p. (Report 144. Cmnd. 4329.)

8198 **National Board for Prices and Incomes.** *Bread prices and pay in the baking industry: second report*. London: H.M.S.O., 1970. v, 47p. (Report 151. Cmnd. 4428.)

8199 **National Board for Prices and Incomes.** *Costs, prices and profitability in the ice-cream manufacturing industry*. London: H.M.S.O., 1970. vi, 16p. (Report 160. Cmnd. 4548.)

8200 **National Board for Prices and Incomes.** *Margarine and compound cooking fats.* London: H.M.S.O., 1970. v, 15p. (Report 147. Cmnd. 4368.)

8201 **National Board for Prices and Incomes.** *Tea prices.* London: H.M.S.O., 1970. vi, 18p. (Report 154. Cmnd. 4456.)

See also: 7827; 8685; 8742–3; 8868; 13,038; 13,042.

b. CHEMICALS AND ALLIED INDUSTRIES

8202 **Goodwin**, Sheila Margaret. *A case study of the internal wage-structure in a chemical works.* 1965. (M.A. (Econ.) thesis, University of Manchester.)

8203 **National Board for Prices and Incomes.** *Prices of household and toilet soaps, soap powders and soap flakes, and soapless detergents.* London: H.M.S.O., 1965. iv, 20p. (Report 4. Cmnd. 2791.)

8204 **National Board for Prices and Incomes.** *Prices of compound fertilisers.* London: H.M.S.O., 1967. 19p. (Report 28. Cmnd. 3228.)

8205 **Cable**, John Reginald. *Methods of wage-fixing in a soap and chemical plant: a case study.* 1969. (M.A. (Econ.) thesis, University of Manchester.)

8206 **National Board for Prices and Incomes.** *Manufacturers' prices of toilet preparations.* London: H.M.S.O., 1969. v, 25p. (Report 113. Cmnd. 4066.)

8207 **National Board for Prices and Incomes.** *Pay of general workers and craftsmen in Imperial Chemical Industries Ltd.* London: H.M.S.O., 1969. v, 30p. (Report 105. Cmnd. 3941.)

8208 **National Board for Prices and Incomes.** *Synthetic organic dyestuffs and organic pigments prices.* London: H.M.S.O., 1969. vi, 14p. (Report 100. Cmnd. 3895.)

See also: 7795; 7827; 8870.

c. IRON, STEEL, AND OTHER METALS

8209 **Munro,** Joseph Edwin Crawford. 'Sliding scales in the iron industry.' *Manchr. Statist. Soc. Trans.* (1885–86), 1–43.

8210 **Evans**, A. Dudley. 'An iron trade sliding scale.' *Econ. J.*, XIX, 73 (March 1909), 122–33.

8211 **Rawson**, S. W. 'War and wages in the iron, coal and steel industries.' *Econ. J.*, XXVI, 102 (June 1916), 174–82.

8212 **Tyler**, John Ecclesfield. 'Wages and hours in the Britannia-metal trade at Sheffield, 1857–8.' *Hunter Archaeol. Soc. Trans.*, v, 1 (January 1938), 33–4.

8213 **Jefferys**, James Bavington. 'The guaranteed weekly wage in the British metal trades.' *Int. Labour Rev.*, LIX, 3 (March 1949), 297–318.

8214 **Adams**, Robert McDonald. *A comparative study of the occupational wage structures of the iron and steel industries of Great Britain and the United States in the last seventy years.* 1957–58. (Ph.D. thesis, University of London.)

8215 **Ostry**, Sylvia Wiseman, **Cole**, H. J. D. and **Knowles**, Kenneth Guy Jack Charles. 'Wage differentials in a large steel firm.' *Oxf. Univ. Inst. Statist. Bull.*, XX, 3 (August 1958), 217–64.

8216 **Clark**, M. Gardner. 'Comparative wage structures in the steel industry of the Soviet Union and western countries.' Industrial Relations Research Association. *Proceedings of the thirteenth annual meeting, St. Louis, Missouri, December 28 and 29, 1960.* p. 266–88. Discussion, p. 289–96.

8217 **National Board for Prices and Incomes.** *Costs and prices of aluminium semi-manufactures.* London: H.M.S.O., 1967. vii, 34p. (Report 39. Cmnd. 3378.)

8218 **National Board for Prices and Incomes.** *Prices of non-alloy bright steel bars.* London: H.M.S.O., 1969. v, 11p. (Report 118. Cmnd. 4903.)

8219 **National Board for Prices and Incomes.** *Steel prices.* London: H.M.S.O., 1969. v, 46p. (Report 111. Cmnd. 4033.)

See also: 7795; 7827; 8163; 8168; 12,987; 13,052.

d. ENGINEERING AND SHIP-BUILDING

8220 **Bowley**, Arthur Lyon and **Wood**, George Henry. 'The statistics of wages in the United Kingdom during the last hundred years. X. Engineering and shipbuilding. A. Trade union standard rates.' *R. Statist. Soc. J.*, LXVIII, 1 (March 1905), 104–37.

8221 **Bowley**, Arthur Lyon and **Wood**, George Henry. 'The statistics of wages in the United Kingdom during the last hundred years. XI. Engineering and shipbuilding. B. Statements of wages from non-trade union sources in general engineering.' *R. Statist. Soc. J.*, LXVIII, 2 (June 1905), 373–91.

8222 **Bowley**, Arthur Lyon and **Wood**, George Henry. 'The statistics of wages in the United Kingdom during the last hundred years. XII. Engineering and shipbuilding. C. Statements of wages from non-trade union sources in shipbuilding and engineering at shipbuilding centres.' *R. Statist. Soc. J.*, LXVIII, 3 (September 1905), 563–614.

8223 **Bowley**, Arthur Lyon and **Wood**, George Henry. 'The statistics of wages in the United Kingdom during the last hundred years. XIII. Engineering and shipbuilding. D. Dockyards and railway centres. With errata and addenda to Part X.' *R. Statist. Soc. J.*, LXVIII, 4 (December 1905), 704–15.

8224 **Bowley**, Arthur Lyon and **Wood**, George Henry. 'The statistics of wages in the United Kingdom during the last hundred years. XIV. Engineering and shipbuilding. E. Averages, index numbers and general results.' *R. Statist. Soc. J.*, LXIX, 1 (March 1906), 148–92.
Discussion, p. 193–6.

8225 **Engineering and Allied Employers' National Federation.** *Wage movements, 1897–1925.* London, 1926. 986p.

8226 **Spicer**, Robert S. *British engineering wages.* London: Arnold, 1928. 159p.

8227 **Shipbuilder and Marine Engine-Builder.** *British shipbuilding wages in 1929* [1931, 1932]. 1930–33. 3 pts.

8228 **Richardson**, H. E. 'Wages of shipwrights in H.M. dockyards, 1496–1788.' *Mar. Mirror*, XXXIII, 4 (October 1947), 265–74.

8229 **Cook**, Stanley and **James**, Robert. 'An experiment in wage assessment.' *Ind. Law Rev.*, II, 11 (April 1948), 274–80.
In engineering works.

8230 **Knowles**, Kenneth Guy Jack Charles and **Robertson**, Donald James. 'Earnings in engineering, 1926–1948.' *Oxf. Univ. Inst. Statist. Bull.*, XIII, 6 (June 1951), 179–200.

8231 **Knowles**, Kenneth Guy Jack Charles and **Robertson**, Donald James. 'Earnings in shipbuilding.' *Oxf. Univ. Inst. Statist. Bull.*, XIII, 11–12 (November–December 1951), 357–65.

8232 **Knowles**, Kenneth Guy Jack Charles and **Robertson**, Donald James. 'Some notes on engineering earnings.' *Oxf. Univ. Inst. Statist. Bull.*, XIII, 7 (July 1951), 223–8.

8233 **Knowles**, Kenneth Guy Jack Charles and **Hill**, Thomas Peter. 'The structure of engineering earnings.' *Oxf. Univ. Inst. Statist. Bull.*, XVI, 9–10 (September–October 1954), 271–328.

8234 **Hill**, Thomas Peter and **Knowles**, Kenneth Guy Jack Charles. 'The variability of engineering earnings.' *Oxf. Univ. Inst. Statist. Bull.*, XVIII, 2 (May 1956), 97–139.

8235 **National Incomes Commission.** *Agreements of November–December 1963 in the engineering and shipbuilding industries.* London: H.M.S.O.
[Interim report.] 1964. vii, 9p. (Report 4 (Interim). Cmnd. 2380.)
[Final report.] 1965. xi, 126p. (Report 4 (Final). Cmnd. 2583.)
Chairman: Sir F. G. Lawrence.

8236 **National Board for Prices and Incomes.** *Wages and conditions in the electrical contracting industry.* London: H.M.S.O., 1966. 32p. (Report 24. Cmnd. 3172.)

8237 **National Board for Prices and Incomes.** *Costs and charges in the motor repairing and servicing industry.* London: H.M.S.O., 1967. v, 38p. (Report 37. Cmnd. 3368.)

8238 **National Board for Prices and Incomes.** *Pay and conditions of limbfitters employed by J. E. Hanger and Company.* London: H.M.S.O., 1967. v, 16p. (Report 30. Cmnd. 3245.)

8239 **National Board for Prices and Incomes.** *Pay and conditions of service of engineering workers: first report on the engineering industry.* London: H.M.S.O., 1967. v, 70p. (Report 49. Cmnd. 3495.)
Reprinted 1968.

8240 **Sloane**, Peter J. 'Wage drift, with reference to case studies in the engineering industry of Central Scotland.' *J. Econ. Studies*, II, 1 (Spring 1967), 23–49; 2 (Autumn 1967), 61–73.

8241 **Sloane**, Peter J. *Wage drift in the engineering industry of Central Scotland: an intra-firm analysis.* 1967–68. (Ph.D. thesis, University of Strathclyde.)

8242 **National Board for Prices and Incomes.** *Increase in prices of mercury hearing-aid batteries manufactured by Mallory Batteries Limited.* London: H.M.S.O., 1968. v, 8p. (Report 64. Cmnd. 3625.)

8243 **National Board for Prices and Incomes.** *Increase in rental charges for equipment hired from IBM United Kingdom Limited.* London: H.M.S.O., 1968. v, 8p. (Report 76. Cmnd. 3699.)

8244 **National Board for Prices and Incomes.** *Pay and conditions of service of staff workers in the engineering industry: statistical supplement.* London: H.M.S.O., 1968. vi, 72p. (Report 49 (Supplement). Cmnd. 3495-I.)

8245 **National Board for Prices and Incomes.** *The prices of Hoover domestic appliances.* London: H.M.S.O., 1968. v, 5p. (Report 73. Cmnd. 3671.)

8246 **National Board for Prices and Incomes.** *Prices of secondary batteries.* London: H.M.S.O., 1968. v, 13p. (Report 61. Cmnd. 3597.)

8247 **Lupton**, Tom. 'Components Limited: a report of a survey of the earnings structure at the factory, with recommendations.' Lerner, S. W., Cable, J. R. and Gupta, S. (eds.). *Workshop wage determination.* Oxford: Pergamon P., 1969. p. 73–87.
An appendix to Chapter 2, 'The engineering industry'.

8248 **National Board for Prices and Incomes.** *Pay and conditions of service of engineering workers: second report on the engineering industry.* London: H.M.S.O., 1969. vi, 39p. (Report 104. Cmnd. 3931.)

8249 **National Board for Prices and Incomes.** *Pay of staff in British Insulated Callenders' Cables Ltd.* London: H.M.S.O., 1969. v, 24p. (Report 125. Cmnd. 4168.)

8250 **Clarke**, J. F. 'The notebook of an engineering craftsman, H. Gardner: earnings data related to 1881–1893.' *NE. Group Study Labour Hist. Bull.*, 4 (November 1970), 33–7. 1 chart.

8251 **National Board for Prices and Incomes.** *Electric motor prices.* London: H.M.S.O., 1970. v, 14p. (Report 139. Cmnd. 4258.)

8252 **National Board for Prices and Incomes.** *Prices of primary batteries proposed by the Ever Ready Company (Great Britain) Ltd.* London: H.M.S.O., 1970. vi, 14p. (Report 148. Cmnd. 4370.)

See also: 4561; 7827; 8073; 8747; 8806; 8817; 8831; 8856; 9157; 12,942.

e. TEXTILES

8253 **British Association for the Advancement of Science.** 'Report of the Committee ...on the regulation of wages by means of lists in the cotton industry.' British Association. *Report of the fifty-seventh meeting... Manchester...August and September, 1887.* London: Murray, 1888. p. 303–20.
Committee: Professors Sidgwick, Foxwell, Munro; A. H. D. Acland; W. Cunningham.
Covers spinning and weaving.

8254 *Return of the rates of wages* [and number of operatives employed] *in the principal textile trades of the United Kingdom, with the report thereon.* London: H.M.S.O., 1889. xxxviii, 152p. (C. 5807.)

8255 *Return of rates of wages* [and number of operatives employed] *in the minor textile trades of the United Kingdom, with report thereon.* London: H.M.S.O., 1890. xxix, 70p. (C. 6161.)

8256 **Merttens**, Frederick. 'The hours and the cost of labour in the cotton industry at home and abroad.' *Manchr. Statist. Soc. Trans.* (1893–94), 125–90.

8257 **Chapman**, Sydney John. 'The regulation of wages by lists in the spinning industry.' *Econ. J.*, IX, 36 (December 1899), 592–9.
Supplementing information contained in the British Association's report on the subject in 1887.

8258 **Bowley**, Arthur Lyon. 'The statistics of wages in the United Kingdom during the last hundred years. IX. Wages in the worsted and woollen manufactures of the West Riding of Yorkshire.' *R. Statist. Soc. J.*, LXV, 1 (March 1902), 102–26.

8259 **Wood**, George Henry. *The history of wages in the cotton trade during the last hundred years.* London, Manchester: Sherratt and Hughes, 1910. 162p.

8260 **Wood**, George Henry. 'The statistics of wages in the United Kingdom during the nineteenth century. XV[–XIX]. The cotton industry.' *R. Statist. Soc. J.*, LXXIII, 1 (January 1910), 39–58; 2 (February 1910), 128–63; 3 (March 1910), 283–315; 4 (April 1910), 411–34; 6 (June 1910), 585–626.
With discussion, p. 626–33.

8261 **Rowe**, John Wilkinson Foster. 'Wages in the cotton industry, 1914–1920.' *Econ. J.*. XXXIV, 134 (June 1924), 200–10.

8262 **Gray**, Edward Mayall. *The weaver's wage: earnings and collective bargaining in the Lancashire cotton weaving industry.* Manchester: Manchester U.P., 1937. xi, 69p.

8263 **Kuczynski**, Jürgen. 'Wages in British-controlled textile factories: a study of wage averages within a capitalist organism.' *New frontiers in wage theory: Keynes, Robinson, Hicks, Rueff.* London: Lawrence and Wishart, 1937. p. 51–63.

8264 **Gray**, Edward Mayall. 'Wages rates and earnings in cotton weaving.' *Manchr. Statist. Soc. Trans.* (1938–39), 1–22.

8265 **Ministry of Labour and National Service.** *Cotton spinning industry: report of a Commission set up to review the wages arrangements and methods of organisation of work, and to make recommendations.* London: H.M.S.O., 1945.
Chairman: Mr Justice Evershed.
Supplement. Appendix IV. 1946.
Supplement. Mule-spinners' wages: report by the Chairman of the Commission. 1946.

8266 **Gibson**, Roland. *Cotton textile wages in the United States and Great Britain: a comparison of trends, 1860–1945.* New York: King's Crown P., 1948. ix, 137p.

8267 **Ministry of Labour and National Service.** Cotton Manufacturing Commission. *Interim report of an enquiry into wages arrangements and methods of organisation of work in the cotton manufacturing industry.* London: H.M.S.O., 1948.
Final report. Part I. 1949.
Final report. Parts II, III and IV. 1949.
Chairman: Ronw Moelwyn Hughes.

8268 **Vincent**, P. D. *New wage structures in cotton.* Manchester, [1950?]. 11p.

8269 **International Labour Office.** *Textile wages: an international study.* Geneva: I.L.O., 1952. v, 126p. (Studies and reports, new series 31.)

8270 **Evans**, Gwenllian. 'Wage rates and earnings in the cotton industry between 1947 and 1951.' *Manchr. Statist. Soc. Trans.* (1952–53), 11–15.

8271 **Evans**, Gwenllian. 'Wage rates and earnings in the cotton industry from 1946 to 1951.' *Manchr. Sch.*, XXI, 3 (September 1953), 224–57.

8272 **Gibson**, I. F. 'The revision of the jute wages-structure.' *Scott. J. Polit. Econ.*, IV, 1 (February 1957), 46–59.
'A revised version of a paper read to the Economics Section of the British Association at its Bristol meeting in September 1955.'

8273 **Collier**, Frances. *The family economy of the working classes in the cotton industry, 1784–1833.* Manchester: Manchester U.P., 1965. x, 94p.
Edited by R. S. Fitton.

8274 **National Board for Prices and Incomes.** *Man-made fibre and cotton yarn prices: first report.* London: H.M.S.O., 1969. v, 14p. (Report 119. Cmnd. 4092.)

8275 **National Board for Prices and Incomes.** *Man-made fibre and cotton yarn prices: second report.* London: H.M.S.O., 1969. vi, 26p. (Report 127. Cmnd. 4180.)
See also: 7827; 8696.

f. CLOTHING AND FOOTWEAR

8276 **Papworth**, Lucy Wyatt and **Zimmern**, Dorothy M. *Clothing and textile trades: summary tables.* London: Women's Industrial Council, 1912. 12, [20]p.

8277 **Crawford**, J. 'The problem of introducing modern systems of wage payment into the boot and shoe industry.' *J. Ind. Econ.*, I, 3 (July 1953), 231–40.

8278 **Knowles**, Kenneth Guy Jack Charles and **Verry**, Monica. 'Earnings in the boot and shoe industry.' *Oxf. Univ. Inst. Statist. Bull.*, XVI, 2–3 (February–March 1954), 29–72.

8279 **National Board for Prices and Incomes.** *Pay and conditions in the clothing manufacturing industries.* London: H.M.S.O., 1969. vi, 65p. With correction. (Report 110. Cmnd. 4002.)
Statistical supplement. 1969. iv, 53p. (Report 110 (Supplement). Cmnd. 4002-I.)
See also: 491; 7827; 8783; 12,935; 12,945; 12,947; 12,974; 13,020; 13,027.

g. BRICKS, POTTERY, GLASS, AND CEMENT

8280 **National Board for Prices and Incomes.** *Portland Cement prices.* London: H.M.S.O., 1967. v, 19p. (Report 38. Cmnd. 3381.)

8281 **National Board for Prices and Incomes.** *Prices of fletton and non-fletton bricks.* London: H.M.S.O., 1967. v, 19p. (Report 47. Cmnd. 3480.)

8282 **National Board for Prices and Incomes.** *Plasterboard prices.* London: H.M.S.O., 1969. v, 24p. (Report 130. Cmnd. 4184.)

8283 **National Board for Prices and Incomes.** *Portland Cement prices.* London: H.M.S.O., 1969. vi, 14p. (Report 133. Cmnd. 4215.)

8284 **National Board for Prices and Incomes.** *Pay and other terms and conditions of employment in the fletton brick industry and the prices charged by the London Brick Company.* London: H.M.S.O., 1970. vi, 40p. (Report 150. Cmnd. 4422.)

8285 **National Board for Prices and Incomes.** *Pay and other terms and conditions of employment of workers in the pottery industry.* London: H.M.S.O., 1970. vi, 118p. (Report 149. Cmnd. 4411.)
See also: 7827.

h. TIMBER AND FURNITURE

8286 **British Furniture Trades Joint Committee.** *Report to the British Furniture Trades Joint Committee by an investigator into wages and working conditions prevailing in certain sections of the furniture manufacturing trade in London during 1938.* London, 1939. 47p.

8287 **National Board for Prices and Incomes.** *Report on an agreement relating to the pay of surveyors and wood-cutting machinists in the saw milling industry.* London: H.M.S.O., 1968. v, 6p. (Report 82. Cmnd. 3768.)
See also: 12,944.

i. PAPER, PRINTING, AND PUBLISHING

8288 **Bowley**, Arthur Lyon and **Wood**, George Henry. 'The statistics of wages in the United Kingdom during the last hundred years. Part V. Printers.' *R. Statist. Soc. J.*, LXII, 4 (December 1899), 708–15.

8289 **National Board for Prices and Incomes.** *Wages, costs and prices in the printing industry.* London: H.M.S.O., 1965. iv, 32p. (Report 2. Cmnd. 2750.)
Reprinted 1970.

8290 **National Board for Prices and Incomes.** *Costs and revenue of national daily newspapers.* London: H.M.S.O., 1967. v, 25p. (Report 42. Cmnd. 3405.)

8291 **National Board for Prices and Incomes.** *Prices of standard newsprint.* London: H.M.S.O., 1967. 21p. (Report 26. Cmnd. 3210.)

8292 **National Board for Prices and Incomes.** *Journalists' pay.* London: H.M.S.O., 1969. v, 29p. (Report 115. Cmnd. 4077.)

8293 **National Board for Prices and Incomes.** *Pay structure within H.M. Stationery Office presses and binderies.* London: H.M.S.O., 1969. vi, 32p. (Report 135. Cmnd. 4219.)

8294 **National Board for Prices and Incomes.** *Costs and revenue of national newspapers.* London: H.M.S.O., 1970. v, 41p. (Report 141. Cmnd. 4277.)
See also: 7827; 8802; 8848; 13,056.

j. OTHER MANUFACTURING

8295 **National Board for Prices and Incomes.** *Price of butyl rubber.* London: H.M.S.O., 1968. v, 7p. (Report 66. Cmnd. 3626.)
See also: 13,049.

5. Construction

8296 **Henshaw**, Richard S. *Notes on labour in the building trade of London, and the rates of wages in twenty-two principal towns of Great Britain.* Bromley: S. Bush, 1892. 8p.

8297 **Bowley**, Arthur Lyon. 'The statistics of wages in the United Kingdom during the last hundred years. VI. Wages in the building trades: English towns.' *R. Statist. Soc. J.*, LXIII, 2 (June 1900), 297–315.

8298 **Bowley**, Arthur Lyon. 'The statistics of wages in the United Kingdom during the last hundred years. VII. Wages in the building trades: Scotland and Ireland.' *R. Statist. Soc. J.*, LXIII, 3 (September 1900), 485–97.

8299 **Bowley**, Arthur Lyon. 'The statistics of wages in the United Kingdom during the last hundred years. VIII. Wages in the building trades: London.' *R. Statist. Soc. J.*, LXIV, 1 (March 1901), 102–12.

8300 **Hicks**, John Richard. 'Wage-fixing in the building industry.' *Economica*, VIII, 23 (June 1928), 159–67.

8301 **Knoop**, Douglas and **Jones**, Gwilym Peredur. 'Masons' wages in medieval England.' *Econ. Hist.*, II, 8 (January 1933), 473–99.

8302 **Knoop**, Douglas and **Jones**, Gwilym Peredur. 'The first three years of the building of Vale Royal Abbey.' *Ars Quat. Coron.*, XLIV (1934), 5–39.

Discussion, p. 39–47.

8303 **Knoop**, Douglas and **Jones**, Gwilym Peredur. 'Notes on three early documents relating to masons.' *Ars Quat. Coron.*, XLIV (1934), 223–35.

III. 'Wage list of the York Minster masons, 1472.' p. 228–35.

8304 **Wigfull**, James Ragg. 'Local plumbers and glaziers.' *Hunter Archaeol. Soc. Trans.*, IV, 4 (March 1937), 331–46.

8305 **Moos**, S. 'Labour costs in housing.' *Oxf. Univ. Inst. Statist. Bull.*, V, 14 (9 October 1943), 225–31.

8306 **Bowen**, Ian. 'Incentives and output in the building and civil engineering industries.' *Manchr. Sch.*, XV, 2 (May 1947), 157–75.

8307 **Ministry of Works.** Division of the Chief Scientific Adviser. Economics Research Section. *Wages, earnings and negotiating machinery in the building industry, 1886–1948.* [1949?]. 38p.

8308 **Ministry of Education.** *Site labour studies in school buildings.* London: H.M.S.O., 1955. 41p. (Building bulletin 12.)

8309 **Phelps Brown**, Ernest Henry and **Hopkins**, Sheila V. 'Seven centuries of building wages.' *Economica*, n.s. XXII, 87 (August 1955), 195–206.

Reprinted in Carus-Wilson, E. M. (ed.). *Essays in economic history.* Vol. II. London: Arnold, 1962. p. 168–78.

8310 **Phelps Brown**, Ernest Henry and **Hopkins**, Sheila V. 'Seven centuries of the prices of consumables, compared with builders' wage rates.' *Economica*, n.s., XXIII, 92 (November 1956), 294–314.

Reprinted in Carus-Wilson, E. M. (ed.). *Essays in economic history.* Vol. II. London: Arnold, 1962. p. 179–96.

8311 **Phelps Brown**, Ernest Henry and **Hopkins**, Sheila V. 'Builders' wage-rates, prices and population: some further evidence.' *Economica*, n.s., XXVI, 101 (February 1959), 18–38.

8312 **National Incomes Commission.** *Report on the agreements of February–March 1963 in electrical contracting, in heating, ventilating and domestic engineering, and in exhibition contracting.* London: H.M.S.O., 1963. viii, 70p. (Report 2. Cmnd. 2098.)

Chairman: Sir Geoffrey Lawrence.

8313 **National Incomes Commission.** *Report on the Scottish plumbers' and Scottish builders' agreements of 1962.* London: H.M.S.O., 1963. viii, 64p. (Cmnd. 1994.)

Chairman: Sir Geoffrey Lawrence.

8314 **National Board for Prices and Incomes.** *Increases in rents of local authority housing.* London: H.M.S.O., 1968. vi, 82p. (Report 62. Cmnd. 3604.)

Statistical supplement. 1968. v, 123p. (Report 62 (Supplement). Cmnd. 3604-I.)

8315 **National Board for Prices and Incomes.** *Pay and conditions in the building industry.* London: H.M.S.O., 1968. vii, 84p. (Report 92. Cmnd. 3837.)

8316 **National Board for Prices and Incomes.** *Pay and conditions in the civil engineering industry.* London: H.M.S.O., 1968. vii, 78p. (Report 91. Cmnd. 3836.)

8317 **National Board for Prices and Incomes.** *Pay and conditions in the construction industry other than building and civil engineering.* London: H.M.S.O., 1968. vii, 60p. (Report 93. Cmnd. 3838.)

8318 **National Board for Prices and Incomes.** *Report on a settlement relating to the pay of certain workers employed in the thermal insulation contracting industry.* London: H.M.S.O., 1968. viiip. (Report 84. Cmnd. 3784.)

8319 **National Board for Prices and Incomes.** *Pay and conditions in the building industry, the civil engineering industry, and the construction industry other than building and civil engineering: statistical supplement.* London: H.M.S.O., 1969. v, 167p. (Reports 91, 92 and 93 (Supplement). Cmnd. 3982.)

8320 **National Board for Prices and Incomes.** *Pay and conditions of workers in the exhibition contracting industry.* London: H.M.S.O., 1969. vii, 53p. (Report 117. Cmnd. 4088.)

See also: 7827; 8831–2; 8748; 8755; 8758; 8769; 8773; 8811; 8827; 9157.

6. Gas, Electricity, and Water

8321 **National Board for Prices and Incomes.** *Electricity and gas tariffs: London Electricity Board and Scottish, South Western and Wales Gas Boards.* London: H.M.S.O., 1965. iv, 27p. (Report 7. Cmnd. 2862.)

8322 **National Board for Prices and Incomes.** *Remuneration of administrative and clerical staff in the electricity supply industry.* London: H.M.S.O., 1965. iv, 30p. (Report 5. Cmnd. 2801.)

8323 **National Board for Prices and Incomes.** *Pay of electricity supply workers.* London:

H.M.S.O., 1967. v, 37p. (Report 42. Cmnd. 3405.)

8324 **National Board for Prices and Incomes.** *The bulk supply tariff of the Central Electricity Generating Board.* London: H.M.S.O., 1968. v, 20p. (Report 59. Cmnd. 3575.)

8325 **National Board for Prices and Incomes.** *Gas prices: first report.* London: H.M.S.O., 1968. v, 25p. (Report 57. Cmnd. 3567.)

8326 **National Board for Prices and Incomes.** *Pay and productivity of industrial employees of the United Kingdom Atomic Energy Authority.* London: H.M.S.O., 1968. 43p. (Report 51. Cmnd. 3499.)

8327 **National Board for Prices and Incomes.** *Pay of staff workers in the gas industry.* London: H.M.S.O., 1968. vi, 30p. (Report 86. Cmnd. 3795.)

8328 **Sallis,** Howard. *Pay and conditions in electricity supply before the status agreement.* London: Electricity Council, 1968. 10p.

Reprinted from *Electricity*, January–February 1968.

8329 **Sallis,** Howard. *Pay and conditions in the British electricity supply industry, 1906–1939.* London: Electricity Council, 1968. 8p.

Reprinted from *Electricity*, November–December 1967.

8330 **National Board for Prices and Incomes.** *Gas prices: second report.* London: H.M.S.O., 1969. v, 123p. (Report 102. Cmnd. 3924.)

8331 **National Board for Prices and Incomes.** *Pay and conditions in the electrical contracting industry.* London: H.M.S.O., 1969. v, 71p. (Report 120. Cmnd. 4097.)

8332 **National Board for Prices and Incomes.** *Pay and conditions in the electrical contracting industry in Scotland.* London: H.M.S.O., 1969. v, 13p. (Report 108. Cmnd. 3966.)

8333 **National Board for Prices and Incomes.** *Costs and efficiency in the gas industry.* London: H.M.S.O., 1970. vi, 61p. (Report 155. Cmnd. 4458.)

8334 **National Board for Prices and Incomes.** *Pay and productivity in the water supply industry.* London: H.M.S.O., 1970. vi, 87p. (Report 152. Cmnd. 4434.)

See also: 7827; 8614; 8660.

7. Transport and Communications

a. RAILWAYS AND LONDON TRANSPORT

8335 **Bureau of Railway Economics,** Washington, D.C. *A comparative study of railway wages and the cost of living in the United States, the United Kingdom and the principal countries of Continental Europe.* Washington, 1912. 77p. (Bulletin 34.)

8336 **London Municipal Society.** Department of Social Economics. *Digest of official statistics: earnings and hours of labour in the railway service in 1907 and later.* London, 1912. 16p. (Statistical and other memoranda, 2nd series, 3.)

8337 **Browne,** K. J. Norman. *British railwaymen's wages: what are the facts? Pre-war concessions and post-war costs.* London: Great Western Railway, 1922. 8p. (Great Western pamphlets 9.)

Reprinted from the *Financial Times*, 26 June 1922.

8338 **Hunter,** George Burton. *Cost of labour on our railways.* Newcastle: privately printed, 1930. [4]p.

Another edition. Newcastle, 1930. [4]p.

'Present wages and conditions cannot be maintained without disaster.'

8339 **Fox,** W. E., and others. *Ten years of railway finance: a study of the railways of Great Britain, their 'watered' capital, their directors, earnings, reserves and dividends, road transport interests and the position of the railway workers.* London: Labour Research Department, 1932. 23p.

8340 **Fox,** W. E. *Seven years of railway finance, 1928–1934.* London: Labour Research Department, 1935. 31p.

A revision of *Ten years of railway finance*, 1932.

8341 **Knowles,** Kenneth Guy Jack Charles and **Cole,** H. J. D. 'Rates and earnings in London transport.' *Oxf. Univ. Inst. Statist. Bull.*, xv, 8 (August 1953), 261–94.

8342 **Peitchinis,** S. G. *The determination of the wages of railwaymen: a study of British experience with a comparative study of Canadian since 1914.* 1960. xiv, 448p. (Ph.D. thesis, University of London.)

8343 **Railway Pay Committee of Inquiry.** *Report.* London: Special Joint Committee on Machinery of Negotiation for Railway Staff, 1960. 94p.

Chairman: C. W. Guillebaud.

8344 **National Board for Prices and Incomes.** *Pay and conditions of service of British Railways staff (conciliation, salaried and workshop grades).* London: H.M.S.O., 1966. iv, 48p. (Report 8. Cmnd. 2873.)

8345 **National Board for Prices and Incomes.** *Proposals by the London Transport Board and British Railways Board for fare increases in the London area.* London: H.M.S.O., 1968. v, 29p. (Report 56. Cmnd. 3561.)

8346 **National Board for Prices and Incomes.** *Proposed increases by British Railways Board in certain country-wide fares and charges.* London: H.M.S.O., 1968. v, 34p. (Report 72. Cmnd. 3656.)

8347 **National Board for Prices and Incomes.** *Proposals by the British Railways Board for fare increases in the London commuter area.* London: H.M.S.O., 1969. vi, 30p. (Report 137. Cmnd. 4250.)

8348 **National Board for Prices and Incomes.** *Proposals by the London Transport Board for fares increases.* London: H.M.S.O., 1969. v, 49p. (Report 112. Cmnd. 4036.)

8349 **National Board for Prices and Incomes.** *London Transport fares.* London: H.M.S.O., 1970. v, 43p. (Report 159. Cmnd. 4540.)

See also: 7827.

b. ROAD

8350 **Hallsworth,** *Sir* Joseph. *Memorandum on the wages of road transport workers.* Manchester: Amalgamated Union of Cooperative and Commercial Employees and Allied Workers, 1920. 26p.

Earlier edition. 1919. 15p.

8351 **National Board for Prices and Incomes.** *Road haulage rates.* London: H.M.S.O., 1965. vi, 23p. (Report 1 (Interim). Cmnd. 2965.)

8352 **National Board for Prices and Incomes.** *Pay and conditions of busmen.* London: H.M.S.O., 1966. iv, 38p. (Report 16. Cmnd. 3012.)

8353 **National Board for Prices and Incomes.** *Road haulage charges: final report.* London: H.M.S.O., 1966. 23p. (Report 14. Cmnd. 2968.)

8354 **National Board for Prices and Incomes.** *Charges, costs and wages in the road haulage industry.* London: H.M.S.O., 1967. v, 41p. (Report 48. Cmnd. 3482.)

Statistical supplement. 1968. iv, 40p. (Report 48 (Supplement). Cmnd. 3482-I.)

8355 **National Board for Prices and Incomes.** *Pay and conditions of busmen employed by the Corporation of Dundee.* London: H.M.S.O., 1968. v, 18p. (Report 85. Cmnd. 3791.)

8356 **National Board for Prices and Incomes.** *Pay and conditions of busmen employed by the Corporation of Wigan.* London: H.M.S.O., 1968. 16p. (Report 95. Cmnd. 3845.)

8357 **National Board for Prices and Incomes.** *Pay and conditions of busmen employed by the Corporations of Belfast, Glasgow and Liverpool.* London: H.M.S.O., 1968. viii, 55p. (Report 69. Cmnd. 3646.)

8358 **National Board for Prices and Incomes.** *Pay of busmen employed by the Corporation of Great Yarmouth.* London: H.M.S.O., 1968. vi, 5p. (Report 96. Cmnd. 3844.)

8359 **National Board for Prices and Incomes.** *Pay of municipal busmen.* London: H.M.S.O., 1968. vi, 60p. (Report 63. Cmnd. 3605.)

8360 **National Board for Prices and Incomes.** *Pay of vehicle maintenance workers in British Road Services.* London: H.M.S.O., 1968. vi, 20p. (Report 90. Cmnd. 3848.)

8361 **National Board for Prices and Incomes.** *Proposed increase in London taxicab fares.* London: H.M.S.O., 1968. v, 25p. (Report 87. Cmnd. 3796.)

8362 **National Board for Prices and Incomes.** *Pay of maintenance workers employed by bus companies.* London: H.M.S.O., 1969. v, 28p. (Report 99. Cmnd. 3868.)

8363 **National Board for Prices and Incomes.** *Costs, charges and productivity of the National Freight Corporation.* London: H.M.S.O., 1971. vi, 45p. (Report 162. Cmnd. 4569.)

See also: 13,017; 13,055.

c. SEA

8364 **Departmental Committee Appointed to Consider the Question of the Extension to Ports Abroad with Home Trade Limits of the Arrangements now in force in the United Kingdom for the Transmission of Seamen's Wages.** *Report, with evidence, appendices and index.* London: H.M.S.O., 1893–94. (C. 7179.)

8365 **Committee on Seamen's Wages.** *Report.* London: H.M.S.O., 1905. 8p. (H.C. 334.)

Chairman: A. Bonar Law.

8366 **Leyland,** John. 'The purser and the seaman's pay.' *Mar. Mirror,* II, 11 (November 1912), 321–4.

8367 **Brooks,** F. W. 'A wage-scale for seamen, 1546.' *Engl. Hist. Rev.,* LX, 237 (May 1945), 234–46.

Note, and text of Trinity House subscription of Kingston-upon-Hull.

8368 **Schoenfeld,** Maxwell P. 'The Restoration seaman and his wages.' *Am. Neptune,* XXV, 4 (October 1965), 278–87.

8369 **National Board for Prices and Incomes.** *Pay and conditions of Merchant Navy Officers.* London: H.M.S.O., 1967. 22p. (Report 35. Cmnd. 3302.)

d. PORT AND INLAND WATER

8370 **Cunningham,** David. 'Rates of wages paid by the Dundee Harbour Trustees during the last twenty-five years.' Industrial Remuneration Conference. *The report of the proceedings and papers.* London: Cassell, 1885. p. 41–6, 514.

Discussion, p. 62–83.

8371 **Departmental Committee on the Checking of Piece-Work Wages in Dock Labour.** *Report.* London: H.M.S.O., 1908. 10p. (Cd. 4380.)

Minutes of evidence. 1908. (Cd. 4381.)

8372 **Ministry of Labour.** Court of Inquiry Concerning Transport Workers' Wages and Conditions of Employment of Dock Labour. *Report and minutes of evidence.* London: H.M.S.O., 1920. xxii, 500p. (Cmnd. 936.)

Appendices, documents, and indexes. 1920. xx, 194p. (Cmd. 937.)

Chairman: Lord Shaw of Dunfermline.

8373 **Ministry of Labour and National Service.** *Port transport industry: report of a Committee of Inquiry into the amount and basis of calculation of the guaranteed wage to be made to dock workers under the Dock Workers (Regulation of Employment) Scheme, 1947.* London: H.M.S.O., 1947. 3p.

Chairman: Hector Hetherington.

8374 **Dawson**, A. A. P. 'The stabilisation of dockworkers' earnings.' *Int. Labour Rev.*, LXIII, 3 (March 1951), 241–65; 4 (April 1951), 364–89.

8375 **Knowles**, Kenneth Guy Jack Charles and **Romanis**, Ann. 'Dockworkers' earnings.' *Oxf. Univ. Inst. Statist. Bull.*, XIV, 9–10 (September–October 1952).

8376 **Ministry of Labour.** *Report of the Committee of Inquiry under Lord Devlin into the wages structure and level of pay for dock workers.* London: H.M.S.O., 1966. 19p. (Cmnd. 3104.)

8377 **Ministry of Labour.** *Report of Inquiry into the locally determined aspects of the system of payment and earnings opportunities of registered dock workers in the Port of Liverpool (including Birkenhead).* London: H.M.S.O., 1967. 16p.
By A. J. Scamp.

8378 **National Board for Prices and Incomes.** *Passenger fares and freight charges of the North of Scotland, Orkney and Shetland Shipping Company Limited.* London: H.M.S.O., 1968. v, 36p. (Report 67. Cmnd. 3631.)

8379 **National Board for Prices and Incomes.** *Pay awards made by the City and County of Bristol to staff employed in its dock undertaking.* London: H.M.S.O., 1968. vii, 18p. (Report 81. Cmnd. 3752.)

8380 **National Board for Prices and Incomes.** *Pay and duties of light-keepers.* London: H.M.S.O., 1969. vi, 25p. (Report 114. Cmnd. 4067.)

e. AIR

8381 **National Board for Prices and Incomes.** *Pay of pilots employed by the British Overseas Airways Corporation.* London: H.M.S.O., 1968. vi, 25p. (Report 88. Cmnd. 3789.)

8382 **National Board for Prices and Incomes.** *Pay of ground staff at aerodromes.* London: H.M.S.O., 1969. vi, 42p. (Report 128. Cmnd. 4182.)

8383 **National Board for Prices and Incomes.** *Pay of pilots employed by the British Overseas Airways Corporation.* London: H.M.S.O., 1969. vi, 25p. (Report 129. Cmnd. 4197.)

f. POSTAL SERVICES AND TELECOMMUNICATIONS

8384 **Postmaster General.** *Report . . . to the Treasury, proposing certain improvements in the pay and regulations of the sorting clerks, and of the telegraphists of the Post Office; and Treasury reply thereto.* 1881. (H.C. 286.)

8385 **Committee Appointed to Inquire into Post Office Wages.**
Part I. *Report, appendices.* London: H.M.S.O., 1904. 43p. (Cd. 2170.)
Part II. *Minutes of evidence, etc.* 1904. (Cd. 2171.)
Chairman: E. R. C. Bradford.

8386 **Treasury** and **Post Office.** Committee on the Pay of Postmen. *Report.* London: H.M.S.O., 1964.
Minutes of evidence. 1964.
Chairman: A. Ll. Armitage.

8387 **National Board for Prices and Incomes.** *Post Office charges.* London: H.M.S.O., 1968. v, 90p. (Report 58. Cmnd. 3574.)

8388 **National Board for Prices and Incomes.** *Post Office charges: inland parcel post and remittance services.* London: H.M.S.O., 1969. vi, 21p. (Report 121. Cmnd. 4115.)

8. Distributive Trades

8389 **Hallsworth**, *Sir* Joseph. *Memorandum on the wages of co-operative shop managers in Yorkshire . . .* Manchester, 1919. 48p.
Supplementary memorandum . . . 1920. 11p.

8390 **Pollard**, Sidney. 'A note on managerial incomes in retail distribution.' *Manchr. Sch.*, XXIV, 1 (January 1956), 68–76.

8391 **Cynog-Jones**, T. W. *The regulation of wages in the retail trades, 1936–57.* London: Union of Shop, Distributive and Allied Workers, 1957. 55p.
Fourth edition.
Previous edition. 1952.
Private circulation.

8392 **Rottenberg**, Simon. 'Monopoly in the labor market: the "bummarees" of London's wholesale meat market.' *Ind. Labor Relat. Rev.*, XIII, 1 (October 1959), 54–63.

8393 **Ministry of Agriculture, Fisheries and Food** and **Department of Agriculture and Fisheries for Scotland.** *Report of the Committee on the remuneration of milk distributors in the United Kingdom.* London: H.M.S.O., 1962. (Cmnd. 1597.)
Chairman: Sir Guy Thorold.

8394 **Tack Research.** *Salesmen's pay incentives and pensions, 1965: a Tack survey.* London: Tack Research, 1965. 360p.

8395 **National Board for Prices and Incomes.** *Coal distribution costs.* London: H.M.S.O., 1966. iv, 18p. (Report 21. Cmnd. 3094.)

8396 **National Board for Prices and Incomes.** *Distribution costs of fresh fruit and vegetables.* London: H.M.S.O., 1967. vii, 24p. (Report 31. Cmnd. 3265.)

8397 **National Board for Prices and Incomes.** *Pay of workers in the retail drapery, outfitting and footwear trades.* London: H.M.S.O., 1967. 36p. (Report 27. Cmnd. 3224.)
Statistical supplement. 1967. 35p. (Report 27 (Supplement). Cmnd. 3224-I.)

8398 **National Board for Prices and Incomes.** *The renumeration of milk distributors (interim report).* London: H.M.S.O., 1967. 6p. (Report 33. Cmnd. 3294.)

8399 **National Board for Prices and Incomes.** *The remuneration of milk distributors (final report).* London: H.M.S.O., 1967. v, 38p. (Report 46. Cmnd. 3477.)

8400 **National Board for Prices and Incomes.** *Costs and charges in the radio and television rental and relay industry.* London: H.M.S.O., 1968. 36p. (Report 52. Cmnd. 3520.)

8401 **National Board for Prices and Incomes.** *Distributors' costs and margins on furniture, domestic electrical appliances and footwear.* London: H.M.S.O., 1968. v, 87p. (Report 97. Cmnd. 3858.)

8402 **National Board for Prices and Incomes.** *Distributors' margins in relation to manufacturers' recommended prices.* London: H.M.S.O., 1968. v, 14p. (Report 55. Cmnd. 3546.)

8403 **National Board for Prices and Incomes.** *Distributors' margins on paint, children's clothing, household textiles and proprietary medicines.* London: H.M.S.O., 1968. vii, 27p. (Report 80. Cmnd. 3737.)

8404 **National Board for Prices and Incomes.** *Pay and productivity in the car delivery industry.* London: H.M.S.O., 1969. vi, 27p. (Report 103. Cmnd. 3929.)

8405 **National Board for Prices and Incomes.** *Smithfield market.* London: H.M.S.O., 1969. vi, 74p. (Report 126. Cmnd. 4171.)

8406 **Tack Research.** *Salesmen's pay and expenses 1969: a Tack survey.* London: Tack Research, 1969. 49p.

8407 **National Board for Prices and Incomes.** *Pay and conditions of workers in the milk industry.* London: H.M.S.O., 1970. vi, 99p. (Report 140. Cmnd. 4267.)

8408 **National Board for Prices and Incomes.** *Prices, profits and costs in food distribution.* London: H.M.S.O., 1971. vi, 87p. (Report 165. Cmnd. 4645.)

See also: 8804; 13,007–10; 13,012–16; 13,022; 13,024; 13,048.

9. Insurance, Banking, and Finance

8409 **Ministry of National Insurance.** *Compensation and superannuation of staffs of approved societies: statement by the Minister of National Insurance and final report of Staffing Advisory Committee.* London: H.M.S.O., 1948. 28p.
Chairman: C. G. Izard.

8410 **Banker.** 'Bank profits and salaries.' *Banker*, XCVI, 301 (February 1951), 85–92.

8411 **Duncan**, G. A. 'The Irish banks' salary problem.' *Banker*, XCVI, 303 (April 1951), 210–15.

8412 **Hunsworth**, John. 'Are salaries too low?' *Bankers' Mag.*, CLXXIV, 1300 (July 1952), 16–23.

8413 **A Special Correspondent.** 'The new pattern of bank salaries.' *Banker*, XCVIII, 316 (May 1952), 283–7.

8414 **A Special Correspondent.** 'Salaries in the clearing banks.' *Banker*, XCVIII, 312 (January 1952), 55–7.

8415 **A Special Correspondent.** 'Bank earnings and salaries.' *Banker*, CIV, 349 (February 1955), 100–9.

8416 **A Special Correspondent.** 'Other people's salaries: a banker's companion.' *Banker*, CVIII, 389 (June 1958), 390–7.

8417 **Bentley**, Charles. 'Bank salaries: the rate for the job.' *Bankers' Mag.*, CXCVI, 1434 (September 1963), 191–3.

8418 **Brooks**, A. G. 'The structure of bank salaries. 2. The Union's proposals.' *Bankers' Mag.*, CC (August 1965), 66–9.

8419 **Ellis**, J. J. 'The structure of bank salaries. 1. The need for re-appraisal.' *Bankers' Mag.*, C (August 1965), 65–6.

8420 **National Board for Prices and Incomes.** *Salaries of Midland Bank staff.* London: H.M.S.O., 1965. vi, 21p. (Report 6. Cmnd. 2839.)

8421 **National Board for Prices and Incomes.** *Rate of interest on building society mortgages.* London: H.M.S.O., 1966. 34p. (Report 22. Cmnd. 3136.)

8422 **A Special Correspondent.** 'Salaries, negotiation and recruitment.' *Banker*, CXVI, 455 (January 1966), 26–31.

8423 **National Board for Prices and Incomes.** *Bank charges.* London: H.M.S.O., 1967. 80p. (Report 36. Cmnd. 3292.)

8424 **National Board for Prices and Incomes.** *Salaries of staff employed by the General Accident Fire and Life Assurance Corporation Limited.* London: H.M.S.O., 1967. v, 17p. (Report 41. Cmnd. 3398.)

8425 **National Board for Prices and Incomes.** *Pay in the London Clearing Banks.* London: H.M.S.O., 1969. vi, 30p. (Report 106. Cmnd. 3943.)

10. Professional and Scientific Services

a. GENERAL WHITE-COLLAR, MANAGERIAL, AND PROFESSIONAL

8426 **Office Management Association.** *Junior clerical wages report: London area.* London: 1935. 12p.

8427 **Graves**, Charles Patrick Ranke. *Other people's money.* London: Nicholson and Watson, 1937. 304p.
On the financial return provided by various professions.

8428 **Institute of Office Management.** *Clerical salaries analysis.*
Published bi-annually from 1942 when the Institute was called the Office Management Association.

8429 **Copeman**, George Henry. *Promotion and pay for executives.* London: Business Publications, Batsford, 1957. 216p.
Revised edition. 1960. 258p.

8430 **Political and Economic Planning.** 'Salaries of graduates in industry.' *Planning*, XXIII, 408 (18 March 1957), 45–67.

8431 **Fogarty**, Michael Patrick. 'The white-collar pay structure in Britain.' *Econ. J.*, LXIX, 273 (March 1959), 55–70.

8432 **Industrial Welfare Society.** *Staff overtime payments.* London: the Society, 1961. 23p. (Survey 82.)

8433 **Institute of Personnel Management.** *Personnel management salaries: report of a survey undertaken in February/March 1961.* London: I.P.M., 1961. 32p.

8434 **Institute of Personnel Management.** *Status and pay of women supervisory staff (on the factory floor).* London: I.P.M., 1961. [38]p. (Information summary 17.)

8435 **Stevenson, Jordan and Harrison, Ltd.** *Survey of senior management remuneration.* London, 1961. 14p.
Private circulation.

8436 **Kemsley,** W. F. F. *Some technical aspects of a postal survey into professional earnings.* [1961 ?2.] 10p. (Social Survey M. 104.)
'. . . based on talks given to the General Applications Section of the Royal Statistical Society on 11th October 1960, and the Bristol Group of the Society on 16th March 1961.' Appeared in *Applied Statistics,* XI, 2 (1962).

8437 **Institute of Personnel Management** and **National Institute of Economic and Social Research.** *Report of joint conference: company salary structure in the U.K. at 1 May 1962.* London: N.I.E.S.R., 1962.

8438 **British Institute of Management.** *Overtime payments to staff.* London: B.I.M., 1965. 12p. (Information note 39.)

8439 **MacNeill,** Hugh. *Salary scales: does your salary administration sail along, or drift?* Dublin: Irish Management Institute, 1965. 8p.

8440 **Management Centre/Europe.** *Management compensation service, United Kingdom: report of a survey on manager remuneration.* Brussels, 1966.

8441 **Scitovsky,** Tibor. 'An international comparison of the trend of professional earnings.' *Am. Econ. Rev.,* LVI, 1 (March 1966), 25–42.

8442 **Business International Corporation.** *Worldwide executive compensation: how international companies set salaries, incentives, benefits.* New York: the Corporation, 1967. 69p. (Research report 67-2.)

8443 **Industrial Society.** *Staff overtime compensation.* London: the Society, 1967. 36p. (Information survey 143.)

8444 **Merrett,** Anthony John and **Monk,** D. A. J. *Inflation, taxation and executive remuneration.* London: Hallam P., 1967. 128p.

8445 **Alfred Marks Bureau.** Statistical Services Division. *The survey of secretarial and clerical salaries conducted by Alfred Marks Bureau Ltd.* London: Alfred Marks Bureau (Statistical Services Division), 1968. 26 leaves.

8446 **Merrett,** Anthony John. *Executive remuneration in the UK.* London: Longmans, 1968. xiv, 108p.

8447 **National Board for Prices and Incomes.** *Office staff employment agencies charges and salaries.* London: H.M.S.O., 1968. vi, 25p. (Report 89. Cmnd. 3828.)

8448 **Social Research Development.** *Work and remuneration of directors.* London: S.R.D., 1968. 12 leaves.

8449 **Associated Industrial Consultants.** Salary Research Unit. *International salaries & fringe benefits, 1968.* London: the Unit, 1969. 162p.

8450 **Institute of Personnel Management.** *Survey of personnel management salaries, 1968.* London: I.P.M., 1969. 40p. (Information report, new series 1.)

8451 **Irish Management Institute.** *Executive salary survey, 1968.* Dublin: the Institute, 1969. 66p. (Management information survey 2.)

8452 **McBeath,** Maurice Gordon. *Management remuneration policy.* London: Business Books, 1969. xi, 189p.

8453 **National Board for Prices and Incomes.** *Salary structures.* London: H.M.S.O., 1969. v, 94p. (Report 132. Cmnd. 4187.)

8454 **National Board for Prices and Incomes.** *Top salaries in the private sector and nationalised industries.* London: H.M.S.O., 1969. v, 86p. (Report 107. Cmnd. 3970.)

8455 **Social Organisation Limited.** *The effective board: a study of the work and remuneration of directors.* London: Social Organisation Ltd., 1969. 31p.

8456 **Institute of Personnel Management.** *Survey of personnel management salaries, 1970.* London: I.P.M., 1970. 54p. (Information report, new series 4.)

8457 **Social Organisation Limited.** *Work, remuneration and motivation of directors.* London: Social Organisation Ltd., 1970. 39p.

See also: 8816; 8872.

b. EDUCATIONAL SERVICES

i. *General*

8458 **Departmental Committee for Inquiring into the Principles which should determine the Fixing of Salaries for Teachers in Secondary and Technical Schools, Schools of Art, Training Colleges, and other Institutions for Higher Education.**
Vol. I. *Report.* London: H.M.S.O., 1918. (Cd. 9140.)
Vol. II. *Summaries of evidence.* 1918. (Cd. 9168.)
Chairman: Sir H. L. Stephen.

8459 **Greenhalgh,** Vivienne C. 'The movement of teachers' salaries, 1920–68.' *J. Educ. Adm. Hist.,* I, 1 (December 1968), 22–36.

8460 **Scottish Education Department.** *Salaries of registered teachers in primary and secondary schools and teachers in further education centres: report of the Arbitral Body, Scotland.* Edinburgh: H.M.S.O., 1969. 12p.
Chairman: G. Honeyman.

8461 **Bibby**, John. 'Rewards and careers.' *Higher Educ. Rev.*, III, 1 (Autumn 1970), 9–18.

ii. *Primary and Secondary*

8462 *Statistics of salaries paid to assistant mistresses in high schools.* London, 1891. 16p.

8463 **Rouse**, William Henry Denham. *Salaries in secondary schools.* London: Columbus, 1899. 6p.
Reprinted from *Contemporary Review.*

8464 **Departmental Committee for Inquiring into the Principles which should determine the Construction of Scales of Salary for Teachers in Elementary Schools.**
Vol. I. *Report.* London: H.M.S.O., 1918. (Cd. 8939.)
Vol. II. *Evidence and memoranda.* 1918. (Cd. 8999.)
Chairman: Sir Harry Stephen.

8465 **Wallace**, David. *Report of the Departmental Committee on the Remuneration of Teachers in Scotland.* London: A. H. Stockwell, 1918. 9p.
A criticism.

8466 **Standing Joint Committee on a Provisional Minimum Scale of Salaries for Teachers in Public Elementary Schools.** *Report.* London: H.M.S.O., 1919. 8p. (Cmd. 443.)
Chairman: Lord Burnham.

8467 **Northern Ireland.** Ministry of Education. *Interim reports of the Departmental Committee on the Salaries of Teachers in Public Elementary Schools.* Belfast: H.M.S.O., 1925. 29p. (Cmd. 48.)
Final report. 1925. 20p. (Cmd. 50.)
Chairmen: R. J. McKeown; J. H. Robb.

8468 **Eyes and Ears**, *pseud. Shall we pay more? On school teachers.* London: Stockwell, 1930. 47p.

8469 **Dunlop**, B. L. *A study of teachers' salary schedules in Great Britain, the United States and Canada; of the underlying principles of schedules; the application of these principles to Canadian teachers' salary schedules.* 1940. v, 207p. (M.A. thesis, University of Alberta.)

8470 **Northern Ireland.** Ministry of Education. Committee on Salaries and Conditions of Service of Teachers. *Salaries of teachers in primary and secondary schools: interim report.* Belfast, 1945. 12p.

8471 **Northern Ireland.** Ministry of Education. Committee on Salaries and Conditions of Service of Teachers. *Salaries of teachers in technical schools: second interim report.* Belfast, 1946. 11p.

8472 **Northern Ireland.** Ministry of Education. Committee on Salaries and Conditions of Service of Teachers. *Salaries of teachers, 1948: report of the Committee.* Belfast, 1948. 9p.

8473 **Conway**, Freda. 'An index of teachers' salaries.' *Oxf. Univ. Inst. Statist. Bull.*, XV, 6–7 (June–July 1953), 237–48.

8474 **Alexander**, *Sir* William Picken. *The Burnham primary and secondary school report, 1954: a commentary.* London: Councils and Education P., 1955. 39p.

8475 **Alexander**, *Sir* William Picken. *The Burnham report, appendix X: allowances for advanced teaching; a commentary.* London: Councils and Education P., 1955. 15p.

8476 **Alexander**, *Sir* William Picken. *Four salary reports: commentaries.* London: Councils and Education P., 1955. 35p.
Reprinted from *Education.*

8477 **Alexander**, *Sir* William Picken. *The Burnham primary and secondary schools report, 1956: a commentary.* London: Councils and Education P., 1956. 43p.

8478 **Alexander**, *Sir* William Picken. *Four salary reports, 1956: commentaries.* London: Councils and Education P., 1956. 55p.

8479 **Gould**, *Sir* Ronald. 'Factors affecting teachers' salaries in England and Wales.' *Yr. Bk. Educ.* (1956), 454–63.

8480 **Ministry of Education.** Burnham Main Committee. *Report of the Burnham Committee representative of associations of local education authorities and associations of teachers on scales of salaries for teachers in primary and secondary schools maintained by local education authorities, England and Wales.* London: H.M.S.O., 1956. viii, 62p.
Later report. 1959. ix, 66p.
Chairman: Sir Thomas Creed.

8481 **Meigh**, H. *Schoolmasters' salaries since the beginning of the 20th century.* London: National Association of Schoolmasters, [1957]. 69p.

8482 **Northern Ireland.** Ministry of Education. Committee on Teachers' Salaries, 1956. *Salaries of teachers, 1956; miscellaneous matters: final report of the committee appointed by the Minister of Education to consider the salaries, allowances and other matters affecting the remuneration of teachers.* Belfast: H.M.S.O., 1957. 16p.

8483 **Alexander**, *Sir* William Picken. *Teachers' salaries. Special allowances for teachers: an analysis of the 1956 Burnham report.* London: Councils and Education P., 1958. 41p.

8484 **Alexander**, *Sir* William Picken. *The Burnham primary and secondary schools report, 1959: a commentary.* London: Councils and Education P., 1959. 36p.

8485 **Alexander**, *Sir* William Picken. *Four salary reports, 1959: commentaries.* London: Councils and Education P., 1959. 48p.

8486 **Alexander**, *Sir* William Picken. *What teachers are paid.* London: Councils and Education P., 1959. 20p.
'Prepared on the instructions of the Executive Council of the Association of Education Committees.'

8487 **Alexander**, *Sir* William Picken. *Teachers' salaries. Opportunity in the teaching profession: an analysis of the Burnham report of 1959.* London: Councils and Education P., 1961. 41p.

8488 **Incorporated Association of Head Masters.** *The salary of the head of a school.* London: the Association, 1961. 8p.

8489 **Alexander,** *Sir* William Picken. *The Burnham primary and secondary schools report, 1961: a commentary.* London: Councils and Education P., 1962. 25p.

8490 **Alexander,** *Sir* William Picken. *Three salary reports, 1961: commentaries.* London: Councils and Education P., 1962. 40p.

8491 **Conway,** Freda. 'School teachers' salaries, 1945–1959.' *Manchr. Sch.*, xxx, 2 (May 1962), 153–79.

8492 **Papworth,** H. D. *The determination of teachers' salaries, with particular reference to secondary schools, 1870–1919.* 1963–64. (M.A. thesis, University of London.)

8493 **Department of Education and Science.** Arbitral Body on Salaries of Teachers in Primary and Secondary Schools. *Report: England and Wales.* London: H.M.S.O., 1965. 24p.
Another report. 1967. 20p.
Chairman: G. Honeyman.

8494 **National Board for Prices and Incomes.** *Scottish teachers' salaries.* London: H.M.S.O., 1966. 26p. (Report 15. Cmnd. 3005.)

8495 **Conway,** Freda. 'Salary indices for school teachers.' *Manchr. Sch.*, xxxv, 1 (January 1967), 69–81.

8496 **Standing Committee on Teachers' Salaries (Northern Ireland).** *Salaries of teachers: primary, secondary and special schools; report of the Standing Committee appointed by the Minister of Education to consider the salaries, allowances and other matters affecting the remuneration of teachers.* Belfast: H.M.S.O., 1967. 15p. (Cmd. 514.)

8497 **Alexander,** *Sir* William Picken. *The Burnham primary and secondary schools report, 1967: a commentary.* London: Councils and Education P., 1968. 17p.

8498 **Department of Education and Science.** *Report of the arbitral body on the payment of teachers in primary and secondary schools: London area.* London: H.M.S.O., 1968. 12p.
Chairman: G. Honeyman.

8499 **Eire.** Department of Education. Tribunal on Teachers' Salaries. *Report.* 1968. (E.61.)

8500 **Scottish Education Department.** *Scottish teachers' salaries memorandum, 1968.* Edinburgh: H.M.S.O., 1968. 68p.
Chairman: Lord Robertson.

8501 **Alexander,** *Sir* William Picken. *The Burnham primary and secondary schools report, 1969: a commentary.* London: Councils and Education P., 1969. 20p.

8502 **Department of Education and Science.** *Scales of salaries for teachers in primary and secondary schools, England and Wales, 1969.* London: H.M.S.O., 1969. vii, 70p.
Chairman: J. S. Wordie.

8503 **House of Commons.** Select Committee on Public Petitions. *Special report from the Committee on Public Petitions.* London: H.M.S.O., 1969. 3p. (1968/69 H.C. 470.)

8504 **MacArthur,** Brian. *The lesson for Britain.* London: National Union of Teachers, 1969. 16p.

8505 **National Union of Teachers.** *Why teachers are underpaid: a survey.* London: N.U.T., 1969. 17p.

8506 **Scottish Education Department.** *Scottish teachers' salaries memorandum, 1970.* Edinburgh: H.M.S.O., 1970. 70p.
Chairman: The Lord Robertson, Q.C.

See also: 8695; 8700; 8702–3.

iii. *Higher*

8507 **Scottish Education Department.** *Structure of further education salaries: report of a Working Party appointed by the Secretary of State for Scotland and the National Joint Council to deal with salaries of teachers in Scotland.* Edinburgh: H.M.S.O., 1955. 24p. (Cmd. 9365.)
Chairman: T. Grainger-Stewart.

8508 **Scottish Education Department.** *Basis of remuneration of part-time further education teachers: report of Working Party appointed by the Secretary of State for Scotland.* Edinburgh: H.M.S.O., 1959. 18p.
Chairman: H. H. Donnelly.

8509 **Bowen,** William G. 'University salaries: faculty differentials.' *Economica*, n.s., xxx, 120 (November 1963), 341–59.
Reprinted in Bowen, W. G. *Economic aspects of education: three essays.* Princeton, N.J.: Industrial Relations Section, Department of Economics, Princeton University, 1964. p. 87–127.

8510 **Mills,** G. 'Dispersion of academic salaries in Great Britain and in the U.S.A.' *Br. J. Ind. Relat.*, II, 2 (July 1964), 251–7.

8511 **National Incomes Commission.** *Remuneration of academic staff in universities and colleges of advanced technology.* London: H.M.S.O., 1964. xii, 100p. (Report 3. Cmnd. 2317.)
Chairman: Sir Geoffrey Lawrence.

8512 **Alexander,** *Sir* William Picken. *Five salary reports, 1965: salary reports for teachers in establishments of further education, for teachers in farm institutes, for teachers in colleges of education, for youth leaders and for inspectors and organisers: a commentary on these salary reports.* London: Councils and Education P., 1965. 26p.

8513 **Department of Education and Science.** *Report of the Committee on scales of salaries for teachers in establishments for further education.* London: H.M.S.O., 1965.
England and Wales, 1965.
Chairman: D. T. Jack.

8514 **Department of Education and Science.** *Report of the Committee on scales of salaries for the teaching staff of colleges of education, England and Wales, 1965.* London: H.M.S.O., 1965.
Chairman: D. T. Jack.

8515 **Department of Education and Science.** *Report of the Committee on scales of salaries for the teaching staff of farm institutes for teachers of agricultural (including horticultural) subjects, England and Wales, 1965.* London: H.M.S.O., 1965.
Chairman: D. T. Jack.

8516 **Department of Education and Science.** Committee on Scales of Salaries for the Teaching Staff of Colleges of Education. *Report of the committee representatives of associations of local education authorities, college of education authorities and of the Association of Teachers in Colleges and Departments of Education on scales of salaries for the teaching staff of colleges of education, England and Wales, 1967.* London: H.M.S.O., 1967. vi, 16p.

8517 **Wiltshire**, Harold and **Percy**, Keith. *Fee structure in LEA adult education: a survey of practice and principles.* London: National Institute of Adult Education (England and Wales); Nottingham: University of Nottingham, Department of Adult Education, 1967. [6], 25p.

8518 **Alexander**, *Sir* William Picken. *A commentary on the Burnham further education report, 1967.* London: Councils and Education P., 1968. 36p.

8519 **Department of Education and Science.** *Report of the arbitral body on salaries for teachers in establishments for further education.* London: H.M.S.O., 1968. 35p.
Chairman: G. Honeyman.

8520 **Department of Education and Science.** *Scales of salaries for teachers in establishments for further education, England and Wales, 1967.* London: H.M.S.O., 1968. vi, 65p.
Chairman: J. S. Wordie.

8521 **Department of Education and Science.** *Scales of salaries for the teaching staff of farm institutes and for teachers of agricultural (including horticultural) subjects, England and Wales, 1967.* London: H.M.S.O., 1968. 48p.

8522 **National Board for Prices and Incomes.** *Standing reference on the pay of university teachers in Great Britain: first report.* London: H.M.S.O., 1968. vi, 59p. (Report 98. Cmnd. 3866.)

8523 **Alexander**, *Sir* William Picken. *Commentaries on three salary reports: Burnham Further Education Report, 1969, Burnham Farm Institutes Report, 1969, Pelham Report, 1969.* London: Councils and Education P., 1969. 23p.

8524 **Department of Education and Science.** *Report of the arbitral body on salaries for teachers in establishments for further education.* London: H.M.S.O., 1969. 40p.

8525 **Department of Education and Science.** *Report of the Committee on scales of salaries for teaching staff of colleges of education: England and Wales, 1969.* London: H.M.S.O., 1969. 24p.
Chairman: J. S. Wordie.

8526 **Department of Education and Science.** *Scales of salaries for teachers in establishments for further education, England and Wales, 1969, being the document, prepared by the Secretary of State for Education and Science under Sections 2 and 4 of the Remuneration of Teachers Act 1965, setting out the scales of salaries and other provisions for determining remuneration of teachers in establishments for further education (other than farm institutes) maintained by local education authorities.* London: H.M.S.O., 1969. 76p.

8527 **Department of Education and Science.** *Scales of salaries for the teaching staff of farm institutes and teachers of agricultural (including horticultural) subjects, England and Wales, 1969, being the documents prepared by the Secretary of State for Education and Science under Section 2 of the Remuneration of Teachers Act 1965.* London: H.M.S.O., 1969.

8528 **Metcalf**, David. 'University salaries: faculty differentials.' *Economica*, n.s., XXXVII, 148 (November 1970), 362–72.

8529 **National Board for Prices and Incomes.** *Pay of university teachers in Great Britain.* London: H.M.S.O., 1970. vi, 47p. (Report 145. Cmnd. 4334.)

8530 **Scottish Education Department.** *Salaries of teachers employed whole-time in further education centres, Scotland: report of the arbitration body.* London: H.M.S.O., 1970. 28p.
Chairman: A. D. Campbell.

c. MEDICAL AND DENTAL SERVICES

i. *General*

8531 **Royal Commission on Doctors' and Dentists' Remuneration, 1957–1960.** *Report.* London: H.M.S.O., 1960. xii, 346p. (Cmnd. 939.)
Supplement to report: further statistical appendix. 1960. 42p. (Cmnd. 1964.)
Written evidence. Vol. 1. 1957. v, 108p.
Written evidence. Vol. 2. 1960. iii, 154p.
Index to oral and written evidence. 1961. 34p.
Chairman: Sir Harry Pilkington.

8532 **Ministry of Health.** Review Body on Doctors' and Dentists' Remuneration. *Third, fourth and fifth reports.* London: H.M.S.O., 1965. 32p. (Cmnd. 2585.)
Chairman: Lord Kindersley.
Third report. *Remuneration of senior hospital medical and dental officers.*
Fourth report. *Consultants in the National Health Service: distinction awards.*
Fifth report. *Remuneration of general medical practitioners.*

8533 **Ministry of Health.** Review Body on Doctors' and Dentists' Remuneration. *Seventh report.* London: H.M.S.O., 1966. iii, 95p. (Cmnd. 2992)

8534 **Department of Health and Social Security.** Review Body on Doctors' and Dentists' Remuneration. *Ninth report.* London: H.M.S.O., 1968. iii, 70p. (Cmnd. 3600.)

8535 **Department of Health and Social Security.** Review Body on Doctors' and Dentists' Remuneration. *Tenth report.* London: H.M.S.O., 1969. v, 19p. (Cmnd. 3884.)

8536 **Department of Health and Social Security.** Review Body on Doctors' and Dentists' Remuneration. *Twelfth report.* London: H.M.S.O., 1970. v, 78p. (Cmnd. 4352.)

Chairman: Lord Kindersley.

Only those reports of the Review Body on Doctors' and Dentists' Remuneration which were published separately are listed above. Of the remainder the following appeared in the House of Commons *Official report* (Hansard): *First report*, 25 March 1963; *Second report*, 1 February 1965; *Sixth report*, 5 August 1965; *Eighth report*, 12 May 1967.

ii. *Doctors*

8537 **Pearse**, James. 'Friendly societies and the medical profession. *Char. Orgn. Rev.*, n.s., xxv, 147 (March 1909), 126–34.

Paper read at a conference convened by the Charity Organisation Society, February 1909.

Discussion, p. 134–5.

8538 **Plender**, *Sir* William. *Report to the Chancellor of the Exchequer on the result of his investigation into existing conditions in respect of medical attendance and remuneration in certain towns.* London: H.M.S.O., 1912. 6p. (Cd. 6305.)

8539 **Northern Ireland.** *Report of the Inter-Departmental Committee on Medical Benefit in Northern Ireland.* Belfast: H.M.S.O., 1930. 26p. (Cmd. 113.)

8540 **Ministry of Health** and **Department of Health for Scotland.** *Report of the Inter-Departmental Committee on Remuneration of General Practitioners.* London: H.M.S.O., 1946. 31p. (Cmd. 6810.)

Chairman: Sir Will Spens.

8541 **Ministry of Health** and **Department of Health for Scotland.** *Report of the Inter-Departmental Committee on the Remuneration of Consultants and Specialists.* London: H.M.S.O., 1948. 30p. (Cmd. 7420.)

Chairman: Sir Will Spens.

8542 **Ministry of Health** and **Department of Health for Scotland.** *Report of the Inter-Departmental Committee on the Remuneration of General Dental Practitioners.* London: H.M.S.O., 1948. 13p. (Cmd. 7402.)

Chairman: Sir Will Spens.

8543 **Ministry of Health** and **Department of Health for Scotland.** National Health Service. *Distribution of remuneration among general practitioners: report of Working Party of representatives of the General Medical Services Committee of the British Medical Association and Health Departments.* London: H.M.S.O., 1952. 8p.

8544 **British Medical Association** and **Northern Ireland**, Ministry of Health and Local Government. Joint Working Party. *Remuneration of general medical practitioners in Northern Ireland: report.* Belfast: H.M.S.O., 1961. 28p.

8545 **British Medical Association** and **Northern Ireland**, Ministry of Health and Local Government. Joint Working Party. *Distribution of Rural Practitioners' Fund and Contingency Fund.* Belfast: H.M.S.O., 1962. 27p.

8546 **Hogarth**, James. *The payment of the general practitioner: some European comparisons.* Oxford, New York: Pergamon P., 1963. xii, 684p.

8547 **Stevens**, Rosemary. 'How we pay our doctors.' *New Soc.*, 37 (13 June 1963), 15–16.

8548 **Lynch**, Harriet. 'Doctors' pay and the public.' *New Soc.*, VIII, 204 (25 August 1966), 301–2. (Society at work.)

8549 **Rees**, M. S. 'The inflation of National Health Service registers of patients and its effect on the remuneration of general practitioners.' *R. Statist. Soc. J.*, Ser. A, CXXXII, 4 (1969), 526–42.

8550 **Glaser**, William Arnold. *Paying the doctor: systems of remuneration and their effects.* Baltimore, Md., London: Johns Hopkins P., 1970. xii, 323p.

iii. *Nurses*

8551 **Department of Health for Scotland.** Scottish Nurses' Salaries Committee. *Interim report.* Edinburgh: H.M.S.O., 1943. 16p. (Cmd. 6425.)

Chairman: T. M. Taylor.

8552 **Department of Health for Scotland.** Scottish Nurses' Salaries Committee. *Second report.* Edinburgh: H.M.S.O., 1943. 28p. (Cmd. 6439.)

8553 **Department of Health for Scotland.** Scottish Nurses' Salaries Committee. *Report of the Mental Nurses Sub-Committee.* Edinburgh: H.M.S.O., 1943. 6p. (Cmd. 6488.)

Chairman: T. M. Taylor.

8554 **Ministry of Health.** Nurses Salaries Committee. *First report: salaries and emoluments of female nurses in hospitals.* London: H.M.S.O., 1943. 42p. (Cmd. 6424.)

Chairman: Lord Rushcliffe.

8555 **Ministry of Health.** Nurses Salaries Committee. *Second report, on the salaries and emoluments of male nurses, public health nurses, district nurses and state registered nurses in nurseries.* London: H.M.S.O., 1943. (Cmd. 6487.)

Chairman: Lord Rushcliffe.

8556 **Department of Health for Scotland.** Scottish Nurses' Salaries Committee. *Third report: supplement to the Second Report.* Edinburgh: H.M.S.O., 1944. 27p. (Cmd. 6505.)
Reprinted 1945.
Chairman: T. M. Taylor.

8557 **Ministry of Health.** Nurses Salaries Committee. *Further recommendations.* London: H.M.S.O., 1944.

8558 **Ministry of Health.** Nurses Salaries Committee. *Report of the Mental Nurses Sub-Committee.* London: H.M.S.O., 1944. (Cmd. 6542.)
Chairman: Lord Rushcliffe.

8559 **Department of Health for Scotland.** Scottish Nurses' Salaries Committee. *Fourth report (mental nurses).* Edinburgh: H.M.S.O., 1945. 30p. (Cmd. 6684.)

8560 **Hospital and Welfare Services Union.** *Origin, constitution and survey of Nurses Salaries Committee.* [London?]: the Union, 1945.

8561 **Department of Health for Scotland.** Scottish Nurses' Salaries Committee. *Fifth report and supplementary report.* Edinburgh: H.M.S.O., 1947. iv, 132p. (Cmd. 7238.)
Chairman: John Wheatley.

8562 **Department of Health for Scotland.** Scottish Nurses' Salaries Committee. *Sixth report and supplementary report (mental nurses).* Edinburgh: H.M.S.O., 1947. ii, 52p. (Cmd. 7239.)
Chairman: John Wheatley.

8563 **National Board for Prices and Incomes.** *Pay of nurses and midwives in the National Health Service.* London: H.M.S.O., 1968. v, 91p. (Report 60. Cmnd. 3585.)

iv. *Other*

8564 **Committee on Salaries and Emoluments of Institutional and Domiciliary Midwives, Non-Medical Supervisors of Midwives and of Pupil Midwives.** *Report.* London: H.M.S.O., 1943. (Cmd. 6460.)
Chairman: Lord Rushcliffe.

8565 **Ministry of Health.** *Salaries of whole-time public health medical officers: interim revision of the Askwith Memorandum.* London: H.M.S.O., 1946. 11p.

8566 **Association of Hospital Treasurers.** Sheffield Branch. *A guide to salaries and wages procedures.* Swansea: the Association, 1965. 52p.

8567 **National Board for Prices and Incomes.** *Pay and conditions of service of ancillary workers in the National Health Service.* London: H.M.S.O., 1971. v, 134p. (Report 166. Cmnd. 4644.)

See also: 8614.

d. RELIGIOUS ORGANISATIONS

8568 **Hammond**, Frederic John. *The starvelings: a study in clerical poverty.* London: Society of SS. Peter and Paul, 1921. 61p.

8569 **Church of England.** National Assembly. *Report of the Committee appointed to consider the Report – C.A. 719 – of the Commission of the House of Bishops on the Remuneration and Housing of the Clergy and other matters.* London, 1945. 15p.

8570 **Fisher**, Geoffrey Francis, Archbishop of Canterbury. *A statement on clerical stipends made to the Church Assembly by the Archbishop of Canterbury on Tuesday, 11th February 1947.* London: Church Assembly, Society for Promoting Christian Knowledge, 1947. 8p.

8571 **Rawlinson**, Alfred Edward John, Bishop of Derby. *The financial straits of the clergy: an address.* Derby: Press and Publications Board of the Church Assembly for the Bishop of Derby, 1947. 9p.

8572 **Wood**, Edward Frederick Lindley, Earl of Halifax. *The crisis in the Church.* London: Press and Publications Board, 1948. 8p.

8573 **Duffield**, Gervase Elwes (ed.). *The Paul Report considered: an appraisal of Mr Leslie Paul's report 'The deployment and payment of the clergy': thirteen essays.* Marcham: Marcham Manor P., 1964. 94p.

8574 **Hunter**, Leslie H. 'The economy of the Church of England and its ministry.' *Q. Rev.*, 641 (July 1964), 310–22.

8575 **Paul**, Leslie Allen. *The deployment and payment of the clergy: a report.* London: Church Information Office, 1964. 311p.
Index. 1964. 13p.
For the Church of England Central Advisory Council of Training for the Ministry.

8576 **Sansbury**, Graham Rogers. *The Paul Report: a study guide.* London: Church Information Office, 1964. 48p.

e. OTHER

8577 **Institute of Chemistry of Great Britain and Ireland.** 'Salary statistics, 1930.' *Journal & Proceedings*, pt. III (June 1931), 197–204.

8578 **Institute of Chemistry of Great Britain and Ireland.** 'Remuneration and status of chemists.' *Journal & Proceedings*, pt. VI (December 1938), 443–6.
Editorial on the need for statistics.

8579 **Institute of Chemistry of Great Britain and Ireland.** 'Salary statistics.' *Journal & Proceedings*, pt. I (February 1938), 36.

8580 **Institute of Chemistry of Great Britain and Ireland.** 'Remuneration statistics.' *Journal & Proceedings*, pt. II (April 1939), 207–14.

8581 **Institute of Chemistry of Great Britain and Ireland.** 'Remuneration statistics.' *Journal & Proceedings*, pt. VI (December 1942), 273–82.

8582 **British Federation of Social Workers** and **National Council of Social Service.** Joint Committee. *Report on salaries and conditions of work of social workers.* London: National Council of Social Service, 1947.

Chairman: T. S. Simey.

8583 **Institute of Chemistry of Great Britain and Ireland.** 'Remuneration statistics, 1948.' *Journal & Proceedings*, pt. II (April 1948), 101–10.

8584 **Taylor**, I. M. S. *A case study in the administration of the wage structure of research and development operatives.* 1957–58. (M.Sc. (Econ.) thesis, University of London.)

8585 **Professional Engineer.** 'What do engineers earn?' *Prof. Engr.*, VI, 4 (October 1959), 128–30.

Contains the results of an enquiry carried out into the earnings of professional engineers in connection with the survey undertaken for the Royal Commission on Doctors' and Dentists' Remuneration by the Government Social Survey.

8586 **Milne**, Joan. 'More about architects' incomes in 1955–56.' *R. Inst. Br. Archit. J.*, 3rd ser., LXVII, 7 (May 1960), 233–5.

8587 **Royal Institute of British Architects.** 'Comparison of professional incomes.' *R. Inst. Br. Archit. J.*, 3rd ser., LXVII, 6 (April 1960), 195–200.

Based on data published in the Report of the Royal Commission on Doctors' and Dentists' Remuneration, 1960. (Cmnd. 939.)

8588 **Abel-Smith**, Brian and **Stevens**, Robert. 'Solicitors in an age of inflation.' *New Soc.*, IX, 225 (19 January 1967), 82–4.

8589 **National Board for Prices and Incomes.** *Agreement made between certain engineering firms and the Draughtsmen's and Allied Technicians' Association.* London: H.M.S.O., 1968. vi, 20p. (Report 68. Cmnd. 3632.)

8590 **National Board for Prices and Incomes.** *Architects' costs and fees.* London: H.M.S.O., 1968. v, 97p. (Report 71. Cmnd. 3653.)

8591 **National Board for Prices and Incomes.** *Remuneration of solicitors.* London: H.M.S.O., 1968. v, 66p. (Report 54. Cmnd. 3529.)

8592 **National Board for Prices and Incomes.** *Pay of salaried staff in Imperial Chemical Industries Ltd.* London: H.M.S.O., 1969. vi, 22p. (Report 109. Cmnd. 3981.)

8593 **National Board for Prices and Incomes.** *Standing reference on the remuneration of solicitors: first report.* London: H.M.S.O., 1969. v, 45p. (Report 134. Cmnd. 4217.)

8594 **National Board for Prices and Incomes.** *Standing reference on the remuneration of solicitors: second report.* London: H.M.S.O., 1971. vi, 79p. (Report 164. Cmnd. 4624.)

11. Miscellanous Services

8595 **Board of Trade.** Labour Department. *Report by Miss Collet, on the money wages of indoor domestic servants.* London: H.M.S.O., 1899. vii, 50p. (C. 9346.)

8596 **Halling**, Daisy and **Lister**, Charles. 'A minimum wage for actors.' *Social. Rev.*, I, 6 (August 1908), 441–51.

8597 **Layton**, Walter Thomas. 'Changes in the wages of domestic servants during fifty years.' *R. Statist. Soc. J.*, LXXI, 3 (September 1908), 515–24.

8598 **Ministry of Labour and National Service.** Catering Wages Commission. *The problems affecting the remuneration of catering workers which result from the practice of giving tips.* London: H.M.S.O., 1947. 4p.

8599 **Bentley**, H. 'A rate for servants' wages made at Easter Sessions, 7 Charles I.' *E. Herts Archaeol. Soc. Trans.*, XIII (1950–54), 167–71.

A literal transcription of an Assize of Wages, 1631, with short introduction.

8600 **Institute of Personnel Management.** *Duties and pay of security personnel.* London: I.P.M., 1961. 25p.

8601 **National Board for Prices and Incomes.** *Laundry and dry cleaning charges.* London: H.M.S.O., 1966. iv, 26p. (Report 20. Cmnd. 3093.)

8602 **Economic Development Committee for Hotels and Catering.** *Service in hotels: a study of the labour costs of providing personal services in hotels with suggestions for cost savings.* London: H.M.S.O., 1968. v, 38p.

8603 **Kotas**, Richard. *A study of labour costs in catering establishments in Greater London area.* 1968–69. (M.Phil. thesis, University of Surrey.)

8604 **Economic Development Committee for Hotels and Catering.** *Why tipping? a report of an enquiry into current practice and opinions on tipping in the industry and some of the likely effects of tipping on management, employees and customers.* London: National Economic Development Office, 1969. 23p.

8605 **National Board for Prices and Incomes.** *Pay of certain employees in the film processing industry.* London: H.M.S.O., 1969. v, 22p. (Report 131. Cmnd. 4185.)

8606 **Kotas**, Richard. *Labour costs in restaurants: a study of labour costs in catering establishments in the Greater London area.* London: Intertext, 1970. 209p.

The author's thesis.

8607 **National Board for Prices and Incomes.** *Costs and revenues of independent television companies.* London: H.M.S.O., 1970. v, 56p. (Report 156. Cmnd. 4524.)

8608 **National Board for Prices and Incomes.** *Costs and charges in the motor repairing and servicing industry.* London: H.M.S.O., 1971. vi, 45p. (Report 163. Cmnd. 4590.)

8609 **National Board for Prices and Incomes.** *Pay and conditions in the contract cleaning trade.* London: H.M.S.O., 1971. vi, 73p. (Report 168. Cmnd. 4637.)

8610 **National Board for Prices and Incomes.** *Pay and conditions of service of workers in the laundry and dry cleaning industry.* London: H.M.S.O., 1971. v, 99p. (Report 167. Cmnd. 4647.)

See also: 5535; 7827; 7959; 8804; 12,990; 12,996–13,000; 13,002–6; 13,011; 13,021; 13,025–6; 13,035; 13,044–5; 13,054.

12. Public Administration

a. GENERAL

8611 **Kahn**, Hilda Renate. 'Payment for political and public service.' *Publ. Adm.*, XXXII, 2 (Summer 1954), 181–201.

8612 **Kahn**, Hilda Renate. *Salaries in the public services in England and Wales, 1946–1951: a vertical and horizontal analysis.* 1958–59. (Ph.D. thesis, University of London.)

8613 **Kahn**, Hilda Renate. *Salaries in the public services in England and Wales.* London: Allen and Unwin, 1962 [i.e. 1963]. 428p.

8614 **National Board for Prices and Incomes.** *The pay and conditions of manual workers in local authorities, the National Health Service, gas and water supply.* London: H.M.S.O., 1967. ix, 80p. (Report 29. Cmnd. 3230.)
Reprinted 1968.
Statistical supplement. 1967. v, 97p. (Report 29 (Supplement). Cmnd. 3230-I.)

8615 **Taylor**, Mike. 'The revolt against low pay in the public services.' *Trade Un. Regist.* (1970), 198–204.

b. NATIONAL GOVERNMENT

8616 **Select Committee on Conditions and Rates of Pay of Customs (Out-door Offices at the Outports).** *Report, etc.* London: H.M.S.O., 1881.

8617 **Grey**, *Sir* Edward. 'Payment of Members of Parliament.' Co-operative Wholesale Societies. *Annual for 1892.* p. 345–59.

8618 **Worthington**, A. H. 'A historical note as to payment of Members of Parliament.' Co-operative Wholesale Societies. *Annual for 1893.* p. 555–60.

8619 **Departmental Committee on Remuneration of the Ordnance Survey Staff.** *Report.* London: H.M.S.O., 1911. 28p. (Cd. 5825.)
Minutes of evidence, etc. 1911. (Cd. 5826.)
Chairman: Lord Ilkeston.

8620 **Conference to Consider Certain Questions Relating to Justices' Clerks' Fees and Salaries.** *Report.* London: H.M.S.O., 1914. 26p. (Cd. 7495.)

8621 **Select Committee on Remuneration of Ministers.** *Report, etc.* London: H.M.S.O., 1920. xvi, 29p.
Chairman: John William Wilson.

8622 **Civil Service National Whitley Council.** Cost of Living Committee. *Report of the Cost of Living Committee appointed by the Civil Service National Whitley Council.* London: H.M.S.O., 1921. 5p. (Cmd. 1107.)
Chairman: R. S. Meiklejohn.

8623 **Treasury**. *Report of the Committee appointed to advise as to the salaries of the principal posts in the Civil Service.* London: H.M.S.O., 1921. 4p. (Cmd. 1188.)

8624 **Shepherd**, Edwin Colston. *The fixing of wages in government employment.* London: Methuen, 1923. xx, 207p.

8625 **Eire.** Seanad Éireann. *Report of the Special Committee on the Remuneration of the Cathaoirleach and Leas-Chathaoirleach.* Dublin: Stationery Office, 1929. 4p.
Cathaoirleach and Leas-Chathaoirleach = Chairman and Vice-Chairman of the Senate.

8626 **Select Committee on Ministers' Remuneration.** *Report, etc.* London: H.M.S.O., 1930. viii, 66p. (H.C. 170.)
Chairman: A. Hayday.

8627 **Hughes**, Edward. 'The salaries of the excise officers and a cost of living index (1795–1800).' *Econ. Hist.*, III, 11 (February 1936), 259–66.

8628 *The administrative class of the Civil Service.* 1945. 2p. (Cmd. 6680.)

8629 **Select Committee on Members' Expenses, Salaries and Pensions.** *Members' expenses: report, etc.* London: H.M.S.O., 1946. xiv, 116p.
Chairman: T. Smith.
Committee appointed 1945.

8630 **Select Committee on Members' Expenses, Salaries and Pensions.** *Members' fund: report, etc.* London: H.M.S.O., 1947. xvi, 51p.
Chairman: S. P. Viant.
Committee appointed 1947.

8631 **Treasury**. Committee on Higher Civil Service Remuneration. *Report.* London: H.M.S.O., 1949. 14p. (Cmd. 7635.)
Chairman: Lord Chorley.

8632 **Latham**, R. C. 'Payment of parliamentary wages: the last phase.' *Engl. Hist. Rev.*, LXVI, 258 (January 1951), 27–50.

8633 **Routh**, Gerald Guy Cumming. *A study of the factors determining the level of pay in the British Civil Service since 1875, with particular reference to the general and minor post office manipulative and engineering grades.* 1951. (Ph.D. thesis, University of London.)

8634 **Treasury**. Committee on Pay and Organisation of Civil Service Medical Staff. *Report.* London: H.M.S.O., 1951. 20p.
Interim reports, 1950 and 1951.
Chairman: Sir Harold Howitt.

8635 **Treasury**. Committee on the Organisation, Structure and Remuneration of the Works Group of Professional Civil Servants. *Report.* London: H.M.S.O., 1951. 28p.
Chairman: Sir Thomas Gardiner.

8636 **Treasury**. Committee on the Organisation, Structure and Remuneration of the Professional Accountant Class in the Civil Service. *Report*. London: H.M.S.O., 1952. 22p.
Chairman: Sir Thomas Gardiner.

8637 **Routh**, Gerald Guy Cumming. 'Civil Service pay, 1875 to 1950.' *Economica*, n.s., XXI, 83 (August 1954), 201–23.

8638 **Select Committee on Members' Expenses, Salaries and Pensions.** *Members' expenses, etc.* London: H.M.S.O., 1954. xxxiv, 85p.
Chairman: C. Davies.
Committee appointed 1953.

8639 **Fairbanks**, J. 'The income of the higher civil servant.' *Administration*, III, 2–3 (Summer–Autumn 1955), 59–68.

8640 **Conway**, Freda. 'Salaries index: executive class civil servants, 1938–1961.' *Manchr. Sch.*, XXXI, 1 (January 1963), 79–83.

8641 **Treasury**. Committee on the Remuneration of Ministers and Members of Parliament. *Report*. London: H.M.S.O., 1964. (Cmnd. 2516.)
Chairman: Sir Geoffrey Lawrence.

8642 **National Board for Prices and Incomes.** *Armed forces pay*. London: H.M.S.O., 1966. iv, 7p. (Report 10. Cmnd. 2881.)

8643 **National Board for Prices and Incomes.** *Pay of industrial civil servants*. London: H.M.S.O., 1966. v, 29p. (Report 18. Cmnd. 3034.)

8644 **National Board for Prices and Incomes.** *Pay of the higher Civil Service*. London: H.M.S.O., 1966. vi, 5p. (Report 11. Cmnd. 2882.)

8645 **National Board for Prices and Incomes.** *London weighting in the non-industrial Civil Service*. London: H.M.S.O., 1967. v, 24p. (Report 44. Cmnd. 3436.)

8646 **Ministry of Defence.** *Service pay and pensions*. London: H.M.S.O., 1968. (Cmnd. 3756.)

8647 **National Board for Prices and Incomes.** *Standing reference on the pay of the armed forces: first report*. London: H.M.S.O., 1968. v, 9p. (Report 70. Cmnd. 3651.)

8648 **National Board for Prices and Incomes.** *Standing reference on the pay of the armed forces: second report*. London: H.M.S.O., 1969. vi, 117p. (Report 116. Cmnd. 4079.)

8649 **National Board for Prices and Incomes.** *Pay and conditions of industrial civil servants*. London: H.M.S.O., 1970. vi, 103p. (Report 146. Cmnd. 4351.)

8650 **National Board for Prices and Incomes.** *Pay of the armed forces: third report*. London: H.M.S.O., 1970. vi, 117p. (Report 142. Cmnd. 4291.)

8651 **National Board for Prices and Incomes.** *Standing reference on the pay of the armed forces: fourth report. The pay of senior officers*. London: H.M.S.O., 1970. vi, 9p. (Report 157. Cmnd. 4513.)

8652 **National Board for Prices and Incomes.** *Standing reference on the pay of the armed forces: fifth report. Separation allowance*. London: H.M.S.O., 1970. iv, 3p. (Report 158. Cmnd. 4529.)

c. LOCAL GOVERNMENT

8653 **Farrer**, Thomas Henry, Baron Farrer. *The London County Council's labour bill*. London: Steel and Jones, 1892. 6p.
'Memorandum for the use of members.' Revised with additions.

8654 **Farrer**, Thomas Henry, Baron Farrer. *The London County Council's wages bill: market rate or fancy rate?* London: Steel and Jones, 1892. 8p.
'Memorandum originally printed for the use of Members . . . and since revised.'

8655 **Hewart**, Beatrice. 'The wages of London Vestry employees.' *Econ. J.*, VIII, 31 (September 1898), 407–14.

8656 **Walsall Advertiser**. *The borough member's wages bill, 1913*. Walsall, 1913. 10p.

8657 **Beardmore**, C. J., **Gunton**, H. E., **Parkin**, M. and **Smith,** R. D. H. *Wages records of local authorities and public boards, by a research group*. London: Institute of Municipal Treasurers and Accountants, 1952. 108p. (Research series.)

8658 **National Board for Prices and Incomes.** *Pay of chief and senior officers in local government service and in the Greater London Council*. London: H.M.S.O., 1967. vi, 50p. (Report 45. Cmnd. 3473.)

8659 **Eire.** Department of Local Government. Review Body on Higher Remuneration in the Public Sector. *Report to Minister for Local Government on findings of Local Authorities' Arbitration Board on claims by local authority engineers and county accountants*. 1969. (K. 100.)

See also: 8820.

d. POLICE, FIREMEN, AND PRISON OFFICERS

8660 *Return of rates of wages paid by local authorities and private companies to police, and to work people employed on roads etc., and at gas and water works; with report thereon*. London: H.M.S.O., 1892. (C. 6715.)

8661 **Home Office.** Committee to Consider the Grant of a Non-Pensionable Addition to the Pay of the Police in England and Wales in Consideration of the Increases in the Cost of Living. *Report*. London: H.M.S.O., 1920. 10p.
Chairman: Arthur Lewis Dixon.

8662 **Vice-Regal Commission on Reorganization and Pay of the Irish Police Forces.** *Report*. Dublin: H.M.S.O., 1920. 20p. (Cmd. 603.)
Chairman: Sir John Ross.

8663 **Prison Officers' Pay Committee.** *Report.* London: H.M.S.O., 1923. (Cmd. 1959.)
Chairman: Lord Stanhope.

8664 **Home Department.** Police Pay (New Entrants) Committee. *Report.* London: H.M.S.O., 1933. 18p. (Cmd. 4274.)
Chairman: Sir George Higgins.

8665 **Home Office** and **Scottish Home Department.** Committee on Remuneration and Conditions of Service of Certain Grades in the Prison Service. *Report.* London: H.M.S.O., 1958. 52p. (Cmnd. 544.)

8666 **County Councils Association.** *Royal Commission on the Police: memorandum of evidence by the County Councils Association on the fourth of the Commission's terms of reference.* London: the Association, 1960. 32p.

8667 **National Board for Prices and Incomes.** *Fire Service pay.* London: H.M.S.O., 1967. v, 26p. (Report 32. Cmnd. 3287.)

8668 **Bugler**, Jeremy. 'Fire; ambulance; pay.' *New Soc.*, XIV, 370 (30 October 1969), 688–99.

F. WOMEN'S WAGES AND EQUAL PAY

See also Part Three, III, F, 3; Part Six, II, C, 4; Part Six, IV, A, 4, a–b; and Part Seven, VI, E.

8669 **Collet**, Clara Elizabeth. *The economic position of educated working women: a discourse delivered in South Place Chapel, Finbsury, E. C. on February 2nd, 1890.* London: E. W. Allen, 1890. 205–16p. (South Place Ethical Society. Publications 25.)

8670 **Webb**, Sidney. 'The alleged differences in the wages paid to men and to women for similar work.' *Econ. J.*, I, 4 (December 1891), 635–62.
Comment on this article by Millicent Garrett Fawcett, *Econ. J.*, II (March 1892), 173–6.

8671 **Smart**, William. *Women's wages.* Glasgow, 1892. 19p.

8672 **Heather-Bigg**, Ada. 'The wife's contribution to family income.' *Econ. J.*, IV, 13 (March 1894), 51–8.
'Read before Section F of the British Association, September 18, 1893.'

8673 **Boucherett**, E. Jessie. *The fall of women's wages in unskilled work.* London, 1899. 16p.

8674 **Bosanquet**, Helen. 'A study in women's wages.' *Econ. J.*, XII, 45 (March 1902), 42–9.

8675 **Webb**, Sidney. 'Women's wages.' Webb, S. and Webb, B. *Problems of modern industry.* 2nd ed. London, New York, Bombay: Longmans, Green, 1902. p. 66–81.
First published in *Economic Journal* (December 1891.)

8676 **Hutchins**, B. Leigh. *Women's wages in England in the nineteenth century.* London, 1906. 11p.

8677 **Women's Industrial Council.** *Women's wages in England in the 19th century.* London, 1906. 11p.

8678 **Bosanquet**, Helen. *The economics of women's work and wages.* London, 1907. 16p.

8679 **Fyfe**, William Hamilton. 'The remuneration of women's work.' *Econ. Rev.*, XVIII, 2 (April 1908), 135–45.

8680 **Smith**, Constance. 'The minimum wage.' *Woman in industry from seven points of view.* London: Duckworth, 1908. p. 25–59.

8681 **Hodgson**, Geraldine Emma. *The parliamentary vote and wages.* London: National Union of Women's Suffrage Societies, 1909. 8p.

8682 **Rathbone**, Eleanor F. 'The problem of women's wages: an enquiry into the causes of the inferiority of women's wages to men's.' *Lpool. Econ. Statist. Soc. Trans.* (1910/11–1911/12), 3–24.

8683 **Zimmern**, Dorothy M. 'The wages of women in industry.' National Conference on the Prevention of Destitution. *Report of the proceedings, 1912.* London: King, 1912. p. 408–19.
Discussion, p. 419–27.

8684 **Christian Social Union.** Oxford University Branch. *Women's wages.* [Oxford?], 1913. 4p. (Leaflets 65.)

8685 **Christian Social Union.** Research Committee. London Branch. *Report of inquiry into the wages of women and girls in the following trades: fruit preserving, pickle making, confectionery, tea packing, coffee and cocoa packing, biscuit making.* Manchester: National Labour Press, [1913]. 12p.

8686 **Rathbone**, Eleanor F. 'The remuneration of women's services.' Gollancz, V. (ed.). *The making of women: Oxford essays in feminism.* London: Allen and Unwin; New York: Macmillan, 1917. p. 100–27.

8687 **Rathbone**, Eleanor F. 'The remuneration of women's services.' *Econ. J.*, XXVII, 105 (March 1917), 55–68.

8688 **Round Table.** 'The remuneration of women's services. II.' Gollancz, V. (ed.). *The making of women: Oxford essays in feminism.* London: Allen and Unwin; New York: Macmillan, 1917. Appendix A. p. 179–214.
Reprinted from *Round Table*, March 1916.

8689 **Fawcett**, Millicent Garrett. 'Equal pay for equal work.' *Econ. J.*, XXVIII, 109 (March 1918), 1–6.

8690 **National Union of Clerks.** *Equal pay for similar duties.* London: the Union, 1918. 16p.
Report of a conference held on 30 October 1918.

8691 **Barton**, Dorothea M. 'The course of women's wages.' *R. Statist. Soc. J.*, LXXXII, 4 (July 1919), 508–44.
With discussion, p. 544–53.
'Read before the Royal Statistical Society, Tuesday, June 17, 1919.'
Also reprinted separately.

8692 **Barton**, Dorothea M. *Equal pay for equal work.* London, 1919. 4p.

8693 **Webb**, Beatrice. *The wages of men and women: should they be equal?* London: Fabian Society, Allen and Unwin, 1919. 79p.

8694 **Barton**, Dorothea M. 'Women's minimum wages.' *R. Statist. Soc. J.*, LXXXIV, 4 (July 1921), 538–67.

Discussion, p. 568–77.

'Read before the Royal Statistical Society, June 21, 1921.'

8695 **London Schoolmasters' Association.** *Equal pay and the teaching profession: an enquiry into . . . the demand for 'equal pay for men and women teachers'.* London: the Association, 1921. 112p.

By G. M. Graves, F. R. A. Jarvis, Alfred N. Pocock.

Third edition. London: National Association of Schoolmasters, 1937. 135p.

8696 **Barton**, Dorothea M. 'Women's wages in the cotton trade.' *Manchr. Statist. Soc. Trans.* (1921–22), 93–118.

1833–1920.

8697 **Edgeworth**, Francis Ysidro. 'Equal pay to men and women for equal work.' *Econ. J.*, XXXII, 128 (December 1922), 431–57.

'Presidential address to Section F of the British Association, Hull, 1922.'

8698 **Edgeworth**, Francis Ysidro. 'Women's wages in relation to economic welfare.' *Econ. J.*, XXXIII, 132 (December 1923), 487–95.

'Read before Section F of the British Association.'

8699 **Sargant Florence**, Philip. 'A statistical contribution to the theory of women's wages.' *Econ. J.*, XLI, 161 (March 1931), 19–37.

8700 **National Association of Schoolmasters.** *Equal pay and the teaching profession: an enquiry into, and the case against, the demand for 'equal pay for men and women teachers of the same professional status'.* London: N.A.S., 1937. 135p.

Third edition, prepared by F. R. A. Jarvis and A. N. Pocock.

First and second editions were published by the London Schoolmasters' Association.

8701 **Open Door International for the Economic Emancipation of the Woman Worker.** *The modern line of attack on women's civil rights.* London, 1937. 11p.

8702 **Evans**, John H. *Equal pay in the teaching profession: being a 'running commentary' on the debate on the amendment to clause 82 of the Education Bill in the House of Commons, March 28th, 1944.* London: London Schoolmasters' Association, 1944. 31p.

Author was President of the London Schoolmasters' Association.

8703 **National Association of Schoolmasters.** *Equal pay in the teaching profession.* London, Chesham: N.A.S., 1944. 14p.

8704 **Tate**, M. C. *Equal work deserves equal pay!* London, [1945?]. 12p.

8705 **Cole**, Margaret Isabel. *The rate for the job: a pamphlet prepared for the Fabian Women's Group and based on the evidence of the Group before the Royal Commission on Equal Pay.* London: Fabian Publications, Gollancz, 1946. 25p. (Research series 110.)

8706 **Royal Commission on Equal Pay,** 1944–46. *Report.* London: H.M.S.O., 1946. 219p. (Cmnd. 6937.)

Minutes of evidence. 1945. 13 pts.

Appendices to minutes of evidence. 1945–46. 4 pts.

Chairman: Sir Cyril Asquith.

8707 **Burton**, Elaine Frances, Baroness Burton of Coventry. *What is she worth? A study of the Report on Equal Pay.* London: Fitzroy Publications, 1947. 11p.

8708 **Douie**, Vera (comp.). *Women: their professional status. A world survey immediately preceding World War II.* London: British Federation of Business and Professional Women, 1947. 78p.

A résumé of the section from the I.L.O. publication *The law and women's work.*

8709 **Williams**, Gertrude. 'Equal pay.' *Polit. Q.*, XVIII, 3 (July–September 1947), 230–9.

8710 **Phelps Brown**, Ernest Henry. 'Equal pay for equal work.' *Econ. J.*, LIX, 235 (September 1949), 384–98.

8711 **Harrod**, Roy Forbes. 'Equal pay for men and women.' *Economic essays.* London: Macmillan, 1952. p. 42–74.

Memorandum submitted to the Royal Commission on Equal Pay, 1945.

8712 **Pigou**, Arthur Cecil. 'Men's and women's wages.' *Essays in economics.* London: Macmillan, 1952. p. 217–26.

'Based on and partly reproducing a memorandum prepared for the Royal Commission on Equal Pay, printed in *Appendix to Minutes of Evidence, IX,* 1946.'

8713 **Clark**, Frederick Le Gros. *The economic rights of women.* Liverpool: Liverpool U.P., 1963. 18p. (Eleanor Rathbone memorial lecture.)

8714 **Klein**, Viola. 'Working wives: the money.' *New Soc.*, II, 40 (4 July 1963), 16.

8715 **Morton**, Jane. 'Equal pay for women in seven years?' *New Soc.*, XII, 306 (8 August 1968), 193–5.

8716 **Greenwood**, John Alfred. *Some problems in the implementation of an equal pay policy.* London: Industrial Educational and Research Foundation, 1969. 32p. (Research paper 2.)

8717 **Mepham**, George James. *Problems of equal pay.* London: Institute of Personnel Management, 1969. 52p.

G. PAYMENT SYSTEMS

In addition to the general literature on payment systems, this section includes material on wage and salary administration and the relationship between effort and remuneration. The technical literature on job evaluation and work study has generally been excluded. Many of the industrial and occupational studies classified at Part Six, III, E contain information on wage systems. See Part Two, I and Part Two, II for the literature dealing with the psychological and sociological aspects of incentives at work and restriction of output. See Part Five, II for the literature dealing with trade unions and productivity. See also Part Five, V, B, 2 for material on profit-sharing.

8718 **Schloss**, David Frederick. *Methods of industrial remuneration.* London: Williams and Norgate, 1892 [i.e. 1891]. xx, 287p.
Second edition. 1894. xx, 287p.
Third edition, revised and enlarged. 1898. xix, 446p.

8719 **Schloss**, David Frederick. 'Why working men dislike piece-work.' *Econ. Rev.*, I, 3 (July 1891), 311–26.

8720 **Schloss**, David Frederick. 'The methods of industrial remuneration.' *Char. Orgn. Rev.*, VIII, 94 (October–November 1892), 373–7.
'Paper read at the meeting of the British Association, Edinburgh, August 1892.'

8721 **Chapman**, Sydney John. 'Some theoretical objections to sliding-scales.' *Econ. J.*, XIII, 50 (June 1903), 186–96.

8722 **Garrard**, Charles Cornfield. *Piecework and bonus systems of wage payment, by Zähler.* 1913. 8p.

8723 **Atkinson**, Henry. *A rational wages system: some notes on the method of paying the worker a reward for efficiency in addition to wages.* London: Bell, 1917. xii, 112p.

8724 **Thomson**, *Sir* William Rowan. *The premium bonus system: a scheme for stimulating and increasing the productive capacity of industrial resources.* Glasgow: McCorquodale, 1917. 99p.

8725 **Cole**, George Douglas Howard. *The payment of wages: a study in payment by results under the wage-system.* London: Fabian Research Department, Allen and Unwin, 1918. vi, 155p. (Trade union series 5.)
New and revised edition. Allen and Unwin, 1928. xxi, 155p.

8726 **Prosser**. J. E. *Piece-rate premium, and bonus.* London: Williams and Norgate, 1919. vii, 122p.

8727 **Scott**, Leslie. 'The grave industrial problem: output and reward.' *Nineteenth Century*, LXXXVI, 513 (November 1919), 812–23.

8728 **Pybus**, Percy J. 'Labour: its output and reward.' Manchester University. *Labour and industry: a series of lectures.* Manchester: Manchester U.P.; London: Longmans, 1920. p. 267–84.
'A lecture given on Tuesday, March 9, 1920.'

8729 **Robertson**, Dennis Holme. 'Economic incentive.' *Economica*, I, 3 (October 1921), 231–45.

8730 **Manning**, Phyllis Amy. *The limits to the effectiveness of the system of payments by results as an incentive to production.* 1924. (M.A. thesis, University of Manchester.)

8731 **Pilkington**, W. G. *Some systems of industrial remuneration.* 1924. (M.Comm. thesis, University of Manchester.)

8732 **Powell**, J. E. *Payment by results.* London: Longmans, 1924. viii, 411p.

8733 *The Bedaux method of wage payment.* Chelmsford: Hoffman Manufacturing Co., 1928. 11p.

8734 **Vernon**, Horace Middleton. 'The effects of a bonus on the output of men engaged in heavy work.' *Natn. Inst. Ind. Psychol. J.*, IV, 5 (January 1929), 267–70.

8735 **Wilson**, Robert. *Methods of remuneration.* London: Pitman, 1931. vii, 101p. (Pitman's economic series.)

8736 **Watson**, William Foster. *Bedaux and other bonus systems explained.* London: the author, 1932. 32p.

8737 **Raphael**, Winifred Jessie Gertrude Spielman. 'The efficiency of efficiency rating systems.' *Hum. Factor*, VII, 6 (June 1933), 201–11.
'Extracts from a paper read at the Conference of the Institute of Public Administration on January 29, 1933, and reprinted by permission of *Public Administration.*'

8738 **Trades Union Congress**. *Bedaux: the T.U.C. examines the Bedaux system.* London: T.U.C., 1933. 16p.

8739 **Watson**, William Foster. 'The worker's point of view. XV. The psychology of the pay envelope.' *Hum. Factor*, VII, 10 (October 1933), 354–64.

8740 **Watson**, William Foster. *The worker and wage incentives: the Bedaux and other systems.* London: Woolf, 1934. 46p. (Day to day pamphlets 20.)

8741 **Garland**, T. O. 'The doctor's point of view. V. Piece-work and time-work.' *Hum. Factor*, X, 5 (May 1936), 183–9.

8742 **Munro**, M. S. 'Incentives in the milk industry.' *Hum. Factor*, XI, 6 (June 1937), 224–9.

8743 **Hall**, Patricia and **Locke**, Henry William. *Incentives and contentment: a study made in a British factory.* London: Pitman, 1938. xii, 190p.
Rowntree Cocoa Works.

8744 **Ewart**, Edwin, **Seashore**, S. E. and **Tiffin**, Joseph. 'A factor analysis of an industrial merit rating scale.' *J. Appl. Psychol.*, XXV, 5 (October 1941), 481–6.

8745 **Davis**, Norah M. 'Some psychological effects on women workers of payment by the individual bonus method.' *Occup. Psychol.*, XVIII, 2 (April 1944), 53–62.
'A paper read at a meeting of the Industrial Section of the British Psychological Society on October 17th, 1943.'

8746 **Harold Whitehead and Staff Ltd.** 'Report on a survey of incentive bonus schemes for indirect working.' *Br. Mgmt. Rev.*, v, 1 (January–March 1944), 81–114.

8747 **McLaine**, William. 'Payment by results in British engineering.' *Int. Labour Rev.*, XLIX, 6 (June 1944), 630–46.

8748 **Ministry of Works.** *Memorandum on payment by results, including schedules of trade operations for which bonus rates have been fixed (Essential Work (Building and Civil Engineering) Order, 1942).* London: H.M.S.O. 1944. 36p.
Third edition.
'Reprinted to amplify the information in the official history of the scheme, *Payment by results in building and civil engineering during the war*, with which this memorandum should be read.'

8749 **Nicholson**, John Leonard. 'Wages and cost of living sliding-scales.' *Oxf. Univ. Inst. Statist. Bull.*, VI, 11 (12 August 1944), 189–91.

8750 **Brown**, Wilfred Banks Duncan. 'Incentives within the factory.' *Occup. Psychol.*, XIX, 2 (April 1945), 82–92.

8751 **Political and Economic Planning.** 'Output and the worker.' *Planning*, 233 (20 April 1945), 1–16.

8752 **Somervell**, Hubert. *Labour shares production: ten years' experience of a novel system of wages based on production.* London: Gee, 1946. 44p.
Reprinted from *The Accountant* with an appendix showing the classification of permanent and temporary workers.

8753 **Cook**, Stanley and **James**, Robert. 'Job specification and a fair wage.' *Econ. J.*, LVII, 227 (September 1947), 387–93.

8754 **Deakin**, F. W. *Equal reward for equal effort.* Sutton Coldfield, 1947. 12p.
Second edition.

8755 **Ministry of Works.** *Payment by results in building and civil engineering during the war: a report on the operation of the payment by results scheme applied under the Essential Work (Building and Civil Engineering) Order, 1941, during the period July 1941 to March 1947.* London: H.M.S.O., 1947. 20p.

8756 **Hunt**, Norman Charles. *A critical examination of methods of industrial remuneration, with special reference to the requirements of British industry.* 1947–48. (Ph.D. thesis, University of Edinburgh.)

8757 **Guest**, C. L. *The technique of industrial labour payment.* London: Macdonald and Evans, 1948. xii, 198p.

8758 **International Labour Office.** 'Payment by results in the building and civil engineering industries in the United Kingdom.' *Int. Labour Rev.*, LVIII, 5 (November 1948), 637–43.

8759 **Mackenzie**, W. *Systems of remuneration of labour in agriculture in relation to efficiency and performance.* 1948. (B.Litt. thesis, University of Oxford.)

8760 **Madge**, Charles. 'Payment and incentives.' *Occup. Psychol.*, XXII, 1 (January 1948), 39–45.
'A paper read to Sections F (Economics and Statistics) and J (Psychology) of the British Association for the Advancement of Science at Dundee on September 2nd, 1947.'

8761 **Lynton**, Rolf Paul. *Incentives and management in British industry.* London: Routledge and Kegan Paul, 1949. viii, 212p.

8762 **Wilkins**, Leslie T. 'Incentives and the young worker.' *Occup. Psychol.*, XXIII, 4 (October 1949), 235–47.

8763 **Abbott**, Albert. *Wages procedures.* London: Office Management Association, 1950. 43p.

8764 **Armstrong**, Jack. *Incentive and quality.* London: Chapman and Hall, 1950. x, 113p.
On industrial production schemes.

8765 **British Institute of Management.** *Wage incentive schemes.* London: B.I.M., 1950. 26p. (Personnel management series 3.)

8766 **Burton**, John Henry. *Wages and salaries recording & distributing methods.* London: Gee, 1950. 48p.

8767 **Dyson**, B. H. *Whether direct individual incentive systems based on time-study, however accurately computed, tend over a period to limitation of output.* London: British Institute of Management, 1950.

8768 **Ministry of Labour and National Service.** Personnel Management Advisory Service. *Merit rating: general survey and company schemes.* London: the Service, 1950. 19p.

8769 **Russon**, Frank. *Bonusing for builders and allied trades.* Birmingham: Normal Tiptaft, 1950. 128p.

8770 **Reed**, S. K. *An investigation into wage incentives and their effect on production, with comparisons between Great Britain and the United States.* 1950–51. (Ph.D. thesis, University of Edinburgh.)

8771 **Hunt**, Norman Charles. *Methods of wage payment in British industry.* London: Pitman, 1951. vii, 160p. (Pitman's higher studies in commerce.)

8772 **Jaques**, Elliott, **Rice**, Albert Kenneth and **Hill**, John Michael Meath. 'The social and psychological impact of a change in method of wage payment. (The Glacier Project V.)' *Hum. Relat.*, IV, 4 (November 1951), 315–41.

8773 **Allen**, Victor Leonard. 'Incentives in the building industry.' *Econ. J.*, LXII, 247 (September 1952), 595–608.

8774 **Campbell**, H. 'Group incentive payment schemes: the effects of lack of understanding and of group size.' *Occup. Psychol.*, XXVI, 1 (January 1952), 15–21.

8775 **Himeimy**, I. A. R. *The difficulties arising from the application of job evaluation and merit rating in certain industrial undertakings: six case studies.* 1952. (M.Sc. (Tech.), University of Manchester.)

8776 **Lamberth**, D. L. *Some effects of bonus payments in interviewer performance.* 1952. 13p. (Social Survey papers. Methodological series M56.)

8777 **Social Survey**. *Incentives in industry: an inquiry carried out in February–March 1952.* [1952.] iii, 24p. (S.S. 185/2.)
By Geoffrey Thomas.

8778 **Stewart**, Alan F. 'Merit-rating incentive schemes.' *Int. Labour Rev.*, LXV, 4 (April 1952), 442–61.

8779 **British Institute of Management**. *Payment of wages: 19 company practices.* London: B.I.M., 1953. 4p.

8780 **Davis**, Norah M. 'Some psychological conflicts caused by group bonus methods of payment.' *Br. J. Ind. Med.*, x, 1 (January 1953), 18–26.

8781 **Davis**, Norah M. 'A study of a merit-rating scheme in a factory.' *Occup. Psychol.*, XXVII, 2 (April 1953), 57–68.

8782 **Wyatt**, Stanley. 'A study of output in two similar factories.' *Br. J. Psychol.*, XLIV, 1 (February 1953), 5–17.

8783 **Tite**, C. B. *Piecework and productivity in the boot and shoe industry.* 1953–54. (Ph.D. thesis, University of Birmingham.)

8784 **Institute of Cost and Works Accountants**. *Employee remuneration and incentives.* London: the Institute, 1954. 70p.

8785 **Tuck**, Raphael Herman. *An essay on the economic theory of rank.* Oxford: Blackwell, 1954. 52p.

8786 **Elliott**, Alexander George Patrick. *Revising a merit rating scheme.* London: Institute of Personnel Management, 1955. 23p. (Occasional papers 7.)

8787 **Ministry of Labour and National Service**. *Wage incentive schemes.* London: H.M.S.O., 1955. 39p.
Second edition.
First published in 1951 as a *Supplement* to the 1944 edition of the *Industrial Relations Handbook*.
The main body of the text of the 1955 edition is included in chapter X of the 1953 edition of the *Industrial Relations Handbook*.

8788 **Robertson**, Donald James. 'The present complexity of wage payments.' *Scott. J. Polit. Econ.*, II, 1 (February 1955), 1–16.
'A version of this article was read to a Study Group of the Manchester Statistical Society in March, 1954.'

8789 **Shimmin**, Sylvia. 'Incentives.' *Occup. Psychol.*, XXIX, 4 (October 1955), 240–4.
A paper read at the 1955 Annual Conference of the British Psychological Society.

8790 **Williams**, Robert Glynne. *Methods of remuneration.* Bristol: Society of Commercial Accountants, 1955. 69p.
Private circulation.

8791 **Dalziel**, Stuart J. 'Work study in industry.' *Polit. Q.*, XXVII, 3 (July–September 1956), 270–83.

8792 **Hill**, John Michael Meath. 'The time-span of discretion in job analysis.' *Hum. Relat.*, IX, 3 (August 1956), 295–323.
Reprinted as *Tavistock pamphlet 1*, 1957.

8793 **Jaques**, Elliott. *Measurement of responsibility: a study of work, payment and individual capacity.* London: Tavistock Publications, 1956. xiii, 143p.

8794 **Vickers**, *Sir* Geoffrey. 'Incentives of labour.' *Polit. Q.*, XXVII, 3 (July–September 1956), 284–93.

8795 **Baldamus**, Wilhelm. 'The relationship between wage and effort.' *J. Ind. Econ.*, v, 3 (July 1957), 192–201.

8796 **Behrend**, Hilde M. 'The effort bargain.' *Ind. Labor Relat. Rev.*, x, 4 (July 1957), 503–15.

8797 **Behrend**, Hilde M. 'Effort-control through bargaining.' *Nature*, CLXXIX, 4570 (1 June 1957), 1106–7.

8798 **Buck**, Leslie J. 'The influence of group size and stability upon the effectiveness of an incentive payment system.' *Occup. Psychol.*, XXXI, 4 (October 1957), 270–80.

8799 **Lupton**, Tom and **Cunnison**, Sheila. 'The cash reward for an hour's work under three piecework incentive schemes.' *Manchr. Sch.*, XXV, 3 (September 1957), 213–69.

8800 **Marriott**, Reginald. *Incentive payment systems: a review of research and opinion.* London: Staples P., 1957. 232p.
Second revised edition. 1961. 291p.
Third revised edition, with a 1968 postscript by Silvia Shimmin. 1968. 317p.
Fourth edition. 1971. 317p.

8801 **Strong**, W. M. *A farmer's guide to incentive schemes.* Newton Abbot: University of Bristol, Department of Economics (Agricultural Economics), 1957. 30p. (Reports 98.)

8802 **Wells**, Frederick Arthur. *Productivity in a printing firm.* London: Duckworth, 1957. 148p.

8803 **British Institute of Management**. *Salary reviews, overtime and shift allowances.* London: B.I.M., 1958. 51p. (Information survey 72.)

8804 **Davison**, James Percy, **Sargant Florence**, Philip, **Gray**, Barbara and **Ross**, N. S. *Productivity and economic incentives.* London: Allen and Unwin, 1958. 306p.
Based on fieldwork investigations.
Contents: 'Past and present incentive study', by P. Sargant Florence, p. 17–37. 'Productivity and earnings in manufacturing', by J. P. Davison and N. S. Ross, p. 38–97. 'Attitudes and reactions of factory workers', by J. P. Davison and N. S. Ross, p. 98–137. 'Incentives and productivity in laundries', by B. Gray, p. 138–69. 'Incentives and shop productivity in co-operative societies', by B. Gray, p. 170–93. 'Additional evidence and extension of incentives to services', by P. Sargant Florence, p. 194–218. 'Trade union and labour reactions to the application of incentives and the industrial relations background in factory C', by N. S. Ross, p. 219–61. 'A summary', p. 262–74. Appendices, p. 275–300.

8805 **Jaques**, Elliott. 'Standard earning progression curves: a technique for examining individual progress in work.' *Hum. Relat.*, XI, 2 (May 1958), 167–90.

8806 **Rothe**, Harold F. and **Nye**, Charles T. 'Output rates among coil winders.' *J. Appl. Psychol.*, XLII, 3 (June 1958), 182–6.

8807 **Shimmin**, Sylvia. 'Workers' understanding of incentive payment systems.' *Occup. Psychol.*, XXXII, 2 (April 1958), 106–10.

A paper read to Section J of the British Association for the Advancement of Science, Dublin, September 1957.

8808 **Spraos**, John. 'Linking wages to productivity?' *Bankers' Mag.*, CLXXXV, 1369 (April 1958), 300–4.

8809 **Behrend**, Hilde M. 'Financial incentives as the expression of a system of beliefs.' *Br. J. Sociol.*, X, 2 (June 1959), 137–47.

8810 **British Institute of Management**. *Staff grading: characteristics of some company schemes and principles of salary determination.* London: B.I.M., 1959. 29p.

8811 **Department of Scientific and Industrial Research**. Information Division. *Incentives in building: how target bonus schemes operate.* London: D.S.I.R., 1959. 16p.

Based on full report of the Building Research Station, 1959.

8812 **Rothe**, Harold F. and **Nye**, Charles T. 'Output rates among machine operators.' *J. Appl. Psychol.*, XLIII, 6 (December 1959), 417–20.

8813 **Shimmin**, Sylvia, **Williams**, Joan E. and **Buck**, Leslie J. *Payment by results: a psychological investigation.* London: Staples P., 1959. x, 162p.

8814 **British Institute of Management**. *An objective approach to pay differentials.* London: B.I.M., 1960. 6p.

8815 **British Institute of Management**. *Payment of wages by cheque.* London: B.I.M., 1960.

8816 **Institute of Office Management**. *Clerical job grading and merit rating.* London: the Institute, 1960. 91p.

Revised and enlarged edition of *Job grading.* 1952.

See also *Grading of clerical work.* 1953 [i.e. 1954].

8817 **Pearson**, *Sir* Reginald. 'From group bonus to straight time pay.' *J. Ind. Econ.*, VIII, 2 (March 1960), 113–21.

Vauxhall Motors Ltd.

8818 **Baldamus**, Wilhelm. *Efficiency and effort: an analysis of industrial administration.* London: Tavistock Publications, 1961. viii, 139p.

8819 **Behrend**, Hilde M. 'A fair day's work.' *Scott. J. Polit. Econ.*, VIII, 2 (June 1961), 102–18.

8820 **Brewer**, E. 'Work study and incentives in a city department.' *Publ. Adm.*, XXXIX, 3 (Autumn 1961), 239–45.

A description of a scheme put into operation in the Water Department of the Oxford City Corporation.

8821 **Department of Scientific and Industrial Research**. *Money for effort.* London: H.M.S.O., 1961. 28p. (Problems of progress in industry 11.)

By T. Lupton.

8822 **Jaques**, Elliott. *Equitable payment: a general theory of work, differential payment, and individual progress.* London: Heinemann, 1961. 336p.

Revised edition. Harmondsworth: Penguin, 1967. 382p.

Second edition. Carbondale, Ill.: Southern Illinois U.P., 1970. 382p.

8823 **Brown**, Wilfred Banks Duncan, Baron Brown. *Piecework abandoned: the effect of wage incentive systems on managerial authority.* London: Heinemann, 1962. viii, 119p.

With special reference to the organisation of the Glacier Metal Company.

8824 **Brown**, Wilfred Banks Duncan, Baron Brown. *Piecework or daywork?* London: Institution of Production Engineers, 1962. 16p.

8825 **Jaques**, Elliott. 'Objective measures for pay differentials.' *Harv. Bus. Rev.*, XL, 1 (January–February 1962), 133–8.

8826 **Marriott**, Reginald. 'An exploratory study of merit rating payment systems in three factories.' *Occup. Psychol.*, XXXVI, 4 (October 1962), 179–214.

8827 **Advisory Service for the Building Industry**. *The principles of incentives for the construction industry.* London: the Service, 1963. 80p.

8828 **Behrend**, Hilde M. 'An assessment of the current status of incentive schemes.' *J. Ind. Relat.*, V, 2 (October 1963), 96–109.

8829 **British Institute of Management**. *Payroll simplification.* London: B.I.M., 1963. 11p.

8830 **Currie**, Russell Mackenzie. *Financial incentives based on work measurement.* London: British Institute of Management, 1963. viii, 124p.

8831 **Fay**, Stephen. 'The Scanlon plan: a new departure.' *New Soc.*, II, 55 (17 October 1963), 18–19. (Work & business.)

At Pressed Steel at Linwood.

8832 **Hickson**, D. J. 'Worker choice of payment system.' *Occup. Psychol.*, XXXVII, 2 (April 1963), 93–100.

8833 **Jaques**, Elliott. 'A system for income equity.' *New Soc.*, II, 63 (12 December 1963), 10–12.

8834 **McKersie**, Robert B. 'Wage payment methods of the future.' *Br. J. Ind. Relat.*, I, 2 (June 1963), 191–212.

8835 **Paterson**, Thomas Thomson. 'The Jaques system: impractical?' *New Soc.*, II, 64 (19 December 1963), 9–11.

8836 **Trades Union Congress**. *An outline of work study and payment by results.* London: T.U.C., 1963. 24p.

8837 **Alderson**, Stanley. 'The Jaquesian general theory.' *Contemp. Rev.*, CCV, 1177 (February 1964), 83–90.

8838 **Bentley**, Fred Richard. *People, productivity and progress: obtaining results through share of production plans.* London: Business Publications, 1964. xi, 162p.
Describes the Rucker Plan.

8839 **Industrial Welfare Society.** *Changing wage systems.* London: the Society, 1964.

8840 **Jaques**, Elliott. *Time-span handbook: the use of time-span of discretion to measure the level of the work in employment roles and to arrange an equitable payment structure.* London: Heinemann, 1964. ix, 133p. (Glacier project series.)

8841 **McBeath**, Maurice Gordon and **Rands**, Denis Nigel. *Salary administration.* London: Business Publications, 1964. xiii, 270p. (Business books.)
Second edition. 1969. xiii, 283p.

8842 **Murray**, William. 'Equitable payment for work?' *Administration*, XII, 3 (Autumn 1964), 226–9.
On Elliott Jaques' work.

8843 **Pym**, Denis. 'Is there a future for wage incentive schemes?' *Br. J. Ind. Relat.*, II, 3 (November 1964), 379–97.

8844 **Trades Union Congress.** *Job evaluation and merit rating.* London: T.U.C., 1964. 20p.
Second edition. 1969. 31p.

8845 **Desmond**, B. *The role of incentive payment systems in industry.* 1964–65. (M.Comm. thesis, National University of Ireland.)

8846 **Fogarty**, Michael Patrick. 'Wage and salary policies for recruitment.' *Br. J. Ind. Relat.*, III, 3 (November 1965), 311–25.
Originally presented as a paper to a conference, at Imperial College, London in April 1965, organized by the Industrial Applications Section of the Royal Statistical Society.

8847 **Jaques**, Elliott. 'National incomes policy.' Brown, W. B. D. and Jaques, E. *Glacier Project papers: some essays on organization and management from the Glacier Project Research.* London: Heinemann, 1965. p. 237–45.
First published in *New Society*, 12 December 1963, under the title, 'A system for income equity'.

8848 **Sidebottom**, A. W. and **Brewer**, E. 'The application of financial incentives: a case report from the paper industry.' *J. Mgmt. Studies*, II, 1 (February 1965), 70–82.
Wolvercote papermill.

8849 **Fox**, Alan. *The time-span of discretion theory: an appraisal.* London: Institute of Personnel Management, 1966. 30p.

8850 **Production Engineering Research Association.** *PERA Symposium, October 1966: executive remuneration and development. Section 8. Incentives for management.* London: the Association, 1966. 42p.

8851 **O'Donoghue**, M. T. *Incentive pay and the worker.* 1966–67. (M.Litt. thesis, Trinity College, Dublin.)

8852 **British Institute of Management.** *Salary administration methods.* London: B.I.M., 1967. 39p.

8853 **Corner**, Desmond Carteret. *Financial incentives in the smaller business.* London: Edutext Publications, 1967. i, 40p. (Occasional papers in social and economic administration 5.)

8854 **De la Mora**, J. *An analysis of incentive schemes in relation to industrial group behaviour.* 1967. (M.Sc. dissertation, University of London.)

8855 **Grinyer**, Peter H. and **Kessler**, Sidney. 'The systematic evaluation of methods of wage payment.' *J. Mgmt. Studies*, IV, 3 (October 1967), 309–20.

8856 **Tozer**, W. *An appraisal of financial incentives, with special reference to engineering and associated firms in the Stroud area.* 1967–68. (M.A. thesis, University of Wales, Bangor.)

8857 **Blyth**, Douglas. *Remuneration and incentives.* Hove: Editype, 1968. 52p. (Editype mini-book 17.)

8858 **Conboy**, Bill. *Payment with what result?* Oxford: Pergamon, 1968. 21p. (Productivity progress.)

8859 **Coventry and District Engineering Employers' Association.** *Wage drift, work measurement and systems of payment.* 1968.

8860 **Jaques**, Elliott. *Progression handbook: how to use earnings progression data sheets for assessing individual capacity, for progression, and for manpower planning and development.* London: Heinemann, 1968. vii, 72p. (Glacier project series [9].)
Supplements the *Time-span handbook.*

8861 **Lupton**, Tom. 'Beyond payment by results?' Pym, D. (ed.). *Industrial society: social sciences in management.* Harmondsworth: Penguin, 1968. p. 294–315.

8862 **McKersie**, Robert B. 'Changing wage payment systems.' Royal Commission on Trade Unions and Employers' Associations. *Two studies in industrial relations.* London: H.M.S.O., 1968. p. 27–65. (Research papers 11.)

8863 **Merrett**, Anthony John and **White**, M. R. M. *Incentive payment systems for managers.* London: Gower P., 1968. xiii, 209p.

8864 **National Board for Prices and Incomes.** *Job evaluation.* London: H.M.S.O., 1968. v, 50p. (Report 83. Cmnd. 3772.)
Supplement. 1968. iii, 65p. (Report 83 (Supplement). Cmnd. 3772-I.)

8865 **National Board for Prices and Incomes.** *Payment by results systems.* London: H.M.S.O., 1968. (Report 65. Cmnd. 3627.)
Supplement. 1968. iv, 112p. (Report 65 (Supplement). Cmnd. 3627-I.)

8866 **Thomason**, George F. *Personnel manager's guide to job evaluation.* London: Institute of Personnel Management, 1968. 49p.

8867 **Thomson**, T. G. 'Job evaluation for non-manual workers: local government staff in Greater London.' *Int. Labour Rev.*, XCVIII, 6 (December 1968), 511–24.

8868 **Turner**, Robert and **Murray**, R. D. *Payment systems for dairy labour in South-West Scotland.* Glasgow: West of Scotland Agricultural College, Economics Department, 1968. 19p. (Farm labour studies 10. West of Scotland Agricultural College. Research bulletins 41.)

8869 **Bolger,** M. D. *The sociological implications of the use of a plant-wide incentive scheme.* 1968–69. (M.A. thesis, University of Leicester.)

8870 **Cable**, John Reginald. *Methods of wage-fixing in a soap and chemical plant: a case study.* 1968–1969. (M.A. (Econ.) thesis, University of Manchester.)

8871 **Nathoo**, S. A. R. *A psychological investigation into the effects of incentive schemes.* 1968–69. (M.Sc. thesis, Trinity College, Dublin.)

8872 **Bayhylle**, J. E. '"White collar measurement": an art or science?' *Ind. Relat. Res. Bull.*, 2 (September 1969), 11–14.

8873 **British Institute of Management**. *Notes on some company-wide incentive schemes: Scanlon, Rucker and Kaiser-Steel.* London: B.I.M., 1969. 13p. (Information note 26.)

8874 **Gordon**, Michael E. 'An evaluation of Jaques' studies of pay in the light of current compensation research.' *Pers. Psychol.*, XXII, 4 (Winter 1969), 369–89.

8875 **Greenwood**, John Alfred. 'Payment by results systems: a case study in control at the workplace with a national piecework price list.' *Br. J. Ind. Relat.*, VII, 3 (November 1969), 399–413.

8876 **Hellriegel**, Don and **French**, Wendell. 'A critique of Jaques' equitable payment system.' *Ind. Relat.*, VIII, 3 (May 1969), 269–79.

8877 **Jaques**, Elliott. 'Fair pay: how to achieve it.' *New Soc.*, XIV, 374 (27 November 1969), 852–4.

8878 **Keal**, John and **Jeffery**, Ray. 'Wage payment system selection: some consultants' views.' *Ind. Relat. Res. Bull.*, 2 (September 1969), 19–22.

A criticism of T. Lupton and D. Gowler, *Selecting a wage-payment system*, 1969.

8879 **Lupton**, Tom. 'The management of earnings and productivity drift.' Farrow, N. (ed.). *Progress of management research.* Harmondsworth: Penguin, 1969. p. 92–105.

8880 **Lupton**, Tom and **Gowler**, Dan. *Selecting a wage payment system.* London: Kogan Page for the Engineering Employers' Federation, 1969. 55p. (Research series.)

8881 **Sutcliffe**, Edward. 'Factory money.' Fraser, R. (ed.). *Work, volume 2: twenty personal accounts.* Harmondworth: Penguin, 1969. p. 287–97.

First published in *New Left Review*, 31 (May–June 1965), 46–50.

Personal account of incentive schemes by a Lancashire factory worker.

8882 **Bayhylle**, J. E. 'Motivating the indirect worker: solving the problem – applying payment by results where no obvious method of work measurement exists.' *Ind. Relat. Res. Bull.*, 3 (February 1970), 19–23.

'This paper has been adapted from a lecture given by the author to P.E.R.A. (Production Engineering Research Association) on 9th September, 1969, at Melton Mowbray, Leicestershire.'

8883 **Easterfield**, T. E. 'Productivity measurements and payment systems.' *Ind. Relat. Res. Bull.*, 3 (February 1970), 5–9.

8884 **Flanders**, Allan David. 'Pay as an incentive.' *Management and unions: the theory and reform of industrial relations.* London: Faber, 1970. p. 72–81.

'A previously unpublished paper read to a British Institute of Management conference at Birmingham in November 1968.'

8885 **Gowler**, Dan. 'Socio-cultural influences on the operation of a wage payment system: an explanatory case study.' Robinson, D. (ed.). *Local labour markets and wage structures.* London: Gower P., 1970. p. 100–26.

8886 **Gowler**, Dan and **Legge**, Karen. 'The wage payment system: a primary infrastructure.' Robinson, D. (ed.). *Local labour markets and wage structures.* London: Gower P., 1970. p. 168–214.

8887 **Keal**, John and **Jeffery**, Ray. 'Changing the system of wage payments.' *Ind. Relat. Res. Bull.*, 4 (September 1970), 23–5.

8888 **Organisation for Economic Co-operation and Development.** *Forms of wage and salary payment for higher productivity: International Management Seminar, Versailles, 26th–29th September 1967. Final report.* Paris: O.E.C.D., 1970. 161p.

See also: 5706; 8277; 12,310; 14,279.

H. INCOME DISTRIBUTION

This section contains material dealing with the share of wages and salaries in the national income as well as with the way in which income is distributed between different groups. In addition, some of the more general works in Part One, IV and Part Five, IV, A also discuss income distribution. Works in these sections, however, tend to be philosophical in nature, while those in this section tend to be statistical in nature. See also Part Six, I; Part Six, III, A; and Part Six, IV, A, 1.

8889 **Brassey**, *Sir* Thomas. 'Has the increase of the products of industry tended most to the benefit of capitalists or to that of the working classes?' Industrial Remuneration Conference. *The report of the proceedings and papers . . .* London: Cassell, 1885. p. 4–23.

Discussion, p. 62–83.

8890 **Wallace**, Alfred Russel. 'How to cause wealth to be more equally distributed.' Industrial Remuneration Conference. *The report of the proceedings and papers* . . . London: Cassell, 1885. p. 368–92.
Discussion, p. 397–418.
Note on this paper by J. S. Nicholson, p. 472–3.

8891 **O'Conor**, W. A. 'One aspect of wealth distribution.' *Manchr. Statist. Soc. Trans.* (1885–86), 61–80.

8892 **Giffen**, Robert. 'The growth and distribution of wealth.' Ward, T. H. (ed.). *The reign of Queen Victoria: a survey of fifty years of progress.* Vol. II. London: Smith, Elder, 1887. p. 1–42.

8893 **Smith**, James Carmichael. *The distribution of the produce.* London: Kegan Paul, 1892. 77p.

8894 **Mallock**, William Hurrell. *Labour and the popular welfare.* London: Black, 1893. xi, 336p.
New edition, with appendix. 1894. xxviii, 357p.

8895 **Dawbarn**, Climenson Yelverton Charles. *The principles of wealth distribution.* London: Simpkin, Marshall, Hamilton, Kent, 1896. xii, 180p.

8896 **Smart**, William. *The distribution of income, being a study of what the national wealth is and of how it is distributed according to economic worth.* London: Macmillan, 1899. xv, 341p.
Second edition. 1912. xix, 345p.

8897 **Hayward**, Julia G. (comp.). *Percentages of the maximum and minimum wage.* Newport: J. E. Southall, 1903. 66p.

8898 **Money**, *Sir* Leo George Chiozza. *Riches and poverty.* London: Methuen, 1905. xx, 338p.
Fourth and cheaper edition. 1908. xvi, 338p.
Tenth and revised edition. 1911. xxiv, 355p.
New and cheaper issue, revised and enlarged. 1913. xxiv, 355p.

8899 **Shaw**, George Bernard. *Socialism and superior brains: a reply to Mr. Mallock.* London: Fabian Society, 1909. 24p. (Fabian tract 146.)
Reprinted. 1910. 59p. (Fabian socialist series VIII.)
A reply to W. H. Mallock's *Critical examination of socialism.*

8900 **British Association.** 'The amount and distribution of income (other than wages) below the income tax exemption limit in the United Kingdom.' *R. Statist. Soc. J.*, LXXIV, 1 (December 1910), 37–66.
Report of a committee consisting of E. Cannan (Chairman), A. L. Bowley (Secretary), F. Y. Edgeworth, H. B. Lees Smith and W. R. Scott.

8901 **London Municipal Society.** Department of Social Economics. *Conspectus of the national income, showing the enormous proportion borne to the total by the incomes of workers receiving £400 a year and under, with appendix relating to the wages of manual labour and services.* London, 1911. 15p. (Monographs 15.)

8902 **London Municipal Society.** Department of Social Economics. *The distribution of wages as illustrated by three great industries: family incomes exceeding and not exceeding £100 according to the latest Board of Trade figures.* London, 1911. 7p. (Monographs 16.)

8903 **London Municipal Society.** Department of Social Economics. *The ratio of the profits earned in United Kingdom as a whole to the wages and salaries paid to employees in the United Kingdom.* London, 1911. 8p. (Monographs 5.)

8904 **Stamp**, Josiah Charles. *British incomes and property.* 1916. xvi, 538p. (D.Sc. (Econ.) thesis, University of London.)

8905 **Bowley**, *Sir* Arthur Lyon. *The division of the product of industry: an analysis of material income before the war.* Oxford: Clarendon P., 1919. 60p.

8906 **Allen**, J. E. 'Some changes in the distribution of the national income during the war.' *R. Statist. Soc. J.*, LXXXIII, 1 (January 1920), 86–115.
Discussion, p. 116–26.

8907 **Bowley**, *Sir* Arthur Lyon. *The change in the distribution of the national income, 1880–1913.* Oxford: Clarendon P., 1920. 27p.
A lecture delivered in Manchester Municipal College of Technology, 13 January 1920.

8908 **Hook**, Alfred. *The workers' share.* London: Labour Publishing Co., 1924. viii, 124p.

8909 **Money**, *Sir* Leo George Chiozza. 'The distribution of wealth.' Tracey, H. (ed.). *The Labour Party, its history, growth, policy, and leaders.* London: Caxton Publishing Co., 1925. Vol. 2. p. 259–73.

8910 **Pethick-Lawrence**, Frederick William. 'Note on the paper by Professor S. N. Procopovitch on the distribution of national income.' *Econ. J.*, XXXVI, 142 (June 1926), 302–5.

8911 **Procopovitch**, S. N. 'The distribution of national income.' *Econ. J.*, XXXVI, 141 (March 1926), 69–82.

8912 **Dutt**, Rajani Palme. *Socialism and the living wage.* London: Communist Party of Great Britain, 1927. 238p.

8913 **Clark**, Colin Grant. 'Bernard Shaw and equality of income.' *Social. Rev.*, n.s., 31 (August 1928), 12–19.
An examination and discussion of the main thesis of Shaw's book: *The intelligent woman's guide to socialism and capitalism.*

8914 **Connor**, L. P. 'On certain aspects of the distribution of income in the United Kingdom in the years 1913 and 1924.' *R. Statist. Soc. J.*, XCI, 1 (1928), 50–66.
Discussion, p. 67–78.
'Read before the Royal Statistical Society, December 20, 1927.'

8915 **Money**, *Sir* Leo George Chiozza. *Product money*. London: Methuen, 1933. xv, 172p.
'A sequel to *Riches and poverty*.'

8916 **Hicks**, Ursula K. 'Some effects of financial policy on the distribution of income in Great Britain since the war.' *Int. Labour Rev.*, XXXIV, 5 (November 1936), 594–617.

8917 **Silverman**, H. H. 'Wages and national income.' *Cert. Acctnt. J.*, XXX, 369 (November 1938), 346–7.
A note based on C. Clark's *National income and outlay* and Bowley's *Wages and income in the United Kingdom since 1860*.

8918 **Kalecki**, Michael. 'The share of wages in the national income.' *Oxf. Univ. Inst. Statist. Bull.*, III, 9 (28 June 1941), 196–8.

8919 **Kalecki**, Michael. 'The burden of the war. B. The burden on wages and other incomes.' *Oxf. Univ. Inst. Statist. Bull.*, IV, 1 (10 January 1942), 10–11.

8920 **Kalecki**, Michael. 'Wages and the national income in 1940 and 1941.' *Oxf. Univ. Inst. Statist. Bull.*, IV, 7 (16 May 1942), 150–3.

8921 **Nicholson**, John Leonard. 'The burden of the war.' *Oxf. Univ. Inst. Statist. Bull.*, IV, 8 (6 June 1942), 166–9.

8922 **Nicholson**, John Leonard. 'The burden of the war. A. Changes in real income.' *Oxf. Univ. Inst. Statist. Bull.*, IV, 1 (10 January 1942), 5–10.

8923 **Nicholson**, John Leonard. 'The distribution of incomes.' *Oxf. Univ. Inst. Statist. Bull.*, IV, 12 (29 August 1942), 225–8.

8924 **Nicholson**, John Leonard. 'Wages and income tax.' *Oxf. Univ. Inst. Statist. Bull.*, IV, 4 (14 March 1942), 87–9.

8925 **Rhodes**, E. C. 'The distribution of incomes.' *Economica*, n.s., IX, 35 (August 1942), 245–56.

8926 **Barna**, Tibor. *Redistribution of incomes through public finance in 1937*. 1943. (Ph.D. thesis, University of London.)

8927 **Kalecki**, Michael. 'Profits, salaries and wages.' *Oxf. Univ. Inst. Statist. Bull.*, V, 8 (5 June 1943), 125–9.

8928 **Nicholson**, John Leonard. 'The distribution of the war burden.' *Oxf. Univ. Inst. Statist. Bull.*, V, 7 (15 May 1943), 105–12.

8929 **Bowley**, Arthur Lyon. 'Distribution of incomes, expenditure and prices.' *Lond. Camb. Econ. Serv. Bull.*, XXII, 3 (July 1944), 54–6.
Examines the 1944 White Paper figures of the distribution of incomes above £250 in the light of Pareto's Law.

8930 **Common Wealth**. *Poverty and inequality*. London, 1944. 25p. (Information bulletins 6.)

8931 **Hilton**, John. *Rich man, poor man*. London: Allen and Unwin, 1944. 174p. (Sir Halley Stewart lectures 1938.)

8932 **Nicholson**, John Leonard. 'The distribution of incomes.' *Oxf. Univ. Inst. Statist. Bull.*, VI, 2 (5 February 1944), 23–9.

8933 **Nicholson**, John Leonard. 'The distribution of the war burden.' *Oxf. Univ. Inst. Statist. Bull.*, VI, 10 (22 July 1944), 153–61.

8934 **Nicholson**, John Leonard. 'Employment and national income during the war.' *Oxf. Univ. Inst. Statist. Bull.*, VII, 14 (13 October 1945), 230–44.

8935 **Kalecki**, Michael. 'The distribution of the national income.' American Economic Association. *Readings in the theory of income distribution*. Philadelphia: Blakiston, 1946; London: Allen and Unwin, 1950. p. 197–217.
Reprinted from *Essays in the theory of economic fluctuations*. London: Allen and Unwin, 1939. p. 13–41.
'This essay is an altered version of the article published in *Econometrica*, April 1938.'

8936 **Booker**, H. S. 'The distribution of income under full employment.' *Manchr. Sch.*, XV, 1 (January 1947), 75–91.

8937 **Cockfield**, F. A. 'The distribution of incomes.' *Economica*, n.s., XIV, 55 (November 1947), 254–82.

8938 **Woodburn**, Arthur. 'The distribution of wealth.' Tracey, H. (ed.). *The British Labour Party: its history, growth, policy, and leaders*. London: Caxton Publishing Co., 1948. Vol. 2. p. 206–22.

8939 **Adler**, Max K. 'The silent revolution.' *Polit. Q.*, XX, 2 (April–June 1949), 146–53.
Rise in workers' share of national income.

8940 **Rhodes**, E. C. 'The distribution of earned and investment incomes in the United Kingdom.' *Economica*, n.s., XVI, 61 (February 1949), 53–65.

8941 **Seers**, Dudley George. *Changes in the cost-of-living and the distribution of income since 1938*. Oxford: Blackwell, 1949. 84p.
Published for the Institute of Statistics, University of Oxford.

8942 **Seers**, Dudley George. 'Income distribution in 1938 and 1947.' *Oxf. Univ. Inst. Statist. Bull.*, XI, 9 (September 1949), 253–68.

8943 **Aims of Industry**. *The earnings of industry: the truth about wages and profits*. London: Hollis and Carter, 1950. 79p.
Another edition. 1951–52.

8944 **Pigou**, Arthur Cecil. 'Control over prices and the distribution of incomes.' *Distr. Bank Rev.*, 96 (December 1950), 1–10.

8945 **Rhodes**, E. C. 'Distribution of incomes in the United Kingdom in 1938 and 1947.' *Economica*, n.s., XVII, 66 (May 1950), 146–58.

8946 **Roy**, A. D. 'The distribution of earnings and of individual output.' *Econ. J.*, LX, 239 (September 1950), 489–505.
'A further statistical note on the distribution of individual output.' *Econ. J.*, LX, 240 (December 1950), 831–6.

8947 **Rhodes**, E. C. 'Distribution of earned and investment incomes in the United Kingdom in 1937–38.' *Economica*, n.s., XVIII, 69 (February 1951), 18–34.

8948 **Rhodes**, E. C. 'The distribution of incomes and the burden of estate duties in the United Kingdom.' *Economica*, n.s., XVIII, 71 (August 1951), 270–7.

8949 **Seers**, Dudley George. *The levelling of incomes since 1938.* Oxford: Blackwell, 1951. 74p.

Originally published in the *Bulletin of the Oxford Institute of Statistics.*

8950 **Hahn**, F. H. *The share of wages: an enquiry into the theory of distribution.* 1951–52. (Ph.D. thesis, University of London.)

8951 **Lydall**, Harold French. 'National survey of personal incomes and savings.' *Oxf. Univ. Inst. Statist. Bull.*, XIV, 11–12 (November–December 1952), 369–92.

Outline of aims, etc.

8952 **Phelps Brown**, Ernest Henry and **Hart**, P. E. 'The share of wages in national income.' *Econ. J.*, LXII, 246 (June 1952), 253–77.

8953 **Rhodes**, E. C. 'The inequality of incomes in the United Kingdom.' *Economica*, n.s., XIX, 74 (May 1952), 168–74.

8954 **Young**, Michael. 'Distribution of income within the family.' *Br. J. Sociol.*, III, 4 (December 1952), 305–21.

8955 **Champernowne**, D. G. 'A model of income distribution.' *Econ. J.*, LXIII, 250 (June 1953), 318–51.

8956 **Lydall**, Harold French. 'National survey of personal incomes and savings.' *Oxf. Univ. Inst. Statist. Bull.*, XV, 2–3 (February 1953), 35–84; 6–7 (June–July 1953), 193–236; 10–11 (October–November 1953), 341–401.

Part II. The distribution of personal incomes.

Part III. The ownership of liquid and non-liquid assets.

Part IV. Personal saving and consumption expenditure.

8957 **Cartter**, Allan Murray. 'Income shares of upper income groups in Great Britain and the United States.' *Am. Econ. Rev.*, XLIV, 5 (December 1954), 875–83.

8958 **Peacock**, Alan Turner and **Browning**, P. R. 'The social services in Great Britain and the redistribution of income.' Peacock, A. T. (ed.). *Income redistribution and social policy: a set of studies.* London: Cape, 1954. p. 139–77.

8959 **Cartter**, Allan Murray. *The redistribution of income in postwar Britain: a study of the effects of the central government fiscal program in 1948–49.* New Haven, Conn.: Yale U.P., 1955. viii, 242p. (Yale studies in economics 3.)

Revision of thesis, Yale University.

8960 **Rhodes**, E. C. 'Earned and investment incomes, U.K., 1952–53.' *Economica*, n.s., XXIII, 89 (February 1956), 62–6.

8961 **Seers**, Dudley George. 'Has the distribution of income become more unequal?' *Oxf. Univ. Inst. Statist. Bull.*, XVIII, 1 (February 1956), 73–86.

8962 **Allen**, R. G. D. 'Changes in the distribution of higher incomes.' *Economica*, n.s., XXIV, 94 (May 1957), 138–53.

8963 **Cole**, Dorothy and **Utting**, J. E. G. 'The distribution of household and individual income.' International Association for Research in Income and Wealth. *Income and wealth: series VI.* London: Bowes and Bowes, 1957. p. 239–68.

8964 **Brittain**, John Ashleigh. *The size distribution of income in the United Kingdom since the mid-thirties.* 1957–58. (Dissertation, University of California, Berkeley.)

8965 **Shaw**, George Bernard. *The case for equality.* London: Shaw Society, 1958. 24p. (Shavian tracts 6.)

8966 **Hill**, Thomas Peter. 'An analysis of the distribution of wages and salaries in Great Britain.' *Econometrica*, XXVII, 3 (July 1959), 355–81.

8967 **Lydall**, Harold French and **Lansing**, John B. 'A comparison of the distribution of personal income and wealth in the United States and Great Britain.' *Am. Econ. Rev.*, XLIX, 1 (March 1959), 43–67.

8968 **Lydall**, Harold French. 'The long-term trend in the size distribution of income.' *R. Statist. Soc. J.*, Ser. A, CXXII, 1 (1959), 1–37.

Discussion, p. 37–46.

'Read before the Royal Statistical Society on November 19th, 1958.'

8969 **Sturmey**, Stanley George. *Income and economic welfare.* London: Longmans, Green, 1959. x, 208p.

8970 **Brittain**, John Ashleigh. 'Some neglected features of Britain's income leveling.' *Am. Econ. Rev.*, L, 2 (May 1960), 593–603.

Discussion by M. Nerlove, 618–22.

8971 **Hill**, Thomas Peter. 'A pilot survey of incomes and savings.' *Oxf. Univ. Inst. Statist. Bull.*, XXII, 2 (May 1960), 131–41.

8972 **Kravis**, Irving B. 'International differences in the distribution of income.' *Rev. Econ. Statist.*, XLII, 4 (November 1960), 408–16.

8973 **Phelps Brown**, Ernest Henry and **Browne**, Margaret H. 'Distribution and productivity under inflation, 1947–57.' *Econ. J.*, LXX, 280 (December 1960), 724–45.

8974 **Lydall**, Harold French and **Tipping**, D. G. 'The distribution of personal wealth in Britain.' *Oxf. Univ. Inst. Statist. Bull.*, XXIII, 1 (February 1961), 83–104.

8975 **El-Sheikh**, R. A.-H. E. *The redistribution of incomes through public finance in the United Kingdom, 1948–1958.* 1961–62. (Ph.D. thesis, University of Leeds.)

8976 **Titmuss**, Richard Morris. *Income distribution and social change: a study in criticism.* London: Allen and Unwin, 1962. 240p.

8977 **De Alessi**, L. 'The redistribution of wealth by inflation: an empirical test with United Kingdom data.' *South. Econ. J.*, XXX, 2 (October 1963), 113–27.

8978 **Toyosaki**, M. 'Contemporary capitalism and law of wage and income distribution.' *Kyoto Univ. Econ. Rev.*, XXXIII, 2 (October 1963), 1–20.

8979 **Clark**, Colin and **Peters**, G. H. 'Income redistribution through taxation and social services: some international comparisons.' International Association for Research in Income and Wealth. *Income and wealth: Series X. Income redistribution and the statistical foundations of economic policy.* London: Bowes and Bowes, 1964. p. 99–120.

8980 **Meade**, James Edward. *Efficiency, equality and the ownership of property.* London: Allen and Unwin, 1964. 92p.

8981 **Nicholson**, John Leonard. 'Redistribution of income in the United Kingdom in 1959, 1957 and 1953.' International Association for Research in Income and Wealth. *Income and wealth: Series X. Income redistribution and the statistical foundations of economic policy.* London: Bowes and Bowes, 1964. p. 121–85.
Also published separately. London: Bowes and Bowes, 1965. x, 65p.

8982 **Walker**, William Michael. *The cultural basis of income distribution in industrial organisations.* 1964–65. (Ph.D. thesis, University of Birmingham.)

8983 **Jaques**, Elliott. 'Economic justice – by law?' Brown, W. B. D. and Jaques, E. *Glacier project papers: some essays on organization and management from the Glacier Project Research.* London: Heinemann, 1965. p. 246–51.
First published in *The Twentieth Century*, Spring 1964.

8984 **Saville**, John. 'Labour and income redistribution.' *Social. Regist.* (1965), 147–62.

8985 **Prest**, A. R. and **Stark**, Thomas. 'Some aspects of income distribution in the U.K. since World War II.' *Manchr. Statist. Soc. Trans.* (1966–67). 27p.

8986 **Blackburn**, Robin. 'Inequality and exploitation.' *New Left Rev.*, 42 (March–April 1967), 3–24.
A version of the first chapter of the book *The incompatibles.*

8987 **Blackburn**, Robin. 'The unequal society.' Blackburn, R. and Cockburn, A. (eds.). *The incompatibles: trade union militancy and the consensus.* Harmondsworth: Penguin in association with *New Left Review*, 1967. p. 15–55.

8988 **Cutright**, P. 'Income redistribution: a cross-national analysis.' *Soc. Forces*, XLVI, 2 (December 1967), 180–90.

8989 **Devine**, Patrick John. *Inter-regional variations in the degree of inequality of income distribution: the United Kingdom, 1949–65.* 1967. 165p. (M.A. (Econ.) thesis, University of Manchester.)

8990 **Nicholson**, R. J. 'The distribution of personal income.' *Lloyds Bank Rev.*, n.s., 83 (January 1967), 11–21.

8991 **Prest**, A. R. and **Stark**, Thomas. 'Some aspects of income distribution in the U.K. since World War II.' *Manchr. Sch.*, XXXV, 3 (September 1967), 217–43.

8992 **Stark**, Thomas. *A survey of the distribution of income in the United Kingdom since World War II.* 1967. 341p. (Ph.D. thesis, University of Manchester.)

8993 **United Nations.** Economic Commission for Europe. *Incomes in post-war Europe: a study of politics, growth and distribution.* New York: U.N., 1967.

8994 **Burkus**, John. 'Some aspects of income redistribution through social security in four Western European countries.' *Int. Labour Rev.*, XCVII, 2 (February 1968), 167–90.

8995 **Dyer**, Christopher. 'A redistribution of incomes in fifteenth-century England?' *Past Pres.*, 39 (April 1968), 11–33.

8996 **Feinstein**, C. H. 'Changes in the distribution of the national income in the United Kingdom since 1860.' Marchal, J. and Ducros, B. (eds.). *The distribution of national income.* London: Macmillan; New York: St. Martin's P., 1968. p. 115–39.
Discussion, p. 139–48.

8997 **Lydall**, Harold French. *The structure of earnings.* Oxford: Clarendon P., 1968. xiii, 394p.

8998 **Peacock**, Alan Turner and **Shannon**, Robin. 'The welfare state and the redistribution of income.' *Westm. Bank Rev.* (August 1968), 30–46.

8999 **Soltow**, Lee. 'Long-run changes in British income inequality.' *Econ. Hist. Rev.*, 2nd ser., XXI, 1 (April 1968), 17–29.

9000 **Thatcher**, A. R. 'The distribution of earnings of employees in Great Britain.' *R. Statist. Soc. J.*, Ser. A, CXXXI, 2 (1968), 133–70.
Discussion, p. 170–80.
'Read before the Royal Statistical Society on Wednesday, December 13th, 1967.'

9001 **Chiswick**, Barry R. 'Minimum schooling legislation and the cross-sectional distribution of income.' *Econ. J.*, LXXIX, 315 (September 1969), 495–507.

9002 **Devine**, Patrick John. 'Inter-regional variations in the degree of inequality of income distribution: the United Kingdom 1949–65.' *Manchr. Sch.*, XXXVII, 2 (June 1969), 141–59.

9003 **Alexander**, Kenneth John Wilson. 'Equality and inquality.' Robertson, D. J. and Hunter, L. C. (eds.). *Labour market issues of the 1970s.* Edinburgh: Oliver and Boyd for the Scottish Economic Society, 1970. p. 133–49.
First appeared in the June 1970 issue of the *Scottish Journal of Political Economy*, p. 249–265.

9004 **Bowen**, Ian. *Acceptable inequalities: an essay on the distribution of income.* London: Allen and Unwin, 1970. 148p.

9005 **Nicholson**, R. J. 'The distribution of personal income.' Open University. Social Sciences Foundation Course Team (ed.). *Understanding society: readings in the social* *sciences*. London: Macmillan for the Open University Press, 1970. p. 264–70.

9006 **Seminar on the Use of Census Data in the Estimation of Income Distributions for Small Areas**, Centre for Environmental Studies, 1970. *Papers from the Seminar on the Use of Census Data in the Estimation of Income Distributions for Small Areas, 21 April 1970*. London: Centre for Environmental Studies, 1970. 71p. (Information paper 17.)

IV. CONDITIONS OF EMPLOYMENT

See also Parts Three and Five where many of the works on trade unionism and collective bargaining contain material on employment conditions.

A. GENERAL CONDITIONS OF WORK

This section includes material dealing with working conditions in general. Material relating primarily to wages is classified at Part Six, III, and that relating to other specific conditions of employment is classified at Part Six, IV, B–D. The emphasis here is on 'working' conditions as opposed to 'living' conditions. Material primarily concerned with the cost of living and such aspects of living conditions as food, clothing, and housing (except tied housing) have generally been excluded. In particular, the literature relating to the debate over the impact of the Industrial Revolution upon workers' living standards has generally been excluded; a good deal of this literature is listed in Arthur J. Taylor (ed.), *The Standard of Living in Britain in the Industrial Revolution* (London: Methuen, 1975). Most general social and economic history texts contain material on working conditions, but it was not possible to analyse the contents of each of these volumes and include the relevant material here. The memoirs and autobiographies of workers also generally contain information on working conditions and these have been included here. See also Part Five, V, B, 1; Part Six, II, D; Part Seven, V, A, 1; and Part Seven, IX, 2.

1. General

9007 **Brassey**, Thomas, Earl Brassey. *Work and wages practically illustrated*. London: Bell and Daldy, 1872. xvi, 296p.
Based on the experience of Thomas Brassey of Bulkeley.

9008 **Brassey**, Thomas, Earl Brassey. *Foreign work and English wages considered with reference to the depression of trade*. London: Longmans, 1879. ix, 417p.

9009 **Donisthorpe**, Wordsworth. *The claims of labour: or serfdom, wagedom and freedom*. London: S. Tinsley, 1880. vi, 52p.
Printed in Guildford.

9010 **Ingram**, John Kells. *Work and the workman: being an address to the Trades' Union Congress in Dublin, September, 1880*. London: Longmans, 1880. 19p.
Second edition. London: Longmans; Dublin: Ponsonby, 1884. 44p.
Reprinted with introduction by Richard T. Ely. Dublin: Eason, 1928. 24p.
Also reprinted in *Statist. Soc. Inq. Soc. Ir. J.*, VIII, 2 (January 1881), 106–23.

9011 **O'Brien**, Charlotte G. 'The Irish "poor man".' *Nineteenth Century*, VIII, 46 (December 1880), 876–87.

9012 **Joule**, Benjamin Saint John Baptist. *A letter to Mr. James H. Tuke: an answer to his pamphlet 'Irish distress and its remedies'*. London: Simpkin, Marshall, 1881. 32p.

9013 **Casey**, Henry James. *The workman: his worth and his future . . .* Manchester: J. Heywood, 1882. 88p.
Fourth edition.

9014 **Rowe**, Richard. *How our working people live*. Strahan, 1882. 242p.

9015 **Sketchley**, J. *The workman's question: why he is poor*. Birmingham: J. Sketchley, [1882?]. 24p.
Later editions. [1886?], 1890.

9016 **Giffen**, Robert. 'The progress of the working classes in the last half century.' *R. Statist. Soc. J.*, XLVI, 4 (December 1883), 593–622.
The President's inaugural address, 20 November 1883.

9017 **Marindin**, Francis Arthur, *Major*. *Workmen's trains on the metropolitan lines: report*. London: H.M.S.O., 1883. (C. 3535.)

9018 **Reid**, R. *How the working classes are to be saved, and pauperism extinguished*. Northampton: the author, 1883. 16p.

9019 **Rogers**, James Edwin Thorold. *Eight chapters on the history of work and wages*. London: Sonnenschein, 1885 [i.e. 1884]. 206p.
'Being a reprint of chapters VIII, XII, XIV, XV, XVII, XVIII, XIX, XX of "Six centuries of work and wages".'
Seventh edition. 1902. 206p.

9020 **Rogers**, James Edwin Thorold. *Six centuries of work and wages: the history of English labour*. London: Sonnenschein, 1884. 2v.
Third edition. 1890. 591p.

9021 **Whittaker**, Thomas. *Life's battles in temperance armour*. London: Hodder and Stoughton, 1884. xi, 379p.
Including factory work.

9022 **Montgomery**, Robert. 'A comparison of some of the economic and social conditions of Manchester and the surrounding districts in 1834 and 1884.' *Manchr. Statist. Soc. Trans.* (1884–85), 1–30.

9023 **Adams**, Edwin. *Wealth, work and want: an examination of the existing social condition*. London: London Literary Society, 1885. 139p.

9024 **Bastable**, C. F. 'Some considerations on the Industrial Remuneration Conference 1885.' *Statist. Soc. Inq. Soc. Ir. J.*, VIII, 8 (July 1885), 623–33.

9025 **Harris**, W. J. 'Do any remediable causes influence prejudicially the well-being of the working classes?' Industrial Remuneration Conference. *The report of the proceedings and papers*. London: Cassell, 1885. p. 221–31.
Discussion, p. 240–50.

9026 **Houldsworth**, W. H. 'The conditions of industrial prosperity.' Industrial Remuneration Conference. *The report of the proceedings and papers*. London: Cassell, 1885. p. 231–5.
Discussion, p. 240–50.

9027 **Jones**, Benjamin. 'Do any remediable causes influence prejudicially the well-being of the working classes?' Industrial Remuneration Conference. *The report of the proceedings and papers*. London: Cassell, 1885. p. 265–304.
Discussion, p. 323–35.

9028 **O'Brien**, James Bronterre. *The rise, progress and phases of human slavery*. London: W. Reeves, 1885. viii, 148p.

9029 **Porter**, Robert Percival. *Bread-winners abroad*. New York: J. S. Ogilvie, 1885. 420p.
In Great Britain.

9030 **Simcox**, Edith. 'Loss or gain of the working classes during the nineteenth century.' Industrial Remuneration Conference. *The report of the proceedings and papers*. London: Cassell, 1885. p. 84–107.
Discussion, p. 119–36.

9031 **Taylor**, Sedley. 'How far do remediable causes influence prejudicially the well-being of the working classes?' Industrial Remuneration Conference. *The report of the proceedings and papers*. London: Cassell, 1885. p. 251–65.
Discussion, p. 323–35.

9032 **Geddes**, Patrick. 'On the conditions of progress of the capitalist and of the labourer.' Oliphant, J. (ed.). *The claims of labour: a course of lectures delivered in Scotland in the summer of 1886, on various aspects of the labour problem*. Edinburgh: Co-operative Printing Co., 1886. p. 74–111.

9033 **Giffen**, Robert. 'Further notes on the progress of the working classes in the last half century.' *R. Statist. Soc. J.*, XLIX, 1 (March 1886), 28–91.
With discussion, p. 92–100.
Read before the Society, 19 January 1886.

9034 **Marcroft**, William. *The Marcroft family: a history of strange events*. Manchester, London: J. Heywood, 1886. 44p.
Revised edition. Rochdale: E. Wrigley, 1889. 108p.

9035 **Simonds**, John Cameron and **McEnnis**, John T. *The story of manual labour in all lands and ages; its past condition, present progress, and hope for the future: a . . . pen-picture of the wage-worker, from a social, political and economical standpoint, together with an account of the unions, guilds, and associations, organized for his benefit and protection*. Chicago: R. S. Peale, 1886. 715p.

9036 **Taylor**, Richard Whately Cooke. *Introduction to a history of the factory system*. London: Bentley, 1886. xviii, 441p.

9037 **Bockett**, F. W. *The workman's life: what it is, and what it might be: an address*. . . London: Reeves and Turner, [1887]. 12p.

9038 **Cudworth**, William. *Condition of the industrial classes of Bradford and District*. Bradford, 1887. 91p.

9039 **Gunton**, George. *Wealth and progress: a critical examination of the labor problem; the natural basis for industrial reform, or how to increase wages without reducing profits or lowering rents: the economic philosophy of the eight hour movement*. New York: Appleton, 1887. xxiii, 382p.
'This book had its origin in a work begun by Ira Steward, completed by the present author, after Mr. Steward's death.'
Published in Great Britain as *Wealth and progress: a critical examination of the wages question and its economic relation to social reform*. London: Macmillan, 1888.
Seventh edition. New York: Appleton, 1897. xxiii, 385p.

9040 **Newman**, R. 'Work and wages in East London now and twenty years ago.' *Char. Orgn. Rev.*, III, 31 (July 1887), 269–75.
'A Paper read on Wednesday, June 1, at the Denison Club . . .'

9041 **Smith**, Hilda Caroline Miall. *The British hive and its working bees*. London: Isbister, 1888. 384p. (Isbister's home library.)

9042 **Gladstone**, William Ewart. *The workman and his opportunities: a discourse delivered . . . Oct. 26th, 1889*. London: Crystal Palace, 1889. 20p.

9043 **Marcroft**, William. *Ups and downs: life in machine-making works*. Oldham, 1889. 90p.

9044 **Valpy**, Robert Arthur (ed.). *An inquiry into the condition and occupations of the people in central London*. London: E. Stanford, 1889. 28p.

9045 **Boseley**, Ira. *The living loom; or, Light on factory life*. London: Bumpus, 1890. xi, 166p.

9046 **Aveling**, Edward Bibbins and **Aveling**, Eleanor Marx. *The factory hell*. Aberdeen, 1891. 24p.
Also London: Socialist League, 1885. (Socialist platform 3.)

9047 **Hobson**, John Atkinson. *Problems of poverty: an inquiry into the industrial condition of the poor*. London: Methuen, 1891. vi, 232p.
Second edition. 1894.
Third edition. 1896.
Fourth edition. 1899.
Fifth edition. 1905.
Sixth edition. 1906. vii, 231p.

9048 **Howell**, George. 'Industrial London.' Co-operative Wholesale Societies. *Annual for 1891*. p. 163–98.
I. Boot and shoe trades.
II. The tailoring trades.

III. The cabinet-making trades.

IV. Artificial flower making.

9049 **Leo XIII**, Pope. *Encyclical letter of our Holy Father, by divine providence Pope Leo XIII, on the condition of labour*. Dublin: Browne and Nolan, 1891. 46p.

'Official translation.'

9050 **Taylor**, Richard Whately Cooke. *The modern factory system*. London: Kegan Paul, 1891. vii, 476p.

9051 **Chamberlain**, Joseph. 'The labour question.' *Nineteenth Century*, XXXII, 189 (November 1892), 677–710.

9052 **Engels**, Friedrich. *The condition of the working class in England in 1844*. London: Sonnenschein, 1892. xix, 298p.

Translated from the German by F. K. Wischnewetzky.

Another edition. New York: Macmillan; London: Blackwell, 1958. xxxi, 386p. Translated and edited by W. H. Chaloner and W. O. Henderson.

9053 **Mann**, Tom. *The duties of co-operators in regard to the hours and conditions of labour . . . paper*. Manchester: Co-operative Union, 1892. 11p.

9054 **Thompson**, Herbert Metford. *The theory of wages and its application to the eight hours question and other labour problems*. London, New York: Macmillan, 1892. xxiv, 140p.

9055 **Dilke**, Charles Wentworth. 'The labour problem. I. Pressing reforms.' *New Rev.*, VIII, 46 (March 1893), 257–72.

9056 **Gould**, E. R. L. 'The social condition of labour.' *Contemp. Rev.*, LXIII (January 1893), 125–52.

9057 **Higgs**, Henry. 'Workmen's budgets.' *R. Statist. Soc. J.*, LVI, 2 (June 1893), 255–85.

Discussion, p. 285–94.

'Read before the Royal Statistical Society, 16th May, 1893.'

9058 **Solly**, Henry. *'These eighty years'; or, the story of an unfinished life*. London: Simpkin and Marshall, 1893. 2v.

Includes work in a counting-house.

9059 **Tuckley**, Henry. *Masses and classes: a study of industrial conditions in England*. Cincinnati: Cranston and Curts; New York: Hunt and Eaton, 1893. 179p.

9060 **Webb**, Sidney. 'The condition of the working class in Great Britain in 1842 and 1892.' Co-operative Wholesale Societies. *Annual for 1893*. p. 537–54.

9061 **Galton**, Frank W. (ed.). *Workers on their industries*. London: Sonnenschein, 1895 [i.e. 1894]. xvi, 239p.

Originally delivered as a course of lectures.

Also London: Swan Sonnenschein, 1896. xvi, 239p.

9062 **Halstead**, Robert. 'The stress of competition from the workman's point of view.' *Econ. Rev.*, IV, 1 (January 1894), 43–58.

9063 **Nyland**, J. *Report on the social condition of the people: the result of fifteen years' researches*. London: J. Davy, 1894. 8p.

9064 **Strachey**, John St. Loe. *Industrial and social life and the Empire*. 1895. viii, 228p.

Published as Part 2 of *The citizen and the state*. Part 2 was by E. J. Mathew.

Second edition. London: Macmillan, 1904. xii, 224p.

Fourth edition. 1913. xii, 239p.

9065 **Diack**, William. 'The rural toilers of the North.' *Westm. Rev.*, CXLV, 4 (April 1896), 446–53.

9066 **Hobson**, John Atkinson. 'Is poverty diminishing?' *Contemp. Rev.*, LXIX (April 1896), 484–99.

Reply: 'Mr. Hobson on poverty', by W. H. Mallock, LXIX (June 1896), 789–804.

9067 **Jay**, Arthur Osborne Montgomery. *A story of Shoreditch, being a sequel to 'Life in darkest London'*. London: Simpkin, Marshall, 1896. 112p.

9068 **Mallock**, William Hurrell. *Classes and masses; or, wealth, wages, and welfare in the United Kingdom: a handbook of social facts for political thinkers and speakers*. London: Black, 1896. xvi, 139p.

Originally appeared in the *Pall Mall Magazine*.

9069 **Davidson**, John Morrison. *The annals of toil, being labour-history outlines, Roman and British*. London: W. Reeves, 1896–98. 4v. (Bellamy library.)

Also published in one volume. 1899. xii, 494p.

9070 **Swank**, J. M. 'The British workingman under Victoria and her immediate predecessors.' *Notes and comments*. Philadelphia: American Iron and Steel Association, 1897. p. 23–33.

9071 **Webb**, Sidney. *Labor in the longest reign, 1837–1897*. London: Fabian Society, 1897. 19p. (Fabian tract 75.)

9072 **Bosanquet**, Helen. 'A hundred years ago.' *The standard of life, and other essays*. London, New York: Macmillan, 1898. p. 191–214.

9073 **Macrosty**, Henry W. 'The recent history of the living wage movement.' *Polit. Sci. Q.*, XIII, 3 (September 1898), 413–41.

9074 **Webb**, Sidney and **Webb**, Beatrice. *Problems of modern industry*. London: Longmans, 1898. vi, 286p.

Second edition. London, New York, Bombay: Longmans, Green, 1902. xxxii, 286p.

Introduction to the second edition reprinted as 'Problems of modern industry' in R. C. K. Ensor (ed.). *Modern socialism*. 2nd ed. London, New York: Harper, 1909. p. 90–113.

New edition. 1920. xxxvi, 286p.

9075 **Batson**, Henrietta M. and **Wyndham**, Percy. 'Town and country labourers.' *Nineteenth Century*, XLVI, 272 (October 1899), 570–90.

I by H. M. Batson, p. 570–82.

II by P. Wyndham, 583–90.

9076 **Blatchford**, Robert. *Dismal England.* London: W. Scott, 1899. 240p.
Articles on social conditions in England.

9077 **Stephens**, William Walker. *Higher life for working people: its hindrances discussed.* London: Longmans, 1899. vii, 132p.

9078 **Story**, Alfred Thomas. *The martyrdom of labour.* London: G. Redway, 1899. viii, 293p.

9079 **Wood**, George Henry. 'Some statistics relating to working class progress since 1860.' *R. Statist. Soc. J.*, LXII, 4 (December 1899), 639–66.
Discussion, p. 667–75.
'Read before the Royal Statistical Society, 19th December, 1899.'

9080 **Hutchinson**, James G. 'British labour: a workman's view.' *Nineteenth Century*, LI, 299 (January 1902), 104–11.

9081 **Rennie**, James. *Seed time and harvest: autobiography of J. Rennie, colporteur.* London: Morgan and Scott, 1902. 61p.
Edited by T. Bowick.
Fifth edition. *Wells and welldiggers.* Edinburgh: Religious Tract and Book Society of Scotland, 1906. 75p.

9082 **Wood**, George Henry. 'The condition of labour, being some account of wages, prices, and the standard of living in foreign countries and our colonies.' Co-operative Wholesale Societies. *Annual for 1902.* p. 247–78.
Includes comparison with Great Britain.

9083 **Ingram**, W. H. *The British workman, being a study of industrial life.* 1903. i, 45p. (M.A. thesis, University of Toronto.)

9084 **Select Committee on Workmen's Trains.** *Report, with proceedings, evidence, and appendix.* London: H.M.S.O., 1902. (H.C. 297.)
1904. (H.C. 305.)
1905. (H.C. 270.)
Chairman: Andrew Bonar Law succeeded by Colonel Bowles.

9085 **Glyde**, C. A. *The misfortune of being a working man.* Keighley, [*c.* 1903]. 24p.
Fifth edition. Shipley, [1908?].

9086 **Board of Trade**. *Statistical charts for St. Louis exhibition. Charts (reduced in size) illustrating the statistics of trade, employment, and conditions of labour in the United Kingdom, prepared for the St. Louis exhibition by the Commercial, Labour, and Statistical Department of the Board of Trade.* London: Darling for H.M.S.O., 1904. v, 37, xxviii p. (Cd. 2145.)

9087 **Chapman**, *Sir* Sydney John. *Work and wages, in continuation of Lord Brassey's 'Work and wages' and 'Foreign work and English wages'.* London: Longmans, 1904–14. 3v.
Vol. 1. Foreign competition. 1904.
Vol. 2. Wages and employment. 1908.
Vol. 3. Social betterment. 1914. viii, 382p.
With a preface to each volume by Earl Brassey.

9088 **Horne**, E. A. *Labour in Scotland in the seventeenth century.* St Andrews: W. C. Henderson, 1905. 23p.

9089 **Meakin**, Budgett. *Model factories and villages: ideal conditions of labour and housing.* London: Fisher Unwin, 1905. 480p.
'With 209 illustrations, many of them from the author's camera.'

9090 **Knight**, J. Martin. 'Industrial conditions at home and abroad.' Co-operative Wholesale Societies. *Annual for 1906.* p. 307–45.

9091 **Robertson**, William Bell. *The slavery of labour: a scientific demonstration of the identity of free and slave labour.* London, New York: Walter Scott Publishing Co., 1906. 53p.
Second edition, altered and enlarged, edited, with an introduction by I. P. Scott. London: Sammels and Taylor, 1906. 63p.

9092 **Norman**, C. H. *Our factory workers: the conditions under which they work.* London, 1907. 15p.

9093 **Sutter**, Julie. *Britain's hope: an open letter concerning the pressing social problems to the Rt. Hon. John Burns.* London: J. Clarke, 1907. 154p.

9094 **Hill**, Thomas. *The church, capital, labour and land: a speech at the Lincoln Diocesan Conference, 1907.* Louth: Goulding, 1908. 16p.

9095 **Johnson**, Arthur Graham. *Leisure for workmen and national wealth.* London: King, 1908. 242p.

9096 **Loane**, M. E. *From their point of view.* London: Arnold, 1908. 309p.
Short papers on the life of the poor.

9097 **St Clair**, Oswald. *Low wages and no wages: an essay on the economic causes of poverty, unemployment and bad trade.* London: Swan Sonnenschein, 1908. 240p.

9098 **Van Dusen**, Harlan Page. *The British workman: how to better his condition and repopulate the rural districts. The need for action and its effect upon the nation.* London: G. B. Moore, 1908. 15p.

9099 **Webb**, Sidney. 'The necessary basis of society.' *Contemp. Rev.*, XCIII (June 1908), 658–68.

9100 **Langdon**, Roger. *The life of Roger Langdon, told by himself.* London: Elliot Stock, 1909. 104p.
'With additions by his daughter, Ellen.'

9101 **Liverpool Economic and Statistical Society**. *How the casual labourer lives: report of the Liverpool Joint Research Committee on the domestic condition and expenditure of the families of certain Liverpool labourers.* Liverpool: the Society, 1909. xxxv, 114p.
Read before the Society.

9102 **Schloesser**, H. H. and **Game**, Clement. *Machinery: its masters and its servants.* London: Fabian Society, 1909. 19p. (Fabian tract 144.)

9103 **Wheatley**, John. *The Catholic working man.* Glasgow: Catholic Socialist Society, 1909. 32p.

9104 **Gompers**, Samuel. *Labor in Europe and America: personal observations from an American viewpoint of life and conditions of working men in Great Britain, France, Holland, Germany, Italy.* New York, London: Harper, 1910. x, 286p.

9105 *Questions for wage-earners and the answers.* London: J. Jeffrey, 1910.

9106 **Clay**, Arthur. 'Public opinion and industrial unrest.' *Nineteenth Century*, LXX, 418 (December 1911), 1005–21.

9107 **Hammond**, John Lawrence Le Breton and **Hammond**, Lucy Barbara. *The village labourer, 1760–1832: a study in the government of England before the Reform Bill.* London: Longmans, 1911. x, 418p.
New edition. 1913.
New edition. 1920. x, 339p.
Fourth edition. 1927. xii, 339p.
Another edition. London: Longmans, Green for the British Publishers Guild, 1948. 2v. (Guild books 239, 240.)
Paperback edition. 1966. 384p.

9108 **Wood**, George Henry. *The wages aspect of poverty.* London, [1911?]. 15p.

9109 **Johnson**, Stewart. 'The relation between large families, poverty, irregularity of earnings and crowding.' *R. Statist. Soc. J.*, LXXV, 5 (April 1912), 539–50.

9110 **Porter**, George Richardson. *The progress of the nation in its various social and economic relations from the beginning of the nineteenth century.* London: Methuen, 1912. xvi, 735p.
'A completely new edition revised and brought up to date by F. W. Hirst.'
Earlier editions. 1836–38, 1847, 1851.

9111 **Poyntz**, Juliet Stuart. 'Introduction: seasonal trades.' Webb, S. and Freeman, A. (eds.). *Seasonal trades, by various writers.* London: Constable, 1912. p. 1–69.

9112 **Washington**, Booker Taliaferro. *The man furthest down: a record of observation and study in Europe.* Garden City, N.Y.: Doubleday, Page, 1912. 390p.
With collaboration of Robert E. Park.
Also published with a different title page by T. Fisher Unwin, London, 1912.

9113 **Webb**, Sidney and **Freeman**, Arnold (eds.). *Seasonal trades, by various writers.* London: Constable, 1912. xi, 410p.
'. . . the outcome of a Seminar at the London School of Economics and Political Science . . .'

9114 **Berry**, George Leonard. *Labour conditions abroad: a review of the social, economic, and political conditions of the workers of France, Germany, England, Switzerland, Italy and Spain.* Rogersville, Tenn.: Technical Trade School Printing Pressmen and Assistants' Union, 1913. 125p.
The author was President of the International Printing Pressmen and Assistants' Union of North America and represented the American Federation of Labor at the British Trades Union Congress in September 1912, the I.P.P.A.U. at the International Printers' Congress in Stuttgart, August 1912 and at the convention of the International Association for Labor Legislation, Zurich, September 1912.

9115 *Labour and industry in 1913.* London: Murray, 1913. 102p. (The Times series.)

9116 *Labour conditions in Ireland: a series of articles.* Belfast, 1913. 18p.

9117 **Watney**, Charles and **Little**, James A. *The workers' daily round.* London: Routledge; New York: Dutton, 1913. xii, 354p.

9118 **Claxton**, William J. *Journeys in industrial England.* London: Harrap, 1914. 192p.

9119 **Tawney**, Richard Henry. *Poverty as an industrial problem.* London: London School of Economics and Political Science, Ratan Tata Foundation, 1914. 20p. (Memoranda on problems of poverty 2.)
Inaugural lecture.

9120 **Young**, P. A. *Living graves.* London, [1914?]. 12p.

9121 **Bowley**, *Sir* Arthur Lyon and **Hurst**, Alexander Robert Burnett. *Livelihood and poverty: a study in the economic conditions of working-class households in Northampton, Warrington, Stanley and Reading.* London: London School of Economics and Political Science, Ratan Tata Foundation, 1915. 222p.

9122 **Cole**, George Douglas Howard. *Labour in war time.* London: Bell, 1915. viii, 316p.

9123 **Kennedy**, J. M. 'Labour and the war.' *Fortn. Rev.*, n.s., XCVII, 580 (April 1915), 722–32.

9124 **Weir**, William. [Letter to] *the Lord Provost of Glasgow, President, Glasgow and West of Scotland Armaments Committee* [on the necessity of changes in the working conditions in industry]. [Glasgow], 1915. 15p.

9125 **Brassey**, Thomas. Earl Brassey. *Work and wages; the reward of labour and the cost of work. Founded on the experiences of the late Mr Brassey . . . A volume of extracts, revised, and partially rewritten.* London: Longmans, 1916. x, 200p.

9126 **Farrar**, Frank Albert. *Factories and great industries, with some account of trade unions, old age pensions, state insurance, the relief of distress, hospitals.* Cambridge: Cambridge U.P., 1916. 90p. (Cambridge industrial and commercial series.)

9127 **Hallsworth**, *Sir* Joseph. *Labour after the war.* Manchester, 1916. 19p.

9128 **Stewart**, Andrew. *British and German industrial conditions: a comparison.* London: Odhams, 1916. 47p.
'Reprinted, with additions, from *Electricity*.'

9129 **Webb**, Sidney and **Freeman**, Arnold. *Great Britain after the war.* London: Workers' Educational Association, 1916. 80p.

9130 **Ashley**, William James. 'Mind and munitions.' Code, G. B. (ed.). *War and the citizen: urgent questions of the day.* London: Hodder and Stoughton, 1917. p. 1–7.
Reprinted from the *Birmingham Street Children's Union Magazine.*

9131 **Bedborough**, George. *Before the war: reprints of some contributions to the 'Labour World', U.S.A., by its London correspondent.* Letchworth: Garden City P., 1917. 71p.

9132 **Clay**, Henry. 'The war and the status of the wage-earner.' Furniss, H. Sanderson (ed.). *The industrial outlook*. London: Chatto and Windus, 1917. p. 61–105.

9133 **De Kay**, John Wesley. *The world allies: a survey of nationalism, labour and world-trade; and a remedy for wage-slavery and war*. Berne: E. Kuhn, 1917. xx, 393p.

9134 **Gordon**, Lionel Smith and **O'Brien**, Francis Cruise. *Starvation in Dublin*. Dublin: Wood Printing Works, 1917. 31p.

9135 **Hammond**, John Lawrence Le Breton and **Hammond**, Lucy Barbara. *The town labourer, 1760–1832: the new civilisation*. London: Longmans, 1917. xi, 346p.
New edition. 1925. ix, 342p.
Left Book Club edition. Gollancz, 1937.
New edition. 1966. 329p.
Another edition. London: Longmans, Green, for the British Publishers Guild, 1949. 2v. (Guild books 410–411).

9136 **Hinkson**, E. W. *The condition of the working man at the beginning of the sixteenth century*. 1918. (M.A. thesis, McMaster University.)

9137 **Watson**, H. Cecil. 'Labour conditions in Dublin and the coming revolution.' *Bett. Bus.*, III, 2 (February 1918), 146–63; III, 3 (May 1918), 244–52.

9138 **Hammond**, John Lawrence Le Breton and **Hammond**, Lucy Barbara. *The skilled labourer, 1760–1832*. London: Longmans, 1919. ix, 397p.
Second edition. London: Longmans, Green, 1920. ix, 403p.

9139 **Fay**, Charles Ryle. *Life and labour in the nineteenth century, being the substance of lectures delivered at Cambridge University in the year 1919*. Cambridge: Cambridge U.P., 1920. viii, 319p.
Second edition. 1933. viii, 308p.
Third edition. 1943.
Fourth edition. 1947. viii, 320p.

9140 **Lynd**, Robert. *The passion of labour*. London: Bell, 1920. viii, 205p.

9141 **Selley**, Ernest and **Dallas**, G. *Farm workers fight for a living wage*. London, 1920. 12p.

9142 **Wilkins**, William George. *The progress of poverty in England*. London, Manchester, 1921. 85p. (Popular histories 1.)

9143 **Clarke**, William Patrick. *My travelogue: sketches and observations made on a tour of the principal cities of Europe shortly after the world war*. Toledo: Kraus and Schreiber, 1922. 117p.
The author was President of the American Flint Glass Workers' Union.

9144 **Camp**, Charles Wellner. *The artisan in Elizabethan literature*. New York: Columbia U.P., 1923. 171p. (Columbia University studies in English and comparative literature.)
Ph.D. thesis, Columbia University, 1924.
Reissue. 1924. 170p.

9145 **Pigou**, Arthur Cecil. 'Employers and economic chivalry.' *Essays in applied economics*. London: King, 1923.
Revised edition. 1924. p. 12–23.

9146 **Stibbons**, Frederick. *Norfolk's 'caddie' poet: his autobiography, impressions, and some of his verses*. Holt: Rounce and Wortley, 1923. 79p.
Ploughboy and caddie.

9147 **Williams**, Gertrude, *Lady*. *Social aspects of industrial problems*. London: King, 1923. xii, 260p.

9148 **David**, Albert Augustus, Bishop of Liverpool. *The worker and his work*. London, 1924. 19p.

9149 **Edwards**, Ness. *The Industrial Revolution in South Wales*. London: Labour Publishing Co., 1924. vii, 108p.

9150 **National Movement Towards a Christian Order of Industry and Commerce.** *The standard of living and the problem of raising it: papers . . . Balliol College, Oxford, January 11th to 14th, 1924*. [York?]: the Movement, [1924?]. 63p. (Christian order of industry series 4.)
Papers by Douglas Knoop, A. M. Carr-Saunders, J. H. Jones, John Lee, the Master of Balliol [A. D. Lindsay].

9151 **Smith**, M. *Statistical data on the situation of the working class of Europe in the first half of 1923*. Moscow, 1924. 38p.

9152 **Bowley**, *Sir* Arthur Lyon and **Hogg**, Margaret Hope. *Has poverty diminished? A sequel to 'Livelihood and poverty'*. London: King, 1925. viii, 236p. (Studies in economics and political science 82.)

9153 **Hammond**, John Lawrence Le Breton and **Hammond**, Lucy Barbara. *The rise of modern industry*. London: Methuen, 1925. xi, 280p.
Second edition. 1926.
Third edition. 1927.
Fourth edition. 1930.
Fifth edition. 1934.
Sixth edition. 1944.
Seventh edition. 1947.
Eighth edition. 1951.
Ninth edition. 1966. xxxi, 303p. With introduction by R. M. Hartwell.

9154 **Hope**, Ellis. *A short history of English life and labour*. London: Nisbet, 1925. 244p.

9155 **Pollock**, *Hon.* Margaret Anna (ed.). *Working days, being the personal records of sixteen working men and women*. London: Cape, 1926. 276p.

9156 **Chisholm**, Cecil. *Vulcan; or the future of labour*. London: Kegan Paul, Trench, Trubner, [1927]. 95p. (To-day and to-morrow.)

9157 **Hicks**, John Richard. *The positions of the skilled and less skilled workman in the engineering and building trades, 1914–25*. 1927. (B.Litt. thesis, University of Oxford.)

9158 **International Association for Social Progress** (**British Section**). *Report on the effects upon labour of modern industrial developments*. London, 1927. 18p.

9159 **Robbins**, Helen. 'A comparison of the effects of the Black Death on the economic organization of France and England.' *J. Polit. Econ.*, XXXVI, 4 (August 1928), 447–79.

'Effects on labor and wages', p. 462–73.

'The statutes of laborers', p. 473–6.

9160 **Collier**, Frances. 'An early factory community.' *Econ. Hist.*, II, 5 (January 1930), 117–24.

9161 **Fang**, Hsien-T'ing. *Triumph of factory system in England*. Tientsin: Nankai University, Committee on Social and Economic Research, 1930. 310p. (Economic history series 2.)

'The present study was completed as a doctoral dissertation for the Graduate School of Yale University in the summer of 1928.'

9162 **Gibberd,** Kathleen. *Workmen's fare: an account of Herbert Richard Haynes, the average working man, and the social and industrial problems arising out of his life*. London: Student Christian Movement P., 1930. 128p.

9163 **Humphrey**, A. W. *The workers' share: a study in wages and poverty*. London: Allen and Unwin, 1930. 92p.

9164 **Mallon**, James Joseph and **Lascelles**, Edward C. T. *Poverty yesterday & to-day*. London: Student Christian Movement, 1930. 100p.

9165 **Davies**, Margaret Llewelyn (ed.). *Life as we have known it, by co-operative working women*. London: Hogarth P., 1931. xxxix, 141p.

By members of the Women's Co-operative Guild.

Contents: 'Memories of seventy years', by Mrs Layton. p. 1–55. 'A plate-layer's wife', by Mrs Wrigley. p. 56–66. 'In a mining village', by Mrs F. H. Smith. p. 67–72. 'A guild office clerk', by M. L. Davies. p. 73–80. 'A felt hat worker', by Mrs Scott. p. 81–101. 'A public-spirited rebel', by Mrs Yearn. p. 102–8. 'Extracts from guildswomen's letters.' p. 109–41.

9166 **Wells**, Herbert George. *The work, wealth and happiness of mankind*. Garden City, N.Y.: Doubleday, Doran, 1931. 2v.

Another edition. London: Heinemann, 1932. xiii, 850p.

New and revised edition. 1934. xiii, 867p.

9167 **Board of Trade**. *Industrial survey*. 1932.

Lancashire area (excluding Merseyside). By University of Manchester. ix, 380p.

South-west of Scotland. By University of Glasgow. vi, 220p.

South Wales. By University College of South Wales and Monmouthshire. 181p.

Merseyside. By University of Liverpool. 174p.

North-East coast area. By Armstrong College, Newcastle upon Tyne. viii, 505p.

9168 **Chambers**, Jonathan David. *Nottinghamshire in the eighteenth century: a study of life and labour under the squirearchy*. London: King, 1932. xi, 377p.

Second edition. Cass, 1969. xxix, 377p.

9169 **Pearse**, Innes Hope and **Williamson**, George Scott. *The case for action: a survey of everyday life under modern industrial conditions*. London: Faber, 1932. xii, 171p.

Second impression. 1932.

Third edition. 1938. xv, 162p.

9170 **Manning**, Phyllis Amy. *The postwar relations of skilled and unskilled labour in the printing, building and engineering industries*. 1932–33. (Ph.D. thesis, University of London.)

9171 **Orwell**, George (*pseud.*). *Down and out in Paris and London*. London: Gollancz, 1933. 288p.

Another edition. Harmondsworth, New York: Penguin Books, 1940. 184p. (No. 297.)

Another edition. London: Secker and Warburg, 1949. 213p.

Another edition. Harmondsworth: Penguin Books in association with Secker and Warburg, 1963. 188p.

9172 **Brown**, John. *I was a tramp*. London: Selwyn and Blount, 1934. 280p.

9173 **Holmes**, Henry N. 'Progress in the conditions of employment in Norwich.' *J. St. Med.*, XLII, 7 (July 1934), 373–90.

Since sixteenth century.

9174 **Jermy**, Louise. *The memories of a working woman*. Norwich: Goose, 1934. 188p.

9175 **Kenyon**, Nora. 'Labour conditions in Essex in the reign of Richard II.' *Econ. Hist. Rev.*, IV, 4 (April 1934), 429–51.

Reprinted in Carus-Wilson, E. M. (ed.). *Essays in economic history*. Vol. II. London: Arnold, 1962. p. 91–111.

9176 **Klingender**, Francis Donald. *The black-coated worker in London*. 1934. (Ph.D. thesis, University of London.)

9177 **Manning**, Henry Edward, Cardinal, Archbishop of Westminster. *The dignity and rights of labour, and other writings on social questions*. London: Burns, Oates, and Washbourne, 1934. ix, 98p.

The dignity and rights of labour was first published in 1874.

9178 **Ministry of Labour**. *Reports of investigations into the industrial conditions in certain depressed areas*. London: H.M.S.O., 1934. (Cmd. 4728.)

9179 **O'Mara**, Patrick. *The autobiography of a Liverpool Irish slummy*. London: M. Hopkinson, 1934. 306p.

9180 **Watson**, William Foster. 'The worker's point of view. XVI. The problem of the small shop.' *Hum. Factor*, VIII, 3 (March 1934), 101–11.

9181 **Worts**, Frederick Robert. *The heroic worker*. London: Harrap, 1934. 179p. (History of England at work, bk. 1.)

9182 **Worts**, Frederick Robert. *The nation at work, from 1603 to the present day.* London: Harrap, 1934. 249p. (History of England at work, bk. 4.)
New edition revised. 1942. 249p.
9183 **Hilton**, Jack. *Caliban shrieks.* London: Cobden-Sanderson, 1935. vii, 166p.
9184 **Holt**, William. *I was a prisoner.* Todmorden: the author, 1935. xi, 134p.
Another edition. London: J. Miles, 1935. 155p.
9185 **Hutt**, George Allen. *This final crisis.* London: Gollancz, 1935. 288p.
9186 **Katin**, Louis. 'The worker's point of view. XXIV. Music at work.' *Hum. Factor*, IX, 7–8 (July–August 1935), 277–80.
9187 **Raphael**, Winifred. 'Boredom and work.' Williams, H. (ed.). *Man and the machine.* London: Routledge, 1935. p. 196–207.
9188 **Sherwood**, Will. 'The trade union view.' Williams, H. (ed.). *Man and the machine.* London: Routledge, 1935. p. 133–57.
9189 **Watson**, William Foster. *Machines and men: an autobiography of an itinerant mechanic.* London: Allen and Unwin, 1935. 226p.
9190 **Watson**, William Foster. 'The worker's point of view. XXI. Important trivialities.' *Hum. Factor*, IX, 2 (February 1935), 68–75.
9191 **Bennett**, Ernest Pendarves Leigh. *The other man's job.* London: Allen and Unwin, 1937. 281p.
Impressions of various types of work.
9192 **Brown**, John. *The road to power.* London: Selwyn and Blount, 1937. 327p.
9193 **House of Industry League**, and others. *Conference on exploitation: a challenge to the churches.* London, 1937. 5 pts.
9194 **Katin**, Louis. 'The worker's point of view. XXXII. Avoiding long journeys for the worker.' *Hum. Factor*, XI, 5 (May 1937), 178–80.
9195 **Common**, Jack (ed.). *Seven shifts.* London: Secker and Warburg, 1938. xi, 271p.
9196 **Titmuss**, Richard Morris. *Poverty and population: a factual study of contemporary social waste.* London: Macmillan, 1938. xxviii, 320p.
9197 **Garratt**, Vero W. *A man in the street.* London: Dent, 1939. xii, 317p.
Autobiographical reminiscences.
9198 **Greenwood**, Walter. *How the other man lives.* London: Labour Book Service, 1939. 256p.
A survey of various occupations from personal interviews.
9199 **Holt**, William. *I haven't unpacked: an autobiography.* London: Harrap, 1939. 287p.
9200 **Kuczynski**, Jürgen. *The condition of the workers in Great Britain, Germany and the Soviet Union, 1932–1938.* London: Gollancz, 1939. 92p.
Also Left Book Club edition.
9201 **Steel**, Frank. *Ditcher's row: a tale of the older charity.* London: Sidgwick and Jackson, 1939. xiii, 299p.
9202 **Goldman**, William. *East End my cradle.* London: Faber, 1940. 317p.
9203 **Morrison**, Herbert Stanley, Baron Morrison of Lambeth. *Mr. Smith and Mr. Schmidt.* London: Collins, 1940. 30p.
9204 **Vernon**, Horace Middleton. 'An experience of munition factories during the Great War.' *Occup. Psychol.*, XVI, 1 (January 1940), 1–13.
9205 **Willis**, R. *Workers' problems in war and peace.* London, 1940. 19p.
9206 **Masefield**, John Edward. *In the mill.* London, Toronto: Heinemann, 1941. 160p.
An autobiographical account of experiences in a factory.
9207 **Ramsbottom**, E. C. 'Changes in labour conditions during the past forty years.' *Manchr. Statist. Soc. Trans.* (1941–42). 38p.
9208 **Jones**, Edna. 'Why I left my factory.' *Nineteenth Century*, CXXXII, 789 (November 1942), 218–23.
9209 **Kuczynski**, Jürgen. *A short history of labour conditions under industrial capitalism.* London: Muller, 1942–47. 8 pt.
Vol. 1. *Great Britain and the Empire.* 1942. 272p.
Vol. 1. pt. 1. *Great Britain.* Second, considerably enlarged, edition. 1944. 191p.
Vol. 1. pt. 1. Third enlarged edition. 1947. 200p.
Vol. 1. pt. 2. *The British Empire.* Second, considerably enlarged edition. 1945. 193p.
Vol. 2. *The United States of America.* 1943. 228p.
Vol. 3, pt. 1. *Germany.* 1945. 268p.
Vol. 3, pt. 2. *Germany under fascism.* 1944. 238p.
Vol. 4. *France.* 1946. 210p.
9210 **Wartime Social Survey.** *Clothing needs in 15 occupational groups: an enquiry into the clothing needs of 4,700 workers in 15 occupational groups, made in March and April 1942, for the Board of Trade.* [1942?] 76p. (Report no. 14, new series.)
9211 **Liberal Party Organisation.** *Status of the worker: the report of the Liberal Status of the Worker Sub-Committee.* London, 1943. 19p.
9212 **Ministry of Labour and National Service.** *Report of the Committee on minimum rates of wages and conditions of employment in connection with special arrangements for domestic help.* London: H.M.S.O., 1943. 9p. (Cmd. 6481.)
Chairman: H. J. W. Hetherington.
9213 **Ord**, Lewis Craven. *Secrets of industry.* London: Allen and Unwin, 1944. 160p.
Also 1949.
9214 **Hiscock**, Eric Charles. *I left the navy.* London: Arnold, 1945. 176p.
Autobiographical reminiscences.
Agricultural labour and work in a war factory.
9215 **Edwards**, Ifan. *No gold on my shovel.* London: Porcupine P., 1947. 224p.

9216 **Fay**, Charles Ryle. 'The industrial scene, 1842.' *Life and labour in the nineteenth century . . .* Cambridge: Cambridge U.P., 1947. p. 171–83.

Earlier editions. 1920, 1933, 1943.

9217 **Reid**, *Sir* George T. 'The human side of industry.' Barker, E. (ed.). *The character of England*. Oxford: Clarendon P., 1947. p. 159–78.

9218 **Beard**, John. *My Shropshire days on common ways*. Birmingham: Cornish, 1948. 241p.

9219 **Copeman**, Fred. *Reason in revolt*. London: Blandford P., 1948. 235p.

Second edition. 1948. 235p.

9220 **Graves**, Elizabeth Mildred and **Furth**, Charles. *Your work and wages*. London: Allen and Unwin, 1948. 24p. (Understanding the modern world.)

9221 **Loughlin**, *Dame* Anne. 'Factory conditions.' Tracey, H. (ed.). *The British Labour Party: its history, growth, policy, and leaders*. London: Caxton Publishing Co., 1948. Vol. 2. p. 77–83.

9222 **Cohen**, Barbara Jones and **Towy-Evans**, Melrhodd Mary. *Working conditions and employee services*. London: Institute of Personnel Management, 1950. 88p.

Second revised edition.

9223 **Donnelly**, Peter. *The yellow rock*. London: Eyre and Spottiswoode, 1950. 215p.

Autobiography including description of factory work in Barrow-in-Furness.

9224 **Turner**, Alan. *Plan for a Christian factory*. Hinckley: S. Walker, 1950. 36p.

Another impression. Derby: the author, 1952. 44p.

Another impression. Hinckley, 1954.

9225 **Amin**, Mohammed S. *The industrial worker in Egypt and Great Britain*. 1951. (Ph.D. thesis, University of Reading.)

9226 **Industrial Welfare Society, National Institute of Industrial Psychology**, and **Royal Society for the Prevention of Accidents.** *People at work: Festival year conferences, Keble College, Oxford, 1951*. London, 1951. 120p.

9227 **Fay**, Charles Ryle. *Round about industrial Britain, 1830–1860*. Toronto: U. of Toronto P., 1952. ix, 227p. (The Toronto lectures.)

9228 **Goodwin**, Michael (ed.). *Nineteenth century opinion: an anthology of extracts from the first fifty volumes of 'The Nineteenth Century', 1877–1901*. Harmondsworth: Penguin, 1951 [i.e. 1952]. 283p.

Section on 'The social conscience', p. 19–82.

9229 **Ministry of Labour and National Service.** *The worker in industry: a series of ten centenary lectures delivered during Festival of Britain Year, 1951*. London: H.M.S.O., 1952. vi, 106p.

9230 **Dyos**, H. J. 'Workmen's fares in South London, 1860–1914.' *J. Transp. Hist.*, I, 1 (May 1953), 3–19.

9231 **Holt**, William. *I still haven't unpacked*. London: Harrap, 1953. 240p.

9232 **Phelps Brown**, Ernest Henry. *Economic growth and human welfare: three lectures*. Delhi: Ranjit Printers and Publishers; Cambridge: Students' Bookshops, 1953. 55p. (Delhi University, Delhi School of Economics. Occasional papers 7.)

Contents:

1. Human personality as a condition of economic development.

2. Some effects of economic growth upon human relations.

3. Some social responses to economic growth.

9233 **Marx-Engels-Lenin-Stalin Institute**, Moscow. *Karl Marx and Frederick Engels on Britain*. Moscow: Foreign Languages Publishing House; London: Lawrence and Wishart, 1953 [i.e. 1954]. xvi, 571p.

9234 **Maule**, Harry Gordon. 'The working environment.' Ling, T. M. (ed.). *Mental health and human relations in industry*. London: H. K. Lewis, 1954. p. 105–28.

9235 **Dahrendorf**, R. *Unskilled labour in British industry*. 1955–56. (Ph.D. thesis, University of London.)

9236 **Coleman**, Donald Cuthbert. 'Labour in the English economy of the seventeenth century.' *Econ. Hist. Rev.*, 2nd. ser, VIII, 3 (April 1956), 280–95.

'Based on a paper read to the Annual Conference of the Economic History Society, April 1955.'

Reprinted in Carus-Wilson, E. M. (ed.). *Essays in economic history*. Vol. II. London: Arnold, 1962. p. 291–308.

9237 **Henderson**, W. O. and **Chaloner**, William Henry. 'Engels and the England of the 1840s.' *Hist. Today*, VI, 7 (July 1956), 448–56.

9238 **British National Conference on Social Work**. Central Studies Committee. *People and work: co-operation for social welfare in industrial communities; a guide to studies for the British National Conference on Social Work, 1960*. London: National Council of Social Service, 1958. 36p.

9239 **Morrissey**, Patrick J. *Working conditions in Ireland and their effect on Irish emigration: an industrial relations study*. New York: P. J. Morrissey, 1958. 79p.

M.B.A. thesis, New York University, 1957.

9240 **Saxena**, R. C. *Labour problems and social welfare*. Meerut: Jai Prakash Nath, 1958. 762p.

Sixth edition.

9241 **Chaloner**, William Henry. 'Mrs. Trollope and the early factory system.' *Vic. Studies*, IV, 2 (December 1960), 159–66.

A discussion of the novel *The life and adventures of Michael Armstrong, the factory boy* (1839–40) and its author.

9242 **Hobsbawm**, Eric John Ernest. 'Custom, wages, and work-load in nineteenth-century industry.' Briggs, A. and Saville, J. (eds.). *Essays in labour history*... London: Macmillan; New York: St Martin's P., 1960. p. 113–39.
Revised edition. 1967.

9243 **Marshall**, John Duncan. 'Nottinghamshire labourers in the early nineteenth century.' *Thoro. Soc. Trans.*, LXIV (1960), 56–73.

9244 **National Council of Social Service.** Central Studies Committee. *People and work: co-operation for social welfare in industrial communities: preparatory studies for the British National Conference on Social Work at the Victoria Rooms, Clifton, Bristol, 10–13th April, 1960.* London: N.C.S.S., 1960. vii, 72p.

9245 **Stewart**, William. *Characters of bygone London.* London: Harrap, 1960. 143p.

9246 **Central Committee of Study Groups.** *Work and leisure: summary of an investigation by the study groups based on H.R.H. The Duke of Edinburgh's Study Conference 1956.* London: the Committee, 1961. 17p.
By Guy Hunter.

9247 **Head**, Peter. *Industrial organisation in Leicester, 1844–1914: a study in changing technology, innovation and conditions of employment.* 1961. (Ph.D. thesis, University of Leicester.)

9248 **Straka**, W. W. *The Scottish industrial labourer during the Anglo-French wars, 1792–1815.* 1961. 139p. (M.A. thesis, McGill University.)

9249 **Clarke**, Ronald Oliver. 'The social aspects of industrial employment.' Roberts, B. C. (ed.). *Industrial relations: contemporary problems and perspectives.* London: Methuen, 1962. p. 166–94.

9250 **Evans**, Eric Wyn. 'British labour and the Common Market.' *Bankers' Mag.*, CXCIV, 1423 (October 1962), 238–45.
The consequences for labour of Britain's joining the Common Market.

9251 **Wedderburn**, Dorothy Cole. 'Poverty in Britain today: the evidence.' *Sociol. Rev.*, n.s., x, 3 (November 1962), 257–82.
Paper read at the Brighton Conference of the British Sociological Association in March 1962.

9252 **Pollard**, Sidney. 'Factory discipline in the Industrial Revolution.' *Econ. Hist. Rev.*, 2nd ser., XVI, 2 (December 1963), 254–71.

9253 **Straka**, W. W. *The Scottish industrial labourer during the age of reform, 1792–1832.* 1963. 346p. (Ph.D. thesis, McGill University.)

9254 **World Marxist Review**. 'Aspects of the conditions of the British working class.' *World Marxist Rev.*, VI, 8 (August 1963), 29–45; 9 (September 1963), 51–64.
'... prepared by a number of Marxists in Great Britain and by members of the staff of *Problems of Peace and Socialism* ...'

9255 **Pollard**, Sidney. 'The factory village in the Industrial Revolution.' *Engl. Hist. Rev.*, LXXIX, 312 (July 1964), 513–31.

9256 **Thomas**, Keith. 'Work and leisure in pre-industrial society.' *Past Pres.*, 29 (December 1964), 50–62.
Paper delivered at the 7th Past and Present Conference, 1964, to start discussion. Summary of discussion, p. 63–6.

9257 **Bugler**, Jeremy. 'Shopfloor struggle for status.' *New Soc.*, VI, 165 (25 November 1965), 19–21.

9258 **Central Committee of Study Groups.** *Status and benefits in industry: being a summary of an investigation by the Study Groups of the Central Committee of Study Groups into conditions of employment for hourly paid and staff workers in industry.* London: Industrial Society, 1966. viii, 45p.

9259 **Daniel**, William Wentworth. 'The rat race.' *New Soc.*, VII, 185 (14 April 1966), 6–9.

9260 **Davies**, Clarice Stella. *Living through the Industrial Revolution.* London: Routledge and Kegan Paul, 1966. x, 243p.

9261 **Derbyshire Archaeological and Natural History Society**. Local History Section. *A memoir of Robert Blincoe, by John Brown, with A brief account of the early textile industry in Derbyshire, by Owen Ashmore, and An introductory note on Robert Blincoe and the early factory system, by A. E. Musson.* Duffield: Derbyshire Archaeological Society, Local History Section, 1966. v, 36, 59p. (Supplements 10.)
Limited edition of 250 copies.

9262 **Hughes**, Mervin. 'A truck shop at Dinas, near Betws-y-Coed, on Telford's London to Holyhead road.' *Caern. Hist. Soc. Trans.*, XXVII (1966), 139–48.

9263 **Pike**, Edgar Royston (comp.). *Human documents of the Industrial Revolution in Britain.* London: Allen and Unwin, 1966. 368p.

9264 **Chapman**, Stanley D. *The early factory masters: the transition to the factory system in the Midlands textile industry.* Newton Abbot: David and Charles, 1967. 256p. (David and Charles industrial history.)
Chap. 9. 'Recruitment of labour for the mills.' p. 156–73.
Chap. 10. 'Labour relations.' p. 174–209.

9265 **Coates**, Ken. 'Wage slaves.' Blackburn, R. and Cockburn, A. (eds.). *The incompatibles: trade union militancy and the consensus.* Harmondsworth: Penguin in association with *New Left Review*, 1967. p. 56–92.

9266 **Coats**, A. W. 'The classical economists and the labourer.' Jones, E. L. and Mingay, G. E. (eds.). *Land, labour and population in the Industrial Revolution: essays presented to J. D. Chambers.* London: Arnold, 1967. p. 100–30.

9267 **Miller**, Edwin (comp.). *Eyewitness: the Industrial Revolution in the North East.* Sunderland: Sunderland College of Education, 1967. 54p.

9268 **Temple**, Simon. *Out at work*. London: Cassell, 1967. 55p. (Working world series, fourth year 59.)

9269 **Alderson**, Frederick. *View North: a long look at Northern England*. Newton Abbot: David and Charles, 1968. 285p.
'Work.' p. 69–90.
'Strike.' p. 147–66.

9270 **Black Arrow Leasing**. *British office standards, analysed by area and industry: a national survey*. Liverpool: Black Arrow Leasing, 1968. 29p.

9271 **Fraser**, Ronald (ed.). *Work: twenty personal accounts*. Harmondsworth: Penguin, in association with *New Left Review*, 1968. 298p.
First published in *New Left Review* 1965–67.

9272 **Andrews**, William. *Master and artisan in Victorian England: the diary of William Andrews and the autobiography of Joseph Gutteridge*. London: Evelyn, Adams and Mackay, 1969. vii, 238p. (Documents of social history.)
Edited with an introduction by Valerie E. Chancellor.

9273 **Aspin**, Christopher. *Lancashire: the first industrial society*. Rossendale: Helmsmore Local History Society, 1969. 190p.

9274 **Bell**, Florence Eveleen Eleanore Olliffe, *Lady*. *At the works: a study of a manufacturing town* (*Middlesbrough*). New York: Kelley, 1969. 19, xv, 272p.
Reprint of the 1907 edition with a new introduction by F. Alderson.
First edition. London: Arnold, 1907. xv, 272p.

9275 **Chaloner**, William Henry. *The skilled artisans during the Industrial Revolution, 1750–1850*. London: Historical Association, 1969. 16p. (Aids for teachers 15.)

9276 **Fraser**, Ronald (ed.). *Work, volume 2: twenty personal accounts*. Harmondsworth: Penguin in association with *New Left Review*, 1969. 365p.
First published in *New Left Review*, 1967–68.

9277 **Hennessey**, Roger Anthony Shaun. *Factories*. London: Batsford, 1969. 96p. (Past-into-present series.)
For secondary schools.

9278 **Lazarus**, Mary Ellen. *Victorian social conditions and attitudes, 1837–71*. London: Macmillan, 1969. 88p. (Sources of history series.)

9279 *Reports from committees of inquiry and a select committee on the conditions of labour in several industries, with minutes of evidence, appendices and an index, 1893–95*. Shannon: Irish U.P., 1969. 583p. (British parliamentary papers, Industrial Revolution, factories, 30.)
Facsimile reprint of first editions, 1893.

9280 *Reports from committees of inquiry on conditions of labour in several industries, with minutes of evidence, appendices and an index, 1893–94*. Shannon: Irish U.P., 1969. 583p. (British parliamentary papers, Industrial Revolution, factories, 29.)
Facsimile reprints of first editions, 1893 and 1894.

9281 **Lupton**, Tom and **Hamilton**, Robert. 'The status of the industrial worker.' Robertson, D. J. and Hunter, L. C. *Labour market issues of the 1970s*. Edinburgh: Oliver and Boyd for the Scottish Economic Society, 1970. p. 151–78.
First appeared in the June 1970 issue of the *Scottish Journal of Political Economy*.

9282 **Mantoux**, Paul. *The Industrial Revolution, in the eighteenth century: an outline of the beginnings of the modern factory system in England*. London: Methuen, 1970. 528p.
Second edition.
Translated from the French edition of 1927.

9283 **Shellard**, Peter. *Factory life, 1774–1885*. London: Evans, 1970. 17p., [40] leaves. (History at source.)
Facsimile documents.

9284 **Ward**, John Towers. *The factory system*. Newton Abbot: David and Charles, 1970. 2v. (Sources for social and economic history.)
Vol. 1. *Birth and growth*. 203p.
Vol. 2. *The factory system and society*. 199p.

9285 **Wedderburn**, Dorothy. 'Workplace inequality.' *New Soc.*, xv, 393 (9 April 1970), 593–5.

See also: 47; 1291; 6334–5; 8019.

2. Social Surveys

a. GENERAL

9286 **Bosanquet**, Helen. 'The "poverty line".' *Char. Orgn. Rev.*, n.s., XIII, 73 (January 1903), 9–23.
A discussion of the classifications used by C. Booth and S. Rowntree.

9287 **Macgregor**, D. H. 'The poverty figures.' British Association for the Advancement of Science. *Reports of meetings*. 1910. p. 686–7.
Criticism of the inquiries by Booth, Rowntree, and Chiozza Money.

9288 **Wells**, Alan Frank. *The local social survey in Great Britain*. London: Allen and Unwin for the Sir Halley Stewart Trust, 1935. 108p. Bibliog. 17p.

9289 **Jones**, David Caradog. *Social surveys*. 1949. 232p.

9290 **Agnihotri**, Vidyadhar. 'Labour surveys: a brief review.' *Indian J. Labour Econ.*, I, 1–2 (April–July 1958), 241–7.
A paper presented at the First All-India Labour Economics Conference held in Lucknow on January 6th, 7th and 8th, 1958.

b. MAYHEW

9291 **Mayhew**, Henry. *London labour and the London poor: a cyclopaedia of the condition and earnings of those that will work, those that cannot work, and those that will not work.* No. 1–63. Vol. 1 and parts of vol. 2 and 3. London, 1851.

No more published.

Another edition. 'With numerous illustrations from photographs.' 1861–62. 4v. A portion of this is a duplicate of the edition of 1851.

Another edition. 1865.

9292 **Mayhew**, Henry. *The street trader's lot: London, 1851; being an account of the lives, miseries, joys & chequered activities of the London street sellers as recorded by their contemporary H. Mayhew; and now recalled . . . by Stanley Rubinstein, together with twenty-five selected contemporary illustrations, and an introduction by M. Dorothy George.* London: Sylvan P., 1947. xxiii, 169p.

9293 **Mayhew**, Henry. *Mayhew's London; being selections from 'London labour and the London poor'.* London: Pilot P., 1949. 569p.

Edited by Peter Quennell.

Reissued London: Kimber, 1951. 569p.

9294 **Mayhew**, Henry. *London's underworld; being selections from 'Those that will not work', the fourth volume of 'London labour and the London poor'.* London: Kimber, 1950. 434p.

Edited by Peter Quennell.

Reprinted London: Spring Books, 1958. 427p.

9295 **Mayhew**, Henry. *Mayhew's characters, edited with a note on the English character by Peter Quennell, selected from 'London labour and the London poor' (which was first published in 1851).* London: Kimber, 1951. 336p.

Reprinted London: Spring Books, 1967. 360p.

9296 **Mayhew**, Henry. *London labour and the London poor: selections.* London: Oxford U.P., 1965. xl, 238p. (World's classics 607.)

Chosen with an introduction by John L. Bradley.

9297 **Mayhew**, Henry. *London street life: selections from the writings of Henry Mayhew.* London: Chatto and Windus, 1966. 176p. (Queen's classics.)

Edited with an introduction by Raymond O'Malley.

9298 **Yeo**, Eileen. [Abstract of a paper on Henry Mayhew as a social investigator.] *Soc. Study Labour Hist. Bull.*, 16 (Spring 1968), 10.

Paper given at a conference of the Society for the Study of Labour History, Birkbeck College, London, 25 November 1967.

An abstract of the discussion which followed the paper appears on p. 11–12.

9299 **Hughes**, J. R. T. 'Henry Mayhew's London.' *J. Econ. Hist.*, XXIX, 3 (September 1969), 526–36.

Review article.

c. BOOTH

9300 **Booth**, Charles. 'The inhabitants of Tower Hamlets (School Board Division), their condition and occupations.' *R. Statist. Soc. J.*, L, 2 (June 1887), 326–91.

With discussion, p. 392–401.

Read before the Society, 17th May 1887.

9301 **Booth**, Charles. 'Condition and occupations of the people of East London and Hackney, 1887.' *R. Statist. Soc. J.*, LI, 2 (June 1888), 276–331.

With discussion, p. 332–9.

Read before the Royal Statistical Society, 15 May 1888.

9302 **Booth**, Charles. *Life and labour.* London: Williams and Norgate, 1889–91. 2v.

Title of vol. 2 is 'Labour and life of the people'.

Second edition. *Labour and life of the people.* 1889–93. 2v. Vol. 2 duplicates vol. 2 of the previous edition.

Another edition. *Life and labour of the people in London.* London: Macmillan, 1892–97. 10v.

Another edition. 1902–3. 17v.

See also *Charles Booth's London: a portrait of the poor at the turn of the century, drawn from his 'Life and labour of the people in London'.* London: Hutchinson, 1969. xxxix, 342p. Edited by Albert Fried and Richard M. Elman.

9303 **Booth**, Charles. 'Life and labour of the people in London: first results of an inquiry based on the 1891 Census.' *R. Statist. Soc. J.*, LVI, 4 (December 1893), 557–93.

Presidential address, 21 November 1893.

9304 **Booth**, Mary. *Charles Booth: a memoir.* London: Macmillan, 1918. vii, 176p.

Facsimile reprint. Farnborough: Gregg, 1968. xi, 176p.

9305 **Simey**, Thomas Spensley and **Simey**, Margaret Bayne. *Charles Booth: social scientist.* London: Oxford U.P., 1960. x, 282p.

9306 **Rubinstein**, David. 'Booth and Hyndman.' *Soc. Study Labour Hist. Bull.*, 16 (Spring 1968), 22–4. (Labour notes and queries.)

d. ROWNTREE

9307 **Rowntree**, Benjamin Seebohm. *Poverty: a study of town life.* London: Macmillan, 1901. xviii, 437p.

Second edition. 1902. xxii, 452p.

Another edition. London: Nelson, 1913. 496p. (Nelson's shilling library.)

New edition. London: Longmans, 1922. 496p.

9308 **Political and Economic Planning.** 'Poverty and progress in York.' *Planning*, 179 (21 October 1941), 1–16.

An issue devoted to Seebohm Rowntree's *Poverty and progress.*

9309 **Rowntree**, Benjamin Seebohm. *Poverty and progress: a second social survey of York.* London: Longmans, 1941. xx, 540p.

9310 **Rowntree**, Benjamin Seebohm and **Lavers**, George Russell. *English life and leisure: a social study*. London: Longmans, Green, 1951. xvi, 482p.

9311 **Rowntree**, Benjamin Seebohm and **Lavers**, George Russell. *Poverty and the welfare state: a third social survey of York dealing only with economic questions*. London: Longmans, Green, 1951. vii, 104p.

9312 **Drinkwater**, R. W. 'Seebohm Rowntree's contribution to the study of poverty.' *Yorks. Bull. Econ. Soc. Res.*, XI, 2 (December 1959), 125–33.

9313 **Wallace**, William. 'A tribute to the life and work of Seebohm Rowntree, C. H.' *Yorks. Bull. Econ. Soc. Res.*, XI, 2 (December 1959), 109–15.

9314 **Briggs**, Asa. *Social thought and social action: a study of the work of Seebohm Rowntree, 1871–1954*. London: Longmans, 1961. x, 371p.

e. NEW SURVEY OF LONDON LIFE AND LABOUR

9315 **Llewellyn-Smith**, *Sir* Hubert. 'The new survey of London life and labour.' *R. Statist. Soc. J.*, XCII, 4 (1929), 530–47.
Discussion, p. 547–58.
'Read before the Royal Statistical Society, June 18, 1929.'

9316 *New survey of London life and labour*. London: King, 1930–35. 9v.
Undertaken by the London School of Economics and Political Science.
Director: Sir Hubert Llewellyn-Smith.
Contents:
1. Forty years of change.
2. London industries, I.
3. Survey of social conditions (1). The eastern area (text).
4. Maps, I.
5. London industries, II.
6. Survey of social conditions (2). The western area (text).
7. Maps, II.
8. London industries, III.
9. Life and leisure.

9317 **Carpenter**, Niles. 'London life and labor.' *Q. J. Econ.*, XLVII, 1 (November 1932), 150–9.
Review of vol. 1 of *New survey of London life and labour*. 1930.

9318 **Thomas**, Brinley. 'The *New Survey of London life and labour*.' *Economica*, n.s., III, 12 (November 1936), 461–75.

9319 **Maynard**, John. 'Conditions of the urban worker, Moscow and London.' *Polit. Q.*, XIII, 3 (July–September 1942), 321–7.

f. OTHER

9320 **Mess**, Henry Adolphus. *Industrial Tyneside: a social survey made for the Bureau of Social Research for Tyneside*. London: Bureau of Social Research for Tyneside, 1928. 184p.

9321 **Jones**, David Caradog. 'The social survey of Merseyside: an analysis of material relating to poverty, overcrowding, and the social services.' *R. Statist. Soc. J.*, XCIV, 2 (1931), 218–50.
Discussion, p. 250–66.
'Read before the Royal Statistical Society, February 17, 1931.'

9322 **Jones**, David Caradog (ed.). *The social survey of Merseyside*. London: U.P. of Liverpool and Hodder and Stoughton, 1934. 3v.
Vol. 1. Compares migrants and non-migrants in a survey of working-class households, 1929–30.
Vol. 1. Chap. 7. Income: amount and adequacy. p. 146–61.
Vol. 2. Chap. 1. The industries of Merseyside. p. 1–12.
Chap. 2. The occupied population. p. 13–24.
Chap. 3. Earnings of different classes. p. 25–32.
Chap. 4. Occupational mobility. p. 33–46.
Chap. 5. Employment in separate industries. p. 47–60.
Chap. 6. The port of Liverpool: its trade and its workers. p. 61–103.

9323 **Carr-Saunders**, Alexander Morris, **Jones**, David Caradog and **Moser**, C. A. *A survey of social conditions in England and Wales as illustrated by statistics*. Oxford: Clarendon P., 1958. xxi, 302p.
First published in 1927, with a new edition in 1937, under the title *A survey of the social structure of England and Wales*.

3. Particular Occupations and Industries

Many of the general works in Part Six, IV, A, 1 also include material on particular industries. Works on the attitudes and behaviour of workers in particular occupations and industries are classified in Part Two. See also Part Three, III, E; Part Five, III; Part Five IV, E; and Part Six, III, E.

a. AGRICULTURE, FORESTRY, AND FISHING

i. *Agriculture and Forestry*

9324 **Kebbel**, Thomas Edward. *The agricultural labourer: a short summary of his position, partly based on the Report of Her Majesty's Commissioners appointed to inquire into the employment of women and children in agriculture, and republished in part from the* Pall Mall Gazette *and the* Cornhill Magazine. London, 1870.
'New edition, brought down to date, with fresh chapters on wages, labour, allotments . . .' London: Allen and Unwin, 1887. xvi, 271p.
'New edition, with a new preface.' London: Swan Sonnenschein, 1893. xvi, 271p.
'Fourth edition, abridged, with a new preface.' Swan Sonnenschein, 1907. vii, 176p.

9325 **Jefferies**, John Richard. *Hodge and his masters*. London: Smith, Elder, 1880. 2v.
Reprinted from *The Standard*.
Another edition. Revised by Henry Williamson. London: Methuen, 1937. xiii, 369p.
Another edition. *A classic of English farming: Hodge and his masters*, edited and with an introduction by Henry Williamson. London: Faber, 1946. 340p.

9326 **Hardy**, Thomas. *The Dorset farm labourer past and present*. Dorchester: Dorset Agricultural Workers' Union, 1884. 21p.

9327 **Heath**, Richard. *The English via dolorosa; or, Glimpses of the history of the agricultural labourer*. London: Marlborough, 1884. 64p.

9328 **Stuart**, H. V. *Observations and statistics concerning the question of Irish agricultural labourers*. London, 1884. 44p.

9329 **Stubbs**, Charles William, Bishop of Truro. *The land and the labourers: a record of facts and experiments in cottage-farming and co-operative agriculture*. London: Swan Sonnenschein, 1884. 186p.
Second edition, with an appendix, 'My small dairy farm', by F. Impey, 1885. 200p.
Another edition. 1891. 228p.

9330 *From the plough-tail to the college steps; being the first twenty-nine years of the life of a Suffolk farmer's boy: an autobiography*. London: Hamilton, Adams, 1885. 166p.

9331 **Saunders**, W. 'Loss or gain of labourers in rural districts.' Industrial Remuneration Conference. *The report of the proceedings and papers*. London: Cassell, 1885. p. 107–14.
Discussion, p. 119–36.

9332 **W.**, A. *Position of the agricultural labourer in the past and in the future, by an agricultural labourer*. London: W. Reeves, 1885. 63p.

9333 **British Quarterly Review**. 'The land and the labourers.' *Br. Q. Rev.*, LXXXIII, 166 (April 1886), 257–80.

9334 **Edinburgh Review**. 'English land, law, and labour.' *Edinb. Rev.*, CLXV, 337 (January 1887), 1–39.
Review article.

9335 **Jessopp**, Augustus. *Arcady for better for worse*. London: Fisher Unwin, 1887. xxv, 251p.
Essays on agricultural life in Norfolk.

9336 **McKenzie**, William John. *Hope for the farm servant, with suggestions for the social and moral elevation of the class*. Elgin: Moray and Nairn Newspaper Co., 1887. 79p.

9337 **Collings**, Jesse. *An address to the agricultural labourers of East Somerset*. Yeovil, 1890. 23p.

9338 **Dodd**, John Theodore. *Local rights and interests of farm labourers*. London: National Press Agency, [1890?].

9339 **Batson**, Henrietta M. 'The rural voter. III. Hodge at home.' *Nineteenth Century*, XXXI, 179 (January 1892), 174–80.

9340 **Bear**, William E. 'The rural voter. II. Farm labourers and their friends.' *Nineteenth Century*, XXXI, 179 (January 1892), 160–73.

9341 **Gammell**, J. S. *A laird among the ploughmen*. Aberdeen, 1892. 15p.

9342 **Jefferies**, John Richard. *The toilers of the field*. London: Longmans, 1892. vi, 327p.

9343 **Thring**, *Lord*. 'The rural voter. I. The law, the land, and the labourers.' *Nineteenth Century*, XXXI, 179 (January 1892), 150–9.

9344 **Arch**, Joseph. 'Lords and labourers.' *New Rev.*, VIII, 45 (February 1893), 129–38.

9345 **Heath**, Richard. 'The cottage homes of England.' *The English peasant*... London: Fisher Unwin, 1893. p. 57–87.
First published in *Leisure Hour*, 1870.

9346 **Heath**, Richard. *The English peasant: studies, historical, local and biographic*. London: Fisher Unwin, 1893. viii, 382p.

9347 **Heath**, Richard. 'The English *Via dolorosa*, or, Glimpses of the history of the agricultural labourer.' *The English peasant*... London: Fisher Unwin, 1893. p. 1–56.
Paper first published in 1884. This edition omits the list of sources.

9348 **Heath**, Richard. 'Walks and talks with English peasants.' *The English peasant*... London: Fisher Unwin, 1893. p. 89–241.
Articles originally published in *Golden Hours*, 1871–92.

9349 **Bear**, William E. 'The farm labourers of Scotland and Ireland.' *Econ. J.*, IV, 16 (December 1894), 707–13.
A summary of the most important points in the Reports of the Assistant Commissioners to the Royal Commission on Labour.

9350 **Verinder**, Frederick. 'The agricultural labourer.' Galton, F. W. (ed.). *Workers on their industries*. London: Sonnenschein, 1895 [i.e. 1894]. p. 153–74.

9351 **Garnier**, Russell Montague. *Annals of the British peasantry*. London: Swan Sonnenschein, 1895. xvi, 460p. (Half-guinea international library.)

9352 **Danvers**, Frederick Charles. 'Agriculture in Essex during the past fifty years, as exemplified by the records of one farm, with special reference to the prices of corn and the conditions of labour.' *R. Statist. Soc. J.*, LX, 2 (June 1897), 251–69.
Discussion, p. 269–77.
'Read before the Royal Statistical Society, 16th March, 1897.'

9353 **Phillimore**, Margaret. 'The agricultural labourer, past and present.' *Econ. Rev.*, VII, 1 (January 1897), 13–24.
'A reply', by John C. Medd, VII, 2 (April 1897), 218–29.
'A rejoinder', by M. Phillimore, VII, 4 (October 1897), 468–79.

9354 **Perrott**, Frank Duerdin. *The Housing of the Working-Classes Act, 1890: an account of the solitary instance of the putting part III of the Act into operation in an English village where the labourers were rack-rented and overcrowded in dilapidated and insanitary dwellings*. Smethwick: Smethwick Telephone Co., 1900. 8p.

9355 **Ord**, Richard. *The Sedgefield country.* Darlington, 1904.
Includes autobiography of John Bevans and account of his early life on a Lincolnshire farm.

9356 **Verney**, F. *The farm labourer as a skilled workman.* London, 1904. 8p.

9357 **Clark**, Joseph. 'The farm labourer as he is.' *Econ. J.*, XVI, 63 (September 1906), 442–4.

9358 **Iselin**, Henry. 'Hop-picking in its relation to casual labour.' *Char. Orgn. Rev.*, n.s., XIX, 112 (April 1906), 193–200.

9359 **Pearson**, A. *The labourers' progress, or the coming revolution.* London: Terry, 1907. viii, 183p.

9360 **Hasbach**, Wilhelm. *A history of the English agricultural labourer.* London: P. S. King, 1908. xvi, 470p. (Studies in economics and political science 15.)
Newly edited by the author and translated from the German by Ruth Kenyon.
Preface by Sidney Webb.
New impression. London: Cass, 1969.

9361 **Pedder**, Digby Coates. *Where men decay: a survey of present rural conditions.* London: Fifield, 1908. x, 151p.

9362 **Beard**, John. *Socialism and the farm labourer.* Birmingham, [*c.* 1910?]. 15p.

9363 **Green**, Frederick Ernest. *A few acres and a cottage.* London: A. Melrose, 1911. viii, 230p.

9364 **Heath**, Francis George. *British rural life and labour.* London: King, 1911. xi, 318p.

9365 **Rowntree**, Benjamin Seebohm. *Land and labour: lessons from Belgium.* London: Macmillan, 1911. xx, 633p.

9366 **Baverstock**, Alban Henry. *The condition of the husbandman.* London, 1912. 8p.

9367 **Baverstock**, Alban Henry. *The English agricultural labourer.* London: Fifield, 1912. vii, 56p.

9368 **Curtler**, W. H. R. 'The landlords, the labourers, and the land.' *Econ. Rev.*, XXII, 3 (July 1912), 290–301.

9369 **Lennard**, Reginald. 'Agricultural labourers and a minimum wage.' *Econ. Rev.*, XXII, 4 (October 1912), 367–79.

9370 **Dunlop**, Olive Jocelyn. *The farm labourer: the history of a modern problem.* London, Leipsic: Fisher Unwin, 1913. 268p.

9371 **Holdenby**, Christopher (*pseud.*). *Folk of the furrow.* London: Smith, Elder, 1913. xvi, 290p.
Another edition. London: Nelson, 1916. 374p. (Nelson's shilling library.)

9372 **Pigou**, Arthur Cecil. 'A minimum wage for agriculture.' *Nineteenth Century*, LXXIV, 442 (December 1913), 1167–84.

9373 **Rowntree**, Benjamin Seebohm and **Kendall**, May. *How the labourer lives: a study of the rural labour problem.* London: Nelson, 1913. 342p.
Reissued 1918.

9374 **Whetham**, William Cecil Dampier and **Whetham**, C. D. 'Agricultural labour and rural housing.' *Edinb. Rev.*, CCXVIII, 445 (July 1913), 42–63.

9375 **Aronson**, Hugh. *The land and the labourer.* London: A. Melrose, 1914. xiv, 290p.

9376 **Inter-Denominational Summer School**, 1914. *Converging views of social reform, no. 3, being a series of lectures on land and labour, given at the Inter-Denominational Summer School held at Swanwich . . . June 20th–29th, 1914.* London: the Collegium, [1914]. 167p.
Edited by Lucy Gardner.

9377 **Macdermott**, G. M. 'Agricultural conditions in Norfolk.' *Econ. Rev.*, XXIV, 4 (October 1914), 398–403.

9378 **Nash**, H. Norman. 'The agricultural labourer in Lincolnshire.' *Econ. Rev.*, XXIV, 3 (July 1914), 247–58.

9379 **Rowntree**, Benjamin Seebohm. *The labourer and the land.* Manchester: National Labour P., 1914. 57p. (Brother Richard's bookshelf 7.)

9380 **Mackenzie**, Kenneth James Joseph. *Agricultural problems: the farm labourer.* Cambridge, [1915?]. 19p.

9381 **Smith**, J. Drummond. 'The housing of the Scottish farm servant.' *Econ. J.*, XXV, 99 (September 1915), 466–74.

9382 **Ashby**, Arthur Wilfred. 'Rural problems.' Furniss, H. Sanderson (ed.). *The industrial outlook.* London: Chatto and Windus, 1917. p. 207–54.

9383 **Green**, Frederick Ernest. 'Agriculture and the minimum wage.' *Nineteenth Century*, LXXXII, 487 (September 1917), 596–608.

9384 **Ponsonby**, T. B. *Agricultural labour: standardisation as a means of improving the conditions of rural employment.* Dublin: Co-operative Reference Library, 1917. 29p.

9385 **Treeves**, *Sir* Frederick. 'Dorset seventy years ago.' *Society of Dorset Men in London Yearbook* (1917–18), 3–13.
1846. With particular reference to the state of the agricultural labourer.

9386 **Board of Agriculture and Fisheries.** *Wages and conditions of employment in agriculture.* London: H.M.S.O., 1919.
Vol. I. *General report.* By Geoffrey Drage. iv, 200p. (Cmd. 24.)
Vol. II. *Reports of investigators.* iv, 504p. (Cmd. 25.)

9387 **Green**, Frederick Ernest. *A history of the English agricultural labourer, 1870–1920.* London: King, 1920. x, 356p.

9388 **Board of Agriculture for Scotland.** *Report on farm workers in Scotland in 1919–20.* Edinburgh: H.M.S.O., 1921. vi, 78p.
By Sir J. Wilson.

9389 *Farm worker: his past and future.* London, [1921?]. 23p.

9390 **Mead**, Isaac. *The life story of an Essex lad, written by himself.* Chelmsford: A. Driver, 1923. 106p.

9391 **Fordham**, Montague and **Fordham**, T. R. *The English agricultural labourer, 1300–1925*. London: Labour Publishing Co., 1925. 63p.

9392 **Wedgwood**, Josiah Clement. *Labour and the farm workers*. London, 1925. 11p.

9393 **Morris**, Marmaduke Charles Frederick. *The British workman, past and present*. London: Oxford U.P., 1928. vi, 166p.

'A description of farm life, about the middle of the last century, in the East Riding of Yorkshire, centering around William Blades, agricultural labourer.'

9394 **Yates**, Norah. *English agriculture and the labourer, 1840–1885, with special reference to the depression of the 'seventies'*. 1930. [iv], 232p. (M.A. thesis, University of Birmingham.)

9395 **Interdepartmental Committee on Agricultural Tied Cottages**. *Report*. London: H.M.S.O., 1932. 33p. (Cmd. 4148.)

Chairman: W. R. Smith.

9396 **Evans**, G. Nesta. 'The artisan and the small farmer in mid-eighteenth century Anglesey.' *Angles. Antiq. Soc. Field Club Trans.* (1933), 81–96.

9397 **Henderson**, R. 'Some aspects of the employment of farm workers in north Northumberland: farming, labour differentiation and the hiring system.' *Sociol. Rev.*, xxv, 2 (July 1933), 175–87.

9398 **Mead**, Isaac. *A retrospect, by an Essex lad*. Chelmsford: A. Driver, 1933. 11p.

9399 **Ashby**, Arthur Wilfred. 'The position and problem of the farm worker in England and Wales.' *Int. Labour Rev.*, xxxi, 3 (March 1935), 311–43.

9400 **Grey**, Edwin. *Cottage life in a Hertfordshire village: 'how the agricultural labourer lived and fared in the late '60's and the '70's'*. St Albans: Fisher, Knight, 1935. 253p.

9401 **Howard**, Louise Ernestine. *Labour in agriculture: an international survey*. London: Oxford U.P., H. Milford, 1935. xiv, 339p.

For the Royal Institute of International Affairs.

9402 **Springall**, Lillie M. *The Norfolk agricultural labourer, 1834–1884*. 1935. (Ph.D. thesis, University of London.)

9403 **Board of Agriculture for Scotland**. *Report of the Committee on farm workers in Scotland*. Edinburgh: H.M.S.O., 1936. 51p. (Cmd. 5217.)

Chairman: L. Caithness.

9404 **Toyne**, W. 'A farm worker's memories.' *Lincs. Mag.*, ii, 12 (July–August 1936), 353–5.

9405 **Postan**, M. M. 'The chronology of labour services.' *R. Hist. Soc. Trans.*, 4th ser., xx (1937), 169–93.

Before fourteenth century.

9406 **Northern Ireland**. *The conditions of employment and wages of agricultural workers in Northern Ireland: report of the Committee appointed by the Ministry of Agriculture*. Belfast: H.M.S.O., 1938. 34p. (Cmd. 199.)

9407 **Kitchen**, Fred. *Brother to the ox: the autobiography of a farm labourer*. London: Dent, 1940. viii, 243p.

9408 **Pedley**, William Hird. *Labour on the land since 1920*. 1940. (B.Litt. thesis, University of Oxford.)

9409 **Phillips**, J. R. E. 'Agricultural workers' budgets.' University College of Wales, Aberystwyth, Department of Agricultural Economics. *Welsh studies in agricultural economics*, 1940. p. 60–9.

Reprinted from the *Welsh Journal of Agriculture*, vol. xvi, 1940.

9410 **Kitchen**, Fred. *Life on the land*. London: Dent, 1941. 276p.

9411 **Pedley**, William Hird. *Labour on the land: a study of the developments between the two great wars*. London: King, 1942. x, 198p.

9412 **Hughes**, Philip Gwyn. *Wales and the drovers: the historic background of an epoch*. London: Foyle's Welsh Co., 1943. 63p.

Reissued 1944.

9413 **Watson**, James A. Scott. 'Land ownership, farm tenancy and farm labor in Britain.' *Agric. Hist.*, xvii, 2 (April 1942), 73–80.

General sketch since the middle ages.

9414 **Batley**, James C. 'Work and wages on the land.' *Ind. Law Rev.*, i, 4 (September 1946), 113–15; 5 (October 1946), 158–60; 6 (November 1946), 188–90; 7 (December 1946), 219–22.

9415 **Butler**, J. B. 'The farm-worker.' Bateson, F. W. (ed.). *Towards a socialist agriculture: studies by a group of Fabians*. London: Gollancz, 1946. p. 136–51.

9416 **Collis**, John Stewart. *While following the plough*. London: Cape, 1946. 232p.

On the author's experiences as an agricultural labourer.

9417 **Hamilton**, Henry (ed.). *Life and labour on an Aberdeenshire estate, 1735–1750, being selections from the Monymusk papers*. Aberdeen: Third Spalding Club, 1946. xl, 184p.

Transcribed and edited by H. Hamilton.

9418 **Joseph**, Shirley. *If their mothers only knew: an unofficial account of life in the Women's Land Army*. London: Faber, 1946. 157p.

9419 **Salt**, A. E. W. 'The agricultural labourer in Hertfordshire.' *Wool. Nat. Field Club Trans.*, xxxii (1946–48), 95–102.

9420 **Hennell**, Thomas Barclay. *The countryman at work*. London: Architectural P., 1947. 80p.

Written and illustrated by T. Hennell.

With a memoir of the author by H. J. Massingham.

9421 **Tilley**, Michael F. *Housing the country worker*. London: Faber, 1947. 152p.

9422 **Mejer**, Eugene. *Agricultural labour in England and Wales*. Sutton Bonington: University of Nottingham, School of Agriculture, Department of Agricultural Economics, 1949, 1951. 2pts.

Part 1. *1900–1920*.

Part 2. *Farm workers' earnings, 1917–1951*.

9423 **Mejer**, Eugene. *Agricultural labour in England and Wales, 1917–1939.* 1951. (M.Sc. (Agric.) thesis, University of Nottingham.)

9424 **Palca**, H. and **Davies**, I. G. R. 'Earnings and conditions of employment in agriculture.' *R. Statist. Soc. J.*, Ser. A, CXIV, 1 (1951), 50–8.

9425 **Bridge**, John W. 'Kent hop-tokens.' *Archaeol. Cant.*, LXVI (1953), 60–3.

9426 **Gooch**, E. G. 'Farm labour since 1894.' *Agriculture*, LXI, 6 (September 1954), 272–5.

9427 **Houston**, George F. B. *A history of the Scottish farm worker, 1800–50.* 1954. (B.Litt. thesis, University of Oxford.)

9428 **Postan**, M. M. *The famulus: the estate labourer in the XIIth and XIIIth centuries.* London, New York: Cambridge U.P. for Economic History Society, 1954. 48p. (Economic history review supplements 2.)

9429 **Bates**, D. N. *The agricultural labourer in West Oxfordshire in the 19th century.* 1956. (M.A. thesis, University of Birmingham.)

9430 **Dovring**, Folke. *Land and labor in Europe, 1900–1950: a comparative survey of recent agrarian history.* London: Batsford; The Hague: Nijhoff, 1956. viii, 480p. (Studies in social life 4.)

'With a chapter on land reform as a propaganda theme, by Karin Dovring.'

Second edition. Nijhoff, 1960.

Third edition. *Land and labor in Europe in the twentieth century* . . . New York: Heinman; The Hague: Nijhoff, 1965. xi, 511p.

9431 **Evans**, George Ewart. *Ask the fellows who cut the hay.* London: Faber, 1956. 250p.

Second edition. 1962. 262p.

On life in the Suffolk village of Blaxhall.

9432 **Bennett**, Richard Albury. *The farm worker.* London: Conservative Political Centre, 1957. 31p. (News and views series.)

9433 **Cowie**, William John Gavin and **Giles**, Anthony Kent. *An inquiry into the accommodation of agricultural workers.* Bristol: University of Bristol, Agricultural Economics Department, 1960. 30, vii p. (Notes on farm economics 89.)

9434 **Evans**, George Ewart. *The horse in the furrow.* London: Faber, 1960. 292p.

9435 **Goodland**, Norman L. 'Farm workers, past and present.' *Q. Rev.*, CCXCIX, 627 (January 1961), 84–96.

9436 **Marshall**, John Duncan. 'The Lancashire rural labourer in the early nineteenth century.' *Lanc. Chesh. Antiq. Soc. Trans.*, LXXI (1961), 90–128.

9437 **Blanckenburg**, P. von. *The position of the agricultural hired worker: a survey carried out in eight European countries.* Paris: Organisation for Economic Co-operation and Development, 1962. 269p.

9438 **Kerr**, Barbara. 'The Dorset agricultural labourer, 1750–1850.' *Dors. Nat. Hist. Archaeol. Soc. Proc.*, LXXXIV (1962), 158–77.

9439 **Lloyd**, T. H. 'Ploughing services on the demesnes of the Bishop of Worcester in the late thirteenth century.' *Univ. Birm. Hist. J.*, VIII, 2 (1962), 189–96.

9440 **Giles**, Anthony Kent and **Cowie**, William John Gavin. *The farm worker: his training, pay and status.* Reading: Crown P., 1964. 43p.

9441 **Jones**, E. L. 'The agricultural labour market in England, 1793–1872.' *Econ. Hist. Rev.*, 2nd ser., XVII, 2 (December 1964), 322–38.

9442 **Barr**, John. 'Tied farm cottages.' *New Soc.*, V, 126 (25 February 1965), 5–8.

9443 **Dunbabin**, J. P. D. 'Labourers and farmers in the late nineteenth century: some changes.' *Soc. Study Labour Hist. Bull.*, 11 (Autumn 1965), 6–8.

Discussion on the paper, p. 9.

A paper given at the May 1965 Conference of the Society for the Study of Labour History.

9444 **Jones**, David J. V. 'Distress and discontent in Cardiganshire, 1814–1819.' *Ceredigion*, V, 3 (1966), 280–9.

9445 **Campbell**, J. 'The Northumbrian agricultural labourer.' *NE. Group Study Labour Hist. Bull.*, 2 (October 1968), 29–40.

A description of sources followed by a bibliography and 'transcripts of a few documents illustrative of labour in agriculture in Northumberland selected from manuscript collections in Northumberland Record Office'.

9446 **Horn**, Pamela L. R. 'Nineteenth century Naseby farm workers.' *Northamps. Past Pres.*, IV, 3 (1968), 167–73.

9447 **Phillips**, Richard. 'The last of the drovers: Dafydd Isaac.' *Hon. Soc. Cymm. Trans.*, (1968), pt. 1, 110–21.

9448 **Evans**, George Ewart. *Where beards wag all: the relevance of the oral tradition.* London: Faber, 1970. 296p.

Includes personal accounts of conditions in agriculture and rural industries.

See also: 8136; 9141; 9146; 9214; 10,189; 11,117; 12,430; 12,434; 12,454; 12,511; 12,621; 14,099; 14,367; 14,389; 14,464; 14,484.

ii. *Fishing*

9449 **Duncan**, Joe. 'Capitalism and the Scots fisherman.' *Social. Rev.*, II, 11 ([January] 1909), 826–33.

9450 **Young**, J. R. 'A brief review of fishery conditions.' *Hum. Factor*, XI, 10 (October 1937), 345–53.

9451 **Tunstall**, Jeremy. 'Distant water fishermen.' *New Soc.*, 27 (4 April 1963), 18–19.

9452 **Anson**, Peter Frederick. *Fisher folk-lore: old customs, taboos and superstitions among fisher folk, especially in Brittany and Normandy, and on the East coast of Scotland.* London: Faith P., 1965. 176p.

9453 **Anson**, Peter Frederick. *Life on low shore: memories of twenty years among fisher folk at Macduff, Banffshire, 1938–1958.* Banff: *Banffshire Journal*, 1969. 152p.

9454 **Martin**, Peter. 'On the trawlers.' Fraser, R. (ed.). *Work, volume 2: twenty personal accounts.* Harmondsworth: Penguin, 1969. p. 70–86.

See also: 14,240.

b. MINING AND QUARRYING

i. *Coal*

9455 **Fitzgerald**, Sarah Jane. *Coals and colliers; or, How we get the fuel for our fires.* London: T. Woolmer, 1881. 192p.

9456 **Harris**, John. *My autobiography.* London: Hamilton, Adams, 1882. x, 124p.
Printed in Penryn.
Including work as a miner.

9457 **Presto**, Jonathan *pseud.* [i.e. Charles Challenger]. *Five years of colliery life: a narrative of facts.* Manchester: Heywood, 1884. 62p.

9458 **Mountjoy**, Timothy. *Life, labours and deliverances.* London, Coventry: A. Chilver, 1887. viii, 110p.

9459 **Haddow**, Robert. 'The miners of Scotland.' *Nineteenth Century*, XXIV, 139 (September 1888), 360–71.

9460 **Hartwig**, Georg Ludwig. *Workers under the ground; or, Mines and mining.* London: Longmans, 1888. 126p.
From *The subterranean world* by the same author.

9461 **Wallace**, William. *Alston Moor: its pastoral people, its mines and miners, from the earliest periods to recent times.* Newcastle-upon-Tyne: Mawson, Swan, 1890. vi, 213p.

9462 **Richardson**, *Sir* Benjamin Ward. *Thomas Sopwith; with excerpts from his diary of fifty-seven years.* London: Longmans, 1891. xii, 400p.
Sopwith was the chief mining agent of the Beaumont family from 1845 to 1871.
Microfilm of the original diary in 167 vols is in Newcastle University Library.

9463 **Woods**, Samuel. *Vision of the mines.* Wigan, 1891.

9464 **Munro**, Joseph Edwin Crawford. 'Wages and hours of working in the coal industry in France, Germany and England.' *Manchr. Statist. Soc. Trans.* (1891–92), 1–10.

9465 **Dueckershoff**, Ernst. *How the English workman lives, by a German coal miner.* London: King, 1899. viii, 97p.
Translated by C. H. d'E. Leppington.

9466 **Metcalfe**, Francis James. *Colliers and I; or, Thirty years' work among Derbyshire colliers.* Manchester: H. H. Ashworth, 1903. 218p.

9467 **Durland**, Kellogg. *Among the Fife miners.* London: Swan Sonnenschein, 1904. 198p.

9468 **Hartley**, Edward R. *Socialism and coal.* London, 1909. 15p. (Pass on pamphlets 13.)

9469 **Dunn**, James. *From coal mine upwards; or, Seventy years of an eventful life.* London: W. Green, 1910. xvii, 227p.
Describes early life in a coal mine in first part of book.

9470 **Steavenson**, C. H. *Colliery workmen sketched at work.* Newcastle-upon-Tyne: A. Reid, 1912. 28p.

9471 **Coal Mining Organisation Committee.** *Report of the Departmental Committee appointed to inquire into the conditions prevailing in the coal mining industry due to the war.* London: H.M.S.O.
Part I. *Report.* 1915. 54p. (Cd. 7939.)
Part II. *Minutes of evidence and index.* 1915. IV, 248p. (Cd. 8009.)
Second general report. 1916. 33p. (Cd. 8147.)
Third general report. 1916. 17p. (Cd. 8345.)
Chairman: Sir Richard Redmayne.

9472 **Keating**, Joseph. *My struggle for life.* London: Simpkin, Marshall, 1916. xv, 308p.
Work in mines.

9473 **Arnot**, Robert Page (comp.). *Facts from the Coal Commission.* London: Labour Research Department, Allen and Unwin, 1919. 40p.

9474 **Arnot**, Robert Page (comp.). *Further facts from the Coal Commission.* London: Labour Research Department, Allen and Unwin, 1919. 47p.
With a preface by R. Smillie and F. Hodges.

9475 **Coal Industry Commission.** London: H.M.S.O.
Vol. I. *Reports and minutes of evidence on the first stage of the inquiry.* 1919. xxiv, 414p. (Cmd. 359.)
Vol. II. . .*on the second stage of inquiry.* 1919. xxii, 415–1219p. (Cmd. 360.)
Vol. III. *Appendices, charts and indexes.* 1919. 318p. (Cmd. 361.)
Chairman: Mr Justice Sankey.

9476 **Coal Industry Commission.** *Interim report by Messrs. R. W. Cooper, J. T. Forgie, and Evan Williams, 20th March 1919.* London: H.M.S.O., 1919. 8p. (Cmd. 86.)

9477 **Coal Industry Commission.** *Interim report by the Honourable Mr. Justice Sankey, G.B.E., (Chairman), Mr. Arthur Balfour, Sir Arthur Duckham, K.C.B., M.I.C.E., and Sir Thomas Royden, Bart., M.P., 20th March, 1919.* London: H.M.S.O., 1919. 14p. (Cmd. 84.)

9478 **Coal Industry Commission.** *Report by Messrs. R. Smillie, Frank Hodges, and Herbert Smith, Sir Leo Chiozza Money, Messrs. R. H. Tawney, and Sidney Webb, 20th March 1919.* London: H.M.S.O., 1919. 20p. (Cmd. 85.)

9479 **Coal Industry Commission.** *Second stage. Reports* [by Mr Justice Sankey and other members of the Commission]. London: H.M.S.O., 1919. 67p. (Cmd. 210.)

9480 **Gibson**, Finlay A. *Statistical summaries and tables submitted . . . to the Commission of Inquiry re miners' wages and hours.* Cardiff: Mining Association of Great Britain, 1919. 61p.

9481 **Henderson**, Hubert Douglas. 'The Reports of the Coal Industry Commission.' *Econ. J.*, XXIX, 115 (September 1919), 265–76.

9482 **Bulman**, Harrison Francis. *Coal mining and the coal miner.* London: Methuen, 1920. xii, 338p.

9483 **Committee Appointed to Inquire into the Position of and Conditions Prevailing in the Coal Industry in Ireland.** *Report.* 1920. (Cmd. 650.)

9484 **Hodges**, Frank. *Nationalization of the mines.* London: Parsons, 1920. 170p. (New era series 1.)

The author was Secretary of the Miners' Federation of Great Britain.

9485 **Hughes**, Emrys. *Socialism and the mining industry . . . ten outline lectures for study circles, with notes and bibliography for class leaders & students.* London: I.L.P. Information Committee, 1923. 24p. (I.L.P. study courses 6.)

9486 **Williams**, D. Jeffrey. *The agony of the mines.* London: National Equine Defence League, 1923. 16p.

On pit-ponies.

9487 **Lloyd George**, David. *Coal and power: the report of an enquiry presided over by the Right Hon. D. Lloyd George.* London: Hodder and Stoughton, 1924. xiv, 139p.

Another edition. With additional appendices and plates. 1924. xiv, 285p.

9488 **McNair**, Arnold Duncan, Baron McNair. *The problem of the coal mines.* London, 1924. 27p. ('The new way' series 8.)

9489 **Dataller**, Roger (*pseud.*). *From a pitman's note book.* London: Cape; New York: L. Macveagh, The Dial P., 1925. 270p.

Sketches of life in a Yorkshire colliery.

9490 **Parry-Jones**, T. J. *The other story of coal.* London: Allen and Unwin, 1925. 160p.

9491 **Hewes**, Amy. 'The task of the English Coal Commission.' *J. Polit. Econ.*, XXXIV, 1 (February 1926), 1–12.

9492 **Jones**, John Harry. 'The report of the Coal Commission.' *Econ. J.*, XXXVI, 142 (June 1926), 282–97.

9493 **Meakin**, Walter. *What it is: a summary of the whole report of the Royal Commission on the Coal Industry.* London: Fleetgate Publications, 1926. 32p.

9494 **National Institute of Industrial Psychology.** 'The Institute's evidence before the Commission on the Coal Industry (1925).' *Natn. Inst. Ind. Psychol. J.*, III, 1 (January 1926), 34–9.

'Presented by the Director at a meeting of the Commission on November 4, 1925.'

9495 **Royal Commission on the Coal Industry**, 1925.

Vol. I. *Report.* London: H.M.S.O., 1926. xiv, 294p. (Cmd. 2600.)

Vols. IIA, IIB, III. *Minutes of evidence, appendices, index.*

Chairman: Sir Herbert Louis Samuel.

9496 **Porter** Alan (ed.). *Coal: a challenge to the national conscience.* London: Hogarth P., 1927. 84p.

By V. A. Demant, A. Porter, Philippe Mairet, Maurice B. Reckitt, Albert Newsome, Egerton Swann, W. T. Symons.

9497 **Ashton**, Thomas Southcliffe. 'The coal-miners of the 18th century.' *Econ. Hist.*, I, 3 (January 1928), 307–34.

'Read before Section F of the British Association at Leeds, 1927.'

9498 **Communist Party of Great Britain.** *Communism and coal.* London: C.P.G.B., 1928. 308p.

Part I. *The economic situation of coal capitalism*, by G. A. Hutt.

Part II. *The miners and their struggle*, by Arthur Horner.

9499 *Report on investigation in the coalfield of South Wales and Monmouth (on the social conditions of the miners' families).* London: H.M.S.O., 1928–29. (Cmd. 3272.)

9500 **Brooke**, Henry. *The lot of the miners.* London: Society for Promoting Christian Knowledge, 1929. 8p. (Major issues of the day 2.)

9501 **Greenwell**, Herbert. 'The employer's point of view. II. The man and the machine.' *Hum. Factor*, VII, 9 (September 1933), 300–6.

Reprinted from the *Colliery Guardian*.

A commentary on the article by J. H. Mitchell, 'The mechanization of the miner', VII, 4 (April 1933), 139–50.

9502 **Mitchell**, J. H. 'The worker's point of view. XIII. The mechanization of the miner.' *Hum. Factor*, VII, 4 (April 1933), 139–50.

Reprinted in *The worker's point of view: a symposium.* London: Hogarth P., 1933. p. 74–91.

9503 **Watkins**, Harold Mostyn. *Coal and men: an economic and social study of the British & American coalfields.* London: Allen and Unwin, 1934. 460p.

9504 **Redmayne**, *Sir* Richard Augustine Studdert. 'Mechanization of the coal-mining industry.' Williams, H. (ed.). *Man and the machine.* London: Routledge, 1935. p. 45–58.

9505 **Stewart**, William Dale. *Mines, machines and men.* London: King, 1935. xii, 180p.

On the condition of the coal industry.

9506 **Varley**, A. 'The miner.' Williams, H. (ed.). *Man and the machine.* London: Routledge, 1935. p. 61–72.

9507 **Jones**, Joseph. *The coal scuttle.* London: Faber, 1936. 168p.

9508 **Williams**, W. H. (ed.). *The miner's two bob.* London: Lawrence, 1936. 97p.
Contents: 'The miners' case', by W. H. Williams; 'The capitalist organization of the coal industry', by a Research Worker; 'The coal trade', by R. Hale; 'The Miners' Federation of Great Britain: its history and organization', by R. Page Arnot.

9509 **Jones**, Jack. *Unfinished journey.* London: Hamish Hamilton, 1937. 318p.

9510 **Massey**, Philip Hubert. *Portrait of a mining town.* London: *Fact*, 1937. 98p. (Fact 8.)
In South Wales.

9511 **Tomlinson**, G. A. W. *Coal-miner.* London: Hutchinson, 1937. 239p.
Reminiscences of an unemployed Nottingham miner.

9512 **Coombes**, Bert Lewis. *I am a miner.* London: *Fact*, 1939. 97p. (Fact 23.)

9513 **Coombes**, Bert Lewis. *These poor hands: the autobiography of a miner working in South Wales.* London: Gollancz, 1939. 286p.
Also Left Book Club edition.

9514 **Dallison**, Buck. *Lookin' back.* London: Rich and Cowan, 1939. 320p.

9515 **Dallison**, Buck. *Still lookin' back.* London: Rich and Cowan, 1941. 254p.
Reminiscences of colliery work in the North of England.

9516 **Ward**, Robert W. L. *Old King Coal.* London: Methuen, 1941. vi, 176p.
On the mining district of South Yorkshire.

9517 **Redmayne**, *Sir* Richard Augustine Studdert. *Men, mines and memories.* London: Eyre and Spottiswoode, 1942. xv, 325p.

9518 **Stephenson**, Tom and **Brannan**, Hugh. *The miners' case.* London: Independent Labour Party, 1942. 18p.

9519 **Coombes**, Bert Lewis. *Those clouded hills.* London: Cobbett Publishing Co., 1944. 72p.
On the lives of coalminers.

9520 **Heinemann**, Margot. *Britain's coal: a study of the mining crisis.* London: Gollancz, 1944. 195p.
Prepared for the Labour Research Department.

9521 **Coombes**, Bert Lewis. *Miners day.* Harmondsworth, New York: Penguin Books, 1945. 128p. (Penguin special S149.)

9522 **Foot**, Robert William. *A plan for coal, being the report to the colliery owners.* London: Mining Association of Great Britain, 1945. vi, 66p.
Also *Supplement, being notes on the draft constitution and covenant with proposals for an arbitration tribunal.* 1945. 17p.

9523 **Jones**, Jack. *Me and mine: further chapters in the autobiography of Jack Jones.* London: Hamish Hamilton, 1946. 428p.

9524 **Pick**, John Barclay. *Under the crust.* London: J. Lane, 1946. 138p.
On the author's experiences as a coalminer.

9525 **Scott**, Hylton. *The history of the miner's bond in Northumberland and Durham, with special reference to its influence on industrial disputes.* 1946. (M.A. thesis, University of Manchester.)

9526 **Shaw**, Sam. *Guttersnipe.* London: Sampson Low, Marston, 1946. x, 209p.
An autobiography including work as a miner.

9527 **Scott**, Hylton. 'The miners' bond in Northumberland and Durham.' *Soc. Antiq. Newc. Tyne. Proc.*, 4th ser., XI (1946–50), 55–78; 87–98.
Part II consists of texts of bonds.

9528 **Agnew**, Derek. *Bevin boy.* London: Allen and Unwin, 1947. 139p.
On the author's experiences as a miner.

9529 **Fay**, Charles Ryle. 'Mining operations.' *Life and labour in the nineteenth century.* Cambridge: Cambridge U.P., 1947. p. 184–97.
Earlier editions. 1920, 1933, 1943.

9530 **Manley**. E. R. *Meet the miner: a study of the Yorkshire miner at work, at home and in public life.* Lofthouse: the Author, 1943. 120p.
Illustrations by the author and Michael Groser.

9531 **Rosenberg**, John Joseph. *Life in a model coal-mining village, by a Bevin boy, Sjt. J. J. Rosenberg.* Manchester: Oxford P., 1947. 106p.

9532 **Lewis**, William John. 'The Cardiganshire miners' drinking song.' *Ceredigion*, II, 1 (1952), 53–4.

9533 **Harrison**, Norman. *Once a miner.* London: Oxford U.P., 1954. vi, 191p.
An account of the author's experiences as a miner.

9534 **Wood**, Oliver. 'A Cumberland colliery during the Napoleonic War.' *Economica*, n.s., XXI, 81 (February 1954), 54–63.

9535 **Hair**, P. E. H. *The social history of British coal-miners, 1800–1845.* 1955. (D.Phil. thesis, University of Oxford.)

9536 **Morris**, J. H. and **Williams**, L. J. 'The discharge note in the South Wales coal industry, 1841–1898.' *Econ. Hist. Rev.*, 2nd ser., x, 2 (December 1957), 286–93.
'The discharge note was a certificate given to each worker who satisfactorily completed his contract of service at one colliery and which had to be produced before he could be engaged at another.'

9537 **Edmonds**, O. P. and **Kerr**, D. S. 'Observations on the occupational life history of the face worker at two collieries.' *Br. J. Ind. Med.*, XVII, 3 (July 1960), 234–7.

9538 **Sigal**, Clancy. *Weekend in Dinlock.* London: Secker and Warburg, 1960. 197p.
Another edition. Harmondsworth: Penguin Books in association with Secker and Warburg, 1962. 198p. (Penguin books 1836.)

9539 **Hitchin**, George. *Pit-yacker.* London: Cape, 1962. 192p.
Autobiography.

9540 **Jencks**, Clinton Edward. *The impact of nationalization on working conditions in British coal mining*. 1963–64. (Dissertation, University of California, Berkeley.)

9541 **Anderson**, D. 'Blundell's Collieries: wages-disputes and conditions of work.' *Hist. Soc. Lanc. Chesh. Trans.*, CXVII (1965), 109–43.

9542 **Hair**, P. E. H. 'The binding of the pitmen of the North-East, 1800–1809.' *Durham Univ. J.*, LVIII, 1 (December 1965), 1–13.

9543 **Jencks**, Clinton Edward. 'Social status of coal miners in Britain since nationalization.' *Am. J. Econ. Sociol.*, XXVI, 3 (July 1967), 301–12.

9544 **Duckham**, Baron F. 'Life and labour in a Scottish colliery 1698–1755.' *Scott. Hist. Rev.*, XLVII, 2 (October 1968), 109–28.

9545 **Griffin**, Alan Ramsay. 'Contract rules in the Notts. & Derbyshire coalfield.' *Soc. Study Labour Hist. Bull.*, 16 (Spring 1968), 12–18.

Appendices contain the contract rules of Blackwell Colliery and of Bestwood Colliery.

9546 **Hair**, P. E. H. 'The Lancashire collier girl, 1795.' *Hist. Soc. Lanc. Chesh. Trans.*, CXX (1968), 63–86.

9547 **Evans**, Chris. 'A miner's life.' Fraser, R. (ed.). *Work, volume 2: twenty personal accounts*. Harmondsworth: Penguin, 1969. p. 41–55.

9548 **Griffin**, Alan Ramsay. 'Checkweighing arrangements at the Butterley Company's collieries, Derbyshire, 1871–73.' *Soc. Study Labour Hist. Bull.*, 18 (Spring 1969), 21–7.

Contains the texts of posters, letters, reports, etc.

9549 **Potts**, A. 'The papers of Henry Havelock Robson, 1858–1929, Durham colliery engineman.' *NE. Group Study Labour Hist. Bull.*, 3 (October 1969), 27–33.

Includes H. H. Robson's account of the Durham Coal Dispute, 1892.

9550 **Gretton**, John. 'Pitfalls.' *New Soc.*, XVI, 415 (10 September 1970), 441–2.

See also: 41; 61; 3155; 10,592; 10,607; 10,611; 10,646–7; 10,656; 10,798; 10,870; 10,956; 11,032–11,033; 11,058; 11,060–2; 11,064–9; 11,075; 11,081; 11,083–4; 11,087–9; 11,091; 11,093; 11,095; 11,097–8; 11,104; 11,106; 11,108; 11,110; 11,125; 11,129; 11,133; 11,542; 11,713; 12,077; 12,104; 12,107; 12,130; 12,139; 12,248; 12,257; 12,260–1; 12,268; 12,290; 12,300; 12,340; 12,351; 12,360; 12,371; 12,378; 12,417; 12,435; 12,462; 12,510; 12,513; 12,562; 12,564; 12,571–2; 12,586; 12,589–90; 12,596; 12,598; 12,604–5; 12,626; 14,590; 14,829.

ii. *Other*

9551 **Price**, Langford Lovell Frederick Rice. '"West Barbary"; or, Notes on the system of work and wages in the Cornish mines.' *R. Statist. Soc. J.*, LI, 3 (September 1888), 494–566.

9552 **Price**, Langford Lovell Frederick Rice. '*West Barbary*': *or notes on the system of work and wages in the Cornish mines*. London: H. Frowde, 1891. 91p.

Reprinted in Burt, R. (ed.). *Cornish mining: essays on the organisation of Cornish miners and the Cornish mining economy*. Newton Abbot: David and Charles, 1969. p. 111–206.

9553 **Burrow**, J. C. *'Mongst mines and miners; or, Underground scenes by flash-light: a series of photographs, with explanatory letterpress, illustrating methods of working in Cornish mines*. London: Simpkin, Marshall; Camborne: Camborne Printing and Stationery Co., 1893. 32p.

Part I. An account of the photographic experiences, by J. C. Burrow.

Part II. A description of the subjects photographed, by William Thomas.

9554 **Departmental Committee on Conditions of Labour in Open Quarries.** *Report*. London: H.M.S.O., 1893–4. (C. 7237.)

9555 **Thomas**, Herbert. *Cornish mining interviews*. Camborne: Camborne Printing Co., 1896. 351p.

The author was editor of *The Cornish Post and Mining News*.

9556 **Departmental Committee on Checkweighing in Chalk Quarries and Cement Works and Limestone Quarries and Lime Works.** *Reports, minutes of evidence, appendices*. London: H.M.S.O., 1908. 37p. (Cd. 4002.)

Chairman: E. F. G. Hatch.

9557 **Lewis**, George Randall. *The stannaries: a study of the English tin miner*. Boston, New York: Houghton, Mifflin, 1908. xviii, 299p. (Harvest economic studies 3.)

Also Cambridge, Mass.: Harvard U.P., 1924.

9558 **Bruff**, Harold John Lexow. *T'ill an' t'oade uns upuv Greenho: an account of the traditions, life and work of the old lead miners of Greenhow Hill in Yorkshire*. York: T. A. J. Waddington, 1920. 108p.

9559 **Bruff**, Harold John Lexow. *T'miners: character sketches of Yorkshire lead-miners*. York: T. A. J. Waddington, 1924. 95p.

9560 **Jenkin**, Alfred Kenneth Hamilton. 'Cornish mines and miners.' *Old Corn.* [1], 1 (April 1925), 9–18.

9561 **Jenkin**, Alfred Kenneth Hamilton. *The Cornish miner: an account of his life above and underground from early times*. London: Allen and Unwin, 1927. 351p.

Second edition. 1948. 351p.

Third edition. 1962. 351p.

9562 **Raistrick**, Arthur. '"Rara avis in terris": the laws and customs of lead mines in West Yorkshire.' *Durham Univ. Phil. Soc. Proc.*, IX (1931–37), 180–90.

9563 **Jenkin**, Alfred Kenneth Hamilton. *Mines and miners of Cornwall*. Truro: Truro Bookshop, 1961–69. 15v.
Vol. 15 published by the Federation of Old Cornwall Societies, Penzance.

9564 **Hunt**, Christopher John. 'The lead miners of the Northern Pennines.' *NE. Group Study Labour Hist. Bull.*, 1 (October 1967), 10–12.
A paper read at Van Mildert College on 13 May 1967.

9565 **Lewis**, William John. *Lead mining in Wales*. Cardiff: U. of Wales P., 1967.
Chap. XI. 'Condition of labour.'

9566 **Hunt**, Christopher John. *The economic and social conditions of lead miners in the Northern Pennines in the eighteenth and nineteenth centuries*. 1968. (M. Litt. thesis, University of Durham.)

9567 **Williamson**, I. A. 'Lead mining in Lancashire.' *Eccles Distr. Hist. Soc. Trans.* (1968–69). 3p.

9568 **Hunt**, Christopher John. *The lead miners of the Northern Pennines, in the eighteenth and nineteenth centuries*. Manchester: Manchester U.P., 1970. ix, 282p.

See also: 11,035; 11,040; 11,055.

c. MANUFACTURING INDUSTRIES

i. *Food, Drink, and Tobacco*

9569 **Daniell**, M. and **Nicol**, R. A. *The truth about chocolate factories; or, modern white slavery*. Bristol, 1889. 15p.

9570 **Fox**, Stephen N. 'Industrial conditions and vital statistics of operative bakers.' *Econ. J.*, IV, 13 (March 1894), 106–11.

9571 **Salmon**, W. 'Corn-milling, ancient and modern.' Galton, F. W. (ed.). *Workers on their industries*. London: Sonnenschein, 1895 [i.e. 1894]. p. 81–94.
The author was President of the London District of the Millers' National Union.

9572 **Ministry of Labour**. Committee of Inquiry into Night Work in the Bread Baking and Flour Confectionery Trade. *Report*. London: H.M.S.O., 1919. 44p. (Cmd. 246.)
Chairman: Sir William MacKenzie.

9573 **Ministry of Labour**. Departmental Committee on Night Baking. *Report*. London: H.M.S.O., 1937. 48p. (Cmd. 5525.)
Chairman: L. Alness.
Minority report by F. Marshall.

9574 **Ministry of Labour and National Service**. Committee on Night Baking. *Report*. London: H.M.S.O., 1951. viii, 84p. (Cmd. 8378.)

9575 **Johnson**, Dennis. 'Factory time.' Fraser, R. (ed.). *Work: twenty personal accounts*. Harmondsworth: Penguin, 1968. p. 11–21.
First published in *New Left Review*, 31 (May–June 1965), 51–7.
Personal account of work in a large Midlands cigarette factory.

See also: 10,789; 10,869; 10,882; 10,885; 11,048; 11,076.

ii. *Engineering, Shipbuilding, and Metal Manufacture*

9576 **Sawyer**, Frederick Ernest. *'Old Clem' celebrations and blacksmiths' lore*. London, 1884. 9p.

9577 **Board of Trade**. Labour Correspondent. *Report as to the condition of nailmakers and small chain makers in South Staffordshire and East Worcestershire*. London: H.M.S.O., 1888. (H.C. 385.)

9578 **Baron**, Joseph. *James Sharples, blacksmith and artist*. London: Jarrold; Manchester: Heywood, 1894. 59p.

9579 **Steadman**, W. C. 'Ship-building.' Galton, F. W. (ed.). *Workers on their industries*. London: Sonnenschein, 1895 [i.e. 1894]. p. 56–66.
The author was Secretary of the London Bargebuilders' Trade Union.

9580 **Steward**, W. Augustus. 'Workers in precious metals.' Galton, F. W. (ed.). *Workers on their industries*. London: Sonnenschein, 1895 [i.e. 1894]. p. 32–55.
The author was Secretary of the London Silver Trades Council.

9581 **Swift**, J. 'Engineering.' Galton, F. W. (ed.). *Workers on their industries*. London: Sonnenschein, 1895 [i.e. 1894]. p. 95–114.

9582 **Best**, Robert Hall, **Davis**, William John and **Perks**, C. *The brassworkers of Berlin and of Birmingham: a comparison*. London: King, 1905. viii, 82p.
Third edition.
Fifth edition. 1910. x, 82p.

9583 **Departmental Committee on Checkweighing in the Iron and Steel Trades**. *Report*. London: H.M.S.O., 1907 [i.e. 1908]. (Cd. 3846.)
Minutes of evidence, etc. 1907 [i.e. 1908]. vi, 129p. (Cd. 3847.)
Chairman: E. F. G. Hatch.

9584 **Departmental Committee on Machinery and Engineering Staffs at Poor Law Institutions**. *Report, appendices*. London: H.M.S.O., 1909. iv, 38p. (Cd. 4502.)
Minutes of evidence, appendices, index. 1909. 139p. (Cd. 4503.)
Chairman: A. Lowry.

9585 **Carter**, George Reginald. 'The cycle industry.' Webb, S. and Freeman, A. (eds.). *Seasonal trades, by various writers*. London: Constable, 1912. p. 107–47.

9586 **Hodge**, John. *Conditions in British iron and steel works*. London, 1912. 8p.

9587 **Home Office**. *Report on the conditions of employment in the manufacturing of tinplates, with special reference to the process of tinning*. London: H.M.S.O., 1912. 27p. (Cd. 6394.)
By Edgar L. Collis and J. Hilditch.

9588 **Hills**, Gordon P. G. 'Notes on some blacksmiths' legends and the observance of St. Clement's Day.' *Hamps. Field Club Archaeol. Soc. Pap. Proc.*, VIII, 1 (1917), 65–82.

9589 **Murray**, K. S. 'Work and wages in the engineering industry.' *Nineteenth Century*, CII, 610 (December 1927), 725–35.

9590 **Fox**, Richard Michael. 'Work and wages in the engineering industry, II.' *Nineteenth Century*, CIII, 612 (February 1928), 201–9.

9591 **Roll**, Erich. *An early experiment in industrial organisation, being a history of the firm of Boulton & Watt, 1775–1805*. London: Longmans, 1930. xvi, 320p.

Chap. III. 'Wages and labour conditions.' p. 189–236.

9592 **Dyson**, B. Ronald. 'The Sheffield cutler and his dialect.' *Yorks. Dial. Soc. Trans.*, V, pt. 33 (1932), 9–36.

9593 **Ferrie**, W. 'The engineer.' Williams, H. (ed.). *Man and the machine*. London: Routledge, 1935. p. 73–82.

9594 **Gregory**, William. 'The steel worker.' Williams, H. (ed.). *Man and the machine*. London: Routledge, 1935. p. 83–98.

9595 **Stirling**, James. 'Steel works.' Common, J. (ed.). *Seven shifts*. London: Secker and Warburg, 1938. p. 53–101.

Personal account.

9596 **Watson**, J. H. 'The big chimney.' Common, J. (ed.). *Seven shifts*. London: Secker and Warburg, 1938. p. 207–45.

Personal account of a blast furnaceman.

9597 **Murphy**, John Thomas. *Victory production! A personal account of seventeen months spent as a worker in an engineering and an aircraft factory; with a criticism of our present methods of production and a plan for its reorganisation*. London: John Lane, The Bodley Head, 1942. 164p.

9598 **Benney**, Mark' (*pseud.*) [i.e. Henry Ernest Degras]. *Over to bombers*. London: Allen and Unwin, 1943. 236p.

An account of work in an aircraft factory.

9599 **Ministry of Labour and National Service.** *Industrial conditions in the cutlery trade: report by the Cutlery Wages Council (Great Britain)*. London: H.M.S.O., 1946. 19p.

Chairman: A. N. Shimmin.

9600 **Jefferys**, Margot and **Jefferys**, James Bavington. 'The wages, hours and trade customs of the skilled engineer in 1861.' *Econ. Hist. Rev.*, XVII, 1 (1947), 27–44.

9601 **Ministry of Labour and National Service.** *Conditions in iron foundries: Joint Advisory Committee report*. London: H.M.S.O., 1947.

Chairman: H. E. Chasteney.

9602 **Stokes**, R. S. 'A shipyard from within.' *Manchr. Sch.*, XVII, 1 (January 1949), 88–96.

The author worked with a shipbuilding firm in preparation for becoming a Welfare Officer.

9603 **Ministry of Labour and National Service.** *Report of the Committee on Conditions in the Drop-forging Industry*. London: H.M.S.O., 1953. 33p.

Chairman: R. Bramley-Harker.

9604 **Ministry of Labour and National Service.** *Conditions in iron foundries: first report of the Joint Standing Committee*. London: H.M.S.O., 1956.

Chairman: T. W. McCullough.

9605 **Fitton**, Robert Sucksmith and **Wadsworth**, Alfred Powell. *The Strutts and the Arkwrights, 1758–1830: a study of the early factory system*. Manchester: Manchester U.P., 1958. xii, 361p.

Chap. IX. 'Workers and welfare', by R. S. Fitton. p. 224–60.

9606 **Butt**, Denis. 'Men and motors, I.' *New Left Rev.*, 3 (May–June 1960), 10–18.

Discusses 'trade union structure and organisation, the tangled pattern of wages, the role of the shop steward, the problem of automation, and the political attitudes of motor workers in the Midlands'.

9607 **Aris**, Stephen. 'Another day on the job: portrait of one man's work in an engineering plant.' *New Soc.*, 2 (11 October 1962), 11.

9608 **Alexander**, Kenneth John Wilson. 'Casual labour and labour casualties.' *Instn. Engrs. Shipbldrs. Scotl. Trans.*, CVIII (1964–65), 68–121.

9609 **Clarke**, J. F. 'Papers of Robert Allen (1883–1966) – Tyneside engineer.' *NE. Group Study Labour Hist. Bull.*, 1 (October 1967), 17–18.

Also loose chart.

9610 **Clarke**, J. F. 'The shipwrights.' *NE. Group Study Labour Hist. Bull.*, 1 (October 1967), 21–40.

9611 **Bugler**, Jeremy. 'The maintenance men.' *New Soc.*, XI, 299 (20 June 1968), 903–5.

9612 **Clarke**, J. F. 'Labour in shipbuilding on the North-East coast 1850–1900.' *NE. Group Study Labour Hist. Bull.*, 2 (October 1968), 3–7. Charts.

A paper read at Rutherford College of Technology on 9 February 1968.

9613 **Slater**, Bryan. 'On the line.' Fraser, R. (ed.). *Work: twenty personal accounts*. Harmondsworth: Penguin, 1968. p. 95–105.

First published in *New Left Review*, 42 (March–April 1967), 56–62.

Account of a panel-beater on a line producing tractors.

9614 **Haas**, James M. 'The introduction of task work into the royal dockyards, 1775.' *J. Br. Studies*, VIII, 2 (May 1969), 44–68.

9615 **McGeown**, Patrick. 'Steelman.' Fraser, R. (ed.). *Work, volume 2: twenty personal accounts*. Harmondsworth: Penguin, 1969. p. 56–69.

First published in *New Left Review*, 45 (September–October 1967), 43–52.

9616 **Pomlet**, Jack. 'The toolmaker.' Fraser, R. (ed.). *Work, volume 2: twenty personal accounts*. Harmondsworth: Penguin, 1969. p. 21–40.

First published in *New Left Review*, 53 (January–February 1969), 68–81.

9617 **Taylor**, Mike. 'The machine-minder.' Fraser, R. (ed.). *Work, volume 2: twenty personal accounts*. Harmondsworth: Penguin, 1969. p. 87–107.

9618 **Ward**, R. A. H. 'A watchmaker's pocket book.' *Hist. Soc. Lanc. Chesh. Trans.*, CXXII (1970), 153–7.

Describes the pocket-book of Richard Wright, a Lancashire watchmaker. It 'contains accounts and other entries covering the years 1713–56, and supplies new information about the "out-work" system which centred on the London watch trade'.

'Extracted and abridged from R. A. H. Ward, *Watchmaking in Liverpool before 1730*, unpublished B. Phil. extended essay (Liverpool University, 1970).'

See also: 8248; 9157; 9170; 10,596; 10,605; 11,046; 11,079; 11,092; 11,123; 11,126; 12,380.

iii. *Textiles*

9619 **Brierley**, Benjamin. *Home memories, and recollections of a life*. Manchester: Heywood; London: Simpkin Marshall, 1886. viii, 99p.

9620 **Myles**, James. *Chapters in the life of a Dundee factory boy: an autobiography*. Dundee: Kidd; Edinburgh: Menzies, 1887. iv, 76p.

9621 **Firth**, J. B. 'Weavers of Bradford, their work and wages.' *Econ. J.*, II, 7 (September 1892), 543–9.

Discusses evidence given before the Royal Commission on Labour.

9622 **Holder**, H. L. 'The weavers of Bradford, their work and wages.' *Econ. J.*, III, 12 (December 1893), 715–19.

Continues further from Firth, J. B. 'The weavers of Bradford...' *Econ. J.*, II, 7 (September 1892.)

9623 **Departmental Committee Appointed to Inquire into the Conditions of Work in Wool-sorting and other Kindred Trades.** *Report*. London: H.M.S.O., 1897. (C. 8506.)

9624 **Rose**, Frank Herbert. *Boggart Mill: a legend of the old factory days*. Manchester, 1907. 19p.

9625 **Committee of Inquiry into the Conditions of Employment in the Linen and other Making-up Trades of the North of Ireland.** *Report and evidence*. London: H.M.S.O., 1912. xxviii, 191p. (Cd. 6509.)

Chairman: Sir Ernest F. G. Hatch.

9626 **Taylor**, George. *The hand loom weavers in the Stockport area, 1784–94*. 1922. (M.A. thesis, University of Manchester.)

9627 **Wood**, George Henry. 'An examination of some statistics relating to the wool textile industry.' *R. Statist. Soc. J.*, XC, 2 (1927), 272–320.

Discussion, p. 320–8.

'Read before the Royal Statistical Society, February 15, 1927.'

9628 **Palmer**, Gladys L. 'Trade custom in the Lancashire cotton industry.' *J. Polit. Econ.*, XXXVI, 3 (June 1928), 391–8.

9629 **Nelson**, Evelyn Gibson. 'The putting-out system in the English framework-knitting industry.' *J. Econ. Bus. Hist.*, II, 3 (May 1930), 467–94.

9630 **Jordan**, W. M. *The silk industry in London, 1760–1830, with special reference to the condition of the wage-earners and the policy of the Spitalfields Acts*. 1930–31. (M.A. thesis, University of London.)

9631 **Whittaker**, James. *I, James Whittaker*. London: Rich and Cowan, 1934. 327p.

An autobiography.

9632 **Jewkes**, John and **Gray**, Edward Mayall. *Wages and labour in the Lancashire cotton spinning industry*. Manchester: Manchester U.P., 1935. xiv, 222p. (Publications of the University of Manchester CCXLII.)

9633 **Ward**, Jim. 'The cotton operative.' Williams, H. (ed.). *Man and the machine*. London: Routledge, 1935. p. 99–111.

9634 **Baxter**, Peter. *Perth: its weavers and weaving and the Weaver Incorporation of Perth*. Perth: Hunter, 1936. 248p.

9635 **Collier**, Frances. 'Workers in a Lancashire factory at the beginning of the nineteenth century.' *Manchr. Sch.*, VII, 1 (1936), 50–4; 2 (1936), 126–31.

9636 **Ministry of Labour**. *Report by a Board of Inquiry into the wages and hours of work in the wool textile industry in Yorkshire (except wool combing)*. London: H.M.S.O., 1936. 44p.

9637 **Weekley**, C. M. 'The Spitalfields silk-weavers.' *Hug. Soc. Lond. Proc.*, XVIII, 4 (1947–52), 284–91.

9638 **Armstrong**, D. L. 'Social and economic conditions in the Belfast linen industry, 1850–1900.' *Irish Hist. Studies*, VII, 28 (September 1951), 235–69.

9639 **Higgens**, Clare W. 'The framework knitters of Derbyshire.' *Derby. Archaeol. Nat. Hist. Soc. J.*, LXXI (1951), 106–14.

9640 **Minchinton**, W. E. 'The petitions of the weavers and clothiers of Gloucestershire in 1756.' *Bris. Glouc. Archaeol. Soc. Trans.*, LXXIII (1954), 216–27.

9641 **Smelser**, Neil Joseph. *Social change in the Industrial Revolution: an application of theory to the Lancashire cotton industry, 1770–1840*. London: Routledge and Kegan Paul, 1959. xii, 440p. (International library of sociology and social reconstruction.)

9642 **Lindsay**, Jean. 'An early industrial community: the Evans cotton mill at Darley Abbey, Derbyshire, 1783–1810.' *Bus. Hist. Rev.*, XXXIV, 3 (Autumn 1960), 277–301.

p. 294–301. 'The workers'.

9643 **Mann**, J. de L. 'Clothiers and weavers in Wiltshire during the eighteenth century.' Pressnell, L. S. (ed.). *Studies in the Industrial Revolution*. London: U. of London, Athlone P., 1960. p. 66–96.

9644 **Bythell**, Duncan. 'The hand-loom weavers in the English cotton industry during the Industrial Revolution: some problems.' *Econ. Hist. Rev.*, 2nd ser., XVII, 2 (December 1964), 339–53.

9645 **Hilton**, George Woodman. 'The controversy concerning relief for the hand-loom weavers.' *Explor. Entrepren. Hist.*, 2nd ser., I, 2 (Winter 1964), 164–86.

9646 **Selley**, Walter Thomas. *A nineteenth century Lancashire weaver's family*. London: Oxford U.P., 1965. 32p. (People of the past.)

9647 **Bythell**, Duncan. *The handloom weavers in the English cotton industry during the Industrial Revolution*. 1967–68. (D.Phil. thesis, University of Oxford.)

9648 **Alexander**, Archibald Wilson and **York**, M. P. *The handloom weavers of Corby*. Corby: Corby Historical Society, 1968. 26p. (Research bulletin 1.)

9649 **Brigg**, Mary. 'Life in East Lancashire, 1856–60: a newly discovered diary of John O'Neil (John Ward), weaver, of Clitheroe.' *Hist. Soc. Lanc. Chesh. Trans.*, CXX (1968), 87–133.

9650 **Chapman**, Stanley D. (ed.). 'Memoirs of two eighteenth-century framework knitters.' *Text. Hist.*, I, 1 (December 1968), 103–18. 'Documents and sources I.'

Biographical memoirs of Caleb Herring and William Felkin, written in the nineteenth century.

9651 **Johnson**, J. 'Cadishead fustian cutting.' *Eccles Distr. Hist. Soc. Trans.* (1968–69). 3p.

9652 **Bythell**, Duncan. *The handloom weavers: a study in the English cotton industry during the Industrial Revolution*. London: Cambridge U.P., 1969. xiv, 302p.

See also: 10,142; 10,662; 11,034; 11,037; 11,044; 11,050; 11,056; 11,082; 11,102; 11,127; 11,131; 12,075; 12,277; 12,349; 12,575; 14,756.

iv. *Leather and Fur*

9653 **Hogg**, Edith F. 'The fur-pullers of South London.' *Nineteenth Century*, XLII, 249 (November 1897), 734–43.

9654 **Bourat**, Marguerite. 'The fur trade.' Webb, S. and Freeman, A. (eds.). *Seasonal trades, by various writers*. London: Constable, 1912. p. 243–81.

See also: 11,063.

v. *Clothing and Footwear*

1. Clothing

See also Part Six, IV, A, 4, a.

9655 **Heather-Bigg**, Ada. 'Women and the glove trade.' *Nineteenth Century*, XXX, 178 (December 1891), 939–50.

9656 **Mundella**, Anthony John. 'The hosiery trade.' Co-operative Wholesale Societies. *Annual for 1893*. p. 479–506.

9657 **Hicks**, Frances. 'Dressmakers and tailoresses.' Galton, F. W. (ed.). *Workers on their industries*. London: Sonnenschein, 1895 [i.e. 1894]. p. 13–31.

The author was Secretary of the Women's Trade Association.

9658 **Black**, Clementina. 'London's tailoresses.' *Econ. J.*, XIV, 56 (December 1904), 555–67.

9659 **Drake**, Barbara. 'The West End tailoring trade.' Webb, S. and Freeman, A. (eds.). *Seasonal trades, by various writers*. London: Constable, 1912. p. 70–91.

9660 **Saunders**, Charlotte K. 'Millinery.' Webb, S. and Freeman, A. (eds.). *Seasonal trades, by various writers*. London: Constable, 1912. p. 210–42.

9661 **Northern Ireland**. Ministry of Labour. *Report of the Committee of Enquiry in the retail bespoke tailoring trade in Northern Ireland*. Belfast: H.M.S.O., 1923. 28p. (Cmd. 21.)

On '(a) Dilution of labour, (b) Employment of day's wage men, and (c) Employment of apprentices.'

9662 **Dobbs**, Sealey Patrick. 'Sweating in the clothing industry.' *Economica*, VII, 19 (March 1927), 74–90.

9663 **Dobbs**, Sealey Patrick. *The clothing workers of Great Britain*. London: Routledge, 1928. xiv, 216p. (Studies in economics and political science 96.)

9664 **Dony**, J. G. *The history of the straw-hat and straw-plaiting industries of Great Britain to 1914, with special reference to the social conditions of the workers engaged in them*. 1941. (Ph.D. thesis, University of London.)

9665 **Hartley**, Marie and **Ingilby**, Joan. *The old hand-knitters of the Dales; with an introduction to the early history of knitting*. Clapham, Lancaster: Dalesman Publishing Co., 1951.

9666 **Newman**, Peter K. 'The early London clothing trades.' *Oxf. Econ. Pap.*, n.s. IV, 3 (October 1952), 243–51.

See also: 8279; 9048.

2. Footwear

9667 **Calver**, Constance. 'The boot and shoe trade.' Webb, S. and Freeman, A. (eds.). *Seasonal trades, by various writers*. London: Constable, 1912. p. 282–311.

9668 **Dare**, M. Paul. 'Medieval shoemakers and tanners of Leicester, Northampton, and Nottingham: a sidelight on the history of footwear crafts in the Midlands as revealed by municipal and occupation records 1196–1670.' *Assd. Archit. Soc. Rep. Pap.*, XXXIX (1928), 141–77.

9669 **Hatley**, Victor Arthur. 'Monsters in Campbell Square: the early history of two industrial premises in Northampton.' *Northamps. Past Pres.*, IV, 1 (1966), 51–9.
See also: 9048; 11,072; 11,116.

vi. *Bricks, Pottery, Glass, and Cement*

9670 **Hoare**, Edward Newenham. 'George Smith.' *Notable workers in humble life.* London: Nelson, 1887. p. 184–219.
Fought to improve conditions in brickyards and on canal boats.
9671 **Thomas**, S. J. 'Pottery.' Galton, F. W. (ed.). *Workers on their industries.* London: Sonnenschein, 1895 [i.e. 1894]. p. 186–200.
The author was Secretary of the Amalgamated Society of Pottery Moulders and Finishers, London.
9672 **Owen**, Harold. *The Staffordshire potter; with a chapter on the dangerous processes in the potting industry by the Duchess of Sutherland.* London: Grant Richards, 1901. viii, 357p.
Facsimile reprint. Bath: Kingsmead Bookshop, 1970. (Kingsmead reprints.)
9673 *When I was a child, by an old potter.* London: Methuen, 1903. xv, 258p.
'With an introduction by R. S. Watson.'
9674 **Clarke**, William Patrick. *Europe's flint glass industry.* Toledo: Kraus and Schreiber, 1921. viii, 84p.
The author was President of the American Flint Glass Workers' Union.
9675 **Ministry of Works**. Committee on Amenities in the Brick Industry. *Report.* London: H.M.S.O., 1947. 13p.
Chairman: A. W. Garrett.
See also: 8284–5; 11,036; 11,038–9; 11,043; 11,047; 11,049; 11,051; 11,121; 11,130; 12,249–50; 12,391; 12,520.

vii. *Timber and Furniture*

9676 **Crooks**, W. 'Cask-making.' Galton, F. W. (ed.). *Workers on their industries.* London: Sonnenschein, 1895 [i.e. 1894]. p. 115–26.
9677 **Crossfield**, Henry. 'Wood engraving.' Galton, F. W. (ed.). *Workers on their industries.* London: Sonnenschein, 1895 [i.e. 1894]. p. 67–80.
9678 **Rose**, Walter. *The village carpenter.* Cambridge: Cambridge U.P., 1937. xxi, 146p.
9679 **Levinson**, Maurice. *The trouble with yesterday.* London: P. Davies, 1946. 193p.
An autobiography.
9680 **Eltringham**, G. J. *The mediaeval carpenter and worker in wood.* 1951–52. (M.A. thesis, University of Sheffield.)
9681 **Cohen**, Max. *What nobody told the foreman.* London: Spalding and Levy, 1953. v, 218p.
The autobiography of a woodworker.
See also: 8286; 9048.

viii. *Paper, Printing, and Publishing*

9682 **Webb**, Sidney and **Linnett**, Amy. 'Women compositors.' *Econ. Rev.*, II, 1 (January 1892), 42–9.
9683 **Rogers**, Frederick. 'The art of bookbinding.' Galton, F. W. (ed.). *Workers on their industries.* London: Sonnenschein, 1895 [i.e. 1894]. p. 127–52.
The author was President of the Vellum Binders' Trade Society.
9684 **Wilson**, Fred. 'Journalism as a profession.' *Westm. Rev.*, CXLVI, 4 (October 1896), 427–36.
'A rejoinder', by W. N. Shansfield (December 1896), 686–8.
9685 **Katin**, Louis. 'The worker's point of view. XX. The change from hand to machine-composing.' *Hum. Factor*, VIII, 11 (November 1934), 416–19.
9686 **Propert**, E. J. *An economic survey of the printing industry in Bristol.* 1934. (M.A. thesis, University of Bristol.)
Chap. III. 'Industrial conditions and relations.'
9687 **Howe**, Ellic. *From craft to industry: aspects of the London printing trade, 1700–1900.* London: North-Western Polytechnic Department of Printing, 1946. 15p.
An address.
9688 **Howe**, Ellic (ed.). *The London compositor: documents relating to wages, working conditions, and customs of the London printing trade, 1785–1900.* London: Bibliographical Society, 1947. 528p.
9689 **Cannon**, I. C. *The social situation of the skilled worker: a study of the compositor in London.* 1961. (Ph.D. thesis, University of London.)
9690 **Doyle**, Robert. 'The print jungle.' Fraser, R. (ed.). *Work: twenty personal accounts.* Harmondsworth: Penguin, 1968. p. 22–33.
First published in *New Left Review*, 40 (November–December 1966), 3–9, and reprinted in Blackburn, R. and Cockburn, A. (eds.). *The incompatibles: trade union militancy and the consensus.* Harmondsworth: Penguin in association with *New Left Review*, 1967. p. 103–12.
9691 **Freeman**, Ronald. 'Producing the news.' *Work: twenty personal accounts.* Harmondsworth: Penguin, 1968. p. 64–77.
First published in *New Left Review*, 32 (July–August 1965), 32–9.
'. . . a journalist's account of an international news agency's factory-like routine.'
9692 **G.**, G. 'Work: the publisher.' *New Left Rev.*, 49 (May–June 1968), 59–64.
Personal account.
See also: 9170; 11,128; 12,279.

ix. *Other Manufacturing*

9693 **Oakeshott**, Grace M. 'Artificial flower-making: an account of the trade, and a plea for municipal training.' *Econ. J.*, XIII, 49 (March 1903), 123–31.

9694 **Viala**, R. 'Labour conditions in the diamond cutting industry.' *Int. Labour Rev.*, LXVI, 4 (October 1952), 354–78.

See also: 9048; 10,615; 11,042; 11,052; 11,054; 11,057; 12,312.

d. CONSTRUCTION

9695 **Barrett**, Daniel William. *Life and work among the navvies.* London: Wells Gardner, 1880. xv, 157p.
Second edition.
Third edition. London: Society for Promoting Christian Knowledge, 1883. xvi, 162p.

9696 **Garnett**, Elizabeth. *Our navvies: a dozen years ago and to-day.* London: Hodder and Stoughton, 1885. vi, 303p.

9697 **Ainslie**, J. *Reminiscences of half a century of plumbers and plumbing.* Edinburgh, 1892.

9698 **Taylor**, H. R. 'Bricklayers.' Galton, F. W. (ed.). *Workers on their industries.* London: Sonnenschein, 1895 [i.e. 1894]. p. 175–85.
The author was Secretary to the Central Committee of the Operative Bricklayers' Society.

9699 **A Working Man**. *The reminiscences of a stone-mason.* London: Murray, 1908. viii, 260p.

9700 **MacGill**, Patrick. *Gleanings from a navvy's scrap book.* 1910.
Second edition. 1911.

9701 **Webb**, Augustus D. 'The building trade.' Webb, S. and Freeman, A. (eds.). *Seasonal trades by various writers.* London: Constable, 1912. p. 312–93.

9702 **MacGill**, Patrick. *Children of the dead end: the autobiography of a navvy.* London: H. Jenkins, 1914. xi, 305p.

9703 **Railway News.** 'The railway navvy.' *Jubilee of the Railway News, 1864–1914.* London: *Railway News*, 1914. p. 26–8.

9704 **Ministry of Labour**. *Report of a Court of Inquiry concerning steel houses.* London: H.M.S.O., 1925. 19p. (Cmd. 2392.)
Chairman: Lord Bradbury.

9705 **Hobbs**, J. Walter. 'The travelling masons and cathedral builders.' *Ars. Quat. Coron.*, XL (1928), 140–57.
Discussion, p. 157–66.

9706 **Gibson**, John. 'The worker's point of view. XI. Re-organization in the building industry.' *Hum. Factor*, VII, 1 (January 1933), 24–6.
Reprinted in *The workers' point of view: a symposium.* London: Woolf, 1933. p. 114–22.

9707 **Knoop**, Douglas and **Jones**, Gwilym Peredur. *The mediaeval mason: an economic history of English stone-building in the later middle ages and early modern times.* Manchester: U. of Manchester, 1933. xii, 294p. (Economic history series 8.)

9708 **Knoop**, Douglas and **Jones**, Gwilym Peredur. *The London mason in the seventeenth century.* Manchester: Manchester U.P.; London: Quatuor Coronati Lodge, No. 2076, 1935. 92p.
'Issued in advance of "Ars Quatuor Coronatorum", vol. XLVIII, part i.'

9709 **Knoop**, Douglas and **Jones**, Gwilym Peredur. 'The impressment of masons for Windsor Castle, 1360–1363.' *Econ. Hist.*, III, 12 (February 1937), 350–61.

9710 **Knoop**, Douglas and **Jones**, Gwilym Peredur. 'The impressment of masons in the middle ages.' *Econ. Hist. Rev.*, VIII, 1 (November 1937), 57–67.

9711 **Knoop**, Douglas and **Jones**, Gwilym Peredur. *The sixteenth century mason.* London: Quatuor Coronati Lodge, 1937. 20p.
'Issued in advance of "Ars Quatuor Coronatorum", vol. L, part iii, 1937.'

9712 **Hilton**, Jack. 'The plasterer's life.' Common, J. (ed.). *Seven shifts.* London: Secker and Warburg, 1938. p. 3–49.
Personal account.

9713 **Knoop**, Douglas and **Jones**, Gwilym Peredur. 'London bridge and its builders: a study of the municipal employment of masons, mainly in the fifteenth century.' *Ars Quat. Coron.*, XLVII (1938), 5–44.

9714 **Knoop**, Douglas and **Jones**, Gwilym Peredur. *The Scottish mason; and, The mason word.* Manchester: Manchester U.P., 1939. x, 114p.
Two studies.

9715 **Skelton**, Thomas. *Clay under clover.* London: Gollancz, 1949. 219p.
Autobiographical reminiscences of a navvy.

9716 **Ball**, Frederick Cecil. *Tressell of Mugsborough.* London: Lawrence and Wishart, 1951. 223p.

9717 **Lloyd**, Roger Bradshaigh. *Railwaymen's gallery.* London: Allen and Unwin, 1953. 116p.
p. 32–45. 'The old English navvy.'

9718 **Mills**, John Orme. 'The tower builders' future.' *New Soc.*, 9 (29 November 1962), 23–5.

9719 **Mitchell**, William Reginald. *The long drag: a story of men under stress during the construction of the Settle–Carlisle line.* Settle: the author, 1962. [32]p.

9720 **Patmore**, J. A. 'A navvy gang of 1851.' *J. Transp. Hist.*, v, 3 (May 1962), 182–9.

9721 **Coleman**, Terry. 'The men who dug England's railways.' *New Soc.*, VI, 151 (19 August 1965), 10–13.
Based on the author's *The railway navvies.*

9722 **Coleman**, Terry. *The railway navvies: a history of the men who made the railways*. London: Hutchinson, 1965. 224p.
First edition published with revisions. Harmondsworth: Penguin, 1968. 256p. (Pelican books.)

9723 **Coleman**, Terry. 'The elite inside the tunnel.' *New Soc.*, VII, 171 (6 January 1966), 6–8.

9724 **Mac Amhlaigh**, Donall. *An Irish navvy: the diary of an exile*. London: Routledge and Kegan Paul, 1966. ix, 182p.
Translated from the Irish by Valentin Iremonger.
This translation originally published 1964.

9725 **Ministry of Technology**. Building Research Station. *Building operatives' work*. London: H.M.S.O., 1966. 2v.
Vol. I. *Report*. By R. E. Jeanes.
Vol. II. *Appendices*.

9726 **Barr**, John. 'Rebuilding an industry?' *New Soc.*, IX, 233 (16 March 1967), 387–8. (Society at work.)

9727 **Gagg**, Max. 'The subby bricklayer.' Fraser, R. (ed.). *Work, volume 2: twenty personal accounts*. Harmondsworth: Penguin, 1969. p. 130–46.

9728 **Mitchell**, Jack. *Robert Tressell and the 'Ragged trousered philanthropists'*. London: Lawrence and Wishart, 1969. xiv, 200p.

9729 **Gretton**, John. 'The lump.' *New Soc.*, XV, 390 (19 March 1970), 469–70.

See also: 8315–17; 8319–20; 8331–2; 9157; 9170; 10,593; 10,886; 11,086; 11,109; 12,382.

e. TRANSPORT AND COMMUNICATIONS

i. *Railways and London Transport*

9730 **Harkness**, Margaret E. 'Railway labour.' *Nineteenth Century*, XII, 69 (November 1882), 721–32.

9731 **Frith**, Henry. *The biography of a locomotive engineer*. London: Cassell, 1891. 254p.

9732 **Amalgamated Society of Railway Servants**. *Return of the hours of duty and rates of wages paid to railway servants on the principal lines in Great Britain, in operation May 1884 and May 1891*. London, 1892.

9733 **Gordon**, William John. *Everyday life on the railroad*. London: Leisure Hour, 1892. 192p. (Leisure Hour library. New series.)
Another edition. 1897. 192p.
Second edition, revised. 1898. 192p.

9734 **Pennington**, Myles. *Railways and other ways, being reminiscences of canal and railway life during a period of sixty-seven years, with characteristic sketches of canal and railway men, early tram roads and railways*. Toronto: Williamson, 1896. 407, 48p.
Canada and Great Britain.

9735 **Snowden**, Keighley. *The railway nerve: a day in the life of an engine driver*. London, 1906. 14p.
Reprinted from the *Pall Mall Magazine*.
'With 12 special photographs.'

9736 **Langdon**, Roger. *The life of Roger Langdon, told by himself; with additions by his daughter Ellen*. London: Elliot Stock, 1909. 104p.
R. Langdon was Station-master of Silverton, Great Western Railway, 1867–94.

9737 **Geddes**, E. C. *Education and advancement of the railway clerk: paper read before the York Railway Lecture & Debating Society, 4th October, 1910*. York, 1910. 22p.
E. C. Geddes was Chief Goods Manager, North Eastern Railway.

9738 *Statement of settlements regarding questions as to rates of wages and hours of labour of railway employees that have been effected under the scheme for conciliation and arbitration*. London: H.M.S.O., 1910. 78p.

9739 **Railway Clerks' Association**. *The life of the railway clerk: some interesting facts and figures*. London: the Association, 1911.
Fifth edition.

9740 **Ferguson**, James. *Experiences of a railway guard: thrilling stories of the rail*. Dundee: privately printed, 1913. 116p.
Second edition.

9741 **Kenney**, Rowland. *Men and rails*. London, Leipsic: Fisher Unwin, 1913. xiii, 263p.

9742 **Railway Clerks' Association**. *The future of the railway service: permanency or dismissal?* London: the Association, 1913.

9743 **Gattie**, Alfred Warwick. *The advantages of economic transport to railway employees*. London: New Transport Co., 1914. 27p.
Paper, South Eastern and Chatham Railway Research Association, 2 March 1914.

9744 **Railway News**. 'Conditions of railway service.' *Jubilee of the Railway News, 1864–1914*. London: *Railway News*, 1914. p. 177–83.

9745 **Williams**, Alfred. *Life in a railway factory*. London: Duckworth, 1915. xiii, 315p.
Facsimile reprint, with new introduction by Leonard Clark. Newton Abbot: David and Charles; New York: Kelley, 1969.

9746 **Browne**, K. J. Norman. *The Brown and other systems of railway discipline*. London: *Railway Gazette*, 1923. 67p.

9747 **Great Western Railway**. *Rates of pay and conditions of service of railway operating staff, 1907–1922*. London: Great Western Railway, 1923. 42p. (Great Western pamphlets 11.)

9748 **Young**, Robert. *Timothy Hackworth and the locomotive*. London: Locomotive Publishing Co., 1923. xxxii, 406p.
p. 293–311. The first engine drivers. Working conditions and methods.

9749 **Chappell**, Henry. *Life on the iron road*. London: John Lane, 1924. viii, 207p.

9750 *The life story of the railwaymen's friend, Miss Emma Saunders of Clifton; or, The lady with the basket*. Bristol, 1927. 31p.
'Compiled by her niece.'

9751 **James**, Samuel Thomas. *The railwayman: his work by night and day on the iron way.* London: Nelson, 1928. 317p.

9752 **Leigh**, Dell. *On the line.* Bungay: R. Clay, 1928. 199p.

Sketches of life on the London and North Eastern Railway.

9753 **Brown**, James Douglas, and others. *Railway labor survey.* New York: Social Science Research Council, Division of Industry and Trade, 1933. 153p.

Reproduced from typescript.

9754 **Stokes**, Arthur. *Fifty years on the railway: yarns by a Methodist signalman.* Birmingham: the author, 1936. 74p.

The author was with the Great Western Railway and worked Solihull box from 1892 to 1936.

9755 **McCulloch**, T. A. 'Working on the railway.' Common, J. (ed.). *Seven shifts.* London: Secker and Warburg, 1938. p. 249–71.

Personal account.

9756 **Earl**, L. A. *Speeding north with the 'Royal Scot': a day in the life of a locomotive man.* London: Oxford U.P., 1939. 160p.

'In collaboration with H. N. Greenleaf.'

9757 **Wrightson**, P. *Barnard Castle in war paint: a stationmaster's diary.* Barnard Castle: the author, 1945. 11p.

9758 **Bishop**, Fred C. *Queen Mary of the iron road.* London: Jarrolds, 1946. 150p.

The autobiography of an engine-driver.

As told to M. C. D. Wilson and A. S. L. Robinson.

9759 **Creswell**, A. J. *On the footplate.* Huddersfield: Quadrant Publications, 1947. 40p.

9760 **Lewis**, Richard Albert. 'Edwin Chadwick and the railway labourers.' *Econ. Hist. Rev.*, 2nd ser., III, 1 (1950), 107–18.

9761 **Kingsford**, P. W. 'The railway clerk in 1851.' *Transp. Sal. Staff J.*, XLVIII, 571 (September 1951), 386–8; 572 (October 1951), 423–5.

9762 **Kingsford**, P. W. *Railway labour, 1830–1870.* 1951. (Ph.D. thesis, University of London.)

9763 **Street**, James William. *I drove the Cheltenham Flyer.* London: Nicholson and Watson, 1951. 154p.

An autobiography.

9764 **McKillop**, Norman. *How I became an engine driver.* London: Nelson, 1953. ix, 116p.

Second edition. 1960.

Career on the London and North Eastern Railway.

9765 **Ransome-Wallis**, Patrick. *Men of the footplate.* London: Ian Allan, 1954. 96p.

Collected memoirs of Walter T. Harris, Percy Cox, Albert Young, Charles H. Simmons.

9766 **Ministry of Labour** and **Ministry of Transport**. *Interim report of the Committee of Enquiry to review the pay and conditions of employment of drivers and conductors of the London Transport Board's Road Services.* London: H.M.S.O., 1963.

Report. 1964. iii, 67p.

Chairman: E. H. Phelps Brown.

9767 **W.**, B. 'Work: guard underground.' *New Left Rev.*, 50 (July–August 1968), 105–12.

On work as a London Transport underground guard.

9768 **Wise**, Hope. 'The signalwoman.' Fraser, R. (ed.). *Work: twenty personal accounts.* Harmondsworth: Penguin, 1968. p. 115–23.

First published in *New Left Review*, 44 (July–August 1967), 46–51.

9769 **McKenna**, Frank (comp.). *A glossary of railwaymen's talk: a compendium of slang terms old and new used by railwaymen together with anecdotes of footplate life at Carlisle Kingmoor, Willesden Junction and Kentish Town; brief recollections of the railwaymen's hostel in Somers Town and the footplate strike of 1955; and a young man's experience of night life in Leicester Square and the Strand.* Oxford: Ruskin College History Workshop, 1970. x, 44p. (History Workshop pamphlets 1.)

See also: 56; 8344; 10,746; 10,770; 10,867; 10,877; 10,883; 11,053; 11,059; 11,067; 11,070–1; 11,074; 11,085; 11,090; 11,094; 11,120; 12,082; 12,113; 12,136; 12,443; 12,445–6; 12,449–52; 12,454; 12,456; 12,542; 12,559; 12,567; 12,574; 12,579; 12,585.

ii. *Road*

9770 **Crowest**, Frederick J. 'The London cabmen: an improvement scheme.' *Westm. Rev.*, CXXXVI, 5 (November 1891), 537–48.

9771 **Wilkins**, William Henry. 'Hansoms and their drivers.' *Nineteenth Century*, XXXIII, 193 (March 1893), 470–9.

9772 **Fox**, W. E. *Taximen and taxi-owners: a study of organisation, ownership, finances and working conditions in the London taxi trade.* London: Labour Research Department, 1935. 24p.

Advocates that taxi-drivers should join the Transport and General Workers' Union.

9773 **Ministry of Labour** and **Ministry of Transport**. *Report of the Committee on the regulation of wages and conditions of service in the road motor transport industry (goods).* London: H.M.S.O., 1937. iv, 56p. (Cmd. 5440.)

Chairman: Sir James B. Baillie.

Minutes of evidence. 1936–37. 10v.

Appendices. 1937.

Index to the evidence. 1937.

9774 **Hargreaves**, J. A. *Labour conditions in the road motor transport industry.* 1938. (B. Litt. thesis, University of Oxford.)

9775 **Katin**, Zelma. *'Clippie': the autobiography of a war time conductress.* London: Gifford, 1944. 124p.
'By Z. Katin in collaboration with Louis Katin.'

9776 **Smith**, George William Quick. *Lorry drivers' wages and conditions of employment: a practical guide which includes points on the law relating to employment, with a ready reckoner.* London: Iliffe, 1948. 74p.

9777 **Courtney**, Edith. *Fares please.* London: Hutchinson, 1957. 208p.

9778 **Bugler**, Jeremy. 'The lorry men.' *New Soc.*, VIII, 201 (4 August 1966), 181–4.

9779 **Jones**, J. W. 'Driving the bus.' Fraser, R. (ed.). *Work: twenty personal accounts.* Harmondsworth: Penguin, 1968. p. 205–18.

9780 **National Board for Prices and Incomes.** *Award relating to terms and conditions of employment in the Road Passenger Transport Department of Rochdale County Borough Council.* v, 17p. With correction. London: H.M.S.O., 1968. (Report 78. Cmnd. 3723.)

See also: 8352; 8355–7.

iii. *Sea*

9781 **Plimsoll**, Samuel. *Cattle ships, being the fifth chapter of Samuel Plimsoll's second appeal for our seamen.* London: Kegan Paul, 1890. 150p.

9782 **Hall**, Benjamin Tom. *Socialism and sailors.* London: Fabian Society, 1893. 15p. (Fabian tract 46.)

9783 **S.**, C. S. *Reminiscences of a midshipman's life, 1850–56.* London, 1893. 2v.

9784 **Departmental Committee on the Question of the Engagement and Discharge of British Seamen at Continental Ports Within the Home Trade Limits.** *Report.* London: H.M.S.O., 1897. (C. 8577.)
Minutes of evidence. 1897. (C. 8578.)

9785 **Admiralty.** Committee appointed to inquire into the Question of Navy Rations, Meal Hours, the Prices paid for 'Savings', and the Management of Canteens. *Report; with appendices.* London: H.M.S.O., 1901. 70p. (Cd. 782.)
Chairman: E. Rice.

9786 **Board of Trade.** Committee on Certain Questions affecting the Mercantile Marine. London: H.M.S.O., 1903.
Part I. *Report.* xiii p. (Cd. 1607.)
Part II. *Minutes of evidence.* (Cd. 1608.)
Part III. *Appendices.* (Cd. 1609.)
Chairman: F. J. Jeune.

9787 **Richards**, Ernest. *In a deep-water ship: a personal narrative of a year's voyage as apprentice in a British clipper ship.* London: A. Melrose, 1907. xi, 241p.

9788 **Reynolds**, Stephen. 'Ships *versus* men in the navy.' *Engl. Rev.*, XII, 46 (September 1912), 281–99.

9789 **Fayle**, Charles Ernest. *The war and the shipping industry.* London: Milford, 1927. xxiv, 472p. (Economic and social history of the world war. British series.)
Chapter XVI. 'Wages and conditions afloat.'

9790 **Jenkin**, Alfred Kenneth Hamilton. 'The Cornish seaman.' *Geogrl. Mag.*, II, 6 (April 1936), 421–40.

9791 **International Labour Office.** 'Organisation for seamen's welfare in Great Britain.' *Int. Labour Rev.*, XLIII, 4 (April 1941), 401–14.

9792 **Mortished**, R. J. P. 'Developments in welfare work for British seamen.' *Int. Labour Rev.*, L, 3 (September 1944), 316–34.

9793 **Jenks**, A. H. *Merchant Navy established service scheme.* 1952–53. (M.A. thesis, University of Liverpool.)

9794 **Masters**, David. *The Plimsoll mark.* London: Cassell, 1955. x, 278p.
A biography of Samuel Plimsoll.

9795 **McGirr**, P. O. M. *The British merchant seaman: aspects of his social setting, occupational hazards and the health and welfare services available to him.* 1955–56. (M.D. thesis, University of Sheffield.)

9796 **Gutman**, Herbert G. 'Documents on Negro seamen during the Reconstruction period.' *Labor Hist.*, VII, 3 (Fall 1966), 307–11.

9797 **Ministry of Labour.** *First report of the Court of Inquiry into certain matters concerning the shipping industry.* London: H.M.S.O., 1966. 18p. (Cmnd. 3025.)
Chairman: Lord Pearson.
Final report. 1967. xi, 130p. (Cmnd. 3211.)

9798 **Milsom**, C. H. *Guide to the merchant navy: entry, conditions, organisations.* Glasgow: Brown, Son and Ferguson, 1968. xiv, 264p.

See also: 8369; 10,718; 10,762; 10,873; 11,099; 11,118; 11,132; 12,071–2; 12,097–8; 12,100–1; 12,103; 12,118; 12,345; 14,077; 14,718.

iv. *Port and Inland Water*

9799 **Potter**, Beatrice. 'The dock life of East London.' *Nineteenth Century*, XXII, 128 (October 1887), 483–99.
Later incorporated in Booth's *Life and labour* . . . 1902. Poverty, vol. 4. chap. I.

9800 **Tillett**, Ben. *A dock labourer's bitter cry, by a docker.* London, 1887.

9801 **Select Committee on the Thames Watermen and Lightermen Bill.** *Special report, with the proceedings.* London: H.M.S.O., 1890. (H.C. 244.)

9802 **H.M. Consuls.** *Reports respecting the working of cargoes on Sundays in foreign ports.* London: H.M.S.O., 1890–1. (C. 6369, 6369-I.)
Part I. *Europe.*
Part II. *America.*

9803 **Booth**, Charles. '[Presidential address, session 1892–93.]' *R. Statist. Soc. J.*, LV, 4 (December 1892), 521–57.
On dock labour.

9804 **Llewellyn-Smith**, Hubert. 'Chapters in the history of London waterside labour. 1. Waterside porters.' *Econ. J.*, II, 8 (December 1892), 593–607.

9805 **Mann**, Tom. *The position of dockers and sailors in 1897, and the International Federation of Ship, Dock, and River Workers.* London, 1897. 14p. (Clarion pamphlets 18.)

9806 **Allen**, A. J. 'Dock labour in Ipswich.' *Econ. Rev.*, XII, 3 (July 1902), 289–98.

9807 **Rathbone**, Eleanor F. 'Report on the results of a special inquiry into the conditions of labour at the Liverpool docks.' *Lpool. Econ. Statist. Soc. Trans.* (1903–4), 15–57.

9808 **Williams**, Richard. 'The Liverpool docks problem.' *Lpool. Econ. Statist. Soc. Trans.* (1910/11 – 1911/12). 44p.
Paginated separately at the end of the volume. Also folding charts. The author was Divisional Officer of Labour Exchanges and Unemployment Insurance, North-Western Division.
Also published separately, 1912.

9809 **Williams**, Richard. 'The organisation of the casual labour market.' *Manchr. Statist. Soc. Trans.* (1911–12), 37–60.

9810 **Williams**, Richard. 'Liverpool docks scheme.' *Progress Civic Soc. Ind.*, VII, 4 (October 1912), 235–47.

9811 **Williams**, Richard. *Map of the British Isles shewing complications arising from present methods of organisation among dockers, waterside workers . . .* London, [1912?]. 8p.

9812 **Williams**, Richard. *Procedure necessitated by the Liverpool and Birkenhead dock labour scheme.* [Liverpool?], 1912. 20p.

9813 **Williams**, Richard. 'The first year's working of the Liverpool Docks Scheme.' *Lpool. Econ. Statist. Soc. Trans.* (1913–14), 1–192.
With folding charts.
Also published separately, 1914.

9814 **Woolf**, Leonard Sidney. 'An experiment in decasualisation: the Liverpool docks scheme.' *Econ. J.*, XXIV, 94 (June 1914), 314–19.

9815 **Ministry of Labour**. Committee on Casual Labour in the Port of London.
Chairman: Mr Justice Roche.
Two interim reports were presented by the Committee in March and July 1919, but neither was published.

9816 **Ministry of Labour**. Court of Inquiry Concerning Transport Workers' Wages and Conditions of Employment of Dock Labour.
Vol. 1. *Report and minutes of evidence.* London: H.M.S.O., 1920. xxii, 500p. (Cmd. 936.)
Vol. 2. *Appendices, documents, and indexes.* 1920. xx, 194p. (Cmd. 937.)
Chairman: Lord Shaw of Dunfermline.

9817 **Shadwell**, Arthur. *The problem of dock labour.* London: Longmans, 1920. 30p.
Reprinted from *The Times*.

9818 **Lascelles**, Edward Charles Ponsonby and **Bullock**, S. S. *Dock labour and decasualisation.* London: King, 1924. xi, 201p. (Studies in economics and political science 74.)

9819 **Ministry of Labour**. Committee on Port Labour. *Port labour inquiry: report.* London: H.M.S.O., 1931. 92p.
Chairman: Donald Maclean.

9820 **Whyte**, William Hamilton. 'Decasualisation of dock labour at the port of Bristol.' *Economica*, XII, 37 (August 1932), 357–64.

9821 **Whyte**, William Hamilton. *Decasualization of dock labour, with special reference to the Port of Bristol.* Bristol: Arrowsmith, 1934. 132p. (University of Bristol studies 2.)

9822 **Ministry of Labour**. Board of Inquiry on Port Labour in Aberdeen and Glasgow. *Report.* London: H.M.S.O., 1937. 63p.
Chairman: J. M. Irvine.

9823 **Ministry of War Transport**. *Dock labour in Merseyside, Manchester and Preston areas: explanatory memorandum.* London: H.M.S.O., 1941.

9824 **Ministry of War Transport**. *Dock labour in the Port of Glasgow: explanatory memorandum.* London: H.M.S.O., 1941.

9825 **Ministry of War Transport**. *Dock labour in the Port of Greenock: explanatory memorandum.* London: H.M.S.O., 1941.

9826 **Ministry of Labour and National Service**. *Port transport industry: report of inquiry held under para. I (4) of the Schedule to the Dock Workers (Regulation of Employment) Act, 1946.* London: H.M.S.O., 1946. 16p.
By Sir John Forster.

9827 **Ministry of Labour and National Service**. *Port transport industry: report of inquiry held under paragraph 5 of the Schedule to the Dock Workers (Regulation of Employment) Act, 1946.* London: H.M.S.O., 1947. 36p.
By John Cameron.

9828 **University of Liverpool.** Department of Social Science. *The dock worker: an analysis of conditions of employment in the Port of Manchester.* Liverpool: U.P. of Liverpool, 1954. 277p. (Social research series.)

9829 **Ministry of Labour and National Service.** *Port transport industry: report of a Committee appointed on July 27, 1955, to inquire into the operation of the Dock Workers (Regulation of Employment) Scheme, 1947.* London: H.M.S.O., 1956. iii, 63p. (Cmd. 9813.)

9830 **Simey**, Thomas Spensley. 'The problem of social change – the docks industry: a case study.' *Sociol. Rev.*, n.s., IV, 2 (December 1956), 157–66.

9831 **National Dock Labour Board.** *Welfare among dock workers: a review published under the authority of the National Board.* London, 1960. 47p. (Educational booklet 4.)

9832 **Ministry of Labour.** *Port transport industry: objections made to the Draft Dock Workers (Regulation of Employment) (Amendment) Order, 1961. Report by the Rt. Hon. The Lord Forster of Harraby, K.B.E., Q.C., of Inquiry held under Paragraph 5 of the Schedule to the Dock Workers (Regulation of Employment) Act, 1946.* London: H.M.S.O., 1961.

9833 **Jensen**, Vernon Horton. 'Hiring arrangements and the rule-making process in certain European ports and in the port of New York.' Industrial Relations Research Association. *Proceedings of the fifteenth annual meeting, 1962.* p. 16–25.
Discussion, p. 49–54.

9834 **Jensen**, Vernon Horton. *Hiring of dock workers and employment practices in the ports of New York, Liverpool, London, Rotterdam, and Marseilles.* Cambridge, Mass.: Harvard U.P., 1964. xiii, 317p. (Wertheim publications in industrial relations.)

9835 **Ministry of Labour.** *First report of the Committee of Inquiry into certain matters concerning the port transport industry.* London: H.M.S.O., 1964. (Cmnd. 2523.)
Final report. 1965. (Cmnd. 2734.)
Chairman: Lord Devlin.

9836 **Ellenger**, V. C. 'The engine that drives the system.' *New Soc.*, v, 130 (25 March 1965), 10–13.

9837 **Ministry of Labour.** *Port transport industry: report of inquiry held under Paragraph 5 of the Schedule of the Dock Workers (Regulation of Employment) Act 1946.* London: H.M.S.O., 1966. 36p.
Chairman: G. Honeyman.

9838 **Ministry of Labour** and **Ministry of Transport.** *Report by Mr. A. J. Scamp of an enquiry into the employment of coal trimmers in the ports of Blyth, Dunston, North Shields, South Shields, Seaham Harbour and Sunderland.* London: H.M.S.O., 1967. 20p.

9839 **Ministry of Labour.** *Reduction to 65 years of the compulsory retirement age of dock workers: report by a Committee appointed by the Minister of Labour.* London: H.M.S.O., 1968. 12p.

9840 **Green**, George. 'A dock labourer in the 1880's: a Liverpool docker's experiences.' *Hist. Today*, XIX, 6 (June 1969), 424–6.
An essay by John Green, written between 1887 and 1890, with an introduction by his great-grandson, George Green.

9841 **Nicholson**, B. 'The first year of Devlin: a review of the docks.' *Trade Un. Regist.* (1969), 211–22.

9842 **Lewis**, William John. *Ceaseless vigil: my lonely years in the lighthouse service.* London: Harrap, 1970. 128p.

9843 **Oram**, Robert Bruce. *The dockers' tragedy.* London: Hutchinson, 1970. xi, 196p.

See also: 9734; 11,114; 11,122; 11,124; 12,355.

v. *Postal Services and Telecommunications*

9844 **Clery**, William Edward. *Civil servitude: an appeal from the Postmaster-General to his masters – the public.* London: The Post Office, 1895. viii, 94p.
Fifth edition.

9845 **Postmen's Federation.** *The Inter-Departmental Committee on Post Office Establishments, being a verbatim report of the evidence given before Lord Tweedmouth and Committee by the representatives of the Postmen's Federation.* London, Glasgow: A. Malcolm, 1896. 656p.
'Published by authority of the Postmen's Federation for private sale.'

9846 **Select Committee on Post Office Servants.** *Report, proceedings.* London: H.M.S.O., 1907. 194p. (H.C. 266.)
Minutes of evidence. 2v. (H.C. 380.)
Chairman: C. E. H. Hobhouse.

9847 **Departmental Committee on Post Office Factories.** *Report.* London: H.M.S.O., 1912. ii, 42p. (Cd. 6027.)
Chairman: C. Norton.

9848 **Select Committee on Post Office Servants (Wages and Conditions of Employment).** *Report appendices.* London: H.M.S.O., 1913. iv, 290p. (H.C. 268.)
Proceedings. 1913.
Minutes of evidence. 2v. 1913. (H.C. 268.)
Appendices. 1913.
Index. 1914.
Chairman: R. D. Holt.

9849 **Committee Appointed to Examine the Issues Arising out of the Report of the Select Committee on Post Office Servants,** 1912–13. *First report.* London: H.M.S.O., 1915. 14p. (Cd. 7995.)
Second report. 1916. (Cd. 8244.)
Chairman: G. S. Gibb.

9850 **Martinuzzi**, L. S. *The history of employment in the British Post Office.* 1952. (B. Litt. thesis, University of Oxford.)

9851 **Kerrigan**, Peter. *What next for Britain's postworkers?* London: Newsletter, 1959. 12p. (Newsletter pamphlets.)

f. GAS, ELECTRICITY, AND WATER

9852 **Popplewell**, Frank. 'The gas industry.' Webb, S. and Freeman, A. (eds.). *Seasonal trades, by various writers.* London: Constable, 1912. p. 148–209.

9853 **Mannion**, Herbert. 'I was in a gas works.' Common, J. (ed.). *Seven shifts.* London: Secker and Warburg, 1938. p. 147–77.
Personal account.

See also: 8328–9; 8614; 10,655; 10,902.

g. DISTRIBUTIVE TRADES

See also Part Seven, V, C.

9854 **Brown**, J. *My experiences as a commercial traveller.* London, 1885. 80p.

9855 **Fender**, C. R. 'A few facts about the "living-in-system".' *Econ. Rev.*, IV, 2 (April 1894), 246–53.

Includes a list of the 97 rules laid down by one London store for its assistants.

9856 **Johnson**, William. *Shop life and its reform.* London: Fabian Society, 1897. 15p. (Fabian tract 80.)

9857 **A Manager.** 'The drapery trade.' *Econ. Rev.*, VII, 1 (January 1897), 42–56.

9858 **Bondfield**, Margaret Grace. 'Conditions under which shop assistants work.' *Econ. J.*, IX, 34 (June 1899), 277–86.

9859 **Hughes**, Henry. *Glimpses of my life 'on the road': extracts from the notebook of a commercial traveller.* London: W. Bensted and Forwood, 1902. 118p.

9860 **Jones**, T. Spencer. *The moral side of living-in.* 1906.

9861 **Hallsworth**, *Sir* Joseph and **Davies**, Rhys John. *The working life of shop assistants: a study of conditions of labour in the distributive trades.* Manchester: the authors, 1910. viii, 198p.

9862 **Select Committee on Shop Assistants.**

Vol. I. *Report and proceedings.* London: H.M.S.O., 1931. iv, 110p. (H.C. 148.)

Vol. II. *Appendices.* 1931. iv, 399p.

Vol. III. *Minutes of evidence.* 1931. iv, 544p.

Special report. 1930. viii, 237p. (H.C. 176.)

Chairman: Charles Buxton.

9863 **Blumenfeld**, Simon. 'A stall in the market.' Common, J. (ed.). *Seven shifts.* London: Secker and Warburg, 1938. p. 181–204.

Personal account.

9864 **Ministry of Labour.** *Retail distributive trades conference. England and Wales. Wages, hours and conditions in the retail distributive trades. Report.* London: H.M.S.O., 1939. 8p.

9865 **Miller**, Glenn W. 'Wages and hours in consumers' co-operatives in Great Britain and the United States.' *Q. J. Econ.*, LV, 2 (February 1941), 294–305.

9866 **Bondfield**, Margaret Grace. 'Welfare in distribution and domestic work.' *Fortnightly*, n.s., CLVII, 938 (February 1945), 112–19.

9867 **Hughes**, John Dennis and **Pollard**, Sidney. 'Labour in British retail trade, 1950.' *Yorks. Bull. Econ. Soc. Res.*, VIII, 2 (November 1956), 109–29.

9868 **Ministry of Labour and National Service.** *Cold store undertakings: report by Hugh Lloyd-Williams, C.B.E., D.S.O., M.C., of enquiry held under paragraphs 1 (4) and 5 of the Schedule to the Dock Workers (Regulation of Employment) Act, 1946.* London: H.M.S.O., 1959.

9869 **Stern**, Walter Marcel. *The porters of London.* London: Longmans, Green, 1960. xvi, 346p.

9870 **Smith**, Raymond. *Sea-coal for London: history of the coal factors in the London market.* London: Longmans, 1961. xiv, 388p.

Foreword by Col. Sir Ralph S. Clarke, Chairman of the Coal Factors' Society.

9871 **Clarke**, William. *The hair pedlar in Devon.* St Peter Port: Toucan P., 1968. 12p.

Notes by J. Stevens Cox.

'First appeared in *The companion to a cigar*, 1850.'

9872 **Powley**, Robert. 'Selling for a living.' Fraser, R. (ed.). *Work: twenty personal accounts.* Harmondsworth: Penguin, 1968. p. 124–39.

First published in *New Left Review*, 33 (September–October 1965), 70–9.

Personal account of a salesman.

9873 **Department of Employment and Productivity** and **Ministry of Transport.** *Report by Sir Jack Scamp, DL, JP, of an inquiry into employment on the loading of coal at Immingham and South Killingholme.* London: H.M.S.O., 1970. 16p.

See also: 8407; 10,182; 10,629; 10,633; 12,131; 12,315–16; 12,319; 12,325; 12,339; 12,344; 12,358; 12,364; 12,366; 12,388–9; 12,395; 12,400; 12,407; 12,410; 12,436; 12,443; 12,445–6; 12,449–12,452; 12,454; 12,456.

h. INSURANCE, BANKING, AND FINANCE

9874 **Minty**, Leonard Le Marchant. 'Before the coming of the manager: the life of the banker's clerk a century ago.' *Inst. Bankers J.*, XLI, 3 (March 1920), 89–95.

9875 **Harris**, George H. *Life assurance salesmanship: a personal adventure.* London: Stone and Cox, 1935. v, 119p.

9876 **Harris**, H. R. *Conditions of employment in English banking: recruitment, training, promotion, staff–management relations.* 1959. (M.A. thesis, University of Nottingham.)

9877 **Smart**, P. E. 'Bankers in fiction.' *Inst. Bankers J.*, LXXXII, 1 (February 1961), 27–34; 2 (April 1961), 87–94; 4 (August 1961), 289–96; LXXXIII, 1 (February 1962), 17–23; 2 (April 1962), 101–8; 4 (August 1962), 241–8; 5 (October 1962), 306–13; 6 (December 1962), 367–74.

9878 **A Special Correspondent.** 'Bank staffs – the next thirty years.' *Banker*, CXIII, 450 (August 1963), 548–53.

9879 **Fry**, Richard. 'The accountant.' Fraser, R. (ed.). *Work: twenty personal accounts.* Harmondsworth: Penguin, 1968. p. 257–70.

9880 **National Board for Prices and Incomes.** *Agreements relating to terms and conditions of employment of staff employed by the Prudential Assurance Company Ltd., and the Pearl Assurance Company Ltd.* London: H.M.S.O., 1968. (Report 74. Cmnd. 3674.)

9881 **Pickerill**, John Bernard. *Wealth of interest: banking as a career.* Reading: Educational Explorers, 1968. 115p. (My life and work series.)

9882 **Hopper**, William. 'The stockbroker.' Fraser, R. (ed.). *Work, volume 2: twenty personal accounts.* Harmondsworth: Penguin, 1969. p. 272–86.

i. PROFESSIONAL AND SCIENTIFIC SERVICES

i. *General White-Collar and Professional*

9883 *Clerks and shop assistants of both sexes: their grievances, position and advancement.* Gateshead: Robert Kelly, 1890. 18p.

9884 **Hutchins**, B. L. 'An enquiry into the salaries and hours of work of typists and shorthand writers.' *Econ. J.*, XVI, 63 (September 1906), 445–9.
Results of an enquiry held by the Association of Typists and Shorthand Writers.

9885 **Cope**, Edward A. *Clerks: their rights and obligations; a complete guide for the clerical worker.* London: Pitman, 1910. vii, 152p. (Pitman's library of practical information.)

9886 **Robinson**, H. M. and **Anderson**, Adelaide Mary. 'Hours and conditions of work in typewriting offices.' *Factories and workshops: annual report.* London: H.M.S.O., 1911. (Cd. 5693.)

9887 **Home Office**. *Report of the Committee appointed to consider the conditions of clerical and commercial employment with a view to advising what steps should be taken, by the employment of women, or otherwise, to replace men withdrawn for service in the military forces.* London: H.M.S.O., 1915. 12p. (Cd. 8110.)
Chairman: Cecil Harmsworth.

9888 **MacDonald**, William. *The intellectual worker and his work.* London: Cape, 1923. 351p.

9889 **Klingender**, Francis Donald. *The condition of clerical labour in Britain.* London: Lawrence, 1935. xxii, 117p.

9890 **Lee**, Stella. *True to type: the autobiography of a cog.* London: Joseph, 1959. 192p.
On the author's experiences of commercial life.

9891 **Kelly**, J. *An investigation into salaries, conditions and duties of first line management in the West of Scotland.* Glasgow: Scottish College of Commerce, Department of Management Studies, 1962.

9892 **Hutchinson**, J. M. *A study of the economic status, trade union affiliations, working conditions and occupational training of clerical workers in Great Britain.* 1963–64. (M.A. (Econ.) thesis, University of Durham.)

9893 **G.**, J. A. 'Work: at the office, 2.' *New Left Rev.*, 38 (July–August 1966), 73–8.
Personal account of a clerk.

9894 **Heathcote**, F. E. 'Are offices fit to work in?' *New Soc.*, VIII, 206 (8 September 1966), 367–8.
'Society at work.'

9895 **Callow**, Philip. 'The clerk.' Fraser, R. (ed.). *Work: twenty personal accounts.* Harmondsworth: Penguin, 1968. p. 55–63.
First published in *New Left Review*, 38 (July–August 1966), 69–73.

9896 **Neville**, Jill. 'Writing the ads.' Fraser, R. (ed.). *Work: twenty personal accounts.* Harmondsworth: Penguin, 1968. p. 156–66.
First published in *New Left Review*, 36 (March–April 1966), 59–64.

9897 **Andemann**, R. 'Managing science.' Fraser, R. (ed.). *Work, volume 2: twenty personal accounts.* Harmondsworth: Penguin, 1969. p. 178–94.

See also: 30; 49; 6091; 9058; 10,139; 10,170; 10,177; 10,180; 12,173.

ii. *Educational Services*

9898 **Ferguson**, John. 'A few observations on the present position of the Irish National School teachers, as regards salaries, pensions, and residences.' *Statist. Soc. Inq. Soc. Ir. J.*, VIII, 5 (August 1882), 359–63.

9899 **Hinder**, Eustace Francis. *The schoolmaster in the gutter, or, a plea for the middle class.* London: E. Stock, 1883. 30p.

9900 **Findlay**, Joseph John. *Teaching as a career for university men.* London: Rivingtons, 1889 [i.e. 1888]. 42p.

9901 **Departmental Committee Appointed to Consider the Desirability of a Fixed Age for the Compulsory Retirement of Professors Serving under the Crown.** *Report, with the evidence.* London: H.M.S.O., 1895. (C. 7889.)

9902 **Kynnersley**, Edmund Mackenzie Sneyd. *H.M.I.: some passages in the life of one of H.M. Inspectors of Schools.* London: Macmillan, 1908. viii, 358p.

9903 **Incorporated Association of Assistant Masters in Secondary Schools.** *Report of an inquiry into the conditions of service of teachers in English and foreign secondary schools.* London: Bell, 1910. xi, 179p.

9904 **Vice-Regal Committee on the Conditions of Service and Remuneration of Teachers in Intermediate Schools, and on the Distribution of Grants from Public Funds for Intermediate Education in Ireland.** *Report.* Dublin: H.M.S.O., 1919. (Cmd. 66.)

9905 **Cleeve**, Marion. *Fire kindleth fire: the professional autobiography of Marion Cleeve, ex-headmistress.* London, Glasgow: Blackie, 1930. xiv, 212p.

9906 **Kynnersley**, Edmund Mackenzie Sneyd. *H.M.I.'s notebook: or recreations of an inspector of schools.* London: Lane, 1930. vii, 280p.

9907 **Chegwidden**, Cuthbert. *Some aspects of the social position of the professional teacher at various periods in the history of education.* 1933. (M.A. thesis, University of Wales, Aberystwyth.)

9908 **Northern Ireland.** *Conditions of service of teachers: final report of the Committee appointed by the Ministry of Education to consider the salaries and conditions of service of teachers.* Belfast: H.M.S.O., 1947. 20p. (Cmd. 243.)

9909 **Tropp**, Asher. 'Factors affecting the status of the school teacher in England and Wales.' International Sociological Association. *Transactions of the Second World Congress of Sociology*, II, 1954. p. 166–74.

9910 **Collison**, Peter. 'Research note: career contingencies of English university teachers.' *Br. J. Sociol.*, XIII, 3 (September 1962), 286–93.

9911 **Scottish Education Department**. Committee on Conditions of Service of Teachers in Further Education in Scotland. *Report*. Edinburgh: H.M.S.O., 1965. 52p.
Chairman: A. G. Rodger.

9912 **Glossop**, J. A. *A study of certain aspects of teaching as a career*. 1965–66. (M.A. thesis, University of London.)

9913 **R.**, H. 'Work: primary school.' *New Left Rev.*, 35 (January–February 1966), 43–8.
Personal account of a primary school teacher.

9914 **S.**, T. 'Work: secondary modern.' *New Left Rev.*, 35 (January–February 1966), 48–55.
Personal account of a secondary modern school teacher.

9915 **Holland**, T. W. H. *Some problems of headmasters*. London: F. L. Allan Memorial Trust, 1969. 50p.

9916 **Turvey**, S. G. 'The schoolteacher.' Fraser, R. (ed.). *Work, volume 2: twenty personal accounts*. Harmondsworth: Penguin, 1969. p. 215–27.

See also: 6090; 6104; 8470–2; 10,752–3; 10,756; 10,760; 10,773–4; 10,780–1; 10,784; 10,815; 10,824–5; 10,828; 10,830; 10,834; 10,839; 10,841; 10,850; 10,855; 11,077–8; 12,094; 12,099; 12,112; 12,221; 12,241.

iii. *Medical Services*

9917 **Hassall**, C. H. *Medical work and medical workers; or healing and healers*. Farnworth: R. Cooke, 1890–

9918 **Holmes**, Jessie. *The private nurse: reminiscences of eight years' private nursing*. London: Fisher Unwin, 1899. 113p.

9919 **A Hospital Nurse**. *'Memories', by a hospital nurse*. Bristol: Wright, 1910. viii, 168p.

9920 **Labour Party**. *Draft report on the nursing profession prepared by a Sub-Committee of the Standing Joint Committee of Industrial Women's Organisations and the Labour Party's Advisory Committee on Public Health, and to be submitted for consultation to a conference of nursing and kindred organisations to be held in the Caxton Hall, Westminster, London, on Friday, January 28th, 1927, at 10 a.m.* London: Labour Party, [1927?]. 36p.

9921 **Royal College of Nursing**. *Memorandum relating to conditions in the nursing profession, for submission to the Inter-Departmental Committee on the Nursing Services*. London: the College, 1938. 43p.

9922 **Carter**, Gladys Beaumont. *A new deal for nurses*. London: Gollancz, 1939. 319p.

9923 **Dickens**, Monica. *One pair of feet*. London: Joseph, 1942. 208p.
Experiences as a probationer nurse in the Second World War.
Abridged in *Daily Express condensed books*. Vol. 2. 1955. p. 447–565.

9924 **Bevington**, Sheila Macfarlane. *Nursing life and discipline: a study based on over five hundred interviews*. London: Lewis, 1943. xii, 89p.

9925 **Northern Ireland**. *Report of the General Nurses Committee for Northern Ireland, appointed by the Minister of Health and Local Government: salaries and conditions of service of nurses and mid-wives in hospitals, other than mental hospitals*. Belfast: H.M.S.O., 1947. 44p. (Cmd. 244.)

9926 **Northern Ireland**. *Report of the Hospital Domestic and General Staffs Committee for Northern Ireland, appointed by the Minister of Health and Local Government: salaries and conditions of service of domestic staff in hospitals*. Belfast: H.M.S.O., 1947. 16p. (Cmd. 247.)

9927 **Northern Ireland**. *Report of the Mental Nurses Committee for Northern Ireland, appointed by the Minister of Health and Local Government: salaries and conditions of service of nurses in mental hospitals and mental deficiency institutions*. Belfast: H.M.S.O., 1947. 40p. (Cmd. 245.)

9928 **Northern Ireland**. *Second report of the General Nurses Committee for Northern Ireland, appointed by the Minister of Health and Local Government. Part I. Salaries and conditions of service of district nurses, domiciliary midwives and public health nurses. Part II. Further recommendations regarding the salaries and conditions of service of nurses and midwives in hospitals, other than mental hospitals*. Belfast: H.M.S.O., 1947. 35p. (Cmd. 252.)

9929 **Northern Ireland**. *Second report of the Mental Nurses Committee for Northern Ireland, appointed by the Minister of Health and Local Government: further recommendations on the salaries and conditions of service of nurses in mental hospitals*. Belfast: H.M.S.O., 1948. 16p. (Cmd. 256.)

9930 **Martindale**, Louisa, the younger. *A woman surgeon*. London: Gollancz, 1951. 253p.
An autobiography.

9931 **Ministry of Health**. Standing Nursing Advisory Committee. *Report on the position of the enrolled assistant nurse within the National Health Service*. London: H.M.S.O., 1953.
Chairman: Miss K. G. Douglas.

9932 **Department of Health for Scotland**. Scottish Health Services Council. *The state enrolled assistant nurse in the National Health Service: report by the Standing Nursing and Midwifery Advisory Committee*. Edinburgh: H.M.S.O., 1955. 12p.
Chairman: Miss E. G. Manners.

9933 **Manchester Regional Hospital Board** and **University of Manchester**. Joint Committee. *The work of the mental nurse: a survey*. Manchester: Manchester U.P., 1955. x, 154p.

9934 **Cardew**, Bruce. *The future of the family doctor*. London: Fabian Society, 1959. 29p. (Research series 208.)

9935 **Collier**, Cecily. *Domestic work in hospitals*. London: Macmillan, 1962. 17p. (*Nursing Times* investigates series.)
Reprinted from *Nursing Times*, March 9th–30th, 1962.

9936 **Deal**, Paula. *Factory nurse*. London: Booker, 1963. 160p.

9937 **Bridger**, H., **Miller**, E. J. and **O'Dwyer**, J. J. *The doctor and sister in industry: a study of change*. London: Macmillan (Journals) Ltd., 1964. 34p.
Reprinted from *Occupational Health*, xv (1963).

9938 **Ferris**, Paul. *The doctors*. London: Gollancz, 1965. 228p.
Revised edition. Harmondsworth: Penguin, 1967. 267p. (Pelican books.)

9939 **Central Health Services Council.** Standing Dental Advisory Committee. Sub-Committee on Dental Technicians. *Dental technicians: report*. London: H.M.S.O., 1968. 16p.

9940 **Raison**, Matthew. 'House-surgeon.' Fraser, R. (ed.). *Work: twenty personal accounts*. Harmondsworth: Penguin, 1968. p. 78–94.

9941 **Williams**, William Owen (comp.). *A study of general practitioners' work load in South Wales, 1965–1966: a survey by 68 doctors*. London: Royal College of General Practitioners, 1970. 19p. (Reports from general practice 12.)

See also: 10,794; 10,807; 11,107; 12,078.

iv. *Other*

9942 **Spray**, Henry. *Lawyers' clerks, real and fictitious: an address*. London: E. Cox, 1894. 15p.

9943 **Lord Chancellor's County Court Staff Committee.** *Report*. London: H.M.S.O., 1920. 31p. (Cmd. 1049.)
Chairman: Rigby Swift.

9944 **Association of Assistant Librarians.** *Report on the hours, salaries, training and conditions of service in British municipal libraries, 1931*. London: the Association, 1932. 39p.
Edited by F. Seymour Smith.

9945 **Departmental Committee on Justices' Clerks.** *Report*. London: H.M.S.O., 1944. 70p. (Cmd. 6507.)
Chairman: Lord Roche.

9946 **National Council of Social Service.** *Salaries and conditions of work of social workers: a report by a joint committee of the British Federation of Social Workers and the National Council of Social Service*. London, 1947. 85p.
Chairman: T. S. Simey.

9947 **Davis**, Peter and **Goddard**, Julie (eds.). *Library staffs, today and tomorrow: proceedings of a course of lectures held during April and May 1963*. London: Association of Assistant Librarians, Greater London Division, 1966. 54p.
Contents: 'Professional and non-professional duties', by K. A. Mallaher; 'Recruitment', by D. D. Haslam; 'In-service training', by J. H. Jones; 'Professional education', by R. Stokes; 'Welfare', by C. W. H. Currie; 'Management', by A. G. D. Collis; 'Summary', by W. S. H. Ashmore.

9948 **B.**, H. 'Work: the laboratory technician.' *New Left Rev.*, 46 (November–December 1967), 55–62.
Personal account.

9949 **L.**, J. 'Work: the railway technician.' *New Left Rev.*, 44 (July–August 1967), 53–8.
Personal account.

9950 **Chancery**, David. 'The solicitor.' Fraser, R. (ed.). *Work: twenty personal accounts*. Harmondsworth: Penguin, 1968. p. 167–84.

9951 **Chesterton**, Keith. 'The programmer.' Fraser, R. (ed.). *Work: twenty personal accounts*. Harmondsworth: Penguin, 1968. p. 232–41.

9952 **Forsyth**, Clint. 'The technician.' Fraser, R. (ed.). *Work: twenty personal accounts*. Harmondsworth: Penguin, 1968. p. 219–31.
First published in *New Left Review*, 41 (January–February 1967), 70–7.

9953 **Jordan**, Peter J. (ed.). *Working conditions in libraries: a survey*. London: Association of Assistant Librarians, 1968. 71p.
Contents: 'Recruitment', by J. Hoyle and G. Crowther; 'Library school', by D. Jones; 'Education', by M. J. Ramsden; 'Training', by P. M. St. J. Brewer; 'Salaries', by F. M. Featherstone; 'Welfare', by F. A. Milligan; 'Working conditions', by G. Crowther.
Results of a survey.

9954 **Playfair**, John. 'The research scientist.' Fraser, R. (ed.). *Work: twenty personal accounts*. Harmondsworth: Penguin, 1968. p. 106–14.

9955 **S.**, W. G. 'Work: the scenic artist.' *New Left Rev.*, 47 (January–February 1968), 52–60.
Personal account.

9956 **Dracup**, Catherine. 'The secretary.' Fraser, R. (ed.). *Work, volume 2: twenty personal accounts*. Harmondsworth: Penguin, 1969. p. 228–39.

9957 **Gotch**, Christopher. 'The architect.' Fraser, R. (ed.). *Work, volume 2: twenty personal accounts*. Harmondsworth: Penguin, 1969. p. 147–64.

9958 **Rodes**, Jon. 'The town planner.' Fraser, R. (ed.). *Work, volume 2: twenty personal accounts*. Harmondsworth: Penguin, 1969. p. 165–77.

9959 **Vince**, Norma. 'Child-care officer.' Fraser, R. (ed.). *Work, volume 2: twenty personal accounts*. Harmondsworth: Penguin, 1969. p. 195–214.

9960 **Wollen**, Douglas. 'Methodist minister.' Fraser, R. (ed.). *Work, volume 2: twenty personal accounts*. Harmondsworth: Penguin, 1969. p. 240–56.

See also: 6124; 8582; 9684; 12,079–80; 12,085; 12,096; 12,194.

j. MISCELLANEOUS SERVICES

i. *Domestic Service*

9961 **James**, *Mrs* A. G. F. Eliot. *Our servants: their duties to us and ours to them.* London: Ward, Lock, 1883. vii, 180p.

9962 **Clifford**, Mary. *Our little servant girls; addressed to their mistresses.* London: Hamilton, Adams, 1884. 24p.

9963 **White**, Henry. *The record of my life.* Cheltenham: published by the author, 1889. 184p.

9964 **Benson**, M. 'In defence of domestic service: a reply.' *Nineteenth Century*, XXVIII, 164 (October 1890), 616–26.

A reply to the article by E. W. Darwin.

9965 **Darwin**, Ellen W. 'Domestic service.' *Nineteenth Century*, XXVIII, 162 (August 1890), 286–96.

9966 **Bulley**, Agnes Amy. 'Domestic service: a social study.' *Westm. Rev.*, CXXXV, 2 (February 1891), 177–86.

9967 **Robinson**, John. 'A butler's view of men-service.' *Nineteenth Century*, XXXI, 184 (June 1892), 925–33.

9968 **Black**, Clementina. 'The dislike to domestic service.' *Nineteenth Century*, XXXIII, 193 (March 1893), 454–6.

9969 **Layard**, George Somes. 'The doom of the domestic cook.' *Nineteenth Century*, XXXIII, 192 (February 1893), 309–19.

9970 **Lewis**, Elizabeth Alicia M. 'A reformation of domestic service.' *Nineteenth Century*, XXXIII, 191 (January 1893), 127–38.

9971 **A Servant**. *The servant's question: how to improve the conditions of domestic service, by a servant.* London, 1894. 17p.

9972 **Rayner**, John. *Employers and their female domestics: their respective rights and responsibilities.* Exmouth: the author, 1895. 84p.

9973 **Mann**, T. G. *The duties of an experienced servant.* London: Stafford Northcote Employment Bureau, 1897. 33p.

9974 **Buckton**, Catherine M. *Comfort and cleanliness: the servant and mistress question.* London: Longmans, 1898. 96p.

9975 **Cowan**, Isabella. *The high estate of service.* Edinburgh: David Douglas, 1898. viii, 29p.

Second edition.

9976 **Veritas**, Amara (*pseud.*) *The servant problem: an attempt at its solution by an experienced mistress.* London: Simpkin, Marshall, 1899. 207p.

9977 **International Congress of Women**, London, 1899. 'Scientific treatment of domestic service.' *Transactions. Vol. VI. Women in industrial life.* London: T. Fisher Unwin, 1900. p. 86–111.

Contributions for Great Britain by Clementina Black, Mrs William Stead, Mrs Walter Ward, Jane Hume Clapperton.

9978 **Wakeman**, Annie. *The autobiography of a charwoman, as chronicled by Annie Wakeman.* London: Macqueen, 1900. x, 304p.

Another edition. London: Routledge, 1906. 123p.

9979 **Salmon**, Lucy Maynard. *Domestic service. 2nd ed. with an additional chapter on domestic service in Europe.* New York and London: Macmillan, 1901. xxvii, 338p.

First edition. New York: Macmillan, 1897.

9980 **Webb**, Catherine. 'An unpopular industry: the results of an inquiry instituted by the Women's Industrial Council into the causes of the unpopularity of domestic service.' *Nineteenth Century*, LIII, 316 (June 1903), 989–1001.

9981 **Butler**, Christina Violet. *Domestic service: an enquiry by the Women's Industrial Council; report.* London: Bell, 1916. 148p.

With a supplementary chapter by Lady Willoughby de Broke.

9982 **S.**, M. *Domestic service, by an old servant.* London: Constable, 1917. 111p.

9983 **Johnson**, William A. *The servant problem: can it be solved? Why not? By an old-established domestic employment agent.* Leyton: E. R. Alexander, 1922. 33p.

9984 **Lanceley**, William. *From hall-boy to house-steward.* London: Arnold, 1925. 190p.

9985 **Marshall**, Dorothy. 'The domestic servants of the eighteenth century.' *Economica*, IX, 25 (April 1929), 15–40.

9986 *Memoirs of Martha: an autobiography elicited by her mistress.* London: A. Barker, 1933. xx, 331p.

9987 **Dickens**, Monica. *One pair of hands.* London: Joseph, 1939. 286p.

9988 **Myers**, Charles Samuel. 'The servant problem.' *Occup. Psychol.*, XIII, 2 (April 1939), 77–88.

9989 **Fremlin**, Celia. *The seven chars of Chelsea.* London: Methuen, 1940. vii, 178p.

9990 **Thomas**, Albert. *Wait and see.* London: Joseph, 1944. 186p.

Autobiography of a domestic servant.

The author was butler to the Principal, Brasenose College, Oxford.

9991 **Stuart**, Dorothy Margaret. *The English abigail.* London: Macmillan, 1946. viii, 220p.

9992 **Hecht**, Joseph Jean. *The domestic servant class in eighteenth century England.* 1948. (Ph.D. dissertation, Harvard University.)

Published London: Routledge and Kegan Paul, 1956. xii, 240p.

9993 **Marshall**, Dorothy. *The English domestic servant in history.* London: G. Philip for the Historical Association, 1949. 29p. (Historical Association publications. General series G 13.)

Reprinted. Historical Association, 1968.

9994 **Plant**, Marjorie. 'The servant problem in eighteenth century Scotland.' *Scott. Hist. Rev.*, XXIX, 2 (October 1950), 143–57.

9995 **Elliott**, Dorothy M. 'The status of domestic work in the United Kingdom with special reference to the National Institute of Houseworkers.' *Int. Labour Rev.*, LXIII, 2 (February 1951), 125–48.

9996 **Rennie**, Jean. *Every other Sunday: the autobiography of a kitchenmaid.* London: Barker, 1955. 231p.

9997 **Tayler**, William. *Diary of William Tayler, footman, 1837.* London: Strathmore Bookshop for the St Marylebone Society, 1962. 63p. (St Marylebone Society. Publications 7.)

Edited by Dorothy Wise, with notes by Ann Cox-Johnson.

9998 **Turner**, Ernest Sackville. *What the butler saw: two hundred and fifty years of the servant problem.* London: Joseph, 1962. 304p.

9999 **Cox-Johnson**, Ann. 'A gentleman's servant's journal.' *Hist. Today*, XIII, 2 (February 1963), 102–7.

Journal of William Tayler, 1807–92.

10,000 **King**, Ernest. *The green baize door; as told to Richard Viner.* London: W. Kimber, 1963. 160p.

Autobiography of a steward.

10,001 **Powell**, Margaret. *Below stairs.* London: P. Davies, 1968. 177p.

Another edition. London: Pan Books, 1970. 159p.

10,002 **Powell**, Margaret. *The treasure upstairs.* London: P. Davies, 1970. 184p.

See also: 12,083; 12,102; 12,126; 14,103.

ii. *Entertainment*

10,003 **Sear,** H. G. *The composer must live!* London: Workers' Music Association, 1944. 47p. (Keynote series 5.)

10,004 **Political and Economic Planning.** 'The football industry.' *Planning*, XVII, 324 (26 February 1951), 157–84; 325 (5 March 1951), 185–208.

Part 2 includes discussion of players' conditions, wages and contracts, etc.

10,005 **Allera**, S. V. and **Nobay**, A. R. 'English professional football.' *Planning*, XXXII, 496 (June 1966), 77–160.

10,006 **Ackers**, Krii. 'The croupiere.' Fraser, R. (ed.). *Work: twenty personal accounts.* Harmondsworth: Penguin, 1968. p. 242–56.

10,007 **Department of Education and Science.** *Report of the Committee on Football.* London: H.M.S.O., 1968. vii, 135p.

Chairman: D. N. Chester.

10,008 **Football Association** and **Football League**. *The professional footballer.* London: the Association and the League, 1968. 49p.

10,009 **O'Casey**, Ronan. 'The actor.' Fraser, R. (ed.). *Work, volume 2: twenty personal accounts.* Harmondsworth: Penguin, 1969. p. 257–71.

See also: 12,500; 12,514; 14,240.

iii. *Other*

10,010 **Inspectors of Factories.** *Report...as to hours of work and dangerous machinery in laundries, and as to their sanitary condition.* London: H.M.S.O., 1894. (C. 7418.)

10,011 **Christian Social Union.** Committee on Laundries. *Report.* [1897?] [4]p.

10,012 **Fabian Society.** *Life in the laundry.* London: Fabian Society, 1902. 15p. (Fabian tract 112.)

Special edition with a supplement 'From the laundry-man's point of view'. 1903. 19p.

10,013 **Joint Committee on the Employment of Barmaids.** *Women as barmaids.* London: King, 1905. iv, 58p.

10,014 **Drake**, Barbara. 'The waiter.' Webb, S. and Freeman, A. (eds.). *Seasonal trades, by various writers.* London: Constable, 1912. p. 92–106.

10,015 **Ministry of Labour.** *Results of an investigation into the rates of wages, the hours of employment and the degree of industrial organization in the light refreshment and dining room (non-licensed) branch of the catering trade: report, appendices.* London: H.M.S.O., 1926. 69p.

10,016 **Ministry of Labour.** *Remuneration, hours of employment, etc. in the catering trade. Report, appendices.* London: H.M.S.O., 1930. xxxii, 207p.

10,017 **Barclay**, Thomas Patrick. *Memoirs and medleys: the autobiography of a bottle-washer.* Leicester: Backus, 1934. xi, 142p.

Edited by James K. Kelly.

Reminiscences of Ruskin, William Morris, Bernard Shaw and early Fabians.

10,018 **St George**, Vivian de Gurr. *St. George of Piccadilly.* London: Werner Laurie, 1935. 174p.

Reminiscences of a shoeblack.

10,019 **Benson**, Charles. *This way, sir! The autobiography of a waiter.* London: P. R. Macmillan, 1959. 117p.

10,020 **Nightingale**, Benedict. 'The catering caper.' *New Soc.*, X, 257 (31 August 1967), 281–3.

10,021 **Morel**, Julian John. *At your service: a career in the hotel and catering industry.* Reading: Educational Explorers, 1968. 119p. (My life and work series.)

10,022 **Nairn**, Tom. 'The nightwatchman.' Fraser, R. (ed.). *Work: twenty personal accounts.* Harmondsworth: Penguin, 1968. p. 34–54.

First published in *New Left Review*, 34 (November–December 1965), 37–49.

See also: 8609–10; 10,129; 10,720; 11,105; 11,779; 12,289; 12,303; 12,448.

k. PUBLIC ADMINISTRATION

i. *General*

10,023 **New Statesman**. 'State and municipal enterprise.' *New States.*, v, 109 (8 May 1915), Supplement. 32p.
Part III of the Draft Report of the Committee of the Fabian Research Department on the Control of Industry.
Mainly by B. and S. Webb.
Chapter IV. 'The position of the employees in the state and municipal service.' p. 18–24.

10,024 **Shanks**, Michael J. (ed.). *The lessons of public enterprise*. London: Cape, 1963. 314p.
'A Fabian Society study.'
Chapter IV. 'Wages.'
Chapter VI. 'Labour relations.'
Chapter IX. 'Staffing and recruitment.'

See also: 8614; 10,745; 10,749; 10,757; 10,759; 10,761; 10,764; 10,772; 10,796; 10,817; 10,826; 10,831; 10,837; 10,842; 12,190; 12,493; 12,541.

ii. *National Government*

10,025 **King**, G. Swinburn. *Stories and anecdotes of the Civil Service*. London: Griffith, Farran, etc., 1884. 127p.

10,026 **Departmental Committee on the Position of the Civil Assistants Employed in the Ordnance Survey**. *Report*. London: H.M.S.O., 1892. (C. 6692.)

10,027 **Departmental Committee on the Conditions of Employment of the Present Members of the Engrossing Staff in the General Register of Sasines**. Edinburgh: H.M.S.O., 1913.
Vol. I. *Report*. 19p. (Cd. 6789.)
Vol. II. *Minutes of evidence, appendices*. 43p. (Cd. 6790.)
Chairman: G. M. Paul.

10,028 **Civil Service National Whitley Council.** *Report of the Joint Committee on the organisation, etc. of the Civil Service*. London: H.M.S.O., 1921. 12p.
Chairman: Sir Malcolm G. Ramsay.

10,029 **Committee on the Conditions of Service of Women Staff Employed in the Navy, Army and Air Force Canteens.** *Report*. London: H.M.S.O., 1931. (Cmd. 3769.)

10,030 **Royal Commission on the Civil Service**, 1929–31.
Report. London: H.M.S.O., 1931. (Cmd. 3909.)
Minutes of evidence. 1929–32.
Chairman: L. Tomlin.

10,031 **Robson**, William Alexander (ed.). *The British civil servant*. London: Allen and Unwin, 1937. 254p.

10,032 **Civil Service National Whitley Council.** Joint General Purposes Committee. Sub-Committee on Promotions Procedure. *Report*. London: H.M.S.O., 1938.

10,033 **Cruickshank**, Charles G. 'Dead-pays in the Elizabethan army.' *Engl. Hist. Rev.*, LIII, 209 (January 1938), 93–7.
'Pay continued in the name of a soldier . . . actually dead or discharged, and appropriated by the officer.'

10,034 **Harris**, Richard William. *Not so humdrum: the autobiography of a civil servant*. London: John Lane, 1939. 271p.

10,035 **Treasury**. *Working conditions in the Civil Service: report by a study group appointed by H.M. Treasury*. London: H.M.S.O., 1947 [i.e. 1948]. 164p. and appendices.

10,036 **Royal Commission on the Civil Service**, 1953–55. *Report*. London: H.M.S.O., 1955. viii, 239p. (Cmd. 9613.)
Chairman: Sir Raymond Edward Priestley.
Introductory factual memorandum on the Civil Service. 1954. vi, 184p.
Supplement . . . Medical and legal staffs. 1954. ii, 13p.
Minutes of evidence. 1954–5.
Appendix I to minutes of evidence: first selection of supplementary statements from witnesses. 1954. 57p.
Appendix II to minutes of evidence: second selection of supplementary statements from witnesses. 1955. 89p.

10,037 **Mackenzie**, W. J. M. 'The Royal Commission on the Civil Service.' *Polit. Q.*, XXVII, 2 (April–June 1956), 129–40.

10,038 **Prives**, Moshe Zalman. *Career in civil service: Canada, Great Britain and the United States*. 1957–8. (Dissertation, McGill University.)

10,039 **Field**, Ronald. *The Civil Service & local government as a career*. London: Batsford, 1964. 136p.

10,040 **Treasury**. *Report of a committee appointed to review the organisation of the scientific Civil Service*. London: H.M.S.O., 1965. 28p.

10,041 **Civil Service Commission**. *Lawyers in the government service*. London: the Commission, 1967. 33p.

10,042 **Committee on the Civil Service**. *Report on the Civil Service*. London: H.M.S.O., 1968. 4v.
Chairman: Lord Fulton.

10,043 **House of Commons**. Select Committee on Customs (Outdoor Officers at the Outports). *Reports from Committees and Commissions on customs officers, civil establishments and Civil Service copyists, with minutes of evidence, appendices and an index, 1881–87*. Shannon: Irish U.P., 1969. 794p. (British parliamentary papers, government, civil service 10.)
Chairman: Sir Matthew Wright Ridley.
Facsimile reprint of first editions, 1881–7.

10,044 **Newens**, Stan. 'Member of Parliament.' Fraser, R. (ed.). *Work, volume 2: twenty personal accounts*. Harmondsworth: Penguin, 1969. p. 311–29.
First published in *New Left Review*, 51 (September–October 1968), 88–94.

See also: 8649; 10,765; 10,771; 10,788; 10,795; 10,844; 10,863; 11,100; 12,176; 12,188; 12,219.

iii. *Local Government*

10,045 **Bywater**, J. A. 'The regulation of wages and conditions of employment of local authority employees.' *Publ. Adm.*, XXIII, 2 (Summer 1945), 92–9.

10,046 **Keast**, Horace. *The local government service: a commentary on the scheme of conditions of service of the National Joint Council*. Leigh-on-Sea: Thames Bank Publishing Co., 1948. 94p.

10,047 **Royal Institute of Public Administration.** *The elements of local government establishment work*. London, 1951. 119p.

10,048 **Warren**, John Herbert. *The local government service*. London: Allen and Unwin, 1952. 222p. (New town and county hall series.)

10,049 **Kinch**, M. B. 'Qualified administrative staff in the local government service; their deployment and opportunities.' *Publ. Adm.*, XLIII, 2 (Summer 1965), 173–90.

10,050 **Bugler**, Jeremy. 'On the dust.' *New Soc.*, XI, 278 (25 January 1968), 113–14.

10,051 **Home Office.** *Workloads in Children's Departments*. London: H.M.S.O., 1969. 82p. (Home Office research studies 1.)
By Eleanor Gray.

See also: 10,775; 10,786; 10,791; 10,799; 10,808; 10,832; 10,865; 11,113; 12,291.

iv. *Police, Prison Officers, and Firemen*

10,052 **Committee of Inquiry on the Royal Irish Constabulary.** *Report*. Dublin: H.M.S.O., 1902. 33p. (Cd. 1087.)
Minutes of evidence. vii, 246p. (Cd. 1094.)
Chairman: Sir Howard Vincent.

10,053 **Committee of Inquiry on the Royal Irish Constabulary and the Dublin Metropolitan Police.** *Report*. London: H.M.S.O., 1914. 36p. (Cd. 7421.)
Minutes of evidence, etc. v, 386p. (Cd. 7637.)
Chairman: Sir David Harrel.

10,054 **Committee Appointed to Enquire into the Conditions of Service and Superannuation of the Warder Classes in Prisons and Criminal Lunatic Asylums.** *Report*. London: H.M.S.O., 1919. 7p. (Cmd. 313.)
Chairman: Sir Thomas Henry Elliott.

10,055 **Committee on the Police Service of England, Wales and Scotland.** *Report*. London: H.M.S.O., 1919. (Cmd. 253.)
Chairman: Lord Desborough.

10,056 **Committee on the Hours, Pay and Conditions of Service of Firemen in Professional Fire Brigades in Great Britain.** *Report*. London: H.M.S.O., 1920. (Cmd. 710.)
Evidence. (Cmd. 876.)
Chairman: Sir William Middlebrook.

10,057 **Home Department.** *Report of the Prison Officers' Pay Committee: report of the committee appointed to inquire into the pay and conditions of service at the prisons and Borstal institutions in England and Scotland and at Broadmoor Criminal Lunatic Asylum*. London: H.M.S.O., 1923. 43p. (Cmd. 1959.)
Chairman: Lord Stanhope.

10,058 **Home Department.** Committee Appointed to Consider Possible Readjustments in the Standard Conditions of Service of the Police Forces in Great Britain. *Report*. London: H.M.S.O., 1924. 3p. (Cmd. 2086.)
Chairman: Lord Desborough.

10,059 **Home Office.** *Approved schools: remuneration and conditions of service. Report of the Committee*. London: H.M.S.O., 1936. 30p.
Chairman: Vivian Leonard Henderson.

10,060 **Home Office.** *Approved schools and remand homes: remuneration and conditions of service. Report of the Committee*. London: H.M.S.O., 1946. 42p.
Chairman: B. J. Reynolds.

10,061 **Home Office.** Police Council. Committee on Local Conditions of Service for the Police. *Report*. London: H.M.S.O., 1947. 16p.
Chairman: S. J. Baker.

10,062 **Home Office.** Committee on Police Conditions of Service. *Home Office memorandum of evidence*. London: H.M.S.O., 1949. vi, 106p.

10,063 **Home Office** and **Scottish Home Department.** *Report of the Committee on Police Conditions of Service. Part I*. London: H.M.S.O., 1949. iv, 123p. (Cmd. 7674.)
Part II. 1949. iv, 124p. (Cmd. 7831.)
Chairman: Lord Oaksey.

10,064 **Home Office** and **Scottish Home Department.** *Statement on pay and conditions of service of police*. London: H.M.S.O., 1949. 10p. (Cmd. 7707.)

10,065 **Scottish Home Department.** Committee on Police Conditions of Service. *Scottish Home Department memorandum of evidence*. Edinburgh: H.M.S.O., 1949. ii, 55p.

10,066 **Home Office** and **Scottish Home Department.** *Report of the Committee on Remuneration and Conditions of Service of Certain Grades in the Prison Service*. London: H.M.S.O., 1958. 52p. (Cmnd. 544.)

10,067 **Royal Commission on the Police.** *Report.* London: H.M.S.O., 1960, 1962. (Cmnd. 122, Cmnd. 1728.)
Chairman: H. Willink.

10,068 **Bradley**, Robert. 'The copper.' Fraser, R. (ed.). *Work: twenty personal accounts.* Harmondsworth: Penguin, 1968. p. 185–204.

10,069 **Government Social Survey.** *The fire service and its personnel.* London: H.M.S.O., 1969. vii, 154p. (SS417/B.)
By Margaret Thomas.
'An enquiry undertaken for the Home Office.'

10,070 **Eire.** Commission on the Garda Síochána. *Report on remuneration and conditions of service.* Dublin: Stationery Office, 1970. 269p. (R.109.)

See also: 10,748; 10,750–1; 10,763; 10,767; 10,778–9; 10,782–3; 10,792; 10,796; 10,801; 10,804; 10,887; 12,217–18; 12,597.

4. Particular Groups and Problems

See also Part Three, III. F.

a. SWEATING

A good deal of the material in Part Six, IV, A, 4, b is also relevant here. See also Part Six, IV, A, 3, c, v, 1; and Part Seven, VI, C.

10,071 **Board of Trade.** Labour Correspondent. *Report on the sweating system at the East End of London.* London: H.M.S.O., 1887. (H.C. 331.)

10,072 **Board of Trade.** Labour Correspondent. *Report on the sweating system in Leeds.* London: H.M.S.O., 1888. (C. 5513.)

10,073 **Harrington**, George Fellows. *The sweating problem and its solution.* London: Ridgway, 1888. 56p.
Printed in Ryde.

10,074 **Potter**, Beatrice. 'East London labour.' *Nineteenth Century*, XXIV, 138 (August 1888), 161–83.
Sweating in the clothing trade.

10,075 **Potter**, Beatrice. 'Pages from a work-girl's diary.' *Nineteenth Century*, XXIV, 139 (September 1888), 301–14.
Sweated labour in the tailoring trade in London.

10,076 **Potter**, Beatrice. 'The sweating system, II.' *Char. Orgn. Rev.*, IV, 37 (January 1888), 12–16.
Discusses the Report to the Board of Trade by J. Burnett.

10,077 **Schloss**, David Frederick. 'The sweating system, I.' *Char. Orgn. Rev.*, IV, 37 (January 1888), 1–12.
Discusses the Report to the Board of Trade by J. Burnett.

10,078 **House of Lords.** Select Committee on the Sweating System.
First report; with proceedings, evidence, and appendix. London: H.M.S.O., 1888. (H.C. 361.)
Second report; with proceedings, evidence, and appendix. 1888. (H.C. 448.)
Third report; with evidence, and appendix. 1889. (H.C. 165.)
Fourth report; with proceedings, evidence, and appendix; and analysis of evidence to the third and fourth reports. 1889. (H.C. 331.)
Indices to the evidence. Part I. First and second reports. 1889. (H.C. 331-I.) *Part II. Third and fourth reports.* 1889. (H.C. 331-II.)
Fifth report; with an appendix. 1890. (H.C. 169.)

10,079 **Campbell**, Helen Stuart. *Prisoners of poverty abroad.* Boston, Mass.: Roberts, 1889. iv, 248p.

10,080 **Schloss**, David Frederick. 'What is "the sweating system"?' *Char. Orgn. Rev.*, V, 50 (February 1889), 49–64.

10,081 **Irwin**, Margaret Hardinge. *Home work amongst women. 1. Shirtmaking, shirtfinishing and kindred trades.* Glasgow, [189–]. 20, xxiii p.

10,082 **Potter**, Beatrice. 'The Lords and the sweating system.' *Nineteenth Century*, XXVII, 160 (June 1890), 885–905.
Discussion of the report of the Select Committee of the House of Lords to inquire into the sweating system.

10,083 **Schloss**, David Frederick. 'The sweating system.' *Fortn. Rev.*, n.s., XLVII, 280 (April 1890), 532–51.

10,084 **Lippington**, C. H. d'E. 'Side lights of the Sweating Commission.' *Westm. Rev.*, CXXXVI, 3 (September 1891), 273–88; 5 (November 1891), 504–16.

10,085 **Schloss**, David Frederick. 'The Jew as a workman.' *Nineteenth Century*, XXIX, 167 (January 1891), 96–109.

10,086 **Schloss**, David Frederick. 'The present position of the "sweating system" question in the United Kingdom.' *Econ. Rev.*, II, 4 (October 1892), 452–9.
'Paper sent by request to the meeting of the American Social Science Association, at Saratoga, August, 1892.'

10,087 **Schloss**, David Frederick. 'The "sweating system" in the United Kingdom, August 1892.' *J. Soc. Sci.*, 30 (October 1892), 65–72.

10,088 **Webb**, Beatrice. *How best to do away with the sweating system.* Manchester: Co-operative Union, 1892. 16p.

10,089 **Gonner**, E. C. K. 'The survival of domestic industries.' *Econ. J.*, III, 9 (March 1893), 23–32.

10,090 **Fabian Society.** *Sweating: its cause and remedy.* London: Fabian Society, 1894. 15p. (Fabian tract 50.)
By H. W. Macrosty.
Issued without the author's name.

10,091 **Irwin**, Margaret Hardinge. 'The problem of home work.' *Westm. Rev.*, CXLVIII, 5 (November 1897), 541–57.

10,092 **March-Phillipps**, Evelyn. *Evils of home work for women.* Manchester: Women's Co-operative Guild, 1898. 7p. (Investigation papers 3.)

10,093 **Angus** (*pseud.*). *Salvation and sweating.* London, [1899?]. 16p.

10,094 **Knightly**, Louisa M., *Lady*. 'Women as home workers.' *Nineteenth Century*, L, 294 (August 1901), 287–92.

10,095 **Webb**, Beatrice. 'The diary of an investigator.' Webb, S. and Webb, B. *Problems of modern industry.* London, New York, Bombay: Longmans, Green, 1902. p. 1–19.

Second edition.

First published in *Nineteenth Century* (September 1888).

Sweating in the tailoring trade.

10,096 **Webb**, Beatrice. 'How to do away with the sweating system.' Webb, S. and Webb, B. *Problems of modern industry.* London, New York, Bombay: Longmans, Green, 1902. p. 139–55.

Second edition.

'A paper read at the twenty-fourth annual congress of Co-operative Societies, held at Rochdale, June 1892.'

10,097 **Women's Industrial Council.** *How to deal with home work.* London, [1902?]. 4p.

10,098 **Tuckwell**, Gertrude Mary. 'The "sweated industries" exhibition.' *Progress Civic Soc. Ind.*, I, 3 (July 1906), 193–203.

10,099 **Women's Industrial Council.** *Home industries of women in London, 1906: interim report of an inquiry by the Investigation Committee.* London, 1906. 45p.

10,100 **Black**, Clementina. *Sweated industry and the minimum wage.* London: Duckworth, 1907. xxiv, 281p.

10,101 **Hutchins**, B. Leigh. 'The control of sweating.' *Econ. Rev.*, XVII, 4 (October 1907), 403–9.

10,102 **Select Committee on Home Work.** *Report.* London: H.M.S.O., 1907. (H.C. 290.)

A formal presentation of the minutes of evidence.

Report, proceedings, minutes of evidence, appendices. 1908. l, 216p. (H.C. 246.)

Chairman: T. Whittaker.

10,103 **Beveridge**, William Henry. 'The curse of casual labour.' *Socialist Rev.*, I, 4 (June 1908), 257–70.

10,104 **Carlyle**, Alexander James. 'Underpayment and sweating in a provincial town.' *Econ. Rev.*, XVIII, 3 (July 1908), 287–301.

A report prepared by a committee organized by the Oxford City branch of the Christian Social Union.

10,105 **Hutchins**, B. Leigh. *Home work and sweating: the causes and the remedies.* London: Fabian Society, 1908. 19p. (Fabian tract 130.)

10,106 **Leppington**, C. H. d'E. 'The fate of the workwoman at home.' *Char. Orgn. Rev.*, n.s., XXIII, 137 (May 1908), 257–70.

10,107 **Money**, Leo George Chiozza. 'Sweating: its cause and cure.' Co-operative Wholesale Societies. *Annual for 1908.* p. 270–94.

10,108 **National Anti-Sweating League.** *Living wage for sweated workers.* London, 1908. 20p.

10,109 **Samuelson**, James. *The lament of the sweated.* London: King, 1908. xii, 68p.

10,110 **Whittaker**, Thomas Palmer. 'A minimum wage for home workers.' *Nineteenth Century*, LXIV, 379 (September 1908), 507–24.

The author was Chairman of the Select Committee to investigate sweating.

10,111 **Women's Industrial Council.** *Home industries of women in London.* London, 1908. 169p.

10,112 **Meyer**, *Lady* Adele and **Black**, Clementina. *Makers of our clothes: a case for trade boards; being the results of a year's investigation into the work of women in London in the tailoring, dressmaking, and underclothing trades.* London: Duckworth, 1909. xv, 304p.

10,113 **Chapman**, Sydney John. 'Home work.' *Manchr. Statist. Soc. Trans.* (1909–10), 79–109.

10,114 **Devlin**, J. *Belfast linen trade: the condition of the home workers.* Belfast, 1910. 35p.

10,115 **Irwin**, Margaret Hardinge. 'The bitter cry of the Irish home worker.' *Nineteenth Century*, LXVIII, 404 (October 1910), 703–18.

10,116 **Freedom of Labour Defence.** *Report of an inquiry into the conditions of home work.* London, 1911. 10p.

10,117 **Mallon**, James Joseph. 'Sweating and the Trade Boards Act.' *Progress Civic Soc. Ind.*, VII, 3 (July 1912), 157–69.

10,118 **Latter**, *Mrs* R. *Sweated labour.* London, Oxford: Mowbray, 1913. iv, 58p. (The Church and citizenship 2.)

10,119 **Pope**, Samuel. *Married women outworkers.* London: H.M.S.O., 1913. 24p. (Cd. 6600.)

10,120 **Willis**, W. N. *White slaves of toil: how women and children are sweated.* London: Pearson, 1914. 208p.

10,121 **De Vesselitsky**, V. *The homeworker and the outlook: a descriptive study of tailoresses and boxmakers.* London: Bell, 1916. xvi, 118p. (Studies in the minimum wage 4.)

With an introduction by R. H. Tawney.

10,122 **Phelps**, Sydney K. 'Sweated home workers.' *Nineteenth Century*, LXXXVII, 519 (May 1920), 929–37.

10,123 **Coleman**, Donald Cuthbert. *The domestic system in industry.* London: Routledge and Kegan Paul for the Historical Association, 1960. 12p. (Aids for teachers series 6.)

See also: 5.

b. WOMEN

A good deal of the material in Part Six, IV, A, 4, a is also relevant here. Sociological and psychological material on women's attitudes to, and behaviour at, work is generally classified in Part Two. See also Part Three, III, F, 3; Part Six, II, C, 4; Part Six, II, D, 7; Part Six, III, F; Part Seven, V, B, 2, b; and Part Seven, VI, E.

i. *General*

10,124 **Jevons**, William Stanley. 'Married women in factories.' *Contemp. Rev.*, XLI (January 1882), 37–53.
See also Whately Cooke Taylor, ' "Married women in factories": a reply'. XLII (September 1882), 428–41.

10,125 **Blackwell**, Elizabeth. *Purchase of women: the great economic blunder. Part 1.* London: John Kensil, 1887. 42p.
No more published.

10,126 **Schloss**, David Frederick. 'Women's work and wages.' *Char. Orgn. Rev.*, III, 33 (September 1887), 337–43.

10,127 **Black**, Clementina. 'A working woman's speech.' *Nineteenth Century*, XXV, 147 (May 1889), 667–71.
Report of a speech by the Secretary of the Nottingham and Leicester Cigar Makers' Union 'in her own words'.

10,128 **'British Weekly' Commissioners.** *Toilers in London.* London, 1889. viii, 264p.

10,129 **Deane**, Lucy. *Women and children in factories, workshops, and laundries, and how to help them.* London: Industrial Law Committee, [189–?]. 14p. ([Pamphlets] 2.)

10,130 **Booth**, E. G. *Women's right to work.* Manchester, [*c.* 1890?]. 8p.

10,131 **Birmingham Ladies' Union of Workers Among Women and Girls.** *Women workers: papers read at a conference.* Birmingham, 1891. 216p.

10,132 **Collet**, Clara Elizabeth. 'Women's work in Leeds.' *Econ. J.*, I, 3 (September 1891), 460–73.

10,133 **Liverpool Ladies' Union of Workers Among Women and Girls.** *Women workers: papers read at a conference convened by the Liverpool Ladies' Union of Workers among Women and Girls, in November, 1891.* Liverpool: Gilbert G. Walmsley, 1892. vii, 267p.

10,134 **Bristol and Clifton Ladies' Association for the Care of Girls.** *Women workers: papers read at a conference convened by the . . . Association . . . November, 1892.* Bristol: Arrowsmith, 1893. 2v.

10,135 **Dilke**, Emilia Frances Strong, *Lady.* 'The industrial position of women.' *Fortn. Rev.*, n.s., LIV, 322 (October 1893), 499–508.

10,136 **Ford**, Isabella O. *Women's wages, and the conditions under which they are earned.* London: Humanitarian League, 1893. 17p. (Publications 8.)

10,137 *Ladies at work: papers on paid employment for ladies, by experts in the several branches.* London: A. M. Innes, 1893. 143p.
'With an introduction by Lady Jenne.'

10,138 **Bulley**, Agnes Amy. 'The employment of women.' *Fortn. Rev.*, n.s., LV, 325 (January 1894), 39–48.
The lady assistant commissioners' report.

10,139 **Bateson**, Margaret (ed.). *Professional women upon their professions: conversations.* London: H. Cox, 1895. xii, 133p.
First published in *Queen.*

10,140 **Dilke**, *Lady* Emilia Frances Strong. *The industrial position of women.* London, [*c.* 1895?]. 15p.

10,141 **Robertson**, C. G. 'Women's work.' *Econ. Rev.*, V, 2 (April 1895), 167–90.

10,142 **Women's Co-operative Guild.** *Investigations into conditions of women's work, outside textile trades, etc.* [1896?] [14]p.

10,143 **Women's Co-operative Guild.** *Report of investigations into conditions of women's work 1895–6.* 1896. 16p.

10,144 **Swank**, J. M. 'The hopeless poor of Great Britain.' *Notes and comments.* Philadelphia: American Iron and Steel Association, 1897. p. 34–47.

10,145 **Booth**, E. G. *Women workers and parliamentary representation.* Manchester, [*c.* 1898?]. 8p.

10,146 **Morten**, H. *The employment of women.* London, [1898?]. 18p.

10,147 **MacDonald**, Margaret E., and others. *Wage earning mothers.* London: Women's Labour League, [190–?]. 32p.

10,148 **Ford**, Isabella O. *Industrial women and how to help them.* London: Humanitarian League, 1900. 12p.

10,149 **Hobhouse**, Emily. 'Women workers: how they live; how they wish to live.' *Nineteenth Century*, XLVII, 277 (March 1900), 471–84.

10,150 **International Congress of Women**, London, 1899. 'The home as workshop.' *Transactions. Vol. VI. Women in industrial life.* London: T. Fisher Unwin, 1900. p. 145–61.
Contributions for Great Britain and Ireland by T. W. Rolleston, A. Ballantyne.

10,151 **Crawford**, Virginia M. 'Philanthropy and wage-paying.' *Econ. J.*, XI, 41 (March 1901), 96–105.

10,152 **Creighton**, Louise. 'The employment of educated women.' *Nineteenth Century*, L, 297 (November 1901), 806–11.

10,153 **Lapham**, Ella Caroline. 'The industrial status of women in Elizabethan England.' *J. Polit. Econ.*, IX, 4 (September 1901), 562–99.

10,154 **Collet**, Clara Elizabeth. *Educated working women: essays on the economic position of women workers in the middle classes.* London: King, 1902. vi, 143p.

10,155 **Women's Labour League.** *Wage earning mothers.* London, [1902?]. 32p.
By Margaret MacDonald.

10,156 **Women's Industrial Council.** *London borough councils and the welfare of women workers.* London, 1903. 4p.

10,157 **Cadbury**, Edward, **Matheson**, M. Cecile and **Shann**, George. *Women's work and wages: a phase of life in an industrial city.* London: Fisher Unwin, 1906. 368p.
Birmingham.

10,158 **Black**, Clementina. 'Legislative proposals.' *Woman in industry from seven points of view.* London: Duckworth, 1908. p. 183–206.

10,159 **Edinburgh Review.** 'The industrial position of women.' *Edinb. Rev.*, CCVIII, 426 (October 1908), 367–89.
Review article.

10,160 **Tennant**, May. 'Infantile mortality.' *Woman in industry from seven points of view.* London: Duckworth, 1908. p. 85–119.
Title in Contents: 'Infant mortality'.

10,161 **Clark**, Victor S. 'Woman and child wage-earners in Great Britain.' *U.S. Bur. Labor Bull.*, 80 (January 1909), 1–85.

10,162 **Hutchins**, B. Leigh. 'Statistics of women's life and employment.' *R. Statist. Soc. J.*, LXXII, 2 (June 1909), 205–37.
With discussion, p. 238–47.
'Read before the Royal Statistical Society, Tuesday, 16th March, 1909.'

10,163 **Hutchins**, B. Leigh. 'Woman's industrial career.' *Sociol. Rev.*, II, 4 (October 1909), 338–48.

10,164 **Swiney**, Frances. 'Women's industries.' *Westm. Rev.*, CLXXI, 4 (April 1909), 383–95.

10,165 **Women's Industrial Council.** *What the Council is and does.* London, 1909. 8p.
Also 1911. 12p.

10,166 **Higgs**, Mary and **Hayward**, Edward Ernest. *Where shall she live? The homelessness of the woman worker.* London: King, 1910. viii, 216p. (National Association for Women's Lodging-Houses.)

10,167 **Collet**, Clara Elizabeth. *Women in industry.* London: Women's Printing Society, 1911. 20p.

10,168 **Hutchins**, B. Leigh. *The working life of women.* London: Fabian Society, 1911. 16p. (Fabian tract 157.)

10,169 **Martin**, Anna. 'The married working woman: a study.' *Nineteenth Century*, LXVIII, 406 (December 1910), 1102–18; LXIX, 407 (January 1911), 108–22.

10,170 **Sheavyn**, Phoebe Anne Beale. 'Professional women.' *The position of women: actual and ideal.* London: Nisbet, 1911.

10,171 **Women's Co-operative Guild.** *Working women and divorce: an account of evidence given on behalf of the Women's Co-operative Guild before the Royal Commission on Divorce.* London: D. Nutt, 1911. 74p.

10,172 **Smith**, Constance. 'The industrial employment of girls.' National Conference on the Prevention of Destitution. *Report of the proceedings . . . 1912.* London: King, 1912. p. 254–9.
Discussion, p. 260–5.

10,173 **Bentinck**, *Lord* Henry Cavendish. *Women's labour.* London, 1913. [4]p.

10,174 **Ramsay**, Nora M. *A working woman's day.* 1913. 7p.

10,175 **Fabian Women's Group.** 'Women in industry.' *New States.*, II, 46 (21 February 1914), Supplement. xvp.
Essays written for the Fabian Women's Group.
Contents: 'Introduction.' B. Webb. p. i–ii. 'Women's wages.' Mrs F. W. Hubback. p. ii–vi. 'Women in trade unionism.' B. L. Hutchins. p. vi–ix. 'The legal minimum wage at work.' J. J. Mallon. p. x–xii. 'A policy for women workers.' Mrs P. Reeves and Mrs C. M. Wilson. p. xii–xv.

10,176 **Morley**, Edith Julia. 'The economic position of women: an account of some work attempted by the Fabian Women's Group.' *Econ. Rev.*, XXIV, 4 (October 1914), 389–97.

10,177 **Collet**, Clara Elizabeth. 'The professional employment of women.' *Econ. J.*, XXV, 100 (December 1915), 627–30.

10,178 **Haslam**, James. 'Women in industry.' Co-operative Wholesale Societies. *Annual, 1915.* p. 419–48.

10,179 **Kinloch-Cooke**, Clement. 'Women and the reconstruction of industry.' *Nineteenth Century*, LXXVIII, 466 (December 1915), 1396–416.

10,180 **Morley**, Edith Julia (ed.). *Women workers in seven professions: a survey of their economic conditions and prospects.* London: Routledge, 1915. xvi, 318p.
Edited for the Fabian Women's Group.
Contents: Teaching, medical profession, nursing, sanitary inspectors and health visitors, Civil Service, clerks and secretaries, acting.

10,181 **Women's Industrial Council.** *Married women's work, being the report of an enquiry undertaken by the Women's Industrial Council.* London: G. Bell, 1915. vi, 292p.
Edited by Clementina Black.

10,182 **Abram**, A. 'Women traders in medieval London.' *Econ. J.*, XXVI, 102 (June 1916), 276–85.

10,183 **Bosanquet**, Helen. 'Women in industry.' *Econ. J.*, XXVI, 102 (June 1916), 209–18.

10,184 **Hutchins**, B. Leigh. 'The position of the woman worker after the war.' *Econ. J.*, XXVI, 102 (June 1916), 183–91.

10,185 **Ministry of Munitions.** Labour Supply Department. *Exhibition of samples of women's work and official photographs at the Whitworth Institute, Oxford Road, Manchester.* London: the Department, 1917. 118p.
'Illustrating the various types of work upon which women are employed in engineering and other industries on munitions of war.'

10,186 **Stone**, *Sir* Gilbert (ed.). *Women war workers: accounts contributed by representative workers.* London: Harrap, 1917. 319p.

10,187 **Anderson**, Adelaide Mary. *Women workers and the health of the nation.* London, 1918. 24p.

10,188 **Collier**, D. J. *The girl in industry.* London: Bell, 1918. xvi, 56p.

10,189 **Hockin,** Olive. *Two girls on the land: war-time on a Dartmoor farm.* London: Arnold, 1918. 158p.

10,190 **Clark**, Alice. *Working life of women in the seventeenth century.* London: Routledge; New York: Dutton, 1919. 335p. (Studies in economics and political science 56.)

New impression. Cass, 1968. 328p.

Also New York: Kelley, 1968. (Reprints of economic classics.)

10,191 **Lawrence**, A. Susan. 'The woman wage earner.' Phillips, M. (ed.). *Women and the Labour Party, by various writers.* London: Headley Bros., 1919. p. 94–101.

10,192 **Cullis**, Winifred. 'The demands of industry upon women from the physiological standpoint.' Muscio, B. (ed.). *Lectures on industrial administration.* London: Pitman, 1920. p. 185–99.

10,193 **Tuckwell**, Gertrude Mary. 'Women in industry.' *Nineteenth Century,* LXXXVII, 516 (February 1920), 331–43.

10,194 **Bowley**, Arthur Lyon. 'Earners and dependants in English towns in 1911.' *Economica,* I, 2 (May 1921), 101–11.

10,195 **Hogg**, Margaret Hope. 'Dependants on women wage-earners.' *Economica,* I, 1 (January 1921), 69–86.

Note, 2 (May 1921), 111–12, by A. L. Bowley.

10,196 **Hutchins**, B. Leigh. 'The present position of industrial women workers.' *Econ. J.,* XXXI, 124 (December 1921), 462–71.

Reprinted. London: Macmillan, 1921.

10,197 **Bondfield**, Margaret Grace. 'Women workers in British industry.' Hogue, R. W. (ed.). *British labour speaks.* New York: Boni and Liveright, 1924. p. 45–69.

10,198 **Tweedy**, Rosamond. '*Consider Her Palaces*': *a study of the housing problem of lower paid single women workers in London.* London: Over Thirty Association, 1936. 39p.

10,199 **Beauchamp**, Joan. *Women who work.* London: Lawrence and Wishart, 1937. 104p.

10,200 **Open Door Council.** *1844–1937: women's ninety-three years minority in industry.* London, 1937. 16p.

10,201 **Stuart-Bunning**, G. H. 'Women in employment.' *Publ. Adm.,* XVIII, 3 (July 1940), 192–7.

10,202 **Collet**, Clara Elizabeth. 'The present position of women in industry.' *R. Statist. Soc. J.,* CV, 2 (1942), 122–4.

'Read and discussed at the Adam Smith Club, January 12th, 1935.'

10,203 **Holmes**, Beatrice Gordon. *In love with life: a pioneer career woman's story.* London: Hollis and Carter, 1944. 207p.

Official in the Federation of Business Women.

10,204 **Scott**, Peggy. *They made invasion possible.* London: Hutchinson, 1944. 148p.

Accounts of their experiences by women on war-work.

10,205 **Florecka**, Irene. *A comparative study of the economic position of women in Great Britain and Poland in the inter-war period.* 1944–5. (Ph.D. thesis, University of Edinburgh.)

10,206 **Strachey**, Mary Anabel Nassau. *Is woman's place in the home?* London, 1947. 15p. (Labour discussion series 9.)

10,207 **Earengey**, Florence. *The legal and economic status of women.* London: National Council of Women of Great Britain, 1949. 18p.

Revised edition. *A milk-white lamb: the legal and economic status of women.* 1953. 64p.

10,208 **Zweig**, Ferdynand. *Women's life and labour.* London: Gollancz, 1952. 190p.

10,209 **Smieton**, *Dame* Mary. 'Problems of women's employment in Great Britain.' *Int. Labour Rev.,* LXIX, 1 (January 1954), 47–59.

10,210 **Christian Economic and Social Research Foundation.** *Young mothers at work.* London: the Foundation, 1960. 16–27p. (Social problems of post-war youth 6.)

Published with number 5 of the series.

10,211 **Klein**, Viola. *Women workers: working hours and services. A survey in 21 countries.* Paris: Organisation for Economic Co-operation and Development, 1965. 100p. (Employment of special groups 1.)

10,212 **National Federation of Business and Professional Women's Clubs of Great Britain and Northern Ireland.** *Justice or prejudice?* Hunstanton: Witley P., 1968. 48p.

10,213 **Seear**, Nancy. 'The position of women in industry.' Royal Commission on Trade Unions and Employers' Associations. *Two studies in industrial relations.* London: H.M.S.O., 1968. p. 1–26. (Research papers 11.)

See also: 77; 9165; 10,620; 10,625; 10,631; 10,644; 10,657; 10,660; 10,674; 10,898; 14,053; 14,063; 14,082.

ii. *Particular Occupations and Industries*

See also Part Six, IV, A, 3, j, i.

10,214 **Harkness**, Margaret E. 'Women as civil servants.' *Nineteenth Century,* x, 55 (September 1881), 369–81.

10,215 **Irwin**, Margaret Hardinge. *Women's employment in shops.* Glasgow, [1895?]. 24p.

10,216 **Harris**, Lillian. *The treatment of women employees in the co-operative movement, being a report of an enquiry into the wages, hours and conditions of women working in co-operative stores in 1895*. Manchester, 1897. 18p.

10,217 **Hobhouse**, Emily. 'Dust-women.' *Econ. J.*, x, 39 (September 1900), 411–20.
Sifting and sorting of refuse.

10,218 **Joint Committee on the Employment of Barmaids.** *The barmaid problem*. London, [*c.* 1900]. 7p.

10,219 **Oakeshott**, Grace M. 'Women in the cigar trade in London.' *Econ. J.*, x, 40 (December 1900), 562–72.

10,220 **Garland**, Charles H. 'Women as telegraphists.' *Econ. J.*, xi, 42 (June 1901), 251–61.

10,221 **Hutchins**, B. Leigh. 'The employment of women in paper mills.' *Econ. J.*, xiv, 54 (June 1904), 235–48.

10,222 **MacDonald**, James Ramsay (ed.). *Women in the printing trades: a sociological study*. London: King, 1904. xvii, 206p.

10,223 **Breckinridge**, Sophonisba P. 'A recent English case on women and the legal profession.' *J. Polit. Econ.*, xxiii, 1 (January 1915), 64–70.

10,224 **Zimmern**, Dorothy M. 'The Civil Service and women.' *Polit. Q.*, 8 (September 1916), 79–103.
Based on a report of an inquiry made on behalf of the Women's Industrial Council.

10,225 **Home Department.** Committee on the Nature and Limits of the Assistance which can be given by Women in the Carrying Out of Police Duties, and as to what ought to be the Status, Pay and Conditions of Service of Women employed on such Duties. *Report*. London: H.M.S.O., 1920. 17p. (Cmd. 877.)
Evidence. 1921. (Cmd. 1133.)
Chairman: Sir John Baird.

10,226 **Phillips**, Marion. *Women and children in the textile industry*. Aberdeen, 1922. 29p.

10,227 **Home Department.** Departmental Committee on the Employment of Police-Women. *Report*. London: H.M.S.O., 1924. 16p. (Cmd. 2224.)
Minutes of evidence, index. 1924.
Chairman: W. C. Bridgeman.

10,228 **Allen**, Mary Sophia. *The pioneer policewoman*. London: Chatto and Windus, 1925. xi, 288p.
Edited by Julie Helen Heyneman.

10,229 **National British Women's Total Abstinence Union.** *Barmaids: facts regarding women's employment in drinking bars*. London, [*c.* 1930]. 18p.

10,230 **Allen**, Mary Sophia and **Heyneman**, Julie Helen. *Woman at the cross roads*. London: Unicorn P., 1934. 176p.
Reminiscences of Mary S. Allen, a policewoman.

10,231 **Treasury.** Committee on Women's Questions. *Report*. London: H.M.S.O., 1934. 10p.
Chairman: Edward Raven.
'To consider various matters arising out of the Report of the Royal Commission on the Civil Service (1929–31) in regard to the position of women in the Civil Service.'

10,232 **Allen**, Mary Sophia. *Lady in blue*. London: Stanley Paul, 1936. 286p.
Reminiscences and a study of the status of women police.

10,233 **A Lady Secretary.** 'The worker's point of view. XXIX. The "shorthanded" myth.' *Hum. Factor*, x, 7–8 (July–August 1936), 284–8.

10,234 **Heal**, *Sir* Ambrose. 'Women chimney-sweepers.' *Notes Quer.*, clxxx, 7 (15 February 1941), 110.

10,235 **Women's Farm and Garden Association.** *Report of an ad hoc sub-committee on women's conditions of employment and wages in agriculture*. London: the Association, 1945. 16p.

10,236 **Civil Service National Whitley Council.** Committee on the Marriage Bar. *Marriage bar in the Civil Service: report*. London: H.M.S.O., 1946. 24p. (Cmd. 6886.)
Chairman: Sir J. A. Barlow.

10,237 **Gladden,** Edgar Norman. 'The woman civil servant in Great Britain.' *Publ. Adm.* (Sydney), n.s., vi, 5 (March 1947), 233–9.

10,238 **Jefferys**, Margot. 'Married women in the higher grades of the Civil Service and government sponsored research organizations.' *Br. J. Sociol.*, iii, 4 (December 1952), 361–4.

10,239 **Woodside**, Moya. 'The woman prison officer 100 years ago.' *Pris. Serv. J.*, i, 3 (July 1961), 13–18.

10,240 **Gail**, Suzanne. 'The housewife.' Fraser, R. (ed.). *Work: twenty personal accounts*. Harmondsworth: Penguin, 1968. p. 140–55.
First published in *New Left Review*, 43 (May–June 1967), 45–54.

See also: 9418; 9546; 9682; 9768; 9775; 9777; 9905; 9918–33; 9935–7; 9956; 9959; 10,013; 10,029; 10,129; 10,139; 10,142; 10,170; 10,177; 10,180; 10,182; 10,189; 11,127.

c. CHILDREN AND YOUTH

Sociological and psychological material on the industrial attitudes and behaviour of young persons is classified in Part Two. See also Part Five, V, B, 1; Part Six, II, A; Part Six, II, C, 5; Part Six, II, D, 7; Part Seven, IV, D, 2, b; and Part Seven, V, B, 2, a.

i. *General*

10,241 **Conway**, M. *Child labour*. Bradford, n.d. 19p.

10,242 **Social-Democratic Federation.** Executive Council. *Campaign against child labour.* London, [189–?]. 4p.

10,243 **Dunckley**, Henry. 'Child labour. II. The half-timers.' *Contemp. Rev.*, LIX (June 1891), 798–802.

10,244 **Manning**, Henry Edward, Cardinal. 'Child labour. I. Minimum age for labour of children.' *Contemp. Rev.*, LIX (June 1891), 794–7.

10,245 **Glasier**, Katherine Bruce. *The cry of the children.* Manchester, 1894. 15p.

10,246 **A Bradford Manufacturer.** 'The factory children.' *Econ. Rev.*, v, 3 (July 1895), 370–9.

10,247 **Hogg**, Edith F. 'School children as wage earners.' *Nineteenth Century*, XLII, 246 (August 1897), 235–44.

10,248 **Bosanquet**, Helen. 'Little drudges and troublesome boys.' *The standard of life, and other studies.* London, New York: Macmillan, 1898. p. 174–82.

10,249 **Hird**, Frank. *The cry of the children: an exposure of certain British industries in which children are iniquitously employed.* London: J. Bowden; New York: M. F. Mansfield, 1898. 96p.

Second edition.

10,250 **Daily News.** *The children's labour question.* London, 1899. 156p.

10,251 **Gorst**, John Eldon. 'School children as wage-earners.' *Nineteenth Century*, XLVI, 269 (July 1899), 8–17.

10,252 **Hogg**, Edith F. 'Children outside the factory laws.' International Congress of Women, London, 1899. *Transactions. Vol. VI. Women in industrial life.* London: T. Fisher Unwin, 1900. p. 71–6.

Discussion, p. 84–5.

10,253 **Hogg**, Edith F. 'Wage-earning children.' *Econ. Rev.*, x, 3 (July 1900), 345–54.

10,254 **Cox**, J. Bell. 'Wage-earning children.' *Char. Orgn. Rev.*, n.s., IX, 53 (May 1901), 238–49.

A paper read at a special meeting of the Council of the Charity Organisation Society, 29 April 1901.

10,255 **Adler**, Nettie. *Wage earning children in England.* London, 1902. 7p.

10,256 **Adler**, Nettie. 'Children as wage-earners.' *Fortn. Rev.*, n.s., LXXIII, 437 (May 1903), 918–27.

Discussion of the Inter-Departmental Committee on the Employment of School Children, *Report* (Cd. 849, 1901) and *Minutes of evidence* (Cd. 895, 1902).

10,257 **Gibb**, Spencer James. *The irregular employment of boys.* London, 1903. 19p.

10,258 **Charity Organisation Review.** 'Trades for invalid children.' *Char. Orgn. Rev.*, n.s., XVI, 93 (September 1904), 152–63.

Papers read at the Guildhall Conference, 7–8 June 1904.

I. 'The Kyrle Workshop for Cripples, Liverpool', by Mrs Frank Fletcher, p. 152–60.

II. 'Special preparation for the teaching of trades', by Miss F. M. Townsend, p. 160–3.

10,259 **Cloete**, J. G. 'The boy and his work.' Urwick, E. J. (ed.). *Studies of boy life in our cities; written by various authors for the Toynbee Trust.* London: Dent, 1904. p. 102–38.

10,260 **Russell**, Charles Edward Bellyse. *Manchester boys: sketches of Manchester lads at work and play.* Manchester: Manchester U.P., 1905. xvi, 176p.

Second edition. 1913. xv, 159p.

10,261 **Sherard**, Robert Harborough. *The child-slaves of Britain.* London: Hurst and Blackett, 1905. xix, 266p.

10,262 **Adler**, Nettie. 'Juvenile wage-earners and their work.' *Progress Civic Soc. Ind.*, I, 3 (July 1906), 204–10.

10,263 **Gibb**, Spencer James. *The problem of boy-work.* London: Wells Gardner, 1906. xi, 96p.

10,264 **Jevons**, H. Winifrid. 'Industrial prospects for boys and girls.' *Char. Orgn. Rev.*, n.s., XX, 117 (September 1906), 125–39.

10,265 **Bray**, Reginald Arthur. *The town child.* London: Unwin, 1907. viii, 334p.

10,266 **Mackirdy**, Olive Christian. *Baby toilers.* London: Hutchinson, 1907. xv, 198p.

10,267 **Adler**, Nettie. 'Child employment and juvenile delinquency.' *Woman in industry from seven points of view.* London: Duckworth, 1908. p. 121–41.

10,268 **Adler**, Nettie. 'Child workers and wage-earners.' *R. Soc. Arts J.*, LVI, 2899 (12 June 1908), 738–47.

Shaw lectures on industrial hygiene, v, delivered 17 March 1908.

10,269 **Alden**, Margaret Elizabeth. *Child life and labour.* London: Headley Bros., 1908. 184p. (Social service handbooks 6.)

Second edition. 1909.

Third edition, revised. 1913. 190p.

10,270 **Dale**, Marianne. *Child labor under capitalism.* London: Fabian Society, 1908. 19p. (Fabian tract 140.)

10,271 **Smith**, Constance Isabella Stuart. *Children as wage-earners.* London: Society for Promoting Christian Knowledge, 1908. 8p. (Pan-Anglican papers S.G. 5a.)

10,272 **Adler**, Nettie and **Tawney**, Richard Henry. *Boy and girl labour.* London, 1909. 17p.

10,273 **Alden**, Percy. 'Child life and labour.' Co-operative Wholesale Societies. *Annual for 1909.* p. 135–59.

10,274 **Baggallay**, F. W. 'Child labour in factories and workshops.' *Econ. Rev.*, XIX, 3 (July 1909), 293–308.

10,275 **Carter**, J. *Infant life and child labour.* Oxford, 1909. 16p.

10,276 **Jackson**, Cyril. *Report of the Poor Law Commission on the subject of boy labour.* London: H.M.S.O., 1909. (Cd. 4632.)

10,277 **Tawney**, Richard Henry. 'The economics of boy labour.' *Econ. J.*, XIX, 76 (December 1909), 517–37.

10,278 **Departmental Committee on the Employment of Children Act**, 1903. *Report.* London: H.M.S.O., 1910. 23p. (Cd. 5229.)
Minutes of evidence, appendices and index. (Cd. 5230.)
Chairman: J. A. Simon.
For the Home Department.

10,279 **Gibb**, Spencer James. *Boy-work and unemployment.* London, 1910. 19p.
Also 1912. 18p.

10,280 **Baron**, Barclay. *The growing generation: a study of working boys and girls in our cities.* London: Student Christian Movement, 1911. xiv, 192p.

10,281 **Gibb**, Spencer James. *The boy and his work.* London, Oxford: Mowbray, 1911. vii, 170p. (Christian Social Union handbooks.)

10,282 **Greenwood**, Arthur. 'Juvenile labour problems.' *Child*, II, 1 (October 1911), 25–34.

10,283 **Keynes**, Margaret Neville. *The problem of boy labour in Cambridge.* Cambridge: Bowes and Bowes, 1911. 23p.

10,284 **Scottish Council for Women's Trades.** *The employment of children.* Glasgow, 1911. 28p.

10,285 **Paton**, J. L. 'The adolescence of the working lad in industrial towns.' *Manchr. Statist. Soc. Trans.* (1911–12), 85–99.

10,286 **Brown**, H. Maughan. 'Schoolboys as wage earners.' *Child*, II, 12 (September 1912), 1026–30.

10,287 **Gibb**, Spencer James. 'Boy labour: some studies in detail.' Whitehouse, J. H. (ed.). *Problems of boy life.* London: King, 1912. p. 52–78.

10,288 **Gibb**, Spencer James and **Whitehouse**, John Howard. 'Boy labour: towards reform.' Whitehouse, J. H. (ed.). *Problems of boy life.* London: King, 1912. p. 79–96.

10,289 **Greenwood**, Arthur. 'Blind-alley labour.' *Econ. J.*, XXII, 86 (June 1912), 309–14.
'Blind-alley labour is boy and girl labour employed in an industry from which it will be ejected towards the end of adolescence ...'

10,290 **Harwood**, W. 'Child labour.' *Child*, III, 2 (November 1912), 131–3.

10,291 **Kennedy**, A. K. Clark. 'Boy labour and the factory system.' Whitehouse, J. H. (ed.). *Problems of boy life.* London: King, 1912. p. 97–122.

10,292 **Paton**, J. L. *The adolescence of the working lad in industrial towns.* London, 1912. [15]p.

10,293 **Tawney**, Richard Henry. 'The economics of boy labour.' Whitehouse, J. H. (ed.). *Problems of boy life.* London: King, 1912. p. 17–51.

10,294 **Whitehouse**, John Howard. 'The supervision of juvenile employment.' Whitehouse, J. H. (ed.). *Problems of boy life.* London: King, 1912. p. 170–3.

10,295 **Home Department.** Night Work Committee. *Report of the departmental committee on the night employment of male young persons in factories and workshops.* London: H.M.S.O., 1912–13. 2v. (Cd. 6503, Cd. 6711.)

10,296 **Adler**, Nettie. 'School children as wage-earners.' *Contemp. Rev.*, CVI (July 1914), 77–86.

10,297 **Freeman**, Arnold. *Boy life and labour: the manufacture of inefficiency.* London: King, 1914. xv, 252p.

10,298 **Greenwood**, Arthur. *The school child in industry: a study of industrial fatigue.* Manchester, 1914. 8p.

10,299 **Keeling**, Frederic. *The present position of the juvenile labour problem.* Manchester, 1914. 20p.

10,300 **Catholic Working Boys' Technical Aid Association.** *The blind alley: some aspects of juvenile employment in Ireland.* Dublin, 1915. 64p.

10,301 **Mundella**, Anthony John. 'The fight for the child.' *Rev. Revs.*, LI, 303 (March 1915), 207–9.

10,302 **Workers' Educational Association.** *Fair play for the children.* London, 1916. 11p.

10,303 **Macartney**, Douglas Halliday. *Boy welfare.* London: King, 1917. 40p.

10,304 **Millin**, S. Shannon. 'Child life as a national asset.' *Statist. Soc. Inq. Soc. Ir. J.*, XIII, 96 (September 1917), 301–16.

10,305 **United States.** Children's Bureau. *Child labor in warring countries: a brief review of foreign reports.* Washington, D.C., 1917. 75p.

10,306 **Gibb**, Spencer James. *Boy-work: exploitation or training?* London: Fisher Unwin, 1919. 223p.

10,307 **King**, O. Bolton. *The employment and welfare of juveniles.* London: Murray, 1925. xii, 244p.

10,308 **Hutt**, W. H. 'The factory system of the early 19th century.' *Economica*, VI, 16 (March 1926), 78–93.
The debate on conditions of child labour in factories.
Reprinted in F. A. Hayek (ed.). *Capitalism and the historians.* London: Routledge and Kegan Paul, 1954.

10,309 **Kenworthy**, William. 'The worker's point of view. XXV. First years at work.' *Hum. Factor*, IX, 9 (September 1935), 321–9.

10,310 **Lestrange**, W. F. *Wasted lives.* London: Routledge, 1936. 128p.
On social conditions in England, with special reference to children and young workers.

10,311 **Gollan**, John. *Youth in British industry: a survey of labour conditions to-day.* London: Gollancz, Lawrence and Wishart, 1937. 344p.
Also Left Book Club edition.

10,312 **Labour Party.** National Conference of Labour Women. *Reports on a Children's Charter and juvenile employment and unemployment, to be presented to the National Conference of Labour Women, Norwich, 1937.* London, 1937. 47p.

10,313 **Industrial Christian Fellowship.** Youth Committee and **Christian Workers' Union.** *Children at work: hours of young people in industry, shops and agriculture.* London: the Fellowship, 1943. 23p.

10,314 **Goodbrand**, James A. 'Some reflexions upon juvenile employment.' *Occup. Psychol.*, XIX, 2 (April 1945), 76–81.

10,315 **London Trades Council.** *Juvenile employment and blind alley labour: the problem and its remedies.* London: the Council, 1945. 15p.

10,316 **Ball**, Frank Norman. 'The re-introduction of child labour: an argument.' *Ind. Law Rev.*, II, 3 (August 1947), 84–8.

10,317 **Gardiner**, A. *The Industrial Revolution and child slavery.* Slaithwaite, 1948. 45p.

10,318 **London Council of Social Service.** *Young workers at meal time: a study in and about the London area.* London: National Council of Social Service for the London Council of Social Service, 1948. 20p.

10,319 **Morgan**, A. E. 'The young worker in British industry.' *Natn. Prov. Bank Rev.*, 24 (November 1953), 1–10.

10,320 **Herford**, Martin Edward Meakin. *Youth at work: a five-year study by an appointed factory doctor.* London: Parrish, 1957. xvi, 154p.

10,321 **Pilkington**, *Sir* Harry. *The boy in industry.* London: The Trustees, Charles Russell Memorial Lecture, 1958. 9p. (The seventh Charles Russell memorial lecture.)

10,322 **Wardle**, David. 'Working class children in Nottingham, from the Blue Books 1842–1862.' *Thoro. Soc. Trans.*, LXX (1966), 105–14.

Includes wages and conditions of children working in the lace and hosiery industries.

See also: 5868; 10,120; 10,161; 10,618; 10,620; 10,631; 10,657; 10,660; 10,925.

ii. *Particular Occupations and Industries*

10,323 **Waugh**, Benjamin. 'Street children.' *Contemp. Rev.*, LIII (June 1888), 825–35.

10,324 **Kirlew**, Gilbert R. 'Facts and figures relating to street children.' *Manchr. Statist. Soc. Trans.* (1888–89), 43–50.

10,325 **Fawcett**, Millicent Garrett. 'The employment of children in theatres.' *Contemp. Rev.*, LVI (December 1889), 822–9.

10,326 **Burke**, Thomas. 'The street-trading children of Liverpool.' *Contemp. Rev.*, LXXVIII (November 1900), 720–6.

10,327 **Campagnac**, Ernest Trafford and **Russell**, Charles Edward Bellyse. 'The education, earnings, and social condition of boys engaged in street-trading in Manchester.' Board of Education. *Special reports on educational subjects.* Vol. 8. London, 1902. p. 653–70.

10,328 **Committee Appointed by the Bishop of Birmingham to Enquire into Street Trading by Children.** *Report.* Birmingham, [1910?]. 10p.

10,329 **Pelham**, Herbert Sidney. *Street trading by children: a paper read to the club workers of the Street Children's Union.* Birmingham: Cornish, 1910. 24p.

10,330 **Medley**, K. I. M. 'Van-boy labour.' *Econ. Rev.*, XXI, 1 (January 1911), 57–62.

10,331 **Post Office.** Standing Committee on Boy Labour. *Report*[s] *of Standing Committee on boy labour in the Post Office, together with instructions issued by the Postmaster General in connection therewith.* London: H.M.S.O., 1911–15. 5v. (Cd. 5504, 5755, 6959, 7556, 8019.)

Chairman: Sir Matthew Nathan.

10,332 **Agenda Club.** *The rough and the fairway: an enquiry into the golf caddie problem.* London: Heinemann, 1912. xi, 163p.

10,333 **Whitehouse**, John Howard. 'Street trading by children.' Whitehouse, J. H. (ed.). *Problems of boy life.* London: King, 1912. p. 163–9.

10,334 **Home Department.** Departmental Committee on the Hours and Conditions of Employment of Van Boys and Warehouse Boys. *Report, appendices.* London: H.M.S.O., 1913. 31p. (Cd. 6886.)

Minutes of evidence, etc. 1913. (Cd. 6887.)

Chairman: G. Bellhouse.

10,335 **Greenwood**, Arthur. 'Agriculture and child labour.' *Polit. Q.*, 6 (May 1915), 119–44.

10,336 **Barrow**, *Mrs* Harrison. 'Girl munition workers.' Code, G. B. (ed.). *War and the citizen: urgent questions of the day.* London: Hodder and Stoughton, 1917. p. 67–73.

Reprinted from the *Birmingham Street Children's Union Magazine.*

10,337 **Hyde**, *Sir* Robert Robertson. 'Boy munition workers.' Code, G. B. (ed.). *War and the citizen: urgent questions of the day.* London: Hodder and Stoughton, 1917. p. 57–65.

Reprinted from the *Birmingham Street Children's Union Magazine.*

10,338 **Lennard**, Reginald. 'The employment of boys in agriculture and the rural exodus.' *Econ. J.*, XXVII, 108 (December 1917), 559–61.

10,339 **Green**, Herbert. 'Child labour in the coal mines of Nottinghamshire and Derbyshire in the nineteenth century: extracts from the reports of the Commissioners, 1842.' *Derby. Archaeol. Nat. Hist. Soc. J.*, 57 (1936), 1–14.

10,340 **Industrial Christian Fellowship.** Youth Committee. *From school to . . . ? Conditions of young people in the distributive trades.* London: the Fellowship, 1936. 27p.

10,341 **Barnard**, E. A. B. 'Chimney-sweepers: their climbing boys.' *Notes Quer.*, CLXXIX, 26 (28 December 1940), 461–2.

10,342 **Emmison**, Frederick George. 'Essex children deported to a Lancashire cotton mill, 1799.' *Essex Rev.*, LIII, 211 (July 1944), 77–81.

10,343 **Phillips**, George Lewis. 'The chimney-sweeper's friend, and climbing-boy's album.' *Hunter Archaeol. Soc. Trans.*, VI, 5 (December 1949), 221–31.

10,344 **Phillips**, George Lewis. 'May-Day is sweeps' day.' *Folk-lore*, LX, 1 (March 1949), 217–27.

10,345 **Phillips**, George Lewis. 'Mrs. Montagu and the climbing-boys.' *Rev. Engl. Studies*, XXV, 99 (July 1949), 237–44.

Elizabeth Montagu, 1720–1800 and her annual entertainment on May Day of young chimney sweeps.

10,346 **Home Office.** Departmental Committee on the Employment of Children as Film Actors, in Theatrical Work and in Ballet. *Report, etc.* 1950. v, 119p. (Cmd. 8005.)

Chairman: D. L. Bateson.

10,347 **Phillips**, George Lewis. 'The abolition of climbing boys.' *Am. J. Econ. Sociol.*, IX (July 1950), 445–62.

10,348 **Musson**, Albert Edward. 'Robert Blincoe and the early factory system.' *Derby. Misc.* (February 1958), 1–7.

On child labour in a cotton mill.

See also: 10,612.

iii. *Education*

See also Part Six, II, B, 3; and Part Seven, IV, E.

10,349 **Sykes**, T. P. 'The factory half-timer.' *Fortn. Rev.*, n.s., XLVI, 276 (December 1889), 823–31.

Child labour and education.

10,350 **Waddington,** R. *The half-time system as it affects the education of girls.* Congleton, 1893. 11p.

10,351 **Home Department.** Departmental Committee on the Conditions of School Attendance and Child Labour. *Report.* London: H.M.S.O., 1893–94. 46p. (H.C. 311.)

10,352 **Wyatt**, Charles Henry. 'Continuation schools.' *Manchr. Statist. Soc. Trans.* (1895–96), 151–74.

10,353 **McMillan**, Margaret. *Child labour and the half-time system.* London: *Clarion* Newspaper Co., 1896. 12p. (Clarion pamphlet 15.)

10,354 **Spencer**, F. H. 'Child labour and the half-time system.' *Econ. Rev.*, VIII, 4 (October 1898), 463–81.

10,355 **Campbell**, A. C. *The granting of certificates of fitness to children and young persons for employment in factories and workshops, with special reference to the system of half-time employment.* London, 1902. 11p.

10,356 **Mansbridge**, Albert. 'Working men and continuation schools.' Sadler, M. E. (ed.). *Continuation schools in England & elsewhere: their place in the educational system of an industrial and commercial state.* Manchester: Manchester U.P., 1907. p. 369–87.

10,357 **Sadler**, Michael Ernest (ed.). *Continuation schools in England & elsewhere: their place in the educational system of an industrial and commercial state.* Manchester: Manchester U.P., 1907. xxvi, 779p. (University of Manchester publications, no. XXIX. Educational series 1.)

Second edition. 1908.

10,358 **Sadler**, M. E. and **Beard**, Mary S. 'English employers and the education of their workpeople.' Sadler, M. E. (ed.). *Continuation schools in England & elsewhere: their place in the educational system of an industrial and commercial state.* Manchester: Manchester U.P., 1907. p. 265–317.

'Returns summarised by M. E. Sadler and Mary S. Beard.'

10,359 **Sandiford**, Peter. 'The half-time system in the textile trades.' Sadler, M. E. (ed.). *Continuation schools in England & elsewhere: their place in the educational system of an industrial and commercial state.* Manchester: Manchester U.P., 1907. p. 318–51.

10,360 **Waddington**, R. *Lancashire's shame; the half-time system: physical, moral and mental effect.* Manchester, [1908?]. 8p.

10,361 **Chesser**, Elizabeth Sloan. 'Half-timers in the factories.' *Westm. Rev.*, CLXXII, 4 (October 1909), 406–9.

10,362 **Jones**, Thomas. 'Unemployment, boy labour and continued education.' *Social. Rev.*, II, 11 (January 1909), 857–70.

10,363 **Bathurst**, Charles. 'Rural continuation schools as affecting the prevention of destitution.' National Conference on the Prevention of Destitution. *Report of the proceedings . . . 1911.* London: King, 1911. p. 283–90.

Discussion, p. 299–307.

10,364 **Greenwood**, Arthur. 'Continuation schools: their organisation and curriculum.' National Conference on the Prevention of Destitution. *Report of the proceedings . . . 1911.* London: King, 1911. p. 276–83.

The author was Head of the Economics Department, Huddersfield Technical College.

Discussion, p. 299–307.

10,365 **Watts**, J. I. 'Effect of continuation and evening schools on the industrial classes.' National Conference on the Prevention of Destitution. *Report of the proceedings . . . 1911.* London: King, 1911. p. 273–6.

The author was Managing Director of Brunner, Mond & Co.

Discussion, p. 299–307.

10,366 **Main**, William. 'The organisation and aim of continuation classes, with special reference to recent developments in Edinburgh.' National Conference on the Prevention of Destitution. *Report of the proceedings . . . 1912.* London: King, 1912. p. 233–40.
Discussion, p. 260–5.

10,367 **Workers' Educational Association.** *Child labour and education: during the war and after.* London: W.E.A., 1915. 28p.

10,368 **Best**, Robert Hall. 'The workshop and the citizen.' Code, G. B. (ed.). *War and the citizen: urgent questions of the day.* London: Hodder and Stoughton, 1917. p. 9–14.
Reprinted from the *Birmingham Street Children's Union Magazine.*

10,369 **Findlay**, Joseph John (ed.). *The young wage-earner and the problem of his education: essays and reports.* London: Sidgwick and Jackson, 1918. 211p.

10,370 **Labour Party.** *Memorandum prepared by the Advisory Committee on Education.* London: Labour Party, 1918. 24p.

10,371 **Brooks**, Leonard. *The London compulsory day continuation schools, January, 1921–July 1922.* 1923. 3v. (M.A. thesis, University of London.)

10,372 **Garland**, William Robert. *Continuation schools, with special reference to the continuative clauses of the Education Act, 1918.* 1925. ix, 270 leaves. (M.Sc. thesis (Econ.), University of London.)

10,373 **Laurie**, A. P. *Education of the adolescent and juvenile employment.* London, [1927?]. 8p.

10,374 **Milne-Watson**, *Sir* David. *Education and industry.* Birmingham, 1927. 12p.

10,375 **Robson**, A. H. *The education of children engaged in industry in England 1833–76.* 1929–30. (Ph.D. thesis, University of London.)

10,376 **Mills**, Nora. 'Child growth under the half-time factory system.' *Roch. Lit. Soc. Trans.*, XVIII (1932–34), 69–72.

10,377 **Bell**, Valentine Augustus. *The function and operation of Junior Instruction Centres.* Loughborough: Association of Technical Institutions, 1934. 15p. (Miscellaneous pamphlets.)
Paper read at the Summer Meeting, 1934.

10,378 **Bell**, Valentine Augustus. *Junior instruction centres and their future: a report to the Carnegie United Kingdom Trust.* Edinburgh: Constable, 1934. xx, 106p.

10,379 **Leslie**, W. *The development of Junior Instruction Centres in the County of Durham.* Loughborough: Association of Technical Institutions, 1935. 28p. (Miscellaneous pamphlets.)
Paper read at the Summer Meeting, 1935.

10,380 **Ward**, Gertrude. 'The education of factory child workers, 1833–1850: a study of the effects of the educational clauses in the Factory Act of 1833.' *Econ. Hist.*, III, 10 (February 1935), 110–24.

10,381 **Northern Ireland.** *The instruction of unemployed juveniles: report of the Committee appointed by the Minister of Labour to advise him on the types of courses of instruction to be provided in accordance with s.80 of the Unemployment Insurance Act (Northern Ireland), 1936.* Belfast: H.M.S.O., 1938. 77p. (Cmd. 193.)

10,382 **Brooksbank**, K. *The day continuation school in England.* 1939. (M.Ed. thesis, University of Manchester.)

10,383 **Hicks**, W. C. R. 'The education of the half-timer, as shown particularly in the case of Messrs. McConnel and Co. of Manchester.' *Econ. Hist.*, III, 14 (February 1939), 222–39.

10,384 **Smith**, May and **Leiper**, Margaret. 'A study of temporarily unemployed girls at a Junior Instruction Centre.' *Occup. Psychol.*, XIV, 2 (April 1940), 82–93.

10,385 **Evans**, Owen E. *Redeeming the time: a survey of the Junior Instruction Centre Movement.* Liverpool: U.P. of Liverpool, 1941. 63p. (New Merseyside series 13.)

10,386 **Lane**, Fearnley. 'In praise of the Day Continuation School.' *Occup. Psychol.*, XVII, 2 (April 1943), 92–7.

10,387 **Scottish Education Department.** *Compulsory day continuation classes: fourth report of the Advisory Council on Education in Scotland.* Edinburgh: H.M.S.O., 1943. 41p.
Second (Interim) Report published as Appendix I to this Report. p. 33–7.

10,388 **Evans**, Leslie Wynne. 'Ironworks schools in South Wales, 1784–1860.' *Sociol. Rev.*, XLIII, 11 (1951), 203–28.

10,389 **Evans**, Leslie Wynne. *The works schools of the Industrial Revolution in Wales.* 1953. 474 leaves. (Ph.D. thesis, University College, Cardiff.)

10,390 **Doherty**, Bernard. 'Compulsory day continuation education: an examination of the 1918 experiment.' *Voc. Asp.*, XVIII, 39 (Spring 1966), 41–56.

10,391 **Evans**, Leslie Wynne. 'Voluntary education in the industrial areas of Wales before 1870.' *Natn. Libr. Wales J.*, XIV, 4 (Winter 1966), 407–23.
On the part played by employers of labour with works schools.

10,392 **Hatley**, Victor Arthur. *The St. Giles' Shoe-School: an incident in the history of shoe manufacturing at Northampton.* Northampton: Northampton Historical Series, 1966. 7p. (Northampton historical series 4.)
Second edition. 1968.

10,393 **Evans**, Leslie Wynne. 'School Boards and the works schools system after the Education Act of 1870.' *Natn. Libr. Wales J.*, XV, 1 (Summer 1967), 89–100.

10,394 **Sanderson**, Michael. 'Education and the factory in industrial Lancashire, 1780–

1840.' *Econ. Hist. Rev.*, 2nd ser., xx, 2 (August 1967), 266–79.

10,395 **Pallister**, Ray. 'Educational investment by industrialists in the early part of the nineteenth century in County Durham.' *Durham Univ. J.*, LXI, 1 (December 1968), 32–8.

10,396 **Jack**, Denis Raymond. *A history of the Royal Dockyard schools, with particular reference to the Portsmouth School.* 1968–69. (M.A. thesis, University of London.)

d. THE UNEMPLOYED: CONDITIONS AND RELIEF

See also Part Three, III, F, 4; Part Six, II, D; Part Six, II, E, 3; Part Six, IV, C, 4; Part Seven, IV, B; Part Seven, IV, D, 2; Part Seven, IV, D, 5; Part Seven, IX, A, 2; and Part Seven, IX, B, 1.

i. *General*

10,397 **May**, Reuben. *The London poor and unemployed: an address at Spencer Place Chapel.* London, 1882.

10,398 **Local Government Board for Ireland.** *Copies of a report . . . dated the 13th day of March 1883, with regard to the distress existing, or apprehended in certain parts of Ireland, and of the reports from Inspectors of the Local Government Board, and other papers enclosed therewith.* [London: H.M.S.O.], 1883. 19p. (H.C. 92.)

Further reports and papers were published as H.C. 145. 15p.

10,399 **Champion**, Henry Hyde. *The facts about the unemployed: an appeal and a warning by 'one of the middle class'.* London: Modern P., 1886. 16p.

Signed H.H.C., i.e. Henry H. Champion.

10,400 **Peek**, Francis. *The workless, the thriftless and the worthless.* London: Isbister, 1888. 96p.

Second edition. 1892. 56p.

10,401 **Shoreditch Vestry.** *Report of a committee to take into consideration the question of the unemployed.* 1888.

10,402 **Burns**, John. 'Labour leaders on the labour question. I. The unemployed.' *Nineteenth Century*, XXXII, 190 (December 1892), 845–63.

10,403 **Burns**, John. *The unemployed.* London: Fabian Society, 1893. 19p. (Fabian tract 47.)

Reprinted 1906.

Written in 1892.

Reprinted, with additions, from *Nineteenth Century*, December 1892.

10,404 **Glasgow City.** *Report of conference on the social condition of the people.* 1893.

10,405 **Mansion House Committee**, London. *Report of the Mansion House Committee appointed . . . 1893, to investigate the existence of distress in London, caused by lack of employment, and to consider the best means of dealing with it.* London, 1893. 147p.

10,406 **Shoreditch Vestry.** *Report of Committee on the unemployed.* 1893.

10,407 **Brewster**, Alice Rollins. 'Early experiments with the unemployed.' *Q. J. Econ.*, IX (October 1894), 88–95.

10,408 **Liverpool City.** *Full report of the Commission of Inquiry into the subject of the unemployed in the City of Liverpool.* Liverpool, 1894. xxii, 119p.

10,409 **Mansion House Committee**, London. *First report . . . on the condition of the unemployed, November 1887 to July 1888.* London, [1894?]. 31p.

10,410 **Charity Organisation Society.** *Winter distress: a paper for the consideration of provincial societies.* London: the Society, 1896. 4p. (Occasional paper 53.)

By N. Masterman.

10,411 **Duckworth**, George H. 'The work of the Select Committee of the House of Commons on Distress from Want of Employment.' *Econ. J.*, VI, 21 (March 1896), 143–53.

10,412 **Woodworth**, Arthur V. *Report of an inquiry into the condition of the unemployed conducted under the Toynbee Trust, Winter 1895–6. Based on information collected from local inquirers by Viscount Fitzharris, B.A.* London: Dent, 1897. 62p.

10,413 **McKenzie**, Frederick Arthur. *Famishing London: a study of the unemployed and unemployable.* London: Hodder and Stoughton, 1903. 88p.

10,414 **Barnett**, Samuel Augustus. *Industrial invalids. I. The unemployed and the unemployable.* Oxford: Christian Social Union, Oxford University Branch, 1904. p. 1–13.

Reprinted from the *Economic Review*, October 1903.

Published with 'The Belgian labour colonies', by H. J. Torr.

10,415 **Manson**, R. T. *Casual labour . . . an address delivered at the Church Congress.* Liverpool, 1904.

10,416 **Benson**, T. D. *The workers' hell and the way out.* London, [1905?]. 16p.

10,417 **Leigh**, Leighton (*pseud.*) [i.e. Constance Sutcliffe *afterwards* Marriott]. *'Brother East and Brother West': a searchlight on the unemployed.* London: Heinemann, 1905. viii, 229p.

10,418 **Motion**, J. R. *The unemployed in Glasgow, 1904–1905.* Glasgow, 1905. 53p.

10,419 **Reason**, Will (ed.). *Our industrial outcasts; by members of the Christian Brotherhood.* London: A. Melrose, 1905. 155p.

10,420 **Clarke**, E. Dillon. 'The experiences of a tramp.' *Econ. J.*, XVI, 62 (June 1906), 284–91.

10,421 **Higgs**, Mary. *Glimpses into the abyss.* London: King, 1906. xiv, 331p.

10,422 **Sirr**, William. *Workless and starving: brief considerations upon the burning question of the day*. Plaistow: Church P., 1906. 15p.

10,423 **Donaldson**, Frederic Lewis. *The unemployed*. London: Society for Promoting Christian Knowledge, 1907. 4p. (Pan-Anglican papers S.A.4d.)

10,424 **Barnett**, Samuel Augustus. 'The problem of distress among the unemployed.' *International*, III, 12 (November 1908), 265–70.

10,425 **Bristol Right-to-Work Committee.** *Unemployed and starving in Bristol*. Bristol, 1908. 16p.

10,426 **Barnett**, Samuel Aguustus, *Canon* and **Barnett**, *Dame* Henrietta Octavia Weston. *Towards social reform*. London, Leipsic: Fisher Unwin, 1909. 352p.

Part II, 'Poverty', includes short articles on the unemployed, relief and the Poor Law.

10,427 **Good**, T. 'Unemployment from the "unemployed" point of view.' *Nineteenth Century*, LXV, 383 (January 1909), 153–62.

10,428 **National Committee to Promote the Break up of the Poor Law.** *The disease of unemployment*. 1909.

10,429 **Ashton**, Thomas Southcliffe. 'The relation between unemployment and sickness.' *Econ. J.*, XXVI, 103 (September 1916), 396–400.

In the Amalgamated Society of Engineers.

10,430 **Little**, Howard. 'The evil of unemployment: a skilled labourer's point of view.' *Nineteenth Century*, XCII, 548 (October 1922), 670–7.

10,431 **Ewart**, R. J. 'Unemployment and public health.' *R. Sanit. Inst. J.*, XLIII, Confer. I (February 1923), 225–30.

10,432 **Higgs**, Mary. *Down and out: studies in the problem of vagrancy, being a revised edition of 'My brother the tramp'*. London: Student Christian Movement, 1924. 110p.

First published as *My brother the tramp*, 1914.

10,433 **Mullins**, George William. *Unemployment: the gateway to a new life*. London: Longmans, 1926. xiii, 140p.

10,434 **Appleton**, William Archibald. *Work or starve*. London: Haycock, 1927. 8p.

Reprinted from the *Daily Mail*.

10,435 **Horsley**, Terence. *The Odyssey of an out-of-work*. London: John Lane, 1931. xiv, 272p.

10,436 **Brockway**, Archibald Fenner. *Hungry England*. London: Gollancz, 1932. 224p.

10,437 **Pearson**, Scott. *To the streets and back*. London: J. Lane, 1932. 244p.

10,438 **Bakke**, Edward Wight. *The unemployed man: a social study*. London: Nisbet, 1933. xviii, 308p.

'In its original form the study formed a part of a dissertation presented to the faculty of the Graduate School of Yale University for the degree of Doctor of Philosophy.'

10,439 **Bentley**, John A. *The submerged tenth: the story of a down and out*. London: Constable, 1933. 170p.

Autobiographical reminiscences.

10,440 **Teeling**, *Sir* Luke William Burke. *The near-by thing; or, living with our unemployed and how they are solving their own problems*. London: Jenkins, 1933. 232p.

10,441 **Beales**, Hugh Lancelot and **Lambert**, Richard Stanton (eds.). *Memoirs of the unemployed*. London: Gollancz, 1934. 287p.

Accounts by unemployed workers of the effects of unemployment.

First published in *The Listener* during the summer of 1933.

Appendices: 'How the workers spend their money', by Ruth Bowley; 'The psychology of the unemployed from the medical point of view', by Morris Robb.

10,442 **Neville-Rolfe**, Sybil Katherine and **Sempkins**, F. A. R. *Poverty and prostitution*. London: British Social Hygiene Council, 1934. 35p. (N.C. 104.)

Contents: 'Economic conditions in relation to prostitution', by S. Neville-Rolfe; 'Unemployment and prostitution of young girls', by F. Sempkins.

10,443 **Greene**, Felix (ed.). *Time to spare: what unemployment means, by eleven unemployed*. London: Allen and Unwin, 1935. 188p.

'With additional chapters by S. P. B. Mais, George Davies, Rev. Cecil Northcott, Prof. V. H. Mottram, Ronald C. Davison, the Master of Balliol [A. D. Lindsay].'

10,444 **Barker**, Reginald J. *Christ in the valley of unemployment*. London: Hodder and Stoughton, 1936. 126p.

10,445 **Burke**, D. *Give no jobs*. London, 1936. 10p.

10,446 **Newsom**, John. *Out of the pit: a challenge to the comfortable*. Oxford: Blackwell, 1936. xviii, 117p.

On the problem of the unemployed.

10,447 **Hanley**, James. *Grey children: a study in humbug and misery*. London: Methuen, 1937. ix, 230p.

On unemployment among miners in South Wales.

10,448 **Oxley**, Will. 'Are you working?' Common, J. (ed.). *Seven shifts*. London: Secker and Warburg, 1938. p. 105–44.

Personal account of an unemployed man.

10,449 **Pilgrim Trust.** *Men without work: a report made to the Pilgrim Trust*. Cambridge: Cambridge U.P., 1938. xii, 447p.

By a committee formed to consider the problem of unemployment.

10,450 **Wilkinson**, Ellen Cicely. *The town that was murdered: the life-story of Jarrow*. London: Gollancz, 1939. 287p.

Also Left Book Club edition.

10,451 **Cohen**, Max. *I was one of the unemployed*. London: Gollancz, 1945. x, 244p.
Foreword by Sir William Beveridge.
Also Left Book Club edition.

10,452 **Mount Street Club.** *Work to do: a survey of the unemployment problem*. Dublin: Mount Street Club, 1945. 120p.
A collection of short articles.

10,453 **Goldthorpe**, Harry. *Room at the bottom*. Bradford: Sunbeam P., 1959. 48p.
The author was Secretary of the Bradford Unemployed Association.

10,454 **Kershaw**, G. R. 'Medical repercussions of redundancy.' *Ass. Ind. Med. Offr. Trans.*, XIII, 2 (July 1963), 67–9.

10,455 **Coulter**, J. A. 'Employment and unemployment: the social repercussions.' *Christus Rex*, XVIII, 4 (October–December 1964), 221–9.

10,456 *The unemployed and the rights of man: a charter for those who are unemployed or sick, or disabled, or aged, or widowed, or orphaned*. Kirkoswald: J. Wilde, 1965. 16p.

10,457 **Keenan**, Jock. 'On the dole.' Fraser, R. (ed.). *Work: twenty personal accounts*. Harmondsworth: Penguin, 1968. p. 271–9.
First published in *New Left Review*, 37 (May–June 1966), 23–8.
Account of an unemployed miner.

10,458 **Waddy**, Stacy. 'On the dole.' *Trade Un. Regist.* (1969), 147–9.

See also: 5860; 5941.

ii. *Labour Colonies and Other Employment Schemes*

10,459 **Charity Organisation Society.** *On the best means of dealing with exceptional distress: the report of a special committee of the Charity Organisation Society*. London: Cassell, 1886. xxvi, 135, xip.

10,460 **Mansion House Conference on the Unemployed.** *Reports and suggestions . . . by the Sub-Committee on Agricultural Colonies*. 1887.

10,461 **Barnett**, Samuel Augustus. 'A scheme for the unemployed.' *Nineteenth Century*, XXIV, 141 (November 1888), 753–63.
Advocates training farms.

10,462 **Gardner**, A. Dunn. 'Some notes on relief works.' *Char. Orgn. Rev.*, IV, 42 (June 1888), 260–6.
'A paper read at the Denison Club on Wednesday, April 11 . . .'

10,463 **Rees**, William Lee. *From poverty to plenty: or, The labour question solved*. London: Wyman, 1888. xvi, 474p.

10,464 **Booth**, William Bramwell. *In darkest England and the way out*. London: International Headquarters of the Salvation Army, 1890, 285, xxxip.

10,465 **Brabazon**, M. J., Countess of Meath. *Brabazon pauper employment scheme*. 1890. 8p.

10,466 **Charity Organisation Society.** *An examination of 'General' Booth's social scheme, adopted by the Council of the London Charity Organisation Society*. London: Swan Sonnenschein, 1890. 102p.
Second edition.
By Sir Charles Stewart Loch.

10,467 **Hyndman**, Henry Mayers. *General Booth's book refuted*. London: Justice Printery, 1890. 16p.
On *In darkest England and the way out*.

10,468 **Loch**, *Sir* Charles Stewart. *An examination of 'General' Booth's social scheme*. London: Swan Sonnenschein, 1890. 102p.
Second edition.
Published for the Charity Organisation Society.

10,469 **Ashley**, William James. 'General Booth's panacea.' *Polit. Sci. Q.*, VI, 3 (September 1891), 537–50.
On *In darkest England and the way out*.

10,470 **Bosanquet**, Bernard. *'In darkest England' on the wrong track*. London: Swan Sonnenschein, 1891. vi, 72p.
A criticism of the work of William Booth.

10,471 **Jay**, Arthur Osborne Montgomery. *Life in darkest London: a hint to General Booth*. London: Webster and Cable, 1891. 146p.

10,472 **Phelps**, Lancelot Ridley. '*In darkest England and the way out*, by General Booth.' *Econ. Rev.*, I, 1 (January 1891), 144–8.

10,473 **Roberts**, W. Hazlitt. *General Booth's scheme, and the municipal alternative, with special reference to labour farms, including a successful English one*. London: Simpkin and Marshall, 1891. 49p.
General Booth's scheme as set forth in his work *In darkest England*.

10,474 **Salvation Army.** *'Darkest England' social scheme*. 1891.

10,475 **Glasgow Association for Improving the Conditions of the People.** *Report on labour colonies*. Glasgow, 1892.
By James Mavor and others.

10,476 **Paton**, John Brown. *Home colonisation*. 1892.

10,477 **Stevenson**, D. M. *Labour colonies and the unemployed: a partial solution of the problem*. Glasgow, 1892.

10,478 **Toynbee Hall Unemployed Committee.** *Draft report*. London: printed for private circulation, 1892. 4 leaves.

10,479 **English Land Colonisation Society.** *Report upon farm labour colonies and farm settlements*. London: the Society, 1893. 34p.

10,480 **Mavor**, James. 'Setting the poor on work.' *Nineteenth Century*, XXXIV, 200 (October 1893), 523–32.
Labour colonies and similar schemes in the seventeenth to nineteenth centuries.

10,481 **Moore**, Harold Edward. 'The unemployed and the land.' *Contemp. Rev.*, LXIII (March 1893), 423–38.
Description of labour colonies.

10,482 **Salvation Army.** *Hadleigh: the story of a great endeavour*. 1893.

10,483 **Toynbee** H. V. 'A winter's experiment.' *Macmillan's Mag.*, LXIX, 409 (November 1893), 54–8.
Work of the Mansion House Committee in the East End of London with the unemployed.

10,484 **Johnson**, *Sir* Samuel George. *Unskilled labour and relief work: a paper read at the second meeting of the Charity Organisation Conference at Rochdale, April 17, 1894.* London: Charity Organisation Society, 1894. 9p.

10,485 **Moore**, Harold Edward. *The land and the unemployed.* London, 1894. 63p.

10,486 **Paton**, John Brown. *Labour for the unemployed on the land.* London: Christian Union for Social Service, 1894. 11p.
Paper read at the second conference held in connection with the English Land Colonisation Society, October 25th, 1894.

10,487 **Robinson**, Thomas and **Burrows**, Joseph. *The next revolution; or, an agricultural remedy for the present distress in the United Kingdom.* London: C. H. Kelly, 1894. 12p.

10,488 **Withy**, Arthur. 'Work for the workless.' *Westm. Rev.*, CXLI, 3 (March 1894), 233–42.

10,489 **Booth**, William Bramwell. *Light in darkest England in 1895: a review of the social operations of the Salvation Army.* London, 1895. 106, xlviip.
Second edition.

10,490 **Conference upon Land, Co-operation and the Unemployed**, Holborn Town Hall, October, 1894. *Report.* 1895.

10,491 **Loch**, Charles Stewart. 'Methods of relief adopted in the metropolis during the winter of 1895.' *Char. Orgn. Rev.*, XII, 132 (January 1896), 2–17.
A paper read at a special meeting of the Council of the Charity Organisation Society on Monday, December 16, 1895.

10,492 **Palgrave**, M. E. 'A social experiment.' *Econ. Rev.*, VI, 2 (April 1896), 251–4.
Walter Hazell's farm for the unemployed at Langley, Essex.

10,493 **Buxton**, Noel. 'Labour homes.' *Econ. Rev.*, VIII, 3 (July 1898), 326–48.

10,494 **Booth**, William Bramwell. *Social reparation, or personal impressions of work for darkest England.* London: International Headquarters of the Salvation Army, 1899. 123p.

10,495 **Hazell**, Walter. 'A test farm for the unemployed.' *Puritan*, I, 1 (February 1899), 39–42.
Account of the author's Test Farm for the Unemployed, near Chesham, Bucks., for training men before emigration to Canada.

10,496 **Booth**, William Bramwell. 'What has come of the "Darkest England" scheme.' *Sun. Strand*, I, 1 (January 1900), 82–93.

10,497 **Hunt**, William H. 'An interesting industrial experiment.' *Westm. Rev.*, CLIV (September 1900), 285–97.
On General Booth's Darkest England Estate at Hadleigh, Essex.

10,498 **Albinson**, J. 'The Scottish labour colony: a difficult problem successfully solved.' *Good Words* (May 1901), 344–9.
A description of the labour colony at Ruthwell, Dumfriesshire. With illustrations.

10,499 **Verinder**, Frederick. *The land question, chiefly in its relation to labour and taxation: a paper . . .* Manchester: Co-operative Printing Society, 1901. 23p.

10,500 **Rider Haggard**, Henry. 'Agriculture and the unemployed question.' *Char. Orgn. Rev.*, n.s., XIII, 78 (June 1903), 287–302.
Given at a special meeting of the Charity Organisation Society, 4 May 1903. With discussion.

10,501 **Beveridge**, William Henry and **Maynard**, H. R. 'The unemployed: lessons from the Mansion House Fund.' *Contemp. Rev.*, LXXXVI (November 1904), 629–38.
Proposed creation of compulsory and permanent colonies for unemployables, and of two kinds of free colony, to be open only in times of distress, for 'genuine casual labourers', and 'regular workers'.

10,502 **Booth**, William Bramwell. *The vagrant and the 'unemployable'. A proposal for the extension of the land and industrial colony system, whereby vagrants may be detained under suitable conditions and compelled to work.* London: The Salvation Army, 1904. 47p.
'With a report and notes by Col. David C. Lamb . . . and contributions upon the subject by Mr. Bramwell Booth and others.'

10,503 **Bosanquet**, Helen. 'Past experience in relief works.' Loch, C. S. (ed.). *Methods of social advance: short studies in social practice by various authors.* London, New York: Macmillan, 1904. p. 79–87.

10,504 **Cowland**, E. M. 'A new unemployed relief scheme.' *Econ. Rev.*, XIV, 2 (April 1904), 213–16.
Account of the scheme in Camberwell where the author worked.

10,505 **Martineau**, John. 'Emigration and want of employment.' Loch, C. S. (ed.). *Methods of social advance: short studies in social practice by various authors.* London, New York: Macmillan, 1904. p. 88–95.

10,506 **Rider Haggard**, Henry. 'Agriculture and the unemployed question: an address.' Loch, C. S. (ed.). *Methods of social advance: short studies in social practice by various authors.* London, New York: Macmillan, 1904. p. 64–78.

10,507 **Booth**, William Bramwell. *The recurring problem of the unemployed; one permanent remedy: emigration – colonisation; proposals for the better distribution of the people.* London: International H.Q. of the Salvation Army, 1905. 54p.

10,508 **Carlile**, Wilson. 'Problem of the unemployed and suggestions for its solution.' *Fortn. Rev.*, n.s., LXXVIII, 468 (December 1905), 1065–73.

Church Army labour homes.

10,509 **London Unemployed Fund**, 1904–5. *Report of central executive committee, presented to the full committee, November 10, 1905*. London: King, 1905. 160p.

10,510 **Pringle**, J. C. 'Labour colonies.' *Econ. Rev.*, xv, 1 (January 1905), 50–73.

10,511 *Report of a temporary colony at Garden City for unemployed workmen mainly from West Ham during February, March & April 1905, carried out by the Trinity College, Oxford, Settlement . . .* London: King, 1905. 28p.

10,512 **Rider Haggard**, *Sir* Henry. *The poor and the land, being a report on the Salvation Army colonies in the United States and at Hadleigh, England, with scheme of national land settlement, and an introduction*. London: Longmans, 1905. xxxvii, 157p.

10,513 **Rider Haggard**, *Sir* Henry. *Report on Salvation Army colonies*. London: H.M.S.O., 1905. (Cd. 2562.)

10,514 **Rowan**, Edgar. *Wilson Carlile and the Church Army*. London: Hodder and Stoughton, 1905. xvi, 487p.

Another edition. 1907. 128p.

Third and revised edition, by A. E. Reffold. London: Church Army Bookroom, 1928. ix, 222p.

10,515 **Tillyard**, Frank. 'Three Birmingham relief funds, 1885, 1886, and 1905.' *Econ. J.*, xv, 60 (December 1905), 505–20.

10,516 **Alden**, Percy. 'Labour colonies.' Co-operative Wholesale Societies. *Annual for 1906*. p. 175–201.

Reprinted by the Friends' Social Union, 1906, under the title *Labour colonies in England and on the Continent*.

10,517 **Charity Organisation Review.** 'Last year's unemployed.' *Char. Orgn. Rev.*, n.s., XIX, 110 (February 1906), 61–84.

'. . . a summary of the means adopted in London for the relief of distress due to want of employment during the winter of 1904–5.'

10,518 **Departmental Committee Appointed to Consider Mr. Rider Haggard's Report on Agricultural Settlements in British Colonies.**

Vol. I. *Report*. London: H.M.S.O., 1906. iii, 41p. (Cd. 2978.)

Vol. II. *Minutes of evidence, etc.* (Cd. 2979.)

Chairman: Lord Tennyson.

10,519 **Fels**, Joseph. 'Farm colonies.' *Fmr. Club J.* (May 1906), 399–420.

10,520 **Manson**, John. *The Salvation Army and the public: a religious, social, and financial study*. London: Routledge; New York: Dutton, 1906. xix, 376p.

Second edition, augmented. 1908.

Third edition. 1908.

Includes a chapter on 'The working of the "social" scheme'.

10,521 **Morrison**, David McLaren. 'The unemployed and trades unions.' *Nineteenth Century*, LIX, 349 (March 1906), 483–7.

10,522 **Roberts**, W. Hazlitt. *Landward ho! A review of the land and unemployed questions, and a solution*. London: Caxton P., [1906]. vi, 101p.

10,523 **Central (Unemployed) Body for London.** *A report upon the work and procedure of the distress committees in London*. London, 1907. 15p.

10,524 **Gunning**, J. *The unemployed: Hollesley Bay farm colony*. 1907.

Reprinted from *A.S.E. Journal*.

The colony set up by the London Central Committee for the Unemployed.

10,525 **Lansbury**, George. 'Hollesley Bay labour colony.' *Commonwealth*, XII, 7 (July 1907), 196–9.

10,526 **Paton**, John Brown. *How to restore our yeoman-peasantry; and, Labour on the land for the unemployed*. London: J. Clarke, 1907. 72p. (Social questions of the day 6.)

10,527 **Charity Organisation Society.** Special Committee on Unskilled Labour. *Report and minutes of evidence, June, 1908*. London: the Society, 1908. 249p.

10,528 **Fels**, Joseph. 'Unemployment and unused town lands.' *St. George*, XI, 44 (October 1908), 230–7.

10,529 **Lansbury**, George. 'Hollesley Bay.' *Social. Rev.*, I, 3 (May 1908), 220–33.

10,530 **M.**, W. A. and **M.**, A. C. H. *The free table: a scheme for the immediate relief of the unemployed*. London: Questall P., 1908. 8p.

10,531 **Morris**, J. C. 'The unemployed.' *Char. Orgn. Rev.*, n.s., XXIV, 142 (October 1908), 219–25.

Based on the 'Return as to the Proceedings of Distress Committees and of the Central Unemployed Body for London under the Unemployed Workmen Act of 1905, for the year ended March 31, 1908'.

10,532 **Society for Organizing Charitable Relief and Repressing Mendicity.** Special Committee on Unskilled Labour. *Report and minutes of evidence, June, 1908*. London: the Society, 1908. 249p.

10,533 **Summerbell**, Thomas. *Afforestation, the unemployed and the land*. London: Independent Labour Party, 1908. 16p.

10,534 **International Emigration Office.** *The surplus, being a restatement of the emigration policy and methods of the Salvation Army, together with a report of last year's work, etc.* 1909.

10,535 **Watts**, J. Hunter. *Self-maintenance for the unemployed*. London, 1909. 15p.

10,536 **Lamb**, David C. 'The labour colony as an agency for the prevention of destitution.' National Conference on the Prevention of Destitution. *Report of the proceedings . . . 1911*. London: King, 1911. p. 501–9.

Discussion, p. 509–16.

10,537 **Lodge**, Richard. 'The Edinburgh Labour Colony at Murieston.' National Conference on the Prevention of Destitution. *Report of the proceedings . . . 1911*. London: King, 1911. p. 499–501.

Discussion, p. 509–16.

10,538 **Smart**, Bolton. 'The Hollesley Bay Labour Colony.' National Conference on the Prevention of Destitution. *Report of the proceedings . . . 1911*. London: King, 1911. p. 482–93.

The author was Superintendent of the Colony.

Discussion, p. 509–16.

10,539 **Grenfell**, Arthur P. *Afforestation and unemployment*. London: Fabian Society, 1912. 16p. (Fabian tract 161.)

10,540 **Twycross**, John. *Colonising England instead of the colonies, no. 1*. London: the author, 1914. 12p.

10,541 **Moore**, Harold Edward. *Farm work for discharged soldiers*. London: King, 1916. 30p.

10,542 **Rothband**, *Sir* Henry Lesser. *The Rothband scheme for the employment of disabled men*. Manchester: J. Heywood, 1917.

10,543 **Rothband**, *Sir* Henry Lesser. *A scheme for finding employment for disabled soldiers & sailors*. Manchester, London: J. Heywood, 1917. 3 pt.

'Extracts from press notices of Mr. Rothband's scheme; extracts from letters containing expressions of opinion on his proposals for a national roll of employers.'

10,544 **Rothband**, *Sir* Henry Lesser. *The Rothband employment scheme for sailors and soldiers disabled in the war. Parliament to the rescue*. Manchester, London: Norbury, Natzio, 1918. 34p.

10,545 **Saunderson**, R. 'The relief of the unemployed.' *Char. Orgn. Rev.*, n.s., XLIX, 290 (February 1921), 116–23.

'The chief purpose of this article is to present a summary of the measures which have been proposed, as well as of the actual sources, official and voluntary, which are available, for the relief of distress due to the present wave of unemployment.'

10,546 **Northcott**, Clarence Hunter. 'Emigration and colonization as a remedy for unemployment.' *Assemblée générale de l'Association internationale pour la lutte contre le chômage, Luxembourg, 9–11 septembre, 1923*. Geneva: S.A. Des Éditions 'Sonor', 1923. p. 57–65.

10,547 **Smith**, Alfred. *A cottage and an acre: the remedy for unemployment*. London: the author, 1923. 31p.

10,548 **Wright**, William and **Penty**, Arthur Joseph. *Agriculture and the unemployed*. London: Labour Publishing Co., 1925. 94p.

10,549 **Pughe**, Thomas St. John Parry. *The problem of migration and unemployment, being a report on a visit to Australia*. London: Simpkin, Marshall, 1928. 31p.

10,550 **Irwin**, Margaret Hardinge. *What are we doing in Scotland for our unemployed girls*. Glasgow, 1929. 19p.

10,551 **Agricola.** *An ordinary man looks at economics: a way to prosperity for farmers and a remedy for unemployment*. Birmingham: Cornish Bros., 1930. 12p.

10,552 **Lester**, William Richard. *Unemployment and the land*. London: United Committee for the Taxation of Land Values, 1930. 16p.

Fifth edition. 1934. 19p.

10,553 *Why not a 'Camp of Refuge' for the unemployed?* London: printed for the author, 1930. 16p.

10,554 **Christian Social Council.** *For the unemployed: a ministry of Christian fellowship*. London: the Council, 1932. 31p.

10,555 **National Council of Social Service.** *Work with the unemployed: an account of some experiments*. London, 1932. 22p.

10,556 **Bournville Village Trust.** *An unemployment relief scheme: notes on an experiment made by the Bournville Village Trust, 1932–33*. Bournville: the Trust, 1933. 14p.

10,557 *The centre; the social centre in relation to unemployment and national health: a study by five independent observers*. London: King, 1933. vii, 29p.

10,558 **National Council of Social Service.** *Unemployment and opportunity: some practical suggestions*. London, 1933. 24p.

10,559 **Williams**, Michael Sims. *Camps for men*. London: Universities' Council for Unemployed Camps, 1933. 55p.

10,560 **Alexandre**, John P. 'The Jersey School at Lincoln (1591–1830 circa): an old-time scheme for relieving unemployment.' *Lincs. Mag.*, I, 9 (January–February 1934), 289–91.

10,561 **Cameron**, Alice Mackenzie. *Civilisation and the unemployed*. London: Student Christian Movement P., 1934. vii, 152p.

Describes organisation of unemployed clubs in Lincoln, 1927–30.

10,562 **Hoyland**, John Somervell. *Digging with the unemployed*. London: Student Christian Movement P., 1934. xi, 100p.

10,563 **Parry**, Elizabeth Annie and **King**, Harold. *New leisure and old learning: being a report on the classes for unemployed men and women held in the David Lewis Club . . . Liverpool, June 1932–March 1934*. Liverpool: U.P. of Liverpool; London: Hodder and Stoughton, 1934. 32p.

10,564 **Shadforth**, William. *In workless civilization and the way out by means of the 'Shadforth unemployment policy'*. London: W. Shadforth, 1934. 94p.

10,565 **Herbert**, George. *Can land settlement solve unemployment?* London: Allen and Unwin, 1935. 129p.

10,566 **Muirhead**, James Fullerton. *Land and unemployment.* London: Oxford U.P., 1935. xix, 211p.
Edited with an introductory note on Henry George, by Garnet Smith.

10,567 **Scott**, John Waugh. *Self-subsistence for the unemployed: studies in a new technique.* London: Faber, 1935. 223p.

10,568 **Shadforth**, William. *In workless civilization and the way out.* Otley: W. Walker, 1935. 23p.
On the Shadforth unemployment policy.

10,569 **Brynmawr**, Brecknockshire. Order of Friends. *An Order of Friends: an account of their activities and ideas.* Hereford, 1936. 47p.

10,570 **Hoyland**, John Somervell. *Digging for a new England: the co-operative farm for unemployed men.* London: Cape, 1936. 224p.

10,571 **National Council of Social Service.** *Unemployment and community service.* London, 1936. 99p.

10,572 **Yates**, P. Lamartine. 'The land and the unemployed industrial worker in Great Britain.' *Int. Labour Rev.*, XXXIV, 3 (September 1936), 339–60.

10,573 **Young Women's Christian Association.** *Opportunity: the YWCA and unemployment.* London, 1936. [12]p.

10,574 **Richmond**, A. C. 'The action of voluntary organisations to provide occupation for unemployed workers in Great Britain.' *Int. Labour Rev.*, XXXVII, 5 (May 1938), 644–51.

10,575 **Ministry of Labour.** Committee on Land Settlement (England and Wales). *Report.* London: H.M.S.O., 1939. 158p.
Chairman: Sir William Dampier.

10,576 **National Council of Social Service.** *Out of adversity: a survey of the clubs for men and women which have grown out of the needs of unemployment.* London, 1939. 63p.

10,577 **Mount Street Club.** *Work to do: a survey of the unemployment problem.* Dublin, 1945. 120p.

10,578 **Fry**, Joan Mary. *Friends lend a hand in alleviating unemployment: the story of a social experiment extending over 20 years, 1926–1946.* London: Friends' Book Centre, 1947. 48p.

10,579 **Mess**, Henry Adolphus. 'Social service with the unemployed.' Mess, H. A., and others. *Voluntary social services since 1918.* London: Kegan Paul, Trench, Trubner, 1947. p. 40–54.

10,580 **Sherwin**, Oscar. 'An eighteenth century Beveridge planner.' *Am. Hist. Rev.*, LII, 2 (January 1947), 281–90.
Patrick Colquhoun, 1745–1816, author of *A treatise on indigence* . . . 1806.

10,581 **Sherwin**, Oscar. 'Thomas Firmin, Puritan precursor of WPA.' *J. Med. Hist.*, XXII, 1 (March 1950), 38–43.
Author of *Some proposals for the employment of the poor* . . . 1681.
WPA – Works Progress Administration.

10,582 **Glen**, W. *The Glasgow Council for Community Service in Unemployment, 1932–1950.* Glasgow: the Council, 1951. 29, [10] leaves.

10,583 **Brown**, John. 'Charles Booth and labour colonies, 1889–1905.' *Econ. Hist. Rev.*, 2nd ser., XXI, 2 (August 1968), 349–60.

e. PRISON LABOUR

10,584 **Treasury.** Committee Appointed to Consider Certain Questions Relating to the Employment of Convicts in the United Kingdom. *Report.* London: H.M.S.O., 1882. (C. 3427.)

10,585 **Home Office.** *Report of the sub-committee appointed to investigate the question of the most suitable place for a harbour of refuge on the East coast of Scotland to be constructed by convicts; together with the report by the Committee on Convict Labour.* London: H.M.S.O., 1884. 221p. (C. 4053.)

10,586 **Home Department.** *Report of the Departmental Committee on the Employment of Prisoners.* London: H.M.S.O.
Part I. *Employment of prisoners.* 1933. iv, 99p. (Cmd. 4462.)
Part II. *Employment on discharge.* 1935. 75p. (Cmd. 4897.)
Chairman: Isidore Salmon.

10,587 **Home Office** and **Scottish Home Department.** *Work for prisoners: report of the Advisory Council on the Employment of Prisoners.* London: H.M.S.O., 1961. 42p.
Chairman: Sir Wilfred Anson.

10,588 **Home Office.** Advisory Council on the Employment of Prisoners. *Work and vocational training in borstals (England & Wales): report.* London: H.M.S.O., 1962 [i.e. 1963]. 32p.
Chairman: Sir Wilfred Anson.

10,589 **Martin**, John Powell. 'Employing ex-prisoners.' *New Soc.*, II, 53 (3 October 1963), 18–19.

10,590 **Home Office** and **Scottish Home and Health Department.** *The organisation of work for prisoners: report of the Advisory Council on the Employment of Prisoners.* London: H.M.S.O., 1964. 15p.
Chairman: Sir Wilfred Anson.

10,591 **Cooper**, M. H. and **King**, R. D. 'Prison work – but how?' *New Soc.*, VI, 153 (2 September 1965), 8–10.

B. HOURS

Many of the general works contained in Part Six, IV, A, 1 and 3–4 also contain material on hours of work. See also Part Seven, V, C.

1. General

10,592 **Durham Coal Trade Arbitration.** *Working hours arbitration, July 1880.* Newcastle, 1880. 74p.

10,593 **Association of Master Builders.** *Comparative statement showing hours worked in the building trade.* Liverpool, 1885.

10,594 **Hadfield**, P. A. and **Gibbins**, Henry de Bettgens. *A shorter working day.* London: Methuen, 1892. (Social questions of to-day.)

10,595 **Mather**, William. *Trade unions and the hours of labour: an article...* Manchester: *Guardian* Printing Works, 1892. 11p.

10,596 **Mather**, William. *The forty-eight hours week: a year's experiment and its results at the Salford Iron Works, Manchester.* Manchester: *Guardian* Printing Works, 1894. 28p.

10,597 **Mather**, William. *A reply to some criticism on Mr. Mather's report of a year's trial of the forty-eight hours week.* London: King, 1894. 8p.

Reprinted from *The Times.*

10,598 **Beardsley**, Charles. 'The effect of an eight hours' day on wages and the unemployed.' *Q.J. Econ.*, IX (July 1895), 450–9.

10,599 **Schlytter**, T. *Continuous industries.* 1910. 10p.

10,600 **Scottish Council for Women's Trades.** *Exempted shops: reports I, II.* Glasgow, 1911. 2v.

10,601 **International Association for Labour Legislation.** *Report . . . on hours of labour in continuous industries.* London, 1912. 26p.

10,602 **Rathbone**, H. P. R. *Some notes on the relation of hours to output.* London, 1917. 19 leaves.

10,603 **United States.** National Industrial Conference Board. *Analysis of British wartime reports on hours of work as related to output and fatigue.* Boston, Mass.: N.I.C.B., 1917. iv, 57p. (Research report 2.)

10,604 **Magnusson**, Leifur. 'Hours of labor in foreign countries.' *Ann. Am. Acad. Polit. Soc. Sci.*, LXXXIII (May 1919), 202–32.

10,605 **Engineering and Allied Employers' National Federation.** *Working hours: report of Joint Investigation Committee appointed by the Engineering and National Employers' Federation, the Shipbuilding Employers' Federation, and the Unions' Negotiating Committee.* London, 1922. 92p.

10,606 **International Labour Office.** *Hours of labour in industry: Great Britain, October 1922.* Geneva: I.L.O., 1923. 31p. (Studies and reports, series D, wages and hours 7.)

10,607 **Ministry of Labour.** *Report by a Court of Inquiry concerning hours of labour of coal tippers and trimmers in South Wales.* London: H.M.S.O., 1923. 7p. (Cmd. 1948.)

Chairman: John A. Compston.

10,608 **Sargant Florence**, Philip. 'The forty-eight hour week and industrial efficiency.' *Int. Labour Rev.*, x, 5 (November 1924), 729–58.

10,609 **International Association for Social Progress.** British Section. *Report on hours of work and their relation to output.* London, 1927. 10p.

10,610 **Medical Research Council.** Industrial Health Research Board. *Two studies on hours of work.* London: H.M.S.O., 1928. 35p. (Report 47.)

10,611 **Booth**, N. H. *Hours of work in the coal-mining industry of Great Britain since the early part of the nineteenth century with special reference to Northumberland and Durham and with an account of certain movements connected therewith.* 1930. (B. Litt. thesis, University of Oxford.)

10,612 **Ministry of Labour.** National Advisory Council for Juvenile Employment (England and Wales). *Fourth report. Hours of employment of boys and girls in unregulated occupations.* London: H.M.S.O., 1932. 21p.

Chairman: Lord Goschen.

10,613 **International Association for Social Progress.** British Section. *Report on new aspects of the problem of hours of work (hours, leisure and employment).* London, 1933. 50p.

Report drafted by P. Sargant Florence.

Chairman of Committee of Enquiry: Lady Hall.

10,614 **Macartney**, Carlile Aylmer. *Hours of work and employment.* London: League of Nations Union, 1934. 94p.

10,615 **Redmayne**, *Sir* Richard Augustine Studdert. *A review of the experimental working of the five days week by Boots Pure Drug Company at Nottingham.* Nottingham, 1934. 70p.

10,616 **Mander**, *Sir* C. A. *Can we reduce hours of labour?* London, [1935?]. [3]p.

10,617 **Vernon**, Horace Middleton. 'The reduction in hours of work.' *Hum. Factor*, IX, 6 (June 1935), 218–25.

10,618 **Home Department.** *Report of the Departmental Committee on the hours of employment of young persons in certain unregulated occupations.* London: H.M.S.O., 1937. 50p. (Cmd. 5394.)

Chairman: W. Byng Kenrick.

10,619 **Stewart**, Michael. *The forty hour week: a case for collective action.* London: New Fabian Research Bureau, 1937. 35p. (Pamphlets 34.)

10,620 **Ministry of Labour and National Service.** *Report on hours of employment of women and young persons in factories during the first five months of the war.* London: H.M.S.O., 1940. (Cmd. 6182.)

10,621 **Sargant Florence**, Philip and **Florence**, Lella. 'A scientific labour policy for industrial plants.' *Int. Labour Rev.*, XLIII, 3 (March 1941), 260–98.

10,622 **Vernon**, Horace Middleton. *Hours of work and their influence on health and efficiency.* London: British Association for Labour Legislation, 1943. 38p.

10,623 **Lambert**, *Dame* Florence. *Labour's case for the forty hour working week.* London: Marx Memorial Library and Workers' School, 1945. 16p. (A Marx House discussion guide.)

10,624 **Stewart**, Michael. 'Hours of labour.' Cole, G. D. H. *British trade unionism today: a survey*. London: Methuen, 1945. p. 143–52.
Earlier edition. 1939.

10,625 **Industrial Welfare Society.** *Part-time employment of women: a review of present-day schemes*. London: the Society, 1955. 25p.

10,626 **McCormick**, Brian J. 'Hours of work in British industry.' *Ind. Labor Relat. Rev.*, XII, 3 (April 1959), 423–33.

10,627 **Ford Motor Company.** *Short report on a survey of working and leisure time*. Dagenham, 1960. 8p.

10,628 **Labour Research Department.** *A forty hour week and three weeks holiday: how the case rests at present in United Kingdom and overseas*. London: L.R.D., 1960. 16p.

10,629 **Industrial Welfare Society.** *Part-time work in the retail distributive trades: a survey of practices in fifty retail stores*. London: the Society, 1961. 38p. (Survey 80.)

10,630 **Clegg**, Hugh Armstrong. *Implications of the shorter working week for management*. London: British Institute of Management, 1962. 12p. (Occasional papers 8.)

10,631 **Ministry of Labour.** Factory Inspectorate. *Hours of employment of women and young persons*. London: H.M.S.O., 1963. 36p. (Safety, health and welfare booklets, new series 23.)

10,632 **Labour Research Department.** *Shorter hours, longer holidays*. London: L.R.D., 1965. 8p.

10,633 **Oxford Consumers' Group.** *Oxford shop hours*. Oxford: Oxford Consumers' Group, 1966. 32p.

10,634 **Roberts**, Benjamin Charles and **Hirsch**, Judith L. 'Factors influencing hours of work.' Roberts, B. C. and Smith, J. R. (eds.). *Manpower policy and employment trends*. London: Bell for the London School of Economics and Political Science, 1966. p. 111–37.

10,635 **Thompson,** Edward Palmer. 'Time, work-discipline, and industrial capitalism.' *Past Pres.*, 38 (December 1967), 56–97.

10,636 **Feldstein**, M. S. 'Estimating the supply curve of working hours.' *Oxf. Econ. Pap.*, n.s., XX, 1 (March 1968), 74–80.

10,637 **Hallaire**, Jean. *Part-time employment: its extent and its problems*. Paris: Organisation for Economic Co-operation and Development, 1968. 106p. (Employment of special groups 6.)

10,638 **Oldfield**, M. H. 'Part-time work.' Wright, H. B. (ed.). *Solving the problems of retirement*. London: Institute of Directors, 1968. p. 92–6.

10,639 **Bienefeld**, M. A. *A study of the course of change in the customary and in the specified or normal hours of work of manual workers in certain British industries and of the factors affecting changes in the specified or normal hours from the eighteenth century to the present day*. 1968–69. (Ph.D. thesis, University of London.)

10,640 **Bienefeld**, M. A. 'The normal week under collective bargaining.' *Economica*, n.s., XXXVI, 142 (May 1969), 172–92.

10,641 **National Board for Prices and Incomes.** *Hours and overtime in the London clearing banks*. London: H.M.S.O., 1970. (Report 143. Cmnd. 4301.)

10,642 **National Board for Prices and Incomes.** *Hours of work, overtime and shift-working*. London: H.M.S.O., 1970. v, 133p. (Report 161. Cmnd. 4554.)
Supplement. 1970. vi, 259p. (Report 161 (Supplement). Cmnd. 4554-I.)

10,643 **Thompson**, Edward Palmer. 'Time and work discipline.' Worsley, P. (ed.). *Modern sociology: introductory readings*. Harmondsworth: Penguin, 1970. p. 221–2.
Excerpt from the author's 'Time, work-discipline, and industrial capitalism' (see 10,635), p. 60–1.

See also: 6304; 7808; 7812; 7817; 7827; 8014; 8016; 8018; 8020; 8165; 8212; 8256; 8302–4; 8336; 9039; 9174; 10,935; 10,972; 12,138; 12,284.

2. Overtime

10,644 **Harris**, Lilian. *Abolition of overtime for women*. Manchester, 1895. 8p.

10,645 **Women's Trade Union League.** *Factory and Workshops Bill: overtime; medical opinion*. London, 1895. 16p.

10,646 **Mines Department.** *Report of a special inquiry into the working of overtime in coal mines in Lancashire*. London: H.M.S.O., 1934. 9p. (Cmd. 4626.)

10,647 **Mines Department.** *Report of a special inquiry into the working of overtime in coal mines in Scotland*. London: H.M.S.O., 1935. 14p. (Cmd. 4959.)

10,648 **Katin**, Louis. 'The worker's point of view. XXXI. When the factory hand stays late.' *Hum. Factor*, XI, 2 (February 1937), 69–73.

10,649 **Knoop**, Douglas and **Jones**, Gwilym Peredur. 'Overtime in the age of Henry VIII.' *Econ. Hist.*, III, 13 (February 1938), 13–20.

10,650 **Buck**, Leslie J. and **Shimmin**, Sylvia. 'Overtime and financial responsibility.' *Occup. Psychol.*, XXXIII, 3 (July 1959), 137–48.

10,651 **Shimmin**, Sylvia and **De La Mare**, Gwynneth. 'Individual differences in overtime working.' *Occup. Psychol.*, XXXVIII, 1 (January 1964), 37–47.

10,652 **Whybrew** E. G. 'Overtime and the reduction of the working week: a comparison of British and Dutch experience.' *Br. J. Ind. Relat.*, II, 2 (July 1964), 149–64.

10,653 **Barnes**, Michael. 'The overtime blight.' *New Soc.*, V, 127 (4 March 1965), 10–13.

10,654 **Whybrew**, E. G. *Overtime working in Britain: a study of its origins, functions and methods of control*. London: H.M.S.O., 1968. vi, 96p. (Royal Commission on Trade Unions and Employers' Associations. Research papers 9.)

10,655 **Sallis**, Howard. *Overtime in electricity supply: its incidence and control in England and Wales 1954–1969*. London: *British Journal of Industrial Relations*, 1970. 91p. (Occasional paper.)

See also: 8438; 8443; 8803; 10,641–2; 12,279; 12,321; 12,333.

3. Shift Work

10,656 **Bulman**, Harrison Francis. *The multiple shift system of working in Northumberland and Durham*. London: Colliery Guardian, 1910. 14p. (Coal trade pamphlets 2.)

10,657 **Home Department.** Departmental Committee on the Employment of Women and Young Persons on the Two-Shift System. *Report*. London: H.M.S.O., 1920. (Cmd. 1037.)

Evidence. 1920. (Cmd. 1038.)

10,658 **Vernon**, Horace Middleton. 'The development of the two-shift system in Great Britain.' *Int. Labour Rev.*, XXIX, 2 (February 1934), 165–80.

10,659 **Vernon**, Horace Middleton. *The shorter working week, with special reference to the two-shift system*. London: Routledge, 1934. viii, 201p.

10,660 **Labour Party.** *The two-shift system for women and young persons, what it means, why we oppose it: a memorandum prepared by the Standing Joint Committee of Industrial Women's Organisations*. London: National Labour P., 1935. 7p.

10,661 **Ministry of Labour.** Committee on Double Day-Shift Working. *Report*. London: H.M.S.O., 1947. 50p. (Cmd. 7147.)

Chairman: J. L. Brierly.

10,662 **Clegg**, Hugh Armstrong and **Cleary**, E. J. *Single and double day shift working in the cotton industry: a paper given at the Cotton Board Conference, Harrogate, Oct. 17–19, 1952*. Manchester: Cotton Board, Industrial Relations Department, 1952. 29p.

10,663 **Wyatt**, Stanley and **Marriott**, Reginald. 'Night work and shift changes.' *Br. J. Ind. Med.*, X, 3 (July 1953), 164–72.

10,664 **Cook**, Frank Patrick. *Shift work*. London: Institute of Personnel Management, 1954. 36p.

10,665 **Ministry of Labour and National Service.** Personnel Management Advisory Service. *Evening shifts*. London: the Ministry, 1954. 8p.

10,666 **Banks**, Olive. 'Continuous shift work: the attitudes of wives.' *Occup. Psychol.*, XXX, 2 (April 1956), 69–84.

10,667 **Brown**, Hilda Grace. *The social consequences of shift work*. Sheffield: the University, 1956. 42p.

10,668 **Eels**, Francis R. 'The economics of shift working.' *J. Ind. Econ.*, V, 1 (November 1956), 51–62.

'. . . based on a paper read to Section F of the British Association at Bristol in September 1955.'

10,669 **Shepherd**, R. D. and **Walker**, J. 'Three-shift working and the distribution of absence.' *Occup. Psychol.*, XXX, 2 (April 1956), 105–11.

10,670 **McDonald**, John Campbell. *Social and psychological effects of night shift work*. 1957–58. (Ph.D. thesis, University of Birmingham.)

10,671 **Eels**, Francis R. 'The effect of the introduction of shift working upon the amount of working capital required.' *Accting. Res.*, IX, 3 (July 1958), 183–92.

10,672 **Brown**, Hilda Grace. *Some effects of shift work on social and domestic life*. Hull: Yorkshire Bulletin of Economic and Social Research, 1959. 54p. (Occasional papers 2.)

10,673 **Walker**, J. 'Shift changes and hours of work.' *Occup. Psychol.*, XXXV, 1–2 (January–April 1961), 1–9.

'A paper read to the Occupational Section of the British Psychological Society in November, 1960.'

10,674 **Hutton**, C. R. *Married women on full-time shiftwork: some domestic and social consequences*. 1961–62. (M.A. thesis, University of London.)

10,675 **Federation of British Industries.** *Shift working: three case studies*. London: F.B.I., 1962. 4p.

10,676 **Industrial Welfare Society.** *Some examples of shift rotas*. London: the Society, 1963. 12p.

10,677 **Industrial Welfare Society**. *Some social and industrial implications of shift work*. London: the Society, 1963. 24p.

10,678 **Aris**, Stephen. 'The future of shift work.' *New Soc.*, III, 66 (2 January 1964), 8–10.

10,679 **De La Mare**, Gwynneth and **Shimmin**, Sylvia. 'Preferred patterns of duty in a flexible shift-working situation.' *Occup. Psychol.*, XXXVIII, 3–4 (July–October 1964), 203–14.

10,680 **Marris**, Robin Lapthorn. *The economics of capital utilisation: a report on multiple shift work*. Cambridge: Cambridge U.P., 1964. xviii, 267p. (Cambridge University, Department of Applied Economics. Monographs 10.)

Assisted by Ian Maclean and Simon Bernau.

10,681 **British Institute of Management.** *Shift work*. London: B.I.M., 1965. 15p. (Information summary 119.)

10,682 **Industrial Welfare Society.** *Shift work in offices.* London: the Society, 1965. 24p. (Information survey 126.)

10,683 **Industrial Society.** *Shift work: current practice in Great Britain.* London: the Society, 1966. 47p. (Information survey 140.)

10,684 **Production Engineering Research Association of Great Britain.** *The benefits and problems of shift working: a P.E.R.A. symposium, 7th and 8th June 1966.* London, 1966.

10,685 **Walker**, J. 'Frequent alternation of shifts on continuous work.' *Occup. Psychol.*, XL, 4 (October 1966), 215–25.

10,686 **Chadwick-Jones**, John K. 'Shift working: physiological effects and social behaviour.' *Br. J. Ind. Relat.*, V, 2 (July 1967), 237–43.

10,687 **Wedderburn**, A. A. I. 'Social factors in satisfaction with swiftly rotating shifts.' *Occup. Psychol.*, XLI, 2–3 (April–July 1967), 85–107.

10,688 **De La Mare**, Gwynneth and **Walker**, J. 'Factors influencing the choice of shift rotation.' *Occup. Psychol.*, XLII, 1 (January 1968), 1–21.

10,689 **Department of Employment and Productivity.** *Introduction of shift working: survey made at the request of the National Joint Advisory Council.* London: H.M.S.O., 1968. 32p.

10,690 **Sergean**, R., **Howell**, D., **Taylor**, Peter John and **Pocock**, S. J. ' "Compensation for inconvenience": an analysis of shift payments in collective agreements in the U.K.' *Occup. Psychol.*, XLIII, 3–4 (1969), 183–92.

10,691 **National Economic Development Office.** *Multiple shiftwork: a problem for decision by management and labour.* London: H.M.S.O., 1970. 28p. (Monograph 1.)
Based on a paper prepared by R. L. Marris.

See also: 8803; 10,642.

C. FRINGE BENEFITS AND OTHER CONDITIONS

Works in this section deal with benefits provided by the employer, including the state when it is acting in its capacity as an employer. Benefits provided by the state to society as a whole are classified at Part Seven, IX. Many of the general works in Part Six, IV, A, 1 and 3–4 also contain material on fringe benefits. See also Part Four, II, A.

1. General

10,692 **Hazell, Watson and Viney.** *Hazell's: being some account of the provident & social institutions connected with Hazell, Watson & Viney, Ld.* London, Aylesbury, 1924. ix, 91p.

10,693 **Cadbury Brothers.** *Bournville works and its institutions: educational, recreational, pensions and other schemes.* Bournville, 1936. 34p.

10,694 **Industrial Welfare Society.** *Employee benefit schemes, July 1949.* London: the Society, 1949. 63p.

10,695 **Durham**, William. *The £.s.d. of welfare in industry: an investigation into the cost of personnel administration and employee benefits.* London: Industrial Welfare Society, 1958. 47p.

10,696 **Institute of Office Management.** *Office staff practices.* London, 1961.
Supplement. 1963.

10,697 **Bates**, James and **Reid**, Graham Livingstone. 'Supplementary labour costs and their effect on wage bills.' *Three Banks Rev.*, 55 (September 1962), 22–39.

10,698 **Reid**, Graham Livingstone. 'The concept of "fringe benefits".' *Scott. J. Polit. Econ.*, IX, 3 (November 1962), 208–18.

10,699 **Rubner**, Alex. *Fringe benefits: the golden chains.* London: Putnam, 1962. xiv, 258p.

10,700 **Reid**, Graham Livingstone and **Bates**, James. 'The cost of fringe benefits for manual workers in British industry.' *Br. J. Ind. Relat.*, I, 3 (October 1963), 348–69.

10,701 **Rubner**, Alex. 'A working definition of fringe-wages.' *J. Ind. Relat.*, VI, 3 (November 1964), 189–202.

10,702 **British Institute of Management.** *Fringe benefits for executives.* London: B.I.M., 1965. 80p. (Information survey.)

10,703 **Holmans**, A. E. 'Public versus private protection against insecurity.' Reid, G. L. and Robertson, D. J. (eds.). *Fringe benefits, labour costs and social security.* London: Allen and Unwin, 1965. p. 145–68.

10,704 **Reid**, Graham Livingstone and **Bates**, James. 'The cost of fringe benefits in British industry.' Reid, G. L. and Robertson, D. J. (eds.). *Fringe benefits, labour costs and social security.* London: Allen and Unwin, 1965. p. 46–91.

10,705 **Reid**, Graham Livingstone and **Robertson**, Donald James (eds.). *Fringe benefits, labour costs and social security.* London: Allen and Unwin, 1965. 336p. (University of Glasgow. Department of Social and Economic Research. Social and economic studies, new series 5.)
Introduction, p. 15–32.
Conclusion, p. 313–27.

10,706 **Reid**, Graham Livingstone. 'Supplementary labour costs in Britain before 1960.' Reid, G. L. and Robertson, D. J. (eds.). *Fringe benefits, labour costs and social security.* London: Allen and Unwin, 1965. p. 33–45.

10,707 **Reid**, Graham Livingstone. 'Supplementary labour costs in Europe and Britain.' Reid, G. L. and Robertson, D. J. (eds.). *Fringe benefits, labour costs and social security.* London: Allen and Unwin, 1965. p. 92–123.

10,708 **Lurie**, Melvin. 'The growth of fringe benefits and the meaning of wage setting by wage comparisons.' *J. Ind. Econ.*, xv, 1 (November 1966), 16–25.

10,709 **Wade**, Michael (ed.). *Personnel manager's guide to employee benefits*. London: Business Publications, 1967. xi, 210p. (Management in action.)

10,710 **Young**, Agnes Freda and **Smith**, J. H. 'Fringe benefits: a local survey.' *Br. J. Ind. Relat.*, v, 1 (March 1967), 63–73.

10,711 **Hand**, Michael. *Staff status for manual workers*. Oxford, London: Pergamon, 1968. 18p. (Productivity progress series.)

See also: 7939; 12,413.

2. Holidays and Vacations

10,712 **Watson**, William Foster. 'The worker's point of view. XXX. Holidays with pay.' *Hum. Factor*, x, 10 (October 1936), 366–71.

10,713 **Ministry of Labour.** Committee to investigate the extent to which holidays with pay are given to employed workpeople, and the possibility of extending the provision of such holidays by statutory enactment or otherwise, and to make recommendations. *Report, appendices*. 1938. 79p. (Cmd. 5724.)
Minutes of evidence. 1937. 13v.
Appendix to the minutes of evidence. 1938.
Index. 1938.
Chairman: Lord Amulree.

10,714 **Industrial Welfare Society.** *Report of Conference on Workers' Holidays, November 30th, 1938*. London: the Society, 1938. 24p.

10,715 **Mackenzie**, William Warrender, Baron Amulree. *Industrial holidays*. London: Royal Society of Arts, 1938. 11p. (Royal Society of Arts. Inaugural address, 1938.)

10,716 **Ministry of Labour.** *Holidays with pay: collective agreements between organisations of employers and workpeople*. London: H.M.S.O., 1939. 85p.

10,717 **Political and Economic Planning.** 'Planning for holidays.' *Planning*, 194 (13 October 1942), 1–15.

10,718 **International Labour Office.** 'Holidays with pay for seafarers: conditions in four merchant navies.' *Int. Labour Rev.*, XLVIII, 6 (December 1943), 733–46.

10,719 **International Labour Office.** 'Holidays with pay in Great Britain.' *Int. Labour Rev.*, LI, 6 (June 1945), 741–9.

10,720 **Ministry of Labour and National Service.** Catering Wages Commission. *The staggering of holidays: report to the Minister of Labour and National Service by the Catering Wages Commission under Section 2 of the Catering Wages Act, 1943*. London: H.M.S.O., 1945. 24p.

10,721 **C.**, C. T. 'Staggered holidays.' *Ind. Law Rev.*, I, 1 (June 1946), 25–31.

10,722 **British Institute of Management.** *Length of holidays for directors and executives*. London: B.I.M., 1955. 15p. (Information survey 62.)

10,723 **British Institute of Management.** *Company holiday arrangements*. London: B.I.M., 1958. 22p. (Information summary 37.)

10,724 **Industrial Welfare Society.** *Employee holidays in British industry*. London: the Society, 1959. 43p. (Information survey 56.)

10,725 **Clegg**, Hugh Armstrong and **Narasimham**, P. S. *Implications for management of longer standard holidays*. London: British Institute of Management, 1963. 22p. (Occasional papers 9.)

10,726 **Industrial Welfare Society.** *The case for staggered holidays*. London: the Society, 1963. 6p.

10,727 **Industrial Welfare Society.** *Holidays: current practices and trends*. London: the Society, 1963. 30p.

10,728 **British Institute of Management.** *Management holidays*. London: B.I.M., 1965. 23p. (Information summary 85.)

10,729 **Cameron** G. C. 'The growth of holidays with pay in Britain.' Reid, G. L. and Robertson, D. J. (eds.). *Fringe benefits, labour costs and social security*. London: Allen and Unwin, 1965. p. 273–99.

10,730 **Industrial Society.** *Holidays: current practices and trends*. London: the Society, 1966. 58p. (Information survey 134.)

10,731 **British Institute of Management.** *Holidays: company practice*. London: B.I.M., 1967. 4p.

10,732 **Martin**, G. C. *Some aspects of the provision of annual holidays for the English working classes down to 1947*. 1967–68. (M.A. thesis, University of Leicester.)

See also: 6304; 10,628; 10,632.

3. Sick Pay

See also Part Two, III; and Part Seven, IX, B, 2.

10,733 **Industrial Welfare Society.** *Sick pay schemes and benevolent funds*. London: the Society, 1957. 20p.

10,734 **Institute of Personnel Management.** *Company sick pay schemes*. London: I.P.M., 1959. 26p. (Information summary.)

10,735 **British Institute of Management.** *Payment for sickness*. London: B.I.M., 1963. 30p. (B.I.M. survey.)

10,736 **James**, Edward. 'Private industrial sick benefits.' *New Soc.*, 34 (23 May 1963), 23–4.

10,737 **Ministry of Labour.** *Sick pay schemes: report of a Committee of the National Joint Advisory Council on occupational sick pay schemes*. London: H.M.S.O., 1964. vi, 65p.
Chairman: A. S. Marre.

10,738 **Reid**, Graham Livingstone. 'Sick pay.' Reid, G. L. and Robertson, D. J. (eds.). *Fringe benefits, labour costs and social security*. London: Allen and Unwin, 1965. p. 200–45.

10,739 **Industrial Society.** *Sick pay.* London: the Society, 1967. 62p.

4. Unemployment Pay

See also Part Six, IV, A, 4, d; Part Seven, IV, D, 5; and Part Seven, IX, B, 1.

10,740 **Gilson,** Mary Barnett and **Riches,** E. J. 'Employers' additional unemployment benefit schemes in Great Britain.' *Int. Labour Rev.*, XXI, 3 (March 1930), 348–94.

10,741 **Industrial Welfare Society.** *Notes on redundancy practice.* London: the Society, 1957. 37p.

10,742 **Industrial Welfare Society.** *Terms of notice survey: supplement on treatment of redundancy.* London: the Society, 1963. 17p.

10,743 **British Institute of Management.** *Redundancy policies.* London: B.I.M., 1966.

10,744 **Department of Employment and Productivity.** *Dealing with redundancies.* London: the Department, 1968. 16p.

5. Pensions

This section includes material on private pension schemes and on pensions provided by the state for its employees. Material on national pension funds is classified at Part Seven, IX, B, 4. Technical material relating to the actuarial aspects of pensions has generally been excluded. See also Part Six, II, C, 6.

10,745 **Select Committee on Union Officers' Superannuation (Ireland) Bill.** *Special report, and report . . . together with the proceedings of the Committee, minutes of evidence, and appendix.* [London: H.M.S.O.], 1882. 115p. (H.C. 353.)

10,746 **MacGregor,** D. *Railway superannuation funds: their operation and suggested improvements.* Edinburgh, 1887. 16p.

10,747 **Select Committee on Perpetual Pensions.** *Report, etc.* London: H.M.S.O., 1887.

10,748 **Select Committee on the City of London Police Bill.** *Report, with the proceedings and evidence.* London: H.M.S.O., 1889. (H.C. 264.)
On pensions.

10,749 **Select Committee on Workmen (Woolwich Arsenal).** *Report; with the proceedings, evidence, appendix and index.* London: H.M.S.O., 1889. (H.C. 197.)
On the right to pensions.

10,750 **Departmental Committee upon Metropolitan Police Superannuation.** *Notes of evidence, and papers.* London: H.M.S.O., 1890. (C. 6075.)

10,751 **Select Committee on Police (Scotland) Bill.** *Report; with the proceedings, evidence, appendix and index.* London: H.M.S.O., 1890. (H.C. 324.)
On pensions.

10,752 **Select Committee on School Board for London (Superannuation) Bill.** *Report; with the proceedings, evidence, appendix and index.* London: H.M.S.O., 1890–91. (H.C. 350.)

10,753 **Select Committee on Elementary Education (Teachers' Superannuation).** *Report; with the proceedings, evidence, appendix and index.* London: H.M.S.O., 1892. (Session 1. H.C. 231.)

10,754 **Select Committee on Greenwich Hospital (Age Pensions).** *Report, with the proceedings, evidence, and appendix.* London: H.M.S.O., 1892. (H.C. 138.)

10,755 **Select Committee on the Superannuation Acts Amendment (No. 2) Bill.** *Report, etc.* London: H.M.S.O., 1892. (Session 1. H.C. 271.)

10,756 **Departmental Committee to Consider the Question of the Superannuation of Teachers in Public Elementary Schools.** *Report.* London: H.M.S.O., 1895. (C. 7636.)

10,757 **Rutherglen,** John H. *The Poor Law Officers' Superannuation Act, 1896, annotated and explained . . . together with a history of the superannuation movement.* London: Knight, 1896. xv, 46p.

10,758 **Standing Committee on Law, etc.** *Report . . . on the Poor Law Officers' Superannuation Bill; with the proceedings.* London: H.M.S.O., 1896. (H.C. 164.)

10,759 **Welch,** F. J. *The Poor Law Officers' Superannuation Act, 1896: a plain handbook for the use of clerks to guardians and poor law officers generally.* London: Shaw, 1896. 39p.

10,760 **Departmental Committee on the National School Teachers (Ireland) Pension Fund.** *Report.* London: H.M.S.O., 1897. 11p. (C. 8471.)

10,761 **F.** 'The new Lunacy Bill and its pension clause.' *Westm. Rev.*, CLI, 6 (June 1899), 663–6.

10,762 **Ainslie,** W. L. *Old age pensions and thrift in connection with the mercantile marine.* London: Shipmasters' Society, 1900. (Papers 65.)

10,763 **Select Committee on the Police Superannuation (Scotland) Bill.** *Special report, and report . . . proceedings . . . minutes of evidence, appendix and index.* London: H.M.S.O., 1901. xiv, 180p. (H.C. 356.)
Chairman: The Lord Advocate.

10,764 **Howell,** C. E. *Report to the Local Government Board for Ireland on the financial provisions of the Poor Law Superannuation (Ireland) Bill, 1901.* Dublin: H.M.S.O., 1902. 8p. (Cd. 925.)

10,765 **Royal Commission on Superannuation in the Civil Service.** *Report.* London: H.M.S.O., 1903. xviiip. (Cd. 1744.)
Minutes of evidence, etc. 1903. (Cd. 1745.)
Chairman: Lord Courtney.

10,766 **Schloss**, David Frederick. *Old age pension schemes in the U.K.* [1905?] 26p.

10,767 **Savill**, Stanley. *The Police Pension Acts – England and Wales.* London: *Police Review*, 1906. 62p.

10,768 **Aston**, John Williams. *The great question of pensions or a small permanent income.* London: King, 1909. 16p.

10,769 **Select Committee on Asylums Officers' Superannuation Bill.** *Reports, proceedings, minutes of evidence, appendices.* London: H.M.S.O., 1909. xvi, 98p. (H.C. 257.)
Chairman: John Henderson.

10,770 **Board of Trade.** Committee appointed to inquire into the constitution, rules, administration and financial position of the superannuation and similar funds of railway companies. *Report.* London: H.M.S.O., 1910. (Cd. 5349.)
Evidence, appendices, index. 1911. (Cd. 5484.)
Chairman: Lord Southwark.

10,771 **Brown**, Herbert D. *Civil service retirement in Great Britain and New Zealand.* Washington: U.S.G.P.O., 1910. 264p. (U.S. Senate documents. 61st Congress, 2nd Session, vol. 58.)

10,772 **Select Committee on the Asylums Officers (Employment, Pensions and Superannuation) Bill.** *Report, proceedings, minutes of evidence, appendices.* London: H.M.S.O., 1911. xxii, 167p. (H.C. 239, 242.)
Index. (H.C. 239, 242–Ind.)
Chairman: Charles Roberts.

10,773 **Departmental Committee on the Superannuation of Teachers.** *Report on the first reference.* London: H.M.S.O., 1914. iii, 16p. (Cd. 7364.)
Report on the second reference. iv, 42p. (Cd. 7365.)
Chairman: E. S. Montagu, then J. W. Wilson.

10,774 **Allen**, Edwin Hopkins. *What will my pension be? The School Teachers (Superannuation) Act, 1918, and the deferred annuities under the Act of 1898 described and explained.* London: Evans, 1919. 45p. (Kingsway series.)

10,775 **Departmental Committee on the Superannuation of Persons Employed by Local Authorities in England and Wales.** *Report.* London: H.M.S.O., 1919. (Cmd. 329.)
Chairman: Ronald C. Norman.

10,776 **Llewellyn**, Richard Llewellyn Jones and **Jones**, Arthur Bassett. *Pensions and the principles of their evaluation.* London: Heinemann, 1919. xxvii, 702p.
'With a section on pensions in relation to the eye, by W. M. Beaumont.'

10,777 **Schooling,** *Sir* William. *Pensions and policies: a plan for employers and employed.* London, 1919. 24p.

10,778 **Savill**, Stanley. *The Police Pensions Act 1921, with notes, exposition, cross references, and index.* London: *Police Review* Publishing Co., 1921. 61p.

10,779 **Stafford**, Percival Herbert. *Police finance, including police pensions.* London, 1921. 48p. (Local government series of financial textbooks.)

10,780 **Select Committee on Teachers in Grant-aided Schools (Superannuation).** *Report,* [etc.]. London: H.M.S.O., 1922. xxiv, 105p. (H.C. 106.)
Chairman: F. D. Acland.

10,781 **Departmental Committee on the Superannuation of School Teachers.** *Report.* London: H.M.S.O., 1923. 72p. (Cmd. 1962.)
Chairman: Lord Emmott.

10,782 **Alban**, *Sir* Frederick John and **Lamb**, Norman Ernest. *Police finance, including police pensions finance.* London: Knight, 1925. 120, viiip.
Second edition of the work by Percival Herbert Stafford.

10,783 **Home Department.** Committee appointed to consider the temporary deductions from police pay and allowances and the rateable deductions for pension. *Report.* London: H.M.S.O., 1925. 6p. (Cmd. 2444.)
Chairman: Lord Lee of Fareham.

10,784 **Barker**, *Sir* Wilberforce Ross. *The superannuation of teachers in England and Wales.* London: Longmans, 1926. viii, 245p.

10,785 **Edwards**, Herbert Horace and **Murrell**, Reginald. *Staff pension schemes in theory and practice.* London: Layton, 1927. 135p.

10,786 **Departmental Committee on the Superannuation of Local Government Employees.** *Report.* London: H.M.S.O., 1928.

10,787 **Robertson**, Bernard and **Samuels**, Harry. *Pension and superannuation funds: their formation and administration explained.* London: Pitman, 1928. x, 134p.
Second edition. 1930. xii, 148p.

10,788 **Nixon**, John. *The authentic history of Civil Service superannuation.* London: King, 1930. 65p.

10,789 **Cadbury Brothers.** *Pension, provident, and benevolent funds: an account of the schemes in operation at Cadbury Brothers Ltd. Bournville.* Bournville: Publication Department, Bournville Works, 1932. 48p.

10,790 **Owen**, Arthur David Kemp. 'Employees' retirement pension schemes in Great Britain.' *Int. Labour Rev.*, XXXII, 1 (July 1935), 80–99.

10,791 **Simonds**, John (ed.). *The Local Government Superannuation Act, 1937.* London: Eyre and Spottiswoode, 1938. xvi, 246p.
New edition, revised, annotated and edited by W. C. Anderson. 1947. xxxii, 272p.

10,792 **Home Office.** Departmental Committee on Police Widows Pensions. *Report.* London: H.M.S.O., 1941. (Cmd. 6312.)
Chairman: Lord Snell.

10,793 **Cohen**, Emmeline W. 'Superannuation.' Robson, W. A. (ed.). *Social security.* London: Allen and Unwin for the Fabian Society, 1943. p. 239–49.
Second edition. 1945.
Third edition. 1948.

10,794 **Ministry of Health.** Nurses Salaries Committee and Midwives Salaries Committee. *Report of the Joint Superannuation Sub-Committee on superannuation of nurses and midwives.* London: H.M.S.O., 1945. (Cmd. 6603.)
Chairman: J. Lythgoe.

10,795 **Civil Service National Whitley Council.** *Pensionability of unestablished Civil Service: report of a Committee of the Civil Service National Whitley Council.* London: H.M.S.O., 1946. (Cmd. 6942.)
Chairman: H. Wilson-Smith.

10,796 **Home Office.** *Police Pensions Bill, 1948. Summary of the main provisions proposed for inclusion in Regulations under Clause I of the Bill.* London: H.M.S.O., 1948. (Cmd. 7312.)

10,797 **Hosking**, Gordon Albert and **Lane**, Ralph Charles Bradley. *Superannuation schemes.* London: Sweet and Maxwell, 1948. viii, 323p.

10,798 **Acton Society Trust.** *The miner's pension.* Claygate: the Trust, 1951. 23p. (Studies in nationalised industry 5.)

10,799 **Crowther**, Frank. *Shaw's guide to superannuation for local authorities.* London: Shaw, 1951. xii, 102p.
Second edition. 1955. xxxii, 206p.
Third edition. By Arthur C. Robb. 1962. xxiv, 433p.
Fourth edition. By Arthur C. Robb. 1966. 439p.

10,800 **British Institute of Management.** *Retirement age for staff employees.* London: B.I.M., 1952. 14p. (Information summary 42.)

10,801 **Home Office.** *Police pensions: report of the Working Party of the Police Council.* London: H.M.S.O., 1952.
Chairman: F. C. Johnson.

10,802 **Crabbe,** Reginald James Williams and **Poyser**, Cyril Alexander. *Pension and widows' and orphans' funds.* Cambridge: Cambridge U.P. for the Institute of Actuaries and the Faculty of Actuaries, 1953. viii, 240p.
A draft published for the Institute in 1950. 255p.

10,803 **Keast**, Horace. 'Modern trends in pension schemes.' *Ind. Law Rev.*, VIII, 2 (October 1953), 115–22.

10,804 **Scottish Home Department.** *Police pensions: report of the Working Party of the Scottish Police Council.* Edinburgh: H.M.S.O., 1953.
Chairman: W. C. Barnes.

10,805 **Paish**, Frank Walter and **Peacock**, Alan Turner. 'The economics of pension funds.' *Lloyds Bank Rev.*, n.s., 34 (October 1954), 14–28.

10,806 **Political and Economic Planning.** 'Providing for pensions.' *Planning*, XX, 364 (24 May 1954), 93–116.

10,807 **Barry**, Hugh Desmond. *Superannuation for the general medical practitioner in the National Health Service in England, Scotland and Wales.* London: Heinemann Medical Books, 1955. 21p.

10,808 **Keast**, Horace. *Local government superannuation: a commentary on the Local Government Superannuation Acts, 1937 and 1953.* London: Knight, 1955. xxvi, 417p.
Second edition.
Looseleaf.
Previous edition by W. G. Gillings and G. H. Forster, 1935.

10,809 **Durham**, William. *Industrial pension schemes.* London: Industrial Welfare Society, 1956. 65p.

10,810 **Hosking**, Gordon Albert. *Pension schemes and retirement benefits.* London: Sweet and Maxwell, 1956. viii, 372p.
Second edition. 1960. xv, 466p.
Third edition. 1968. xiv, 412p.

10,811 **Raphaël**, Marios. *The origins of public superannuation schemes in England, 1684–1859.* 1956–57. (Ph.D. thesis, University of London.)

10,812 **Phillips**, William. *Pension scheme precedents.* London: Sweet and Maxwell, 1957. [583]p.
Various paging.
First supplement. To July 1, 1961. 1961. [54]p.

10,813 **Seldon**, Arthur. *Pensions in a free society.* London: Institute of Economic Affairs, 1957. vi, 42p.

10,814 **Government Actuary.** *Occupational pension schemes.* London: H.M.S.O., 1958. 28p.
1966. vii, 60p.
1968. v, 44p.

10,815 **Scottish Education Department.** *Pensions for the widows, children and dependants of teachers in Scotland: report of the Working Party.* Edinburgh: H.M.S.O., 1958. (Cmd. 527.)

10,816 **A Special Correspondent.** 'What future for pension schemes?' *Banker*, CVIII, 392 (September 1958), 589–97.

10,817 **Government Actuary.** *Report on the National Health Service Superannuation Scheme, 1948–1955.* London: H.M.S.O., 1959. iii, 24p.
. . . 1955–1962. 1967. 20p.

10,818 **Industrial Welfare Society.** *Executive disability pensions.* London: the Society, 1959. 22p.

10,819 **Honohan,** W. A. 'Providing for old age through private channels.' *Statist. Soc. Inq. Soc. Ir. J.*, xx, 3 (1959–60), 178–93.
Discussion, p. 193–8.

10,820 **Acton Society Trust.** *Retirement: a study of current attitudes and practices.* London: the Trust, 1960. 69p.
Prepared for publication by Rosemary Stewart from material collected by W. A. Martin, R. Holmes, G. Pitt.

10,821 **Industrial Welfare Society.** *Preparation for retirement: report of a three-day conference, 1960.* London: the Society, 1960. 20p.

10,822 **Pilch,** Michael and **Wood,** Victor. *Pension schemes.* London: Hutchinson, 1960. 223p.
Foreword by Lord Beveridge.

10,823 **Seldon,** Arthur. *Pensions for prosperity.* London: Barrie and Rockliff for the Institute of Economic Affairs, 1960. 48p. (Hobart papers 4.)
Revised and enlarged version in Institute of Economic Affairs, *Radical reaction*, 1961. p. 197–247.

10,824 **University Grants Committee.** Committee on the Superannuation of University Teachers. *Report.* London: H.M.S.O., 1960. iv, 55p.
Chairman: Sir Edward Hale.

10,825 **Government Actuary.** *Report on the Teachers Superannuation Scheme (England and Wales), 1948 to 1956.* London: H.M.S.O., 1961. (H.C. 269.)
. . . *1956–61.* 1966. (H.C. 41.)
. . . *1961–1966.* 1969. (H.C. 128.)

10,826 **Ministry of Health.** *National Health Service Superannuation Scheme (England and Wales): an explanation.* London: H.M.S.O., 1961.
Other editions. 1962, 1963, 1965, 1967.

10,827 **Eiref,** Z. *The income tax aspects of retirement benefit schemes.* 1961–62. (LL.M. thesis, University of London.)

10,828 **Government Actuary.** *Report on the Teachers Superannuation Scheme (Scotland), 1948–1956.* Edinburgh: H.M.S.O., 1962. (H.C. 100.)
. . . *1956–1961.* 1966. (H.C. 47.)
. . . *1961–66.* 1970. (H.C. 203.)

10,829 **Parrack,** N. S. 'With-profit pensions.' *Inst. Actuar. Students' Soc. J.*, XVI, 6 (March 1962), 452–67.

10,830 **Scottish Education Department.** *Pensions for teachers' widows: report of the Working Party on pensions for widows, widowers, children and other dependants of teachers in Scotland.* Edinburgh: H.M.S.O., 1962.
Chairman: H. H. Donnelly.

10,831 **Scottish Home and Health Department.** *Health service superannuation scheme in Scotland: a broad outline.* Edinburgh: H.M.S.O., 1962. 28p.
Another edition. 1964.

10,832 **Shaw and Sons, Ltd.** *The local government superannuation scheme: an explanation.* London: Shaw, 1962. 32p.

10,833 **Taylor,** Basil. 'Pension rights: a study in inequality.' *Westm. Bank Rev.* (November 1962), 19–28.

10,834 **Treasury.** *Report by the Government Actuary on the '1926 scheme', relating to teachers in contributory service in schools which are not grant-aided.* London: H.M.S.O., 1962. (H.C. 311.)

10,835 **Tronchin-James,** Nevil. *Arbitrary retirement.* London: Cassell, 1962. 122p.

10,836 **Pilch,** Michael and **Wood,** Victor. *New trends in pensions.* London: Hutchinson, 1964. 223p.

10,837 **Raphaël,** Marios. *Pensions and public servants: a study of the origins of the British system.* Paris: Mouton, 1964. 171p. (Publications of the Social Sciences Centre, Athens, 3.)
Revision of Ph.D. thesis, University of London, 1957.

10,838 **British Institute of Management.** *Company pension schemes: some recent developments.* London: B.I.M., 1965. 61p. (B.I.M. survey.)

10,839 **Department of Education and Science.** Official Working Party on Pensions for Widows, Widowers, Children and Other Dependants of Teachers in England and Wales. *Family pensions benefits for teachers in England and Wales: report.* London: H.M.S.O., 1965. 43p.
Chairman: W. D. Pile.

10,840 **Insurance Institute of London.** Advanced Study Group No. 177. *The effect on occupational pension schemes of future increases in the benefits of the state scheme: report.* London: Insurance Institute, 1965. 60p.

10,841 **Macdonald,** C. R. *Fifty years of the F.S.S.U.* London: Federated Superannuation System for Universities, 1965. v, 153p.

10,842 **Rhodes,** Gerald. *Public sector pensions.* London: Allen and Unwin for the Royal Institute of Public Administration, 1965. 320p.
Also published Toronto: U. of Toronto P., 1965.

10,843 **Talbot,** J. E. *Provision for retirement.* London: Institute of Chartered Accountants in England and Wales, 1965. 40p.

10,844 **Treasury.** *Digest of law and regulations affecting the superannuation of members of the Civil Service, governors of colonies and the judiciary.* London: H.M.S.O., 1965. iii, 715p.

10,845 **Wiseman,** Jack. 'Occupational pension schemes.' Reid, G. L. and Robertson, D. J. (eds.). *Fringe benefits, labour costs and social security.* London: Allen and Unwin, 1965. p. 169–99.

10,846 **Labour Research Department.** *Guide to company pension schemes.* London: L.R.D., 1966. 16p.

10,847 **Mass-Observation.** *A survey on pensions: first report.* London: Mass-Observation Ltd., 1966. 19 leaves.
Prepared for Noble Lowndes Holdings Ltd.

10,848 **Ministry of Labour.** National Joint Advisory Council. *Preservation of pension rights on change of employment: report of a Committee.* London: H.M.S.O., 1966. 68p.
Chairman: A. M. Morgan.

10,849 **British Institute of Management.** *Company retirement policies.* London: B.I.M., 1967. 51p.

10,850 **Department of Education and Science.** *Allocation of pension under the Teachers' Superannuation Regulations.* London: H.M.S.O., 1967. iii, 27p.

10,851 **Industrial Society.** *Pension funds: papers presented at conference, April 1967.* London: the Society, 1967. 55p.

10,852 **Pilch**, Michael and **Wood**, Victor. *Pension scheme practice.* London: Hutchinson, 1967. 192p.

10,853 **Beveridge**, W. E. 'Problems in preparing for retirement.' Wright, H. B. (ed.). *Solving the problems of retirement.* London: Institute of Directors, 1968. p. 68–73.

10,854 **Cannon**, Les. 'A trades union leader's view on the problems of retirement.' Wright, H. B. (ed.). *Solving the problems of retirement.* London: Institute of Directors, 1968. p. 37–43.

10,855 **Department of Education and Science.** *University teachers' superannuation: report of a working party.* London: H.M.S.O., 1968. vi, 69p.
Chairman: Sir G. Maddes.

10,856 **Gaselee**, John. 'Flexibility in retirement policy and employees' pensions.' Wright, H. B. (ed.). *Solving the problems of retirement.* London: Institute of Directors, 1968. p. 83–91.

10,857 **Institute of Directors.** *Directors' pensions.* London: the Institute, 1968. 58p.

10,858 **Mitchell**, John Keith. *Pension schemes.* London: Stone and Cox, 1968. 107p.

10,859 **National Association of Schoolmasters.** *Superannuation: a summary.* Hemel Hempstead: N.A.S., 1968. 24p.
Private circulation.

10,860 **Sawtell**, Roger A. 'One company's experience.' Wright, H. B. (ed.). *Solving the problems of retirement.* London: Institute of Directors, 1968. p. 97–100.

10,861 **Tyzack**, J. E. V. 'Dealing with the inevitable.' Wright, H. B. (ed.). *Solving the problems of retirement.* London: Institute of Directors, 1968. p. 44–51.

10,862 **Clark**, Frederick Le Gros and **Faubert**, Carole. *Fringe benefits for pensioners: a study of company post retirement schemes.* London: Institute of Personnel Management, 1969. 32p. (Information report 2 [new series].)

10,863 **Select Committee on Perpetual Pensions.** *Select Committee reports on perpetual pensions and reports from the Commissioners on Civil Establishments, with minutes of evidence, appendices and index, 1887–92.* Shannon: Irish U.P., 1969. 782p. (British parliamentary papers, government, civil service, 12.)
Commission chairman: Sir Matthew Wright Ridley.
Facsimile reprints of first editions, 1887–92.

10,864 **Warden**, James. *The case for private pensions.* London: Aims of Industry, 1969. 11p.

10,865 *The local government superannuation scheme: an explanation.* London: Shaw, 1970. ii, 32p.

See also: 3614; 8394; 8409; 8646; 14,872–3; 14,997; 15,013; 15,026.

6. Health and Welfare Schemes

This section contains material dealing with the provision of specific health and welfare schemes by employers. Works describing the general state of health and welfare in industry are classified at Part Six, IV, D. See also Part Four, II, A.

10,866 **Navvy Mission Society.** *Canteens among the navvies.* London: the Society, [1895?]. 11p. ([Publications] 50.)
Privately printed.

10,867 **Bayley**, G. B. 'Railway companies' provident funds.' *Jubilee of the Railway News, 1864–1914.* London: *Railway News*, 1914. p. 184–7.

10,868 **Hutton**, Joseph Edmund. *Welfare and housing: a practical record of war-time management.* London: Longmans, 1918. viii, 192p.
The author was Director of the Labour and Catering Department of Vickers.

10,869 **Cadbury Brothers.** *The factory & recreation: recreational and social schemes at Bournville Works.* Bournville: Publication Department, 1925.
Also later editions.

10,870 **Mining Association of Great Britain.** *The other side of the miner's life: a sketch of welfare work in the mining industry.* London: the Association, 1936. 30p.

10,871 **Gardiner**, C. G. *Canteens at work.* London: Oxford U.P., 1941. xii, 104p.

10,872 **Industrial Welfare Society.** *Canteens in industry.* London: the Society, 1942. 70p.

10,873 **Ministry of Labour and National Service.** *Welfare outside the factory and seamen's welfare in port, August 1941 to August 1942.* London: H.M.S.O., 1942. (Cmd. 6411.)

10,874 **Labour Research Department.** *Works canteens and the catering trade.* London: L.R.D., 1943. 48p.

10,875 **Curtis-Bennett**, *Sir* Francis Noel. *The food of the people, being the history of industrial feeding.* London: Faber, 1949. 320p.

10,876 **Hampton**, Jack. *Factory canteens and their management in Great Britain.* London: Hill, 1952. 126p.

10,877 **Salmon**, John Leslie. *A proud heritage: the story of the Railway Convalescence Homes.* London: Railway Convalescence Homes, 1954. 100p.

10,878 **New**, James G. *Office and works catering.* London: Business Publications, Batsford, 1957. 175p.

10,879 **Elliott**, Alexander George Patrick. 'Company welfare schemes.' Reid, G. L. and Robertson, D. J. (eds.). *Fringe benefits, labour costs and social security.* London: Allen and Unwin, 1965. p. 300–12.

10,880 **Kingsley**, Roger and **Kingsley**, Mary. *An industrial day nursery: the personnel manager's guide.* London: Institute of Personnel Management, 1969. 24p.

10,881 **Institute of Personnel Management.** *Company day nurseries.* London: I.P.M., 1970. 29 leaves. (Information note.)
Prepared by J. West.

7. Other

10,882 **Cadbury Brothers.** *The educational scheme connected with the Bournville works, Messrs. Cadbury Brothers, Ltd., including the programme of the Bournville Works School.* Bournville, 1913. 52p.

10,883 **Sime**, W. *'Repta' records: a brief history of the Railway Employees' Privilege Ticket Association.* Derby, 1926. 120p.

10,884 **Schwenning**, G. T. 'British dismissal gratuities.' *Soc. Forces*, XIII (March 1935), 436–52.

10,885 **Cadbury Brothers.** *Children's allowances: an account of the scheme in force at Cadbury Brothers, Ltd.* Bournville: Publications Department, 1938. 4p.

10,886 **Lee**, Charles Edward. *Workmen's fares: survey of the provision of cheap daily conveyance of workmen between suburban homes and their places of business.* London: *Railway Gazette*, 1944. 8p.
Reprinted from *Railway Gazette*.

10,887 **Home Office.** *Police rent and supplementary allowances: report of the Committee of the Police Council.* London: H.M.S.O., 1948.
Chairman: J. H. Burrell.

10,888 **Industrial Welfare Society.** *Employment of pregnant women and maternity leave of absence.* London: the Society, 1957. 18p.

10,889 **Tack Management Consultants Ltd.** *Salemen's cars, expenses and allowances, 1963.* London: Tack Management Consultants, 1963. 163p. (Tack surveys.)

10,890 **British Institute of Management.** *Retirement/bonuses/gifts. Bonus to employees on retirement, quite apart from the provisions of the company pension scheme.* London: B.I.M., 1965. 3p.

10,891 **Irish Management Institute.** Membership Services Division. *The executive car as a fringe benefit: a survey of current practice of 20 companies in the private sector of industry in Ireland.* Dublin: the Institute, 1969. [12]p. (Management information survey 1.)

D. SAFETY, HEALTH, AND WELFARE

This section contains works describing the general state of safety, health, and welfare in industry. Works dealing with the techniques of medical practice or of accident prevention have generally been excluded. Many of the general works contained in Part Six, IV, A, 1 and 3–4 also contain material on safety, health, and welfare. See also Part Two, III; Part Six, IV, C, 6; Part Seven, V, B; and Part Seven, IX, B, 3.

1. General

10,892 **Lincoln**, David Francis. *Health in schools and workshops.* London: Ward and Locke, 1881. 148p. ('Long-life' series 12.)
New edition, edited by George Black. 1888. 148p.

10,893 **Thwaite**, Benjamin Howarth. *Our factories, workshops and warehouses, their sanitary and fire-resisting arrangements.* London: E. and F. N. Spon, 1882 [i.e. 1881]. xii, 270p.

10,894 **Lakeman**, James B. *Health in the workshop.* London: Clowes, 1884. 101p. (International Health Exhibition, 1884. Handbook.)

10,895 **MacNicoll**, Edward Day. *Health saving in the industrial world.* Manchester: J. Heywood, 1887. 16p.

10,896 **Arlidge**, John Thomas. *The hygiene, diseases, and mortality of occupations.* London: Percival, 1892. xx, 568p.

10,897 **Bertillon**, Jacques. 'Morbidity and mortality according to occupation.' *R. Statist. Soc. J.*, LV, 4 (December 1892), 559–600.

10,898 **Mallet**, *Mrs* C. *Dangerous trades for women.* London: Reeves, 1893. 22p. (Humanitarian League. Publications 9.)

10.899 **Smith**, W. *An address . . . on diseases incident to work-people in chemical and other industries.* London, 1893. 34p.

10,900 **Thatcher**, T. *Health and high pressure in business with a few words on . . . compulsory early closing . . .* Bristol, 1894. 26p.

10,901 **Mallet**, *Mrs* C. *Dangerous trades.* London, [*c.* 1895?]. 16p.

10,902 **Departmental Committee Appointed to Inquire into and report upon certain Miscellaneous Dangerous Trades.** *Interim report; with appendix.* London: H.M.S.O., 1896. (C. 8149.)
Second interim report: electrical generating works. 1897. (C. 8522.)
Third interim report: certain miscellaneous trades. 1899. (C. 9073.)
Fourth interim report: supplementary report and evidence on the manufacture and use of grind-stones and on file-cutting. 1899. (C. 9420.)
Final report. 1899. (C. 9509.)

10,903 **Sherard**, Robert Harborough. *The white slaves of England, being true pictures of certain social conditions in the kingdom of England in the year 1897*. London: J. Bowden, 1897. 370p.
Another edition. 1898. 319p.
Dangerous trades.

10,904 **Burns**, John. *Labour's death roll: the tragedy of toil*. London: Clarion Newspaper Co., 1899. 24p. (Clarion pamphlet 29.)
From the *Co-operative Annual*, 1899.

10,905 **Burns**, John. 'Risks and casualties of labour.' Co-operative Wholesale Societies. *Annual for 1899*. p. 383–408.

10,906 **Calder**, John. *The prevention of factory accidents*. London: Longmans, 1899. xvi, 325p.
The author was an Inspector of Factories.

10,907 **Clarke**, Charles Allen. *The effects of the factory system*. London: Grant Richards, 1899. viii, 178p.
Third edition, with added matter. Dent, 1913. xvi, 159p.

10,908 **Clarke**, Charles Allen. *Effects of the factory system on health*. Bolton, 1899. 2 pts. in 1.

10,909 **Parry**, Leonard Arthur. *The risks and dangers of various occupations and their prevention*. London: Scott, Greenwood, 1900. vii, 196p.

10,910 **Oliver**, *Sir* Thomas (ed.). *Dangerous trades: the historical, social and legal aspects of industrial occupations as affecting health, by a number of experts*. London: Murray, 1902. xxiii, 891p.

10,911 **Smith**, Constance. 'Dangerous trades.' *Econ. Rev.*, xv, 4 (October 1905), 434–50.

10,912 **Tozer**, William H. 'Completed cases of incapacity from injury during the year ending 30th June, 1904, deduced from the annual returns of certified schemes under the Workmen's Compensation Acts, 1897 and 1900.' *R. Statist. Soc. J.*, LXVIII, 4 (December 1905), 735–7.

10,913 **Crum**, F. S. 'Occupation mortality statistics of Sheffield, England, 1890–1907.' *J. Am. Statist. Ass.*, XI (December 1908), 309–18.

10,914 **Oliver**, *Sir* Thomas. *Diseases of occupation, from the legislative, social, and medical points of view*. London: Methuen, 1908. xix, 427p. (The new library of medicine.)
Third edition, revised. 1916. xix, 476p.

10,915 **Royal Society of Arts.** *Shaw lectures on industrial hygiene, delivered before the Royal Society of Arts in November and December, 1907; and February and March, 1908*. London: printed by W. Trounce, 1908. 63p.
Also published in the *Royal Society of Arts Journal*, LVI (12 June 1908), 738–47.

10,916 **Greer**, William Jones. *Industrial diseases and accidents*. Bristol: Arrowsmith, 1909. xiii, 326p.

10,917 **Lever**, William Hesketh. *Royal Institute of Public Health: ... address by the president ...* Liverpool, 1910. livp.
On occupational diseases.

10,918 **Verney**, Harry. 'On the recent considerable increase in the number of reported accidents in factories.' *R. Statist. Soc. J.*, LXXIII, 2 (February 1910), 95–118.
With discussion, p. 119–25.
'Read before the Royal Statistical Society, January 18, 1910.'

10,919 **Verney**, Harry. 'Industrial accidents.' *Manchr. Statist. Soc. Trans.* (1910–11), 17–79.

10,920 **Dearden**, William Francis. 'Work of the certifying surgeon and its relation to other branches of preventive medicine.' National Conference on the Prevention of Destitution. *Report of the proceedings ... 1911*. London: King, 1911. p. 434–44.
Discussion, p. 472–81.

10,921 **Departmental Committee on Accidents in Places under the Factory and Workshop Acts.** *Report*. London: H.M.S.O., 1911. v, 64p. (Cd. 5535.)
Minutes of evidence, etc. (Cd. 5540.)
Chairman: F. D. Acland.

10,922 **National Association of Manufacturers of the United States of America.** *Accident prevention and relief: an investigation of the subject in Europe with special attention to England and Germany, together with recommendations for action in the United States of America*. New York, 1911. xxxvi, 481p.
By Ferd. C. Schwedtman and James A. Emery.

10,923 **Allan**, Francis J. 'The use of underground rooms as workplaces.' National Conference on the Prevention of Destitution. *Report of the proceedings ... 1912*. London: King, 1912. p. 76–9.
Discussion, p. 88–96.

10,924 **Brockelbank**, T. A. *Mammon's victims: a revelation to the nation. A text book for workers and coroners*. London: C. W. Daniel, 1912. 92p.

10,925 **Greenwood**, Arthur. 'The medical supervision of juvenile workers.' National Conference on the Prevention of Destitution. *Report of the proceedings ... 1912*. London: King, 1912. p. 245–53.
Discussion, p. 260–5.

10,926 **Lawrence**, Sidney C. 'Health conditions in factories and other workplaces.' National Conference on the Prevention of Destitution. *Report of the proceedings ... 1912*. London: King, 1912. p. 85–8.
Discussion, p. 88–96.

10,927 **Phillips**, M. E. *Dangerous trades*. London, 1912. 15p.

10,928 **Oliver**, *Sir* Thomas. *Lead poisoning from the industrial, medical, and social points of view: lectures delivered at the Royal Institute of Public Health*. London: H. K. Lewis, 1914. x, 294p.

10,929 **Thompson**, William Gilman. *The occupational diseases: their causation, symptoms, treatment, and prevention.* New York and London: D. Appleton, 1914. xxvi, 724p.

10,930 **Departmental Committee on Lighting in Factories and Workshops.** *First report.* London: H.M.S.O., 1914–16.
Vol. I. *Report and appendices.* (Cd. 8000.)
Vol. II. *Evidence, etc.* (Cd. 8001.)
Second report. 1921. (Cmd. 1418.)
Third report. 1922. (Cmd. 1686.)

10,931 **Oliver**, *Sir* Thomas. *Occupations from the social, hygienic and medical points of view.* Cambridge: Cambridge U.P., 1916. x, 110p. (Cambridge public health series.)

10,932 **Shadwell**, Arthur. 'The welfare of factory workers.' *Edinb. Rev.*, CCXXIV, 458 (October 1916), 361–81.
Review article.

10,933 **Webb**, Sidney. 'The coming educational revolution. II. Health and employment.' *Contemp. Rev.*, CX (December 1916), 724–33.

10,934 **Walton**, Cecil. *Welfare study: what it is.* Glasgow: Maclure, MacDonald, 1917. 24p.

10,935 **Bentinck**, *Lord* Henry Cavendish. *Industrial fatigue and the relation between hours of work and output, with a memorandum on sickness.* London: King, 1918. 41p.

10,936 **Kober**, George Martin and **Hanson**, William C. (eds.). *Diseases of occupation and vocational hygiene.* London: Heinemann, 1918. xxi, 918p.
Printed in America.

10,937 **Medical Research Council.** Industrial Fatigue Research Board. *Incidence of industrial accidents upon individuals with special reference to multiple accidents.* London: H.M.S.O., 1919. (Report 4.)
By Major Greenwood and H. M. Woods.
Reissued 1953.

10,938 **Bellhouse**, Gerald. 'Accident prevention and "safety first".' Manchester University. *Labour and industry: a series of lectures.* Manchester: Manchester U.P.; London: Longmans, 1920. p. 147–67.
'A lecture given on Tuesday, January 27, 1920.'

10,939 **Collis**, Edgar Leigh (ed.). *The industrial clinic: a handbook dealing with health at work.* London: John Bale, Sons and Danielsson, 1920. vii, 239p. (Modern clinic manuals.)
By several writers.

10,940 **Hill**, Leonard. 'Atmospheric conditions and efficiency.' Berriman, A. E., and others. *Industrial administration: a series of lectures.* Manchester: Manchester U.P.; London: Longmans, Green, 1920. p. 99–132.

10,941 **Kent**, A. F. Stanley. 'Industrial fatigue.' Berriman, A. E., and others. *Industrial administration: a series of lectures.* Manchester: Manchester U.P.; London: Longmans, Green, 1920. p. 185–95.

10,942 **Legge**, Thomas Morison. 'Occupational diseases.' Berriman, A. E., and others. *Industrial administration: a series of lectures.* Manchester: Manchester U.P.; London: Longmans, Green, 1920. p. 79–98.

10,943 **Collis**, Edgar Leigh and **Greenwood**, Major, the younger. *The health of the industrial worker.* London: Churchill, 1921. xx, 450p.
With a chapter on 'Reclamation of the disabled' by A. J. Collis.

10,944 **International Labour Office.** 'The health of the British population judged by the examination of recruits in 1917 & 1918.' *Int. Labour Rev.*, I, 2 (February 1921), 91–107 (241–57).

10,945 **Wilson**, Robert McNair. *The care of human machinery.* London: Oxford U.P., 1921. xi, 238p. (Oxford medical publications.)

10,946 **Greenwood**, Major, the younger. *Influence of industrial employment upon general health.* London, 1922. 17p.

10,947 **Rusher**, Edward A. 'The statistics of industrial morbidity in Great Britain: a retrospect and a scheme for development.' *R. Statist. Soc. J.*, LXXXV, 1 (January 1922), 27–71.
With discussion, p. 71–86.
'Read before the Royal Statistical Society, December 20, 1921.'

10,948 **Hope**, Edward William. *Industrial hygiene and medicine.* London: Baillière, 1923. viii, 766p.
With W. Hanna and C. O. Stallybrass.

10,949 **Macassey**, *Sir* Lynden. 'Industrial hygiene.' *Natn. Inst. Ind. Psychol. J.*, I, 7 (July 1923), 294–304.
'Being the Presidential Address to Section V of the Congress of the Royal Institute of Public Hygiene, delivered at Scarborough, May 17th, 1923.'

10,950 **Industrial Welfare Society.** *Memorandum on accident prevention.* London: the Society, 1924. 22, viii p.

10,951 **Dearden**, William Francis. *What medical science can do for industry.* Manchester: Association of Certifying Factory Surgeons, 1925. 16p. (Health and industry series 1.)

10,952 **Oliver**, *Sir* Thomas. *The health of the workers.* London: Faber and Gwyer, 1925. 226p. (Modern health books.)

10,953 **Medical Research Council.** Industrial Fatigue Research Board. *Contribution to the study of the human factor in the causation of accidents.* London: H.M.S.O., 1926. (Report 34.)
Re-issued 1952.
By E. M. Newbold.

10,954 **Stephenson**, A. 'Accidents in industry.' *Natn. Inst. Ind. Psychol. J.*, III, 4 (October 1926), 194–200.
'This article is based on a paper read before Section J (Psychology) at the British Association Meeting in Oxford, 1926.'
Reviews methods of accident prevention.

10,955 **Lockhart**, Leonard Phipps. *A short manual of industrial hygiene.* London: Murray, 1927. xiv, 114p.

10,956 **New Health Society.** *Artificial sunlight in industrial health . . . the Sherwood Colliery demonstration.* 1928. 30p.

10,957 **Nixon, J. W.** 'Some problems of statistics of accidents as illustrated by the British statistics.' *Int. Labour Rev.*, XVIII, 6 (December 1928), 731–59.

10,958 **Hill**, A. Bradford. 'An investigation of sickness in various industrial occupations.' *R. Statist. Soc. J.*, XCII, 2 (1929), 183–230.

Discussion, p. 230–8.

'Read before the Royal Statistical Society, February 19, 1929.'

10,959 **Chesmore**, Stuart. *Daily danger.* London: Nelson, 1933. viii, 263p. (Nelsonian library 20.)

An account of various professions and occupations.

10,960 **Yule**, G. Udny. 'On some points relating to vital statistics, more especially statistics of occupational mortality.' *R. Statist. Soc. J.*, XCVII, 1 (1934), 1–72.

Discussion, p. 73–84.

'Read before the Royal Statistical Society, November 21st, 1933.'

10,961 **Lockhart**, Leonard Phipps. *Modern factory practice: costs and output in relation to health.* London: Monotype Corporation, 1936. 16p.

'The text of a speech delivered at the thirty-sixth annual congress of the British Federation of Master Printers at Cliftonville.'

10,962 **Kuczynski**, Jürgen. 'Intensity of work versus safety measures.' *New frontiers in wage theory: Keynes, Robinson, Hicks, Rueff.* London: Lawrence and Wishart, 1937. p. 64–71.

10,963 **Political and Economic Planning.** 'Industry and health.' *Planning*, IV, 92 (9 February 1937), 1–14.

10,964 **Stocks**, Percy. 'The effects of occupation and of its accompanying environment on mortality.' *R. Statist. Soc. J.*, CI, 4 (1938), 669–96.

Discussion, p. 696–708.

'Read before the Royal Statistical Society, May 17th, 1938.'

10,965 **Industrial Safety Survey.** 'The organisation of safety services in industrial undertakings in Great Britain.' *Ind. Saf. Surv.*, XV, 6 (November–December 1939), 149–57.

Based largely on information supplied by G. Stevenson Taylor, H.M. Deputy Chief Inspector of Factories, and H. G. Winbolt, Assistant Secretary of the National Safety First Association.

10,966 **Vernon**, Horace Middleton. 'To what extent is the health of industrial workers dependent on occupation?' *Occup. Psychol.*, XIII, 1 (January 1939), 10–24.

10,967 **Levy**, Hermann Joachim. *War effort and industrial injuries.* London: Fabian Society, 1940. 16p. (Fabian tracts 253.)

10,968 **Medical Research Council.** Industrial Health Research Board. *Industrial health in war: a summary of research findings capable of immediate application in furtherance of the national effort.* London: H.M.S.O., 1940. 36p. (Emergency report 1.)

10,969 **Wells**, A. Q., **Hyde**, W. and **Witts**, L. H. 'Industrial health.' Barnett House, Oxford. Survey Committee. *A survey of the social services in the Oxford district.* Vol. 2. London: Oxford U.P., 1940. p. 226–39.

10,970 **Medical Research Council.** Industrial Health Research Board. *The personal factor in accidents.* London: H.M.S.O., 1942. 19p. (Emergency report 3.)

10,971 **Burnet**, James. *Outlines of industrial medicine, legislation, and hygiene.* Bristol: Wright, 1943. 87p.

Second edition. 1953. 122p.

10,972 **International Association for Labour Legislation.** British Section. *Report on welfare and health in relation to hours of work and output in war-time.* London: the Association, 1943. 34p.

10,973 **Ministry of Labour and National Service.** *Conference on Industrial Health, Caxton Hall, Westminster, 9th, 10th and 11th April, 1943: report of proceedings.* London: H.M.S.O., 1943. 107p.

10,974 **Hughes**, Therle. *Welfare at work.* London: British Council, 1944. 32p. (Britain advances 17.)

10,975 **Hyde**, Robert Robertson. 'Medical services in industry in Great Britain.' *Int. Labour Rev.*, LI, 4 (April 1945), 433–58.

Supplements the information contained in the account of the Industrial Health Conference of 1943, published *Int. Labour Rev.*, XLVIII, 4 (October 1943), 447–65.

10,976 **Medical Research Council.** Industrial Health Research Board. *Health research in industry: proceedings of a conference on industrial health research, held at the London School of Hygiene and Tropical Medicine.* London: H.M.S.O., 1945.

10,977 **Socialist Medical Association.** Industrial Health Committee. *Health and safety committees in industry: their origin, growth, development.* London: S.M.A., 1945. 11p.

10,978 **Medical Research Council.** Industrial Health Research Board. *The incidence of neurosis among factory workers.* London: H.M.S.O., 1947. (Report 90.)

By Russell Fraser.

10,979 **Industrial Law Review.** 'Index of industrial injuries.' *Ind. Law Rev.*, III, 2 (October 1948), 133–56; 3 (January 1949), 192–213.

A guide.

10,980 **Schuster**, *Sir* George. 'Human relations in industry.' *Br. Med. J.* (11 September 1948), 505–10.
'Read in opening a discussion in the Section of Occupational Health at the Annual Meeting of the British Medical Association, Cambridge, 1948.'

10,981 **Committee of Inquiry into the Health, Welfare, and Safety in Non-Industrial Employment.** *Report.* London: H.M.S.O., 1949. (Cmd. 7664.)
Chairman: Sir Ernest Gowers.

10,982 **Industrial Welfare Society.** *Works lavatories.* London, 1949. 81p.
Compiled by the Association for Planning and Regional Reconstruction in co-operation with the Industrial Welfare Society, Inc.

10,983 **Plumbe**, Charles Conway. *Factory well-being.* London: Seven Oaks P., 1949. vi, 138p.

10,984 **Stewart**, Donald. 'Occupational health.' Massey, A. (ed.). *Modern trends in public health.* London: Butterworth, 1949. p. 386–418.

10,985 **White**, Albert Arnold. *The aftercare of illness in industry.* 1950–51. (M.D. thesis, University of Aberdeen.)

10,986 **Herbert**, *Sir* Alfred. *Safety in industry.* Coventry: Alfred Herbert Ltd., 1951. [7]p. (Productivity in British industry 15.)
Reprinted from *The Engineer*, October 27 and November 3, 1950.

10,987 **Medical Research Council.** *Occupational factors in the aetiology of gastric and duodenal ulcers, with an estimate of their incidence in the general population.* London: H.M.S.O., 1951. (Special report series 276.)
By R. Doll and F. Avery-Jones.

10,988 **Lane**, R. E. 'The effect of environment on the health and efficiency of the industrial worker.' Ministry of Labour. *The worker in industry: a series of ten centenary lectures delivered during Festival of Britain year.* London: H.M.S.O., 1952. p. 17–27.

10,989 **Matthew**, T. U. 'The human factor in accident prevention.' Ministry of Labour. *The worker in industry: a series of ten centenary lectures delivered during Festival of Britain Year.* London: H.M.S.O., 1952. p. 88–100.

10,990 **Richardson**, I. M. *Age and work: a study of 489 men in heavy industry.* 1952–53. (M.D. thesis, University of Edinburgh.)

10,991 **Plumbe**, Charles Conway. *Factory health, safety and welfare encyclopaedia.* London: National Trade P., 1953. xii, 328p.

10,992 **Charley**, Irene Hannah. *The birth of industrial nursing: its history and development in Great Britain.* London: Baillière, Tindall and Cox, 1954. xii, 224p.

10,993 **Ling**, Thomas Mortimer. 'Psychological and occupational effects of illness and accident.' Ling, T. M. (ed.). *Mental health and human relations n industry.* London: H. K. Lewis, 1954. p. 47–68.

10,994 **MacFarlane**, Donald Ian. *Safety in industry: an introduction to the protection of personnel.* London: Iliffe, 1955. 71p.
Reprinted from *Machine Shop Magazine.*

10,995 **Ministry of Labour and National Service.** National Joint Advisory Council. Industrial Safety Sub-Committee. *Industrial accident prevention: a report.* London: H.M.S.O., 1956. iv, 36p.
Chairman: Dame Mary Smieton.

10,996 **Whitfield**, J. W. 'Men, machines and accidents.' *Min. Electl. Mech. Engr.*, XXXVII, 431 (August 1956), 34–42.
The 8th W. M. Thornton Lecture.

10,997 **Moore**, I. R. *The incidence and prevention of industrial accidents in Ireland.* 1956–57. (M.D. thesis, Trinity College, Dublin.)

10,998 **Socialist Medical Association.** *Men at work.* London, 1957. 16p.
Industrial accidents.

10,999 **Ministry of Labour and National Service.** *Survey in Halifax: report by H.M. Factory Inspectorate and recommendations of the Industrial Health Advisory Committee.* London: H.M.S.O., 1958.
Chairman: Iain Macleod.

11,000 **Royal Society for the Prevention of Accidents.** *Work accident statistics. Part I. Accident definition and investigation.* London: RoSPA, 1958. 23p. (Safety organization pamphlet 4.)

11,001 **Stevenson**, J. *The economic effect of industrial accidents, with special reference to Northern Ireland.* 1958–59. (M.Sc. (Econ.) thesis, Queen's University, Belfast.)

11,002 **Hogg**, Garry Lester. *Dangerous trades.* London: Phoenix House, 1959. 144p.

11,003 **Hunter**, Donald. *Health in industry.* Harmondsworth: Penguin Books, 1959. 288p. (Pelican books A441.)

11,004 **Ministry of Labour and National Service.** Factory Inspectorate. *Canteens and messrooms for small factories.* London: H.M.S.O., 1959. 48p. (Safety, health and welfare, new series 2.)

11,005 **Ministry of Labour and National Service.** Factory Inspectorate. *Cloakroom accommodation and washing facilities in factories.* London: H.M.S.O., 1959. 33p. (Safety, health and welfare, new series 5.)

11,006 **Silcock**, H. 'The comparison of occupational mortality rates.' *Populat. Studies*, XIII, 2 (November 1959), 183–92.

11,007 **Ministry of Labour.** *Health at work: a description of medical services in fourteen British factories.* London: Ministry of Labour and Central Office of Information, 1960. 76p.

11,008 **Schilling**, Richard Selwyn Francis (ed.). *Modern trends in occupational health.* London: Butterworth, 1960. ix, 313p. (Modern trends series.)

11,009 **Williams**, John Lewis. *Accidents and ill-health at work*. London: Staples, 1960. 516p.

11,010 **Browne**, Richard Charles. *Health in industry: a guide for engineers, executives and doctors*. London: Arnold, 1961. vii, 157p.

Based on lectures given at the University of Durham.

11,011 **Royal Society for the Prevention of Accidents.** *Works accident statistics. Part 2. Records and analysis*. London: RoSPA, 1961. 38p. (Safety organization pamphlet 6.)

11,012 **Cherns**, A. B. 'Accidents at work.' Welford, A. J., Argyle, M., Glass, D. V. and Morris, J. N. (eds.). *Society: problems and methods of study*. London: Routledge and Kegan Paul, 1962. p. 247–67.

11,013 **Institution of Mechanical Engineers.** *Factory working conditions*. London: the Institution, 1962. 30p.

11,014 **Rudd**, J. 'The statistics of accidents collected by H.M. Factory Inspectorate, Ministry of Labour.' *R. Statist. Soc. J.*, Ser. A, cxxv, 1 (1962), 144–50.

11,015 **Council of Europe.** Partial Agreement [in the social and public health field]. Social Committee. *Training of supervisory staff in accident prevention*. Strasbourg: C. of E., 1963.

Report of the Sub-Committee.

11,016 **Institute of Directors.** *Better factories*. London: the Institute, 1963. 279p.

11,017 **Institute of Directors.** *Better offices*. London: the Institute, 1964. 216p.

11,018 **Trades Union Congress.** *Health at work*. London: T.U.C., 1965.

11,019 **Archer**, Bruce. 'Murderous machines.' *New Soc.*, ix, 248 (29 June 1967), 953–4.

11,020 **Belmont**, Solomon. *Safety at work*. London: Cassell, 1967. 58p. (Working world series. Fourth year 61.)

11,021 **World Congress on the Prevention of Occupational Diseases**, London, 1964. [Proceedings of the congress held in] *London, 13–18 July 1964, organised by the Royal Society for the Prevention of Accidents in collaboration with the Committee on the Prevention of Occupational Risks of the International Social Security Association and in co-operation with the International Labour Office*. London: RoSPA, 1967. viii, 301p.

Also available in Spanish, French and German.

11,022 **Confederation of British Industry.** *Industrial safety organisation: report of a meeting held on October 11, 1967, London*. London: C.B.I., 1968. iii, 42p.

11,023 **Industrial Safety Advisory Council.** Sub-Committee for Joint Consultation on Safety. *Works safety committees in practice – some case studies: interim report*. London: H.M.S.O., 1968. 40p.

11,024 **Royal Society for the Prevention of Accidents.** *Occupational safety committees: joint consultation can prevent accidents*. London: the Society, 1968. 16p.

Revised edition.

11,025 **Anisulowo**, S. A. *Cyclical variations in industrial accidents among immigrant workers in Great Britain*. 1968–69. (M. Soc. Sc. dissertation, University of Birmingham.)

11,026 **Baker**, Frank, **McEwan**, Peter J. M. and **Sheldon**, Alan (eds.). *Industrial organizations and health*. London: Tavistock Publications.

Vol. 1. *Selected readings*. 1969. xvi, 699p.

11,027 **McCullough**, Winifred. *Physical working conditions*. London: Gower P., 1969. xiv, 162p. (Industrial Society. Handbook of employee amenities in factory and office.)

11,028 **Carr**, C. F. 'The pattern of accident causation.' *Ind. Law Soc. Bull.*, 8 (September 1970), 1–3.

The author was H.M. Deputy Chief Inspector of Factories.

11,029 **Hale**, A. R. and **Hale**, M. 'Accidents in perspective.' *Occup. Psychol.*, xliv (1970), 115–21.

11,030 **Johnson**, William George. *New approaches to safety in industry*. London: Industrial and Commercial Techniques, 1970. 43p.

11,031 **Powell**, Philip. 'By accident or design?' *Ind. Law Soc. Bull.*, 8 (September 1970), 4–5.

The author was Head of Accident Research, National Institute of Industrial Psychology.

2. Particular Occupations and Industries

11,032 **Campbell**, George L. *Miners' insurance funds: their origin and extent*. London: Waterlow, 1880. 17p.

11,033 **Neison**, Francis G. P. *The rate of fatal and non-fatal accidents in and about mines and on railways*. London, 1880.

11,034 **Brown**, G. T. *Report on anthrax or woolsorters' disease*. London: H.M.S.O., 1881. 2p. (C. 3022.)

11,035 *Two special reports on the use of gunpowder in slate or ironstone mines*. London: H.M.S.O., 1881. (C. 2876.)

11,036 **Observer** (*pseud.*). *White-lead workers; being an examination of the recent parliamentary papers, showing that the proposed legislation cannot remedy the state of affairs under the old stack process, and calling attention to the true remedy*. London: Hamilton, Adams, 1883. 32p.

11,037 *Report on the effects of heavy sizing in cotton weaving upon the health of the operatives employed*. London: H.M.S.O., 1884. (C. 3861.)

11,038 **Arlidge**, John Thomas. *The pottery manufacture in its sanitary aspects*. Hanley: Allbut and Daniel, 1892. 18p.

11,039 **Barrett-Lennard**, J. 'White-lead manufacture and its alleged dangers.' *Fortn. Rev.*, n.s., liii, 316 (April 1893), 591–2.

Letter in reply to article by V. Nash.

11,040 **Robinson**, W. *Lead miners and their diseases.* Newcastle, 1893.

11,041 **Departmental Committee Appointed to Inquire into the Conditions of Labour in the Various Lead Industries, into the Dangers to Work People Employed Therein, and to Propose Remedies.** *Report, with evidence, appendices, and index.* London: H.M.S.O., 1893–94. (C. 7239, 7239-I.)

11,042 **Departmental Committee on the Conditions of Labour in Chemical Works, the Dangers to Life and Health of the Workpeople Employed Therein, and the Proposed Remedies.** *Report, with evidence and appendix.* London: H.M.S.O., 1893–94. (C. 7235.)

11,043 **Departmental Committee on the Conditions of Labour in Potteries, the Injurious Effects upon the Health of the Workpeople, and the Proposed Remedies.** *Report, with appendices.* London: H.M.S.O., 1893–94. (C. 7240.)

11,044 **Inspector of Factories.** *Report . . . upon the conditions of work in flax mills and linen factories, and upon the mortality amongst textile operatives, etc., in the United Kingdom; with appendices.* London: H.M.S.O., 1893–94. (C. 7287.)

11,045 **Select Committee on Steam Engines (Persons in Charge) Bill.** *Special report and report, with the proceedings.* London: H.M.S.O., 1895. (H.C. 274.)

11,046 **Departmental Committee on the Conditions of Labour in the Manufacture of Brass, and of Kindred Amalgams.** *Report.* London: H.M.S.O., 1896. (C. 8091.)

11,047 **Farrington**, F. L. and **Wilson**, Bertram. 'The potters and lead-poisoning.' *Econ. Rev.*, VIII, 4 (October 1898), 521–4.

11,048 **Inspectors of Factories Appointed to Inquire into the Conditions of Work of the Fish Curing Trade of the United Kingdom.** *Reports.* London: H.M.S.O., 1898. (C. 8753.)

11,049 **Tuckwell**, Gertrude Mary. 'Commercial manslaughter.' *Nineteenth Century*, XLIV, 258 (August 1898), 253–8.

Occupational disease. Potteries.

11,050 **Inspectors of Factories.** *Report . . . on the prevention of accidents from machinery in the manufacture of cotton.* London: H.M.S.O., 1899. (C. 9456.)

By W. A. Beaumont and H. S. Richmond.

11,051 *Report on the employment of lead in the manufacture of pottery, its influence upon the health of the workpeople, with suggestions as to the means which might be adopted to counteract its evil effects* [with appendices]. London: H.M.S.O., 1899. (C. 9207.)

11,052 *The use of phosphorus in the manufacture of lucifer matches: reports.* London: H.M.S.O., 1899. (C. 9188.)

11,053 **Royal Commission on Accidents to Railway Servants.**

Part I. *Report.* London: H.M.S.O., 1900. 14p. (Cd. 41.)

Part II. *Minutes of evidence, etc.* 1900. (Cd. 42.)

Chairman: Lord Hereford.

11,054 **Wood**, George Henry. 'Report on the manufacture of matches.' *Econ. J.*, XII, 48 (December 1902), 556–60.

'A report prepared at the request of the Fabian Society in reply to a schedule of questions submitted by the International Labour Office.'

11,055 **Haldane**, J. S., **Martin**, Joseph S. and **Thomas**, R. Arthur. *Report on the health of Cornish miners.* London: H.M.S.O., 1904. 107p. (Cd. 2091.)

11,056 *Report upon the conditions of work in flax and linen mills as affecting the health of the operatives employed therein.* London: H.M.S.O., 1904. (Cd. 1997.)

11,057 *Report on the manufacture of paints . . . containing lead, as affecting the health of the operatives employed.* London: H.M.S.O., 1905. (Cd. 2466.)

By T. M. Legge, H.M. Medical Inspector of Factories.

11,058 *Tragedies of the mine: thirty years' explosions in South Wales.* London, 1905. 48p.

11,059 **Committee on Railway Employment Safety Appliances.** *First, second reports.* London: H.M.S.O., 1907. 13p. (Cd. 3638.)

Third, fourth reports. 1908. 11p. (Cd. 4213.)

Fifth, sixth, seventh, eighth reports. 1910. 7p. (Cd. 5359.)

Chairman: H. A. Yorke.

11,060 **Royal Commission on Mines.** *First report.* London: H.M.S.O., 1907. (Cd. 3548.)

Minutes of evidence; with index and appendices.

Vol. I. 1907. (Cd. 3549.)
Vol. II. 1908. (Cd. 3873.)
Vol. III. 1908. (Cd. 4349.)
Vol. IV. 1909. (Cd. 4667.)
Vol. V. 1911. (Cd. 5642.)

Second report. 1909. (Cd. 4820.)

Third report (Pit ponies). 1911. (Cd. 5561.)

Chairman: Lord Monkswell.

'To enquire into certain questions relating to the health and safety of miners, and the administration of the Mines Act.'

11,061 **Departmental Committee on Rescue and Aid in the Case of Accidents in Mines.** *Report.* London: H.M.S.O., 1911. 5p. (Cd. 5550.)

Chairman: C. F. G. Masterman.

11,062 **Martin**, Joseph S. and **Jones**, D. Rocyn. *Report to the Right Honourable the Secretary of State for the Home Department on an outbreak of glanders among the horses, and the alleged insanitary condition of the collieries, belonging to the Ebbw Vale Steel, Iron and Coal Company, Limited, in the County of Monmouth.* London: H.M.S.O., 1911. 16p. (Cd. 5713.)

11,063 **Ponder**, Constant. *Report to the Worshipful Company of Leathersellers on the incidence of anthrax amongst those engaged in the hide, skin, and leather industries, with an inquiry into certain measures aiming at its prevention.* London: Worshipful Company of Leathersellers, 1911. vii, 88p.

11,064 **Burns**, Daniel. *Safety in coal mines: a textbook of fundamental principles for firemen and other workers in mines.* London: Blackie, 1912. 158p.

11,065 **Departmental Committee on the Testing of Miners' Safety Lamps.** *Report.* London: H.M.S.O., 1912. 6p. (Cd. 6387.)

11,066 **Glasier**, Katherine Bruce, **Richardson**, T., and others. *Baths at the pithead and the works.* London: Women's Labour League, 1912. 16p.

Third edition of *Miners' baths*, enlarged and completely revised.

11,067 **Money**, *Sir* Leo George Chiozza. 'Sympathy – in patches.' *Things that matter: papers upon subjects which are, or ought to be, under discussion.* London: Methuen, 1912. p. 176–82.

On dangers to the workman in mining and on the railways.

11,068 **Departmental Committee Appointed to Consider the Provision of Washing and Drying Accommodation at Mines Under the Coal Mines Act, 1911.** *Report.* London: H.M.S.O., 1913. 11p. (Cd. 6724.)

Chairman: William Walker.

11,069 **Horton**, Frederick Waters. *Coal mine accidents in the United States and foreign countries.* 1913. 102p. (U.S.A. Bureau of Mines. Bulletin 69.)

11,070 **Edwards**, W. R. 'The development of first aid to the injured amongst railway employees.' *Jubilee of the Railway News, 1864–1914.* London: *Railway News*, 1914. p. 188–90.

11,071 **Great Western Railway.** *The 'Safety' movement.* London, 1914. 47p.

11,072 **Smith**, J. W. G. *Consumption and the boot and shoe industry; with supplementary report.* London, 1915. 2 pts.

11,073 **Collis**, Edgar Leigh. *The protection of the health of munition workers.* London, 1917. 11p.

11,074 **Great Western Railway.** *The 'Safety' movement: an interesting experiment for railwaymen.* London, 1918. 7p.

By Edward S. Hadley.

11,075 **Chappell**, Edgar Leyshon and **Fraser**, James Alexander Lovat. *Pithead and factory baths.* Cardiff: Welsh Housing and Development Association, 1920. xv, 93p.

11,076 **Cadbury Brothers.** *Health in the factory: an account of the work of the medical & dental departments at Bournville Works.* Bournville, 1922. 32p.

Later editions. 1925, 1936.

11,077 **Hart**, J. Y. 'An investigation of sickness data of public elementary school teachers in London, 1904–1919.' *R. Statist. Soc. J.*, LXXXV, 3 (May 1922), 349–92.

Discussion, p. 392–411.

'Read before the Royal Statistical Society, March 21, 1922.'

11,078 **Hart**, J. Y. 'A note on the rates of sickness of elementary school teachers recruited from London and the provinces.' *R. Statist. Soc. J.*, LXXXVI, 3 (May 1923), 420–2.

11,079 **Home Office.** Committee to enquire into the circumstances and causes of accidents in shipbuilding and ship repairing, and to report what further measures for their prevention are desirable. *Report, appendices.* London: H.M.S.O., 1924. 68p.

Chairman: Godfrey Lampson Tennyson Locker-Lampson.

11,080 **Home Office.** Departmental Committee on Silicosis (Medical Arrangements). *Report.* London: H.M.S.O., 1929. 19p.

Chairman: John Crosthwaite Bridge.

11,081 **Ministry of Health.** *Investigation in the coalfields of South Wales and Monmouth.* London: H.M.S.O., 1929. 10p. (Cmd. 3272.)

11,082 **Home Office.** Departmental Committee on Dust in Card Rooms in the Cotton Industry. *Report.* London: H.M.S.O., 1932. 96p.

Chairman: John Jackson.

11,083 **Mitchell**, J. H. 'The worker's point of view. X. Pit-head baths: their effect on the worker.' *Hum. Factor*, VI, 12 (December 1932), 454–66.

Reprinted in *The worker's point of view: a symposium.* London: Hogarth P., 1933. p. 92–106.

11,084 **Williams**, Enid Mary. *The account of an investigation into the health of old and retired coalminers in South Wales.* 1932. (M.D. thesis, University of Wales, Cardiff.)

11,085 **Campbell**, C. Douglas. 'Trade fluctuations and accidents to railway employees.' *Manchr. Sch.*, IV, 2 (1933), 69–81.

11,086 **National Employers' Mutual General Insurance Association.** *Accident prevention in the building and allied trades.* London, 1933. 195p.

11,087 **Williams**, Enid Mary. *Health of old and retired coalminers in South Wales.* Cardiff: U. of Wales P. Board, 1933. ix, 108p.

11,088 **Mitchell**, J. H. 'A note on pithead baths.' *Hum. Factor*, VIII, 5 (May 1934), 193–7.

11,089 **Dickson**, D. Elliot. 'The morbid miner.' *Edinb. Med. J.*, n.s. (4th), XLIII, 11 (November 1936), 696–705.
Paper read before the Edinburgh Medico-Sociological Club, October 1935.

11,090 **Medical Research Council.** Industrial Health Research Board. *An investigation into the sickness experience of London transport workers, with special reference to digestive disturbances.* London: H.M.S.O., 1937. (Report 79.)
By A. Bradford Hill.

11,091 **Mines Department.** *Explosions in mines: a comparison between Great Britain and France. A report by Major H. M. Hudspeth, D.S.O., M.C., H.M. Deputy Chief Inspector of Mines.* London: H.M.S.O., 1937. (Cmd. 5566.)

11,092 **Home Office.** Factory Department. *Report on conferences between employers, operatives and inspectors concerning fencing of machinery, other safety precautions, health and welfare in tinplate factories.* London: H.M.S.O., 1938. 12p.

11,093 **Royal Commission on Safety in Coal Mines.** *Report.* London: H.M.S.O., 1938. xxxii, 520p. (Cmd. 5890.)
Chairman: Lord Rockley.

11,094 **Ministry of Labour.** *London Central busmen: conferences between representatives of the London Passenger Transport Board, the Transport and General Workers' Union and the Medical Research Council, under the chairmanship of Sir John Forster, on the effects of working conditions upon the health of London Central busmen.* London: H.M.S.O., 1939.

11,095 **Thomas**, Ivor. 'Safety in mines.' *Polit. Q.*, x, 2 (April–June 1939), 244–53.

11,096 **Vernon**, Horace Middleton. *The health and efficiency of munition workers.* London: Oxford U.P., 1940. 138p. (Oxford medical publications.)

11,097 **Medical Research Council.** *Chronic pulmonary disease in South Wales coal miners. I. Medical studies.* London: H.M.S.O., 1942. (Special report series 243.)

11,098 **Davies**, David James. *Silicosis and the Welsh miner.* Caernarfon, Cardiff: Swyddfa'r Blaid, 1945.

11,099 **Ministry of Labour and National Service** and **Ministry of War Transport.** *Seamen's welfare in ports: report of the Committee appointed by the Minister of Labour and National Service and the Minister of War Transport in 1943.* London: H.M.S.O., 1945. 52p.
Chairman: H. G. White.

11,100 **Bashford**, *Sir* Henry. 'Health and welfare in the Civil Service.' *Hlth. Soc. Welf.* (1945–46), 95–8.

11,101 **McLaughlin**, Arthur Ivan Granville. 'Medical and nursing services in factories.' *Hlth. Soc. Welf.* (1945–46), 117–24.

11,102 **Ministry of Labour and National Service.** *Cotton industry: interim reports of the Joint Advisory Committee of the cotton industry. 1. Sanitary accommodation, washing facilities, accommodation for clothing, medical and welfare services, decoration and vacuum cleaning. 2. Dust in card rooms.* London: H.M.S.O., 1946.

11,103 **Amor**, A. J. 'The duties of an industrial medical officer in a large factory.' *Hlth. Soc. Welf.* (1947), 55–62.

11,104 **Morris**, J. N. 'Coal miners.' *Lancet*, CCLIII (September 1947), 341–6.

11,105 **Maule**, Harry Gordon. *A study in the laundry industry of the general conditions of work and management which may influence the health and well-being of laundry operatives.* 1949. (Ph.D. thesis, University of London.)

11,106 **National Coal Board.** *Notes on miners' welfare.* London: N.C.B., 1949.

11,107 **Industrial Injuries Advisory Council.** Sub-Committee. *Tuberculosis and other communicable diseases in relation to nurses and other health workers.* London: H.M.S.O., 1950. 20p. (Cmd. 8093.)
Chairman: A. W. Garrett.
Time limits. 1952. 12p. (Cmd. 8511.)
Pneumoconiosis. 1953. 24p. (Cmd. 8866.)
Raynaud's Phenomenon. 1954. 16p. (Cmd. 9347.)

11,108 **Medical Research Council.** *The social consequences of pneumoconiosis among coalminers in South Wales.* London: H.M.S.O., 1951. viii, 54p. (Memorandum 25.)
By P. Hugh-Jones and C. M. Fletcher.

11,109 **Ministry of Labour and National Service.** *Welfare arrangements on building sites.* London: H.M.S.O., 1951. 29p.

11,110 **Paterson**, Thomas Thomson and **Willett**, F. J. 'An experiment in the reduction of accidents in a colliery.' *Sociol. Rev.*, XLIII, 6 (1951), 107–26.

11,111 **Roberts**, C. G. *The health of executives.* London, 1951. 17p.

11,112 **Thomas**, Geoffrey. *The employment of men with pneumokoniosis.* [London]: Central Office of Information, [1951?]. 36p. (Social Survey. Report 73.)
'An inquiry carried out at the request of Pneumokoniosis Research Unit of the Medical Research Council in February 1946.'

11,113 **Bell**, J. H. *The relationship between occupation and health as shown by an investigation into the health of sewermen in Glasgow.* 1951–52. (M.D. thesis, University of Glasgow.)

11,114 **National Dock Labour Board.** *Welfare among dock workers: a review – July 1947 to December 1951.* London: the Board, 1952. 30p.

11,115 **Wiggans**, K. C. 'Job and health in a shipyard town.' *Sociol. Rev.*, XLIV, 5 (1952), 73–92.
Describes a survey made in Wallsend.

11,116 **Yekutiel**, M. P. *The history of pulmonary tuberculosis in the boot and shoe industry, and its relation to social conditions, including a comparison with other industries.* 1953–54. (D.Phil. thesis, University of Oxford.)

11,117 **King**, Howard Frederick. 'An age-analysis of some agricultural accidents.' *Occup. Psychol.*, XXIX, 4 (October 1955), 245–53.

11,118 **Ministry of Transport and Civil Aviation.** Marine Department. *Seafarers and their ships: the story of a century of progress in the safety of ships and the well-being of seamen.* London: H.M.S.O., 1955. 96p.

11,119 **Baker**, H. C. *Psychological factors in industrial accidents.* 1955–56. (M.A. thesis, University of Liverpool.)

11,120 **British Transport Commission.** London Transport Executive. *Health in industry: a contribution to the study of sickness absence experience in London Transport.* London: Butterworth for the London Transport Executive, 1956. 177p.

11,121 **Ministry of Labour and National Service.** Factory Inspectorate. *Industrial health survey of the pottery industry in Stoke-on-Trent.* London: H.M.S.O., 1959.

11,122 **Griffiths**, *Sir* Hugh Ernest. *The health of the dock worker: a lecture given at the National Week-end Conference, University of Leeds, September 26th & 27th 1959.* London: National Dock Labour Board, 1960. 18 leaves. (Education booklets 2.)

Private circulation.

Loose-leaf.

11,123 **National Council of Associated Iron Ore Producers.** *The iron ore industry of Great Britain.* Kettering: the Council, 1960. 136p.

Chap. IX. 'Britain's iron ore industrial organisation.'

Chap. X. 'Safety, education and welfare.'

11,124 **National Dock Labour Board.** *Welfare among dock workers: a review published under the authority of the National Board.* London: the Board, 1960. 47p.

Title on cover: *Welfare among dock workers, 1940–1960.*

11,125 **Liddell**, Francis Douglas Kelly. 'Coalminers' morbidity.' *R. Statist. Soc. J.*, Ser. A, CXXV, 1 (1962), 1–19.

With discussion, p. 19–30.

Read before the Society, 17th November, 1961.

11,126 **Ministry of Labour.** Factory Inspectorate. Joint Standing Committee on Health, Safety and Welfare in the Drop Forging Industry. *Conditions in the drop forging industry, 1954–1964: report.* London: H.M.S.O., 1966. v, 61p.

11,127 **Mekky**, S. I. *A comparative study of the health of women employed in the English and Egyptian cotton industries.* 1967–68. (Ph.D. thesis, University of London.)

11,128 **Fairley**, Michael Charles. *Safety, health and welfare in the printing industry.* Oxford: Pergamon, 1968. xv, 138p. (Library of industrial and commercial education and training.)

11,129 **Hair**, P. E. H. 'Mortality from violence in British coal-mines, 1800–50.' *Econ. Hist. Rev.*, 2nd ser., XXI, 3 (December 1968), 545–61.

11,130 **International Symposium on Health Conditions in the Ceramic Industry,** Stoke-on-Trent, 1968. *Health conditions in the ceramic industry: an international symposium organized by the North Staffordshire Medical Institute (J. T. Arlidge Section of Occupational Health) and the British Occupational Hygiene Society, Stoke-on-Trent, 27 March to 29 March 1968.* Oxford: Pergamon, 1969. xxviii, 254p.

Edited by C. N. Davies.

11,131 **Department of Employment and Productivity.** *Wool textile industry: developments in safety, health and welfare 1948–1968.* London: H.M.S.O., 1970. 32p.

11,132 **Department of Trade and Industry.** *Safety of seamen: report of the Steering Committee on the safety of merchant seamen.* London: H.M.S.O., 1970. 20p.

Chairman: M. J. Service.

11,133 **Forster**, Eric. *The death pit: the untold story of mass death in a mine.* Newcastle-upon-Tyne: Graham, 1970. 88p.

The story of the West Stanley Colliery explosion of 1909.

Based on a series of six articles by the same author originally published in the *Newcastle Evening Chronicle* in 1969.

See also: 10,902; 10,956; 11,542; 14,590.

PART SEVEN

THE STATE AND ITS AGENCIES

I. GENERAL

This section includes general works on such topics as labour law, trade unions and the state, and government policy. See also Part One, IV; Part Three, III, A; Part Five, I; and Part Five, IV, A.

11,134 **Howell**, George. *A handy-book of the labour laws.* London, 1876.
'With introductions, notes and . . . forms for the use of workmen.'
Third edition, revised. London: Macmillan, 1895. xii, 338p.

11,135 **Hancock**, William Neilson. 'On the law reforms which have been successfully advocated by the Trades Union Congress and the further reforms which they now seek.' *Statist. Soc. Inq. Soc. Ir. J.*, VIII, 2 (January 1881), 170–8.

11,136 **Ogilvie**, S. C. *The working-man and the state.* London, 1881. 16p.

11,137 **Jevons**, William Stanley. *The state in relation to labour.* London: Macmillan, 1882. vi, 166p. (The English citizen, his rights and responsibilities.)
Second edition. 1887.
Third edition. 1894. xxix, 171p. Edited with an introduction by Michael Cabebé.
Fourth edition. 1910. xviii, 174p. Edited with an introduction by Francis W. Hirst.
Fourth edition reprinted. New York: Kelley, 1968. (Reprints of economic classics.)

11,138 **Davis**, J. E. *Labour and labour laws.* London, 1883. 48p.

11,139 **Stone**, W. H. *Legislation as affecting the labouring classes.* Guildford, 1885. 22p.

11,140 **Howell**, George. 'Trades Union Congresses and social legislation: a record of mutual self-help by associative effort.' *Contemp. Rev.*, LVI (September 1889), 401–20.

11,141 **N.** 'The rights of labour.' *Westm. Rev.*, CXXXIV, 1 (July 1890), 95–103.
Proposes state tribunals to protect labour.

11,142 **Bradlaugh**, Charles. *Labor and law.* London: R. Forder, 1891. lxiii, 217p.
With a memoir of the author by John M. Robertson, and two portraits.

11,143 **Brentano**, Lujo. *The relation of labor to the law of to-day.* New York: Putnam, 1891. viii, 306p.
Translated from the German by Porter Sherman.
With an introduction by the translator.

11,144 **Howell**, George. 'Liberty for labour.' Mackay, T. (ed.). *A plea for liberty: an argument against socialism.* London: Murray, 1891. p. 109–41.
On legislation affecting labour.
Revised edition. 1892.

11,145 **Rumsey**, Almaric. *Handbook for employers and employed.* London: Swan Sonnenschein, 1892. xiv, 330p. (Legal handbooks.)

11,146 **Brown**, R. *The tyranny of government inspection as it affects manufacturers . . . and workers.* Glasgow, 1894. 12p.

11,147 **Guyot**, Yves. *The state control of labour: an address delivered at Antwerp, July 21st, 1894.* London: Liberty and Property Defence League, 1895. 22p.

11,148 **Cohen**, Simon. *A great scheme for a national aid organization for the improvement of the condition of trade, labour, and welfare of humanity, and extinction of pauperism.* London: Simon Cohen, 1896. 31p.

11,149 **Nunn**, E. W. *Capital and labour and state control.* Manchester, 1897. 7p.

11,150 **Webb**, Sidney. *Labor in the longest reign, 1837–1897.* London: Fabian Society, 1897. 20p. (Fabian tract 75.)
Reprinted with alterations from the Co-operative Wholesale Society's Annual for 1893.
Second edition reprinted. 1899.
Another edition. London: Grant Richards, 1897. 62p.

11,151 **Edinburgh Review.** 'The state and condition of labour.' *Edinb. Rev.*, CLXXXVII, 384 (April 1898), 277–99.
Review article on Webbs' *Industrial democracy; The labour question*, by Paul de Rousiers; *The labour problem*, by G. Drage and *Report of the Chief Labour Correspondent of the Board of Trade on the strikes and lock-outs of 1896*, 1897 (C. 8643).

11,152 **Minton-Senhouse,** Robert Metcalfe. *Work and labour; being a compendium of the law affecting the conditions under which manual work of the working classes is performed in England.* London: Sweet and Maxwell, 1904. xcviii, 379p.

11,153 **Ashley,** William James. 'The present position of social legislation in England.' *Econ. Rev.*, XVIII, 4 (October 1908), 391–411.

'A paper prepared for the Pan-Anglican Congress, June 22, 1908, with some additions and notes.'

11,154 **International Association for Labour Legislation.** British Section. *Report on the administration of labour laws in the United Kingdom.* London, 1908. 47p.

11,155 **Steel-Maitland,** *Sir* Arthur Herbert Drummond Ramsay. 'Labour.' Harris, J. E., 5th Earl of Malmesbury (ed.). *The new order: studies in Unionist policy.* London: Francis Griffiths, 1908. p. 335–76.

11,156 **Conacher,** H. M. 'The state as an agent for securing distributive justice.' *Econ. Rev.*, XX, 4 (October 1910), 368–86.

11,157 **Dolan,** Winifred. *History of social reform during one hundred years.* London: Love and Malcomson, 1910. 112p.

11,158 **International Association for Labour Legislation.** *First comparative report on the administration of labour laws: inspection in Europe.* London: King, 1911. xv, 109p.

Printed in Basle.

11,159 **Tillyard,** Frank. 'Non-parliamentary industrial legislation.' *Econ. J.*, XXV, 99 (September 1915), 360–8.

Explanation of provisional order, statutory orders, determinations and bye-laws.

11,160 **Greenwood,** John Henry. *A handbook of industrial law: a practical legal guide for trade union officers and others.* London: U. of London P., 1916. xv, 288p.

11,161 **Tillyard,** *Sir* Frank. *Industrial law.* London: Black, 1916. xx, 626p.

Second edition. 1928. xxiv, 582p.

11,162 **Radford,** George. *Labour and the state.* [c. 1920.] 8p.

11,163 **De Montgomery,** Bo Gabriel. *British and continental labour policy: the political labour movement and labour legislation in Great Britain, France and the Scandinavian countries, 1900–1922.* London: Kegan Paul, Trench, Trubner, 1922. xxvii, 575p.

11,164 **Rich,** Theodore. *Labour trusts: their pretensions, their methods and their influence on the state.* London: Boswell Printing and Publishing Co., 1922. 32p.

11,165 **Gutteridge,** H. C. 'The interpretation and administration of labour laws in England.' *Int. Labour Rev.*, x, 2 (August 1924), 209–35.

11,166 **Labour Party.** *Legislation for the workers: Labour government's output of new labour laws.* London: Labour Publications Department, 1924. 18p. (Can Labour rule? 8.)

11,167 **National Movement Towards a Christian Order of Industry and Commerce.** *The regularisation of industry: papers . . . Trinity College, Cambridge, July 4th to 7th, 1924.* [York?]: the Movement, [1924?]. 71p. (Christian order of industry series 5.)

Papers by J. R. Bellerby, A. L. Bowley, H. D. Henderson, J. H. Jones, Sydney W. Pascall, D. H. Robertson.

11,168 **Slesser,** *Sir* Henry Herman and **Henderson,** Arthur. *Industrial law.* London: Benn, 1924. xxxvi, 947p.

11,169 **Colyer,** William Thomas. *Anti-labour legislation: why the workers should demand their repeal.* London: Communist Party of Great Britain, 1925. 22p.

11,170 **Slesser,** *Sir* Henry Herman. 'The place of industrial law in English jurisprudence.' *Economica*, v, 13 (March 1925), 28–37.

11,171 **Troup,** *Sir* Charles Edward. *The Home Office.* London and New York: Putnam, 1925. [xii], 267p. (Whitehall series.)

Chapter XI. 'Industrial laws.' p. 156–77.

11,172 **Burns,** Eveline Mabel. *Wages and the state.* 1926. ix, 443 leaves. (Ph.D. thesis, University of London.)

11,173 **Mackenzie,** A. L. 'Some aspects of recent legislation.' *Publ. Adm.*, IV (1926), 232–42.

'Lecture delivered under the joint auspices of the Glasgow School of Social Study and the Institute of Public Administration, 11th March, 1926.'

Includes Factory Acts, Workmen's Compensation Acts, Insurance Acts, Shop Acts.

11,174 **League of Nations Union.** *Towards industrial peace, being the report of the proceedings of a conference organized by the League of Nations Union and held at the London School of Economics, February 1–4, 1927 on systems of fixing minimum wages . . ., and, methods of conciliation and arbitration.* London: King, 1927. 283p.

Contents include: Systems of fixing minimum wages: the trade boards system; other methods of fixing minimum wages; joint industrial councils – present position; joint industrial councils – proposals for re-organization; industrial arbitration; conciliation schemes; industrial relations.

11,175 **Pipkin,** Charles Wooten. *The idea of social justice: a study of legislation and administration and the labour movement in England and France between 1900 and 1926.* New York: Macmillan, 1927. xvii, 595p.

11,176 **Hill,** R. L. *The attitude of the Tory Party to labour questions, 1832–46.* 1928. (B.Litt. thesis, University of Oxford.)

11,177 **Richardson**, John Henry. 'What has been done by British fact-finding bodies in industrial relations.' *Acad. Polit. Sci. Proc.*, XIII, 1 (June 1928), 20, 34.

11,178 **Marlow**, George Stanley Withers. *Law and industry*. London: Baillière, 1929. vii, 319p. (Industrial chemistry series.)

11,179 **Cochrane**, L. *Note on the differences between the provisions of international labour conventions adopted prior to 1926 . . . and existing British legislation on the same subjects*. London, [1930?]. 16p.

11,180 **Price**, T. W. *Soviet legislation and theory in Great Britain from 1906 to 1914*. 1930. (B.Litt. thesis, University of Oxford.)

11,181 **Worts,** Frederick Robert. *Work, wealth and government in England*. London: Heinemann, 1930. 208p.

11,182 **Hobson**, Samuel George. *The house of industry: a new estate of the realm*. London: King, 1931. xxviii, 113p.

Proposes a national economic planning body with union participation.

11,183 **Pipkin**, Charles Wooten. *Social politics and modern democracies*. New York: Macmillan, 1931. 2v.

Vol. 1. Great Britain.

Vol. 2. France.

Industrial legislation.

11,184 **Roberts**, Frederick. *Guide to industrial and social legislation, with special reference to the local government service*. London: Gee, 1931. xiii, 318p.

11,185 **Samuels**, Harry. *The law relating to industry*. London: Pitman, 1931. xvii, 241p.

Second edition. *Industrial law*. 1939. xxi, 249p.

Third edition. *Industrial law*. 1948. xix, 252p.

Fourth edition. *Industrial law*. 1949. xxi, 228p.

Fourth edition, revised and reprinted. *Industrial law*. 1953. xix, 228p.

11,186 **Slifer**, Walter L. *British coal miners and the government, 1840–1860*. 1931. (Ph.D. dissertation, University of Pennsylvania.)

11,187 **Milne-Bailey**, Walter. *Trade unions and the state*. London: Allen and Unwin, 1934. 395p.

Based on the author's Ph.D. thesis, University of London.

11,188 **Macpherson**, C. B. *Voluntary associations within the state, 1900–1934, with special reference to the place of trade unions in relation to the state in Great Britain*. 1935. (M.A. thesis, University of London.)

11,189 **Duffy**, Luke J. *The Conditions of Employment Act handbook*. Dublin: Labour Party, 1936. 43p.

11,190 **Young Women's Christian Association of Great Britain.** *The worker and the law: a practical guide to industrial law, social insurance, etc*. London, 1936. 34p.

11,191 **Mackenzie**, William Warrender, Baron Amulree. *Inaugural address: the state and the worker*. London: Royal Society of Arts, 1937. 12p.

By the Chairman of the Council. Delivered before the Royal Society, 3 November 1937.

11,192 **Mackenzie**, William Warrender, Baron Amulree. *The state and the worker*. London: Society for the Encouragement of Arts, Manufactures and Commerce, 1937. 12p.

11,193 **Ball**, Frank Norman. *Statute law relating to employment*. Southend-on-Sea: Thames Bank Publishing Co., 1939. xxxii, 293p.

Third edition. Leigh-on-Sea, 1949. xii, 383p.

11,194 **Bondfield**, Margaret Grace. 'Industrial welfare in my time.' *Fortnightly*, n.s., CLVI, 936 (December 1944), 378–83.

Industrial legislation.

11,195 **Fisk**, William L. *Twenty years of English labor legislation*. 1946. (Ph.D. dissertation, Ohio State University.)

11,196 **International Labour Office.** 'Collaboration of employers and workers with government departments in Great Britain.' *Int. Labour Rev.*, LIV, 5–6 (November–December 1946), 321–30.

11,197 **Thomas**, Maurice Walton. 'How it began: the origins of industrial law.' *Ind. Law Rev.*, I, 1 (June 1946), 5–14; 2 (July 1946), 46–54; 4 (September 1946), 97–105; 5 (October 1946), 140–8; 6 (November 1946), 178–87; 7 (December 1946), 212–18; 8 (January 1947). 245–51; 10 (March 1947), 309–17.

11,198 **Conservative and Unionist Central Office.** *The industrial charter: a statement of Conservative industrial policy*. London: Conservative and Unionist Central Office, 1947. 40p.

By a committee appointed at the Conservative Party Conference in October 1946.

Popular edition. 1947. 11p.

11,199 **Cooper**, *Sir* William Mansfield. *Outlines of industrial law*. London: Butterworth, 1947. lix, 344, 17p.

Second edition. 1954. lxi, 378, 21p.

Third edition, by W. M. Cooper and John C. Wood. 1958. lxvi, 413, 21p.

Fourth edition, by W. M. Copper and J. C. Wood. 1962. lxx, 423, 23p.

Fifth edition, by W. M. Cooper and J. C. Wood. 1966. lxxvi, 445, 26p.

11,200 **Levy**, Hermann. 'The scope of industrial law.' *Ind. Law Rev.*, II, 2 (July 1947), 34–40.

11,201 **National Union of Conservative and Constitutional Associations.** Conservative Political Centre. *Conservative social and industrial reform, 1800–1945*. London, 1947. 60p.

By Charles E. Bellairs.

11,202 **Sachs**, Eric. *The law of employment: a summary of the rights of employers and employees*. London: Pitman, 1947. ix, 69p.

11,203 **Mortished**, R. J. P. 'The Industrial Relations Act, 1946; an outline of the Act, with some comparisons with other countries.' *Statist. Soc. Inq. Soc. Ir. J.* (1947–48), 671–87.
Discussion, p. 687–90.

11,204 **Robson**, William Alexander. 'Nationalized industries and industrial law.' *Ind. Law Rev.*, II, 8 (January 1948), 192–6.

11,205 **Winterbottom**, Allan. 'Trade unions and labour under the law.' Tracey, H. (ed.). *The British Labour Party: its history, growth, policy, and leaders.* London: Caxton Publishing Co., 1948. Vol. 2. p. 239–50.

11,206 **Mortished**, R. J. P. 'The Industrial Relations Act, 1946.' King, F. C. (ed.). *Public administration in Ireland.* Vol. II. Dublin: Parkside P., 1949. p. 75–89.

11,207 **Vries**, Carl Wilhelm de and **Vries**, Jan Pieter Marie Laurens de (eds.). *Texts concerning early labour legislation. I. 1791–1848.* Leiden: Brill, 1949. 52p. (Textus minores, vol. 5.)

11,208 **Rolfe**, Sidney E. 'The trade unions, freedom and economic planning.' Industrial Relations Research Association. *Proceedings of the third annual meeting, Chicago, Illinois, December 28–29, 1950.* p. 338–51.

11,209 **Kahn-Freund**, Otto. 'Report on some fundamental characteristics of labour law in Great Britain.' Congresso Internazionale di Diritto del Lavoro, Trieste, 1951. *Atti.* Trieste: Editrice Università di Trieste, 1952. p. 175–205.

11,210 **Schmitthoff**, Clive M. 'The rule of law in industrial relations.' *Ind. Law Rev.*, VII, 2 (October 1952), 84–100.
Based on a lecture given under the auspices of the West Midlands Advisory Council for Technical, Commercial and Art Education at Birmingham on 30th June 1952.

11,211 **Quinn**, K. P. J. *The Industrial Relations Act, 1946.* 1952–53. (M.A. thesis, National University of Ireland.)

11,212 **Conservative and Unionist Party.** Conservative Industrial Department. *Trade unions and the government.* London: Conservative Political Centre, 1954. 22p. (Trade union services series 8.)
Revised edition. 1963. 19p. (New trade union series 7.)

11,213 **Kahn-Freund**, Otto. 'Legal framework.' Flanders, A. and Clegg, H. A. (eds.). *The system of industrial relations in Great Britain.* Oxford: Blackwell, 1954. p. 42–127.
'Table of statutes and cases' appears on pages 365–71.

11,214 **Gayler**, Joshua Leonard. *Industrial law.* London: English Universities P., 1955. xxvi, 362p.

11,215 **Rogow**, Arnold Austin. *The Labour government and British industry, 1945–1951.* Oxford: Blackwell, 1955. xiii, 196p.
With the assistance of Peter Shore.
Chap. V. 'Industry and labour.' p. 101–17.

11,216 **Sethur**, Frederick. 'Trade unionism and central planning in Western Europe.' *Sth. Econ. J.*, XXII, 2 (October 1955), 221–9.

11,217 **Rimel**, M. M. 'Modern industrial law.' *Ind. Law Rev.*, X, 4 (April 1956), 257–66.
'This article contains the subject matter of a lecture given by the author to the Mansfield Law Club on 8th December, 1955.'

11,218 **Payne**, John. 'Men at work.' Archer, P. (ed.). *Social welfare and the citizen.* Harmondsworth: Penguin, 1957. p. 225–41.

11,219 **Trades Union Congress.** *Industrial law: an introduction for trades union officers.* London: T.U.C., 1957. 40p.
New edition.

11,220 **Frankel**, Marvin. 'Joint industrial planning in Great Britain.' *Ind. Labor Relat. Rev.*, XI, 3 (April 1958), 429–45.

11,221 **Kahn-Freund**, Otto. 'Labour law.' Ginsberg, M. (ed.). *Law and opinion in England in the 20th century.* London: Stevens, 1959. p. 215–63.

11,222 **Parsons**, Owen Henry. *Tory war on trade unionism.* London: Labour Research Department, 1959. 16p.

11,223 **Roberts**, Benjamin Charles. 'Industrial relations.' Ginsberg, M. (ed.). *Law and opinion in England in the 20th century.* London: Stevens, 1959. p. 364–89.

11,224 **Allen**, Victor Leonard. *Trade unions and the government.* London: Longmans, 1960. xii, 326p.

11,225 **Macdonald**, Donald Farquhar. *The state and the trade unions.* London: Macmillan; New York: St Martin's P., 1960. vii, 199p.

11,226 **Mack**, John A. 'Trade unions and the state.' *Scott. J. Polit. Econ.*, VII, 1 (February 1960), 47–64.

11,227 **O'Donovan**, Tim. *Above the law? The case for a Royal Commission on trade unions.* London: Johnson, 1960. 86p.

11,228 **Welton**, Harry. *The trade unions, the employers, and the state.* London: Pall Mall P., 1960. 178p.

11,229 **Evans**, Hywell. *Governmental regulation of industrial relations: a comparative study of United States and British experience.* Ithaca, N.Y.: Cornell University, New York State School of Industrial and Labor Relations, 1961. vii, 116p.

11,230 **Lincoln**, John Abraham. 'Trade unions and the labour market. Part 2. Human rights in industry.' Seldon, A. (ed.). *Agenda for a free society: essays on Hayek's 'The constitution of liberty'.* London: Hutchinson for the Institute of Economic Affairs, 1961. p. 155–68.

11,231 **Thomson**, Andrew William John. *The courts and labor in Britain and the United States, 1880–1910: a study in the legal effects of class structure.* Ithaca, N.Y., 1961. vi, 335 leaves. (M.S. thesis, Cornell University.)

11,232 **Aikin**, Olga L. 'Legal perspectives.' Roberts, B. C. (ed.). *Industrial relations: contemporary problems and perspectives.* London: Methuen, 1962. p. 195–226.

11,233 **Conference on Labour Law in Europe with Special Reference to the Common Market**, London, 1962. *Labour law in Europe, with special reference to the Common Market: a report of a conference held on June 7 and 8, 1962, under the joint auspices of the Federal Trust for Education and Research, the British Institute of International and Comparative Law, the Institute of Advanced Legal Studies, the Industrial Law Society (British Section of the International Association of Labour Law).* London: Stevens for the British Institute of International and Comparative Law, 1962. vi, 92p. (*International and Comparative Law Quarterly.* Supplementary publications 5.)

11,234 **Barres**, Stephen J. 'The origins of modern labor law.' *Am. J. Econ. Sociol.*, XXII, 2 (April 1963), 279–86.

11,235 **Beever**, R. Colin. 'The consequences for labour and social policy.' *Polit. Q.*, XXXIV, 1 (January–March 1963), 78–87.
The consequences of Britain's joining the European Economic Community.

11,236 **Fridman**, Gerald Henry Louis. *The modern law of employment.* London: Stevens, 1963. clxii, 1065p.
First supplement, to 1 March 1964. 1964. [73], xxp.
Second supplement, to 31 Dec. 1966. 1967. [119]p.

11,237 **Brown**, E. D. *Some aspects of European social and labour law.* 1963–64. (LL.M. dissertation, University of London.)

11,238 **Mitchell**, Ewan (*pseud.*) [i.e. Greville Ewan Janner]. *The personnel manager's lawyer and employer's guide to the law.* London: Business Publications, 1964. xxi, 276p.
Second edition. 1967. xii, 303p.

11,239 **Sams**, K. I. 'Government and trade unions: the situation in Northern Ireland.' *Br. J. Ind. Relat.*, II, 2 (July 1964), 258–70.

11,240 **Brown**, Wilfred Banks Duncan. 'Legislation.' Brown, W. B. D. and Jaques, E. *Glacier Project papers: some essays on organization and management from the Glacier Project Research.* London: Heinemann, 1965. p. 215–36.

11,241 **Bryant**, Robert. *A modern view of the law relating to employment.* Oxford, London: Pergamon, 1965. ix, 116p. (Commonwealth and international library. Pergamon modern legal outlines.)

11,242 **Wedderburn**, Kenneth William. 'Labour courts?' *New Soc.*, VI, 167 (9 December 1965), 9–11.

11,243 **Wedderburn**, Kenneth William. *The worker and the law.* Harmondsworth: Penguin, 1965. 368p. (Pelican books.)
New edition. London: MacGibbon and Kee, 1966. 360p.
Second edition. Penguin, 1971. 587p.

11,244 **Abbott**, Stephen. *Industrial relations: Conservative policy.* London: Conservative Political Centre, 1966. 18p.

11,245 **Conservative and Unionist Party.** Conservative Industrial Department. Trade Unionists' National Advisory Committee. *Industrial advance: a report from the Conservative Trade Unionists' National Advisory Committee together with evidence to the Royal Commission on Trade Unions and Employers' Associations.* London: Conservative Political Centre, 1966. 20p.

11,246 **Industrial Society.** *Legal problems of employment.* London: Industrial Society, 1966. iv, 98p.
Fourth edition.
Previous edition. 1960.

11,247 **McCarthy**, Charles. 'Trade unions and economic planning in Ireland.' *Int. Labour Rev.*, XCIV, 1 (July 1966), 54–72.

11,248 **Robertson**, Norman. 'Trade unions and economic planning.' *Bankers' Mag.*, CCI (January 1966), 26–31.

11,249 **Wootton**, Graham. *Workers, unions and the state.* London: Routledge and Kegan Paul, 1966. xi, 173p.
Also New York, Schocken Books, 1967. xi, 173p.

11,250 **Wedderburn**, Kenneth William. *Cases and materials on labour law.* Cambridge: Cambridge U.P., 1967. xxix, 784p. (Cambridge legal case books.)

11,251 **Conservative Political Centre.** *Fair deal at work: the Conservative approach to modern industrial relations.* London: C.P.C., 1968. 67p.

11,252 **Drake**, Charles Dominic. 'Wage-slave or entrepreneur?' *Mod. Law Rev.*, XXXI, 4 (July 1968), 408–23.
On some difficulties in labour law.

11,253 **Jenkins**, Clive and **Mortimer**, James Edward. *The kind of laws the unions ought to want.* Oxford, London: Pergamon P., 1968. viii, 184p. (Commonwealth and international library. Social administration, training, economics and production division.)

11,254 **Johnston**, G. A. 'The influence of international labour standards on legislation and practice in the United Kingdom.' *Int. Labour Rev.*, XCVII, 5 (May 1968), 465–87.

11,255 **Kahn-Freund**, Otto. *Labour law: old tradition and new attitudes.* Toronto, Vancouver: Clarke, Irwin, 1968. xii, 92p. (W. M. Martin lectures, 1967.)

11,256 **O'Higgins**, Paul. 'Industrial legislation.' *New Soc.*, XI, 287 (28 March 1968), 452–5. (The origins of the social services 9.)

11,257 **Roberts**, Benjamin Charles. 'Fair deal at work.' *Br. J. Ind. Relat.*, VI, 3 (November 1968), 360–3.

A review of the pamphlet *Fair deal at work: the Conservative approach to modern industrial relations* (11,251).

11,258 **Seyfarth, Shaw, Fairweather & Geraldson.** *Labor relations and the law in the United Kingdom and the United States: a comparative study.* Ann Arbor, Mich.: Program in International Business, Graduate School of Business Administration, University of Michigan, 1968. xxvi, 634p. (Michigan international labor studies 1.)

11,259 **Thomson**, Andrew William John. *The reaction of the American Federation of Labor and the Trades Union Congress to labor law, 1900–1935.* Ithaca, N.Y., 1968. 2v. (Ph.D. thesis, Cornell University.)

11,260 **Wedderburn**, Kenneth William. 'L'état actuel du droit du travail et de la sécurité sociale dans la domaine de l'enseignement et de la recherche, ainsi que les rapports de cette discipline avec les sciences connexes: rapport national.' Congrès International de Droit du Travail et de la Sécurité Sociale, 6ième, Stockholm, 1966. *Actes.* Stockholm: Almqvist and Wiksell, 1968. Vol. III. 46p.

Text in English.

11,261 **Whincup**, Michael Hynes. *Industrial law.* London: Heinemann for the Institute of Supervisory Management, 1968. xv, 128p. (Supervisor's bookshelf.)

11,262 **Woodcock**, George. *The trade union movement and the government: a lecture delivered in the University of Leicester, 29 April 1968.* Leicester: Leicester U.P., 1968. 20p. (Woodcock lectureship 1968.)

11,263 **Stainton**, Douglas Carter. *Aspects of trade union interest in judicial reform 1867–1882.* 1968–69. (M.Phil. thesis, University of Southampton.)

11,264 **Brodetsky**, P. 'The legal basis.' McCarthy, W. E. J. (ed.). *Industrial relations in Britain: a guide for management and unions.* London: Lyon, Grant and Green, 1969. p. 55–81.

11,265 **Brown**, Douglas. *The law of employment in a nutshell.* London: Sweet and Maxwell, 1969. xii, 93p. (Nutshell series.)

11,266 **Carby-Hall**, Joseph Roger. *Principles of industrial law.* London: Knight, 1969. lxiv, 567p.

11,267 **Chander**, Harish. *Impact of labour legislations on industrial peace and economic development: a comparative study of India and the U.K.* 1969. (Dip. in Law, University of London.)

11,268 **Department of Employment and Productivity.** *In place of strife: a policy for industrial relations.* London: H.M.S.O., 1969. 40p. (Cmnd. 3888.)

11,269 **Drake**, Charles Dominic. *Labour law.* London: Sweet and Maxwell, 1969. xxiii, 311p. (Concise college texts.)

11,270 **Industrial Law Society.** 'Report of the Society's meeting on the White Paper *In place of strife.*' *Ind. Law Soc. Bull.*, 4 (April 1969), 27–32.

20 March 1969.

11,271 **Jenks**, Clarence Wilfred. *Britain and the I.L.O.: Davies Memorial Lecture, London, 4 February 1969.* London: David Davies Memorial Institute of International Studies, 1969. 20p.

11,272 **Kahn-Freund**, Otto. 'Industrial relations and the law – retrospect and prospect.' *Br. J. Ind. Relat.*, VII, 3 (November 1969), 301–16.

Sidney Ball lecture 1969, delivered on 26 February 1969 at Oxford.

11,273 **Kahn-Freund**, Otto. 'Labour law and public opinion.' Aubert, V. (ed.). *Sociology of law: selected readings.* Harmondsworth: Penguin, 1969. p. 80–9.

Excerpt from 'Labour law' in M. Ginsberg (ed.). *Law and opinion in England in the twentieth century.* London: Stevens, 1959. p. 215–27.

11,274 **Kilroy-Silk**, Robert. 'Legislating on industrial relations.' *Parl. Aff.*, XXII, 3 (Summer 1969), 250–7.

On *In place of strife.*

11,275 **Parsons**, Owen Henry. *Strikes and trade unions: government White Paper explained.* London: Labour Research Department, 1969. 20p.

11,276 **Paynter**, Will. 'The law and industrial relations: the future in Britain.' *Ind. Law Soc. Bull.*, 5 (July 1969), Supplement, 24–34.

A paper presented at the Industrial Law Society's Conference on Industrial Conflict and the Law, Nottingham, 11–13 July 1969.

11,277 **Samuels**, Harry. *The law and the employer.* London: Industrial Society, 1969. 19p.

11,278 **Sapper**, Laurie. *A practical guide to your job and the law.* London: Rapp and Whiting, 1969. 175p.

11,279 **Sim**, Raymond Studdart and **Powell-Smith**, Vincent. *Casebook on industrial law.* London: Butterworths, 1969. xxv, 387p.

11,280 **Stewart**, Margaret. *Britain and the ILO: the story of fifty years.* London: H.M.S.O., 1969. vi, 117p.

Published for the Department of Employment and Productivity.

11,281 **Thomas**, Griffith Bowen. 'The role of the state.' McCarthy, W. E. J. (ed.). *Industrial relations in Britain: a guide for management and unions.* London: Lyon, Grant and Green, 1969. p. 85–101.

11,282 **Wedderburn**, Kenneth William. 'The background to the present situation in Britain.' *Ind. Law Soc. Bull.*, 5 (July 1969), Supplement, 2–9.
A paper presented at the Industrial Law Society's Conference on Industrial Conflict and the Law, Nottingham, 11–13 July 1969.

11,283 **Wedderburn**, Kenneth William. 'British unions, beware.' *New Soc.*, XIV, 375 (4 December 1969), 900–1.

11,284 **Clegg**, Hugh Armstrong. 'The role of government agencies.' Robertson, D. J. and Hunter, L. C. (eds.). *Labour market issues of the 1970s.* Edinburgh: Oliver and Boyd for the Scottish Economic Society, 1970. p. 189–202.
First appeared in the June 1970 issue of the *Scottish Journal of Political Economy.*

11,285 **Conservative Party.** *Fair deal takes shape.* London, 1970.

11,286 **Cronin**, John B. and **Grime**, Robert P. *Labour law.* London: Butterworths, 1970. xlviii, 500p.

11,287 **Department of Employment and Productivity.** *Industrial Relations Bill: consultative document.* London: D.E.P., 1970. 27p.

11,288 **Grunfeld**, Cyril. 'The future role of the law.' Robertson, D. J. and Hunter L. C. (eds.). *Labour market issues of the 1970s.* Edinburgh: Oliver and Boyd for the Scottish Economic Society, 1970. p. 89–114.
First appeared in the June 1970 issue of the *Scottish Journal of Political Economy.*

11,289 **Grunfeld**, Cyril. 'Labor relations and the role of law in Great Britain.' Kamin, A. (ed.). *Western European labor and the American corporation.* Washington, D.C.: Bureau of National Affairs, 1970. p. 169–207.

11,290 **Jenkins**, Peter. *The battle of Downing Street.* London: Knight, 1970. xiv, 171p.

11,291 **Keenan**, Dennis J. and **Crabtree**, Cyril. *Essentials of industrial law.* London: Pitman, 1970. vii, 468p.

11,292 **McCarthy**, William Edward John. *The role of government in industrial relations: report of a conference at Ditchley Park, 14–17 June 1968.* Enstone: Ditchley Foundation, 1970. 19p. (Ditchley paper 15.)

11,293 **McCartney**, J. B. 'Ireland and labor relations law.' Kamin, A. (ed.). *Western European labor and the American corporation.* Washington, D.C.: Bureau of National Affairs, 1970. p. 269–304.

11,294 **Parsons**, Owen Henry. *The Tory threat to the unions: an analysis of the consultative document.* London: Labour Research Department, 1970. 28p.

11,295 **Paynter**, Will. 'Trade unions and government.' *Polit. Q.*, XLI, 4 (October–December 1970), 444–54.

11,296 **Summers**, Clyde W. 'Labor relations and the role of law in Western Europe.' Kamin, A. (ed.). *Western European labor and the American corporation.* Washington, D.C.: Bureau of National Affairs, 1970. p. 145–67.

11,297 **Whittingham**, T. G. and **Gottschalk**, Andrew W. 'Proposals for change in the British system of industrial relations: an evaluation.' *J. Ind. Relat.*, XII, 1 (March 1970), 52–71.
On *In place of strife.*

11,298 **Wood**, John. 'Whither labour law now?' *Br. J. Ind. Relat.*, VIII, 3 (November 1970), 305–12.

See also: 21; 110; 185; 211.

II. ROYAL COMMISSIONS

This section includes material relating to the five Royal Commissions which have been established in the United Kingdom to inquire into industrial relations. The reports of the first two Commissions were published before 1880, and hence should be excluded from this bibliography. An exception has been made, however, and they have been included here but comment on them published before 1880 has not. Works on legislation resulting from Royal Commission reports are not included here but are classified with the subject with which they deal. Other Royal Commission reports are classified with the subject to which they pertain.

A. ROYAL COMMISSION ON THE ORGANIZATION AND RULES OF TRADE UNIONS AND OTHER ASSOCIATIONS, 1867–69

11,299 **Royal Commission on the Organization and Rules of Trade Unions and Other Associations,** 1867–69. [Reports, minutes of evidence, etc.]
Command papers, nos. 3873, 3893, 3910, 3952, 3952-I, 3980, 3980-I–VI, 4123, 4123-I.
For further details see P. Ford and G. Ford, *Select list of British parliamentary papers, 1833–1899*, Oxford: Blackwell, 1953. p. 71.

11,300 **Stirling**, James. *Trade unionism: with remarks on the report of the Commissioners on trades' unions.* Glasgow: J. Maclehose, 1889. 56p.
Reprinted from the second edition. 1869.

11,301 **Harrison**, Frederic. *Autobiographic memoirs.* London: Macmillan, 1911. 2v.
The author was a member of the Royal Commission of 1867–69.

11,302 **Smith**, Edwin G. *The establishment of the British Royal Commission of 1867–69 to investigate trade unionism.* 1932. (Ph.D. dissertation, University of Pennsylvania.)

11,303 **McCready**, Herbert W. 'British labour and the Royal Commission on Trade Unions, 1867–9.' *Univ. Tor. Q.*, xxiv, 4 (July 1955), 390–409.

11,304 **Hanson**, C. G. 'The Royal Commission on Trade Unions 1867–69.' *NE. Group Study Labour Hist. Bull.*, 3 (October 1969), 6.

Summary of a paper read to the Group at Rutherford College of Technology, 24 January 1969.

B. ROYAL COMMISSION ON LABOUR LAWS, 1874–75

11,305 *First report of the Commissioners appointed to inquire into the working of the Master and Servant Act, 1867, and the Criminal Law Amendment Act, 34 & 35 Vict. Cap. 32, and for other purposes; together with minutes of evidence.* London: H.M.S.O., 1874. 165p. (C. 1094).

Second and final report of the Commissioners appointed to inquire into the working of the Master and Servant Act, 1867, and the Criminal Law Amendment Act, 34 & 35 Vict. Cap. 32, and for other purposes. London: H.M.S.O., 1875. iv, 29p. (C. 1157.)

Appendix to second and final report... containing notes of cases, minutes of evidence taken before the Commissioners, and other papers. London: H.M.S.O., 1875. 125p. (C. 1157-I.)

Running titles: Labour Laws Commission; Royal Commission on Labour Laws.

C. ROYAL COMMISSION ON LABOUR, 1891–94

11,306 **Mann**, Tom. 'The Labour Commission and its duties.' *New Rev.*, iv, 23 (April 1891), 293–303.

11,307 **Rae**, John. 'The Labour Commission.' *Econ. J.*, i, 3 (September 1891), 520–4; i, 4 (December 1891), 810–13; ii, 5 (March 1892), 179–83; ii, 6 (June 1892), 387–92; ii, 7 (September 1892), 552–8; ii, 8 (December 1892), 731–5; iii, 9 (March 1893), 164–9; iii, 10 (June 1893), 339–42.

A series of reports on the decisions of the Commission.

11,308 **Royal Commission on Labour,** 1891–94. [Reports, minutes of evidence, etc.]

Command papers nos. C. 6708, C. 6708-I–VI, C. 6795, C. 6795-I–XII, C. 6894, C. 6894-I–XXV, C. 7063, C. 7063-I–XIV, C. 7421, C. 7421-I.

For further details see P. Ford and G. Ford, *Select list of British parliamentary papers, 1833–1899,* Oxford: Blackwell, 1953, p. 72–3.

11,309 **Drage**, Geoffrey. 'Mrs. Sidney Webb's attack on the Labour Commission.' *Nineteenth Century*, xxxvi, 211 (September 1894), 452–67.

11,310 **Price**, Langford Lovell Frederick Rice. 'The Report of the Labour Commission.' *Econ. J.*, iv, 15 (September 1894), 444–56.

'A paper read before Section F of the British Association at Oxford, August 1894.'

11,311 **Spyers**, T. G. *The labour question: an epitome of the evidence and report of the Royal Commission on Labour.* London: Sonnenschein, 1894. viii, 248p.

11,312 **Webb**, Beatrice. 'The failure of the Labour Commission.' *Nineteenth Century*, xxxvi, 209 (July 1894), 2–22.

D. ROYAL COMMISSION ON TRADE DISPUTES AND TRADE COMBINATIONS, 1903–06

11,313 **Geldart**, William Martin. 'The Report of the Royal Commission on Trade Disputes.' *Econ. J.*, xvi, 62 (June 1906), 189–211.

11,314 **Royal Commission on Trade Disputes and Trade Combinations,** 1903–06. *Report, appendices.* 1906. iv, 132p. (Cd. 2825.)

Minutes of evidence, appendices, index. 1906. (Cd. 2826.)

Chairman: Lord Dunedin.

E. ROYAL COMMISSION ON TRADE UNIONS AND EMPLOYERS' ASSOCIATIONS, 1965–68

11,315 **Barratt Brown**, Michael. 'The trade union question.' *Polit. Q.*, xxxviii, 2 (April–June 1967), 156–64.

On evidence of the T.U.C. to the Royal Commission on Trade Unions and Employers' Associations, 1966.

11,316 **British Journal of Industrial Relations.** 'The Royal Commission on Trade Unions and Employers' Associations, 1965–1968: a summary of the report and recommendations.' *Br. J. Ind. Relat.*, vi, 3 (November 1968), 275–86.

11,317 **Campbell**, John Ross. 'The movement and the Commission: delusions about Donovan.' *Marxism Today*, xii, 9 (September 1968), 264–72.

11,318 **Cherns**, A. B. 'The Donovan report and associated research papers.' *Occup. Psychol.*, xlii, 4 (October 1968), 239–54.

11,319 **Cooley**, M. J. 'Trade unionism: the TUC's view.' *Marxism Today*, xii, 5 (May 1968), 143–7.

On the T.U.C.'s evidence to the Royal Commission on Trade Unions and Employers' Associations.

11,320 **Crossley**, John Rodney. 'The Donovan report: a case study in the poverty of historicism.' *Br. J. Ind. Relat.*, VI, 3 (November 1968), 296–302.

11,321 **Feather**, Victor. 'The Royal Commission's analysis: a trade union appraisal.' *Br. J. Ind. Relat.*, VI, 3 (November 1968), 339–45.

11,322 **Fox**, Alan. 'Waiting for management.' *New Soc.*, XI, 299 (20 June 1968), 901–3.

11,323 **Goodman**, J. F. B. 'The report of the Royal Commission on Trade Unions and Employers' Associations in Britain, and its implications.' *J. Ind. Relat.*, X, 3 (November 1968), 222–32.

11,324 **Grunfeld**, Cyril. 'Donovan: the legal aspects.' *Br. J. Ind. Relat.*, VI, 3 (November 1968), 316–29.

11,325 **Henderson**, Joan. *Indicators for action: a guide to the report of the Royal Commission on Trade Unions and Employers' Associations.* London: Industrial Society, 1968.

11,326 **Industrial Law Society.** 'Report of Industrial Law Society Conference on the Donovan Commission report.' *Ind. Law Soc. Bull.*, 3 (December 1968), 13–55.
13–15 September 1968.

11,327 **Institute of Personnel Management.** *Report of the Royal Commission on Trade Unions and Employers' Associations: comment on some of the report's main conclusions and recommendations.* London: the Institute, 1968. 6p.

11,328 **Keeler**, W. R. C. 'The Royal Commission's analysis: a management appraisal.' *Br. J. Ind. Relat.*, VI, 3 (November 1968), 330–8.

11,329 **Marsh**, Arthur I. *After Donovan? An assessment of the Royal Commission on Trade Unions and Employers' Associations, 1965–1968.* Oxford: Pergamon P., 1968. 20p. (Productivity progress.)

11,330 **Parsons**, Owen Henry. *The Donovan report: trade unions, strikes and negotiations.* London: Labour Research Department, 1968. 24p.

11,331 **Ramelson**, Bert. *Donovan exposed: a critical analysis of the report of the Royal Commission on Trade Unions.* London: Communist Party of Great Britain, 1968. 16p.

11,332 **Reid**, Graham Livingstone. 'An economic comment on the Donovan report.' *Br. J. Ind. Relat.*, VI, 3 (November 1968), 303–15.

11,333 **Roberts**, Benjamin Charles. 'Reforming industrial relations.' *Lloyds Bank Rev.*, n.s., 90 (October 1968), 22–38.

11,334 **Robertson**, Donald James. 'The implications of the proposed new look in industrial relations.' *Br. J. Ind. Relat.*, VI, 3 (November 1968), 287–95.
A discussion of the Report of the Royal Commission on Trade Unions and Employers' Associations, 1968, first given as a talk at a meeting of the British Universities Industrial Relations Association on 30 June 1968.

11,335 **Robertson**, Norman and **Sams**, K. I. 'The Donovan Commission: a critical appraisal.' *Bankers' Mag.*, CCVI, 1496 (November 1968), 265–70.

11,336 **Royal Commission on Trade Unions and Employers' Associations,** 1965–68. *Report.* London: H.M.S.O., 1968. ix, 352p. (Cmnd. 3623.)
Chairman: Lord Donovan.

11,337 **Royal Commission on Trade Unions and Employers' Associations.** *Minutes of evidence*, 1–69. London: H.M.S.O., 1966–68. 66 pts.
Index to published evidence together with a list of research papers. London: H.M.S.O., 1968. 30p.

11,338 **Royal Commission on Trade Unions and Employers' Associations.** *Selected written evidence submitted to the Royal Commission: Confederation of British Industry, the Trades Union Congress and others.* London: H.M.S.O., 1968. v, 670p.

11,339 **Royal Commission on Trade Unions and Employers' Associations.** *Research papers.* London: H.M.S.O., 1966–68. 11 v.
These have been classified in this bibliography according to subject.

11,340 **Trades Union Congress.** *Action on Donovan: interim statement by the T.U.C. General Council in response to the report of the Royal Commission on Trade Unions and Employers' Associations.* London: T.U.C., 1968. 48p.

11,341 **Turner**, Herbert Arthur. 'The Royal Commission's research papers.' *Br. J. Ind. Relat.*, VI, 3 (November 1968), 346–59.

11,342 **Banks**, Robert Frederick. 'The reform of British industrial relations: the Donovan report and the Labour Government's policy proposals.' *Relat. Ind.*, XXIV, 2 (April 1969), 333–82.

11,343 **Bretten**, G. R. 'Reform of the British system of industrial relations.' *Labor Law J.*, XX, 2 (February 1969), 113–19.

11,344 **Clegg**, Hugh Armstrong. 'The Donovan report and trade union history.' *Soc. Study Labour Hist. Bull.*, 18 (Spring 1969), 12–13.
Abstract of a paper read at a conference of the Society for the Study of Labour History, Birkbeck College, London, 23 November 1968.

11,345 **Doughty**, George H. 'The Donovan report: a sugar coated pill with a bitter centre.' *Trade Un. Regist.* (1969), 41–52.

11,346 **Engineering Employers' Federation.** *The Donovan report: an assessment by the Engineering Employers' Federation.* London: the Federation, 1969. 39p.

11,347 **Kilroy-Silk**, Robert. 'The problem of industrial relations.' *Manchr. Sch.*, XXXVII, 3 (September 1969), 249–57.

11,348 **Kilroy-Silk**, Robert. 'The Royal Commission on Trade Unions and Employers' Associations.' *Ind. Labor Relat. Rev.*, XXII, 4 (July 1969), 544–58.

11,349 **McGregor**, Peter. *Trade unions after Donovan.* London: Liberal Publications Department, 1969. 16p. (Liberal focus 2.)

11,350 **Thomson**, Andrew William John. 'The next step in industrial relations.' *Scott. J. Polit. Econ.*, XVI, 2 (June 1969), 212–24.

11,351 **Trades Union Congress.** *Engineering and shipbuilding: report of a conference of affiliated unions to discuss the conditions and recommendations of the Donovan Commission on Trade Unions and Employers' Associations, Congress House, London, March 17th 1969.* London: T.U.C., 1969. 86p. (Post-Donovan conferences.)

11,352 **Turner**, Herbert Arthur. 'The Donovan report.' *Econ. J.*, LXXIX, 313 (March 1969), 1–10.

11,353 **Verma**, Pramod. 'Industrial relations in Britain: a review of the report of the Royal Commission on Trade Unions and Employers' Associations.' *Indian J. Ind. Relat.*, IV, 4 (April 1969), 527–38.

11,354 **Bonenfant**, Jean-Charles. 'Le rapport Woods et le rapport Donovan.' *Relat. Ind.*, XXV, 1 (January 1970), 3–11.

III. THE DEPARTMENT OF EMPLOYMENT AND ITS PREDECESSORS

A. UNITED KINGDOM

11,355 **Bradlaugh**, Charles. 'A starved government department.' *New Rev.*, III, 18 (November 1890), 438–46.

The Labour Statistical Department of the Board of Trade.

11,356 **Schloss**, David Frederick. 'The reorganisation of our Labour Department.' *R. Statist. Soc. J.*, LVI, 1 (March 1893), 44–65. Discussion, p. 65–70.

'Read before the Royal Statistical Society, 17th January, 1893.'

11,357 **Board of Trade.** *Report on the work of the Labour Department since its formation, with supplement of labour statistics.* London: H.M.S.O., 1894. (C. 7565.)

11,358 **Committee Appointed to Consider the Position and Duties of the Board of Trade and of the Local Government Board.** *Report.* London: H.M.S.O., 1904. vip. (Cd. 2121.)

Chairman: Lord Jersey.

11,359 *Memorandum with respect to the re-organisation of the Board of Trade.* London: H.M.S.O., 1918. 7p. (Cd. 8912.)

11,360 **Phillips**, T. 'Work of the Employment and Insurance Department of the British Ministry of Labor.' United States Department of Labor. Bureau of Labor Statistics. *Proceedings of the Ninth Annual Meeting of the International Association of Public Employment Services held at Buffalo, New York, September 7–9, 1921.* Washington: Government Printing Office, 1922. p. 38–59. (Bulletin of the United States Bureau of Labor Statistics 311.)

11,361 **Smith**, *Sir* Hubert Llewellyn. *The Board of Trade.* London, New York: Putnam, 1928. 288p. (Whitehall series.)

11,362 **Hyde**, Francis Edwin. *No Gladstone at the Board of Trade.* London: Cobden-Sanderson, 1934. xxviii, 256p.

11,363 **Bondfield**, Margaret and **Elliott**, Dorothy. 'The Ministry of Labour and industrial relations in Great Britain.' Gannett, F. E. and Catherwood, B. F. (eds.). *Industrial and labour relations in Great Britain: a symposium.* New York: the editors, 1939. p. 31–42.

Margaret Bondfield was Minister of Labour under the MacDonald Government, and Dorothy Elliott was National Woman Officer, National Union of General and Municipal Workers of Great Britain.

11,364 **Bevin**, Ernest. *Outline of the functions and work of the Ministry of Labour and National Service: report of speech delivered... at the London County Council on Thursday, July 30th, 1942.* London, 1942. 12p.

11,365 **Stokes**, D. Scott. 'The administration in 1945 of some tribunals appointed by the Minister of Labour and National Service.' *Publ. Adm.*, XXIV, 3 (Autumn 1946), 156–65.

11,366 **Stokes**, D. Scott. 'The administration in 1945 of some tribunals appointed by the Minister of Labour.' Pollard, R. S. W. (ed.). *Administrative tribunals at work.* London: Stevens, 1950. p. 19–35.

11,367 **Harrison**, Enid Mary. *The development of the regional organization of the Ministry of Labour and National Service.* 1952. (B.Litt. thesis, University of Oxford.)

11,368 **Prouty**, Roger Warren. *The transformation of the Board of Trade, 1830–1855.* 1954. 373p. (Ph.D. thesis, Columbia University.)

11,369 **Committee on Administrative Tribunals and Enquiries.** *Memoranda submitted by government departments in reply to a questionnaire of November 1955. Vol. I. Ministry of Education, Ministry of Labour and National Service, National Assistance Board, Ministry of Pensions and National Insurance.* London: H.M.S.O., 1956.

11,370 **Ministry of Labour and National Service.** *Staffing and organization of the Factory Inspectorate.* London: H.M.S.O., 1956. 48p. (Cmd. 9879.)

11,371 **Caldwell**, J. A. M. 'The genesis of the Ministry of Labour.' *Publ. Adm.*, XXXVII, 4 (Winter 1959), 367–91.

A shortened version of the Haldane Silver Medal Essay, 1958.

Based partly on research undertaken for a doctoral dissertation, University of Nottingham.

11,372 **Ministry of Labour and National Service.** *Duties, organization and staffing of the medical branch of the Factory Inspectorate.* London: H.M.S.O., 1959. (Cmnd. 736.)

11,373 **Ince**, *Sir* Godfrey Herbert. *The Ministry of Labour and National Service.* London: Allen and Unwin; New York: Oxford U.P., 1960. 216p. (New Whitehall series.)

11,374 **Towy-Evans**, M. 'The Personnel Management Advisory Service in Great Britain.' *Int. Labour Rev.*, LXXXI, 2 (February 1960), 125–39.

11,375 **Shanks**, Michael. 'Public policy and the Ministry of Labour.' Roberts, B. C. (ed.). *Industrial relations: contemporary problems and perspectives.* London: Methuen 1962., p. 258–85.

11,376 **Jenkins**, Peter. 'The Ministry of Labour.' *New Soc.*, II, 52 (26 September 1963), 13–14.

B. EIRE

11,377 **Administration.** 'The Department of Industry and Commerce.' *Administration*, IX, 2 (Summer 1961), 120–46.

'Labour Division,' p. 130–4.

11,378 **Ó Cearbhaill**, Tadhg. 'The Department of Labour and the future.' *Administration*, XV, 2 (Summer 1967), 138–43.

'Address to the Connolly Study Group of IT and GWU [Irish Transport and General Workers' Union] at Cork, 15 April, 1967.'

11,379 **Ó Cearbhaill**, Tadhg. 'The role of the Department of Labour.' *Administration*, XV, 1 (Spring 1967), 1–5.

'Address made to the Liberty Study Group of the ITGWU [Irish Transport and General Workers' Union] at La Touche Hotel, Greystones, 4 February, 1967.'

IV. REGULATION OF MANPOWER

A. GENERAL

See also Part Six, II, C–D.

11,380 **International Labour Office.** *The compulsory employment of disabled men.* Geneva: I.L.O., 1921. 34p. (Studies and reports, series E, 2.)

11,381 **George**, Mary Dorothy. 'The London coal-heavers: attempts to regulate waterside labour in the eighteenth and nineteenth centuries.' *Econ. Hist.*, I, 2 (May 1927), 229–48.

11,382 **Political and Economic Planning.** 'An employment policy.' *Planning*, I, 4 (6 June 1933), 3–11.

Comment by J. J. Mallon, p. 12–13.

11,383 **Political and Economic Planning.** 'A new employment policy.' *Planning*, II, 30 (3 July 1934), 1–12.

11,384 **Political and Economic Planning.** 'Man-power policy.' *Planning*, VI, 133 (1 November 1938), 1–13.

11,385 **Ady**, P. 'Colonial industrialisation and British employment.' *Rev. Econ. Studies*, XI, 1 (Winter 1943), 42–51.

'This paper attempts to outline those aspects of British post-war employment policy which are related to Britain's role as a colonial power . . .'

11,386 **Sargant Florence**, P. 'Incentives and government policy.' *Polit. Q.*, XVIII, 4 (October–December 1947), 283–95.

11,387 **Farrar**, C. *The manpower policy of the British government, 1945–1950.* 1952. (Ph.D. thesis, University of London.)

11,388 **Rolfe**, Sidney E. *The allocation of manpower under United Kingdom planning, 1945–49, with special references to the cotton textile industry.* 1952. (Thesis, University of Chicago.)

11,389 **Phillips**, N. *The Disabled Persons (Employment) Act, 1944: a study of its administration with special reference to the north-west region of the Ministry of Labour and National Service.* 1954–55. (M.A. (Econ.) thesis, University of Manchester.)

11,390 **Montgomery**, Robert John. *Some problems of educational administrations since 1944: the manpower committee and after.* 1959–60. (M.A. thesis, University of London.)

11,391 **Boyfield**, Ray. 'Great Britain.' Organisation for Economic Co-operation and Development. Manpower and Social Affairs Directorate. Social Affairs Division. *International Trade Union Seminar on Active Manpower Policy, Vienna, 17th–20th September 1963. Supplement to the final report.* Paris, O.E.C.D., [1963?]. p. 29–69.

11,392 **Macgougan**, J. 'Ireland.' Organisation for Economic Co-operation and Development. Manpower and Social Affairs Directorate. Social Affairs Division. *International Trade Union Seminar on Active Manpower Policy, Vienna, 17th–20th September 1963. Supplement to the final report.* Paris: O.E.C.D., [1963?]. p. 149–51.

11,393 **Moser**, C. A. and **Layard**, P. R. G. 'Planning the scale of higher education in

Britain: some statistical problems.' *R. Statist. Soc. J.*, Ser. A, CXXVII, 4 (1964), 473–513.

Reprinted in Reprint Series, Unit for Economic and Statistical Studies on Higher Education, no. 1, 1965.

11,394 *Selected readings in employment and manpower, compiled for Subcommittee on Employment and Manpower, Senate Committee on Labor and Public Welfare, US. 88th Congress, 2nd Session.* Washington: U.S.G.P.O., 1964.

Vol. 1. *Exploring the dimensions of the manpower revolution.*

Vol. 2. *Convertibility of space and defense resources to civilian needs: a search for new employment potentials.*

Vol. 3. *The role of apprenticeship in manpower development: United States and Western Europe.*

Vol. 4. *Lessons from foreign labor market policies.*

11,395 **Dunnett**, *Sir* James. 'Manpower research at the Ministry of Labour.' Berners-Lee, C. M. (ed.). *Models for decision.* London: English Universities P., 1965. p. 64–70.

11,396 **Eire.** *White paper on manpower policy.* Dublin, 1965. (I. 118.)

11,397 **Eire.** Department of Finance. Inter-Departmental Committee on Administrative Arrangements for Implementing Manpower Policy. *Report.* Dublin, 1965. 51p. (F. 70.)

11,398 **Eire.** National Industrial Economic Council. *Comments on Report of Inter-Departmental Committee on Administrative Arrangements for Implementing Manpower Policy.* Dublin, 1965. 8p. (F. 66/9.)

11,399 **Ministry of Labour.** 'Labour mobility: the role of the Ministry of Labour.' *Br. J. Ind. Relat.*, III, 2 (July 1965), 143–52.

11,400 **Crossley**, John Rodney. *Manpower policy and employment trends.* London: G. Bell, 1966.

11,401 **Earl**, Lewis Harold, **Linton**, J. H. and **Mullady**, P. M. *Manpower policy and programs in five western European countries: France, Great Britain, the Netherlands, Sweden and West Germany.* Washington: United States Department of Labor, Manpower Administration, 1966.

11,402 **Farrimond**, H. L. *Determining present and future requirements.* London: Ministry of Labour, 1966.

11,403 **Stieber**, Jack. *Manpower adjustments to automation and technological change in Western Europe.* 1966.

United States National Commission on Technology, Automation and Economic Progress. Appendix Volume III to the Report of the Commission.

11,404 **Stephens**, Leslie. 'Personnel advice from government.' *New Soc.*, VII, 195 (23 June 1966), 14–15. (Trends in personnel management 3.)

11,405 **Agnew**, J. A. 'Developments in manpower policy.' *Administration*, XV, 4 (Winter 1967), 333–9.

'Lecture given at the Institute of Public Administration, 8 June 1967.'

11,406 **Eire.** *White paper on manpower policy laid by the Minister for Industry and Commerce before each House of the Oireachtas, October 1965.* Dublin, 1967. 6p. (Pr. 8543.)

11,407 **International Labour Office.** *Manpower adjustment programmes.* Geneva: I.L.O., 1967.

Vol. 1. *France, Federal Republic of Germany, United Kingdom.* 207p. (Labour and automation bulletin 4.)

11,408 **O'Donoghue**, M. 'Manpower educational activities of the Irish E.I.P. team.' Organisation for Economic Co-operation and Development. Directorate for Scientific Affairs. *Manpower forecasting in educational planning: report of the Joint EIP/MRP meeting, Paris, December 1965.* Paris: O.E.C.D., 1967. p. 57–69.

11,409 **Stieber**, Jack. 'Implications of West European manpower programs for the United States.' Industrial Relations Research Association. *Proceedings of the twentieth annual winter meeting: the development and use of manpower, Washington, D.C., December 28–29, 1967.* p. 297–306.

Discussion, p. 324–38.

Concluding remarks, p. 339–41.

11,410 **Howenstine**, Emanuel Jay. *Compensatory employment programmes: an international comparison of their role in economic stabilisation and growth.* Paris: Organisation for Economic Co-operation and Development, 1968. 481p. (Developing job opportunities 3.)

11,411 **Crossley**, John Rodney. 'Theory and methods of national manpower policy.' Robertson, D. J. and Hunter, L. C. (eds.). *Labour market issues of the 1970s.* Edinburgh: Oliver and Boyd for the Scottish Economic Society, 1970. p. 11–30.

First appeared in the June 1970 issue of the *Scottish Journal of Political Economy.*

11,412 **Hansen**, Gary B. 'Manpower policies: lessons for the U.S. from foreign experience. The British experience.' Industrial Relations Research Association. *Spring meeting 1970.* p. 523–33.

Reprinted from the August 1970 issue of *Labor Law Journal.* Discussion of this and other papers by Leonard J. Hausman, p. 552–4.

Discussion of this and other papers by Michael E. Borns, p. 554–7.

11,413 **Organisation of Economic Co-operation and Development.** *Manpower policy in the United Kingdom.* Paris: O.E.C.D., 1970. 230p. (O.E.C.D. reviews of manpower and social policies 7.)

B. GENERAL LEVEL OF EMPLOYMENT

This section includes works dealing with employment and unemployment as a problem of public policy. See also Part Six, II, C–D; Part Six, IV, A, 4, d; Part Seven, IV, E, 1–2; and Part Seven, IX, B, 1.

11,414 **Fabian Society.** *The government organisation of unemployed labour: report made by a committee to the Fabian Society, and ordered to be printed for the information of members.* London: Standring, 1886. 23p.

By S. Webb and F. Podmore.

Issued without the authors' names.

11,415 **Charity Organisation Society.** *Municipal workshops.* London: the Society, 1892. (Occasional paper 29.)

11,416 **Board of Trade.** *Report on agencies and methods for dealing with the unemployed; with map.* London: H.M.S.O., 1893. (C. 7182.)

11,417 **Charity Organisation Review.** 'The State and the unemployed.' *Char. Orgn. Rev.*, IX, 107 (December 1893), 439–63.

11,418 **Home Office.** *Report of the work of the unemployed in the demolition of Millbank Prison.* London: H.M.S.O., 1893. (H.C. 419.)

11,419 **Mallock**, William Hurrell. 'Social remedies of the Labour Party.' *Fortn. Rev.*, n.s., LIII, 316 (April 1893), 504–24.

Municipal employment for the unemployed; eight-hours movement.

11,420 **Select Committee** appointed to inquire into what results have followed upon the recommendations by the Select Committee of 1876–77 for the Employment of meritorious Soldiers, Sailors, and Marines in Civil Departments, and to inquire what further measures are desirable in order to provide Employment for them. *Report, with evidence, appendix, and index.* London: H.M.S.O., 1894. (H.C. 258.)

Report in the following Session, with proceedings, evidence, and appendix. 1895. (H.C. 338.)

11,421 **Dallas**, Duncan Campbell. *How to solve the unemployed problem by co-operative organisation of the unemployed with state control.* London: Twentieth Century P., 1895. 16p.

11,422 **Mackay**, Thomas. 'Relief by means of employment.' *Econ. Rev.*, VI, 2 (April 1896), 183–92.

11,423 *Report on the practice of public authorities in the United Kingdom in giving out contracts to associations of workmen; with appendices relating to foreign countries.* London: H.M.S.O., 1896. (C. 8233.)

11,424 **Rawlinson**, *Sir* Robert. *Public works in Lancashire for the relief of distress among the unemployed during the cotton famine, 1863–66, carried out under the supervision of Mr. Robert Rawlinson . . . with an appendix on the sewering of towns and draining of houses.* London: King, 1898. 136p.

11,425 **Cowie**, Archibald Greig. *The sea services of the empire as fields for employment.* London: Treherne, 1903. x, 456p.

11,426 **London Municipal Society.** *Notes on labour and its relationship to municipalities.* London, 1904. 8p. (Municipal reform pamphlets 2.)

11,427 **Keir Hardie**, James. *John Bull and his unemployed: a plain statement on the law of England as it affects the unemployed.* London: Independent Labour Party, 1905. 16p.

11,428 **Maintenance and Employment Society.** *The draft of a Bill to provide work and maintenance for the people of the U.K. of Great Britain and Ireland, without any increase of taxation or rates.* London, 1905. 45p.

11,429 **Moore**, Harold Edward. *Our heritage in the land, with introduction and scheme for state aid, by Sir William Mather.* London: King, 1906. viii, 136p.

11,430 **Abbott**, Edith. 'Municipal employment of unemployed women in London.' *J. Polit. Econ.*, XV, 9 (November 1907), 513–30.

11,431 **Hazell**, A. P. and **Cook,** W. *Work for the unemployed: a national highway for military and motor traffic. A practical proposal.* London: Twentieth Century P., 1908.

11,432 **Ritzema**, T. P. *Land nationalisation: the remedy for poverty and unemployment: report of an address.* Blackburn, 1908. 8p.

11,433 **Strachey**, John St. Loe. *The government and the unemployed.* London, 1908. 7p. (British Constitution Association. Leaflets 21.)

11,434 **Lansbury**, George. 'Unemployment: the next step.' Crooks, W., and others. *Social ideals: papers on social subjects.* London: R. Culley, 1909.

11,435 **Webb**, Sidney. 'The problem of unemployment in the United Kingdom, with a remedy by organization and training.' *Ann. Am. Acad. Polit. Soc. Sci.*, XXXIII, 2 (March 1909), 196–215.

General title of this issue is *Labor and wages.*

11,436 **Jackson**, Cyril. *Unemployment and trade unions.* London: Longmans, Green, 1910. xii, 92p.

11,437 **Lloyd George**, David. *The problem of unemployment: a speech delivered . . . in the Queen's Hall on December 31st, 1909.* London: Liberal Publication Department, 1910. 16p.

11,438 **Dearle**, Norman Burrell. 'The building trades and the reorganisation of public work.' National Conference on the Prevention of Destitution. *Report of the proceedings . . . 1911.* London: King, 1911. p. 534–41.

Discussion, p. 542–50.

11,439 **Edinburgh Review.** 'The right to work.' *Edinb. Rev.*, CCXIII, 435 (January 1911), 180–99.

'The object of this article is to state and to examine the claim, recently made in certain quarters, and definitely formulated in the Unemployed Workmen Bill of 1908, that every workman not in employment has a right to work.'

11,440 **Fay**, Charles Ryle. 'The right to work.' *Econ. Rev.*, XXI, 1 (January 1911), 7–18.

11,441 **Wood**, George Henry. 'The regularisation of the public demands.' National Conference on the Prevention of Destitution. *Report of the proceedings . . . 1911*. London: King, 1911. p. 528–34.
Discussion, p. 542–50.

11,442 **Webb**, Sidney. *How the government can prevent unemployment*. London: National Committee for the Prevention of Destitution, 1912. 12p.

11,443 **Webb**, Sidney. *The war and the workers: handbook of some immediate measures to prevent unemployment and relieve distress*. London: Fabian Society, 1914. 22p. (Fabian tract 176.)

11,444 **Rowntree**, Benjamin Seebohm. 'Prevention and compensation of unemployment.' *Int. Labour Rev.*, IV, 3 (December 1921), 3–15 (455–67).

11,445 **Trades Union Congress** and **Labour Party.** Joint Committee on Unemployment. *Unemployment: a Labour policy*. London: T.U.C. and Labour Party, 1921. 48p.

11,446 **General Federation of Trade Unions.** *Methods of relieving unemployment*. London, 1922. 12p.

11,447 **Macgregor**, D. H. 'Public authorities and unemployment.' *Economica*, III, 7 (January 1923), 10–18.

11,448 **Rowntree**, Benjamin Seebohm. 'Some necessary steps toward a solution of the unemployment problem.' *Polit. Sci. Q.*, XXXVIII, 2 (June 1923), 189–218.

11,449 **International Labour Office.** 'Prevention of unemployment, with special reference to Great Britain.' *Int. Labour Rev.*, x, 4 (October 1924), 653–64.

11,450 **Irish Labour Party and Trade Union Congress.** *Unemployment, 1922–1924: the record of the government's failure*. Dublin, 1924. 16p.

11,451 *Memorandum on the provision of work for unemployment*. London: H.M.S.O., 1924. (Cmd. 2196.)

11,452 **Young**, E. Hilton. Unemployment. I. 'The "Trade Facilities" Act.' *Nineteenth Century*, XCV, 566 (April 1924), 512–22.

11,453 **Citrine**, Walter McLennan. 'The problem of unemployment.' Tracey, H. (ed.). *The book of the Labour Party: its history, growth, policy, and leaders*. London: Caxton Publishing Co., 1925. Vol. 2. p. 90–106.

11,454 **Hawtrey**, Ralph George. 'Public expenditure and the demand for labour.' *Economica*, V, 13 (March 1925), 38–48.
'Read at the Economic Club on February 10th, 1925.'

11,455 **Milne-Watson**, *Sir* David. *Gas and electricity in relation to unemployment and industrial depression: . . . a protest against state subsidies*. London, 1925. 15p.

11,456 **Davison**, *Sir* Ronald Conway. *The unemployed: old policies and new*. London: Longmans, Green, 1929. xiii, 292p.

11,457 **Fabian Society.** Labour Research Department. *Direct building: a study of building by direct labour under local authorities*. London, 1929. 74p.

11,458 **Hunter**, *Sir* George Burton. *The responsibility of the Labour Party for unemployment*. Newcastle-upon-Tyne, 1929. 8p.

11,459 **Keynes**, John Maynard and **Henderson**, Hubert Douglas. *Can Lloyd George do it? An examination of the Liberal pledge*. London: *The Nation and Athenæum*, 1929. 44p.

11,460 **Labour Party.** *Labour's reply to Lloyd George: how to conquer unemployment*. London: Labour Party, 1929. 30p.

11,461 **Liberal Party.** Liberal Industrial Inquiry. *We can conquer unemployment: Mr. Lloyd George's pledge*. London: Cassell, 1929. 64p.

11,462 '*We can conquer unemployment.*' *Memorandum by Ministers on certain proposals relating to unemployment*. London: H.M.S.O., 1929. 54p. (Cmd. 3331.)

11,463 **Cole**, George Douglas Howard. 'Cheaper money, rationalisation and employment.' *Gold, credit & employment: four essays for laymen*. London: Allen and Unwin, 1930. p. 139–65.
Reprinted from the *New Statesman*, December 1929–February 1930.

11,464 **Cole**, George Douglas Howard. 'The government and the unemployed.' *Gold, credit & unemployment: four essays for laymen*. London: Allen and Unwin, 1930. p. 99–135.
Reprinted from *The New Leader*, December 1929–January 1930.

11,465 **Dennithorne**, John. *The unemployed in relation to industry, the state and the community: a plea for absorption, and for an amendment in regard to unemployment insurance together with a note on the need for friendly clubs among the unemployed*. Dowlais: [the author?, *c*. 1930]. 12p.

11,466 **Lloyd George**, David, **Lothian**, Marquess of, and **Rowntree**, Benjamin Seebohm. *How to tackle unemployment: the Liberal plans as laid before the government and the nation*. London: Press Printers, 1930. 104p.

11,467 **Muir**, John Ramsay Bryce. *Unemployment: how to deal with it. A practical survey*. London: Liberal Publication Department, 1930. 32p.

11,468 *Statement of the principal measures taken by His Majesty's Government in connection with unemployment*. London: H.M.S.O., 1930. 22p. (Cmd. 3746.)

11,469 **Angell**, *Sir* Norman and **Wright**, Harold. *Can governments cure unemployment?* London: Dent, 1931. xii, 147p.

11,470 **Dawes**, George Walter. *A national and empire policy to relieve unemployment.* Birmingham: Moody, 1931. 7p.

11,471 **Walker**, Louis Carlisle. *Distributed leisure: an approach to the problem of over-production and underemployment.* New York, London: Century, 1931. ix, 246p.

11,472 **Federated Employers' Press.** *Municipal Building Departments: an analysis of 'direct labour'. Arguments, methods, facts and figures.* London: Federated Employers' P., 1932. 75p.

11,473 **Bevin**, Ernest. *My plan for 2,000,000 workless.* London: Clarion P., [*c.* 1933]. 28p.

Appendix 1: 'The ways and means of E. B.'s proposals', by Colin Clark.

11,474 **Creedy**, Frederick. *The secret of steady employment.* New York, London: Putnam, 1933. 125p.

11,475 **Garrard**, Charles Cornfield. *A short way with unemployment.* Birmingham: Cornish, 1933. 48p.

11,476 **Vallance**, Aylmer. 'The problem of employment.' *Lloyds Bank Rev.*, n.s., IV, 37 (March 1933), 86–98.

11,477 **Hill**, Arthur Cheney Clifton and **Lubin**, Isador. *The British attack on unemployment.* Washington, D.C.: The Brookings Institution, 1934. xiv, 325p. (The Institute of Economics of the Brookings Institution. Publication 51.)

With specimen forms and card.

11,478 **Crossley**, Anthony Crommelin, and others. *Planning for employment: a preliminary study by some Members of Parliament.* London: Macmillan, 1935. xii, 97p.

11,479 **Lloyd George**, David. *Organising prosperity: a scheme of national reconstruction, being the memorandum on unemployment and reconstruction submitted to the government.* London: Nicholson and Watson, 1935. vii, 107p.

11,480 **Milhaud**, Edgard (ed.). *Ending the unemployment and trade crisis, by the introduction of purchasing certificates and the establishment of an international clearing system.* London: Williams and Norgate, 1935. 354p.

By E. Milhaud, Ulrich von Beckerath, Heinrich Rittershausen and others.

Translated by G. Spiller.

11,481 **Snowden**, Philip. *Mr. Lloyd George's 'New deal'.* London: Nicholson and Watson, 1935. 47p.

11,482 *Absorption of the unemployed into industry: discussions between the Minister of Labour and representatives of certain industries.* London: H.M.S.O., 1936. 10p. (Cmd. 5317.)

11,483 **King**, J. W. *To hell with the dole: how to abolish unemployment.* Scarborough, 1936. 19p.

11,484 **Davison**, *Sir* Ronald Conway. *British unemployment policy: the modern phase since 1930.* London: Longmans, Green, 1938. x, 136p.

11,485 **Hannington**, Walter. *Ten lean years: an examination of the record of the National Government in the field of unemployment.* London: Gollancz, 1940. 287p.

Also Left Book Club edition.

11,486 **Hill**, Polly. *The unemployment services: a report prepared for the Fabian Society.* London: Routledge, 1940. xiv, 226p.

11,487 **Wolman**, Leo. 'The meaning of employment and unemployment.' Warren, R. B., Wolman, L. and Clay, H. *The state in society: a series of public lectures delivered under the auspices of McGill University, Montreal, January 23, 1939–February 10, 1939.* London, New York: Oxford U.P., 1940. p. 65–77.

11,488 **Workers' Educational Association.** *Can we conquer unemployment?* London: W.E.A., 1940. 20p. (Topics for discussion 5.)

11,489 **Wyatt**, Thomas William and **Jones**, David Caradog. *Post-war poverty and unemployment can be prevented.* Birkenhead: J. Woolman, 1940. 24p.

11,490 **Burns**, Eveline Mabel. *British unemployment programs, 1920–1938: a report prepared for the Committee on Social Security.* Washington: Committee on Social Security, Social Science Research Council, 1941. xx, 385p.

11,491 **Wyatt**, Thomas William and **Jones**, David Caradog. *Britain's 'new order': a plea for a sane post-war employment policy.* Birkenhead: J. Woolman, 1941. 32p.

11,492 **Brayshaw**, Shipley Neave. *Post-war employment for all: a paper given to a conference of Quaker employers, with additional notes and explanations.* London: Allen and Unwin, 1942. 44p.

11,493 **Burchardt**, F. A. 'Output and employment policy.' *Oxf. Univ. Inst. Statist. Bull.*, IV, 2 (31 January 1942), 29–40.

11,494 **Kotzin**, Charles. *Memorandum on the international unemployment problem and its effect on post war planning.* St Albans: Fisher, Knight, 1942.

11,495 **Bevan**, Aneurin. 'Plan for work.' Fabian Society. *Plan for Britain: a collection of essays.* London: Routledge, 1943. p. 34–52.

11,496 **Beveridge**, *Sir* William Henry. 'Freedom from idleness.' Fabian Society. *Plan for Britain: a collection of essays.* London: Routledge, 1943. p. 83–100.

11,497 **Beveridge**, *Sir* William Henry. 'Maintenance of employment.' *The pillars of security, and other war-time essays and addresses.* London: Allen and Unwin, 1943. p. 41–52.

'Address to Engineering Industries Association, 30th July, 1942.'

11,498 **Beveridge**, *Sir* William Henry. 'The pillars of security. I. The assumption of employment.' *The pillars of security, and other war-time essays and addresses.* London: Allen and Unwin, 1943. p. 98–104.

First published *Observer*, 3 January 1943; *Daily Herald*, 23 January 1943.

11,499 **Cole**, George Douglas Howard. *The means to full employment.* London: Gollancz, 1943. 175p.

11,500 **Conway**, Edward Sidney. *Post-war employment.* London: Cape, 1943. 143p.

11,501 **Harrod**, R. F. 'Full employment and security of livelihood.' *Econ. J.*, LIII, 212 (December 1943), 321–42.

11,502 **Political and Economic Planning.** 'Employment for all.' *Planning*, 206 (11 May 1943), 1–31.
A modified version also published as a pamphlet under the same title.

11,503 **Robinson,** Joan Violet. *The problem of full employment: an outline for study circles.* London: Workers' Educational Association, 1943. 31p. (W.E.A. study outline 10.)
Revised edition. W.E.A. and Workers' Educational Trade Union Committee, 1949. 36p. (W.E.A. study outline 18.)

11,504 **Schumacher**, E. F. *Export policy and full employment.* London: Fabian Publications and Gollancz, 1943. 33p. (Research series 77.)
Revised edition. 1944. 33p.

11,505 **Wootton**, Barbara. *Full employment.* London: Fabian Publications and Gollancz, 1943. 27p. (Research series 74.)

11,506 **Association of British Chambers of Commerce.** *Employment policy: observations of the Association of British Chambers of Commerce on the government proposals.* London: the Association, 1944. 15p.

11,507 **Beveridge**, *Sir* William Henry. *Full employment in a free society: a report.* London: Allen and Unwin, 1944. 429p.
Reissue. New York: W. W. Norton, 1945.
Fourth impression with a new preface. London: Allen and Unwin, 1953. viii, 429p.

11,508 **Beveridge**, *Sir* William Henry. *Full employment in a free society.* London: Liberal Publication Department, 1944. 7p.
An outline, by the author, of his report.

11,509 **Beveridge**, *Sir* William Henry. *Full employment in a free society: a summary.* London: *New Statesman and Nation*, 1944. 48p.

11,510 **Beveridge**, *Sir* William Henry. 'The government's employment policy.' *Econ. J.*, LIV, 214 (June–September 1944), 161–76.
'This article, with some additions and changes, represents an address to the Royal Economic Society at the Annual Meeting of the Society on June 22, 1944. It is printed, with verbal changes as a Postscript to the *Report on Full Employment in a Free Society* . . . Allen and Unwin.'

11,511 **Cashmore**, F. R. *Social settlement and full employment.* Warrington, 1944. 45p.

11,512 **Cohen**, N. F. *Jobs for all after the war? Full Employment Council set up in the Medway district.* Chatham, 1944. 16p.

11,513 **Cole**, George Douglas Howard. *How to obtain full employment.* London: Odhams P., 1944. 24p. (Post war discussion pamphlets 4.)

11,514 **Conservative and Unionist Party Organisation.** *Employment policy: debate on the government's White Paper in the House of Commons 21st, 22nd and 23rd June, 1944.* London, 1944. 36p.
Account of the debate with extracts.

11,515 **Fabian Society.** *The prevention of general unemployment: evidence submitted to Sir William Beveridge in connection with his investigation into unemployment, by a group of Fabians.* London: Fabian Publications and Gollancz, 1944. 20p. (Research series 79.)

11,516 **Hawtrey**, Ralph George. 'Livelihood and full employment.' *Econ. J.*, LIV, 215–16 (December 1944), 417–22.
Reply to article by R. F. Harrod, December 1943.

11,517 **Kaldor**, Nicholas. 'The quantitative aspects of the full employment problem in Britain.' Beveridge, Sir W. *Full employment in a free society.* London: Allen and Unwin, 1944.
Appendix C. p. 344–401.

11,518 **Kalecki**, Michael. 'Three ways to full employment.' Oxford University. Institute of Statistics. *The economics of full employment.* Oxford: Blackwell, 1944. p. 39–58.

11,519 **Kalecki**, Michael. 'The White Paper on employment policy.' *Oxf. Univ. Inst. Statist. Bull.*, VI, 8 (10 June 1944), 131–5.
On Cmd. 6527.

11,520 **Liberal Party.** Permanent Policy Committee. *The government's employment policy examined.* London, 1944. 7p.

11,521 **London Chamber of Commerce.** *Report . . . on the government white paper on employment policy.* London, 1944. 8p.

11,522 **Ministry of Labour and National Service.** *Government memorandum on a policy for maintaining a high level of employment.* London: H.M.S.O., 1944. 31p. (Cmd. 6527.)

11,523 **Molson**, Arthur Hugh Elsdale. *Full employment and the budget.* London: Signpost P., 1944. 20p. (Signpost booklets.)

11,524 **Political and Economic Planning.** *Employment for all.* London: P.E.P., 1944. 33p. (Pamphlets 3.)

11,525 **Rowntree**, Benjamin Seebohm. *The price of full employment.* London: Liberal Publication Department, 1944. 11p.

11,526 **Schumacher**, E. F. 'Public finance: its relation to full employment.' Oxford University. Institute of Statistics. *The economics of full employment.* Oxford: Blackwell, 1944. p. 85–125.

11,527 **Thorneycroft**, George Edward Peter, Baron Thorneycroft and **Molson**, Arthur Hugh Elsdale. *Employment policy.* London: Tory Reform Committee, 1944. 7p. (Bulletins 2.)

11,528 **Worswick**, George David Norman. 'The stability and flexibility of full employment.' Oxford University. Institute of Statistics. *The economics of full employment*. Oxford: Blackwell, 1944. p. 59–84.

11,529 **Berridge**, William A. 'Observations on Beveridge's *Full employment in a free society and some related matters*.' *Polit. Sci. Q.*, LX, 2 (June 1945), 176–87.

11,530 **Jones**, David Caradog (ed.). *Full employment and state control: a symposium on the degree of control essential*. London: Cape, 1945. 146p.

Contents: 'Some lessons of the war', by Allan G. B. Fisher; 'Stability in a mixed economy', by D. J. Morgan; 'Basis for a higher standard of living', by R. A. S. Paget; 'The cure of unemployment', by T. W. Wyatt; 'A study of full employment', by J. R. Bellerby; 'The economics of full employment', by H. Stanley Jevons; 'A broad comparison of essentials', by D. Caradog Jones; 'The government employment policy', by D. Caradog Jones; 'Postscript on Beveridge'.

11,531 **Kalecki**, Michael. 'The maintenance of full employment after the transition period: a comparison of the problem in the United States and the United Kingdom.' *Int. Labour Rev.*, LII, 5 (November 1945), 449–64.

11,532 **Marsh**, Arnold. *Full employment in Ireland*. Dublin: Browne and Nolan, 1945. x, 278p.

In collaboration with a committee.

11,533 **Newman**, Tom Seth. *Guide to the government's employment policy*. London: Hearts of Oak Benefit Society, 1945. 28p.

11,534 **Pigou**, Arthur Cecil. *Lapses from full employment*. London: Macmillan, 1945. viii, 72p.

11,535 *The problem of unemployment: Beveridge fails to solve it, what will?* London, 1945. 14p.

11,536 **Robinson**, Edward Austin Gossage. 'Sir William Beveridge on full employment.' *Econ. J.*, LV, 217 (April 1945), 70–6.

On *Full employment in a free society*.

11,537 **Ross**, Charles Herbert. *The new plan for remedying unemployment*. Ellenhall: the author, 1945. 98p.

11,538 **Smithies**, Arthur. 'Full employment in a free society.' *Am. Econ. Rev.*, XXXV, 3 (June 1945), 354–67.

On W. H. Beveridge, *Report on full employment in a free society*. London: Allen and Unwin, 1944; published in America as *Full employment in a free society*. New York: Norton, 1945.

11,539 **Young**, Michael Dunlop and **Prager**, Theodor. *There's work for all*. London: Nicholson and Watson, 1945. 128p. (The new democracy.)

11,540 **Abbati**, Alfred Henry. *Towards full employment*. London: Baskerville P., 1946. 71p.

11,541 **Benham**, Frederic. 'Full employment and international trade.' *Economica*, n.s., XIII, 51 (August 1946), 159–68.

'The substance of an Inaugural lecture delivered at the London School of Economics on 22nd January, 1946 . . .'

11,542 **Board of Trade.** *Provision of employment in South Wales for persons suspended from the mining industry on account of silicosis and pneumoconiosis*. London: H.M.S.O., 1946. 6p. (Cmd. 6719.)

11,543 **Conservative Party.** Committee on Policy and Political Education. Sub-Committee on Industry. *Work: a report on the future of British industry*. London: Conservative Political Centre, 1946. 46p.

First published 1944.

11,544 **Fisher**, Allan George Barnard. *International implications of full employment in Great Britain*. London, New York: Royal Institute of International Affairs, 1946. vii, 201p.

11,545 **Jewkes**, John. 'Second thoughts on the British White Paper on employment policy.' National Bureau of Economic Research. *Economic research and the development of economic science and public policy: twelve papers . . .* New York: N.B.E.R., 1946. (Twenty-fifth anniversary series 3.) p. 111–32.

Also published in *Manchester School*, XIV, 2 (May 1946), 65–84.

White Paper published May 1944.

11,546 **Richardson**, John Henry. 'Livelihood and full employment.' *Econ. J.*, LVI, 221 (March 1946), 139–43.

11,547 **Worswick**, George David Norman (ed.). *Jobs for all: talks and discussions on full employment, and its effect on industry at home and abroad, broadcast in the Home Service of the B.B.C.* Worcester: Littlebury, 1946. 78p.

11,548 **Booker**, H. S. 'Have we a full employment policy?' *Economica*, n.s., XIV, 53 (February 1947), 37–47.

11,549 **Morgan**, Edward Victor. *The conquest of unemployment*. London: Sampson Low, Marston, 1947. xii, 182p.

11,550 **Winternitz**, J. *The problem of full employment: a Marxist analysis*. London: Lawrence and Wishart, 1947. 32p.

11,551 **Frank**, W. F. 'Full employment and industrial law.' *Ind. Law Rev.*, III, 2 (October 1948), 110–32.

11,552 **Gaitskell**, Hugh. 'Full employment policy.' Tracey, H. (ed.). *The British Labour Party: its history, growth, policy, and leaders*. London: Caxton Publishing Co., 1948. Vol. 2. p. 50–63.

11,553 **Åkerman**, Gustav. 'Unemployment and unemployment policy in England.' *Kyklos*, III, 1 (1949), 23–35.

A summary of the author's work *Engelsk arbetslöshet och arbetslöshets politik*. Stockholm, 1947.

11,554 **Croome**, Honor. 'Liberty, equality and full employment.' *Lloyds Bank Rev.*, n.s., 13 (July 1949), 14–32.

11,555 **Council of Europe.** *Full employment objectives in relation to the problem of European co-operation.* Strasbourg: C. of E., 1951. 68p.

11,556 **Wood**, John B. *Employment.* London: Conservative Political Centre, 1951. 36p. (Discussion series.)

11,557 **Gould**, Julius. 'Full employment: a discussion of some recent literature.' *Br. J. Sociol.*, III, 2 (June 1952), 178–82.
Principal works discussed are R. H. S. Crossman (ed.), *New Fabian essays*; R. Turvey (ed.), *Wages policy under full employment*; E. H. Phelps-Brown and B. C. Roberts, 'Wages policy in Great Britain', *Lloyds Bank Review* (January 1952); P. F. Drucker, *The new society*; and F. Zweig, *Productivity and trade unions.*

11,558 **Gruber**, Karl. *Conditions of full employment.* London: Hodge, 1952. vi, 141p.
Translated from the German by Jean Meyer.

11,559 **Pigou**, Arthur Cecil. 'Employment policy.' *Essays in economics.* London: Macmillan, 1952. p. 85–107.
Reprint of article from *Agenda*, August 1944, entitled 'Employment policy and Sir William Beveridge.'

11,560 **Röpke**, W. *The economics of full employment: an analysis of the UN report on national and international measures for full employment.* New York: American Enterprise Association, 1952. 34p.

11,561 **United Nations.** Economic and Social Council. 14th Session. *Full employment: implementation of full employment policies. Replies of governments to the full employment questionnaire covering the period 1951–52, submitted under resolutions 221E (IX), 290 (XI) and 371B (XIII) of the Economic and Social Council.* New York: U.N., 1952. 246p. (E/2232.)

11,562 **Sultan**, Paul E. 'Full employment on trial: a case study of British experience.' *Can. J. Econ. Polit. Sci.*, XIX, 2 (May 1953), 210–21.

11,563 **United Nations.** Economic and Social Council. *Full employment: analysis of replies of governments to the questionnaire on full employment, balance of payments and related policies, 1952–1953. Report by the Secretariat.* New York: U.N., 1953. 24p. (E/2445.)
Addendum. 27p. (E/2445/Add. 1.)

11,564 **Hilton**, William Samuel. *Building by direct labour: a national survey.* London: Amalgamated Union of Building Trade Workers, 1954. 191p.

11,565 **United Nations.** Secretary General. *Full employment: implementation of full employment, economic development, and balance of payments policies; replies of governments to the questionnaire on full employment, economic development, the balance of payments, and economic trends, objectives and policies in 1953 and 1954.* New York: U.N., 1954. 165p. (E/2565.)

11,566 **United Nations.** Economic and Social Council. *World economic situation. Agenda item 2 (XX). Full employment: Implementation of full employment and balance of payments policies. Replies from governments to the questionnaire on full employment and balance of payments, submitted under resolution 520B (VI) of the General Assembly and resolutions 221E (IX), 290 (XI) and 371B (XIII) of the Economic and Social Council.* New York: U.N., 1955. 113p.

11,567 **Vaizey**, John Ernest. *The trade unionist and full employment.* London: Workers' Educational Association, 1955. 32p.

11,568 **Treasury.** *Economic implications of full employment.* London: H.M.S.O., 1956. 13p. (Cmd. 9725.)

11,569 **Treasury.** *Must full employment mean ever-rising prices? A popular version of the White Paper 'The economic implications of full employment'.* London: H.M.S.O., 1956. 24p.

11,570 **British Hospitals Contributory Schemes Association.** Conference, Coventry, 1956. *Full employment and the unfit: address delivered by the Earl of Verulam; also address by the President of the Association (Henry Lesser), and a report of speeches made at the conference dinner, October 11th and 12th, 1956.* Bristol: the Association, 1957. 28p.

11,571 **Burton**, H. 'Full employment, inflation and economic policy.' *Publ. Fin.*, XII, 1 (1957), 67–77.

11,572 **Jack**, D. T. 'Some current international economic problems. II. Economic implications of full employment.' *S. Afr. J. Econ.*, XXV, 1 (March 1957), 11–24.
Public lecture.

11,573 **Please**, S. 'Structural unemployment and government policy.' *Int. Labour Rev.*, LXXV, 2 (February 1957), 119–36.
'... written with special reference to the United Kingdom.'

11,574 **Miernyk**, William H. 'British and American approaches to structural unemployment.' *Ind. Labor Relat. Rev.*, XII, 1 (October 1958), 3–19.

11,575 **Jay**, Douglas Patrick Thomas. *Unemployment: the Douglas Jay report.* London: Labour Party, 1959. 10p.

11,576 **Wellens**, John. *The bulge: its industrial impact. A national plan.* Grasscroft, nr. Oldham: John Wellens Organisation, 1959. [40]p.
On the problems arising from the high birth-rate of the years 1942–50.

11,577 **Iles**, Dennis John and **Tucker**, Cyrial Albert. *Problems of full employment.* London: Routledge and Kegan Paul, 1960. x, 265p.

11,578 **Ministry of Labour.** *Security and change: progress in provision for redundancy.* London: H.M.S.O., 1961. 37p.

11,579 **Hancock**, Keith J. 'The reduction of unemployment as a problem of public policy, 1920–29.' *Econ. Hist. Rev.*, 2nd ser., xv, 2 (December 1962), 328–43.

11,580 **Miernyk**, William H. 'Labor market lessons from abroad.' *Labor Law J.*, XIII, 6 (June 1962), 429–38.

11,581 **Freeman**, Robert (ed.). *The black spots: a tax policy for unemployment.* London: Aims of Industry, 1963. 15p. (Aims of Industry booklet.)

11,582 **Green**, Alfred L. *A study and appraisal of manpower programs as related to a policy of full employment in France, Great Britain, The Netherlands, Sweden.* Albany, N.Y.: New York (State) Division of Employment, 1963. 119p.

11,583 **United States**. Department of Labor. Bureau of Employment Security. *Experience of other countries in dealing with technological unemployment.* Washington, D.C.: Manpower Administration, Bureau of Employment Security, 1963. vi, 42p. (B.E.S. report no. ES-220.)

By M. T. Kastanek.

11,584 **Kaldor**, Nicholas. 'The lessons of the British experiment since the war: full employment and the welfare state.' *Essays on economic policy.* Vol. 1. London: Duckworth, 1964. p. 96–108.

'A paper read at the Centenary Congress of the Société Royale d'Economie Politique de Belgique, Brussels, 1955.'

11,585 **Kaldor**, Nicholas. 'The quantitative aspects of the full employment problem in Britain. *Essays on economic policy.* Vol. 1. London: Duckworth, 1964. p. 23–82.

'A memorandum prepared for Sir William Beveridge's Committee on Full Employment and published as Appendix C to *Full Employment in a free society*, by Sir William Beveridge (London, 1944).'

11,586 **Paish**, Frank Walter. 'The two Britains.' *Banker*, CXIV, 456 (February 1964), 88–98.

11,587 **Farrell**, Michael James. *Fuller employment?* London: Institute of Economic Affairs, 1965. 71p. (Hobart papers 34.)

11,588 **Andersen**, Bent. *Work or support: an economic and social analysis of substitute permanent employment.* Paris: Organisation for Economic Co-operation and Development, 1966. 124p. (Employment of special groups.)

11,589 **MacKay**, Donald Iain, **Forsyth**, David J. C. and **Kelly**, David M. 'The discussion of public works programmes, 1917–1935: some remarks on the labour movement's contribution.' *Int. Rev. of Soc. Hist.*, XI, 1 (1966), 8–17.

11,590 **Skidelsky**, R. J. A. *The Labour government and the unemployment question, 1929–31.* 1966–67. (D.Phil. thesis, University of Oxford.)

11,591 **Eire.** National Industrial Economic Council. *Report on full employment.* Dublin: Stationery Office, 1967. 129p. (Report 18.)

11,592 **Fogarty**, Michael. 'Half a million workless for ever?' *New Soc.*, x, 268 (16 November 1967), 695–6.

11,593 **Wittrock**, Jan. *Reducing seasonal unemployment in the construction industry: methods of stabilising construction activity and employee income.* Paris: Organisation for Economic Co-operation and Development, 1967. 282p. (Developing job opportunities 4.)

'United Kingdom', p. 209–22.

11,594 **Burrows**, Paul. 'Manpower policy and the structure of unemployment in Britain.' *Scott. J. Polit. Econ.*, xv, 1 (February 1968), 68–83.

11,595 **Sherman**, Alfred. *Londoners foot the bill: failures in direct labour building.* London: Aims of Industry, 1968. 15p.

11,596 **Sumner**, M. T. 'The costs of Professor Paish.' *Oxf. Univ. Inst. Econ. Statist. Bull.*, XXX, 4 (November 1968), 299–313.

11,597 **Hughes**, John. 'Unemployment: the Labour record and prospect for 1969.' *Trade Un. Regist.* (1969), 124–32.

11,598 **Buckley**, Louis F. 'Employment, unemployment, and manpower policy in Western Europe.' Kamin, A. (ed.). *Western European labor and the American corporation.* Washington, D.C.: Bureau of National Affairs, 1970. p. 395–417.

11,599 **Griffiths**, A. R. G. 'The Irish Board of Works in the famine years.' *Hist. J.*, XIII, 4 (1970), 634–52.

11,600 **United States.** Department of Labor. Manpower Administration. *Special job creation for the hard-to-employ in Western Europe.* Washington, D.C.: U.S.G.P.O., 1970. 44p. (Manpower research monograph 14.)

C. WAR AND RECONSTRUCTION

See also Part Six, II, C, 4.

1. First World War

See also Part Three, III, B, 4.

11,601 **Hamilton**, *Sir* Ian Standish Monteith. *National life and national training.* Birmingham: Birmingham and Midland Institute, 1912. 32p. (Presidential address, 1912.)

Another edition. London: King, 1913. 55p.

Reprinted from *Army Review*.

11,602 *Steps taken for the prevention and relief of distress due to the war: memoranda, appendices* London: H.M.S.O., 1914. 52p. (Cd. 7603.)

Chairman: H. Samuel.

11,603 **Henderson**, H. D. 'The influence of the war on employment.' *Econ. J.*, XXIV, 96 (December 1914), 593–603; XXV, 97 (March 1915), 104–8; 98 (June 1915), 256–61.

11,604 **British Association for the Advancement of Science.** 'Interim report of the Conference on outlets for labour after the war.' *Reports of Meetings.* 1915.

Deals particularly with the employment of women.

The greater part of the transactions of the conference were published as *Credit, industry, and the war*, edited by A. W. Kirkaldy, 1915.

11,605 **Cole**, George Douglas Howard and **Mellor**, William. *The price of dilution of labour: an open letter to the members of the A.S.E. Conference, 30th December, 1915.* London: Co-operative Printing Society, 1915. 8p.

11,606 **Government Committee on War Organisation of the Distributing Trades in Scotland.** *First report.* Edinburgh: H.M.S.O., 1915. 11p. (Cd. 7987.)

Second report. 1916. 4p. (Cd. 8220.)

Chairman: J. Dundas White.

11,607 **Home Department.** Committee appointed to consider the conditions of clerical and commercial employment with a view to advising what steps should be taken, by the employment of women or otherwise, to replace men withdrawn for service in the military forces. *Report.* London: H.M.S.O., 1915. 12p. (Cd. 8110.)

Chairman: Cecil Harmsworth.

11,608 **Home Department.** Committee appointed to consider the conditions of retail trade which can best secure that the further enlistment of men or their employment in other national services may not interfere with the operations of that trade. *Report.* London: H.M.S.O., 1915. 10p. (Cd. 8113.)

Chairman: C. Harmsworth.

11,609 **Kennedy**, J. M. 'Labour, conscription, and finance.' *Fortn. Rev.*, n.s., XCVIII, 587 (November 1915), 947–57.

11,610 **Lee**, Arthur. *The need of compulsory national service.* London: National Service League, 1915. 16p.

11,611 **Local Government Board.** Committee on the Provision of Employment for Sailors and Soldiers Disabled in the War. *Report.* London: H.M.S.O., 1915. 8p. (Cd. 7915.)

Chairman: G. H. Murray.

11,612 **Ministry of Munitions.** *Report on the causes and circumstances of the apprehended differences affecting munition workers in the Clyde district.* London: H.M.S.O., 1915. 5p. (Cd. 8136.)

By Lord Balfour of Burleigh and L. Macassey.

11,613 **Ministry of Munitions.** *Return of cases heard before Munitions Tribunals from their inception up to and including 27th November, 1915.* London: H.M.S.O., 1915. 6p. (Cd. 8143.)

. . . 1st July, 1916. 1916. 9p. (Cd. 8360.)

11,614 **Money**, *Sir* Leo George Chiozza. 'Recruiting and organisation for war.' *Fortn. Rev.*, n.s., XCVII, 581 (May 1915), 865–73; n.s., XCVIII, 584 (August 1915), 363–77.

11,615 **Round Table.** 'The industrial situation.' *Round Table*, 20 (September 1915), 724–48.

11,616 **Round Table.** 'The war and industrial organization.' *Round Table*, 19 (June 1915), 559–88.

11,617 **Slesser**, *Sir* Henry Herman. *Opinion on the Munitions of War Act, 1915.* 1915. 16p.

11,618 **Ministry of Munitions.** Memoranda. 1–21.

1. *Sunday labour.* 1915. (Cd. 8132.)
2. *Welfare supervision.* 1915. (Cd. 8151.)
3. *Industrial canteens.* 1919. (Cd. 8133); Appendices (Cd. 8199, 8370, 8798).
4. *Employment of women.* 1916. (Cd. 8185.)
5. *Hours of work.* 1916. (Cd. 8186.)
6. *Appendix to no. 3.* 1916. (Cd. 8199.)
7. *Industrial fatigue and its causes.* 1916. (Cd. 8213.)
8. *Special industrial diseases.* 1916. (Cd. 8214.)
9. *Ventilation and lighting of munitions factories.* 1916. (Cd. 8215.)
10. *Sickness and injury.* 1916. (Cd. 8216.)
11. *Investigations of workers' food and suggestions as to dietary. 2nd appendix to no. 3.* 1916. (Cd. 8370.)
12. *Statistical information concerning output in relation to hours of work.* 1916. (Cd. 8344.)
13. *Juvenile employment.* 1916. (Cd. 8362.)
14. *Washing facilities and baths.* 1916. (Cd. 8387.)
15. *Effects of industrial conditions upon eyesight.* 1916. (Cd. 8409.)
16. *Medical certificates for munitions workers.* 1917. (Cd. 8522.)
17. *Health and welfare of munitions workers outside the factory.* 1917.
18. *Further statistical information concerning output in relation to hours of work, with special reference to the influence of Sunday labour.* Appendix to no. 5. 1917. (Cd. 8628.)
19. *Investigation of workers' food and suggestions as to dietary. 2nd appendix to no. 3.* Rev. ed. 1917. (Cd. 8798.)
20. *Weekly hours of employment. Supplementary to no. 5.* 1917. (Cd. 8801.)
21. *Investigation of industrial accidents.* 1918. (Cd. 9046.)

11,619 **Alden**, Percy. 'The dilution of labour.' *Contemp. Rev.*, CX (September 1916), 325–33.

11,620 **Board of Trade.** *Report on increased employment of women during the war in the United Kingdom.* London: H.M.S.O., 1916. 33p.
1917. 13p.
1919. 16p. (Cd. 9164.)

11,621 **British Association for the Advancement of Science.** *Labour, finance, and the war, being the results of inquiries, arranged by the Section of Economic Science and Statistics.* London: British Association, 1916. vii, 344p.
Edited by A. W. Kirkaldy.
Contents
I. 'Some thoughts on reconstruction after the war,' by A. W. Kirkaldy.
II. 'Industrial unrest.'
III. 'The replacement of men by women in industry.'
IV. 'The effects of the war on credit, currency and finance.'
V. 'Land settlement', by C. Turnor.

11,622 **British Association for the Advancement of Science.** 'Replacement of men by women in industry: abstract of report.' *Reports of Meetings.* 1916. p. 276–7.

11,623 **Clifford,** William George. *The ex-soldier, by himself: a practical study of the past and future of the ex-soldier problem, with special reference to the situation created by the World War.* London: Black, 1916. viii, 300p.

11,624 **Cole,** George Douglas Howard and **Slesser,** *Sir* Henry Herman. *The Munitions Act and the restoration of trade union customs.* London: Joint Committee on Labour Problems after the War, 1916. 11p.
Memorandum prepared for the Advisory Committee on the Restoration of Trade Union Conditions.

11,625 **Cole,** George Douglas Howard and **Mellor,** William. *Safeguards for dilution: what circulars L2 and L3 mean.* London, 1916. 12p.
'Prepared for the Executive Council of the Amalgamated Society of Engineers.'

11,626 **A Correspondent.** 'The dilution of skilled labour.' *Econ. J.*, XXVI, 101 (March 1916), 28–34.

11,627 **Cosens,** Monica. *Lloyd George's munition girls.* London: Hutchinson, 1916. 160p.

11,628 **Cox,** Harold. 'Industrial reconstruction.' *Edinb. Rev.*, CCXXIII, 456 (April 1916), 393–413.
Review article, on F. W. Taylor, *The principles of scientific management*; R. F. Hoxie, *Scientific management and labor*; Ministry of Munitions, *Memoranda of the Health of Munition Workers Committee*, 1916.

11,629 **Departmental Committee on Juvenile Education in Relation to Employment after the War.** *Interim report.* London: H.M.S.O., 1916. 4p. (Cd. 8374.)
Final report. 1917. 42p. (Cd. 8512.)
Evidence and appendices. (Cd. 8577.)

11,630 **Departmental Committee on Land Settlement for Sailors and Soldiers.** *Final report. Part I.* London: H.M.S.O., 1916. 30p. (Cd. 8182.)
Chairman: H. C. W. Verney.
Final report. Part II. Appendices. 39p. (Cd. 8277.)
Minutes of evidence. (Cd. 8347.)
Chairman: H. Hobhouse.
Interim report was not printed.

11,631 **Derby,** Earl of. *Report on recruiting by the Earl of Derby, K.G., Director-General of Recruiting.* London: H.M.S.O., 1916. 8p. (Cd. 8149.)

11,632 **Fayle,** Charles Ernest. *Industrial reconstruction.* London: Garton Foundation, 1916. 23p.
A commentary on, and condensation of, the 1916 edition of the Foundation's *Memorandum of the industrial situation after the war.*

11,633 **Fyfe,** Thomas Alexander. *Employers and workmen: a handbook explanatory of their duties and responsibilities under the Munitions of War Acts 1915 and 1916.* London, Edinburgh: Hodge, 1916. 95p.
Second edition. 1917. 269p.
Third edition. *Employers & workmen under the Munition of War Acts, 1915–1917.* 1918. 364p.

11,634 **Garton Foundation.** *Memorandum on the industrial situation after the war.* London: the Foundation, 1916. 96p.
Revised and enlarged edition. Harrison, 1919. 175p.
Also American edition. Philadelphia: U.S. Shipping Board Emergency Fleet Corporation, [1918?]. 76p.

11,635 **Joint Committee on Labour Problems after the War.** *The problem of demobilization.* London: Co-operative Printing Society, 1916. 8p.

11,636 **Lehfeldt,** R. A. 'British industry after the war.' *Econ. J.*, XXVI, 103 (September 1916), 306–12.

11,637 **Ministry of Munitions.** *Notes on the employment of women on munitions of war, with an appendix on training of munitions workers.* London: the Ministry, 1916. 94p., illus.
Photographs and written descriptions of work being done by women in munitions factories.

11,638 **Pigou,** Arthur Cecil. 'Labour problems after the war.' *Contemp. Rev.*, CX (September 1916), 334–45.

11,639 **Quarterly Review.** 'The recruiting crisis.' *Q. Rev.*, CCXXV, 447 (April 1916), 566–84.

11,640 *Report on recruiting in Ireland.* London: H.M.S.O., 1916. (Cd. 8168.)

11,641 **Scott,** Leslie. 'Ex-service men on the land: report of departmental committee.' *Econ. J.*, XXVI, 103 (September 1916), 324–7.

11,642 **Snowden** Philip. *The Military Service Acts.* Manchester: Independent Labour Party, 1916. 16p.
Two editions.

11,643 **Surveyors' Institution.** *Unemployment after the war: housing emergency schemes. Part 1. Urban.* London, 1916. 27p.

11,644 **War Office.** *Women's war work in maintaining the industries and export trade of the United Kingdom.* London: H.M.S.O., 1916. 93p.

11,645 **Webb**, Sidney. *When peace comes: the way of industrial reconstruction.* London: Fabian Society, 1916. 32p. (Fabian tract 181.)

Reproduced with slight additions, from articles in the *Daily News*, 28 July, 3, 12, 19, 26 August, 5 September, 1916.

Fuller statement in S. Webb and Arnold Freeman, *Great Britain after the war.*

11,646 **Addison**, Christopher. *British workshops and the war.* London: Unwin, 1917. 52p.

A speech delivered to the House of Commons on 28 June 1917 by the Minister of Munitions.

11,647 **Board of Agriculture and Fisheries.** *British agriculture: the nation's opportunity, being the Minority Report of the Departmental Committee on the Employment of Sailors and Soldiers on the Land.* London: Murray, 1917. 168p.

11,648 **Carter**, Huntly (ed.). *Industrial reconstruction: a symposium on the situation after the war and how to meet it.* London: Fisher Unwin, 1917. xv, 295p.

'This book contains the results of an inquiry recently undertaken to ascertain the opinions held by a large number of distinguished public persons on . . . the industrial situation . . .'

Most of the contributions appeared serially in the *New Age*, November 1916 to April 1917.

11,649 **Chapman**, Sydney John. 'The state and labour.' Dawson, W. H. (ed.). *After-war problems.* London: Allen and Unwin, 1917. p. 137–48.

11,650 **Engineer.** 'Government and labour.' *Natn. Rev.*, LXIX, 414 (August 1917), 716–27.

On the suggested amendments to the Munitions of War Act, and the Interim Report of the Sub-Committee on Relations between Capital and Labour.

11,651 **Hobson**, John Atkinson. *Forced labour.* London: National Council for Civil Liberties, 1917. 15p.

11,652 **Joint Committee on Labour Problems after the War.** *The problem of unemployment after the war.* London: Co-operative Printing Society, 1917. 7p.

11,653 **Joint Committee on Labour Problems after the war.** *Restoration of trade union customs after the war.* London: Co-operative Printing Society, 1917. 14p.

11,654 **Kirkaldy**, Adam Willis (ed.). *Industry and finance: war expedients and reconstruction; being the results of enquiries arranged by the Section of Economic Science and Statistics of the British Association, during the years 1916 and 1917.* London: Pitman, 1917. viii, 371p.

'The replacement of men by women in industry during the war.' p. 24–145.

'Women workers in agriculture', by E. N. Thomas. p. 146–59.

'Workshop committees: suggested lines of development', by C. G. Renold. p. 160–86.

11,655 **Ministry of Munitions.** *The boy in industry.* London: H.M.S.O., 1917. 46p.

11,656 **Ministry of Munitions.** Committee to consider and advise on questions of industrial fatigue, hours of labour, and other matters affecting the personal health and physical efficiency of workers in munitions factories and workshops. *Interim report: industrial efficiency and fatigue.* London: H.M.S.O., 1917. 121p. (Cd. 8511.)

Chairman: G. Newman.

Final report: industrial health and efficiency. 1918. 182p. (Cd. 9065.)

11,657 **Ministry of Munitions.** Health of Munitions Workers Committee. *Health of the munitions workers.* London: H.M.S.O., 1917. 138p.

11,658 **Snowden**, Philip. *Labour in chains: the peril of industrial conscription.* Manchester, London: National Labour P., 1917. 16p.

11,659 **Swanwick, H. M.** 'The war in its effect upon women.' Co-operative Wholesale Societies. *Annual, 1917.* p. 231–56.

11,660 **Walter**, Henriette R. *Munition workers in England and France: a summary of reports issued by the British Ministry of Munitions.* New York: Russell Sage Foundation, 1917. 48p. (Industrial relations series.)

A summary of the twenty-one memoranda of the Health of Munitions Workers Committee of the Ministry of Munitions.

11,661 **Webb**, Sidney. 'British labor under war pressure.' *N. Am. Rev.*, CCV (June 1917), 874–85.

11,662 **Webb**, Sidney James. *The restoration of trade union conditions.* London: Nisbet, 1917. 109p.

11,663 **Zimmern**, Alfred Eckhard. 'Labour and the war.' Cook, Sir E. and Villiers, M. E., Dowager Countess of Jersey (eds.). *Britain's part in the war.* London: Victoria League, 1917. p. 46–52.

11,664 **Robinson**, *Mrs* Annot. 'The substituted labour of women 1914–1917.' *Manchr. Statist. Soc. Trans.* (1917–18), 59–79.

Gives detailed information for Manchester area.

11,665 **Barrett**, Robert Le Moyne. *British industrial experience during the war.* Washington, D.C.: U.S.G.P.O., 1918. 2v. in 1. (65 Congress, 1st session. Senate. Doc. 114.)

11,666 **Benn**, Ernest John Pickstone. 'The higher direction of industry.' *Contemp. Rev.*, CXIII, 630 (June 1918), 671–9.

11,667 **Cockerell**, Douglas. *A national scheme for vocational training for able-bodied soldiers and sailors.* London: Arts and Crafts Exhibition Society, 1918. 15p.

11,668 **Gray**, Howard Levi. *War time control of industry: the experience of England.* New York: Macmillan, 1918. xv, 307p.

11,669 **Greenwood**, Major, the younger. *A report on the causes of wastage of labour in munitions factories employing women.* London: printed under the authority of H.M.S.O. by Sir Joseph Causton and Sons, 1918. 76p. (National Health Insurance Medical Research Committee. Special report series 16.)

11,670 **Hammond**, Matthew Brown. 'Lessons from English war experience in the employment of labor.' *Am. Econ. Rev.*, VIII, 1 (March 1918), Supplement, 147–57.

11,671 **Hitchcock**, Curtice Nelson. 'British labor policy and its implications for the solution of American war problems.' *Acad. Polit. Sci. Proc.*, VII, 4 (February 1918), 771–84.

11,672 **Labour Party.** *Labour and the new social order: a report on reconstruction.* London: Labour Party, 1918. 22p.

Draft report.

Issued in revised form later in the year. 23p.

11,673 **Labour Party.** Advisory Committee on the Machinery of Government. *The juvenile worker at the end of the war.* London, 1918. 6p.

11,674 **Lloyd George**, David. *The great crusade: extracts from speeches delivered during the war.* London and New York: Hodder and Stoughton, 1918. viii, 215p.

Arranged by F. L. Stevenson.

11,675 **Ministry of Labour.** *Reports on reconstruction from English sources.* Philadelphia: United States Shipping Board Emergency Fleet Corporation, Industrial Relations Division, 1918.

Reprinted.

11,676 **Ministry of Munitions.** Mr Justice McCardie's Committee of Enquiry (1) to investigate and report on the labour conditions which have rendered the embargo necessary, and to advise upon the administration of the scheme; (2) to consider and report as to what further measures should be adopted in view of these conditions, to maintain and where necessary increase the output of munitions due regard being given to the public interest, in the most effective and economical use of labour, money and material. *Interim report.* London: H.M.S.O., 1918. 12p.

11,677 **Ministry of Reconstruction.** *Final report of the committee on substitute labour.* London: H.M.S.O., 1918. 8p. (Cd. 9228.)

11,678 **Ministry of Reconstruction.** *Juvenile employment during the war and after: the report of an inquiry.* London: H.M.S.O., 1918. 114p.

11,679 **Ministry of Reconstruction.** Civil War Workers' Committee. *First (interim) report.* London: H.M.S.O., 1918. (Cd. 9117.)

Chairman: Gerald Bellhouse.

11,680 **Ministry of Reconstruction.** Civil War Workers' Committee. *Second, Third, Fourth and Fifth interim reports.* London: H.M.S.O., 1918. 27p. (Cd. 9192.)

Second interim report. Unemployment insurance.

Third interim report. Holidays for munition workers after the war.

Fourth interim report. Arrangements upon cessation of war work.

Fifth interim report.

11,681 **Ministry of Reconstruction.** Civil War Workers' Committee. *Final report. Substitute labour.* London: H.M.S.O., 1918. 8p. (Cd. 9228.)

11,682 **Ministry of Reconstruction.** Women's Advisory Committee. *Interim report of the sub-committee on the co-ordination of the vocational training of women.* London: H.M.S.O., 1918. 8p.

Chairman: A. S. Lawrence.

11,683 **Ministry of Reconstruction.** Women's Employment Committee. *Report.* London: H.M.S.O., 1918. 116p. (Cd. 9239.)

Chairman: John W. Hills.

11,684 **Monkhouse**, O. E. *The employment of women in munition factories.* London, 1918. 9p.

11,685 **National Alliance of Employers and Employed.** *Demand for a central statutory board to regulate demobilization schemes.* London: Co-operative Printing Society, 1918. 14p.

11,686 **National Liberal Party.** *Liberal policy in the task of political and social reconstruction.* London: Liberal Publishing Department, 1918. 130p.

11,687 **Stoker**, William Henry and **Bentwich**, Herbert. *The Military Service Acts practice, with notes of cases and tribunal decisions.* London: Stevens, 1918. xxiv, 187p.

11,688 **Ministry of Munitions.** *History of the Ministry of Munitions.* [London], 1918–22. 8v.

Issued in parts. 'Confidential. For official information only.'

I. *Industrial mobilisation, 1914–1915.*
II. *General organization for munitions supply.*
III. *Finance and contracts.*
IV. *The supply and control of labour, 1915–1916.*
V. *Wages and welfare.*
VI. *Man power and dilution.*
VII. *The control of materials.*
VIII. *Control of industrial capacity and equipment.*

11,689 **Angell**, *Sir* Norman. *The British revolution and the American democracy: an interpretation of the British labour programmes.* New York: Huebsch, 1919. xix, 319p.

11,690 **Arnold**, E. V. *The industrial upheaval.* Cardiff, 1919. 15p.

11,691 **Carter**, Huntly (ed.). *The limits of state industrial control: a symposium on the present situation and how to meet it.* London: Unwin, 1919. 292p.

11,692 **Committee on Women in Industry.** *Report.* London: H.M.S.O., 1919. (Cmd. 167.)

11,693 **Friedman**, Elisha Michael. *Labor and reconstruction in Europe.* New York: Dutton, 1919. xix, 216p.

11,694 **Garton Foundation.** *The pledge to the trade unions.* London: the Foundation, 1919. 8p. (Tracts for the times 1.)

A digest of comments received upon 'Tracts for the times'. 1919. 8p. (Postscript to *Tracts for the times* 1.)

11,695 **Greenwood**, Major. 'Problems of industrial organisation.' *R. Statist. Soc. J.*, LXXXII, 2 (March 1919), 186–209.

With discussion, p. 210–21.

'Read before the Royal Statistical Society, February 18, 1919.'

11,696 **Hammond**, Matthew Brown. *British labor conditions and legislation during the war.* New York: Oxford U.P., 1919. ix, 335p. (Carnegie Endowment for International Peace. Preliminary economic studies of the war 14.)

11,697 **Home Office.** *Substitution of women for men during the war: reports by H.M. Inspectors of Factories showing the position in certain industries at the end of 1918.* London: H.M.S.O., 1919. 142p.

11,698 **Home Office.** *Substitution of women in non-munition factories during the war.* London: H.M.S.O., 1919. 52p.

11,699 **Lanchester**, Frederick William. *The aftermath of the war: economic and industrial problems.* Birmingham: Buckler and Webb, 1919. 28p.

'Presidential address to members of the Vesey Club.'

11,700 **Ministry of Reconstruction.** Women's Advisory Committee. *Report of the sub-committee appointed to consider the position after the war of women holding temporary appointments in government departments.* London: H.M.S.O., 1919. 8p. (Cmd. 199.)

Chairman: Mrs Granville Streatfield.

11,701 *Report of provisional joint committee presented to meeting of Industrial Conference, Central Hall, Westminster, April 4, 1919.* London: H.M.S.O., 1919. 20p. (Cmd. 139.)

With appendices. 1920. 16, xivp. (Cmd. 501.)

Chairman: Sir Thomas Munro.

11,702 **Treasury.** Committee appointed . . . to consider and make recommendations upon certain questions with regard to recruitment for the Civil Service after the war. London: H.M.S.O., 1919.

Interim report. 6p. (Cmd. 34.)
Second interim report. 5p. (Cmd. 35.)
Third interim report. 7p. (Cmd. 36.)
Final report. 15p. (Cmd. 164.)
Chairman: Lord Gladstone.

11,703 **United States.** Department of State. *Report on labour situation in Great Britain.* Washington, 1919. 43p.

11,704 **United States.** National Industrial Conference Board. European Commission. *Interim report . . . July 1919.* Boston, Mass.: N.I.C.B., 1919. iii, 34p.

11,705 **War Cabinet Committee.** *Report on women in industry.* London: H.M.S.O., 1919. 341p. (Cmd. 135.)

Appendices and summaries. 235p. (Cmd. 167.)

Chairman: Sir James Richard Atkin.

11,706 **Committee on Re-employment of Ex-servicemen.** *Interim report.* London: H.M.S.O., 1920. 16p. (Cmd. 951.)

Chairman: T. W. Phillips.

11,707 **London County Council.** *The Council and the war.* London: Oldham's P., 1920. 65p.

Includes manpower planning.

11,708 **Treasury.** Committee on the appointment of ex-service men to posts in the Civil Service. *Report.* London: H.M.S.O., 1920. 10p.

Second interim report. 1921. 4p.
Third interim report. 1921. 27p.
Chairman: L. Lytton.

11,709 **British Association for the Advancement of Science.** *British labour: replacement and conciliation, 1914–21, being the result of conferences and investigations by committees of Section F of the British Association.* London: British Association, 1921. xxxv, 266p.

Part I, on replacement, co-ordinated and revised by L. Grier and A. Ashley.

Part II, on conciliation, edited by A. W. Kirkaldy.

11,710 **International Institute of Agriculture.** *The maintenance of the agricultural labour supply in England and Wales during the war.* Rome, 1922. 121p.

By J. K. Montgomery.

11,711 **Macassey**, *Sir* Lynden Livingstone. *Labour policy: false and true.* London: Butterworth, 1922. 320p.

The author was one of the Dilution Commissioners during 1914–18.

11,712 **Select Committee on the Civil Service (Employment of Conscientious Objectors).** *Report* [etc.] London: H.M.S.O., 1922. xiv, 39p. (H.C. 69)

Chairman: Captain Bowyer.

11,713 **Cole**, George Douglas Howard. *Labour in the coal-mining industry, 1914–1921.* Oxford: Clarendon P., 1923. xiv, 274p. (Economic and social history of the world war. British series.)
For the Carnegie Endowment for International Peace.

11,714 **King's Roll National Council.** *Interim report on the employment of disabled ex-service men.* London: H.M.S.O., 1923. 14p. (Cmd. 1919.)

11,715 **Wolfe**, Humbert. *Labour supply and regulation.* Oxford: Clarendon P., 1923. xiv, 422p. (Economic and social history of the world war. British series.)

11,716 **Lindsay**, Alexander Dunlop. 'The organisation of labour in the army in France during the war and its lessons.' *Econ. J.*, XXXIV, 133 (March 1924), 69–82.

11,717 **Scott**, William Robert and **Cunnison**, James. *The industries of the Clyde Valley during the war.* Oxford: Clarendon P., 1924. xvi, 224p. (Economic and social history of the world war. British series.)
Chapter VIII. 'Labour.' p. 138–61.

11,718 *Statistics relating to financial provisions for the relief of unemployment (including post-war resettlement of ex-members of His Majesty's Forces) from the Armistice.* London: H.M.S.O., 1924. (Cmd. 2082.)

11,719 **Hamilton**, Mary Agnes. *Mary Macarthur: a biographical sketch.* London: Parsons, 1925. 209p.
Member of the Central Munitions Labour Supply Committee.

11,720 **Bowley**, *Sir* Arthur Lyon. *Some economic consequences of the great war.* London: Butterworth, 1930. 251p. (Home university library of modern knowledge.)
Chapter VII. 'Displacement of labour.'

11,721 **Lloyd George**, David. 'The Ministry of Munitions: establishment and labour problems.' *War memoirs.* Vol. I. London: Nicholson and Watson, 1933. Chap. IX. p. 237–353.
New edition. Vol. I. London: Odhams, 1938. Chap. IX. p. 143–210.

11,722 **Addison**, Christopher. *Four and a half years: a personal diary from June, 1914 to January, 1919.* London: Hutchinson, 1934. 2v.
The author was Undersecretary of the Ministry of Munitions and later Minister, December 1916 to July 1917. From July 1917 to 1919 he was Minister of Reconstruction.

11,723 **Morgan**, D. J. 'Labour in the army in two wars.' *Econ. J.*, LX, 237 (March 1950), 175–7.
Discusses E. H. Phelps Brown, 'Morale, military and industrial', *Econ. J.*, LIX, 233, p. 40–55, and 'The organisation of labour in the army in France during the war and its lessons', *Econ. J.*, XXXIV, 133, p. 69–82.

11,724 **Douglas**, Roy. 'Voluntary enlistment in the First World War and the work of the Parliamentary Recruiting Committee.' *J. Mod. Hist.*, XLII, 4 (December 1970), 564–85.

See also: 17; 8449.

2. Second World War

See also Part Three, III, B, 5.

11,725 **Ministry of Labour and National Service.** *Control of Employment Act, 1939. Report to the Minister of Labour and National Service on a Draft Control of Employment (Advertisements) Order, 1940, by a Committee appointed under Section I (I) of the Act.* London: H.M.S.O., 1940. 8p. (H.C. 107.)
Chairman: W. T. Davies.

11,726 **Political and Economic Planning.** 'Economic priorities in war.' *Planning*, 161 (13 February 1940), 1–11.

11,727 **Burchardt**, F. A. 'The White Paper on industrial and labour policy.' *Oxf. Univ. Inst. Statist. Bull.*, III, 11 (9 August 1941), 235–42.

11,728 **Cole**, George Douglas Howard. 'The man-power problem.' *Polit. Q.*, XII, 2 (April–June 1941), 154–66.

11,729 **Flanders**, Allan David. *The battle for production.* London: International Publishing Co., 1941. 46p.

11,730 **Ministry of Labour and National Service.** *Man-power: memorandum on the principal new measures to be introduced by His Majesty's government in pursuance of their man-power policy.* London: H.M.S.O., 1941. 4p. (Cmd. 6324.)

11,731 **Ministry of Labour and National Service.** Committee on Skilled Men in the Services. *Interim report.* London: H.M.S.O., 1941. 7p. (Cmd. 6307.)
Second report and a memorandum by the War Office. 1942. 74p. (Cmd. 6339.)
Chairman: W. H. Beveridge.

11,732 **Murphy**, Mary E. 'The war and British workers.' *Harv. Bus. Rev.*, XX, 1 (Autumn 1941), 92–106.
Government activities vis-à-vis labour.

11,733 **Thomson**, George Walker. 'The war structure of the British engineering industry.' *Int. Labour Rev.*, XLIV, 3 (September 1941), 275–82.

11,734 **Treasury.** Committee on the Calling Up of Civil Servants. *Interim report.* London: H.M.S.O., 1941. 6p. (Cmd. 6301.)
Chairman: Lord Kennet.

11,735 **United States.** Department of Labour. Wage and Hour Division. *War time regulation of hours of labor and labor supply in Great Britain.* Washington, 1941. 82p.
'Combines an early monograph, *Regulating hours of labor in Great Britain*, with a discussion of war-time developments in such closely related supply questions as unemployment, training, dilution, and industrial conscription.'

11,736 **Worswick**, George David Norman. 'The release of labour from the cotton industry.' *Oxf. Univ. Inst. Statist. Bull.*, III, 7 (17 May 1941), 135–40.

11,737 **Wunderlich**, Frieda. *British labor and the war.* New York: Graduate Faculty of Political and Social Science, New School for Social Research, 1941. 67p. (Studies on war and peace 8. *Social Research*, Supplement III.)

11,738 **Advertising Service Guild.** *An enquiry into British war production . . . a report prepared by Mass-Observation for the Advertising Service Guild.* London: Murray.

Part 1: *People in production.* 1942. x, 410p. (Change: bulletin of the Advertising Service Guild 3.)

11,739 **Advertising Service Guild.** *People in production.* Harmondsworth, New York: Penguin, 1942. 280p. (Penguin special 117.)

An abridgement of part 1 of *An enquiry into British war production.*

11,740 **Argonaut** (*pseud.*). *Give us the tools: a study of the hindrances to full war production and how to end them.* London: Secker and Warburg, 1942. 191p.

11,741 **Biddle**, Eric Harbeson. *Manpower: a summary of the British experience.* Chicago: Public Administration Service, 1942. viii, 28p. (Publication 84.)

11,742 **Biddle**, Eric Harbeson. *The mobilization of the home front: the British experience and its significance for the United States.* Chicago: Public Administration Service, 1942. 47p. (Publication 81.)

A report for the American Public Welfare Association.

11,743 **Coppock**, Richard and **Heumann**, Harry. *Design for labour.* London: Dent, 1942. 31p. (Design for Britain series 13.)

11,744 **Crippen**, Harlan R. 'Workers and jobs in wartime Britain.' *Sci. Soc.*, VI, 3 (Summer 1942), 208–26.

11,745 **Eves**, Edward Victor. 'The organisation of man-power.' *Publ. Adm.*, XX, 1 (January–June 1942), 19–27.

Prize-winning essay, Haldane Essay Competition, 1941–42.

11,746 **International Labour Office.** *Wartime transference of labour in Great Britain.* Montreal: I.L.O., 1942. iv, 163p. (Studies and reports, series C, 24.)

11,747 **Political and Economic Planning.** 'Part-time employment.' *Planning*, 185 (10 February 1942), 1–16.

11,748 **Riches**, E. J. *Labour conditions in war contracts, with special reference to Canada, Great Britain and the United States.* Montreal: International Labour Office, 1942. 59p. (Studies and reports, series D, 23.)

11,749 **Tuckett**, Angela. *Civil liberty and the industrial worker.* London, 1942. 40p. (National Council for Civil Liberties. Civil liberty in wartime 1.)

11,750 **Wartime Social Survey.** *Women's registration and call-up: an inquiry among 2798 women for the Ministry of Labour and National Service.* London, 1942. 22, 4p.

11,751 **Bunn**, Margaret. 'Mass Observation: a comment on *People in production.*' *Manchr. Sch.*, XIII, 1 (October 1943), 24–37.

11,752 **Colyer**, William Thomas. *Military and industrial conscription.* London: Fellowship of Conscientious Objectors, 1943. 7p.

11,753 **Douie**, Vera. *The lesser half: a survey of the laws, regulations and practices introduced during the present war which embody discrimination against women.* London: Women's Publicity Planning Association, 1943. 100p.

11,754 **Kalecki**, Michael. 'Labour in the war industries. A. Sources of manpower in the British war sector in 1941 and 1942.' *Oxf. Univ. Inst. Statist. Bull.*, V, 11 (7 August 1943), 173–8.

11,755 **Kalecki**, Michael. 'Labour in the war industries in Britain and U.S.A. A. Sources of manpower in the British war sector.' *Oxf. Univ. Inst. Statist. Bull.*, V, 1 (9 January 1943), 1–11.

11,756 **Mitchell**, J. Howie. 'Part-time labour in munitions work.' *Occup. Psychol.*, XVII, 3 (July 1943), 119–25.

11,757 **National Union of Conservative and Constitutional Associations.** Central Committee on Post-War Reconstruction. *Demobilisation and resettlement, being the first interim report of the Conservative Sub-Committee on Demobilisation and Resettlement.* London, 1943. 31p. (Looking ahead.)

11,758 **Nicholson**, K. L. 'Substitution of women for men in industry.' *Oxf. Univ. Inst. Statist. Bull.*, V, 5 (3 April 1943), 85–7

11,759 **Political and Economic Planning.** 'Part-time work in an aircraft factory.' *Planning*, 205 (20 April 1943), 22–4

Experience of Parnall Aircraft Ltd.

11,760 **Samuel**, Wynne. *Transference must stop: half a million Welshmen were transferred to England and transference goes on.* Caernarfon: Swyddfa'r Blaid, 1943. 11p.

11,761 **University of Oxford.** Nuffield College. *Employment policy and organization of industry after the war: a statement.* London: Oxford U.P., 1943. 70p.

The outcome of a series of private conferences held under the auspices of Nuffield College.

11,762 **Wartime Social Survey.** *Workers and the war: a collection of short reports on inquiries made by the Regional Organisation of the War-time Social Survey.* London, 1943. 34p.

11,763 **Davison**, *Sir* Ronald Conway. *Remobilisation for peace.* London: Pilot P., 1944. 56p. (Target for tomorrow.)

11,764 **Hooks**, Janet Montgomery. *British policies and methods in employing women in wartime.* Washington, D.C.: U.S.G.P.O., 1944. 43p. (Bulletin of the Women's Bureau 200.)

11,765 **International Labour Office.** 'The employment of prisoners of war in Great Britain.' *Int. Labour Rev.*, XLIX, 2 (February 1944), 191–6.

11,766 **Ministry of Information.** *Manpower: the story of Britain's mobilisation for war.* London: H.M.S.O., 1944. 60p.

11,767 **Ministry of Labour and National Service.** *Re-allocation of manpower between civilian employments during any interim period between the defeat of Germany and the defeat of Japan.* London: H.M.S.O., 1944. 10p. (Cmd. 6568.)
Reprinted 1945.

11,768 **Ministry of Labour and National Service.** *Re-allocation of manpower between the armed forces and civilian employment during any interim period between the defeat of Germany and the defeat of Japan.* London: H.M.S.O., 1944. 4p. (Cmd. 6548.)

11,769 **National Union of Conservative and Constitutional Associations.** Central Committee on Post-war Reconstruction. *Work: the future of British industry, being a report by the Conservative Sub-Committee on Industry.* London, 1944. 46p. (Looking ahead.)
Second impression. 1946.

11,770 **Political and Economic Planning.** *Demobilisation and employment.* London: P.E.P., 1944. 33p. (Pamphlets 2.)
A modified version published in *Planning*, 217 (4 February 1944), 1–19.

11,771 **Political and Economic Planning.** 'Reconstruction plans.' *Planning*, 227 (10 November 1944), 1–19.

11,772 **Pritt**, Denis Nowell. *Defence regulation 1AA: analysis and criticism.* London: National Council for Civil Liberties, 1944. 21p.

11,773 *Statistics relating to the war effort of the United Kingdom.* London: H.M.S.O., 1944. 64p. (Cmd. 6564.)

11,774 **Treasury.** *Recruitment to established posts in the Civil Service during the reconstruction period. Statement of government policy and Civil Service National Whitley Council's report.* London: H.M.S.O., 1944. 23p. (Cmd. 6567.)
Chairman: J. A. Barlow.

11,775 **Ince**, *Sir* Godfrey Herbert. 'Mobilisation of man-power in Great Britain for the Second Great War.' *Manchr. Statist. Soc. Trans.* (1944–45). 36p.

11,776 **Fabian Society.** *Labour: control and decontrol; a report to the Fabian Economics Committee.* London: Fabian Publications and Gollancz, 1945. 29p. (Research series 106.)

11,777 **Industrial Welfare Society.** *Plan for reinstatement.* London: the Society, 1945. 24p.

11,778 **Medical Research Council.** Industrial Health Research Board. *A study of women on war work in four factories.* London: H.M.S.O., 1945. (Report 88.)
By S. Wyatt, assisted by R. Marriott, W. M. Dawson, Norah M. Davis, D. E. R. Hughes and F. G. L. Stock.

11,779 **Ministry of Labour and National Service.** Catering Wages Commission. *The rehabilitation of the catering industry: report to the Minister of Labour and National Service on an enquiry by the Catering Wages Commission under Section 2 of the Catering Wages Act, 1943.* London: H.M.S.O., 1945. 48p.
Chairman: Hartley Shawcross.

11,780 **Political and Economic Planning.** 'The disabled ex-servicemen.' *Planning*, 238 (17 August 1945), 1–18.

11,781 **Political and Economic Planning.** 'Framework of a Four Year Plan.' *Planning*, 235 (8 June 1945), 1–20.

11,782 **Political and Economic Planning.** 'Resettlement.' *Planning*, 239 (7 September 1945), 1–20.

11,783 **Radcliffe**, R. A. C. 'The ex-Serviceman in civil employment.' *Occup. Psychol.*, XIX, 1 (January 1945), 1–5.

11,784 **Samuels**, Harry. *The Essential Work Order.* London: Stevens, 1945. 38p. (This is the law.)

11,785 **Treasury.** *The scientific Civil Service: reorganisation and recruitment during the reconstruction period.* London: H.M.S.O., 1945. 16p. (Cmd. 6679.)

11,786 **Ince**, *Sir* Godfrey Herbert. 'Mobilisation of man-power.' *Publ. Adm.*, XXIV, 1 (Spring 1946), 3–14.

11,787 **Ince**, *Sir* Godfrey Herbert. 'The mobilisation of manpower in Great Britain for the Second Great War.' *Manchr. Sch.*, XIV, 1 (January 1946), 17–52.
Read before the Manchester Statistical Society on 14 March 1945.

11,788 **Political and Economic Planning.** 'Manpower stocktaking.' *Planning*, 253 (2 August 1946), 1–14.

11,789 **Home Office.** Central Advisory Council. Committee on the Transfer of Members of the National Fire Service to Fire Brigades. *Interim report.* London: H.M.S.O., 1947. 12p.
Chairman: A. S. Hutchinson.

11,790 **Wishart**, John. 'Statistical aspects of demobilization in the Royal Navy.' *R. Statist. Soc. J.*, CX, 1 (1947), 27–44.
Discussion, p. 44–50.
Read before the Royal Statistical Society, 19 December 1946.

11,791 **Davies**, Rhys John. *Bond or free: Mr. J. Rhys Davies, M.P., here re-states the supreme issue of personal liberty menaced by the Control of Engagement Order, 1947.* London: Nigel Cragoe, 1948. 7p.

11,792 **Hancock**, *Sir* William Keith and **Gowing**, M. M. *British war economy.* London: H.M.S.O., 1949. xvii, 583p. (History of the Second World War. United Kingdom civil series.)

11,793 **Rolfe**, Sidney E. 'Manpower allocation in Great Britain during World War II.' *Ind. Labor Relat. Rev.*, v, 2 (January 1952), 173–94.

11,794 **Ince**, *Sir* Godfrey Herbert. *The re-distribution of man-power in Great Britain following the Second Great War*. Manchester: Manchester Statistical Society, 1953. 36p. (Papers series.)

11,795 **United States.** Women's Bureau. *Womanpower committees during World War II: United States and British experience*. Washington, D.C.: Women's Bureau, 1953. 73p. (Bulletin 244.)

11,796 **Rolfe**, Sidney E. 'Manpower allocation under British planning, 1945–1949.' *Am. Econ. Rev.*, XLIV, 3 (June 1954), 354–68.

11,797 **Inman**, P. *Labour in the munitions industries*. London: H.M.S.O., Longmans, Green, 1957. xv, 461p. (History of the Second World War. United Kingdom civil series. War production series.)

11,798 **Parker**, Henry Michael Denne. *Manpower: a study of war-time policy and administration.* London: H.M.S.O., Longmans, Green, 1957. xix, 535p. (History of the Second World War, United Kingdom civil series. General series.)

11,799 **White**, Rudolph Albert. *A comparative analysis of manpower mobilization in Great Britain and the United States during World War II*. 1958–59. (Dissertation, University of Alabama.)

3. National Service

See also Part Three, III, B, 5.

11,800 **Ministry of Defence** and **Ministry of Labour and National Service.** *Increase in the length of full-time National Service with the armed forces*. London: H.M.S.O., 1950. (Cmd. 8026.)

11,801 **Ministry of Labour and National Service.** *Effects of National Service on the education and employment of young men: report on the enquiry*. London: H.M.S.O., 1955.

11,802 **Ministry of Labour and National Service.** *National Service*. London: H.M.S.O., 1955. (Cmd. 9608.)

11,803 **War Office.** *Report of the Committee on the Employment of National Service Men in the United Kingdom*. London: H.M.S.O., 1956. (Cmnd. 35.)

Committee: Sir John Wolfenden, W. D. Gross, Sir Frederick Hooper.

11,804 **Ministry of Defence.** *Report of the Advisory Committee on Recruiting*. London: H.M.S.O., 1958. iv, 70p. (Cmnd. 545.)

11,805 *Recruiting: Government's comments on Report of Advisory Committee on Recruiting (Cmnd. 545)*. London: H.M.S.O., 1958. 13p. (Cmnd. 570.)

11,806 **Thomis**, Malcolm Ian. *The labour movement in Great Britain and compulsory military service*. 1959. (M.A. thesis, University of London.)

11,807 **Ministry of Labour and National Service.** *Call up of men to the forces, 1957–60*. London: H.M.S.O., 1967. (Cmnd. 175.)

See also: 716.

D. LABOUR MOBILITY

See also Part Six, II, E.

1. Vocational Guidance Services

There is a vast literature on vocational guidance but most of it is outside the scope of this bibliography. This section only includes material which is concerned with describing the nature and development of vocational guidance services. The more psychological literature on the techniques of vocational guidance is specifically excluded. See also Part Six, II, A; and Part Seven, IV, D, 2, b.

11,808 **Stott**, Mary Boole. *Report on the present position of vocational guidance and vocational selection*. London: Women's Employment Publishing Co., 1925. 95p.

11,809 **Clift**, Charles E. 'Vocational guidance in Great Britain.' *Int. Labour Rev.*, xv, 4 (April 1927), 547–67.

11,810 **Simmonds**, H. A. T. *Vocational guidance in secondary schools*. 1930–31. (M.A. thesis, University of London.)

11,811 **Allen**, E. P. 'Vocational guidance: the Birmingham experiment.' *Hum. Factor*, VI, 5 (May 1932), 170–3.

11,812 **Parkinson**, C. A. A. 'Vocational guidance for secondary schools.' *Hum. Factor*, VI, 6 (June 1932), 198–208.

'Reprinted in an abbreviated form from the *Kent Education Gazette*.'

11,813 **Macrae**, Angus. *The case for vocational guidance: three lectures*. London: Pitman, 1934. vii, 92p.

11,814 **Ministry of Labour.** National Advisory Councils for Juvenile Employment. *Joint report on the organisation and development of the Vocational Guidance Service of Great Britain*. London: H.M.S.O., 1934. 34p.

11,815 **Tribe**, Frank Newton. 'The national system of vocational guidance.' *Publ. Adm.*, XII, 1 (January 1934), 20–32.

An address to the Institute of Public Administration, November 1933.

11,816 **Hunt**, E. Patricia and **Smith**, Percival. 'Vocational guidance research: ten years' work by the Birmingham Education Committee.' *Occup. Psychol.*, XII, 4 (Autumn 1938), 302–7.

11,817 **Macdonald**, Allan. 'A scheme of vocational guidance for use in an educational area.' *Occup. Psychol.*, XII, 4 (Autumn 1938), 291–301.

'Describes a large-scale experiment in vocational guidance at present being carried out in Edinburgh with the co-operation of the Edinburgh Education Committee and the Ministry of Labour.'

'A paper read to the Extended General Meeting of the British Psychological Society, held at St. Andrews in April, 1938.'

11,818 **Rodger,** Alec. 'Planning for vocational guidance.' *Occup. Psychol.*, XIII, 1 (January 1939), 1–9.

'Based on the second part of a lecture given at a General Meeting of the British Psychological Society in January, 1938.'

11,819 **Child**, H. A. T. 'The Friends' Appointments Board: an experiment in the organization of vocational guidance.' *Occup. Psychol.*, XV, 4 (October 1941), 199–208.

11,820 **Hunt**, E. Patricia. 'The Birmingham experiments in vocational selection and guidance.' *Occup. Psychol.*, XVII, 2 (April 1943), 53–63. (Essays presented to Dr Myers IX.)

'From a collection of essays by past and present members of the Staff [of the National Institute of Industrial Psychology] on the Institute's 21st Anniversary.'

11,821 **Child**, H. A. T. 'Industrial planning and vocational guidance.' *Occup. Psychol.*, XVIII, 2 (April 1944), 69–75. (Essays presented to Dr Myers XVIII.)

'From a collection of essays by past and present members of the Staff, presented on the Institute's 21st anniversary.'

11,822 **Rodger**, Alec. 'The man and his job: from war to peace.' *Occup. Psychol.*, XVIII, 2 (April 1944), 63–8.

'Reprinted from *The Lancet*, September 4th, 1943.'

11,823 **Hunt**, E. Patricia and **Smith**, Percival. 'Vocational psychology and choice of employment.' *Occup. Psychol.*, XIX, 3 (July 1945), 109–16.

A resumé of a report published by the Birmingham Education Committee.

11,824 **Meiklejohn**, John. 'Vocational guidance in a Scottish county area.' *Occup. Psychol.*, XIX, 4 (October 1945), 201–11.

11,825 **Reeves**, Joan Wynn and **Wilson**, V. W. 'Vocational guidance in Warrington.' *Occup. Psychol.*, XXIII, 2 (April 1949), 97–111.

11,826 **Hunt**, H. J. *Vocational guidance in England and Wales*. 1953–54. (M.A. (Educ.) thesis, University of Bristol.)

11,827 **Floud**, Jean E. and **Halsey**, A. H. 'Education and occupation: English secondary schools and the supply of labour.' *Yr. Bk. Educ.* (1956), 519–32.

'A substantial part of this essay is based on a paper "Social aspects of vocational guidance" in the forthcoming *Problèmes de Sociologie du Travail* (*II*) ed. Pierre Naville (Paris).'

11,828 **Northern Ireland.** Ministry of Labour and National Insurance. Committee of Enquiry on Vocational Guidance and Youth Employment Services for Young Persons. *Vocational guidance and employment services for young people in Northern Ireland: report*. Belfast: H.M.S.O., 1959. 24p. (Cmd. 394.)

11,829 **De**, S. *A comparative study of vocational guidance in various countries*. 1959–60. (Ph.D. thesis, University of London.)

11,830 **Rodger**, Alec and **Cavanagh**, Peter. 'Personnel selection and vocational guidance.' Welford, A. J., Argyle, M., Glass, D. V. and Morris, J. N. (eds.). *Society: problems and methods of study*. London: Routledge and Kegan Paul, 1962. p. 217–34.

Revised edition. 1967.

11,831 **Avent**, Catherine. *A careers advisory service for technical institutions*. London: Association of Technical Institutions, 1964. 12p.

11,832 **Teasdale**, J. R. *Industrial rehabilitation and vocational guidance*. 1965–66. (M.A. thesis, University of Hull.)

11,833 **Crinnion**, John. 'Ministry of Labour Occupational Guidance Units.' *Occup. Psychol.*, XLI, 2–3 (April–July 1967), 121–6.

'A paper read at a meeting of the Occupational Psychology Section of the British Psychological Society held on 14th June 1967.'

11,834 **Glenn**, M. J. *Vocational guidance in West Hartlepool, with special reference to the occupational interests of secondary school children*. 1968–69. (M. Ed. thesis, University of Durham.)

11,835 **Confederation of British Industry.** *Careers guidance: a report of a C.B.I. working party*. London: C.B.I., 1969. 17p.

11,836 **White**, G. C., **Raphael**, L. H. and **Crinnion,** John. 'Vocational guidance at the Department of Employment: the work of psychologists.' *Occup. Psychol.*, XLIV (1970), 229–36.

See also: 34.

2. Employment Services

See also Part Six, II, E, 6; and Part Six, IV, A, 4, d.

a. EMPLOYMENT EXCHANGES

11,837 **Scammell**, E. T. *A national labour bureau with affiliated labour registries*. Exeter, 1893. 16p.

11,838 **Urwick**, E. J. 'The St. Pancras Labour Bureau.' *Econ. Rev.*, III, 4 (October 1893), 562–5.

11,839 **Baldock**, G. Yarrow. *Municipal labour bureaux: what they are and what they ought to be. A paper.* London, 1900. 4p.

11,840 **London Reform Union.** *Metropolitan borough councils and labour bureaux.* 1902. (Leaflet N.S. 2.)

11,841 **Nunn**, T. Hancock. 'Municipal labour bureaux.' *Char. Orgn. Rev.*, n.s., XIII, 77 (May 1903), 238–47.
Discusses 'the utility, true function, and line of development of Labour Bureaux in England'.

11,842 **Nunn**, T. Hancock. 'Municipal labour bureaux.' Loch, C. S. (ed.). *Methods of social advance: short studies in social practice by various authors.* London, New York: Macmillan, 1904. p. 96–106.

11,843 **Beveridge**, William Henry. 'Labour bureaux.' *Econ. J.*, XVI, 63 (September 1906), 436–9.
Discussion of the report by A. Lowry, one of the Assistant Inspectors of the Local Government Board.

11,844 **Lowry**, Arthur. *Labour bureaux: report made to the President of the Local Government Board.* London: H.M.S.O., 1906. 32p. (H.C. 86.)

11,845 **Beveridge**, William Henry. 'Labour exchanges and the unemployed.' *Econ. J.*, XVII, 65 (March 1907), 66–81.

11,846 **Macgregor**, D. H. 'Labour exchanges and unemployment.' *Econ. J.*, XVII, 68 (December 1907), 585–9.
Takes up points from the article by W. H. Beveridge, March 1907.

11,847 **Good**, T. 'Unemployment, insurance and labour exchanges.' *Westm. Rev.*, CLXXI, 5 (May 1909), 544–51.

11,848 **Parry**, G. A. 'Labour exchanges here and abroad.' *Westm. Rev.*, CLXXII, 3 (September 1909), 237–44.

11,849 **Beveridge**, *Sir* William Henry. *Labour exchanges in the United Kingdom.* Villeneuve-St Georges: Imp. Coopérative Ouvrière Pr. 1910. 37p. (Conférence internationale du Chômage, Paris, 18–21 September, 1910. Rapport 26.)

11,850 **Mundella**, Anthony John. *Labour exchanges and education.* [1910?] 8p.

11,851 **Clapham**, L. 'Work of the Labour Exchanges in relation to women's employment.' National Conference on the Prevention of Destitution. *Report of the proceedings . . . 1911.* London: King, 1911. p. 405–12.
The author was Organising Officer for Women's Employment in the Board of Trade Labour Exchanges.
Discussion, p. 417–32.

11,852 **Jackson**, Gilbert E. 'The Labour Exchange and the fisheries.' *Econ. J.*, XXI, 84 (December 1911), 624–7.

11,853 **Rey**, Charles Fernand. 'The national system of Labour Exchanges.' National Conference on the Prevention of Destitution. *Report of the proceedings . . . 1911.* London: King, 1911. p. 394–404.
The author was General Manager, Board of Trade Labour Exchanges.
Discussion, p. 417–32.

11,854 **Rowntree**, Arnold S. 'The advantage of the Labour Exchange to the large employer.' National Conference on the Prevention of Destitution. *Report of the proceedings . . . 1911.* London: King, 1911. p. 413–17.
Discussion, p. 417–32.

11,855 **Rowntree**, Benjamin Seebohm and **Lasker**, Bruno. 'Labour exchanges in 1910.' *Bull. Trim. Ass. Int. Lutte Chôm.*, I, 2 (Octobre–December 1911), 397–409.

11,856 **Beveridge**, William Henry and **Rey**, Charles Fernand. 'Labour exchanges.' *Q. J. Int. Ass. Unempl.*, III, 3 (July–September 1913), 766–825.

11,857 **Jones**, David Caradog. 'Labour exchanges in practice: a critical appreciation.' *Q. J. Int. Ass. Unempl.*, III, 3 (July–September 1913), 831–45.

11,858 **Keeling**, Frederic Hillersdon. 'Towards the solution of the casual labour problem.' *Econ. J.*, XXIII, 89 (March 1913), 1–18.
A consideration of the Labour Exchanges Act.

11,859 **Liverpool Fabian Society.** *Industrial conditions after the war: the place of the labour exchanges.* Liverpool, 1916. 15p. (Tracts 14.)

11,860 **Ministry of Labour.** Committee on the Work of the Employment Exchanges. *Report.* London: H.M.S.O., 1920. 32p. (Cmd. 1054.)
Minutes of evidence. 1921. iv, 461p. (Cmd. 1140.)
Chairman: George N. Barnes.

11,861 **Seymour**, John Barton. *The British Employment Exchange.* London: King, 1928. x, 292p.

11,862 **International Labour Office.** 'The use of the Employment Exchange service in Great Britain as a labour clearing house.' *Int. Labour Rev.*, XXIV, 4 (October 1931), 410–17.

11,863 **Chegwidden**, *Sir* Thomas Sidney and **Myrddin-Evans**, *Sir* Guildhaume. *The employment exchange service of Great Britain: an outline of the administration of placing and unemployment insurance.* London: Macmillan, 1934. xiv, 310p.
Another edition. New York: Industrial Relations Counselors, 1934. xiv, 310p.

11,864 **Allen**, R. G. D. and **Thomas**, Brinley. 'The London building industry and its labour recruitment through employment exchanges.' *Econ. J.*, XLVII, 187 (September 1937), 465–82.

11,865 **Anderson**, Cornelia M. 'A view of the British employment exchanges.' *Harv. Bus. Rev.*, XVI, 1 (Autumn 1937), 93–104.

11,866 **Political and Economic Planning.** 'Employment exchanges.' *Planning*, 163 (12 March 1940), 1–15.

11,867 **Ministry of Labour and National Service.** *Report of the Committee on Higher Appointments.* London: H.M.S.O., 1945. 62p. (Cmd. 6576.)

Chairman: Lord Hankey.

11,868 **Warrington**, S. *A national employment service: Great Britain's experience.* 1947. (Ph.D. thesis, University of London.)

11,869 **International Labour Office.** *National employment services: Great Britain.* Geneva: I.L.O., 1952. iv, 189p. (Handbooks on national employment services.)

11,870 **Cleary**, E. J. 'The placings service of the Ministry of Labour.' *Sociol. Rev.*, n.s., IV, 2 (December 1956), 191–8.

11,871 **Baron**, L. D. A. 'United Kingdom.' Organisation for Economic Co-operation and Development. Manpower and Social Affairs Directorate. Social Affairs Division. *The public employment services and management: International Management Seminar, Madrid, 23rd–26th March 1965. Supplement to the final report.* Paris: O.E.C.D., 1966. p. 65–77.

11,872 'Case studies of services of the United Kingdom employment service to management.' Organisation for Economic Co-operation and Development. Manpower and Social Affairs Directorate. Social Affairs Division. *The public employment services and management: International Management Seminar, Madrid, 23rd–26th March 1965. Supplement to the final report.* Paris: O.E.C.D., 1966. p. 201–7.

11,873 **Hunter**, Laurence. 'Cost and benefits in the operation of a public employment service.' Organisation for Economic Co-operation and Development. Manpower and Social Affairs Directorate. Social Affairs Division. *The public employment services and management: International Management Seminar, Madrid, 23rd–26th March 1965. Supplement to the final report.* Paris: O.E.C.D., 1966. p. 153–72.

11,874 **Organisation for Economic Cooperation and Development.** *The public employment services and management: International Management Seminar, Madrid, 23rd–26th March 1965. Final report.* Paris: O.E.C.D., Manpower and Social Affairs Directorate, Social Affairs Division, 1966. 158p. (International seminars, 1965, no. 1.)

The seminar papers were published as a *Supplement* to the *Report*.

11,875 **Organisation for Economic Co-operation and Development.** Manpower and Social Affairs Directorate. Social Affairs Division. *Promoting the placement of older workers.* Paris: O.E.C.D., 1967. 96p.

11,876 **Eire.** Department of Labour. *The placement and guidance service: report by the Institute of Public Administration.* 1968. (V. 4.)

b. YOUTH EMPLOYMENT SERVICE

See also Part Six, II, A; Part Six, II, C, 5; Part Six, II, D, 7; Part Six, IV, A, 4, c; Part Seven, IV, D, 1; and Part Seven, V, B, 2, a.

11,877 **Chamberlain**, Norman. 'Labour exchanges and boy labour.' *Econ. Rev.*, XIX, 4 (October 1909), 400–9.

'Boy labour – which must throughout be held to include Girl labour . . .'

11,878 **Birmingham Education Committee.** *Report of the special sub-committee on the institution of a juvenile employment bureau and care committee in Birmingham.* Birmingham: Percival Jones, 1910. 36p.

11,879 **Keeling**, Frederic Hillersdon. *The Labour Exchange in relation to boy and girl labour.* London: King, 1910. vi, 76p.

11,880 **Knowles**, G. W. *Junior labour exchanges: a plea for closer co-operation between labour exchanges and educational authorities.* London, 1910. 32p.

11,881 **Adler**, Nettie. 'The limitation of juvenile labour.' National Conference on the Prevention of Destitution. *Report of the proceedings . . . 1911.* London: King, 1911. p. 247–53.

The author was a member of the London County Council.

Discussion, p. 265–72.

11,882 **Denman**, Richard D. 'Working of the London Juvenile Advisory Committee.' National Conference on the Prevention of Destitution. *Report of the proceedings . . . 1911.* London: King, 1911. p. 238–46.

Discussion, p. 265–72.

11,883 **Gordon**, Maria Matilda Ogilvie. 'Juvenile employment bureaux.' *Contemp. Rev.*, XCIX (June 1911), 723–32.

11,884 **Gordon**, Maria Matilda Ogilvie. 'The social organisation of adolescence.' National Conference on the Prevention of Destitution. *Report of the proceedings . . . 1911.* London: King, 1911. p. 253–64.

Discussion, p. 265–72.

11,885 **Greenwood**, Arthur. *Juvenile labour exchanges and aftercare.* London: King, 1911. xi, 112p.

Introduction by Sidney Webb.

11,886 **Greenwood**, Arthur. 'The organisation of the juvenile labour market.' *Progress Civic Soc. Ind.*, VI, 2 (April 1911), 97–105.

11,887 **Peck**, J. W. 'Juvenile employment: the Edinburgh method of co-operation between the education authority and the labour exchange.' National Conference on the Prevention of Destitution. *Report of the proceedings . . . 1911.* London: King, 1911. p. 219–37.

The author was Clerk to the School Board of Edinburgh.

Discussion, p. 265–72.

11,888 **Birmingham.** *Explanatory statement on the scheme for school care committees and juvenile employment exchanges.* Birmingham, 1912. 11p.

11,889 **Birmingham Education Committee.** *Report on the Birmingham system of care committees and juvenile employment bureaux.* Birmingham, 1912. 35p.

11,890 **Bray,** Reginald Arthur. 'The function of the Juvenile Advisory Committee.' National Conference on the Prevention of Destitution. *Report of the proceedings... 1912.* London: King, 1912. p. 225–33.

Discussion, p. 260–5.

11,891 **Greenwood,** Arthur. 'Juvenile labour exchanges.' *Bull. Trim. Ass. Int. Lutte Chôm.*, II, 1–2 (janvier–juin 1912), 177–96.

11,892 **Jevons,** H. Winifred. 'The industrial training and placing of juveniles in England.' *J. Polit. Econ.*, XXI, 3 (March 1913), 243–54.

11,893 **Ministry of Labour.** National Advisory Council for Juvenile Employment (England and Wales). *First report.* London: H.M.S.O., 1929. 16p.

Chairman: Lord Shaftesbury.

11,894 **Cross,** T. K. 'Social service or bureaucracy – a problem for the Juvenile Employment Departments and Bureaux.' *Hum. Factor*, x, 10 (October 1936), 347–50.

11,895 **Board of Education** and **Scottish Education Department.** *Youth registration in 1942.* London: H.M.S.O., 1943. 28p. (Cmd. 6446.)

11,896 **Ministry of Labour.** Committee on the Juvenile Employment Service. *Report.* London: H.M.S.O., 1945. 63p.

Chairman: Sir Godfrey H. Ince.

11,897 **Rodger,** Alec. 'The Juvenile Employment Service: four comments for the Ince Report.' *Occup. Psychol.*, XX, 2 (April 1946), 74–80.

Comments on the *Report* of the Committee on Juvenile Employment Service, 1945.

11,898 **Ministry of Labour and National Service.** Central Juvenile Employment Executive. *Memorandum on the exercise by Local Education Authorities of their power to provide a juvenile employment service.* London: H.M.S.O., 1947. 14p.

11,899 **Dawson,** Joan M. *The juvenile employment service.* 1948. (M.A. thesis, University of London.)

11,900 **Ministry of Labour and National Service.** *Youth employment service: memorandum on the exercise by Local Education Authorities in England and Wales and Education Authorities in Scotland of their powers under Section 10 of the Employment and Training Act, 1948.* London: H.M.S.O., 1948. 12p.

11,901 **Parker,** Henry Michael Denne. 'Vocational guidance for juveniles in the United Kingdom.' *Int. Labour Rev.*, LVII, 1–2 (January–February 1948), 15–25.

11,902 **Rodger,** Alec. 'School records: a further comment on the Ince Report.' *Occup. Psychol.*, XXII, 1 (January 1948), 46–9.

11,903 **Ministry of Labour and National Service.** National Youth Employment Council. *Report on the work of the Youth Employment Service, 1947–50.* London: H.M.S.O., 1950.

...*1950–53.* 1954.
...*1953–56.* 1956. 38p.
...*1956–59.* 1959.
...*1959–62.* 1962.
...*1962–65.* 1965.
...*1965–68.* 1968. 72p.

11,904 **Heginbotham,** Herbert. *The Youth Employment Service.* London: Methuen, 1951. x, 222p.

11,905 **Frere,** K. H. B. 'Dual control in the Youth Employment Service.' *Publ. Adm.*, XXXI, 2 (Summer 1953), 145–53.

Haldane Essay Prize essay, 1952.

'A rejoinder', by H. Heginbotham, XXXI, 3 (Autumn 1953), 265–8.

11,906 **James,** Robert. 'The Youth Employment Service.' *Ind. Law. Rev.*, VIII, 1 (July 1953), 52–61.

11,907 **Canner,** H. E. *The Juvenile Employment Service in Manchester, 1910–1939.* 1958. (M.Ed. thesis, University of Manchester.)

11,908 **International Labour Office.** 'Vocational guidance and youth placement in Great Britain.' *Int. Labour Rev.*, LXXX, 3 (September 1959), 250–61.

11,909 **London County Council.** Education Department. *From school to work: the work of the Youth Employment Service in London, 1955–58.* London: L.C.C., 1959. 24p.

11,910 **Northern Ireland.** *Vocational guidance and employment services for young persons in Northern Ireland: report of the Committee of Enquiry.* Belfast: H.M.S.O., 1959. 24p. (Cmd. 394.)

11,911 **Ministry of Labour.** Central Youth Employment Executive. *Interim report on the National Youth Employment Council on the employment and training of young people, April 1959–October 1961.* London: H.M.S.O., 1961. 21p.

Chairman: Lord Coleraine.

11,912 **Aja,** K. A. *A critical survey of the Youth Employment Service, with special reference to vocational guidance.* 1962. (M.Sc.Tech. thesis, University of Manchester.)

11,913 **Rodger,** Alec. 'Arranging jobs for the young.' *New Soc.*, 10 (6 December 1962), 21–3.

11,914 **Jenks,** Richard E. 'The Youth Employment Service – why, what, and how.' *Statist. Soc. Inq. Soc. Ir. J.*, XXI, 1 (1962–63), 71–80.

11,915 **Burgess,** Tyrrell. 'A day in social work. V. The Youth Employment Officer.' *New Soc.*, 21 (21 February 1963), 23.

11,916 **Jahoda**, Gustav and **Chalmers**, Alastair D. 'The Youth Employment Service: a consumer perspective.' *Occup. Psychol.*, XXXVII, 1 (January 1963), 20–43.

11,917 **France**, G. H. *Experiments in an ongoing Youth Employment Service.* 1963–64. (M.Sc. thesis, University of Edinburgh.)

11,918 **Aja**, K. A. *A study of the utilisation of manpower in the Youth Employment Service.* 1964–65. (Ph.D. thesis, University of London.)

11,919 **Cook**, G. *Development and administration of the Youth Employment Service since 1945.* 1965. (M.A. (Econ.) thesis, University of Manchester.)

11,920 **Jenks**, Richard E. 'The organization and functions of a youth employment service.' *Administration*, XIII, 1 (Spring 1965), 59–68.

11,921 **Ministry of Labour.** Central Youth Employment Executive. *The future development of the Youth Employment Service: report of a working party of the National Youth Employment Council.* London: H.M.S.O., 1965. iv, 92p.
Chairman: Countess of Albemarle.

11,922 **A Study Group.** *The Youth Employment Service.* London: Fabian Society, 1966. 28p. (Young Fabian pamphlet 14.)

11,923 **Beetham**, David. *Immigrant school leavers and the Youth Employment Service in Birmingham.* London: Institute of Race Relations, 1967. 51p. (Special series.)

11,924 **Beetham**, David. *Immigrant school leavers and the Youth Employment Service in Birmingham.* 1967. 95p. (M.A. thesis, University of Manchester.)

11,925 **Inner London Education Authority.** Youth Employment Service. *Careers guidance in Inner London 1964 to 1966: the work of the Youth Employment Service during three years ending 31 August 1967.* London: I.L.E.A., 1968. 28p.

3. Regional Manpower Planning

See also Part Six, II, C, 2; Part Six, II, D, 5; and Part Seven, IV, C.

11,926 **Hall**, A. D. 'The Development Act and unemployment.' National Conference on the Prevention of Destitution. *Report of the proceedings . . . 1911.* London: King, 1911. p. 517–21.
The author was a member o. the Development Commission.
Discussion, p. 542–50.

11,927 **Colyer**, William Thomas. *The worker's passport: a study of the legal restrictions on migrant workers.* London: Labour Research Department, 1928. 100p.
Prepared for the Labour Defence Council.

11,928 **Labour Party.** *The distress in South Wales: report of Labour Committee of Inquiry.* London: Labour Party, 1928. 18p.

11,929 **Inter-Departmental Committee on Migration Policy.** *Report.* London: H.M.S.O., 1934. 93p. (Cmd. 4689.)
Chairman: Malcolm MacDonald.

11,930 **Political and Economic Planning.** 'Regional development, 1.' *Planning*, 53 (18 June 1935), 1–13.

11,931 **Political and Economic Planning.** 'Regional planning, 2.' *Planning*, 59 (8 October 1935), 1–15.

11,932 **Edgeworth**, Kenneth Essex. *A plan for the distressed areas.* London, 1936. 11p.

11,933 **Labour Party.** Distressed Areas Commission. *Central Scotland: report of the Commission.* London, 1937. 24p.

11,934 **Labour Party.** Distressed Areas Commission. *Durham and the North East Coast: report of the Commission.* London, 1937. 28p.

11,935 **Labour Party.** Distressed Areas Commission. *Labour and the distressed areas: a programme of immediate action. Interim report of the Commission.* London, 1937. 15p.

11,936 **Labour Party.** Distressed Areas Commission. *South Wales: report of the Commission.* London, 1937. 32p.

11,937 **Witcutt**, William Purcell. *The dying lands: a fifty years' plan for the distressed areas.* London: Distributist League, 1937. 46p.

11,938 **Stewart**, Margaret. *Taking work to the workers: unemployment and the development areas.* London: Fabian Publications and Gollancz, 1946. 29p. (Fabian research series 116.)

11,939 **Sykes**, Joseph. 'Remedies for localised unemployment.' *Manchr. Sch.*, XIX, 1 (January 1951), 71–88.

11,940 **Sykes**, Joseph. 'Social aspects of the control of industrial location.' *Sociol. Rev.*, n.s., II, 2 (December 1954), 229–38.

11,941 **Sykes**, Joseph. 'Some results of distribution of industry policy.' *Manchr. Sch.*, XXIII, 1 (January 1955), 1–21.

11,942 **Robson**, Peter. 'Growth of employment and diversification of industry in the development areas.' *Oxf. Econ. Pap.*, n.s., VIII, 1 (February 1956), 60–77.

11,943 **Odber**, A. J. 'Local unemployment and the 1958 Act.' *Scott. J. Polit. Econ.*, VI, 3 (November 1959), 211–28.
An examination of the Distribution of Industry (Industrial Finance) Act, 1958, and a discussion of what further action may be necessary to deal with the problem of local unemployment.

11,944 **Peacock**, Alan Turner and **Dosser**, Douglas G. M. 'The new attack on localized unemployment.' *Lloyds Bank Rev.*, n.s., 55 (January 1960), 17–28.
'The need for new policies, especially to help labour mobility.' (Townroe.)

11,945 **United States.** Bureau of Labor Statistics. *Foreign labor information: aid to labor surplus areas in Great Britain, Belgium, the Federal Republic of Germany, and Sweden.* Washington, D.C.: U.S.G.P.O., 1960. 40p. (Foreign labour information 20.)

11,946 **Jones**, Lyndon Hamer. 'Industrial location and unemployment.' *Contemp. Rev.*, CCIII, 1165 (February 1963), 71–6.

11,947 **Select Committee on Estimates.** Session 1962–63. Seventh report. *Administration of the Local Employment Act, 1960.* London: H.M.S.O., 1963. 278p.

11,948 **Simpson**, David. 'Investment, employment, and government expenditures in the Highlands, 1951–1960.' *Scott. J. Polit. Econ.*, X, 3 (November 1963), 259–84.

11,949 **Aiad**, A. A. *A study of some aspects of government policy with regard to regional unemployment in Great Britain. 1934–1962.* 1964. (M.A. (Econ.) thesis, University of Manchester.)

11,950 **Holmans**, A. E. 'Industrial Development Certificates and the control of the growth of employment in South-East England.' *Urb. Studies*, I, 2 (November 1964), 138–52.

Uses figures from the period 1950 to 1962.

11,951 **Richardson**, H. W. and **West**, E. G. 'Must we always take work to the workers?' *Lloyds Bank Rev.*, n.s., 71 (January 1964), 35–48.

11,952 **Jay**, Douglas. 'Distribution of industry policy and related issues.' *Econ. J.*, LXXV, 300 (December 1965), 736–41.

11,953 **Needleman**, L. 'What are we going to do about the regional problem?' *Lloyds Bank Rev.*, n.s., 75 (January 1965), 45–58.

11,954 **Goodman**, J. F. B. and **Samuel**, Peter James. 'The motor industry in a development district: a case study of the labour factor.' *Br. J. Ind. Relat.*, IV, 3 (November 1966), 336–65.

11,955 **Miernyk**, William H. 'Experience under the British Local Employment Acts of 1960 and 1963.' *Ind. Labour Relat. Rev.*, XX, 1 (October 1966), 30–49.

11,956 **Schnitzer**, Martin. *Programs for relocating workers used by governments in selected countries.* Washington, D.C.: U.S.G.P.O., 1966. 76p. (U.S. Congress. Joint Economic Committee. Economic policies and practices. Paper 8.)

11,957 **Thirlwall**, A. P. 'The Local Employment Acts 1960 and 1963: a progress report.' *Yorks. Bull. Econ. Soc. Res.*, XVIII, 1 (May 1966), 49–63.

11,958 **Thirlwall**, A. P. 'Migration and regional unemployment: some lessons for regional planning.' *Westm. Bank Rev.* (November 1966), 31–44.

An argument for more control over the movement of labour.

11,959 **Brown**, Arthur Joseph. 'The "green paper" on the development areas.' *Natn. Inst. Econ. Rev.*, 40 (1967), 26–33.

'A discussion of the proposals for a regional employment premium, including an appendix on regional multipliers.' (Townroe.)

11,960 **Department of Economic Affairs** and **Treasury.** *The development areas: a proposal for a regional employment premium.* London: H.M.S.O., 1967. 20p. (Cmnd. 3310.)

11,961 **Metcalf**, David and **Cowling**, Keith. 'Regional wage inflation in the United Kingdom.' *Distr. Bank Rev.*, 162 (June 1967), 46–60.

The case for a regional employment tax.

11,962 **Organisation for Economic Co-operation and Development.** Manpower and Social Affairs Directorate. Social Affairs Division. *Government financial aids to geographical mobility in OECD countries.* Paris: O.E.C.D., 1967. 36p. (Labour mobility.)

11,963 **Thirlwall**, A. P. 'The impact of the British Local Employment Acts of 1960 and 1963.' *Ind. Labor Relat. Rev.*, XX, 4 (July 1967), 667–70.

11,964 **Thirlwall**, A. P. *Regional unemployment and public policy in Great Britain, 1948 to 1964.* 1967–68. (Ph.D. thesis, University of Leeds.)

11,965 **Hutton**, J. P. and **Hartley**, Keith. 'A regional payroll tax.' *Oxf. Econ. Pap.*, n.s., XX, 3 (November 1968), 417–26.

11,966 **MacKay**, Donald Iain. 'Regional policy and labour reserves in Scotland, II.' *J. Econ. Studies*, III, 1 (March 1968), 65–72.

11,967 **Mair**, Douglas. 'Regional policy and labour reserves in Scotland, I.' *J. Econ. Studies*, III, 1 (March 1968), 55–63.

11,968 **Allen**, E. 'The regional problem in retrospect.' *NE. Group Study Labour Hist. Bull.*, 3 (October 1969), 3–5.

A paper read to the Group at Rutherford College of Technology, 8 November 1968.

11,969 **Hughes**, J. T. 'Employment projection and urban development.' Cullingworth, J. B. and Orr, S. C. (eds.). *Regional and urban studies: a social science approach.* London: Allen and Unwin, 1969. p. 213–41.

11,970 **Hunter**, Laurence Colvin. 'Planning and the labour market.' Cullingworth, J. B. and Orr, S. C. (eds.). *Regional and urban studies: a social science approach.* London: Allen and Unwin, 1969. p. 50–79.

11,971 **Livesey**, F. 'The uses of occupational data in regional planning.' *Urb. Studies*, VII, 2 (June 1970), 137–52.

11,972 **Lloyd**, P. E. 'The impact of development area policies on Merseyside 1949–1967.' Lawton, R. and Cunningham, C. M. (eds.). *Merseyside: social and economic studies.* London: Longmans, 1970. p. 374–410.

11,973 **Schnitzer**, Martin. *Regional unemployment and the relocation of workers: the experience of Western Europe, Canada and the United States.* New York, London: Praeger, 1970. xv, 255p. (Praeger special studies in international economics and development.)

See also: 65.

4. Industrial Manpower Planning and the Selective Employment Tax

See also Part Six, II, B, 3; Part Six, II, C, 3; Part Six, II, D, 6; Part Seven, IV, C; and Part Seven, IV, E, 2.

11,974 **Industrial Transference Board.** *Report.* London: H.M.S.O., 1928. 83p. (Cmd. 3156.)

11,975 **Smith**, Cyril Stanley. *Planned transfer of labour, with special reference to the coal industry.* 1960–61. (Ph.D. thesis, University of London.)

11,976 **Evans**, Eric Wynn. 'The pay-roll tax and the labour market.' *Inst. Bankers J.*, LXXXII, 4 (August 1961), 270–5.

11,977 **Brittenden**, Frederick Henry. *A guide to the Selective Employment Tax.* London: Butterworth, 1966. vi, 81p.
Second edition. 1967. ix, 148p.

11,978 **Butler**, E. B. and **Gidlow**, R. 'The Selective Employment Tax.' *Moor. Wall Street* (Autumn 1966), 58–86.

11,979 **Corner**, Desmond Carteret and **Meyer**, F. V. 'Two discriminatory effects of the selective employment subsidy.' *Bankers' Mag.*, CCII (July 1966), 13–14.

11,980 **Hawtrey**, *Sir* Ralph. 'The employment tax and the balance of payments.' *Bankers' Mag.*, CCII (July 1966), 7–12.

11,981 **Hutton**, J. P. and **Hartley**, Keith. 'The Selective Employment Tax and the labour market.' *Br. J. Ind. Relat.*, IV, 3 (November 1966), 289–303.

11,982 **Newlay**, Simon. *The economic consequences of Mr. Kaldor.* London: Aims of Industry, 1966. 13p.
'This booklet examines the implications for industry of the 1966 Budget and in particular the selective employment tax.'

11,983 **Oppenheimer**, Peter M. 'Economic theory and the Selective Employment Tax.' *Westm. Bank Rev.* (November 1966), 16–30.

11,984 **Treasury**. *Selective employment tax.* London: H.M.S.O., 1966. 12p. (Cmd. 2986.)

11,985 **Corner**, Desmond Carteret and **Fletcher**, C. H. 'The attitude of businesses to Selective Employment Tax.' *Bankers' Mag.*, CCIV (July 1967), 7–9.

11,986 **Economic Development Committee for the Distributive Trades.** *Selective employment tax in the distributive trades.* London: National Economic Development Office, 1967. 4p.

11,987 **Evans**, Eric Wynn. 'The S.E.T. and the labour market.' *Bankers' Mag.*, CCIV (October 1967), 190–3.

11,988 **Corner**, Desmond Carteret and **Fletcher**, C. H. 'Some effects of Selective Employment Tax on the construction and service industries.' *Oxf. Univ. Inst. Econ. Statist. Bull.*, XXXI, 1 (February 1969), 47–54.

11,989 **Foley**, B. J. and **Harvey**, M. G. 'A replacement for S.E.T.' *Bankers' Mag.*, CCX, 1516 (July 1970), 13–16.

11,990 **McLean**, A. A. 'Selective Employment Tax: impact on prices and the balance of payments.' *Scott. J. Polit. Econ.*, XVII, 1 (February 1970), 1–17.

11,991 **Sleeper**, R. D. 'Manpower redeployment and the Selective Employment Tax.' *Oxf. Univ. Inst. Econ. Statist. Bull.*, XXXII, 4 (November 1970), 273–99.

11,992 **Treasury.** *Effects of the Selective Employment Tax; first report: the distributive trades.* London: H.M.S.O., 1970. 328p.
Chairman: W. B. Reddaway.

5. Redundancy Payments

See also Part Six, II, D, 7; Part Six, IV, A, 4, d; Part Six, IV, C, 4; Part Seven, IV, E, 1–2; and Part Seven, V, A.

11,993 **Please**, S. 'The economics of redundancy compensation.' *Distr. Bank Rev.*, 145 (March 1963), 15–34.

11,994 **Evans**, Eric Wynn. 'Redundancy policy and the redeployment of labour.' *Natn. Prov. Bank Rev.*, 66 (May 1964), 8–12.

11,995 **Ministry of Labour.** *The redundancy payments scheme: a guide to the Redundancy Payments Act 1965.* London: the Ministry, 1965. 32p.

11,996 **Wiseman**, Jack and **Hartley**, Keith. 'Redundancy and public policy.' *Moor. Wall Street* (Spring 1965), 45–66.

11,997 **Labour Research Department.** *Short guide to the Redundancy Payments Act.* London: L.R.D., 1966. 16p.

11,998 **Samuels**, Harry and **Stewart-Pearson**, Neville. *Redundancy payments: an annotation and guide to the Redundancy Payments Act, 1965.* London: Knight, 1965 [i.e. 1966]. xiv, 125p.
Second edition. 1970. xv, 197p.
Contains the text of the Act.

11,999 **Ministry of Labour.** *The redundancy payments scheme: a revised guide to the Redundancy Payments Act 1965.* London: the Ministry, 1967. 32p.

12,000 **Whincup**, Michael Hynes. *Redundancy and the law: a short guide to the law on dismissal with and without notice, and rights under the Redundancy Payments Act, 1965.* Oxford, London: Pergamon P., 1967. vii, 79p. (Commonwealth and international library. Supervisory studies.)

12,001 **Labour Research Department.** *Redundancy pay and the High Court.* London: L.R.D., 1968. 8p.
Reprinted from *Labour Research*, April 1968.

12,002 **Drake,** Charles Dominic. 'Labour mobility and the law.' *Ind. Law Soc. Bull.*, 5 (July 1969), 2–22.

12,003 **Freedland,** Mark R. 'Labour mobility and redundancy payments: a comment.' *Ind. Law Soc. Bull.*, 5 (July 1969), 23–5.

12,004 **Rideout,** Roger William. *Reforming the Redundancy Payments Act.* London: Institute of Personnel Management, 1969. 48p.

12,005 **McCormick,** Charles E. 'The Redundancy Payments Act in the practice of the Industrial Tribunals.' *Br. J. Ind. Relat.*, VIII, 3 (November 1970), 334–49.

See also: 13,313.

E. TRAINING AND RETRAINING

This section includes material on government support for vocational and industrial training narrowly defined. It generally excludes material on education more broadly defined, the educational system and planning, and non-industrially based adult and worker education. Many popular management and professional journals also include material on training but this has not been included. See also Part Three, III, L; Part Six, II, B, 3; and Part Six, IV, A, 4, c, iii.

1. General

12,006 **Waterer,** Clarence. 'Unemployment and its cure: a suggested scheme for military and technical instruction.' *Westm. Rev.*, CLXXI, 2 (February 1909), 154–9.

12,007 **King,** William. *An economic and social analysis of the effects of state-aid for industrial training and professional education, with special reference to the Swansea and Aberystwyth districts.* 1921. (M.A. thesis, University of Wales, Aberystwyth.)

12,008 **Brereton,** Maud Adeline Cloudesley. *Unemployed or reserve? A call to England to make good in peace as she made good in war.* London: Knapp, Drewett, 1930. 31p.

12,009 **Pitman,** *Sir* Isaac James and **Miles,** R. A. *The employer and the new Education Act; prepared from findings of the committee of inquiry appointed by the Council of the British Association for Commercial and Industrial Education.* London: B.A.C.I.E., 1938. 24p.

12,010 **Jones,** M. A. B. 'The emergency training scheme for teachers: an adventure in administration.' *Publ. Adm.*, XXVI, 2 (Summer 1948), 92–9.

12,011 **Lawrence,** P. *The influence of the Technical Instruction Acts on the development of the Local Education Authority in England.* 1957–58. (M.A. (Econ.) thesis, University of Manchester.)

12,012 **British Association for Commercial and Industrial Education.** *Cmnd. 1892: the next step. Report of the BACIE conference, London, 15 January, 1963.* London: B.A.C.I.E., 1963. 78p.

12,013 **Cameron,** G. C. 'Retraining the redundant.' *New Soc.*, IV, 107 (15 October 1964), 12–14.

12,014 **Gordon,** Margaret S. *Retraining and labor market adjustment in Western Europe: report submitted to Office of Manpower, Automation, and Training, U.S. Dept. of Labor.* Berkeley, Calif.: University of California, Institute of Industrial Relations, 1964. Pagination varies.
Also *Retraining and labor market adjustment in Western Europe.* Washington, D.C.: Office of Manpower, Automation and Training, 1965. xvi, 226p. (Manpower automation research monograph 4.)

12,015 **Entwistle,** R. *Industrial training policy: a study of influences on government intervention, 1958–1962.* 1965. (M.A. (Econ.) thesis, University of Manchester.)

12,016 **Federation of British Industries.** *Education in transition: the implications for industry of the government reports on education and training, 1959–1964.* London: F.B.I., 1965.

12,017 **Gordon,** Margaret S. *Retraining programs at home and abroad.* Berkeley, Calif.: U. of California, Institute of Industrial Relations, 1965. 11p.

12,018 **Jones,** Gareth. 'Opportunity for skill.' Bow Group. *The Conservative challenge.* London: Batsford, Conservative Political Centre, 1965. p. 82–95.

12,019 **Gordon,** Margaret S. 'The comparative experience with retraining programmes in the United States and Europe.' Stieber, J. (ed.). *Employment problems of automation and advanced technology: an international perspective.* London: Macmillan; New York: St Martin's P., 1966. p. 254–77.
Discussion, p. 294–7.

12,020 **Hollander,** Samuel. 'The role of the state in vocational training: the classical economists' view.' *Sth. Econ. J.*, XXXIV, 4 (April 1968), 513–25.

12,021 **Wellens,** John. 'The need for and the function of legislation in industrial training.' Hutchings, D. (ed.). *Education for industry: Symposium on the Integration of Further Education and Industrial Training.* London: Longmans, 1968. p. 11–18.

12,022 **Foley,** B. J. *The development of, and case for, a positive government training policy in the United Kingdom.* 1968–69. (M.A. thesis, University of Liverpool.)

12,023 **Ziderman**, Adrian. 'Costs and benefits of adult retraining in the United Kingdom.' *Economica*, n.s., XXXVI, 144 (November 1969), 363–76.

12,024 **Administration.** 'AnCO – the industrial training authority.' *Administration*, XVIII, 1 (Spring 1970).
Special issue on An Chomhairle Oiliuna (AnCO).

See also: 12,070.

2. Industrial Training Boards and Government Training Centres

See also Part Seven, IV, D, 4.

12,025 **Ministry of Labour.** *Industrial training: government proposals.* London: H.M.S.O., 1962. 6p. (Cmnd. 1892.)

12,026 **British Association for Commercial and Industrial Education.** *The Industrial Training Act: report of the Bacie conference, London, 29 April, 1964.* London: B.A.C.I.E., 1964. 36p.

12,027 **Engineering Employers' Federation.** Lancashire and Cheshire Regional Committee. *The Industrial Training Act, 1964: main provisions and obligations. Proceedings of a conference held on Wednesday, 27th October, 1965, at the Houldsworth Hall, Deansgate, Manchester.* [Manchester?]: the Committee, 1966. 31 leaves.
Chairman: H. G. G. Gregory.
Speaker: F. Metcalfe.

12,028 **British Association for Commercial and Industrial Education.** *Industrial training boards: progress report no. 2.* London: B.A.C.I.E., 1967.

12,029 **British Industrial Research Associations.** *Report of Industrial Training Act Symposium, 16th November 1966.* Cambridge: British Welding Research Association, for the Committee of Directors of Research Associations, 1967. ii, 53p.

12,030 **Hansen**, Gary B. *Britain's Industrial Training Act: its history, development and implications for America.* Washington, D.C.: National Manpower Policy Task Force, 1967. 76p.

12,031 **McCormick**, Brian J. and **Manley**, P. S. 'The Industrial Training Act.' *Westm. Bank Rev.* (February 1967), 44–56.

12,032 **Page**, Graham Terry. *The Industrial Training Act and after.* London: Deutsch, 1967. 357p.

12,033 **Stretch**, J. A. *Some implications of the Industrial Training Act, 1964.* 1967. (M.Sc. thesis, University of Manchester.)

12,034 **Bretten**, G. R. 'Industrial training in Britain.' *Labor Law J.*, XIX, 6 (June 1968), 358–63.

12,035 **British Association for Commercial and Industrial Education.** *Is it working? The Industrial Training Act in retrospect: papers presented at the B.A.C.I.E. Spring Conference 1967.* London: B.A.C.I.E., 1968. 26p.

12,036 **Bury**, M. O. 'The responsibilities of industry and of Industrial Training Boards.' Hutchings, D. (ed.). *Education for industry: Symposium on the Integration of Further Education and Industrial Training.* London: Longmans, 1968. p. 19–28.

12,037 **Confederation of British Industry.** *The operation of the Industrial Training Act: a survey by the CBI.* London: C.B.I., 1968.

12,038 **Industrial Society.** *Some notes on the operation of the Industrial Training Act 1964 as at end February 1968.* London: the Society, 1968. 57 leaves. (Information survey & report series 129.)

12,039 **Giles**, W. J. *A critical assessment of the initial impact of the Industrial Training Act, 1964, on selected industrial training schemes.* 1968–69. (M.A. thesis, University of Nottingham.)

12,040 **Garbutt**, D. *Training costs, with reference to the Industrial Training Act.* London: Gee, 1969. 204p.

12,041 **Jury**, Geoffrey M. 'Industrial training boards.' *New Soc.*, XIII, 349 (5 June 1969), 875–6.

12,042 **Lees,** Dennis and **Chiplin**, Brian. 'The economics of industrial training.' *Lloyds Bank Rev.*, 96 (April 1970), 29–41.
On the 1964 Industrial Training Act.

12,043 **Livesey**, F. 'The operations of Government Training Centres.' *Oxf. Univ. Inst. Econ. Statist. Bull.*, XXXIII, 1 (February 1970), 33–45.

12,044 **Mukherjee**, Santosh. 'Changing manpower needs: a study of Industrial Training Boards.' *PEP Broad.*, XXXVI, 523 (November 1970). iv, 123p.

12,045 **Toft**, K. S. 'A training board for banking, insurance and finance.' *Bankers' Mag.*, CCIX, 1512 (March 1970), 124–6.

3. Disabled Workers

See also Part Six, II, C, 7; and Part Seven, IX, B, 3.

12,046 **International Labour Office.** 'The industrial training of disabled men in the United Kingdom.' *Int. Labour Rev.*, II, 2–3 (May–June 1921), 117–30 (247–60).

12,047 **Select Committee on the Training and Employment of Disabled Ex-Service-Men.** *Report, proceedings, minutes of evidence, appendices.* London: H.M.S.O., 1922. xlvi, 447p.
Chairman: Sir John Davidson.
Extracts from report. 1923.

12,048 **Ministry of Health, Home Office,** and **Scottish Office.** Inter-Departmental Committee on the Rehabilitation of Persons injured by Accidents. *Report.* London: H.M.S.O., 1937.
Final report. 1939.

12,049 **Levy,** Hermann. *Back to work? The case of the partially disabled worker.* London: Gollancz and Fabian Society, 1941. 24p. (Research series 56.)

12,050 **Eagar,** Waldo McGillycuddy. 'Blind welfare in England and Wales.' Robson, W. A. (ed.). *Social security.* London: Allen and Unwin, 1943. p. 173–83.
Second edition. 1945.
Third edition. 1948.

12,051 **Inter-Departmental Committee on the Rehabilitation and Resettlement of Disabled Persons.** *Report.* London: H.M.S.O., 1943. 51p. (Cmd. 6415.)
Chairman: G. Tomlinson.
The interim report of 1942 was not published.

12,052 **International Labour Office.** 'Rehabilitation and resettlement of disabled persons in Great Britain.' *Int. Labour Rev.*, XLVIII, 1 (July 1943), 43–55.

12,053 **Ministry of Fuel and Power.** *Report of the advisory committee on the treatment and rehabilitation of coal miners in the Wales region suffering from pneumokoniosis.* London: H.M.S.O., 1944.
Chairman: William Jones.

12,054 **Ministry of Labour and National Service.** Standing Committee on Rehabilitation and Resettlement of Disabled Persons. *Report.* London: H.M.S.O., 1946.
Chairman: Sir H. Wiles.
Second report. 1948.

12,055 **Malisoff,** Harry. 'The British Disabled Persons (Employment) Act.' *Ind. Labor Relat. Rev.*, v, 2 (January 1952), 249–57.

12,056 **Maule,** Harry Gordon. 'A report on the study of the rehabilitation services of Great Britain.' *Occup. Psychol.*, XXVI, 4 (October 1952), 225–33.
Based on the Chairman's address to the Industrial Section of the British Psychological Society.

12,057 **Buxton,** W. L. 'Industrial rehabilitation units: a British experiment.' *Int. Labour Rev.*, LXVII, 6 (June 1953), 535–48.

12,058 **Political and Economic Planning.** 'The disabled worker.' *Planning*, XX, 368 (26 July 1954), 173–88.

12,059 **Usdane,** William Miller. *A comparative study of vocational rehabilitation legislation for the severely handicapped orthopedic civilian in Great Britain and the United States.* 1955. 717p. (Ph.D. thesis, New York University.)

12,060 **Ministry of Labour and National Service.** *Report of the Committee of Inquiry on the rehabilitation, training and resettlement of disabled persons.* London: H.M.S.O., 1956. v, 126p. (Cmd. 9883.)
Chairman: Lord Piercy.

12,061 **Vandyk,** Neville D. 'The Piercy Report.' *Ind. Law Rev.*, XI, 3 (January 1957), 148–58.
On *The rehabilitation, training and resettlement of disabled persons* (Cmd. 9883), 1956.

12,062 **Edwards,** J. L. 'Remploy: an experiment in sheltered employment for the severely disabled in Great Britain.' *Int. Labour Rev.*, LXXVII, 2 (February 1958), 147–59.

12,063 **European Seminar on Sheltered Employment, The Hague, 1959.** *European Seminar on Sheltered Employment, 1959, August 31–September 8, The Hague, Netherlands.* The Hague: Nederlandse Centrale Vereniging voor Gebrekkigenzorg, [1959?]. 171p.

12,064 **Ministry of Labour and National Service.** Resettlement Advisory Board. *Progress report, 1957–59.* London: H.M.S.O., 1959. (Cmnd. 789.)

12,065 **Northern Ireland.** *The question of sheltered employment: a report by the Central Advisory Council on the Employment of the Disabled.* Belfast: H.M.S.O., 1960. v, 25p. (H.C. 1401.)

12,066 **Ministry of Labour.** *Report of the Working Party on Workshops for the Blind.* London: H.M.S.O., 1962. xi, 143p.
Chairman: J. G. Stewart.

12,067 **British Council for Rehabilitation of the Disabled.** *The handicapped school-leaver: report of a working party commissioned by the British Council for Rehabilitation of the Disabled under the chairmanship of Elfred Thomas, and in Scotland under the chairmanship of Professor Thomas Ferguson.* London: the Council, 1964. 172p.

12,068 **Medical Research Council.** *The industrial rehabilitation of long-stay schizophrenic patients: a study of 45 patients at an Industrial Rehabilitation Unit.* London: H.M.S.O., 1964. vi, 42p. (Memoranda 42.)
By J. K. Wing, D. H. Bennett and John Denham.

12,069 **Black,** Bertram J. *Industrial therapy for the mentally ill: observations on developments in Western Europe and significance for programs in the U.S.* New York: printed at Alfro Work Shops, 1965. 77p.
'Report of Project MH-1405, supported by the National Institute of Mental Health, U.S. Public Health Service, Department of Health, Education, and Welfare.'

12,070 **Reubens,** Beatrice G. *The hard-to-employ: European programs.* New York, London: Columbia U.P., 1970. xxiii, 420p.

See also: 11,380; 11,389.

V. REGULATION OF TERMS AND CONDITIONS OF EMPLOYMENT

A. INDIVIDUAL EMPLOYEE–EMPLOYER RELATIONSHIP

1. General

This section includes general works on such topics as the law surrounding the contract of employment and the payment of wages. More specialised references relating to discipline and dismissal are included in Part Seven, V, A, 2; those dealing with redundancy payments are in Part Seven, IV, D, 5; and those dealing with the employers' liability for industrial injury are in Part Seven, IX, B, 3. See also Part Six, IV, A, 1.

12,071 **Abbott**, Charles, Baron Tenterden. *A treatise of the law relative to merchant ships and seamen.* London: E. and R. Brooke, 1802. xxvii, 418p.
Fourteenth and last edition. Edited by J. P. Aspinall, B. Aspinall and H. S. Moore. London: Shaw, 1901. cii, 1356, 87p.

12,072 **Kay**, Joseph. *The law relating to shipmasters and seamen, their appointment, duties, powers.* London, 1875. 2v.
Second edition, by J. W. Mansfield and G. W. Duncan. London: Stevens and Hayes, 1894. xcvi, 825p.

12,073 **Smith**, James Walter. *A handy book on the law of master and servant.* London: Effingham Wilson, 1880. 89, xxvp. (Wilson's legal handy books.)
Earlier printings, 1860, etc.
New edition. 1892. 127p. Re-written.
New edition, by G. F. Emery. 1908. 137p.
Revised edition, by G. F. Emery. 1925. 150p.

12,074 **Baker**, Charles Edmund. *The law of master and servant.* London: Warne, 1881. 176p.

12,075 **Bates**, Arthur Henry. 'Irish linen laws and proposed amendments thereof.' *Statist. Soc. Inq. Soc. Ir. J.*, VIII, 3 (December 1881), 203–16.

12,076 **Fraser**, Patrick, Lord Fraser. *Treatise on master and servant according to the law of Scotland.* Edinburgh: T. and T. Clark, 1882 [i.e. 1881]. lix, 834p.
Third edition.
Previous editions, 1846, 1872.

12,077 **Atherley-Jones**, Llewellyn Arthur. *The miners' manual: a legal hand-book for employer and employed.* London: Cassell, 1882. viii, 108p.

12,078 **Greenwood**, James. *A concise handbook of the laws relating to medical men.* London: Baillière, 1882. xvi, 214p.
'Together with a preface and a chapter on the law relating to lunacy practice, by L. S. Forbes-Winslow.'

12,079 **Dalton**, James. *The Solicitors' Remuneration Act, 1881, with scale of charges.* London: Drake, 1883. ix, 78p.

12,080 **Evans**, Patrick Fleming. *Solicitors' Remuneration Act, 1881, and the General Order made in pursuance thereof.* London: Maxwell, 1883. v, 94p.
With notes and tables.

12,081 **Macdonell**, *Sir* John. *The law of master and servant.* London: Stevens, 1883. xxxiv, 717p.
Second edition, by Edward A. Mitchell Innes. 1908. lxxxvi, 899p.

12,082 **Stretton**, Clement Edwin. *A few remarks on railway servants and the law.* Leicester: J. and T. Spencer, 1883. 8p.
Fourth edition.

12,083 **Eversley**, William Pinder. *The law of the domestic relations, including husband and wife, parent and child, guardian and ward, infants, and master and servant.* London: Stevens and Haynes, 1885. xlix, 1097p.
Second edition. 1896. xcv, 1011p.
Third edition. 1906. cx, 1051p.
Fourth edition, by Alexander Cairns. London: Sweet and Maxwell, 1926. lvi, 976p.
Fifth edition, by Alexander Cairns. London: Sweet and Maxwell, 1937. lv, 884p.
Sixth edition, by L. I. Stranger-Jones. London: Sweet and Maxwell, 1951. l, 743p.

12,084 **Fottrell**, *Sir* George and **Fottrell**, John George. *A handy guide to the Labourers (Ireland) Acts, 1883 & 1885, together with the text of these several acts, and a table of procedure.* Dublin: M. H. Gill, 1885. 178, xivp.

12,085 **Incorporated Law Society of the United Kingdom.** *A digest of the Solicitors' Remuneration Act, 1881 and of the opinion of the Council of the Incorporated Law Society on points and questions which have arisen in actual practice down to the end of 1884.* London: the Society, 1885. 56p.

12,086 **Paterson**, James. *Notes on the law of master and servant, with all the authorities.* London: Shaw, 1885. xx, 135p.

12,087 **Roberts**, *Sir* Walworth Howland and **Wallace**, George. *The duty and liability of employers.* London: Reeves and Turner, 1885. xlviii, 551p.
Third edition.
Fourth edition. *The common law and statutory duty and liability of employers.* By the authors and Arthur Harington Graham. London: Butterworth, 1908. lxxxii, 1014, 120p.

12,088 **Smith**, Charles Manley. *A treatise on the law of master and servant.* London: H. Sweet, 1885. lxvii, 803p.
Fourth edition.
Earlier editions, 1852, 1860, 1870.
Fifth edition, by Ernest Manley Smith. Sweet and Maxwell, 1902. xcviii, 823p.
Sixth edition, by E. M. Smith. With notes on the Canadian law by A. C. Forster Boulton. London: Sweet and Maxwell; Toronto: Carswell, 1906. xcvi, 823p.
Seventh edition, by C. M. Knowles. Sweet and Maxwell, 1922. lx, 381p.
Eighth edition, by C. M. Knowles. Sweet and Maxwell, 1931. lxviii, 392p.

12,089 **Redgrave**, Alexander. *Report of Alexander Redgrave, Esq., C.B., H.M. Chief Inspector of Factories, upon the truck system in Scotland.* London: H.M.S.O., 1887. 20p. (C. 4982.)

12,090 **Bradlaugh**, Charles. *Workmen and their wages: the Truck Law and how to enforce it.* West Bromwich: *Labour Tribune*, 1888. 27p.

12,091 **Power**, John Danvers. *The Truck Acts, 1831 & 1887.* London: Stevens, 1888. 24p.

12,092 **Austin**, H. Evans. *The law relating to apprentices, including those bound according to the custom of the city of London.* London: Reeves and Turner, 1890. xvi, 216p.
With appendices containing a digest of statutes, precedents of indentures, etc.

12,093 **A Barrister.** *Servants and masters: the law of disputes, rights and remedies in plain language.* London: H. Cox, 1892. vii. 36p.
Second edition. 1894. vii, 36p.
Third edition, edited by Judge Gye. 1904. vii, 36p.

12,094 **Disney**, Henry William. *The law relating to schoolmasters.* London: Stevens, 1893. vi, 128p.

12,095 **Fox**, Stephen N. and **Black**, Clementina. *The Truck Acts: what they do, and what they ought to do.* London: Women's Trade Union Association, 1894. 15p.

12,096 **White,** Archer Moresby. *A treatise on the constitution and government of solicitors: their rights and duties.* London: Sonnenschein, 1894. xxxix, 495p.

12,097 **White**, James Dundas. *The Merchant Shipping Acts, 1894, with notes, appendices, and index.* London: Eyre and Spottiswoode, 1894. xvi, 628p.
Second edition. *The Merchant Shipping Acts, 1894–1897.* 1897. xvi, 637p.
Third edition. 1906. xliv, 690p.
Fourth edition. 1908. l, 813p.

12,098 **Mansfield**, *Hon.* John William and **Duncan**, George William. *The Merchant Shipping Act, 1894.* London: Stevens and Hayes, 1895. viii, 415p.
'Being a supplement to Kay's *Law relating to shipmasters and seamen.*'

12,099 **Montgomery**, John. *The tenure of office of assistant masters in secondary schools administered under schemes of the Charity Commission.* London: Roberts, 1895. 24p.
Another edition. London: Reeves, 1895. 24p.

12,100 **Scrutton**, *Sir* Thomas Edward. *The Merchant Shipping Act, 1894.* London: Clowes, 1895. xlii, 753p.
Edited with notes and references to decided cases, by T. E. Scrutton.

12,101 **Temperley**, Robert. *The Merchant Shipping Act, 1894 (57 & 58 Vict. c. 60); with an introduction, notes.* London: Stevens, 1895. lxxx, 714p.

12,102 **Baylis**, Thomas Henry. *Rights, duties and relations of domestic servants, and their masters and mistresses.* London: Sampson Low, 1896. xv, 64p.
Fifth edition.
First published 1857.
Sixth edition, with supplement. 1906. 69p.

12,103 **Heney,** Frank St. Maur. *The Merchant Shipping Consolidation Act, 1894.* Dublin: Sealy, 1896. xii, 645p.
With introductory digest, notes, appendix and a general index.

12,104 *Memorandum on the law relating to truck with an appendix of statutes and decided cases, and on the checkweighing clauses in the Coal Mines Regulation Acts, with an appendix of decided cases.* London: H.M.S.O., 1896. (C. 8048.)

12,105 **Standing Committee on Trade, etc.** *Report . . . on the Truck Bill; with the proceedings.* London: H.M.S.O., 1896. (H.C. 196.)

12,106 **M'Neil**, Allan. *Master and servant.* Edinburgh: G. Wilson, 1897. xi, 55p. (Popular law series 4.)

12,107 *Memorandum relating to the Truck Acts for the use of Her Majesty's Inspectors of Mines and Factories.* London: H.M.S.O., 1897. (C. 8330.)

12,108 **Parkyn,** Ernest Albert. *The law of master and servant, with a chapter on apprenticeship.* London: Butterworth, 1897. xxxi, 214p.

12,109 **Wilson**, Mona. 'The Truck Act of 1896.' *Econ. Rev.*, VII, 3 (July 1897), 385–90.

12,110 **Graham**, Arthur Harington. *Master and servant: a complete handbook relating to the law between master and servant.* London: Ward, Lock, 1899. 128p. (Ward, Lock and Co's legal handbooks.)

12,111 **Haldane**, Richard Burdon. 'The labourer and the law.' *Contemp. Rev.*, LXXXIII (March 1903), 362–72.

12,112 **Organ**, Thomas Arthur. *The law relating to schools and teachers.* Leeds: E. J. Arnold, 1903. xvi, 566p.
A manual for the use of members of school boards.

12,113 **Edgar,** W. W. *Railway labour legislation in Great Britain and Canada.* 1904. 41p. (M.A. thesis, University of Toronto.)

12,114 **Umpherston,** Francis Albert. *The law of master and servant.* Edinburgh: W. Green, 1904. xxxv, 331p.

12,115 **McGregor,** J. P. *The doctrine of common employment in England and in Canada: a study in comparative jurisprudence.* 1905. 65p. (M.A. thesis, University of Toronto.)

12,116 **Ruegg,** Alfred Henry. *The laws regulating the relation of employer and workman in England: a course of six lectures.* London: Clowes, 1905. viii, 199p.

12,117 **Barrett,** William and **MacCann,** Hugh J. *The law of the labourers and the labourers question . . including the full text of the Labourers – Ireland – Acts.* Dublin: Sealy and Bryers, 1906. 250p.

12,118 **Cole,** Sanford Darley. *The Merchant Shipping Act, 1906: practical handbook for shipowners, masters, and all connected with the mercantile marine; containing the complete text of the Act.* Glasgow: J. Brown, 1907. ix, 90p.

12,119 **Holdsworth,** William Andrews. *The law of master and servant.* London: Routledge, 1907. xi, 231p.

New edition, revised and enlarged by J. R. McIlraith.

Earlier editions, 1873, 1875.

12,120 **Jackson,** Thomas Chalice. *The law of master and servant.* London: Macdonald and Martin, 1907. viii, 180p.

12,121 **Departmental Committee on the Truck Acts.** Vol. I. *Report, appendices.* London: H.M.S.O., 1908. iv, 142p. (Cd. 4442.)

Vols. II–III. *Minutes of evidence.* 1908. (Cd. 4443, 4444.)

Vol. IV. *Précis of evidence, appendices.* 1909. (Cd. 4568.)

Chairman: T. Shaw.

12,122 **Henle,** Fred T. H. 'The right and duty to work.' *Social. Rev.,* II, 7 (September 1908), 546–60.

Examination of the law, past and present.

12,123 **Moulder,** Priscilla E. 'The Truck Act in Shetland.' *Social. Rev.,* II, 12 (February 1909), 926–9.

12,124 **Myer,** Ernest Alexander. *Apprenticeship law: a practical handbook.* London: Stevens, 1910. viii, 76p.

12,125 **Kerly,** *Sir* Duncan Mackenzie and **Kenrick,** George Harry Blair. *Bar Final examination, 1912: special subjects. 1. Carriers. 2. Master and servant.* London: Sweet and Maxwell; Edinburgh: W. Green, 1911. 122p.

1. By D. M. Kerly.

2. By G. H. B. Kenrick.

'Reprinted from the second edition of the Encyclopaedia of the laws of England.'

12,126 **Casswell,** Joshua David. *The law of domestic servants, with a chapter on the National Insurance Act, 1911.* London: Jordan, 1913. xix, 126p.

Second edition. 1914. xix, 126p.

12,127 **Baty,** Thomas. *Vicarious liability: a short history of the liability of employers, principals, partners, associations and trade-union members.* Oxford: Clarendon P., 1916. 244p.

12,128 **Woolwich District Trades and Labour Council** and **Woolwich Labour Representation Association.** *Memorandum on industrial and civil liberties.* [1916?] 7p. (Memoranda 1.)

12,129 **Ewer,** Monica. *Civil liberties 1918.* London: National Council of Civil Liberties, 1918. 19p.

Chap. IV. 'Industrial freedom.'

12,130 **Cockburn,** John Henry. *The law of checkweighing.* London: Stevens, 1919. xiv, 136p.

12,131 **Committee Appointed to Consider the Question of the Regulation of Street Trading in the Metropolitan Police District.** *Report.* London: H.M.S.O., 1922. (Cmd. 1624.)

12,132 **Davies,** Edward John. *The development of a master's civil vicarious liability in tort for the acts of his servants to third parties.* 1923. (LL.B. thesis, University of Wales.)

12,133 **Pigou,** Arthur Cecil. 'Long and short hirings.' *Essays in applied economics.* London: King, 1923.

Revised edition. 1924. p. 24–33.

From the *Contemporary Review,* September 1922.

12,134 **Garsia,** Marston and **Featherstone,** Belford Kinchant. *The law relating to master and servant in a nutshell.* London: Sweet and Maxwell, 1925. v, 34p.

Second edition, by M. Garsia. 1933. v, 50p.

12,135 **Marlow,** George Stanley Withers. *Contracts of service.* London, 1925. 25p.

12,136 **Eire.** Dáil Éireann. Special Committee on the Railways (Existing Officers and Servants) Bill, 1926. *Special report.* 1926. (T. 41.)

12,137 **Cassidy,** Harry M. 'The emergence of the free labor contract in England.' *Am. Econ. Rev.,* XVIII, 2 (June 1928), 201–26.

12,138 **Open Door Council.** *Restrictive legislation and the industrial woman worker.* London, 1928. 16p.

12,139 **Ashton,** Thomas Southcliffe and **Sykes,** Joseph. *The coal industry of the eighteenth century.* Manchester: Manchester U.P., 1929. ix, 268p. (Publications of the University of Manchester CXCII. Economic history series 5.)

Chap. VI. 'The miners' bond in the North of England.'

Second edition. 1964. ix, 268p.

12,140 **Batt**, Francis Raleigh. *The law of master and servant.* London: Pitman, 1929. xxvii, 384p.
Second edition. 1933. xxxiv, 488p.
Third edition. 1939. xxxvii, 531p.
Fourth edition, by J. Crossley Vaines. 1950. xxxvi, 520p.
Fifth edition, by George J. Webber. 1967. cix, 698p.

12,141 **Diamond**, Arthur Sigismund. *The law of the relation between master and servant.* London: Stevens, 1932. lxvi, 348p.
Second edition. *The law of master and servant.* London: Stevens, Sweet and Maxwell, 1946. xl, 318p.
Supplement to second edition, by Barry Credlow. 1952.

12,142 **Shields**, Bernard Francis. *The labour contract.* London: Burns, Oates, 1936. xvi, 152p.

12,143 **Home Office.** *Memorandum on the Truck Acts.* London: H.M.S.O., 1937. 14p.

12,144 **Robson**, William Alexander and **Gold**, Joseph. 'Common employment: reflections on the doctrine in the light of *Wilsons and Clyde Coal Company Ltd. v. English.*' *Mod. Law Rev.*, I, 3 (December 1937), 224–30.
W. A. Robson, p. 224–5.
J. Gold, p. 225–30.

12,145 **Unger**, J. 'Common employment: reflections on two recent cases.' *Mod. Law Rev.*, II, 1 (June 1938), 43–8.

12,146 **Chapman**, Stephen. 'Common employment: a vindication.' *Mod. Law Rev.*, II, 4 (March 1939), 291–5.

12,147 **Samuels**, Harry. *The industrial worker's guide to his rights and duties.* London: Pitman, 1943. 40p.
Second edition. 1944. 40p.

12,148 **Osmond**, Michael. *The law relating to master and servant in a nutshell.* London: Sweet and Maxwell, 1945. iv, 41p.
Supplement. 1953. 7p.

12,149 **Kahn-Freund**, Otto. 'Spare-time activities of employees.' *Mod. Law Rev.*, IX, 2 (July 1946), 145–53.
Hivac, Ltd. v. *Park Royal Scientific Instruments, Ltd.* [1946].

12,150 **Lewis**, W. Arthur. 'Spare-time activities of employees: an economist's comment on *Hivac, Ltd. v. Park Royal Scientific Instruments Ltd.* [1946] 1 All E.R. 350.' *Mod. Law Rev.*, IX, 3 (October 1946), 280–3.

12,151 **Moxon**, Gerald Richard. 'Preparing a works handbook.' *Ind. Law Rev.*, I, 4 (September 1946), 106–12.

12,152 **Swales**, H. Douglas. 'Spare time employment.' *Ind. Law Rev.*, I, 1 (June 1946), 18–21.

12,153 **Grunfeld**, Cyril. 'General and temporary employers.' *Ind. Law Rev.*, II, 7 (December 1947), 177–83.
Reproduced from the *Modern Law Review.*

12,154 **Ministry of Labour and National Service.** *Memorandum on the Truck Acts.* London: H.M.S.O., 1947. 7p.

12,155 **Kahn-Freund**, Otto. 'The tangle of the Truck Acts.' *Ind. Law Rev.*, IV, 1 (July 1949), 2–9.

12,156 **Keast**, Horace. 'A commentary on the Truck Acts.' *Ind. Law Rev.*, III, 3 (January 1949), 220–4.

12,157 **Winfield**, P. H. 'The abolition of the doctrine of common employment.' *Camb. Law J.*, X, 2 (1949), 191–5.

12,158 **Ashton-Cross**, D. I. C. 'Suggestions regarding the liability of corporations for the torts of their servants.' *Camb. Law J.*, X, 3 (1950), 419–22.

12,159 **Mostyn**, Frederick Evelyn. *The Truck Acts and industry.* London: Thames Bank Publishing Co., 1950. xi, 140p.

12,160 **James**, Robert. 'Industrial rights and duties.' *Ind. Law Rev.*, V, 4 (April 1951), 276–84.

12,161 **Keast**, Horace. 'Reform of the Truck Acts.' *Ind. Law Rev.*, VI, 2 (October 1951), 112–19.

12,162 **Badcock**, Julian. 'Copyrights, patents and employment.' *Ind. Law Rev.*, VI, 3 (January 1952), 170–7.

12,163 **Frank**, W. F. 'The right to work.' *Ind. Law Rev.*, VI, 4 (April 1952), 247–65.

12,164 **Paines**, Douglas H. 'Contracts of service.' *Ind. Law Rev.*, VI, 4 (April 1952), 284–8.

12,165 **Banks**, N. D. 'Invitees and the temporary employer.' *Ind. Law Rev.*, VIII, 1 (July 1953), 27–36.

12,166 **Paines**, Douglas H. 'The employer's right of search and arrest.' *Ind. Law Rev.*, VII, 3 (January 1953), 196–202.

12,167 **Banks**, N. D. 'Interference in contractual relationships.' *Ind. Law Rev.*, VIII, 4 (April 1954), 255–63.

12,168 **Jackson**, Edward. 'The delegation by employers of their statutory duties.' *Ind. Law Rev.*, VIII, 3 (January 1954), 181–92.

12,169 **Pinson**, Barry. 'The liability of employers for the torts of their professional servants.' *Ind. Law Rev.*, VIII, 4 (April 1954), 274–80.

12,170 **Simon**, Daphne. 'Master and servant.' Saville, J. (ed.). *Democracy and the labour movement.* London: Lawrence and Wishart, 1954. p. 160–200.

12,171 **Van Dijk**, R. H. *The liability in tort of employers for their servants and contractors considered in English and Dutch law.* 1954–55. (Ph.D. thesis, University of Cambridge.)

12,172 **Banks**, N. D. 'Damages for breach of contracts of service.' *Ind. Law Rev.*, X, 2 (October 1955), 97–105.

12,173 **Keast**, Horace. 'Arbitration for professional workers.' *Ind. Law Rev.*, X, 2 (October 1955), 129–33.

12,174 **Smith**, P. V. H. 'The law and apprentices.' *Ind. Law Rev.*, X, 2 (October 1955), 120–8.

12,175 **Cairns**, Mary Bell. 'The employer and

the Army.' *Ind. Law Rev.*, XI, 1 (July 1956), 29–36.

12,176 **Christoph**, James Bernard. *The political rights of British civil servants.* 1956. 562p. (Ph.D. thesis, University of Minnesota.)

12,177 **D.**, H. 'Crook *v.* Derbyshire Stone Co.' *Ind. Law Rev.*, XI, 1 (July 1956), 37–41.

12,178 **Frank**, W. F. 'The right to work reconsidered.' *Ind. Law Rev.*, X, 3 (January 1956), 172–7.

12,179 **Garland**, Patrick. 'The right to property found by employees.' *Ind. Law Rev.*, X, 3 (January 1956), 195–201.

12,180 **Jackson**, Edward. 'Homes for employees – not caught by the Rent Act: a discussion and a precedent.' *Ind. Law Rev.*, X, 4 (April 1956), 278–85.

12,181 **Marriott**, T. W. 'The contract of service and the loaned employee.' *Ind. Law Rev.*, X, 3 (January 1956), 178–82.

12,182 **Nevin**, John. 'Servants' references.' *Ind. Law Rev.*, X, 4 (April 1956), 267–77.

'The purpose of this article is to gather into one place the rules which are scattered through various parts of the law about the characters or references of servants.'

12,183 **Paines**, Douglas H. 'Inventions by servants.' *Ind. Law Rev.*, X, 3 (January 1956), 202–5.

12,184 **Hilton**, George Woodman. *The truck system in Great Britain.* 1956–57. (Thesis, University of Chicago.)

12,185 **Hilton**, George Woodman. 'The British truck system in the nineteenth century.' *J. Polit. Econ.*, LXV, 3 (June 1957), 237–56.

12,186 **Keast**, Horace. 'Payment of wages by cheque.' *Ind. Law Rev.*, XI, 4 (April 1957), 224–32.

12,187 **Ryder**, F. R. 'Wage payments and the Truck Acts.' *Banker*, CVII, 373 (February 1957), 118–21.

12,188 **Blair**, Leo C. L. 'The civil servant – a status relationship?' *Mod. Law Rev.*, XXI, 3 (May 1958), 265–76.

12,189 **Hilton**, George Woodman. 'The Truck Act of 1831.' *Econ. Hist. Rev.*, 2nd ser., X, 3 (April 1958), 470–9.

12,190 **Blair**, Leo C. L. *The legal status of the governmental employee.* 1958–59. (Ph.D. thesis, University of Edinburgh.)

12,191 **González Blanco y Garrido**, José Patrocinio. *Protection of wages; legal protection of the servant's wages: a comparative analysis of minimum wages, the principles of 'equal pay for equal work', the principles underlying truck legislation, legislation against assignment and attachment of wages, and preference of payment of wages in the master's bankruptcy.* Geneva: *La Tribune de Genève*, 1959. 332p.

12,192 **Hargrove**, B. 'The Truck Acts in modern industrial law.' *Ind. Law Rev.*, XIII, 4 (April 1959), 221–9.

12,193 **Hilton**, George Woodman. *The truck system, including a history of the British Truck Acts, 1465–1960.* Cambridge: Heffer, 1960. xi, 166p.

12,194 **Pollard**, Robert Spence Watson and **Palmer**, Arthur. *Law and the power engineer.* London: Electrical Power Engineers Association, 1960. 75p.

Second edition. 1966. 77p.

With the assistance of J. Ashton.

12,195 **Coleman**, John Vincent. *An employer's duties at common law in Ireland.* Dublin: Figgis, 1961. 92p.

12,196 **Institute of Directors.** *The law at work.* London: the Institute, 1961. 40p.

12,197 **Megrah**, Maurice. 'Bank advances for wages.' *Banker*, CXI, 426 (August 1961), 562–4.

12,198 **Ministry of Labour.** *Report of the Committee on the Truck Acts.* London: H.M.S.O., 1961. 35p.

Chairman: David Karmel.

12,199 **Dix**, Dorothy Knight. *Contracts of employment in relation to the Contracts of Employment Act, 1963.* London: Butterworth, 1963. xxii, 123p.

12,200 **Parsons**, Owen Henry. *A guide to the Contracts of Employment Act.* London: Labour Research Department, 1963. 16p.

12,201 **Rutter**, Ernest George and **Ottaway**, Kathleen. *Contracts of Employment Act, 1963: a layman's guide.* London: Industrial Welfare Society, 1963. 24p.

Second edition revised. 1964. 25p.

12,202 **Wood**, John Crossley. 'Attachment of wages.' *Mod. Law Rev.*, XXVI, 1 (January 1963), 51–7.

12,203 **Aldridge**, Trevor Martin. *Service agreements.* London: Oyez, 1964. 88p. (Oyez practice notes 52.)

12,204 **Co-operative Union.** *Contracts of employment: a guide for co-operative societies on the operation of the Contracts of Employment Act, 1963.* Manchester: Co-operative Union, 1964. 26p.

12,205 **Hudson**, A. H. 'La responsabilité civile du travailleur envers l'employeur, ses collègues de travail et les tiers: rapport national.' Congrès International de Droit du Travail et de la Securité Sociale, 5ième, Lyon, 1963. *Actes.* Lyon, [1965]. Vol. III. p. 1167–88.

Text in English.

12,206 **Miller**, I. P. *Development of the common law of master and servant in Scotland from the close of the Industrial Revolution period to the present day.* 1965–66. (Ph.D. thesis, University of Glasgow.)

12,207 **Dix**, Dorothy Knight. *Contracts of employment, including redundancy payments.* London: Butterworths, 1966. xxvi, 292p.

Second edition.

Previous edition published as *Contracts of employment in relation to the Contracts of Employment Act, 1963.* 1963.

12,208 **Industrial Society.** *Staff agreements and letters of appointment.* London: the Society, 1966. 45p.

12,209 **Kahn-Freund**, Otto. 'A note on status and contract in British labour law.' *Mod. Law Rev.*, XXX, 6 (November 1967), 635–44.

12,210 **Bugler**, Jeremy. 'The workers' court.' *New Soc.*, XI, 295 (23 May 1968), 747.
Describes a hearing of the Industrial Tribunals.

12,211 **Clark**, Geoffrey de Nnyst. 'La différenciation entre les diverses catégories de travailleurs (travailleurs manuels et non manuels, personnel de surveillance, cadres, personnel de la fonction publique, etc.) tant au regard de la loi et des conventions collectives que de la pratique professionnelle en général: rapport national.' Congrès International de Droit du Travail et de la Securité Sociale, 6ième, Stockholm, 1966. *Actes.* Stockholm: Almqvist and Wiksell, 1968. Vol. II. 18p.
Text in English.

12,212 **Dix**, Dorothy Knight. *Dix on contracts of employment, with special reference to the Redundancy Payments and Contracts of Employment Acts.* London: Butterworths, 1968. xxxii, 351p.
Third edition.
Previous edition. 1966.

12,213 **Bragg**, R. J. *A historical study of the legal contractual capacity of an infant in commerce and industry.* 1968–69. (LL.M. thesis, University of Hull.)

12,214 **Chapman**, V. R. 'Employment and the Race Relations Act, 1968.' *Ind. Law Soc. Bull.*, 4 (April 1969), 3–12.

See also: 12,341; 12,356.

2. Discipline and Dismissal

12,215 **Dilke**, *Sir* Charles Wentworth. *Fines and deductions.* Huddersfield, 1896. 11p.

12,216 **Board of Trade.** Committee on Continuous Discharge Certificates for Seamen.
Part I. *Report.* London: H.M.S.O., 1900. 8p. (Cd. 133.)
Part II. *Minutes of evidence, appendix, index.* 1900. (Cd. 136.)
Chairman: Lord Dudley.

12,217 **Home Department.** Committee on the Claims of the Men Dismissed from the Police and Prison Services on Account of the Strike in 1919. *Report.* London: H.M.S.O., 1924. 35p. (Cmd. 2297.)
Chairman: Sir William Mackenzie.

12,218 **Mackenzie**, William Lyon. *Dismissal of Constables Hill and Moore from Kilmarnock police force: report to the Secretary for Scotland by William Lyon Mackenzie, Esq., K.C., of inquiry held under the Tribunals of Inquiry (Evidence) Act, 1921.* London: H.M.S.O., 1926. 44p. (Cmd. 2659.)

12,219 **Hsiang-jui Kung.** *Civil service discipline in modern democracies: an essay on the code of official conduct in England, U.S.A. and France.* 1938. (M.Sc. thesis, University of London.)

12,220 **Hawkins**, Everett Day. *Dismissal compensation: voluntary and compulsory plans used in the United States and abroad.* Princeton, N.J.: Princeton U.P., 1940. xvii, 390p.

12,221 **Sinclair**, A. *The problem of tenure of assistant masters in secondary schools.* 1940. (M.Ed. thesis, University of Manchester.)

12,222 **Ball**, Frank Norman. *Reinstatement in civil employment.* Leigh-on-Sea: Thames Bank Publishing Co., 1946. viii, 114p.

12,223 **Industrial Law Review.** 'Reinstatement law: recent decisions.' *Ind. Law Rev.*, I, 12 (May 1947), 381–6; II, 1 (June 1947), 2–8.

12,224 **Keast**, Horace. 'Reflections on compensation codes.' *Ind. Law Rev.*, V, 3 (January 1951), 193–9.

12,225 **Pinson**, Barry. 'The action for wrongful dismissal.' *Ind. Law Rev.*, VIII, 1 (July 1953), 45–51.

12,226 **Nevin**, John. 'The summary dismissal of employees.' *Ind. Law Rev.*, IX, 2 (October 1954), 99–108.

12,227 **International Labour Office.** 'Dismissal procedures. V. United Kingdom.' *Int. Labour Rev.*, LXXX, 4 (October 1959), 347–61.

12,228 **Sharan**, Navendra Kishore. *A study of the working of disciplinary procedures in a number of business concerns.* 1960. iv, 391p. (Ph.D. thesis, University of Manchester.)

12,229 **Meyers**, Frederic. 'Job protection in France and Britain.' *Labor Law J.*, XIII, 7 (July 1962), 566–75.
Proceedings of the Industrial Relations Research Association spring meeting 1962, p. 566–75.
Reprinted by the Institute of Industrial Relations, University of California, Los Angeles. Reprint 116.

12,230 **Moonman**, Eric. *Security of employment.* London: Industrial Welfare Society, 1963. 14p.

12,231 **Meyers**, Frederic. *Ownership of jobs: a comparative study.* Los Angeles: Institute of Industrial Relations, University of California, 1964. ix, 114p. (Monograph series 11.)

12,232 **Plumridge**, M. D. *Disciplinary practices in industry.* 1965. (M.Sc. thesis, University of London.)

12,233 **Wood**, John Crossley. 'The settlement of disputes concerning the exercise of disciplinary powers by the employer, including dismissal.' Congrès International de Droit du Travail et de la Securité Sociale, 5ième, Lyon, 1963. *Actes.* Lyon, [1965]. Vol. II. p. 771–80.

12,234 **Avins**, A. *Employee misconduct as cause for discipline or dismissal in the British Commonwealth.* 1965–66. (Ph.D. thesis, University of Cambridge.)

12,235 **Ganz**, G. 'Public law principles applicable to dismissal from employment.' *Mod. Law Rev.*, xxx, 3 (May 1967), 288–302.

12,236 **Ministry of Labour.** National Joint Advisory Council. Committee on Dismissal Procedures. *Dismissal procedures: report.* London: H.M.S.O., 1967. v, 65p.
Chairman: N. Singleton.

12,237 **Organisation of Employers' Federations and Employers in Developing Countries.** *Dismissal procedures: United Kingdom.* London: the Federation, 1967. 15p. (Occasional paper.)
A reprint, omitting footnotes, of an article appearing in the *International Labour Review*, LXXX, 4 (October 1959), 347–61.

12,238 **Kay**, Maurice. 'Shop stewards, union members and their job security: two disappointing reports.' *Ind. Law Soc. Bull.*, 3 (December 1968), 4–10.
Comments on *Dismissal procedures*, a report of the Committee of the National Joint Advisory Council, and chapter IX of the report of the Royal Commission on Trade Unions and Employers' Associations.

12,239 **Levy**, Herman Miles. *The role of law in the United States and England in protecting the worker from discharge and discrimination.* 1968. [12], iv, 100 leaves. (Diploma in Law thesis, University of Oxford.)

12,240 **Stephenson**, C. P. *How to dismiss an employee.* London: C. & M. G. S. Publications, 1968. 80p.

12,241 **Draffan**, P. G. *A study of the law relating to the appointment and dismissal of elementary school teachers from 1870.* 1968–69. (M.Ed. thesis, University of Newcastle-upon-Tyne.)

12,242 **Clark**, Geoffrey de Nnyst. 'Unfair dismissal and reinstatement.' *Mod. Law Rev.*, XXXII, 5 (September 1969), 532–46.

12,243 **Levy**, Herman Miles. 'The role of the law in the United States and England in protecting the workers from discharge and discrimination.' *Int. Comp. Law Q.*, XVIII (July 1969), 558–617.

12,244 **Anderman**, S. D. 'Voluntary dismissal procedures and the proposed legislation on unfair dismissals.' *Br. J. Ind. Relat.*, VIII, 3 (November 1970), 350–68.

12,245 **Clark**, Geoffrey de Nnyst. 'Remedies for unjust dismissal: proposals for legislation.' *PEP Broad.*, XXXVI, 518 (June 1970), v, 103p.

12,246 **Council of Europe.** Partial Agreement [in the social and public health field]. Social Committee. *Safeguard of workers against arbitrary dismissal.* Strasbourg: C. of E., 1970.

12,247 **Freedland**, Mark R. *The application of the general principles of the law of contract to the termination of the employment relationship.* 1970. (D.Phil. thesis, University of Oxford.)

See also: 10,884.

B. SAFETY, HEALTH, AND WELFARE

This section includes the literature relating to the governmental regulation of safety, health, and welfare. Literature describing the conditions of safety, health, and welfare is classified in Part Six, IV, D. See also Part Five, V, B, 1; and Part Seven, IX, B, 3.

1. General

12,248 **Charley**, *Sir* W. T. *Conservative legislation for the working classes. No. 1. Mines and factories.* London: National Union, 1882. 16p.
Third edition.
Another edition. 1891. 11p.

12,249 *Report upon the precautions which can be enforced under the Factory Act, and as to the need for further powers for the protection of persons employed in whitelead works.* London: H.M.S.O., 1882. (C. 3263.)

12,250 *Communications addressed to the Secretary of State on the subject of white lead poisoning, with report by the Chief Inspector of Factories upon the same subject.* London: H.M.S.O., 1883. (C. 3516.)
In continuation of C. 3263 of 1882.

12,251 **Crabtree**, G. *Factory commission: the legality of its appointment questioned.* London, 1883. 20p.

12,252 **Finlayson**, Archibald W. 'Falling trade and factory legislation.' *Nineteenth Century*, XIII, 76 (June 1883), 971–7.

12,253 **National Union of Conservative and Unionist Associations.** *Notes on Conservative legislation for the working classes: unions and factories.* London, 1884. 8p. (Publications 94.)

12,254 **Redgrave**, Alexander. *The Factory & Workshop Act, 1878.* London: Shaw, 1885. 271 p
Third edition.
Earlier edition. 1878.
Fourth edition. *The Factory and Workshop Acts, 1878 to 1891*... By A. Redgrave and Jasper A. Redgrave. 1891. xxxvii, 292p.
Fifth edition. By A. Redgrave and J. A. Redgrave. 1893. xxxvii, 298p.
Sixth edition. *The Factory Acts*, by J. A. Redgrave and H. S. Scrivener. 1895. xliv, 356p.
Seventh edition. By J. A. Redgrave and H. S. Scrivener. 1898. xlviii, 378p.
Eighth edition. By H. S. Scrivener and C. F. Lloyd. London: Shaw, Butterworth, 1902. lvi, 352, 54p.
Ninth edition. By H. S. Scrivener and C. F. Lloyd. Butterworth, Shaw; 1902. lvi, 370, 53p.
Tenth edition. *The Factory and Truck Acts.* By H. S. Scrivener and C. F. Lloyd. Butterworth, Shaw, 1904. lxiii, 366, 69p.
Eleventh edition. By Charles F. Lloyd. Shaw, Butterworth, 1909. xxxvi, 414, 86p.
Twelfth edition. *The Factory, Truck and*

Shop Acts. By C. F. Lloyd. Shaw, Butterworth, 1916. xxxix, 93p.

Thirteenth edition. By C. F. Lloyd. Butterworth, 1924. xxxiv, 637, 99p.

Fourteenth edition. *Redgrave's Factory Acts*. By Joseph Owner. Butterworth, Shaw, 1931. xxxii, 694, 109p.

Fifteenth edition. *Redgrave and Owner's Factories, Truck and Shops Acts*. By J. Owner. Butterworth, Shaw, 1939. xlvii, 1062p.

Supplements 1943– .

Sixteenth edition. By J. Owner. Butterworth, Shaw, 1945. xlvii, 1189p.

Supplement. By John Thompson and Harold R. Rogers. Butterworth, Shaw, 1948. xiv, 60p.

Second cumulative supplement. 1949. xii, 157p.

Seventeenth edition. *Redgrave's Factories, Truck and Shops Acts*. By J. Thompson and H. R. Rogers. Butterworth, 1949. lix, 1279p.

Supplement. 1951. xi, 137p.

Eighteenth edition. By J. Thompson and H. R. Rogers. Butterworth, Shaw, 1952. lxiii, 1417p.

Nineteenth edition. By J. Thompson and H. R. Rogers. Butterworth, Shaw, 1956. lxxvi, 1366p.

Supplement. 1960. xvii, 152p.

Twentieth edition. By Ian Fife and E. Anthony Machin. Butterworth, 1962. lxxxviii, 1445p.

Twenty-first edition. By I. Fife and E. A. Machin. Butterworth, Shaw, 1966. lxiv, 15, 1400p.

12,255 **Hodder**, Edwin. *The life and work of the Seventh Earl of Shaftesbury, K.G.* London [etc.]: Cassell, 1886. 3v.

'Popular edition'. 1887. xv, 792p.

12,256 **Edinburgh Review**. 'The Seventh Earl of Shaftesbury.' *Edinb. Rev.*, CLXV, 338 (April 1887), 354–87.

Review article on *The life and work of the Seventh Earl of Shaftesbury, K.G.*, by Edwin Hodder, 1886.

12,257 **Atherley-Jones**, Llewellyn Arthur. *The miners' handy book to the Coal Mines Regulation Act, 1887*. West Bromwich: *Labour Tribune* Office, 1888. 106p.

Reprinted from *Labour Tribune*.

12,258 **Chadwick**, *Sir* Edwin. *Preventive legislation as against curative legislation*. 1888. 8p.

12,259 **Croft**, W. R. *The history of the factory movement, or Oastler and his time*. Huddersfield: G. Whitehead, 1888. 141p.

12,260 **Miners' National Union.** *Coal Mines Regulation Act, 1887*. Newcastle, 1888.

Reprinted, with introduction.

12,261 **Boyd**, Robert Nelson. *Coal pits and pitmen: a short history of the coal trade, and the legislation affecting it*. London: Whittaker, 1892. viii, 256p.

Second edition, revised and enlarged. 1895. xii, 356p.

12,262 **Gibbins**, Henry de Bettgens. 'The factory reformers.' *English social reformers*. London: Methuen, 1892. p. 109–51.

An account of Richard Oastler, Lord Shaftesbury and Robert Owen.

12,263 **Jeans**, Victorine. *Factory Act legislation: its industrial and commercial effects, actual and prospective*. London: Fisher Unwin, 1892. 96p.

Cobden Prize Essay, 1891.

12,264 **Garcke**, Emile and **Fells**, John Manger. *Summary of the Factory & Workshop Acts, 1878–91, for the use of manufacturers and managers*. London: Crosby Lockwood, 1893. 40p.

Reprinted from the fourth edition of *Factory accounts* by the same authors.

12,265 **Nash**, Vaughan. 'The Home Office and the deadly trades.' *Fortn. Rev.*, n.s., LII, 314 (February 1893), 169–83.

12,266 **The Times.** 'Lord Shaftesbury.' *Eminent persons: biographies reprinted from 'The Times'*. Vol. III. London: Macmillan, *The Times* Office, 1893. p. 262–77.

12,267 **Taylor**, Richard Whately Cooke. *The factory system and the Factory Acts*. London: Methuen, 1894. viii, 184p. (Social questions of to-day.)

12,268 **Walmesley**, Oswald. *Guide to mining laws of the world*. London: Eyre and Spottiswoode, 1894. 331p.

12,269 **Austin**, H. Evans. *The law relating to factories and workshops, being the Factory and Workshop Acts, 1878–1895, together with the Shop Hours Acts, 1892–1895, the Truck Acts, 1831 & 1887, orders of the Secretary of State made under the Factory Acts, with explanatory notes and a copious index*. London: Knight, 1895. xxxvi, 364p.

Second edition. 1901. xlvii, 464p.

12,270 **Blot** (*pseud.*). *The new Factory Act and its victims*. London, [1895?]. 5 leaves.

12,271 **Davies**, David Samuel and **Yabbicom**, Thomas Henry. *Notes on the Factory and Workshop Acts, 1878, 1891, 1895*. London: Sanitary Publishing Co., 1895. 16p.

12,272 **Departmental Committee on Factory Statistics.** *Report*. London: H.M.S.O., 1895. (C. 7608.)

12,273 **Z.** 'The new Factory Act.' *Econ. J.*, V, 19 (September 1895), 471–3.

12,274 **Abraham**, May Edith and **Davies**, Arthur Llewelyn. *The law relating to factories and workshops, including laundries and docks*. London: Eyre and Spottiswoode, 1896. xiv, 283p.

Part I. A practical guide to the law and its administration, by M. E. Abraham.

Part II. The Acts . . . with explanatory notes by A. L. Davies.

Second edition. 1897. xvi, 295p.

Third edition. 1901. xv, 336p.

Fourth edition. 1902. xiv, 381p.

Fifth edition. 1905. xiii, 414p.

Sixth edition, by Roland Burrows. 1908. xvi, 627p.

12,275 **Drage**, Geoffrey. *The labour problem.* London: Smith, Elder, 1896. xv, 424p.

12,276 **Roe**, E. M. *The Factory & Workshop Acts explained and simplified.* London: Simpkin, Marshall, 1896. viii, 111p.

Another edition. *The Factory and Workshop Acts.* 1897. viii, 111p.

12,277 **Committee Appointed to Inquire into the Working of the Cotton Cloth Factories Act, 1889.** *Report.* London: H.M.S.O., 1897. (C. 8348.)

Evidence, appendices, index. (C. 8349.)

12,278 **Nash**, Rosalind. *The law relating to health in factories and workshops.* Manchester: Women's Co-operative Guild, 1897. 20p. (Public health papers.)

12,279 **Bradby**, L. Barbara and **Black,** Anne. 'Women compositors and the Factory Acts.' *Econ. J.*, IX, 34 (June 1899), 261–6.

12,280 **Belderson**, S. W. 'Factory Acts and state employees.' *Westm. Rev.*, CLIV, 2 (August 1900), 177–81.

12,281 **Fox**, Stephen N. 'Factories and Workshops Bill.' *Econ. J.*, X, 38 (June 1900), 258–61.

Discussion of the recent Bill.

12,282 **Bowstead**, William. *The law relating to factories and workshops, as amended and consolidated by the Factory and Workshop Act, 1901.* London: Sweet and Maxwell, 1901. xxvi, 343p.

12,283 **C.**, E. *Statute mongery: the results, the remedy.* London: King, 1901. 29p.

12,284 **Harrison**, Amy. 'The inspection of women's workshops in London: a study in factory legislation.' *Econ. Rev.*, XI, 1 (January 1901), 32–46.

12,285 **Webb**, Beatrice (ed.). *The case for the Factory Acts.* London: Grant Richards, 1901. xvi, 233p.

12,286 **Wilson**, Mona. 'Factory and Workshops Acts Amendment and Consolidation Bill.' *Econ. J.*, XI, 43 (September 1901), 453–4.

12,287 **Wilson**, Mona. 'The Factory and Workshops Acts Amendment Bill.' *Econ. J.*, XI, 42 (June 1901), 268–71.

12,288 **Women's Trade Union League.** *Factory and workshop legislation: opinions of H.M. Inspectors, 1895–1900.* London, [1901?]. 15p.

12,289 **Bowstead**, William. *The law relating to laundries under the Factory and Workshop Act, 1901.* London: Sweet and Maxwell, 1902. xv, 80p.

12,290 **Cockburn**, John Henry. *The law of coal, coal mining, and the coal trade, and of the holding, working, and trading with minerals generally.* London: Stevens, 1902. lv, 930p.

12,291 **Kaye**, James Robert. *The duties of local authorities . . . under the Factory and Workshop Act, 1901.* London: Sanitary Publishing Co., 1902. 43p.

12,292 **Ruegg**, Alfred Henry and **Mossop**, Leonard. *The law of factories and workshops.* London: Stevens, 1902. xl, 573p.

12,293 **Tuckwell**, Gertrude Mary. *The anomalies of our factory laws.* London, 1902. [9]p.

12,294 **Williams**, Charles Willoughby and **Musgrave**, Charles E. *The Factory and Workshop Act, 1901: its general effect and parliamentary history, with notes and other information, including the full text of the Act.* London: Effingham Wilson, 1902. 196p.

12,295 **Wood**, George Henry. 'Factory legislation, considered with reference to the wages, etc., of the operatives protected thereby.' *R. Statist. Soc. J.*, LXV, 2 (June 1902), 284–320.

Discussion, p. 321–4.

12,296 **Edinburgh Review.** 'The past and future of factory legislation.' *Edinb. Rev.*, CXCVII, 403 (January 1903), 174–201.

Review article.

12,297 **Harrison**, Amy. *English factory legislation considered with regard to its economic effects and methods of administration.* 1903. 3 pts. (D.Sc. (Econ.) thesis, University of London.)

12,298 **Hutchins**, B. Leigh and **Harrison**, Amy. *A history of factory legislation.* London: King, 1903. xviii, 372p. (London School of Economics and Political Science. Studies in economics and political science 10.)

Preface by Sidney Webb.

Appendix A. 'The course of women's wages during the nineteenth century', by George H. Wood, with a bibliography.

Appendix B. 'Orders in Council.'

Appendix C. 'Bibliography of factory legislation.'

'New edition.' 1907.

Second edition, revised, with a new chapter. 1911. xvi, 298p.

Third edition. 1926. xvi, 298p.

Third edition, reprinted. London: Cass, 1966. xvi, 298p.

12,299 **Tuckwell**, Gertrude Mary. *Industrial work and industrial laws.* London: Industrial Law Committee, 1903. 44p.

With a chapter on public health by Nora De Chaumont.

12,300 **Atherley-Jones**, Llewellyn Arthur and **Bellot**, Hugh Hale Leigh. *The miner's guide to the Coal Mines Regulation Acts, and the law of employers and workmen.* London: Methuen, 1904. xv, 262p.

Second edition, revised and enlarged. 1910. xv, 374p.

Third edition. *The miner's guide to the law relating to coal mines.* 1914. xii, 384p.

12,301 **Tennant**, *Mrs* H. J. *The case for factory legislation: a comparison of English and foreign industrial regulations.* London, [1904?]. [8]p.

12,302 **Ward**, Leonard. 'The effect, as shown by statistics, of British statutory regulations directed to the improvement of the hygienic conditions of industrial occupations.' *R. Statist. Soc. J.*, LXVIII, 3 (September 1905), 435–518.
Discussion, p. 518–25.
'Read before the Royal Statistical Society, 16th May, 1905.'
Howard Medal Prize Essay.

12,303 **Austin**, H. Evans. *The law relating to laundries, charitable, reformatory & public institutions under the Factory and Workshop Act, 1901, as amended by the Factory & Workshop Act, 1907.* London: Wyman, 1907. xxiv, 149p.
'With introduction, notes, and a copious index.'

12,304 **Committee on Government Factories and Workshops.** *Report.* London: H.M.S.O., 1907. vi, 21p. (Cd. 3626.)
Chairman: G. H. Murray.

12,305 **Anderson**, Adelaide Mary. 'Factory and workshop law.' *Woman in industry from seven points of view.* London: Duckworth, 1908. p. 143–81.

12,306 **Hutchins**, B. L. 'Gaps in our factory n.s., XXIV, 143 (November 1908), 255–71.

12,307 **Leppington**, C. H. d'E. 'The prospects of home-work legislation.' *Char. Orgn. Rev.*, n.s., XXIV, 143 (November 1908), 255–71.

12,308 **Markham**, Violet Rosa. *The Factory and Shop Acts of the British dominions: a handbook . . . together with a general view of the English law.* London: Eyre and Spottiswoode, [1908]. viii, 173p.

12,309 **X, Y** and **Z.** 'The comedy and tragedy of factory inspection.' *Social. Rev.*, I, 3 (May 1908), 181–93.

12,310 **Hatch**, *Sir* Ernest Frederick George. *Piecework wages: methods of applying the 'Particulars' section of the Factory and Workshop Act, 1901: report.* London: H.M.S.O., 1909. 19p. (Cd. 4842.)
See also *Foundries.* 1913. 7p. (Cd. 6990.)

12,311 **Hutchins**, B. Leigh. 'Gaps in our factory legislation.' Webb, B., and others. *Socialism and national minimum.* London: Fifield, 1909. p. 50–64.
'With a postscript on the Report of the Select Committee on Home Work.'

12,312 **Ruegg**, Alfred Henry. *Report as to the application of the Factory and Workshop Act, 1901, to florists' workshops.* London: H.M.S.O., 1909. 8p. (Cd. 4932.)

12,313 **Webb**, Beatrice. 'The economics of factory legislation.' Webb, B., and others. *Socialism and national minimum.* London: Fifield, 1909. p. 5–49.

12,314 *Summary of report on the administration of the Factory and Workshop Act, 1901, by local authorities in respect of workshops, outwork, etc. in 1908.* London: H.M.S.O., 1910. (Cd. 5110.)

12,315 **Keith**, James, Baron Keith of Avonholm. *The Shops Act, 1912, with the regulations issued by the Secretary for Scotland, and the provisions of the Factory and Workshop Act, 1901, incorporated thereunder, explained and annotated.* Edinburgh, London: W. Green, 1912. xxiii, 119p.

12,316 **Leavis**, W. *The new Shop Act: shopkeepers' and assistants' guide.* London, 1912. 16p.

12,317 **Streatfield**, *Mrs* Deane. 'Some necessary amendments to the Factory Acts.' National Conference on the Prevention of Destitution. *Report of the proceedings . . . 1912.* London: King, 1912. p. 428–34.
Discussion, p. 434–42.

12,318 **Greenwood**, Arthur. 'Next steps in factory and workshop reform.' *Polit. Q.*, 3 (September 1914), 38–70.

12,319 **Hallsworth**, *Sir* Joseph. *Memorandum on the labour and public health laws affecting commercial employees.* Manchester, 1915. 28p.

12,320 **International Labour Office.** *Prevention of anthrax among industrial workers: memorandum on the disinfection station established in Great Britain for disinfection of wool and hair.* London: H.M.S.O., 1921. 15p. (Studies and reports, series F, 3.)

12,321 **Anderson**, Adelaide Mary. *Women in the factory: an administrative adventure, 1893–1921.* London: Murray; New York: Dutton, 1922. xiii, 316p.
Printed in Great Britain.
'Story of the woman inspectorate of factories and workshops from its beginning in 1893 . . . until . . . 1921.'

12,322 **Tillyard**, *Sir* Frank. *The worker and the state: wages, hours, safety and health.* London: Routledge, 1922. 297p. (London School of Economics. Ratan Tata Foundation.)
Second edition, revised and enlarged. London: Routledge, 1936. x, 307p.
Third edition. 1948. xii, 302p.

12,323 **Hammond**, John Lawrence Le Breton and **Hammond**, Lucy Barbara. *Lord Shaftesbury.* London, Bombay, Sydney: Constable, 1923. xii, 313p. (Makers of the nineteenth century.)

12,324 **Wightman**, Evelyn Miriam. *The 7th Earl of Shaftesbury as a social reformer.* 1923. [xii], 230p. (M.A. thesis, University of Birmingham.)

12,325 **Hallsworth**, *Sir* Joseph. *Commercial employees & protective legislation.* London: Labour Publishing Co., 1924. 96p.

12,326 **Association of Certifying Factory Surgeons.** *Factory legislation and medical service.* Manchester: the Association, 1925. 14p. (Health and industry series 3.)
Extracted from the 1924 Annual Report of the Association.

12,327 **Sanders**, W. Stephen. 'The welfare of the worker.' Tracey, H. (ed.). *The book of the Labour Party: its history, growth, policy, and leaders.* London: Caxton Publishing Co., 1925. vol. 2. p. 70–89.

12,328 **Williams**, Dorothy M. *Lord Shaftesbury: the story of his life and work for industrial England, 1801–1885.* London: Teachers and Taught, 1925. 61p.

12,329 **Bready**, J. Wesley. *Lord Shaftesbury and social-industrial progress.* London: Allen and Unwin, 1926. 446p.

12,330 **Mess**, Henry Adolphus. *Factory legislation and its administration, 1891–1924.* London: King, 1926. xii, 228p. (Studies in economics and political science 84.)

Based on the author's thesis of the same title, 1926. (Ph.D. thesis, University of London.)

12,331 **Trades Union Congress.** General Council. *New factory legislation.* London: T.U.C., 1926. 32p.

12,332 **Smith**, Constance. 'Anthony Ashley Cooper, Seventh Earl of Shaftesbury, 1801–85.' Martin, H. (ed.). *Christian social reformers of the nineteenth century.* London: Student Christian Movement, 1927. p. 75–106.

12,333 **Squire**, Rose E. *Thirty years in the public service: an industrial retrospect.* London: Nisbet, 1927. 238p.

Factory inspection.

12,334 **National Institute of Industrial Psychology.** 'The Home Office Industrial Museum.' *Natn. Inst. Ind. Psychol. J.*, IV, 4 (October 1928), 224–7.

'A permanent exhibition of methods, arrangements, and appliances for promoting the safety, health, and welfare of industrial workers in the manufacturing and other industries which come within the sphere of Home Office administration.'

12,335 **Johnson**, Dorothy Catherine. 'Lord Shaftesbury, 1801–1885, Lord Ashley, 1811–1851.' *Pioneers of reform.* London: Methuen, 1929. p. 100–21.

12,336 **Ritzmann**, F. 'Accident prevention and factory inspection.' *Int. Labour Rev.*, XIX, 5 (May 1929), 639–46.

12,337 **Baylis**, Gertrude. *The factory system and the Factory Acts, 1802–1850.* 1930. (M.A. thesis, University of Birmingham.)

12,338 **Home Office.** Departmental Committee to consider and report what additions to the Factory Inspectorate are required, whether any changes in its organization are desirable, and what other measures, if any, can be taken to enable the Factory Department to discharge adequately its existing duties and the further duties foreshadowed by the Government's Factory Bill of 1926. *Report, appendices.* 1930. 44p.

Chairman: V. L. Henderson.

12,339 **Hallsworth**, *Sir* Joseph. *Protective legislation for shop & office employees.* London: Harrap, 1932. 210p.

New edition, revised. 1935. 244p.

Third edition, revised. 1939. 253p.

12,340 **Mines Department.** *Miners' Welfare Fund. Departmental Committee of Inquiry 1931: report to the Secretary for Mines.* London: H.M.S.O., 1933. 93p. (Cmd. 4236.)

Chairman: Lord Chelmsford.

12,341 **Owner**, Joseph. *Handbook to the Factory Acts and Truck Acts.* London: Pitman, 1933. xi, 120p.

Second edition. 1939. xi, 151p.

Third edition. 1945. vii, 152p.

12,342 **International Labour Office.** 'Factory inspection in Great Britain, 1929–1933.' *Int. Labour Rev.*, XXX, 6 (December 1934), 820–9.

A survey of five annual reports of the Chief Inspector of Factories and Workshops.

12,343 **Robson**, William Alexander. 'The Factory Acts, 1833–1933: a centenary of pride and shame.' *Polit. Q.*, V, 1 (January–March 1934), 55–73.

12,344 **Wilkinson**, William Elmslie. *The Shops Acts, 1912 to 1934.* London: Solicitors' Law Stationery Society, 1934. xvi, 175p.

Second edition . . . *1912 to 1936.* 1937.

Third edition . . . *1912 to 1938.* 1947. Edited by G. M. Butts.

Fourth edition. *The Shops Act, 1950.* 1961. Edited by Roderick Davies.

See also Davies, R. *The Offices, Shops and Railway Premises Act, 1963.* 1965.

12,345 **Gobert**, Ernest E. 'A government office centenary.' *Naut. Mag.*, CXXXV, 3 (September 1935), 219–23.

General Register Office of Merchant Seamen.

12,346 **Bellhouse**, *Sir* Gerald. 'The Factory Acts.' *Nineteenth Century*, CXX, 717 (November 1936), 582–94.

12,347 **Bowring**, *Sir* John. *Speech . . . on the Factories Regulation Act* . . . London, 1936. 4p.

12,348 **Clark**, J. R. *Employers' guide to the Conditions of Employment Act.* Dublin, 1936. 12p.

12,349 **Launder**, W. B. *Report on conferences between employers, operatives and inspectors concerning fencing of machinery and other safety precautions, first aid and temperature in woollen and worsted factories.* London: Home Office, 1936. 17p.

12,350 **Andrews**, John Bertram. *British factory inspection: a century of progress in administration of labor laws.* Washington: U.S. G.P.O., 1937. vi, 56p. (U.S. Department of Labor, Division of Labor Standards. Bulletin 11.)

12,351 **Flight**, A. T. *Legislation relating to mining, XIX century (1840–1887).* 1937. (Ph.D. thesis, University of London.)

12,352 **Frazier**, Rowland Wynne and **Butts**, George Manning. *The Factories Act, 1937*. London: Solicitors' Law Stationery Society, 1937. xxx, 315p.

12,353 **Katin**, Louis. 'The worker's point of view. XXXIII. The factory inspector and the worker.' *Hum. Factor*, XI, 6 (June 1937), 230–2.

12,354 **'Labourer.'** 'The Factories Bill.' *Polit. Q.*, VIII, 2 (April–June 1937), 240–7.

12,355 **Macdonald**, K. *The Docks Regulations – Factories Act 1937 – explained*. Glasgow: Brown, Son and Ferguson, 1937. 72p.
Second edition. 1948. 72p.

12,356 **Maddock**, Herbert Leslie. *The Factories Act, 1937: a practical explanation of the effect of the new legislation together with the annotated text of the 1937 Act, the text of other important Acts, the Truck Acts annotated, regulations . . .* London: Eyre and Spottiswoode, 1937. xxviii, 684p.
In collaboration with Sir Gerald Bellhouse.

12,357 **Samuels**, Harry. *The Factories Act, 1937*. London: Stevens, 1937. xii, 584p.
Second edition. 1939. xxi, 702p.
Supplement. 1943. 60p.
Third edition. 1943.
Fourth edition. *Factory law*. 1948. xii, 674p.
Fifth edition. *Factory law*. 1951. xxviii, 719p.
Supplement. 1953.
Sixth edition. *Factory law*. 1957. xxx, 734p.
Supplement. 1960. vii, 71p.
Seventh edition. *Factory law*. London: Knight, 1962. xxxv, 779p.
Eighth edition. *Factory law*. Knight, 1969. xxxv, 825p.

12,358 **Samuels**, Harry. *Law relating to shops*. London: Pitman, 1937. xiv, 130p.
Second edition. *The law . . .* London: Knight, 1952. xii, 72p.
Third edition. Knight, 1964. xiv, 91p.

12,359 **Blelloch**, D. H. 'A historical survey of factory inspection in Great Britain.' *Int. Labour Rev.*, XXXVIII, 5 (November 1938), 614–59.

12,360 **Davies**, Daniel. 'Mining legislation and mines inspection.' *Q. Rev.*, CCLXXI, 537 (July 1938), 27–41.
Since 1661.

12,361 **Home Office.** *A guide to the Factories Act, 1937*. London, 1938. 51p.

12,362 **Northern Ireland.** Ministry of Labour. *Factories Bill (Northern Ireland), 1938: memorandum showing the extent to which the Bill differs from the existing law*. Belfast: H.M.S.O., 1938. 18p. (Cmd. 196.)

12,363 **Rackham**, Clara Dorothea. *Factory law*. London: Nelson, 1938. 160p. (Discussion books 7.)

12,364 **Stevenson**, Alan Leslie. *The Shops Acts, 1912–1936, and the Factories Act, 1937, so far as it relates to the powers and duties of local authorities*. London: Hadden, Best, 1938. 320p.

12,365 **Lord Privy Seal's Office.** *A.R.P. in industry: a review and amplified description of the Civil Defence Act, as it affects owners and occupiers of industrial and commercial establishments*. London: H.M.S.O., 1939. 16p.

12,366 **Northern Ireland.** *Report of the Shops Acts Committee*. Belfast: H.M.S.O., 1939. 64p. (Cmd. 202.)

12,367 **Northern Ireland.** Ministry of Labour. *Guide to the Factories Act, Northern Ireland, 1938*. Belfast, 1939. 50p.

12,368 **Shallcross**, Ruth Enalda. *Industrial homework: an analysis of homework regulation, here and abroad*. New York: Industrial Affairs Publ. Co., 1939. xvi, 257p.
Issued also as a Ph.D. thesis, Bryn Mawr College.

12,369 **Taylor**, G. Stevenson. 'Safety provisions of the British Factories Act, 1937.' *Ind. Saf. Surv.*, XV, 2 (March–April 1939), 29–34.

12,370 **Djang Tien Kai.** *Factory inspection in Great Britain*. 1940. (Ph.D. thesis, University of London.)
Published London: Allen and Unwin, 1942. 255p. (Studies in political science and sociology 2.)

12,371 **Davies**, Daniel. 'Some aspects of mining reform.' *Q. Rev.*, CCLXXVI, 547 (January 1941), 103–13.

12,372 **Ministry of Labour and National Service.** *Welfare work outside the factory, June 1940 to August 1941*. London: H.M.S.O., 1941. (Cmd. 6310.)

12,373 **Wilson**, *Sir* Duncan R. 'Factory inspection: a thirty-five years retrospect.' *R. Statist. Soc. J.*, CIV, 3 (1941), 209–24.
Discussion, p. 224–34.
'Read before the Royal Statistical Society on May 20th 1941.'

12,374 **Wilson**, *Sir* Duncan R. 'The work of the Departmental Committee on Lighting in Factories.' *Occup. Psychol.*, XV, 1 (January 1941), 1–9.

12,375 **Walker**, Kenneth O. 'The classical economists and the Factory Acts.' *J. Econ. Hist.*, I, 2 (November 1941), 168–77.

12,376 **McLaughlin**, Arthur Ivan Granville. 'Factory law in relation to health and welfare.' Rolleston, *Sir* H. D. and Moncrieff, *Sir* A. A. (eds.). *Industrial medicine*. London: Eyre and Spottiswoode, 1944. p. 174–84.
Published on behalf of *The Practitioner*.

12,377 **Higham**, Florence M. G. *Lord Shaftesbury: a portrait*. London: S.C.M. Press, 1945. 127p.

12,378 **Miners' Welfare Commission.** *Mining people*. London: H.M.S.O., 1945.
An account of the work of the Commission, 1920–1945.

12,379 **Driver**, Cecil. *Tory radical: the life of Richard Oastler*. New York: Oxford U.P., 1946. ix, 597p.

12,380 **Whiteside**, J. 'The Factory Act of 1937 in relation to the engineering and shipbuilding industries.' *Instn. Engrs. Shipbldrs. Scotl. Trans.*, XC (1946–47), 172–202.

The author was H.M. Superintending Inspector of Factories.

12,381 **Sorenson**, Lloyd Rushford. *The English factory inspectors and the development of factory legislation, 1833–1844*. 1947. (Thesis, University of Illinois.)

12,382 **Ministry of Labour and National Service.** *Revision of the Building Regulations: report by the Commissioner appointed to hold an inquiry with respect to The Draft Code in relation to safety, health and welfare*. London: H.M.S.O., 1948.

By G. G. Honeyman.

12,383 **Thomas**, Maurice Walton. *The development of factory legislation from 1833–47: a study of legislative and administrative evolution*. 1948. (Ph.D. (Econ.) thesis, University of London.)

12,384 **Thomas**, Maurice Walton. 'Development of the Inspectorate.' *Ind. Law Rev.*, II, 9 (February 1948), 228–46.

A chapter from the author's book *The early factory legislation*.

12,385 **Thomas**, Maurice Walton. *The early factory legislation: a study in legislative and administrative evolution*. Leigh-on-Sea: Thames Bank Publishing Co., 1948. xiii, 470p.

12,386 **Thomas**, Maurice Walton. 'Health and safety.' *Ind. Law Rev.*, II, 8 (January 1948), 200–21.

A chapter from the author's book *The early factory legislation*.

12,387 **Barnett**, G. P. 'The engineer and the Factories Act.' *Ind. Law Rev.*, III, 4 (April 1949), 278–89.

A talk given to the Engineering-Legal Society by the Chief Inspector of Factories, 27 January 1949.

12,388 **Keast**, Horace. 'The Gowers Committee: workplace inspectorates.' *Ind. Law Rev.*, IV, 1 (July 1949), 10–14.

12,389 **Pain**, Peter. 'The Gowers Report on Health, Welfare and Safety in Non-industrial Employment.' *Ind. Law Rev.*, IV, 2 (October 1949), 80–5.

Paper given at the Haldane Society Conference on 'Safety at Work and Industrial Law', 15 October 1949.

12,390 **Duffy**, John. 'Early factory legislation: a neglected aspect of British humanitarianism.' McCulloch, S. C. (ed.). *British humanitarianism: essays honoring Frank J. Klingberg*. Philadelphia: Church Historical Society, 1950. p. 66–83.

12,391 **Ministry of Labour and National Service.** *Report of Public Inquiry into the Draft Pottery (Health and Welfare) Special Regulations, under the Provisions of the Factories Acts, 1937 and 1948*. London: H.M.S.O., 1950.

By Eric Sachs.

12,392 **Pain**, Peter. 'The law of fire prevention and fire protection in relation to industrial premises.' *Ind. Law Rev.*, IV, 3 (January 1950), 136–42; 4 (April 1950), 210–19.

12,393 **Ward**, A. E. W. 'The Industrial Injuries Act.' *Ind. Law Rev.*, IV, 4 (April 1950), 224–41.

An address to the Engineering-Legal Society, 14 March 1950.

12,394 **Hunt**, Francis William. *Your factory and the law*. London: Seven Oaks P., 1951. ix, 164p.

12,395 **Northern Ireland.** Ministry of Home Affairs. Committee on Shops Legislation. *Report*. Belfast: H.M.S.O., 1951. 60p.

12,396 **Treasury**. *Industrial health services: report of the Committee of Inquiry*. London: H.M.S.O., 1951. iv, 35p. (Cmd. 8170.)

Chairman: E. T. Dale.

12,397 **Wrottesley**, A. J. F. 'Factory law and industry.' *Ind. Law Rev.*, VI, 2 (October 1951), 104–11.

With special reference to food, including biscuit factories.

12,398 **Pain**, Peter. 'Reform of industrial safety law.' *Ind. Law Rev.*, VI, 4 (April 1952), 279–83.

'Lecture given at a Conference of the Haldane Society on "Accidents at Work" . . . on 5th April 1952.'

12,399 **Sorenson**, Lloyd Rushford. 'Some classical economists, *laissez-faire*, and the Factory Acts.' *J. Econ. Hist.*, XII, 3 (Summer 1952), 247–62.

12,400 **Stevenson**, Alan Leslie. *The Shops Act, 1950, and the Factories Act, 1937 as amended by the Factories Act, 1948 (so far as it relates to the powers and duties of local authorities), fully annotated with regulations and memoranda issued thereunder*. London: Hadden, Best, 1952. lxiii, 341p.

12,401 **Turner-Samuels**, David Jessel. 'Industrial Injuries Acts, 1946–1948.' *Ind. Law Rev.*, VI, 4 (April 1952), 266–78.

'The text of a lecture given at a conference of the Haldane Society on 5th April 1952.'

12,402 **Wrottesley**, A. J. F. 'The nature of responsibility under the Factories Acts.' *Ind. Law Rev.*, VII, 2 (October 1952), 101–8.

12,403 **Cairns**, Mary Bell. 'The enforcement of factory regulations by local authorities.' *Ind. Law Rev.*, VIII, 2 (October 1953), 82–97.

12,404 **Keating**, Donald. 'Safe means of access.' *Ind. Law Rev.*, VII, 4 (April 1953), 272–7.

Under the Factories Act, 1937.

12,405 **Morrison**, E. A. 'What is a factory?' *Ind. Law Rev.*, VIII, 1 (July 1953), 37–44.

12,406 **Symons**, W. G. 'Some problems of labour inspection in European countries.' *Int. Labour Rev.*, LXVIII, 1 (July 1953), 47–64.

12,407 **Cairns**, Mary Bell. 'Some legal reflections upon the Gowers Report 1949.' *Ind. Law Rev.*, IX, 2 (October 1954), 116–25.
On health, welfare and safety in non-industrial employment.

12,408 **Eley**, J. Lloyd. 'Safe system of working.' *Ind. Law Rev.*, IX, 2 (October 1954), 109–15.

12,409 **McKown**, Robert. *Comprehensive guide to factory law: a classified guide to the requirements of the Factories Acts and other legislation affecting factory occupiers.* London: Chantry Publications, 1954. 111p.
New and revised edition. 1961. 124p.
Third edition, revised and enlarged. London: Godwin for *The Builder*, 1965. viii, 157p.
Fourth edition. Godwin, 1968. viii, 163p.

12,410 **Northern Ireland.** *Report of the Joint Select Committee on Shop Acts, together with proceedings of the Committee and minutes of evidence.* Belfast: H.M.S.O., 1954. 294p. (H.C. 1107.)

12,411 **O'Dwyer**, J. J. 'The contribution of the industrial medical officer.' Ling, T. M. (ed.). *Mental health and human relations in industry.* London: H. K. Lewis, 1954. p. 129–40.

12,412 **Stafford**, B. 'The Factory Acts.' King, F. C. (ed.). *Public administration in Ireland.* Dublin: Civics Institute of Ireland, 1954. p. 148–60.

12,413 **Herford**, Martin Edward Meakin. *The opportunities of the appointed factory doctor, with special reference to the problem of the young worker in industry.* 1954–55. (M.D. thesis, University of Bristol.)

12,414 **Jackson**, Edward. 'How securely can a dangerous part of machinery be fenced?' *Ind. Law Rev.*, IX, 3 (January 1955), 202–7.

12,415 **Leeds Journal**. *Health and welfare in factories: the Factory Acts.* Leeds: Leeds Incorporated Chamber of Commerce, 1955. 72p.
Supplement to *The Leeds Journal*, January 1955.

12,416 **McCullough**, T. W. 'Some recent judgments on machinery cases.' *Ind. Law Rev.*, XI, 1 (July 1956), 6–11.
An address given to the Engineering Legal Society, 5 April 1956.

12,417 **Sinha**, Ganesh Prasad. *Economics of labor welfare funds in the coal industries of the United States, Great Britain and India.* Ithaca, N.Y., 1956. xiv, 319 leaves. (Ph.D. thesis, Cornell University.)

12,418 **Aspinall**, K. J. 'What does "dangerous" mean?' *Ind. Law Rev.*, XII, 2 (October 1957), 97–203.

12,419 **Godfrey**, Gerald M. 'Safety in factories: recent developments. 1. Dangerous machinery.' *Ind. Law Rev.*, XII, 1 (July 1957), 24–35.

12,420 **Godfrey**, Gerald M. 'Safety in factories: recent developments. 2. Conditions of work.' *Ind. Law Rev.*, XII, 2 (October 1957), 77–86.

12,421 **Pain**, Peter. 'Responsibility for fire at industrial premises: recent developments in the law.' *Ind. Law Rev.*, XII, 1 (July 1957), 1–13.

12,422 **Ward**, John Towers. *The factory movement, c. 1830–1850.* 1957. (Ph.D. thesis, University of Cambridge.)

12,423 **Jones**, W. T. *A survey of the health services of Tyneside industry, together with a plan for their development.* 1957–58. (M.D. thesis, University of Edinburgh.)

12,424 **Blaug**, Mark. 'The classical economists and the Factory Acts – a re-examination.' *Q.J. Econ.*, LXXII, 2 (May 1958), 221–6.

12,425 **Edmonds**, Edward L. 'Education and early factory inspectors.' *Voc. Asp.*, X (1958), 85–95.

12,426 **Marriott**, T. W. 'The provision of tools & equipment: the duties of an employer.' *Ind. Law Rev.*, XII, 4 (April 1958), 200–8.

12,427 **Mayson**, Christopher F. 'Electrical safety legislation.' *Ind. Law Rev.*, XII, 3 (January 1958), 181–92.

12,428 **Robson**, A. P. W. *The factory controversy, 1830–1853.* 1958. (Ph.D. thesis, University of London.)

12,429 **Cracknell**, D. G. 'Supervision of workmen.' *Ind. Law Rev.*, XIV, 1 (July 1959), 2–9.

12,430 **Fife**, Ian Braham and **Machin**, Edward Anthony. *Agriculture – safety, health and welfare.* London: Butterworth, 1959. x, 83p.
Reprint of Butterworth's annotated legislation service statutes supplement 113.

12,431 **Ministry of Labour.** Factory Inspectorate. *Guide to statistics collected by H.M. Factory Inspectorate.* London: H.M.S.O., 1960. 39p.

12,432 **Ward**, John Towers. 'Leeds and the factory reform movement.' *Thores. Soc. Publs.*, XLVI, 2 (1960), 87–118.

12,433 **Lean**, Garth. 'The dangerous earl: Lord Shaftesbury.' *Brave men choose.* London: Blandford P., 1961. p. 39–69.

12,434 **Abaelu**, J. N. *A study of labour standards and their use in farm planning.* 1961–62. (M.Sc. thesis, University of London.)

12,435 **Cassell**, A. J. *Her Majesty's Inspectors of Mines, 1843–1862.* 1961–62. (M.Sc. (Econ.) thesis, University of Southampton.)

12,436 **Allsop**, Peter Henry Bruce (ed.). *Encyclopaedia of factories, shops and offices: law and practices.* London: Sweet and Maxwell; Edinburgh: Green, 1962. 6 pts. (Local government library.)

Up-dated by releases, no. 1, 1962– .

12,437 **Ministry of Labour.** *The Factories Act, 1961: a short guide.* London: H.M.S.O., 1962. 23p.

12,438 **Ministry of Labour.** Factory Inspectorate. *Organisation of industrial health services.* London: H.M.S.O., 1962. 36p. (Safety, health and welfare booklets. New series 21.)

12,439 **Ward**, John Towers. *The factory movement, 1830–1855.* London: Macmillan; New York: St Martin's P., 1962. xi, 515p.

12,440 **Ward**, John Towers. 'The factory reform movement in Scotland.' *Scott. Hist. Rev.*, XLI, 2 (October 1962), 100–23.

12,441 **Ward**, John Towers. 'Matthew Balme, 1813–1884, factory reformer.' *Brad. Antiq.*, X, n.s., VIII (1962), 217–28.

12,442 **British Journal of Industrial Safety.** 'The development of factory safety legislation.' *Br. J. Ind. Saf.*, VI, 64 (Summer 1963), 27–33.

Expanded version of an article first published in the *Journal* in 1949, I, 2.

12,443 **Fife**, Ian Braham and **Machin**, Edward Anthony. *The Offices, Shops and Railway Premises Act 1963; with introductions and annotations by Ian Fife and E. Anthony Machin, being a reprint of 'Butterworth's annotated legislation service, statutes supplement no. 138'.* London: Butterworths, 1963. xiv, 108p.

12,444 **Howells**, R. W. L. '*Priestley v. Fowler* and the Factory Acts.' *Mod. Law Rev.*, XXVI, 4 (July 1963), 367–95.

12,445 **Samuels**, Alec. 'Offices, Shops and Railway Premises Act, 1963.' *Mod. Law Rev.*, XXVI, 5 (September 1963), 539–42.

Discussion of the Act.

12,446 **Samuels**, Harry and **Stewart-Pearson**, Neville. *The Offices, Shops and Railway Premises Act, 1963.* London: Knight, 1963. xvii, 129p.

Noter-up and supplement. 1965. vii, 71p.

12,447 **Best**, Geoffrey Francis Andrew. *Shaftesbury.* London: Batsford, 1964. 139p.

Chap. IV. 'Satanic millowners, and some others.' p. 80–105.

12,448 **Davis**, Maurice Alexis John. *Law and hairdressing.* London: Independent P., 1964. viii, 238p.

12,449 **Mair**, Lawrence. *Health, safety and welfare in offices, shops and railway premises.* London: Shaw, 1964. ix, 245p.

With the text of the Offices, Shops and Railway Premises Act, 1963, and related statutory instruments.

Second edition. 1968. ix, 292p.

12,450 **Ministry of Labour.** *The Offices, Shops and Railway Premises Act, 1963: a genera guide.* London: H.M.S.O., 1964. 46p.

12,451 **Mitchell**, Ewan (*pseud.*) [i.e. Grevill Ewan Janner]. *Your office and the law.* London: Business Publications, 1964. xii, 286p (A 'business book'.)

12,452 **Davies**, Roderick. *The Offices, Shops an Railway Premises Act, 1963.* London: Oyez 1965. xliii, 299p.

12,453 **Eagger**, Arthur Austin. *Venture in industry the Slough Industrial Health Service, 1947 1963.* London: Lloyd-Luke (Medica Books), 1965. xi, 193p.

12,454 **Fife**, Ian Braham and **Machin**, Edwar Anthony. *Redgrave's offices and shops, togethe with agricultural and railway safety.* London Butterworth, Shaw, 1965. lviii, 570p.

12,455 **Mitchell**, Ewan (*pseud.*) [i.e. Grevill Ewan Janner]. *Your factory and the law.* London: Business Publications, 1965. xii, 264p

Second edition. London: Business Books 1969. xii, 438p.

12,456 **Royal Society for the Prevention o Accidents.** *The ABC of the Offices, Shops an Railway Premises Act, 1963.* London: th Society, 1965. 28p.

12,457 **Carr**, C. F. *The legal responsibilities o management.* London: British Institute c Management, 1966. 7p.

B.I.M. Industrial Safety Forum London, November 1966.

12,458 **Henderson**, Joan and **Cornford**, Brian *The manager's responsibility for safety* London: Industrial Society, 1966. 27p (Notes for managers 12.)

12,459 **MacLeod**, Roy M. 'Social policy and th "floating population": the administratio of the Canal Boats Acts 1877–1899.' *Pas Pres.*, 35 (December 1966), 101–32.

12,460 **Ministry of Labour.** *Report by the Commissioner appointed to hold an inquiry wit respect to the Draft Construction (Workin Places) Regulations and the Draft Construction (Health and Welfare) Regulation* London: H.M.S.O., 1966. iii, 58p.

12,461 **Ministry of Labour.** Industrial Healt Advisory Committee. *Appointed factory docto service: report by a Sub-Committee.* London H.M.S.O., 1966. 28p.

Chairman: N. Singleton.

12,462 **Macdonagh**, Oliver O. G. M. 'Coa mines regulation: the first decade, 1842 1852.' Robson, R. (ed.). *Ideas and institutions of Victorian Britain: essays in honour o George Kitson Clark.* London: Bell, 1967 p. 58–86.

12,463 **Dawson**, Keith and **Wall**, Peter. *Factor reform.* London: Oxford U.P., 1968. 41p (Society and industry in the 19th century: a documentary approach.)

12,464 **O'Higgins**, Paul. 'Dead or injured a work.' *New Soc.*, XII, 322 (28 Novembe 1968), 798–9. (Society at work.)

12,465 **O'Higgins**, Paul. 'Factory legislation

New Soc., XI, 288 (4 April 1968), 490–2. (The origins of the social services 10.)

12,466 **Foster**, John. 'The making of the first six Factory Acts.' *Soc. Study Labour Hist. Bull.*, 18 (Spring 1969), 4–5.

Summary of a paper read to a meeting of the Scottish Labour History Society, Edinburgh, 23 February 1969.

A summary of the discussion which followed appears on p. 5.

12,467 **Martin**, Bernice. 'Leonard Horner: a portrait of an Inspector of Factories.' *Int. Rev. of Soc. Hist.*, XIV, 3 (1969), 412–43.

12,468 **Sinclair**, R. C. *Judicial interpretation of the Factory Acts: a critical appraisal.* 1969. (LL.M. thesis, Queen's University of Belfast.)

12,469 **Barry**, R. P. 'Present and future role of the safety adviser.' *Ind. Law Soc. Bull.*, 8 (September 1970), 6–7.

The author was Manager, Accident Prevention Section, British Steel Corporation.

12,470 **Carson**, W. G. 'Some sociological aspects of strict liability and the enforcement of factory legislation.' *Mod. Law Rev.*, XXXIII, 4 (July 1970), 396–412.

12,471 **Howells**, R. W. L. 'Future patterns of enforcement of the safety codes.' *Ind. Law Soc. Bull.*, 8 (September 1970), 7–12.

12,472 **Ward**, John Towers. 'The factory movement.' Ward, J. T. (ed.). *Popular movements c. 1830–1850.* London: Macmillan, 1970. p. 54–77.

See also: 1391; 13,451; 14,538.

2. Particular Groups

a. YOUNG WORKERS

See also Part Six, II, C, 5; and Part Six, IV, A, 4, c.

12,473 **Tuckwell**, Gertrude Mary. *The state and its children.* London: Methuen, 1894. vi, 164p. (Social questions of to-day.)

12,474 **Hall**, William Clarke. *The Queen's reign for hildren.* London: Unwin, 1897. xvi, 208p.

Chap. I. 'The employer and the child.'

12,475 **Dowdall**, H. Chaloner. 'The new Liverpool bye-laws regulating street trading.' *Econ. Rev.*, IX, 4 (October 1899), 503–14.

Details of the laws, especially those affecting children.

12,476 **Committe on Wage-earning Children.** *Report of Committee on Wage-earning Children; a statement of the existing laws for their protection, with suggestions of possible amendments.* London: printed by G. Reynolds, 1900. 16p.

12,477 **London County Council.** *Employment of children out of school hours.* London, 1900. 12p.

12,478 **Inter-Departmental Committee on the Employment of School Children.** *Report.* London: H.M.S.O., 1901. 25p. (Cd. 849.)

Minutes of evidence, appendices and index. 1902. xii, 485p. (Cd. 895.)

Chairman: Henry H. S. Cunynghame.

12,479 **Dowdall**, H. Chaloner. 'The operation of the Liverpool bye-laws regulating street trading by children.' *Econ. Rev.*, XII, 3 (July 1902), 330–3.

12,480 **Ireland.** Inter-Departmental Committee on the Employment of Children during School Age, especially in Street-trading in the large centres of population in Ireland. *Report; with evidence and appendices.* Dublin: A. Thom for H.M.S.O., 1902. xv, 187p. (Cd. 1144.)

Chairman: Sir Frederic F. J. Cullinan.

12,481 **Peacock**, Robert. 'Employment of children with special reference to street trading by children.' International Congress for the Welfare and Protection of Children, 3rd, London, 1902. *Report of the proceedings.* London: King, 1902. p. 191–202.

Discussion, p. 214–18.

The author was Chief Constable of the City of Manchester.

12,482 **Committee on Wage-Earning Children.** *Employment of Children Act, 1903.* London: the Committee, 1903.

Comments on the Act.

12,483 **Home Department.** *Employment of Children Act, 1903. Report to His Majesty's principal secretary of state for the Home Department on the byelaws made by the London County Council under the Employment of Children Act, 1903, by Chester Jones.* London: Darling for H.M.S.O., 1906. 28p. (Cd. 2809.)

12,484 **Board of Trade.** Labour Department. 'Laws regulating the employment of children and young persons in factories and workshops in the United Kingdom, Germany and Switzerland.' Sadler, M. E. (ed.). *Continuation schools in England and elsewhere: their place in the educational system of an industrial and commercial state.* Manchester: Manchester U.P., 1907. p. 352–68.

12,485 **Lovejoy**, Owen R. 'Child labor legislation in England.' *Chautauquan*, XLVI (April 1907), 217–25.

12,486 **International Association for Labour Legislation.** *Report on the employment of children in the United Kingdom.* London, 1908. 32p.

By Constance Smith.

Second edition. 1909. 32p.

12,487 **Dewar**, David. *The Children Act, 1908, and other Acts affecting children in the United Kingdom.* Edinburgh, London: W. Green, 1910 [i.e. 1909]. vii, 418p.

12,488 **Inter-Departmental Committee on Partial Exemption from School Attendance.** *Report.* London: H.M.S.O., 1909.

Vol. I. *Report.* (Cd. 4791.)

Vol. II. *Evidence, etc.* (Cd. 4887.)

12,489 **Home Department.** Departmental Committee on the Employment of Children Act, 1903. *Report.* London: H.M.S.O., 1910. 23p. (Cd. 5229.)

Minutes of evidence, appendices and index. viii, 555p. (Cd. 5230.)

Chairman: J. A. Simon.

12,490 **Buckmaster**, Stanley Owen. *Employment of Children Act, 1903. Report to His Majesty's principal secretary of state for the Home department, on the byelaws made on the 29th of January, 1910, by the London County Council under the Employment of Children Act, 1903.* London: H.M.S.O., 1911. 18p. (Cd. 5497.)

12,491 **Garnett**, William Hubert Stuart. *Children and the law.* London: Murray, 1911. xxiv, 255p.

12,492 **O'Connell**, John Robert. 'The juvenile street trader and the state: the problem of the waifs and strays.' *Statist. Soc. Inq. Soc. Ir. J.*, XII, 91 (December 1911), 489–507.

12,493 **Standing Committee on Boy Labour in the Post Office.** *First report.* London: H.M.S.O., 1911. 18p. (Cd. 5504.)

Second report. 1912. 22p. (Cd. 5755.)

Third report. 1913. 20p. (Cd. 6959.)

Fourth report. 1914. 31p. (Cd. 7556.)

Fifth report. 1915. 22p. (Cd. 8019.)

Chairman: Sir Matthew Nathan.

12,494 **Pope**, Samuel. *Employment of Children Act, 1903. Report to His Majesty's principal secretary of state for the Home Department on the byelaw made by the Devon County Council under the Employment of Children Act, 1903, and on the objections thereto.* London: H.M.S.O., 1913. 15p. (Cd. 6988.)

12,495 **Holland**, Robert Wolstenholme. *The law relating to the child, its protection, education, and employment.* London: Pitman, 1914. xxiv, 142p.

'With introduction on the laws of Spain, Germany, France and Italy.'

12,496 **International Association for Labour Legislation.** *Child labour in the United Kingdom: a study of the development and administration of the law relating to the employment of children.* London: King, 1914. xxxii, 326p.

By Frederic Keeling.

Prepared on behalf of the British Section of the International Association for Labour Legislation.

12,497 **Keeling**, Frederic Hillersdon. *Child labour in the United Kingdom: a study of the development and administration of the law relating to the employment of children.* London: King, 1914. xxxii, 326p.

Prepared on behalf of the British Section of the International Association for Labour Legislation.

12,498 **Standing Committee on Bills, A.** *Report on the Children (Employment and School Attendance) Bill with the proceedings of the Committee.* London: J. B. Nichols, 1914. 13p.

12,499 **Webb**, Sidney. 'The coming educational revolution. I. Half-time for adolescents.' *Contemp. Rev.*, CX (November 1916), 584–93.

12,500 **Board of Education.** Committee appointed to advise the Board as to the rules which they should make with reference to licences to children to take part in entertainments under the Prevention of Cruelty to Children Act, 1904, as amended by Section 13 (2) of the Education Act, 1918. *Report.* London: H.M.S.O., 1919. 18p. (Cmd. 484.)

Chairman: F. H. Oates.

12,501 **Jones**, Chester. *Report on the byelaws . . . under the Employment of Children Act, 1903, and the Education Act, 1918, and on the objections thereto.* London: H.M.S.O., 1921. 15p. (Cmd. 1122.)

12,502 **Departmental Committee to Enquire into the Working of the Provisions of the Factory and Workshops Acts for the Medical Examination of Young Persons as to their Fitness for Employment in Factories.** *Report, appendices.* London: H.M.S.O., 1924. 24p. (Cmd. 2135.)

Chairman: Rhys J. Davies.

12,503 **Ministry of Labour.** National Advisory Council for Juvenile Employment (England and Wales). *Third report. Provision of courses of instruction for unemployed girls and boys.* London: H.M.S.O., 1930. 18p. (Cmd. 3638.)

Chairman: Lord Shaftesbury.

12,504 **Robson**, Adam Henry. *The education of children engaged in industry in England, 1833–1876.* London: Kegan Paul, 1931. xi, 240p.

Factory Acts and other legislation.

12,505 **Abbott**, Grace (ed.). *The child and the state . . . select documents, with introductory notes.* Chicago, Ill.: U. of Chicago P., 1938. 2v. (University of Chicago social service series, edited by the faculty of the School of Social Service Administration.)

Vol. 1. Legal status in the family. Apprenticeship and child labor.

Vol. 2. The dependent and the delinquent child. The child of unmarried parents.

12,506 **Northern Ireland.** Ministry of Labour. *The instruction of unemployed juveniles.* 1938. 77p.

12,507 **Committee on Wage-Earning Children.** *Industrial protection of youth.* London, 1940. 8p.

Second edition.

Addendum. 1943. 6p.

12,508 **Phillips**, George Lewis and **Cole**, Arthur H. *England's climbing boys: a history of the long struggle to abolish child labor in chimney-sweeping.* Boston, Mass.: Harvard Graduate School of Business Administration, 1949.

61p. (Kress Library of Business and Economics. Publication 5.)

12,509 **International Labour Office.** 'The development of labour legislation on young workers in the United Kingdom.' *Int. Labour Rev.*, LXVII, 1 (January 1953), 64–91.

12,510 **Petherick**, Florence R. *The movement for the abolition of child labor in the mines of England.* 1954. (Ph.D. dissertation, Boston University.)

12,511 **Scottish Education Department.** Committee on the Employment of Children in the Potato Harvest. *Report.* Edinburgh: H.M.S.O., 1956. 16p. (Cmd. 9738.)

12,512 **James**, T. E. *The development of the law relating to children in the nineteenth and twentieth centuries.* 1957–58. (Ph.D. thesis, University of London.)

12,513 **Gillan**, D. J. *The effect of industrial legislation on the social and educational condition of children employed in coal mines, between 1840 and 1876, with special reference to Durham County.* 1967–68. (M.Ed. thesis, University of Durham.)

12,514 **Home Office.** *The law on performances by children: a guide to the Children (Performances) Regulations 1968 and related statutory provisions.* London: H.M.S.O., 1968. lv, 32p.

12,515 **Purves**, Gladstone Dougal. *Mudlarks and ragged schools: Lord Shaftesbury and the working children.* London: H. A. Humphrey, 1968. 61p. (Patch studies.)

See also: 12,524; 12,534–5.

b. WOMEN WORKERS

See also Part Six, IV, A, 4, b.

12,516 **Liberty and Property Defence League.** *Women and factory legislation: debate in the House of Lords on clause 16, Factories and Workshops Bill.* London, 1891. 7p.

Reprinted from *Hansard's parliamentary debates.*

12,517 **March-Phillipps**, Evelyn. 'Factory legislation for women.' *Fortn. Rev.*, n.s., LVII, 341 (May 1895), 733–44.

12,518 **Nash**, Rosalind. *Reduction of hours of work for women: some points in the time regulations of the Factory Act.* Manchester: Women's Co-operative Guild, [1895]. 7p. (Investigation papers 1.)

12,519 **Tuckwell**, Gertrude Mary. *Women's work and factory legislation: the Amending Act of 1895.* London, 1895. 18p.

12,520 **Boucherett**, Jessie and **Blackburn**, Helen. *The condition of working women, and the Factory Acts.* London: Elliot Stock, 1896. 84p.

'Report on the work of women in the white lead trade at Newcastle-on-Tyne, March, 1895, by H. O. Moore and E. Hare.'

12,521 **Brownlow**, Jane M. E. *Women and factory legislation.* Congleton: Women's Emancipation Union, 1896. 7p.

12,522 **Society for Promoting the Employment of Women.** *Factory and Workshops Bill.* [1896?] 6p.

12,523 **Webb**, Beatrice. *Women and the Factory Acts.* London: Fabian Society, 1896. 16p. (Fabian tract 67.)

12,524 **Brooke**, Emma Frances. *A tabulation of the factory laws of European countries in so far as they relate to the hours of labour, and to special legislation for women, young persons, and children.* London: G. Richards, 1898. 52p.

12,525 **Wilson**, Mona. *Our industrial laws: working women in factories, workshops, shops and laundries, and how to help them.* London: Duckworth, 1899. 79p.

Edited by Mrs H. J. Tennant.

New edition, revised and corrected. 1903. 79p.

12,526 **Independent Labour Party.** City of London Branch. *Labour laws for women.* London, 1900. 24p. (City Branch pamphlets 2.)

Third edition.

12,527 **Webb**, Beatrice. 'Special legislation for women.' International Congress of Women, London, 1899. *Transactions. Vol. VI. Women in industrial life.* London: T. Fisher Unwin, 1900. p. 40–3.

Discussion, p. 54–8.

12,528 **British Association for the Advancement of Science.** 'Women's labour.' *Reports of meetings.* 1901, p. 399–402; 1902, p. 286–313; 1903, p. 315–64.

Reports of the committee appointed to investigate the economic effect of legislation regulating women's labour. Chairman: E. W. Brabrook.

12,529 **Webb**, Beatrice. 'Women and the Factory Acts.' Webb, S. and Webb, B. *Problems of modern industry.* 2nd ed. London, New York, Bombay: Longmans, Green, 1902. p. 82–101.

'Reproduced with some additions, from papers read at the Nottingham Conference of the National Union of Women Workers (October 1895), and the Fabian Society (January 1896.)'

12,530 **Vynne**, Nora and **Blackburn**, Helen. *Women under the Factory Act.* London, Oxford: Williams and Norgate, 1903. viii, 205p.

Part I. Position of the employer.

Part II. Position of the employed . . . 'with the assistance of H. W. Allason . . . on certain technical points of law'.

12,531 **British Association for the Advancement of Science.** 'Women's labour: third and final report of the committee... appointed to investigate the economic effect of legislation regulating women's labour.' *Report of the seventy-third meeting... held at Southport in September 1903.* London: J. Murray, 1904. p. 315–64.
'Drawn up by the Secretary', A. L. Bowley.

12,532 **Harrison,** Amy. *Women's industries in Liverpool: an enquiry into the economic effects of legislation regulating the labour of women.* London: Williams and Norgate, 1904. 65p.

12,533 **Tuckwell,** Gertrude Mary. 'The regulation of women's work.' *Woman in industry from seven points of view.* London: Duckworth, 1908. p. 1–23.

12,534 **Harvey,** E. C. *Labour laws for women and children in the United Kingdom.* London: Women's Industrial Council, 1909. 24p.

12,535 **International Labour Office.** 'New British legislation affecting women an young persons.' *Int. Labour Rev.*, 1, (January 1921), 121–6.

12,536 **Blainey,** Joan. *The woman worker and restrictive legislation.* Bristol, London: Arrowsmith, 1928. 112p.
Published for the London and National Society for Women's Service.

12,537 **Open Door Council.** *Statutory and trade union restrictions on the employment of women.* Arkley: Open Door Council, 1957. 28p.

C. HOURS

This section includes the literature relating to the governmental regulation of hours of work. Other literature, describing and discussing hours of work, is classified in Part Six, IV, B.

12,538 **Charteris,** Francis Wemyss, Earl of Wemyss and March and **Sutherst, T.** *Shop hours regulation: correspondence between the Earl of Wemyss... and T. Sutherst.* London: Liberty and Property Defence League, 1885. 11p.

12,539 **Millar,** J. F. 'Legislative regulation of shop hours.' Industrial Remuneration Conference. *The report of the proceedings and papers.* London: Cassell, 1885. p. 507–14.
'Revised by Malcolm Guthrie.'
An appendix to the proceedings and papers.

12,540 **Select Committee on the Shop Hours Regulation Bill.** *Report, proceedings, evidence, appendix and index.* London: H.M.S.O., 1886. (H.C. 155.)

12,541 **Select Committee on Sunday Postal Labour.** *Reports, with the proceedings, evidence, appendix, and index.* London: H.M.S.O., 1887. (H.C. 274.)

12,542 *Return of weekly-paid servants who were, during July 1886 and January 1887, on duty on the railways of the United Kingdom for more than twelve hours at a time, or who, after being so on duty, were allowed to resume work with less than eight hours rest.* London: H.M.S.O., 1888. (H.C. 143.)
... *September 1889 and March 1890.* 1890. (C. 6158.)
... *December 1890.* 1891. (C. 6400.)
... *December 1891.* 1892. (C. 6796.)
... *Glasgow and South Western, North British, and Caledonian Railway Companies, in November 1890.* (H.C. 149.)

12,543 **Bradlaugh,** Charles. 'The eight hours movement.' *New Rev.* 1, 2 (July 1889), 125–39.

12,544 **Champion,** Henry Hyde. 'An eight-hour law.' *Nineteenth Century,* XXVI, 151 (September 1889), 509–22.

12,545 **Cox,** Harold. 'The eight hours question.' *Nineteenth Century,* XXVI, 149 (July 1889), 21–34.

12,546 **Fabian Society.** *An eight hours bill.* London: Fabian Society, 1889. 16p. (Fabian tract 9.)
By Sidney Webb.
Issued without the author's name.
Revised edition. 1890. 16p.

12,547 **Hyndman,** Henry Mayers. 'Eight-hours the maximum working day.' *New Rev.*, 1, 3 (August 1889), 266–87.
A reply to the paper by C. Bradlaugh in the July 1889 issue.

12,548 **Webb,** Sidney. 'The limitation of the hours of labour.' *Contemp. Rev.*, LVI (December 1889), 859–83.

12,549 **Westminster Review.** 'Some economic aspects of the eight hours' movement.' *Westm. Rev.*, CXXXII, 1 (July 1889), 44–55.

12,550 **Bradlaugh,** Charles. 'Regulation by statute of the hours of labour.' *Fortn. Rev.*, n.s., XLVII, 279 (March 1890), 440–60.

12,551 **Burt,** Thomas. *Parliament and the regulation of hours of labour.* London, 1890. 23p.

12,552 **Champion,** Henry Hyde. *The parliamentary eight hours day...* London: Reeves, 1890. 16p.

12,553 **Haldane,** Richard Burdon. 'The eight hours question.' *Contemp. Rev.*, LVII (February 1890), 240–55.

12,554 **Hyndman,** Henry Mayers and **Bradlaugh,** Charles. *Eight hours' movement: verbatim report of a debate....* London: Freethought Publishing Co., 1890. 48p.

12,555 **Leatham,** James. *An eight hours day with ten hours' pay: how to get it and how to keep it.* Aberdeen: the author, 1890. 41p.

12,556 **Macdonald,** J. A. Murray. 'The case for the eight hours day.' *Nineteenth Century,* XXVII, 158 (April 1890), 553–65.

12,557 **Munro,** Joseph Edwin Crawford. *The probable effects on wages of a general reduction in the hours of labour.* London, 1890. 14p.

12,558 **Ramsey**, Laon. 'A plea for an eight hours day.' *Westm. Rev.*, CXXXIV, 6 (December 1890), 642–55.

12,559 **Board of Trade.** *Letter addressed . . . to the Secretary of the Railway Companies Association on the subject of the hours of duty of signalmen, drivers and guards, with reply of the Association thereto.* London: H.M.S.O., 1891. (C. 6266.)

12,560 **Fabian Society.** *The case for an eight hours bill.* London: Fabian Society, 1891. 15p. (Fabian tract 23.)
By Sidney Webb.
Issued without the author's name.

12,561 **Hadfield**, *Sir* Robert Abbott and **Gibbins**, Henry de Bettgens. *A shorter working-day.* London: Methuen, 1891. viii, 184p. (Social questions of to-day 9.)

12,562 **Munro**, Joseph Edwin Crawford. *The economic effects of an eight hours day for coal miners.* London, 1891. 4p.

12,563 **Naylor**, James. 'An artisan's view of the eight-hours question.' *Econ. Rev.*, I, 3 (July 1891), 370–4.

12,564 **Percy**, Cornelius McLeod. *Miners and the eight hour movement.* Wigan, 1891. 30p.

12,565 **Rae**, John. 'The balance sheet of short hours.' *Contemp. Rev.*, LX (October 1891), 499–520.

12,566 *Return of weekly-paid servants who were, during December 1890, on duty for more than ten hours at a time, or who, after being so on duty, were allowed to resume work with less than eight hours' rest.* London: H.M.S.O., 1891. (C. 6388.)
. . . *December 1891*. 1892. (C. 6797.)

12,567 **Select Committee on Railway Servants (Hours of Labour).** *Report, proceedings, evidence, appendix and index.* London: H.M.S.O., 1891. (H.C. 342.)
Special report [in the following Session on allegations that workers were dismissed for giving evidence] *with proceedings, evidence and appendix.* 1892. (H.C. 125.)
Report, with proceedings, evidence, appendix and index. 1892. (H.C. 246.)

12,568 **Shaw**, George Bernard. *The legal eight hours question: a public debate between Mr. Geo. Bernard Shaw and Mr. G. W. Foote at the Hall of Science, London, Jan. 14 & 15, 1891. Verbatim report (corrected by both disputants).* London: Forder, 1891. 77p.

12,569 **Symes**, J. E. 'Some economic aspects of the eight-hour movement.' *Econ. Rev.*, I, 1 (January 1891), 51–6.

12,570 **Webb**, Sidney and **Cox**, Harold. *The eight hours day.* London: W. Scott, 1891. viii, 280p.

12,571 **Whitefield**, W. *The miners' eight hours bill.* Bristol, 1891. 16p.

12,572 **Brooks**, George. *An open letter to W. Mather on the subject of his proposal for regulating the working-hours of miners.* London: Clowes, 1892. 20p.

12,573 **Buxton**, Sydney C. 'Legal limitation of hours.' *A handbook to political questions of the day, and the arguments on either side.* 8th ed. London: Murray, 1892. p. 379–432.
Also in 9th edition. 1892. p. 379–432; in 11th edition. 1903. p. 158–199.

12,574 **Channing**, F. A. *Overwork on railways and the remedy: draft report of the Select Committee on Railway Servants (Hours of Labour) proposed by F. A. Channing, M.P.* London, 1892. 24p.

12,575 **Fogg**, William. *Workers in cotton factories and the eight hours' day: an address delivered on November 16th, 1892.* Manchester: J. Heywood, 1892. 24p.

12,576 **London United Trade Committee of Carpenters and Joiners.** *Epitome of the eight hours' movement, 1891.* London, 1892.

12,577 **Marchant**, James Robert Vernam. *The Shop Hours Act, 1892, with notes and a form.* London: Effingham Wilson, 1892. 64p. (Wilson's legal handy books.)

12,578 **Mather**, William. 'Labour and the hours of labour: the industrial problem of the day.' *Contemp. Rev.*, LXII (November 1892), 609–31.

12,579 *Return of instances, since 1884, in which the Inspectors of the Board of Trade have reported that the hours of the railway servants on duty, on the occasion of accidents, have been unduly long, stating the name, date, and nature of such accidents, the railways on which they occurred, and giving passages in such reports relating to unduly long hours.* London: H.M.S.O., 1892. (H.C. 251.)

12,580 **Select Committee on the Shop Hours Bill.** *Report, special report, proceedings, evidence, appendix and index.* London: H.M.S.O., 1892. (H.C. 287.)

12,581 **Blanchard**, J. T. 'The eight hours question.' *Westm. Rev.*, CXXXIX, 5 (May 1893), 526–53.

12,582 **Fabian Society.** *Eight hours by law: a practical solution.* London: Fabian Society, 1893. 15p. (Fabian tract 48.)
By Henry W. Macrosty.
Issued without the author's name.

12,583 **Rae**, John. 'The eight-hours' day and the unemployed.' *Contemp. Rev.*, LXIII (June 1893), 790–808.

12,584 **Robertson**, John McKinnon. *The eight hours question.* London: Sonnenschein, 1893. vi, 150p.

12,585 **Standing Committee on Trade, etc.** *Report on the Railway Servants (Hours of Labour) Bill, with the proceedings.* London: H.M.S.O., 1893. (H.C. 124.)

12,586 **Bainbridge**, Emerson. 'The eight hours bill for miners: its economic effect.' *Contemp. Rev.*, LXVI (October 1894), 457–74.

12,587 **Rae**, John. 'The eight hours day and foreign competition.' *Contemp. Rev.*, LXV (February 1894), 189–206.

12,588 **Rae**, John. *Eight hours for work.* London: Macmillan, 1894. xii, 340p.

12,589 **Thomson,** Walter Trevelyan. 'The miners' eight-hours question.' *Westm. Rev.*, CXLI, 6 (June 1894), 593–600.

12,590 **Munro**, Joseph Edwin Crawford. 'The economic effects of an eight hours' day for coal miners.' National Liberal Club. Political Economy Circle. *Transactions*, II (1895), 1–14.

12,591 **Select Committee on Shops (Early Closing) Bill.** *Report, with the proceedings, evidence, appendix, and index.* London: H.M.S.O., 1895. (H.C. 273.)

12,592 **Shaxby**, W. J. *An eight-hours day: the case against trade-union and legislative interference.* London: *The Liberty Review* Publishing Co., 1898. vii, 133p.

12,593 **House of Lords.** Select Committee on the Early Closing of Shops. *Report, proceedings, minutes of evidence.* London: H.M.S.O., 1901. xvi, 213p. (H.C. 369.)

Index. 1902. (H.C. 369 – Ind.) 45p.

Chairman: Lord Avebury.

12,594 **Webb**, Sidney. 'The regulation of the hours of labour.' Webb, S. and Webb, B. *Problems of modern industry.* 2nd ed. London, New York, Bombay: Longmans, Green, 1902. p. 102–38.

First published in *Contemporary Review* (December 1889).

12,595 **British Association for Labour Legislation.** *Reports on the legal limitation of hours of work in industry and commerce in the United Kingdom.* London, 1906. 42p.

By S. Sanger and others.

12,596 **Miners' Eight Hour Day Committee.** Departmental Committee appointed to inquire into the probable economic effect of a limit of eight hours to the working day of coal miners. *First report.* London: H.M.S.O., 1907.

Part I. *Report.* iiip. (Cd. 3426.)

Part II. *Minutes of evidence and appendices thereto taken on the first day.* iv, 142p. (Cd. 3427.)

Part III. *Minutes of evidence...second to eleventh days inclusive.* vii, 237p. (Cd. 3428.)

Final report.

Part I. *Report and appendices.* 87p. (Cd. 3505.)

Part II. *Minutes of evidence and appendices thereto taken on the twelfth to twenty-seventh days inclusive, and index to the whole of the evidence.* ix, 390p. (Cd. 3506.)

12,597 **Select Committee on the Police Forces (Weekly Rest Day) Bill.** *Report, with the proceedings of the Committee, evidence, appendix, and index.* London: H.M.S.O., 1908. (H.C. 353,354.)

1909. (H.C. 132.)

Chairman: J. E. Ellis.

12,598 **Rose**, Frank Herbert. 'The Collier's Charter: the eight hours day and what it means.' Co-operative Wholesale Societies. *Annual for 1909.* p. 269–96.

12,599 **Turner**, Ben. 'Should half-time labour be abolished?' *Social. Rev..* III, 13 (March 1909), 19–24.

12,600 **Barnes**, George Nicoll. 'The limitation of the hours of work.' National Conference on the Prevention of Destitution. *Report of the proceedings . . . 1912.* London: King, 1912. p. 445–51.

Discussion, p. 463–73.

12,601 **Gossip**, Alexander. 'The limitation of overtime.' National Conference on the Prevention of Destitution. *Report of the proceedings . . . 1912.* London: King, 1912. p. 451–6.

Discussion, p. 463–73.

12,602 **Gregory**, James. 'Richard Oastler and the Ten Hours Factory Movement.' *Brad. Antiq.*, n.s., III (1912), 411–31.

12,603 **Sanger**, Sophy. 'The limitation of hours from the international point of view.' National Conference on the Prevention of Destitution. *Report of the proceedings . . . 1912.* London: King, 1912. p. 456–62.

Discussion, p. 463–73.

12,604 **Home Office.** *Hours of employment of winding enginemen: report on the draft regulations under the Coal Mines Act, 1911, for the hours of employment of winding enginemen.* London: H.M.S.O., 1913. 6p. (Cd. 6710.)

By A. H. Ruegg.

12,605 *Report on the draft regulations, under the Coal Mines Act, 1911, for the hours of employment of winding enginemen.* London: H.M.S.O., 1913. 6p. (Cd. 6710.)

By A. H. Ruegg for the Home Office.

12,606 **Pope**, Samuel. *Report on the proposed general early closing order (under Section 5 of the Shops Act, 1912) for the Borough of Blackpool.* London: H.M.S.O., 1914. (Cd. 7082.)

12,607 **Pope**, Samuel. *Report on the proposed early closing order for the Borough of Nelson.* London: H.M.S.O., 1915. (Cd. 7868.)

12,608 **Gibb**, Spencer James. *A plea for the regulation of the hours of boy-work.* Manchester, 1918. [4] p.

12,609 **Dutt**, Rajani Palme. *The legal regulation of hours.* London: Labour Research Department, 1919. 16p. (Memorandum 9.)

12,610 **Freedom of Labour Defence.** *The Shops (Early Closing) Bill.* 1920. 4p.

12,611 **Shipowners' Parliamentary Committee.** *The Hours of Employment Bill, 1919.* London, 1920. 16p.

12,612 **Eire.** Dáil Éireann. *Interim report of the Special Committee to consider the Shop Hours (Drapery Trades, Dublin and Districts) Amendment Bill, 1925.* 1925. (T. 37.)

Final report. 1926. (T. 38.)

12,613 **Eire** Dáil Éireann. *Report of the Conference of Members representing the Dáil and the Seanad on certain amendments made by the Seanad to the Shop Hours (Drapery Trades, Dublin and Districts) Bill, 1926.* 1926. (T. 44.)

12,614 **Departmental Committee on the Working of the Shops (Early Closing) Acts, 1920 and 1921.** *Report.* London: H.M.S.O., 1927. 63p. (Cmd. 3000.)
Chairman: Sir W. W. Mackenzie.

12,615 **Early Closing Association.** *The Home Office inquiry . . . into the working of the Shops (Early Closing) Acts . . . evidence of first witness, Captain A. Larking . . .* London, 1927. 7p.

12,616 **Eire.** Seanad Éireann. *Report of the Conference between the two Houses on the Shop Hours (Drapery Trades, Dublin and Districts) Bill, 1926.* [1927?] (R. 39.)

12,617 **Home Department.** Committee on Employment of Women and Young Persons on the Two-Shift System. *Report . . . by the Departmental Committee appointed to enquire into the working of the temporary provisions contained in Section 2 of the Employment of Women, Young Persons and Children Act, 1920, and orders made thereunder.* London: H.M.S.O., 1935. 97p. (Cmd. 4914.)
Chairman: Sir Malcolm Delevingne.

12,618 **Hodgson,** J. S. *The movements for shorter hours, 1840 to 1875.* 1940. (D.Phil. thesis, University of Oxford.)

12,619 **Home Office** and **Scottish Home Department.** *Closing hours of shops: report by a Committee of Enquiry.* London: H.M.S.O., 1947. 39p. (Cmd. 7105.)
Chairman: Sir Ernest Arthur Gowers.

12,620 **Home Office** and **Scottish Home Department.** *Health, welfare, and safety in non-industrial employment; hours of employment of juveniles: report by a Committee of Enquiry.* London: H.M.S.O., 1949. 115p. (Cmd. 7664.)
Chairman: Sir Ernest Arthur Gowers.

12,621 **Eire.** Dáil Éireann. Special Committee on the Agricultural Workers (Weekly Half-Holidays) Bill, 1950. *Report.* 1951. ixp. (T. 129.)

12,622 **Langenfelt,** Gösta. *The historic origin of the eight hours day: studies in English traditionalism.* Stockholm: Almqvist and Wiksell, 1954. 151p. (Kungl. Vitterhets historie och Antikvitets Akademens. Handlingar 87.)

12,623 **Cowherd,** Raymond Gibson. *The humanitarians and the ten hour movement in England.* Boston, Mass.: Baker Library, Harvard Graduate School of Business Administration, 1956. 27p. (Publication of the Kress Library of Business and Economics 10.)
Bibliographical appendix: the writings of John Fielden, Richard Oastler, Michael T. Sadler, by Arthur H. Cole.

12,624 **Ministry of Transport and Civil Aviation.** *'Crush hour' travel in Central London: report of the first year's work of the Committee for Staggering of Working Hours in Central London.* London: H.M.S.O., 1958.
Chairman: J. Fitzgerald.

12,625 **Gill,** John Clifford. *The ten hours parson: Christian social action in the eighteen-thirties.* London: Society for the Promotion of Christian Knowledge, 1959. xiv, 210p.
About G. S. Bull.

12,626 **McCormick,** Brian J. and **Williams,** James Eccles. 'The miners and the eight-hour day, 1863–1910.' *Econ. Hist. Rev.,* 2nd ser., XII, 2 (December 1959), 222–38.

12,627 **Rottenberg,** Simon. 'Legislated early shop closing in Britain.' *J. Law Econ.,* IV (October 1961), 118–30.

12,628 **Home Office** and **Scottish Home and Health Department.** *Retail trading hours: suggested provisions for amending the Shops Act, 1950 (with explanatory notes).* London: H.M.S.O., 1965. 20p.

12,629 **Langenfelt,** Gösta. 'The eight hours' day: a history and a legend.' *Z. Angl. Am.,* XIII, 2 (1965), 167–73.

12,630 **Aydelotte,** William O. 'The conservative and radical interpretations of early Victorian social legislation.' *Vic. Studies,* XI, 2 (December 1967), 225–36.

12,631 **Board of Trade.** *Flight time limitations: the avoidance of excessive fatigue in aircrews.* London: H.M.S.O., 1967. 12p.

12,632 **Duffy,** A. E. P. 'The Eight Hour Day Movement in Britain, 1886–1893.' *Manchr. Sch.,* XXXVI, 3 (September 1968), 203–22; 4 (December 1968), 345–63.

12,633 **Department of Employment and Productivity.** National Joint Advisory Council. *Hours of employment of women and young persons employed in factories: report of a working party of the National Joint Advisory Council on Part VI of the Factories Act 1961 and associated legislation.* London: H.M.S.O., 1969. v, 53p.
Chairman: C. J. Maston.

12,634 **Stewart,** Robert. 'The Ten Hours and sugar crises of 1844: government and the House of Commons in the age of reform.' *Hist. J.,* XII, 1 (1969), 35–57.

See also: 9039; 12,518; 12,524; 13,172; 14,847.

VI. REGULATION OF WAGES AND SALARIES

A. EARLY WAGE REGULATION

This section includes works on the state's attempts to regulate wages prior to the twentieth century.

12,635 **McArthur,** Ellen A. '"The boke longyng to a Justice of the Peace" and the assessment of wages.' *Engl. Hist. Rev.,* IX, 34 (April 1894), 305–14.

12,636 **Hewins,** W. A. S. 'The regulation of wages by the Justices of the Peace.' *Econ. J,* VIII, 31 (September 1898), 340–6.

12,637 **Leonard**, E. M. 'The relief of the poor by the state regulation of wages.' *Engl. Hist. Rev.*, XIII, 49 (January 1898), 91–3.

12,638 **McArthur**, Ellen A. 'A fifteenth-century assessment of wages.' *Engl. Hist. Rev.*, XIII, 50 (April 1898), 299–302.

12,639 **Tingey**, J. C. 'An assessment of wages for the county of Norfolk in 1610.' *Engl. Hist. Rev.*, XIII, 51 (July 1898), 522–7.

12,640 **Hutchins**, B. Leigh. 'The regulation of wages by guilds and town authorities.' *Econ. J.*, X, 39 (September 1900), 404–11.

12,641 **McArthur**, Ellen A. 'The regulation of wages in the sixteenth century.' *Engl. Hist. Rev.*, XV, 59 (July 1900), 445–55.

12,642 **Putnam**, Bertha Haven. *The enforcement of the Statutes of Labourers during the first decade after the Black Death, 1349–1359.* New York, 1908. ix, 224, 480p. (Ph.D. thesis, Columbia University.)
Published also as *Studies in history, economics and public law*, XXXII.

12,643 **Tawney**, Richard Henry. 'The assessment of wages in England by the Justices of the Peace.' *Vjschr. Soz. Wirt.*, XI (1913), 307–37; 533–64.

12,644 **Heaton**, H. 'The assessment of wages in the West Riding of Yorkshire in the seventeenth and eighteenth centuries.' *Econ. J.*, XXIV, 94 (June 1914), 218–35.

12,645 **Putnam**, Bertha Haven. 'Maximum wage-laws for priests after the Black Death, 1348–1381.' *Am. Hist. Rev.*, XXI, 1 (October 1915), 12–32.
'A paper read at the meeting of the American Historical Association in Chicago, December 29, 1914.'

12,646 **Holdsworth**, *Sir* William Searle. 'A neglected aspect of the relations between economic and legal history.' *Econ. Hist. Rev.*, I, 1 (January 1927), 114–23.

12,647 **Putnam**, Bertha Haven. 'Northamptonshire wage assessments of 1560 and 1667.' *Econ. Hist. Rev.*, I, 1 (January 1927), 124–34.

12,648 **Waterman**, Elizabeth L. 'Some new evidence on wage assessments in the eighteenth century.' *Engl. Hist. Rev.*, XLIII, 171 (July 1928), 398–408.

12,649 **Derry**, T. K. 'The repeal of the apprenticeship clauses of the Statute of Apprentices.' *Econ. Hist. Rev.*, III, 1 (January 1931), 67–87.

12,650 **Hindmarsh**, Nora M. *The regulation of wages in England under the Statute of Artificers.* 1931–32. (Ph.D. thesis, University of London.)

12,651 **Levett**, A. E. 'Note on the Statutes of Labourers.' *Econ. Hist. Rev.*, IV, 1 (October 1932), 77–80.

12,652 **Kelsall**, Roger Keith. 'Two East Yorkshire wage assessments, 1669, 1679.' *Engl. Hist. Rev.*, LII, 206 (April 1937), 283–9.

12,653 **Kelsall**, Roger Keith. *Wage regulation under the Statute of Artificers.* London: Methuen, 1938. xii, 132p.

12,654 **Kelsall**, Roger Keith. 'Statute wages during a Yorkshire epidemic, 1679–81.' *Yorks. Archaeol. J.*, XXXIV, pt. 135 (1939), 310–16.

12,655 **Kelsall**, Roger Keith. 'A century of wage assessment in Herefordshire.' *Engl. Hist. Rev.*, LVII, 225 (January 1942), 115–19.
1666–1762.

12,656 **Mendenhall**, T. C. 'A Merioneth wage assessment of 1601.' *Merion. Hist. Rec. Soc. J.*, II (1953–56), 204–8.

12,657 **Reed**, Michael. 'Early seventeenth century wages assessments for the Borough of Shrewsbury.' *Shrops. Archaeol. Soc. Trans.*, LV (1954–56), 136–42.

12,658 **Bindoff**, S. T. 'The making of the Statute of Artificers.' Bindoff, S. T., Hirstfield, J. and Williams, C. H. (eds.). *Elizabethan government and society: essays presented to Sir John Neale.* London: U. of London, the Athlone P., 1961. p. 56–94.

12,659 **Clapham**, J. H. 'The Spitalfields Acts, 1773–1824.' *Econ. J.*, XXVI, 104 (December 1961), 459–71.

12,660 **Zupko**, Ronald Edward. *Statutes of Labourers in the reign of Edward III.* 1962–63. (Dissertation, University of Chicago.)

B. MODERN INCOMES POLICIES

This section includes works dealing with the government's attempts to regulate wages in the twentieth century. The general reports of the National Board for Prices and Incomes have been classified here; those dealing with specific industries, occupations, and topics have been classified at Part Six, III. See also Part Six, I; and Part Six, III, A.

12,661 **Cole**, George Douglas Howard and **Cole**, Margaret I. *The regulation of wages during and after the war.* London: Labour Research Department, 1918. 23p. (Memorandum 7.)

12,662 **Edinburgh Review**. 'The government and wages.' *Edinb. Rev.*, CCXXXI, 472 (April 1920), 374–92.

12,663 **Bibby**, John Pye. 'A note on "The public regulation of wages in Great Britain".' *Econ. J.*, XXXIX, 156 (December 1929), 645–6.
On 12,665.

12,664 **Clay**, Henry. 'The public regulation of wages in Great Britain.' *Nature*, CXXIV, 3123 (7 September 1929), 377–81.

12,665 **Clay**, Henry. 'The public regulation of wages in Great Britain.' *Econ. J.*, XXXIX, 155 (September 1929), 323–43.
'Presidential address to Section F of the British Association, South Africa, 1929.'

12,666 **Clay**, Henry. 'Public regulation of wages in Great Britain.' British Association for the Advancement of Science. *Reports of meetings*. 1929. p. 119–37.

12,667 **Bellerby**, John Rotherford and **Isles**, Keith Sydney. 'Wages policy and the gold standard in Great Britain.' *Int. Labour Rev.*, XXII, 2 (August 1930), 137–54.

12,668 **Isles**, Keith Sydney. *Wages policy and the price level*. 1933–34. (M.Sc. thesis, University of Cambridge.)
Published London: King, 1934. xiv, 256p.

12,669 **Morgan-Webb**, *Sir* Charles. 'Industrial relations in the monetary system of Great Britain.' Gannett, F. E. and Catherwood, B. F. (eds.). *Industrial and labour relations in Great Britain: a symposium*. New York: the editors, 1939. p. 281–95.

12,670 **Robinson**, Austin. 'The problems of wage policy in war-time.' *Econ. J.*, XLIX, 196 (December 1939), 640–55.

12,671 **Flanders**, Allan David. *Wage policy in war-time*. London: International Publishing Co., 1941. 24p.
Special supplement to *Socialist Vanguard Commentary*.

12,672 **McGregor**, Alexander Grant. *Is democracy finished? . . . the common-sense wage policy for Britain*. London, [1941?]. 12p.

12,673 *Statement by His Majesty's Government on price stabilisation and industrial policy*. London: H.M.S.O., 1941. 4p. (Cmd. 6294.)

12,674 **Lidbury**, C. A. 'A national wages policy.' *Ind. Law Rev.*, I, 2 (July 1946), 43–5; 4 (September 1946), 116–18.

12,675 **Steindl**, J. 'Reconstruction and wage policy.' *Oxf. Univ. Inst. Statist. Bull.*, VIII, 9 (September 1946), 285–93.

12,676 **Lidbury**, C. A. 'A national wages policy.' *Ind. Law Rev.*, I, 9 (February 1947), 257–92.
The whole issue is devoted to this article.
Reissued in book form. Leigh-on-Sea: Thames Bank Publishing Co., 1947. 43p.

12,677 **Morgan**, Edward Victor. 'A rational plan for wages.' *Banker*, LXXXI, 253 (February 1947), 82–8.

12,678 **Owen**, Henry. 'A national wages policy: the trade union point of view.' *Ind. Law Rev.*, I, 11 (April 1947), 351–4.

12,679 **Singer**, Hans Wolfgang. 'Wage policy in full employment.' *Econ. J.*, LVII, 228 (December 1947), 438–55.

12,680 **Richardson**, John Henry. 'Wage policy in full employment.' *Econ. J.*, LVIII, 231 (September 1948), 421–5.
Comment on article by H. W. Singer, followed by Singer's rejoinder.

12,681 *Statement on personal incomes, costs and prices*. London: H.M.S.O., 1948. 4p. (Cmd. 7321.)

12,682 **Worswick**, George David Norman and **Martin**, K. 'Prices and wages policy.' *Oxf. Univ. Inst. Statist. Bull.*, X, 3 (March 1948), 84–93.

12,683 **Finch**, C. D. *Some problems in wages policy*. 1949. (Ph.D. thesis, University of London.)

12,684 **Gracie**, James Johnstone. *A fair day's pay*. London: Management Publications Trust, 1949. xi, 103p.
'A plea for a national wages policy.'

12,685 **McKitterick**, Thomas Edward Maurice. *Wages policy?* London: Fabian Publications, Gollancz, 1949. 29p. ('The challenge of 1950.' 'Challenge' series 3.)

12,686 **Nigam**, S. B. L. *A study of the methods of state regulation of wages, with special reference to their possible applications in India*. 1949. (Ph.D. thesis, University of London.)

12,687 **Pigou**, Arthur Cecil. *Wage statistics and wage policy*. London: Oxford U.P., 1949. 44p. (Stamp memorial lecture.)

12,688 **Flanders**, Allan David. *A policy for wages*. London: Fabian Publications, Gollancz, 1950. 31p. (Fabian tract 281.)
A revised version of five articles written for the Journal of the Inland Revenue Staff Federation.

12,689 **Flanders**, Allan. 'Wages policy and full employment in Britain.' *Oxf. Univ. Inst. Statist. Bull.*, XII, 7–8 (July–August 1950), 225–42.

12,690 **Guillebaud**, Claude William. 'Problems of wages policy.' Ministry of Labour and National Service. *The worker in industry: a series of ten centenary lectures delivered during Festival of Britain year*. London: H.M.S.O., 1952. p. 43–54.

12,691 **McKelvey**, Jean Trepp. 'Trade union wage policy in postwar Britain.' *Ind. Labor Relat. Rev.*, VI, 1 (October 1952), 3–19.

12,692 **Phelps Brown**, Ernest Henry and **Roberts**, Benjamin Charles. 'Wages policy in Great Britain.' *Lloyds Bank Rev.*, n.s., 23 (January 1952), 17–31.

12,693 **Pigou**, Arthur Cecil. 'Wage statistics and wage policy.' *Essays in economics*. London: Macmillan, 1952. p. 29–64.
Reprint of the University of London Stamp memorial lecture. London: Oxford U.P., 1949.

12,694 **Worswick**, George David Norman. 'Personal income policy.' Worswick, G. D. N. and Ady, P. H. (eds.). *The British economy 1945–1950*. Oxford: Clarendon P., 1952. p. 313–35.

12,695 **Political and Economic Planning.** 'Fixing wages: a contrast from Holland.' *Planning*, XX, 371 (27 September 1954), 233–48.

12,696 **Political and Economic Planning.** 'Fixing wages: some British methods.' *Planning*, XX, 375 (20 December 1954), 301–14.

12,697 **Driscoll**, James. *National wages policy*. London: Bow Group, 1955. p. 1–15. (Bow Group pamphlet.)

Published with G. Engle, *The audience of politics*.

One of the series of Spring Lectures.

12,698 **Hawtrey**, *Sir* Ralph George. *Cross purposes in wage policy*. London: Longmans, Green, 1955. x, 148p.

12,699 **Hicks**, John Richard. 'The economic foundation of wage policy: address.' *Advmt. Sci.*, XII, 46 (September 1955), 199–208.

Reprinted in *Econ. J.*, LXV, 259 (September 1955), 389–404.

'Presidential address delivered to Section F of the British Association, Bristol, September 1955.'

12,700 **Nomvete**, B. D. *British wages policy, 1940–1950: a study of the decisions of the National Arbitration Tribunal*. 1955. (M.A. (Econ.) thesis, University of Manchester.)

12,701 **Phelps Brown**, Ernest Henry. 'Wage policy and wage differences.' *Economica*, n.s., XXII, 88 (November 1955), 349–54.

12,702 **Richardson**, John Henry. 'Wage policy and a labour standard.' *Econ. J.*, LXVI, 263 (September 1956), 431–41.

12,703 **Robertson**, Donald James. 'Trade unions and wage policy.' *Polit. Q.*, XXVII, 1 (January–March 1956), 19–30.

12,704 **Clegg**, Hugh Armstrong and **Chester**, Theodore Edward. *Wage policy and the health service*. Oxford: Blackwell, 1957. 142p.

12,705 **Flanders**, Allan David. 'Wage movements and wage policy in postwar Britain.' *Ann. Am. Acad. Polit. Soc. Sci.*, CCCX (March 1957), 87–98.

12,706 **Jack**, D. T. 'Is a wages policy desirable and practicable?' *Econ. J.*, LXVII, 268 (December 1957), 585–90.

'This formed the first contribution to a Discussion on the above topic at the Annual General Meeting of the Royal Economic Society held on July 4, 1957.' The second contribution, by Roberts, was published in the London and Cambridge Economic Service.

12,707 **Robertson**, Donald James. 'Wage policy in Britain: a comment.' *Current Econ. Comment*, XIX, 1 (February 1957), 55–7.

12,708 **Turner**, Herbert Arthur. *Wage policy abroad, and conclusions for Britain*. London: Fabian Society, 1957. 36p. (Fabian research series 189.)

12,709 **Alexander**, Kenneth John Wilson and **Hughes**, John Dennis. *A socialist wages plan: the politics of the pay packet*. London: *Universities and Left Review*, [1958?]. 65p. (*Universities and Left Review* and *New Reasoner*. New left discussion booklets.)

12,710 **Council on Prices, Productivity and Incomes.** *First report*. London: H.M.S.O., 1958. iv, 75p.

Second report, August 1958. 1958. iv, 39p.
Third report, July 1959. 1959. iv, 54p.
Fourth report, July 1961. 1961. iv, 31p.

12,711 **Dow**, J. C. R. 'Organizing an opposition to price inflation.' *Scott. J. Polit. Econ.*, v, 2 (June 1958), 175–9.

Originally written for submission to the Council on Prices, Productivity and Incomes.

12,712 **Flanders**, Allan David. 'Can Britain have a wage policy.' *Scott. J. Polit. Econ.*, v, 2 (June 1958), 114–25.

Comment by A. D. Campbell, p. 165–7.
Comment by D. T. Jack, p. 162–4.
Comment by Harry G. Johnson, p. 149–53.
Comment by B. C. Roberts, p. 154–9.

12,713 **Roberts**, Benjamin Charles. *National wages policy in war and peace*. London: Allen and Unwin, 1958. 180p.

12,714 **Robertson**, Donald James. 'The inadequacy of recent wage policies in Britain.' *Scott. J. Polit. Econ.*, v, 2 (June 1958), 99–113.

Comment by A. D. Campbell, p. 165–7.
Comment by D. T. Jack, p. 162–4.
Comment by Harry G. Johnson, p. 149–53.

12,715 **Turner**, Herbert Arthur. 'The inadequacy of recent wage theorising.' *Scott. J. Polit. Econ.*, v, 2 (June 1958), 169–74.

Discusses views of D. J. Robertson, A. Flanders, J. R. Parkinson, and others.

12,716 **Worswick**, George David Norman. 'Prices, productivity, and incomes.' *Oxf. Econ. Pap.*, n.s., x, 2 (June 1958), 246–64.

'This is a shortened version of a paper written at the request of the Council on Prices, Productivity, and Incomes in November 1957.'

12,717 **Roberts**, Benjamin Charles. *Wages, prices and politics*. Madison, Wis.: University of Wisconsin, Industrial Relations Research Center, 1959. p. 385–92. (Reprint series 59/6.)

Sidney Hillman Foundation Lectures, University of Wisconsin, February 1959.

12,718 **Guillebaud**, Claude William. *Wage determination and wages policy*. Welwyn: Nisbet, 1960. 31p. (Economic monographs.)

Second edition. *Wage determination and wages policy: a lecture and postscript*. 1967. 79p.

12,719 **Hicks**, John Richard. 'Economic foundations of wage policy.' Galenson, W. and Lipset, S. M. (eds.). *Labor and trade unionism: an interdisciplinary reader*. New York, London: Wiley, 1960. p. 178–91.

Presidential address to Section F of the British Association, Bristol, September 1955.

From *Econ. J.*, LXV, 259 (September 1955), 389–404.

12,720 **Phelps Brown**, Ernest Henry. 'Wage policy and wage differences.' Galenson, W. and Lipset, S. M. (eds.). *Labor and trade unionism: an interdisciplinary reader*. New York, London: Wiley, 1960. p. 18–22.
From *Economica* (November 1955).
On B. Wootton, *The social foundations of wage policy*.

12,721 **Corina**, John G. *The British experiment in wage restraint, with special reference to 1948–50*. 1961. (D.Phil. thesis, University of Oxford.)

12,722 **Round Table.** 'Towards a wage policy: inflation in the U.K. and the remedy.' *Round Table*, 204 (September 1961), 337–46.

12,723 **Clegg**, Hugh Armstrong. 'A policy for incomes.' *Lloyds Bank Rev.*, n.s., 64 (April 1962), 1–16.

12,724 **Derrick**, Paul. 'Incomes policy.' *Contemp. Rev.*, CCII, 1161 (October 1962), 178–81.

12,725 **Dicks-Mireaux**, L. A. and **Shepherd**, J. R. 'The wages structure and some implications for income policy.' *Natn. Inst. Econ. Rev.*, 22 (November 1962), 38–48.

12,726 **Donoughue**, Bernard. 'Wage policies in the public sector.' *Planning*, XXVIII, 467 (19 November 1962), 365–99.

12,727 **Jasay**, A. E. 'Paying ourselves more money.' *Westm. Bank Rev.* (May 1962), 2–13.

12,728 **Johnston**, Thomas L. 'Pay policy after the pause.' *Scott. J. Polit. Econ.*, IX, 1 (February 1962), 1–16.

12,729 **Knowles**, Kenneth Guy Jack Charles and **Robinson**, Derek. 'Wage rounds and wage policy.' *Oxf. Univ. Inst. Statist. Bull.*, XXIV, 2 (May 1962), 269–329.

12,730 *National Incomes Commission*. London: H.M.S.O., 1962. 4p. (Cmd. 1844.)

12,731 **Pollard**, Sidney. 'Paying whom more money?' *Westm. Bank Rev.* (August 1962), 32–8.
Presents a different crisis viewpoint from that of A. E. Jasay in the issue for May 1962.

12,732 **The Times.** *Towards a national incomes policy: five special articles from 'The Times'*. London: Times Publishing Co., 1962. 22p.

12,733 **Treasury.** *Incomes policy: the next step*. London: H.M.S.O., 1962. 6p. (Cmnd. 1626.)

12,734 **Turner**, Herbert Arthur. *Wage policy and economic development*. Manchester: Manchester Statistical Society, 1962. 22p.
Read 12 December 1962.

12,735 **Westminster Bank Review.** 'Wages policy at home and abroad.' *Westm. Bank Rev.* (November 1962), 29–38.

12,736 **Turner**, Herbert Arthur. 'Wage policy and economic development.' *Manchr. Statist. Soc. Trans.* (1962–63). 22p.

12,737 **Economist Intelligence Unit.** *Trade unions and incomes policy*. London: E.I.U., [1963?]. 10p. (Trend supplement 42/1.)

12,738 **Frank**, W. F. 'The drift towards a British national wages policy.' Palmer, E. E. (ed.). *Current law and social problems*. Vol. 3. Toronto: U. of Toronto P., 1963. p. 61–100.

12,739 **Jenkins**, Peter. 'Is a wages policy possible?' *New Soc.*, 14 (3 January 1963), 9–11.

12,740 **Johnston**, Thomas L. 'Controlling government's wage and manpower bill.' *Scott. J. Polit. Econ.*, X, 1 (February 1963), 86–101.

12,741 **Merrett**, Anthony John and **Sykes**, Allen. 'Insurance policy and company profitability.' *Distr. Bank Rev.*, 147 (September 1963), 18–30.

12,742 **Robinson**, Derek. 'Wage rates, wage income and wage policy.' *Oxf. Univ. Inst. Statist. Bull.*, XXV (February 1963), 47–76.

12,743 **Stamp**, Maxwell and **Feather**, Victor. 'Is an effective incomes policy possible?' *Moor. Wall Street* (Spring 1963), 5–27.
'A correspondence.'

12,744 **Stewart**, Michael and **Winsbury**, Rex. *An incomes policy for Labour*. London: Fabian Society and Young Fabian Group, 1963. 33p. (Fabian tract 350. Socialism in the sixties.)

12,745 **Corina**, John. 'Incomes policy.' Hall, P. G. (ed.). *Labour's new frontiers*. London: Deutsch, 1964. p. 38–57.

12,746 **Corina**, John. 'Labour and incomes policy.' *New Soc.*, IV, 112 (19 November 1964), 8–9.

12,747 **The Economist**. *Salaries: are you better off? A discussion of the changed position of salary-earners in the past few years and the implications for incomes policy*. London: *Economist*, 1964. 12p.
Two articles reprinted from *The Economist*, 23 and 30 May, 1964. p. 813–15, 926–9.

12,748 **Federation of British Industries.** *The search for a national incomes policy*. London: F.B.I., 1964. 13p.

12,749 **Fogarty**, Michael Patrick. 'The National Incomes Commission: the wider implications of its award in the universities' case.' *Br. J. Ind. Relat.*, II, 3 (November 1964), 360–78.

12,750 **Hall**, *Sir* Robert. 'Incomes policy: state of play.' *Three Banks Rev.*, 61 (March 1964), 3–23.

12,751 **Kaldor**, Nicholas. 'A positive policy for wages and dividends.' *Essays on economic policy*. Vol. 1. London: Duckworth, 1964. p. 111–27.
'Memorandum submitted to the Chancellor of the Exchequer on 21 June 1950.'

12,752 **McCarthy**, William Edward John. 'The price of wage restraint.' *New Soc.*, III, 75 (5 March 1964), 12–13.

12,753 **Oettinger**, Martin P. 'Collective bargaining, wage restraint, and national economic policy: a comparative study of the United States and Western Europe.' *West. Econ. J.*, II, 3 (Summer 1964), 233–55.

12,754 **Organisation for Economic Co-operation and Development.** *Policies for prices, profits and other non-wage incomes: a report on price guidance and control, incomes policy for profits and other non-wage incomes, prepared for the Economic Policy Committee by its Working Party on Costs of Production and Prices.* Paris: O.E.C.D., 1964. 78p.

12,755 **Taylor**, Basil. 'A note on profits versus wage restraint.' *Westm. Bank Rev.* (May 1964), 30–3.

12,756 **Marris**, Robin Lapthorn. 'Incomes policy and the rate of profit in industry.' *Manchr. Statist. Soc. Trans.* (1964–65). 28p.

12,757 **Association of Cinematograph, Television and Allied Technicians, Association of Scientific Workers, Association of Supervisory Staffs, Executives and Technicians, Draughtsmen's and Allied Technicians' Association,** and **Society of Technical Civil Servants.** *A declaration of dissent: technicians' unions and incomes policy.* Richmond, Surrey: D.A.T.A., 1965. 15p.

12,758 **Boddy**, David. 'The incomes policy and the printing industry.' *Scott. J. Polit. Econ.*, XII, 3 (November 1965), 309–28.

12,759 **Browne**, Margaret H. 'Industrial labour and incomes policy in the Republic of Ireland.' *Br. J. Ind. Relat.*, III, 1 (March 1965), 46–66.

12,760 **Campbell**, John Ross. 'The development of incomes policy in Britain.' *Marxism Today*, IX, 3 (March 1965), 69–75.

12,761 **Carruthers**, James Pirrie. *With good intent.* London: Neame, 1965. 16p. (Take home books.)

12,762 **Clegg**, Hugh Armstrong. 'The lessons of NIC.' *New Soc.*, V, 128 (11 March 1965), 7–9.

12,763 **Coates**, Ken. 'Incomes policy. II. A strategy for the unions.' *Social. Regist.* (1965), 175–83.

12,764 **Cyriax**, George. 'Can the incomes policy work?' *Banker*, CXV, 477 (November 1965), 711–17.

12,765 **Department of Economic Affairs.** *Machinery of prices and incomes policy.* London: H.M.S.O., 1965. 4p. (Cmnd. 2577.)

12,766 **Department of Economic Affairs.** *Prices and incomes policy.* London: H.M.S.O., 1965. 11p. (Cmnd. 2639.)

12,767 **Department of Economic Affairs.** *Prices and incomes policy: an early warning system.* London: H.M.S.O., 1965. 12p. (Cmnd. 2808.)

12,768 **Derrick**, Paul. 'A new approach to an incomes policy.' *Contemp. Rev.*, CCVI, 1193 (June 1965), 316–22.

12,769 **Edelman**, Jacob Murray and **Fleming**, Robben Wright. *The politics of wage-price decisions: a four-country analysis.* Urbana, Ill.: U. of Illinois P., 1965. 331p.

Condensed version of this book published in 1964 for the American Foundation on Automation and Employment.

12,770 **Fabian Group.** *A plan for incomes.* London: Fabian Society, 1965. 41p. (Socialism in the sixties. Research series 247.)

By John Hughes and Ken Alexander.

12,771 **Hawtrey**, *Sir* Ralph George. *An incomes policy.* London: Woolwich Polytechnic, Department of Economics and Management, 1965. 29p. (Woolwich economic papers 4.)

12,772 **Institute of Economic Affairs.** *Policy for incomes?* London: I.E.A., 1964 [i.e. 1965]. 66p. (Hobart papers 29.)

Part I. *The limits of incomes policies*, by F. W. Paish.

Part II. *Incomes policies in Europe*, by Jossleyn Hennessy.

Second edition. 1966.

Third edition. 1967. 76p.

Fourth edition. 1968. 79p.

12,773 **Layton**, Christopher. 'Incomes mythology.' *New Soc.*, V, 122 (28 January 1965), 8–10.

12,774 **Lloyd**, M. H. 'Farm prices and incomes today.' *Lloyds Bank Rev.*, n.s., 75 (January 1965), 31–44.

12,775 **Murray**, L. 'Non-wage incomes: British experience and policy problems.' Organisation for Economic Co-operation and Development. Manpower and Social Affairs Directorate. Social Affairs Division. *Non-wage incomes and prices policy: papers for a trade union seminar. Supplement to the report.* Paris: O.E.C.D., 1965. p. 105–21.

12,776 **Organisation for Economic Co-operation and Development.** *Report by the Austrian joint team which visited the United Kingdom from 16th – 20th November, 1964, to study economic planning, labour market and incomes policy.* Paris: O.E.C.D., 1965. 23p. (Programme for employers and unions national missions, 1964, report 10.)

12,777 **Rowthorne**, Bob. 'The trap of an incomes policy.' *New Left Rev.*, 34 (November–December 1965), 3–11.

12,778 **Saunders**, Christopher Thomas. 'Incomes policy and equity.' *Westm. Bank Rev.* (February 1965), 2–12.

12,779 **Topham**, Anthony J. 'Incomes policy. I. The background to the argument.' *Social. Regist.* (1965), 163–74.

12,780 **Williams**, Bruce Rodda. 'Prices and incomes.' *Distr. Bank Rev.*, 154 (June 1965), 3–18.

12,781 **Allen**, Victor Leonard. *Militant trade unionism: a re-analysis of industrial action in an inflationary situation.* London: Merlin P., 1966. 175p.

12,782 **Behrend**, Hilde, **Lynch**, Harriet and **Davies**, Jean. *A national survey of attitudes to inflation and incomes policy.* London: Edutext Publications, 1966. 27p. (Occasional papers in social and economic administration 7.)

12,783 **Behrend**, Hilde. 'Price images, inflation and national incomes policy.' *Scott. J. Polit. Econ.*, XII, 3 (November 1966), 273–96.

Deals with 'the problem of learning prices and price-judgements, and of re-learning them when prices change', and discusses 'the practical implications of the findings for national incomes policy'.

Comment, by H. M. Begg and J. A. Stewart, XV, 1 (February 1968), 84–96.

Rejoinder, by H. Behrend, p. 97–100.

12,784 **Clark**, Colin. *An incomes policy.* London: Aims of Industry, [1966?]. 8p. (Study 12.)

12,785 **Cliff**, Tony and **Barker**, Colin. *Incomes policy, legislation and shop stewards.* Harrow Weald: London Industrial Shop Stewards Defence Committee, 1966. 136p.

12,786 **Confederation of British Industry.** *Prices and incomes standstill.* London: C.B.I., 1966. 10p.

12,787 **Corina**, John Gordon. *Incomes policy: problems and prospects.* London: Institute of Personnel Management, 1966. 2 pts. (Industrial relations series.)

Part 1. The labour market. 35p.

Part 2. The development of incomes policy. 82p.

12,788 **Department of Economic Affairs.** *Prices and incomes policy: return to an Order of the House of Lords dated July 28th, 1966, for a paper relating to the prices and incomes policy of Her Majesty's Government.* London: H.M.S.O., 1966. 48p. (H.L. 81.)

12,789 **Department of Economic Affairs.** *Prices and incomes standstill.* London: H.M.S.O., 1966. 8p. (Cmnd. 3073.)

12,790 **Department of Economic Affairs.** *Prices and incomes standstill: period of severe restraint.* London: H.M.S.O., 1966. 10p. (Cmnd. 3150.)

12,791 **Derrick**, Paul. *A socialist incomes policy.* London: Voice of the Unions, 1966. 48p.

12,792 **Goodwin**, Dennis. 'In defence of trade union rights.' *Marxism Today*, X, 9 (September 1966), 361–71.

12,793 **Jaques**, Elliott. *National incomes policy: a democratic plan.* K. H. Services, 1966. 8p. (King-Hall newsletter.)

12,794 **Jenkins**, Peter. 'Next steps in incomes policy' *New Soc.*, VII, 173 (20 January 1966), 6–8.

12,795 **Kassalow**, Everett M. 'National wage policies: lessons to date, Europe and the U.S.A.' Industrial Relations Research Association. *Proceedings of the nineteenth annual winter meeting, San Francisco, December 28–29, 1966.* p. 125–38.

12,796 **McKersie**, Robert B. 'Incomes policy in Great Britain.' Industrial Relations Research Association. *Proceedings of the nineteenth annual winter meeting, San Francisco, December 28–29, 1966.* p. 139–48.

12,797 **Ministry of Housing and Local Government** and **Welsh Office.** *Prices and incomes policy: and 'early warning' system.* London: H.M.S.O., 1966. 4p.

Joint circular.

12,798 **National Board for Prices and Incomes.** *General report, April 1965 to July 1966.* London: H.M.S.O., 1966. (Report 19. Cmnd. 3087.)

12,799 **National Board for Prices and Incomes.** *Productivity and pay during the period of severe restraint.* London: H.M.S.O., 1966. (Report 23. Cmnd. 3167.)

12,800 **Nieuwenhuysen**, J. P. 'Thoughts on an incomes policy for Australia.' *J. Ind. Relat.*, VIII, 1 (March 1966), 1–12.

12,801 **Organisation for Economic Co-operation and Development.** *Non-wage incomes and prices policy: trade union policy and experience. Background report for a trade union seminar.* Paris: O.E.C.D., Manpower and Social Affairs Directorate, Social Affairs Division, 1966. 191p. (International seminars 1965–2.)

12,802 **Phelps Brown**, Ernest Henry. 'Guidelines for growth and for incomes in the United Kingdom: some possible lessons for the United States.' Shultz, G. P. and Aliber, R. Z. (eds.). *Guidelines, informal controls, and the market place: policy choices in a full employment economy.* Chicago, London: U. of Chicago P., 1966. p. 143–63.

12,803 **Ramelson**, Bert. *Incomes policy: the great wage freeze trick.* London: Communist Party of Great Britain, 1966. 21p.

12,804 **Robertson**, Donald James. 'Guideposts and norms: contrasts in the U.S. and U.K. wage policy.' *Three Banks Rev.*, 72 (December 1966), 3–29.

12,805 **Sergeant**, Winsley and **Roydhouse**, E. *Prices and wages freeze: a narrative guide to the Prices and Incomes Act 1966 together with the text of the Act, the narrative guide by Winsley Sergeant, annotations to the Act by E. Roydhouse.* London: Butterworths, 1966. vi, 53, 95p.

12,806 **Sloane**, K. 'Co-operation and coercion in wages and income policies.' *J. Ind. Relat.*, VIII, 1 (March 1966), 13–24.

12,807 **Smith**, David C. *Incomes policies: some foreign experiences and their relevance for Canada.* Ottawa: Queen's Printer, 1966. vii, 207p. (Economic Council of Canada. Special study 4.)

12,808 **Smith**, Henry. 'Problems of planning incomes.' *Lloyds Bank Rev.*, n.s., 79 (January 1966), 30–40.

12,809 **Sturmthal**, Adolf. 'Some tentative generalizations about European incomes policies.' Industrial Relations Research Association. *Proceedings of the nineteenth annual winter meeting, San Francisco, December 28–29, 1966.* p. 106–15.

12,810 **Turner**, Herbert Arthur and **Zoeteweij**, Herbert. *Prices, wages and incomes policies in industrialised market economies.* Geneva: International Labour Office, 1966. iv, 172p.

12,811 **Anderson**, W. C. 'The prices and incomes policy and the public services.' *Publ. Adm.*, XLV, 3 (Autumn 1967), 261–8.

'An address by the General Secretary of NALGO to the Annual General Meeting of the Royal Institute [of Public Administration] on 28 April 1967.'

12,812 **Banks**, Robert Frederick. 'Wages Councils and incomes policy.' *Br. J. Ind. Relat.*, v, 3 (November 1967), 338–58.

12,813 **Barr**, John. 'Report on the P.I.B. 1. Wages.' *New Soc.*, x, 270 (30 November 1967), 779–81.

12,814 **Barr**, John. 'Report on the P.I.B. 2. Prices.' *New Soc.*, x, 272 (14 December 1967), 858–9.

12,815 **Behrend**, Hilde, **Lynch**, Harriet, **Thomas**, Howard and **Davies**, Jean. *Incomes policy and the individual.* Edinburgh, London: Oliver and Boyd, 1967. vii, 72p.

12,816 **Corina**, John. 'Can an incomes policy be administered?' *Br. J. Ind. Relat.*, v, 3 (November 1967), 287–310.

A paper presented at the first World Congress of the International Industrial Relations Association, Geneva, 1967.

12,817 **Corina**, John. 'Incomes policy: an international survey.' *Politico*, XXXII, 3 (September 1967), 462–88.

12,818 **Davies**, Bryan L. 'Incomes policy: the British experience.' *Labor Law J.*, XVIII, 7 (July 1967), 427–39.

12,819 **Davies**, John. 'Incomes policy in the U.K.' *Incomes policy: report of the 12th Conference on economic and industrial problems, held at Fiuggi from May 20 to 22, 1966.* Rome: General Confederation of Italian Industries, Research Department, 1967.

12,820 **Department of Economic Affairs.** *Prices and incomes policy after 30th June 1967.* London: H.M.S.O., 1967. 8p. (Cmnd. 3235.)

12,821 **Inter-American Conference of Ministers of Labor.** Permanent Technical Committee on Labor Matters. *The European experience with income and price policies: possible implications for Latin America.* Viña del Mar, Chile, 1967. 30p. (UP/Ser.H/V.)

12,822 **Jackson**, Joseph Michael. 'Wages: just reward or efficient allocator.' *Br. J. Ind. Relat.*, v, 3 (November 1967), 375–85.

12,823 **Keeler**, W. R. C. 'The relationship of plant productivity agreements to incomes policy.' *Br. J. Ind. Relat.*, v, 1 (March 1967), 40–7.

12,824 **Kelvin**, R. P. 'Incomes policy: what our readers think.' *New Soc.*, IX, 237 (13 April 1967), 532–5.

12,825 **Kelvin**, R. P. 'The *New Society* incomes policy survey.' *New Soc.*, IX, 231 (2 March 1967), 315–18.

12,826 **Kelvin**, R. P. 'What sort of incomes policy?' *New Soc.*, IX, 236 (6 April 1967), 491–4.

Based on an Opinion Research Centre Survey.

12,827 **McKersie**, Robert B. 'The British Board for Prices and Incomes.' *Ind. Relat.*, VI, 3 (May 1967), 267–84.

12,828 **Marshall**, John Leslie. *Freeze, 'severe restraint' – and what then?* London: Aims of Industry, 1967. 16p. (Studies 16.)

12,829 **National Board for Prices and Incomes.** *Second general report, July 1966 to August 1967.* London: H.M.S.O., 1967. (Report 40. Cmnd. 3394.)

12,830 **Robinson**, Derek. 'Low paid workers and incomes policy.' *Oxf. Univ. Inst. Econ. Statist. Bull.*, XXIX, 1 (February 1967), 1–29.

12,831 **Robinson**, Derek. 'National wage and incomes policies and trade unions: issues and experiences.' Barkin, S., and others (eds.). *International labor.* New York, Evanston, London: Harper and Row, 1967. p. 216–46.

12,832 **Romanis**, Anne. 'Cost inflation and incomes policy in industrial countries.' *IMF Staff Pap.*, XIV, 1 (March 1967), 169–209.

12,833 **Seear**, Nancy. *Policies for incomes.* London: Liberal Publication Department for the Unservile State Group, 1967. 22p. (Unservile state papers 13.)

12,834 **Smith**, David C. *Incomes and wages–price policies: some issues and approaches.* Kingston, Ont.: Queen's University, Industrial Relations Centre, 1967. 107p. (Reprint series 9.)

Reprint of chapters 1, 2, 3 and 9 of the author's *Incomes policies: some foreign experiences and their relevance for Canada.*

12,835 **Stalley**, D. J. 'Prices and incomes policy in the United Kingdom.' *J. Ind. Relat.*, IX, 2 (July 1967), 155–67.

12,836 **Ulman**, Lloyd. 'Under severe restraint: British incomes policy.' *Ind. Relat.*, VI, 3 (May 1967), 213–66.

12,837 **Zoeteweij**, Bert. 'Incomes policies abroad: an interim account.' *Ind. Labor Relat. Rev.*, XX, 4 (July 1967), 650–64.

12,838 **Mitchell**, Daniel Jesse Brody. *Incomes policy, costs, and the balance-of-payments: the cases of Britain and Australia.* 1967–68. (Dissertation, Massachusetts Institute of Technology.)

12,839 **Blackaby**, Frank and **Artis**, Michael. 'On incomes policy.' *Distr. Bank Rev.*, 165 (March 1968), 28–44.

12,840 **Campbell**, John Ross and **Ramelson**, Bert. 'British state monopoly capitalism and its impact on trade unions and wages.' *Marxism Today*, XII, 1 (January 1968), 7–14; 2 (February 1968), 50–8.

A paper prepared for a symposium on the 50th anniversary of Lenin's *Imperialism* and the centenary of Marx's *Capital*, and organised at Prague in October 1967 by the *World Marxist Review*. With a postscript.

12,841 **Corina**, John Gordon. 'Can an incomes policy be administered?' Roberts, B. C. (ed.). *Industrial relations: contemporary issues.* London: Macmillan; New York: St Martin's P., 1968. p. 257–91.

12,842 **Crossley**, John Rodney. 'Wage structure and the future of the incomes policy.' *Scott. J. Polit. Econ.*, XV, 2 (June 1968), 109–28.

12,843 **Department of Economic Affairs.** *Productivity, prices and incomes policy in 1968 and 1969.* London: H.M.S.O., 1968. 16p. (Cmnd. 3590.)

12,844 **Douty**, H. M. 'Productivity bargaining in Britain.' *Mon. Labor Rev.*, XCI, 5 (May 1968), 1–6.

12,845 **Gray**, H. Peter. 'Depreciation or incomes policy?' *Manchr. Sch.*, XXXVI, 1 (March 1968), 49–61.

12,846 **Jacobs**, Eric. 'Aubrey Jones.' *New Soc.*, XI, 283 (29 February 1968), 299–300.

12,847 **Jones**, Aubrey. 'The National Board for Prices and Incomes.' *Polit. Q.*, XXXIX, 2 (April–June 1968), 122–33.

12,848 **Jones**, Aubrey. 'Prices and incomes policy.' *Econ. J.*, LXXVIII, 312 (December 1968), 799–806.

'Address to the Annual Meeting of the Royal Economic Society, July 4, 1968.'

12,849 **Jones**, Aubrey. 'Wage relativities.' Smith, A. D. (ed.). *The labour market and inflation.* London: Macmillan; New York: St Martin's P., 1968. p. 115–20.

12,850 **Laffer**, Kingsley. 'Whither arbitration? Problems of incomes policies in Australia and overseas.' *J. Ind. Relat.*, X, 3 (November 1968), 206–21.

'A paper given to the Economic Society of Aust. and N.Z., N.S.W. Branch, 20/6/68.'

12,851 **Lipton**, Michael. 'A real incomes policy?' *New Soc.*, XII, 313 (26 September 1968), 441–2.

12,852 **McCarthy**, William Edward John. 'Incomes policy and the budget.' *New Soc.*, XI, 284 (7 March 1968), 334–5.

12,853 **McGahey**, Mick. *The case for higher wages.* London: Communist Party of Great Britain, 1968. 20p.

12,854 **National Board for Prices and Incomes.** *Third general report, August 1967 to July 1968.* London: H.M.S.O., 1968. v, 70p. (Report 77. Cmnd. 3715.)

12,855 **Robinson**, Derek. 'Implementing an incomes policy.' *Ind. Relat.*, VIII, 1 (October 1968), 73–90.

12,856 **Saunders**, Christopher Thomas. 'Macro-economic aspects of incomes policy.' Smith, A. D. (ed.). *The labour market and inflation.* London: Macmillan; New York: St Martin's P., 1968. p. 10–23.

12,857 **Smith**, David C. 'Incomes policy.' Caves, R. E. (ed.). *Britain's economic prospects.* Washington: Brookings Institution; London: Allen and Unwin, 1968. p. 104–44.

12,858 **Thakur**, S. N. 'Income policy: its prerequisites and implications.' *Indian J. Labour Econ.*, X, 4 (January 1968), C-52–C-54.

A paper given at a conference.

12,859 **Tress**, Ronald Charles. 'Incomes policy in the United Kingdom.' Marchal, J. and Ducros, B. (eds.). *The distribution of national income.* London: Macmillan; New York: St Martin's P., 1968. p. 681–97.

Discussion, p. 712–25.

12,860 **Williams**, Bruce Rodda. 'Incomes policies.' *J. Ind. Relat.*, X, 2 (July 1968), 97–103.

12,861 **Lewis**, P. N. *An examination of British incomes policy.* 1968–69. (M.A. thesis, University of Liverpool.)

12,862 **Bosanquet**, Nicholas. *Pay, prices and Labour in power.* London: Fabian Society, 1969. 25p. (Young Fabian pamphlet 20.)

12,863 **Corina**, John Gordon and **Meyrick**, A. J. *The performance of incomes and prices policy in the United Kingdom, 1958–1968.* Geneva: International Institute for Labour Studies, 1969. 46p. (International educational materials exchange, Eur. IV/9.)

12,864 **Crossley**, John Rodney. 'Incomes policy and sharing in capital gains.' *Br. J. Ind. Relat.*, VII, 3 (November 1969), 336–62.

'This article was presented as a paper at a Conference co-sponsored by the Foundadation on Automation and Employment, held in the Hebrew University, Jerusalem, April 1969.'

12,865 **Department of Employment and Productivity.** *Productivity, prices and incomes policy after 1969.* London: H.M.S.O., 1969. 43p. (Cmnd. 4237.)

12,866 **Douty**, H. M. 'Some aspects of British wage policy.' *Sth. Econ. J.*, XXXVI, 1 (July 1969), 74–81.

12,867 **Hillery**, Patrick J., and others. 'Incomes policy.' *Administration*, XVII, 3 (Autumn 1969), 231–70.
'. . . texts of addresses delivered at a seminar organised by the IPA at Galway on 8 May 1969.'
1. By Patrick J. Hillery. p. 231–5.
2. By W. J. L. Ryan. p. 235–45.
3. By Charles R. Cuffe. p. 246–59.
4. By E. J. Gray. p. 253–63.
5. By Donald Nevin. p. 263–70.

12,868 **Industrial Law Society.** 'Report of the Society's Conference on the Prices and Incomes Policy and the Law.' *Ind. Law Soc. Bull.*, 4 (April 1969), 21–7.
8 February 1969.

12,869 **Mitchell**, Daniel Jesse Brody. 'A simplified approach to incomes policy.' *Ind. Labor Relat. Rev.*, XXII, 4 (July 1969), 512–27.

12,870 **Mouly**, Jean. 'Changing concepts of wage policy.' *Int. Labour Rev.*, C, 1 (July 1969), 1–22.

12,871 **National Board for Prices and Incomes.** *Fourth general report, July 1968 to July 1969.* London: H.M.S.O., 1969. iv, 84p. (Report 122. Cmnd. 4130.)

12,872 **National Board for Prices and Incomes.** *100 PIB reports summarised.* London: N.B.P.I., 1969. ii, 140p.
Supplement covering reports 101 to 122 1969. i, 50p.

12,873 **Paish**, Frank Walter. *Rise and fall of incomes policy.* London: Institute of Economic Affairs, 1969. 64p. (Hobart paper 47.)

12,874 **Topham**, Tony. 'Municipal busmen, productivity and the incomes policy.' *Trade Un. Regist.* (1969), 201–10.

12,875 **Turner**, Herbert Arthur and **Jackson**, D. A. S. 'On the stability of wage differences and productivity-based wage policies: an international analysis.' *Br. J. Ind. Relat.*, VII, 1 (March 1969), 1–18.

12,876 **Ulman**, Lloyd. 'Wage-price policies: some lessons from abroad.' *Ind. Relat.*, VIII, 3 (May 1969), 195–213.

12,877 **Woodward**, Joan. 'How the PIB should work.' *New Soc.*, XIII, 331 (30 January 1969), 168–9. (Society at work.)

12,878 **Tweedie**, David Philip. *Management and incomes policy.* 1969–70. (Ph.D. thesis, University of Edinburgh.)

12,879 **Burns**, D. E. and **Yeomans**, K. A. 'Incomes policy in the control of inflation: an appraisal.' *Lough. J. Soc. Studies*, 9 (June 1970), 5–23.

12,880 **Eire**, Department of Finance. National Industrial Economic Council. *Report on incomes and prices policy.* 1970. (F. 66/28. Report 27.)

12,881 **Lipsey**, Richard G. and **Parkin**, J. Michael. 'Incomes policy: a re-appraisal.' *Economica*, n.s., XXXVII, 146 (May 1970), 115–38.

12,882 **Mitchell**, Joan. 'The National Board for Prices and Incomes.' *Publ. Adm.*, XLVIII, 1 (Spring 1970), 57–67.

12,883 **Parkin**, J. Michael. 'Incomes policy: some further results on the determination of the rate of change of money wages.' *Economica*, n.s., XXXVII, 148 (November 1970), 386–401.

12,884 **Rezler**, Julius. 'Recent wages and incomes policies based on productivity in the United Kingdom and the United States.' Kamin, A. (ed.). *Western European labor and the American corporation.* Washington, D.C.: Bureau of National Affairs, 1970. p. 341–9.

12,885 **Robinson**, Olive. 'Incomes policy and the salariat.' *Bankers' Mag.*, CCX, 1516 (July 1970), 17–22.

12,886 **Silkin**, Samuel C. 'Prices, incomes, and productivity: a policy for Britain.' Kamin, A. (ed.). *Western European labor and the American corporation.* Washington, D.C.: Bureau of National Affairs, 1970. p. 325–8.

12,887 **Topham**, Tony. 'The Labour Government's incomes policy and the trade unions.' *Trade Un. Regist.* (1970), 116–26.

12,888 **Turner**, Herbert Arthur. 'Collective bargaining and the eclipse of incomes policy: retrospect, prospect and possibilities.' *Br. J. Ind. Relat.*, VIII, 2 (July 1970), 197–212.
'This paper was presented to the Manchester Industrial Relations Society as the First Lerner Memorial Lecture on 26 February 1970 at Manchester University.'

12,889 **National Board for Prices and Incomes.** *Fifth and final general report, July 1969 to March 1971.* London: H.M.S.O., 1971, iv, 31p. (Report 170. Cmnd. 4649.)
Supplement. 1971, ii, 204p. (Report 170 (Supplement). Cmnd. 4469-I.)

See also: 8847

C. WAGES COUNCILS AND MINIMUM WAGE LEGISLATION

See also Part Six, III, E; and Part Six, IV, A, 3 for particular industries and groups. See also Part Six, IV, A, 4, a.

12,890 **Veritas** (*pseud.*). *The living wage and the land question.* [189–?] 14p.

12,891 **Davis**, William John. *Minimum rate of wage for brassworkers.* Birmingham, 1892.

12,892 *Catholic Church and the 'living wage'.* London, 1893. 20p.

12,893 **Morris**, A. *Civilization's missing link.* London, 1894. 28p.

12,894 **Oldroyd**, M. *A living wage.* London, 1894. 39p.

12,895 **Phelps**, Lancelot Ridley. 'The plea for a living wage.' *Econ. Rev.*, IV, 4 (October 1894), 519–25.

12,896 **Baylee**, J. Tyrrell. 'The minimum wage and the Poor Law.' *Westm. Rev.*, CLII, 6 (December 1899), 628–40.

12,897 **Jeffreys**, W. Rees. 'Wages and Conciliation Boards.' Co-operative Wholesale Societies. *Annual for 1903.* p. 291–320.

12,898 **M.**, J. *Scheme for a national minimum wage.* Manchester, 1903. 32p.

12,899 **Fabian Society.** *The case for a legal minimum wage.* London: Fabian Society, 1906. 19p. (Fabian tract 128.)
By W. Stephen Sanders.
Issued without the author's name.
See also Fabian Society, *Socialism and national minimum: papers by Mrs. Sidney Webb and Miss B. L. Hutchins, and reprint of Tract no. 128.*

12,900 **Carpenter**, Edward. 'The minimum wage: a benefit to employers as well as workers; with some remarks on its effect on foreign trade.' National Conference on Sweated Industries, 1907. *Report.* p. 58–63.

12,901 **Lees-Smith**, Hastings Bernard. 'Economic theory and proposals for a legal minimum wage.' *Econ. J.*, XVII, 68 (December 1907), 504–12.

12,902 **National Anti-Sweating League.** *Report of conference on a minimum wage, held at the Guildhall, London, on October 24th, 25th, & 26th, 1906.* London, 1907. 97p.

12,903 **Webb**, Sidney and **Webb**, Beatrice. 'The free trade controversy in relation to industrial parasitism and the policy of a national minimum.' Ensor, R. C. K. *Modern socialism.* 2nd ed. London, New York: Harper, 1907. p. 229–41.
Originally appeared as an appendix to *Industrial democracy* (1897).

12,904 **Jones**, John Harry. 'Legal minimum wage.' *Lpool. Econ. Statist. Soc. Trans.* (1907–8), 51–62.

12,905 **MacDonald**, James Ramsay. 'Sweating and wages boards.' *Nineteenth Century*, LXIV, 381 (November 1908), 748–62.

12,906 **MacDonald**, Margaret E. 'Sweated industries and wages boards.' *Econ. J.*, XVIII, 69 (March 1908), 140–5.
Looks at the example of Australian and N.Z. experience, to decide for the British case.

12,907 **Smith**, Constance Isabella Stuart. *The case for wages boards.* London: National Anti-Sweating League, 1908. viii, 94p.

12,908 **Jones**, John Harry. 'A legal minimum wage.' *Lpool. Econ. Statist. Soc. Trans.* (1908–9), 51–67.

12,909 **Fabian Society.** 'The case for a legal minimum wage.' Webb, B., and others. *Socialism and national minimum.* London: Fifield, 1909. p. 65–91.

12,910 **Fabian Society.** *Socialism and national minimum: papers by Mrs. Sidney Webb and Miss B. L. Hutchins, and reprint of Tract No. 128.* London: Fabian Society, 1909. 91p. (Fabian socialist series VI.)

12,911 **Mallon**, James Joseph. *The Trade Boards Act.* London, [*c.* 1909?]. 4p.

12,912 **Parry**, G. A. 'Two labour remedies.' *Westm. Rev.*, CLXXII, 6 (December 1909), 623–31.

12,913 **Philips**, Mary E. 'The working of wages boards.' *Econ. Rev.*, XIX, 1 (January 1909), 17–25.

12,914 **Women's Industrial Council.** *The case for and against a legal minimum wage for sweated workers.* London, 1909. 24p.

12,915 **Buxton**, C. R. *Minimum wages for agricultural labourers.* London, 1910. 12p.

12,916 **Holcombe**, A. N. 'The British Minimum Wages Act of 1909.' *Q. J. Econ.*, XXIV, 3 (May 1910), 574–88.
Text of the Act, p. 578–88.

12,917 **Mallon**, James Joseph. *Extending the Trade Boards Act.* London, [1910?]. 10p.

12,918 **Women's Co-operative Guild.** *A minimum wage scale for co-operative women and girl employees.* Manchester, 1910. 12p.

12,919 **McCale**, H. *The state regulation of wages.* London, 1911. 14p.

12,920 **Morton**, John A. J. *A national minimum wage and the organisation of industry.* Warrington, 1911. 16p.

12,921 **Asquith**, Herbert Henry. *The Coal Mines – Minimum Wage – Act, explained by Mr. Asquith in a speech made in Westminster Hall, March 28th, 1912.* London: National Press Agency, 1912.

12,922 *Coal Mines Minimum Wage Act, 1912, together with the Prime Minister's speeches on the first and second reading and an introduction by 'an old parliamentary hand'.* London, 1912. 30p.

12,923 **Cotterill**, Charles Clement. *A living wage a national necessity: how best to get it.* London: Fifield, 1912. 86p.

12,924 **Ensor**, Robert Charles Kirkwood. 'The practical case for a legal minimum wage.' *Nineteenth Century*, LXXII, 426 (August 1912), 264–75.

12,925 **Hubbard**, Evelyn. 'The minimum wage: past and present.' *Econ. J.*, XXII, 86 (June 1912), 303–9.

12,926 **Keeble**, Samuel Edward. *A legal minimum wage.* London, 1912. 16p.

12,927 **Mallon**, James Joseph. 'The work of the trade boards.' National Conference on the Prevention of Destitution. *Report of the proceedings . . . 1912.* London: King, 1912. p. 402–8.
Discussion, p. 419–27.

12,928 **Northumberland Miners' Mutual Confident Association.** *Coal Mines (Minimum Wage) Act, 1912.* Newcastle, 1912. 499p.

12,929 **Snowden**, Philip. *The living wage.* London: Hodder and Stoughton, 1912. xvi, 189p.

12,930 **Webb**, Sidney. 'The economic theory of a

legal minimum wage.' *J. Polit. Econ.*, xx, 10 (December 1912), 973–98.

Reprinted for private circulation. 1912.

12,931 **Wise**, E. F. 'Wage boards in England.' *Am. Econ. Rev.*, II, 1 (March 1912), 1–20.

Reprinted. London: G. Allen, 1912. 20p.

12,932 **Independent Labour Party** and **Fabian Society.** *War against poverty: the case for the national minimum.* London, 1913. vi, 89p.

12,933 **Mackay**, Thomas. 'The minimum wage.' *The dangers of democracy: studies in the economic questions of the day.* London: Murray, 1913. p. 156–83.

First published in the *Quarterly Review.*

12,934 **Mann**, Tom. *The labourer's minimum wage.* Manchester, 1913. 14p.

12,935 **Moore**, S. C. 'The Trades Board Act at work.' *Econ. J.*, XXIII, 91 (September 1913), 442–7.

Clothing trade of Hebden Bridge, Yorkshire.

12,936 **National Committee for the Prevention of Destitution.** *The case for the national minimum.* London, 1913. v, 89p.

Preface by Beatrice Webb.

12,937 **Select Committee on the Trade Boards Act Provisional Orders Bill.** *Report, proceedings, minutes of evidence.* London: H.M.S.O., 1913. vi, 61p. (H.C. 209.)

Report, special report, proceedings, minutes of evidence, appendices. 1914. vi, 194p. (H.C. 317.)

Chairman: J. Compton-Rickett.

12,938 **Wright**, Thomas (ed.). *Sweated labour and the Trade Boards Act.* London: Catholic Social Guild, 1913. 78p. (Catholic studies in social reform 2.)

Second edition.

12,939 **Keeling,** Frederic. 'The Trades Board Act.' *Econ. J.*, XXIV, 93 (March 1914), 157–61.

12,940 **Money**, *Sir* Leo George Chiozza. 'The minimum wage in practice.' *The future of work, and other essays.* London: Fisher Unwin, 1914. p. 174–94.

12,941 **Smith**, Constance. 'The working of the Trade Boards Act in Great Britain and Ireland.' *J. Polit. Econ.*, XXII, 7 (July 1914), 605–29.

12,942 **Tawney**, Richard Henry. *Establishment of minimum rates in the chain-making industry under the Trade Boards Act of 1909.* London: Bell, 1914. 157p. (London School of Economics. Ratan Tata Foundation. Studies in the minimum wage 1.)

12,943 **Abbott**, Edith. 'Progress of the minimum wage in England.' *J. Polit. Econ.*, XXIII, 3 (March 1915), 268–77.

12,944 **Bulkley**, Mildred Emily. *The establishment of legal minimum rates in the boxmaking industry under the Trade Boards Act of 1909.* London: Bell, 1915. xii, 95p. (Studies in the minimum wage 3.)

12,945 **Tawney**, Richard Henry. *The establishment of the minimum rates in the tailoring industry under the Trade Boards Act of 1909.* London: Bell, 1915. xiii, 274p. (London School of Economics. Ratan Tata Foundation. Studies in the minimum wage 2.)

12,946 **Le Rossignol**, James E. 'Some phases of the minimum wage question.' *Am. Econ. Rev.*, VII, 1 (March 1917), Supplement, 251–81.

With discussion.

12,947 **Better Business.** 'The constitution, procedure and determinations of the trade board in the Irish shirtmaking industry.' *Bett. Bus.*, III, 4 (August 1918), 289–315.

An 'enquiry . . . carried out at the request of the Irish-Women's Association by two women students of Belfast University'.

12,948 **Simplex**, E. (*pseud.*). *The minimum wage stunt.* Keighley, 1918. 32p.

12,949 **Baker**, J. *Some methods of regulating wages.* London, 1919. 13p.

12,950 **O'Connell**, *Sir* John Robert. 'Trades boards as a means of adjusting wages disputes and promoting trade interests.' *Statist. Soc. Inq. Soc. Ir. J.*, XIII, 97 (October 1919), 695–714.

12,951 **Milner**, Dennis. *Higher production by a bonus on national output: a proposal for a minimum income for all varying with national productivity.* London: Allen and Unwin, 1920. 128p.

12,952 **Willis**, *Sir* Walter Addington. *Trade boards at work: a practical guide to the operation of the Trade Boards Act.* London: Nisbet, 1920. xiv, 112p.

12,953 **Mallon**, James Joseph. 'Trade boards and minimum rates of wages.' *Manchr. Statist. Soc. Trans.* (1920–21), 13–27.

12,954 **International Labour Office.** 'Minimum wage legislation for low-paid industries in Europe.' *Int. Labour Rev.*, IV, 2 (November 1921), 108–38 (320–50).

12,955 **Labour Party.** *Agricultural workers' wages: the Labour Party's fight for the Agricultural Wages Board.* London, 1921. 30p.

12,956 **Piddington**, Albert Bathurst. *The next step: a family basic income.* London: Macmillan, 1921. iv, 64p.

12,957 **Cambridge University Settlement.** *Trade boards.* London: the Settlement, 1922. 2 pts. (Cambridge House bulletins 26, 27.)

12,958 **Ministry of Labour.** *Statement of the government's policy in the administration of the Trade Board Acts, 1909 and 1918.* London: H.M.S.O., 1922. 6p. (Cmd. 1712.)

A brief summary of the Cave Report on Trade Boards.

12,959 **Ministry of Labour.** Committee appointed to enquire into the working and effects of the Trade Boards Acts. *Report.* London: H.M.S.O., 1922. 55p. (Cmd. 1645.)
Minutes of evidence, appendices, index. 1922. 1050p.
Documents annexed to the evidence submitted by Mr. Humbert Wolfe. 59–112p.
Chairman: Viscount Cave.

12,960 **Mitchell**, Andrew Ackworth. *The breakdown of minimum wage, and a memorandum on unemployment.* Glasgow: Maclehose, 1922. 23p.

12,961 **Northern Ireland.** Ministry of Labour. *Report of the Advisory Committee on Trade Boards, appointed to advise the Minister of Labour as to the application of the Trade Boards Acts to Northern Ireland.* Belfast: H.M.S.O., 1922. 37p. (Cmd. 7.)

12,962 **Pigou**, Arthur Cecil. 'Trade boards and the Cave Committee.' *Econ. J.*, XXXII, 127 (September 1922), 315–24.

12,963 **Trades Union Congress** and **Labour Party.** *Trade boards and the Cave Report.* London: T.U.C. and Labour Party, 1922. 23p.

12,964 **Anti-Socialist Union.** *The minimum wage: is it practical?* London, [1923?]. 16p.

12,965 **Batten**, Edward. *A fair wage: some reflections on the minimum wage and some economic problems of to-day.* London: Pitman, 1923. ix, 90p.

12,966 **Dewson**, Mary Williams. *The Cave Report on the British Trade Board Acts, 1909–1922: the success of minimum wage legislation.* New York, 1923. 108p.

12,967 **National Consumers' League.** *Cave Report on the British Trade Board Acts.* New York: Steinberg P., 1923. 108p.
Largely a reprint of the Cave Report of April 1922.

12,968 **Pigou**, Arthur Cecil. 'A minimum wage for agriculture.' *Essays in applied economics.* London: King, 1923.
Revised edition. 1924. p. 41–58.
'Reproduced with modifications from *The Nineteenth Century*, December, 1913.'

12,969 **Pigou**, Arthur Cecil. 'Trade boards and the Cave Committee.' *Essays in applied economics.* London: King, 1923.
Revised edition. 1924. p. 59–69.
From *Economic Journal*, September 1922.

12,970 **Sells**, Dorothy McDaniel. *The British trade boards system.* London: King, 1923. vi, 293p. (London School of Economics and Political Science. Studies in economics and political science 70.)

12,971 **Sells**, Dorothy McDaniel. 'The economic effects of the British trade boards system.' *Int. Labour Rev.*, VIII, 2 (August 1923), 191–220.

12,972 **Sells**, Dorothy McDaniel. *An enquiry into the operation of the British trade boards system.* 1923. (Ph.D. thesis, University of London.)

12,973 **Shimmin**, Arnold N. 'The English trade board system.' *Welt. Arch.*, XIX, 3 (July 1923), 419–28.

12,974 **Harris**, J. *The working and effects of trade boards in the linen industry of Northern Ireland.* 1924. (M.Com.Sc. thesis, Queen's University of Belfast.)

12,975 **Mallon**, James Joseph. 'Trade boards.' Hogue, R. W. (ed.). *British labour speaks.* New York: Boris and Liveright, 1924. p. 267–82.

12,976 **Brent**, S. E. *The causeway of capital and labour, comprising minimum wages for every worker based on the cost of living, etc.* London: King, 1925. ix, 109p.

12,977 **Hallsworth**, *Sir* Joseph. *The legal minimum.* London: Labour Publishing Co., 1925. 95p.

12,978 **Rolfe**, Herbert (ed.). *The Agricultural Wages – Regulation – Act 1924.* Hereford: Adams, 1925. 95p.
With comments.

12,979 **Brailsford**, Henry Noel, **Hobson**, John Atkinson, **Jones**, Arthur Creech and **Wise**, E. F. *The living wage.* London: Independent Labour Party Publication Department, 1926. 55p.
A report submitted to the National Administrative Council of the I.L.P.

12,980 **Burns**, Eveline Mabel. *Wages and the state: a comparative study of the problems of state wage regulation.* London: King, 1926. ix, 443p. (London School of Economics and Political Science. Studies in economics and political science 86.)

12,981 **Fisher**, Allan George Barnard. *Some problems of wages and their regulation in Great Britain since 1918.* London: King, 1926. xvii, 281p. (Studies in economics and political science 83.)
Reprinted. New York: Kelley, 1966. xvii, 281p. (Reprints of economic classics.)

12,982 **International Labour Office.** 'Minimum wages and the International Labour Conference.' *Int. Labour Rev.*, XV, 5 (May 1927), 669–80.

12,983 **Richardson**, John Henry. *A study on the minimum wage.* 1927. (Ph.D. thesis, University of London.)
With 11 subsidiary papers.
Published London: Allen and Unwin, 1927. 198p.

12,984 **Broada**, Rudolf. *Minimum wage legislation in various countries.* Washington, D.C., 1928. v, 125p. (U.S. Bureau of Labor Statistics. Bulletin 467.)

12,985 **Fletcher**, I. G. *A study of the minimum wage in its economic aspects.* 1928. ii, 78p. (M.A. thesis, University of Manitoba.)

12,986 **Pribram**, Karl. 'The regulation of minimum wages as an international problem.' *Int. Labour Rev.*, XVII, 3 (March 1928), 317–31.

12,987 *Report on an inquiry into a proposal to alter the description of the hollow-ware making trade contained in the appendix to order III of the Schedule to the Trade Boards Provisional Orders Confirmation Act, 1913.* London: H.M.S.O., 1928. 28p.

12,988 **Harris,** J. *The Irish trade boards system.* 1930. (D.Sc. thesis, Queen's University of Belfast.)

12,989 **Orr,** John. *The economic basis of the minimum wage in agriculture.* Cambridge, 1930. 10p.

12,990 **Ministry of Labour.** *A public enquiry with regard to the Draft Special Order applying the Trade Boards Acts, 1909 and 1918, to the catering trade: report, appendices.* London: H.M.S.O., 1931. 33p.

By Sir A. Colefax.

12,991 **Shields,** Bernard Francis. 'The minimum wage.' *Statist. Soc. Inq. Soc. Ir. J.* (1934–35), 61–79.

12,992 **Cole,** George Douglas Howard. *Living wages: the case for a new Minimum Wage Act.* London: Gollancz, New Fabian Research Bureau, 1938. 32p. (New Fabian Research Bureau research pamphlet 42.)

12,993 **Hetherington,** *Sir* Hector. 'The working of the British trade board system.' *Int. Labour Rev.*, XXXVIII, 4 (October 1938), 472–80.

12,994 **Mallon,** James Joseph. 'Industrial relations and the British trade board system.' Gannett, F. E. and Catherwood, B. F. (eds.). *Industrial and labour relations in Great Britain: a symposium.* New York: the editors, 1939. p. 74–86.

The author was Honorary Secretary of the Trades Boards Advisory Council of the Trades Union Congress.

12,995 **Sells,** Dorothy McDaniel. *British wage boards: a study in industrial democracy.* Washington, D.C.: Brookings Institution, 1939. xv, 389p. (Institute of Economics of the Brookings Institution. Publication 77.)

'This study may be regarded as essentially a sequel to the author's *British trade boards system*, London, 1923.'

12,996 **Bevin,** Ernest. *Square meals and square deals.* London: Labour Party, 1943. 13p.

Speech in the House of Commons on the Catering Wages Bill, with a list of members who voted against it.

12,997 **Palmer,** H. Cecil. *The implications of the Catering Wages Bill.* London: Society of Individualists, 1943. 37p. (Post-war questions 22.)

12,998 **Ministry of Labour and National Service.** Catering Wages Commission. *Report of the Catering Wages Commission on the recommendation for the establishment of a wages board for industrial catering, and correspondence.* London: H.M.S.O., 1944. 8p. (Cmd. 6509.)

Chairman: W. Hartley Shawcross.

12,999 **Ministry of Labour and National Service.** Catering Wages Commission. *Report of the Catering Wages Commission on the recommendation for the establishment of a wages board for unlicensed non-residential catering establishments.* London: H.M.S.O., 1944. 14p. (Cmd. 6569.)

13,000 **Ministry of Labour and National Service.** Catering Wages Commission. *Report on an enquiry under Section 2 (I) (a) of the Catering Wages Act into existing methods of regulating the remuneration and conditions of employment of workers employed by the Crown in catering undertakings.* London: H.M.S.O., 1944. 9p.

Chairman: W. Hartley Shawcross.

13,001 **Mallon,** James Joseph. 'Trade boards.' Cole, G. D. H. *British trade unionism today: a survey . . .* London: Methuen, 1945. p. 133–42.

Earlier edition. 1939.

13,002 **Ministry of Labour and National Service.** Catering Wages Commission. *Report of the Catering Wages Commission on their recommendation for the establishment of a wages board for licensed non-residential establishments.* London: H.M.S.O., 1945. 10p. (Cmd. 6612.)

13,003 **Ministry of Labour and National Service.** Catering Wages Commission. *Report of the Catering Wages Commission on their recommendation for the establishment of a wages board for licensed residential establishments and licensed restaurants.* London: H.M.S.O., 1945. 12p. (Cmd. 6601.)

13,004 **Ministry of Labour and National Service.** Catering Wages Commission. *Report of the Catering Wages Commission on their recommendation for the establishment of a wages board for unlicensed residential establishments.* London: H.M.S.O., 1945. 8p. (Cmd. 6706.)

13,005 **Ministry of Labour and National Service.** Catering Wages Commission. *Report by the Catering Wages Commission recommending variation of the field of operation of catering wages boards to include certain catering activities of local authorities.* London: H.M.S.O., 1946. 12p. (Cmd. 6776.)

13,006 **Ministry of Labour and National Service.** *Report of a Commission of Inquiry on an application for the establishment of a wages council for the hairdressing trade.* London: H.M.S.O., 1947. 12p.

Chairman: G. G. Honeyman.

13,007 **Ministry of Labour and National Service.** *Report of a Commission of Inquiry on an application for the establishment of a wages council for the retail drapery, outfittings and footwear trades.* London: H.M.S.O., 1947. 15p.

Chairman: G. G. Honeyman.

13,008 **Ministry of Labour and National Service.** *Report of a Commission of Inquiry on an application for the establishment of a wages council for the retail food trades.* London: H.M.S.O., 1947. 39p.
Chairman: G. G. Honeyman.

13,009 **Ministry of Labour and National Service.** *Report of a Commission of Inquiry on an application for the establishment of a wages council for the retail furnishing and allied trades.* London: H.M.S.O., 1947. 19p.
Chairman: G. G. Honeyman.

13,010 **Ministry of Labour and National Service.** *Report of a Commission of Inquiry on the question whether a wages council should be established with respect to workers and their employers in the retail bookselling, newsagency, stationery, tobacco and confectionery trades.* London: H.M.S.O., 1947. 27p.
Chairman: G. G. Honeyman.

13,011 **Ministry of Labour and National Service.** Catering Wages Commission. *Report by the Catering Wages Commission recommending variation of the field of operation of catering wages boards in regard to canteens provided by dock authorities.* London: H.M.S.O., 1947. 4p. (Cmd. 7191.)
Chairman: R. Moelwyn Hughes.

13,012 **Northern Ireland.** Ministry of Labour and National Insurance. *Establishment of a wages council for the retail food trades.* Belfast: H.M.S.O., 1947. 18p.

13,013 **Ministry of Labour and National Service.** *Report of a Commission of Inquiry on a Draft Order for the establishment of a wages council for the retail drapery, outfitting and footwear trades (Great Britain).* London: H.M.S.O., 1948. 8p.
Chairman: G. G. Honeyman.

13,014 **Ministry of Labour and National Service.** *Report of a Commission of Inquiry on a Draft Order for the establishment of a wages council for the retail food trades (Scotland).* London: H.M.S.O., 1948. 5p.
Chairman: G. G. Honeyman.

13,015 **Ministry of Labour and National Service.** *Report of a Commission of Inquiry on a Draft Order for the establishment of a wages council for the retail furnishing and allied trades (Great Britain).* London: H.M.S.O., 1948. 11p.
Chairman: G. G. Honeyman.

13,016 **Ministry of Labour.** *Report of a Commission of Inquiry on an application for the establishment of a wages council for the retail drapery, outfitting and footwear trades, Great Britain.* London: H.M.S.O., 1948. 15p.
Chairman: G. G. Honeyman.

13,017 **Northern Ireland.** Ministry of Labour and National Insurance. *Establishment of a wages council with respect to road haulage workers and their employers.* Belfast: H.M.S.O., 1948. 19p.

13,018 **Routh**, Gerald Guy Cumming. 'State intervention in the regulation of wages and working conditions in Great Britain and South Africa.' *S. Afr. J. Econ.*, XVII, 3 (September 1949), 289–305.

13,019 **Mallon**, James Joseph. *Industry and a minimum wage.* London: British Institute of Management, 1950. p. 5–8.
Published with *Universities and management* by Lord Lindsay of Birker. p. 9–14.
Papers from the 54th Oxford Management Conference, Harrogate, November 1949.

13,020 **Ministry of Labour and National Service.** *Report of a Commission of Inquiry on an application for the establishment of a wages council for the rubber proofed garment making industry.* London: H.M.S.O., 1950. 15p.
Chairman: V. R. Aronson.

13,021 **Ministry of Labour and National Service.** Catering Wages Commission. *Report on an inquiry into the operation of the Catering Wages Act, 1943, in the hotel industry.* London: H.M.S.O., 1950. pagination varies. (Cmd. 8004.)

13,022 **Ministry of Labour and National Service.** *Report of a Commission of Inquiry on the question of the establishment of a wages council for the wholesale and retail bread and flour confectionery distributive trades.* London: H.M.S.O., 1950 [i.e. 1951]. 16p.
Chairman: H. S. Kirkaldy.

13,023 **Wrottesley**, A. J. F. 'Wages councils.' *Ind. Law Rev.*, VI, 1 (July 1951), 43–8.

13,024 **Ministry of Labour and National Service.** *Report of a Commission of Inquiry on a Draft Order for the establishment of a wages council for the retail bread and flour confectionery trade (England and Wales).* London: H.M.S.O., 1952. 7p.
Chairman: H. S. Kirkaldy.

13,025 **Wrottesley**, A. J. F. 'The Catering Wages Act.' *Ind. Law Rev.*, VI, 3 (January 1952), 187–92.

13,026 **McCormick**, Brian J. *Labour relations in the catering industry with special reference to the operation of the Catering Wages Act, 1943.* 1956. (M.A. (Econ.) thesis, University of Manchester.)

13,027 **Ministry of Labour and National Service.** *Report of a Commission of Inquiry appointed in 1955 to consider an application for the establishment of a wages council for the rubber proofed garment making industry.* London: H.M.S.O., 1956. 15p.
Chairman: H. S. Kirkaldy.

13,028 **Bayliss**, Frederick Joseph. 'The independent members of British wages councils and boards.' *Br. J. Sociol.*, VIII, 1 (March 1957), 1–25.

13,029 **Bowlby,** Roger Louis. 'Union policy toward minimum wage legislation in postwar Britain.' *Ind. Labour Relat. Rev.*, XI, 1 (October 1957), 72–84.

Comment by F. J. Bayliss, XII, 1 (October 1958), 113–119.

Reply by R. J. L. Bowlby, 119–23.

13,030 **McCormick,** Brian J. and **Turner,** Herbert Arthur. 'The legal minimum wage, employers and trade unions: an experiment.' *Manchr. Sch.*, XXV, 3 (September 1957), 284–316.

13,031 **Bowlby,** Roger Louis. *The statutory regulation of minimum wages in Great Britain.* 1957–58. (Dissertation, University of Texas.)

13,032 **Guillebaud,** Claude William. *The wages councils system in Great Britain.* London: Nisbet, 1958. 31p.

Reprinted from *Industrial labour in India.*

13,033 **Bayliss,** Frederick Joseph. 'British wages councils and full employment.' *Int. Labour Rev.*, LXXX, 55 (November 1959), 410–29.

13,034 **Hawtrey,** E. 'The enforcement of statutory minimum wages in Great Britain.' *Int. Labour Rev.*, LXXIX, 4 (April 1959), 380–97.

13,035 **Ministry of Labour and National Service.** Catering Wages Commission. *Final report.* London: H.M.S.O., 1959. (H.C. 277.)

13,036 **Bayliss,** Frederick Joseph. *The history and working of British wages councils.* 1959–60. (Ph.D. thesis, University of Nottingham.)

13,037 **Saxena,** C. J. N. *Wages boards in Britain and the application of their procedure in India.* 1959–60. (M.Sc.(Econ.) thesis, University of London.)

13,038 **Ministry of Labour.** *Report of the Commission of Inquiry on the Sugar Confectionery and Food Preserving Wages Council (Great Britain).* London: H.M.S.O., 1961.

Chairman: G. G. Honeyman.

13,039 **Armstrong,** Eric George Abbott. *Minimum wage and public contracts laws in Great Britain and in the U.S.A.* 1961–62. (M.Com. thesis, University of Birmingham.)

13,040 **Armstrong,** Eric George Abbott. 'Public policy on minimum wage legislation in Britain and America: a comparison.' *Scott. J. Polit. Econ.*, X, 2 (June 1963), 243–52.

13,041 **Bayliss,** Frederick Joseph. *British wages councils.* Oxford: Blackwell 1962 [i.e. 1963]. x, 177p.

13,042 **Ministry of Labour.** *Report of a Commission of Inquiry on the question whether the Baking Wages Council (Scotland) should be abolished.* London: H.M.S.O., 1963. 20p.

Chairman: Harold Stewart Kirkaldy.

13,043 **Malik,** M. A. *Some economic effects of minimum wage regulation in the United States and Great Britain in the post-war period.* 1963–64. (Dissertation, University of Michigan.)

13,044 **Ministry of Labour.** *Report of a Commission of Inquiry on the Licensed Residential Establishment and Licensed Restaurant Wages Council.* London: H.M.S.O., 1964. 28p.

13,045 **Northern Ireland.** Ministry of Labour and National Insurance. *Report of a Commission of Inquiry on the question whether a wages council should be established with respect to any of the workers and their employers engaged in the catering industry in Northern Ireland.* Belfast: H.M.S.O., 1964. 18p.

Chairman: R. D. C. Brooks.

13,046 **Armstrong,** Eric George Abbott. *The operation of minimum wage legislation in Birmingham.* 1965–66. (Ph.D. thesis, University of Birmingham.)

13,047 **Armstrong,** Eric George Abbott. 'Minimum wages in a fully employed city.' *Br. J. Ind. Relat.*, IV, 1 (March 1966), 22–38.

13,048 **Armstrong,** Eric George Abbott. 'Shopkeepers and the minimum wage: a Birmingham case study.' *Ind. Soc.*, XLIX (June 1967), 20–3.

Account of a survey by questionnaire.

13,049 **Ministry of Labour.** *Report of a Commission of Inquiry on the Hair, Bass and Fibre Wages Council (Great Britain) and the Brush and Broom Wages Council (Great Britain).* London: H.M.S.O., 1967. 31p.

13,050 **McCormick** Brian J. 'The Royal Commission, low paid workers and the future of the wages councils.' *J. Econ. Studies*, III, 3–4 (December 1968), 83–91.

13,051 **Department of Employment and Productivity.** *A national minimum wage: an inquiry. Report of an Inter-Departmental Working Party.* London: H.M.S.O., 1969. vii, 89p.

13,052 **Department of Employment and Productivity.** *Report of a Commission of Inquiry on a draft order to abolish the Cutlery Wages Council (Great Britain).* London: H.M.S.O., 1969. 19p.

Chairman: A. H. Thomas.

13,053 **West,** E. G. 'Britain's evolving minimum wage policy: an economic assessment.' *Moor. Wall Street* (Autumn 1969), 52–66.

13,054 **Davis,** Maurice Alexis John. *The Hairdressing Wages Order explained.* London: Guild of Hairdressers, 1970. 96p.

13,055 **Department of Employment and Productivity.** *Report of a Commission of Inquiry on a draft order varying the field of operation of the Road Haulage Wages Council.* London: H.M.S.O., 1970. 6p.

Chairman: John Crossley Wood.

See also: 5; 3736; 10,175; 12,812.

D. FAIR WAGES RESOLUTIONS

13,056 **Select Committee** appointed to inquire whether the present system of issuing invitations for Tenders and of making Contracts for Government Printing and Binding, sufficiently secures compliance with the Resolution of the House of Commons on February 13, 1891. *Report, with the proceedings.* London: H.M.S.O., 1895. (H.C. 362.)
Report... 1896. (H.C. 230.)
On fair wages and sub-letting.

13,057 **Dew**, George. *Government and municipal contracts: fair wages movement.* London, 1896. 14p.

13,058 **Select Committee on Government Contracts (Fair Wages Resolution).** *Report, with the proceedings, evidence, appendix and index.* London: H.M.S.O., 1896. (H.C. 277.)
Report... 1897. (H.C. 334.)

13,059 **Z.** ' "Fair wages" in government contracts.' *Econ. J.*, VI, 21 (March 1896), 153–4.

13,060 **Fabian Society.** *The economics of direct employment, with an account of the fair wages policy.* London: Fabian Society, 1898. 15p. (Fabian tract 84.)
By Sidney Webb.
Issued without the author's name.
Reprinted in Ensor, R. C. K. *Modern socialism.* 2nd ed. London, New York: Harper, 1907. p. 242–64.

13,061 **Committee on Fair Wages.** *Report, appendices.* London: H.M.S.O., 1908. iv, 52p. (Cd. 4422.)
Minutes of evidence, etc. (Cd. 4423.)

13,062 **Leppington**, C. H. d'E. 'The "fair wages" controversy.' *Char. Orgn. Rev.*, n.s., XXVI, 155 (November 1909), 308–20.

13,063 **Trades Union Congress.** *The fair wage clause.* London: T.U.C., 1935. 15p.

13,064 **Denman**, *Sir* Richard D. 'Sydney Buxton and the Fair Wages Clause.' *Polit. Q.*, XVIII, 2 (April 1947), 161–8.

13,065 **Kahn-Freund**, Otto. 'Legislation through adjudication: the legal aspect of fair wages clauses and recognised conditions.' *Mod. Law Rev.*, XI, 3 (July 1948), 269–89; 4 (October 1948), 429–48.

E. EQUAL PAY FOR WOMEN

See also Part Six, II, C, 4; Part Six, III, F; and Part Six, IV, A, 4, b.

13,066 **Blackman**, Janet. 'Equal pay, 1970.' *Trade Un. Regist.* (1970), 109–15.

13,067 **Freedland**, Mark R. 'The Equal Pay (No. 2) Bill 1970: some problems of interpretation likely to arise.' *Ind. Law Soc. Bull.*, 7 (July 1970), 3–4.

13,068 **Seear**, Beatrice Nancy. 'Equal Pay (No. 2) Bill 1970.' *Ind. Law Soc. Bull.*, 7 (July 1970), 1–2.

13,069 **Sloane**, Peter J. and **Chiplin**, Brian. 'The economic consequences of the Equal Pay Act 1970.' *Ind. Relat. J.* (December 1970), 8–29.

VII. REGULATION OF FRIENDLY SOCIETIES, TRADE UNIONS, AND EMPLOYERS' ASSOCIATIONS

A. FRIENDLY SOCIETIES

See also Part Three, II.

13,070 **Pratt**, William Tidd. *The law of friendly societies.* London: Shaw, 1881. xii, 303p.
Tenth edition, enlarged, by E. W. Brabrook.
Earlier editions. 1850, 1853, 1854, 1858, 1862, 1867, 1873, 1876.
Eleventh edition. 1888. xii, 360p.
Twelfth edition. 1894. xii, 352p.
Thirteenth edition. 1897. l, 303p.
Fourteenth edition, by J. D. S. Sim. 1909. lxxv, 314, 28p.
Fifteenth edition. *Pratt's friendly, and industrial & provident societies.* London: Butterworth, Shaw, 1931. xxxv, 241, 25p. Entirely rewritten and re-arranged by Mervyn Mackinnon.

13,071 **Daly**, James Dominick. *Club law and the law of unregistered friendly societies: a handbook.* Nottingham: F. Goodliffe, 1889. 65p.
Second edition. London: Butterworths, 1889. xii, 135p.
Third edition, by HerbertM alone. London: Butterworth, 1923. xvi, 276, 10p.
Fourth edition, by C. J. Collinge. London: Butterworth, Shaw, 1936. xxix, 228p.
Fifth edition. *Daly's club law,* by C. J. Collinge. London: Butterworth, Shaw, 1954. xxviii, 174p.

13,072 *Memorandum on valuations of friendly societies.* London: H.M.S.O., 1891. 8p.
Second edition.

13,073 **Fowke**, Villiers de Saussure. *Industrial and Provident Societies Act, 1893, with a history of the legislation dealing with industrial and provident societies.* London: Jordan, 1894. xxxii, 188p.

13,074 **Gray**, J. C. *The Industrial and Provident Societies Act, 1893.* Manchester: Cooperative Union, 1894. 170p.
With an introduction by J. C. Gray.

13,075 **Fuller**, Frank Baden. *The law relating to friendly societies, comprising the Friendly Societies Acts, 1875 to 1893, as amended by the Friendly Societies Act, 1895, together with an appendix, containing model rules and the forms appended to the Treasury regulations, 1896.* London: Clowes, 1896. xxii, 280p.
Second edition. 1898. xxix, 282p.
Third edition. Stevens, 1910. xlvii, 534p.
Fourth edition. Stevens, 1926. xlvli, 684p.

13,076 **Diprose**, John (comp.). *Reports of law cases affecting friendly societies.* Manchester: Order of Oddfellows, 1897. xx, 669p.
Assisted by J. Gammon.

13,077 **Brookhouse**, John Charles. *A simple handbook of friendly society law.* London: Diprose, Bateman, 1910. 72p.

13,078 **Gray**, J. C. *The Industrial and Provident Societies Act, 1893, and Amendment Act, 1913.* Manchester: Co-operative Union, 1927. 182p.
With an introduction to the Act of 1893 by J. C. Gray, and to the Amendment Act, 1913, by A. Whitehead.

13,079 **Paines**, Douglas H. 'Forming a works friendly society.' *Ind. Law Rev.*, VIII, 2 (October 1953), 98–102.

13,080 **Pinson**, Barry. 'Trusts for the benefit of employees.' *Ind. Law Rev.*, VII, 3 (January 1953), 169–75.

13,081 **Registry of Friendly Societies.** *Guide to the Friendly Society Acts and the Industrial Assurance Acts.* London: H.M.S.O., 1962. ix, 192p.

13,082 **Southern**, Robert and **Rose**, Paul Bernard. *Handbook to the Industrial and Provident Societies Acts, 1893 to 1961.* Manchester: Co-operative Union, 1961 [i.e. 1962]. 228p.
Second edition.
Previous edition. 1938.

13,083 **Chappenden**, William Jeffrey. *Handbook to the Industrial and Provident Societies Act, 1965.* Manchester: Co-operative Union, 1966. xi, 230p.
First supplement. 1970. iv, 71p.

B. TRADE UNIONS

See also Part Three, III; Part Seven, I; and Part Seven, VIII, B.

1. General

13,084 **Mundella**, Anthony John and **Howell**, George. 'Industrial association.' Ward, T. H. (ed.). *The reign of Queen Victoria: a survey of fifty years of progress.* Vol. II. London: Smith, Elder, 1889. p. 43–82.

13,085 **Lyttelton**, Alfred. 'The law of trade combinations.' Mackay, T. (ed.). *A policy of free exchange: essays by various writers on the economical and social aspects of free exchange and kindred subjects.* London: Murray, 1894. p. 275–92.

13,086 **Devonshire**, *Duke of* and **Holland**, Bernard. 'On some legal disabilities of trade unions.' *Nineteenth Century*, XXXVII, 217 (March 1895), 393–408.
'Prefatory note only' by the Duke of Devonshire, p. 393–4.

13,087 **Samuel**, J. *The legislative history of trade unionism.* London, 1899. 8p.

13,088 **Bell**, Richard. *The law and trade unions.* London, 1901. 95p.

13,089 **Cohen**, Herman Joseph and **Howell**, George. *Trade union law and cases: a text book relating to trade unions and to labour.* London: Sweet and Maxwell, 1901. xiii, 250p.
Second edition. 1907. xiv, 198p.
Third edition. Stevens and Haynes, 1913. xx, 259p.

13,090 *The law and trade unions: a brief review of recent litigation.* London, 1901. 95p.

13,091 **Woodward**, William. 'The British workman and his competitors.' *Nineteenth Century*, XLIX, 289 (March 1901), 456–60.
Trades Union Control Act demanded.

13,092 **Hunt**, Donald Robert Chalmers. *The law relating to trade unions.* London: Butterworth, 1902. xxxiii, 309p.
With an appendix of statutes.

13,093 **Maidstone**, A. F. *Trade unions and the law: a policy for the future suggested.* London, [1902?]. 7p.

13,094 **Clynes**, John Robert. *Trade unions and the law.* Oldham, 1903. 14p.

13,095 **Cohen**, Herman Joseph. *Recent trade union cases.* London, 1903. 19p.

13,096 **Mitchell**, I. *Trade union law and its administration.* London, 1903. 15p.

13,097 **Edwards**, Clement. *Trade unions and the law.* Wrexham, 1904. 24p.

13,098 **Assinder**, George Frederick. *The legal position of trade unions.* London: Stevens, 1905. 59p.
Second edition. 1912. v, 145p.

13,099 **Beveridge**, William Henry. 'The reform of trade union law.' *Econ. Rev.*, XV, 2 (April 1905), 129–49.

13,100 **Pennant**, David Falconer. *Trade unions and the law.* London: Stevens, 1905. xxxi, 146p.

13,101 **Draper**, Warwick H. *Trade unions and the law.* London: Stevens, 1906. 31p.
A paper read in March 1906 to members of the Hampshire House Social Club and the Peel Institute.

13,102 **Maxwell**, Herbert. 'Why lift trades unions above the law?' *Nineteenth Century*, LIX, 351 (May 1906), 871–84.

13,103 **Quarterly Review.** 'Trade-unions and the law.' *Q. Rev.*, CCIV, 407 (April 1906), 481–98.
Review article. Includes *History of trade unionism* by S. and B. Webb.

13,104 **Jevons**, T. Seton. *The law of trade unions, being a text book concerning trade unions and labour.* London: Effingham Wilson, 1907. vii, 144p. (Wilson's legal handy books.)

13,105 **Romanes**, J. H. *The evolution of the law of trade unions.* Glasgow, 1907. 16p.

13,106 **Barker**, Ernest. 'The rights and duties of trade unions.' *Econ. Rev.*, XXI, 2 (April 1911), 127–52.

13,107 **Bell**, *Sir* Hugh. *Trade union regulations.* London, 1911. 22p.

13,108 **Greenwood**, John Henry. *The law relating to trade unions.* London: Stevens, 1911. xx, 302p.
A supplement to the law relating to trade unions including the Trade Unions Act, 1913. 1913. xii, 117p.

13,109 **Greenwood**, John Henry. 'Trade unions and the law.' *Westm. Rev.*, CLXXVI, 6 (December 1911), 609–19.
An examination of the basis on which the existing law rests.

13,110 **Finlay**, T. A. 'Labour associations in their relation to the state.' *Statist. Soc. Inq. Soc. Ir. J.*, XII, 92 (December 1912), 511–22.

13,111 **Glasgow.** Faculty of Procurators. Parliamentary Bills Committee. *Report . . . on the Trades Unions (No. 2) Bill, 1912.* Glasgow, 1912. 7p.

13,112 **Slesser**, *Sir* Henry Herman and **Clark**, William Smith. *The legal position of trade unions.* London: King, 1912. xxiv, 268p.
Second edition. 1913. xliv, 268p.

13,113 **Mackay**, Thomas. 'Trade unions and the law.' *The dangers of democracy: studies in the economic questions of the day.* London: Murray, 1913. p. 90–115.
First published in the *Quarterly Review.*

13,114 **Geldart**, William Martin. *Trade unions, trade lists and the law.* London, 1914. 14p.

13,115 **Smith**, Herbert Arthur. *The law of associations, corporate and unincorporate.* Oxford: Clarendon P., 1914. xv, 168p.

13,116 **Slesser**, *Sir* Henry Herman. *An introduction to trade union law.* London, 1919. 45p.

13,117 **Slesser**, *Sir* Henry Herman. *The law relating to trade-unions.* London: Labour Publishing Co., 1921. 149p. (Trade union manuals 1.)
Four lectures delivered in 1920.

13,118 **Slesser**, *Sir* Henry Herman and **Baker**, Charles. *Trade union law.* London: Nisbet, 1921. xxvi, 333p.
Second edition, with supplement. 1926. 42, 333p.
Third edition. 1927. xxvii, 424p.

13,119 **Asquith**, *Sir* Cyril. *Trade union law for laymen.* London: Cassell, 1927. ix, 101p.

13,120 **Henderson**, Arthur. *Trade union law.* Oxford: Ruskin College, 1927. 39p. (Ruskin College study courses 2.)
Second edition, revised. 1928. 47p.

13,121 **Henderson**, Arthur. *Trade unions and the law.* London: Benn, 1927. 286p.

13,122 **Hewitt**, Edgar Percy. *Trade unions and the law: their history, present position and suggested reform.* London: Solicitor's Law Stationery Society, 1927. 40p.
Reprinted from the *Solicitors' Journal.*

13,123 **Marriott**, John Arthur Ransome. 'The trade union problem.' *Nineteenth Century*, CI, 599 (January 1927), 1–13.

13,124 **Sophian**, Theodore John. *Trade union law and practice.* London: Stevens, 1927. xxiv, 429p.

13,125 **Haslam**, Alec Leslie. *The law relating to combinations.* 1928–29. (D.Phil. thesis, University of Oxford.)
Published as *The law relating to trade combinations.* London: Allen and Unwin, 1921. 215p.

13,126 **Hedges**, Robert Yorke and **Winterbottom**, Allan. *The legal history of trade unionism.* London: Longmans, 1930. xix, 170p.

13,127 **Robson**, William Alexander. 'The future of trade union law.' *Polit. Q.*, I, 1 (January 1930), 86–103.

13,128 **Rothschild**, V. Henry. 'Government regulation of trade unions in Great Britain.' *Columb. Law Rev.*, XXXVIII, 1 (January 1938), 1–48; 8 (December 1938), 1335–92.

13,129 **Strauss**, Henry. *Trade unions and the law.* London: McCorquodale, [*c.* 1945]. 77p.

13,130 **Thompson**, William Henry. 'Trade unions and the law today.' Cole, G. D. H. *British trade unionism today: a survey.* London: Methuen, 1945. p. 124–32.
Earlier edition. 1939.

13,131 **Samuels**, Harry. *The law of trade unions.* London: Stevens, 1946. xv, 93p.
Second edition. 1946. xv, 96p.
Third edition. 1948. xv, 96p.
Fourth edition. 1949. xv, 96p.
Fifth edition. *Trade union law.* 1956. xv, 95p.
Sixth edition. *Trade union law.* 1959. xviii, 108p.
Seventh edition. *Trade union law.* London: Knight, 1966. xvii, 100p.

13,132 **Liu**, Chia-Chi. *Trade union law in the United Kingdom, the United States, and the Republic of China.* 1948–49. (M.Litt. thesis, University of Cambridge.)

13,133 **Algar**, Douglas J. 'The trades unions.' Berry, A. and Wilson, D. (eds.). *Conservative Oxford.* [Oxford?]: Oxford University Conservative Association, 1949. p. 41–4.

13,134 **Citrine**, Norman Arthur. *Trade union law.* London: Stevens, 1950. xliv, 700p.
Based on *Trade union law* by Sir Henry Slesser and Charles Baker.
Second edition. 1960. xliv, 656p.
Third edition, by M. A. Hickling. 1967. lxiv, 772p.

13,135 **Conservative and Unionist Party.** Conservative Industrial Department. *Trade unions and the law.* London: Conservative Political Centre, 1953. 23p. (Trade union series 2.)

Revised edition. 1963. 19p. (New trade union series 2.)

13,136 **Mortished**, R. J. P. 'Irish trade union law.' King, F. C. (ed.). *Public administration in Ireland.* Vol. III. Dublin: Civics Institute of Ireland, 1954. p. 161–83.

13,137 **Sykes**, Edward I. 'Trade union autonomy in Great Britain.' *Univ. Qd. Law J.*, II, 4 (December 1955), 336–48.

13,138 **Vester**, Horatio and **Gardner**, Anthony Herbert. *Trade unions and the law.* London: Methuen, 1955. viii, 120p.

13,139 **Fletcher-Cooke**, C. F. 'Trade unionism and liberty.' Conservative Political Centre. National Summer School, Oxford, 1956. *Liberty in the modern state.* London: the Centre, 1957. p. 69–76.

13,140 **Epstein**, M. *Trade unions before the courts.* 1958. iii, 67p. (LL.M. thesis, Dalhousie University.)

13,141 **Frank**, W. F. 'Trade union law in the British welfare state.' *Louis. Law Rev.*, XVIII, 2 (February 1958), 271–92.

13,142 **Inns of Court Conservative and Unionist Society.** *A giant's strength: some thoughts on the constitutional and legal position of trade unions in England.* London: the Society, Johnson, 1958. 86p.

13,143 **Pritt**, Denis Nowell and **Freeman**, Richard. *The law versus the trade unions.* London: Lawrence and Wishart, 1958. 128p.

13,144 **Vester**, Horatio and **Gardner**, Anthony Herbert. *Trade union law and practice.* London: Sweet and Maxwell, 1958. xxx, 300p.

13,145 **Lloyd**, Dennis. 'The law of associations.' Ginsberg, M. (ed.). *Law and opinion in England in the 20th century.* London: Stevens, 1959. p. 99–115.

13,146 **Registry of Friendly Societies.** *Guide to the Trade Union Acts.* London: H.M.S.O., 1960. v, 42p.

13,147 **Cotton**, John. 'Trade unions and the law.' *Planning*, XXX, 479 (23 March 1964), 121–48.

13,148 **Frank**, W. F. 'How to reform trade union law.' *New Soc.*, IV, 111 (12 November 1964), 13–14.

13,149 **Hoyer-Miller**, Gurth. *Trade unions and the law.* London: New Orbits Group, 1964. 21p.

13,150 **Rideout**, Roger William. 'Trade unions: some social and legal problems.' *Hum. Relat.*, XVII, 1 (February 1964), 73–95; 2 (May 1964), 169–98.

Reprinted. London: Tavistock P., 1964. 54p. (Tavistock pamphlet 6.)

13,151 **Wedderburn**, Kenneth William. 'The TUC and trade union law.' *New Soc.*, IV, 101 (3 September 1964), 8–9.

13,152 **Grunfeld**, Cyril. *Modern trade union law.* London: Sweet and Maxwell, 1966. xii, 517p.

13,153 **Sethi**, R. B. and **Dwivedi**, R. N. *Law of trade unions.* Allahabad: Law Book Co., 1966.

Second edition.

13,154 **Abrahams**, Gerald. *Trade unions and the law.* London: Cassell, 1968. xix, 254p.

13,155 **Pelling**, Henry. 'British trade unions, workers and the law.' *Soc. Study Labour Hist. Bull.*, 17 (Autumn 1968), 26.

Abstract of a paper given at a Conference of the Society for the Study of Labour History, Birkbeck College, London, 3 May 1968.

13,156 **Pelling**, Henry. 'Trade unions, workers and the law.' *Popular politics and society in late Victorian Britain: essays.* London: Macmillan; New York: St Martin's P., 1968. p. 62–81.

13,157 **Brown**, Douglas. *Trade union law in a nutshell.* London: Sweet and Maxwell, 1969. xi, 64p. (Nutshell series.)

13,158 **Coates**, Ken and **Topham**, Tony. *The law versus the unions.* Nottingham: Institute for Workers' Control, 1969. 22p. (I.W.C. pamphlet series 15.)

13,159 **Donovan**, Terence Norbert, Baron Donovan. 'Trade unions and the law in Britain.' *Administration*, XVII, 3 (Autumn 1969), 271–83.

'Text of the Munster and Leinster Bank Lecture 1969, delivered on 11 April 1969 at University College, Galway.'

13,160 **Kahn-Freund**, Otto. 'Trade unions, the law and society.' *Mod. Law Rev.*, XXXIII, 3 (May 1970), 241–67.

'This is – with slight variations – the Gaitskell Memorial Lecture of 1970, delivered at the University of Nottingham on January 23, 1970. The Lecture was mainly intended for non-lawyers.'

13,161 **Pritt**, Denis Nowell. *Employers, workers and trade unions.* London: Lawrence and Wishart, 1970. 174p.

Book 1 of the author's *Law, class and society.*

See also: 2301; 12,127.

2. Legal Status

This section includes material on such subjects as the Combination Laws; the protection of union funds, and, in particular, the Taff Vale case; and the freedom of unions to organise. Material relating to the Trade Disputes Act of 1906 is classified in Part Seven, VIII, B unless it is exclusively concerned with the question of legal status. See also Part Three, III, B, 2–3; Part Seven, VII, B, 3–4; and Part Seven, VIII, B.

13,162 **Manchester Typographical Society.** *Verbatim report of the actions for libel against the officers of the Manchester Typographical Society.* Manchester, 1892.

13,163 *Case of Temperton v. Russell and others.* 1895. 19p.

13,164 **Amalgamated Society of Railway Servants.** *Labour's right to combine.* London, 1897. 48p.

13,165 **Wallas**, Graham. *The life of Francis Place, 1771–1854.* London: Longmans, 1898. viii, 415p.

Revised edition. London: Allen and Unwin, 1918. xiv, 415p.

13,166 **Barlow**, Montague. 'The Taff Vale Railway case.' *Econ. J.*, XI, 41 (March 1901), 130–1.

Supplement. 43 (September 1901), 447–9.

13,167 **Lushington**, Godfrey. 'Trade unions and the House of Lords.' *Natn. Rev.*, XXXVIII, 226 (December 1901), 540–63.

Quinn *v.* Leatham; Taff Vale.

13,168 **Adams**, W. G. S. 'The incorporation of trade unions: the position in England.' *J. Polit. Econ.*, XI, 1 (December 1902), 89–92.

13,169 **Amalgamated Society of Railway Servants.** *The Taff Vale case and the injunction.* London, 1902. 55p.

'Private.'

13,170 **Edwards**, Clement. 'Should trade unions be incorporated?' *Nineteenth Century*, LI, 300 (February 1902) 233–51.

Taff Vale.

13,171 **MacDonald**, James Ramsay. *The law and trade union funds: a plea for 'Ante-Taff Vale'.* London: Independent Labour Party; Leicester: Co-operative Printing Works, [1903?]. 16p.

13,172 **Wood**, George Henry. 'Social movements and reforms of the nineteenth century.' Co-operative Wholesale Societies Ltd. *Annual for 1903.* p. 193–222.

Includes the repeal of the Combination Laws, and the movement for the 'Ten hours bill'.

13,173 **Howell**, George. 'The Taff Vale case: its history, its gravity, and its lessons.' Co-operative Wholesale Societies Ltd. *Annual for 1904.* p. 123–44.

13,174 **Atherley-Jones**, Llewellyn Arthur. 'Trade disputes.' *Contemp. Rev.*, LXXXIX (May 1906), 628–37.

Taff Vale.

13,175 **Cohen**, Herman Joseph. 'Problems of labour. II. Total immunity of trade union funds.' *Fortn. Rev.*, n.s., LXXX, 479 (November 1906), 925–41.

13,176 **Seager**, Henry R. 'The legal status of trade unions in the United Kingdom, with conclusions applicable to the United States.' *Polit. Sci. Q.*, XXII, 4 (December 1907), 611–29.

13,177 **Bryan**, James W. *The development of the English law of conspiracy.* Baltimore, Md.: Johns Hopkins P., 1909. 161p. (Johns Hopkins University studies in historical and political science. Series XXVII, nos. 3, 4, 5.)

13,178 **Ervine**, St. John Greer. *Francis Place, the tailor of Charing Cross.* London: Fabian Society, 1912. 27p. (Fabian tract 165. Biographical series 1.)

13,179 **Irish Transport and General Workers' Union.** National Executive Council. *P. T. Daly's libel action: a report of the legal proceedings against 'The Voice of Labour' and the Irish Transport and General Workers' Union.* Dublin, 1925. 36p.

13,180 **George**, Mary Dorothy. 'The Combination Laws reconsidered.' *Econ. Hist.*, I, 2 (May 1927), 214–28.

13,181 **Gray**, J. L. 'The law of combination in Scotland.' *Economica*, VIII, 24 (December 1928), 332–50.

13,182 **Johnson**, Dorothy Catherine. 'Francis Place, 1771–1854.' *Pioneers of reform.* London: Methuen, 1929. p. 81–99.

13,183 **George**, Mary Dorothy. 'Revisions in economic history. IV. The Combination Laws.' *Econ. Hist. Rev.*, VI, 2 (April 1936), 172–8.

13,184 **International Association for Social Progress.** British Section. *Report . . . on liberty of trade unions and professional associations.* London, 1936. 30p.

13,185 **Cole**, George Douglas Howard. 'A study in legal repression, 1789–1834.' *Persons & periods: studies.* London: Macmillan, 1938. p. 120–42.

Published initially, in part, as a chapter in G. D. H. Cole, and others, *The book of martyrs of Tolpuddle, 1834–1934.* London: Trades Union Congress, 1934.

13,186 **Beighle**, Howard Clyde. *An investigation of the position of labor as modified by the Combination Laws.* 1940. (M.A. thesis, University of Washington.)

13,187 **Kahn-Freund**, Otto. 'The illegality of a trade union.' *Mod. Law Rev.*, VII, 4 (November 1944), 192–205.

13,188 **Braun**, Kurt. *The right to organize and its limits: a comparison of policies in the United States and selected European countries.* Washington, D.C.: Brookings Institution, 1950. xiii, 331p.

13,189 **Kuhn**, James W. 'Combination laws of 1799 and 1800.' *Labor Law J.*, VII, 1 (January 1956), 19–23.

13,190 **Martin**, Ross M. 'Legal personality and the trade union.' Webb, L. C. (ed.). *Legal personality and political pluralism.* Melbourne: Melbourne U.P., for the Australian National University, 1958. p. 93–142.

13,191 **Pittet**, D. G. *The incorporation of trade unions.* 1958, ii, 65p. (LL.M. thesis, Dalhousie University.)

13,192 **Hall**, J. Sexton. 'The legal status of the registered trade union.' *Ind. Law Rev.*, XIII, 3 (January 1959), 136–49.

13,193 **Saville**, John. 'Trade unions and free labour: the background to the Taff Vale decision.' Briggs, A. and Saville, J. (eds.). *Essays in labour history*. London: Macmillan; New York: St Martin's P., 1960. p. 317–50.

Revised edition. 1967.

13,194 **Slesser**, *Sir* Henry Herman. 'Trade unions and the labour market. Part 1. The legal status of trade unions.' Seldon, A. (ed.). *Agenda for a free society: essays on Hayek's 'The Constitution of Liberty'*. London: Hutchinson for the Institute of Economic Affairs, 1961. p. 139–53.

13,195 **Slesser**, *Sir* Henry Herman. 'The legality of trade unionism.' *The art of judgment and other studies*. London: Stevens, 1962.

13,196 **Thomas**, W. E. S. 'Francis Place and working-class history.' *Hist. J.*, v, 1 (1962), 61–70.

13,197 **Montague**, Ruth. *The freedom to organise and its protection by law in Great Britain, the United States of America and the Federal Republic of Germany*. 1966–67. (Ph.D. thesis, University of Edinburgh.)

3. Government and Administration

This section includes material on the law relating to the internal affairs of trade unions, for example, on the exclusion or expulsion of workers from membership. Material on the powers of professional bodies to discipline their members is classified at Part Three, III, E, 9. Material on the case of *Rookes* v. *Barnard* is classified in Part Seven, VIII, B. See also Part Three, III, G; Part Seven, VII, B, 2; and Part Seven, VII, B, 4.

13,198 **Jameson**, John. *Jameson v. The Typographical Association, before Mr. Justice Romer, Royal Courts of Justice, July 28–30, 1948*. London, 1949. 77p.

Transcript of the shorthand notes of the Association of Official Shorthand-writers.

13,199 **Thomas**, Trevor C. 'Expulsions from trade unions.' Megarry, R. E. (ed.). *The law in action: a series of broadcast talks*. London: Stevens, 1954. p. 43–63.

Broadcast B.B.C. Third Programme, 14 February 1954.

13,200 **Lloyd**, Dennis. 'Damages for wrongful expulsion from a trade union: Bonsor *v.* Musicians' Union.' *Mod. Law Rev.*, XIX, 2 (March 1956), 121–35.

13,201 **Thomas**, Trevor C. 'Trade unions and their members.' *Camb. Law J.* (April 1956), 67–79.

About the legal rights of expulsion.

On the case of Bonsor *v.* Musicians' Union.

13,202 **Grunfeld**, Cyril. *Trade unions and the individual*. London: Fabian Society, 1957. 32p. (Fabian research series 193.)

13,203 **Wedderburn**, Kenneth William. 'The Bonsor affair: a post-script.' *Mod. Law Rev.*, XX, 2 (March 1957), 105–23.

On the case of Bonsor *v.* Musicians' Union.

13,204 **Rideout**, Roger William. *The right to membership of trade unions*. 1957–58. (Ph.D. thesis, University of London.)

13,205 **Hickling**, M. A. *The law relating to internal relations of trade unions*. 1958–59. (Ph.D. thesis, University of London.)

13,206 **Clegg**, Hugh Armstrong. 'The rights of British trade-union members.' Harrington, M. and Jacobs, P. (eds.). *Labor in a free society*. Berkeley, Calif.: U. of California P., 1959. p. 119–38.

13,207 **Grodin**, Joseph R. *Comparison of British and American law relating to internal trade union affairs*. 1959–60. (Ph.D. thesis, University of London.)

13,208 **Grodin**, Joseph R. *Union government and the law: British and American experiences*. Los Angeles: Institute of Industrial Relations, University of California, 1961. 209p. (Industrial relations monographs 8.)

13,209 **Hewitt**, Cecil Rolph. *All those in favour? An account of the High Court action against the Electrical Trades Union and its officers for ballot-rigging in the election of union officials (Byrne & Chapple v. Foulkes & others, 1961)*. London: Deutsch, 1962. 255p.

Prepared from the official court transcript by C. H. Rolph, i.e. C. R. Hewitt.

13,210 **Rideout**, Roger William. 'Protection of the right to work.' *Mod. Law Rev.*, XXV, 2 (March 1962), 137–48.

13,211 **Grunfeld**, Cyril. *Trade unions and the individual in English law: a study of recent developments*. London: Institute of Personnel Management, 1963. 60p. (Industrial relations series 1.)

13,212 **Rideout**, Roger William. *The right to membership of a trade union*. London: Athlone P., 1963. xliv, 243p. (University of London legal series 5.)

13,213 **Grunfeld**, Cyril. 'Les relations internes entre les syndicats et leur membres: rapport national.' Congrès International de Droit du Travail et de la Securité Sociale, 5ième, Lyon, 1963. *Actes*. Lyon, [1965]. Vol. 1. p. 253–81.

Text in English.

13,214 **Rookes**, Douglas. *Conspiracy*. London: Johnson Publications, 1966. xiv, 287p.

Includes text of Mr Justice Sachs' summing-up, House of Lords Judgments, and the Trade Disputes Act, 1965.

13,215 **Hendy**, J. 'Trade unions and their members.' *Ind. Law Soc. Bull.*, 7 (July 1970), 5–8.

4. Political Action

See also Part Three, III, B, 3–5; Part Three, III, H; and Part Seven, VII, B, 2–3.

13,216 **Anderson**, W. C. *Parliament and trade union history: an argument for political independence.* Hyde, [1907?]. 19p.

13,217 **Henderson**, Arthur and **MacDonald**, James Ramsay. 'Trade unions and parliamentary representation.' *Contemp. Rev.*, XCV (February 1909), 173–9.

13,218 **Cox**, Harold. 'The position of trade unions.' *Q. Rev.*, CCXIII, 425 (October 1910), 567–84.
Review article on the reports of the judgments given in the Osborne case, and other works.

13,219 **Cox**, Harold. 'The story of the Osborne case.' *Nineteenth Century*, LXVIII, 404 (October 1910), 569–86.

13,220 *Enemies of the red flag. Socialism and the Osborne judgment.* London, [1910?]. 8p.

13,221 **Geldart**, William Martin. *The Osborne judgment and after.* [1910.] 32p.
Reprinted from the *Manchester Guardian*, September and October 1910.

13,222 **Geldart**, William Martin. 'Trade unions and parliamentary representation.' *Econ. J.*, XX, 79 (September 1910), 480–4.

13,223 **Horwill**, Herbert W. 'The payment of labor representatives in the British House of Commons.' *Polit. Sci. Q.*, XXV, 2 (June 1910), 317–27.

13,224 **MacDonald**, James Ramsay. 'The Osborne judgment and trade unions.' *Contemp. Rev.*, XCVIII (November 1910), 535–42.

13,225 **Osborne**, Walter V. *My case: the causes and effects of the Osborne judgment.* London: E. Nash, 1910. vi, 116p.

13,226 **Osborne**, Walter V. *Trade union funds and party politics.* Walthamstow, 1910. 16p.

13,227 **Geldart**, William Martin. 'Legal powers and limitations of trade unions.' *Econ. Rev.*, XXI, 3 (July 1911), 248–66.

13,228 **Osborne**, Walter V. *Trade Union (No. 2) Bill: trade unions and party politics.* Walthamstow, 1911. 16p.

13,229 **Osborne**, Walter V. and **Judge**, Mark H. *Trade unions and the law.* London: King, 1911. 37p.

13,230 **Webb**, Sidney. 'The Osborne revolution.' *Engl. Rev.*, VII, 26 (January 1911), 380–93.

13,231 **Osborne**, Walter V. *Sane trade-unionism.* London, Glasgow: Collins' Clear-Type P., 1913. 264p. (The nation's library.)

13,232 **Osborne**, Walter V. 'The Taff Vale judgement, and after.' *Jubilee of the Railway News, 1864–1914.* London: *Railway News*, 1914. p. 192–4.

13,233 **Clynes**, John Robert. *Speech delivered . . . at Leeds on the Trade Disputes and Trades Unions Bill.* London, 1927. 14p.

13,234 **European Economic and Political Survey.** 'British Trade Disputes and Trade Unions Act.' *Europ. Econ. Polit. Survey*, II (31 August 1927), 785–91.

13,235 **Ferguson**, Lewis Buchanan. *The Trade Disputes and Trade Unions Act, 1927.* London: Butterworth, 1927, xv, 99p.
'Annotated, with four introductory chapters and notes.'

13,236 **Henderson**, Arthur. *The government's attack on trade union law: an analysis of the Trade Disputes and Trade Unions Bill 1927.* London, [1927?]. 33p.

13,237 **Hogg**, Douglas McGarel, Viscount Hailsham. *The Trade Disputes Bill.* London: National Union of Conservative and Unionist Associations, 1927. 10p. ([Publication] 2720.)
A speech made on 13 May 1927.

13,238 **Laski**, Harold Joseph and **Benn**, Ernest John Pickstone. *The Trades Disputes and Trade Unions Bill.* London: King, 1927. 19p. (Present day papers 12.)

13,239 **Muir**, John Ramsay Bryce. *Trade unionism and the Trade Union Bill.* London: Liberal Industrial Enquiry, 1927. 172p.
'With an appendix on the legal position of trade unions, by W. A. Jowitt . . . A. D. McNair . . . and Hubert Phillips.'

13,240 **Robson**, William Alexander. *The Trade Disputes and Trades Unions Bill: an analysis and commentary.* London: Fabian Society, 1927. 8p. (Fabian tract 222.)

13,241 **Thompson**, William Henry. *The Trade Union Bill.* London, 1927. 16p.

13,242 **Mason**, Alpheus Thomas. '[British Trade Disputes Act of 1927.]' *Am. Polit. Sci. Rev.*, XXII, 1 (February 1928), 143–53.

13,243 **Millis**, H. A. 'The British Trade Disputes and Trade Unions Act, 1927.' *J. Polit. Econ.*, XXXVI, 3 (June 1928), 305–29.

13,244 **National Union of Conservative and Unionist Associations.** *The Trade Disputes Act popularly explained.* London, [1928?].

13,245 **Macrae-Gibson**, J. H. 'The British Civil Service and the Trade Unions Act of 1927.' *Am. Polit. Sci. Rev.*, XXIII, 4 (November 1929), 922–9.

13,246 **Edwards**, A. C. *The Tory Act and the Labour Bill as affecting trade-union rights.* London, 1931. 23p.

13,247 **Edwards**, A. C. *The Trade Union Bill: right or privilege?* London, 1931. 42p.

13,248 **Witte**, Edwin E. 'British trade union law since the Trade Disputes and Trade Union Act of 1927.' *Am. Polit. Sci. Rev.*, XXVI, 2 (April 1932), 345–51.

13,249 **Arnot**, Robert Page. *Exit the Trade Disputes Act.* London: Labour Research Department, 1946. 11p.

13,250 **Sires**, Ronald V. 'The repeal of the Trade Disputes and Trade Unions Act of 1927.' *Ind. Labor Relat. Rev.*, VI, 2 (January 1953), 227–38.

13,251 **Ford**, H. A. J. 'Trade union law and aid to political parties.' *J. Ind. Relat.*, II, 1 (April 1960), 20–30.

13,252 **Gwyn**, William Brent. *Democracy and the cost of politics in Britain.* London: U. of London, Athlone P., 1962. vii, 256p.
Chap. VII. Osborne case.

13,253 **Grunfeld**, Cyril. 'Political independence in British trade unions: some legal aspects.' *Br. J. Ind. Relat.*, I, 1 (February 1963), 23–42.

13,254 **Shefftz**, Melvin Charles. 'The Trade Disputes and Trade Unions Act of 1927: the aftermath of the General Strike.' *Rev. Polit.*, XXIX, 3 (July 1967), 387–406.

C. EMPLOYERS' ASSOCIATIONS

See also Part Four, I.

13,255 **Badcock**, Julian K. 'The law relating to employers' associations.' *Ind. Law Rev.*, VII, 3 (January 1953), 186–95.

13,256 **McRobie**, George. 'Some aspects of the law relating to trade associations.' *Ind. Law Rev.*, VIII, 3 (January 1954), 193–202.

VIII. REGULATION OF COLLECTIVE BARGAINING AND INDUSTRIAL CONFLICT

See also Part Five, I; and Part Five, IV.

A. COLLECTIVE AGREEMENTS

13,257 **Industrial Council.** *Report on the methods of securing the due fulfilment of industrial agreements, and of enforcing agreements throughout particular trades or districts.* London: H.M.S.O., 1913. 22p. (Cd. 6952.)
Minutes of evidence, etc. 1913. (Cd. 6953.)
Chairman: G. Askwith.

13,258 **Tillyard**, Frank and **Robson**, William Alexander. 'The enforcement of the collective bargain in the United Kingdom.' *Econ. J.*, XLVIII, 189 (March 1938), 15–25.

13,259 **Hamburger**, L. 'The extension of collective agreements to cover entire trades and industries.' *Int. Labour Rev.*, XL, 2 (August 1939), 153–94.

13,260 **Kahn-Freund**, Otto. 'Collective agreements under war legislation.' *Mod. Law Rev.*, VI, 3 (April 1943), 112–43.

13,261 **Badcock**, Julian K. 'Collective agreements.' *Ind. Law Rev.*, VI, 1 (July 1951), 13–21.

13,262 **Keast**, Horace. 'Enforcement of voluntary wage agreements.' *Ind. Law Rev.*, VII, 3 (January 1953), 203–11.

13,263 **Kahn-Freund**, Otto. 'Report on the legal status of collective bargaining and collective agreements in Great Britain.' Kahn-Freund, O. (ed.). *Labour relations and the law: a comparative study.* London: Stevens; Boston, Mass.: Little, Brown, 1965. p. 21–39.

13,264 **McCartney**, J. B. 'The contractual or non-contractual nature of collective agreements in Great Britain and in Eire.' Kahn-Freund, O. (ed.). *Labour relations and the law: a comparative study.* London: Stevens; Boston, Mass.: Little, Brown, 1965. p. 40–7.

13,265 **Adell**, B. L. *The legal status of collective agreements in England, the United States and Canada.* 1966. xv, 409p. (D.Phil. thesis, University of Oxford.)

13,266 **Selwyn**, Norman M. *Legal aspects of collective agreements.* 1967. 247p. (LL.M. thesis, University of Manchester.)

13,267 **Bernier**, Jean. 'L'extension des conventions collectives dans le droit du travail: France, Grande Bretagne et Canada. [The extension of collective agreements: France, Great Britain and Canada.]' *Relat. Ind.*, XXIV, 1 (January 1969), 141–63.
A summary of this article in English is given on p. 163–6.

13,268 **Lyman**, E. H. *The legal status of collective bargaining agreements in the United States, the United Kingdom and the Republic of Ireland.* 1969. (LL.M. thesis, Queen's University of Belfast.)

13,269 **Selwyn**, Norman M. 'Collective agreements and the law.' *Mod. Law Rev.*, XXXII, 4 (July 1969), 377–96.

13,270 **Horgan**, John M. 'Collective agreements and the law in the Republic of Ireland: a case study in legal enforceability.' *Ind. Relat. J.* (December 1970), 30–40.

13,271 **Lewis**, Roy. 'The legal enforceability of collective agreements.' *Br. J. Ind. Relat.*, VIII, 3 (November 1970), 313–33.

13,272 **Pain**, Peter. 'Are collective bargains contracts? (b).' *Ind. Law Soc. Bull.*, 7 (July 1970), 15.

13,273 **Selwyn**, Norman M. 'Are collective bargains contracts? (a).' *Ind. Law Soc. Bull.*, 7 (July 1970), 13–14.

B. STRIKES AND LOCKOUTS

Material on the Trade Disputes Act of 1906 is included here unless it is exclusively concerned with the question of the legal status of trade unions when it is classified at Part Seven, VII, B, 2. See also Part Seven, VII, B, 1–2.

13,274 **Sayer**, Joseph R. and **Savill**, Stanley. *Labour disputes before magistrates.* London: Shaw, 1888. xxiv, 220p.
'Handbook on the rights of employers and workmen in their relationship as such.'

13,275 **Curran**, P., and others. *The law of intimidation: what does it mean?* Plymouth, 1890. 36p.

13,276 **Neville**, Reginald James Neville. *Strikes: a concise statement of the criminal law relating to . . . offences occurring during disputes between employers and employed.* London: Clowes, 1890. viii, 40p.

13,277 **Labour Protection Association.** *The law relating to picketing as laid down by recent judgments.* London: the Association, 1899. 13p.

13,278 **Employers' Parliamentary Council.** *The law relating to labour unions as regards their legal liabilities in connection with picketing.* London, 1901. 15p.

13,279 **Miners' Federation of Great Britain.** *In the High Court of Justice . . . the Denaby and Cadeby Main Collieries, Ltd.* v. *the Yorkshire Miners' Association and others.* Manchester, 1904. 720p.

13,280 **Cohen**, Herman Joseph. *The law relating to strikes and lockouts.* London, 1905. 16p.

13,281 **Miners' Federation of Great Britain.** *In the Supreme Court of Judicature . . . Denaby and Cadeby Main Collieries, Ltd.* v. *the Yorkshire Miners' Association, and G. Cragg and ten others.* Manchester, 1905. 513, 22p.

13,282 **Edwards**, A. C. *Trade Disputes Bill: privilege or right?* London, 1906. 10p.

13,283 **Edwards**, Clement. 'The Government Trade Disputes Bill.' *Nineteenth Century*, LX, 356 (October 1906), 587–93.

13,284 **Joel**, J. Edmondson. 'Trade disputes and the law of molestation and conspiracy.' *Westm. Rev.*, CLXV, 6 (June 1906), 605–15.

13,285 **Miners' Federation of Great Britain.** *In the House of Lords . . . between the Denaby and Cadeby Main Collieries, Ltd. and the Yorkshire Miners' Association and others.* Manchester, 1906. 448p.

13,286 **Fellows**, Alfred. 'The Trade Disputes Act and freedom of contract.' *Fortn. Rev.*, n.s., LXXXII, 489 (September 1907), 403–16.

13,287 **Whittaker**, *Sir* Thomas Palmer. *The recent strikes and the Trade Disputes Act 1906.* London: Liberal Publication Department, 1912. 12p.
Reprinted, with slight alterations, from the *Westminster Gazette.*

13,288 **Geldart**, William Martin. 'Trade unions, trade lists and the law.' *Econ. Rev.*, XXIII, 2 (April 1913), 128–39.
On Vacher and Sons *v.* The London Society of Compositors.

13,289 **Geldart**, William Martin. 'The present law of trade disputes and trade unions.' *Polit. Q.*, 2 (May 1914), 17–61.
Reprinted. London: Oxford U.P., 1914. 61p.

13,290 **Labour Research Department.** *The right to strike.* London, [1924?]. 12p.

13,291 **Clay**, Henry. 'Administrative aspects of state labour policy.' *Publ. Adm.*, IV (1926), 189–204.
Discussion, p. 204–7.
Lecture delivered before the Institute of Public Administration, 25 March 1926.

13,292 **Goodhart**, Arthur Lehman. *The legality of the general strike in England.* Cambridge: Heffer, 1927. 24p.
Reprinted from *Yale Law Journal.*

13,293 **Conservative Party.** *All you want to know about the Trade Disputes Act.* London, 1946. 36p. (Publications 3882.)

13,294 **Keeton**, G. W. 'The background of the Trades Disputes Act, 1906.' *Ind. Law Rev.*, I, 2 (July 1946), 33–40.

13,295 **Wrottesley**, A. J. F. 'Strikes and the law.' *Ind. Law Rev.*, V, 4 (April 1951), 257–64.

13,296 **Wrottesley**, A. J. F. 'The D. C. Thomson case.' *Ind. Law Rev.*, VII, 4 (April 1953), 260–71.

13,297 **Delany**, V. T. H. 'Immunity in tort and the Trade Disputes Act: a new limitation?' *Mod. Law Rev.*, XVIII, 4 (July 1955), 338–43.

13,298 **Abrahamson**, Max W. 'Trade Disputes Act: strict interpretation in Ireland.' *Mod. Law Rev.*, XXIV, 5 (September 1961), 596–603.

13,299 **Meyers**, Frederic. 'A comparative study of the law of the strike: Britain, France and the United States.' *Symposium on Labor Relations Law.* Baton Rouge, La.: Claitor's Bookstore, 1961. p. 515–31.

13,300 **Wedderburn**, Kenneth William. 'The right to threaten strikes.' *Mod. Law Rev.*, XXIV, 5 (September 1961), 572–91; XXV, 5 (September 1962), 513–30.

13,301 **Aikin**, Olga L. 'A "go slow" or a "work to rule"?' *Br. J. Ind. Relat.*, I, 2 (June 1963), 260–1.
'A legal note.'

13,302 **Coates**, Ken. 'The right to strike.' *New Left Rev.*, 24 (March–April 1964), 58–61.
Rookes *v.* Barnard.

13,303 **Frank**, W. F. 'The right to strike reconsidered.' *J. Bus. Law* (July 1964), 199–210.
Rookes *v.* Barnard.

13,304 **Lincoln**, John Abraham. *Journey to coercion: from Tolpuddle to Rookes* v. *Barnard.* London: Institute of Economic Affairs, 1964. 78p.

13,305 **Parsons**, Owen Henry. *The meaning of Rookes* v. *Barnard: trade unions hamstrung.* London: L.R.D. Publications, 1964. 24p.

13,306 **Wedderburn**, Kenneth William. 'The Lords and the right to strike.' *New Soc.*, III, 70 (30 January 1964), 16–17. (Welfare & work.)
On Rookes *v.* Barnard.

13,307 **McCartney**, J. B. 'Strike law and the constitution of Eire: a note on the case-law.' Kahn-Freund, O. (ed.). *Labour relations and the law: a comparative study.* London: Stevens; Boston, Mass.: Little, Brown, 1965. p. 154–69.

13,308 **Wedderburn**, Kenneth William. 'The law and industrial conflict in Great Britain.' Kahn-Freund, O. (ed.). *Labour relations and the law: a comparative study.* London: Stevens; Boston, Mass.: Little, Brown, 1965. p. 127–53.

13,309 **Healy**, B. P. J. *The operation of the Trade Disputes Act 1906 and 1965.* 1966. (LL.M. thesis, University of London.)

13,310 **Hickling**, M. A. 'Restoring the protection of the Trade Disputes Act: some forgotten aspects.' *Mod. Law Rev.*, XXIX, 1 (January 1966), 32–41.

13,311 **Thomson**, Andrew William John. 'The injunction in trades disputes in Britain before 1910.' *Ind. Labor Relat. Rev.*, XIX, 2 (January 1966), 213–23.

13,312 **Wedderburn**, Kenneth William. 'Strike law and the labour injunction: the British experience, 1850–1966.' Carrothers, A. W. R. and Palmer, E. E. (eds.). *Report of a study on the labour injunction in Ontario.* [Toronto: Ontario Department of Labour], 1966. Vol. 2. p. 603–84.

13,313 **Wedderburn**, Kenneth William. 'Trade Disputes Act 1965, Redundancy Payments Act 1965.' *Mod. Law Rev.*, XXIX, 1 (January 1966), 53–67.

Discussion of the Acts.

13,314 **Christie**, Innis M. *The liability of strikers in the law of tort: a comparative study of the law in England and Canada.* Kingston, Ont.: Queen's University, Industrial Relations Centre, 1967. xxii, 198p. (Research series 5.)

13,315 **Hanson**, C. G. 'Trade union law reform and unofficial strikes.' *Westm. Bank Rev.* (August 1968), 47–61.

13,316 **Monson**, Weldon P. 'The case of Rookes *v.* Barnard (House of Lords 1964).' *Labor Law J.*, XIX, 1 (January 1968), 50–54.

'. . . discusses in detail here the English case of Rookes *v.* Barnard – its implications in Anglo-American industrial relations and judicial thought.'

13,317 **Casey**, J. P. 'The injunction in labour disputes in Eire.' *Int. Comp. Law Q.*, XVIII, 2 (April 1969), 347–59.

13,318 **O'Higgins**, Paul and **Partington**, Martin. 'Industrial conflict: judicial attitudes.' *Mod. Law Rev.*, XXXII, 1 (January 1969), 53–8.

13,319 **Phelps Brown**, Ernest Henry. 'Unofficial strikes and the law.' *Three Banks Rev.*, 83 (September 1969), 3–19.

13,320 **McErlean**, J. R. *The criminal law and emergency and special legislation in relation to trade disputes in the United Kingdom.* 1970. (Ll.M. thesis, Queen's University of Belfast.)

See also: 12,093; 13,214; 14,476.

C. CONCILIATION, ARBITRATION, AND INQUIRY

Material on private conciliation and arbitration is listed in Part Five, IV, A and E. Works on conciliation and arbitration by the state are listed here.

13,321 **Wright**, Carroll Davidson. *Industrial conciliation and arbitration.* Boston, Mass.: Rand, Aberg, 1881. 173p.

'Compiled from material in the possession of the Massachusetts Bureau of Statistics of Labor, by direction of the Massachusetts Legislature, Chapter 43, Resolves of 1881.'

13,322 **Board of Trade.** Sea Fishing Trade Committee. *Report of a committee appointed under a minute of the Board of Trade, to inquire into and report whether any and what legislation is desirable with a view to placing the relations between the owners, masters and crews of fishing vessels on a more satisfactory basis; together with the minutes of evidence taken on the inquiry.* London: Eyre and Spottiswoode for H.M.S.O., 1883. xxi, 238p. (C. 3432.)

13,323 **Ashley**, William James. 'Methods of industrial peace.' *Econ. Rev.*, II, 3 (July 1892), 297–317.

'A public lecture delivered before the University of Toronto, January 23, 1892.'

13,324 **Schloss**, David Frederick. 'State promotion of industrial peace.' *Econ. J.*, III, 10 (June 1893), 218–25.

13,325 **North**, S. N. D. 'Industrial arbitration: its methods and its limitations.' *Q. J. Econ.*, X (July 1896), 407–30.

13,326 **Standing Committee on Trade, etc.** *Report . . . on the Conciliation (Trade Disputes) Bill and the Boards of Conciliation (No. 2) Bill; with the proceedings.* London: H.M.S.O., 1896. (H.C. 281.)

13,327 **Webb**, Sidney and **Webb**, Beatrice. 'Arbitration in labour disputes.' *Nineteenth Century*, XL, 237 (November 1896), 743–58.

13,328 **Board of Trade.** *Proceedings under the Conciliation (Trade Disputes) Act, 1896: first report.* London: H.M.S.O., 1897. (C. 8533.)

Second report. 1899. (H.C. 275.)

13,329 **Fabian Society.** *State arbitration and the living wage.* London: Fabian Society, 1897. 16p. (Fabian tract 83.)

Second edition, revised. 1903.

By H. W. Macrosty.

Issued without the author's name.

13,330 **Z.** 'Compulsory arbitration.' *Econ. J.*, IX, 33 (March 1899), 85–7.

13,331 **Edinburgh Review.** 'Conciliation and arbitration in trade disputes.' *Edinb. Rev.*, CXCI, 391 (January 1900), 1–21.
Review article on the Conciliation Act, 1896; Fifth and final report of the Royal Commission on Labour, June 1894; Second report of the Board of Trade of proceedings under the Conciliation (Trade Disputes) Act, 1896, 11 July 1899.

13,332 **Thomas**, G. P. *Compulsory arbitration: is it feasible?* London, 1900. 16p.

13,333 **Mallock**, William Hurrell. 'Labour unrest as a subject of official investigation.' *Nineteenth Century*, LXXI, 424 (June 1912), 1029–45.

13,334 **Hamilton**, W. F. *Compulsory arbitration in industrial disputes.* London: Butterworth, 1913. 129p.

13,335 **Constable**, W. G. 'The compulsory settlement of industrial disputes.' *Edinb. Rev.*, CCXIX, 447 (January 1914), 195–211.
Australia, New Zealand, U.S., England and Canada.

13,336 **Compton**, Wilson. 'Wage theories in industrial arbitration.' *Am. Econ. Rev.*, VI, 2 (June 1916), 324–42.

13,337 **Mote**, Carl Henry. *Industrial arbitration: a world-wide survey of natural and political agencies for social justice and industrial peace.* Indianapolis, Ind.: Bobbs-Merrill, 1916. 351, xlvp.

13,338 **United States.** Board of Mediation and Conciliation. *Railway strikes and lockouts: a study of arbitration and conciliation laws of the principal countries of the world providing machinery for the peaceable adjustment of disputes between railroads and their employees, and laws of certain countries for the prevention of strikes.* Washington: U.S.G.P.O., 1916. 367p.
Chapter VII. Great Britain.

13,339 **Cannan**, Edwin. 'Industrial unrest.' *Econ. J.*, XXVII, 108 (December 1917), 453–70.
Discussion of reports of Commission of Enquiry into Industrial Unrest.

13,340 **Committee on Production** and **Special Arbitration Tribunal** (Section 1 (2) Munitions of War Act, 1917). *Memorandum on proceedings of the Committee on Production, May 1917–April 1918.* London: H.M.S.O., 1918. 9p. (Cd. 9126.)

13,341 **Moses**, Milton. 'Compulsory arbitration in Great Britain during the war.' *J. Polit. Econ.*, XXVI, 9 (November 1918), 882–900.

13,342 **Committee on Production** and **Special Arbitration Tribunal** (Section 1 (2) Munitions of War Act, 1917). *Memorandum on proceedings of the Committee on Production, May 1918–November 1918.* London: H.M.S.O., 1919. 8p. (Cmd. 70.)

13,343 **Ministry of Labour.** Industrial Relations Department. *Conciliation Act and Industrial Courts Act.* London: H.M.S.O., 1920. 462p. (H.C. 221.)

13,344 **Stoker**, William Henry. *The Industrial Courts Act, 1919, and conciliation and arbitration in industrial disputes.* London: Stevens, 1920. vii, 56p.

13,345 **International Labour Office.** 'Conciliation and arbitration in Great Britain.' *Int. Labour Rev.*, I, 3 (March 1921), 91–110 (371–90).

13,346 **Mackenzie**, *Sir* William Warrender. 'The British Industrial Court.' *Int. Labour Rev.*, III, 1–2 (July–August 1921), 41–50.
The author was President of the Court at the time of writing.

13,347 **Douglas**, Paul H. 'The practice and theory of labour adjustment.' *J. Polit. Econ.*, XXXI, 2 (April 1923), 288–93.
Review article on Askwith, *Industrial problems and disputes* and Feis, *The settlement of wage disputes.*

13,348 **Mackenzie**, *Sir* William Warrender. *The Industrial Court: practice and procedure.* London: Butterworth, 1923. viii, 44, 8p.

13,349 **Morris**, *Sir* Harold. 'The Industrial Court and its working.' *Economica*, VIII, 22 (March 1928), 16–27.

13,350 **Mackenzie**, William Warrender, Baron Amulree. *Industrial arbitration.* London: Institute of Arbitrators, 1929.

13,351 **Mackenzie**, William Warrender, Baron Amulree. *Industrial arbitration in Great Britain.* London: Oxford U.P., 1929. x, 233p.

13,352 **Rankin**, Mary Theresa. *Arbitration principles and the Industrial Court: an analysis of decisions 1919–1929.* London: King, 1931. viii, 178p.

13,353 **Sprigge**, John Joshua. *A Bill to provide a public service for conciliation.* London: Williams and Norgate, 1931. 60p.

13,354 **Chang**, Ducksoo. *British methods of industrial peace: a study of democracy in relation to labor disputes.* 1937. (Thesis, Columbia University.)

13,355 **Carver**, Thomas Nixon. *Memorandum on the question: what legislation is best designed to reduce existing antagonisms, to conciliate the interests of employers and employees, to co-ordinate the special activities of all enterprises and to harmonize the interests of producers and consumers?* Paris, Liège (printed), 1938. 446p. (Université Libre de Bruxelles. Enquêtes sociologiques 4.)

13,356 **Cole**, George Douglas Howard. *A memorandum on the question: what legislation is best designed to reduce existing antagonisms, to conciliate the interests of employers and employees, to co-ordinate the special activities of all enterprises and to harmonize the interests of producers and consumers?* Paris, Liège (printed), 1938. (Université Libre de Bruxelles. Enquêtes sociologiques 4.)

13,357 **Hugh-Jones**, E. M. 'The state and

industrial order.' *Q. J. Econ.*, LIII, 2 (February 1939), 194–212.

On machinery in England for dealing with industrial disputes.

13,358 **Morris**, *Sir* Harold. 'The Industrial Court of Great Britain.' Gannett, F. E. and Catherwood, B. F. (eds.). *Industrial and labour relations in Great Britain: a symposium.* New York: the editors, 1939. p. 43–73.

The author was President of the Industrial Court.

13,359 **Sharp**, Ian Gordon. *A study of the practice and procedure of arbitration and conciliation as a voluntary principle in some British industries, with an account of state action in this field.* 1940. (Ph.D. thesis, University of London.)

13,360 **Burton**, *Sir* Montague. *The middle path: talks on collective security, arbitration and other aspects of international and industrial relations.* Leeds: Petty, 1943. 76p.

13,361 **Wilson**, *Sir* Horace. 'William Warrender Mackenzie, Baron Amulree of Strathbraan: his influence on industrial relations.' *R. Soc. Arts J.* (18 January 1946), 106–13.

Amulree Memorial Lecture, 1945.

13,362 **Flexner**, Jean Atherton. 'Arbitration of labour disputes in Great Britain.' *Ind. Relat. Rev.*, I, 3 (April 1948), 421–30.

13,363 **Badcock**, Julian K. 'The Industrial Court.' *Ind. Law Rev.*, V, 2 (October 1950), 104–10.

13,364 **Relations Industrielles.** Étude comparative sur la législation de conciliation et d'arbitrage.' *Relat. Ind.*, VI, 3 (June 1951), 72–8.

13,365 **Sharp**, Ian Gordon. *Industrial conciliation and arbitration in Great Britain.* London: Allen and Unwin, 1950 [i.e. 1951]. 466p.

Based on the author's Ph.D. thesis, University of London, 1940.

13,366 **Alexander**, J. R. W. *Conciliation and arbitration in industrial disputes.* Cambridge: Heffer for Chartered Institute of Secretaries, 1952. 20p.

13,367 **McKelvey**, Jean Trepp. 'Legal aspects of compulsory arbitration in Great Britain.' *Cornell Law Q.*, XXXVII, 3 (Spring 1952), 403–18.

13,368 **McKelvey**, Jean Trepp. 'Union attitudes toward compulsory arbitration in Great Britain.' *Arbit. J.*, VII, 2 (1952), 102–10.

13,369 **Turner**, Herbert Arthur. *Arbitration: a study of industrial experience.* London: Fabian Publications, 1952. 28p. (Fabian research series 153.)

13,370 **Adams**, W. S. 'Lloyd George and the labour movement.' *Past Pres.*, 3 (February 1953), 55–64.

13,371 **Forster**, *Sir* John. 'The Industrial Court. II. The Industrial Court to-day.' *Br. J. Adm. Law.*, I, 2 (September 1954), 37–40.

13,372 **Hendy**, J. 'Arbitration in industrial disputes.' *Marxist Q.*, I, 4 (October 1954), 231–41.

13,373 **Mackenzie**, *Sir* William Warrender. 'The Industrial Court. I. The development of industrial arbitration.' *Br. J. Adm. Law*, I, 2 (September 1954), 35–7.

'Based on an article by Sir William Mackenzie, K.C., K.B.E., the then President of the Court, in the *International Labour Review*, vol. III, nos. 1–2 (1921).'

13,374 **Lockwood**, David. 'Arbitration and industrial conflict.' *Br. J. Sociol.*, VI, 4 (December 1955), 335–47.

13,375 **Newman**, Theodore. *The development of wage determination criteria in government arbitration and fact finding.* 1956 [i.e. 1955]. v, 173 leaves. (M.S. thesis, Cornell University.)

13,376 **Rankin**, Mary Theresa. 'The Scottish cases before the Industrial Disputes Tribunal, 1951–53.' *Scott. J. Polit. Econ.*, II, 3 (October 1955), 218–30.

13,377 **Janaki Amma**, A. C. *A comparative study of the principles, practical working, and effects of the compulsory arbitration of industrial disputes.* 1955–56. (Ph.D. thesis, University of London.)

13,378 **Banks**, N. D. 'Conciliation and the settlement of industrial disputes.' *Ind. Law Rev.*, XI, 1 (July 1956), 42–50.

13,379 **FitzGerald**, Maureen. 'Outlook on industrial relations.' *Ind. Law Rev.*, XIII, 2 (October 1958), 76–81.

13,380 **Frank**, W. F. 'The state and industrial arbitration in the United Kingdom.' *Louis. Law Rev.*, XIX, 3 (April 1959), 617–43.

13,381 **Armstrong**, Eric. 'Why the British shelved compulsory arbitration.' *Calif. Mgmt. Rev.*, II, 4 (Summer 1960), 45–53.

13,382 **Handsaker**, Morrison and **Handsaker**, Marjorie L. 'Arbitration in Great Britain.' *Ind. Relat.*, I, 1 (October 1961), 117–36.

13,383 **Reiss**, M. *Compulsory arbitration as a method of settling industrial disputes, with special reference to British experience since 1940.* 1964. (B.Litt. thesis, University of Oxford.)

13,384 **Chamber of Commerce of the United States of America.** *Compulsory arbitration: a brief study.* Washington: Chamber of Commerce, [1965?]. 27p.

13,385 **Smith**, Henry. 'The wage fixers.' Lees, D. S., and others. *Freedom or free-for-all: essays in welfare, trade and choice.* London: Institute of Economic Affairs, 1965. p. 157–200.

The collection is 'Volume 3 of the Hobart Papers' and was first published under the general series title *Hobart papers 1961–3.* The above essay was first published as *Hobart paper* 18. 1962. 47p.

13,386 **McCarthy**, William Edward John and **Clifford**, B. A. 'The work of Industrial Courts of Inquiry.' *Br. J. Ind. Relat.*, IV, 1 (March 1966), 39–58.

13,387 **McCarthy**, William Edward John. 'Compulsory arbitration in Britain: the work of the Industrial Disputes Tribunal.' Royal Commission on Trade Unions and Employers' Associations. *Three studies in collective bargaining*. London: H.M.S.O., 1968. (Research papers 8.) p. 31–44.

13,888 **Bartlett**, A. F. *Industrial conciliation and arbitration in the United Kingdom, other than emergency and special legislation*. 1970. (Ll.M. thesis, Queen's University of Belfast.)

13,389 **Commission on Industrial Relations.** *First general report*. London: H.M.S.O., 1970. v, 25p. (Report 9. Cmnd. 4417.)

See also: 232; 12,700.

IX. EMPLOYMENT AND SOCIAL SECURITY

A. THE DEVELOPMENT OF SOCIAL SECURITY

1. General

This section primarily contains general historical accounts of the development of the welfare state and textbooks on social administration. General works relating primarily to the post-1945 period are classified in Part Seven, IX, A, 5.

13,390 **Blackley**, William Lewery. 'National insurance, considered economically and practically.' *Manchr. Statist. Soc. Trans.* (1879–80), 23–42.

13,391 **Ede**, W. Moore. *State relief and other artificial obstacles to thrift*. [*c*. 1890.] 15p.

13,392 **Clarke**, John Joseph. *Social administration, including the Poor Laws*. London: Pitman, 1922. 364p.
Second edition. 1935. xi, 776, lxxvip.
Third edition. 1939. x, 784p.
Fourth edition. *Social administration*. 1946. x, 774p.

13,393 **Plummer** Alfred. 'Some aspects of the history and theory of social insurance.' *Economica*, 20 (June 1927), 203–23.

13,394 **Cohen**, Percy. *The British system of social insurance: a history and description of health insurance*. London: P. Allan; New York: Columbia U.P., 1932. 278p.

13,395 **Wickwar**, William Hardy. *The social services: a historical survey*. London: Cobden-Sanderson, 1936. 268p.
With the collaboration of K. Margaret Wickwar.
Revised edition. London: Bodley Head, 1949. 302p.

13,396 **De Schweinitz**, Karl. *England's road to social security: from the Statute of Laborers in 1349 to the Beveridge Report of 1942*. Philadelphia: U. of Pennsylvania P.; London: Oxford U.P., 1943. x, 281p.

13,397 **Cole**, Margaret Isabel. *Social services and the Webb tradition*. London: Fabian Publications, 1946. 12p. (Webb memorial lectures 1946.)

13,398 **Mendelsohn**, Ronald S. *The evolution of social security: the record of four British counties*. 1950–51. 614 leaves. (Ph.D. thesis, University of London.)
See also: 14,277.

13,399 **Aggarwala**, Krishna C. 'The development of the social security services in the United Kingdom.' *India Q.*, VIII, 1 (January–March 1952), 42–62.

13,400 **Raup**, Ruth M. *The change in Britain from local to national assistance, 1930–1950*. 1952. (B.Litt. thesis, University of Oxford.)

13,401 **Clarke**, John Joseph. *Social welfare; being an abridgement of 'Social administration'*. London: Pitman, 1953. x, 420p.

13,402 **Raynes**, Harold Ernest. *Social security in Britain: a history*. London: Pitman, 1957. vii, 244p.
Second edition. 1960 [i.e. 1961]. viii, 264p.

13,403 **Woodard**, C. *The Charity Organisation Society and the rise of the welfare state*. 1960–61. (Ph.D. thesis, University of Cambridge.)

13,404 **Bruce**, Maurice. *The coming of the welfare state*. London: Batsford, 1961. xi, 307p.
Second edition. 1965. xi, 308p.
Third edition. *The coming of the welfare state, with a comparative essay on American and English welfare programs*. London: Batsford; New York: Schocken, 1966. xxiv, 308p.
Fourth edition, re-set. 1968. 374p.

13,405 **Mowat**, Charles Loch. *The Charity Organization Society, 1869–1913: its ideas and work*. London: Methuen, 1961. xii, 188p.

13,406 **Gilbert**, Bentley Brinkerhoff. *The evolution of national insurance in Great Britain: the origins of the welfare state*. London: Joseph, 1966. 497p.

13,407 **Lubove**, Roy (ed.). *Social welfare in transition: selected English documents, 1834–1909*. Pittsburgh, Penn.: U. of Pittsburgh P., 1966. xiii, 334p.
Introductory essays by John Duffy and Samuel Mencher.

13,408 **Rimlinger**, Gaston Victor. 'Welfare policy and economic development: a comparative historical perspective.' *J. Econ. Hist.*, XXVI, 4 (December 1966), 556–71.
Discussion by G. C. Bjork, 572–6.
Includes Great Britain.

13,409 **Evans**, Lloyd and **Pledger**, Philip J. (comps.). 'Blessed are the poor'. *Contemporary sources and opinions in modern British history*. London, New York: F. Warne, 1967. Vol. 1. p. 133–95.

13,410 **Mencher**, Samuel. *Poor law to poverty program: economic security policy in Britain and the United States*. Pittsburgh, Penn.: U. of Pittsburgh P., 1967. xix, 476p.

13,411 **Williams**, Gertrude, *Lady*. *The coming of the welfare state*. London: Allen and Unwin, 1967.

13,412 **New Society.** *The origins of the social services*. London: *New Society*, [1968]. 34p. (Social studies readers.)
Articles reprinted from *New Society*.

13,413 **Pelling**, Henry. 'The working class and the origins of the welfare state.' *Popular politics and society in late Victorian Britain: essays*. London: Macmillan; New York: St Martin's P., 1968. p. 1–18.
'. . . first delivered, in rather different form, to an Anglo-French conference on Social History in April 1966.'

13,414 **Rooke**, Patrick John. *The growth of the social services*. London: Weidenfeld and Nicolson, 1968. 144p. (British social and economic history since 1760.)

13,415 **Young**, Agnes Freda. *Social services in British industry*. London: Routledge and Kegan Paul, 1968. xiv, 258p. (International library of sociology and social reconstruction.)

13,416 **Rodgers**, Brian. *The battle against poverty*. London: Routledge and Kegan Paul, 1968–69. 2v.
Vol. 1. *From pauperism to human rights*. 1968. xii, 83p.
Vol. 2. *Towards a welfare state*. 1969. x, 84p.

See also: 19; 45.

2. Poor Law

See also Part Six, IV, A, 4, d.

a. GENERAL

See also Part Seven, IX, A, 2, d–e.

13,417 **Aschrott**, Paul Felix. *The English poor law system, past and present*. London: Knight, 1888. xviii, 332p.
Translated from the German by H. Preston-Thomas.
Second edition. 1902. xx, 376p.

13,418 **Mackay**, Thomas. *The English poor: a sketch of their social and economic history*. London: Murray, 1889. xi, 299p.

13,419 **Rhodes**, John Milson. 'Pauperism, past and present.' *Manchr. Statist. Soc. Trans.* (1890–91), 61–112.
Reprinted. London: Knight, 1891.

13,420 **Green**, G. *The history of the Poor Law*. London, 1893. 16p.

13,421 **Hoare**, H. N. Hamilton. *On the development of the English Poor Law*. London: W. Ridgway, 1893. 28p.

13,422 **Green**, G. *History of the Poor Laws, with other lectures*. Manchester, 1894. 80p.

13,423 **Wallas**, Graham. 'The history of the Poor Law.' Co-operative Wholesale Societies. *Annual for 1894*. p. 262–85.

13,424 **Lonsdale**, Sophia. *The English Poor Laws . . . lectures* . . . London: King, 1897. 85p.
Third edition, revised and enlarged. *The English Poor Laws: their history, principles and administrations*. 1902. viii, 89p.

13,425 **Nicholls**, *Sir* George. *A history of the English Poor Law*. London: King, 1898–1899. 3v.
New edition, containing the revisions made by the author and a biography by H. G. Willink.
Vol. I. *A.D. 924 to 1714*.
Vol. II. *A.D. 1714 to 1853*.
Vol. III. *From 1834 to the present time* . . . by T. Mackay.
Originally published 1854. 2v.
Reissued. 1904.
Reissued. London: Cass, 1967 [i.e. 1968].

13,426 **Chance**, William. 'Pauperism in Kensington, past and present.' *Char. Orgn. Rev.*, n.s., VII, 41 (May 1900), 243–58.

13,427 **Wilson**, David H. 'The economic causes of pauperism.' *Westm. Rev.*, CLXV, 2 (February 1906), 135–47.

13,428 **Charity Organisation Review.** 'Poor relief in a country village, 1786–1906.' *Char. Orgn. Rev.*, n.s., XXI, 124 (April 1907), 186–90.

13,429 **Bailward**, William Amyas. *The reports of the Poor Laws Commissions of 1834 and 1909*. London, 1909. 16p.

13,430 **Mackay**, Thomas. 'The theory, necessity and limits of state action in respect of the relief of the poor.' *Char. Orgn. Rev.*, n.s., XXVI, 156 (December 1909), 379–86; [XXVII], 157 (January 1910), 6–16.
A lecture delivered to Newcastle-upon-Tyne Economic Society on 24 November 1909.

13,431 **Tawney**, Richard Henry. 'The theory of pauperism.' *Sociol. Rev.*, II, 3 (October 1909), 361–74.
'A paper read before the Sociological Society, May 24th, 1909.'

13,432 **Bosanquet**, Helen. 'The historical basis of English Poor-Law policy.' *Econ. J.*, XX, 78 (June 1910), 182–94.

13,433 **Webb**, Sidney and **Webb**, Beatrice. *English Poor Law policy*. London: Longmans, 1910. xv, 379p.
Reprinted. With a new introduction by W. A. Robson. London: Cass, 1963. (English local government series 10.)

13,434 **Ashby**, Arthur Wilfred. *One hundred years of Poor Law administration in a Warwickshire village*. Oxford: Clarendon P., 1912. 190p. (Oxford studies in social and legal history 3.)
The village of Tysoe.

13,435 **Chadwick**, William Edward. *The church, the state, and the poor: a series of historical sketches.* London: R. Scott, 1914. viii, 223p.

13,436 **Walker**, Gladstone. *The evolution of the English Poor Law.* London, 1917. 8p.

13,437 **Poock**, Anselm. 'English Poor Law: its history and modern developments.' *Manchr. Statist. Soc. Trans.* (1919–20), 1–33.

13,438 **Leach**, Robert Alfred. *The evolution of Poor Law administration.* Great Malvern, 1924. 15p.

13,439 **Webb**, Sidney and **Webb**, Beatrice. *English Poor Law history.* London: Longmans, 1927–29. 3v.

Part 1. *The old Poor Law.*

Part 2. *The last hundred years.* 2v.

Reprinted, with a new introduction by W. A. Robson. London: Cass, 1963. (English local government series 7, 8, 9.)

13,440 **Sathyagirinathan**, P. G. 'Dickens and the Poor Law.' *Mys. Univ. Half-y. J.*, n.s., Section A, III, 2 (March 1943), 115–28.

13,441 **Flynn-Hughes**, Cledwyn. 'The Bangor workhouse.' *Caern. Hist. Soc. Trans.*, V (1945), 88–100.

13,442 **Flynn-Hughes**, Cledwyn. 'The workhouses of Caernarvonshire, 1760–1914.' *Caern. Hist. Soc. Trans.*, VII (1946), 88–100.

13,443 **Fay**, Charles Ryle. 'The old Poor Law and the new.' *Life and labour in the nineteenth century.* Cambridge: Cambridge U.P., 1947. p. 89–108.

Earlier editions, 1920, 1933, 1943.

13,444 **Zagday**, M. I. 'Bentham and the Poor Law.' Keeton, G. W. and Schwarzenberger, G. (eds.). *Jeremy Bentham and the law.* London: Stevens, 1948. p. 58–67.

13,445 **Lloyd Prichard**, Muriel Florence. *The treatment of poverty in Norfolk from 1700 to 1850.* 1949–50. (Ph.D. thesis, University of Cambridge.)

13,446 **Jones**, J. Fitzroy. 'Aspects of Poor Law administration, seventeenth to nineteenth centuries, from Trull Overseers' accounts.' *Som. Archaeol. Nat. Hist. Soc. Proc.*, XCV (1950), 72–105.

13,447 **Pike**, W. *The administration of the Poor Law in the rural area of Surrey, 1830–1850.* 1950. (M.A. thesis, University of London.)

13,448 **Purton**, Rowland W. C. 'Leyton poor rate.' *Essex Rev.*, LX, 238 (April 1951), 81–3.

13,449 **Austen**, F. W. 'Overseers' accounts and proceedings in Vestry, Ramsden Bellhouse.' *Essex Rev.*, LXII, 247 (July 1953), 41–6.

The author's name is given incorrectly at the head of the article as J. W. Austen.

13,450 **Tupling**, G. H. 'Searching the parish records. 3. Overseers' accounts.' *Amat. Hist.*, I, 9 (December 1953–January 1954), 269–72.

13,451 **Mackey**, Howard. *Humanitarian opposition to the economists on the Poor Law and factory legislation, 1802–1847.* 1955. 238p. (Ph.D. thesis, Lehigh University.)

13,452 **Skinner**, K. E. *Poor Law administration in Glamorgan, 1750–1850.* 1955–56. (M.A. thesis, University of Wales.)

13,453 **Pierce**, E. M. *Town–country relations in England and Wales in the pre-railway age as revealed by the Poor Law Unions.* 1956–57. (M.A. thesis, University of London.)

13,454 **Kent County Archives Office.** *The poor: a collection of examples from original sources in the Kent Archives Office, from the sixteenth to the nineteenth century.* Maidstone: Kent County Council, 1964. xviii, 189p. (Kentish sources 4.)

Edited by Elizabeth Melling.

13,455 **Kratz**, Marjorie Thiel. *The Poor Law medical officer and the administration of medical relief in England, 1832–42.* 1965–66. (Dissertation, University of Oregon.)

13,456 **Rose**, Michael E. *The administration of the Poor Law in the West Riding of Yorkshire (1820–55).* 1965–66. (D.Phil. thesis, University of Oxford.)

13,457 **Bagley**, John Joseph and **Bagley**, Alexander. *The English Poor Law.* London: Macmillan; New York: St Martin's P., 1966. 74p. (Sources of history.)

13,458 **Mullineux**, Constance Elsie. *Pauper and poorhouse: a study of the administration of the Poor Laws in a Lancashire parish.* Swinton, Lancs.: Public Library, 1966. xvii, 47p.

The Parish of Worsley.

13,459 **Rose**, Michael E. 'The Anti-Poor Law movement in the North of England.' *Nth. Hist.*, I (1966), 60–91.

13,460 **Webb**, John (ed.). *Poor relief in Elizabethan Ipswich.* Ipswich: Suffolk Records Society, 1966. 167p. (Publications vol. 60.)

13,461 **Midwinter**, E. C. *Social administration in Lancashire, 1830–1860: poor law, public health and police.* 1966–67. (D.Phil. thesis, University of York.)

13,462 **Pack**, L. F. C. *A study of the evolution of the methods of poor relief in the Winchester area, 1720–1845.* 1966–67. (M.A. thesis, University of Southampton.)

13,463 **Kuczynski**, Jürgen. 'Pauperization theory: 100 years after.' *Soc. Study Labour Hist. Bull.*, 15 (Autumn 1967), 9–10.

Abstract of a paper given at a conference of the Society for the Study of Labour History, Birkbeck College, London, 20 May 1967.

An abstract of the discussion following the paper appears on p. 10–11.

13,464 **Neate**, Alan Robert. *The St. Marylebone Workhouse and Institution, 1730–1965.* London: St Marylebone Society, 1967. 43p. (Publications 9.)

13,465 **Hopkin**, N. D. *The old and the new Poor Law in East Yorkshire, c. 1760–1850.* 1967–68. (M.Phil. thesis, University of Leeds.)

13,466 **Hennock,** E. P. 'The Poor Law era.' *New Soc.*, XI, 283 (29 February 1968), 301–3. (The origins of the social services 5.)

13,467 **Davies**, A. M. E. *Poverty and its treatment in Cardiganshire, 1750–1850.* 1968–69. (M.A. thesis, University of Wales, Aberystwyth.)

13,468 **Hampshire Archivists' Group.** *Poor Law in Hampshire through the centuries: a guide to the records.* Portsmouth: the Group, 1970. 78p. (Publication 1.)

See also: 18; 12,637.

b. 'OLD'

See also Part Seven, IX, A, 2, d–e.

13,469 **Leonard**, E. M. *The early history of English poor relief.* Cambridge: Cambridge U.P., 1900. xviii, 397p.

Reprinted. London: Cass, 1965. xviii, 397p.

13,470 **M.**, T. 'Note on the gradual introduction of the Poor Law of Elizabeth.' *Char. Orgn. Rev.*, n.s., VIII, 48 (December 1900), 369–79.

13,471 **Blease**, Walter Lyon. 'The Poor Law in Liverpool, 1681–1834.' *Hist. Soc. Lanc. Chesh. Trans.*, LXI (1909), 97–182.

13,472 **Leppington,** C. H. d'E. 'How the Poor Law was introduced into Warwickshire.' *Char. Orgn. Rev.*, n.s., XXVIII, 166 (October 1910), 268–75; 167 (November 1910), 315–22.

13,473 **Wilkins**, Henry John. *Transcription of the 'Poor Book' of the Tithings of Westbury-on-Trym, Stoke Bishop & Shirehampton from A.D. 1656–1698.* Bristol: Arrowsmith, 1910. xx, 284p.

With introduction and notes by H. J. Wilkins.

13,474 **Boone**, Gladys. *The Poor Law of 1601, with some consideration of modern developments of the Poor Law problem.* 1917. [ii], 147p. (M.A. thesis, University of Birmingham.)

13,475 **Teignmouth**, *Lord.* 'The "dole" system a century ago.' *Engl. Rev.*, XXXIX, 5 (November 1924), 630–8.

13,476 **Dodd**, A. H. 'The old Poor Law in North Wales.' *Archaeol. Cambrensis*, 7th ser., VI (June 1926), 111–32.

13,477 **Marshall**, Dorothy. *The English poor in the eighteenth century: a study in social and administrative history.* London: Routledge, 1926. xi, 292p.

Reissued. London: Routledge and Kegan Paul, 1969. xvi, 292p.

13,478 **Hampson**, Ethel Mary. 'Settlement and removal in Cambridgeshire, 1662–1834.' *Camb. Hist. J.*, II, 3 (1928), 273–89.

13,479 **Jennings**, H. R. 'Poor Law administration in the 18th century.' *R. Instn. Corn. J.*, XXII, 3 (1928), 338–49.

13,480 **Rideout**, Eric Hardwicke. 'Poor Law administration in North Meols in the eighteenth century.' *Hist. Soc. Lanc. Chesh. Trans.*, LXXXI (1929), 62–109.

13,481 **Hampson**, Ethel Mary. *Pauperism and vagrancy in Cambridgeshire to 1834.* 1930–31. (Ph.D. thesis, University of Cambridge.)

13,482 **Emmison**, Frederick George. 'Poor relief accounts of two rival parishes in Bedfordshire, 1563–1598.' *Econ. Hist. Rev.*, III, 1 (January 1931), 102–16.

13,483 **Anderson**, Kitty. *The treatment of vagrancy and the relief of the poor and destitute in the Tudor period, based upon the local records of London to 1552 and Hull to 1576.* 1932–33. (Ph.D. thesis, University of London.)

13,484 **Emmison**, Frederick George. *The relief of the poor at Eaton Socon, 1706–1834.* Apsley Guise: Bedfordshire Historical Record Society, 1933. (Bedfordshire Historical Record Society publications 15.)

13,485 **Hampson**, Ethel Mary. *The treatment of poverty in Cambridgeshire, 1597–1834.* Cambridge: Cambridge U.P., 1934. xx, 308p. (Cambridge studies in economic history.)

13,486 **Oldham**, C. R. 'Oxfordshire Poor Law papers.' *Econ. Hist. Rev.*, IV, 4 (April 1934), 470–4; V, 1 (October 1934), 87–97.

'This article is the outcome of a systematic attempt to catalogue the Poor Law papers of Oxfordshire prior to 1834.'

13,487 **Thomas**, *Sir* Benjamin Bowen. 'The old Poor Law in Arduwy-Uwch-Artro.' *Board Celt. Studies Bull.*, VII, 2 (May 1934), 153–91.

13,488 **Dakyns**, A. L. 'Bentham's influence in municipal and Poor Law reform.' *Publ. Adm.*, XIII, 1 (January 1935), 44–50.

13,489 **Allin**, William Egbert. *Poor Law administration in Glamorganshire before the Poor Law Amendment Act of 1834.* 1936. (M.A. thesis, University of Wales, Cardiff.)

13,490 **Cutlack**, S. A. 'The Gnosall records, 1679 to 1837: Poor Law administration.' *Collns. Hist. Staffs.* (1936), 1–141.

13,491 **Southam**, Herbert. 'Loxley, Co. Warwick: overseers' accounts.' *Notes Quer.*, CLXX (22–30 May 1936), 384–5.

1798–1820. Extracts and comments.

13,492 **Marshall**, Dorothy. 'Revisions in economic history. VII. The old Poor Law, 1662–1795.' *Econ. Hist. Rev.*, VIII, 1 (November 1937), 38–47.

Reprinted in Carus-Wilson, E. M. (ed.). *Essays in economic history.* London: Arnold, 1954. p. 295–305.

13,493 **Dangerfield**, M. E., **Marshall**, O., **Stringer**, E. R. and **Welch**, V. E. 'Chichester workhouse.' *Sx. Archaeol. Colln.*, LXXIX (1938), 131–67.

13,494 **Parker**, W. A. *The bishops and the Poor Law, 1782–1834.* 1939. (M.A. Comm., University of Manchester.)

13,495 **Hinton**, F. H. 'Notes on the administration of the relief of the poor of Lacock, 1583 to 1834.' *Wilts. Mag.*, XLIX, 173 (December 1940), 166–218.

13,496 **Owen**, Geraint Dyfnallt. 'The Poor Law system in Carmarthenshire during the eighteenth and early nineteenth centuries.' *Hon. Soc. Cymm. Trans.* (1941), 71–86.

13,497 **McNaulty**, Mary. *Some aspects of the history of the administration of the Poor Laws in Birmingham between 1730 and 1834.* 1942. ix, 182p. (M.A. thesis, University of Birmingham.)

13,498 **Pool**, Anne (ed.). 'The relief of the poor in the 18th century.' *Old Corn.*, III, 12 (Winter 1942), 487–91.
Examples from overseers' accounts of Lelant and Lyndgvan.

13,499 **Bond**, M. F. 'Windsor's experiment in poor-relief, 1621–1829.' *Berks. Archaeol. J.*, XLVIII (1944–45), 31–42.

13,500 **Flynn-Hughes**, Cledwyn. 'Aspects of the old Poor Law administration and policy in Amlwch parish, 1770–1837.' *Angles. Antiq. Soc. Field Club Trans.* (1945), 48–60.

13,501 **Hopkirk**, Mary. 'The administration of poor relief, 1604–1834, illustrated from the parochial records of Danbury.' *Essex Rev.*, LVIII, 231 (July 1949), 113–21.

13,502 **Fessier**, Alfred. 'The official attitude towards the sick poor in seventeenth-century Lancashire.' *Hist. Soc. Lanc. Chesh. Trans.*, CII (1950), 85–113.

13,503 **Allen**, A. F. 'An early Poor Law account.' *Archaeol. Cant.*, LXIV (1951), 74–84.
Shorne, nr. Gravesend, Kent.

13,504 **Keith-Lucas**, Brian. 'A local Act for social insurance in the eighteenth century.' *Camb. Law J.*, XI, 2 (1952), 191–7.
The Devon Poor Act, 1769.

13,505 **Elton**, G. R. 'An early Tudor poor law.' *Econ. Hist. Rev.*, 2nd ser., VI, 1 (August 1953), 55–67.

13,506 **Emmison**, Frederick George. 'The care of the poor in Elizabethan Essex: recently discovered records.' *Essex Rev.*, LXII, 248 (September 1953), 7–28.
The author was County Archivist of Essex.

13,507 **Mitchelson**, Noel. *The old Poor Law in East Yorkshire.* York: East Yorkshire Local History Society, 1953. 16p. (E.Y. local history series 2.)

13,508 **Thomas**, Emlyn George. *The parish overseer in Essex, 1597–1834.* 1955–56. (M.A. thesis, University of Exeter.)

13,509 **Goodman**, P. H. 'Eighteenth century Poor Law administration in the parish of Oswestry.' *Shrops. Archaeol. Soc. Trans.*, LVI (1957–60), 328–40.
'This paper is a publication of the University of Birmingham Extra-Mural Research Group studying the history of Oswestry . . .'

13,510 **Rilling**, John Robert. *The administration of poor relief in the counties of Essex and Somerset during the personal rule of Charles I, 1629–1640.* 1958–59. (Dissertation, Harvard University.)

13,511 **Tierney**, Brian. *Medieval Poor Law: a sketch of canonical theory and its application in England.* Berkeley, Calif.: California U.P.; London: Cambridge U.P., 1959. xi, 169p.

13,512 **Coats**, A. W. 'Economic thought and Poor Law policy in the eighteenth century.' *Econ. Hist. Rev.*, 2nd ser., XIII, 1 (August 1960), 39–51.

13,513 **Flinn**, M. W. 'The Poor Employment Act of 1817.' *Econ. Hist. Rev.*, 2nd ser., XIV, 1 (August 1961), 82–92.

13,514 **Pound**, J. F. 'An Elizabethan census of the poor: the treatment of vagrancy in Norwich, 1570–1580.' *Univ. Birm. Hist. J.*, VIII, 2 (1962), 135–61.

13,515 **Blaug**, Mark. 'The myth of the old Poor Law and the making of the new.' *J. Econ. Hist.*, XXIII, 2 (June 1963), 151–84.

13,516 **Styles**, Philip. 'The evolution of the law of settlement.' *Univ. Birm. Hist. J.*, IX, 1 (1963), 33–63.

13,517 **Blaug**, Mark. 'The Poor Law Report re-examined.' *J. Econ. Hist.*, XXIV, 2 (June 1964), 229–45.

13,518 **Body**, G. A. *The administration of the Poor Laws in Dorset 1760–1834, with special reference to agrarian distress.* 1964–65. (Ph.D. thesis, University of Southampton.)

13,519 **Burne**, R. V. H. 'The treatment of the poor in the eighteenth century in Chester.' *Ches. N. Wales Archit. Archaeol. Hist. Soc. J.*, n.s., LII (1965), 33–48.

13,520 **Oxley**, G. W. *Administration of the old 'poor law' in the West Derby hundred of Lancashire, 1607–1837.* 1965–66. (M.A. thesis, University of Liverpool.)

13,521 **Beier**, A. L. 'Poor relief in Warwickshire 1630–1660.' *Past Pres.*, 35 (December 1966), 77–100.

13,522 **Davies**, C. S. L. 'Slavery and Protector Somerset: the Vagrancy Act of 1547.' *Econ. Hist. Rev.*, XIX, 3 (December 1966), 533–49.
'In Edward VI's first year there was passed the most savage act in the grim history of English vagrancy legislation, imposing slavery as a punishment for the refusal to work. Two years later . . . the same Parliament repealed the act . . .'

13,523 **Edmonds**, G. C. 'Accounts of the 18th-century overseers of the poor of Chalfont St. Peter.' *Rec. Bucks.*, XVIII (1966), 3–23.

13,524 **Lightning**, Ronald Herbert. *Ealing and the poor: the Poor Law, the work-houses and poor relief in the parish of St. Mary Ealing, from 1722 to 1800.* London: Ealing Local History Society, 1966. 61p. (Members' papers 7.)

13,525 **Williams**, D. Elwyn. 'The Poor Law in operation in the parish of Rumney, 1825–30.' *Hon. Soc. Cymm. Trans.* (1966), pt. 2, 341–71.

13,526 **Neumann**, Mark Donald. *Aspects of poverty and Poor Law administration in Berkshire, 1782–1834.* 1967–68. (Dissertation, University of California, Berkeley.)

13,527 **Avery**, David. *Edmonton Workhouse Committee 1732–37: a paper read to the Edmonton Hundred Historical Society on Wednesday 3rd September 1965.* London: Edmonton Hundred Historical Society, 1968. 30p. (Occasional papers. New series 14.)

13,528 **Caplan**, N. 'Sussex Poor Law administration, 1801.' *Sx. Notes Quer.*, XVII, 3 (May 1968), 82–8.

13,529 **Marshall**, John Duncan. *The old Poor Law, 1795–1834.* London: Macmillan, 1968. 50p. (Studies in economic history.)
Prepared for the Economic History Society.

13,530 **Clark**, Dorinda. *The early days of Retford workhouse.* Retford: Eaton Hall College of Education, 1969. [18]p. (Monograph 3.)

13,531 **Huzel**, James P. 'Malthus, the Poor Law, and population in early nineteenth century England.' *Econ. Hist. Rev.*, 2nd ser., XXII, 3 (December 1969), 430–52.
'The purpose of this article is to dispute the contention of Malthus that the Old Poor Law operated institutionally to promote population growth.'

13,532 **Poynter**, John Riddoch. *Society and pauperism: English ideas on poor relief, 1795–1834.* London: Routledge and Kegan Paul, 1969. xxvi, 367p. (Studies in social history.)

13,533 **Taylor**, James Stephen. 'The mythology of the Old Poor Law.' *J. Econ. Hist.*, XXIX, 23 (June 1969), 292–7.

13,534 **Taylor**, James Stephen. 'Poverty in a west Devon parish (Bradford) in the last years of the Old Poor Law.' *Devon. Ass. Advmt. Sci. Lit. Art Rep. Trans.*, CI (1969), 161–82.

13,535 **Thomas**, W. K. 'Crabbe's workhouse.' *Huntington Libr. Q.*, XXXII, 2 (February 1969), 149–61.
On Crabbe's description of a workhouse in his poem *The Village*, 1783 and his selectivity in representing what he had seen in order to create a feeling of charity towards the poor in his readers.

13,536 **Lane**, Joan. *Poor Law administration in Butlers Marston, Warwickshire, 1713–1822.* 1970. (M.A. thesis, University of Wales, Cardiff.)

13,537 **Whicher**, D. S. *The administration of poor relief, with special reference to Watford, 1601–1836.* 1970. (Dip. in Pub. Admin., University of London.)

See also: 16.

c. 'NEW'

See also Part Seven, IX, A, 2, d–e.

13,538 **Owen**, *Sir* Hugh. *Manual for overseers, assistant overseers, collectors of poor rates and vestry clerks, as to their powers, duties, and responsibilities.* London, 1871.
Fourth edition. 1878.
Fifth edition. Knight, 1880. viii, 280p.
Sixth edition. 1882. viii, 286p.
Seventh edition. 1884. viii, 293p.
Eighth edition. 1887. viii, 316p.

13,539 **Dickins**, Thomas. 'The border-land of pauperism.' *Manchr. Statist. Soc. Trans.* (1879–80), 77–89.

13,540 **Fry**, Danby Palmer. *The Union Assessment Acts, 1860 to 1880, and the Rating Act, 1874.* London: Knight, 1880. viii, 268p.
Sixth edition.
Seventh edition, by R. C. Glen and A. D. Laurie, 1887. xxvii, 439p.
Eighth edition, by R. C. Glen. 1897. xxix, 431p.
Previous editions. Second, 1862. Fourth, 1864. Fifth, 1870.

13,541 **P.**, T. S. *Why pay poor rates? Or the abolition of poor rates a social necessity.* London: W. Ridgway, 1880. iii, 34p.

13,542 **Twining**, Louisa. *Recollections of workhouse visiting and management during twenty-five years.* London: Kegan Paul, 1880. xx, 217p.

13,543 **O'Conor**, W. A. 'Poor Laws.' *Manchr. Statist. Soc. Trans.* (1880–81), 97–122.

13,544 **Chapman**, J. *Three essays on the Poor Law with introductions: the workhouse; the tramp question; and out-door relief.* Macclesfield, 1881. 46p.

13,545 **Fowle**, Thomas Welbanke. *The Poor Law.* London: Macmillan, 1881. 163p. (The English citizen.)
Second edition. 1890. vi, 175p.

13,546 **Lumley**, William Golden. *Lumley's Union Assessment Committee Acts, 1862–1880.* London: Shaw, 1881. ciii, 221p.
Tenth edition, by W. C. Glen.
Earlier editions. 1862, 1863, 1864, 1866, 1870.
Eleventh edition. *Lumley's Union Assessment Acts.* 1895. xcii, 200p. By W. C. Ryde.

13,547 **Murray**, Henry. *Poor-law administration and proposed legislative amendments.* Edinburgh: Bell and Bradfute, 1881. 24p.

13,548 **Owen**, *Sir* Hugh. *The Pauper Inmates Discharge and Regulation Act, 1871.* London: Knight, 1882. 56p.
Third edition.
First edition. 1871.
Second edition. 1871.
Fourth edition. 1884. 60p.

13,549 **Owen**, *Sir* Hugh. *The Poor Rate Assessment and Collection Act, 1869.* London: Knight, 1882. vii, 90p.
Earlier editions. 1869, 1870, 1872.

13,550 **Symonds**, John Fish. *A handbook on the law of settlement and removal of union poor, as amended by the 39 & 40 Vict., c. 61, with a collection of statutes.* London: Shaw, 1882. xii, 182p.
Second edition. 1887. xxvii, 222p.
Third edition. 1891. xxxii, 256p.
Fourth edition. *The law of settlement and removal*, by Joshua Scholefield and Gerard R. Hill. London: Butterworth, 1903. xxiv, 226, 18p.

13,551 **Lifford**, *Lord*. 'The "canker-worm" – outdoor relief.' *Nineteenth Century*, XIII, 73 (March 1883), 453–7.

13,552 **Peek**, Francis. *Social wreckage: a review of the laws of England as they affect the poor.* London: W. Isbister, 1883. lx, 279p.
Third edition. 1888 [i.e. 1887]. l, 256p.

13,553 **Mason**, M. H. *Classification of girls and boys in workhouses, and the legal powers of boards of guardians for placing them beyond the workhouse.* London: Hatchards, 1884. 32p.

13,554 **Allen**, J. H. 'Outdoor relief.' *Char. Orgn. Rev.*, I, 11 (16 November 1885), 441–6.
A paper read at a special meeting of Council, 26 October 1885.

13,555 **Bristol.** Committee to Inquire into the Condition of the Poor. *Report.* London, 1885. 244p.

13,556 *Indoor paupers, by one of them.* London: Chatto and Windus, 1885. 123p.

13,557 **Westminster Review.** 'The work of women as Poor Law Guardians.' *Westm. Rev.*, n.s., LXVII, 2 (April 1885), 386–95.
Review article.

13,558 **Barnett**, Samuel Augustus. 'Distress in East London.' *Nineteenth Century*, XX, 117 (November 1886), 678–92.

13,559 **Macdonell**, G. P. 'The state and the unemployed.' *Br. Q. Rev.*, LXXXIII, 166 (April 1886), 348–64.
On the first report of the Commissioners on Poor Laws, 1834.

13,560 **Montague**, Francis Charles. *The old Poor Law and the new socialism; or pauperism and taxation.* London: Cassell, Petter and Galpin, 1886. 66p. (Cobden Club pamphlet.)

13,561 **Symonds**, John Fish. *Relieving officer.* London: Shaw, 1886. 123p. (Shaw's Poor Law officers' handbooks.)
New edition.
Fourth edition. 1898. 120, 6p.
Fifth edition. London: Butterworth, 1904. xxiv, 149p.

13,562 **Twining**, Louisa. 'Workhouse cruelties.' *Nineteenth Century*, XX, 117 (November 1886), 709–14.

13,563 **Biggs**, Caroline Ashurst. *Some notes upon the election of Guardians of the Poor.* London, 1887. 14p.

13,564 **Biggs**, Caroline Ashurst. *Women as Poor Law Guardians.* 1887. 4p.
Reprinted from *Englishwoman's Review*.

13,565 **Charity Organisation Society.** 'Report regarding applications made at the St. Giles' Casual Ward on the 5th, 7th, 8th and 9th November.' *Char. Orgn. Rev.*, III, 36 (December 1887), 449–53.
Report of an investigation into a new system of relief by tickets.

13,566 **Holland**, John R. 'Emigration and the Poor Law.' *Char. Orgn. Rev.*, III, 32 (August 1887), 303–8.
'A Paper read at a special meeting of the Council of the Charity Organisation Society on Monday, July 11 . . .'
Discussion, p. 326–7.

13,567 **Phelps**, Lancelot Ridley. *Poor Law and charity: a paper read in the common room of Keble College, March 9th, 1887.* Oxford: Blackwell, 1887. 16p.

13,568 **Twining**, Louisa. *A letter on some matters of Poor Law administration, addressed (by kind permission) to the Right Hon. the President of the Local Government Board.* London: Ridgway, 1887. 70p.

13,569 **Brigg.** Union. Board of Guardians. *Report of the Committee appointed by the Board of Guardians to endeavour to devise means for a more efficient and economical administration of out relief, in this Union, presented to the Guardians . . . on the 23rd February, 1888.* Brigg, 1888.

13,570 **Charity Organisation Review.** 'The relief of vagrants and of the unemployed in Germany and England.' *Char. Orgn. Rev.*, IV, 39 (March 1888), 81–92.
Compares the two systems.

13,571 **Craigie**, P. G. 'The English poor rate: some recent statistics of its administration and pressure.' *R. Statist. Soc. J.*, LI, 3 (September 1888), 450–85.
Discussion, p. 486–93.
Read before the Royal Statistical Society, 19 June 1888.

13,572 **Crowder**, A. G. *Statement of Mr. A. G. Crowder, Guardian of the Poor of St. George's-in-the-East, London East, for the information of the House of Lords Select Committee on Poor Law Relief, April, 1888.* London, 1888. 40p.

13,573 **House of Lords.** Select Committee on Poor Law Relief. *Report, with proceedings, minutes of evidence, appendix and index.* London: H.M.S.O., 1888. (H.C. 363.)
Facsimile reprint published. Shannon: Irish U.P., 1970. (British parliamentary papers, poor law, 27.)

13,574 **Manning**, Henry Edward, Cardinal. 'A pleading for the worthless.' *Nineteenth Century*, XXIII, 133 (March 1888), 321–30.

13,575 **Peek**, Francis. 'The workless, the thriftless and the worthless.' *Contemp. Rev.*, LIII (January 1888), 39–52; (February 1888), 276–85.

13,576 **Brooke**, C. E. *The organisation of relief in the parish.* 1889. 4p.

13,577 **Edinburgh Review.** 'The relief of the destitute.' *Edinb. Rev.*, CLXIX, 346 (April 1889), 398–415.
Review article on the Poor Law.

13,578 **Mackenzie**, William Warrender. *The overseers' handbook*. London: Shaw, 1889. xv, 214p.
Second edition. 1893. xv, 276p.
Third edition. 1895. xvii, 310p.
Fourth edition. 1896. xxiv, 360p.
Fifth edition. 1901. xxiv, 379p.
Sixth edition, by W. W. Mackenzie and H. J. Comyns. London: Shaw, Butterworth, 1906. xxxi, 502, 113p.
Seventh edition. Shaw, Butterworth, 1910. xxxv, 528, 146p.
Eighth edition. Butterworth, Shaw, 1915. xxxviii, 576, 183p.
Ninth edition, by W. C. Howe and F. J. Ogden. Butterworth, 1925. lvi, 480, 159p.
Tenth edition. *Mackenzie's rating and valuation officers' handbook*, by F. J. Phillips. Butterworth, 1932. lii, 269, 31p.

13,579 **Twining**, Louisa. *Poor relief in foreign countries, and out-door relief in England*. London: Cassell, 1889. 63p.

13,580 **Booth**, Charles. *Enumeration and classification of paupers, and state pensions for the aged*. London, 1890. 44p.

13,581 **Bourne**, H. Clarence. 'Pride and prejudice.' *Char. Orgn. Rev.*, VI, 61 (January 1890), 19–24.

13,582 **Dodd**, F. S. *Poor law reform*. Oxford, 1890. 19p.

13,583 **Dodd**, John Theodore. *Casual paupers' and how we treat them*. London, 1890. 8p.
Reprinted from *Charity*.

13,584 **Howell**, George. 'Pauperism: its nature and extent, its causes and remedies. A review of Poor Law administration.' Co-operative Wholesale Societies. *Annual for 1890*. p. 187–208.

13,585 **Lowell**, *Mrs* C. R. *The economic and moral effects of public outdoor relief*. 1890. 11p.

13,586 **Macmorran**, Alexander and **Macmorran**, Michael Stewart Johnstone. *The Poor Law Statutes, comprising the statutes in force relating to the poor; and to guardians . . . from 1879 to 1889 inclusive . . . with notes and index*. London: Shaw and Sons, 1890.
A continuation of *The statutes in force relating to the Poor Laws* . . . by W. C. Glen, 1873–79.

13,587 **Pell**, Albert. *Out-relief: a paper*. London: Knight, 1890. 16p.

13,588 *The powers and duties of Poor Law Guardians in times of exceptional distress*. [*c.* 1890?] 8p.

13,589 **Sheen**, Alfred. *The workhouse and its medical officer*. Bristol, 1890. vi, 80p.
Second edition.

13,590 **Webb**, Sidney. 'The reform of the Poor Law.' *Contemp. Rev.*, LVIII (July 1890), 95–120.
Reprinted in Webb, S. and Webb, B. *Problems of modern industry*. 2nd ed. London, New York, Bombay: Longmans, Green, 1902. p. 156–91.

13,591 **Webb**, Sidney. *The reform of the Poor Law*. London: Fabian Society, 1890. 20p. (Fabian tract 17.)
The great part reprinted from an article in *Contemporary Review*, July 1890.

13,592 **Booth**, Charles. 'Enumeration and classification of paupers, and state pensions for the aged.' *R. Statist. Soc. J.*, LIV, 4 (December 1891), 600–43.
Discussion, LV, 1 (March 1892), 56–79.
'A correction.' LV (2 June 1892), 287–94.
Extracts from *Pauperism and the endowment of old age*, correcting errors in the figures in the above paper.

13,593 **Charity Organisation Review.** 'The Poor Law as an obstacle to thrift and voluntary insurance.' *Char. Orgn. Rev.*, VII, 75 (March 1891), 113–25.

13,594 **Costelloe**, Benjamin Francis Conn. *The reform of the Poor Law*. London: Catholic Truth Society, 1891. 16p.

13,595 **Mackay**, Thomas. 'The interest of the working class in the Poor Law.' *Char. Orgn. Rev.*, VII, 84 (December 1891), 446–54.
'A paper read at the South-Eastern Poor Law Conference on Monday, November 2 . . .'

13,596 **Booth**, Charles. *Pauperism: a picture; and, Endowment of old age: an argument*. London: Macmillan, 1892. viii, 355p.
Another edition. London: Macmillan, 1892. 188p.

13,597 **Bosanquet**, Bernard. 'The limitations of the Poor Law.' *Econ. J.*, II, 6 (June 1892), 369–71.
Reply to Marshall, A. 'The Poor Law in relation to state-aided pensions.' *Econ. J.*, II (March 1892), 186–91.

13,598 **Dumsday**, William Henry. *The relieving officers' handbook, being a complete and practical guide to the law relating to the powers, duties, and liabilities of relieving officers*. London: Hadden, Best, [1892?]. xxii, 211p.
Second edition. 1912. xxx, 264p.
Third edition. 1923. xxx, 285p.
Fourth edition, by W. H. Dumsday and John Moss. 1929. xxxii, 365p.
Fifth edition, by W. H. Dumsday and John Moss. 1930. xxxii, 362p.
Sixth edition, by W. H. Dumsday and John Moss. 1935. xxxiii, 416p.
Seventh edition, by John Moss. 1938. xxx, 447p.

13,599 **Fowle**, Thomas Welbanke. *The Poor Law, friendly societies and old age destitution*. Oxford: Parker, 1892. 23p.

13,600 **Loch**, Charles Stewart. 'Returns as an instrument in social science.' *Char. Orgn. Rev.*, VIII, 93 (September 1892), 333–44.
'A paper read . . . to the Economic Section of the British Association, Edinburgh, 1892.'

13,601 **Mackenzie**, William Warrender. *The Poor Law Guardian: his power and duties.* London: Shaw, 1892. xii, 328p.
Third edition.
Fourth edition. 1895. xii, 360p.

13,602 **Marshall**, Alfred. 'The Poor Law in relation to state-aided pensions.' *Econ. J.*, II, 5 (March 1892), 186–91.

13,603 **Marshall**, Alfred. 'Poor-Law reform.' *Econ. J.*, II, 6 (June 1892), 371–9.
Reply to Bosanquet, B. 'The limitations of the Poor Law.' *Econ. J.*, II, 6 (June 1892), 369–71.

13,604 **Rutherglen**, John H. *Poor Law administration in Kensington.* London, 1892. 42p.

13,605 **Barnett**, Samuel Augustus. 'Poor Law reform.' *Contemp. Rev.*, LXIII (March 1893), 322–34.

13,606 **Chance**, William. 'The administration of the Poor Law in a country union.' *Char. Orgn. Rev.*, IX, 98 (March 1893), 73–81.

13,607 **Charity Organisation Society.** *The state and the unemployed, with notes regarding the action of vestries in different parts of London, 1892–3.* London, 1893. 30p.

13,608 **Dodd**, John Theodore. 'What can the government do for the poor at once?' *New Rev.*, IX, 51 (August 1893), 191–200.

13,609 **Fabian Society.** *A plea for Poor Law reform.* London: Fabian Society, 1893. 3p. (Fabian tract 44.)
By Frederick Whelen.
Issued without the author's name.
Revised. 1907. 3p.

13,610 **Loch**, Charles Stewart. 'Some controverted points in the administration of poor relief.' *Econ. J.*, III, 11 (September 1893), 425–42; III, 12 (December 1893), 583–99.
Discusses views expressed by Alfred Marshall in March and September 1892 issues of *Economic Journal*.

13,611 **Mackay**, Thomas. *On the co-operation of charitable agencies with the Poor Law.* London, 1893. 12p.

13,612 **Phelps**, Lancelot Ridley. 'Old-age pensions.' *Econ. Rev.*, III, 4 (October 1893), 475–85.

13,613 **Select Committee on the Local Government Provincial Order (Poor Law) Bill.** *Report, with the proceedings.* London: H.M.S.O., 1893. (H.C. 256.)

13,614 **Twining**, Louisa. *Recollections of life and work, being the autobiography of Louisa Twining.* London: Arnold, 1893. xiv, 291p.

13,615 **Wilkinson**, John Frome. 'The English Poor Law and old age.' *Contemp. Rev.*, LXIV (November 1893), 670–80.

13,616 **Booth**, Charles. *The aged poor in England and Wales: condition.* London, New York: Macmillan, 1894. vi, 527p.
By C. Booth and others.

13,617 **Booth**, Charles. 'Statistics of pauperism in old age.' *R. Statist. Soc. J.*, LVII, 2 (June 1894), 235–45.
Discussion, p. 246–53.
'Abstract of a paper read before the Royal Statistical Society, 20th March, 1894.'

13,618 **Dodd**, John Theodore. *To Boards of Guardians in rural districts. The winter's distress: how to provide for the unemployed.* London: National Press Agency, 1894. 7p.

13,619 **Hunter**, W. A. 'Outdoor relief: is it so very bad?' *Contemp. Rev.*, LXV (March 1894), 305–25.

13,620 **Loch**, Charles Stewart. 'Mr. Charles Booth on the aged poor.' *Econ. J.*, IV, 15 (September 1894), 468–87.
A discussion of *The aged poor in England and Wales*, by Charles Booth. London: Macmillan, 1894.

13,621 **Loch**, Charles Stewart. 'The statistics of metropolitan pauperism.' *Char. Orgn. Rev.*, X, 114 (July 1894), 313–57.
'A paper . . . read at a Special Meeting of the Council . . . May 21, 1894.'

13,622 **Masterman**, N. 'Poor relief in the Isle of Man.' *Char. Orgn. Rev.*, X, 115 (August 1894), 414–19.
'A Paper read to the Council on June 25, 1894 . . .'

13,623 **Oakeshott**, Joseph Francis. *The humanizing of the Poor Law.* London: W. Reeves, 1894. 40p. (Humanitarian League. Publications 13.)
Another edition. London: Fabian Society, 1894. 23p. (Fabian tract 54.)
New and revised edition. Fabian Society, 1905. 23p.

13,624 *Plain words on out-relief.* London: Knight, 1894. 65p.

13,625 **A Barrister.** *An elementary ABC guide to the Poor Law.* London: Eyre and Spottiswoode, 1895. vii, 32p.

13,626 **Cannan**, Edwin. 'The stigma of pauperism.' *Econ. Rev.*, V, 3 (July 1895), 380–91.

13,627 **Chance**, *Sir* William. *The better administration of the Poor Law.* London: Swan Sonnenschein, 1895. xii, 260p. (Charity organisation series.)

13,628 **Drage**, Geoffrey. *The problem of the aged poor.* London: Black, 1895. xvii, 375p.

13,629 **Lonsdale**, Sophia. *The evils of a lax system of outdoor relief.* 1895. 8p.

13,630 **Lubbock**, Gertrude. *Some poor relief questions, with the arguments on both sides, together with the summary of the report of the Royal Commission on the Aged Poor.* London: Murray, 1895. x, 329p.

13,631 **Royal Commission on the Aged Poor** appointed to consider whether any alterations in the system of Poor Law relief are desirable in the case of persons whose destitution is occasioned by incapacity for work resulting from old age, or whether assistance could otherwise be afforded in those cases.
Vol. I. *Report*. London: H.M.S.O., 1895. (C. 7684.)
Vol. II. *Minutes of evidence*. (C. 7684-I.)
Vol. III. *Minutes of evidence*. (C. 7684-II.)
Chairman: C. T. Ritchie.
Facsimile reprint published Shannon, Irish U.P., 1970 in 2 vols. (British parliamentary papers, poor law, 28, 29.)

13,632 **Select Committee on Distress from Want of Employment.** *First report, with proceedings and evidence*. London: H.M.S.O., 1895. (H.C. 111.)
Second report, with an appendix. 1895. (H.C. 253.)
Third report, with proceedings, evidence, appendix and index. 1895. (H.C. 365.)
Report in the following Session, with proceedings, evidence, appendix, and index. 1896. (H.C. 321.)
Facsimile reprint published Shannon, Irish U.P., 1970 in 2 vols. (British parliamentary papers, industrial relations, 23, 24.)

13,633 **Tallack**, William. *Poor relief and the diminution of pauperism: a British desideratum. The following letter appeared in the 'Times' London, January 25th 1895: The problem of poor relief*. London: Wertheimer and Lea (printed), 1895. 4p.
No title page.

13,634 **Vulliamy**, Arthur Frederick. *The law of settlement and removal of paupers*. London: Knight, 1895. xii, 274p.
Second edition. 1906. xvi, 336p.

13,635 **Walker**, H. *Memorandum on Poor Law reform*. 1895. 7p.

13,636 **Wilkins**, H. *Memorandum on the administration of the Poor Law*. London, 1895. 32p.

13,637 **Yule**, G. Udny. 'On the correlation of total pauperism with proportion of out-relief.' *Econ. J.*, V, 20 (December 1895), 603–11.
'Revised from a paper read before Section P of the British Association, September 1895.'

13,638 **Rooke**, George. 'On the report of the Royal Commission on the Aged Poor, 26th February, 1895.' *Manchr. Statist. Soc. Trans.* (1895–96), 29–55.

13,639 **Booth**, Charles. 'Poor Law statistics.' *Econ. J.*, VI, 21 (March 1896), 70–4.
Reply to C. S. Loch and G. Udny Yule.

13,640 **Bousfield**, W. R. 'The unemployed.' *Contemp. Rev.*, LXX (December 1896), 835–52.
On reports of Select Committee on Distress from Want of Employment, 1895–6.

13,641 **Chambers**, George Frederick. *A handy digest of cases relating to Poor Law matters, comprising all the recent and many of the old cases*. London: Knight, 1896. vii, 112p.

13,642 **Chance**, William. 'State administration of relief.' *Char. Orgn. Rev.*, XII, 135 (April 1896), 138–49.
'An address delivered by...[the] Hon. Secretary of the Central Poor Law Conferences, on January 24, 1895, at a meeting convened in Bermondsey by The St. Olave's Committee of The Charity Organisation Society.'

13,643 **Dumsday**, William Henry. *Hadden's overseers' handbook*. London: Hadden, Best, 1896. xxxi, 348p.
Second edition. 1900. xxix, 391p.
Third edition. 1906. xlii, 435p.
Fourth edition. 1920. xlvii, 485p.
First edition 'by the author of *Hadden's Local Government Act, 1894*' [i.e. W. H. Dumsday].

13,644 **Galton**, Francis. 'Application of the method of percentiles to Mr. Yule's data on the distribution of pauperism.' *R. Statist. Soc. J.*, LIX, 2 (June 1896), 392–6.
'Remarks on Mr. Galton's note', by G. U. Yule, p. 396–8.

13,645 **Willink**, Henry George. *The principles of the English Poor Law*. London, 1896. 27p.

13,646 **Yule**, G. Udny. 'Notes on the history of pauperism in England and Wales from 1850, treated by the method of frequency-curves; with an introduction on the method.' *R. Statist. Soc. J.*, LIX, 2 (June 1896), 318–49.
Discussion, p. 350–7.
'Read before the Royal Statistical Society, 21st April, 1896.'

13,647 **Yule**, G. Udny. 'On the correlation of total pauperism with proportion of out-relief.' *Econ. J.*, VI, 24 (December 1896), 611–23.

13,648 **Baylee**, J. Tyrrell. 'The problems of pauperism: the unemployed.' *Westm. Rev.*, CXLVII, 3 (March 1897), 274–85.

13,649 **Chance**, William. *Children under the Poor Law*. London: Swan Sonnenschein, 1897. xii, 443p.

13,650 **Chance**, William. 'The Elberfeld and English Poor Law systems: a comparison.' *Econ. J.*, VII, 27 (September 1897), 332–45.

13,651 **Clifford**, Mary. *Poor-Law work: suggestions & new departures*. London: Nisbet; Bristol: Rose and Harris, 1897. 51p.
Second edition.

13,652 **Davey**, Herbert. *The Poor Law Act, 1897, with notes and appendix*. London, 1897. 51p.

13,653 **Henning**, James. *The church in a workhouse*. London: Christian Knowledge Society, 1897. 24p.

13,654 **Lansbury**, George. *The principle of the*

English Poor Law. London, 1897. 16p.

13,655 **Phelps**, Lancelot Ridley. 'Modern criticisms of the Poor Law.' *Econ. Rev.*, VII, 3 (July 1897), 374–84.

13,656 **McDougall**, A. 'The English Poor Law, with special reference to progress in its administration during the Queen's reign.' *Manchr. Statist. Soc. Trans.* (1897–98), 9–31.

13,657 **Archbold**, John Frederick. *The Poor Law*. London: Shaw and Sons, 1898. lii, 1078, 140p.

Fifteenth edition. By James Brooke Little. Sixth edition. 1850. lv, 807p.

Sixteenth edition. *Archbold's Poor Law*. Butterworth, Shaw, 1930. xliii, 490, 65p. By E. Gilbert Woodward.

13,658 **Chadwick,** William Edward. *The relief of the deserving poor: a record of experience, with some suggestions*. London: Society for Promoting Christian Knowledge, 1898. 32p.

13,659 **Clifford**, Mary. *Out-relief*. London: National Union of Women Workers, 1898. 14p. (Tracts 1.)

'. . . a paper read on April 22nd, 1896, before the General Council of the National Union of Women Workers.'

13,660 **Drage**, Geoffrey. 'Poor Law reform.' *Econ. Rev.*, VIII, 1 (January 1898), 77–87.

13,661 **Standing Committee on Law, etc.** *Report on the Poor Law (Scotland) Bill, with the proceedings*. London: H.M.S.O., 1898. (H.C. 234.)

13,662 **Barnett**, Samuel Augustus. 'Charity *versus* outdoor relief.' *Nineteenth Century*, XLVI, 273 (November 1899), 818–26.

13,663 **Booth**, Charles. 'Poor Law statistics as used in connection with the old age pension question.' *Econ. J.*, IX, 34 (June 1899), 212–23.

13,664 **Chance**, William. 'The decrease of old age pauperism.' *Char. Orgn. Rev.*, n.s., VI, 34 (October 1899), 177–200; 36 (December 1899), 312–3.

'In this article I hope to show, by the example of certain typical unions, how old age pauperism is decreasing, and should continue to decrease under our existing Poor Law.'

13,665 **Daily Chronicle.** *Down with the workhouse*. London, 1899. 5 pts.

13,666 **Davey**, Sydney. *The law relating to casual paupers*. London: Hadden, Best, 1899. 91p.

13,667 **Dodd**, John Theodore. *A lecture on Poor Law administration, with particular reference to out-relief in Oxford*. Oxford, 1899. 7p.

13,668 **Rigby**, E. A. *The powers and duties of guardians of the poor*. London, [1899?]. 20p.

13,669 **Select Committee on the Aged Deserving Poor.** *Report, with the proceedings, evidence, appendix and index*. London: H.M.S.O., 1899. (H.C. 296.)

13,670 **Stansfeld**, Ina. *Industrial training of girls in the separate and district schools in the metropolitan district*. London: H.M.S.O., 1899. 125p. (Cd. 237.)

13,671 **Bosanquet**, Helen. *Why not a 'national' authority for dealing with unemployment?* London: National Poor Law Reform Association, [19—?]. 5p.

13,672 **Cox**, J. C. *Outdoor relief: the heritage of the poor*. London, 1900. 24p.

13,673 **Departmental Committee on the Aged Deserving Poor.** *The financial aspects of the proposals made by the Select Committee of 1899: report*. London: H.M.S.O., 1900. l, 93p. (Cd. 67.)

Chairman: E. W. Hamilton.

13,674 **Dodd**, John Theodore. 'Indiscriminate indoor relief.' *Econ. Rev.*, x, 1 (January 1900), 62–74.

13,675 **Irish Women's Suffrage and Local Government Association.** *Papers read at a conference of women Poor Law Guardians and other ladies . . . on the 19th of April, 1900*. Dublin: the Association, 1900. 48p.

Papers read . . . 12th of May, 1903. 1903. 52p.

13,676 **Mackay**, Thomas. 'How far is pauperism a necessary element in a civilized community?' *Econ. Rev.*, x, 4 (October 1900), 417–33.

13,677 **Poor-Law Officers' Journal.** *Poor Law administration: aged deserving poor*. Manchester, [1900?]. 16p.

13,678 **Quarterly Review.** 'Poor Law reform.' *Q. Rev.*, CXCI, 381 (January 1900), 155–75.

Review article.

13,679 **Toynbee**, C. M. 'Poverty and the Poor Law.' *Econ. Rev.*, x, 3 (July 1900), 316–22.

13,680 **Wilson**, J. C. 'Poor-Law statistics.' *Econ. Rev.*, x, 2 (April 1900), 206–27.

13,681 **Ashworth**, T. E. *An account of the Todmorden Poor Law riots of November, 1838 and the Plug plot of August, 1842*. Todmorden, 1901. 25p.

13,682 **Fuller**, S. D. *Charity and the Poor Law*. London: Swan Sonnenschein, 1901. 68p.

13,683 **Greenwood**, Major, the elder. *The law relating to the Poor Law medical service and vaccination*. London: Baillière, 1901. 94p.

13,684 **Mackay**, Thomas. *Public relief of the poor: six lectures*. London: Murray, 1901. vi 214p.

13,685 **Martineau**, John. *The English country labourer and the Poor Law in the reign of Queen Victoria: a paper*. London: Skeffington, 1901. 32p.

13,686 **Smith**, Percival Gordon. *Hints and suggestions as to the planning of Poor Law buildings*. London: Knight, 1901. viii, 151p.

13,687 **Twining**, Louisa. 'Some thoughts on the Poor Law and poverty.' *Econ. Rev.*, XI, 3 (July 1901), 308–15.

13,688 **Little**, James Brooke. *The Poor Law statutes, comprising the statutes in force relating to the poor, and to guardians, overseers and other Poor Law authorities and officers, from Elizabeth to end of Victoria, with notes and cases.* London: Shaw, 1901–02. 3v.

13,689 **Bailward**, William Amyas. *Poor Law and charity: a paper.* London: King, 1902. 31p.

13,690 **Chance**, *Sir* William. 'Principles and practice of the English Poor Law.' *Char. Orgn. Rev.*, n.s., XII, 70 (October 1902), 185–203.

'A paper read at the South Wales Poor Law Conference on June 6, 1902 . . .'

13,691 **Lander**, Beatrice. 'The relief of the poor in Jersey.' *Econ. J.*, XII, 46 (June 1902), 192–201.

13,692 **Longbotham**, A. T. *The English Poor Law and its administration in the Halifax Union.* Halifax, 1902. 30p.

13,693 **Mackay**, Thomas. 'The Poor Law and the economic order.' *Econ. Rev.*, XII, 3 (July 1902), 278–88.

A paper read at the meeting of the British Association at Glasgow, 1901.

13,694 **Brabrook**, Edward William. *Outdoor Relief (Friendly Societies) (No. 2) Bill, 1900: report to the Treasury.* London: H.M.S.O., 1903. 3p. (H.L. 60.)

13,695 **Chance**, *Sir* William. 'A decade of London pauperism, 1891–1901.' *R. Statist. Soc. J.*, LXVI, 3 (September 1903), 534–70.

Discussion, p. 571–81.

'Supplementary note (with tables)', LXVI, 4 (March 1903), 731–4.

'Read before the Royal Statistical Society, 16th June, 1903.'

13,696 **Charity Organisation Review.** 'Poor Law reform.' *Char. Orgn. Rev.*, n.s., XIII, 76 (April 1903), 176–84.

13,697 **Mackay**, Thomas. 'The reform of the Poor Law.' *Char. Orgn. Rev.*, n.s., XIV, 84 (December 1903), 317–26.

A paper read at a special meeting of the Council of the Charity Organisation Society, 7 December 1903.

13,698 **Sellers**, Edith. 'Shifting scenes in rural workhouses.' *Nineteenth Century*, LIV, 322 (December 1903), 1000–12.

13,699 **Local Government Board.** *The unemployed: outline of Mr. Long's scheme proposed at the Conference of Metropolitan Guardians held at the Local Government Board.* 1904.

13,700 **Mackay**, Thomas. 'Poor Law reform.' Loch, C. S. (ed.). *Methods of social advance: short studies in social practice by various authors.* London, New York: Macmillan, 1904. p. 158–68.

13,701 **South Metropolitan Board of Guardians.** *Report of a conference . . . to consider the best means of . . . finding employment for the respectable unemployed . . .* London, 1904. 14p.

13,702 **Vulliamy**, Arthur Frederick. *The duties of relieving officers and the administration of out-relief.* London: Knight, 1904. xvi, 195, xxxixp. (Local government library 4.)

13,703 **Bentham**, F. H. *The position of the Poor Law in the problem of poverty.* London, 1905. 25p.

13,704 **Colchester-Wemyss**, M. W. 'Another Board of Guardians: a reply to Miss Sellars.' *Nineteenth Century*, LVIII, 346 (December 1905), 974–9.

13,705 **Dean**, C. W. *Vagrancy: memorandum as to present law relating to casual paupers.* 1905. [5]p.

13,706 **Graham**, James Edward. *The law relating to the poor and to parish councils.* Edinburgh: G. A. Morton, 1905. xii, 699p.

New edition. Edinburgh, London: Hodge, 1922. xxvi, 394p.

13,707 *A peep behind the scenes on a Board of Guardians.* [1905?] 32p.

13,708 **Sellers**, Edith. 'How Poor Law Guardians spend their money.' *Nineteenth Century*, LVIII, 343 (September 1905), 403–15.

13,709 **Toynbee**, H. V. 'The problem of the unemployed.' *Econ. Rev.*, XV, 3 (July 1905), 291–305.

13,710 **Barrow**, F. H. 'Church and Poor Law reform.' *Westm. Rev.*, CLXV, 4 (April 1906), 387–400.

13,711 **Carlile**, Wilson and **Carlile**, Victor Wilson. *The Continental outcast: land colonies and Poor Law relief.* London: Fisher Unwin, 1906. ix, 143p.

13,712 **Crowder**, A. G. *Statement . . . for the information of the Royal Commission on the Poor Laws and Relief of Distress.* London, 1906. 16p.

13,713 **Davy**, J. S. *Report to the President of the Local Government Board on the Poplar Union.* London: H.M.S.O., 1906. 75p. (Cd. 3240.)

Transcript of shorthand notes taken at the inquiry held by J. S. Davy . . . 1906. iv, 405p. (Cd. 3274.)

13,714 **Dearle**, Norman Burrell. 'The Poor Law and the unemployed.' *Econ. J.*, XVI, 61 (March 1906), 141–6.

13,715 **Departmental Committee on Vagrancy.** Vol. I. *Report.* London: H.M.S.O., 1906. (Cd. 2852.)

Vol. II. *Minutes of evidence, index.* (Cd. 2891.)

Vol. III. *Appendices, etc.* (Cd. 2892.)

Chairman: J. L. Wharton.

13,716 **Dodd**, John Theodore. *Poor Law and the Poor Law Commission.* 1906. 7p.

13,717 **Edinburgh Review.** 'The Royal Poor Law Commission, 1905, and the condition of the poor.' *Edinb. Rev.*, CCIII, 416 (April 1906), 488–516.

Review article.

13,718 **Fabian Society.** *The abolition of Poor Law Guardians.* London: Fabian Society, 1906. 23p. (Fabian tract 126. New heptarchy series 5.)

By E. R. Pease.

13,719 **Loch**, Charles Stewart. 'Statistics of population and pauperism in England and Wales, 1861–1901.' *R. Statist. Soc. J.*, LXIX, 2 (June 1906), 289–312.
Discussion, p. 313–20.
'Read before the Royal Statistical Society, March 20th 1906.'

13,720 **Pease**, Edward Reynolds. *The abolition of Poor Law Guardians.* London: Fabian Society, 1906. 24p. (Fabian tract 126.)

13,721 **Quarterly Review.** 'The employed and the Poor Law.' *Q. Rev.*, CCIV, 406 (January 1906), 228–47.
Review article.

13,722 **Webb**, Beatrice. *The relation of Poor-Law medical relief to the public health authorities.* Bristol: Wright, [1906?]. 16p.
Reprinted from *Public Health*, December 1906.

13,723 **Barnett**, *Dame* Henrietta Octavia Weston. *The ethics of the Poor Law.* Derby, [1907?]. 6p.

13,724 **Chance**, *Sir* William. 'The increasing burden of Poor Law relief.' *Char. Orgn. Rev.*, n.s., XXI, 125 (May 1907), 230–42.
'Read at the Hampshire Poor Law Conference at Winchester, March 1907.'

13,725 **Crosse**, Gordon. 'The Poplar workhouse inquiry.' *Econ. Rev.*, XVII, 1 (January 1907), 46–53.

13,726 **Dumsday**, William Henry. *The workhouse officers' handbook.* London: Hadden, Best, 1907. xxviii, 338p.

13,727 **Fust**, *Sir* Herbert Jenner. *Poor Law Orders.* London: King, 1907. xxiii, 822p.
Supplement. *Poor Law Orders: the Relief Regulation Order, 1911 and the Boarding Out Order, 1911.* 1912. viii, 119p.

13,728 **Sellers**, Edith. 'Foreign remedies for English Poor Law defects.' *Nineteenth Century*, LXII, 369 (November 1907), 770–86.

13,729 **Webb**, Sidney. 'What shall we do with the Poor Law?' *Unit. Par. Mag.*, V, 68 (1907). 4p.

13,730 **Booth**, William. 'Suggestions for Poor Law reform. I. Classification.' *Progress Civic Soc. Ind.*, III, 4 (October 1908), 243–54.

13,731 **Chance**, *Sir* William. *Old age pensions and the Poor Law.* London, 1908. 14p.

13,732 **Charteris**, F. R. *The Poor Law and pauperism.* London, 1908. 15p.

13,733 **Cook**, J. Basil. 'An examination of the amount of indoor pauperism in three metropolitan boroughs and of the causes which led to this pauperism.' *R. Statist. Soc. J.*, LXXI, 1 (March 1908), 147–74.

13,734 **Davey**, Herbert. *Poor Law settlement and removal.* London: Stevens, 1908. xxix, 364p.
Second edition. 1913. xxxvi, 449p.
Third edition. 1925. xxxvi, 376p.

13,735 **Dearmer**, Percy. *The reform of the Poor Law.* London: Mowbray, 1908. 14p. (Christian Social Union. Pamphlet 16.)

13,736 **Dodd**, John Theodore. *Mistakes of the Local Government Board and of other 'authorities' in Poor Law administration, being a memorandum laid before the Poor Law Commission.* Oxford: Parker; London: Simpkin, Marshall, 1908. 12p.

13,737 **Dodd**, John Theodore. 'The social and economic advantage of maintaining outdoor relief.' *Progress Civic Soc. Ind.*, III, 1 (January 1908), 1–10.

13,738 *London County Council and Poor Law administration.* 1908. 16p.

13,739 **Macnamara**, Thomas James. *Children under the Poor Law: a report to the President of the Local Government Board.* London: H.M.S.O., 1908. 25p.

13,740 **Moore**, G. W. 'Relief by the community.' *Leic. Lit. Phil. Soc. Trans.*, 9th ser., XII, 1 (January 1908), 49–59.

13,741 **Paton**, John Brown. 'Suggestions for Poor Law reform. II. Administration.' *Progress Civic Soc. Ind.*, III, 4 (October 1908), 254–61.

13,742 **Walsh**, *Hon.* Gerald. *Dock labour in relation to Poor Law relief: report to the President of the Local Government Board.* London: H.M.S.O., 1908. 46p. (Cd. 4391.)

13,743 **Booth**, William. *The Salvation Army and Poor Law reform.* London, 1909. xxxvi, 64p.

13,744 **Bosanquet**, Bernard. 'The reports of the Poor Law Commission. I. The majority report.' *Sociol. Rev.*, II, 2 (April 1909), 109–26.

13,745 **Bosanquet**, Helen. *The Poor Law report of 1909: a summary explaining the defects of the present system and the principal recommendations of the Commission, so far as relates to England and Wales.* London: Macmillan, 1909. vi, 263p.

13,746 **Bosanquet**, Helen. *Reform of the Poor Law.* London, 1909. 15p.

13,747 **British Constitution Association.** *Poor-Law reform, not revolution.* London, 1909. 12p. (Poor Law papers 1.)

13,748 **Charles Knight and Co.** *The suggested new Poor Law: Knight's synopsis of the majority and minority reports of the Royal Commission on the Poor Laws and Relief of Distress, adapted to meet the special requirements of members of local authorities and local officials.* London: Knight, 1909. vii, 195p.

13,749 **Davey**, Herbert. *The Poor Law Acts, 1894–1908, revised and annotated, with notes of the decisions of the courts, and of the orders of the Local Government Board and other departments.* London: Hadden and Best, 1909. xxiv, 400p.

13,750 **Downes**, *Sir* Arthur Henry. *Memorandum on the reports of the Royal Commission on the Poor Laws and Relief of Distress.* London: King, 1909. 15p.

13,751 **Edinburgh Review.** 'The Poor Law report of 1909.' *Edinb. Rev.*, CCIX, 428 (April 1909), 439–73.
Review article.

13,752 **Fabian Society.** *Break up the Poor Law and abolish the workhouse, being Part I of the minority report of the Poor Law Commission.* London: Fabian Society, 1909. 601p.
By Sidney and Beatrice Webb.
Issued without the authors' names.

13,753 **Fabian Society.** *The remedy for unemployment, being Part II of the minority report of the Poor Law Commission.* London: Fabian Society, 1909. 345p.
By Sidney and Beatrice Webb.
Issued without the authors' names.

13,754 **Gorst,** *Sir* John Eldon. 'The reports on the Poor Law.' *Sociol. Rev.*, II, 3 (July 1909), 217–27.
On reports of the Royal Commission.

13,755 **Hamilton,** C. J. *The Poor Law controversy.* London, 1909. 11p.

13,756 **Hamilton,** C. J. 'The principles of the Poor Law: a contrast between 1834 and 1909.' *Char. Orgn. Rev.*, n.s., XXVI, 151 (July 1909), 23–46.
Paper read at the Annual Conference of Charity Organisation and Kindred Societies, Malvern and Worcester, 1909.
Discussion, p. 47–55.

13,757 **Hawkins,** C. B. and **Nicholson,** Joseph Shield. *Poor Law Commission: what it proposes; full summary of both reports.* London, Manchester: *Daily News*, 1909. 48p.

13,758 **Hill,** Octavia. *Memorandum on the report of the Royal Commission on the Poor Laws and Relief of Distress.* London: King, 1909. 4p.
Reprinted from the official report.

13,759 **Hutchins,** B. Leigh. *Working women and the Poor Law.* London, 1909. 12p.

13,760 **Jones,** Thomas. 'The reports of the Poor Law Commission: some first impressions.' *Econ. Rev.*, XIX, 22 (April 1909), 137–48.

13,761 **Lansbury,** George. *Socialism for the poor: the end of pauperism.* London: Clarion P., 1909. 19p. (Pass on pamphlets 12.)

13,762 **Loch,** Charles Stewart. 'The report of the Royal Commission on the Poor Law and the Relief of Distress.' *Char. Orgn. Rev.*, n.s., XXV, 146 (February 1909), 61–77.
A survey of the report.

13,763 **Macrosty,** *Mrs. What the minority report means to women.* London, 1909. 7p.

13,764 **McVail,** J. C. *Report on Poor Law medical relief in certain unions in England and Wales.* London: H.M.S.O., 1909. 338p.

13,765 **Moorhouse,** W. *The Royal Commission on the Poor Law and Relief of Distress.* Wakefield, 1909. 21p.

13,766 **Muirhead,** John Henry. *By what authority: the principles in common and at issue in the reports of the Poor Law Commission.* London: King, 1909. vi, 102p.

13,767 **National Committee to Promote the Break-up of the Poor Law.** *The failure of the Poor Law.* London, 1909. 11p.

13,768 **National Committee to Promote the Break-up of the Poor Law.** *How the minority report deals with children.* London, 1909. 15p.

13,769 **National Committee to Promote the Break-up of the Poor Law.** *How the minority report deals with the sick, the infirm, and the infants.* London, 1909. 15p.

13,770 **National Committee to Promote the Break-up of the Poor Law.** *How the minority report deals with unemployment.* London, 1909. 15p.

13,771 **National Committee to Promote the Break-up of the Poor Law.** *Minority report of the Poor Law Commission. Vol. 1. Break-up of the Poor Law.* London, 1909. ix, 601p.
Vol. 2. The unemployed. 1909. vii, 345p.

13,772 **National Committee to Promote the Break-up of the Poor Law.** *The new charter of the poor: what is meant by the break-up of the Poor Law.* London, 1909. 7p.

13,773 **National Committee to Promote the Break-up of the Poor Law.** *The scheme of reform (unemployment).* London, 1909.

13,774 *New Poor Law or no Poor Law: a description of the majority & minority reports of the Poor Law Commission.* London: Dent, 1909. xiii, 176p.
'With an introductory note by Canon Barnett.'

13,775 **Nunn,** T. Hancock. *A council of social welfare: a note and memorandum in the report of the Royal Commission on the Poor Laws.* London, 1909. 115p.

13,776 *The Poor Law Commission and the medical profession, by a medical practitioner.* London: A. C. Fifield, 1909. 16p.

13,777 **Royal Commission on the Poor Laws and Relief of Distress.** *Report.* London: H.M.S.O., 1909. xiii, 1238p. (Cd. 4499.)
Report on Ireland. 1909. v, 88p. (Cd. 4630.)
Report on Scotland. 1909. ix, 314p. (Cd. 4922.)
Appendix [i.e. reports, memoranda, evidence]. 1909–10. 50v.
Chairman: Lord George Hamilton.
For further details see P. Ford and G. Ford, *A breviate of parliamentary papers, 1900–1916: the foundation of the welfare state.* Oxford: Blackwell, 1957, p. 248–65; and *General index to the bills, reports and papers printed by order of the House of Commons and to the reports and papers presented by command 1900 to 1948–49,* London: H.M.S.O., 1960, p. 556–7.

13,778 **Sellers,** Edith. 'Poor relief in the days to come.' *Nineteenth Century*, LXV, 387 (May 1909), 875–90.
On the majority report of the Royal Commission on the Poor Law.

13,779 **The Times.** *The report of the Poor Law Commission.* London: *The Times,* 1909. 48p.
A summary.
'Reprinted from *The Times.*'

13,780 **Turnor,** Christopher Hatton. *Memorandum on the report of the Poor Law Commission.* 1909. 8p.
Made for the Poor Law Committee of the Royal Agricultural Society.

13,781 **Webb,** Sidney and **Webb,** Beatrice (eds.). *The break-up of the Poor Law; being Part One of the minority report of the Poor Law Commission.* London, [etc.]: Longmans, Green, 1909. xvii, 601p.

13,782 **Webb,** Sidney. 'The economic aspects of Poor Law reform.' *Engl. Rev.,* III, 11 (October 1909), 501–16.

13,783 **Webb,** Beatrice. *The Poor Law medical officer and his future.* London, 1909. 8p.

13,784 **Webb,** Sidney. *Poor Law reform: an address.* London: Political Committee of the National Liberal Club, 1909. 8p.

13,785 **Webb,** Sidney and **Webb,** Beatrice (eds.). *The public organisation of the labour market; being Part Two of the minority report of the Poor Law Commission.* London, [etc.]: Longmans, Green, 1909. xiii, 345p.

13,786 **Webb,** Sidney. 'The reports of the Poor Law Commission. II. The end of the Poor Law.' *Sociol. Rev.,* II, 2 (April 1909), 127–39.

13,787 **Wyrall,** Everard. '*The spike.*' London: Constable, 1909. 72p.
An account of the workhouse casual ward.

13,788 **Dickson,** T. A. 'The report of the Royal Commission on the Poor Laws and the Relief of Distress.' *Survey. Instn. Trans.,* XLII (1909–10), 363–422.

13,789 **Becket-Overy,** H., and others. *The medical proposals of the minority report.* London, 1910. 16p.

13,790 **Booth,** Charles. *Poor Law reform, being memoranda submitted in April and December 1907 to the Royal Commission on the Poor Laws and Relief of Distress, with some additional notes.* London: Macmillan, 1910. 92p.
'With an appendix embodying memoranda by Dr. Arthur Downes and Miss Octavia Hill, which were published in the report of the Poor Law Commission.'
New issue, with additional remarks. 1911. 136p.

13,791 **Booth,** Charles. *Reform of the Poor Law by the adaptation of the existing Poor Law areas and their administration.* 1910. 38p.

13,792 **Bosanquet,** Helen. *Prevention and cure.* London, [1910?]. 4p.

13,793 **Bund,** John William Willis. *Seven reasons for supporting the minority report of the Poor Law Commission.* London, 1910. 4p.

13,794 **Chance,** *Sir* William. *Poor Law reform; 'via tertia': the case for the Guardians.* London: King, 1910. 95p.

13,795 **Clay,** *Sir* Arthur Temple Felix. *The principles of Poor Law reform: a paper.* London: British Constitution Association, 1910. 38p. (Miscellaneous pamphlets.)

13,796 **Dalton,** James Henry Chesshyre. *Poor Law reform.* Cambridge, 1910. 23p.

13,797 **Dodd,** John Theodore. *The majority report of the Poor Law Commission, and why we should reject it.* London, 1910. 19p.

13,798 **Dodd,** John Theodore. *The poor and their rights: how to obtain them under existing legislation.* London: King, 1910. 28p.

13,799 **Greenwood,** Major. *The policy of the English Poor Law and its proposed medical reform.* London, [1910?]. 19p.

13,800 **Hamilton,** C. J. *The method of Poor Law reform.* London, [1910?]. 14p.

13,801 **Hamilton,** C. J. 'The Poor Law controversy.' *Econ. J.,* XX, 79 (September 1910), 472–9.
Title on contents page is given as 'Reform of the Poor Laws'.

13,802 **Hamilton,** *Lord* George. 'A statistical survey of the problems of pauperism.' *R. Statist. Soc. J.,* LXXIV, 1 (December 1910), 1–34.
Presidential address, 15 November 1910.

13,803 **Humphry,** A. M. *What is really meant by the break up of the Poor Law.* London, [1910?]. 8p.

13,804 **Keay,** J. H. *Poor Law reform in its medical aspects.* London, 1910. 14p.

13,805 **Kenyon,** Ruth. 'Social conditions and the principles of 1834.' *Econ. Rev.,* XX, 2 (April 1910), 146–64; 3 (July 1910), 277–300.

13,806 **Lansbury,** George and **Quelch,** H. *The Poor Law minority report.* London, 1910. 15p.

13,807 **Leppington,** C. H. d'E. 'The minority report and the unemployed.' *Char. Orgn. Rev.,* n.s., [XXVII], 160 (April 1910), 192–205.

13,808 **London Reform Union.** *The reform of the Poor Law in London and the equalisation of rates.* London, 1910. 23p.

13,809 **Macgregor,** D. H. 'The poverty figures.' *Econ. J.,* XX, 80 (December 1910), 569–72.

13,810 *The minority report: a criticism.* London: King, 1910. 32p.
'. . . a summary of which appeared in the *Times* of 19th June 1910.'

13,811 **Muirhead,** John Henry. *The starting point of Poor Law reform; being articles upon the principles in common and at issue in the reports of the Poor Law Commission, with a plea for agreement as to first steps.* London: King, 1910. viii, 102p.
Second edition of the author's *By what authority,* 1909.

13,812 **National Committee for the Prevention of Destitution.** *Lessons on the minority report.* London, 1910. 47p.

13,813 **National Committee for the Prevention of Destitution.** *The new charter of the poor: what is meant by the break-up of the Poor Law.* London, 1910. 8p.

13,814 **National Committee for the Prevention of Destitution.** *The Poor Law: its failure; what is meant by breaking it up. Why you should support the minority report.* London, 1910. 20p.

13,815 **Nunn**, T. Hancock. *The minority report.* London, [1910?]. 18p.

13,816 **Parkinson**, H. *The problem of Poor Law reform.* London, 1910. 18p.

13,817 **Phelps**, Lancelot Ridley. *The majority report and the unemployed.* London: National Poor Law Reform Association, [1910?]. 15p.

13,818 **Phelps**, Lancelot Ridley. 'The majority report and the unemployed: a lecture.' *Char. Orgn. Rev.*, n.s., [XXVII], 160 (April 1910), 177–91.

13,819 **Pilditch**, *Sir* Philip Edward. *Why London should prefer the principle of the majority report.* London, [1910?]. 4p.

13,820 **Toke**, Leslie Alexander St. Lawrence. *Pauperism and the nation. Part 2. The minority report.* London, [1910?]. 32p.

13,821 **Wakefield**, Henry Russell, Bishop of Birmingham, and others. *Nine lectures on the report of the Royal Commission on the Poor Laws and Relief of Distress* . . . Sheffield, 1910. 56p.

13,822 **Wakefield**, Henry Russell, Bishop of Birmingham. *Poor Law reform: an address.* London: Political Committee of the National Liberal Club, 1910. 14p.

13,823 **Wakefield**, Henry Russell, Bishop of Birmingham. *The sphere of voluntary agencies under the minority report.* London, 1910. 23p.

13,824 **Webb** Beatrice. *A letter describing the principles of the minority report and the work of the National Commission for the Prevention of Destitution.* London, [1910?]. 8p.

13,825 **Webb**, Beatrice. *The minority report in relation to public health and the medical profession.* London, 1910. 23p.

13,826 **Webb**, Sidney and **Webb**, Beatrice. 'A national crusade against destitution.' Co-operative Wholesale Societies. *Annual for 1910.* p. 143–68.

13,827 **Williams**, Ethel Mary Nucella. *Report on the condition of the children who are in receipt of the various forms of Poor Law relief in England and Wales.* London: H.M.S.O., 1910. 285p.

13,828 **Williams**, W. M. J. 'Pensions and the Poor Law.' Co-operative Wholesale Societies. *Annual for 1910.* p. 169–90.

13,829 **Webb**, Sidney. 'The economics of the existing (or of any) Poor Law.' *Manchr. Statist. Soc. Trans.* (1910–11), 1–15.

13,830 **Abbott**, Edith. 'English Poor Law reform.' *J. Polit. Econ.*, XIX, 1 (January 1911), 47–59.

13,831 **Booth**, Charles. *Comments on proposals for the reform of the Poor Law.* 1911. 23p.

13,832 **Carter**, Henry. *Destitution: can we end it?* London, 1911. 64p.

13,833 **Chance**, William. 'The returns of pauperism.' *Char. Orgn. Rev.*, n.s., XXX, 177 (September 1911), 209–15.

Describes the existing nature of returns and makes proposals for a new form of return.

13,834 **County Councils Association.** *County Councils Association's proposals for Poor Law administration, after consideration of majority and minority reports; containing also views of Royal Commissioners on the scheme.* London: King, 1911. vii, 86p.

13,835 **Departmental Committee on the Administration of Outdoor Relief.** *Report.* London: H.M.S.O., 1911. 62p. (Cd. 5525.)

Chairman: S. B. Provis.

13,836 **Freeman**, Arnold. 'The place of charge and recovery in the minority report of the Royal Commission on the Poor Laws.' *Econ. J.*, XXI, 82 (June 1911), 294–301.

13,837 **National Committee for the Prevention of Destitution.** *The charter of the poor.* London, 1911. 24p.

13,838 **National Committee for the Prevention of Destitution.** *Index to the minority report of the Poor Law Commission.* London, 1911. 89p.

13,839 **National Committee for the Prevention of Destitution.** *An outline of the proposal to break up the poor law, on the lines of the minority report of the Poor Law Commission.* London, 1911. 14p.

13,840 **Robinson**, M. Fothergill. *The Poor Law enigma.* London: Murray, 1911. x, 189p.

13,841 **Stearns**, Lucy B. *Two schemes to prevent pauperism.* London: S. W. Sprigg, 1911. 20p.

13,842 **Tillyard**, Frank. 'The increase in male adult pauperism.' *Econ. J.*, XXI, 84 (December 1911), 630–6.

13,843 **Unionist Social Reform Committee.** *Poor Law report.* [*c.* 1911.] 26p.

13,844 **Webb**, Sidney and **Webb**, Beatrice. *The prevention of destitution.* London: Longmans, 1911. vi, 348p.

Reprinted. 1920. xvi, 348p.

13,845 **Bailward**, William Amyas. 'Some recent developments of poor relief.' *Econ. J.*, XXII, 88 (December 1912), 542–53.

13,846 **Blease**, Walter Lyon. *The Poor Law and parochial government in Liverpool.* Liverpool: Liverpool U.P.; London: Constable, 1912.

13,847 **Everest**, H. B. *A practical treatise showing how the case paper system can be worked.* London: Hadden, Best, 1912. 92p.

13,848 **Hills**, John Waller and **Woods**, Maurice. *Poor Law reform: a practical programme; the scheme of the Unionist Social Reform Committee explained.* London: West Strand Publishing Co., 1912. 63p.

13,849 **Lloyd**, Charles Mostyn. *The abolition oj the Poor Law*. London, 1912. 19p.

13,850 **Percival**, Tom. *Poor Law children*. London: Shaw, 1912. xv, 409p.

13,851 **Poor Law Officers' Journal**. *The Poor Law and the coal strike...together with an appendix – containing the Local Government Board's circular letter ... 19th March, 1912, on exceptional unemployment*. London, 1912. 15p.

13,852 **Roberts**, George Joseph. *A practical guide to Poor Law prosecutions, together with full police court procedure and the necessary forms and documents*. London: C. Knight, 1912. xix, 168p.

13,853 **Scurfield**, Harold. *Royal Commission on the Poor Laws and Relief of Distress: a course of nine lectures delivered on the report of the above-named Commission in Sheffield, during the winter of 1909–10*. Sheffield: W. C. Long, 1912. 56p. (*Sheffield Weekly News* reprints.)

15,854 **Wallis**, *Mrs* Ransome. *Back to the source: a suggestion founded on the recommendations of the Royal Commission on the Poor Law (1908) respecting rescue work*. London: King, 1912. 26p.

13,855 **Banbury**, E. *Poor Law reform*. 1913. 20p.

13,856 **Departmental Committee on Poor Law Orders.** *First report*. London: H.M.S.O., 1913. 89p. (Cd. 6968.)

Chairman: S. B. Provis.

13,857 **Dodd**, John Theodore. *Letter to the Right Honourable John Burns, M.P., President of the Local Government Board* [upon the draft Poor Law Institutions Order]. London: King, 1913. xi, 30p.

13,858 **Dodd**, John Theodore. *Suggestions for amendment of consolidated orders and for improvement in Poor Law administration*. London: King, 1913. 23p.

13,859 **Mackay**, Thomas. 'The reform of the Poor Law.' *The dangers of democracy: studies in the economic questions of the day*. London: Murray, 1913. p. 294–321.

First published in the *Quarterly Review*. Criticism of the report of the Royal Commission and the minority report.

13,860 **Bailward**, William Amyas. *Some recent developments of poor relief*. London: King, 1914. 46p.

Reprinted from *Economic Journal*, December 1912, with postscript, 1914.

13,861 **Dodd**, John Theodore. *Letter to the Right Hon. Herbert Samuel, M.P., President of the Local Government Board, upon the New Poor Law Institutions Order, suggesting an amending order and explanatory circular*. London: King, 1914. vi, 28p.

13,862 **Drage**, Geoffrey. *The state and the poor*. London, Glasgow: Collins' Clear-Type P., 1914. 264p. (The nation's library.)

13,863 **Dumsday**, William Henry. *The Poor Law Institutions Order, 1913, and the Poor Law Institutions (Nursing) Order, 1913, with introduction, notes and explanations*. London: Hadden, Best, 1914. 235p.

13,864 **Shaw and Sons.** *Shaw's annotated edition of the Poor Law Institutions Order, 1913*. London: Shaw, 1914. 116p.

13,865 **Walker**, Gladstone. *The Poor-Law – indispensable*. London: Poor-Law Publications Co., 1914. 26p.

13,866 **Dodd,** John Theodore. *The war against destitution*. London, 1915. 7p.

13,867 **Graham**, James Edward and **Forbes**, James Wright. *Digest of arbitration decisions by the Local Government Board, 1898 to 1914, under the powers conferred by the Poor Law, Scotland, Act, 1898*. Paisley: A. Gardner, 1915. xxxix, 104p.

13,868 **Chance**, *Sir* William. 'Unsolved problems of the English Poor Law.' Dawson, W. H. (ed.). *After-war problems*. London: Allen and Unwin, 1917. p. 291–310.

13,869 **Lansbury**, George. *Your part in poverty*. London: Allen and Unwin, 1917. 126p.

13,870 **Lewis**, William Gibson. *'Reconstruction' of the Poor Law: 'the devoted work of the guardians'*. London: W. G. Lewis, 1918. viii, 80p.

13,871 **Local Government Committee.** *Report on transfer of functions of Poor Law authorities in England and Wales*. London: H.M.S.O., 1918. 26p. (Cd. 8917.)

Chairman: Sir Donald Maclean.

13,872 **Parr**, R. J. *Reconstructing local government*. London, 1918. 12p.

13,873 **Webb**, Beatrice. *The abolition of the Poor Law*. London: Fabian Society, 1918. 11p. (Fabian tract 185.)

13,874 **Maidenhead.** Union. *Report of the Committee appointed by the Guardians of the Maidenhead Union to examine and report on the old documents accumulated at the Poor Law Institution, Maidenhead*. Maidenhead, 1919. 42p.

13,875 *Our silent Poor-Law service*. Liverpool, 1919. 15p.

13,876 **Webb**, Beatrice. 'The end of the Poor Law.' Phillips, M. (ed.). *Women and the Labour Party, by various women writers*. London: Headley Bros., 1919. p. 50–6.

13,877 **Blyth**, M. E. *The passing of the poor*. London: Society for Promoting Christian Knowledge, 1920. 126p.

13,878 **Lloyd**, Charles Mostyn. *The present state of the Poor Law*. London, 1920. 8p.

13,879 **Lloyd**, Charles Mostyn. *The scandal of the Poor Law*. London: Fabian Society, 1920. 19p. (Fabian tract 195.)

13,880 **Warburg**, F. S. 'Of old-age pensions, out-relief, and other matters.' *Char. Orgn. Rev.*, n.s., XLVIII, 285 (September 1920), 63–6.

Résumé of some of the information obtained from a questionnaire sent out by the Charity Organisation Society.

13,881 **Curtis,** *Sir* Richard James. *The English Poor Law system and the work of the Birmingham Board of Guardians.* Birmingham: Hudson, 1922. 7p.
Address to the Birmingham Rotary Club, 30 October 1922.

13,882 **Ministry of Health.** *Special enquiry into the expenditure of the Guardians of the Parish of Poplar Borough: report.* London: H.M.S.O., 1922. 32p.
By H. I. Cooper.
Reprinted. 1924.

13,883 **Scurr,** John. *The rate protest of Poplar.* London: Caledonian P., 1922. 15p.

13,884 **Chance,** *Sir* William. *The Ministry of Health and the Poor Law.* London: King, 1923. 12p.

13,885 **Ministry of Health.** *Public inquiry into the administration of relief in the Sheffield Union: report.* London: H.M.S.O., 1932. 13p.
By Sir Arthur Lowry.

13,886 **Yeoman,** John Brown. *Some poor history and the Wirrall Union.* Chester: W. H. Evans, 1923. 40p.

13,887 *Memorandum on the rescission of the Poplar Order.* London: H.M.S.O., 1924. 14p. (Cmd. 2052.)

13,888 **Lloyd,** Charles Mostyn. 'The Poor Law.' Tracey, H. (ed.). *The Labour Party: its history, growth, policy, and leaders.* London: Caxton Publishing Co., 1925. Vol. 3. p. 3–18.

13,889 **Central Committee of Poor Law Conferences.** *'Provisional proposals for a measure of Poor Law reform': deputation to the Rt. Hon. A. Neville Chamberlain . . . from the Central Committee of Poor Law Conferences at the Ministry of Health . . . March 9, 1926. Verbatim report.* London, 1926. 16p.

13,890 **Charity Organisation Society.** *Poor Law commissioners for London.* London, 1926. 10p.

13,891 **Curtis,** *Sir* James. 'The English Poor Law system.' *Publ. Adm.*, IV (1926), 52–62.
Read before the Birmingham Group of the Institute of Public Administration.

13,892 **Hart,** *Sir* W. E. 'The reform of the Poor Law.' *Publ. Adm.*, IV (1926), 223–31.
Paper read to the Nottingham Group of the Institute of Public Administration.

13,893 **Marshall,** Dorothy. *The English Poor Laws.* 1926. (Ph.D. thesis, University of Cambridge.)

13,894 **Metropolitan Boroughs' Standing Joint Committee.** *Report of special sub-committee: proposals for the reform of the Poor Law.* London, 1926. 5p.

13,895 **Poor Law Officers' Journal.** *The government Bill to consolidate the enactments relating to the relief of the poor in England and Wales.* London, 1926. viii, 152p.

13,896 **Poor Law Officers' Journal.** *West Ham: an impartial study of the facts.* London, 1926. 16p.

13,897 *West Ham Union Board of Guardians: report on their administration for the period 20th July to 30th October, 1926.* London: H.M.S.O., 1926. 16p. (Cmd. 2786.)
Chairman: Alfred Woodgate.
Second report. Period 1st November, 1926 to 31st May, 1927. 1927. 10p. (Cmd. 2900.)
Third report. Period 1st June, 1927, to 31st May, 1928. 1928. 12p. (Cmd. 3142.)

13,898 *Bedwellty Union Board of Guardians: report, period ending 30th September, 1927.* London: H.M.S.O., 1927. 12p. (Cmd. 2976.)
Second report. Period ending 31st March, 1928. 1928. 8p. (Cmd. 3141).

13,899 *Chester-le-Street Union Board of Guardians: report on the administration for the period 30th August, 1926, to 31st December, 1926.* London: H.M.S.O., 1927. 14p. (Cmd. 2818.)
Chairman: Charles S. Shortt.
Second report. Period 1st January, 1927 to 30th June, 1927. 1927. 7p. (Cmd. 2937.)
Third report. Period 1st July, 1927, to 31st December, 1927. 1928. 9p. (Cmd. 3072.)

13,900 **Marshall,** H. J. *Socialism and the Poor Law.* London, 1927. 21p.

13,901 **Marshall,** H. J. *The West Ham Board of Guardians: what the new board found on taking over and what they have done since.* London, [1927?]. 19p.

13,902 **Moss,** John. *Poor Law Act, 1927.* London: Butterworth, Shaw, 1927. xxix, 304p.
'With an introduction . . . an annotated index, tables of comparison . . .'

13,903 **Poor Law Officers' Journal.** *Board of Guardians (Default) Act in operation.* London, 1927. 17p.

13,904 **Scurr,** John, *The reform (!) of the Poor Law.* London, 1927. 16p.

13,905 **Sophian,** Theodore John. *The Poor Law Act, 1927.* London: Sweet and Maxwell, Stevens, 1927. xix, 134p.

13,906 **Walker,** Gladstone. *Poor Law reform.* London, 1927. 16p.

13,907 **Woodward,** Edward Gilbert and **Woodward,** Edward Robert. *The Poor Law Act, 1927, with introduction, notes and cross references.* London: Hadden, Best, 1927. xiv, 167p.

13,908 **Davey,** Herbert and **Smith,** Alfred James. *The Poor Law Statutes – annotated, being the Consolidating Poor Law Act of 1927, as recently amended.* London: Stevens, 1928. 463p.
With explanatory notes.

13,909 **Higgs,** Mary. *Casuals and their casual treatment.* London: King, 1928. 30p.

13,910 **Webb,** Beatrice. *The English Poor Law: will it endure?* London: Oxford U.P., 1928. 32p. (Barnett House papers 11.)

13,911 **Davey,** Herbert. *A supplement to Davey's Poor Law Statutes Consolidated, containing the Poor Law and miscellaneous administrative provisions of the Local Government Act, 1929, annotated.* London: Stevens, 1929. vii, 96p.

13,912 **Noordin**, R. M. *Through a workhouse window, being a brief summary of three years spent by the youngest member of a Board of Guardians*. London: Palmer, 1929. 216p.

13,913 **Mackinnon**, J. M. *The English Poor Law of 1834, with special reference to its working between 1834 and 1847: a study in social pathology*. 1929–30. (M.A. thesis, University of London.)

13,914 **Blyth**, M. E. *The Poor-Law and the people*. London: Law and Local Government Publications, 1930. 22p.

13,915 **Davey**, Herbert. *The Poor Law Statutes and Orders, being the Consolidated Poor Law Act of 1930, with other enactments relating to powers and duties of the Poor Law authorities*. London: Stevens, 1930. 507p.

13,916 **Departmental Committee on the Relief of the Casual Poor.** *Report*. London: H.M.S.O., 1930. 99p. (Cmd. 3640.)

Chairman: L. R. Phelps.

13,917 **Glen**, Randolph Alexander. *Glen's Poor Law Act, 1930, together with the unrepealed sections of the Poor Law Act, 1927, the Audit . . . Act, 1927, and the Poor Law provisions of the Local Government Act, 1929*. London: Eyre and Spottiswoode, 1930. xxx, 130p.

With an index specially compiled by H. A. C. Sturgess.

13,918 **Jennings**, *Sir* William Ivor. *The Poor Law Code, being the Poor Law Act, 1930, and the Poor Law Orders now in force*. London: Knight, 1930. lxxxviii, 302p.

Annotated with an introduction.

13,919 **London Municipal Society.** *The new Poor Law for London*. London, 1930. 16p. (Pamphlets 37.)

Revised edition.

13,920 **Ministry of Health.** *Poor Law: report of a special inquiry into various forms of test work*. London: H.M.S.O., 1930. 44p. (Cmd. 3585.)

13,921 **Peterken**, W. B. *Practical procedure in reference to the administration of Poor Law relief*. London: Knight, 1930. 47p.

13,922 **Beales**, Hugh Lancelot. 'The New Poor Law.' *History*, n.s., xv, 60 (January 1931), 308–19.

Reprinted in Carus-Wilson, E. M. (ed.). *Essays in economic history*. Vol. III. London: Arnold, 1962. p. 179–87.

13,923 **Bonsor**, George F. *Our workhouse million*. London: *Efficiency Magazine*, 1931. 143p.

13,924 **Roff**, Tom Walter. *The pinch of poverty*. London: Student Christian Movement P., 1931. v, 72p.

'With an appendix on the extent of poverty and the provision for meeting it, by E. E. Parnell.'

13,925 **Wake**, Joan. *Memorandum of the British Record Society: records of Boards of Guardians, 1834–1930. Suggestions for the selection of those which should be preserved*. London: British Record Society, 1931. 9p.

In collaboration with S. Peyton.

13,926 **Exley**, C. H. *The guide to poor relief*. Liverpool: Meek, Thomas, 1932. 160p.

Second edition. 1932. 160p.
Third edition. 1932. 191p.
Fourth edition. 1935. 386p.

13,927 **Glen**, Randolph Alexander. *Glen's law relating to public assistance, being the Poor Law Act, 1930, the Public Assistance and Relief Regulation Orders of 1930, 1931 & 1932, Mental Disability, the Children and Young Persons Act 1932, the 'Needs Test', other Poor Law enactments and regulations, cases and departmental decisions, and three administrative schemes*. London: Law and Local Government Publications, 1933. xliii, 786p.

By R. A. Glen, assisted by E. Bright Ashford and Alexander P. L. Glen.

13,928 **Carr-Saunders**, *Sir* Alexander Morris. *A century of pauperism*. London, 1934. 4p.

13,929 **Cuttle**, George. *The legacy of rural guardians: a study of conditions in mid-Essex*. Cambridge: Heffer, 1934. viii, 384p.

Administration of Poor Laws since 1895.

13,930 **Atkinson**, William C. 'Luis Vives and poor relief.' *Dublin Rev.*, CXCVII (July 1935), 93–103.

English and Dutch conditions compared.

13,931 **Slater**, Gilbert. 'The relief of the poor.' Laski, H. J., Jennings, W. I. and Robson, W. A. (eds.). *A century of municipal progress, 1835–1935*. London: Allen and Unwin, 1935. p. 332–69.

Published under the auspices of the National Association of Local Government Officers.

13,932 **Jennings**, *Sir* William Ivor. *The Poor Law Code and the law of unemployment assistance*. London: Knight, 1936. xl, 488p.

Second edition.

13,933 **Albery**, William. 'Terrors of the Poor Law at Horsham, 1834–36.' *Sx. County Mag.*, xv, 7 (July 1941), 231–5.

13,934 **Flynn-Hughes**, Cledwyn. *The development of the Poor Laws in Caernarvonshire and Anglesey, 1815–1914*. 1945. 2v. (M.A. thesis, University of Wales, Bangor.)

13,935 **Beales**, Hugh Lancelot. 'The passing of the Poor Law.' *Polit. Q.*, XIX, 4 (October–December 1948), 312–22.

13,936 **Morgan**, John S. 'The break-up of the Poor Law in Britain, 1907–47: an historical footnote.' *Can. J. Econ. Polit. Sci.*, XIV, 22 (May 1948), 209–19.

13,937 **Clarke**, Joan Simeon. 'The break-up of the Poor Law.' Cole, M. I. (ed.). *The Webbs and their work*. London: Muller, 1949. p. 101–15.

13,938 **Hodgkinson**, Ruth Gladys. *The medical services of the new Poor Law, 1834–1871*.

1951. 2v. (Ph.D. thesis, University of London.)

13,939 **Thomas**, J. E. *Poor Law administration in West Glamorgan, 1834–1930*. 1951. (M.A. thesis, University of Wales, Swansea.)

13,940 **Stanley-Morgan**, Robert. 'The Poor Law unions and their records.' *Amat. Hist.*, II, 1 (August–September 1954), 11–15.

13,941 **Watkinson**, Walter Reginald. *The relieving officer looks back: the last years of the Poor Law in Holderness*. Withernsea: A. E. Lunn, 1955. 38p.

13,942 **Ross**, E. M. *Women and Poor Law administration, 1857–1909*. 1955–56. (M.A. thesis, University of London.)

13,943 **Baker**, G. F. *The care and education of children in union workhouses of Somerset, 1834–1870*. 1959–60. (M.A. thesis, University of London.)

13,944 **Boyson**, Rhodes. *The history of the Poor Law administration in North East Lancashire, 1834–1871*. 1960. x, 452p. (M.A. thesis, University of Manchester.)

13,945 **Boyson**, Rhodes. 'The new Poor Law in North-East Lancashire, 1834–71.' *Lanc. Chesh. Antiq. Soc. Trans.*, LXX (1960), 35–56.

13,946 **Jones**, T. D. *Poor Law and public health administration in the area of Merthyr Tydfil Union, 1834–1894*. 1961. (M.A. thesis, University of Wales, Cardiff.)

13,947 **Marshall**, John Duncan. 'The Nottinghamshire reformers and their contribution to the new Poor Law.' *Econ. Hist. Rev.*, 2nd ser., XIII, 3 (April 1961), 382–96.

13,948 **Brocklebank**, J. A. H. 'The new Poor Law in Lincolnshire.' *Lincs. Hist.*, II, 9 (1962), 21–33.

13,949 **Roberts**, David. 'How cruel was the Victorian Poor Law?' *Hist. J.*, VI, 1 (1963), 97–107.

13,950 **Lewis**, Richard Albert. 'William Day and the Poor Law Commissioners.' *Univ. Birm. Hist. J.*, IX, 22 (1964), 163–96.

13,951 **Proctor**, Winifred. 'Poor Law administration in Preston Union, 1838–1848.' *Hist. Soc. Lanc. Chesh. Trans.*, CXVII (1965), 145–66.

13,952 **Edsale**, Nicholas Cranford. *The new Poor Law and its opponents, 1834–44*. 1965–66. (Dissertation, Harvard University.)

13,953 **Rose**, Michael E. 'The allowance system under the new Poor Law.' *Econ. Hist. Rev.*, 2nd ser., XIX, 3 (December 1966), 607–20.

13,954 **Caplan**, Maurice. *The administration of the Poor Law in the Unions of Southwell and Basford, 1836–71*. 1966–67. (Ph.D. thesis, University of Nottingham.)

13,955 **Russell**, V. J. *Poor Law administration, 1840–1843, with particular reference to the Cardiff Union*. 1966–67. (M.A. thesis, University of Wales, Cardiff.)

13,956 **Hodgkinson**, Ruth Gladys. *The origins of the National Health Service: the medical services of the new Poor Law 1834–1871*. London: Wellcome Historical Medical Library, 1967. xix, 714p. (Publications, new series, vol. II.)

'The work was in its original form approved for the Ph.D. degree by the University of London . . .', 1951.

13,957 **Midwinter**, E. C. 'State intervention at the local level: the new Poor Law in Lancashire.' *Hist. J.*, X, 1 (1967), 106–12.

13,958 **Victorian Society.** Annual Conference, 4th, London, 1966. *The Victorian poor*. London: the Society, 1967. 57p.

13,959 **Henriques**, Ursula. 'How cruel was the Victorian Poor Law?' *Hist. J.*, XI, 2 (1968), 365–71.

13,960 **Richardson**, Stanley Ivor. *A history of the Edmonton Poor Law Union 1837–1854, based on the minutes of the Board of Guardians of the Edmonton Poor Law Union, volumes 1–15*. London: Edmonton Hundred Historical Society, 1968. 87p. (Occasional papers, new series, 12.)

13,961 **Maltby**, A. *The Poor Law Commission, 1905–1909: an investigation of its task and achievement*. 1968–69. (M.A. thesis, University of Liverpool.)

13,962 **Mishra**, R. C. *A history of the relieving officer in England and Wales from 1834 to 1948*. 1968–69. (Ph.D. thesis, University of London.)

13,963 **Beresford**, Peter. 'The relieving officer: Poor Law personified.' *New Soc.*, XIV, 371 (6 November 1969), 721–3.

13,964 **Brown**, J. 'The appointment of the 1905 Poor Law Commission.' *Inst. Hist. Res. Bull.*, XLII (1969), 239–42.

13,965 **Handley**, Michael David. *Local administration of the Poor Law in the Great Boughton and Wirral Unions and the Chester Local Act Incorporation, 1834–71*. 1969. (M.A. thesis, University of Wales, Bangor.)

13,966 **McCord**, Norman. 'The implementation of the 1834 Poor Law Amendment Act on Tyneside.' *Int. Rev. of Soc. Hist.*, XIV, 1 (1969), 90–108.

13,967 **Caplan**, Maurice. 'The Poor Law in Nottinghamshire, 1836–71.' *Thoro. Soc. Trans.*, LXXIV (1970), 82–98.

13,968 **Fraser**, Derek. 'Poor Law politics in Leeds 1833–1855.' *Thores. Soc. Publs.*, LIII, 1 (1970), 23–49.

13,969 **Grace**, Ray. 'The Hendon and Pwllheli Unions, 1835–1871.' *NE. Group Study Labour Hist. Bull.*, 4 (November 1970), 15–16.

Summary of a paper read at the Group's half-day school on 'The Poor Law Amendment Act in the North East' on 16 May 1970 at Durham.

13,970 **McCord**, Norman. 'The introduction of the 1834 Poor Law Amendment Act on Tyneside.' *NE. Group Study Labour*

Hist. Bull., 4 (November 1970), 12–13.
Summary of a paper read at the Group's half-day school on 'The Poor Law Amendment Act in the North East' on 16 May 1970 at Durham.

13,971 **Mawson**, Pamela. 'Poor Law administration in South Shields, 1836–1847.' *NE. Group Study Labour Hist. Bull.*, 4 (November 1970), 13–15.
Summary of a paper read at the Group's half-day school on 'The Poor Law Amendment Act in the North East' on 16 May 1970 at Durham.

13,972 **Rose**, Michael E. 'The anti-Poor Law agitation.' Ward, J. T. (ed.). *Popular movements* c. *1830–1850*. London: Macmillan, 1970. p. 78–94.

13,973 **Rose**, Michael E. 'The new Poor Law in an industrial area.' Hartwell, R. M. (ed.). *The industrial revolution*. Oxford: Blackwell, 1970. p. 121–43.

See also: 9126; 12,896.

d. SCOTLAND

13,974 **Hancock**, William Neilson. 'On the Scotch Branch of the poor removal question.' *Statist. Soc. Inq. Soc. Ir. J.*, VIII, 2 (January 1881), 178–81.

13,975 *Western Highlands and islands of Scotland: reports from Messrs. Peterkin and Campbell, General Superintendents of Poor, to the Board of Supervision, Edinburgh, as to alleged destitution in the Western Highlands and islands*. London: H.M.S.O., 1883. 10p. (C. 3600.).
Reports by Alexander Campbell and W. A. Peterkin.

13,976 **Lamond**, Robert Peel. *The Scottish Poor Laws: their history, policy and operation*. Glasgow: W. Hodge, 1892. xvi, 398p.
New edition, enlarged.

13,977 **Loch**, Charles Stewart. 'Poor relief in Scotland: its statistics and development.' *R. Statist. Soc. J.*, LXI, 2 (June 1898), 271–365.
Discussion, p. 366–70.
'Read before the Royal Statistical Society, 19th April 1898.'

13,978 **Ross**, *Rev.* H. *The resources of the poor in Glasgow*. Glasgow, 1898. 16p.

13,979 **Local Government Board for Scotland.** Departmental Committee to inquire into the system of Poor Law medical relief, and into the rules and regulations for the management of poor houses.
Vol. I. *Report, with supplement*. Edinburgh: H.M.S.O., 1904. (Cd. 2008.)
Vol. II. *Minutes of evidence, appendices and index*. (Cd. 2022.)

13,980 **Baird**, Alexander. 'How Poor Law Guardians spend their money in Scotland.' *Nineteenth Century*, LVIII, 344 (October 1905), 674–6.

13,981 **Local Government Board.** *Report on the methods of administering poor relief in certain large town parishes of Scotland*. Glasgow: H.M.S.O., 1905. xxxi, 43p. (Cd. 2524.)
Chairman: R. B. Barclay.

13,982 **Mackay**, George A. *Practice of the Scottish Poor Law*. Edinburgh: W. Green, 1907. xii, 242p.

13,983 **Local Government Board for Scotland.** *Report as to the proceedings of Distress Committees in Scotland from the date of their appointment to the 15th May 1906*. Glasgow: H.M.S.O., 1907. 21p. (Cd. 3431.)
...*for the year ended 15th May 1907*. 1907. 22p. (Cd. 3830.)
...*for the year ended 15th May 1908*. 1908. 19p. (Cd. 4478.)
By G. Falconar-Stewart.
...*for the year ended 15th May 1909*. 1909. 21p. (Cd. 4946.) By A. Murray.

13,984 **Glasse**, J. *Poor Law amendment*. Edinburgh, 1908. 16p.

13,985 **Glasgow Herald.** *The Royal Commission: Scottish Poor Law reform*. [1909?] 50p.

13,986 **Scottish National Committee to Promote the Break-up of the Poor Law.** *The minority report for Scotland*. Glasgow: the Committee, 1909. vii, 79p.

13,987 **Chalmers**, Thomas. *Doctor Chalmers and the Poor Laws: a comparison of Scotch and English pauperism, and evidence before the Committee of the House of Commons*. Edinburgh: David Douglas, 1911. xii, 235p.
Preface by Mrs George Kerr and introduction by Miss Grace Chalmers Wood.

13,988 *Scottish Poor Law reform: case for reform and the scope thereof*. Glasgow, [1911?]. 31p.

13,989 **Cormack**, Alexander Allan. *Poor relief in Scotland: an outline of the growth and administration of the Poor Laws in Scotland, from the Middle Ages to the present day*. Aberdeen: Wyllie, 1923. xi, 215p.

13,990 **Cormack**, Alexander Allan. *Poor relief in Scotland: the old and the new*. Glasgow: Hodge, 1926. 24p.
A lecture.
Reprinted from *Poor Law and Local Government Magazine*.

13,991 **Burn**, W. L. 'The Scottish Poor Law and the Poor Law (Amendment) Act, 1834.' *Publ. Adm.*, x, 4 (October 1932), 388–96.

13,992 **Birnie**, Arthur. 'The Edinburgh Charity Workhouse, 1740–1845.' *Old Edinb. Club Book*, XXII (1938), 38–55.

13,993 **Department of Health for Scotland.** *Report of the Departmental Committee on Poor Law in Scotland*. Edinburgh: H.M.S.O., 1938. 40p. (Cmd. 5803.)

13,994 **Hamilton**, Thomas. *Poor relief in South Ayrshire, 1700–1845*. Edinburgh, London: Oliver and Boyd, 1942. xi, 155p.

13,995 **Henderson**, W. O. 'The cotton famine in Scotland and the relief of distress, 1862–1864.' *Scott. Hist. Rev.*, xxx, 2 (October 1951), 154–64.

13,996 **Lindsay**, J. *The operation of the Poor Law in the north-east of Scotland, 1745–1845*. 1962. (Ph.D. thesis, University of Aberdeen.)

See also: 13,661.

e. IRELAND

13,997 **Hancock**, William Neilson. 'Some further information as to migratory labourers from Mayo to England, and as to importance of limiting law taxes and law charges in proceedings affecting small holders of land.' *Statist. Soc. Inq. Soc. Ir. J.*, VIII, 1 (April 1880), 61–78.

13,998 **McCabe**, F. *Copy of Dr. McCabe's report on the state of Belfast workhouse.* [London: H.M.S.O.], 1880. 6p. (H.C. 359. Sess. 2.)

13,999 *Belfast workhouse.* [London: H.M.S.O.], 1881. 33p. (H.C. 123.)

Copies of papers and correspondence relating to Belfast workhouse.

14,000 **Dodd**, W. H. 'A common poor fund for the metropolis.' *Statist. Soc. Inq. Soc. Ir. J.*, VIII, 2 (January 1881), 159–64.

14,001 **Hancock**, William Neilson. 'On the anomalous differences in the Poor-Laws of Ireland and of England: an address to the Trades Union Congress.' *Statist. Soc. Inq. Soc. Ir. J.*, VIII, 2 (January 1881), 123–42.

Also published separately. Dublin: R. D. Webb, 1880. 21p.

14,002 **Local Government Board.** Inspectors. *Reports . . . on the subject of apprehended distress in the Ennistymon and Corrofin Unions, dated the 6th and 10th days of November 1882 respectively.* [London: H.M.S.O.], 1882. 5p. (H.C. 426.)

14,003 **Shackleton**, Abraham. 'On the anomalous differences in the Poor-Laws of Ireland and of England with reference to outdoor relief, area of taxation, etc.' *Statist. Soc. Inq. Soc. Ir. J.*, VIII, 4 (January 1882), 282–8.

14,004 **Field**, William. *Suggestions for the improvement of the Irish Poor Law.* Dublin: R. D. Webb, 1883. 26p.

14,005 **Sandiford**, T. Henry. *Permanent reduction of the poor-rates in Ireland, by three pence in the pound. To be effected by the formation of a new public health service.* Dublin: Hodges, Figgis, 1884. 12p.

14,006 **Poor Relief (Ireland) Inquiry Commission.** *Report and evidence, with appendices.* Dublin: H.M.S.O., 1887. xxiv, 246p. (C. 5043.)

14,007 **Hackett**, Edward Augustus. *The Irish grand jury system, with a note on the Irish Poor Law system, 1898.* London: King, 1898. 40p.

14,008 **British Medical Association.** *Reports on the Poor Law medical system in Ireland.* London, 1904. 63p.

14,009 **Evatt**, *Sir* George Joseph Hamilton. *A report on the Poor Law medical system in Ireland, with special reference to the dispensary medical service.* London, 1904.

Supplement to the *British Medical Journal.*

14,010 **Dawson**, Charles. 'Suggested substitutes for the present Poor Law system.' *Statist. Soc. Inq. Soc. Ir. J.*, XI, 86 (December 1906), 428–38.

14,011 **Vice-Regal Commission on Poor Law Reform in Ireland.**

Vol. I. *Report.* Dublin: H.M.S.O., 1906. ix, 82p. (Cd. 3202.)

Vol. II. *Appendix.* (Cd. 3203.)

Vol. III. *Minutes of evidence, index.* (Cd. 3204.)

Chairman: W. L. Micks.

14,012 **Finlay**, T. A. 'Ethics and economics of poor relief.' *Statist. Soc. Inq. Soc. Ir. J.*, XII, 87 (December 1907), 43–51.

14,013 **Jones**, Thomas. 'Pauperism and poverty.' *Statist. Soc. Inq. Soc. Ir. J.*, XII, 90 (December 1910), 358–70.

14,014 **Parkinson**, H. *The prevention of destitution in Ireland.* Dublin, [*c.* 1910]. 30p.

14,015 **Martin**, Lester. *The amazing philanthropists; being extracts from the letters of L. Martin.* London: Sidgwick and Jackson, 1916. 290p.

Edited and arranged by S. R. Day.

14,016 **Maguire**, J. 'Poor Law reform.' *Statist. Soc. Inq. Soc. Ir. J.*, XV, 100 (October 1925), 134–42.

14,017 **Eason**, Charles. 'Report of the Irish Poor Law Commission.' *Statist. Soc. Inq. Soc. Ir. J.*, XVI, 102 (October 1928), 17–32.

Discussion, p. 33–43.

14,018 **Eire.** Seanad Éireann. *Report of the Special Committee re Poor Law relief.* 1929. (R. 48.)

14,019 **Meghen**, P. J. 'Building the workhouses.' *Administration*, III, 1 (Spring 1955), 40–6.

14,020 **McGrath**, B. *Introduction of the Poor Law to Ireland, 1831–38.* 1964–65. (M.A. thesis, National University of Ireland.)

3. Early National Insurance Schemes

This section includes the material dealing with proposals for a national system of social insurance; with the National Insurance Act, 1911; and with subsequent measures up to the time of the Beveridge Report.

14,021 **Blackley**, William Lewery. 'The House of Lords and national insurance.' *Nineteenth Century*, VIII, 41 (July 1880), 107–18.

Discussion of objections to national insurance raised in the House of Lords, and reaction of the press.

14,022 **Carnarvon**, *Earl of.* 'A few more words on national insurance.' *Nineteenth Century*, VIII, 43 (September 1880), 384–93.

14,023 **Tremenheere**, Hugh Seymour. 'State aid and control in industrial assurance.' *Nineteenth Century*, VIII, 42 (August 1880), 275–93.

14,024 **Mackay**, Thomas. *Working class insurance.* London: E. Stanford, 1890. vi, 78p.

14,025 **Doyle**, J. A. 'Pauperism and national insurance.' *Char. Orgn. Rev.*, IX, 99 (April 1893), 111–18.

14,026 **Atkinson**, Alexander. *The national insurance and pension scheme as formulated by A. Atkinson.* Bradford: J. Dale, 1894. 16p.

14,027 **Henderson**, Edward Piercy. *The insurance question plainly treated for plain people.* London: Effingham Wilson, 1900. iv, 40p.
Supplements, for private circulation only, 1902, 1903, 1909, 1910, 1911.

14,028 **Blackley**, William Lewery. *Thrift & national insurance as a security against pauperism.* London: Kegan Paul, 1906. ix, 151p.
'With a memoir of the late Rev. Canon Blackley and reprint of his essays by M. J. J. Blackley.'

14,029 **Brabrook**, *Sir* Edward. 'Social insurances.' *R. Statist. Soc. J.*, LXXI, 4 (December 1908), 601–9.
Discussion, p. 612–18.
'Read before the Royal Statistical Society, 17th November, 1908.'

14,030 **Slesser**, *Sir* Henry Herman. *A Bill to provide for the more effectual prevention of destitution and the better organisation of public assistance.* London, 1910. 19p.

14,031 **Billing**, Noel Pemberton. 'Confusion worse confounded.' *Nineteenth Century*, LXVIII, 412 (June 1911), 1157–62.

14,032 **Booth**, E. G. *The Insurance Bill and women wage-earners.* Manchester, [1911?]. [4]p.

14,033 **Cooke**, Oswald Hayward. *The National Insurance Act explained.* Chester: Taplen and Paddock, 1911. 48p.
Second edition, revised. 1912. 52p.
Third edition. London: Murray and Evenden, 1912. 52p.

14,034 **Evans**, David Owen. *The Insurance Bill made clear: a guide for the million.* London: D. Nutt, 1911. 94p.

14,035 **Evans**, *Sir* Laming Worthington. *The National Insurance Bill: summary.* London: National Union of Conservative and Constitutional Associations, 1911. 88p.
Fourth edition with notes.

14,036 **Fabian Society.** *The Insurance Bill and the workers: criticisms and amendments of the National Insurance Bill, prepared by the Executive Committee.* London: Fabian Society, 1911. 19p.

14,037 **Fabian Society.** Fabian Women's Group. *How the National Insurance Bill affects women.* London, [1911?]. 20p.

14,038 **Fabian Society.** Fabian Women's Group. *The National Insurance Bill: a criticism.* London: Fabian Women's Group, Executive Committee, 1911. 28p.
Preface by Mrs Bernard Shaw.

14,039 **Foley**, Frank S. *The National Insurance Act, 1911, as it affects employers and workmen.* London, Manchester: Sherratt and Hughes, 1911. 61p.

14,040 **Hillier**, Alfred P. 'National insurance and the commonweal.' *Nineteenth Century*, LXX, 414 (August 1911), 339–49.

14,041 **Liberal Publication Department.** *The National Insurance Bill: its proposals summarised and explained.* London, 1911. 32p.

14,042 **Lloyd George**, David. *The people's insurance.* London: Hodder and Stoughton, 1911. 161p.
Third edition, 'containing the text of the National Insurance Act, 1911, together with explanations of the Insurance Commissioners'. 1912. vii, 303p.

14,043 **Loch**, *Sir* Charles Stewart. *The National Insurance Bill: a paper.* London: Charity Organisation Society, 1911. 48p.

14,044 **London and Suburban Traders' Federation.** *A plain summary of part I of the National Insurance Bill, as it will affect traders, shopkeepers, and employees generally.* London, 1911. 11p.
Prepared by A. W. J. Groos.

14,045 **Money**, *Sir* Leo George Chiozza. *A nation insured: the National Insurance Act explained.* London: Liberal Publication Department, 1911. 68p.
Third edition. 1912. 78p.

14,046 **National Council of Women of Great Britain.** *Domestic servants under the National Insurance Bill.* London, 1911. [4] p.

14,047 **Rees**, Joseph Aubrey. *The ABC of the national insurance scheme.* London: Stead's Publishing House, 1911. 64p.
Second edition. 1911. 63p.
Fourth edition. *The ABC of the National Insurance Act.* 1912. 71p.

14,048 **Reid**, J. *The economics of the Insurance Act.* Middlesbrough, [1911?]. 8p.

14,049 **Roberts**, A. Carson. 'The government scheme of national insurance.' *Nineteenth Century*, LXIX, 412 (June 1911), 1141–56.

14,050 **Roberts**, Harry. 'The Insurance Bill, the doctors, and national policy.' *Nineteenth Century*, LXX, 413 (July 1911), 152–62.

14,051 **Schuster**, Ernest Joseph. 'National insurance against invalidity and old age: a reply to Mr. Carson Roberts.' *Nineteenth Century*, LXIX, 408 (February 1911), 351–68.

14,052 **Society for Organizing Charitable Relief and Repressing Mendicity.** *The National Insurance Bill.* London, 1911. 48p.

14,053 **Stocks**, H. 'Women and state insurance.' *Econ. Rev.*, XXI, 4 (October 1911), 439–45.

14,054 **Watts**, John Henry. *The National Insurance Bill.* London: Stevens, 1911. 286p.
'With introduction and notes.'

14,055 **Appleton**, William Archibald. *National Insurance Act: the critical position of trade unions. An appeal to organized workers.* London: Wyman, 1912. 4p.

14,056 **Ashley**, Annie. *The social policy of Bismarck: a critical study, with a comparison of German and English insurance legislation.* London: Longmans, Green, 1912. xi, 95p. (Birmingham studies in social economics and adjacent fields 3.)

14,057 **A Barrister-at-Law.** *Popular guide to national insurance: the new Act fully analysed and explained.* London: *Daily Chronicle*, 1912. 30p.
Second edition revised to date.

14,058 **Browne**, *Sir* Edmond and **Wood**, *Sir* Howard Kingsley. *The law of national insurance.* London: Sweet and Maxwell, 1912. xlvii, 444p.
Second edition. 1912. xlvii, 436, 42p.
With introduction and notes.

14,059 **Carr**, Arthur Strettell Comyns, **Garnett**, William Hubert Stuart and **Taylor**, James Henry (eds.). *National insurance.* London: Macmillan, 1912. xxx, 504p.
Second edition. 1912. xxxii, 587p.
Third edition. 1912. xxxii, 748p.
Fourth edition. 1913. xliii, 1284p.
Includes the text and schedules of the National Insurance Act, 1911.

14,060 **Clarke**, Orme Bigland. *The National Insurance Act, 1911; being a treatise on the scheme of national health insurance and insurance against unemployment created by that Act, with the incorporated enactments, full explanatory notes, tables and examples.* London: Butterworth, 1912. c, 338, 52p.
Second edition. 1913. civ, 467, 65p.

14,061 **Committee Appointed to Consider and Advise with regard to the Application of the National Insurance Act to Outworkers.**
Vol. I. *Report.* London: H.M.S.O., 1912. 21p. (Cd. 6178.)
Vol. II. *Minutes of evidence, appendices, index.* (Cd. 6179.)
Chairman: E. F. G. Hatch.

14,062 **Daily News.** *Sixty points about the Insurance Act.* London, [1912?]. iv, 60p.

14,063 **Earengey**, William George. *Woman under the Insurance Act.* London: Women's Freedom League, 1912. 31p.

14,064 **Evans**, *Sir* Laming Worthington. *The National Insurance Act, 1911: summary . . . with explanatory chapters and full index.* London: National Conservative Union, 1912. 152p.

14,065 **Federation of Master Cotton Spinners' Associations.** *The National Insurance Act.* Manchester, 1912.

14,066 **Fraser**, James Alexander Lovat. *The National Insurance Act, 1911.* London: Waterlow, 1912. xii, 216p.

14,067 **Freedom of Labour Defence.** *The Insurance Act and home work.* [1912?] [4]p.

14,068 **Gadd**, Henry Wippell. *A guide to the National Insurance Act. 1911.* London: Effingham Wilson, 1912. vi, 140p. (Wilson's legal handy books.)
With notes and index.

14,069 **Gough**, George W. 'The economics of the Insurance Act.' *Engl. Rev.*, XI, 44 (July 1912), 634–44.

14,070 **Haldane**, Richard Burdon, Viscount Haldane. *The national insurance scheme: a speech delivered . . . in the House of Lords, on December 11th, 1911.* London: Liberal Publication Department, 1912. 24p.

14,071 **Insurance Tax Protest League.** *Mr. Lloyd George's root mistake: the great miscalculations of the Insurance Act.* London, [1912?]. 4p.

14,072 **Inter-Departmental Committee on Employment under the Crown.**
First report. London: H.M.S.O., 1912. 20p. (Cd. 6234.)
Second report. 1912. 4p. (Cd. 6315.)
Third report. 1913. 11p. (Cd. 7176.)
Chairman: M. Nathan.

14,073 **Inter-Departmental Committee on Outdoor Staff.** *Report.* London: H.M.S.O., 1912. 9p. (Cd. 6231.)
Chairman: F. Mowatt.

14,074 **Inter-Departmental Committee on the Appointment of the Audit Staff.** *First report.* London: H.M.S.O., 1912. 7p. (Cd. 6232.)
Second report. 1912. 3p. (Cd. 6243.)
Chairman: H. J. Gibson.

14,075 **McCurdy**, Charles Albert and **Lees-Smith**, Hastings Bertrand. *The people's guide to the Insurance Act: the Act complete with introduction and full explanatory notes.* London: Liberal Insurance Committee, 1912. 175p.
Second and revised edition.

14,076 **Macnamara**, Thomas James. *The great Insurance Act: addresses to working men.* London: Hodder and Stoughton, 1912. xiv, 54p.

14,077 **McVie**, Angus. *Seamen and the National Insurance Act: a short practical guide to the position of seafarers and the special provisions that have been made for all classes serving in the British Mercantile Marine.* Glasgow: James Brown, 1912. 27p.

14,078 **Money**, *Sir* Leo George Chiozza. *Insurance versus poverty.* London: Methuen, 1912. xxiii, 396p.

14,079 **Money**, *Sir* Leo George Chiozza. *The truth about insurance.* London: *Daily Chronicle*, 1912. 11p.
Reprinted from the *Daily Chronicle.*

14,080 **Moorhouse**, Edward Albert and **Woodhouse**, James R. *National Insurance Act, 1911: a handbook for employers, with specimen account forms for working the Act.* Liverpool: *Daily Post & Mercury*, 1912. 44p.
Second edition. 1912. iv, 65p.

14,081 **Moran**, Clarence Gabriel. *The alphabet of the National Insurance Act, 1911.* London: Methuen, 1912. vi, 164p.

14,082 **National Council of Women of Great Britain.** Committee to Further Women's Interests under the National Insurance Act. *Women and local insurance committees.* London, [1912?]. [4]p.

14,083 **Pringle**, Arthur Stanley. *The National Insurance Act, 1911, explained, annotated, and indexed.* Edinburgh, London: W. Green, 1912. xx, 544p.

14,084 **Samuel**, Horace Barnett. *The Insurance Act and yourself.* London: T. Murby, 1912. 112p.

14,085 **Smith**, Thomas. *Everybody's guide to the Insurance Act.* London: Knight, 1912. vii, 304p.
Second edition. 1912. viii, 357p.
Third edition. *Everybody's guide to the Insurance Acts, 1911–1913.* 1914. xii, 506, xvip.

14,086 **Smith**, Thomas. *A householder's help to the National Insurance Act.* London: Knight, 1912.

14,087 **Smith**, Thomas. *Knight's guide to the Insurance Act for employers and cashiers.* London: Knight, 1912. 11p.

14,088 **Spens**, William Patrick, Baron. *National Insurance Act, 1911, being a King's Printer's copy of the Act, and a reprint of official explanatory memoranda relating thereto, bound up with an index to the Act.* London: Solicitors' Law Stationery Society, 1912. lvii, 170p.

14,089 **Stone**, *Sir* Gilbert. *Questions and answers on national insurance: a practical and clear handbook for all.* London: Butterworth, Shaw, 1912. xxi, 224p.

14,090 **Amend the Act League.** *Unionists and insurance.* London, 1913. 15p.

14,091 **Croasdell**, William Carlyle. *The National Insurance Act: how it works and what it secures.* London: Ganes, 1913. 99p.

14,092 **Cunnison**, James. 'Some factors affecting the incidence of the national insurance contributions.' *Econ. J.*, XXIII, 91 (September 1913), 367–78.

14,093 **Edinburgh Review.** 'National insurance and national character.' *Edinb. Rev.*, CCXVIII, 445 (July 1913), 22–41.
Compares Germany and England.

14,094 **Gowers**, Ernest Arthur. *Report by the Chief Inspector to the National Insurance Commission (England) on an inquiry into the reasons why certain insured persons became deposit contributors.* London: H.M.S.O., 1913. 9p. (Cd. 7034.)

14,095 **Lloyd George**, David. *Benefits of the Insurance Act: a speech delivered . . . at Sutton-in-Ashfield, on August 9th, 1913.* London: Liberal Publication Department, 1913. 14p.

14,096 **Macnamara**, Thomas James. *The great Insurance Act: a year's experience. A comment.* London: Liberal Publication Department, 1913. 15p.

14,097 **Rubinow**, Isaac Max. *Social insurance.* London: Williams and Norgate; New York: H. Holt, 1913. vii, 525p.

14,098 **Watts**, John Henry. *The law relating to national insurance, with an explanatory introduction, the text of the National Insurance Act, 1911, annotated, and appendices containing regulations.* London: Stevens, 1913. vii, 664p.

14,099 **Ashby**, Arthur Wilfred. 'The incidence of the insurance tax on British agriculture.' *Econ. Rev.*, XXIV, 1 (January 1914), 39–47.

14,100 **Committee Appointed to Consider and Advise with regard to the Application of the National Insurance Act to Outworkers in Ireland.**
Vol. I. *Report.* London: H.M.S.O., 1914. 23p. (Cd. 7685.)
Vol. II. *Evidence and appendices.* 1914. (Cd. 7686.)
Chairman: Sir Ernest F. G. Hatch.

14,101 **Fabian Research Department.** 'The working of the Insurance Act.' *New Statesman*, II, 49 (14 March 1914), Supplement. 31p.
Interim report of Committee of Enquiry (Chairman, Sidney Webb).

14,102 **Inter-Departmental Committee Appointed to Consider Proposals for Facilitating the Payment through the Post of Benefits under the National Insurance Act.** *Report.* London: H.M.S.O., 1914. 11p. (Cd. 7245.)
Chairman: T. H. Elliott.

14,103 **Lloyd**, James Henry. *Domestic servants and the Insurance Acts: a guide for mistresses and servants.* London: Pitman, 1914. v, 30p.

14,104 **Webb**, Sidney and **Gardner**, Rose. 'The Insurance Act at work.' *Contemp. Rev.*, CVI (July 1914), 41–51.

14,105 **Fabian Society**. 'Industrial insurance.' *New Statesman* (13 March 1915), Supplement. 32p.

14,106 **Departmental Committee on Approved Society Finance and Administration.** *Interim report.* London: H.M.S.O., 1916. 39p. (Cd. 8251.)
Further report. 1916. ix, 88p. (Cd. 8396.)
Final report. 1917. 17p. (Cd. 8451.)
Chairman: G. H. Ryan.

14,107 **Committee of Inquiry into the Scheme of Out-of-work Donation.** *Interim report.* London: H.M.S.O., 1919. (Cmd. 196.)
Final report. 1919. (Cmd. 305.)
Evidence. 1919. (Cmd. 407.)
Chairman: Lord Aberconway.

14,108 *National health and unemployment insurance: complete information for the employer.* Liverpool: H. T. Woodrow, 1920. 78p.

14,109 **Departmental Committee on Approved Societies' Administration Allowance.** *Reports.* London: H.M.S.O., 1921. iii, 20p. (Cmd. 1291.)
Chairman: Sir Walter S. Kinnear.

14,110 **Daily News.** *National health and unemployment insurance: the schemes popularly explained.* London: *Daily News*, 1922. 32p.

14,111 **Inter-Departmental Committee on Health and Unemployment Insurance.** *First and second interim reports.* London: H.M.S.O., 1922. 10p. (Cmd. 1644.)

Chairman: Alfred W. Watson.

First interim report. *Grant towards administration expenses of associations under Section 17 of the Unemployment Insurance Act, 1920.*

Second interim report. *Possibility of introducing combined card for health and unemployment insurance contributions in July 1922.*

Third interim report. Reduction of administrative expenses. 1923. 11p. (Cmd. 1821.)

14,112 **Beveridge,** *Sir* William Henry. *Insurance for all and everything.* London: *Daily News*, 1924. 40p. ('The new way' series 7.)

14,113 **Cohen,** Joseph Lewis. *Social insurance unified, and other essays.* London: King, 1924. 157p.

14,114 **Gordon,** Alban. *Social insurance: what it is and what it might be.* London: Fabian Society, Allen and Unwin, 1924. x, 150p.

14,115 **Inter-Departmental Committee on the Co-ordination of Administrative and Executive Arrangements for the Grant of Assistance from Public Funds on Account of Sickness, Destitution and Unemployment.** *Report.* London: H.M.S.O., 1924. 167p. (Cmd. 2011.)

Chairman: H. B. Betterton.

14,116 **Daily News.** *National health and unemployment insurance.* London: 'Daily News', 1925. 48p.

14,117 **Inter-Departmental Committee on Migration and Social Insurance.** *Report.* London: H.M.S.O., 1926. 32p. (Cmd. 2608.)

Chairman: Sir Donald Maclean.

14,118 **Ormerod,** James Redman. *National insurance: its inherent defects.* London, 1930. 46p.

14,119 **Dearnley,** Irvine Hubert. *The 'needs test' for unemployment insurance, transitional payments and public assistance.* London: Shaw, 1931. 6, 62p.

14,120 **Emanuel,** Montague Rousseau. *Insurance; chapter on national health insurance and pensions, by B. A. Harwood.* London: Virtue, 1933. xxxi, 523p.

Second edition of *Insurance: law, theory and practice.* London: Virtue, 1931. xxvii, 556p.

Third edition. 1935. xxxii, 544p.

Fourth edition. 1936. xxxii, 576p.

14,121 **Exley,** C. H. *The guide to the law and administration of the needs test.* Liverpool: Meek, Thomas, 1933. 86p.

14,122 **International Labour Office.** 'Operation of laws providing benefits in case of injury, sickness, old age, and death in Great Britain.' *Int. Labour Rev.*, XXIX, 1 (January 1934), 108–15.

14,123 **Political and Economic Planning.** 'How to build up social security.' *Planning*, 50 (7 May 1935), 3–12.

14,124 **Political and Economic Planning.** 'What are the social services?' *Planning*, 64 (17 December 1935), 1–14.

14,125 **Warburton,** Edward and **Butler,** Carl. *'Disallowed': the tragedy of the means test.* London: Wishart, 1935. vii, 160p.

14,126 **Gibbon,** *Sir* Gwilym. 'The public social services.' *R. Statist. Soc. J.*, C, 4 (1937), 495–545.

Discussion, p. 546–57.

'Read before the Royal Statistical Society, May 24th, 1937.'

14,127 **Political and Economic Planning.** 'Industrial assurance criticised.' *Planning*, V, 104 (27 July 1937), 1–14.

14,128 **Political and Economic Planning.** *The report on the British social services: a survey of the existing public social services in Great Britain with proposals for future development.* London: P.E.P., 1937. 210p.

14,129 **Stevens,** *Sir* Bertram Sydney Barnsdale. *Contributory health and pensions insurance in Great Britain: report.* Sydney, 1937. 20p. (New South Wales parliamentary papers. Session 1937–38. Vol. 5.)

14,130 **Kulp,** C. A. *Social insurance coordination: an analysis of German and British organization.* Washington, D.C., 1938. xiv, 333p.

14,131 **Sakmann,** Marianne. *Unemployment and health insurance in Great Britain, 1911–1937.* Washington, D.C.: U.S.G.P.O., 1938. v, 44p. (U.S. Social Security Board. Bureau of Research and Statistics. Bureau report 3.)

14,132 **Ford,** Percy. *Incomes, means tests and personal responsibility.* London: King, 1939. ix, 86p.

14,133 **Waldheim,** Harald von. 'War policy of the British and German social insurance schemes.' *Publ. Adm.*, XIX, 1 (January 1941), 36–50.

14,134 **Harris,** Richard William. *How do I stand in regard to national health insurance? unemployment benefit and allowances? and old age and widows' pensions?* London: Wells Gardner, 1942. 158p.

14,135 **Hennock,** E. P. 'Social security: a system emerges.' *New Soc.*, XI, 284 (7 March 1968), 336–8. (The origins of the social services 6.)

4. The Beveridge Report

14,136 **Beveridge,** *Sir* William Henry. *Social insurance and allied services: the Beveridge Report in brief.* London, 1942. 63p.

14,137 **Cole,** George Douglas Howard. *Beveridge explained: what the Beveridge Report on social security means.* London: *New Statesman and Nation*, 1942. 48p.

14,138 **Fabian Society.** Social Security Sub-

Committee. *Social security: evidence submitted to the Interdepartmental Committee on Social Insurance and Allied Services.* London: Fabian Society, 1942. 28p.

14,139 **Gibbon,** *Sir* Gwilym. 'The Beveridge Report.' *R. Statist. Soc. J.*, CV, 4 (1942), 336–40.

14,140 **Hill,** Walter. 'Great Britain's social services.' *Banker*, LXIV, 203 (December 1942), 139–44.
On cover: 'Background to Beveridge'.

14,141 **Industrial Life Offices' Association.** *The Beveridge Report: preliminary observations of the industrial life offices.* London: the Association, 1942. 16p.

14,142 **Inter-Departmental Committee on Social Insurance and Allied Services.** *Social insurance and allied services: report by Sir William Beveridge.* London: H.M.S.O., 1942. 299p. (Cmd. 6404.)
Appendix G. Memoranda from organisations. (Cmd. 6405.)

14,143 **National Council of Women of Great Britain.** *Memorandum for submission to the Interdepartmental Committee on Social Insurance and Allied Services.* 1942. 9p.

14,144 **Political and Economic Planning.** 'Planning for social security.' *Planning*, 190 (14 July 1942), 1–52.

14,145 **Treasury.** *Social insurance and allied services: the Beveridge Report in brief.* London: H.M.S.O., 1942.

14,146 **Hicks,** John Richard and **Hicks,** Ursula K. 'The Beveridge Plan and local government finance.' *Manchr. Statist. Soc. Trans.* (1942–43). 36p.

14,147 **Abbott,** Edith and **Bompas,** K. *The woman citizen and social security: a criticism of the . . . Beveridge Report.* London, 1943. 20p.

14,148 **Beveridge,** *Sir* William Henry. 'Four questions on the Plan.' *The pillars of security, and other war-time essays and addresses.* London: Allen and Unwin, 1943. p. 76–8.
'Points from Address at Savoy Hotel, 9th December, 1942.'

14,149 **Beveridge,** *Sir* William Henry. 'The Government proposals and the Beveridge Report.' *The pillars of security, and other war-time essays and addresses.* London: Allen and Unwin, 1943. p. 126–37.
First published *Observer*, 24 February and 7 March, *Daily Herald*, 1 and 8 March, 1943.

14,150 **Beveridge,** *Sir* William Henry. 'Plan for social security.' *The pillars of security, and other war-time essays and addresses.* London: Allen and Unwin, 1943. p. 53–8.
'Radio Address, 2nd December, 1942.'

14,151 **Beveridge,** *Sir* William Henry. 'Social security: some trans-Atlantic comparisons.' *R. Statist. Soc. J.*, CVI, 4 (1943), 305–21.
Discussion, p. 322–32.
'Read before the Royal Statistical Society, October 12th, 1943.'

14,152 **Beveridge,** *Sir* William Henry. 'Social security and social policy.' *The pillars of security, and other war-time essays and addresses.* London: Allen and Unwin, 1943. p. 138–50.
'Addresses under the auspices of the Liberal Party at Caxton Hall, 3rd March, 1943.'

14,153 **Beveridge,** *Sir* William Henry. 'Third time lucky? Summary of Report by Sir William Beveridge on social insurance and allied services.' *The pillars of security, and other war-time essays and addresses.* London: Allen and Unwin, 1943. p. 59–75.
The first appearance, as a whole, of the author's summary of his Report. It appeared in part as an article in the February 1943 number of *Britain Today*, published by the British Council.

14,154 **British Institute of Public Opinion.** *The Beveridge Report and the public: what Britain thinks of the Beveridge Report, as shown by a Gallup Poll.* London: the Institute, 1943. 16p.

14,155 **Bunbury,** *Sir* Henry. 'Administration of the proposals in the Beveridge Report.' *Publ. Adm.*, XXI, 2 (July 1943), 80–2.
'An extract from an Address given at a Regional Meeting of the American Public Welfare Association, 7th March, 1943, and published in the April issue of *Public Welfare.*'

14,156 **Burns,** Eveline Mabel. 'The Beveridge Report.' *Am. Econ. Rev.*, XXXIII, 3 (September 1943), 512–33.

14,157 **Clarke,** Joan Simeon and **Coward,** L. E. (eds.). *Beveridge quiz.* London, 1943. 48p.

14,158 **Clarke,** Joan Simeon. *Social security.* London: Association for Education in Citizenship, 1943. 23p. (Unless we plan now 14.)

14,159 **Clarke,** R. W. B. 'The Beveridge Report and after.' Robson, W. A. *Social security.* London: Allen and Unwin for the Fabian Society, 1943. p. 272–327.
Second edition. 1945.
Third edition. 1948.

14,160 **Clarke,** R. W. B. 'Social security housekeeping.' Robson, W. A. (ed.). *Social security.* London: Allen and Unwin for the Fabian Society, 1943. p. 328–72.
Second edition. 1945.
Third edition. 1948.

14,161 **Cole,** George Douglas Howard. *The Beveridge plan: where are we now?* London: *New Statesman and Nation*, 1943. 15p.
Reprinted, with additions, from *New Statesman and Nation.*

14,162 **Cole,** George Douglas Howard. *Notes for a speech on the Beveridge Plan.* 1943. 7 leaves.
Mimeographed.
Prepared for the Social Security League.

14,163 **Communist Party of Great Britain.** *Memorandum on the Beveridge Report and what must be done.* London, 1943. 26p.

14,164 **Davison**, *Sir* Ronald Conway. *Insurance for all and everything: a plain account and a discussion of the Beveridge Plan.* London: Longmans, Green, 1943. 32p.

14,165 **Davison**, *Sir* Ronald Conway. *Social security: the story of British social progress and the Beveridge Plan.* London: Harrap, 1943. 62p.

14,166 **Fabian Society.** Social Security Sub-Committee. 'Memorandum of evidence submitted to the Beveridge Committee.' Robson, W. A. (ed.). *Social security.* London: Allen and Unwin for the Fabian Society, 1943. Appendix. p. 406–34.

14,167 **Kaldor**, Nicholas. 'The Beveridge Report. II. The financial burden.' *Econ. J.*, LIII, 209 (April 1943), 10–27.

14,168 **Kaldor**, Nicholas. 'The economic implications of the Beveridge plan.' Kaldor, N., and others. *Planning for abundance.* London: National Peace Council, 1943. (Peace aims pamphlet 21.) p. 22–8.

14,169 **Kalecki**, Michael. 'The economic implications of the Beveridge Plan.' *Oxf. Univ. Inst. Statist. Bull.*, v, Supplement 4 (20 February 1943), 2–7.

14,170 **Labour Party**. *Beveridge Report: summary of principles and proposals.* London, 1943. 16p.

14,171 **Labour Research Department.** *Beveridge Report: industrial assurance.* London: L.R.D., 1943. 32p.

14,172 **Labour Research Department.** *Beveridge Report: what it means; a brief and clear analysis showing how it affects various sections, what changes it proposes, its financial basis.* London: L.R.D., 1943. 16p.

14,173 **Mass-Observation.** 'Social security and parliament.' *Polit. Q.*, XIV, 3 (July–September 1943), 245–55.

Attitudes to the Beveridge Report, etc.

14,174 **National Federation of Employees' Approved Societies.** *The Beveridge Report on the social insurance and allied services: memorandum.* London, 1943. 23p.

14,175 **Nicholson**, John Leonard. 'The benefits and costs of the Beveridge Plan.' *Oxf. Univ. Inst. Statist. Bull.*, v, Supplement 4 (20 February 1943), 7–18.

14,176 **Nisbet**, J. W. *The Beveridge Plan: a symposium.* London: Society of Individualists, 1943. 55p. (Post-war questions.)

14,177 **Owen**, Arthur David Kemp. 'The Beveridge Report. I. Its proposals.' *Econ. J.*, LIII, 209 (April 1943), 1–9.

14,178 **Owen**, Arthur David Kemp. 'From Poor Law to Beveridge Report.' *Foreign Aff.*, XXI, 4 (July 1943), 743–55.

Chiefly since 1834.

14,179 **Pakenham**, F. 'The Beveridge Report: some reflections.' *Dublin Rev.*, CCXII (January 1943), 21–31.

14,180 **Political and Economic Planning.** 'After the Beveridge Report.' *Planning*, 205 (20 April 1943), 1–21.

14,181 **Pollard**, Robert Spence Watson. *Beveridge in brief.* London, 1943. 42p.

14,182 **Robson**, William Alexander. 'The Beveridge Report: an evaluation.' *Polit. Q.*, XIV, 2 (April–June 1943), 150–63.

14,183 **Robson**, William Alexander. 'Introduction: present principles.' Robson, W. A. (ed.). *Social security.* London: Allen and Unwin for the Fabian Society, 1943. p. 9–34.

Second edition. 1945.

Third edition. 1948.

14,184 **Robson**, William Alexander (ed.). *Social security.* London: Allen and Unwin for the Fabian Society, 1943. 447p.

Second edition. 1945. 472p.

Third edition. 1948. 475p.

14,185 **Saxton**, Clifford Clive. *Beveridge Report criticised.* London: Harrap, 1943. 32p.

14,186 **Scheu**, F. J. *Labor and the Beveridge plan.* New York, 1943. 128p.

14,187 **Singer**, Hans Wolfgang. *Can we afford 'Beveridge'?* London: Gollancz, Fabian Publications, 1943. 21p. (Research series 72.)

14,188 **Socialist Party of Great Britain.** *Beveridge re-organises poverty.* London, [1943?]. 20p.

14,189 **Society to Promote Human Equality.** 'The Beveridge Report.' *Human Equality*, 32 (February 1943), 3–8; 33 (May 1943), 2–5.

14,190 **Stewart**, M. C. 'Industrial assurance.' *Oxf. Univ. Inst. Statist. Bull.*, v, Supplement 4 (20 February 1943), 18–24.

14,191 **Summers**, Spencer and **Beveridge**, *Sir* William Henry. 'Finance of the Beveridge Report: questions and answers.' Beveridge, *Sir* W. H. *The pillars of security, and other war-time essays and addresses.* London: Allen and Unwin, 1943. p. 117–25.

Questions by S. Summers; answers by Sir William Beveridge.

14,192 **Watt**, Lewis. *A Catholic view of the Beveridge Plan.* Oxford: Catholic Social Guild, 1943. 24p.

14,193 **Williams**, Gertrude. 'Finance of the social services.' Robson, W. A. (ed.). *Social security.* London: Allen and Unwin for the Fabian Society, 1943. p. 213–38.

Second edition. 1945.

Third edition. 1948.

14,194 **Wootton**, Barbara. 'Before and after Beveridge.' *Polit. Q.*, XIV, 4 (October–December 1943), 357–63.

14,195 **Bailey**, Jack. *How the Beveridge Plan will help women.* Manchester: Co-operative Union, 1944. 20p.

14,196 **Beveridge**, *Sir* William Henry. *Beveridge on Beveridge: recent speeches of Sir William Beveridge.* London: Social Security League, 1944. 40p.

Edited by Joan S. Clarke.

14,197 **Clarke**, Joan Simeon. *Social security guide: the White Paper and the Beveridge Report compared.* London: Social Security League, 1944. 16p.

14,198 **National Deposit Friendly Society.** *Social security: a voluntary friendly society's comments on the Beveridge Report.* London, 1944. 16p.

14,199 **Nicholson**, John Leonard. 'The government's plans for social insurance.' *Oxf. Univ. Inst. Statist. Bull.*, VI, 15 (4 November 1944), 241–9.
Discusses Cmd. 6550 and Cmd. 6551.

14,200 **Palmer**, H. Cecil. *The debit side of the Beveridge Report.* London: Discussion Groups Association, 1944. 12p.

14,201 **Prain**, Alex M. *The Beveridge Report answered.* London, Glasgow: Collins, 1944. 14p.

14,202 **Smyth**, J. L. *Social security.* London: Odhams P., 1944. 24p. (Post war discussion pamphlets 1.)

14,203 **Social Security League.** *Social security guide: the White Paper and the Beveridge Report compared.* London, 1944. 18p.

14,204 **Wootton**, Barbara. *Social security and the Beveridge Plan.* London, 1944. 16p. (Common Wealth popular library 4.)

14,205 **Beveridge,** *Sir* William Henry. 'Summary of the Report on Social Insurance and Allied Services.' *Hlth. Soc. Welf.* (1944–45), 36–46.

14,206 **Beveridge,** *Sir* William Henry. *Contributions for social insurance: a reconsideration of rates.* 1945.
Reprinted from *The Times.*

14,207 **Beveridge,** *Sir* William Henry. *Power and influence.* London: Hodder and Stoughton, 1953. xi, 447p.
An autobiography.

14,208 **Beveridge**, Janet, Baroness Beveridge. *Beveridge and his plan.* London: Hodder and Stoughton, 1954. 239p.

14,209 **Moos**, Siegfried. 'A pioneer of social advance: William Henry Beveridge, 1879–1963.' *Durham Univ. J.*, LVI, 1 (December 1963), 2–13.
Reprinted. Durham: University of Durham, Department of Social Studies, 1963. 13p.

14,210 **George**, V. *Social security: Beveridge and after.* London: Routledge and Kegan Paul; New York: Humanities P., 1968. xiv, 258p.

5. Post-Beveridge Developments

This section includes general works relating primarily to the post-1945 period. General historical accounts of the development of the welfare state and textbooks on social administration are classified in Part Seven, IX, A, 1.

14,211 **Griggs**, C. H. *White Paper on social insurance. Part 1. Administration of benefits by approved societies.* London, 1944. 8p.

14,212 **House of Commons.** *Social insurance and industrial injury insurance: debates on the government's White Papers in the House of Commons.* London: Conservative and Unionist Party Organisation, 1944. 30p.

14,213 **Labour Party.** *Preliminary observations on the government White Paper on social insurance, workmen's compensation and a national health service.* London, 1944. 11p.

14,214 **Labour Research Department.** *Social insurance: the government plan explained, compared with 'Beveridge' and with present practices.* London: L.R.D., 1944. 19p.

14,215 **Office of the Minister of Reconstruction.** *Social insurance.* London: H.M.S.O., 1944. 2 pts.
Part I. 64p. (Cmd. 6550). Sets out the government's proposals for social insurance generally.
Part II. *Workmen's compensation: proposals for an industrial injury insurance scheme.* 31p. (Cmd. 6551.)

14,216 **Office of the Minister of Reconstruction.** *Social insurance, including industrial injury insurance: brief guide to the government's plan.* London: H.M.S.O., 1944. 31p.

14,217 **Arman**, F. Marcus. 'National insurance and national assistance local offices.' *Publ. Adm.*, XXIII, 4 (Winter 1945), 125–37.
'This article attempts to forecast and discuss the administration of those services for which the Minister of National Insurance will be responsible to Parliament.'

14,218 **Lafitte**, François. *Britain's way to social security.* London: Pilot P., 1945. 110p. (Target for to-morrow series.)

14,219 **National Union of Conservative and Constitutional Associations.** Central Committee on Post-War Reconstruction. *The national insurance plan.* London, 1945. 19p.

14,220 **Newman**, Tom Seth. *Guide to the government's proposals for a national health service.* London: Hearts of Oak Benefit Society, 1945. 20p.

14,221 **Newman**, Tom Seth. *Guide to the government's proposals for national insurance.* London: Hearts of Oak Benefit Society, 1945. 31p.

14,222 **Newman**, Tom Seth. *The story of friendly societies and social security, past, present and future.* London: Hearts of Oak Benefit Society, 1945. 40p.

14,223 **Political and Economic Planning.** 'Forward to social security.' *Planning*, 232 (23 March 1945), 1–16.

14,224 **Booker**, H. S. 'Lady Rhys Williams' proposals for the amalgamation of direct taxation with social insurance.' *Econ. J.*, LVI, 222 (June 1946), 230–43.
On her book *Something to look forward to* (London: Macdonald, 1943). Her proposals are here compared with those in the Beveridge Report.

14,225 **Industrial Law Review.** [Special issue on national insurance.] I, 3 (August 1946).

14,226 **Labour Party.** *A guide to the National Insurance Act, 1946.* London, 1946. 35p.

By Alban Gordon and others.

14,227 **Northern Ireland.** *National Insurance Bill (Northern Ireland): explanatory memorandum by the Ministry of Labour and National Insurance.* Belfast: H.M.S.O., 1946. 11p. (Cmd. 237.)

14,228 **Potter,** Douglas Charles Loftus. *The National Insurance Act, 1946.* London: Butterworth, 1946. v, 269p.

With general introduction and annotations.

Reprinted from *Butterworths' emergency legislation service.*

Second edition. *National insurance.* By D. C. L. Potter and D. H. Stansfield. 1949. xix, 553p.

14,229 **Gazdar,** John. *National insurance.* London: Stevens, 1947. ix, 74p.

Second edition. 1949. vii, 96p. (This is the law.)

14,230 **Lesser,** Henry. 'Some practical aspects of supplementary benefit schemes.' *Ind. Law Rev.*, II, 5 (October 1947), 127–35.

14,231 **Lesser,** Henry. 'Supplementary schemes under Section 27 of the National Insurance Act.' *Ind. Law Rev.*, II, 3 (August 1947), 64–70.

14,232 **Levy,** Hermann Joachim. 'Sociology and health.' *Ind. Law Rev.*, II, 6 (November 1947), 140–57.

An abstract of three lectures delivered at a Summer School at Oxford organized by the Central Council for Health Education.

14,233 **Ministry of National Insurance.** *Absorption of staffs of approved societies: statement by the Minister of National Insurance and interim report of a Staffing Advisory Committee.* London: H.M.S.O., 1947. 30p.

Chairman: A. G. Lee.

14,234 **Newman,** Tom Seth. *Digest of British social insurance ... national insurance, industrial insurance, family allowances.* London: Stone and Cox, 1947. xxx, 322p.

Supplements. 1947– .

14,235 **Allen,** W. P. 'The system of social insurance.' Tracey, H. (ed.). *The British Labour Party: its history, growth, policy, and leaders.* London: Caxton Publishing Co., 1948. Vol. 2. p. 95–107.

14,236 **Ball,** Frank Norman. *National insurance and industrial injuries.* Leigh-on-Sea: Thames Bank Publishing Co., 1948. xvi, 508p.

With the text of the Ministry of National Insurance Act, 1944; the Family Allowances Act, 1945; the National Insurance–Industrial Injuries–Act, 1946, and the National Insurance Act, 1946, and comments upon them.

14,237 **Gibbs,** Edmund Reginald. *National insurance and social service for everyman.* Oxford: Pen-in-Hand, 1948. 69p. (Everyman's guide series 2.).

14,238 **Industrial Law Review.** 'Index of national insurance.' *Ind. Law Rev.*, III, I (July 1948), 20–81.

A guide to the national insurance scheme.

14,239 **Lafitte,** François. *Social insurance: the national scheme.* London: Bureau of Current Affairs, 1948. 20p. (Current affairs 57.)

14,240 **National Insurance Advisory Committee.** *National Insurance Act, 1946: report on the insurance of share fishermen under that Act.* London: H.M.S.O., 1948. 12p. (H.C. 137.)

Seasonal workers. 1949. 14p. (H.C. 262.)

Seasonal workers. 1952. 25p. (Cmd. 8558.)

Time limits. 1952. 20p. (Cmd. 8483.)

Entertainment industry. 1952. 21p. (Cmd. 8549.)

Hospital in-patients. 1952. 14p. (Cmd. 8600.)

Credits for training courses. 1953. 12p. (Cmd. 8860.)

Availability question. 1953. 24p. (Cmd. 8894.)

Liability for contributions of persons with small incomes. 1955. 21p. (Cmd. 9432.)

14,241 *The new national health and insurance schemes explained.* London: Dawn P., 1948. 31p. (Dawn Press survey 2.)

14,242 **Newman,** Tom Seth. *News Chronicle guide to national insurance as affecting married women.* London: *News Chronicle* Publications Department, 1948. 40p.

14,243 **Owen,** David. *News Chronicle guide to the National Insurance Act, 1946.* London: *News Chronicle* Publications Department, 1948. 32p.

Revised edition. 1949. 48p.

14,244 **Willcock,** H. D. *The 'Family guide to the National Insurance Scheme'.* [London], 1948. i, 44p. (Social Survey N.S. 121.)

'An inquiry made by the Social Survey for the Ministry of National Insurance.'

14,245 **Willoughby,** Gertrude. 'Social security in France and Britain.' *Polit. Q.*, XIX, I (January–March 1948), 49–59.

14,246 **Bayne,** A. W. 'The principles of social insurance.' King, F. C. (ed.). *Public administration in Ireland.* Vol. II. Dublin: Parkside P., 1949. p. 236–46.

14,247 **Eire.** Department of Social Welfare. *The welfare plan: Ireland's new social security proposals at-a-glance.* Dublin: Stationery Office, 1949. 23p.

14,248 **Eire.** Department of Social Welfare. *White Paper containing government proposals for social security.* Dublin: Stationery Office, 1949. 66p. (K. 54.)

14,249 **Peacock,** Alan Turner. 'The national insurance funds.' *Economica*, n.s., XVI, 63 (August 1949), 228–42.

14,250 **Rhodes**, Harold Vale. *Setting up a new government department: an account of the formation of the Ministry of National Insurance.* London: British Institute of Management, 1949. 47p. (Occasional papers 3.)

14,251 **Wootton**, Barbara. 'Record of the Labour Government in the social services.' *Polit. Q.*, xx, 2 (April–June 1949), 101–12.

14,252 **Wunderlich**, Frieda. 'New trends in social insurance.' *Soc. Res.*, xvi, 1 (March 1949), 31–44.

14,253 **Statistical and Social Inquiry Society of Ireland.** 'Symposium on social security.' *Statist. Soc. Inq. Soc. Ir. J.* (1949–50), 247–69.

14,254 **Lewis**, Barbara and **Condie**, R. H. B. 'The British social security program.' *J. Polit.*, xii, 2 (May 1950), 323–47.

14,255 **Newman**, Tom Seth and **Davies**, William Tudor. *National Insurance Acts: tribunals.* London: Stone and Cox, 1950. 23p.

14,256 **Oades**, B. C. 'The Ministry of National Insurance.' Milward, G. E. (ed.). *Large-scale organisations: a first-hand account of the day-to-day organisation and management of large industrial undertakings and public services.* London: Macdonald and Evans for the Institute of Public Administration, 1950. p. 34–50.

14,257 **Peacock**, Alan Turner. 'National insurance and economic policy.' *Banker*, xcv, 299 (December 1950), 373–8.

14,258 **Clancy**, T. J. *Social security and Ireland.* 1950–51. (M. Econ. Sc. thesis, National University of Ireland.)

14,259 **Burns**, Eveline Mabel. 'Social security in a period of full employment.' Industrial Relations Research Association. *Proceedings of the fourth annual meeting, December 1951.* p. 240–52.
Discussion, p. 253–60.

14,260 **Marsh**, David Charles. *National insurance and assistance in Great Britain.* London: Pitman, 1950 [i.e. 1951]. xii, 187p.

14,261 **Ministry of National Insurance.** *National insurance scheme: proposed changes.* London: H.M.S.O., 1951. 4p. (Cmd. 8208.)

14,262 **Gazdar**, John. 'National insurance: a survey.' *Ind. Law Rev.*, vi, 3 (January 1952), 178–86.

14,263 **Harrison**, Enid. 'The work of the National Insurance Advisory Committee.' *Publ. Adm.*, xxx, 2 (Summer 1952), 149–58.

14,264 **Palmer**, C. *The British Socialist ill-fare state: an examination of its political, social, moral, and economic consequences.* Caldwell, Idaho: Caxton Printers, 1952. xxxviii, 618p.

14,265 **Peacock**, Alan Turner. *The economics of national insurance.* London: Hodge, 1952. 126p.

14,266 **Political and Economic Planning.** 'Poverty ten years after Beveridge.' *Planning*, xix, 344 (4 August 1952), 21–40.

14,267 **Abel-Smith**, Brian. *The reform of social security.* London: Fabian Publications, Gollancz, 1953. 41p. (Research series 161.)

14,268 **Hagenbuch**, Walter. 'The rationale of the social services.' *Lloyds Bank Rev.*, n.s., 29 (July 1953), 1–16.

14,269 **Ministry of National Insurance.** National Insurance Advisory Committee. *The availability question: report.* London: H.M.S.O., 1953. 24p. (Cmd. 8894.)

14,270 **Powell**, John Enoch. 'Conservatives and social services.' *Polit. Q.*, xxiv, 2 (April–June 1953), 156–66.

14,271 **Treasury**. *The Ministry of Pensions: proposed transfer of functions.* London: H.M.S.O., 1953. 11p. (Cmd. 8842.)

14,272 **Vandyk**, Neville D. 'The Minister of National Insurance as a judicial authority.' *Publ. Adm.*, xxxi, 4 (Winter 1953), 331–43.

14,273 **Vandyk**, Neville D. 'National insurance adjudication.' *Ind. Law Rev.*, vii, 3 (January 1953), 176–85.

14,274 **Wootton**, Barbara. 'The Labour Party and social services.' *Polit. Q.*, xxiv, 1 (January–March 1953), 55–67.

14,275 **Jenkins**, E. *The constitution, working and practice of administrative tribunals under the National Insurance and Industrial Injuries Acts, 1946.* 1953–54. (Ph.D. thesis, University of London.)

14,276 **Crew**, F. A. E. 'The welfare state: a eugenic appraisal.' *Eug. Rev.*, xlvi, 2 (July 1954), 81–90.

14,277 **Mendelsohn**, Ronald S. *Social security in the British Commonwealth: Great Britain, Canada, Australia, New Zealand.* London: Athlone P., 1954. xv, 391p.
See also: 13,398.

14,278 **O'Sullivan**, J. J. 'The new social welfare scheme.' King, F. C. (ed.). *Public administration in Ireland.* Vol. iii. Dublin: Civics Institute of Ireland, 1954. p. 129–47.

14,279 **Peacock**, Alan Turner and **Browning**, P. R. 'The social services in Great Britain and the redistribution of income.' Peacock, A. T. (ed.). *Income redistribution and social policy: a set of studies.* London: Cape, 1954. p. 139–77.

14,280 **Political and Economic Planning.** 'Social security: lessons from America.' *Planning*, xx, 370 (13 September 1954), 217–31.

14,281 **Safford**, Archibald. 'The creation of case law under the National Insurance and National Insurance (Industrial Injuries) Acts.' *Mod. Law Rev.*, xvii, 3 (May 1954), 197–210.
'A University of London special Lecture in Law delivered at the London School of Economics and Political Science on October 27, 1953.'

14,282 **Vaizey**, John Ernest. *The cost of social services*. London: Fabian Publications, 1954. 24p. (Fabian research series 166.)

14,283 **Vandyk**, Neville D. 'The National Insurance Advisory Committee and national insurance regulations: a further note.' *Ind. Law Rev.*, IX, 1 (July 1954), 34–43.

14,284 **Vandyk**, Neville D. 'The national Insurance Advisory Committee and time limits for claims.' *Ind. Law Rev.*, VIII, 3 (January 1954), 203–14.

14,285 **Walker**, David. 'National insurance contributions, 1946–1955.' *Manchr. Sch.*, XXIII, 3 (September 1955), 228–44.

14,286 **Sheridan**, L. A. 'National insurance adjudication.' *Statist. Soc. Inq. Soc. Ir. J.* (1955–56), 29–41.

14,287 **Sheridan**, L. A. 'Late national insurance claims: cause for delay.' *Mod. Law Rev.*, XIX, 4 (July 1956), 341–64.

14,288 **Basuraychaudhuri**, Nirmalchandra. *Some aspects of the welfare state in Britain and India*. 1956–57. (Ph.D. thesis, University of London.)

14,289 **International Labour Office.** *Systems of social security: Great Britain*. Geneva: I.L.O., 1957. xi, 73p.

Compiled by the Ministry of Pensions and National Insurance and the Ministry of Health.

14,290 **Political and Economic Planning.** 'Free trade and social security.' *Planning*, XXIII, 412 (15 July 1957), 141–55.

European Economic Community and the effects.

14,291 **Prentice**, R. E. 'National insurance.' Archer, P. (ed.). *Social welfare and the citizen*. Harmondsworth: Penguin, 1957. p. 24–45.

14,292 **Abel-Smith**, Brian. 'Social security.' Ginsberg, M. (ed.). *Law and opinion in England in the 20th century*. London: Stevens, 1959. p. 347–63.

14,293 **Halsbury**, Hardinge Stanley Giffard, *1st Earl*. *National insurance*. London: Butterworth, 1959. 27, 649–918p.

Reprint of the material on national insurance from Vol. 27 of *The laws of England*, third edition.

14,294 **Duff**, C. R. *A study of the provisions of the Welfare Services Act (Northern Ireland), 1949, and the Children and Young Persons Act (Northern Ireland), 1950*. 1959–60. (M.Sc. thesis, Queen's University, Belfast.)

14,295 **Hood**, Katherine. *Room at the bottom: national insurance in the welfare state*. London: Lawrence and Wishart, 1960. 72p.

14,296 **Utley**, H. W. *Administrative tribunals in the national insurance scheme*. 1960–61. (M.A. thesis, University of Hull.)

14,297 **Fogarty**, Michael Patrick. *Under-governed and over-governed*. London: Chapman, 1962. 135p.

14,298 **Abel-Smith**, Brian. 'Beveridge II: another viewpoint.' *New Soc.*, 22 (28 February 1963), 9–11.

14,299 **Burns**, Eveline Mabel. 'Social security in Britain: twenty years after Beveridge.' *Ind. Relat.*, II, 2 (February 1963), 15–32.

14,300 **Labour Party**. National Executive Committee. *New frontiers for social security: a statement of comprehensive and radical proposals for the reform of our social security services*. London, 1963. 19p.

14,301 **Ministry of Pensions and National Insurance**. *Proposed changes in the national insurance schemes*. London: H.M.S.O., 1963. (Cmnd. 1934.)

Earlier editions, 1957 (Cmnd. 295), 1960 (Cmnd. 1196).

14,302 **Reid**, Graham Livingstone. 'Social security in Britain and the Six.' *Banker*, CXIII, 448 (June 1963), 409–16.

14,303 **Seldon**, Arthur. 'Beveridge: 20 years after.' *New Soc.*, 20 (14 February 1963), 9–12.

14,304 **Stevenson**, J. *Social security in Northern Ireland, with special reference to a selected group of industries*. 1963–64. (Ph.D. thesis, Queen's University, Belfast.)

14,305 **Abel-Smith**, Brian. 'Social security.' Hall, P. G. (ed.). *Labour's new frontiers*. London: Deutsch, 1964. p. 119–29.

14,306 **Farley**, Desmond. *Social insurance and social assistance in Ireland*. Dublin: Institute of Public Administration, 1964. xii, 182p.

14,307 **Kaim-Caudle**, Peter Robert. *Social security in Ireland and Western Europe*. Dublin: Economic Research Institute, 1964. [iv], 48p. (Papers 20.)

14,308 **Ministry of Pensions and National Insurance.** *Memorandum on the National Insurance [etc.] Bill, 1964 and report by the Minister of Pensions and National Insurance on her review of the rates and amounts of national insurance benefit*. London: H.M.S.O., 1964. (Cmnd. 2518.)

14,309 **Hemming**, M. F. W. 'Social security in Britain and certain other countries.' *Natn. Inst. Econ. Rev.*, 33 (August 1965), 48–67.

14,310 **Howe**, Geoffrey. *In place of Beveridge*. London: Conservative Political Centre, 1965. (Conservative new tasks 8.)

14,311 **Joseph**, *Sir* Keith Sinjohn. *A new strategy for social security*. London: Conservative Political Centre, 1966. 10p. ([Publications] 336.)

14,312 **Ministry of Social Security.** *Earnings-related short-term benefits and other proposed changes in the national insurance schemes*. London: H.M.S.O., 1966. 8p. (Cmnd. 2887.)

14,313 **Noble Lowndes Group.** *Social security and pension practice in Western Europe*. London: Noble Lowndes and Partners, 1966. 58p.

Third edition.

14,314 **Paige**, Deborah C. and **Jones**, Kit. *Health and welfare services in Britain in 1975*. London: Cambridge U.P., 1966. ix, 142p.

14,315 **Ministry of Social Security.** *Memorandum on the National Insurance (No. 2) Bill*. London: H.M.S.O., 1967. 10p. (Cmnd. 3320.)

14,316 **Wedderburn**, Dorothy. 'How adequate are our cash benefits?' *New Soc.*, x, 263 (12 October 1967), 512–16.

14,317 **Fabian Society.** *Social services for all?* London: the Society, 1968. 4 pts. (Fabian tracts 382, 383, 384, 385.)

14,318 **O'Higgins**, Paul. 'Les problèmes juridiques relatifs à la fixation des prestations de la sécurité sociale, notamment en fonction des modifications du coût de la vie et des salaires: rapport national.' Congrès International de Droit du Travail et de la Sécurité Sociale, 6ième, Stockholm, 1966. *Actes*. Stockholm: Almqvist and Wiksell, 1968. Vol. 1. 5p.
Text in English.

14,319 **Rodgers**, Barbara. 'A new plan for social security.' *New Soc.*, xii, 316 (17 October 1968), 560–2.

14,320 **Atkinson**, A. B. *Poverty in Britain and the reform of social security*. London: Cambridge U.P., 1969. 224p. (University of Cambridge. Department of Applied Economics. Occasional paper 18.)

14,321 **Chambers**, *Sir* Paul. *Forward from Beveridge: the Beveridge memorial lecture, 1969, given at the Senate House, University of London on 20th March 1969*. London: Institute of Statisticians, 1969. 16p.

14,322 **Department of Health and Social Security.** *Explanatory memorandum on the National Superannuation and Social Insurance Bill 1969*. London: H.M.S.O., 1969. 28p. (Cmnd. 4222.)

14,323 **Department of Health and Social Security.** *Memorandum on the National Insurance (No. 2) Bill 1969*. London: H.M.S.O., 1969. 15p. (Cmnd. 4076.)

14,324 **Department of Health and Social Security.** *National superannuation and social insurance: proposals for earnings-related social security*. London: H.M.S.O., 1969. 64p. (Cmnd. 3883.)

14,325 **Department of Health and Social Security.** *Social insurance: proposals for earnings-related short-term and invalidity benefits*. London: H.M.S.O., 1969. 20p. (Cmnd. 4124.)

14,326 **Government Actuary.** *National Insurance (No. 2) Bill 1969. Report by the Government Actuary on the financial provisions of the Bill*. London: H.M.S.O., 1969. 12p. (Cmnd. 4074.)

14,327 **Government Actuary.** *National Superannuation and Social Insurance Bill 1969. Report by the Government Actuary on the financial provisions of the Bill*. London: H.M.S.O., 1969. 36p. (Cmnd. 4223.)

14,328 **Christopher**, Anthony, **Polanyi**, George, **Seldon**, Arthur and **Shenfield**, Barbara. *Policy for poverty: a study of the urgency of reform in social benefits and of the advantages and limitations of a reverse income tax in replacement of the existing structure of state benefits*. London: Institute of Economic Affairs, 1970. 95p. (Research monographs 20.)

14,329 **Confederation of British Industry.** *Earnings-related social security: the National Superannuation and Social Insurance Bill*. London: C.B.I., 1970. 25p.

B. PARTICULAR ASPECTS

Many of the works included in Part Seven, IX, A also contain material on the particular aspects of social security classified below. See also Part Three, II; and Part Three, III, G, 6.

1. Unemployment Benefit

See also Part Three, III, F, 4; Part Six, II, D; Part Six, IV, A, 4, d; Part Six, IV, C, 4; and Part Seven, IV, B.

14,330 **Board of Supervision (Scotland).** *Unemployed (Scotland): report by the Board of Supervision to Her Majesty's Secretary for Scotland, on the measures taken by the local authorities of the principal centres of population of Scotland, for the relief of the ablebodied unemployed during the winter of 1893–94*. London: H.M.S.O., 1894. 74p. (C. 7410.)

14,331 **London Reform Union.** *Report on the unemployed*. London: the Union, [1896]. 7p. (Pamphlet 75.)

14,332 **Clay**, *Sir* Arthur Temple Felix. *The unemployed and legislation*. London, [190–]. 13p.

14,333 **Clay**, *Sir* Arthur Temple Felix. 'The unemployed and the Unemployed Workmen Act.' *Mon. Rev.*, xxi, 63 (December 1905), 78–102.

14,334 **Lees-Smith**, Hastings Bertrand. 'The Unemployed Workmen Bill.' *Econ. J.*, xv, 58 (June 1905), 248–54.
Discussion of the Bill.

14,335 *Unemployed Workmen Act, 1905 (5 Edw. 7, c.18), and the orders issued by the Local Government Board thereunder, with the explanatory circulars and notes*. London: Shaw, 1905. 76p.

14,336 **Association of Municipal Corporations.** *Unemployed Workmen Act, 1905: summary of information received from towns as to number of applications and how dealt with*. London, 1906. [13]p.

14,337 **Bradshaw**, Lewis. *How to avoid the red peril of the unemployed; the Unemployed Act and its failure; the Labour Party and their new Bill; a criticism and an alternative*. Kettering: Northants Publishing Co., 1907. 32p.

14,338 **MacDonald**, James Ramsay. *The new unemployed Bill of the Labour Party*. London: Independent Labour Party, 1907. 15p.

14,339 **Beveridge**, William Henry. 'The Unemployed Workmen Act in 1906–7.' *Sociol. Rev.*, I, 1 (January 1908), 79–83.

Discussion of the Local Government Board's report on the administration of the Act.

14,340 **Dearle,** Norman Burrell. 'The working of the Unemployed Workmen Act, 1905, in relation to the London building trade.' *Econ. J.*, XVIII, 69 (March 1908), 101–10.

14,341 **Wallace**, Alfred Russel. 'The remedy for unemployment.' *Social. Rev.*, I (June 1908), 310–20; (July 1908), 390–400.

14,342 **Jones**, John Harry. 'The unemployed workmen Bill of the Labour Party.' *Lpool. Econ. Statist. Soc. Trans.* (1908–9), 9–18.

14,343 **Schloss**, David Frederick. *Insurance against unemployment*. London: King, 1909. x, 132p.

14,344 **Spender**, Harold. 'Unemployment insurance.' *Contemp. Rev.*, XCV (January 1909), 24–36.

14,345 **Gibbon**, Ioan Gwilym. 'Compulsory insurance against unemployment.' *Econ. J.*, XX, 78 (June 1910), 172–81.

14,346 **Llewellyn-Smith**, Hubert. 'Economic security and unemployment insurance.' *Econ. J.*, XX, 80 (December 1910), 513–29.

Part of the address given to the Economic Science and Statistics Section of the British Association for the Advancement of Science, Sheffield, 1910.

14,347 **Ashley**, William James. 'The National Insurance Bill. Part II. Unemployment.' *Econ. J.*, XXI, 82 (June 1911), 266–74.

14,348 **Gibbon**, Ioan Gwilym. *Unemployment insurance: a study of schemes of assisted insurance. A record of research in the Department of Sociology in the University of London*. London: King, 1911. xvii, 354p.

The author's D.Sc. (Econ.) thesis, University of London, 1911.

14,349 **Gibbon**, Ioan Gwilym. 'Unemployment insurance: the proposals of the government of the United Kingdom.' *Revue Internationale du Chômage*, I, 1 (Troisième Trimestre 1911), 131–44.

Published by l'Association Internationale pour la Lutte Contre la Chômage, Paris.

Opinions on the proposals: J. A. Hobson, p. 145–6; B. S. Rowntree and Bruno Lasker, p. 147–8.

14,350 **Lennard**, Reginald. 'The government's scheme for insurance against unemployment.' *Econ. J.*, XXI, 83 (September 1911), 335–45.

14,351 **London and District Right to Work Council.** *Lloyd George and unemployment insurance: an exposure of the unemployment proposals of the National Insurance Bill, and how it will affect the workers*. London: the Council, [1911?]. 8p.

14,352 **Unionist Social Insurance Committee.** *Insurance against loss of wages through unemployment*. London, 1911. 30p.

By L.W.E.

14,353 **Dawes**, James Arthur. *Unemployment insurance: part II of the National Insurance Act, 1911, indexed and classified*. London: Liberal Publications Department, 1912. 18p.

14,354 **Foerster**, Robert F. 'The British National Insurance Act.' *Q. J. Econ.*, XXVI, 2 (February 1912), 275–312.

14,355 **Porritt**, Edward. 'The British National Insurance Act.' *Polit. Sci. Q.*, XXVII, 2 (June 1912), 260–80.

14,356 **Bailward**, William Amyas. *Some impressions of the first six months' working of compulsory insurance against unemployment in England*. London, 1913. 16p.

14,357 **Beveridge**, William Henry. *Unemployment insurance. Proceedings of the Board of Trade under Part II of the National Insurance Act, 1911. First report, appendices*. London: H.M.S.O., 1913. viii, 82p. (Cd. 6965.)

14,358 **Bailward**, William Amyas. 'Some impressions of the first six months' working of compulsory insurance against unemployment in England.' *Char. Orgn. Rev.*, n.s., XXXV, 209 (May 1914), 246–60.

Prepared primarily for, but not delivered at, an International Congress on Unemployment at Ghent, 1913.

14,359 **Bailward**, William Amyas. 'Some impressions of the first six month's [*sic*] working of compulsory insurance against unemployment in England.' *Q. J. Int. Ass. Unempl.*, IV, 2 (April–June 1914), 489–98.

The author was Chairman of the Bethnal Green Board of Guardians, and Delegate of the London Charity Organisation Society.

14,360 **Beveridge**, William Henry and **Rey**, Charles Fernand. 'State unemployment insurance in the United Kingdom.' *Q. J. Int. Ass. Unempl.*, IV, 1 (January–March 1914), 136–87.

14,361 **Committee on Audit of Unemployment Benefit of Associations having arrangements under Section 106 of the National Insurance Act, 1911.** *Report*. London: H.M.S.O., 1916. (Cd. 8412.)

14,362 **Ministry of Labour.** *Interim report of the Committee of Inquiry into the scheme of out-of-work donation*. London: H.M.S.O., 1919. 6p. (Cmd. 196.)

Final report. 1919. 18p. (Cmd. 305.)

Evidence. 1919. (Cmd. 407.)

Chairman: Lord Aberconway.

14,363 **Daily News.** *The Unemployment Insurance Act, 1920: explanation and summary*. London, 1920. 16p.

14,364 **International Labour Office.** *British legislation on unemployment insurance.* Geneva: I.L.O., 1920. 15p. (Studies and reports, series C, 1.)

14,365 **Association of British Chambers of Commerce.** *Unemployment Insurance Act, 1920: report of meeting of representatives of Chambers of Commerce to consider the question of co-operation between the Chambers and the National Federation of Employees' Approved Societies in the administration of the Unemployment Insurance Act, 1920.* London, 1921. 8p.

14,366 **Cohen,** Joseph Lewis. *Insurance against unemployment, with special reference to British and American conditions.* London: King, 1921. 536p.

14,367 **Committee to Inquire into and Report upon the Extent to which the Unemployment Insurance Act might be made Applicable and Beneficial to Agricultural Workers.** *Report.* London: H.M.S.O., 1921. 18p. (Cmd. 1344.)
Chairman: R. Henry Rew.

14,368 **Lesser,** Henry. *Unemployment insurance with special reference to individual firms and industries.* London, 1921. 31p.

14,369 **Northcott,** Clarence Hunter. 'Unemployment relief measures in Great Britain.' *Polit. Sci. Q.*, XXXVI, 3 (September 1921), 420–32.

14,370 **Ministry of Labour.** *Report on the administration of Section 18 of the Unemployment Insurance Act, 1920 (special schemes of unemployment insurance by industries), and on the action taken with a view to investigating the possibility of developing unemployment insurance by industries.* London: H.M.S.O., 1922. 44p. (Cmd. 1613.)

14,371 **Northern Ireland.** Ministry of Labour. Committee of Enquiry on Unemployment Insurance and Employment Exchanges. *Interim report.* Belfast: H.M.S.O., 1922. 7p. (Cmd. 2.)
Final report. 19p. (Cmd. 11.)
Chairman: Major D. G. Shillington.

14,372 **Rowntree and Co., Ltd.** *Unemployment benefits: regulations.* York, 1922. 16p.

14,373 **Trades Union Congress** and **Labour Party.** *Unemployment insurance by industry.* London: National Joint Council, 1922. 32p.

14,374 *Unemployment insurance: report of a Committee on Ministerial Reductions under Section 17 (b) of the Unemployment Insurance Act, 1920, appointed at a Conference of societies administering under Section 17 of the Act, convened by the Amalgamated Union of Building Trade Workers, and held in London on 18 May 1922.* London: Twentieth Century P., 1922. 22p.

14,375 **Cohen,** Joseph Lewis. *Insurance by industry examined: an enquiry into the recent working of the British scheme of unemployment insurance and an examination of proposals which have been suggested to take its place.* London: King, 1923. 120p.

14,376 **Drage,** Geoffrey. 'The dole and demoralisation.' *Q. Rev.*, CCXL, 476 (July 1923), 183–204.
Review article on official documents.

14,377 **Ministry of Labour.** *Memorandum on the proposal to use unemployment benefits in aid of (a) wages on relief work, or (b) wages in industry.* London: H.M.S.O., 1923. 8p.

14,378 **Ministry of Labour.** Departmental Committee on Out-Workers in Relation to Unemployment Insurance. *Report.* London: H.M.S.O., 1923. 14p.
Chairman: Sir David James Shackleton.

14,379 **Trades Union Congress** and **Labour Party.** *The administration of the Unemployment Insurance Acts.* London: T.U.C. and Labour Party, 1923. 24p.

14,380 **Lyon,** Charles E. 'Financial aspects of unemployment in England.' *Ann. Am. Acad. Polit. Soc. Sci.*, CXI (January 1924), 363–71.

14,381 **Morley,** Felix. *Unemployment relief in Great Britain: a study in state socialism.* Boston, New York: Houghton, Mifflin, 1924. xviii, 203p. (Hart, Schaffner and Marx prize essays 38.)
Also London: Routledge, 1924. (Studies in economics and political science 77.) With a different title page.

14,382 **National Confederation of Employers' Organisations.** *Report on unemployment insurance, submitted to the Minister of Labour in reply to the Minister's letter to the Confederation dated 28 November 1922.* London, 1924. 30p.

14,383 **National Confederation of Employers' Organisations.** *Unemployment Insurance (No. 2) Bill, 1924: memorandum by the Confederation.* London, 1924. 8p.

14,384 **Astor,** John Jacob, and others. *Unemployment insurance in Great Britain: a critical examination.* London: Macmillan, 1925. 68p.
'By the authors of *The Third winter of unemployment* and *Is unemployment inevitable?*'
By a committee of J. J. Astor and others under the chairmanship of W. T. Layton.

14,385 **Milne-Bailey,** Walter. 'Work or maintenance.' Tracey, H. (ed.). *The book of the Labour Party: its history, growth, policy, and leaders.* London: Caxton Publishing Co., 1925. Vol. II. p. 107–31.

14,386 **Newman,** Tom Seth and **Lee,** A. G. *Guide to unemployment insurance.* London: *Daily News*, 1925. 47p.
Revised edition. London: Fleetgate Publications, 1929. 47p.

14,387 **Emmerson,** *Sir* Harold Corti and **Lascelles,** Edward Charles Ponsonby. *Guide to the Unemployment Insurance Acts.* London: Longmans, 1926. viii, 172p.
Revised and enlarged edition. 1928. x, 244p.
Third edition. 1930. viii, 262p.
Fourth edition. 1935. vi, 280p.
Fifth edition. 1939. vii, 292p.

14,388 **Labour Party.** *On the dole – or off! What to do with Britain's workless workers?* London: Labour Party, 1926. 32p.

Report on the prevention of unemployment by the Joint Committee representing the General Council of the Trades Union Congress, the National Executive Committee of the Labour Party, and the Executive Committee of the Parliamentary Labour Party.

14,389 **Ministry of Agriculture and Fisheries** and **Scottish Office.** *Report of the inter-departmental committee on agricultural unemployment insurance.* London: H.M.S.O., 1926. 107p.

Chairman: Sir R. Henry Rew.

14,390 **Northern Ireland.** *Unemployment insurance (agreement): memorandum explaining financial resolution.* Belfast: H.M.S.O., 1926. 6p. (Cmd. 57.)

14,391 **Petch,** Arthur William (comp.). *Unemployment Acts, 1920–1925: an explanatory memorandum.* Manchester, 1926. 23p.

14,392 **Trades Union Congress** and **Labour Party.** *Unemployment insurance: principles of labour policy.* London, [1926?]. 20p.

14,393 **Wolman,** Leo. *English experience with unemployment insurance.* New York, [1926?]. 15p.

14,394 **Beveridge,** *Sir* William Henry. 'Unemployment insurance in the war and after.' Hill, Sir N., and others. *War and insurance.* London: Humphrey Milford, Oxford U.P.; New Haven: Yale U.P., 1927. (Economic and social history of the world war. British series.) p. 229–50.

14,395 **Blundun,** P. Y. 'Administrative aspects of social insurance: unemployment insurance.' *Publ. Adm.*, v, 4 (October 1927), 358–72.

14,396 **International Association for Social Progress.** British Section. *Memorandum on unemployment insurance in Great Britain.* London: Co-operative Printing Society, 1927. 14p.

14,397 **Ministry of Labour.** Departmental Committee on Unemployment Insurance. *Report.* London: H.M.S.O., 1927.

Vol. I. *Report, appendices.* 96p.

Vol. II. *Minutes of evidence.*

Chairman: Lord Blanesburgh.

14,398 **Price,** J. F. G. 'Unemployment insurance.' *Publ. Adm.*, v, 3 (July 1927), 260–75.

'Paper read before the Institute of Public Administration on 20th January, 1927.'

The author was Principal Assistant Secretary, Ministry of Labour.

14,399 **Trades Union Congress.** National Joint Council. *Special national conference on unemployment insurance and the report of the Blanesburgh Committee.* London: T.U.C., 1927. 14p.

14,400 **Eire.** Committee on the Relief of Unemployment. *First interim report; Final report.* Dublin: Stationery Office, 1927, 1928. 27p.

Bound in one volume.

14,401 **Crew,** Albert. *The Unemployment Insurance Acts, 1920–1927.* London: Jordan, 1928. xvi, 195p.

Assisted by R. J. Blackham.

With the texts of the Acts.

Another edition. *The Unemployment Insurance Acts, 1920–1930.* London: Jordan, 1930. xviii, 220p.

Assisted by R. J. Blackham and Archibald Forman.

14,402 **Hannington,** Walter and **Llewelyn,** E. *How to get unemployment benefit.* London: National Unemployed Workers' Committee Movement, 1928. 11p.

14,403 **Departmental Committee on Procedure and Evidence for the Determination of Claims for Unemployment Insurance Benefit.** *Report.* London: H.M.S.O., 1929. 60p. (Cmd. 3415.)

Chairman: Sir Harold Morris.

14,404 **Ministry of Labour.** National Advisory Councils for Juvenile Employment (England and Wales, and Scotland). *Second reports. Age of entry into unemployment insurance as affected by the school-leaving age.* London: H.M.S.O., 1929. 23p. (Cmd. 3427.)

Chairman (England and Wales): Lord Shaftesbury.

Chairman (Scotland): Lord Elgin.

14,405 **Northern Ireland.** *Unemployment insurance: memorandum on financial resolution.* Belfast: H.M.S.O., 1929. 7p. (Cmd. 102.)

14,406 **Wolman,** Leo. 'Some observations on unemployment insurance.' *Am. Econ. Rev.*, XIX, 1 (March 1929), Supplement, 23–9.

14,407 **Beveridge,** *Sir* William Henry. *The past and present of unemployment insurance.* London: Oxford U.P., 1930. 47p. (Barnett House papers 13.)

14,408 **Carr,** *Sir* Arthur Strettell Comyns. *Escape from the 'dole': unemployment insurance or employment assurance?* London: Faber, 1930. 38p. (Criterion miscellany 19.)

14,409 **Davison,** *Sir* Ronald Conway. *Unemployment insurance in Great Britain.* Rome, 1930. 8p.

14,410 **Davison,** *Sir* Ronald Conway. *What's wrong with unemployment insurance.* London: Longmans, Green, 1930. 73p.

14,411 **Gibson,** R. S. 'The incentive to work as affected by unemployment insurance and the Poor Law respectively.' *Manchr. Sch.*, I, 1 (1930), 21–7.

14,412 **Northern Ireland.** *Unemployment Fund: memorandum on the financial resolution to be proposed relative to the Unemployment Fund.* Belfast: H.M.S.O., 1930. [2]p. (Cmd. 112.)

14,413 **Northern Ireland.** *Unemployment Insurance (Amendment) Bill (Northern Ireland), 1929: memorandum explanatory of the Bill, including financial memorandum.* Belfast: H.M.S.O., 1930. 12p. (Cmd. 109.)

14,414 **Smyth,** J. L. *Unemployment insurance.* London, 1930. [7]p.

14,415 **Unemployment Grants Committee.** *Report to August 30th, 1930.* London: H.M.S.O., 1930. 16p. (Cmd. 3744.)

Report for the period 1st September, 1930 to 31st December, 1931. 1932. 11p. (Cmd. 4029.)

Final report, 20th December, 1930 to 31st August, 1932. 1933. 35p. (Cmd. 4354.)

Chairman: Lord St Davids.

14,416 **Elliot,** Walter. 'Unemployment insurance.' *Lloyds Bank Rev.*, n.s., II, 14 (April 1931), 127–36.

14,417 **Gilson,** Mary Barnett. *Unemployment insurance in Great Britain: the national system and additional benefit plans.* New York: Industrial Relations Counselors, 1931. xiii, 560p.

14,418 **Maurette,** Fernand. 'Is unemployment insurance a cause of permanent unemployment?' *Int. Labour Rev.*, XXIV, 6 (December 1931), 663–84.

A critical analysis of the theory of Jacques Rueff which was based on conditions in Great Britain and put forward in the following:

1. [J. Rueff.] *L'assurance chômage, cause du chômage permanent.* Paris, 1931. vii, 41p. Reprinted from *Revue d'économie politique*, March–April 1931, with a preface by Charles Rist.

2. J. Rueff. 'Les variations du chômage en Angleterre.' *Revue politique et parlementaire,* 10 December 1925.

3. At the meeting of the Société d'économie politique of 5 May 1931.

14,419 **Northern Ireland.** *Unemployment insurance: memorandum on the financial resolution proposed relative to unemployment insurance and the Unemployment Fund.* Belfast: H.M.S.O., 1931. [2]p. (Cmd. 126.)

14,420 **Witmer,** Helen Leland. 'Some effects of the English Unemployment Insurance Acts on the number of unemployed relieved under the Poor Law.' *Q.J. Econ.*, XLV, 2 (February 1931), 262–88.

14,421 **Royal Commission on Unemployment Insurance,** 1930–32.

First report. London: H.M.S.O., 1931. 74p. (Cmd. 3872.)

Final report. 1932. 529p. (Cmd. 4185.)

Minutes of evidence. 1931–32.

Appendices. 1931–32.

Chairman: Holman Gregory.

14,422 **Cohen,** Joseph Lewis. 'Unemployment insurance and public assistance.' *Int. Labour Rev.*, XXVI, 6 (December 1932), 777–96.

A revised version of the general report presented to a Technical Commission of the International Association for Social Progress, London, July 1932.

14,423 **International Association for Social Progress.** *Report of the British Section on unemployment insurance and public assistance.* London, 1932. 40p.

14,424 **News Chronicle.** *News-Chronicle summary of the final report of the Royal Commission on Unemployment Insurance.* London, 1932. 72p.

14,425 **Stewart,** Bryce M. 'Some phases of European unemployment insurance experience.' *Acad. Polit. Sci. Proc.*, XIV, 4 (January 1932), 493–514.

14,426 **Metropolitan Life Insurance Company.** Social Insurance Section. *British experience with unemployment insurance.* New York, 1932–33. 6 pts. (Monographs 7–12.)

14,427 **Fabian Society.** *Royal Commission on Unemployment Insurance, December 1930–November 1932: an abridgement of the minority report signed by the Labour members of the Commission, Councillor W. Asbury and Councillor Mrs. C. D. Rackham.* London: Fabian Society, 1933. 73p.

Abridged from the *Final report* of the Royal Commission on Unemployment Insurance (Cmd. 4185), 1932.

14,428 **Fuss,** Henri and **Tait,** D. Christie. 'Unemployment benefits and measures for occupying the unemployed in Great Britain.' *Int. Labour Rev.*, XXVII, 5 (May 1933), 595–619.

14,429 **Gilson,** Mary Barnett. *Unemployment insurance.* Chicago, Ill.: U. of Chicago P., 1933. 30p. (Public policy pamphlets 3.)

14,430 **Hilton,** John. 'The state and the unemployed: the report of the Royal Commission on Unemployment Insurance.' *Polit. Q.*, IV, 1 (January–March 1933), 16–29.

14,431 **Low,** *Sir* Stephen Philpot and **Coules,** St. Vincent Froude. *Unemployment insurance.* London: Pitman, 1933. xi, 123p.

14,432 **Mellor,** William. 'The claim of the unemployed.' Addison, C., and others. *Problems of a socialist government.* London: Gollancz, 1933. p. 113–49.

14,433 **Ministry of Labour.** Departmental Committee on the Operation of the Anomalies Regulations. *Report.* London: H.M.S.O., 1933. 18p. (Cmd. 4346.)

14,434 **National Liberal Federation.** *Report of the National Liberal Federation Committee on Unemployment Insurance and the report of the Liberal Women's Unemployment Enquiry Group.* London, 1933. 20p.

14,435 **Alderson,** Bernard. *Social questions.* Birmingham: Journal Printing Offices, 1934. 54p.

Housing, slum reform, means test, unemployment insurance.

Articles reprinted from the *Birmingham Mail.*

14,436 **Beveridge,** *Sir* William Henry. 'Lessons for the present from the British experience with unemployment.' *Acad. Polit. Sci. Proc.*, xv, 4 (January 1934), 378–84.

14,437 **Connolly,** James. *An easy guide to the new Unemployment Act.* London: National Unemployed Workers' Movement, 1934. 19p.

14,438 **Davison,** *Sir* Ronald Conway. 'The new scheme of unemployment relief.' *Polit. Q.*, v, 3 (July–September 1934), 376–83.

14,439 **Davison,** *Sir* Ronald Conway. *The new Unemployment Act popularly explained: a simple description of insurance benefit, the new unemployment assistance scheme, training and voluntary occupation.* London: Longmans, Green, 1934. 32p.

14,440 **Glen,** Randolph Alexander. *Law relating to unemployment assistance.* London: Law and Local Government Publications, 1934. xii, 176p.

Edited by E. Bright Ashford, assisted by Alexander P. L. Glen.

14,441 **Harris,** C. 'The Unemployment Bill.' *Nineteenth Century*, cxv, 683 (January 1934), 38–49.

14,442 **Hetherington,** Hector James Wright. 'Public assistance.' *Sociol. Rev.*, xxvi, 1 (January 1934), 1–21.

14,443 **Hohman,** Helen Fisher. 'The status of unemployment insurance in Great Britain.' *J. Polit. Econ.*, xlii, 6 (December 1934), 721–52.

14,444 **McGlynn,** Edna M. *Unemployment insurance in England.* 1934. (Ph.D. dissertation, Boston College.)

14,445 **National Congress and March Council.** *Next steps in the fight against the new Unemployment Act.* London, 1934. 8p.

14,446 **Northern Ireland.** *Unemployment Bill (Northern Ireland), 1934: memorandum by the Minister of Labour explanatory of the Bill.* Belfast: H.M.S.O., 1934. 24p. (Cmd. 158.)

14,447 **Northern Ireland.** *Unemployment: memorandum by the Ministry of Finance.* Belfast: H.M.S.O., 1934. 8p. (Cmd. 159.)

14,448 **Stevenson,** E. F. *Unemployment relief: the basic problem.* London: Allen and Unwin, 1934. 284p.

14,449 **Tribe,** *Sir* Frank Newton. *The educational provisions of the Unemployment Bill.* Loughborough: Association of Technical Institutions, 1934. 11p. (Miscellaneous pamphlets.)

Paper read at the Annual General Meeting, 1934.

14,450 **United States.** National Industrial Conference Board. *Unemployment insurance: lessons from British experience.* New York: N.I.C.B., 1934. viii, 30p. (Studies 207.)

14,451 **Wilson,** Elizabeth C. 'Unemployment insurance and the stability of wages in Great Britain.' *Int. Labour Rev.*, xxx, 6 (December 1934), 767–96.

14,452 **Wolfenden,** Hugh Herbert. *Unemployment funds: a survey and proposal; a study of unemployment insurance and other types of funds for the financial assistance of the unemployed.* Toronto: Macmillan, 1934. xviii, 229p.

14,453 **Bakke,** Edward Wight. *Insurance or dole? The adjustment of unemployment insurance to economic and social facts in Great Britain.* New Haven, Conn.: Yale U.P., for Institute of Human Relations, 1935. xii, 280p.

Continues the report of findings begun in the author's study *The unemployed man* first published in 1933.

14,454 **Heliograph** (*pseud.*). *Sunlight on unemployment insurance.* Richmond: F. B. Bacon, 1935. 28p.

14,455 **Huntington,** Emily H. 'British health and unemployment insurance and standards of living.' *Essays in social economics in honor of Jessica Blanche Peixotto.* Berkeley, Calif.: U. of California P., 1935. p. 165–90.

14,456 **Kraus,** Hertha. *Aiding the unemployed: a survey of methods and trends in 24 foreign countries.* [Albany, N.Y.]: State of New York, Temporary Emergency Relief Administrations, 1935. 104p.

14,457 *Memorandum on the Unemployment Assistance (Determination of Need and Assessment of Needs) Regulations, 1934.* London: H.M.S.O., 1935. 32p. (Cmd. 4791.)

14,458 **Ministry of Labour.** Unemployment Insurance Statutory Committee. *Draft Unemployment Insurance (Anomalies) (Seasonal Workers) Order, 1935: report.* 1935. 13p.

Report. 1936. 4p.

Chairman: W. H. Beveridge.

14,459 **Ministry of Labour.** Unemployment Insurance Statutory Committee. *Report of the Unemployment Insurance Statutory Committee, in accordance with Section 20 of the Unemployment Insurance Act, 1934, on the question of the insurance against unemployment of persons engaged in employment in agriculture.* London: H.M.S.O., 1935. 73p. (Cmd. 4786.)

Chairman: W. H. Beveridge.

14,460 **Political and Economic Planning.** 'Inquest on the Unemployment Act.' *Planning*, 47 (26 March 1935), 1–13.

14,461 **Tipping,** G. A. *Unemployment and unemployment insurance in Northern Ireland.* 1935. (Ph.D. thesis, Queen's University of Belfast.)

14,462 **Hannington,** Walter. *Why do they march? Explaining what the new unemployment assistance scales and regulations will mean.* London: National Unemployed Workers' Movement, 1936. 12p.

14,463 **McKenzie,** G. Grant. *Unemployment assistance guide.* London: Labour Party, 1936. 55p.

14,464 **Ministry of Labour.** Unemployment Insurance Statutory Committee. *Extension of unemployment insurance to private gardeners.* London: H.M.S.O., 1936. 8p.
Chairman: W. H. Beveridge.

14,465 **Ministry of Labour.** Unemployment Insurance Statutory Committee. *Remuneration limit for insurance of non-manual workers: report.* London: H.M.S.O., 1936. 36p.
Chairman: W. H. Beveridge.

14,466 **Ministry of Labour.** Unemployment Insurance Statutory Committee. *Report of the Unemployment Statutory Committee, in accordance with section 57/1 of the Unemployment Insurance Act, 1935, on remuneration limit of insurance for non-manual workers.* London: H.M.S.O., 1936. 36p.
Chairman: W. H. Beveridge.

14,467 **Political and Economic Planning.** 'Unemployment assistance reviewed.' *Planning*, IV, 75 (19 May 1936), 1–10.

14,468 **Smyth**, J. L. *Notes on the Unemployment Assistance Regulations, 1936.* London, 1936. [4]p.

14,469 **Bakke**, Edward Wight. 'Basic realities in a system of unemployment benefit.' Murdock, G. P. (ed.). *Studies in the science of society.* New Haven, Conn.: Yale U.P., 1937. p. 29–41.

14,470 **Beveridge**, *Sir* William Henry. *The Unemployment Insurance Statutory Committee.* London: London School of Economics and Political Science, 1937. 55p. (Political pamphlet 1.)

14,471 **Hilton**, John. 'The public services in relation to the problem of unemployment.' *Publ. Adm.*, XV, 1 (January 1937), 3–9.
Inaugural address of the London Winter Session of the Institute of Public Administration, October 1936.

14,472 **Ministry of Labour.** *Summary of the Unemployment Insurance Acts 1935 and 1936.* London: H.M.S.O., 1937. 31p.

14,473 **Stamford**, Paul Tutt. 'Unemployment assistance in Great Britain.' *Am. Polit. Sci. Rev.*, XXXI, 3 (June 1937), 433–54.

14,474 **Stevens**, *Sir* Bertram Sydney Barnsdale. *Unemployment insurance and unemployment assistance in Great Britain: report:* Sydney, 1937. 25p. (New South Wales parliamentary papers. Session 1937–38. Vol. 5.)

14,475 **Stoddart**, S. A. *News Chronicle guide to unemployment insurance – Unemployment Insurance Acts, 1920 to 1936.* London: *News Chronicle* Publications Dept., 1937. 56p.
Revised edition of *Guide to unemployment insurance*, by Tom S. Newman and A. G. Lee.

14,476 **Swanish**, Peter T. *Trade disputes disqualification clause under the British Unemployment Insurance Acts.* Chicago, Ill.: U. of Chicago P., 1937. ix, 73p. (Studies in business administration, vol. VIII, no. 1.)

14,477 **Cohen**, Percy. *Unemployment insurance and assistance in Britain.* London: Harrap, 1938. 272p.

14,478 **Matscheck**, Walter. *Administration of unemployment insurance and the public employment service in Great Britain.* [Washington? 1938?] 181 leaves.
Foreword signed: Joseph P. Harris, Director of Research, Committee on Public Administration, Social Science Research Council.

14,479 **Northern Ireland.** *Unemployment Insurance Bill (Northern Ireland), 1938: memorandum by the Minister of Labour explanatory of the Bill.* Belfast: H.M.S.O., 1938. [4]p. (Cmd. 188.)

14,480 **University of Liverpool.** Department of Social Science. Statistics Division. *Unemployment assistance in Liverpool: a report on co-operation between the Unemployment Assistance Board, the local authority and voluntary associations in Liverpool.* Liverpool: Liverpool U.P.; London: Hodder and Stoughton, 1938. 64p.

14,481 **Northern Ireland.** *Unemployment Insurance Bill (Northern Ireland), 1939: memorandum by the Minister of Labour explanatory of the Bill.* Belfast: H.M.S.O., 1939. 4p. (Cmd. 209.)

14,482 **White**, R. Clyde. 'The British unemployment assistance program.' *Soc. Forces*, XVII (May 1939), 478–86.
'Read at the joint meeting of the American Sociological Society and the American Association for Labor Legislation, Dec. 29, 1938.'

14,483 **Ackroyd**, E. and **Hall**, R. L. 'Public assistance and unemployment assistance.' Barnett House, Oxford. Survey Committee. *A survey of the social services in the Oxford district.* Vol. 2. London: Oxford U.P., 1940. p. 91–108.

14,484 **Cohen**, Wilbur Joseph. *Unemployment insurance and agricultural labor in Great Britain.* Washington: Committee on Social Security, Social Science Research Council, 1940. viii, 32p. (Pamphlet series 2.)

14,485 **Millett**, John David. *The Unemployment Assistance Board: a case study in administrative autonomy.* London: Allen and Unwin, 1940. 300p.

14,486 **Northern Ireland.** *Unemployment Insurance Bill (Northern Ireland), 1940: memorandum by the Minister of Labour explanatory of the Bill.* Belfast: H.M.S.O., 1940. [2]p. (Cmd. 213.)

14,487 **Northern Ireland.** *Determination of Needs Bill (Northern Ireland), 1941: memorandum explanatory of the Bill.* Belfast: H.M.S.O., 1941. 5p. (Cmd. 214.)

14,488 **'Regionaliter.'** 'Administrative justice: a study of unemployment insurance courts and military service hardship committees.' *Polit. Q.*, XII, 4 (October–December 1941), 442–54.

14,489 **Grant**, E. A. 'The relief of unemployment.' *Banker*, LXIV, 203 (December 1942), 144–52.

14,490 **Rackham**, Clara Dorothea. 'Unemployment insurance.' Robson, W. A. (ed.). *Social security*. London: Allen and Unwin for the Fabian Society, 1943. p. 113–25.

Second edition. 1945. p. 122–34.

Third edition. 1948.

14,491 **Willard**, J. W. *Some aspects of the administration of unemployment insurance in Canada with comparative notes on the other British Dominions and Great Britain*. 1943. 117p. (M.A. thesis, University of Toronto.)

14,492 **Hidaka**, K. *The administration of unemployment assistance*. 1945. iv, 194p. (M.A. thesis, Queen's University, Kingston, Ontario.)

14,493 **Ministry of Labour and National Service.** *Tables relating to employment and unemployment in Great Britain 1939, 1945 and 1946. Regional and industrial analysis of persons insured against unemployment*. London: H.M.S.O., 1947.

. . . *1947*. 1948.

14,494 **Tillyard**, *Sir* Frank. '"Out of work donation": the true dole.' *Ind. Law Rev.*, III, 1 (July 1948), 12–19.

A chapter of the author's book *Unemployment insurance in Great Britain, 1911–48*.

14,495 **O'Sullivan**, J. J. 'Unemployment insurance.' King, F. C. (ed.). *Public administration in Ireland*. Vol. II. Dublin: Parkside P., 1949. p. 225–35.

14,496 **Tillyard**, *Sir* Frank and **Ball**, Frank Norman. *Unemployment insurance in Great Britain, 1911–48*. Leigh-on-Sea: Thames Bank Publishing Co., 1949. ix, 233p.

14,497 **International Labour Office.** *Unemployment insurance schemes*. Geneva: I.L.O., 1955. iv, 254p.

14,498 **Malisoff**, Harry. *Cost estimation methods in unemployment insurance, 1909–1957*. New York: New York State Department of Labor, Division of Employment, Bureau of Research and Statistics, 1958. 153p.

14,499 **Steer**, W. S. 'The origins of social insurance.' *Devon. Ass. Advmt. Sci. Lit. Art Rep. Trans.*, XCVI (1964), 303–17.

'The purpose of this paper is to describe the system of voluntary social insurance which the country magistrates of Devon succeeded in introducing in 1769, and the efforts of the Devon Bench in 1787, which almost achieved success, to promote a nation-wide compulsory social insurance scheme.'

14,500 **Gilbert**, Bentley Brinkerhoff. 'Winston Churchill versus the Webbs: the origins of British unemployment insurance.' *Am. Hist. Rev.*, LXXI, 3 (April 1966), 846–62.

14,501 **Burrows**, H. P. *Selected problems in the economics of unemployment insurance*. 1966–67. (D. Phil. thesis, University of York.)

14,502 **Hauser**, Mark M. and **Burrows**, Paul. *The economics of unemployment insurance*. London: Allen and Unwin, 1969. xvii, 213p. (University of York. Studies in economics 3.)

14,503 **Thirlwall**, A. P. 'Unemployment compensation as an automatic stabiliser.' *Oxf. Univ. Inst. Econ. Statist. Bull.*, XXXI, 1 (February 1969), 23–37.

14,504 **Bakke**, Edward Wight. 'The environment of unemployment.' Worsley, P. (ed.). *Modern sociology: introductory readings*. Harmondsworth: Penguin, 1970. p. 223–7.

Excerpts from E. Wight Bakke, *The unemployed man: a social study*. London: Nisbet, 1933. p. 62–72.

2. Sickness Benefit

This section includes works primarily concerned with state benefits for the sick. More general works relating to the administration and functioning of the National Health Service are excluded. General works on the National Insurance Act are to be found in Part Seven, IX, A, 3. See also Part Six, IV, C, 3.

14,505 **Loch**, Charles Stewart. 'Sickness insurance: some pros and contras.' *Char. Org. Rev.*, n.s., XXVIII, 166 (October 1910), 256–68.

Revised and expanded version of a paper read at the Section of Medical Sociology of the British Medical Association, London, July 1910.

14,506 **Alden**, Percy. 'The National Insurance Bill in relation to sickness and invalidity.' *Progress Civic Soc. Ind.*, VI, 3 (July 1911), 157–64.

14,507 **Brabrook**, *Sir* Edward William. 'State invalidity insurance.' *Econ. J.*, XXI, 81 (March 1911), 1–5.

14,508 **Richards**, Harold Meredith. *Public health and national insurance*. London: King, 1911. 71p.

14,509 **Sale**, Charles V. *National Health Insurance: proposals for an alternative to the Government Bill*. London: King, 1911. 27p.

14,510 **Schuster**, Ernest Joseph. *National health insurance: the parliamentary Bill examined and compared with the German scheme*. London: Murray, 1911. 26p.

Reprinted from the *Journal of Comparative Legislation*.

Second edition, revised and enlarged. 1911. 32p.

14,511 **Bray**, J. Dyer. *The doctors and the Insurance Act: a statement of the medical-man's case against the Act*. Manchester: T. Griffiths, 1912. vii, 82p.

14,512 **Dawes**, James Arthur. *National Health insurance: part I of the National Insurance Act, 1911, indexed and summarised.* London: Liberal Publication Department, 1912. 81p.

14,513 **Edwards**, W. Dudley. 'The National Insurance Act, 1911 (Part 1), as applying to Ireland.' *Statist. Soc. Inq. Soc. Ir. J.*, XII, 92 (December 1912), 569–82.

14,514 **Lowry**, Ernest Ward. *Can the doctors work the Insurance Act?* London: Watts, 1912. 64p.

14,515 **Rhodes**, Milson Russen. *A national medical service . . . as placed before the British Medical Association.* Manchester: C. Sever, 1912. 20p.

14,516 **Richards**, John Theodore. *National health insurance: a plain exposition of the Act for employers and employed.* London: Pull, 1912. 14p.

14,517 **Committee Appointed to Consider the Extension of Medical Benefit under the National Insurance Act to Ireland.** *Report.* London: H.M.S.O., 1913. 15p. (Cd. 6963.)

Appendices, minutes of evidence, etc. 1913. iv, 192p. (Cd. 7039.)

Chairman: Lord Ashby St Ledgers.

14,518 **Orriss**, W. Gerald. *The National Health Insurance Act: an alternative scheme.* London: King, 1913. 20p.

14,519 **Pope**, Samuel. *Report on the objections raised against the Draft Special Order including married women outworking within the provisions of Part 1 of the National Insurance Act.* London: H.M.S.O., 1913. 24p. (Cd. 6600.)

14,520 **Departmental Committee on Sickness Benefit Claims under the National Insurance Act**. *Report.* London: H.M.S.O., 1914. vii, 87p. (Cd. 7687.)

Minutes of evidence, appendices. Vols. I–IV. (Cd. 7688, 7689, 7690, 7691.)

Index.

Chairman: C. Schuster.

14,521 **Lloyd**, James Henry (ed.). *National Insurance Acts, 1911 and 1913: medical and sanatorium benefit regulations.* London: Pitman, 1914. 232p.

14,522 **Willis**, *Sir* Walter Addington. *National health insurance through approved societies; being a practical legal treatise incorporating the operative orders and regulations.* London: U. of London P., 1914. xxx, 494p.

14,523 **Rubinow**, Isaac Max. 'Standards of sickness insurance.' *J. Polit. Econ.*, XXIII, 3 (March 1915), 221–51; 4 (April 1915), 327–64; 5 (May 1915), 437–64.

14,524 **Faculty of Insurance.** *Report of the Commission of Investigation into National Health Insurance.* London: Faculty of Insurance, 1917. iii, 31p.

14,525 **Browne**, *Sir* Edmond and **Wood**, *Sir* Howard Kingsley. *The law of national health insurance: the National Insurance (Health) Acts, 1911 to 1918.* London: Insurance Publishing Co., 1919. 415p.

The texts with a commentary.

14,526 **McKail**, David and **Jones**, William. *A public medical service.* London: Fabian Society, Allen and Unwin, 1919. 72p.

14,527 **Hoffman**, Frederick Ludwig. *National health insurance and the friendly societies: an address delivered in abstract before the Fraternal Congress, Chicago, Ill., August 23, 1920.* Newark, N.J.: Prudential Insurance Company of America, 1921. viii, 101p.

14,528 **Macara**, *Sir* Charles Wright. 'The National Health Insurance Act.' *Recollections.* London: Cassell, 1921. p. 217–28.

14,529 **Harris**, Richard William and **Sack**, Leonard Shoeten. *Medical insurance practice: a work of reference to the medical benefit provisions of the National Health Insurance Acts.* London: Scientific P., 1922. xvi, 327p.

Second and revised edition. 1924. xii, 347p.

Fourth edition. London: British Medical Association, 1937. xv, 383p.

14,530 **National Health Insurance Joint Committee.** *Government of Ireland Act, 1920: report of the Departmental Committee on the Application of the Act to National Health Insurance.* London: H.M.S.O., 1922. 27p. (Cmd. 1575.)

Chairman: Sir Alfred W. Watson.

14,531 **Gray**, *Sir* Alexander. *Some aspects of national health insurance.* London: King, 1923. 29p.

14,532 **Harris**, Henry John. *National health insurance in Great Britain. 1911 to 1921.* Washington, D.C., 1923. iv, 103p. (U.S. Bureau of Labor Statistics bulletin 312.)

14,533 **Morgan**, Gerald. *Public relief of sickness.* London: Allen and Unwin, 1923. 195p.

Chap. VI. 'Cash relief and medical treatment by compulsory insurance: England.' p. 74–93.

14,534 **Aggs**, William Hanbury. *The National Health Insurance Act, 1924.* London: Sweet and Maxwell, Stevens, 1924. xxii, 175p.

14,535 **Wood**, *Sir* Howard Kingsley and **Newman**, Tom Seth. *National health insurance manual.* London: Vail, 1924. 206p.

Fourth edition.

Revised edition by T. S. Newman and A. G. Lee. London: McCorquodale, 1930. 245p.

Another revised edition. 1934. 358p.

14,536 **Eire.** Commission on the Relief of the Sick and Destitute Poor, Including the Insane Poor. *Report.* Dublin: Stationery Office, 1925. 163p.

Minutes of evidence, 27th May, 1925. 24p.

Minutes of evidence, 2nd June, 1925. 18p.

14,537 **Newman**, Tom Seth and **Lee**, A. G. *Guide to national health insurance.* London: *Daily News*, 1925. 48p.
Revised edition. 1929. 48p.
Revised edition. London: *News-Chronicle* Publications Dept., 1933. 55p.
Fourth edition. London: *News Chronicle*, 1936. 63p.

14,538 **Dearden**, William Francis. *The need for a state factory medical service.* Manchester: Association of Certifying Factory Surgeons, 1926. 20p. (Health and industry series 2.)

14,539 **Royal Commission on National Health Insurance.** *Report.* London: H.M.S.O., 1926. xii, 394p. (Cmd. 2596.)
Minutes of evidence.
Appendices.

14,540 **Northern Ireland.** Ministry of Labour. *National Health Insurance Bill: memorandum explanatory of the Bill.* Belfast: H.M.S.O., 1927. 16p. (Cmd. 82.)

14,541 **Watson**, *Sir* Alfred William. 'National health insurance: a statistical review.' *R. Statist. Soc. J.*, XC, 3 (1927), 433–73.
Discussion, p. 473–86.
'Read before the Royal Statistical Society, March 15, 1927.'

14,542 **Watson**, *Sir* Alfred William. 'National health insurance and friendly societies during the war.' Hill, *Sir* N., and others. *War and insurance.* London: Humphrey Milford, Oxford U.P.; New Haven, Conn.: Yale U.P., 1927. (Economic and social history of the world war. British series.) p. 171–225.

14,543 **Duffy**, Luke J. 'National health insurance from the workers' standpoint.' *Statist. Soc. Inq. Soc. Ir. J.*, XVI, 102 (October 1928), 49–59.

14,544 **Eason**, Charles. *Review of the report of the Commission on the Relief of the Sick & Destitute Poor, including the Insane Poor, appointed by the Government of the Irish Free State.* Dublin: Eason and Son, 1928. 29p.

14,545 **Eason**, J. C. M. 'Statement of the views of employers in the Irish Free State on the system of national health insurance.' *Statist. Soc. Inq. Soc. Ir. J.*, XVI, 102 (October 1928), 60–7.

14,546 **Riordan**, R. G. 'National health insurance.' *Statist. Soc. Inq. Soc. Ir. J.*, XVI, 102 (October 1928), 44–8.

14,547 **British Medical Association.** *National formulary for national health insurance purposes.* London: B.M.A., 1929. 79p.
Compiled by the Insurance Acts Committee.

14,548 **Newman**, Tom Seth and **Lee**, A. G. *National health insurance manual.* London: McCorquodale, 1930. 245p.
Revised edition of the work by Sir Howard Kingsley Wood and T. S. Newman.
Revised edition. 1934. 358p.

14,549 **Northern Ireland.** *National Health Insurance Bill (Northern Ireland), 1931: memorandum explanatory of the Bill.* Belfast: H.M.S.O., 1931. [2]p. (Cmd. 127.)

14,550 **McCleary**, George Frederick. *National health insurance.* London: Lewis, 1932. 185p.

14,551 **Northern Ireland.** *National Health Insurance and Contributory Pensions Bill: memorandum by the Ministry of Labour explanatory of the Bill.* Belfast: H.M.S.O., 1932. 8p. (Cmd. 140.)

14,552 **Foster**, Wilfred Justus and **Taylor**, Frederick George. *National health insurance.* London: Pitman, 1934. xi, 263p.
Second edition. 1935. xv, 278p.
Third edition. 1937. xv, 288p.

14,553 **Northern Ireland.** *National Health Insurance and Contributory Pensions Bill, 1935: memorandum explanatory of the Bill by the Ministry of Labour.* Belfast: H.M.S.O., 1935. 8p. (Cmd. 166.)

14,554 **Northern Ireland.** *National Health Insurance (Juvenile Contributors and Young Persons) Bill: memorandum explanatory of the Bill by the Ministry of Labour.* Belfast: H.M.S.O., 1937. 3p. (Cmd. 184.)

14,555 **Bull**, Susan L. *An historical and critical analysis of British health insurance.* 1938. (M.Sc. thesis, University of London.)

14,556 **Orr**, Douglass Winnett and **Orr**, Jean Walker. *Health insurance with medical care: the British experience.* New York: Macmillan, 1938. xvi, 271p.

14,557 **Ministry of Health.** *National health insurance and contributory pensions insurance: an outline of the schemes in the United Kingdom of Great Britain and Northern Ireland.* London: H.M.S.O., 1939. 34p.

14,558 **Northern Ireland.** *National Health Insurance and Contributory Pensions Bill (Northern Ireland) 1941: memorandum explanatory of the Bill by the Minister of Labour.* Belfast: H.M.S.O., 1941. [2]p. (Cmd. 215.)

14,559 **Clarke**, Joan Simeon. 'National health insurance.' Robson, W. A. (ed.). *Social security.* London: Allen and Unwin for the Fabian Society, 1943. p. 75–112.
Second edition. 1945.
Third edition. 1948.

14,560 **Levy**, Hermann Joachim. 'The economic history of sickness and medical benefit since the Puritan Revolution.' *Econ. Hist. Rev.*, XIV, 2 (1944), 135–60.

14,561 **Levy**, Hermann Joachim. *National health insurance: a critical study.* Cambridge: Cambridge U.P., 1944. x, 366p. (Economic and social studies 4.)

14,562 **Harris**, Richard William. *National health insurance in Great Britain, 1911–1946.* London: Allen and Unwin, 1946. 224p.

14,563 **Keast**, Horace. 'Sick leave pay under national insurance.' *Ind. Law. Rev.*, III, 2 (October 1948), 157–9.

14,564 **Newman**, Tom Seth. *News Chronicle guide to the National Health Service Act, 1946.* London: *News Chronicle* Publications Dept., 1948. 31p.

14,565 **Cudmore**, J. S. *Comparative study of health insurance and public medical care schemes in Germany, Great Britain, the United States of America, and Canada.* 1951. viii, 384p. (Ph.D. thesis, University of Toronto.)

14,566 **Willmott**, Phyllis and **Willmott**, Peter. 'Off work through illness.' *New Soc.*, 15 (10 January 1963), 16–18.

14,567 **Rai Choudhuri**, Sunil. *Sickness insurance in India and Britain.* Calcutta: World P., 1966. xvi, 318p.

14,568 **Mapes**, Roy. 'The pattern of insured absence.' *J. Mgmt. Studies*, IV, 1 (February 1967), 89–94.

3. Industrial Injury and Workmen's Compensation

This section includes material not only on workmen's compensation but also on the employer's responsibilities to employees injured at work. Many of the general works in Part Seven, V, A, 1 on the individual employee–employer relationship also contain material on the employer's liability for industrial injury. See also Part Six, II, C, 7; Part Six, IV, d; Part Seven, IV, E, 3; and Part Seven, V, B.

14,569 **Bramwell**, George William Wilsher, Baron Bramwell. *Employers' liability: letter from Lord Justice Bramwell to Sir Henry Jackson.* London: King, 1880. 16p.

14,570 **Howell**, George. *National industrial insurance and employers' liability, . . . being a series of papers.* London: King, 1880. 32p.

14,571 **Smith**, Horace. *The Employers' Liability Act, 1880.* London: Stevens, 1880. 13p.

A supplement to *A treatise on the law of negligence.* 1880.

14,572 **Sym**, John David. *An analysis of the Employers' Liability Act, 1880, 43 & 44 Victoria, cap. 42.* Edinburgh: Bell and Bradfute, 1880. 54p.

Second edition. 1885. 114p.

14,573 **Beven**, Thomas. *The law of the employers' liability for the negligence of servants causing injury to fellow servants, together with the Employers' Liability Act, 1880, with notes.* London: Waterlow and Layton, 1881. xiii, 137, xp.

14,574 **Black**, Charles Augustus Harold. *Employers & Workmen Act, 1875; and Employers' Liability Act, 1880, annotated and arranged.* Chesterfield: W. Edmunds; London, Derby: Bemrose, 1881. 22p.

14,575 **Howell**, George. *Employers' Liability Act, 1880 . . . with introduction and notes.* London, [1881?]. 16p.

14,576 **Innes**, George Rose. *Employers and employed: the Employers' Liability Act, 1880, and the alterations in the law effected thereby.* London: Effingham Wilson, 1881. 25p.

14,577 *Proposals for government insurance through the Post Office against fatal accidents from any cause.* Manchester, 1881. viii, 44p.

14,578 **Ruegg**, Alfred Henry. *A treatise upon the Employers' Liability Act 1880 (43 & 44 Vict. cap. 42).* London: Butterworths, 1882 [i.e. 1881]. xii, 131p.

Second edition. 1892. xii, 255p.

14,579 **Turner**, Edmond R. *A treatise on the Employers' Liability Act, 1880, 43 & 44 Victoria, cap. 42; to which is added a chapter on Lord Campbell's Act, 9 & 10 Victoria, cap. 93, and the Act amending the same, 27 & 28 Victoria, cap. 95.* London: Clowes, 1882. xvi, 182p.

14,580 **A Barrister-at-Law.** *The Act relating to the liability of employers, rendered into plain English, and revised with explanatory notes.* London: F. E. Longley, 1883. 8p.

14,581 **Burt**, Thomas. *Mr. Burt's address on the Employers' Liability Amendment Bill.* Newcastle, 1883. 14p.

14,582 **Westminster Review.** 'The Employers' Liability Act, 1880: accidents and accident insurance.' *Westm. Rev.*, n.s., LXIII, 1 (January 1883), 54–71.

Review article.

14,583 **Field**, Joshua Leslie. *The new Employers' Liability Act.* Manchester: J. Heywood, 1886. 35p.

14,584 **Select Committee on the Employers' Liability Act (1880) Amendment Bill.** *Report, with the proceedings, evidence, appendix, and index.* London: H.M.S.O., 1886. (H.C. 192.)

14,585 **Spens**, Walter Cook and **Younger**, Robert Tannahill. *Employers and employed: being (1) an exposition of the law of reparation for physical injury; (2) the Employers' Liability Act, 1880, annotated . . . and (3) suggested amendment of the law as to the liability of employers; with appendices and indices.* Glasgow: Maclehose, 1887. xxiv, 611p.

14,586 **Bradlaugh**, Charles. *Employers' Liability Bill: letter.* London, 1888. 23p.

14,587 **Standing Committee on Law, etc.** *Report . . . on the Employers' Liability for Injuries to Workmen Bill; with proceedings.* London: H.M.S.O., 1888. (H.C. 275.)

14,588 **Westminster Review.** 'The flaw in the Employers' Liability Bill.' *Westm. Rev.*, CXXXI, 5 (May 1889), 492–500.

14,589 **Firth**, Thomas Williams Staples. *On the law relating to the liability of employers for injuries suffered by their servants in the course of their employment.* London: Stevens, 1890. 48p. (Sir Henry James prize essay.)

14,590 **Campbell**, George L. *Miners' thrift and employers' liability: a remarkable experience.* Wigan: Strowger, 1891.

A paper read before Section F (Economic Science and Statistics) of the British Association for the Advancement of Science, at the Annual Meeting, held at Cardiff, in July 1891.

14,591 **Mozley-Stark**, Augustus. *The Employers' Liability Act and how to give notice of injury under it.* London: E. W. Allen, 1891. 15p.

'Reprinted with additions from *The navvy's and general labourer's guide.*'

14,592 **Provand**, A. D. 'Employers' liability.' *Nineteenth Century*, XXXIV, 201 (November 1893), 698–720.

14,593 **Wolff**, Henry William. 'Accident insurance.' *Econ. Rev.*, V, 3 (July 1895), 296–318.

14,594 **Browne**, Edmond. *Employers' liability: past and prospective legislation, with special reference to 'contracting out'.* London, 1896. 32p.

14,595 **Barlow**, Montague. 'The insurance of industrial risks.' *Econ. J.*, VII, 27 (September 1897), 354–67.

'Being the substance of a lecture delivered at the London School of Economics, on Wednesday, July 7, 1897.'

14,596 **Brown**, S. S. *On compensation for accidents to workmen in the U.K.* 1897. 15p.

14,597 **Fabian Society.** *The Workmen's Compensation Act.* London: Fabian Society, 1897. 20p. (Fabian tract 82.)

By C. R. Allen.

Issued without the author's name.

14,598 **Green**, Charles H. *Employers' liability: its history, limitations and extension.* London: T. J. W. Buckley, 1897. 21p.

The author was Chief Inspector for the Ocean Accident and Guarantee Corporation Limited.

14,599 **Inglis**, John. *On the Workmen's Compensation Act of 1897: paper read before the Civic Society of Glasgow.* 1897. 16p.

14,600 **Jones**, M. B. *Handbook to the Workmen's Compensation Act, 1897.* Cardiff, 1897. 78p.

14,601 **Londonderry**, Theresa. 'The "Conservative" Compensation (Workmen's) Bill of 1897.' *Nineteenth Century*, XLII, 247 (September 1897), 349–52.

14,602 **M'Neil**, Allan. *Employers' liability.* Edinburgh: G. Wilson, 1897. viii, 55p. (Popular law series 5.)

14,603 **Nash**, Rosalind. *The Accidents Compensation Act, 1897.* Leicester, 1897. 13p.

14,604 **Roberts Jones**, Morris. *Handbook to the Workmen's Compensation Act, 1897.* Cardiff: Tudor Printing Works, *1897*. 80p.

14,605 **Willis**, *Sir* Walter Addington. *The Workmen's Compensation Act, 1897, with copious notes and an appendix containing the Employers' Liability Act, 1880.* London: Butterworth, 1897. 76p.

Thirty-seventh edition. *Willis's Workmen's Compensation Acts, 1925 to 1943.* 1945. clvi, 1206, 101p.

Supplement. 1946. viii, 88p.

14,606 **Wolff**, Henry William. *Employers' liability: what ought it to be?* London: King, 1897. 114p.

14,607 **Wolff**, Henry William. 'The Workmen's Compensation Act.' *Econ. Rev.*, VII, 4 (October 1897), 432–49.

14,608 *Workmen's Compensation Act, 1897, with full extracts from the statutes therein referred to.* London, 1897. iv, 26, 14p.

14,609 **Flux**, A. W. 'Compensation for industrial accidents.' *Manchr. Statist. Soc. Trans.* (1897–98), 267–306.

14,610 **Beven**, Thomas. *The law of employers' liability and workmen's compensation.* London: Waterlow and Layton, 1898. xxxvi, 326, xxxp.

Second edition. 1899. xlv, 424p.

Third edition. 1902. lxv, 570, lviiip.

Fourth edition. Stevens and Haynes, 1909. lxxxiii, 953p.

14,611 **Brown**, H. *Injuries to workmen and compensation: the new liability and the old.* Glasgow, 1898. 18p. (Glasgow Insurance Society. Transactions, 4th series, no. 7.)

14,612 **Browne**, Edmond. *Workmen's compensation: the Act explained.* London, 1898. 32p.

14,613 **Flux**, A. W. 'Compensation Acts in Europe.' *Econ. J.*, VIII, 32 (December 1898), 559–63.

Comparison with England.

14,614 **Flux**, A. W. *Compensation for industrial accidents.* Manchester, 1898. [40]p.

14,615 **Glegg**, Arthur Thomson. *Commentary on the Workmen's Compensation Act, 1897.* Edinburgh: W. Green, 1898. viii, 152p.

Second edition. 1899. x, 172p.

14,616 **Hanna**, Henry. *The Workmen's Compensation Act, 1897, as applied to Ireland, with full explanation, notes.* Dublin: J. Falconer, 1898. viii, 166p.

14,617 **Hill**, William Ellis. *Law and practice relating to workmen's compensation and employers' liability.* London: Waterlow, 1898. 2 pts.

14,618 **Minton-Senhouse**, Robert Metcalfe and **Emery**, George Frederick. *Accidents to workmen, being a treatise on the Employers' Liability Act, 1880, Lord Campbell's Act, the Workmen's Compensation Act, 1897, and matters relating thereto.* London: Effingham Wilson, 1898. lii, 378p.

Second edition, by R. M. Minton-Senhouse. London: Sweet and Maxwell, 1902. lxviii, 432p.

14,619 **Minton-Senhouse**, Robert Metcalfe and **Emery**, George Frederick. *A handbook to the Workmen's Compensation Act, 1897.* London, Derby: Bemrose, 1898. vii, 184p.

With the text of the Act.

Second edition. [1899?] vii, 184p.

14,620 **Minton-Senhouse**, Robert Metcalfe and **Emery**, George Frederick. *The people's guide to the Workmen's Compensation Act.* London: Christian Knowledge Society, 1898. 32p.
Also, with different title-page. London, Derby: Bemrose, 1898.

14,621 **Mozley-Stark**, Augustus. *The duties of an arbitrator under the Workmen's Compensation Act, 1897, with notes on the Act and rules.* London: Stevens, 1898. viii, 136p.

14,622 **Pattinson**, Hubert Foden. *A treatise on the workmen's new Compensation Act, 1897, with notes.* London: R. Browning, 1898. 16p.

14,623 **Robinson**, Arthur. *Employer's liability under the Workmen's Compensation Act, 1897 and the Employers' Liability Act, 1880.* London: Stevens, 1898. xii, 125p.
Second edition, by A. Robinson and J. D. Stuart Sim. 1898. xii, 248p.

14,624 **Ruegg**, Alfred Henry. *The Employers' Liability Act, 1880, and the Workmen's Compensation Act, 1897.* London: Butterworth, 1898. xx, 369, 19p.
Third edition.
Fourth edition. 1899. xxii, 412, 22p.
Fifth edition. 1901. xxvi, 462, 26p.
Sixth edition. 1903. xxxii, 558, 32p.
Seventh edition. 1907. xxxvii, 732, 42p.
Eighth edition. With the Canadian notes, by F. A. C. Redden. 1910. lxxiii, 980, 64p.

14,625 **Taylor**, Alexander. *The Workmen's Compensation Act, 1897. With introduction and notes.* Glasgow, Edinburgh: Hodge, 1898. xxiii, 105p.

14,626 **Thomson**, Robert Tickell. 'The Workmen's Compensation Act, 1897.' *Nineteenth Century*, XLIII, 256 (June 1898), 899–914.

14,627 **Wilson**, Mona. 'Employers' liability and workmen's compensation.' *Westm. Rev.*, CXLIX, 2 (February 1898), 194–203.

14,628 **Wolff**, Henry William. *Employers' liability and workmen's compensation.* London, 1898. 64p.

14,629 **Aggs**, William Hanbury. *Handbook for workmen on the Workmen's Compensation Act, 1897.* Liverpool: Young, 1899. 40p.

14,630 **Minton-Senhouse**, Robert Metcalfe. *The case law of the Workmen's Compensation Act, 1897, intended to supplement Part III of 'Accidents to workmen'.* London: Effingham Wilson, 1899. xxii, 44p.
Second edition. 1900. xxvi, 100p.

14,631 *Workmen's compensation rights . . ., by an insurance expert.* London: Simpkin, Marshall, 1899. 32p.

14,632 **Carlisle**, Ernest J. 'Employers' liability and compensation to workmen in case of accidents.' *Manchr. Statist. Soc. Trans.* (1899–1900), 141–70.

14,633 **Parsons**, Albert and **Bertram**, *Sir* Thomas Anton. *The Workmen's Compensation Acts, 1897 and 1900.* London: Clowes, 1900. xviii, 156p.
Second edition. 1902. xxvii, 215p.
Third edition, by A. Parsons and Raymund Allen. London: Butterworth, 1907. xxxiv, 366p.
Fourth edition, by A. Parsons and R. Allen. Butterworth, 1910. xliv, 471p.
Fifth edition, by A. Parsons. Butterworth, 1914. xlvii, 449, 28p.

14,634 **Sexton**, *Sir* James. *A criticism of the Workmen's Compensation Act.* Liverpool, 1900. 15p.

14,635 **Walton**, Frederick Parker. *The new laws of employers' liability in England and France, and their bearing on the law of Quebec.* Montreal: C. Theoret, 1900. vi, 67p.
With the text of the two Acts.

14,636 **Barlow**, Montague. 'The insurance of industrial risks, 1897–1901.' *Econ. J.*, XI, 43 (September 1901), 345–53.

14,637 **Bowstead**, William. *The law relating to workmen's compensation under the Workmen's Compensation Acts, 1897 and 1900. London:* Sweet and Maxwell, 1901. xviii, 313p.
'With an appendix containing the rules, regulations, and orders under the Acts, and forms.'

14,638 **Campbell**, Thomas Joseph. *Workmen's compensation: a popular synopsis of the Acts and cases.* Dublin: Hodges, Figgis, 1901. viii, 128p.
Second edition.
Third edition. London: Sweet and Maxwell, 1902. viii, 150p.

14,639 **Elliott**, Adshead. *The Workmen's Compensation Acts. Being an annotated study of the Workmen's Compensation Act, 1897, and the Workmen's Compensation Act, 1900. With an introduction by Judge Parry.* 2nd ed. Manchester: Sherratt and Hughes; London: Stevens and Haynes, 1901. xxxii, 378p.
Third edition revised. Manchester: Sherratt and Hughes; London: Stevens and Haynes, 1903. xxxi, 444p.
Fourth edition. London, Manchester: Sherratt and Hughes, 1907. xxxi, 582p.
Fifth edition. London, Manchester: Sherratt and Hughes, 1909. xxix, 728p.
Sixth edition. London, Manchester: Sherratt and Hughes, 1912. xxxviii, 862p.
Seventh edition. London, Manchester: Sherratt and Hughes, 1915. xlviii, 804p.
Eighth edition. By Montague Berryman. London: Sweet and Maxwell, 1925. xxxiv, 775p.
Ninth edition. By Montague Berryman. London: Sweet and Maxwell, 1926. xxxviii, 792p.

14,640 **Thomson**, Robert Tickell. *The Workmen's Compensation Act, 1897: a plea for revision.* London: Effingham Wilson, 1901. v, 96p.

14,641 **Wilson**, Mona. 'Contracting-out from the Workmen's Compensation Act.' *Econ. J.*, XI, 41 (March 1901), 23–30.

14,642 **Baylee**, J. Tyrrell. 'The Workmen's

Compensation Act: what it is and what it might be.' *Westm. Rev.*, CLVII, 1 (January 1902), 68–72.

14,643 **Bowstead**, William. *Outline of the law relating to workmen's compensation under the Workmen's Compensation Acts, 1897 and 1900.* London: Simpkin, Marshall, 1902. 64p.

14,644 **Departmental Committee Appointed to inquire into the Notification of Industrial Accidents.** *Report, appendix.* London: H.M.S.O., 1902. iv, 124p. (Cd. 998.)
Chairman: H. Cunynghame.

14,645 **Glegg**, Arthur Thomson and **Robertson**, Maxwell Alexander. *Digest of cases decided under the Workmen's Compensation Acts, 1897 and 1900 . . . down to the end of August 1902.* Edinburgh: W. Green, 1902. xvi, 244p.
With the Acts annotated and indexed.

14,646 **Low**, A. M. 'The English Workingmen's Compensation Act.' *J. Soc. Sci.*, 40 (December 1902), 19–30.

14,647 **Dawbarn**, Climenson Yelverton Charles. *Employers' liability to their servants at common law, and under the Employers' Liability Act, 1880, and the Workmen's Compensation Acts, 1897 and 1900.* London: Sweet and Maxwell, 1903. xxxii, 299p.
Second edition.
With the text of the Acts.
Third edition. *Employers' liability to their servants at common law, and under the Employers' Liability Act, 1880, and the Workmen's Compensation Act, 1906.* London: Sweet and Maxwell; Toronto: Carswell, 1907. xl, 528, 31p.
With notes on the Canadian law, by A. C. Forster Boulton.
Fourth edition. London: Sweet and Maxwell, 1911. xxxix, 714, 34p.

14,648 **Minton-Senhouse**, Robert Metcalfe. *Digest of workmen's compensation cases, being a digest of the reports of cases known as 'Workmen's compensation cases'.* London: W. Clowes, 1903. xii, 57p.

14,649 **Neave**, Frederick George. *The law relating to injuries to workmen.* London: Effingham Wilson, 1903. viii, 111p. (Wilson's legal handy books.)
Second edition. 1910. xv, 146p.
Third edition, revised. 1926. xv, 160p.
Fourth edition, revised by F. G. Neave in collaboration with Grange Turner. 1930. xix, 172p.

14,650 **Gladwell**, Sidney William. 'A statistical view of the Workmen's Compensation Act Committee's report.' *R. Statist. Soc. J.*, LXVII, 4 (December 1904), 675–8.

14,651 **Home Office.** Departmental Committee appointed to inquire into the law relating to compensation for injuries to workmen.
Vol. I. *Report & appendices.* London: H.M.S.O., 1904. 236p. (Cd. 2208.)
Vol. II. *Minutes of evidence with index.* 1904. v, 404p. (Cd. 2334.)
Vol. III. *Supplementary appendix.* 1905. iii, 50p. (Cd. 2458.)
Chairman: Sir Kenelm Digby.

14,652 **Tozer**, William H. 'Five years' experience of the effect of the Workmen's Compensation Acts, with especial reference to schemes certified thereunder.' *R. Statist. Soc. J.*, LXVII, 2 (June 1904), 228–48.
With discussion, p. 249–56.
Read before the Society, 19 April 1904.

14,653 **Gow**, John Robertson. *Employers' liability.* London, 1905. (Transactions of the Insurance and Actuarial Society of Glasgow, series 5, no. 17.)

14,654 **Weber**, Adna F. 'Employers' liability and accident insurance.' Commons, J. R. (ed.). *Trade unions and labor problems.* Boston, Mass.: Ginn, 1905. p. 546–73.
First published *Political Science Quarterly*, XVII (1902), 256–83.
Reprinted. New York: Kelley, 1967.

14,655 **Barber**, W. *Notes and explanations of the Workmen's Compensation Act, 1906.* Bradford, 1906. 16p.

14,656 **Baylis**, Thomas Henry. *Workmen's Compensation Act, 1906, which includes domestic servants and others.* London: Sampson Low, 1907. xv, 83p.
Seventh edition of *The rights, duties and relations of domestic servants.*
Contains an analysis of the Act in Supplement B.

14,657 **Beaumont**, William Mardon. *Injuries of the eyes of the employed and the Workmen's Compensation Act: problems in prognosis.* London: H. K. Lewis, 1907. viii, 160p.

14,658 **Benthall**, A. *Précis of the Workmen's Compensation Act, 1906.* London, [1907?]. 10p.

14,659 **Cole**, Sanford Darley. *Seamen and compensation: a short practical guide to the law of compensation for accidents to seafarers under the new Act.* Glasgow: J. Brown, 1907. 24p.
Second edition, revised and enlarged. Glasgow: J. Brown; London: Simpkin, Marshall, 1911. 34p.

14,660 **Departmental Committee Appointed to Consider whether the Post Office should provide Facilities for Insurance under the Workmen's Compensation Acts.** *Report.* London: H.M.S.O., 1907. 11p. (Cd. 3568.)
Minutes of evidence, appendices, index. (Cd. 3569.)
Chairman: Lord Farrer.

14,661 **Departmental Committee on Compensation for Industrial Diseases.** *Report.* London: H.M.S.O., 1907. 24p. (Cd. 3495.)
Minutes of evidence, appendices, index. (Cd. 3496.)
Second report. 1908. (Cd. 4386.)
Evidence and appendix. (Cd. 4387.)
Chairman: H. Samuel.

14,662 **Edwards**, Clement. *Compensation Act, 1906. Who pays? To whom, to what, and when it applies.* London: Chatto and Windus, 1907. vi, 126p.

14,663 **Emery**, George Frederick. *Compensation for accidents to seamen, being a guide to the Workmen's Compensation Act, 1906, so far as it affects the mercantile marine of the world.* London: Bemrose, 1907. viii, 82p.

14,664 **Emery**, George Frederick. *A handbook to the Workmen's Compensation Act, 1906.* London: Bemrose, Effingham Wilson, 1907. viii, 102p.

14,665 **Emery**, George Frederick. *People's guide to the Workmen's Compensation Act, 1906.* London: Christian Knowledge Society, 1907. 54p.

14,666 **Firminger**, Ferdinand Leopold. *The Workmen's Compensation Act, 1906, and the County Court Rules relating thereto, with notes.* London: Eyre and Spottiswoode, 1907. xxiv, 386p.

Second edition. *The Workmen's Compensation Acts, 1906 and 1909, and the County Court rules relating thereto, with notes.* London: Stevens, 1910. xv, 575p.

14,667 **Foot**, Alfred. *The practice of insurance against accidents and employers' liability lectures.* London: Smith and Ebbs, 1907. 206p.

Second edition. 1908. 215p.

Third edition, with Acts of Parliament. 1909. 215p.

14,668 **Haslam**, Thomas Penman. *The new Compensation Act, 1906: are you in it?* Wolverhampton: Whitehead, 1907. 24p.

14,669 **Hill**, William Ellis. *Law of workmen's compensation and employers' liability.* London: Waterlow, 1907. xxiii, 483p.

14,670 **Hill**, William Ellis. *The Workmen's Compensation Act, 1906.* London: Waterlow, 1907. xi, 72p.

'With explanatory notes and index.'

Second edition. 1907. xi, 74p. 'With explanatory notes, list of employés and servants within the act, and index.'

14,671 **Knowles**, Charles Matthew. *The law relating to compensation for injuries to workmen, being an exposition of the Workmen's Compensation Act, 1906, and of the case law relevant thereto.* London: Stevens, 1907. xxxv, 278p.

Second edition.... *including the Workmen's Compensation rules and forms, 1907.* 1907. xliii, 460p.

Third edition. . . . *with the Workmen's Compensation (Anglo-French Convention) Act, 1909, and certain relevant provisions of the National Insurance Act, 1911.* 1912. lxi, 590p.

Fourth edition. 1924. lxxi, 502p.

14,672 **Lynn**, Henry. *The Workmen's Compensation Act, 1906, with explanatory notes and decided cases.* London: Jordan, 1907. xvi, 194p.

Second edition. 1907. xvi, 210p.

Third edition. 1909. xx, 282p.

14,673 **MacCleery**, James Carlisle. *Plain facts about workmen's compensation.* London, 1907. 23p.

14,674 **Nelham**, Thomas Ambrose. *Workmen's Compensation Act, 1906, explained with special reference to domestic servants, clerks, shopmen, and other work-people.* Manchester: Meredith, Ray, Littler, 1907. 52p.

Second issue. Manchester: Meredith, 1907. 55p.

14,675 **Snowden**, Philip. *The new Workmen's Compensation Act made plain.* London: Independent Labour Party, 1907. 15p.

14,676 **Umpherston**, Francis Albert. *A commentary on the Workmen's Compensation Act, 1906.* Edinburgh: Green, 1907. xxv, 369p.

'With comparative tables of the Workmen's Compensation Acts, 1897, 1900, and 1906, and Acts of Sederunt arranged by J. Hossell Henderson.'

14,677 **Walbrook**, Angus Fraser Oakley. *The Workmen's Compensation Act, 1906: handy notes for employers.* London: Walbrook, 1907. 15p.

14,678 **Wihl**, Oscar Morris. *Compensation for man and maid: a full explanation of the Workmen's Compensation Act, 1906.* London: Gee, 1907. xii, 103p.

14,679 **Kelly**, Richard J. *The Workmen's Compensation Act, 1906: the new law of master and servant.* Dublin: Sealy and Bryers, 1908. xv, 369p.

'With . . . a chapter on the relation of the Act to Seamen, by W. H. Boyd.'

Second edition.

14,680 **Aronson**, Victor Rees. *The Workmen's Compensation Act, 1906.* London, Leipsic: Fisher Unwin, 1909. xii, 559p.

14,681 **Barnett**, Henry Norman. *Accidental injuries to workmen, with reference to Workmen's Compensation Act, 1906.* London: Rebman, 1909. vii, 376p.

With article on injuries to the organs of special sense by Cecil E. Shaw, and legal introduction by Thomas J. Campbell.

14,682 **Collie**, *Sir* Robert John. *A simple remedy for a grave abuse.* London, 1909. 43p.

14,683 **Cooke**, Charles Taylor. *Handbook to the Workmen's Compensation Act, 1906, written for employers and workmen, with explanations, containing the most recent decisions.* Warrington, London: Mackie, 1909. 32p.

14,684 **Greenwood**, John Henry. *Amount o, compensation and review of weekly payments under the Workmen's Compensation Act, 1906.* London: Jordan, 1909. ix, 72p.

14,685 **Lawes**, Edward Thornton Hill. *The law of compensation for industrial diseases, being an annotation of Section 8 of the Workmen's Compensation Act, 1906, with chapters upon the powers and duties of certifying surgeons and medical referees . . . and including a special treatise upon every disease to which the Act now applies.* London: Stevens, 1909. xii, 288, 18p.

14,686 **Beverley**, Frank. *A digest of cases decided under the Workmen's Compensation Acts, 1897–1906, with the Acts of 1906 and 1909 and orders extending the provisions of the Act of 1906 to additional industrial diseases.* London: Stevens, 1910. xx, 152p.

Second edition. 1912. xxviii, 187, 32p.

14,687 **Darker**, George Fitzjames. *Bodily injuries: an index to the English law relating to bodily harm.* London: Winkley, 1910. 259p.

14,688 **Knocker**, Douglas (ed.). *Accidents in their medico-legal aspect.* London: Baillière, Tindall and Cox, Butterworth, 1910. xxviii, 1254p.

'By leading medical and surgical authorities.'

14,689 **Collie**, *Sir* Robert John. *Medico-legal aspect of the British Workmen's Compensation Act, 1906 . . . A paper read at Brussels.* London: Baillière, 1911. 41p.

11ième Congrès international des maladies professionelles.

14,690 *Employers and the compensation law, by an accident claims inspector.* London, Manchester: Sherratt and Hughes, 1911. 31p.

14,691 **Annan**, William. *The duties of employers under the National Insurance Act, 1911, with tables, specimen rulings, and appendices.* Edinburgh, London: Hodge, 1912. 231p.

14,692 **Collie**, *Sir* Robert John. *Medico-legal examinations and the Workmen's Compensation Act, 1906.* London: Baillière, 1912. 128p.

Second edition. *Medico-legal examinations and the Workmen's Compensation Act, 1906, as amended by subsequent Acts.* 1922. 157p.

14,693 **Dawbarn**, Climenson Yelverton Charles. *Workmen's compensation appeals, 1910–1911: a critical commentary on the workmen's compensation law for the past legal year.* London: Sweet and Maxwell, 1912. xiii, 128p.

With the text of the Workmen's Compensation Act, 1906.

14,694 **Dawbarn**, Climenson Yelverton Charles. *Workmen's compensation appeals: the case law for the legal years 1910–11 and 1911–12.* London: Sweet and Maxwell; Toronto: Carswell, 1912. xv, 199p.

With the text of the Workmen's Compensation Act, 1960.

14,695 **Knocker**, Douglas. *Workmen's compensation digest, containing every reported decision of present authority in the House of Lords and the Supreme Court of Judicature in England decided up to May 15th, 1912, and in the Court of Session in Scotland and the Supreme Court of Judicature in Ireland reported up to May 15th, 1912, under the Workmen's Compensation Acts, 1897, 1900, and 1906.* London: Butterworth, 1912. xxvii, 455, 38p.

Second edition. *Butterworth's digest of leading cases on workmen's compensation, being a second edition of Knocker's 'Digest of Workmen's compensation cases'*, by Sidney Henry Noakes. 1933. lxxxvi, 479, 30p.

Second cumulative supplement, by R. Marven Everett. 1942. vii, 18p.

14,696 **Lord**, J. W. *Employers' liability and workmen's compensation laws.* 1912. 22p.

14,697 **MacKendrick**, Archibald. *Malingering and its detection under the Workmen's Compensation and other Acts.* Edinburgh: Livingstone, 1912. 94p.

14,698 **Money**, *Sir* Leo George Chiozza. 'The breaking of a man.' *Things that matter: papers upon subjects which are, or ought to be, under discussion.* London: Methuen, 1912. p. 109–22.

On the law relating to Workmen's Compensation.

14,699 **Packer**, L. *History and operation of workmen's compensation in Great Britain.* Washington, 1912. 71p.

14,700 **Robertson**, F. J. *National health insurance.* Edinburgh, 1912. 16p.

14,701 **Steel-Maitland**, Arthur Drummond. 'The Workmen's Compensation Act in relation to industrial disease.' National Conference on the Prevention of Destitution. *Report of the proceedings . . . 1912.* London: King, 1912. p. 79–85.

Discussion, p. 88–96.

14,702 **Boyd**, James Harrington. *Workmen's compensation and industrial insurance under modern conditions . . . including a full text of the statutes in force January 1, 1913, in Germany, England and the several states of America.* Indianapolis, Ind.: Bobbs-Merrill, 1913. 2v.

14,703 **Charles Knight and Co.** *Knight's handbook for the use of Health Insurance Committees, and all other local authorities, approved societies, and medical practitioners affected by the National Insurance Act, 1911.* London: Knight, 1913. xii, 377p.

14,704 **Craig**, William Thomson. *Case law of workmen's compensation, collected from the decisions of the House of Lords and the Courts of the United Kingdom.* Edinburgh: W. Green, 1913. 12 pts.

14,705 **Dawbarn**, Climenson Yelverton Charles. *Workmen's compensation appeals: thr case law for the legal year 1912–13.* London: Sweet and Maxwell; Toronto: Carswell, 1913. xvi, 131p.

With the text of the Workmen's Compensation Act, 1906.

14,706 **Departmental Committee Appointed to inquire and report whether the following Diseases can be properly added to those enumerated in the Third Schedule of the Workmen's Compensation Act, 1906, namely, Cowpox, Dupuytren's Contraction, Clonic Spasm of the Eyelids apart from Nystagmus, and Writers' Cramp.** *Report.* London: H.M.S.O., 1913. 10p. (Cd. 6956.)

Minutes of evidence, appendices, index. (Cd. 6957.)

Chairman: E. J. Griffith.

14,707 **Rowntree**, Herbert. *Common law liability for accidental injury or damage.* London: *Post Magazine* P., 1913. 137p.
Third edition. *Post Magazine*, 1924. 219p.
Fourth edition. London: Buckley P., 1935. x, 356p.
'Supplement to Chapter XI, comprising a commentary upon the House of Lords Judgment in Rose v. Ford.' 1937. 13p.
Sixth edition. Buckley P., 1947. 295p.
Seventh edition. 'Including a revised and extended section upon the liability of employers for accidents to employees.' Buckley P., 1951. xxx, 378p.

14,708 **Scanlan**, John James. *The mutilated hand and the Workmen's Compensation Act, 1906, having a special reference to 'missing' fingers; based on a series of cases examined.* London: Scientific P., 1913. vii, 90p.

14,709 **Thomas**, George Nathaniel William. *Leading cases in workmen's compensation.* London: Butterworth, 1913. xvii, 122, 21p.

14,710 **Cousins**, *Sir* Harry. *The Workmen's Compensation Act, 1906, and the Consolidated Workmen's Compensation Rules, 1913: instances and methods of payment into court.* Cardiff, London: *Western Mail*, 1914. 41p.

14,711 **Stone**, *Sir* Gilbert and **Groves**, Keith Grimble. *Stone's insurance cases . . . together with all cases upon workmen's compensation and employers' liability.* London: Reports and Digests Syndicate, 1914. 2v.

14,712 **Chartres**, John Smith. *Judicial interpretations of the law relating to workmen's compensation.* London: Butterworth, 1915. l, 753p.

14,713 **Wells**, William T. W. *Workmen's compensation insurance: average cost of claims settlements under the Workmen's Compensation Act, 1906.* Edinburgh: H. and J. Pillans and Wilson, 1915. 83p.

14,714 **MacKendrick**, Archibald. *Back injuries and their significance under the Workmen's Compensation and other Acts.* Edinburgh: Livingstone, 1916. viii, 173p.

14,715 **Blanchard**, Ralph Harrub. *Liability and compensation insurance, industrial accidents and their prevention, employers' liability, workmen's compensation insurance of employers' liability and workmen's compensation.* New York, London: D. Appleton, 1917. xii, 394p.

14,716 **Chatterton**, George. *Extracts from the Workmen's Compensation Act, 1906, with table of redemption values of weekly payments.* Manchester: Marsden, 1917. 51p.

14,717 **Wilkinson**, William Elmslie. *The law of workmen's compensation.* 1918. (Ll.D. thesis, University of London.)

14,718 **Departmental Committee on Compensation for Disabled Sailors and Soldiers under the Workmen's Compensation Act, 1906.** *Report.* London: H.M.S.O., 1919. 8p. (Cmd. 49.)
Chairman: Lord Peel.

14,719 **Departmental Committee on Workmen's Compensation.** *Report.* London: H.M.S.O., 1920. 86p. (Cmd. 816.)
Minutes of evidence. 1920. 2v. (Cmd. 908, 909.)
Chairman: Holman Gregory.

14,720 **Parkinson**, Jacob. *Workmen's accidents and compensation: the Workmen's Compensation Act from the workingman's standpoint.* Lytham: N. King, 1920. 52p.
Second edition.

14,721 **Golding**, Cecil Edward. *Workmen's compensation insurance, with a summary of the statutory law relating thereto.* London: Pitman, 1922. vii, 104p.
Second edition. 1929. vii, 108p.

14,722 **Ruegg**, Alfred Henry and **Stanes**, Henry Percy. *The Workmen's Compensation Act, 1906.* London: Butterworth, 1922. liv, 525, 29p.
Ninth edition of the chapters on the Act contained in *The Employers' Liability Act . . . and the Workmen's Compensation Act*, by A. H. Ruegg.

14,723 **Thompson**, William Henry. *Workmen's compensation: an outline of the Acts.* London: Labour Publishing Co., 1922. 96p.
Second edition. *Workmen's compensation, 1924.* 1924. 110p.

14,724 **Clark**, George. *In the Court of Appeal: history of a famous trial; the Workmen's Compensation Act, 1897, and re an arbitration between George Clark and the Gas Light & Coke Coy.* Chadwell Heath: G. Clark, 1923. 15p.

14,725 **Cohen**, Joseph Lewis. *Workmen's compensation in Great Britain.* London: *Post Magazine*, 1923. 232p.

14,726 **Rowntree**, Herbert. *An analysis of the Workmen's Compensation Act, 1923.* London: *Post Magazine*, 1923. 74p.

14,727 **Welson**, James Bevan and **Bryant**, F. W. *Workmen's compensation insurance: its principles and practice.* London: *Post Magazine*, 1923. 176p.
Second edition. 1930. 209p.

14,728 **Downey**, Ezekiel Henry. *Workmen's compensation.* New York: Macmillan, 1924. xxv, 223p. (Social science text-books.)

14,729 **International Labour Office.** 'Alien workers under workmen's compensation legislation in the British Empire.' *Int. Labour Rev.*, IX, 5 (May 1924), 708–28.

14,730 **Newman**, Tom Seth. *Handbook to the Workmen's Compensation Acts, 1906–1923.* London: Vail, 1924. 50p.
Another edition. London: *Daily News*, 1925. 48p.

14,731 **Parry**, Cuthbert L. *Workmen's Compensation Acts, 1906 to 1923: computation of . . . earnings and compensation.* London: *Post Magazine*, 1924. 26p.

14,732 **Connolly**, Thomas James Doull. *Handbook on the Workmen's Compensation Acts, 1906–1923.* Edinburgh: Hodge, 1925. xlii, 752p.

14,733 **Eire.** Department of Industry and Commerce. *Report of Departmental Committee on Workmen's Compensation.* Dublin: Stationery Office, 1925. 84p.
Second report. 1929. 15p.

14,734 **Umpherston**, Francis Albert. *Workmen's Compensation Act, 1925, and relative Act of Sederunt.* Edinburgh, Glasgow: Hodge, 1926. 97p.

14,735 **Hughes**, Hector. 'Workmen's compensation: some suggested reforms.' *Statist. Soc. Inq. Soc. Ir. J.*, xv, 101 (October 1927), 299–309.

14,736 **Turner-Samuels**, Moss and **Geddes**, Douglas. *The Workmen's Compensation Act, 1925, as amended by the Workmen's Compensation Act, 1926, and the Workmen's Compensation Rules, 1926.* London: Solicitors' Law Stationery Society, 1927. iii, 282p.

14,737 **Edwards**, A. G. *The Workmen's Compensation Acts: an outline of certain anomalies which appear to exist in the position of workmen, when the provisions of the 1925 Act are compared with those of the 1906 Act.* London, 1928. 12p.

14,738 **Home Office.** Departmental Committee on Compensation for Silicosis. *Report.* London: H.M.S.O., 1928. 41p.
Chairman: Vivian Leonard Henderson.

14,739 **Connolly**, Thomas James Doull. *Workmen's compensation.* Edinburgh: Green, 1929. viii, 176p. (Popular law series 4.)

14,740 **Eire.** Dáil Éireann. Special Committee on the Workmen's Compensation (Increase of Compensation) Bill, 1929. *Report; together with the proceedings of the Special Committee.* Dublin: Stationery Office, 1929. 7p.

14,741 **Robinson**, *Sir* Harry Perry. *The Employers' Liability Assurance Corporation, Ltd., 1880–1930.* London: the Corporation, 1930. viii, 177p.

14,742 **Robson**, William Alexander. 'Industrial relations and the state: a reform of workmen's compensation.' *Polit. Q.*, I, 4 (September–December 1930), 511–30.

14,743 **Kessler**, Henry Howard. *Accidental injuries: the medico-legal aspects of workmen's compensation and public liability.* London: H. Kimpton, 1931. 718p.
Printed in America.
Second edition enlarged. 1941. 803p.

14,744 **Davie**, Paul Christopher. *Silicosis and asbestosis compensation schemes.* London: Solicitors' Law Stationery Society, 1932. 176p.

14,745 **Home Office.** *Memorandum on the Workmen's Compensation Acts, 1925–1931.* London: H.M.S.O., 1932. 23p.
. . . *1925–38.* 1938. 23p.
. . . *1925–40.* 1940.
. . . *1925–43.* 1944. 18p.
. . . *1925–45.* 1946. 19p.

14,746 **Home Office.** Departmental Committee on Compensation for Industrial Diseases. *Report.* London: H.M.S.O., 1932. 16p.
Chairman: Sir Humphry Davy Rolleston.
Second report. 1933. 21p.
Third report. 1936. 16p.

14,747 **Collie**, *Sir* Robert John. *Workmen's compensation: its medical aspect.* London: Arnold, 1933. vii, 160p.

14,748 **International Labour Office.** 'Disablement benefit under the British health insurance scheme.' *Int. Labour Rev.*, XXVIII, 2 (August 1933), 192–213.
'The present report is not intended to give a general outline of the provisions concerning disablement benefit in Great Britain, but is limited to showing the experience in regard to disablement benefit during recent years.'

14,749 **Walker**, George Frederick. *The injured workman.* Bristol: J. Wright, 1933. xix, 190p.
With the collaboration of J. Harvey Robson, R. E. Jowett, Stanley Ritson and John Foster.

14,750 **Macloughlin**, Richard F. *Workmen's Compensation Act, 1934: a summary and explanation of the important alterations in the law introduced by this Act.* Dublin: Eason, 1934. 8p.

14,751 **Spafford**, Christopher Housian. *The legal aspect of industrial diseases: Sections 43 and 44 of the Workmen's Compensation Act, 1925.* London: Butterworth, 1934. xxxiv, 263, 9p.

14,752 **Henderson**, Arthur. 'Workmen's compensation.' *Nineteenth Century*, CXX, 718 (December 1936), 728–35.

14,753 **Board of Trade.** Committee on Compulsory Insurance. *Report.* London: H.M.S.O., 1937. 82p. (Cmd. 5528.)
Minutes of evidence. 1937. 325p.
Chairman: Sir Felix Cassel.

14,754 **International Labour Office.** *Workmen's compensation for silicosis in the Union of South Africa, Great Britain and Germany.* Geneva: I.L.O., 1937. 147p. (Studies and reports, series F (Industrial hygiene), 16.)
Also *Supplement.*

14,755 **Home Office.** Departmental Committee on Certain Questions Arising under the Workmen's Compensation Acts. *Report.* London: H.M.S.O., 1938. iv, 115p. (Cmd. 5657.)
Chairman: William Stewart.

14,756 **Home Office.** Departmental Committee on Compensation for Card Room Workers. *Report.* London: H.M.S.O., 1939. 32p.
Chairman: W. D. Ross.

14,757 **Nixon**, John Alexander. *Medical referees under the Workmen's Compensation Acts.* London, 1939. 16p.
Reprinted from *The Lancet.*

14,758 **Wilson**, *Sir* Arnold Talbot. 'Workmen's compensation.' *Polit. Q.*, x, 2 (April–June 1939), 232–43.

14,759 **Wilson**, *Sir* Arnold Talbot and **Levy**, Hermann Joachim. *Workmen's compensation.* London: Oxford U.P., 1939, 1941. 2v.

Vol. 1. *Social and political development.* 1939. xxi, 328p.

Vol. 2. *The need for reform.* 1941. xii, 384p.

14,760 **Levy**, Hermann Joachim. *War effort and industrial injuries.* London: Fabian Society, 1940. 16p. (Fabian tract 253.)

14,761 **Thompson**, William Henry. *Workmen's Compensation: the new Act explained.* London: Muller, 1940.

With the text of the Workmen's Compensation, Supplementary Allowances, Act 1940.

14,762 **Chambers**, Rosalind C. 'Some aspects of workmen's compensation.' *Mod. Law Rev.*, v, 2 (November 1941), 113–17.

'...by a social scientist with experience of welfare work.'

14,763 **Jordan**, Henry H. *Workmen's compensation and the physician: a manual for the use of general practitioners and insurance carriers.* London: Oxford U.P., 1941. xi, 180p.

'With a discussion of traumatic neuroses [by] Paul H. Hoch.'

14,764 **Chambers**, Rosalind C. 'Workmen's compensation.' Robson, W. A. (ed.). *Social security.* London: Allen and Unwin for the Fabian Society, 1943. p. 55–74.

Second edition. 1945.

Third edition. 1948.

14,765 **Parsons**, Owen Henry. *Workmen's compensation: accidents at work. A commentary on the government plan.* London: Labour Research Department, [1943?]. 24p.

14,766 **Shillman**, Bernard J. *The law relating to employers' liability and workmen's compensation in Ireland.* Dublin: Dollard, Printinghouse, 1943. xxxvi, 502p.

Second edition.

14,767 **Russell-Jones**, A. 'Workmen's compensation: common law remedies and the Beveridge Report.' *Mod. Law. Rev.*, VII, 1–2 (April 1944), 13–25.

14,768 **Thompson**, William Henry. *Workmen's compensation up-to-date.* London: Labour Research Department, 1944. 71p.

14,769 **Burn**, W. L. 'Workmen's compensation: the new proposals.' *Nineteenth Century*, CXXXVII, 815 (January 1945), 20–8.

14,770 **Home Office.** *Workmen's compensation: interim report of the Departmental Committee on Alternative Remedies (Contributory Negligence).* London: H.M.S.O., 1945. 7p. (Cmd. 6580.)

Chairman: Sir Walter T. Monckton.

Second interim report. 1945. 8p. (Cmd. 6642.)

14,771 **Royal Commission on Workmen's Compensation.** *Report.* London: H.M. S.O., 1945. 7p. (Cmd. 6588.)

Minutes of evidence. 1939–40. 11 pts.

Chairman: Sir Hector Hetherington.

'The proceedings of the Commission were suspended in July 1940. This Report gives a brief outline of the Commission's work, and states: "Two recent events seem to indicate that our continued existence is no longer necessary. The Government have published in the second of two White Papers on Social Insurance their proposals for replacing the existing system of Workmen's Compensation by a new Scheme of Industrial Injury Insurance, and they have appointed a Committee under the Chairmanship of Sir Walter Monckton, K.C.V.O., K.C. to consider certain questions relative to 'alternative remedies', the major problem of principle still remaining over. In these circumstances we feel that any further reports by us would serve no useful purpose."' (Ford.)

14,772 **Samuels**, Harry. *Compensation and common law: lecture.* London: Co-operative Printing Society, 1945. 12p.

14,773 **Levy**, Hermann Joachim. 'Compensation for industrial injury.' *Hlth. Soc. Welf.* (1945–46), 113–17.

14,774 **Ball**, Frank Norman. 'Elementary law of industry. 1. The workmen's compensation scheme.' *Ind. Law Rev.*, I, 2 (July 1946), 59–62.

14,775 **Ministry of National Insurance.** *Memorandum on the effect of the Family Allowances Act, 1945, on the Workmen's Compensation Acts, 1925–1945.* London: H.M.S.O., 1946. 9p.

14,776 **Northern Ireland.** *National Insurance (Industrial Injuries) Bill (Northern Ireland): explanatory memorandum by the Ministry of Labour and National Insurance.* Belfast: H.M.S.O., 1946. 7p. (Cmd. 235.)

14,777 **Parsons**, Owen Henry. 'The Monckton Report on Alternative Remedies.' *Ind. Law Rev.*, I, 5 (October 1946), 131–5.

14,778 **Samuels**, Harry and **Pollard**, Robert Spence Watson. *Industrial injuries.* London: Stevens, 1946. vii, 87p. (This is the law.)

Second edition. 1950. viii, 104p.

14,779 **Shannon**, Norman Pasquilla and **Potter**, Douglas Charles Loftus. *The National Insurance—Industrial Injuries—Act, 1946.* London: Butterworth, 1946. v, 238p.

Reprinted from *Butterworth's emergency legislation service–annotated.*

Second edition. *National insurance—industrial injuries*, by D. C. L. Potter and D. H. Stansfeld. 1950. xix, 392p.

14,780 **Ministry of National Insurance.** *Report of the Departmental Committee on Industrial Diseases.* London: H.M.S.O., 1948. 15p. (Cmd. 7557.)

Chairman: Edgar T. Dale.

14,781 **Tillyard,** *Sir* Frank. 'Fifty years of workmen's compensation.' *Ind. Law Rev.*, II, 10 (March 1948), 250–60.

14,782 **Newman**, Tom Seth and **Prior**, Thomas W. *News Chronicle guide to Industrial Injuries Act: National Insurance, Industrial Injuries, Act, 1946.* London: *News Chronicle* Publications Department, 1949. 32p.

14,783 **Pollard**, Robert Spence Watson. *Introducing the National Insurance—Industrial Injuries—Acts, 1946 and 1948.* London: Law Society, 1949. 42p.

. . . *1946 to 1953.* 1954 [i.e. 1955]. 45p.

14,784 **Trades Union Congress.** *Guide to the Industrial Injuries Acts and Regulations.* London: T.U.C., 1949. 166p.

14,785 **Mallalieu**, William C. 'Joseph Chamberlain and workmen's compensation.' *J. Econ. Hist.*, x, 1 (May 1950), 45–57.

14,786 **Munkman**, John Henry. *Employer's liability at common law.* London: Butterworth, 1950. xxxvi, 339p.

Second edition. 1952. liv, 478p.
Third edition. 1955. lviii, 496p.
Fourth edition. 1959. lxii, 534p.
Fifth edition. 1962. lxvi, 582p.
Fifth edition, Supplement. 1964. xi, 19p.
Sixth edition. 1966. lxxiv, 611p.

14,787 **Keast**, Horace. *Case-law on national insurance and industrial injuries.* Hadleigh: Thames Bank Publishing Co., 1952. xvi, 194, xip.

14,788 **Pain**, Peter. 'The employer's duty to provide a safe system of work.' *Ind. Law Rev.*, VII, 2 (October 1952), 109–117.

14,789 **Schwarzer**, William W. 'Wages during temporary disability: partial impossibility in employment contracts.' *Ind. Law Rev.*, VIII, 1 (July 1953), 12–26.

14,790 **Redmond**, P. W. D. *History of the responsibility of a master at common law for the safety of his servants.* 1953–54. (LL.M. thesis, University of Liverpool.)

14,791 **Dean**, R. 'Injuries to workmen caused by fellow employees.' *Ind. Law Rev.*, VIII, 4 (April 1954), 245–54.

14,792 **Smith**, P. V. H. 'Contributory negligence and the employer's liability.' *Ind. Law Rev.*, IX, 1 (July 1954), 15–33.

14,793 **Somers**, Herman Miles and **Somers**, Anne Ramsay. *Workmen's compensation: prevention, insurance, and rehabilitation of occupational disability.* London: Chapman and Hall; New York: Wiley, 1954. xv, 341p.

14,794 **Taylor**, Eric. *An examination of the operation of the National Insurance (Industrial Injuries) Act, 1946.* 1954. viii, 298p. (LL.M. thesis, University of Manchester.)

14,795 **Jackson**, Edward. 'Liability for lifting gear.' *Ind. Law Rev.*, x, 2 (October 1955), 106–19.

14,796 **Smith**, P. V. H. 'Contributory negligence: apportionment of liability.' *Ind. Law Rev.*, IX, 3 (January 1955), 216–17.

On Laszczyk *v.* National Coal Board, 1954.

14,797 **Banks**, N. D. 'Master's indemnity from negligent servant.' *Ind. Law Rev.*, x, 4 (April 1956), 247–56.

14,798 **Jolowicz**, J. A. 'The right to indemnity between master and servant.' *Camb. Law J.* (April 1956), 101–11.

14,799 **Marriott**, T. W. 'Romford Ice and Cold Storage Co. Ltd., *v.* Lister: a problem of ethics.' *Ind. Law Rev.*, XI, 1 (July 1956), 18–23.

'. . . the defendant Lister, by his negligence injured a fellow servant, and the employers were called upon to compensate that employee . . . They did so by the hand of their insurers, who, having indemnified the employers were entitled to all the rights of the employers against Lister. They exercised these rights in the name of their insured.'

14,800 **Marriott,** T. W. 'Pneumoconiosis.' *Ind. Law Rev.*, XIII, 1 (July 1958), 2–11.

14,801 **Ford**, H. A. J. 'Legal liability for industrial accidents.' *J. Ind. Relat.*, I, 2 (October 1959), 90–7.

14,802 **Marriott**, T. W. 'Falls from other people's ladders.' *Ind. Law Rev.*, XIII, 4 (April 1959), 204–11.

Duties of an employer to his employees when they are working on other persons' premises.

14,803 **Ministry of Labour and National Service.** *Lister* v. *The Romford Ice and Cold Storage Co., Ltd.: report of the Inter-departmental Committee.* London: H.M.S.O., 1959.

Chairman: P. H. St John Wilson.

14,804 **Moloney**, W. J. 'The accident problem.' *Administration*, VII, 1 (Spring 1959), 32–40.

At Bord na Mona.

14,805 **Rose**, Paul Bernard. 'Diseases under the National Insurance (Industrial Injuries) Act, 1946.' *Ind. Law Rev.*, XIV, 1 (July 1959), 10–14.

14,806 **Raychaudhuri**, Sunil. *Industrial injuries schemes in India and Britain: a comparative study.* 1959–60. (Ph.D. thesis, University of London.)

Published as *Social security in India and Britain: a study of the industrial injury schemes in the two countries.* Calcutta: World P., 1962. 328p.

14,807 **Rose**, Paul Bernard. 'Comparative schemes for industrial injuries insurance in France & Britain.' *Ind. Law Rev.*, XIV, 2 (October 1959), 66–79; 3 (January 1960), 118–33; 4 (April 1960), 181–97.

14,808 **Fricke**, Graham L. 'General practice in industry.' *Mod. Law Rev.*, XXIII, 6 (November 1960), 653–9.
Admissibility, relevance and effect of evidence that a system of work is one customarily prevailing in a particular industry in actions brought by employees for negligent failure to provide a safe system, with special reference to Cavanagh *v.* Ulster Weaving Co. Ltd.

14,809 **Hurley**, D. M. *Comparative conflict of laws: workmen's compensation and industrial injuries.* 1960–61. (Ll.M. dissertation, University of London.)

14,810 **Parsons**, Owen Henry. *Guide to the Industrial Injuries Act.* London: L.R.D. Publications, 1961. 68p.

14,811 **Vester**, Horatio and **Cartwright**, Hilary Ann. *Industrial injuries.* London: Sweet and Maxwell, 1961. 2v.

14,812 **Auld**, R. E. *Compensation for industrial accidents.* 1962–63. (Ph.D. thesis, University of London.)

14,813 **Taylor**, Alan Broughton. *Liability and effective compensation for bodily injuries sustained in accidents.* 1962–63. (B.Litt. thesis, University of Oxford.)

14,814 **Gordon**, Margaret S. 'Industrial injuries insurance in Europe and the British Commonwealth before World War II.' Cheit, E. F. and Gordon, M. S. (eds.). *Occupational disability and public policy.* New York, London: Wiley, 1963. p. 191–220.

14,815 **Gordon**, Margaret S. 'Industrial injuries insurance in Europe and the British Commonwealth since World War II.' Cheit, E. F. and Gordon, M. S. (eds.). *Occupational disability and public policy.* New York, London: Wiley, 1963. p. 221–53.

14,816 **Whincup**, Michael Hynes. *The general principles of employers' liability at common law and under the Factories Act, 1961.* Birmingham: Institute of Industrial Supervisors, 1963. 44p.
Second enlarged and revised edition. 1964. 57p.

14,817 **Whitmore**, Edward. *Employers' liability insurance.* London: Pitman, 1962 [i.e. 1963]. xxiv, 231p. (Insurance handbook 13.)

14,818 **Smith**, Harry. *The responsibilities of employers and others for the maintenance and support of injured workmen and their families, including the families of deceased workmen, during the half century before 1840.* 1964. (M.A. thesis, University of London.)

14,819 **Young**, Agnes Freda. *Industrial injuries insurance: an examination of British policy.* London: Routledge and Kegan Paul, 1964. xi, 180p. (International library of sociology and social reconstruction.)

14,820 **Crossley Yaines**, J. 'Les rapports de l'employeur avec la sécurité sociale à l'occasion des accidents du travail et des maladies professionnelles: rapport national.' Congrès International de Droit du Travail et de la Sécurité Sociale, 5ième, Lyon, 1963. *Actes.* Lyon, [1965]. Vol. III. p. 1555–70.
Text in English.

14,821 **Bell**, John. *How to get industrial injuries benefits.* London: Sweet and Maxwell, 1966. xv, 275p.

14,822 **Kaim-Caudle**, Peter Robert. 'Compensation for occupational injury.' *Administration*, XIV, 1 (Spring 1966), 24–37.

14,823 **Reid**, Judith. 'Industrial injuries and the teabreak.' *Mod. Law Rev.*, XXIX, 4 (July 1966), 389–96.

14,824 **Clifford**, Frank. *What to do if you have an accident at work or on the road.* London: Mitchell, 1967. 72p.

14,825 **Heather**, A. D. *The extent of the existing statutory protection for workers against injuries from machinery.* 1967–68. (Ll.M. thesis, University of Nottingham.)

14,826 **Hanes**, David Gordon. *The first British Workmen's Compensation Act, 1897.* New Haven, Conn.: Yale U.P., 1968. xi, 124p. (Yale college series 8.)
'The author's honors thesis, Yale, class of 1966.'
Appendix 1. Employers' Liability Act, 1880 (43 and 44 Vict., ch. 42).

14,827 **Ingram**, John Thornton. *Industrial dermatoses and the Industrial Injuries Act.* London: Churchill, 1968. v, 42p.

14,828 **Curson**, Christopher. 'Compensation for accidents at work: can we learn from Canada?' *Ind. Law Soc. Bull.*, 6 (December 1969), 1–6.

14,829 **House of Commons.** Select Committee on Employers' Liability for Injuries to their Servants. *Select Committee and other reports on employers' liability for injuries to their servants and the insurance of persons employed in mines, with proceedings, minutes of evidence, appendices, indices, 1876–86.* Shannon: Irish U.P., 1970. 1094p. (British parliamentary papers, industrial relations, 19.)
Facsimile reprint of first editions, 1876–86.

14,830 **Society of Labour Lawyers.** *Occupational accidents and the law.* London: Fabian Society, 1970. 16p. (Research series 280.)

14,831 **Woolf**, A. D. 'Enforcement? The asbestosis case.' *Ind. Law Soc. Bull.*, 8 (September 1970), 12–13.

4. Pensions

This section includes material on the economic, social, and political aspects of national pension funds. Material on private pension funds and on pensions provided by the state for its employees is classified at Part Six, IV, C, 5. Material on the actuarial basis of pension funds and their administration is generally excluded. See also Part Six, II, C, 6.

14,832 **Ede**, W. Moore. *A scheme for national pensions.* London, 1889. 15p.

14,833 **Cooper**, Edward. 'A national pension fund.' *Fortn. Rev.*, n.s., L, 298 (6 October 1891), 516–24.

14,834 **Ede**, W. Moore. 'National pensions: one way out of darkest England.' *Contemp. Rev.*, LIX (April 1891), 580–96.

14,835 **Ede**, W. Moore. *A national pensions scheme.* London, 1891. 24p.

14,836 **Hardy**, R. P. *Old age pensions.* London, 1891. 16p.

14,837 **Newton**, A. W. 'Insurance against old age.' *Char. Orgn. Rev.*, VII, 79 (July 1891), 275–8; 80 (August 1891), 313–6.
Discusses the various kinds of schemes suggested, and costs.

14,838 **Beale**, *Sir* William Phipson. *Pensions for old age: a consideration of some of the objections raised to various pension schemes.* London: Eighty Club, 1892. 26p.

14,839 **Brooks**, J. G. 'Old age pensions in England.' *Q. J. Econ.*, VI (July 1892), 417–35.

14,840 **Chamberlain**, Joseph and **Loch**, *Sir* Charles Stewart. *Pauperism and old-age pensions.* London: Spottiswoode, 1892. 8p.
Correspondence reprinted from *The Times*.

14,841 **Ede**, W. Moore. 'Pensions for the aged.' *Econ. Rev.*, II, 2 (April 1892), 179–91.
'Read before the Political Economy Circle of the National Liberal Club, February 24, 1892.'

14,842 **Fremantle**, *Sir* Charles W. 'Address [as President of Section F of the British Association].' *R. Statist. Soc. J.*, LV, 3 (September 1892), 415–36.
On old-age pensions, etc.

14,843 **Fremantle**, *Sir* Charles W. 'Old-age pensions and pauperism.' *Char. Orgn. Rev.*, VIII, 93 (September 1892), 319–31.
'Address to the Economic Science and Statistics Section of the British Association . . . Edinburgh, 1892.'

14,844 **Loch**, *Sir* Charles Stewart. *Old age pensions and pauperism: an inquiry as to the bearing of the statistics of pauperism quoted by the Rt. Hon. J. Chamberlain, M.P., and others, in support of a scheme for national pensions.* London: Swan Sonnenschein, 1892. 59p.

14,845 **M.** *A prosperous kingdom; or, a vision of the possible: the problem of pensions for old age discussed and how to empty the workhouse.* London: G. Slater, 1892. 53p.

14,846 **Mackay**, Thomas. 'National pensions.' *Char. Orgn. Rev.*, VIII, 88 (April 1892), 125–33.
'An address delivered to the Council and members of the Council Charity Organisation Society, on Monday, March 21, 1892 . . .'
Report of discussion, p. 152–8.

14,847 *Pensions for all at sixty and an eight hours day, by the Chairman of a Yorkshire School Board.* London: Sampson Low, 1892. ix, 45p.

14,848 **Scanlon**, Thomas. 'Mr. Chamberlain's pension scheme: a friendly society view of it.' *Westm. Rev.*, CXXXVII, 4 (April 1892), 357–63.

14,849 **Sharp**, David. *A scheme for a national system of rest-funds, or pensions, for working people.* London: G. Philip, 1892. 16p.

14,850 **Spender**, John Alfred. *The state and pensions in old age.* London: Sonnenschein, 1892. xxvi, 165p.

14,851 **Taylor**, William. *State pensions: a paper read before the Bath Liberal Association, on March 18th, 1892.* Bristol: W. Lewis, 1892. 10p.

14,852 **Tullis**, John. *Old age pensions: a scheme for the formation of a citizens' national union. A contribution towards the solution of the problem of pauperism.* Glasgow: printed for the author by Brodie and Salmond, 1892. 40p.
On the cover: London, King.

14,853 **Wilkinson**, John Frome. *Pensions and pauperism.* London: Methuen, 1892. 127p.
'With notes by T. E. Young.'

14,854 **Sowerbutts**, Eli. 'Considerations in relation to state insurance of old age pensions, and other benefits.' *Manchr. Statist. Soc. Trans.* (1892–93), 101–14.

14,855 **Calverley**, Mary. 'Thrift and old-age pensions.' *Char. Orgn. Rev.*, IX, 96 (January 1893), 1–7.

14,856 **Everett**, R. L. 'Old age pensions.' Co-operative Wholesale Societies. *Annual for 1893.* p. 464–78.

14,857 **Ormerod**, James Redman. *A scheme for the formation of pension assurance societies.* Warrington: N. Leach, 1893. 16p.

14,858 **Richardson**, J. Hall. 'Old age pay for the million.' *Westm. Rev.*, CXXXIX, 4 (April 1893), 362–8.

14,859 **Robertson**, John. *New light is thrown on the question of old age pensions by the proposed formation of the Glasgow Mutual Aid Association.* Glasgow, 1893. 6p.

14,860 **Chamberlain**, Joseph. *Friendly societies and 'old-age' pensions: important speech by the Rt. Hon. Joseph Chamberlain, M.P., to a representatives' meeting of friendly societies, in the Town Hall, Birmingham, 6th December, 1894.* Handsworth: *Handsworth Chronicle*, 1894. 20p.

14,861 **Chance**, *Sir* William. *State-aided pensions for old age.* London, [1894?]. 31p.

14,862 **Society of Inspectors of Poor for Scotland.** *Report of committee on old age pensions and pauperism, Dec. 1893, adopted by Society, 31st Jan. 1894.* Glasgow, 1894. 8p.

14,863 **Bowack**, W. M. *Poverty and old age in relation to the state.* Edinburgh, 1895. 32p.

14,864 **Ede**, W. Moore. 'Pensions for the aged.' National Liberal Club. Political Economy Circle. *Transactions,* II (1895), 15–27.

14,865 **Loch**, *Sir* Charles Stewart. 'Some economic issues in regard to old-age pensions.' *Econ. J.*, V, 19 (September 1895), 347–68.

14,866 **Mackay**, Thomas. 'Old age pensions and the state.' *Char. Orgn. Rev.*, XI, 121 (February 1895), 37–51.

'A paper read at a meeting of the Society of Arts on February 22, 1893. Reprinted from the *Journal of the Society of Arts.*'

14,867 **Tyler**, L. *Old age allowances.* Cardiff, 1895. 18p.

14,868 **Williams**, J. W. 'Old age pensions.' *Westm. Rev.*, CXLIV, (August 1895), 193–202.

14,869 **Baylee**, J. Tyrrell. 'The problems of pauperism and old age pensions.' *Westm. Rev.*, CXLV, 1 (January 1896), 67–74.

14,870 **Fabian Society**. *The case for state pensions in old age.* London: Fabian Society, 1896. 15p. (Fabian tract 73.)

By George Turner.

First issued without the author's name.

14,871 **Paulin**, D. *Old age pensions and pauperism.* London, 1896. 32p.

14,872 **Rutherglen**, John H. *The Poor Law Officers' Superannuation Act, 1896.* London: Knight, 1896. xv, 46p.

'Annotated and explained by J. H. Rutherglen . . . Together with a history of the superannuation movement.'

14,873 **Fatkin**, Thomas. *Observations on the Poor Law Officers Superannuation Act for the consideration of the Leeds Board of Guardians.* Leeds: printed by Goodall and Suddick, 1897. 18p.

14,874 **Martineau**, John. *Pensions and voluntary effort.* London, 1897. 8p.

14,875 **Shackleton**, Joseph. *Social amelioration: a treatise upon Mr. A. Atkinson's national pension scheme.* Bradford: J. S. Toothill, 1897. 266p.

'Edited and revised by "Theodore".'

14,876 **Birkmyre**, William. *Old age pensions.* Glasgow, [1898?]. 39p.

Third edition. Glasgow: Aird and Coghill, [189–?]. 44p.

14,877 **Burdett**, *Sir* Henry. 'Old age pensions.' *R. Statist. Soc. J.*, LXI, 4 (December 1898), 597–624.

Abstract of pension scheme, p. 625–7. Discussion, p. 628–39.

'Read before the Royal Statistical Society, 15th November, 1898.'

14,878 **Departmental Committee on Old Age Pensions.** *Report, with evidence, appendices, and index.* London: H.M.S.O., 1898. (C. 8911.)

14,879 **Holland**, Bernard. 'Old age pensions.' *Econ. J.*, VIII, 31 (September 1898), 333–9.

On the report of the Committee on Old Age Pensions.

14,880 **Holland**, *Hon.* Lionel Reginald. *Suggestion for a scheme of old age pensions, with an introductory chapter dealing with the report of the Committee on Old Age Pensions.* London: Arnold, 1898. xxxix, 110p.

14,881 **Newman**, Philip L. 'Super-annuation.' Co-operative Wholesale Societies. *Annual for 1898.* p. 349–89.

14,882 **Pilling**, William. *Old age pensions: scheme for the establishment of a government superannuation fund.* London: Chapman and Hall, 1898. viii, 50p.

14,883 **Stephens**, William Walker. *Old age annuities for men and women.* Edinburgh, 1898. 14p.

14,884 **Alexander**, L. C. *Industrial superannuation versus pauper pensions.* London, 1899. 23p.

14,885 **Bailward**, William Amyas. *A reply to Mr. Charles Booth's latest proposal concerning old-age pensions and the aged poor.* London, 1899. 5p.

14,886 **Booth**, Charles. *Old age pensions: verbatim report . . . of the proceedings at a conference held in . . . Birmingham . . . 1899 . . . and addressed by . . . C. Booth.* Birmingham, [1899?]. 16p.

14,887 **Booth**, Charles. *Old age pensions and the aged poor: a proposal.* London: Macmillan, 1899. xi, 75p.

Another edition. London: Macmillan, 1906. v, 84p.

14,888 **Booth**, Charles. *Pensions for all in old age: argument.* London, New York: Macmillan, 1899. 47p.

'Reprinted for the use of the National Committee [of Organised Labour for Promoting Old Age Pensions for All].'

An abridged edition of *Old age pensions and the aged poor.*

14,889 **Booth**, Charles. *A reply to Old-age pensions and the aged poor: a proposal.* London, 1899. 7p.

14,890 **Committee on Old-age Pensions.** *Old-age pensions and poor relief.* London, 1899. 6p. (Papers 8.)

14,891 **Edinburgh Review.** 'Old age relief.' *Edinb. Rev.*, CXC, 380 (October 1899), 332–55.

Review article.

14,892 **Fabian Society.** *Old age pensions at work.* London: Fabian Society, 1899. 4p. (Fabian tract 89.)

By J. Bullock.

Issued without the author's name.

14,893 **King**, George. 'Old age pensions.' *Ins. Act. Soc. Glasg. Trans.*, 4th ser., 12 (13 March 1899), 283–304.

14,894 **Loch**, *Sir* Charles Stewart. 'Old age pensions.' *Econ. J.*, IX, 36 (December 1899), 520–40.

14,895 **Loch**, *Sir* Charles Stewart. *Old age pensions: mistakes and misstatements.* London, 1899. 20p.

14,896 **Metcalfe**, John. *The case for universal old age pensions.* London: Simpkin, Marshall, 1899. viii, 220p.

Introduction by Charles Booth.

14,897 **Spender**, A. Edmund. 'A state crutch for old-age pensions: an alternative suggestion.' *Westm. Rev.*, CLII, 1 (July 1899), 44–9.

14,898 **Trist**, John. 'Old age pensions.' *Westm. Rev.*, CLII, 5 (November 1899), 533–47.

14,899 **Veale**, E. W. *Old age pensions: a suggested solution.* Bristol, 1899. 8p.

14,900 **Wolff**, Henry William. 'Old age pensions.' *Econ. Rev.*, IX, 3 (July 1899), 321–41.

14,901 **Wright**, John Cooke. *Old age pensions: a paper . . . read at the . . . North Midland District Poor Law Conference.* London: King, 1899. 20p.

14,902 **Wright**, W. Chapman. 'The landlords to pay old-age pensions.' *Westm. Rev.*, CLI, 5 (May 1899), 501–8.

14,903 **Buxton**, Sydney C. 'Old age pensions.' *Supplement to the ninth edition of A handbook to political questions of the day and the arguments on either side.* London: Murray, 1900. p. 7–19.

Also in eleventh edition. 1903. p. 314–26.

14,904 **Fitzpatrick**, P. *Fitzpatrick's old age pension scheme.* South Shields: E. Sword, 1900. 16p.

'Issued under the auspices of No. 14 Branch of the National Amalgamated Union of Labour.'

14,905 **Glyde**, C. A. *Britain's disgrace: an urgent plea for old age pensions.* Keighley, [1900?]. 32p.

14,906 **MacGregor**, W. D. 'Old-age pensions.' *Westm. Rev.*, CLIV, 3 (September 1900), 276–84.

14,907 **National Committee of Organised Labour for Promoting Old Age Pensions for All.** *Old age pensions: a memorandum . . . to the Right Hon. A. J. Balfour, M.P. by F. Rogers, March 5th, 1900; and a speech delivered by the Archbishop of Canterbury* . . . London: the Committee, 1900. 15p.

14,908 **Whitcombe**, J. *Observations on the circular letter of the Local Government Board . . . 1900* . . . London, 1900. 10p.

14,909 **Sinclair**, *Sir* John George Tollemache, and others. *Old-age pensions . . . with criticisms on the Charity Organisation Society.* London, [1901?]. 26p.

14,910 **D.**, E. 'Old age pensions.' *Char. Orgn. Rev.*, n.s., XI, 62 (February 1902), 85–96.

Discusses three kinds of pension schemes which have been put forward.

14,911 **Eastick**, C. B. *A working man's ideal scheme of old age pensions.* London: the author, 1902. 20p.

14,912 *England's shame! how wealthy Christian England treats her aged deserving poor.* Sheffield, 1902. [iii], 11, [iv]p.

14,913 **Perrott**, Frank Duerdin. *The government and old age pensions.* Smethwick: Telephone Co., [1902]. [9]p.

14,914 **Rogers**, Frederick. *Society and its worn-out workers.* London, 1902. 16p.

14,915 **Committee on Old-age Pensions.** *Old-age pensions: the case against old-age pension schemes; a collection of short papers.* London, New York: Macmillan 1903. 247p.

14,916 **Rogers**, Frederick. *Old age pensions: are they desirable and practicable? Pro – F. Rogers, Con – F. Millar.* London: Isbister, 1903. xiii, 226p. (Pro and con series 1.)

14,917 **Select Committee on the Aged Pensioners Bill.** *Reports, etc.* London: H.M.S.O., 1904. xvi, 571p.

Chairman: G. Lawson.

14,918 **Tullis**, John. *The Citizen's National Union, being an old age pension scheme revised & brought into line with the fiscal question of to-day.* Paisley: A. Gardner, 1904. 32p.

14,919 **Barnes**, G. *Old age pensions.* London, 1905. 16p.

14,920 **Tebbutt**, Joseph Henry. *The B.B.B., or, every Briton's blue book on old age pensions.* London: Bemrose, 1905. 80p.

14,921 **Burt**, Thomas. 'Old age pensions.' *Nineteenth Century*, LX, 355 (September 1906), 372–87.

14,922 **Rogers**, Frederick. *A plea for old-age pensions.* London: C. H. Kelly, 1906. 18p. (Social tracts for the times 2.)

14,923 **Root**, John Wilson. *Old age pensions.* Liverpool: J. W. Root, 1906. 22p.

14,924 *£4 a week for life; or, the problem of advancing age and its solution.* Gillingham: A. W. Hoyle, 1907. 63p.

14,925 **Harrison**, . *The Walsall old-age pension scheme.* Walsall, 1907. 8p.

14,926 **Publishers' Syndicate Amalgamated.** *Old age pensions: an appeal on behalf of the aged poor.* Coventry: the Syndicate, [1907?]. 33p.

14,927 **Snowden**, Philip. *Old age pensions this year.* London: Independent Labour Party. 1907. 15p.

14,928 **Sutherland**, William. *Old age pensions in theory and practice.* London: Methuen, 1907. x, 227p.

14,929 **Tebbutt**, Joseph Henry. *Old age pensions: an appeal on behalf of the aged poor.* Coventry: Publishers' Syndicate Amalgamated, 1907. 33p.

14,930 **Webb**, Sidney. *Paupers and old age pensions.* London: Fabian Society, 1907. 15p. (Fabian tract 135.)

Reprinted, with revision, from the *Albany Review*, August 1907.

14,931 **Barlow**, *Sir* Clement Anderson Montague and **Gomme**, *Sir* George Laurence. *The Old Age Pensions Act, 1908, together with the regulations made thereunder, official circulars, and financial instructions by the Treasury.* London: Eyre and Spottiswoode, 1908. 180p.

14,932 **Brabrook**, Edward William. 'Old age pensions. I. The dangers of the non-contributory principle.' *Sociol. Rev.*, I, 3 (July 1908), 291–4.

14,933 **Burleigh**, Bennet. *An address on old-age pensions.* London: National Liberal Club, Political Committee, 1908. 21p.

14,934 **Burleigh**, Bennet. *Old age pensions: a national scheme: ways and means.* London, 1908. 21p.

14,935 **Casson**, William Augustus. *Old-age Pensions Act, 1908, together with the text of the regulations made thereunder and official circulars and instructions for the guidance of pension authorities by the Local Government Boards of England, Scotland, and Ireland, annotated and explained, with historical introduction.* London: Knight, 1908. xxvii, 135p.

Second edition. *Old Age Pensions Act . . .* 1908. xxviii, 171p.

Third edition. 1908. xxx, 185p.

14,936 **Emery**, George Frederick. *The people's guide to the Old Age Pensions Act, 1908.* London, Derby: Bemrose, 1908. 39p.

14,937 **Evans**, David Owen. *Old Age Pensions Act, 1908, with notes. Together with the statutory regulations and official circulars issued by the Local Government Boards of England, Scotland, and Ireland, and financial instructions of the Treasury. With an introduction by D. Lloyd-George.* London: Sweet and Maxwell, 1908. x, 224p.

14,938 **Hobson**, John Atkinson. 'Old age pensions. II. The responsibility of the state to the aged poor.' *Sociol. Rev.*, I, 3 (July 1908), 295–9.

14,939 **Johnston**, W. J. and **Muldoon**, J. *Old age pensions in Ireland.* Dublin: Eason, 1908. 96p.

14,940 **Kelly**, Richard J. *Old Age Pensions Act, 1908.* Dublin: Sealy, Bryers and Walker, 1908. viii, 103p.

14,941 **Kettle**, Thomas Michael and **Sheehy**, R. J. *The Old Age Pensions Act, 1908: a popular handbook.* Dublin: Maunsel, 1908. 116p.

14,942 *Law of old age pensions.* London, [1908?]. 16p.

14,943 **Leach**, Robert Alfred. *The Old Age Pensions Act, 1908.* London, 1908. viii, 84p.

14,944 **Lecky**, William Edward Hartpole. *Old-age pensions.* London: Longmans, 1908. 24p.

Reprinted from *The Forum.*

14,945 **Rogers**, Frederick. 'Old age pensions.' *Progress Civic Soc. Ind.*, III, 2 (April 1908), 79–86.

14,946 **Rolfe**, Douglass Horace Boggis. *Handbook to the Old Age Pensions Act, 1908.* London: Waterlow and Layton, 1908. 130, xp.

14,947 **Ehrlich**, Eugen. 'The old-age pension scheme.' *Econ. Rev.*, XIX, 1 (January 1909), 49–53.

A comparison of the German and English schemes.

14,948 **Marr**, Vyvyan. *Some financial and statistical considerations of the old age pension scheme.* London, 1909. 16p.

14,949 **National Committee of Organised Labour for Promoting Old Age Pensions for All.** *Ten years' work for old age pensions, 1899–1909.* London: the Committee, 1909. pagination varies.

A collection of the pamphlets, leaflets, and reports published by the Committee during the years mentioned.

14,950 **Stead**, Francis Herbert. *How old age pensions began to be.* London: Methuen, 1909. vii, 328p.

14,951 **Roberts**, A. Carson. *A compendium of national pension schemes and a proposed scheme for amending the Act of 1908.* London, 1910. 73p.

14,952 **Roberts**, A. Carson. 'How to improve and extend our national pension scheme.' *Nineteenth Century*, LXVIII, 406 (December 1910), 957–77; LXIX, 410 (April 1911), 614–35.

14,953 **Ellis**, Charles Cleveland. *The Old Age Pensions Acts, 1908 and 1911, and regulations made thereunder.* Edinburgh and Glasgow: William Hodge, 1911. xi, 120p.

14,954 **Pilter**, *Sir* J. *Contributory scheme for old age pensions.* Beccles, [1911?]. 12p.

14,955 *Memorandum on old age pensioners and aged pauperism.* London: H.M.S.O., 1913. 41p. (Cd. 7015.)

14,956 **Hoare**, Henry J. *Old age pensions: their actual working and ascertained results in the United Kingdom.* London: King, 1915. xi, 196p.

14,957 **National Conference of Representatives of the National Free Church Council, Friendly Societies, Trade Unions, etc.**, Newcastle-on-Tyne, August 1917. *Old age pensions.* [1917?] 4p.

14,958 **Dennison**, J. L. *Reconstruction of old age pensions: plain facts.* [1919?] 24p.

14,959 **Departmental Committee on Old Age Pensions.** *Report.* London: H.M.S.O., 1919. 19p. (Cmd. 410.)

Evidence and appendices. (Cmd. 411.)

Chairman: Sir W. Ryland D. Adkins.

14,960 **Ministry of Pensions.** Departmental Committee on the Machinery and Administration of the Ministry of Pensions. *Report, etc.* London: H.M.S.O., 1921. 156p.

Chairman: G. C. Tryon.

14,961 **Bailey**, F. *Pensions at sixty.* London, 1924. 16p.

14,962 **Waterworth**, John W. *The new old-age pension Act, clearly explained.* London: Independent Labour Party, 1924. 15p.

14,963 **Barker**, Wilberforce Ross. 'The Widows, Orphans and Old Age Contributory Pensions Bill.' *Nineteenth Century*, XCVIII, 581 (July 1925), 19–31.

14,964 **Labour Joint Publications Department.** *Pensions for the aged and the mothers.* London, [*c.* 1925]. 15p.

14,965 **Northern Ireland.** Ministry of Labour. *Widows', Orphans' and Old Age Contributory Pensions Bill: memorandum explanatory of the Bill.* Belfast: H.M.S.O., 1925. (Cmd. 46.) 8p.

14,966 **Shillaker**, J. F. 'The state's dependents.' Tracey, H. (ed.). *The book of the Labour Party: its history, growth, policy, and leaders.* London: Caxton Publishing Co., 1925. Vol. 2. p. 226–44.

14,967 **Wilkinson**, William Elmslie. *The new pensions scheme explained.* London: Simpkin, Marshall, 1925. 31p.

14,968 **Eire.** *Old age pensions. Report of Committee of Enquiry.* 1926. (R 28.)

14,969 **International Labour Office.** 'The new British Pensions Act.' *Int. Labour Rev.*, XIII, 3 (March 1926), 361–81; 4 (April 1926), 506–22.

14,970 **Leach**, Robert Webber. *Widows', Orphans' and Old Age Contributory Pensions Act, 1925, the Old Age Pensions Acts, 1908–24, and relevant provisions of the National Health Insurance Act, 1924.* London: Law and Local Government Publications, 1926. 198p.

14,971 **Conyngton**, Mary Katherine. *Public service retirement systems: United States, Canada, and Europe. January 1929.* Washington, D.C.: U.S.G.P.O., 1929. vii, 223p. (Bulletin of the United States Bureau of Labor Statistics 477. Workmen's insurance and compensation series.)

Issued also as House doc. 476, 70th Congress, 2nd Session.

14,972 **Burns**, Eveline Mabel. 'State pensions and old age dependency in Great Britain.' *Polit. Sci. Q.*, XLV, 2 (June 1930), 181–213.

14,973 **Macdonald**, Thomas Pringle and **Davie**, George. *Handbook of widows', orphans', and old age contributory pensions.* Edinburgh, London: Hodge, 1930. 104p.

14,974 **Newman**, Tom Seth and **Lee**, A. G. *Guide to widows', orphans', and old age pensions.* London: *Daily News*, 1930. 64p.

Fifth edition. London: *News Chronicle*, 1936. 64p.

14,975 **Social Service Review.** 'Some old age pension questions in England.' *Soc. Serv. Rev.*, IV (June 1930), 262–81.

14,976 **Witmer**, Helen Leland. 'Influence of old age pensions on public poor relief in England and Wales.' *Soc. Serv. Rev.*, IV (December 1930), 587–607.

14,977 **Edgar**, W. S. *Old age pensions: a study of opinion on the subject of state aid to necessitous old age in Great Britain.* 1932. 212p. (M.A. thesis, McGill University.)

14,978 **Political and Economic Planning.** *The exit from industry: a survey of the provision for old age and for retirement from gainful occupation in the United Kingdom.* London: P.E.P., 1935. 52p.

14,979 **Newman**, Tom Seth and **Lee**, A. G. *News Chronicle guide to Widows', Orphans' and Old Age Pensions – Voluntary Contributions – Act, 1937.* London: *News Chronicle* Publications Department, 1937. 80p.

14,980 **Northern Ireland.** *Widows', Orphans' and Old Age Contributory Pensions (Voluntary Contributors) Bill, 1937: memorandum explanatory of the Bill by the Ministry of Labour.* Belfast: H.M.S.O., 1937. 10p. (Cmd. 182.)

14,981 **Sacks**, B. 'The passage of the British Old Age Pension Act of 1908.' *S.-West. Soc. Sci. Q.*, XVII (March 1937), 331–41.

14,982 **Colville**, David John, Baron Clydesmuir. *Labour's pension plan.* London: National Conservative Union, 1938. 11p. (No. 3668.)

14,983 **Committee on Pensions for Unmarried Women.** *Report.* London: H.M.S.O., 1939. iv. 78p. (Cmd. 5991.)

Chairman: C. T. Le Quesne.

14,984 **Northern Ireland.** *Old Age and Widows' Pensions Bill (Northern Ireland): memorandum explanatory of the Bill by the Ministry of Labour.* Belfast: H.M.S.O., 1940. 6p. (Cmd. 212.)

14,985 **Wilson**, *Sir* Arnold Talbot and **Mackay**, G. S. *Old age pensions: an historical and critical study.* London: Oxford U.P., 1941. xx, 238p.

14,986 **Clarke,** Joan Simeon. 'Widows', orphans' and old age pensions.' Robson, W.A. (ed.). *Social security.* London: Allen and Unwin for the Fabian Society, 1943. p. 156–72.

Second edition. 1945.

Third edition. 1948.

14,987 **Cohen**, Emmeline W. 'Superannuation.' Robson, W. A. (ed.). *Social security.* London: Allen and Unwin for the Fabian Society, 1943. p. 239–49.

Second edition. 1945. p. 249–59.

14,988 **Ferill**, Everett W. *The background of old age pension legislation in England, 1878–1908.* 1947. (Thesis, University of Illinois.)

14,989 **Lee**, Jennie. 'Pensioners of the state.' Tracey, H. (ed.). *The British Labour Party: its history, growth, policy, and leaders.* London: Caxton Publishing Co., 1948. Vol. 2. p. 142–53.

14,990 **McLernon**, Sylvia G. *Government provision for the aged in Great Britain, Canada and New Zealand.* 1948–49. (D.Pol.Sc. thesis, Radcliffe University.)

Published Rochester, N.Y.: U. of Rochester P., 1954.

14,991 **Hohman**, Helen Fisher. 'Income maintenance for the aged in Great Britain.' Industrial Relations Research Association. *Proceedings of the fourth annual meeting, December 1951*. p. 220–39.
Discussion, p. 253–60.

14,992 **Garibian**, V. S. and **Wiles**, P. J. D. 'Pensions and rising prices.' *Oxf. Econ. Pap.*, n.s., IV, 2 (July 1952), 131–48.

14,993 **Peacock**, Alan Turner. 'Social security and inflation: a study of the economic effects of an adjustable pensions scheme.' *Rev. Econ. Studies*, XX, 3 (1952–53), 169–73.

14,994 **Melling**, Ernest. *Pensioners' progress: the story of the fight for the aged people of Great Britain*. Blackburn: National Federation of Old Age Pensions Associations, [1953?]. 35p.

14,995 **Keast**, Horace. *Knight's commentary on the Superannuation Benefit Regulations, 1954*. London: Knight, 1954. 112p.

14,996 **Little**, Leo T. 'The economics of dependency: burden of pensions in perspective.' *Banker*, CII, 341 (June 1954), 334–40.

14,997 **Moss**, John. *The Local Government Superannuation Act, 1953, annotated and explained together with the main regulations and the Local Government Superannuation Act, 1937, as an appendix, and full index*. London: Hadden, Best, 1954. xi, 160p.

14,998 **Paish**, Frank Walter and **Peacock**, Alan Turner. 'Economics of dependence (1952–1982).' *Economica*, n.s., XXI, 84 (November 1954), 279–99.

14,999 **Sires**, Ronald V. 'The beginnings of British legislation for old-age pensions.' *J. Econ. Hist.*, XIV, 3 (Summer 1954), 229–53.

15,000 **Treasury.** *Report of the Committee on the Economic and Financial Problems of the Provision for Old Age*. London: H.M.S.O., 1954. (Cmd. 9333.)

15,001 **Abel-Smith**, Brian and **Townsend**, Peter Brere. *New pensions for the old*. London: Fabian Publications, 1955. 27p. (Research series 171.)

15,002 **Little**, Leo T. 'The superannuated state: who pays for pensions.' *Banker*, CIV, 348 (January 1955), 17–24.

15,003 **Titmuss**, Richard M. 'Pension systems and population change.' *Polit. Q.*, XXVI, 2 (April–June 1955), 152–66.
Reprinted in *Essays on 'the welfare state'*. London: Allen and Unwin, 1958. p. 56–74.

15,004 **Fabian Society.** *Plan for industrial pensions* [by] *a group of trade unionists*. London: Fabian Society, 1956. 11p. (Fabian tract 303.)
Preface by Margaret Cole.

15,005 **Peace**, T. H. 'Pensions for the self-employed: the plan and its limitations.' *Banker*, CVI, 365 (June 1956), 354–8.

15,006 **Labour Party.** *National superannuation: Labour's policy for security in old age*. London: Labour Party, 1957. 122p.

15,007 **Peacock**, Alan Turner. 'The economics of national superannuation.' *Three Banks Rev.*, 35 (September 1957), 2–22.

15,008 **Round Table.** 'Economics of old age: a study of national pensions.' *Round Table*, 188 (September 1957), 342–9.

15,009 **Shanks**, Michael J. 'Superannuation for all? State schemes and the alternatives.' *Banker*, CVII, 380 (September 1957), 589–96.

15,010 **Shenfield**, Barbara Estelle. *Social policies for old age: a review of social provision for old age in Great Britain*. London: Routledge and Kegan Paul, 1957. viii, 236p. (International library of sociology and social reconstruction.)

15,011 **Association of British Chambers of Commerce.** *National superannuation: a critical review of the proposals of the Labour Party*. London: the Association, 1958. 32p.

15,012 **Black**, J. 'A note on the economics of national superannuation.' *Econ. J.*, LXVIII, 270 (June 1958), 338–52.
With special reference to *National superannuation: Labour's policy for security in old age*, 1957.

15,013 **Charles Knight and Co.** *Employee's guide* [*to*] *Local Government Superannuation Acts, 1937–1953, Local Government Superannuation (Benefits) Regulations, 1954 and 1955, and other supplementary regulations*. London: Knight, 1958. 24p.

15,014 **Ministry of Pensions and National Insurance.** *Provision for old age: the future development of the National Insurance Scheme*. London: H.M.S.O., 1958. 23p. (Cmnd. 538.)

15,015 **Powell**, John Enoch. 'Pensions -- will the good impede the best?' *Banker*, CVIII, 394 (November 1958), 705–9.

15,016 **Carpenter**, Niles. *Programs for older people in Great Britain*. Buffalo, N.Y.: U. of Buffalo, 1959. 288–363p. (University of Buffalo studies, v. 24, no. 4. Monographs in sociology 7.)

15,017 **Institute of Actuaries.** Council and **Faculty of Actuaries in Scotland.** *National pensions*, London, 1959. 11p.

15,018 **Labour Party.** *2 pension plans: Labour & Tory plans compared*. London: Labour Party, 1959. 12p.

15,019 **Liberal Party.** Pensions Committee. *Security for our pensioners*. 1959. 28p.

15,020 **Seldon**, Arthur. 'Pensions in a prosperous society.' *Contemp. Rev.* (October 1959), 134–46.
Analyses the pension plans of the three main political parties.

15,021 **Wiseman**, Jack. 'Pensions in Britain.' *Finanzarchiv*, XIX, 3 (1959), 427–40.
Discussion of Conservative, Labour and Liberal plans for retirement pensions.

15,022 **British Institute of Management.** *Government pension scheme 1961.* London: B.I.M., 1960. 20p.
One-day conference, 1960.

15,023 **Industrial Welfare Society.** *Further papers on government pension proposals: the implications for industry and commerce of the National Insurance Bill, 1959.* London: the Society, 1960. 28p.
Contributors: F. Lafitte, G. W. Pingstone, A. W. Morling, C. A. Poyser.

15,024 **Institute of Directors.** *State pensions: should you contract out?* London: the Institute, 1960. 10p.

15,025 **International Labour Office.** 'The evolution of state pension schemes in Great Britain.' *Int. Labour Rev.*, LXXXI, 5 (May 1960), 456–79.

15,026 **Charles Knight and Co.** *Employee's guide [to the] Local Government Superannuation Acts, 1937–1953, Local Government Superannuation (Benefits) Regulations, 1954 and 1955, National Insurance Act, 1959 and regulations made thereunder, and other supplementary regulations.* London: Knight, 1961. 30p.

15,027 **Forster**, George Henry. *Graduated national pensions as affecting local authorities.* London: Knight, 1961. xiii, 432p.
Supplement. 1961. vi, 166p.

15,028 **Gration**, David Thomas. *The graduated pension scheme – and how to work it.* Manchester: Co-operative Union, 1961. 8p.
Reprinted from the *Co-operative Review*.

15,029 **Ministry of Pensions and National Insurance.** *Retirement pensions.* London: the Ministry, 1961. 19p.

15,030 **Wedderburn**, Dorothy Cole. 'Economic aspects of ageing.' *Int. Soc. Sci. J.*, XV, 3 (1963), 394–409.

15,031 **Gibson**, Geoffrey. 'The income guarantee.' *New Soc.*, IV, 113 (26 November 1964), 10–11.

15,032 **Registrar of Non-participating Employments.** *Contractiong out of the graduated pension scheme, National Insurance Acts 1959 and 1963.* London: H.M.S.O., 1964. 23p.

15,033 **A Special Correspondent.** 'Retirement – in 2011.' *Banker*, CXIV, 456 (February 1964), 110–13.

15,034 **Wedderburn**, Dorothy Cole. 'Pensions, equality and socialism.' *New Left Rev.*, 24 (March–April 1964), 68–81.

15,035 **Ashworth**, Philip. 'New policies for pensions.' Bow Group. *The Conservative challenge.* London: Batsford, Conservative Political Centre, 1965. p. 28–42.

15,036 **Collins**, Doreen. 'The introduction of old age pensions in Great Britain.' *Hist. J.*, VIII, 2 (1965), 246–59.

15,037 **Gilbert**, Bentley Brinkerhoff. 'The decay of nineteenth-century provident institutions and the coming of old age pensions in Great Britain.' *Econ. Hist. Rev.*, 2nd ser., XVII, 3 (April 1965), 551–63.

15,038 **Ratcliff**, A. R. N. 'The cost of pensions.' Burn, D., Seale, J. R., and Ratcliff, A. R. N. *Lessons from central forecasting.* London: Institute of Economic Affairs, 1965. p. 42–62.

15,039 **Wedderburn**, Dorothy Cole. 'The old and the poor.' *New Soc.*, VI, 147 (22 July 1965), 7–8.
Based on *The aged in the welfare state* by Peter Townsend and Dorothy Wedderburn.

15,040 **Ministry of Pensions and National Insurance.** *Financial and other circumstances of retirement pensioners: report on an enquiry by the Ministry of Pensions and National Insurance with the co-operation of the National Assistance Board.* London: H.M.S.O., 1966. x, 210p.

15,041 **Windsor Davies**, T. 'Pensions for the future.' *New Soc.*, VII, 187 (28 April 1966), 12–13.

15,042 **Gilling-Smith**, Gordon Douglas. *The complete guide to pensions and superannuation.* Harmondsworth: Penguin, 1967. 480p. (Pelican books.)
Second edition. 1968. 480p.

15,043 **Ministry of National Insurance.** *Report of the National Insurance Advisory Committee in accordance with section 88 (3) of the National Insurance Act 1965 on the question of the earnings limit for retirement pensions.* London: H.M.S.O., 1967. 39p. (Cmnd. 3197.)

15,044 **Department of Health and Social Security.** *The new pensions scheme: latest facts and figures with examples.* London: H.M.S.O., 1969. 32p.

15,045 **Department of Health and Social Security.** *Pensions – the way forward: the new earnings-related scheme. A summary of the Government White Paper 'National superannuation and social insurance'.* London: H.M.S.O., 1969. 22p.

15,046 **Department of Health and Social Security.** *Terms for partial contracting out of the National Superannuation Scheme.* London: H.M.S.O., 1969. 18p. (Cmnd. 4195.)

15,047 **Lynes**, Tony. *Labour's pension plan.* London: Fabian Society, 1969. 33p. (Fabian tract 396.)

15,048 **Titmuss**, Richard. 'Superannuation for all: a broader view.' *New Soc.*, XIII, 335 (27 February 1969), 315–17.

15,049 **Walley**, *Sir* John. 'Pensions reform in Great Britain.' *Polit. Q.*, XL, 1 (January–March 1969), 66–78.
The author was Deputy Secretary, Ministry of Pensions and National Insurance, 1958–66.

15,050 **Atkinson**, A. B. 'National superannuation: redistribution and value for money.' *Oxf. Univ. Inst. Econ. Statist. Bull.*, XXXII, 3 (August 1970), 171–85.

15,051 **Fisher**, Paul. 'Minimum old-age pensions. I. Their adequacy in terms of consumer expenditures, assistance benefits and poverty standards.' *Int. Labour Rev.*, CII, 1 (July 1970), 51–78.

15,052 **Fisher**, Paul. 'Minimum old-age pensions. II. Their adequacy in terms of average earnings, minimum wages and national income, and some problems of adjustment.' *Int. Labour Rev.*, CII, 3 (September 1970), 277–317.

15,053 **Lynes**, Tony. 'Parties and pensions.' *New Soc.*, XV, 390 (19 March 1970), 480–1. (Society at work.)

15,054 **Pole**, J. D. 'The burden of pensions.' *Bankers' Mag.*, CCX, 1521 (December 1970), 260–3.

15,055 **Prest**, A. R. 'Some redistributional aspects of the National Superannuation Fund.' *Three Banks Rev.*, 86 (June 1970), 3–22.

15,056 **Williams**, Patricia Mary. *The development of old age pensions policy in Great Britain, 1878–1925.* 1970. (Ph.D. (Econ.) thesis, University of London.)

INDEX

An asterisk (*) denotes that the work indicated appears twice in the bibliography.

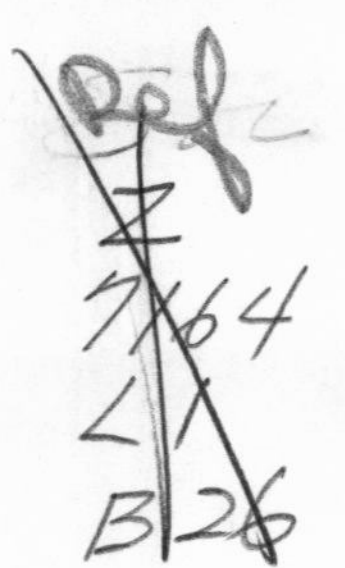